Tax Formula for Indivi...

Income (broadly conceived)	$xx,xxx
Less: Exclusions.......................................	(x,xxx)
Gross income	$xx,xxx
Less: Deductions *for* adjusted gross income	(x,xxx)
Adjusted gross income.................................	$xx,xxx
Less: The greater of—	
Total itemized deductions	
or standard deduction	(x,xxx)
Less: Personal and dependency exemptions	(x,xxx)
Taxable income	$xx,xxx
Tax on taxable income	$ x,xxx
Less: Tax credits (including Federal income tax	
withheld and other prepayments of Federal	
income taxes)	(xxx)
Tax due (or refund)....................................	$ xxx

Basic Standard Deduction Amounts

	Standard Deduction Amount	
Filing Status	2005	2006
Single	$ 5,000	$ 5,150
Married, filing jointly	10,000	10,300
Surviving spouse	10,000	10,300
Head of household	7,300	7,550
Married, filing separately	5,000	5,150

Amount of Each Additional Standard Deduction

Filing Status	2005	2006
Single	$1,250	$1,250
Married, filing jointly	1,000	1,000
Surviving spouse	1,000	1,000
Head of household	1,250	1,250
Married, filing separately	1,000	1,000

Personal and Dependency Exemption

2005	2006
$3,200	$3,300

West Federal Taxation

Individual Income Taxes

2007 EDITION

General Editors

William H. Hoffman, Jr.
J.D., Ph.D., CPA

James E. Smith
Ph.D., CPA

Eugene Willis
Ph.D., CPA

Contributing Authors

James H. Boyd
Ph.D., CPA
Arizona State University

D. Larry Crumbley
Ph.D., CPA
Louisiana State University

Steven C. Dilley
J.D., Ph.D., CPA
Michigan State University

William H. Hoffman, Jr.
J.D., Ph.D., CPA
University of Houston

David M. Maloney
Ph.D., CPA
University of Virginia

Gary A. McGill
Ph.D., CPA
University of Florida

William A. Raabe
Ph.D., CPA
Ohio State University

Boyd C. Randall
J.D., Ph.D.
Brigham Young University

W. Eugene Seago
J.D., Ph.D., CPA
Virginia Polytechnic
Institute and State University

James E. Smith
Ph.D., CPA
College of William and Mary

Eugene Willis
Ph.D., CPA
University of Illinois,
Urbana-Champaign

Australia · Brazil · Canada · Mexico · Singapore · Spain · United Kingdom · United States

THOMSON
★
SOUTH-WESTERN

West Federal Taxation: Individual Income Taxes, 2007 Edition
William H. Hoffman, Jr., James E. Smith, Eugene Willis

VP/Editorial Director
Jack W. Calhoun

Publisher
Rob Dewey

Acquisitions Editor
Daniel Jones

Senior Developmental Editor
Craig Avery

Marketing Manager
Chris McNamee

Senior Production Project Manager
Tim Bailey

Manager of Technology, Editorial
Vicky True

Technology Project Editor
Kelly Reid

Web Coordinator
Scott Cook

Manufacturing Coordinator
Doug Wilke

Art Director
Michelle Kunkler

Internal Designer
Diane Gliebe/Design Matters

Cover Designer
Craig Ramsdell

Cover Images
© Getty Images, Inc.

Production
LEAP Publishing Services, Inc.

Composition
Cadmus Professional Communications

Printer
Quebecor World
Versailles, KY

For more information about our products, contact us at:

Thomson Learning Academic Resource Center

1-800-423-0563

Professional Edition ISBN: 0-324-39960-X
Student Edition with CD ISBN: 0-324-39961-8
Loose Leaf Edition ISBN: 0-324-31383-7
Instructor's Edition ISBN: 0-324-37953-6

ISSN: 0272-0329
2007 Annual Edition

For permission to use material from this text or product, submit a request online at http://www.thomsonrights.com.

Thomson Higher Education
5191 Natorp Boulevard
Mason, OH 45040
USA

To the Student
The Leadership You Trust—The Innovation You Expect—The Service You Deserve

West Federal Taxation (WFT) is the most trusted and largest selling brand in college taxation. We are focused exclusively on providing the most useful, comprehensive, and up-to-date tax texts, online study aids, tax preparation tools, and print study guides to help you succeed in your tax courses and beyond.

More than just a textbook, the *WFT* series provides a dynamic learning experience in and out of the classroom. Built around the areas students have identified as the most important, our total integrated solution will offer you options in the way you learn.

Student Workflow

READ

Learning Objectives
Chapter Outlines
Chapter Introductions
Examples
Concept Summaries

TEST

Book Companion Web Site Quizzing
WebTutor ToolBox
ThomsonNOW™ for West Federal Taxation

STUDY

Key Terms
Study Guide
Discussion Questions
Book Companion Web Site
ThomsonNOW™ for West Federal Taxation

PRACTICE

Practice Sets
Research Problems
Cumulative Problems
Comprehensive Tax Return Problems
TurboTax
TaxBrain
Thomson RIA Checkpoint®
ThomsonNOW™ for West Federal Taxation

Today, the *WFT* series provides the most innovative solutions on the market. With integration of TurboTax, RIA Checkpoint®, TaxBrain®, and Deloitte Tax LLP, materials, *WFT* exposes you to the professional knowledge and tools you will use now and in your future career.

FREE RESOURCES AND STUDY TOOLS

- **Free TurboTax software** is included with every new copy of your text and provides access to tools for all your homework.
- **Free Online Access to TaxBrain® Tax Preparation Software,** which is used by more than 2,500 tax professionals every year. You can use TaxBrain® to work the income tax form problems in the text, developing your skills as you master course information. To access, log on to **http://www.taxbrain.com**. Take advantage of a 20% filing discount when filing your 2005 return with TaxBrain®—enter promotional code **SWL947**.
- **Exclusive Free Access to RIA's Checkpoint® Student Edition Online Tax Research Database.** Each *new* copy of the text contains an RIA Checkpoint® Student Edition access code, allowing you access to content from the research database most widely used by tax professionals. As you use Checkpoint® to complete problems within the text, you are building research skills and familiarity with the database—valuable preparation for your professional future.
- **Free Tutorial for RIA's Checkpoint®.** This self-paced tutorial from RIA orients you to Checkpoint® features and walks you through the application of RIA research strategies—giving you a running start on your class assignments that use Checkpoint®.
- **ThomsonNOW for** *West Federal Taxation.* This powerful, fully integrated online teaching and learning system provides you with the ultimate in flexibility, control, and results.
  - One place to find all of your assignments! Homework, quizzing, and self-assessment can all be accessed in one convenient location.
  - Improve your grades by accessing chapter materials through integrated eBooks and Personalized Learning Paths.
  - Save valuable time by accessing your assignments from any computer.
- **Book Companion Web Site – http://wft.swlearning.com**
  - **Tax newsletters** published twice a month written by the text authors.
  - **NewsEdge** pulls from full text articles from over 1,200 online news sources on a continuous basis and includes the following features: topic organization, personalization with the "Select My Topics/View My Topics" feature, 30-day archive, links to full online articles, and robust search functionality. NewsEdge also offers access to "Company News by Ticker," which includes stock detail, charts, and financials.
  - **Tax Tips for the Recent Graduate** introduces the college graduate to some common tax considerations that could be beneficial in reducing the dreaded "tax-bite."
  - **Tax Legislation Updates** is a resource available to instructors and their students that provides up-to-the-minute tax information and major changes to the tax law. Tax Legislation Updates are posted as needed on the *WFT* Web site.
  - **Download a Study Guide Chapter FREE before You Buy! Get one chapter of the print Study Guide free online.** The Study Guide contains **questions and problems with solutions for self-study**, as well as **chapter highlights** that point you to the right place in the text for further study. Order it from your bookstore (ISBN 0-324-39951-0) or buy it online at **http://wft.swlearning.com.**

For over 29 years, the *West Federal Taxation (WFT)* Series has guided more than 1.5 million students through the ever changing field of Federal taxation. With commitment to leadership, innovation, and service, we will continue to play a part in your success both now and in the future.

About the Editors

William H. Hoffman Jr. earned B.A. and J.D. degrees from the University of Michigan and M.B.A. and Ph.D. degrees from The University of Texas. He is a licensed CPA and attorney in Texas. His teaching experience includes: The University of Texas (1957-1961), Louisiana State University (1961-1967), and the University of Houston (1967-1999). Professor Hoffman has addressed many tax institutes and conferences and has published extensively in academic and professional journals. His articles appear in *The Journal of Taxation, The Tax Adviser, Taxes—The Tax Magazine, The Journal of Accountancy, The Accounting Review,* and *Taxation for Accountants.*

James E. Smith is the John S. Quinn Professor of Accounting at the College of William and Mary. He has been a member of the Accounting Faculty for over thirty years. He received his Ph.D. degree from the University of Arizona.

Professor Smith has served as a discussion leader for Continuing Professional Education programs for the AICPA, Federal Tax Workshops, and various state CPA societies. He has conducted programs in over 40 states for approximately 25,000 CPAs. He has been the recipient of the AICPAs' Outstanding Discussion Leader Award and the American Taxation Association/Arthur Andersen Teaching Innovation Award.

Other awards received by him include the Virginia Society of CPAs' Outstanding Accounting Educator Award and the James Madison University's Outstanding Accounting Educator Award. He was the President of the Administrators of Accounting Programs Group (AAPG) in 1991-1992. He was the faculty adviser for the William and Mary teams that received first place in the Andersen Tax Challenge in 1994, 1995, 1997, 2000, and 2001 and in the Deloitte & Touche Tax Case Study Competition in 2002, 2004, and 2005.

Eugene Willis is the Arthur Andersen Alumni Professor of Accountancy Emeritus at the University of Illinois (Urbana-Champaign). He joined the Illinois faculty in 1975 after receiving his Ph.D. from the University of Cincinnati. His articles have appeared in leading academic and professional journals, including *The Accounting Review, The Journal of the American Taxation Association, The Journal of Accountancy,* and *The Journal of Taxation.* Professor Willis is co-director of the National Tax Education Program, a continuing education program co-sponsored by the American Institute of CPAs and the University of Illinois.

CONTENTS

PART 1: INTRODUCTION AND BASIC TAX MODEL

PART 2: GROSS INCOME

PART 4: SPECIAL TAX COMPUTATION METHODS, PAYMENT PROCEDURES, AND TAX CREDITS

PART 5: PROPERTY TRANSACTIONS

PART 6: ACCOUNTING PERIODS, ACCOUNTING METHODS, AND DEFERRED COMPENSATION

PART 7: CORPORATIONS AND PARTNERSHIPS

APPENDIXES

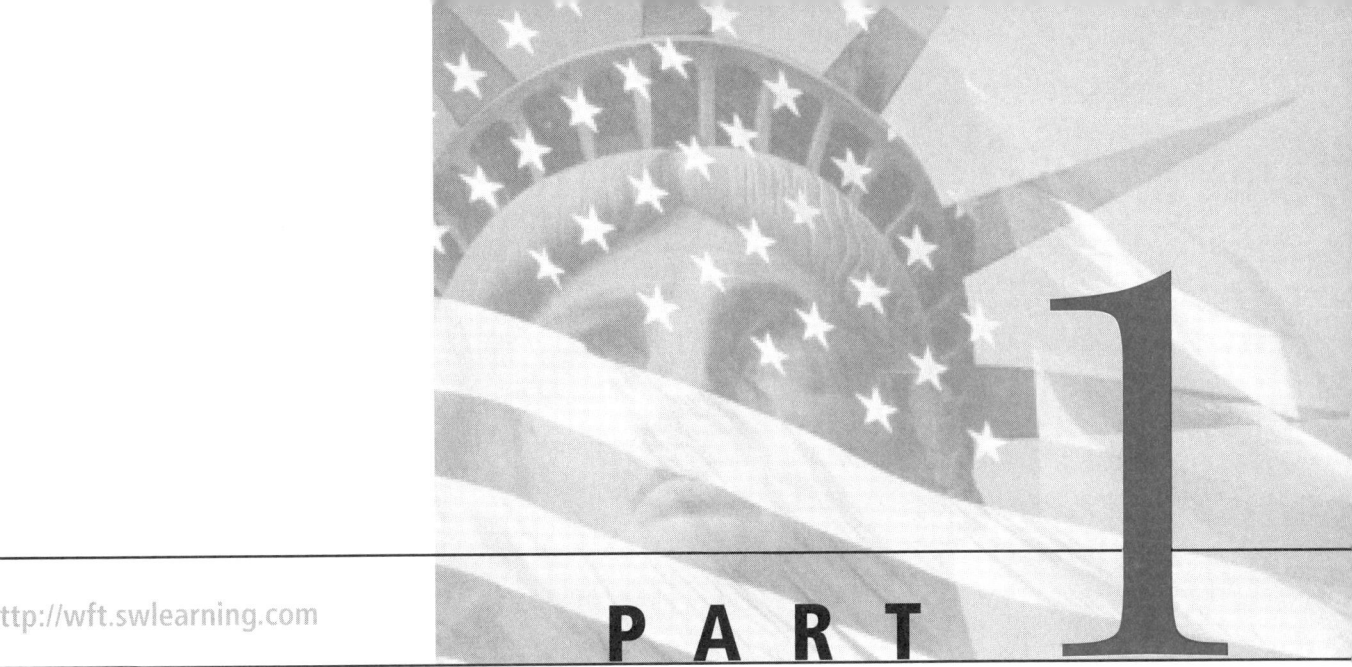

PART 1

Introduction and Basic Tax Model

Part I provides an introduction to taxation in the United States. Although the primary orientation of this text is income taxation, other types of taxes are also discussed briefly. The purposes of the Federal tax law are examined, and the legislative, administrative, and judicial sources of Federal tax law, including their application to the tax research process, are analyzed. Part I concludes with the introduction of the basic tax model for the individual taxpayer.

CHAPTER 1
An Introduction to Taxation and
Understanding the Federal Tax Law

CHAPTER 2
Working with the Tax Law

CHAPTER 3
Tax Determination; Personal and
Dependency Exemptions; An Overview
of Property Transactions

CHAPTER 1

An Introduction to Taxation and Understanding the Federal Tax Law

LEARNING OBJECTIVES

After completing Chapter 1, you should be able to:

LO.1

Understand some of the history and trends of the Federal income tax.

LO.2

Know some of the criteria for selecting a tax structure; understand the components of a tax structure.

LO.3

Identify the different taxes imposed in the United States at the Federal, state, and local levels.

LO.4

Understand the administration of the tax law, including the audit process utilized by the IRS.

LO.5

Appreciate some of the ethical guidelines involved in tax practice.

LO.6

Recognize the economic, social, equity, and political considerations that justify various aspects of the tax law.

LO.7

Describe the role played by the IRS and the courts in the evolution of the Federal tax system.

OUTLINE

The primary objective of this chapter is to provide an overview of the Federal tax system. Among the topics discussed are the following:

- The history of the Federal income tax in brief.
- The types of taxes imposed at the Federal, state, and local levels.
- Some highlights of tax law administration.
- Tax concepts that help explain the reasons for various tax provisions.
- The influence that the Internal Revenue Service (IRS) and the courts have had in the evolution of current tax law.

Why does a text devoted primarily to the Federal individual income tax discuss state and local taxes? A simple illustration shows the importance of non-Federal taxes.

EXAMPLE 1

Rick is employed by Flamingo Corporation in San Antonio, Texas, at a salary of $64,000. Rick's employer offers him a chance to transfer to its New York City office at a salary of $82,000. A quick computation indicates that the additional taxes (Federal, state, and local) involve approximately $12,000. ■

Although Rick must consider many nontax factors before he decides on a job change, he should also evaluate the tax climate. How do state and local taxes compare? For example, neither Texas nor San Antonio imposes an income tax, but New York State and New York City both do. Consequently, what appears to be an $18,000 pay increase is only $6,000 when the additional taxes of $12,000 are taken into account.

LO.1

Understand some of the history and trends of the Federal income tax.

History of U.S. Taxation

Early Periods

The concept of an income tax can hardly be regarded as a newcomer to the Western Hemisphere. An income tax was first enacted in 1634 by the English colonists in the Massachusetts Bay Colony, but the Federal government did not adopt this form of taxation until 1861. In fact, both the Federal Union and the Confederate

States of America used the income tax to raise funds to finance the Civil War. Although modest in its reach and characterized by broad exemptions and low rates, the income tax generated $376 million of revenue for the Federal government during the Civil War.

When the Civil War ended, the need for additional revenue disappeared, and the income tax was repealed. Once again the Federal government was able to finance its operations almost exclusively from customs duties (tariffs). It is interesting to note that the courts held that the Civil War income tax was not contrary to the Constitution.

When a new Federal income tax on individuals was enacted in 1894, its opponents were prepared and were able to successfully challenge its constitutionality. The U.S. Constitution provided that "No Capitation, or other direct, Tax shall be laid, unless in Proportion to the Census or Enumeration herein before directed to be taken." In *Pollock v. Farmers' Loan and Trust Co.*, the U.S. Supreme Court found that taxes on the income of real and personal property were the legal equivalent of a tax on the property involved and, therefore, required apportionment.[1]

A Federal corporate income tax, enacted by Congress in 1909, fared better in the judicial system. The U.S. Supreme Court found this tax to be constitutional because it was treated as an excise tax.[2] In essence, it was a tax on the right to do business in the corporate form. As such, it was likened to a form of the franchise tax.[3] The corporate form of doing business had been developed in the late nineteenth century and was an unfamiliar concept to the framers of the U.S. Constitution. Since a corporation is an entity created under law, jurisdictions possess the right to tax its creation and operation. Using this rationale, many states still impose franchise taxes on corporations.

The ratification of the Sixteenth Amendment to the U.S. Constitution in 1913 sanctioned both the Federal individual and corporate income taxes and, as a consequence, neutralized the continuing effect of the *Pollock* decision.

Revenue Acts

Following ratification of the Sixteenth Amendment, Congress enacted the Revenue Act of 1913. Under this Act, the first Form 1040 was due on March 1, 1914. The law allowed various deductions and personal exemptions of $3,000 for a single individual and $4,000 for married taxpayers. Rates ranged from a low of 2 percent to a high of 6 percent. The 6 percent rate applied only to taxable income in excess of $500,000![4]

Various revenue acts were passed between 1913 and 1939. In 1939, all of these revenue laws were codified into the Internal Revenue Code of 1939. In 1954, a similar codification of the revenue law took place. The current law is entitled the Internal Revenue Code of 1986, which largely carries over the provisions of the 1954 Code. To date, the Code has been amended several times since 1986. This matter is discussed further in Chapter 2 under Origin of the Internal Revenue Code.

Historical Trends

The income tax has proved to be a major source of revenue for the Federal government. Figure 1–1, which contains a breakdown of the major revenue sources,[5] demonstrates the importance of the income tax. *Estimated* income tax collections from individuals and corporations amount to 55 percent of the total receipts.

---

[1]3 AFTR 2602, 15 S.Ct. 912 (USSC, 1895). See Chapter 2 for an explanation of the citations of judicial decisions.

[2]*Flint v. Stone Tracy Co.*, 3 AFTR 2834, 31 S.Ct. 342 (USSC, 1911).

[3]See the discussion of state franchise taxes later in the chapter.

[4]This should be contrasted with the highest 2006 tax rate of 35%, which applies once taxable income exceeds $336,550.

[5]Budget of the United States Government for Fiscal Year 2006, Office of Management and Budget (Washington, D.C.: U.S. Government Printing Office, 2005).

FIGURE 1–1	Federal Budget Receipts—2006
Individual income taxes	44%
Corporation income taxes	11
Social insurance taxes and contributions	38
Excise taxes	3
Other	4
	100%

The need for revenues to finance the war effort during World War II converted the income tax into a *mass tax*. For example, in 1939, less than 6 percent of the U.S. population was subject to the Federal income tax. In 1945, over 74 percent of the population was subject to the Federal income tax.[6]

Certain changes in the income tax law are of particular significance in understanding the Federal income tax. In 1943, Congress passed the Current Tax Payment Act, which provided for the first pay-as-you-go tax system. A pay-as-you-go income tax system requires employers to withhold for taxes a specified portion of an employee's wages. Persons with income from other than wages must make quarterly payments to the IRS for estimated taxes due for the year.

One trend that has caused considerable concern is the increasing complexity of the Federal income tax laws. In the name of tax reform, Congress has added to this complexity by frequently changing the tax laws. Most recent legislation continues this trend. Increasingly, this complexity forces many taxpayers to seek the assistance of tax professionals. At this time, therefore, substantial support exists for tax law simplification.

LO.2

Know some of the criteria for selecting a tax structure; understand the components of a tax structure.

Criteria Used in the Selection of a Tax Structure

In the eighteenth century, Adam Smith identified the following *canons of taxation*, which are still considered when evaluating a particular tax structure:[7]

- *Equality.* Each taxpayer enjoys fair or equitable treatment by paying taxes in proportion to his or her income level. Ability to pay a tax is the measure of how equitably a tax is distributed among taxpayers.
- *Convenience.* Administrative simplicity has long been valued in formulating tax policy. If a tax is easily assessed and collected and its administrative costs are low, it should be favored. An advantage of the withholding (pay-as-you-go) system is its convenience for taxpayers.
- *Certainty.* A tax structure is *good* if the taxpayer can readily predict when, where, and how a tax will be levied. Individuals and businesses need to know the likely tax consequences of a particular type of transaction.
- *Economy.* A *good* tax system involves only nominal collection costs by the government and minimal compliance costs on the part of the taxpayer. Although the government's cost of collecting Federal taxes amounts to less than one-half of 1 percent of the revenue collected, the complexity of our current tax structure imposes substantial taxpayer compliance costs.

By these canons, the Federal income tax is a contentious product. *Equality* is present as long as one accepts ability to pay as an ingredient of this component.

[6]Richard Goode, *The Individual Income Tax* (Washington, D.C.: The Brookings Institution,1964), pp. 2–4.

[7]*The Wealth of Nations*, Book V, Chapter II, Part II (New York: Dutton, 1910).

TAX *in the News*	ADAM SMITH STOPPED TOO SOON

On July 2, 2001, the American Institute of Certified Public Accountants (AICPA) issued suggestions on Federal tax policy. Titled *Guiding Principles of Good Tax Policy: A Framework for Evaluating Tax Proposals*, the monograph sets forth 10 tax principles that are commonly used as indicators of desirable tax policy.

The first four principles are adapted from Adam Smith's *The Wealth of Nations*. The other six are summarized below:

- The tax system should be simple.
- The tax should be neutral in terms of its effect on business decisions.

- The tax system should not reduce economic growth and efficiency.
- The tax should be clear and readily understood so that taxpayers know about it and when it applies.
- The tax should be structured so as to minimize noncompliance.
- The tax system should enable the IRS to predict the amount and timing of revenue production.

Source: *Adapted from a Tax Policy Concept Statement issued by the Tax Division of the AICPA.*

Convenience exists due to a heavy reliance on pay-as-you-go procedures. *Certainty* probably generates the greatest controversy. In one sense, certainty is present since a mass of administrative and judicial guidelines exists to aid in interpreting the tax law. In another sense, however, certainty does not exist since many questions remain unanswered and frequent changes in the tax law by Congress lessen stability. *Economy* is present if only the collection procedure of the IRS is considered. Economy is not present, however, if one focuses instead on taxpayer compliance efforts and costs.

The Tax Structure

Tax Base

A tax base is the amount to which the tax rate is applied. In the case of the Federal income tax, the tax base is *taxable income*. As noted later in the chapter (Figure 1–2), taxable income is gross income reduced by certain deductions (both business and personal).

Tax Rates

Tax rates are applied to the tax base to determine a taxpayer's liability. The tax rates may be proportional or progressive. A tax is *proportional* if the rate of tax remains constant for any given income level.

EXAMPLE 2

Bill has $10,000 of taxable income and pays a tax of $3,000, or 30%. Bob's taxable income is $50,000, and the tax on this amount is $15,000, or 30%. If this constant rate is applied throughout the rate structure, the tax is proportional. ∎

A tax is *progressive* if a higher rate of tax applies as the tax base increases. The Federal income tax, Federal gift and estate taxes, and most state income tax rate structures are progressive.

EXAMPLE 3

If Cora, a married individual filing jointly, has taxable income of $10,000, her tax for 2006 is $1,000 for an average tax rate of 10%. If, however, Cora's taxable income is $50,000, her tax will be $6,745 for an average tax rate of 13.5%. The tax is progressive since higher rates are applied to greater amounts of taxable income. ∎

Incidence of Taxation

The degree to which various segments of society share the total tax burden is difficult to assess. Assumptions must be made concerning who absorbs the burden of paying the tax. For example, since dividend payments to shareholders are not deductible by a corporation and are generally taxable to shareholders, the same income is subject to a form of double taxation. Concern over double taxation is valid to the extent that corporations are *not* able to shift the corporate tax to the consumer through higher commodity prices. Many research studies have shown a high degree of shifting of the corporate income tax, converting it into a consumption tax that is borne by the ultimate purchasers of goods.

The progressiveness of the U.S. Federal income tax rate structure for individuals has varied over the years. As late as 1986, for example, there were 15 rates, ranging from 0 to 50 percent. These later were reduced to two rates of 15 and 28 percent. Currently, there are six rates ranging from 10 to 35 percent.

<table>
<tr><td>**LO.3**
Identify the different taxes imposed in the United States at the Federal, state, and local levels.</td></tr>
</table>

Major Types of Taxes

Property Taxes

Correctly referred to as **ad valorem taxes** because they are based on value, property taxes are a tax on wealth, or capital. In this regard, they have much in common with death taxes and gift taxes discussed later in the chapter. Although property taxes do not tax income, the income actually derived (or the potential for any income) may be relevant insofar as it affects the value of the property being taxed.

Property taxes fall into *two* categories: those imposed on realty and those imposed on personalty, or assets other than land and buildings. Both have added importance since they usually generate a deduction for Federal income tax purposes (see Chapter 10).

Ad Valorem Taxes on Realty. Property taxes on realty are used exclusively by states and their local political subdivisions, such as cities, counties, and school districts. They represent a major source of revenue for *local* governments, but their importance at the *state* level has waned over the past few years. Some states, for example, have imposed freezes on upward revaluations of residential housing.

How realty is defined can have an important bearing on which assets are subject to tax. This is especially true in jurisdictions that do not impose ad valorem taxes on personalty. Primarily a question of state property law, **realty** generally includes real estate and any capital improvements that are classified as fixtures. Simply stated, a *fixture* is something so permanently attached to the real estate that its removal will cause irreparable damage. A built-in bookcase might well be a fixture, whereas a movable bookcase would not be a fixture. Certain items such as electrical wiring and plumbing cease to be personalty when installed in a building and become realty.

The following are some of the characteristics of ad valorem taxes on realty:

- Property owned by the Federal government is exempt from tax. Similar immunity usually is extended to property owned by state and local governments and by certain charitable organizations.
- Some states provide for lower valuations on property dedicated to agricultural use or other special uses (e.g., wildlife sanctuaries).
- Some states partially exempt the homestead, or personal residence, portion of property from taxation. Additionally, modern homestead laws normally protect some or all of a personal residence (including a farm or ranch) from the actions of creditors pursuing claims against the owner.
- Lower taxes may apply to a residence owned by a taxpayer age 65 or older.

TAX *in the News*	A FEW PIGS AND CHICKENS MAY NOT BE ENOUGH

Mel Gibson, the director of *The Passion of the Christ*, applied for an agricultural use exemption for 17 acres of his 75.7-acre estate in Greenwich, Connecticut. The $17.7 million estate features a 28-room mansion, pool, tennis court, and two guesthouses. In addition, it also includes a barn where Gibson has kept sheep, donkeys, and some chickens. The town officials, however, found that the property was not being held for a bona fide productive farming activity and turned down Gibson's request for an agricultural use exemption. Securing the exemption would have saved Gibson $10,000 per year in ad valorem property taxes.

Source: *Associated Press, "Ol' Mel Gibson Didn't Have a Farm,"* Houston Chronicle, *January 17, 2005, p. A2.*

- When non-income-producing property (e.g., a personal residence) is converted to income-producing property (e.g., a rental house), typically the appraised value increases.
- Some jurisdictions extend immunity from tax for a specified period of time (a *tax holiday*) to new or relocated businesses. A tax holiday can backfire, however, and cause more harm than good. If it is too generous, it can damage the local infrastructure (e.g., less funding for public works and education).

Unlike the ad valorem tax on personalty (see below), the tax on realty is difficult to avoid. Since real estate is impossible to hide, a high degree of taxpayer compliance is not surprising. The only avoidance possibility that is generally available is associated with the assessed value of the property. For this reason, the assessed value of the property—particularly, a value that is reassessed upward—may be subject to controversy and litigation.

Four methods are currently in use for assessing the value of real estate:

1. Actual purchase or construction price.
2. Contemporaneous sales prices or construction costs of comparable properties.
3. Cost of reproducing a building, less allowance for depreciation and obsolescence from the time of actual construction.
4. Capitalization of income from rental property.

Because all of these methods suffer faults and lead to inequities, a combination of two or more is not uncommon. For example, when real estate values and construction costs are rising, the use of actual purchase or construction price (method 1) places the purchaser of a new home at a definite disadvantage compared with an owner who acquired similar property years before. As another illustration, if the capitalization of income (method 4) is used for property subject to rent controls (e.g., New York City), the property may be undervalued.

The history of the ad valorem tax on realty has been marked by inconsistent application due to a lack of competent tax administration and definitive guidelines for assessment procedures. In recent years, however, some significant improvements have occurred. Some jurisdictions, for example, have computerized their reassessment procedures so that they will have an immediate effect on all property located within the jurisdiction. Nevertheless, the property tax area continues to be controversial.

Ad Valorem Taxes on Personalty. **Personalty** can be defined as all assets that are not realty. It may be helpful to distinguish between the *classification* of an asset (realty or personalty) and the *use* to which it is put. Both realty and personalty can be either business use or personal use property. Examples include a residence (realty that is personal use), an office building (realty that is business use), surgical instruments (personalty that is business use), and regular wearing apparel (personalty that is personal use).[8]

Personalty can also be classified as tangible property or intangible property. For ad valorem tax purposes, intangible personalty includes stocks, bonds, and various other securities (e.g., bank shares).

The following generalizations may be made concerning the ad valorem taxes on personalty:

- Particularly with personalty devoted to personal use (e.g., jewelry, household furnishings), taxpayer compliance ranges from poor to zero. Some jurisdictions do not even attempt to enforce the tax on these items. For automobiles devoted to personal use, many jurisdictions have converted from value as the tax base to arbitrary license fees based on the weight of the vehicle. Some jurisdictions also consider the vehicle's age (e.g., automobiles six years or older are not subject to the ad valorem tax because they are presumed to have little, if any, value).
- For personalty devoted to business use (e.g., inventories, trucks, machinery, equipment), taxpayer compliance and enforcement procedures are measurably better.
- Which jurisdiction possesses the authority to tax movable personalty (e.g., railroad rolling stock) always has been and continues to be a troublesome issue.
- A few states levy an ad valorem tax on intangibles such as stocks and bonds. Taxpayer compliance may be negligible if the state lacks a means of verifying security transactions and ownership.

Transaction Taxes

Transaction taxes, which characteristically are imposed at the manufacturer's, wholesaler's, or retailer's level, cover a wide range of transfers. Like many other types of taxes (e.g., income taxes, death taxes, and gift taxes), transaction taxes usually are not within the exclusive province of any level of taxing authority (Federal, state, local government). As the description implies, these levies place a tax on transfers of property and normally are determined by multiplying the value involved by a percentage rate.

Federal Excise Taxes. Long one of the mainstays of the Federal tax system, Federal **excise taxes** had declined in relative importance until recently. In recent years, Congress substantially increased the Federal excise taxes on such items as tobacco products, fuel and gasoline sales, telephone usage, and air travel. Other Federal excise taxes include the following:

- Manufacturers' excise taxes on trucks, trailers, tires, firearms, sporting equipment, and coal and the gas guzzler tax on automobiles.[9]
- Alcohol taxes.
- Miscellaneous taxes (e.g., the tax on wagering).

The list of transactions covered, although seemingly impressive, has diminished over the years. At one time, for example, there was a Federal excise tax on admission to amusement facilities (e.g., theaters) and on the sale of such items as leather goods, jewelry, furs, and cosmetics.

When reviewing the list of both Federal and state excise taxes, one should recognize the possibility that the tax laws may be trying to influence social behavior.

---

[8]The distinction, important for ad valorem and for Federal income tax purposes, often becomes confused when personalty is referred to as "personal" property to distinguish it from "real" property. This designation does not give a complete picture of what is involved. The description "personal"

residence, however, is clearer, since a residence can be identified as being realty. What is meant, in this case, is realty that is personal use property.
[9]The gas guzzler tax is imposed on the manufacturers of automobiles and progresses in amount as the mileage ratings per gallon of gas decrease.

For example, the gas guzzler tax is intended as an incentive for the automobile companies to build fuel-efficient cars.

State and Local Excise Taxes. Many state and local excise taxes parallel the Federal version. Thus, all states tax the sale of gasoline, liquor, and tobacco products; however, unlike the Federal version, the rates vary significantly. For gasoline products, for example, compare the 31 cents per gallon imposed by the state of Washington with the 7.5 cents per gallon levied by the state of Georgia. For tobacco sales, contrast the 5 cents per pack of 20 cigarettes in effect in North Carolina with the $2.46 per pack applicable in the state of Rhode Island. Given the latter situation, is it surprising that the smuggling of cigarettes for resale elsewhere is so widespread?

Other excise taxes found at some state and local levels include those on admission to amusement facilities and on the sale of playing cards, oleomargarine products, and prepared foods. Most states impose a transaction tax on the transfer of property that requires the recording of documents (e.g., real estate sales).[10] Some extend the tax to the transfer of stocks and other securities.

Over the last few years, two types of excise taxes imposed at the local level have become increasingly popular: the hotel occupancy tax and the rental car "surcharge." Since they tax the visitor who cannot vote, they are a political windfall and are often used to finance special projects that generate civic pride (e.g., convention centers, state-of-the-art sports arenas). These levies can be significant, as demonstrated by Houston's hotel tax of 17 percent and Boston's car rental tax of 28.7 percent.

General Sales Taxes. The distinction between an excise tax and a general **sales tax** is easy to make. One is restricted to a particular transaction (e.g., the 18.4 cents per gallon Federal excise tax on the sale of gasoline), while the other covers a multitude of transactions (e.g., a 5 percent tax on *all* retail sales). In actual practice, however, the distinction is not always that clear. Some state statutes exempt certain transactions from the application of the general sales taxes (e.g., sales of food to be consumed off the premises, sales of certain medicines and drugs). Also, it is not uncommon to find that rates vary depending on the commodity involved. Many states, for example, allow preferential rates for the sale of agricultural equipment or apply different rates (either higher or lower than the general rate) to the sale of automobiles. With many of these special exceptions and classifications of rates, a general sales tax can take on the appearance of a collection of individual excise taxes.

A **use tax** is an ad valorem tax, usually at the same rate as the sales tax, on the use, consumption, or storage of tangible property. The purpose of a use tax is to prevent the avoidance of a sales tax. Every state that imposes a general sales tax levied on the consumer also has a use tax. Alaska, Delaware, Montana, New Hampshire, and Oregon have neither tax.

EXAMPLE 4

The jurisdiction where Susan resides imposes a 5% general sales tax, but the neighboring state has no sales or use tax at all. Susan purchases an automobile for $20,000 from a dealer located in the neighboring state. Has she saved $1,000 in sales taxes? The state use tax is designed to pick up the difference between the tax paid in another jurisdiction and what would have been paid in the state in which Susan resides. ∎

The use tax is difficult to enforce for many purchases and is therefore often avoided. In some cases, for example, it may be worthwhile to make purchases

---

[10]This type of tax has much in common with the stamp tax levied by Great Britain on the American colonies during the pre-Revolutionary War period in U.S. history.

through an out-of-state mail-order business. In spite of shipping costs, the avoidance of the local sales tax that otherwise might be incurred can lower the cost of such products as computer components. Some states are taking steps to curtail this loss of revenue. For items such as automobiles (refer to Example 4), the use tax probably will be collected when the purchaser registers the item in his or her home state.

ETHICAL Considerations   MAKING GOOD USE OF OUT-OF-STATE RELATIVES

Marcus, a resident of Texas, has found the ideal gift for his wife in celebration of their upcoming wedding anniversary—a $22,000 diamond tennis bracelet. However, Marcus is appalled at the prospect of paying the state and local sales tax of $1,815 (combined rate of 8.25 percent). He, therefore, asks his aunt, a resident of Montana, to purchase the bracelet. The jewelry store lists the aunt as the buyer and ships the bracelet to her. Prior to the anniversary, Marcus receives the bracelet from his aunt. Is Marcus able to save $1,815 on the present for his wife? What can go wrong?

Local general sales taxes, over and above those levied by the state, are common. It is not unusual to find taxpayers living in the same state but paying different general sales taxes due to the location of their residence.

EXAMPLE 5

Pete and Sam both live in a state that has a general sales tax of 3%. Sam, however, resides in a city that imposes an additional general sales tax of 2%. Even though Pete and Sam live in the same state, one is subject to a rate of 3%, while the other pays a tax of 5%. ∎

For various reasons, some jurisdictions will suspend the application of a general sales tax. New York City does so to stimulate shopping. Illinois has permanently suspended the tax on construction materials used to build power-generating plants. Texas does so annually on clothing right before the beginning of the school year. Such suspensions are similar to the tax holidays granted for ad valorem tax purposes. As state revenues have declined in recent years, many states have had misgivings about the advisability of scheduling further sales tax holidays. Turning off the spigot could be political suicide, however. These holidays are extremely popular with both merchants and shoppers, and their termination could cause severe voter backlash at the polls.

Severance Taxes. **Severance taxes** are an important source of revenue for many states. These transaction taxes are based on the notion that the state has an interest in its natural resources (e.g., oil, gas, iron ore, coal). Therefore, a tax is imposed when the natural resources are extracted.

Death Taxes

A **death tax** is a tax on the right to transfer property or to receive property upon the death of the owner. Consequently, a death tax falls into the category of an excise tax. If the death tax is imposed on the right to pass property at death, it is classified as an **estate tax**. If it taxes the right to receive property from a decedent, it is termed an **inheritance tax**. As is typical of other types of excise taxes, the value of the property transferred provides the base for determining the amount of the death tax.

The Federal government imposes only an estate tax. State governments, however, levy inheritance taxes, estate taxes, or both.

At the time of her death, Wilma lived in a state that imposes an inheritance tax but not an estate tax. Mary, one of Wilma's heirs, lives in the same state. Wilma's estate is subject to the Federal estate tax, and Mary is subject to the state inheritance tax. ■

EXAMPLE 6

The Federal Estate Tax. The Revenue Act of 1916 incorporated the estate tax into the tax law. Never designed to generate a large amount of revenue, the tax was originally intended to prevent large concentrations of wealth from being kept within a family for many generations. Whether this objective has been accomplished is debatable. Like the income tax, estate taxes can be reduced through various planning procedures.

The gross estate includes property the decedent owned at the time of death. It also includes property interests, such as life insurance proceeds paid to the estate or to a beneficiary other than the estate if the deceased-insured had any ownership rights in the policy. Quite simply, the gross estate represents property interests subject to Federal estate taxation.[11] All property included in the gross estate is valued as of the date of death or, if the alternate valuation date is elected, six months later.[12]

Deductions from the gross estate in arriving at the taxable estate include funeral and administration expenses, certain taxes, debts of the decedent, casualty losses[13] incurred during the administration of the estate, transfers to charitable organizations, and, in some cases, the marital deduction. The *marital deduction* is available for amounts actually passing to a surviving spouse (a widow or widower).

Once the taxable estate has been determined and certain taxable gifts have been added to it, the estate tax can be computed. From the amount derived from the appropriate tax rate schedules, various credits should be subtracted to arrive at the tax, if any, that is due.[14] Although many other credits are also available, probably the most significant is the *unified transfer tax credit*. The main reason for this credit is to eliminate or reduce the estate tax liability for modest estates. For 2006, the amount of the credit is $780,800. Based on the estate tax rates, the credit covers a tax base of $2 million.

EXAMPLE 7

Ned made no taxable gifts before his death in 2006. If Ned's taxable estate amounts to $2 million or less, no Federal estate tax is due because of the application of the unified transfer tax credit. Under the tax law, the estate tax on a taxable estate of $2 million is $780,800. ■

The Federal estate tax has often been criticized for imposing a hardship on small businesses and, in particular, on family farms. Many believe that the need to pay the estate tax on the death of a major owner often forces the heirs to dissolve and liquidate the family business. In the Tax Relief Reconciliation Act of 2001, Congress responded to this criticism and scheduled a phaseout of the Federal estate tax, to be accomplished over a 10-year period by increasing the amount of the credit at periodic intervals. Consequently, the Federal estate tax is due to be eliminated in 2010. For budgetary reasons, the Act included a "sunset" provision that reinstates the Federal estate tax (as it was prior to the phaseout) as of January 1, 2011. Although the Republicans in Congress have tried to enact legislation that would repeal the sunset provision, their efforts have not been successful. As it stands now, therefore, the Federal estate tax is scheduled to end and then begin again. Obviously, this is a situation that cannot last, as it makes meaningful estate planning impossible. (Sunset provisions are discussed further later in the chapter.)

---

[11]For further information on these matters, see *West Federal Taxation: Corporations, Partnerships, Estates, and Trusts.*

[12]See the discussion of the alternate valuation date in Chapter 14.

[13]For a definition of casualty losses, see the Glossary of Tax Terms in Appendix C.

[14]For tax purposes, it is always crucial to appreciate the difference between a deduction and a credit. A *credit* is a dollar-for-dollar reduction of tax liability.

A *deduction*, however, only benefits the taxpayer to the extent of his or her tax bracket. An estate in a 50% tax bracket, for example, would need $2 of deductions to prevent $1 of tax liability from developing. In contrast, $1 of credit neutralizes $1 of tax liability.

State Death Taxes. As noted earlier, states usually levy an inheritance tax, an estate tax, or both. The two forms of death taxes differ according to whether the tax is imposed on the heirs or on the estate.

Characteristically, an inheritance tax divides the heirs into classes based on their relationship to the decedent. The more closely related the heir, the lower the rates imposed and the greater the exemption allowed. Some states completely exempt from taxation amounts passing to a surviving spouse.

Gift Taxes

Like a death tax, a **gift tax** is an excise tax levied on the right to transfer property. In this case, however, the tax is imposed on transfers made during the owner's life and not at death. Also, a gift tax applies only to transfers that are not supported by full and adequate consideration.

EXAMPLE 8

Carl sells property worth $20,000 to his daughter for $1,000. Although property worth $20,000 has been transferred, only $19,000 represents a gift, since this is the portion not supported by full and adequate consideration. ■

The Federal Gift Tax. First enacted in 1932, the Federal gift tax was intended to complement the estate tax. If lifetime transfers by gift were not taxed, it would be possible to avoid the estate tax and escape taxation entirely.

Only taxable gifts are subject to the gift tax. For this purpose, a taxable gift is measured by the fair market value of the property on the date of transfer less the *annual exclusion per donee* and, in some cases, less the *marital deduction,* which allows tax-free transfers between spouses. Each donor is allowed an annual exclusion of $12,000 in 2006 ($11,000 in 2005) for each donee.[15]

EXAMPLE 9

On December 31, 2005, Louise (a widow) gives $11,000 to each of her four married children, their spouses, and her eight grandchildren. On January 2, 2006, she repeats the procedure, giving $12,000 to each recipient. Due to the annual exclusion, Louise has not made a taxable gift, although she transferred $176,000 [$11,000 (annual exclusion) × 16 (donees)] in 2005 and $192,000 [$12,000 (annual exclusion) × 16 (donees)] in 2006, for a total of $368,000 ($176,000 + $192,000). ■

A special election applicable to married persons allows one-half of the gift made by the donor-spouse to be treated as being made by the nondonor-spouse (*gift splitting*). This election to split the gifts of property made to third persons has the effect of increasing the number of annual exclusions available. Also, it allows the use of the nondonor-spouse's unified transfer tax credit and may lower the tax brackets that will apply.

The gift tax rate schedule is the same as that applicable to the estate tax. The schedule is commonly referred to as the *unified transfer tax schedule.*

The Federal gift tax is *cumulative* in effect. What this means is that the tax base for current taxable gifts includes past taxable gifts. Although a credit is allowed for prior gift taxes, the result of adding past taxable gifts to current taxable gifts is to force the donor into a higher tax bracket.[16] Like the Federal estate tax rates, the Federal gift tax rates are progressive (see Example 3 earlier in this chapter).

---

[15]The purpose of the annual exclusion is to avoid the need to report and pay a tax on *modest* gifts. Without the exclusion, the IRS could face a real problem of taxpayer noncompliance. The annual exclusion is indexed as the level of inflation warrants. The exclusion was $3,000 through 1981, $10,000 from 1982 to 2000, and $11,000 from 2001 to 2005.

[16]For further information on the Federal gift tax, see *West Federal Taxation: Corporations, Partnerships, Estates, and Trusts.*

The unified transfer tax credit is available for all taxable gifts; the amount of this credit for 2006 is $345,800. There is, however, only one unified transfer tax credit, and it applies both to taxable gifts and to the Federal estate tax. In a manner of speaking, therefore, once the unified transfer tax credit has been exhausted for Federal gift tax purposes, it is no longer available to insulate a decedent from the Federal estate tax, except to the extent of the excess of the credit amount for estate tax purposes over that for gift tax purposes.

As noted above, the Tax Relief Reconciliation Act of 2001 proposes to phase out the Federal estate tax. The reason for the elimination of the estate tax does not apply to the gift tax. Unlike death, which is involuntary, the making of a gift is a voluntary parting of ownership. Thus, the ownership of a business can be transferred gradually without incurring drastic and immediate tax consequences. As a result, the Federal gift tax is to be retained with the unified transfer tax credit frozen at $345,800 (which covers a taxable gift of $1 million).

Even though a larger unified transfer tax credit is available for transfers by death ($780,800 for 2006), lifetime gifts continue to be attractive. If income-producing property is involved (e.g., marketable securities, rental real estate), a gift may reduce income taxes for the family unit by shifting income to lower-bracket donees. If the gift involves property that is expected to appreciate in value (e.g., life insurance policies, real estate, artworks), future increases in value will be assigned to the donee and will not be included in the donor's estate. Also important is that due to the annual exclusion ($12,000 per donee in 2006), some of the gift is not subject to any gift tax. Recall that the gift-splitting election enables married donors to double up on the annual exclusion.

State Gift Taxes. The states currently imposing a state gift tax are Connecticut, Louisiana, North Carolina, and Tennessee. Most of the laws provide for lifetime exemptions and annual exclusions. Like the Federal gift tax, the state taxes are cumulative in effect. But unlike the Federal version, the amount of tax depends on the relationship between the donor and the donee. Like state inheritance taxes, larger exemptions and lower rates apply when the donor and donee are closely related to each other.

Income Taxes

Income taxes are levied by the Federal government, most states, and some local governments. The trend in recent years has been to place greater reliance on this method of taxation. This trend is not consistent with what is happening in other countries, and in this sense, our system of taxation is somewhat different.

Income taxes generally are imposed on individuals, corporations, and certain fiduciaries (estates and trusts). Most jurisdictions attempt to assure the collection of income taxes by requiring pay-as-you-go procedures, including withholding requirements for employees and estimated tax prepayments for all taxpayers.

Federal Income Taxes. Chapters 3 through 19 deal with the application of the Federal income tax to individuals. The procedure for determining the Federal income tax applicable to individuals is summarized in Figure 1–2.

The application of the Federal corporate income tax does not require the computation of adjusted gross income (AGI) and does not provide for the standard deduction and personal and dependency exemptions. All allowable deductions of a corporation fall into the business-expense category. In effect, therefore, the taxable income of a corporation is the difference between gross income (net of exclusions) and deductions.

Chapter 20 summarizes the rules relating to corporations. For an in-depth treatment of the Federal income tax as it affects corporations, estates, and trusts, see *West Federal Taxation: Corporations, Partnerships, Estates, and Trusts*, 2007 Edition, Chapters 2 through 9, 12, and 19.

FIGURE 1–2	Formula for Federal Income Tax on Individuals
Income (broadly conceived)	$ xx,xxx
Less: Exclusions (income that is not subject to tax)	(x,xxx)
Gross income (income that is subject to tax)	$ xx,xxx
Less: Certain business deductions (usually referred to as deductions *for* adjusted gross income)	(x,xxx)
Adjusted gross income	$ xx,xxx
Less: The greater of certain personal and employee deductions (usually referred to as *itemized deductions*)	
or	
The standard deduction (including any additional standard deduction)	(x,xxx)
and	
Less: Personal and dependency exemptions	(x,xxx)
Taxable income	$ xx,xxx
Tax on taxable income (see the Tax Tables and Tax Rate Schedules in Appendix A)	$ x,xxx
Less: Tax credits (including Federal income tax withheld and other prepayments of Federal income taxes)	(xxx)
Tax due (or refund)	$ xxx

State Income Taxes. All but the following states impose an income tax on individuals: Alaska, Florida, Nevada, South Dakota, Texas, Washington, and Wyoming.

Some of the characteristics of state income taxes are summarized as follows:

- With few exceptions, all states require some form of withholding procedures.
- Most states use as the tax base the income determination made for Federal income tax purposes.
- A minority of states go even further and impose a flat rate upon AGI as computed for Federal income tax purposes. Several apply a rate to the Federal income tax liability. This is often referred to as the piggyback approach to state income taxation. Although the term *piggyback* does not lend itself to precise definition, in this context, it means making use, for state income tax purposes, of what was done for Federal income tax purposes.
- Some states are somewhat eroding the piggyback approach by "decoupling" from selected recent tax reductions passed by Congress. Many, for example, are not accepting for state income tax purposes the adjustments allowed by the Jobs and Growth Tax Relief Reconciliation Act (JGTRRA) of 2003. The purpose of the decoupling is to retain state revenue that would otherwise be lost. In other words, the state cannot afford to allow its taxpayers the same deduction for state purposes as is allowed for Federal purposes.
- Because of the tie-ins to the Federal return, a state may be notified of any changes made by the IRS upon audit of a Federal return. In recent years, the exchange of information between the IRS and state taxing authorities has increased.
- Most states allow a deduction for personal and dependency exemptions. Some states substitute a tax credit for a deduction.
- A diminishing minority of states allow a deduction for Federal income taxes.
- Most states allow their residents some form of tax credit for income taxes paid to other states.
- The objective of most states is to tax the income of residents and those who regularly conduct business within the state (e.g., nonresidents who commute

---

TAX *in the News*	**USING THE INCOME TAX RETURN AS A "USE TAX" REMINDER**

Many consumers do not pay state and local sales tax on out-of-state purchases made online or through mail-order catalogs. In such cases, the consumer has an obligation to pay the taxing authority an equivalent use tax. Because the use tax often is not paid, either inadvertently or deliberately, some states are resorting to less subtle enforcement measures.

New York has added a separate line on its income tax return for the reporting of use taxes. The line cannot be left blank—either an amount *or* a notation of "zero" must be entered. As to the amount option, the taxpayer should list the actual amount due *or* an estimate based on a table. The table is prepared by the state and reflects the average Internet purchases for various income levels.

---

to work). These states also purport to tax the income of nonresidents who earn income within the state on an itinerant basis. In practice, however, the only visitors actually taxed are highly paid athletes and entertainers. This so-called *jock tax* has been much criticized as being discriminatory due to its selective imposition.

- The due date for filing generally is the same as for the Federal income tax (the fifteenth day of the fourth month following the close of the tax year).
- Some states have occasionally instituted amnesty programs that allow taxpayers to pay back taxes (and interest) on unreported income with no (or reduced) penalty.

Nearly all states have an income tax applicable to corporations. It is difficult to determine those that do not because a state franchise tax sometimes is based in part on the income earned by the corporation.[17]

Local Income Taxes. Cities imposing an income tax include, but are not limited to, Baltimore, Cincinnati, Cleveland, Detroit, Kansas City (Mo.), New York, Philadelphia, and St. Louis. The application of a city income tax is not limited to local residents.

Employment Taxes

Classification as an employee usually leads to the imposition of **employment taxes** and to the requirement that the employer withhold specified amounts for income taxes. The rules governing the withholding for income taxes are discussed in Chapter 13. The material that follows concentrates on the two major employment taxes: FICA (Federal Insurance Contributions Act—commonly referred to as the Social Security tax) and FUTA (Federal Unemployment Tax Act). Both taxes can be justified by social and public welfare considerations: FICA offers some measure of retirement security, and FUTA provides a modest source of income in the event of loss of employment.

Employment taxes come into play only if two conditions are satisfied. First, is the individual involved an *employee* (as opposed to *self-employed*)? The differences between an employee and a self-employed person are discussed in Chapter 9.[18] Second, if the individual involved is an employee, is he or she covered under FICA or FUTA or both? The coverage of both of these taxes is summarized in Exhibit 13–2 in Chapter 13.[19]

---

[17]See the discussion of franchise taxes later in the chapter.

[18]See also Circular E, *Employer's Tax Guide*, issued by the IRS as Publication 15.

[19]Chapter 13 includes coverage on the self-employment tax (the Social Security and Medicare taxes for self-employed persons).

FICA Taxes. The FICA tax rates and wage base have increased steadily over the years. It is difficult to imagine that the initial rate in 1937 was only 1 percent of the first $3,000 of covered wages. Thus, the maximum tax due was only $30!

Currently, the FICA tax has two components: Social Security tax (old age, survivors, and disability insurance) *and* Medicare tax (hospital insurance). The Social Security tax rate is 6.2 percent for 2005 and 2006, and the Medicare tax rate is 1.45 percent for these years. The base amount for Social Security is $90,000 for 2005 and $94,200 for 2006. There is no limit on the base amount for the Medicare tax. The employer must match the employee's portion for both the Social Security tax and the Medicare tax.

A spouse employed by another spouse is subject to FICA. However, children under the age of 18 who are employed in a parent's trade or business are exempted.

FUTA Taxes. The purpose of the FUTA tax is to provide funds that the states can use to administer unemployment benefits. This leads to the somewhat unusual situation of one tax being handled by both Federal and state governments. The end result of such joint administration is to compel the employer to observe a double set of rules. Thus, state and Federal returns must be filed and payments made to both governmental units.

In 2006, FUTA applies at a rate of 6.2 percent on the first $7,000 of covered wages paid during the year to each employee. The Federal government allows a credit for FUTA paid (or allowed under a merit rating system) to the state. The credit cannot exceed 5.4 percent of the covered wages. Thus, the amount required to be paid to the IRS could be as low as 0.8 percent (6.2% − 5.4%).

States follow a policy of reducing the unemployment tax on employers who experience stable employment. Thus, an employer with little or no employee turnover might find that the state rate drops to as low as 0.1 percent or, in some states, even to zero. The reason for the merit rating credit is that the state has to pay fewer unemployment benefits when employment is steady.

FUTA differs from FICA in the sense that the incidence of taxation falls entirely upon the employer. A few states, however, levy a special tax on employees to provide either disability benefits or supplemental unemployment compensation, or both.

Other U.S. Taxes

To complete the overview of the U.S. tax system, some missing links need to be covered that do not fit into the classifications discussed elsewhere in this chapter.

Federal Customs Duties. One tax that has not yet been mentioned is the tariff on certain imported goods.[20] Generally referred to as customs duties or levies, this tax, together with selective excise taxes, provided most of the revenues needed by the Federal government during the nineteenth century. In view of present times, it is remarkable to note that tariffs and excise taxes alone paid off the national debt in 1835 and enabled the U.S. Treasury to pay a surplus of $28 million to the states.

In recent years, tariffs have served the nation more as an instrument for carrying out protectionist policies than as a means of generating revenue. Thus, a particular U.S. industry might be saved from economic disaster, so the argument goes, by imposing customs duties on the importation of foreign goods that can be sold at lower prices. Protectionists contend that the tariff thereby neutralizes the competitive edge held by the producer of the foreign goods.[21]

---

[20]Less-developed countries that rely principally on one or more major commodities (e.g., oil, coffee) are prone to favor *export* duties as well.

[21]The North American Free Trade Agreement (NAFTA), enacted in 1993, substantially reduced the tariffs on trade between Canada, Mexico, and the United States. The General Agreement on Tariffs and Trade (GATT) legislation enacted in 1994 also reduced tariffs on selected commodities among 124 signatory nations.

Protectionist policies seem more appropriate for less-developed countries whose industrial capacity has not yet matured. In a world where a developed country should have everything to gain by encouraging international free trade, such policies may be of dubious value. History shows that tariffs often lead to retaliatory action on the part of the nation or nations affected.

Miscellaneous State and Local Taxes. Most states impose a franchise tax on corporations. Basically, a **franchise tax** is levied on the right to do business in the state. The base used for the determination of the tax varies from state to state. Although corporate income considerations may come into play, this tax most often is based on the capitalization of the corporation (either with or without certain long-term indebtedness).

Closely akin to the franchise tax are **occupational taxes** applicable to various trades or businesses, such as a liquor store license, a taxicab permit, or a fee to practice a profession such as law, medicine, or accounting. Most of these are not significant revenue producers and fall more into the category of licenses than taxes. The revenue derived is used to defray the cost incurred by the jurisdiction in regulating the business or profession in the interest of the public good.

Proposed U.S. Taxes

Considerable dissatisfaction with the U.S. Federal income tax has led to several recent proposals that, to say the least, are rather drastic in nature. One proposal would retain the income tax but with substantial change. Two other proposals would replace the Federal income tax with an entirely different system of taxation.

The Flat Tax. Former Representative Dick Armey (R–Tex.) once proposed a **flat tax** that would replace the current graduated income tax with one rate, 17 percent. Large personal exemptions (e.g., approximately $30,000 for a family of four) would allow many low- and middle-income taxpayers to pay no tax. All other deductions would be eliminated, and no tax would be imposed on income from investments.

Various other versions of the flat tax have been suggested that would retain selected deductions (e.g., interest on home mortgages and charitable contributions) and not exclude all investment income from taxation.

The major advantage of the flat tax is its simplicity. Everyone agrees that the current Federal income tax is unbelievably complex. Consequently, compliance costs are disproportionately high. For this reason, among others, Steve Forbes, a former candidate for the Republican presidential nomination and editor of *Forbes* magazine, has been a major proponent of the flat tax approach.

Political considerations are a major obstacle to the enactment of a flat tax in its pure form (i.e., as proposed by Representative Armey). Special interest groups, such as charitable organizations and mortgage companies, are not apt to be complacent over the elimination of a tax deduction that benefits their industry. In addition, there is uncertainty as to the economic effects of the tax.

It is interesting to note that Russia's attempt at a progressive income tax was quite disastrous. Not only did high rates drive capital out of the country but also failure to report income was rampant. In early 2000, the income tax was repealed and replaced with a 13 percent flat tax. To date, the flat tax has worked quite well. Several Baltic states (Estonia, Latvia, and Slovakia) have followed Russia's example, and Poland and the Czech Republic are considering the adoption of a flat tax.

Value Added Tax. The **value added tax (VAT)** is one of two proposals that would replace the Federal income tax. Under the VAT, a business would pay the tax (approximately 17 percent) on all of the materials and services required to manufacture its product. In effect, the VAT taxes the increment in value as goods move through production and manufacturing stages to the marketplace. Moreover, the

VAT paid by the producer will be reflected in the selling price of the goods. Thus, the VAT is a tax on consumption.

The United States is the only country in the OECD (Organization for Economic Cooperation and Development) that does not have a VAT. Approximately 136 countries around the world use a VAT, ranging from 5 percent in Japan to 25 percent in Denmark. Instead, the United States relies heavily on income taxes.

Sales Tax. A national sales tax is favored by former Representative Bill Archer (R–Tex.), who was the long-time chairman of the House Ways and Means Committee. This tax differs from a VAT in that it would be collected on the final sale of goods and services. Consequently, it is collected from the consumer and not from businesses that add value to the product. Like the VAT, the national sales tax is intended to replace the Federal income tax.

The current proposal for a national sales tax, called the "Fair Tax," is sponsored by former House Majority Leader Tom DeLay (R–Tex.). It would tax all purchases, including food and medicine, at approximately 23 percent. Exempt items include business expenses, used goods, and the costs of education.

Critics contend that both forms of consumption taxes, a VAT and a national sales tax, are regressive. They impose more of a burden on low-income taxpayers who must spend larger proportions of their incomes on essential purchases. The proposals would attempt to remedy this inequity by granting some sort of credit, rebate, or exemption to low-income taxpayers.

In terms of taxpayer compliance, a value added tax is preferable to a national sales tax. Without significant collection efforts, a national sales tax could easily be circumvented by resorting to a barter system of doing business.

Tax Administration

LO.4

Understand the administration of the tax law, including the audit process utilized by the IRS.

Internal Revenue Service

The responsibility for administering the Federal tax laws rests with the Treasury Department. Administratively, the IRS is part of the Department of the Treasury and is responsible for enforcing the tax laws. The Commissioner of Internal Revenue is appointed by the President and is responsible for establishing policy and supervising the activities of the entire IRS organization.

The Audit Process

Selection of Returns for Audit. Due to budgetary limitations, only a small minority of tax returns are audited. For the fiscal year ended September 30, 2004, the IRS audited only 0.78 percent of all individual income tax returns (about one in every 129 returns filed). Nevertheless, the number of individual income tax returns being audited has increased significantly over the past four years.

The IRS utilizes mathematical formulas and statistical sampling techniques to select tax returns that are most likely to contain errors and to yield substantial amounts of additional tax revenues upon audit. The mathematical formula yields what is called a Discriminant Information Function (DIF) score. It is the DIF score given to a particular return that may lead to its selection for audit.

To update the DIF components, the IRS selects a cross section of returns, which are subject to various degrees of inspection (i.e., information return verification, correspondence, and face-to-face audits with filers). The results of these audits highlight areas of taxpayer noncompliance and enable the IRS to use its auditors more productively. In recent years, IRS audits have resulted in an increasing number of "no change" results (see below). This indicates that the IRS is not always choosing the right returns to audit (i.e., the ones with errors).

Though the IRS does not openly disclose all of its audit selection techniques, the following observations may be made concerning the probability of selection for audit:

- Certain groups of taxpayers are subject to audit much more frequently than others. These groups include individuals with large amounts of gross income, self-employed individuals with substantial business income and deductions, and taxpayers with prior tax deficiencies. Also vulnerable are cash businesses (e.g., cafés and small service businesses) where the potential for tax avoidance is high.

E X A M P L E   10

Jack owns and operates a liquor store on a cash-and-carry basis. Since all of Jack's sales are for cash, he might well be a prime candidate for an audit by the IRS. Cash transactions are easier to conceal than those made on credit. ■

- If information returns (e.g., Form 1099, Form W–2) are not in substantial agreement with reported income, an audit can be anticipated.
- If an individual's itemized deductions are in excess of norms established for various income levels, the probability of an audit is increased.
- Filing of a refund claim by the taxpayer may prompt an audit of the return.
- Information obtained from other sources (e.g., informants, news items) may lead to an audit. Recently, for example, the IRS advised its agents by Internet to be on the alert for newspaper accounts of large civil court judgments. The advice was based on the assumption that many successful plaintiffs were not reporting as income the punitive damages portion of awards, which is taxable.

The tax law permits the IRS to pay rewards to persons who provide information that leads to the detection and punishment of those who violate the tax laws. The rewards may not exceed 15 percent of the taxes, fines, and penalties recovered as a result of such information.

E X A M P L E   11

After 15 years of service, Rita is discharged by her employer, Dr. Smith. Shortly thereafter, the IRS receives an anonymous letter stating that Dr. Smith keeps two separate sets of books, one of which substantially understates his cash receipts. ■

E X A M P L E   12

During a divorce proceeding, it is revealed that Leo, a public official, kept large amounts of cash in a shoe box at home. This information is widely disseminated by the news media and comes to the attention of the IRS. Needless to say, the IRS would be interested in knowing whether these funds originated from a taxable source and, if so, whether they were reported on Leo's income tax returns. ■

Types of Audits. Once a return is selected for audit, the taxpayer is notified. If the issue involved is minor, the matter often can be resolved simply by correspondence (a **correspondence audit**) between the IRS and the taxpayer.

E X A M P L E   13

During 2004, Janet received dividend income from Green Corporation. In early 2005, Green Corporation reported the payment on Form 1099–DIV (an information return for reporting dividend payments), the original being sent to the IRS and a copy to Janet. When preparing her income tax return for 2004, Janet apparently overlooked this particular Form 1099–DIV and failed to include the dividend on Schedule B, Interest and Dividend Income, of Form 1040. In 2006, the IRS sends a notice to Janet calling her attention to the omission and requesting a remittance for additional tax, interest, and penalty. Janet promptly mails a check to the IRS for the requested amount, and the matter is closed. ■

Other examinations are generally classified as either office audits or field audits. An **office audit** usually is restricted in scope and is conducted in the facilities of the IRS. In contrast, a **field audit** involves an examination of numerous items reported on the return and is conducted on the premises of the taxpayer or the taxpayer's representative.

Upon the conclusion of the audit, the examining agent issues a Revenue Agent's Report (RAR) that summarizes the findings. The RAR will result in a refund (the tax was overpaid), a deficiency (the tax was underpaid), or a *no change* (the tax was correct) finding. If, during the course of an audit, a special agent accompanies (or takes over from) the regular auditor, this means the IRS suspects fraud. If the matter has progressed to an investigation for fraud, the taxpayer should retain competent counsel.

Settlement Procedures. If an audit results in an assessment of additional tax and no settlement is reached with the IRS agent, the taxpayer may attempt to negotiate a settlement with the IRS. If an appeal is desired, an appropriate request must be made to the Appeals Division of the IRS. The Appeals Division is authorized to settle all disputes based on the *hazard of litigation* (the probability of favorable resolution of the disputed issue or issues if litigated). In some cases, a taxpayer may be able to obtain a percentage settlement or a favorable settlement of one or more disputed issues.

If a satisfactory settlement is not reached within the administrative appeal process, the taxpayer may wish to litigate the case in the Tax Court, a Federal District Court, or the Court of Federal Claims. However, litigation is recommended only as a last resort because of the legal costs involved and the uncertainty of the final outcome. Tax litigation considerations are discussed more fully in Chapter 2.

Statute of Limitations

A **statute of limitations** is a provision in the law that offers a party a defense against a suit brought by another party after the expiration of a specified period of time. The purpose of a statute of limitations is to preclude parties from prosecuting stale claims. The passage of time makes the defense of such claims difficult since witnesses may no longer be available or evidence may have been lost or destroyed. Found at the state and Federal levels, such statutes cover a multitude of suits, both civil and criminal.

For our purposes, the relevant statutes deal with the Federal income tax. The two categories involved cover both the period of limitations applicable to the assessment of additional tax deficiencies by the IRS and the period that deals with claims for refunds by taxpayers.

Assessment by the IRS. Under the general rule, the IRS may assess an additional tax liability against a taxpayer within *three years* of the filing of the income tax return. If the return is filed early, the three-year period begins to run from the due date of the return (usually April 15 for a calendar year individual taxpayer). If the taxpayer files the return late (i.e., beyond the due date), the three-year period begins to run on the date filed.

If a taxpayer omits an amount of gross income in excess of 25 percent of the gross income reported on the return, the statute of limitations is increased to six years.

EXAMPLE 14	For 2001, Mark, a calendar year taxpayer, reported gross income of $400,000 on a timely filed income tax return. If Mark omitted more than $100,000 (25% × $400,000), the six-year statute of limitations would apply to the 2001 tax year. ∎

The six-year provision on assessments by the IRS applies only to the omission of income and does not cover other factors that might lead to an understatement of tax liability, such as overstatement of deductions and credits.

There is *no* statute of limitations on assessments of tax if *no return* is filed or if a *fraudulent* return is filed.

Limitations on Refunds. If a taxpayer believes that an overpayment of Federal income tax was made, a claim for refund should be filed with the IRS. A *claim for refund*, therefore, is a request to the IRS that it return to the taxpayer the excessive income taxes paid.[22]

A claim for refund generally must be filed within *three years* from the date the return was filed *or* within *two years* from the date the tax was paid, whichever is later. Income tax returns that are filed early are deemed to have been filed on the date the return was due.

Interest and Penalties

Interest rates are determined quarterly by the IRS based on the existing Federal short-term rate. Currently, the rates for tax refunds (overpayments) for individual taxpayers are the same as those applicable to assessments (underpayments). For the first quarter (January 1–March 31) of 2006, the rates are 7 percent for refunds and assessments.[23]

For assessments of additional taxes, the interest begins running on the unextended due date of the return. With refunds, however, no interest is allowed if the overpayment is refunded to the taxpayer within 45 days of the date the return is filed. For this purpose, returns filed early are deemed to have been filed on the due date.

In addition to interest, the tax law provides various penalties for lack of compliance by taxpayers. Some of these penalties are summarized as follows:

- For a *failure to file* a tax return by the due date (including extension—see Chapter 3), a penalty of 5 percent per month up to a maximum of 25 percent is imposed on the amount of tax shown as due on the return. Any fraction of a month counts as a full month.
- A penalty for a *failure to pay* the tax due as shown on the return is imposed in the amount of 0.5 percent per month up to a maximum of 25 percent. Again, any fraction of a month counts as a full month. During any month in which both the failure to file penalty and the failure to pay penalty apply, the failure to file penalty is reduced by the amount of the failure to pay penalty.

EXAMPLE 15

Adam files his tax return 18 days after the due date of the return. Along with the return, he remits a check for $1,000, which is the balance of the tax he owed. Disregarding the interest element, Adam's total penalties are as follows:

[22]Generally, an individual filing a claim for refund should use Form 1040X.
[23]The rates applicable after March 31, 2006, were not available when this text went to press.

Failure to pay penalty (0.5% × $1,000)		$ 5
Plus:		
Failure to file penalty (5% × $1,000)	$50	
Less failure to pay penalty for the same period	(5)	
Failure to file penalty		45
Total penalties		$50

Note that the penalties for one full month are imposed even though Adam was delinquent by only 18 days. Unlike the method used to compute interest, any part of a month is treated as a whole month. ■

- A *negligence* penalty of 20 percent is imposed if any of the underpayment was for intentional disregard of rules and regulations without intent to defraud. The penalty applies to just that portion attributable to the negligence.

EXAMPLE 16

Cindy underpaid her taxes for 2005 in the amount of $20,000, of which $15,000 is attributable to negligence. Cindy's negligence penalty is $3,000 (20% × $15,000). ■

- Various fraud penalties may be imposed. *Fraud* is a deliberate action on the part of the taxpayer evidenced by deceit, misrepresentation, concealment, etc. For possible fraud situations, refer to Examples 11 and 12.

Tax Practice

The area of tax practice is largely unregulated. Virtually anyone can aid another in complying with the various tax laws. If a practitioner is a member of a profession, such as law or public accounting, he or she must abide by certain ethical standards. Furthermore, the Internal Revenue Code imposes penalties upon the preparers of Federal tax returns who violate proscribed acts and procedures.

LO.5

Appreciate some of the ethical guidelines involved in tax practice.

Ethical Guidelines. The American Institute of CPAs has issued numerous pronouncements dealing with CPAs engaged in tax practice. Originally called "Statements on Responsibilities in Tax Practice," these pronouncements were intended to be only *guides* to action. In 2000, however, the AICPA redesignated the pronouncements as "Statements on Standards for Tax Services" and made them *enforceable* as part of its Code of Professional Conduct. They include the provisions summarized below.

- Do not take questionable positions on a client's tax return in the hope that the return will not be selected for audit by the IRS. Any positions taken should be supported by a good-faith belief that they have a realistic possibility of being sustained if challenged. The client should be fully advised of the risks involved and of the penalties that will result if the position taken is not successful.
- A practitioner can use a client's estimates if they are reasonable under the circumstances. If the tax law requires receipts or other verification, the client should be so advised. In no event should an estimate be given the appearance of greater accuracy than is the case. For example, an estimate of $1,000 should not be deducted on a return as $999.
- Every effort should be made to answer questions appearing on tax returns. A question need not be answered if the information requested is not readily available, the answer is voluminous, or the question's meaning is uncertain. The failure to answer a question on a return cannot be justified on the grounds that the answer could prove disadvantageous to the taxpayer.

- Upon learning of an error on a past tax return, advise the client to correct it. <u>Do not, however, inform the IRS of the error.</u> If the error is material and the client refuses to correct it, consider withdrawing from the engagement. This will be necessary if the error has a carryover effect and prevents the current year's tax liability from being determined correctly.

ETHICAL *Considerations*   **WHEN THE IRS DOES NOT KNOW**

Al Garth is a longtime client and a golfing companion as well. In reviewing the information he furnishes you to prepare his income tax return for 2005, you find no reference to the Honda SUV he won in the annual club tournament. When you inquire about the matter, Al tells you that the club treasurer says that the club does not report these awards to the IRS and has told him to "proceed accordingly." What course of action should you take?

Statutory Penalties Imposed on Tax Return Preparers. In addition to ethical constraints, a tax return preparer may be subject to certain statutorily sanctioned penalties, including the following:

- Various penalties involving procedural matters. Examples include failing to furnish the taxpayer with a copy of the return; endorsing a taxpayer's refund check; failing to sign the return as a preparer; failing to furnish one's identification number; and failing to keep copies of returns or maintain a client list.
- Penalty for understatement of a tax liability based on a position that lacks any realistic possibility of being sustained. If the position is not frivolous, the penalty can be avoided by disclosing it on the return.
- Penalty for any willful attempt to understate taxes. This usually results when a preparer disregards or makes no effort to obtain pertinent information from a client.
- Penalty for failure to exercise due diligence in determining eligibility for, or the amount of, an earned income tax credit.

Understanding the Federal Tax Law

LO.6

Recognize the economic, social, equity, and political considerations that justify various aspects of the tax law.

The Federal tax law is a mosaic of statutory provisions, administrative pronouncements, and court decisions. Anyone who has attempted to work with this body of knowledge would have to admit to its complexity. For the person who has to trudge through a mass of rules to find the solution to a tax problem, it may be of some consolation to know that the law's complexity can generally be explained. Whether sound or not, there is a reason for the formulation of every rule. Knowing these reasons, therefore, is a considerable step toward understanding the Federal tax law.

The Federal tax law has as its *major objective* the raising of revenue. But although the fiscal needs of the government are important, other considerations explain certain portions of the law. Economic, social, equity, and political factors also play a significant role. Added to these factors is the marked impact the IRS and the courts have had and will continue to have on the evolution of Federal tax law. These matters are treated in the remainder of the chapter, and, wherever appropriate, the discussion is referenced to subjects covered later in the text.

Revenue Needs

The foundation of any tax system has to be the raising of revenue to cover the cost of government operations. Ideally, annual outlays should not exceed anticipated revenues, thereby leading to a balanced budget with no resulting deficit.

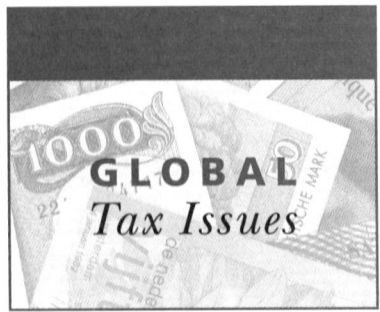

GLOBAL Tax Issues

OUTSOURCING OF TAX RETURN PREPARATION

The use of foreign nationals to carry out certain job assignments for U.S. businesses is an increasingly popular practice. Outsourcing such activities as telemarketing to India, for example, usually produces the same satisfactory result but at a much lower cost.

Outsourcing is also being applied to the preparation of tax returns. During 2003, an estimated 100,000 to 150,000 Federal and state income tax returns were outsourced to India by U.S. firms. Not only can this practice be expected to continue, but it probably will increase in volume. Outsourcing tax return preparation does not violate Federal law and is compatible with accounting ethical guidelines as long as three safeguards are followed: First, the practitioner must make sure that client confidentiality is maintained. Second, the practitioner must verify the accuracy of the work that has been outsourced. Third, the practitioner must inform clients, preferably in writing, when any third-party contractor is used to provide professional services.

Practitioners justify the outsourcing practice as a means of conserving time and effort that can be applied toward more meaningful tax planning on behalf of their clients.

When enacting tax legislation, a deficit-conscious Congress often has been guided by the concept of revenue neutrality. The concept means that the changes made will neither increase nor decrease the net result reached under the prior rules. Revenue neutrality does not mean that any one taxpayer's tax liability will remain the same. Since the circumstances involved will differ, one taxpayer's increased tax liability could be another's tax savings. Although revenue-neutral tax reform does not reduce deficits, at least it does not aggravate the problem.

In addition to making changes in the tax law revenue neutral, several other procedures can be taken to mitigate any revenue loss. When tax reductions are involved, the full impact of the legislation can be phased in over a period of years.[24] Or, as an alternative, the tax reduction can be limited to a period of years. When the period expires, the prior law is reinstated through a sunset provision. Most of the major tax bills recently passed by Congress have contained numerous sunset provisions. They provide some semblance of revenue neutrality as some of the bills include tax cuts that were not offset by new sources of revenue. It remains to be seen, however, whether Congress will allow the sunset provisions to take effect and, thereby, kill the tax cuts that were enacted.

Economic Considerations

Using the tax system in an effort to accomplish economic objectives has become increasingly popular in recent years. Generally, proponents of this goal use tax legislation to amend the Internal Revenue Code in ways designed to help control the economy or encourage certain activities and businesses.

Control of the Economy. Congress has used depreciation write-offs as a means of controlling the economy. Theoretically, shorter asset lives and accelerated methods should encourage additional investment in depreciable property acquired for business use. Conversely, longer asset lives and the required use of the straight-line method of depreciation dampen the tax incentive for capital outlays.

Another approach that utilizes depreciation as a means of controlling capital investment is the amount of write-off allowed upon the acquisition of assets. This is

---

[24]An example of a gradual phase-in is the increase in the unified transfer tax credit (discussed earlier in this chapter), which does not become fully implemented at $3.5 million until year 2009.

the approach followed by the § 179 election to expense assets. It also was the approach used by Congress on occasions in provisions that permitted additional first-year depreciation (see Chapter 8).

A change in the tax rate structure has a more immediate impact on the economy. With lower tax rates, taxpayers are able to retain additional spendable funds. If lower tax rates are accompanied by the elimination of certain deductions, exclusions, and credits, however, the overall result may not be lower tax liabilities.

Encouragement of Certain Activities. Without passing judgment on the wisdom of any such choices, it is quite clear that the tax law does encourage certain types of economic activity or segments of the economy. For example, the favorable treatment allowed research and development expenditures can be explained by the desire to foster technological progress. Under the tax law, such expenditures can be either deducted in the year incurred or capitalized and amortized over a period of 60 months or more. In terms of the timing of the tax savings, these options usually are preferable to capitalizing the cost with a write-off over the estimated useful life of the asset created. If the asset developed has an indefinite useful life, no write-off would be available without the two options allowed by the tax law.

Is it desirable to encourage the conservation of energy resources? Considering the world energy situation and our own reliance on foreign oil, the answer to this question has to be yes. The concern over energy usage was a prime consideration in the enactment of legislation to make various tax savings for energy conservation expenditures available to taxpayers.

Is preserving the environment a desirable objective? Ecological considerations explain why the tax law permits a 60-month amortization period for costs incurred in the installation of pollution control facilities.

Is it wise to stimulate U.S. exports of services? Along this line, Congress has deemed it advisable to establish incentives for U.S. citizens who accept employment overseas. Such persons receive generous tax breaks through special treatment of their foreign-source income and certain housing costs.

Is saving desirable for the economy? Saving leads to capital formation and thereby makes funds available to finance home construction and industrial expansion. The tax law encourages saving by according preferential treatment to private retirement plans. Not only are contributions to Keogh (H.R. 10) plans and certain Individual Retirement Accounts (IRAs) deductible, but income from the contributions accumulates free of tax. As noted below, the encouragement of private-sector pension plans can also be justified under social considerations.

Encouragement of Certain Industries. No one can question the proposition that a sound agricultural base is necessary for a well-balanced national economy. Undoubtedly, this can explain why farmers are accorded special treatment under the Federal tax system. Among the benefits are the election to expense rather than capitalize certain soil and water conservation expenditures and fertilizers and the election to defer the recognition of gain on the receipt of crop insurance proceeds.

Encouragement of Small Business. At least in the United States, a consensus exists that what is good for small business is good for the economy as a whole. Whether valid or not, this assumption has led to a definite bias in the tax law favoring small business.

In the corporate tax area, several provisions can be explained by the desire to benefit small business. One provision permits the shareholders of a small business corporation to make a special election that generally will avoid the imposition of the corporate income tax.[25] Furthermore, such an election enables the corporation to pass through its operating losses to its shareholders.

---

[25]Known as the S election, it is discussed in Chapter 20.

Social Considerations

Some provisions of the Federal tax law, particularly those dealing with the income tax of individuals, can be explained by social considerations. Some notable examples and their rationales include the following:

- Certain benefits provided to employees through accident and health plans financed by employers are nontaxable to employees. Encouraging such plans is considered socially desirable since they provide medical benefits in the event of an employee's illness or injury.
- Most premiums paid by an employer for group term insurance covering the life of the employee are nontaxable to the employee. These arrangements can be justified on social grounds in that they provide funds for the family unit to help it adjust to the loss of wages caused by the employee's death.
- A contribution made by an employer to a qualified pension or profit sharing plan for an employee may receive special treatment. The contribution and any income it generates are not taxed to the employee until the funds are distributed. Such an arrangement also benefits the employer by allowing a tax deduction when the contribution is made to the qualified plan. Private retirement plans are encouraged to supplement the subsistence income level the employee otherwise would have under the Social Security system.[26]
- A deduction is allowed for contributions to qualified charitable organizations. The deduction attempts to shift some of the financial and administrative burden of socially desirable programs from the public (the government) to the private (the citizens) sector.
- A tax credit is allowed for amounts spent to furnish care for certain minor or disabled dependents to enable the taxpayer to seek or maintain gainful employment. Who could deny the social desirability of encouraging taxpayers to provide care for their children while they work?
- Various tax credits, deductions, and exclusions are designed to encourage taxpayers to obtain additional education.[27]
- A tax deduction is not allowed for certain expenditures deemed to be contrary to public policy. This disallowance extends to such items as fines, penalties, illegal kickbacks, bribes to government officials, and gambling losses in excess of gains. Social considerations dictate that the tax law should not encourage these activities by permitting a deduction.

Many other examples could be cited, but the conclusion would be unchanged. Social considerations do explain a significant part of the Federal tax law.

Equity Considerations

The concept of equity is relative. Reasonable persons can, and often do, disagree about what is fair or unfair. In the tax area, moreover, equity is most often tied to a particular taxpayer's personal situation. To illustrate, compare the tax positions of those who rent their personal residences with those who own their homes. Renters receive no Federal income tax benefit from the rent they pay. For homeowners, however, a large portion of the house payments they make may qualify for the Federal interest and property tax deductions. Although renters may have difficulty understanding this difference in tax treatment, the encouragement of home ownership can be justified on both economic and social grounds.

---

[26]The same rationale explains the availability of similar arrangements for self-employed persons (the H.R. 10, or Keogh, plan). See Chapter 19.

[27]These provisions can also be justified under the category of economic considerations. No one can take issue with the conclusion that a better educated workforce carries a positive economic impact.

TAX *in the News* — **TREATING EVERYONE THE SAME**

As noted in the text, a Federal income tax deduction for state and local income taxes paid is allowed to mitigate the effect of having the same income taxed twice. But what if a state does not impose an income tax and, instead, derives comparable amounts of revenue from a general sales tax? Is it fair to deny a deduction to residents of this state just because the state imposes a tax on sales rather than on income?

In the American Jobs Creation Act of 2004, Congress resolved this purported inequity by allowing a Federal income tax deduction for state and local general sales taxes. However, a taxpayer who is subject to both state income and sales taxes must make a choice. One or the other, but not both, can be claimed as a deduction. Furthermore, the sales tax option is available only for taxable years beginning after December 31, 2002, and before January 1, 2006. [Note: An extension by Congress is probable but by no means certain.]

In the same vein, compare the tax treatment of a corporation with that of a partnership. Although the two businesses may be of equal size, similarly situated, and competitors in the production of goods or services, they are not treated comparably under the tax law. The corporation is subject to a separate Federal income tax; the partnership is not. Whether the differences in tax treatment can be justified logically in terms of equity is beside the point. The point is that the tax law can and does make a distinction between these business forms.

Equity, then, is not what appears fair or unfair to any one taxpayer or group of taxpayers. Some recognition of equity does exist, however, and explains part of the law. The concept of equity appears in tax provisions that alleviate the effect of multiple taxation and postpone the recognition of gain when the taxpayer lacks the ability or wherewithal to pay the tax. Provisions that mitigate the effect of the application of the annual accounting period concept and help taxpayers cope with the eroding results of inflation also reflect equity considerations.

Alleviating the Effect of Multiple Taxation. The income earned by a taxpayer may be subject to taxes imposed by different taxing authorities. If, for example, the taxpayer is a resident of New York City, income might generate Federal, state of New York, and city of New York income taxes. To compensate for this apparent inequity, the Federal tax law allows a taxpayer to claim a deduction for state and local income taxes. The deduction does not, however, neutralize the effect of multiple taxation, since the benefit derived depends on the taxpayer's Federal income tax rate. Only a tax credit, rather than a deduction, would eliminate the effects of multiple taxation on the same income.

Equity considerations can explain the Federal tax treatment of certain income from foreign sources. Since double taxation results when the same income is subject to both foreign and U.S. income taxes, the tax law permits the taxpayer to choose between a credit and a deduction for the foreign taxes paid.

The Wherewithal to Pay Concept. The **wherewithal to pay** concept recognizes the inequity of taxing a transaction when the taxpayer lacks the means with which to pay the tax. It is particularly suited to situations in which the taxpayer's economic position has not changed significantly as a result of the transaction.

An illustration of the wherewithal to pay concept is the provision of the tax law dealing with the treatment of gain resulting from an involuntary conversion. An involuntary conversion occurs when property is destroyed by casualty or taken by a public authority through condemnation. If gain results from the conversion, it need not be recognized if the taxpayer replaces the property within a specified period of time. The replacement property must be similar or related in service or use to that involuntarily converted.

EXAMPLE 17

Some of the pasture land belonging to Ron, a rancher, is condemned by the state for use as a game preserve. The condemned pasture land cost Ron $120,000, but the state pays him $150,000 (its fair market value). Shortly thereafter, Ron buys more pasture land for $150,000. ■

In Example 17, Ron has a realized gain of $30,000 [$150,000 (condemnation award) − $120,000 (cost of land)]. It would be inequitable to force Ron to pay a tax on this gain for two reasons. First, without disposing of the property acquired (the new land), Ron would be hard-pressed to pay the tax. Second, his economic position has not changed.

A warning is in order regarding the application of the wherewithal to pay concept. If the taxpayer's economic position changes in any way, tax consequences may result.

EXAMPLE 18

Assume the same facts as in Example 17, except that Ron reinvests only $140,000 of the award in new pasture land. Now, Ron has a taxable gain of $10,000. Instead of ending up with only replacement property, Ron now has $10,000 in cash. ■

Mitigating the Effect of the Annual Accounting Period Concept. For purposes of effective administration of the tax law, all taxpayers must report to and settle with the Federal government at periodic intervals. Otherwise, taxpayers would remain uncertain as to their tax liabilities, and the government would have difficulty judging revenues and budgeting expenditures. The period selected for final settlement of most tax liabilities, in any event an arbitrary determination, is one year. At the close of each year, therefore, a taxpayer's position becomes complete for that particular year. Referred to as the annual accounting period concept, its effect is to divide each taxpayer's life, for tax purposes, into equal annual intervals.

The finality of the annual accounting period concept could lead to dissimilar tax treatment for taxpayers who are, from a long-range standpoint, in the same economic position.

EXAMPLE 19

José and Alicia, both sole proprietors, have experienced the following results during the past three years:

	Profit (or Loss)	
Year	José	Alicia
2004	$50,000	$150,000
2005	60,000	60,000
2006	60,000	(40,000)

Although José and Alicia have the same profit of $170,000 over the period from 2004 to 2006, the finality of the annual accounting period concept places Alicia at a definite disadvantage for tax purposes. The net operating loss procedure offers Alicia some relief by allowing her to apply some or all of her 2006 loss to the earlier profitable years (in this case, 2004). Thus, with a net operating loss carryback, Alicia is in a position to obtain a refund for some of the taxes she paid on the $150,000 profit reported for 2004. ■

The same reasoning used to support the deduction of net operating losses can explain the special treatment the tax law accords to excess capital losses and excess charitable contributions.[28] Carryback and carryover procedures help mitigate the effect of limiting a loss or a deduction to the accounting period in which it was

---

[28]The tax treatment of these items is discussed in Chapters 7, 10, and 16.

realized. With such procedures, a taxpayer may be able to salvage a loss or a deduction that might otherwise be wasted.

The installment method of recognizing gain on the sale of property allows a taxpayer to spread tax consequences over the payout period.[29] The harsh effect of taxing all the gain in the year of sale is thereby avoided. The installment method can also be explained by the wherewithal to pay concept since recognition of gain is tied to the collection of the installment notes received from the sale of the property. Tax consequences, then, tend to correspond to the seller's ability to pay the tax.

Coping with Inflation. Because of the progressive nature of the income tax, a wage adjustment to compensate for inflation can increase the income tax bracket of the recipient. Known as *bracket creep*, its overall impact is an erosion of purchasing power. Congress recognized this problem and began to adjust various income tax components, such as tax brackets, standard deduction amounts, and personal and dependency exemptions, through an indexation procedure. Indexation is based upon the rise in the consumer price index over the prior year.

Political Considerations

A large segment of the Federal tax law is made up of statutory provisions. Since these statutes are enacted by Congress, is it any surprise that political considerations influence tax law? For purposes of discussion, the effect of political considerations on the tax law is divided into the following topics: special interest legislation, political expediency situations, and state and local government influences.

Special Interest Legislation. There is no doubt that certain provisions of the tax law can largely be explained by the political influence some pressure groups have had on Congress. Is there any other realistic reason that, for example, prepaid subscription and dues income is not taxed until earned while prepaid rents are taxed to the landlord in the year received?

The American Jobs Creation Act of 2004 included several good examples of special interest legislation. One provision, sponsored by former Senator Zell Miller (D–Ga.), suspended the import duties on ceiling fans. The nation's largest seller of ceiling fans is Home Depot, which is based in Atlanta, Georgia. Another provision, sponsored by House Speaker Dennis Hastert (R–Ill.), reduced the excise taxes on fishing tackle boxes. Representative Hastert's district includes Plano Molding, a major manufacturer of tackle boxes. The justification for this change was that it placed tackle boxes on a more level playing field with toolboxes (which are not subject to tax). Allegedly, fishermen had been buying and converting toolboxes to avoid the excise tax!

Special interest legislation is not necessarily to be condemned if it can be justified on economic, social, or some other utilitarian grounds. At any rate, it is an inevitable product of our political system.

Political Expediency Situations. Various tax reform proposals rise and fall in favor with the shifting moods of the American public. That Congress is sensitive to popular feeling is an accepted fact. Therefore, certain provisions of the tax law can be explained by the political climate at the time they were enacted.

Measures that deter more affluent taxpayers from obtaining so-called preferential tax treatment have always had popular appeal and, consequently, the support of Congress. Provisions such as the alternative minimum tax, the imputed interest rules, and the limitation on the deductibility of interest on investment indebtedness can be explained on this basis.

---

[29]Under the installment method, each payment received by the seller represents both a recovery of capital (the nontaxable portion) and profit from the sale (the taxable portion). The tax rules governing the installment method are discussed in Chapter 18.

Other changes explained at least partially by political expediency include the lowering of individual income tax rates, the increase in the personal and dependency exemptions, and the increase in the amount of the earned income credit.

State and Local Government Influences. Political considerations have played a major role in the nontaxability of interest received on state and local obligations. In view of the furor that has been raised by state and local political figures every time any modification of this tax provision has been proposed, one might well regard it as next to sacred.

Somewhat less apparent has been the influence state law has had in shaping our present Federal tax law. Such was the case with community property systems. The nine states with community property systems are Louisiana, Texas, New Mexico, Arizona, California, Washington, Idaho, Nevada, and Wisconsin. The rest of the states are classified as common law jurisdictions.[30] The difference between common law and community property systems centers around the property rights possessed by married persons. In a common law system, each spouse owns whatever he or she earns. Under a community property system, one-half of the earnings of each spouse is considered owned by the other spouse.

EXAMPLE 20

Al and Fran are husband and wife, and their only income is the $80,000 annual salary Al receives. If they live in New Jersey (a common law state), the $80,000 salary belongs to Al. If, however, they live in Arizona (a community property state), the $80,000 is divided equally, in terms of ownership, between Al and Fran. ■

At one time, the tax position of the residents of community property states was so advantageous that many common law states actually adopted community property systems. Needless to say, the political pressure placed on Congress to correct the disparity in tax treatment was considerable. To a large extent this was accomplished in the Revenue Act of 1948, which extended many of the community property tax advantages to residents of common law jurisdictions.

The major advantage extended was the provision allowing married taxpayers to file joint returns and compute the tax liability as if the income had been earned one-half by each spouse. This result is automatic in a community property state, since half of the income earned by one spouse belongs to the other spouse. The income-splitting benefits of a joint return are now incorporated as part of the tax rates applicable to married taxpayers. See Chapter 3.

Influence of the Internal Revenue Service

LO.7

Describe the role played by the IRS and the courts in the evolution of the Federal tax system.

The influence of the IRS is apparent in many areas beyond its role in issuing the administrative pronouncements that make up a considerable portion of our tax law. In its capacity as the protector of the national revenue, the IRS has been instrumental in securing the passage of much legislation designed to curtail the most flagrant tax avoidance practices (to close *tax loopholes*). In its capacity as the administrator of the tax law, the IRS has sought and obtained legislation to make its job easier (to attain administrative feasibility).

The IRS as Protector of the Revenue. Innumerable examples can be given of provisions in the tax law that stem from the direct influence of the IRS. Usually, such provisions are intended to prevent a loophole from being used to avoid the tax consequences intended by Congress. Working within the letter of existing law, ingenious taxpayers and their advisers devise techniques that accomplish indirectly what cannot be accomplished directly. As a consequence, legislation is enacted to

[30]In Alaska, spouses can choose to have the community property rules apply. Otherwise, property rights are determined under common law rules.

close the loopholes that taxpayers have located and exploited. Some tax law can be explained in this fashion and is discussed in the chapters to follow.

ETHICAL *Considerations*   **DEDUCTING UNCOLLECTED CHARGES FOR SERVICES RENDERED**

Dr. Taylor is a cash basis, calendar year taxpayer who maintains a dental practice as a sole proprietor. For tax year 2006, he claims $36,500 as a bad debt deduction. After performing the dental procedures and billing the patients repeatedly, he has been unable to collect the amounts due. He feels quite certain that the patients involved will never pay their bills. Comment on the propriety of Dr. Taylor's deduction.

In addition, the IRS has secured from Congress legislation of a more general nature that enables it to make adjustments based on the substance, rather than the formal construction, of what a taxpayer has done. For example, one such provision permits the IRS to make adjustments to a taxpayer's method of accounting when the method used by the taxpayer does not clearly reflect income.[31]

Tina, a cash basis taxpayer, owns and operates a pharmacy. All drugs and other items acquired for resale, such as cosmetics, are charged to the purchases account and written off (expensed) for tax purposes in the year of acquisition. As this procedure does not clearly reflect income, it would be appropriate for the IRS to require that Tina establish and maintain an ending inventory account. ■

EXAMPLE 21

Administrative Feasibility. Some tax law is justified on the grounds that it simplifies the task of the IRS in collecting the revenue and administering the law. With regard to collecting the revenue, the IRS long ago realized the importance of placing taxpayers on a pay-as-you-go basis. Elaborate withholding procedures apply to wages, while the tax on other types of income may be paid at periodic intervals throughout the year. The IRS has been instrumental in convincing the courts that accrual basis taxpayers should in most cases pay taxes on prepaid income in the year received and not when earned. The approach may be contrary to generally accepted accounting principles, but it is consistent with the wherewithal to pay concept.

Of considerable aid to the IRS in collecting revenue are the numerous provisions that impose interest and penalties on taxpayers for noncompliance with the tax law. Provisions such as the penalties for failure to pay a tax or to file a return that is due, the negligence penalty for intentional disregard of rules and regulations, and various penalties for civil and criminal fraud serve as deterrents to taxpayer noncompliance.

One of the keys to an effective administration of our tax system is the audit process conducted by the IRS. To carry out this function, the IRS is aided by provisions that reduce the chance of taxpayer error or manipulation and therefore simplify the audit effort that is necessary. An increase in the amount of the standard deduction, for example, reduces the number of individual taxpayers who will choose the alternative of itemizing their personal deductions.[32] With fewer deductions to check, the audit function is simplified.[33]

---

[31]See Chapter 18.
[32]For a discussion of the standard deduction, see Chapter 3.
[33]The same justification was given by the IRS when it proposed to Congress the $100 limitation on personal casualty and theft losses. Imposition of the limitation eliminated many casualty and theft loss deductions and, as a consequence, saved the IRS considerable audit time. Later legislation, in addition to retaining the $100 feature, limits deductible losses to those in excess of 10% of a taxpayer's adjusted gross income. See Chapter 7.

Influence of the Courts

In addition to interpreting statutory provisions and the administrative pronouncements issued by the IRS, the Federal courts have influenced tax law in two other respects.[34] First, the courts have formulated certain judicial concepts that serve as guides in the application of various tax provisions. Second, certain key decisions have led to changes in the Internal Revenue Code.

Judicial Concepts Relating to Tax. A leading tax concept developed by the courts deals with the interpretation of statutory tax provisions that operate to benefit taxpayers. The courts have established the rule that these relief provisions are to be narrowly construed against taxpayers if there is any doubt about their application.

Important in this area is the *arm's length* concept. Particularly in dealings between related parties, transactions may be tested by looking to whether the taxpayers acted in an arm's length manner. The question to be asked is: Would unrelated parties have handled the transaction in the same way?

EXAMPLE 22

Rex, the sole shareholder of Silver Corporation, leases property to the corporation for a yearly rent of $6,000. To test whether the corporation should be allowed a rent deduction for this amount, the IRS and the courts will apply the arm's length concept. Would Silver Corporation have paid $6,000 a year in rent if it had leased the same property from an unrelated party (rather than from Rex)? Suppose it is determined that an unrelated third party would have paid an annual rent for the property of only $5,000. Under these circumstances, Silver Corporation will be allowed a deduction of only $5,000. The other $1,000 it paid for the use of the property represents a nondeductible dividend. Accordingly, Rex will be treated as having received rent income of $5,000 and dividend income of $1,000. ∎

Judicial Influence on Statutory Provisions. Some court decisions have been of such consequence that Congress has incorporated them into statutory tax law. For example, many years ago the courts found that stock dividends distributed to the shareholders of a corporation were not taxable as income. This result was largely accepted by Congress, and a provision in the tax statutes now covers the issue.

On occasion, however, Congress has reacted negatively to judicial interpretations of the tax law.

EXAMPLE 23

Nora leases unimproved real estate to Wade for 40 years. At a cost of $200,000, Wade erects a building on the land. The building is worth $100,000 when the lease terminates and Nora takes possession of the property. Does Nora have any income either when the improvements are made or when the lease terminates? In a landmark decision, a court held that Nora must recognize income of $100,000 upon the termination of the lease. ∎

Congress felt that the result reached in Example 23 was inequitable in that it was not consistent with the wherewithal to pay concept. Consequently, the tax law was amended to provide that a landlord does not recognize any income either when the improvements are made (unless made in lieu of rent) or when the lease terminates.

Summary

In addition to its necessary revenue-raising objective, the Federal tax law has developed in response to several other factors:

---

[34]A great deal of case law is devoted to ascertaining congressional intent. The courts, in effect, ask: What did Congress have in mind when it enacted a particular tax provision?

- *Economic considerations.* The emphasis here is on tax provisions that help regulate the economy and encourage certain activities and types of businesses.
- *Social considerations.* Some tax provisions are designed to encourage (or discourage) certain socially desirable (or undesirable) practices.
- *Equity considerations.* Of principal concern in this area are tax provisions that alleviate the effect of multiple taxation, recognize the wherewithal to pay concept, mitigate the effect of the annual accounting period concept, and recognize the eroding effect of inflation.
- *Political considerations.* Of significance in this regard are tax provisions that represent special interest legislation, reflect political expediency, and exhibit the effect of state and local law.
- *Influence of the IRS.* Many tax provisions are intended to aid the IRS in the collection of revenue and the administration of the tax law.
- *Influence of the courts.* Court decisions have established a body of judicial concepts relating to tax law and have, on occasion, led Congress to enact statutory provisions to either clarify or negate their effect.

These factors explain various tax provisions and thereby help in understanding why the tax law developed to its present state. The next step involves learning to work with the tax law, which is the subject of Chapter 2.

KEY TERMS

Ad valorem taxes, 1–6	Franchise tax, 1–17	Revenue neutrality, 1–24
Correspondence audit, 1–19	FUTA tax, 1–16	Sales tax, 1–9
Death tax, 1–10	Gift tax, 1–12	Severance taxes, 1–10
Employment taxes, 1–15	Inheritance tax, 1–10	Statute of limitations, 1–20
Estate tax, 1–10	National sales tax, 1–18	Sunset provision, 1–24
Excise taxes, 1–8	Occupational taxes, 1–17	Use tax, 1–9
FICA tax, 1–16	Office audit, 1–19	Value added tax (VAT), 1–17
Field audit, 1–19	Personalty, 1–7	Wherewithal to pay, 1–27
Flat tax, 1–17	Realty, 1–6	

PROBLEM MATERIALS

DISCUSSION QUESTIONS

1. Irene, a middle management employee, is offered a pay increase by her employer. As a condition of the offer, Irene must move to another state. What tax considerations should Irene weigh before making a decision on whether to accept the offer?

2. The Federal income tax was first enacted during the Civil War, but it was never challenged in the U.S. Supreme Court until the mid-1890s. Comment on whether this statement is correct, incorrect, or misleading.

3. The effect of the Sixteenth Amendment to the U.S. Constitution was to affirm what the U.S. Supreme Court had held in its prior decisions regarding the Federal income tax. Do you agree?

4. World War II converted the Federal income tax into a *mass tax.* Explain.

5. How does the pay-as-you-go procedure apply to wage earners? To persons who have income from other than wages?

6. In terms of Adam Smith's canon of *certainty*, how does the Federal income tax fare?

7. Are the following taxes *proportional* or *progressive*?
   a. Federal estate tax.
   b. FUTA tax.
   c. Ad valorem tax on personalty.
   d. Hotel occupancy tax.

Issue ID

8. Until recently, Hunter College has relied on privately owned dormitories to provide housing for its out-of-state students. After a successful fund-raising campaign, the board of regents is considering purchasing and operating most of the privately owned dormitories. The city where Hunter College is located opposes the project. Why?

Issue ID

9. The Adams Independent School District desires to sell a parcel of unimproved land that it does not need. Its three best offers are as follows: from State Department of Public Safety (DPS), $2.3 million; from Second Baptist Church, $2.2 million; and from Baker Chevrolet Company, $2.1 million. DPS would use the property for a new state highway patrol barracks; Second Baptist would start a church school; and Baker would open a car dealership. If you are the financial adviser for the school district, which offer would you prefer? Why?

Issue ID

10. Before she entered a nursing home, Doris signed a deed transferring title to her personal residence to her only son, Walt. Walt has never filed the deed with the county clerk's office and continues to pay the property taxes in his mother's name. Walt and his family are the only occupants of the property. Is there an explanation for Walt's actions?

11. The commissioners for Colby County are actively negotiating with Eagle Industries regarding the location of a new manufacturing facility in the county. As Eagle is considering several other sites, a "generous tax holiday" may be needed to influence its choice. The local school district is opposed to any "generous tax holiday."
    a. In terms of a "generous tax holiday," what might the proposal entail?
    b. Why should the school district be opposed?

12. The Mayo family is selected for ABC's *Extreme Makeover: Home Edition*. The program gives the Mayos' California home the royal treatment, increasing the living area from 1,200 square feet to about 4,300—more than doubling the value of the property. Do you envision any tax problems?

13. Franklin County is in dire financial straits and is considering a number of sources for additional revenue. Evaluate the following possibilities in terms of anticipated taxpayer compliance:
    a. A property tax on business inventories.
    b. A tax on intangibles (i.e., stocks and bonds) held as investments.
    c. A property tax on boats used for recreational purposes.

14. After his first business trip to a major city, Herman is alarmed when he reviews his credit card receipts. Both the hotel bill and the car rental charge are in excess of the price he was quoted. Was Herman overcharged, or is there an explanation for the excess amounts?

Issue ID

15. Jared wants to give his wife a $30,000 diamond necklace for her birthday. To avoid the state and local general sales tax of 8.5%, he asks his aunt (who lives in New Hampshire) to make the purchase. Has Jared saved $2,550 (8.5% × $30,000)?

16. a. What is a sales tax holiday? What purpose might it serve?
    b. If a state anticipates a revenue shortfall, an easy solution is to cancel any scheduled sales tax holidays. Please assess the validity of this statement.

Issue ID

17. Velma lives in Wilson County, which is adjacent to Grimes County. Although the retail stores in both counties are comparable, Velma drives an extra 10 miles to do all of her shopping in Grimes County. Why might she do this?

Issue ID

18. During a social event, Muriel and Earl are discussing the home computer each recently purchased. Although the computers are identical makes and models, Muriel is

surprised to learn that she paid a sales tax, while Earl did not. Comment as to why this could happen.

19. On a recent shopping trip to a warehouse discount store, Ruby bought goods worth $400. Although the state and local general sales tax is 7%, she was charged less than $28 (7% × $400) in tax. Why?

20. What was the original objective for the Federal estate tax? Is this objective being accomplished?

21. Oscar, age 70, wants all of his property to eventually pass to Natalie, age 30, his recent bride. From a tax standpoint, would it be cheaper for Oscar to make the transfers to Natalie by gift or at death? Explain.

22. Beverly is surprised to learn that the gifts she made to family members in the current year will result in a Federal gift tax. Similar gifts made in past years have not generated any gift tax.   *Issue ID*
    a. What is the plausible explanation for this change in result?
    b. Could Beverly also be subject to a state gift tax? Explain.

23. a. What is the purpose of the unified transfer tax credit?
    b. Is the same amount available for both the Federal gift tax and the estate tax? Explain.
    c. Does the use of the credit for a gift affect the amount of credit available for the estate tax? Explain.

24. Marcus and Lottie are husband and wife and have five married daughters and 13 minor grandchildren. For year 2006, what is the maximum amount Marcus and Lottie can give their family (include the sons-in-law) without using any of their unified transfer tax credit?

25. The Tax Relief Reconciliation Act of 2001 purports to phase out the Federal estate tax but retains the Federal gift tax.
    a. What is the justification for rescinding the Federal estate tax?
    b. If the Federal estate tax is to be eliminated, why not also eliminate the Federal gift tax?

26. As the Federal estate tax is scheduled to be phased out, making lifetime gifts unnecessarily incurs a transfer tax that could have been avoided by passing the property by death.
    a. Evaluate this statement. In what way is it correct? Incorrect? Misleading?
    b. What could be some justifications for lifetime giving?

27. Compare the Federal income tax on corporations with that applicable to individual taxpayers in terms of the following:
    a. Determination of AGI.
    b. Availability of the standard deduction.
    c. Nature of deductions allowed.

28. Mike Barr was an outstanding football player in college and expects to be drafted by the NFL in the first few rounds. Mike has let it be known that he would prefer to sign with a club located in Florida, Texas, or Washington. Mike sees no reason why he should have to pay state income tax on his player's salary! Is Mike under any delusions? Explain.   *Issue ID*

29. A state that uses a "piggyback" approach to its income tax has "decoupled" from a recent change in the Internal Revenue Code.
    a. What does this mean?
    b. Why might it have occurred?

30. A question on a state income tax return asks the taxpayer if he or she made any out-of-state Internet or mail-order catalog purchases during the year. The question requires a yes or no answer, and if the taxpayer answers yes, the amount of such purchases is to be listed.   *Issue ID*
    a. Does such an inquiry have any relevance to the state income tax? If not, why is it being asked?
    b. Your client, Harriet, wants to leave the question unanswered. As the preparer of her return, how do you respond?

31. As to those states that impose an income tax on individuals, comment on the following:
    a. Use of withholding procedures.
    b. Treatment of Federal income taxes paid.
    c. Due date for filing.
    d. Handling of personal and dependency exemptions.
    e. Credit for income taxes paid to other states.
    f. Availability of an amnesty program.

32. Contrast FICA and FUTA as to the following:
    a. Purpose of the tax.
    b. Upon whom imposed.
    c. Governmental administration of the tax.
    d. Reduction of tax based on a merit rating system.

33. At a social event you attend in April, you overhear a guest remark that she is glad that "the payroll bit is over with for a while."
    a. What was the guest referring to?
    b. Was her statement entirely correct? Explain.

34. Errol and Keith live in Massachusetts, and each is a contractor. They have the same number of employees. Errol handles outdoor landscaping (including pool construction), and Keith remodels kitchens. How would you expect their annual FUTA expenses to compare?

35. Regarding the proposal for a "flat tax," comment on the following:
    a. Justification for.
    b. Major obstacles to enactment.

36. Regarding the value added tax (VAT), comment on the following:
    a. Popularity of this type of tax.
    b. Nature of the tax.

37. In 2004, a bill was introduced in Congress that would replace the current income tax with a national sales tax, called the "Fair Tax."
    a. Describe the mechanics of the "Fair Tax" approach.
    b. What, if any, might be the shortcomings of this approach?

Issue ID 38. Serena operates a lawn maintenance service in southern California. As most of her employees are itinerant, they are paid on a day-to-day basis. Because of cash-flow problems, Serena requires her customers to pay cash for the services she provides.
    a. What are some of the tax problems Serena might have?
    b. Assess Serena's chances of audit by the IRS.

 39. Assess the probability of an audit in each of the following independent situations:
    a. As a result of a jury trial, Linda was awarded $3.5 million because of job discrimination. The award included $3 million for punitive damages.
    b. Mel operates a combination check-cashing service and pawnshop. He recently broke up with his companion of 18 years and married her teenage daughter.
    c. Gavin operates a valet parking service for several upscale restaurants and nightclubs. Gavin is paid by the customers and not by the establishments he works for.
    d. Dr. Fair just fired the accountant who maintained the records for the dental clinic he operates. The accountant received no severance pay or retirement benefits although she had been employed by the clinic for more than 15 years.
    e. Mario is employed as a mechanic by a Honda dealership. He also buys, repairs, and sells cars on his own.

40. With regard to the IRS audit process, comment on the following:
    a. Percentage of individual returns audited.
    b. Availability of an "informant's fee."
    c. DIF score.
    d. Relevance of information returns (e.g., Form 1099).
    e. Type of audit (i.e., correspondence, office, field).
    f. Special agent joins the audit team.
    g. Function of the Appeals Division.

41. Regarding the statute of limitations on additional assessments of tax by the IRS, determine the applicable period in each of the following situations. Assume a calendar year individual with no fraud or substantial omission involved.
    a. The income tax return for 2005 was filed on February 24, 2006.
    b. The income tax return for 2005 was filed on June 28, 2006.
    c. The income tax return for 2005 was prepared on April 7, 2006, but was never filed. Through some misunderstanding between the preparer and the taxpayer, each expected the other to file the return.
    d. The income tax return for 2005 was never filed because the taxpayer thought no additional tax was due or a refund was available.

42. Brianna, a calendar year taxpayer, files her income tax return for 2005 on February 7, 2006. Although she makes repeated inquiries, she does not receive her refund from the IRS until May 27, 2006. Is Brianna entitled to interest on the refund? Explain.

43. On a Federal income tax return filed five years ago, Andy inadvertently omitted a large amount of gross income.
    a. Andy seeks your advice as to whether the IRS is barred from assessing additional income tax in the event he is audited. What is your advice?
    b. Would your advice differ if you are the person who prepared the return in question? Explain.
    c. Suppose Andy asks you to prepare his current year's return. Would you do so? Explain.

44. Samantha files her income tax return 65 days after the due date of the return without obtaining an extension from the IRS. Along with the return, she remits a check for $10,000, which is the balance of the tax she owes. Disregarding the interest element, what are Samantha's penalties for failure to file and for failure to pay?

45. In March 2006, Jim asks you to prepare his Federal income tax returns for tax years 2003, 2004, and 2005. In discussing this matter with him, you discover that he also has not filed for tax year 2002. When you mention this fact, Jim tells you that the statute of limitations precludes the IRS from taking any action as to this year.
    a. Is Jim correct about the application of the statute of limitations? Why?
    b. If Jim refuses to file for 2002, should you prepare returns for 2003 through 2005?

46. Ethan owns and operates a janitorial maintenance service for commercial properties. He has instructed his new accountant that around year-end the books of the business should be kept open longer for some transactions and closed earlier for others.
    a. What does Ethan have in mind?
    b. When the accountant objects to the procedure, Ethan assures him that no distortion will occur. Because the practice has been followed in past years, the result is a "washout." Explain Ethan's reasoning and comment on the propriety of what is occurring.

47. With regard to the concept of revenue neutrality, comment on the following:
    a. A tax cut that is accompanied by a revenue offset.
    b. A tax cut that is phased in over a period of years.
    c. A tax cut that contains a sunset provision.

48. Some tax rules can be justified on multiple grounds (e.g., economic, social, etc.). In this connection, comment on the possible justification for the rules governing the following:
    a. Pension plans.
    b. Education.
    c. Home ownership.

49. Discuss the possible justifications for the following provisions of the tax law:
    a. The preferential treatment allowed U.S. citizens who work overseas.
    b. The election to expense, rather than capitalize and depreciate, certain property acquisitions.
    c. The deferral of gain recognition on the receipt of crop insurance proceeds.
    d. An election that enables certain corporations to avoid the corporate income tax and pass losses through to their shareholders.
    e. The tax treatment of premiums paid by an employer on group life insurance for employees.

50. Allowing a taxpayer a deduction for Federal income tax purposes for state income taxes paid eliminates the double taxation of the same income. Do you agree? Why or why not?

51. One of Jane Colby's orchards is being condemned by the Georgia Department of Corrections for use as a prison farm. She paid $25,000 for the property 18 years ago and is receiving an award of $200,000. Shortly after the condemnation, Jane purchases another orchard. Discuss her tax consequences if the cost of the replacement property is:
    a. $20,000.
    b. $190,000.
    c. $205,000.

52. In what manner does the tax law mitigate the effect of the annual accounting period concept with the income recognition treatment allowed for installment sales?

53. How does the tax law cope with the impact of inflation?

Issue ID

54. Renee is the sole shareholder of Bronze Corporation. During the year, she leases property to Bronze for an annual rent of $24,000. Under what circumstances might this arrangement be subject to challenge by the IRS?

55. Edward leases real estate to Janet for a period of 20 years. Janet makes capital improvements to the property. When the lease expires, Edward reclaims the property, including the improvements made by Janet.
    a. Under current law, at what point does Edward recognize income as a result of Janet's improvements?
    b. Has the law in (a) always been the rule?
    c. What is the justification, if any, for the current rule?

CHAPTER 2

Working with the Tax Law

LEARNING OBJECTIVES

After completing Chapter 2, you should be able to:

LO.1
Distinguish between the statutory, administrative, and judicial sources of the tax law and understand the purpose of each source.

LO.2
Locate and work with the appropriate tax law sources.

LO.3
Have an awareness of electronic and paper tax services.

LO.4
Understand the tax research process.

LO.5
Communicate the results of the tax research process in a client letter and a tax file memorandum.

LO.6
Apply tax research techniques and planning procedures.

LO.7
Be aware of taxation on the CPA examination.

LO.1

Distinguish between the statutory, administrative, and judicial sources of the tax law and understand the purpose of each source.

Tax Sources

Understanding taxation requires a mastery of the sources of the *rules of tax law*. These sources include not only legislative provisions in the form of the Internal Revenue Code, but also congressional Committee Reports, Treasury Department Regulations, other Treasury Department pronouncements, and court decisions. Thus, the *primary sources* of tax information include pronouncements from all three branches of government: legislative, executive, and judicial.

In addition to being able to locate and interpret the sources of the tax law, a tax professional must understand the relative weight of authority within these sources. The tax law is of little significance, however, until it is applied to a set of facts and circumstances. This chapter, therefore, both introduces the statutory, administrative, and judicial sources of tax law and explains how the law is applied to individual and business transactions. It also explains how to apply research techniques and use planning procedures effectively.

A large part of tax research focuses on determining the intent of Congress. Although Congress often claims simplicity as one of its goals, a cursory examination of the tax law indicates that it has not been very successful in achieving this objective. Commenting on his 48-page tax return, James Michener, the author, said, "it is unimaginable in that I graduated from one of America's better colleges, yet I am totally incapable of understanding tax returns." David Brinkley, the television news commentator, observed that "settling a dispute is difficult when our tax regulations are all written in a foreign tongue whose language flows like damp sludge leaking from a sanitary landfill."

Frequently, uncertainty in the tax law causes disputes between the Internal Revenue Service (IRS) and taxpayers. Due to these *gray areas* and the complexity of the tax law, a taxpayer may have more than one alternative for structuring a business transaction. In structuring business transactions and engaging in other tax planning activities, the tax adviser must be cognizant that the objective of tax planning is not necessarily to minimize the tax liability. Instead a taxpayer should maximize his or her after-tax return, which may include maximizing nontax as well as noneconomic benefits.

Statutory Sources of the Tax Law

Origin of the Internal Revenue Code. Before 1939, the statutory provisions relating to Federal taxation were contained in the individual revenue acts enacted by Congress. Because dealing with many separate acts was inconvenient and confusing, in 1939 Congress codified all of the Federal tax laws. Known as the Internal Revenue Code of 1939, the codification arranged all Federal tax provisions in a logical sequence and placed them in a separate part of the Federal statutes. A further rearrangement took place in 1954 and resulted in the Internal Revenue Code of 1954, which continued in effect until 1986 when it was replaced by the Internal Revenue Code of 1986. Although Congress did not recodify the law in the Tax Reform Act (TRA) of 1986, the magnitude of the changes made by TRA of 1986 did provide some rationale for renaming the Federal tax law the Internal Revenue Code of 1986.

The following observations help clarify the codification procedure:

- Neither the 1939 nor the 1954 Code substantially changed the tax law existing on the date of its enactment. Much of the 1939 Code, for example, was incorporated into the 1954 Code; the major change was the reorganization and renumbering of the tax provisions.
- Although the 1986 Code resulted in substantial changes, only a minority of the statutory provisions were affected.[1]
- Statutory amendments to the tax law are integrated into the Code. For example, the Taxpayer Relief Act (TRA) of 1997, the Internal Revenue Service Restructuring and Reform Act of 1998, the Tax Relief Reconciliation Act of 2001, the Job Creation and Worker Assistance Act of 2002, the Jobs and Growth Tax Relief Reconciliation Act (JGTRRA) of 2003, the Working Families Tax Relief Act of 2004, the American Jobs Creation Act of 2004, and the Energy Tax Incentives Act of 2005 all became part of the Internal Revenue Code of 1986. In view of the frequency with which tax legislation has been enacted in recent years, it appears that the tax law will continue to be amended frequently.

The Legislative Process. Federal tax legislation generally originates in the House of Representatives, where it is first considered by the House Ways and Means Committee. Tax bills originate in the Senate when they are attached as riders to other legislative proposals.[2] If acceptable to the House Ways and Means Committee, the proposed bill is referred to the entire House of Representatives for approval or disapproval. Approved bills are sent to the Senate, where they are considered by the Senate Finance Committee.

---

[1] This point is important in assessing judicial decisions interpreting provisions of the Internal Revenue Code of 1939 and the Internal Revenue Code of 1954. If the same provision was included in the Internal Revenue Code of 1986 and has not been subsequently amended, the decision has continuing validity.

[2] The Tax Equity and Fiscal Responsibility Act of 1982 originated in the Senate, and its constitutionality was unsuccessfully challenged in the courts. The Senate version of the Deficit Reduction Act of 1984 was attached as an amendment to the Federal Boat Safety Act.

TAX *in the News*   PRISON INMATES' TAX FRAUD

A cartoon shows two cell mates in prison talking about the earned income tax credit (EITC) and dependency exemptions:

"Do you qualify for the EITC this year, Lou?"

"But, of course, Ed!"

"And will you be taking the small business credit, Lou?"

"I feel I've earned it, Ed!"

"And still 750 dependents like last year, Lou?"

"Let's make it an even 800, Ed!"

Although the IRS was able to stop the issuance of 78 percent of fraudulent inmate refunds in 2004, about $14.7 million in erroneous refunds was paid to prisoners. Schemes include using stolen Social Security numbers, filing false forms, and claiming fraudulent tax credits.

Source: *Adapted from Wesley Elmore, "Ways and Means Panel Examines Tax Fraud by Prison Inmates," Tax Notes (July 4, 2005): 65.*

The next step is referral from the Senate Finance Committee to the entire Senate. Assuming no disagreement between the House and Senate, passage by the Senate results in referral to the President for approval or veto. The passage of JGTRRA of 2003 required the vote of Vice President Dick Cheney to break a 50–50 tie in the Senate. If the bill is approved or if the President's veto is overridden, the bill becomes law and part of the Internal Revenue Code of 1986.

House and Senate versions of major tax bills frequently differ. One reason bills are often changed in the Senate is that each individual senator has considerable latitude to make amendments when the Senate as a whole is voting on a bill referred to it by the Senate Finance Committee.[3] In contrast, the entire House of Representatives either accepts or rejects what is proposed by the House Ways and Means Committee, and changes from the floor are rare. When the Senate version of the bill differs from that passed by the House, the Joint Conference Committee, which includes members of both the House Ways and Means Committee and the Senate Finance Committee, is called upon to resolve the differences. The deliberations of the Joint Conference Committee usually produce a compromise between the two versions, which is then voted on by both the House and the Senate. If both bodies accept the bill, it is referred to the President for approval or veto. Former Senator Daniel Patrick Moynihan observed that it is common in the last hours of Congress for the White House and lawmakers to agree on a "1,200-page monster, we vote for it; nobody knows what is in it." Figure 2–1 summarizes the typical legislative process for tax bills.

The role of the Joint Conference Committee indicates the importance of compromise in the legislative process. As an example of the practical effect of the compromise process, consider Figure 2–2, which shows what happened to a limitation on contributions by taxpayers to their education Individual Retirement Accounts (now Coverdell Education Savings Accounts) in the Taxpayer Relief Act of 1997.

Referrals from the House Ways and Means Committee, the Senate Finance Committee, and the Joint Conference Committee are usually accompanied by Committee Reports. These Committee Reports often explain the provisions of the proposed legislation and are therefore a valuable source for ascertaining the *intent of Congress.* What Congress had in mind when it considered and enacted tax legislation is, of course, the key to interpreting such legislation by taxpayers, the IRS, and the courts. Since Regulations normally are not issued immediately after a statute is enacted, taxpayers often look to Committee Reports to determine congressional intent.

---

[3]During the passage of the Tax Reform Act of 1986, Senate leaders tried to make the bill *amendment proof* to avoid the normal amendment process.

FIGURE 2–1   **Legislative Process for Tax Bills**

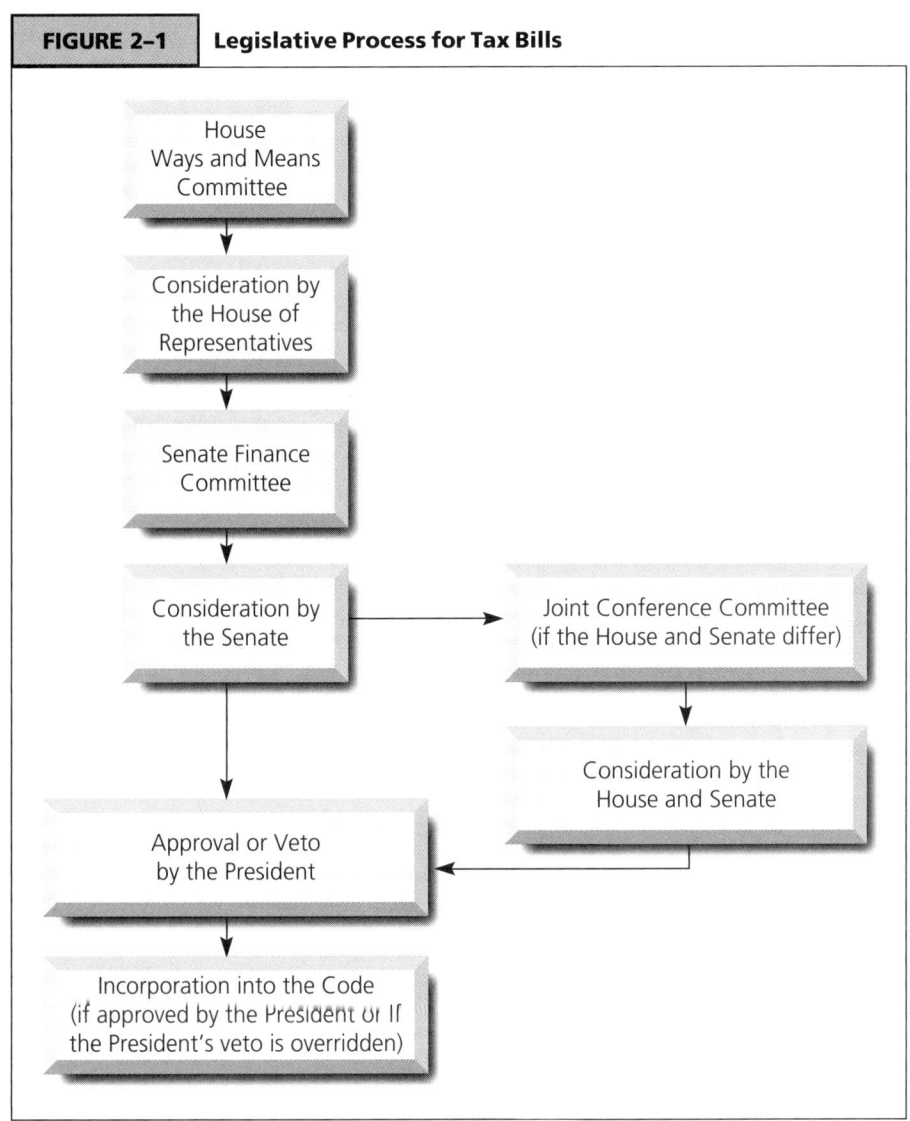

FIGURE 2–2   **Example of Compromise in the Joint Conference Committee**

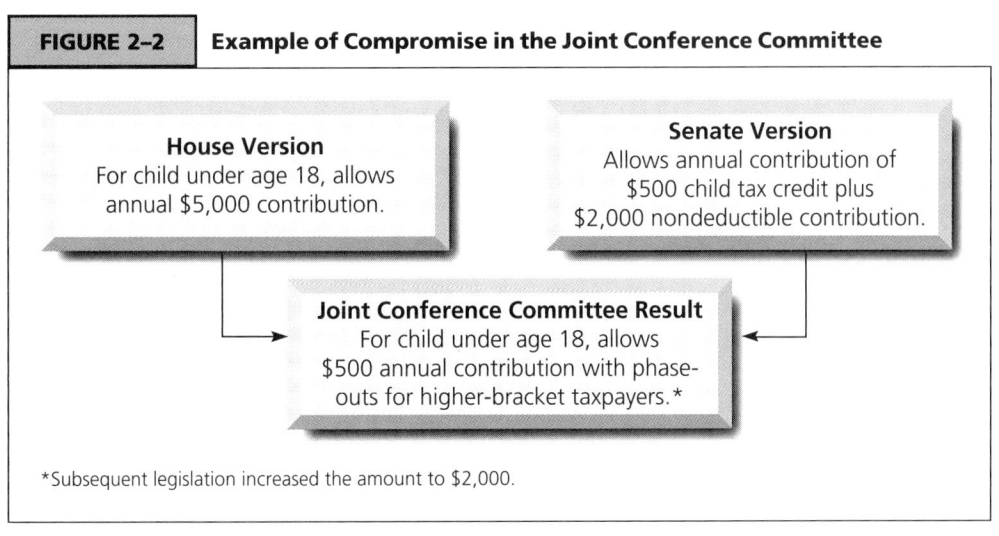

*Subsequent legislation increased the amount to $2,000.

Arrangement of the Code. The Internal Revenue Code of 1986 is found in Title 26 of the U.S. Code. In working with the Code, it helps to understand the format. Note, for example, the following partial table of contents:

> Subtitle A. Income Taxes
> > Chapter 1. Normal Taxes and Surtaxes
> > > Subchapter A. Determination of Tax Liability
> > > > Part I. Tax on Individuals
> > > > > Sections 1–5
> > > > Part II. Tax on Corporations
> > > > > Sections 11–12

In referring to a provision of the Code, the *key* is usually the Section number. In citing Section 2(a) (dealing with the status of a surviving spouse), for example, it is unnecessary to include Subtitle A, Chapter 1, Subchapter A, Part I. Merely mentioning Section 2(a) will suffice, since the Section numbers run consecutively and do not begin again with each new Subtitle, Chapter, Subchapter, or Part. Not all Code Section numbers are used, however. Notice that Part I ends with Section 5 and Part II starts with Section 11 (at present there are no Sections 6, 7, 8, 9, and 10).[4]

Tax practitioners commonly refer to some specific areas of income tax law by their Subchapters. Some of the more common Subchapter designations include Subchapter C ("Corporate Distributions and Adjustments"), Subchapter K ("Partners and Partnerships"), and Subchapter S ("Tax Treatment of S Corporations and Their Shareholders"). In the last situation in particular, it is much more convenient to describe the subject of the applicable Code provisions (Sections 1361–1379) as S corporation status rather than as the "Tax Treatment of S Corporations and Their Shareholders."

Citing the Code. Code Sections often are broken down into subparts.[5] Section 2(a)(1)(A) serves as an example.

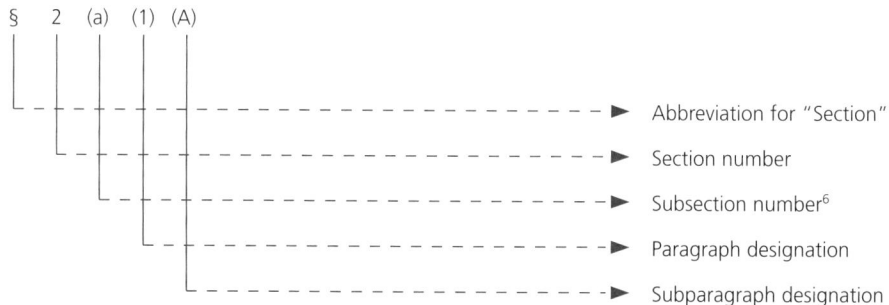

Broken down by content, § 2(a)(1)(A) becomes:

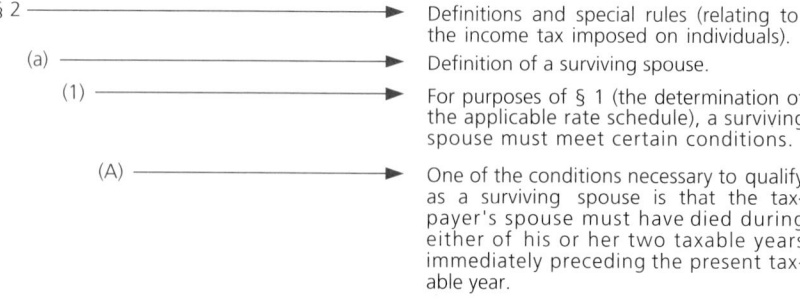

§ 2	→	Definitions and special rules (relating to the income tax imposed on individuals).
(a)	→	Definition of a surviving spouse.
(1)	→	For purposes of § 1 (the determination of the applicable rate schedule), a surviving spouse must meet certain conditions.
(A)	→	One of the conditions necessary to qualify as a surviving spouse is that the taxpayer's spouse must have died during either of his or her two taxable years immediately preceding the present taxable year.

---

[4]When the 1954 Code was drafted, some Section numbers were intentionally omitted so that later changes could be incorporated into the Code without disrupting its organization. When Congress does not leave enough space, subsequent Code Sections are given A, B, C, etc., designations. A good example is the treatment of §§ 280A through 280H.

[5]Some Code Sections do not require subparts. See, for example, §§ 211 and 241.

[6]Some Code Sections omit the subsection designation and use the paragraph designation as the first subpart. See, for example, §§ 212(1) and 1222(1).

Throughout the text, references to the Code Sections are in the form given above. The symbols "§" and "§§" are used in place of "Section" and "Sections." Unless otherwise stated, all Code references are to the Internal Revenue Code of 1986. The following table summarizes the format that will be used:

Complete Reference	Text Reference
Section 2(a)(1)(A) of the Internal Revenue Code of 1986	§ 2(a)(1)(A)
Sections 1 and 2 of the Internal Revenue Code of 1986	§§ 1 and 2
Section 2 of the Internal Revenue Code of 1954	§ 2 of the Internal Revenue Code of 1954
Section 12(d) of the Internal Revenue Code of 1939[7]	§ 12(d) of the Internal Revenue Code of 1939

Administrative Sources of the Tax Law

The administrative sources of the Federal tax law can be grouped as follows: Treasury Department Regulations, Revenue Rulings and Revenue Procedures, and various other administrative pronouncements (see Exhibit 2–1). All are issued by either the U.S. Treasury Department or the IRS.

ETHICAL *Considerations* — **THE PRESIDENT AND THE IRS**

President Franklin Delano Roosevelt once said, "I am wholly unable to figure out the amount of tax." In a letter to the then Commissioner of the IRS, Roosevelt said, "as this is a problem in higher mathematics, may I ask the Bureau [IRS] to let me know the amount of the balance due."

When a friend of FDR was ordered to pay $420,000 in tax penalties, the President called the Commissioner within earshot of reporters and told him to cut the penalties to $3,000. One listener, David Brinkley, recalled years later: "Nobody seemed to think it was news or very interesting." Evaluate the President's actions.

Treasury Department Regulations. Regulations are issued by the U.S. Treasury Department under authority granted by Congress.[8] Interpretive by nature, they provide taxpayers with considerable guidance on the meaning and application of the Code. Regulations may be issued in *proposed, temporary,* or *final* form. Regulations carry considerable authority as the official interpretation of tax statutes. They are an important factor to consider in complying with the tax law.

Since Regulations interpret the Code, they are arranged in the same sequence as the Code. A number is added at the beginning, however, to indicate the type of tax or administrative, procedural, or definitional matter to which they relate. For example, the prefix 1 designates the Regulations under the income tax law. Thus, the Regulations under Code § 2 are cited as Reg. § 1.2 with subparts added for further identification. The numbering patterns of these subparts often have no correlation with the Code subsections. The prefix 20 designates estate tax Regulations; 25 covers gift tax Regulations; 31 relates to employment taxes; and 301 refers to procedure and administration. This list is not all-inclusive.

---

[7]§ 12(d) of the Internal Revenue Code of 1939 is the predecessor to § 2 of the Internal Revenue Code of 1954 and the Internal Revenue Code of 1986. Keep in mind that the 1954 Code superseded the 1939 Code and the 1986 Code has superseded the 1954 Code. Footnote 1 of this chapter explains why references to the 1939 or 1954 Code are included.

[8]§ 7805.

EXHIBIT 2-1	Administrative Sources	

Source	Location	Authority**
Regulations	*Federal Register**	Force and effect of law.
Temporary Regulations	*Federal Register** *Internal Revenue Bulletin* *Cumulative Bulletin*	May be cited as a precedent.
Proposed Regulations	*Federal Register** *Internal Revenue Bulletin* *Cumulative Bulletin*	Preview of final Regulations.
Revenue Rulings Revenue Procedures Treasury Decisions Actions on Decisions	*Internal Revenue Bulletin* *Cumulative Bulletin*	Do not have the force and effect of law.
General Counsel Memoranda Technical Advice Memoranda	*Tax Analysts' Tax Notes;* RIA's *Internal* *Memoranda of the IRS;* CCH's *IRS Position* *Reporter*	May not be cited as a precedent.
Letter Rulings	Research Institute of America and Commerce Clearing House tax services	Applicable only to taxpayer addressed. No precedential force.

*Finalized, Temporary, and Proposed Regulations are published in soft-cover form by several publishers.

**Each of these sources may be substantial authority for purposes of the accuracy-related penalty in § 6662. Notice 90–20, 1990–1 C.B. 328.

New Regulations and changes to existing Regulations are usually issued in proposed form before they are finalized. The interval between the proposal of a Regulation and its finalization permits taxpayers and other interested parties to comment on the propriety of the proposal. **Proposed Regulations** under Code § 2, for example, are cited as Prop.Reg. § 1.2. The Tax Court indicates that Proposed Regulations carry little weight—no more than a position advanced in a written brief prepared by a litigating party before the Tax Court. **Finalized Regulations** have the force and effect of law.[9]

Sometimes the Treasury Department issues **Temporary Regulations** relating to matters where immediate guidance is important. These Regulations are issued without the comment period required for Proposed Regulations. Temporary Regulations have the same authoritative value as final Regulations and may be cited as precedents. Temporary Regulations must also be issued as Proposed Regulations and automatically expire within three years after the date of issuance.[10] Temporary Regulations and the simultaneously issued Proposed Regulations carry more weight than traditional Proposed Regulations. An example of a Temporary Regulation is Temp.Reg. § 1.274–5T(k), which excludes cars, trucks, and vans that are qualified nonpersonal use vehicles from the substantiation requirements for exception treatment to the depreciation limits on luxury passenger automobiles.

Proposed, Temporary, and final Regulations are published in the *Federal Register*, in the *Internal Revenue Bulletin* (I.R.B.), and by major tax services. Final Regulations are issued as Treasury Decisions (TDs).

Regulations may also be classified as *legislative, interpretive,* or *procedural.* This classification scheme is discussed under Assessing the Validity of a Treasury Regulation later in the chapter.

[9]*F. W. Woolworth Co.,* 54 T.C. 1233 (1970); *Harris M. Miller,* 70 T.C. 448 (1978);   [10]§ 7805(e).
and *James O. Tomerlin Trust,* 87 T.C. 876 (1986).

Revenue Rulings and Revenue Procedures. Revenue Rulings are official pronouncements of the National Office of the IRS.[11] They typically provide one or more examples of how the IRS would apply a law to specific fact situations. Like Regulations, Revenue Rulings are designed to provide interpretation of the tax law. However, they do not carry the same legal force and effect as Regulations and usually deal with more restricted problems. Regulations are approved by the Secretary of the Treasury, whereas Revenue Rulings generally are not.

Although letter rulings (discussed below) are not the same as Revenue Rulings, a Revenue Ruling often results from a specific taxpayer's request for a letter ruling. If the IRS believes that a taxpayer's request for a letter ruling deserves official publication because of its widespread impact, the letter ruling will be converted into a Revenue Ruling and issued for the information and guidance of taxpayers, tax practitioners, and IRS personnel. Names, identifying descriptions, and money amounts are changed to conceal the identity of the requesting taxpayer. Revenue Rulings also arise from technical advice to District Offices of the IRS, court decisions, suggestions from tax practitioner groups, and various tax publications.

Revenue Procedures are issued in the same manner as Revenue Rulings, but deal with the internal management practices and procedures of the IRS. Familiarity with these procedures can increase taxpayer compliance and help the IRS administer the tax laws more efficiently. A taxpayer's failure to follow a Revenue Procedure can result in unnecessary delay or, in a discretionary situation, can cause the IRS to decline to act on behalf of the taxpayer.

Both Revenue Rulings and Revenue Procedures serve an important function by providing *guidance* to IRS personnel and taxpayers in handling routine tax matters. Revenue Rulings and Revenue Procedures generally apply retroactively and may be revoked or modified by subsequent rulings or procedures, Regulations, legislation, or court decisions.

Revenue Rulings and Revenue Procedures are published weekly by the U.S. Government in the *Internal Revenue Bulletin* (I.R.B.). Semiannually, the bulletins for a six-month period are gathered together and published in a bound volume called the *Cumulative Bulletin* (C.B.).[12] The proper form for citing Revenue Rulings and Revenue Procedures depends on whether the item has been published in the *Cumulative Bulletin* or is only available in I.R.B. form. Consider, for example, the following transition:

Temporary Citation	Rev.Rul. 2005–48, I.R.B. No. 32, 259. *Explanation:* Revenue Ruling Number 48, appearing on page 259 of the 32nd weekly issue of the *Internal Revenue Bulletin* for 2005.
Permanent Citation	Rev.Rul. 2005–48, 2005–1 C.B. 259. *Explanation:* Revenue Ruling Number 48, appearing on page 259 of Volume 1 of the *Cumulative Bulletin* for 2005.

Note that the page reference of 259 is the same for both the I.R.B. (temporary) and C.B. (permanent) versions of the ruling. The IRS numbers the pages of the I.R.B.s consecutively for each six-month period so as to facilitate their conversion to C.B. form.

Revenue Procedures are cited in the same manner, except that "Rev.Proc." is substituted for "Rev.Rul." Some recent Revenue Procedures dealt with the following matters:

---

[11]§ 7805(a).

[12]Usually, only two volumes of the *Cumulative Bulletin* are published each year. However, when Congress has enacted major tax legislation, other volumes may be published containing the congressional Committee Reports supporting the Revenue Act. See, for example, the two extra volumes for 1984 dealing with the Deficit Reduction Act of 1984. The 1984–3 *Cumulative Bulletin*, Volume 1, contains the text of the law itself; 1984–3, Volume 2, contains the Committee Reports. There are a total of four volumes of the *Cumulative Bulletin* for 1984: 1984–1; 1984–2; 1984–3, Volume 1; 1984–3, Volume 2.

- The condition under which a credit card issuer may treat credit card cash advance fees as creating or increasing original issue discount on a pool of credit card loans.
- The maximum values of employer-provided vehicles first made available to employees for personal use in 2005 for which the vehicle cents-per-mile valuation rule applies.
- Advice to taxpayers not to provide identical paper documents after submitting electronically or magnetically filed tax returns.

Letter Rulings. **Letter rulings** are issued for a fee upon a taxpayer's request and describe how the IRS will treat a *proposed* transaction for tax purposes. They apply only to the taxpayer who asks for and obtains the ruling, but post-1984 letter rulings may be substantial authority for purposes of the accuracy-related penalty.[13] Letter rulings can be useful to taxpayers who wish to be certain of how a transaction will be taxed before proceeding with it. Letter rulings also allow taxpayers to avoid unexpected tax costs. Although the procedure for requesting a ruling can be quite cumbersome, sometimes requesting a ruling is the most effective way to carry out tax planning. Nevertheless, the IRS limits the issuance of individual rulings to restricted, preannounced areas of taxation. The main reason the IRS will not rule in certain areas is that they involve fact-oriented situations. Thus, a ruling may not be obtained on many of the problems that are particularly troublesome for taxpayers.[14] The IRS issues over 2,000 letter rulings each year.

The law now requires the IRS to make individual rulings available for public inspection after identifying details are deleted.[15] Published digests of private letter rulings can be found in *Private Letter Rulings* (published by RIA), BNA *Daily Tax Reports,* and Tax Analysts & Advocates *Tax Notes. IRS Letter Rulings Reports* (published by Commerce Clearing House) contains both digests and full texts of all letter rulings. *Letter Ruling Review* (published by Tax Analysts) is a monthly publication that selects and discusses the more important letter rulings issued each month. In addition, computerized databases of letter rulings are available through several private publishers.

Letter rulings are issued multidigit file numbers, which indicate the year and week of issuance as well as the number of the ruling during that week. Consider, for example, Ltr.Rul. 200530033, which waived the 60-day rollover requirement for distributions from an Individual Retirement Account and granted a 60-day extension.

2005	30	033
Year 2005	30th week of issuance	33rd ruling issued during the 30th week

Other Administrative Pronouncements. *Treasury Decisions* (TDs) are issued by the Treasury Department to promulgate new Regulations, amend or otherwise change existing Regulations, or announce the position of the Government on selected court decisions. Like Revenue Rulings and Revenue Procedures, TDs are published in the *Internal Revenue Bulletin* and subsequently transferred to the *Cumulative Bulletin.*

The IRS publishes other administrative communications in the *Internal Revenue Bulletin* such as Announcements, Notices, LRs (Proposed Regulations), and Prohibited Transaction Exemptions.

---

[13]Notice 90–20, 1990–1 C.B. 328. In this regard, letter rulings differ from Revenue Rulings, which are applicable to *all* taxpayers. A letter ruling may later lead to the issuance of a Revenue Ruling if the holding affects many taxpayers. In its Agents' Manual, the IRS indicates that letter rulings may be used as a guide with other research materials in formulating a District Office position on an issue. The IRS is required to charge a taxpayer a fee for letter rulings, determination letters, etc.

[14]Rev.Proc. 2005–68, I.R.B. No. 41, 694 contains a list of areas in which the IRS will not issue advance rulings. From time to time, subsequent Revenue Procedures are issued that modify or amplify Rev.Proc. 2005–68.

[15]§ 6110.

Like letter rulings, **determination letters** are issued at the request of taxpayers and provide guidance on the application of the tax law. They differ from letter rulings in that the issuing source is the Area Director rather than the National Office of the IRS. Also, determination letters usually involve *completed* (as opposed to proposed) transactions. Determination letters are not published and are made known only to the party making the request.

The following examples illustrate the distinction between letter rulings and determination letters:

EXAMPLE 1

The shareholders of Red Corporation and Green Corporation want assurance that the consolidation of the corporations into Blue Corporation will be a nontaxable reorganization. The proper approach is to request the National Office of the IRS to issue a letter ruling concerning the income tax effect of the proposed transaction. ∎

EXAMPLE 2

Chris operates a barber shop in which he employs eight barbers. To comply with the rules governing income tax and payroll tax withholdings, Chris wants to know whether the barbers working for him are employees or independent contractors. The proper procedure is to request a determination letter on their status from the appropriate Area Director. ∎

Several internal memoranda that constitute the working law of the IRS now must be released. These General Counsel Memoranda (GCMs), Technical Advice Memoranda (TAMs), and Field Service Advices (FSAs) are not officially published, and the IRS indicates that they may not be cited as precedents by taxpayers.[16] However, these working documents do explain the IRS's position on various issues.

The National Office of the IRS releases **Technical Advice Memoranda (TAMs)** weekly. TAMs resemble letter rulings in that they give the IRS's determination of an issue. However, they differ in several respects. Letter rulings deal with proposed transactions and are issued to taxpayers at their request. In contrast, TAMs deal with completed transactions. Furthermore, TAMs arise from questions raised by IRS personnel during audits and are issued by the National Office of the IRS to its field personnel. TAMs are often requested for questions relating to exempt organizations and employee plans. TAMs are not officially published and may not be cited or used as precedent.[17] They are assigned file numbers according to the same procedure used for letter rulings. For example, TAM 200528026 refers to the 26th TAM issued during the 28th week of 2005.

The Office of Chief Counsel prepares Field Service Advice (FSAs) to help IRS employees. They are issued in response to requests for advice, guidance, and analysis on difficult or significant tax issues. FSAs are not binding on either the taxpayer to whom they pertain or on the IRS. For example, FSA 200233016 states that § 269 may be used to disallow foreign tax credits and deductions that arise from a series of reorganizations if the underlying transaction's principal purpose is to secure tax benefits.

Field Service Advices are being replaced by a new form of field guidance called Technical Expedited Advice Memoranda (TEAMs). The purpose of TEAMs is to expedite legal guidance to field agents as disputes are developing. FSAs are reverting to their original purpose of case-specific development of facts.

A TEAM guidance differs from a TAM in several ways, including a mandatory presubmission conference involving the taxpayer. In the event of a tentatively adverse conclusion for the taxpayer or the field, a conference of right is offered to the taxpayer and to the field; once the conference of right is held, no further conferences are offered.

---

[16]These are unofficially published by the publishers listed in Exhibit 2–1. Such internal memoranda for post-1984 may be substantial authority for purposes of the accuracy-related penalty. Notice 90–20, 1990–1 C.B. 328.

[17]§ 6110(j)(3). Post-1984 TAMs may be substantial authority for purposes of avoiding the accuracy-related penalty. Notice 90–20, 1990–1 C.B. 328.

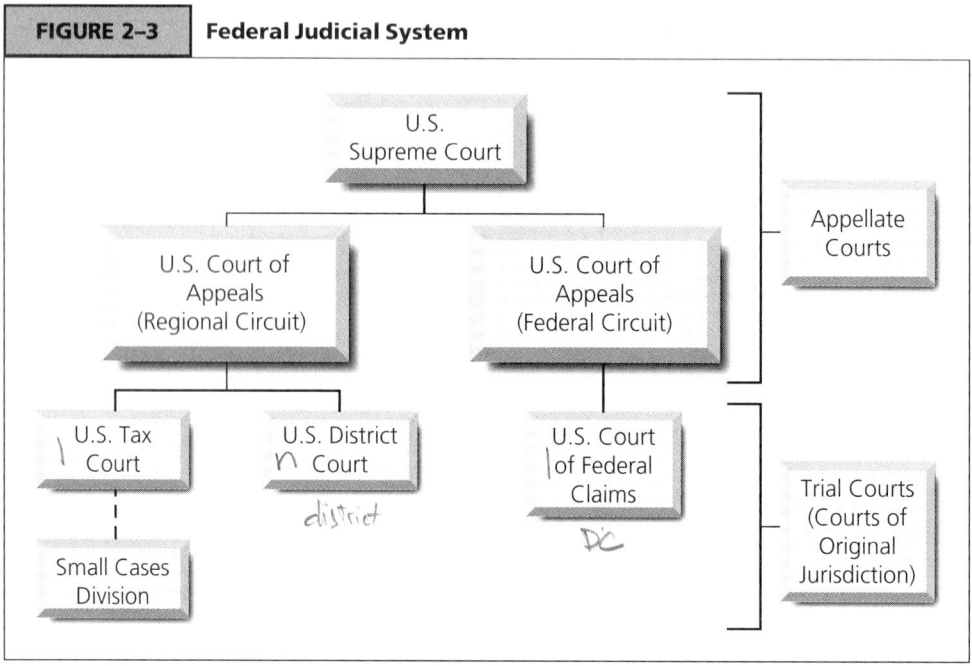

FIGURE 2–3 | **Federal Judicial System**

Judicial Sources of the Tax Law

The Judicial Process in General. After a taxpayer has exhausted some or all of the remedies available within the IRS (i.e., no satisfactory settlement has been reached at the agent or at the Appeals Division level), the dispute can be taken to the Federal courts. The dispute is first considered by a **court of original jurisdiction** (known as a trial court) with any appeal (either by the taxpayer or the IRS) taken to the appropriate appellate court. In most situations, the taxpayer has a choice of any of *four trial courts:* a **Federal District Court**, the **U.S. Court of Federal Claims**, the **U.S. Tax Court**, or the **Small Cases Division** of the U.S. Tax Court. The trial and appellate court system for Federal tax litigation is illustrated in Figure 2–3.

The broken line between the U.S. Tax Court and the Small Cases Division indicates that there is no appeal from the Small Cases Division. The jurisdiction of the Small Cases Division is limited to cases involving amounts of $50,000 or less. The proceedings of the Small Cases Division are informal (e.g., no necessity for the taxpayer to be represented by a lawyer or other tax adviser). Special trial judges rather than Tax Court judges preside over these proceedings. The decisions of the Small Cases Division are not precedents for any other court decision and are not reviewable by any higher court. Proceedings can be more timely and less expensive in the Small Cases Division. Some of these cases can now be found on the U.S. Tax Court Internet Web site.

American law, following English law, is frequently *made* by judicial decisions. Under the doctrine of *stare decisis,* each case (except in the Small Cases Division) has precedential value for future cases with the same controlling set of facts. Most Federal and state appellate court decisions and some decisions of trial courts are published. More than 6 million judicial opinions have been published in the United States; over 130,000 cases are published each year.[18] Published court decisions are organized by jurisdiction (Federal or state) and level of court (trial or appellate).

A decision of a particular court is called its holding. Sometimes a decision includes dicta or incidental opinions beyond the current facts. Such passing

---

[18]Mersky and Dunn, *Fundamentals of Legal Research,* 8th ed. Westbury, N.Y.:(The Foundation Press, 2002), p. 11.

TAX *in the News*   **THE TAX GAP INCREASES**

A cartoon shows a Tax Court judge talking to Mr. Van Gogh: "The IRS is facing a $312 billion tax gap, and you expect this court to believe that you only have income from the sale of one painting?! Really, Mr. Van Gogh!"

According to an IRS study, the tax gap for individuals was between $312 billion and $353 billion in 2001. In other words, individual taxpayers failed to pay up to $353 billion of what they owed in taxes in that year.

The IRS refers to the difference between the amount of taxes owed and the amount collected as the "tax gap."

In contrast, the tax gap created by abusive corporate tax shelters is estimated to be around $30 billion a year, only a fraction of the gap for individuals. IRS Commissioner Mark Everson does not know if the individual tax gap is caused by the complexity of the tax Code or by deliberate evasion on the part of taxpayers.

Source: *Adapted from Allen Kenney, "New IRS Estimates Show Slight Widening of Tax Gap," Tax Notes (April 4, 2005): 7–8.*

---

remarks, illustrations, or analogies are not essential to the current holding. Although the holding has precedential value under *stare decisis*, dicta are not binding on a future court.

Trial Courts. The differences among the various trial courts (courts of original jurisdiction) can be summarized as follows:

- *Number of courts.* There is only one Court of Federal Claims and only one Tax Court, but there are many Federal District Courts. The taxpayer does not select the District Court that will hear the dispute but must sue in the one that has jurisdiction where the taxpayer resides.
- *Number of judges.* District Courts have various numbers of judges, but only one judge hears a case. The Court of Federal Claims has 16 judges, and the Tax Court has 19 regular judges. The entire Tax Court, however, reviews a case (the case is sent to court conference) only when more important or novel tax issues are involved. Most cases are heard and decided by one of the 19 judges.
- *Location.* The Court of Federal Claims meets most often in Washington, D.C., whereas a District Court meets at a prescribed seat for the particular district. Each state has at least one District Court, and many of the more populous states have more than one. Choosing the District Court usually minimizes the inconvenience and expense of traveling for the taxpayer and his or her counsel. Although the Tax Court is officially based in Washington, D.C., the various judges travel to different parts of the country and hear cases at predetermined locations and dates. This procedure eases the distance problem for the taxpayer, but it can mean a delay before the case comes to trial and is decided.
- *Jurisdiction of the Court of Federal Claims.* The Court of Federal Claims has jurisdiction over any claim against the United States that is based upon the Constitution, any Act of Congress, or any regulation of an executive department. Thus, the Court of Federal Claims hears nontax litigation as well as tax cases. This forum appears to be more favorable for issues having an equitable or pro-business orientation (as opposed to purely technical issues) and for those requiring extensive discovery.[19]
- *Jurisdiction of the Tax Court and District Courts.* The Tax Court hears only tax cases and is the most popular forum. The District Courts hear a wide variety of nontax cases, including drug crimes and other Federal violations, as well as tax cases. Some Tax Court judges have been appointed from IRS or Treasury Department positions. For these reasons, some people suggest that the Tax Court has more expertise in tax matters.

---

[19]T. D. Peyser, "The Case for Selecting the Claims Court to Litigate a Federal Tax Liability," *The Tax Executive* (Winter 1988): 149.

CONCEPT SUMMARY *2–1*

Federal Judicial System: Trial Courts

Issue	U.S. Tax Court	U.S. District Court	U.S. Court of Federal Claims
Number of judges per court	19*	Varies	16
Payment of deficiency before trial	No	Yes	Yes
Jury trial available	No	Yes	No
Types of disputes	Tax cases only	Most criminal and civil issues	Claims against the United States
Jurisdiction	Nationwide	Location of taxpayer	Nationwide
IRS acquiescence policy	Yes	Yes	Yes
Appeal route	U.S. Court of Appeals	U.S. Court of Appeals	U.S. Court of Appeals for the Federal Circuit

*There are also 14 special trial judges and 9 senior judges.

- *Jury trial.* The only court in which a taxpayer can obtain a jury trial is a District Court. But since juries can only decide questions of fact and not questions of law, even taxpayers who choose the District Court route often do not request a jury trial. In that event, the judge will decide all issues. Note that a District Court decision is controlling only in the district in which the court has jurisdiction.
- *Payment of deficiency.* For the Court of Federal Claims or a District Court to have jurisdiction, the taxpayer must pay the tax deficiency assessed by the IRS and sue for a refund. A taxpayer who wins (assuming no successful appeal by the Government) recovers the tax paid plus appropriate interest. For the Tax Court, however, jurisdiction is usually obtained without first paying the assessed tax deficiency. In the event the taxpayer loses in the Tax Court (and does not appeal or an appeal is unsuccessful), the deficiency must be paid with appropriate interest. With the elimination of the deduction for personal (consumer) interest, the Tax Court route of delaying payment of the deficiency can become expensive. For example, to earn 7 percent after tax in 2006, a taxpayer with a 35 percent marginal tax rate would have to earn 10.77 percent. By paying the tax, a taxpayer limits underpayment interest and penalties on the underpayment.
- *Termination of running of interest.* A taxpayer who selects the Tax Court may deposit a cash bond to stop the running of interest. The taxpayer must deposit both the amount of the tax and any accrued interest. If the taxpayer wins and the deposited amount is returned, the Government does not pay interest on the deposit.
- *Appeals.* Appeals from a District Court or a Tax Court decision are to the U.S. Court of Appeals for the circuit in which the taxpayer resides. Appeals from the Court of Federal Claims go to the Court of Appeals for the Federal Circuit. Few Tax Court cases are appealed, and when appeals are made, most are filed by the taxpayer rather than the IRS.
- *Bankruptcy.* When a taxpayer files a bankruptcy petition, the IRS, like other creditors, is prevented from taking action against the taxpayer. Sometimes a bankruptcy court may settle a tax claim.

For a summary of the Federal trial courts, see Concept Summary 2–1.

FIGURE 2–4   **The Federal Courts of Appeals**

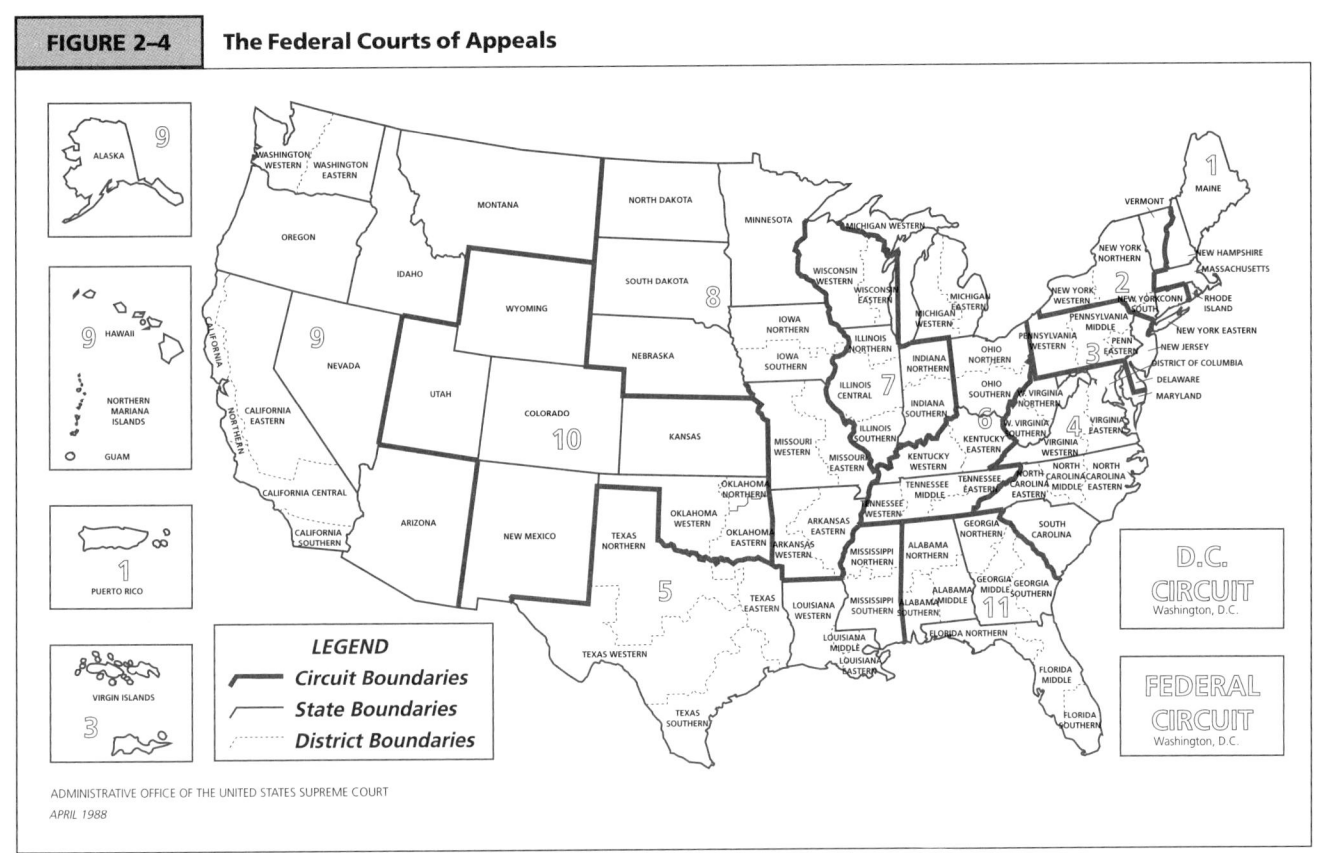

ADMINISTRATIVE OFFICE OF THE UNITED STATES SUPREME COURT
APRIL 1988

Appellate Courts. The losing party can appeal a trial court decision to a **Circuit Court of Appeals.** The 11 geographic circuits, the circuit for the District of Columbia, and the Federal Circuit[20] appear in Figure 2–4. The appropriate circuit for an appeal depends on where the litigation originated. For example, an appeal from New York goes to the Second Circuit.

If the Government loses at the trial court level (District Court, Tax Court, or Court of Federal Claims), it need not (frequently does not) appeal. The fact that an appeal is not made, however, does not indicate that the IRS agrees with the result and will not litigate similar issues in the future. The IRS may decide not to appeal for a number of reasons. First, if the current litigation load is heavy, the IRS may decide that available personnel should be assigned to other, more important cases. Second, the IRS may determine that this case is not a good one to appeal. Perhaps the taxpayer is in a sympathetic position or the facts are particularly strong in his or her favor. In that event, the IRS may wait to test the legal issues involved with a taxpayer who has a much weaker case. Third, if the appeal is from a District Court or the Tax Court, the Court of Appeals of jurisdiction could have some bearing on whether the IRS chooses to go forward with an appeal. Based on past experience and precedent, the IRS may conclude that the chance for success on a particular issue might be more promising in another Court of Appeals. If so, the IRS will wait for a similar case to arise in a different jurisdiction.

[20]The Court of Appeals for the Federal Circuit was created, effective October 1, 1982, by P.L. 97–164 (4/2/82) to hear decisions appealed from the Claims Court (now the Court of Federal Claims).

The Federal Circuit at the appellate level provides the taxpayer with an alternative forum to the Court of Appeals for his or her home circuit. Appeals from both the Tax Court and the District Court go to a taxpayer's home circuit. When a particular circuit has issued an adverse decision, the taxpayer may prefer the Court of Federal Claims route, since any appeal will be to the Federal Circuit.

District Courts, the Tax Court, and the Court of Federal Claims must abide by the **precedents** set by the Court of Appeals of jurisdiction. A particular Court of Appeals need not follow the decisions of another Court of Appeals. All courts, however, must follow the decisions of the **U.S. Supreme Court.**

This pattern of appellate precedents raises an issue for the Tax Court. Because the Tax Court is a national court, it decides cases from all parts of the country. For many years, the Tax Court followed a policy of deciding cases based on what it thought the result should be, even though its decision might be appealed to a Court of Appeals that had previously decided a similar case differently. A number of years ago this policy was changed in the *Golsen*[21] decision. Now the Tax Court will decide a case as it feels the law should be applied *only* if the Court of Appeals of appropriate jurisdiction has not yet passed on the issue or has previously decided a similar case in accord with the Tax Court's decision. If the Court of Appeals of appropriate jurisdiction has previously held otherwise, the Tax Court will conform under the *Golsen* rule even though it disagrees with the holding.

EXAMPLE 3

Emily lives in Texas and sues in the Tax Court on Issue A. The Fifth Circuit Court of Appeals is the appellate court of appropriate jurisdiction. It has already decided, in a case involving similar facts but a different taxpayer, that Issue A should be resolved against the Government. Although the Tax Court feels that the Fifth Circuit Court of Appeals is wrong, under its *Golsen* policy it will render judgment for Emily. Shortly thereafter, Rashad, a resident of New York, in a comparable case, sues in the Tax Court on Issue A. Assume that the Second Circuit Court of Appeals, the appellate court of appropriate jurisdiction, has never expressed itself on Issue A. Presuming the Tax Court has not reconsidered its position on Issue A, it will decide against Rashad. Thus, it is entirely possible for two taxpayers suing in the same court to end up with opposite results merely because they live in different parts of the country. ■

Appeal to the U.S. Supreme Court is by **Writ of Certiorari.** If the Court agrees to hear the case, it will grant the Writ (*Cert. granted*). Most often, it will deny jurisdiction (*Cert. denied*). For whatever reason or reasons, the Supreme Court rarely hears tax cases. The Court usually grants certiorari to resolve a conflict among the Courts of Appeals (e.g., two or more appellate courts have assumed opposing positions on a particular issue) or where the tax issue is extremely important. The granting of a Writ of Certiorari indicates that at least four members of the Supreme Court believe that the issue is of sufficient importance to be heard by the full Court.

The *role* of appellate courts is limited to a review of the record of trial compiled by the trial courts. Thus, the appellate process usually involves a determination of whether the trial court applied the proper law in arriving at its decision. Rarely will an appellate court disturb a lower court's fact-finding determination.

Both the Code and the Supreme Court indicate that Federal appellate courts are bound by findings of facts unless they are clearly erroneous.[22] This aspect of the appellate process is illustrated by a decision of the Court of Appeals for the District of Columbia involving whether a taxpayer was engaged in an activity for profit under § 183.[23] This appeals court specifically held that the "Tax Court's findings of facts are binding on Federal courts of appeals unless clearly erroneous." The court

---

[21]*Jack E. Golsen*, 54 T.C. 742 (1970).

[22]§§ 7482(a) and (c). *Comm. v. Duberstein*, 60–2 USTC ¶9515, 5 AFTR2d 1626, 80 S.Ct. 1190 (USSC, 1960). See Rule 52(a) of the Federal Rules of Civil Procedure.

[23]*Dreicer v. Comm.*, 81–2 USTC ¶9683, 48 AFTR2d 5884, 665 F.2d 1292 (CA–DC, 1981).

applauded the Tax Court for the thoroughness of its factual inquiry but could "not place the stamp of approval upon its eventual legal outcome." In reversing and remanding the decision to the Tax Court, the appellate court said that "the language of § 183, its legislative history and the applicable Treasury regulation combine to demonstrate that the court's [Tax Court's] standard is erroneous as a matter of law." The appeals court held that this taxpayer's claims of deductibility were to be evaluated by proper legal standards.

An appeal can have any of a number of possible outcomes. The appellate court may approve (affirm) or disapprove (reverse) the lower court's finding, or it may send the case back for further consideration (remand). When many issues are involved, a mixed result is not unusual. Thus, the lower court may be affirmed (*aff'd*) on Issue A and reversed (*rev'd*) on Issue B, while Issue C is remanded (*rem'd*) for additional fact finding.

When more than one judge is involved in the decision-making process, disagreements are not uncommon. In addition to the majority view, one or more judges may concur (agree with the result reached but not with some or all of the reasoning) or dissent (disagree with the result). In any one case, of course, the majority view controls. But concurring and dissenting views can have an influence on other courts or, at some subsequent date when the composition of the court has changed, even on the same court.

Knowledge of several terms is important in understanding court decisions. The term *plaintiff* refers to the party requesting action in a court, and the *defendant* is the party against whom the suit is brought. Sometimes a court uses the terms *petitioner* and *respondent*. In general, "petitioner" is a synonym for "plaintiff," and "respondent" is a synonym for "defendant." At the trial court level, a taxpayer is normally the plaintiff (or petitioner), and the Government is the defendant (or respondent). If the taxpayer wins and the Government appeals as the new petitioner (or appellant), the taxpayer becomes the new respondent.

Judicial Citations—General. Having briefly described the judicial process, it is appropriate to consider the more practical problem of the relationship of case law to tax research. As previously noted, court decisions are an important source of tax law. The ability to cite and locate a case is, therefore, a must in working with the tax law. Judicial citations usually follow a standard pattern: case name, volume number, reporter series, page or paragraph number, court (where necessary), and the year of the decision.

> **LO.2**
>
> Locate and work with the appropriate tax law sources.

Judicial Citations—The U.S. Tax Court. A good starting point is with the Tax Court. The Tax Court issues two types of decisions: Regular and Memorandum. The Chief Judge decides whether the opinion is issued as a Regular or Memorandum decision. The distinction between the two involves both substance and form. In terms of substance, *Memorandum* decisions deal with situations necessitating only the application of already established principles of law. *Regular* decisions involve novel issues not previously resolved by the court. In actual practice, however, this distinction is not always preserved. Not infrequently, Memorandum decisions will be encountered that appear to warrant Regular status and vice versa. At any rate, do not conclude that Memorandum decisions possess no value as precedents. Both represent the position of the Tax Court and, as such, can be relied on.

The Regular and Memorandum decisions issued by the Tax Court also differ in form. Memorandum decisions are officially published in mimeograph form only. Regular decisions are published by the U.S. Government in a series entitled *Tax Court of the United States Reports* (T.C.). Each volume of these *Reports* covers a six-month period (January 1 through June 30 and July 1 through December 31) and is given a succeeding volume number. But, as is true of the *Cumulative Bulletin*, there is usually a time lag between the date a decision is rendered and the date it appears in bound form. A temporary citation may be necessary to help the researcher locate a recent Regular decision. Consider, for example, the temporary and permanent citations for *Estate of Leona Engelman*, a decision filed on July 24, 2003:

Temporary Citation	{ *Estate of Leona Engelman*, 121 T.C. ___, No. 4 (2003). *Explanation:* Page number left blank because not yet known.
Permanent Citation	{ *Estate of Leona Engelman*, 121 T.C. 54 (2003). *Explanation:* Page number now available.

Both citations tell us that the case will ultimately appear in Volume 121 of the *Tax Court of the United States Reports*. But until this volume is bound and made available to the general public, the page number must be left blank. Instead, the temporary citation identifies the case as being the 4th Regular decision issued by the Tax Court since Volume 120 ended. With this information, the decision can easily be located in either of the special Tax Court services published by Commerce Clearing House (now owned by the Dutch company Wolters Kluwer) or Research Institute of America (formerly by Prentice-Hall). Once Volume 121 is released, the permanent citation can be substituted and the number of the case dropped. Starting in 1999, both Regular decisions and Memorandum decisions are published on the U.S. Tax Court Web site (**http://www.ustaxcourt.gov**).

Before 1943, the Tax Court was called the Board of Tax Appeals, and its decisions were published as the *United States Board of Tax Appeals Reports* (B.T.A.). These 47 volumes cover the period from 1924 to 1942. For example, the citation *Karl Pauli*, 11 B.T.A. 784 (1928), refers to the 11th volume of the *Board of Tax Appeals Reports*, page 784, issued in 1928.

If the IRS loses in a decision, it may indicate whether it agrees or disagrees with the results reached by the court by publishing an **acquiescence** ("A" or "*Acq.*") or **nonacquiescence** ("NA" or "*Nonacq.*"), respectively. Until 1991, acquiescences and nonacquiescences were published only for certain Regular decisions of the Tax Court, but the IRS has expanded its acquiescence program to include other civil tax cases where guidance is helpful. The acquiescence or nonacquiescence is published in the *Internal Revenue Bulletin* and the *Cumulative Bulletin* as an *Action on Decision*. The IRS can retroactively revoke an acquiescence.

Most often the IRS issues nonacquiescences to adverse decisions that are not appealed. In this manner, the Government indicates that it disagrees with the result reached, despite its decision not to seek review of the matter in an appellate court. A nonacquiescence provides a warning to taxpayers that a similar case cannot be settled administratively. A taxpayer will incur fees and expenses appealing within the IRS even though the IRS may be unwilling to litigate a fact pattern similar to a nonacquiescence decision.[24]

Although Memorandum decisions were not published by the U.S. Government until recently (they are now published on the U.S. Tax Court Web site), they were—and continue to be—published by Commerce Clearing House (CCH) and Research Institute of America (RIA [formerly by Prentice-Hall]). Consider, for example, the three different ways that *Jack D. Carr* can be cited:

Jack D. Carr, T.C.Memo. 1985–19
The 19th Memorandum decision issued by the Tax Court in 1985.
Jack D. Carr, 49 TCM 507
Page 507 of Vol. 49 of the CCH *Tax Court Memorandum Decisions*.
Jack D. Carr, RIA T.C.Mem.Dec. ¶85,019
Paragraph 85,019 of the RIA *T.C. Memorandum Decisions*.

---

[24]G. W. Carter, "Nonacquiescence: Winning by Losing," *Tax Notes* (September 19, 1988): 1301–1307.

Note that the third citation contains the same information as the first. Thus, ¶85,019 indicates the following information about the case: year 1985, 19th T.C. Memo. decision.[25] Although the RIA citation does not specifically include a volume number, the paragraph citation indicates that the decision can be found in the 1985 volume of the RIA Memorandum decision service.

Starting in 2001, U.S. Tax Court Summary Opinions are published on the U.S. Tax Court Web site, with the warning that they may not be treated as precedent for any other case. For example, *James A. Wiese*, filed on July 19, 2005, is cited as follows:

James A. Wiese, T.C. Summary Opinion, 2005–91.

In 2005, the U.S. Supreme Court held that decisions of the Small Cases Division must be made public.

Judicial Citations—The U.S. District Court, Court of Federal Claims, and Courts of Appeals.

District Court, Court of Federal Claims, Courts of Appeals, and Supreme Court decisions dealing with Federal tax matters are reported in both the CCH *U.S. Tax Cases* (USTC) and the RIA *American Federal Tax Reports* (AFTR) series. Federal District Court decisions, dealing with *both* tax and nontax issues, also are published by West Publishing Company in its *Federal Supplement Series* (F.Supp.). Volume 999, published in 1998, is the last volume of the *Federal Supplement Series*. It is followed by the *Federal Supplement Second Series* (F.Supp.2d). The following examples illustrate three different ways of citing a District Court case:

Simons-Eastern Co. v. U.S., 73–1 USTC ¶9279 (D.Ct. Ga., 1972).

Explanation: Reported in the first volume of the *U.S. Tax Cases* (USTC) published by Commerce Clearing House for calendar year 1973 (73–1) and located at paragraph 9279 (¶9279).

Simons-Eastern Co. v. U.S., 31 AFTR2d 73–640 (D.Ct. Ga., 1972).

Explanation: Reported in the 31st volume of the second series of the *American Federal Tax Reports* (AFTR2d) published by RIA and beginning on page 640. The "73" preceding the page number indicates the year the case was published but is a designation used only in recent decisions.

Simons-Eastern Co. v. U.S., 354 F.Supp. 1003 (D.Ct. Ga., 1972).

Explanation: Reported in the 354th volume of the *Federal Supplement Series* (F.Supp.) published by West Publishing Company and beginning on page 1003.

In all of the preceding citations, note that the name of the case is the same (Simons-Eastern Co. being the taxpayer), as is the reference to the Federal District Court of Georgia (D.Ct. Ga.) and the year the decision was rendered (1972).[26]

Decisions of the Court of Federal Claims[27] and the Courts of Appeals are published in the USTCs, AFTRs, and a West Publishing Company reporter called the *Federal Second Series* (F.2d). Volume 999, published in 1993, is the last volume of the *Federal Second Series*. It is followed by the *Federal Third Series* (F.3d). Beginning with October 1982, the Court of Federal Claims decisions are published in another West Publishing Company reporter entitled the *Claims Court Reporter* (abbreviated Cl.Ct.). Beginning with Volume 27 on October 30, 1992, the name of the reporter changed to the *Federal Claims Reporter* (abbreviated as Fed.Cl.). The following examples illustrate the different forms:

---

[25]In this text, the RIA citation for Memorandum decisions of the U.S. Tax Court is omitted. Thus, *Jack D. Carr* would be cited as 49 TCM 507, T.C.Memo. 1985–19.

[26]In this text, the case would be cited in the following form: *Simons-Eastern Co. v. U.S.*, 73–1 USTC ¶9279, 31 AFTR2d 73–640, 354 F.Supp. 1003 (D.Ct. Ga., 1972). Prentice-Hall Information Services is now owned by Research Insti-

tute of America. Although recent volumes contain the RIA imprint, many of the older volumes continue to have the P-H imprint.

[27]Before October 29, 1992, the Court of Federal Claims was called the Claims Court. Before October 1, 1982, the Court of Federal Claims was called the Court of Claims.

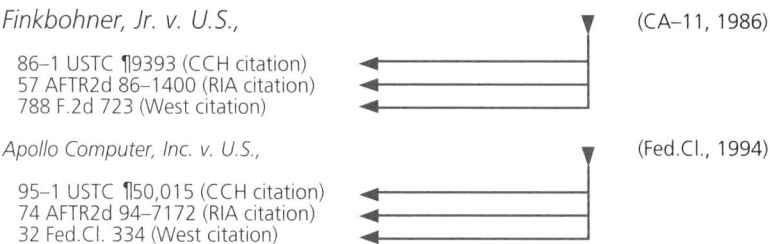

Finkbohner, Jr. v. U.S.,   (CA–11, 1986)

86–1 USTC ¶9393 (CCH citation)
57 AFTR2d 86–1400 (RIA citation)
788 F.2d 723 (West citation)

Apollo Computer, Inc. v. U.S.,   (Fed.Cl., 1994)

95–1 USTC ¶50,015 (CCH citation)
74 AFTR2d 94–7172 (RIA citation)
32 Fed.Cl. 334 (West citation)

Note that *Finkbohner, Jr.* is a decision rendered by the Eleventh Circuit Court of Appeals in 1986 (CA–11, 1986), while *Apollo Computer, Inc.* was issued by the Court of Federal Claims in 1994 (Fed.Cl., 1994).

Judicial Citations—The U.S. Supreme Court.

Like all other Federal tax decisions (except those rendered by the Tax Court), Supreme Court decisions are published by Commerce Clearing House in the USTCs and by RIA (formerly by Prentice-Hall) in the AFTRs. The U.S. Government Printing Office also publishes these decisions in the *United States Supreme Court Reports* (U.S.) as does West Publishing Company in its *Supreme Court Reporter* (S.Ct.) and the Lawyer's Co-operative Publishing Company in its *United States Reports, Lawyer's Edition* (L.Ed.). The following illustrates the different ways the same decision can be cited:

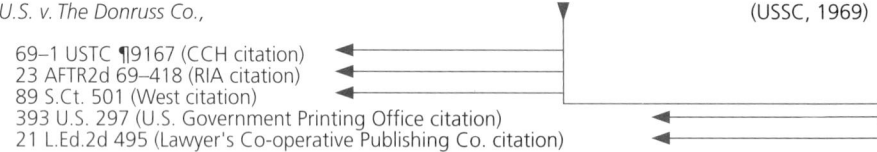

U.S. v. The Donruss Co.,   (USSC, 1969)

69–1 USTC ¶9167 (CCH citation)
23 AFTR2d 69–418 (RIA citation)
89 S.Ct. 501 (West citation)
393 U.S. 297 (U.S. Government Printing Office citation)
21 L.Ed.2d 495 (Lawyer's Co-operative Publishing Co. citation)

The parenthetical reference (USSC, 1969) identifies the decision as having been rendered by the U.S. Supreme Court in 1969. In this text, the citations of Supreme Court decisions will be limited to the CCH (USTC), RIA (AFTR), and West (S.Ct.) versions. For a summary, see Concept Summary 2–2.

Other Sources of the Tax Law

Other sources of tax information that a tax practitioner may need to consult include tax treaties and tax periodicals.

Tax Treaties. The United States signs certain tax treaties (sometimes called tax conventions) with foreign countries to render mutual assistance in tax enforcement

CONCEPT SUMMARY 2–2

Judicial Sources

Court	Location	Authority
U.S. Supreme Court	S.Ct. Series (West)	Highest authority
	U.S. Series (U.S. Gov't.)	
	L.Ed.2d (Lawyer's Co-op.)	
	AFTR (RIA)	
	USTC (CCH)	
U.S. Courts of Appeal	Federal 3d (West)	Next highest appellate court
	AFTR (RIA)	
	USTC (CCH)	
Tax Court (Regular decisions)	U.S. Gov't. Printing Office	Highest trial court*
	RIA/CCH separate services	
Tax Court (Memorandum decisions)	RIA T.C.Memo. (RIA)	Less authority than Regular T.C. decision
	TCM (CCH)	
U.S. Court of Federal Claims**	Federal Claims Reporter (West)	Similar authority as Tax Court
	AFTR (RIA)	
	USTC (CCH)	
U.S. District Courts	F.Supp.2d Series (West)	Lowest trial court
	AFTR (RIA)	
	USTC (CCH)	
Small Cases Division of Tax Court	U.S. Tax Court Web site***	No precedent value

*Theoretically, the Tax Court, Court of Federal Claims, and District Courts are on the same level of authority. But some people believe that since the Tax Court hears and decides tax cases from all parts of the country (i.e., it is a national court), its decisions may be more authoritative than a Court of Federal Claims or District Court decision.

**Before October 29, 1992, the U.S. Claims Court.

***Starting in 2001.

and to avoid double taxation. The Technical and Miscellaneous Revenue Act of 1988 provided that neither a tax law nor a tax treaty takes general precedence. Thus, when there is a direct conflict, the most recent item will take precedence. A taxpayer must disclose on the tax return any position where a treaty overrides a tax law.[28] There is a $1,000 penalty per failure to disclose for individuals and a $10,000 per failure penalty for corporations.[29]

Tax Periodicals. The various tax periodicals are another source of tax information. The easiest way to locate a journal article pertinent to a tax problem is through Commerce Clearing House's *Federal Tax Articles*. This multivolume service includes a subject index, a Code Section number index, and an author's index. The RIA (formerly P-H) tax service also has a topical "Index to Tax Articles" section that is organized using the RIA paragraph index system. Also, beginning in 1992, *The Accounting & Tax Index* is available in three quarterly issues plus a cumulative year-end volume covering all four quarters. The original *Accountant's Index* started in 1921 and ended in 1991.

[28]§ 7852(d).   [29]Reg. §§ 301.6114–1, 301.6712–1, and 301.7701(b)(7).

The following are some of the more useful tax periodicals:

The Journal of Taxation
Warren, Gorham and Lamont
395 Hudson Street
4th Floor
New York, NY 10014

Tax Law Review
Warren, Gorham and Lamont
395 Hudson Street
4th Floor
New York, NY 10014

Trusts and Estates
249 W. 17th Street
New York, NY 10011

Oil, Gas, and Energy Quarterly
Matthew Bender & Co.
1275 Broadway
Albany, NY 12204

The International Tax Journal
Aspen Publishing, Inc.
1185 Avenue of the Americas
New York, NY 10036

TAXES—The Tax Magazine
Commerce Clearing House, Inc.
2700 Lake Cook Road
Riverwood, IL 60015

National Tax Journal
725 15th Street NW
Suite 600
Washington, D.C. 20005

The Tax Adviser
Harborside Financial Center
201 Plaza III
Jersey City, NJ 07311-3881

The Practical Accountant
One State Street Plaza
New York, NY 10004

Estate Planning
Warren, Gorham and Lamont
395 Hudson Street
4th Floor
New York, NY 10014

Taxation for Accountants
Warren, Gorham and Lamont
395 Hudson Street
4th Floor
New York, NY 10014

The Tax Executive
1200 G Street NW
Suite 300
Washington, D.C. 20005

Journal of Corporate Taxation
Warren, Gorham and Lamont
395 Hudson Street
4th Floor
New York, NY 10014

Journal of Taxation for Individuals
Warren, Gorham and Lamont
395 Hudson Street
4th Floor
New York, NY 10014

The Tax Lawyer
American Bar Association
750 N. Lake Shore Drive
Chicago, IL 60611

Journal of the American Taxation Association
American Accounting Association
5717 Bessie Drive
Sarasota, FL 34233

Tax Notes
6830 Fairfax Drive
Arlington, VA 22213

LO.3

Have an awareness of electronic and paper tax services.

Working with the Tax Law—Tax Research Tools

As the later discussion of tax research makes clear, a crucial part of the research process is the ability to locate appropriate sources of the tax law. Both electronic and paper-based research tools are available to aid in this search.

Electronic versus Paper Tax Research Tools

Computerized tax research tools have replaced paper resources in most tax practices. As will be described shortly, there are two chief ways to conduct tax research using computer resources: (1) online and CD-ROM subscription services and (2) online free Internet sites.

Accessing tax documents through electronic means offers a number of advantages over a strictly paper-based approach:

- Materials generally are available to the practitioner faster through an electronic system, as delays related to typesetting, proofreading, production, and distribution of the new materials are substantially reduced. Online services are updated daily and can be accessed from remote locations.
- Some tax documents, such as so-called slip opinions of trial-level court cases and interviews with policymakers, are available only through electronic means.
- Commercial subscriptions to electronic tax services are likely to provide, at little or no additional cost, additional tax sources to which the researcher would not have access through stand-alone purchases of traditional paper resources. For example, the full texts of letter rulings are quite costly to acquire in a paper-based format, but electronic publishers may bundle the rulings with other material for a reasonable cost.
- When consulting a topical or annotated paper tax service, a user is relying on someone else's judgment while searching the topical index. The keyword that the researcher is searching for may not have been used by the editor.
- A computerized tax service allows a user to create his or her own keywords and indexes. The software will electronically scan entire files and retrieve all of the documents that contain those words.
- A computerized tax service may retrieve documents that are no longer in print and may obtain regularly published documents to which a researcher does not otherwise have access.
- Most computerized services allow a user to retrieve documents in order of relevance or in the order listed by database sources. Although this can be useful, just because a document is placed high on the relevance list does not mean it is valid law. Reading the primary sources, validating their authority, and checking the citator are essential in reaching a correct answer.

As indicated above, computerized tools allow the tax library to reflect the tax law itself, including its dynamic and daily changes. Nevertheless, electronic research should not become an end in itself. Using electronic means to locate tax sources cannot substitute for developing and maintaining a thorough knowledge of the tax law or for logical and analytical review in addressing open tax research issues.

Tax Services

Whether in electronic or paper form, tax services are key research tools for the tax practitioner. The major tax services available are as follows:

Standard Federal Tax Reporter, Commerce Clearing House.

United States Tax Reporter, Research Institute of America (entitled *Federal Taxes* prior to July 1992).

Federal Tax Coordinator 2d, Research Institute of America.

Tax Management Portfolios, Bureau of National Affairs.

Federal Income, Gift and Estate Taxation, Warren, Gorham and Lamont.

CCH's Federal Tax Service, Commerce Clearing House.

Mertens Law of Federal Income Taxation, Callaghan and Co.

In this text, it is not feasible to teach the use of any particular tax service; this ability can be obtained only by practice.[30] However, several important observations

---

[30]The representatives of the various tax services are prepared to provide the users of their services with printed booklets and individual instruction on the use of the materials.

about the use of tax services cannot be overemphasized. First, always check for current developments. The main text of any paper-based service is not revised frequently enough to permit reliance on that portion as the *latest* word on any subject. Where current developments can be found depends, of course, on which service is being used. Commerce Clearing House's *Standard Federal Tax Reporter* service contains a special volume devoted to current matters. Both RIA's *U.S. Tax Reporter* and *Federal Tax Coordinator 2d* integrate the new developments into the body of the service throughout the year. Second, when dealing with a tax service synopsis of a Treasury Department pronouncement or a judicial decision, remember there is no substitute for the original source.

To illustrate, do not base a conclusion solely on a tax service's commentary on a potentially relevant court case such as *Simons-Eastern Co. v. U.S.* If the case is vital to the research, look it up. The facts of the case may be distinguishable from those involved in the problem being researched. This is not to say that the case synopsis contained in the tax service is wrong; it might just be misleading or incomplete.

Electronic Services

Virtually all of the major commercial tax publishers and most of the primary sources of the law itself, such as the Supreme Court and some of the Courts of Appeals, provide tax materials in electronic formats. Competitive pressures have rewarded tax practitioners who have developed computer literacy skills, and the user-friendliness of the best of the tax research software is of great benefit to both the daily and the occasional user. Exhibit 2–2 summarizes the most popular of the electronic tax services on the market today.

In using these resources, usually, the law is found using one of the following strategies:

- *Search* various databases using keywords that are likely to be found in the underlying documents, as written by Congress, the judiciary, or administrative sources.
- *Link* to tax documents for which all or part of the proper citation is known (e.g., Code Section, court decision).

EXHIBIT 2–2   Electronic Tax Services

Electronic Tax Service	Description
CCH	Includes the CCH tax service, primary sources including treatises, and other subscription materials. Ten to 20 discs and online.
RIA	Includes the RIA topical *Coordinator* and the annotated tax service formerly provided by Prentice-Hall. The citator has elaborate document-linking features, and major tax treatises are provided. One to 10 discs and online.
WESTLAW	Code, Regulations, *Cumulative Bulletins*, cases, citators, and editorial material. About a dozen discs and online.
Kleinrock's	A single disc with tax statutory, administrative, and judicial law. Another single disc provides tax forms and instructions for Federal and state jurisdictions.

July 3-8
Nikki 9-12
Mike 13-18.

Vn items: 18 - 21

September 2006						
Mo	Tu	We	Th	Fr	Sa	Su
4	5	6	7	8	1	2 3
11	12	13	14	15	16	17
18	19	20	21	22	23	24
25	26	27	28	29	30	

October 2006						
Mo	Tu	We	Th	Fr	Sa	Su
2	3	4	5	6	7	1 8
9	10	11	12	13	14	15
16	17	18	19	20	21	22
23	24	25	26	27	28	29
30	31					

November 2006						
Mo	Tu	We	Th	Fr	Sa	Su
6	7	1 8	2 9	3 10	4 11	5 12
13	14	15	16	17	18	19
20	21	22	23	24	25	26
27	28	29	30			

October 2006

Monday	Tuesday	Wednesday	Thursday	Friday	Saturday	Sunday
16	17	18	19	20	21	22
03:00 PM - 04:00 PM Quarterly meeting	10:30 AM - 11:00 AM Discuss Martini's scope -- Location: Brett's office. -- Chair: Morris Vu		10:00 AM - 11:00 AM Dev Tech Meeting -- Room: 17th Floor Board Room/Dalla s@maverickcap -- Chair: John Daug hety			Paint house
23	24	25	26	27	28	29
	09:00 AM - 10:00 AM Dev Status meeting -- Room: 17th Floor Board Room/Dalla s@maverickcap -- Location: 17th floor board room -- Chair: Kim Brandl				Study	Study
30	31	1	2	2		
	07:00 PM - 08:00 PM Acct Test	10:00 AM - 11:00 AM Dev Tech Meeting -- Room: 17th Floor Board Room/D... s@mav...				

- *Browse* the tax databases, examining various tables of contents and indexes in a traditional manner or using cross-references in the documents to jump from one tax law source to another.

CD-ROM Services.

The CD has been a major source of electronic tax data for about a decade. Data compression techniques continue to allow more tax materials to fit on a single disc every year. CCH, RIA, WESTLAW, and others offer vast tax libraries to the practitioner, often in conjunction with a subscription to traditional paper-based resources or accompanied by newsletters, training seminars, and ongoing technical support.

At its best, a CD-based tax library provides the archival data that make up a permanent, core library of tax documents. For about $300 a year, the tax CD is updated quarterly, providing more comprehensive tax resources than the researcher is ever likely to need. The CD is comparable in scope to a paper-based library of a decade ago costing perhaps $20,000 to establish and $5,000 per year in perpetuity to maintain. If the library is contained on a small number of discs, it also can offer portability through use on notebook computers.

Online Systems.

An online research system allows a practitioner to obtain virtually instantaneous use of tax law sources by accessing the computer of the service provider. Online services generally employ price-per-search cost structures, which can be as much as $200 per hour, significantly higher than the cost of CD materials. Thus, unless a practitioner can pass along related costs to clients or others, online searching generally is limited to the most important issues and to the researchers with the most experience and training in search techniques.

Perhaps the best combination of electronic tax resources is to conduct day-to-day work on a CD system, so that the budget for the related work is known in advance, and augment the CD search with online access where it is judged to be critical. Exhibit 2–3 provides details on the contents of the most commonly used commercial online tax services.

EXHIBIT 2–3   Online Tax Services

Online Service	Description
LEXIS/NEXIS	Federal and state statutory, administrative, and judicial material. Extensive libraries of newspapers, magazines, patent records, and medical and economic databases, both U.S. and foreign-based.
RIA	Includes the RIA tax services, major tax treatises, Federal and state statutes, administrative documents, and court opinions. Extensive citator access, editorial material, and practitioner aids.
CCH	Includes the CCH tax service, primary sources including treatises, and other subscription materials. Tax and economic news sources, extensive editorial material, and practitioner support tools.
WESTLAW	Federal and state statutes, administrative documents, and court opinions. Extensive citator access, editorial material, and gateways to third-party publications. Extensive government document databases.

The Internet. The Internet provides a wealth of tax information in several popular forms, sometimes at no direct cost to the researcher. Using so-called browser software that often is distributed with new computer systems and their communication devices, the tax professional can access information provided around the world that can aid the research process.

- *Home pages (sites) on the World Wide Web (WWW)* are provided by accounting and consulting firms, publishers, tax academics and libraries, and governmental bodies as a means of making information widely available or of soliciting subscriptions or consulting engagements. The best sites offer links to other sites and direct contact to the site providers. One of the best sites available to the tax practitioner is the Internal Revenue Service's *Digital Daily*, illustrated in Exhibit 2–4. This site offers downloadable forms and instructions, "plain English" versions of Regulations, and news update items. Exhibit 2–5 lists some of the Web sites that may be most useful to tax researchers and their Internet addresses as of press date.

EXHIBIT 2–4	The IRS's *Digital Daily*

- *Newsgroups* provide a means by which information related to the tax law can be exchanged among taxpayers, tax professionals, and others who subscribe to the group's services. Newsgroup members can read the exchanges among other members and offer replies and suggestions to inquiries as desired. Discussions address the interpretation and application of existing law, analysis of proposals and new pronouncements, and reviews of tax software.
- *E-mail capabilities* are available to most tax professionals through an employer's equipment or by a subscription providing Internet access at a low and usually fixed cost for the period. E-mail allows for virtually instantaneous sending and receiving of messages, letters, tax returns and supporting data, spreadsheets, and other documents necessary to solve tax problems.

EXHIBIT 2–5   **Tax-Related Web Sites**

Web Site	WWW Address at Press Date (Usually preceded by http://www.)	Description
Internal Revenue Service	**irs.gov/**	News releases, downloadable forms and instructions, tables, and e-mail
Court opinions	The site at **law.emory.edu/caselaw** allows the researcher to link to the site of the jurisdiction (other than the Tax Court) that is the subject of the query.	
Tax Analysts	**taxanalysts.com**	Policy-oriented readings on the tax law and proposals to change it, moderated bulletins on various tax subjects
Tax Sites Directory	**taxsites.com**	References and links to tax sites on the Internet, including state and Federal tax sites, academic and professional pages, tax forms, and software
Tax laws online	Regulations are at **cfr.law.cornell.edu/cfr/** and the Code is at **uscode.house.gov/search/criteria.php** and **www4.law.cornell.edu/uscode/**	
Commercial tax publishers	For instance, **tax.com** and **cch.com**	Information about products and services available for subscription and newsletter excerpts
Large accounting firms and professional organizations	For instance, the AICPA's page is at **aicpa.org**, Ernst and Young is at **ey.com**, and KPMG is at **kpmg.com**	Tax planning newsletters, descriptions of services offered and career opportunities, and exchange of data with clients and subscribers
Thomson South-Western	**wft.swlearning.com**	Informational updates, newsletters, support materials for students and adopters, and continuing education
U.S. Tax Court decisions	**ustaxcourt.gov**	Recent U.S. Tax Court decisions

NOTE: Caution: addresses change frequently.

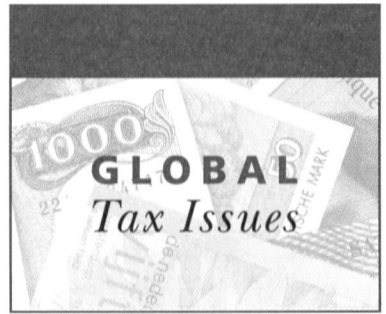

DATA WAREHOUSING REDUCES GLOBAL TAXES

Many global companies are using data warehouses to collect data, which can be analyzed and used to minimize their global tax liabilities. "You take all of your tax data and dump it into a data warehouse," says Michael S. Burke of KPMG's e-tax solutions. "Next, it's applying a tool to define user requirements—compliance, real time analysis, etc." The company can then manipulate all of this information to reduce compliance costs, facilitate planning for value added taxes, and minimize time spent dealing with international tax problems.

For example, a company wishes to implement an e-procurement technique that would save it $100 million in expenses and increase taxable income. That could mean that about $40 million in additional taxes would go to the U.S. Treasury and state treasuries. By looking at the tax laws worldwide, the company may decide to base the operation in Bermuda, Ireland, or the Philippines where the tax will be only $20 million. That's a savings of $20 million, which is not taxable.

Source: *Adapted from Jay Weinstein, "Internet Tax Solutions Proliferate,"* Global Finance, *January 2001, pp. 74–75.*

In many situations, solutions to research problems benefit from, or require, the use of various electronic tax research tools. A competent tax professional must become familiar and proficient with these tools and be able to use them to meet the expectations of clients and the necessities of work in the modern world.[31]

Working with the Tax Law—Tax Research

LO.4

Understand the tax research process.

Tax research is the method by which a tax practitioner, student, or professor determines the best available solution to a situation that possesses tax consequences. In other words, it is the process of finding a competent and professional conclusion to a tax problem. The problem may originate from completed or proposed transactions. In the case of a completed transaction, the objective of the research is to determine the tax result of what has already taken place. For example, was the expenditure incurred by the taxpayer deductible or not deductible for tax purposes? When dealing with proposed transactions, the tax research process is directed toward the determination of possible alternative tax consequences. To the extent that tax research leads to a choice of alternatives or otherwise influences the future actions of the taxpayer, it becomes the key to effective tax planning.

Tax research involves the following procedures:

- Identifying and refining the problem.
- Locating the appropriate tax law sources.
- Assessing the validity of the tax law sources.
- Arriving at the solution or at alternative solutions with due consideration given to nontax factors.
- Effectively communicating the solution to the taxpayer or the taxpayer's representative.
- Following up on the solution (where appropriate) in light of new developments.

---

[31]For a more detailed discussion of the use of electronic tax research in the modern tax practice, see Raabe, Whittenburg, Sanders, and Bost, *West's Federal Tax Research*, 7th ed. (Thomson/South-Western, 2006).

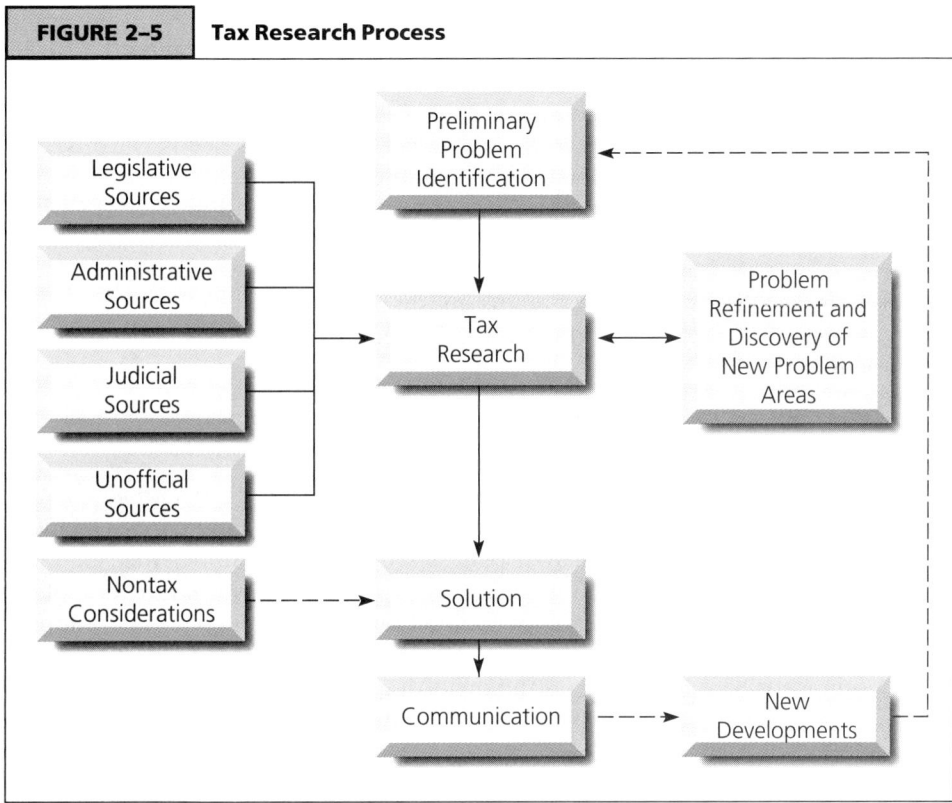

FIGURE 2–5   **Tax Research Process**

This process is depicted schematically in Figure 2–5. The broken lines reflect the steps of particular interest when tax research is directed toward proposed, rather than completed, transactions.

Identifying the Problem

Problem identification must start with a compilation of the relevant facts involved.[32] In this regard, *all* of the facts that may have a bearing on the problem must be gathered because any omission could modify the solution reached. To illustrate, consider what appears to be a very simple problem.

EXAMPLE 4

Early in December, Fred and Megan review their financial and tax situation with their son, Sam, and daughter-in-law, Dana, who live with them. Fred and Megan are in the 28% tax bracket in 2006. Both Sam and Dana are age 21. Sam, a student at a nearby university, owns some publicly traded stock that he inherited from his grandmother. A current sale would result in approximately $8,000 of gross income ($19,000 amount realized − $11,000 adjusted basis). At this point, Fred and Megan provide about 55% of Sam and Dana's support. Although neither is now employed, Sam has earned $960 and Dana has earned $900. The problem: Should the stock be sold, and would the sale prohibit Fred and Megan from claiming Sam and Dana as dependents? Would the stock sale in 2006 result in a tax liability for Sam and Dana? ■

Refining the Problem

Initial reaction is that Fred and Megan in Example 4 could *not* claim Sam and Dana as dependents if the stock is sold, since Sam would then have gross income of more

---

[32]For an excellent discussion of the critical role of facts in carrying out tax research, see R. L. Gardner, D. N. Stewart, and R. G. Worsham, *Tax Research* *Techniques* (New York: The American Institute of Certified Public Accountants, 2000), Chapter 2.

than the exemption amount under § 151(d).[33] However, after 2004, the test for whether a child qualifies for dependency status is first conducted under the *qualifying child* requirements. Only if these requirements cannot be satisfied is the test for dependency status conducted under the *qualifying relative* requirements. The gross income test is applicable only under the qualifying relative status.[34] Thus, Sam could sell the stock without penalizing the parents with respect to the gross income test. Under the qualifying child provision, however, Sam must not have provided more than one-half of his own support.[35] Hence, the $19,000 of proceeds from the sale of the stock might lead to the failure of the not self-supporting requirement, depending on how much Sam spends for his support.

Assume, however, that further fact gathering reveals the following additional information:

- Sam does not really need to spend the proceeds from the sale of the stock.
- Sam receives a sizable portion of his own support from a scholarship.

With these new facts, additional research leads to § 152(f)(5) and Regulation § 1.152–1(c), which indicate that a scholarship received by a student is not included for purposes of computing whether Sam is self-supporting under the qualifying child provision. Further, if Sam does not spend the proceeds from the sale of the stock, the unexpended amount is not counted for purposes of the not self-supporting test. Thus, it appears that the parents would not be denied the dependency exemptions for Sam and Dana, as the qualifying child requirements appear to be satisfied for Sam and the qualifying relative requirements appear to be satisfied for Dana.

Locating the Appropriate Tax Law Sources

Once the problem is clearly defined, what is the next step? Although the next step is a matter of individual judgment, most tax research begins with the index volume of the tax service, a keyword search on an online tax service, or a CD-ROM search as described earlier. If the problem is not complex, the researcher may bypass the tax service or online service and turn directly to the Internal Revenue Code and Treasury Regulations. For the beginner, the latter procedure saves time and will solve many of the more basic problems. If the researcher does not have a personal copy of the Code or Regulations, resorting to the appropriate volume(s) of a tax service or a CD-ROM will be necessary.[36]

Assessing the Validity of the Tax Law Sources

Once a source has been located, the next step is to assess it in light of the problem at hand. Proper assessment involves careful interpretation of the tax law with consideration given to its relevance and validity. In connection with validity, an important step is to check for recent changes in the tax law.

Interpreting the Internal Revenue Code. The language of the Code often is difficult to comprehend fully. Contrary to many people's suspicions, the Code is not written deliberately to confuse. Unfortunately, though, it often has that effect. The Code is intended to apply to more than 200 million taxpayers, many of whom are willing to exploit any linguistic imprecision to their benefit—to find a "loophole" in popular parlance. Many of the Code's provisions are limitations or restrictions involving two or more variables. Expressing such concepts algebraically

---

[33]§ 152(d)(2). See the related discussion in Chapter 3.
[34]Compare § 152(c) for qualifying child with § 152(d) for qualifying relative.
[35]§ 152(c)(1)(D).
[36]Several of the major tax services publish paperback editions of the Code and Treasury Regulations that can be purchased at modest prices. These editions

are usually revised twice each year. For an annotated and abridged version of the Code and Regulations that is published annually, see James E. Smith, *West's Internal Revenue Code of 1986 and Treasury Regulations: Annotated and Selected* (Thomson/South-Western, 2007).

TAX *in the News*   **INTERNAL REVENUE CODE: INTERPRETATION PITFALLS**

One author has noted 10 common pitfalls in interpreting the Code:

1. Determine the limitations and exceptions to a provision. Do not permit the language of the Code Section to carry greater or lesser weight than was intended.
2. Just because a Section fails to mention an item does not necessarily mean that the item is excluded.
3. Read definitional clauses carefully.
4. Do not overlook small words such as *and* and *or*. There is a world of difference between these two words.
5. Read the Code Section completely; do not jump to conclusions.

6. Watch out for cross-referenced and related provisions, since many Sections of the Code are interrelated.
7. At times Congress is not careful when reconciling new Code provisions with existing Sections. Conflicts among Sections, therefore, do arise.
8. Be alert for hidden definitions; terms in a particular Code Section may be defined in the same Section or in a separate Section.
9. Some answers may not be found in the Code; therefore, a researcher may have to consult the Regulations and/or judicial decisions.
10. Take careful note of measuring words such as *less than 50 percent, more than 50 percent,* and *at least 80 percent.*

Source: *Adapted by permission from Henry G. Wong, "Ten Common Pitfalls in Reading the Internal Revenue Code,"* Journal of Business Strategy *(July–August 1972): 30–33. Reprinted with permission by Faulkner & Gray, Inc., 11 Penn Plaza, New York, NY 10001.*

---

would be more direct; using words to accomplish this task instead is often quite cumbersome. Among the worst such attempts was former § 341(e) relating to so-called collapsible corporations. One sentence had more than 450 words (twice as many as in the Gettysburg Address). Within this same subsection was another sentence of 300 words. Research has shown that in one-third of the conflicts reaching the Tax Court, the court could not discern the intent of Congress by simply reading the statute. Yet the overriding attitude of the Tax Court judges is that the statute comes first. Even when the statute is unworkable, the court will not rewrite the law.[37]

Assessing the Validity of a Treasury Regulation. Treasury Regulations are the official interpretation of the Code and are entitled to great deference. Occasionally, however, a court will invalidate a Regulation or a portion thereof on the grounds that the Regulation is contrary to the intent of Congress. Usually, the courts do not question the validity of Regulations because of the belief that "the first administrative interpretation of a provision as it appears in a new act often expresses the general understanding of the times or the actual understanding of those who played an important part when the statute was drafted."[38]

Keep the following observations in mind when assessing the validity of a Regulation:

- IRS agents must give the Code and the Regulations issued thereunder equal weight when dealing with taxpayers and their representatives.
- Proposed Regulations provide a preview of future final Regulations, but they are not binding on the IRS or taxpayers.
- In a challenge, the burden of proof is on the taxpayer to show that the Regulation varies from the language of the statute and has no support in the Committee Reports.

---

[37]T. L. Kirkpatrick and W. B. Pollard, "Reliance by the Tax Court on the Legislative Intent of Congress," *The Tax Executive* (Summer 1986): 358–359.

[38]*Augustus v. Comm.*, 41–1 USTC ¶9255, 26 AFTR 612, 118 F.2d 38 (CA–6, 1941).

- If the taxpayer loses the challenge, a 20 percent negligence penalty may be imposed.[39] This accuracy-related penalty applies to any failure to make a reasonable attempt to comply with the tax law and any disregard of rules and Regulations.[40]
- Final Regulations can be classified as procedural, interpretive, or legislative. **Procedural Regulations** neither establish tax laws nor attempt to explain tax laws. Procedural Regulations are *housekeeping-type instructions* indicating information that taxpayers should provide the IRS as well as information about the internal management and conduct of the IRS itself.
- Some **interpretive Regulations** rephrase and elaborate what Congress stated in the Committee Reports that were issued when the tax legislation was enacted. Such Regulations are *hard* and *solid* and almost impossible to overturn because they clearly reflect the intent of Congress. An interpretive Regulation is given less deference than a legislative Regulation, however. The Supreme Court has told lower courts to analyze Treasury Regulations carefully before accepting the Treasury's interpretation.[41]
- In some Code Sections, Congress has given the *Secretary or his delegate* the authority to prescribe Regulations to carry out the details of administration or to otherwise complete the operating rules. Under such circumstances, Congress effectively is delegating its legislative powers to the Treasury Department. Regulations issued pursuant to this type of authority possess the force and effect of law and are often called **legislative Regulations** (e.g., consolidated return Regulations).
- Courts tend to apply a legislative reenactment doctrine. A particular Regulation is assumed to have received congressional approval if the Regulation was finalized many years earlier and Congress has not amended the Code Section pertaining to that Regulation.

Assessing the Validity of Other Administrative Sources of the Tax Law.
Revenue Rulings issued by the IRS carry less weight than Treasury Department Regulations. Revenue Rulings are important, however, in that they reflect the position of the IRS on tax matters. In any dispute with the IRS on the interpretation of tax law, therefore, taxpayers should expect agents to follow the results reached in any applicable Revenue Rulings. A 1986 Tax Court decision, however, indicated that Revenue Rulings "typically do not constitute substantive authority for a position."[42] Most Revenue Rulings apply retroactively unless a specific statement indicates the extent to which a ruling is to be applied without retroactive effect.[43]

Actions on Decisions further tell the taxpayer the IRS's reaction to certain court decisions. Recall that the IRS follows a practice of either acquiescing (agreeing) or nonacquiescing (not agreeing) with selected judicial decisions. A nonacquiescence does not mean that a particular court decision is of no value, but it does indicate that the IRS may continue to litigate the issue involved.

Assessing the Validity of Judicial Sources of the Tax Law.
The judicial process as it relates to the formulation of tax law has already been described. How much reliance can be placed on a particular decision depends upon the following variables:

- The higher the level of the court that issued a decision, the greater the weight accorded to that decision. A decision rendered by a trial court (e.g., a Federal District Court) carries less weight than one issued by an appellate court

[39]§§ 6662(a) and (b)(1).
[40]§ 6662(c).
[41]*U.S. v. Vogel Fertilizer Co.*, 82–1 USTC ¶9134, 49 AFTR2d 82–491, 102 S.Ct. 821 (USSC, 1982); *National Muffler Dealers Assn., Inc.*, 79–1 USTC ¶9264, 43 AFTR2d 79–828, 99 S.Ct. 1304 (USSC, 1979).

[42]*Nelda C. Stark*, 86 T.C. 243 (1986). See also *Ann R. Neuhoff*, 75 T.C. 36 (1980). For a different opinion, however, see *Industrial Valley Bank & Trust Co.*, 66 T.C. 272 (1976).
[43]Rev.Proc. 87–1, 1987–1 C.B. 503.

(e.g., the Fifth Circuit Court of Appeals). Unless Congress changes the Code, decisions by the U.S. Supreme Court represent the last word on any tax issue.

- More reliance is placed on decisions of courts that have jurisdiction in the area where the taxpayer's legal residence is located. If, for example, a taxpayer lives in Texas, a decision of the Fifth Circuit Court of Appeals means more than one rendered by the Second Circuit Court of Appeals. This result occurs because any appeal from a U.S. District Court or the Tax Court would be to the Fifth Circuit Court of Appeals and not to the Second Circuit Court of Appeals.[44]

- A Tax Court Regular decision carries more weight than a Memorandum decision since the Tax Court does not consider Memorandum decisions to be binding precedents.[45] Furthermore, a Tax Court *reviewed* decision carries even more weight. All of the Tax Court judges participate in a reviewed decision.

- A Circuit Court decision where certiorari has been requested and denied by the U.S. Supreme Court carries more weight than a Circuit Court decision that was not appealed. A Circuit Court decision heard *en banc* (all the judges participate) carries more weight than a normal Circuit Court case.

- A decision that is supported by cases from other courts carries more weight than a decision that is not supported by other cases.

- The weight of a decision also can be affected by its status on appeal. For example, was the decision affirmed or overruled?

In connection with the last two variables, the use of a citator is invaluable to tax research.[46] A **citator** provides the history of a case and lists subsequently published opinions that refer to the case being assessed. Reviewing these references enables the tax researcher to determine whether the decision in question has been reversed, affirmed, followed by other courts, or distinguished in some way. If one intends to rely on a judicial decision to any significant degree, "running" the case through a citator is imperative. Citators and their use are discussed in Appendix E.

Assessing the Validity of Other Sources. *Primary sources* of tax law include the Constitution, legislative history materials, statutes, treaties, Treasury Regulations, IRS pronouncements, and judicial decisions. In general, the IRS considers only primary sources to constitute substantial authority. However, a researcher might wish to refer to *secondary materials* such as legal periodicals, treatises, legal lopinions, General Counsel Memoranda, and written determinations. In general, secondary sources are not authority.

Although the statement that the IRS regards only primary sources as substantial authority generally is true, there is one exception. In Notice 90–20,[47] the IRS expanded the list of substantial authority *for purposes of* the accuracy-related penalty in § 6662 to include a number of secondary materials (e.g., letter rulings, General Counsel Memoranda, the Bluebook). "Authority" does not include conclusions reached in treatises, legal periodicals, and opinions rendered by tax professionals.

A letter ruling or determination letter is substantial authority *only* for the taxpayer to whom it is issued, except as noted above with respect to the accuracy-related penalty.

Upon the completion of major tax legislation, the staff of the Joint Committee on Taxation (in consultation with the staffs of the House Ways and Means and Senate Finance Committees) often will prepare a General Explanation of the Act, commonly known as the Bluebook because of the color of its cover. The IRS will not accept this detailed explanation as having legal effect, except as noted above

---

[44]Before October 1, 1982, an appeal from the then-named U.S. Court of Claims (the other trial court) was directly to the U.S. Supreme Court.

[45]*Severino R. Nico, Jr.*, 67 T.C. 647 (1977).

[46]The major citators are published by Commerce Clearing House, RIA, and Shepard's Citations, Inc. These citators are available in published and electronic formats. WESTLAW has a citator that is available only in electronic format. See Appendix E.

[47]1990–1 C.B. 328; see also Reg. § 1.6661–3(b)(2).

with respect to the accuracy-related penalty. The Bluebook does, however, provide valuable guidance to tax advisers and taxpayers until Regulations are issued. Some letter rulings and General Counsel Memoranda of the IRS cite Bluebook explanations.

Arriving at the Solution or at Alternative Solutions

Example 4 raised the question of whether a taxpayer would be denied dependency exemptions for a son and a daughter-in-law if the son sold some stock near the end of the year. A refinement of the problem supplies additional information:

- Sam and Dana anticipate filing a joint return.

Section 152(b)(2) indicates that a taxpayer is not permitted a dependency exemption for a married dependent if the married individual files a joint return. Initial reaction is that a joint return by Sam and Dana would be disastrous to the parents. However, more research uncovers two Revenue Rulings that provide an exception if neither the dependent nor the dependent's spouse is required to file a return but does so solely to claim a refund of tax withheld. The IRS asserts that each spouse must have gross income of less than the exemption amount.[48] Therefore, if Sam sells the stock and he and Dana file a joint return, the parents would lose the dependency exemption for both Sam and Dana.

If the stock is not sold until January, both dependency exemptions are available to the parents in 2006 even if Sam and Dana file a joint return. However, under § 151(d)(2) a personal exemption is not available to a taxpayer who can be claimed as a dependent by another taxpayer (whether actually claimed or not). Thus, if the parents can claim Sam and Dana as dependents, Sam and Dana would lose their personal exemptions on their tax return.

Communicating Tax Research

LO.5

Communicate the results of the tax research process in a client letter and a tax file memorandum.

Once the problem has been researched adequately, the researcher may need to prepare a memo, letter, or oral presentation setting forth the result. The form such a communication takes could depend on a number of considerations. For example, does the employer or professor recommend a particular procedure or format for tax research memos? Is the memo to be given directly to the client, or will it first go to the researcher's employer? Who is the audience for the oral presentation? How long should you talk? Whatever form it takes, a good tax research communication should contain the following elements:

- A clear statement of the issue.
- In more complex situations, a short review of the fact pattern that raises the issue.
- A review of the pertinent tax law sources (e.g., Code, Regulations, Revenue Rulings, judicial authority).
- Any assumptions made in arriving at the solution.
- The solution recommended and the logic or reasoning supporting it.
- The references consulted in the research process.

In short, a good tax research communication should tell the audience what was researched, the results of that research, and the justification for the recommendation made.[49]

Illustrations of the memos for the tax file and the client letter associated with Example 4 appear in Figure 2–6, Figure 2–7, and Figure 2–8.

---

[48]Rev.Rul. 54–567, 1954–2 C.B. 108; Rev.Rul. 65–34, 1965–1 C.B. 86.

[49]See Chapter 6 of the publication cited in Footnote 32. For oral presentations, see W. A. Raabe and G. E. Whittenburg, "Talking Tax: How to Make a Tax Presentation," *The Tax Adviser* (March 1997): 179–182.

FIGURE 2–6	Tax File Memorandum

August 16, 2006

TAX FILE MEMORANDUM

FROM: John J. Jones
SUBJECT: Fred and Megan Taxpayer
          Engagement: Issues

Today I talked to Fred Taxpayer with respect to his August 12, 2006 letter requesting tax assistance. He wishes to know if his son, Sam, can sell stock worth $19,000 (basis = $11,000) without the parents losing the dependency exemptions for Sam and Sam's wife, Dana. Fred would also like to know the effect on Sam and Dana's tax liability in 2006 if the stock is sold.

Fred Taxpayer is married to Megan, and Sam is a full-time student at a local university. Sam inherited the stock from his grandmother about five years ago. If he sells the stock, he will save the proceeds from the sale. Sam does not need to spend the proceeds if he sells the stock because he receives a $5,500 scholarship that he uses for his own support (i.e., to pay for tuition, books, and fees). Although neither Sam nor Dana is currently employed, Sam has earned income of $960, and Dana has earned income of $900. Fred and Megan are in the 28% tax bracket and furnish approximately 55% of Sam and Dana's support.

ISSUE: If the stock is sold, would the sale prohibit Fred and Megan from claiming Sam and Dana as dependents? I told Fred that we would have an answer for him within two weeks.

Working with the Tax Law—Tax Planning

LO.6
Apply tax research techniques and planning procedures.

Tax research and tax planning are inseparable. The *primary* purpose of effective *tax planning* is to reduce the taxpayer's total tax bill. This statement does not mean that the course of action selected must produce the lowest possible tax under the circumstances. The minimization of tax liability must be considered in context with the legitimate business goals of the taxpayer.

A *secondary* objective of effective tax planning is to reduce or defer the tax in the current tax year. Specifically, this objective aims to accomplish one or more of the following: eradicating the tax entirely; eliminating the tax in the current year; deferring the receipt of income; converting ordinary income into capital gains; converting active to passive income; converting passive to active expense; proliferating taxpayers (i.e., forming partnerships and corporations or making lifetime gifts to family members); eluding double taxation; avoiding ordinary income; or creating, increasing, or accelerating deductions. However, this second objective should be approached with considerable reservation and moderation. For example, a tax election in one year may reduce taxes currently, but saddle future years with a disadvantageous tax position.

Nontax Considerations

There is an honest danger that tax motivations may take on a significance that does not correspond to the true values involved. In other words, tax considerations may impair the exercise of sound business judgment by the taxpayer. Thus, the tax planning process can become a medium through which to accomplish ends that are socially and economically objectionable. All too often, planning seems to lean toward the opposing extremes of placing either too little or too much emphasis on tax considerations. The happy medium—a balance that recognizes the significance of taxes, but not beyond the point where planning detracts from the exercise of good business judgment—turns out to be the promised land that is too infrequently reached.

The remark is often made that a good rule is to refrain from pursuing any course of action that would not be followed were it not for certain tax

FIGURE 2–7   **Tax File Memorandum**

August 26, 2006
TAX FILE MEMORANDUM
FROM: John J. Jones
SUBJECT: Fred and Megan Taxpayer
Engagement: Conclusions

See the Tax File Memorandum dated August 16, 2006, which contains the facts and identifies the tax issues.

Section 152(a) provides that in order for a taxpayer to take a dependency exemption, the potential dependent must satisfy either the qualifying child requirements or the qualifying relative requirements (see Chapter 3). Fred and Megan provide about 55% of the support of their son, Sam, and their daughter-in-law, Dana. If Sam should sell the stock in 2006, he would not need to spend the proceeds for support purposes (i.e., would save the proceeds). Thus, the stock sale would not affect his qualifying as not self-supporting under § 152(c)(1)(D). In calculating the percentage of support provided by Fred and Megan, a $5,500 scholarship received by Sam is not counted in determining the amount of support Sam provides for himself [see § 152(f)(5) and Reg. § 1.152–1(c)]. Note, however, that if the $5,500 had been provided by student loans, it would have been included in calculating support [*Philip J. McCauley*, 56 T.C. 48 (1971)].

Section 152(d)(1)(B) provides that in order to qualify for a dependency exemption as a qualifying relative, the potential dependent's gross income must be less than the exemption amount (i.e., $3,300 in 2006). Without the stock sale, the gross income of both Sam ($960) and Dana ($900) will be below the exemption amount in 2006. The $5,500 Sam receives as a scholarship is excluded from his gross income under § 117(a) because he uses the entire amount to pay for his tuition, books, and fees at a local university.

Although the gross income test is not applicable to Sam (as a qualifying child), it is applicable to Dana, the daughter-in-law (a qualifying relative). [See Concept Summary 3–1.] A key issue is whether the stock sale that will produce $8,000 of recognized gain for Sam and Dana will cause the gross income test to be violated for Dana. Since the $8,000 recognized gain is from the sale of Sam's separately owned asset and they do not live in a community property state, Dana should qualify as a dependent because her gross income would be only $900.

Sam must not be self-supporting under the qualifying child requirements. So, if the stock is sold, he must limit his spending of the sales proceeds such that he continues to be supported by his parents. Since he plans on not spending any of the sales proceeds, this should not be an issue.

The stock sale would result in the parents' loss of the dependency exemptions for Sam and Dana if they file a joint return for 2006 [see § 152(b)(2)]. The joint return requirement does not apply, however, if the dependent files a joint return solely to claim a refund and neither spouse had a tax liability on a separate return (Rev.Rul. 65–34, 1965–1 C.B. 86). However, sale of the stock would keep this exception from applying.

From a tax planning perspective, Sam can choose to sell the stock in 2006. However, if this choice is made, Sam and Dana need to file separate returns so as not to violate the absence of a joint return provision. Under these circumstances, the sale will not interfere with Fred and Megan's ability to claim dependency exemptions for Sam and Dana on their 2006 return. Note, however, that neither Sam nor Dana will be permitted to take a personal exemption deduction on their 2006 tax return since they are claimed as dependents on someone else's return [see § 151(d)(2)]. However, this disallowance of the personal exemption deduction will not produce any significant negative tax consequences since Dana's tax liability would be $0 and Sam's would be only $385. Alternatively, Sam could delay the sale of the stock until 2007. In this case, Sam and Dana's tax liability in 2006 would be $0. The disallowance of the personal exemption deductions by Sam and Dana will not produce any negative tax consequences since both Sam and Dana's tax liability would be $0.

considerations. This statement is not entirely correct, but it does illustrate the desirability of preventing business logic from being *sacrificed at the altar of tax planning*.

Tax Avoidance and Tax Evasion

A fine line exists between legal tax planning and illegal tax planning—tax avoidance versus tax evasion. **Tax avoidance** is merely tax minimization through legal techniques. In this sense, tax avoidance is the proper objective of all tax planning. Tax evasion, while also aimed at the elimination or reduction of taxes, connotes the use of subterfuge and fraud as a means to an end. Popular usage—probably because of the common goals involved—has so linked these two concepts that many individuals are no longer aware of the true distinctions between them. Consequently, some taxpayers have been deterred from properly taking advantage of

FIGURE 2–8	Client Letter

Hoffman, Smith, and Willis, CPAs
5191 Natorp Boulevard
Mason, Ohio 45040

August 30, 2006

Mr. and Ms. Fred Taxpayer
111 Boulevard
Williamsburg, Virginia 23185

Dear Mr. and Ms. Taxpayer:

This letter is in response to your request for us to review your family's financial and tax situation. Our conclusions are based upon the facts as outlined in your August 12th letter. Any change in the facts may affect our conclusions.

You provide over 50% of the support for your son, Sam, and his wife, Dana. The scholarship Sam receives is not included in determining support. If the stock is not sold, you will qualify for a dependency exemption for both Sam and Dana.

If the stock is sold, a gain of approximately $8,000 will result. If Sam and Dana then file a joint return, you would lose the dependency exemption for Sam as a qualifying child and would lose the dependency exemption for Dana as a qualifying relative. You can avoid the loss of these two dependency exemptions if Sam and Dana file separate returns. This would result in a tax liability of $0 for Dana and $385 for Sam.

From a family tax planning and tax avoidance perspective, Sam should not sell the stock in 2006. Delaying the stock sale will enable you to claim dependency exemptions for both Sam and Dana and will enable Sam and Dana to have a $0 tax liability for 2006.

Should you need more information or need to clarify our conclusions, do not hesitate to contact me.

Sincerely yours,

John J. Jones, CPA
Partner

planning possibilities. The now classic words of Judge Learned Hand in *Commissioner v. Newman* reflect the true values the taxpayer should have:

> Over and over again courts have said that there is nothing sinister in so arranging one's affairs as to keep taxes as low as possible. Everybody does so, rich or poor; and all do right, for nobody owes any public duty to pay more than the law demands: taxes are enforced extractions, not voluntary contributions. To demand more in the name of morals is mere cant.[50]

As Denis Healy, a former British Chancellor, once said, "The difference between tax avoidance and tax evasion is the thickness of a prison wall."

ETHICAL *Considerations*   A TOILET PAPER TAX?

A Florida legislator has proposed a 2 cents per-roll tax on toilet paper to pay for wastewater treatment and help small towns upgrade their sewer systems. Many of these small towns have experienced such tremendous growth in population that their municipal infrastructure cannot accommodate it. If this bill were to pass, the extra two pennies could bring in $50 million a year.

Is this a good idea? Would such a toilet paper tax be fair?

---

[50]*Comm. v. Newman*, 47–1 USTC ¶9175, 35 AFTR 857, 159 F.2d 848 (CA–2, 1947).

TAX *in the News*   THE DISAPPEARING TAXPAYERS

Should income taxes be increased, not decreased, especially on the bottom 50 percent of taxpayers? Should the tax base be expanded? Recent tax data lend credence to such unpopular opinions.

In 2002, 91 percent of the individual income tax was raised from 32 percent of the taxpayers. The top 1 percent of taxpayers paid 34 percent of all Federal income taxes while the bottom 50 percent of taxpayers paid less than 4 percent. Of the 130 million returns processed, at least 44 million owed no tax, and many of those received an earned income credit.

In 2003, earned income credit claims totaled more than $34 billion. Fraudulent or mistaken earned income credit claims amount to as much as $10 billion annually.

Another problem is that the Internet is helping taxpayers to disappear. In a recent *New Yorker* magazine cartoon, two dogs are sitting in front of a computer screen: one tells the other, "On the Internet, nobody knows that you are a dog." Similarly, in order to collect a tax, the government must know who is liable to pay the tax. Taxpayers are becoming increasingly more difficult to identify as anonymous electronic money and uncrackable encryption techniques are developed.

If too many taxpayers disappear via the Internet, will the government's deficit grow larger?

Follow-up Procedures

Because tax planning usually involves a proposed (as opposed to a completed) transaction, it is predicated upon the continuing validity of the advice based upon the tax research. A change in the tax law (either legislative, administrative, or judicial) could alter the original conclusion. Additional research may be necessary to test the solution in light of current developments (refer to the broken lines at the right in Figure 2–5).

Tax Planning—A Practical Application

Returning to the facts of Example 4, what could be done to protect the dependency exemptions for the parents? If Sam and Dana refrain from filing a joint return, both could be claimed by the parents.

An obvious tax planning tool is the installment method. Could the securities be sold using the installment method under § 453 so that most of the gain is deferred into the next year? Under the installment method, certain gains may be postponed and recognized as the cash proceeds are received. The problem is that the installment method is not available for stock traded on an established securities market.[51]

A little more research, however, indicates that Sam might be able to sell the stock and postpone the recognition of gain until the following year by selling short an equal number of substantially identical shares and covering the short sale in the subsequent year with the shares originally held. Selling short means that Sam sells borrowed stock (substantially identical) and repays the lender with the stock held on the date of the short sale. This *short against the box* technique would allow Sam to protect his $8,000 profit and defer the closing of the sale until the following year.[52] However, additional research indicates that 1997 tax legislation provides that the short against the box technique will no longer produce the desired postponement of recognized gain. That is, at the time of the short sale, Sam will have a recognized gain of $8,000 from a constructive sale. Note the critical role

---

[51]See Chapter 18 for a discussion of installment sales.

[52]§§ 1233(a) and 1233(b)(2). See Chapter 16 for a discussion of short sales.

of obtaining the correct facts in attempting to resolve the proper strategy for the taxpayers.

Throughout this text, most chapters include observations on Tax Planning Considerations. Such observations are not all-inclusive but are intended to illustrate some of the ways in which the material covered can be effectively utilized to minimize taxes.

Taxation on the CPA Examination

LO.7

Be aware of taxation on the CPA examination.

The CPA examination has changed from a paper-and-pencil exam to a computer-based exam with increased emphasis on information technology and general business knowledge. The 14-hour exam has four sections, and taxation is included in the 3-hour Regulation section. The taxation part of the Regulation section covers:

- Federal tax procedures and accounting issues.
- Federal taxation of property transactions.
- Federal taxation—individuals.
- Federal taxation—entities.

Each exam section includes both multiple-choice questions and case studies called simulations. The multiple-choice part consists of three sequential testlets, each containing 24 to 30 questions. These testlets are groups of questions prepared to appear together. In addition, each exam section includes a testlet which consists of two simulations. A candidate may review and change answers within each testlet but cannot go back after exiting a testlet. Candidates take different, but equivalent exams.

Simulations are small case studies designed to test a candidate's tax knowledge and skills using real-life work-related situations. The simulations range from 30 to 50 minutes in length and complement the multiple-choice questions. Simulations include a four-function pop-up calculator, a blank spreadsheet with some elementary functionality, and authoritative literature appropriate to the subject matter. The taxation database includes authoritative excerpts that are necessary to complete the tax case study simulations (e.g., *Internal Revenue Code* and Federal tax forms). Examples of such simulations follow.

EXAMPLE 5

The *tax citation type* simulation requires the candidate to research the *Internal Revenue Code* and enter a Code Section and subsection. For example, Amber Company is considering using the simplified dollar-value method of pricing its inventory for purposes of the LIFO method that is available to certain small businesses. What Code section is the relevant authority in the *Internal Revenue Code* to which you should turn to determine whether the taxpayer is eligible to use this method? To be successful, the candidate needs to find § 474. ■

EXAMPLE 6

A *tax form completion* simulation requires the candidate to fill out a portion of a tax form. For example, Green Company is a limited liability company (LLC) for tax purposes. Complete the income section of the 2005 IRS Form 1065 for Green Company using the values found and calculated on previous tabs along with the following data:

Ordinary income from other partnerships	$ 5,200
Net gain (loss) from Form 4797	2,400
Management fee income	12,000

The candidate is provided with page 1 of Form 1065 on which to record the appropriate amounts. ■

KEY TERMS

Acquiescence, 2–18

Circuit Court of Appeals, 2–15

Citator, 2–33

Court of original jurisdiction, 2–12

Determination letters, 2–11

Federal District Court, 2–12

Finalized Regulations, 2–8

Interpretive Regulations, 2–32

Legislative Regulations, 2–32

Letter rulings, 2–10

Nonacquiescence, 2–18

Precedents, 2–16

Procedural Regulations, 2–32

Proposed Regulations, 2–8

Revenue Procedures, 2–9

Revenue Rulings, 2–9

Small Cases Division, 2–12

Tax avoidance, 2–36

Tax research, 2–28

Technical Advice Memoranda (TAMs), 2–11

Temporary Regulations, 2–8

U.S. Court of Federal Claims, 2–12

U.S. Supreme Court, 2–16

U.S. Tax Court, 2–12

Writ of Certiorari, 2–16

PROBLEM MATERIALS

DISCUSSION QUESTIONS

1. A large part of tax research consists of determining what?

2. Why do taxpayers often have more than one alternative for structuring a business transaction? *Complexity of tax law & diff interpretation.*

3. To what day in 2005 did the average taxpayer have to work in order to pay his or her taxes for the year?

4. Where does Federal tax legislation generally originate?

5. In which title and subtitle of the U.S. Code is the income tax portion of the Internal Revenue Code of 1986 found?

Communications

6. Paul Bishop operates a small international firm named Teal, Inc. A new treaty between the United States and France conflicts with a Section of the Internal Revenue Code. Paul asks you for advice. If he follows the treaty position, does he need to disclose this on his tax return? If he is required to disclose, are there any penalties for failure to disclose? Prepare a letter in which you respond to Paul. Teal's address is 100 International Drive, Tampa, FL 33620.

7. Interpret this Regulation citation: Reg. § 1.183–1(c)(3).

8. Explain how Regulations are arranged. How would the following Regulations be cited?
   a.   Finalized Regulations under § 442.
   b.   Proposed Regulations under § 318.
   c.   Temporary Regulations under § 446.
   d.   Legislative Regulations under § 1501. *rephrase — indicate info, taxpayer should provide IRS.*

9. Distinguish between legislative, interpretive, and procedural Regulations. *Given to IRS by Congress*

10. In the citation Rev.Rul. 73–329, 1973–2 C.B. 302, to what do the 329 and the 302 refer?

11. Rank the following items from the highest authority to the lowest in the Federal tax law system:
    a.   Interpretive Regulation.
    b.   Legislative Regulation.
    c.   Letter ruling.
    d.   Revenue Ruling.
    e.   Internal Revenue Code.
    f.   Proposed Regulation.

12. Interpret each of the following citations:
    a. Prop.Reg. § 1.280A–3(c)(4).
    b. Rev.Rul. 67–74, 1967–1 C.B. 194.
    c. Ltr.Rul. 200409001.

13. Barbara Brown calls you on the phone. She says that she has found a 1991 letter ruling that agrees with a position she wishes to take on her tax return. She asks you about the precedential value of a letter ruling. Draft a memo for the tax files outlining what you told Barbara.

Communications

14. Sammie is considering writing the IRS to determine whether a retirement plan maintained by an association of churches qualifies as a church plan under § 414(e). Outline some relevant tax issues Sammie faces in making this decision.

Issue ID

15. What are the major differences between letter rulings and determination letters?

16. What are the differences between Technical Advice Memoranda (TAMs) and Technical Expedited Advice Memoranda (TEAMs)?

17. Caleb receives a 90-day letter after his discussion with an appeals officer. He is not satisfied with the $92,000 settlement offer. Identify the relevant tax research issues facing Caleb.

Issue ID

18. Which of the following would be considered advantages of the Small Cases Division of the Tax Court?
    a. Appeal to the U.S. Tax Court is possible.
    b. A hearing of a deficiency of $65,000 is considered on a timely basis.
    c. Taxpayer can handle the litigation without using a lawyer or certified public accountant.
    d. Taxpayer can use other Small Cases Division decisions for precedential value.
    e. The actual hearing is conducted informally.
    f. Travel time will probably be reduced.

19. List an advantage and a disadvantage of using the U.S. District Court as the trial court for Federal tax litigation. *Adv : trial by Jury . Disadv : Tax must be paid first.*

20. Dwain Toombs is considering litigating a tax deficiency of approximately $311,000 in the court system. He asks you to provide him with a short description of his alternatives indicating the advantages and disadvantages of each. Prepare your response to Dwain in the form of a letter. His address is 200 Mesa Drive, Tucson, AZ 85714.

Communications

21. List an advantage and a disadvantage of using the U.S. Court of Federal Claims as the trial court for Federal tax litigation.

22. A taxpayer lives in Michigan. In a controversy with the IRS, the taxpayer loses at the trial court level. Describe the appeal procedure under the following different assumptions:
    a. The trial court was the Small Cases Division of the U.S. Tax Court. *None*
    b. The trial court was the U.S. Tax Court. *6th Circuit Court of Appeals → Supreme Crt.*
    c. The trial court was a U.S. District Court. *Same (b)*
    d. The trial court was the U.S. Court of Federal Claims. *US Court of Appeals → Supreme Crt.*

23. Suppose the U.S. Government loses a tax case in the U.S. District Court but does not appeal the result. What does the failure to appeal signify?

24. Because the U.S. Tax Court is a national court, it always decides the same issue in a consistent manner. Assess the validity of this statement.

25. For the U.S. Tax Court, U.S. District Court, and U.S. Court of Federal Claims, indicate the following:
    a. Number of regular judges per court.
    b. Availability of a jury trial.
    c. Whether the deficiency must be paid before the trial.

26. In which of the following states could a taxpayer appeal the decision of a U.S. District Court to the Eleventh Circuit Court of Appeals?
    a. Alaska.
    b. Arkansas.
    c. Florida.

    d.   New York.

    e.   Texas.

27. What precedents must each of these courts follow?

    a.   U.S. Tax Court.

    b.   U.S. Court of Federal Claims.

    c.   U.S. District Court.

28. What is the Supreme Court's policy on hearing tax cases?

29. In assessing the validity of a prior court decision, discuss the significance of the following on the taxpayer's issue:

    a.   The decision was rendered by the U.S. District Court of Wyoming. Taxpayer lives in Wyoming. *US District Court of WY.*

    b.   The decision was rendered by the U.S. Court of Federal Claims. Taxpayer lives in Wyoming.

    c.   The decision was rendered by the Second Circuit Court of Appeals. Taxpayer lives in California.

    d.   The decision was rendered by the U.S. Supreme Court. *Done until new law.*

    e.   The decision was rendered by the U.S. Tax Court. The IRS has acquiesced in the result.

    f.   Same as (e) except that the IRS has issued a nonacquiescence as to the result.

acquiesce: submit, comply w/ contest. Agree.

30. In the citation *The Carborundum Co.*, 74 T.C. 730 (1980), what do the 74 and the 730 refer to?

31. What is the difference between a Regular decision, a Memorandum decision, and a Summary Opinion of the U.S. Tax Court?

32. Referring to the citation only, determine which court issued these decisions:

    a.   *Estate of Albert Strangi*, 115 T.C. 478 (2000).

    b.   *Moline Properties*, 319 U.S. 436 (1943).

    c.   *Estate of Morton B. Harper*, T.C.Memo. 2002–121.

    d.   *Azar Nut Co.*, 931 F.2d 314 (CA–5, 1991).

33. Interpret each of the following citations:

    a.   54 T.C. 1514 (1970).

    b.   408 F.2d 1117 (CA–2, 1969).

    c.   69–1 USTC ¶9319 (CA–2, 1969).

    d.   23 AFTR2d 69–1090 (CA–2, 1969).

    e.   293 F.Supp. 1129 (D.Ct. Miss., 1967).

    f.   67–1 USTC ¶9253 (D.Ct. Miss., 1967).

    g.   19 AFTR2d 647 (D.Ct. Miss., 1967).

    h.   56 S.Ct. 289 (USSC, 1935).

    i.   36–1 USTC ¶9020 (USSC, 1935).

    j.   16 AFTR 1274 (USSC, 1935).

    k.   422 F.2d 1336 (Ct.Cls., 1970).

34. Explain the following abbreviations:

a. CA–2.	f. *Cert. denied.*	k. F.3d.
b. Fed.Cl.	g. *acq.*	l. F.Supp.
c. *aff'd.*	h. B.T.A.	m. USSC.
d. *rev'd.*	i. USTC.	n. S.Ct.
e. *rem'd.*	j. AFTR.	o. D.Ct.

35. Give the Commerce Clearing House citation for the following courts:

    a.   Small Cases Division of the Tax Court.

    b.   Federal District Court.

    c.   U.S. Supreme Court.

    d.   U.S. Court of Federal Claims.

    e.   Tax Court Memorandum decision.

36. Where can you locate a published decision of the U.S. Court of Federal Claims?

37. Which of the following items can probably be found in the *Cumulative Bulletin*?
    a. Action on Decision.
    b. Small Cases Division of the U.S. Tax Court decision.
    c. Letter ruling.
    d. Revenue Procedure.
    e. Finalized Regulation.
    f. U.S. Court of Federal Claims decision.
    g. Senate Finance Committee Report.
    h. Acquiescences to Tax Court decisions.
    i. U.S. Circuit Court of Appeals decision.

38. Ashley has to prepare a research paper discussing the credit for child and dependent care expenses for her tax class. Explain to Ashley how she can research this credit.

    Issue ID

39. Where can a researcher find the current Internal Revenue Code of 1986?

40. Which of the following would be considered differences between the Research Institute of America and Commerce Clearing House citators?
    a. Distinguishes between the various issues in a particular court decision.
    b. Lists all court decisions that cite the court decision being researched.
    c. Allows a researcher to determine the validity of a Revenue Ruling.
    d. Indicates whether a court decision is explained, criticized, followed, or overruled by a subsequent decision.
    e. Pinpoints the exact page on which a decision is cited by another case.

41. You inherit a tax problem that was researched five months ago. You believe the answer is correct, but you are unfamiliar with the general area. How would you find some recent articles dealing with the subject area? How do you evaluate the reliability of the authority cited in the research report? How do you determine the latest developments pertaining to the research problem?

    Decision Making

42. Discuss the advantages of computerized tax research versus paper tax research.

43. What are the three ways that most electronic tax services can be entered?

PROBLEMS

44. Tom, an individual taxpayer, has just been audited by the IRS and, as a result, has been assessed a substantial deficiency (which has not yet been paid) in additional income taxes. In preparing his defense, Tom advances the following possibilities:
    a. Although a resident of Kentucky, Tom plans to sue in a U.S. District Court in Oregon that appears to be more favorably inclined toward taxpayers.
    b. If (a) is not possible, Tom plans to take his case to a Kentucky state court where an uncle is the presiding judge.
    c. Since Tom has found a B.T.A. decision that seems to help his case, he plans to rely on it under alternative (a) or (b).
    d. If he loses at the trial court level, Tom plans to appeal either to the U.S. Court of Federal Claims or to the U.S. Second Circuit Court of Appeals because he has relatives in both Washington, D.C., and New York. Staying with these relatives could save Tom lodging expense while his appeal is being heard by the court selected.
    e. Whether or not Tom wins at the trial court or appeals court level, he feels certain of success on an appeal to the U.S. Supreme Court.

    Evaluate Tom's notions concerning the judicial process as it applies to Federal income tax controversies.

45. Using the legend provided, identify the governmental unit that produces the following tax sources:

Legend

T = U.S. Treasury Department
NO = National Office of the IRS
AD = Area Director of the IRS
NA = Not applicable

---

    a.   Proposed Regulations.
    b.   Revenue Procedures.
    c.   Letter rulings.
    d.   Determination letters.
    e.   Technical Advice Memoranda.
    f.   Treasury Decisions.
    g.   Revenue Rulings.
    h.   Small Cases Division decisions.

46. Using the legend provided, classify each of the following statements (more than one answer per statement may be appropriate):

Legend

D = Applies to the U.S. District Court
T = Applies to the U.S. Tax Court
C = Applies to the U.S. Court of Federal Claims
A = Applies to the U.S. Circuit Court of Appeals
U = Applies to the U.S. Supreme Court
N = Applies to none of the above

---

    a.   Decides only Federal tax matters.
    b.   Decisions are reported in the F.3d Series.
    c.   Decisions are reported in the USTCs.
    d.   Decisions are reported in the AFTRs.
    e.   Appeal is by Writ of Certiorari.
    f.   Court meets most often in Washington, D.C.
    g.   A jury trial is available.
    h.   Trial court.
    i.   Appellate court.
    j.   Appeal is to the Federal Circuit and bypasses the taxpayer's particular circuit court.
    k.   Has a Small Cases Division.
    l.   The only trial court where the taxpayer does not have to pay the tax assessed by the IRS first.

47. Using the legend provided, classify each of the following citations as to the type of court:

Legend

D = Applies to the U.S. District Court
T = Applies to the U.S. Tax Court
C = Applies to the U.S. Court of Federal Claims
A = Applies to the U.S. Circuit Court of Appeals
U = Applies to the U.S. Supreme Court
N = Applies to none of the above

---

    a.   Temp.Reg. § 1.79–4T.
    b.   *Whipple Chrysler Plymouth*, 31 TCM 230 (1972).
    c.   *Keller v. Comm.*, 723 F.2d 58 (CA–10, 1983).
    d.   *Borge v. Comm.*, 395 U.S. 933 (1969).
    e.   *Allen Leavell*, 104 T.C. 140 (1995).
    f.   *Shaffstall Corp. v. U.S.*, 639 F.Supp. 1041 (S.D. Ind., 1986).

g. *Mernard, Inc. v. Comm.*, T.C.Memo. 2004–207.
h. Rev.Rul. 84–68, 1984–1 C.B. 31.
i. 3 B.T.A. 1042 (1926).

48. Using the legend provided, classify each of the following tax sources:

Legend
P = Primary tax source
S = Secondary tax source
B = Both
N = Neither

a. Sixteenth Amendment to the Constitution.
b. Tax treaty between the United States and France.
c. Revenue Ruling.
d. General Counsel Memoranda (1989).
e. U.S. District Court decision.
f. *Tax Notes* article.
g. Temporary Regulations (issued 2004).
h. U.S. Tax Court Memorandum decision.
i. Small Cases Division of the U.S. Tax Court decision.
j. Senate Finance Committee report.

49. Using the legend provided, classify each of the following citations as to publisher:

Legend
RIA = Research Institute of America
CCH = Commerce Clearing House
W   = West Publishing Company
U.S. = U.S. Government
O   = Others

a. 103 T.C. 80.
b. 69 TCM 3042.
c. 839 F.Supp. 933.
d. 56 AFTR2d 85–5926.
e. 92–1 USTC ¶50,186.
f. RIA T.C.Mem.Dec. ¶80,582.
g. Rev.Proc. 92–16, 1992–1 C.B. 673.
h. Rev.Proc. 77–37, 1977–2 C.B. 568.
i. 110 S.Ct. 589.
j. 493 U.S. 203.

50. Using the legend provided, classify each of the following statements:

Legend
A = Tax avoidance
E = Tax evasion
N = Neither

a. Terry writes a $250 check for a charitable contribution on December 28, 2006, but does not mail the check to the charitable organization until January 10, 2007. She takes a deduction in 2006.
b. Robert decides not to report interest income from a bank because the amount is only $11.75.
c. Jim pays property taxes on his home in December 2006 rather than waiting until February 2007.

d. Jane switches her investments from taxable corporate bonds to tax-exempt municipal bonds.

e. Ted encourages his mother to save most of her Social Security benefits so that he
will be able to claim her as a dependent.

RESEARCH PROBLEMS

Note: Solutions to Research Problems can be prepared by using the **RIA Checkpoint**®
Student Edition online research product, which is available to accompany this text. It is
also possible to prepare solutions to the Research Problems by using tax research materials found in a standard tax library.

Research Problem 1. In *Bank One Corp.*, 120 T.C. 174 (2003), what was the position of the
court with respect to the mark-to-market rule?

Research Problem 2. Determine what is covered in the following subchapters in Chapter 1,
Subtitle A of the Internal Revenue Code of 1986:
a. B.
b. D.
c. F.
d. K.
e. P.

Research Problem 3. Locate the following items and give a brief summary of the results.
a. Prop. Reg. § 1.864(b)–1(b)(2)(ii)(E).
b. Rev.Proc. 2005–50, I.R.B. No. 32,272.
c. FSA 200228005.
d. IRC § 32(c)(2)(A).
e. *Ramirez-Ota v. Comm.*, T.C. Summary Opinion, 2002–27.

Research Problem 4. Determine how the term *person* is defined in the Internal Revenue
Code of 1986. Specify the Code Section in which the term is defined.

Research Problem 5. Locate the April 2005 issue of *The Tax Adviser* and find the article by
Robert A. Briskin. What are the title and page numbers of the article he wrote? Define
"incidental property."

Research Problem 6. Determine the reliability of the following items:
a. *FRGC Investment, LLC*, T.C.Memo. 2002–276.
b. *Donald L. Evans*, 54 T.C. 40 (1970).
c. Rev.Rul. 77–137, 1977–1 C.B. 178.

Research Problem 7. Locate the following tax services in your library and indicate the
name of the publisher and whether the service is organized by topic or Code Section:
a. *United States Tax Reporter.*
b. *Standard Federal Tax Reporter.*
c. *Federal Tax Coordinator 2d.*
d. *Mertens Law of Federal Income Taxation.*
e. *Tax Management Portfolios.*
f. *Federal Income, Gift and Estate Taxation.*
g. *Federal Tax Service.*

Research Problem 8. In the tax publications matrix below, place an X if a court decision
can be found in the publication. There may be more than one X in a row for a particular
court.

Court	U.S. Govt. Printing Office	West Publishing Company				Research Institute of America			Commerce Clearing House	
		Federal Supp.2d	Federal 3d	Federal Claims Reporter	S.Ct.	BTA Memo.	T.C.Memo.	AFTR	T.C. Memo.	USTC
U.S. Supreme Court	✗				✓			✓		✗
Circuit Court of Appeals			✗					✓		✓
Court of Federal Claims				✓				✓		✓
District Court		✓						✓		✓
Tax Court (Regular decisions)	✓									
Tax Court (Memo decisions)							✓		✓	
Board of Tax Appeals						✓				
BTA Memo.						✓				

Research Problem 9. Complete the following citations:

a. *Betty R. Carraway,* T.C.Memo. 1994–___.

b. *Robert E. Imel,* 61 T.C. ___ (1973).

c. *Higgins v. Comm.,* 312 U.S. 212 (___).

d. Rev.Rul. 68–378, 1968–___ C.B. ___.

e. *Dye v. U.S.,* 121 F.3d 1399 (___, 1997).

f. Rev.Proc. 2003–85, ___ C.B. 1184.

g. *Talen v. U.S.,* 355 F.Supp.2d 22 (D.D.C., ___).

Research Problem 10. Find *Kathryn Bernal,* 120 T.C. 102 (2003) and answer the following questions:

a. What was the docket number?

b. When was the dispute filed?

c. Who is the respondent?

d. Who was the attorney for the taxpayers?

e. Who was the judge who wrote the opinion?

f. What was the disposition of the dispute?

Research Problem 11. Determine the disposition of the following decisions at the Supreme Court level.

a. *Adda v. Comm.,* 10 T.C. 272 (1948), *aff'd* 171 F.2d 457 (CA–4, 1948).

b. *Comm. v. Nubar,* 185 F.2d 584 (CA–4, 1950), *rev'g* 13 T.C. 566.

c. *U.S. v. Henderson,* 375 F.2d 36 (CA–5, 1967).

Research Problem 12. Determine the reliability of the following items:

a. Rev.Proc. 2000–15, 2000–1 C.B. 447.

b. *Jacquelyn Hayman,* T.C.Memo. 1992–228.

c. Rev.Proc. 80–27, 1980–1, C.B. 677.

Research Problem 13. During 2005, Frank lived with and supported a 20-year-old woman who was not his wife. He resides in a state that has a statute that makes it a misdemeanor for a man and woman who are not married to each other to live together. May Frank

Decision Making

claim his *friend* as a dependent assuming he satisfies the normal tax rules for the deduction? Should Frank consider moving to another state?

Partial list of research aids:
§ 152(f)(3).
John T. Untermann, 38 T.C. 93 (1962).
S.Rept. 1983, 85th Cong., 2d Sess., reprinted in the 1958 Code Cong. & Adm. News 4791, 4804.

Internet *Activity*

Use the tax resources of the Internet to address the following questions. Do not restrict your search to the World Wide Web, but include a review of newsgroups and general reference materials, practitioner sites and resources, primary sources of the tax law, chat rooms and discussion groups, and other opportunities.

Research Problem 14.   Go to each of the following Internet locations:
  a. Several primary sources of the tax law, including the U.S. Supreme Court, a Circuit Court of Appeals, the Internal Revenue Service, and final Regulations.
  b. Sources of proposed Federal tax legislation.
  c. A collection of tax rules for your state.

Research Problem 15.   Go to the U.S. Tax Court Internet site:
  a. What different types of cases can be found on the site?
  b. What is a Summary Opinion? Find one.
  c. What is a Memorandum Opinion? Find one.
  d. Find the "Rules and Practices and Procedures."
  e. Is the site user-friendly? E-mail suggested improvements to the webmaster.

CHAPTER 3

Tax Determination; Personal and Dependency Exemptions; An Overview of Property Transactions

LEARNING OBJECTIVES

After completing Chapter 3, you should be able to:

LO.1
Understand and apply the components of the Federal income tax formula.

LO.2
Apply the rules for arriving at personal exemptions.

LO.3
Apply the rules for determining dependency exemptions.

LO.4
Use the proper method for determining the tax liability.

LO.5
Identify and work with kiddie tax situations.

LO.6
Recognize the filing requirements and the proper filing status.

LO.7
Possess an overview of property transactions.

LO.8
Identify tax planning opportunities associated with the individual tax formula.

Individuals are subject to Federal income tax based on taxable income. This chapter explains how taxable income and the income tax of an individual taxpayer are determined.

To compute taxable income, it is necessary to understand the tax formula in Figure 3–1. Although the tax formula is rather simple, determining an individual's taxable income can be quite complex. The complexity stems from the numerous provisions that govern the determination of gross income and allowable deductions.

FIGURE 3–1   Tax Formula

Income (broadly conceived)	$xx,xxx
Less: Exclusions	(x,xxx)
Gross income	$xx,xxx
Less: Deductions *for* adjusted gross income	(x,xxx)
Adjusted gross income	$xx,xxx
Less: The greater of total itemized deductions *or* the standard deduction	(x,xxx)
Personal and dependency exemptions	(x,xxx)
Taxable income	$xx,xxx
Tax on taxable income (see Tax Tables or Tax Rate Schedules)	$ x,xxx
Less: Tax credits (including income taxes withheld and prepaid)	(xxx)
Tax due (or refund)	$ xxx

After computing taxable income, the appropriate rates must be applied. This requires a determination of the individual's filing status, since different rates apply for single taxpayers, married taxpayers, and heads of household. The basic tax rate structure is progressive, with rates for 2006 ranging from 10 percent to 35 percent.[1] For comparison, the lowest rate structure, which was in effect in 1913–1915, ranged from 1 to 7 percent, and the highest, in effect during 1944–1945, ranged from 23 to 94 percent.

Once the individual's tax has been computed, prepayments and credits are subtracted to determine whether the taxpayer owes additional tax or is entitled to a refund.

When property is sold or otherwise disposed of, a gain or loss may result, which can affect the determination of taxable income. Although property transactions are covered in detail in Chapters 14–17, an understanding of certain basic concepts helps in working with some of the materials to follow. The concluding portion of this chapter furnishes an overview of property transactions, including the distinction between realized and recognized gain or loss, the classification of such gain or loss (ordinary or capital), and the treatment for income tax purposes.

Tax Formula

LO.1
Understand and apply the components of the Federal income tax formula.

Most individuals compute taxable income using the tax formula shown in Figure 3–1. Special provisions govern the computation of taxable income and the tax liability for certain minor children who have unearned income in excess of specified amounts. These provisions are discussed later in the chapter.

Before illustrating the application of the tax formula, a brief discussion of its components is helpful.

Components of the Tax Formula

Income (Broadly Conceived). This includes all the taxpayer's income, both taxable and nontaxable. Although it is essentially equivalent to gross receipts, it does not include a return of capital or receipt of borrowed funds.

EXAMPLE 1

Dave needed money to purchase a house. He sold 5,000 shares of stock for $100,000. He had paid $40,000 for the stock. In addition, he borrowed $75,000 from a bank. Dave has income that is taxable of $60,000 from the sale of the stock ($100,000 selling price − $40,000 return of capital). He has no income from the $75,000 borrowed from the bank because he has an obligation to repay that amount. ■

Exclusions. For various reasons, Congress has chosen to exclude certain types of income from the income tax base. The principal income exclusions are discussed in Chapter 5. A partial list of these exclusions is shown in Exhibit 3–1.

Gross Income. The Internal Revenue Code defines gross income broadly as "except as otherwise provided . . ., all income from whatever source derived."[2] The "except as otherwise provided" refers to exclusions. Gross income includes, but is not limited to, the items in the partial list in Exhibit 3–2. It does not include unrealized gains. Gross income is discussed in Chapters 4 and 5.

---

[1]Prior to the Tax Relief Reconciliation Act of 2001, the tax rates ranged from 15% to 39.6%. The Act established 10% as the new lowest bracket. Later legislation lowered the top rate to 35%.

[2]§ 61(a).

| **EXHIBIT 3–1** | **Partial List of Exclusions from Gross Income** |

Accident insurance proceeds
Annuities (cost element)
Bequests
Child support payments
Cost-of-living allowance (for military)
Damages for personal injury or sickness
Gifts received
Group term life insurance, premium paid by employer (for coverage up to $50,000)
Inheritances
Interest from state and local (i.e., municipal) bonds
Life insurance paid on death

Meals and lodging (if furnished for employer's convenience)
Military allowances
Minister's dwelling rental value allowance
Railroad retirement benefits (to a limited extent)
Scholarship grants (to a limited extent)
Social Security benefits (to a limited extent)
Veterans' benefits
Welfare payments
Workers' compensation benefits

| **EXHIBIT 3–2** | **Partial List of Gross Income Items** |

Alimony
Annuities (income element)
Awards
Back pay
Bargain purchase from employer
Bonuses
Breach of contract damages
Business income
Clergy fees
Commissions
Compensation for services
Death benefits
Debts forgiven
Director's fees
Dividends
Embezzled funds
Employee awards (in certain cases)
Employee benefits (except certain fringe benefits)
Estate and trust income
Farm income
Fees
Gains from illegal activities
Gains from sale of property
Gambling winnings
Group term life insurance, premium paid by employer (for coverage over $50,000)

Hobby income
Interest
Jury duty fees
Living quarters, meals (unless furnished for employer's convenience)
Mileage allowance
Military pay (unless combat pay)
Notary fees
Partnership income
Pensions
Prizes
Professional fees
Punitive damages
Rents
Rewards
Royalties
Salaries
Severance pay
Strike and lockout benefits
Supplemental unemployment benefits
Tips and gratuities
Travel allowance (in certain cases)
Wages

CITIZENSHIP IS NOT TAX-FREE

Gross income from "whatever source derived" includes income from both U.S. and foreign sources. This approach to taxation, where the government taxes its citizens and residents on their worldwide income regardless of where earned, is referred to as a *global system*. Income earned by U.S. citizens outside the United States can be subject to additional taxes, however, because all countries maintain the right to tax income earned within their borders. Consequently, the U.S. tax law includes various mechanisms to alleviate the double taxation that arises when income is subject to tax in multiple jurisdictions. These mechanisms include the foreign tax deduction, the foreign tax credit, the foreign earned income exclusion for U.S. citizens and residents working abroad, and various tax treaty provisions.

Most industrialized countries use variants of the global system. An alternative approach is the *territorial system*, where a government taxes only the income earned within its borders. Hong Kong and Guatemala, for example, use a territorial approach.

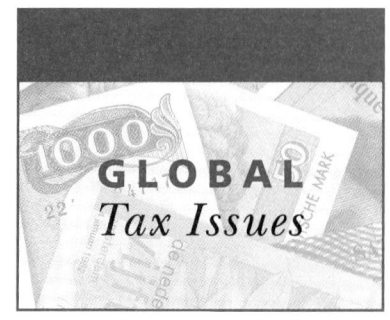

GLOBAL
Tax Issues

EXAMPLE 2

Beth received the following amounts during the year:

Salary	$30,000	✓
Interest on savings account	900	✓
Gift from her aunt	10,000	✗
Prize won in state lottery	1,000	✓
Alimony from ex-husband	12,000	✓
Child support from ex-husband	6,000	✗
Damages for injury in auto accident	25,000	✗
Increase in the value of stock held for investment	5,000	✗

Review Exhibits 3–1 and 3–2 to determine the amount Beth must include in the computation of taxable income and the amount she may exclude. Then check your answer in footnote 3.[3]

Deductions for Adjusted Gross Income. Individual taxpayers have two categories of deductions: (1) deductions *for* adjusted gross income (deductions to arrive at adjusted gross income) and (2) deductions *from* adjusted gross income.

Deductions *for* adjusted gross income (AGI) include ordinary and necessary expenses incurred in a trade or business, one-half of self-employment tax paid, alimony paid, certain payments to an Individual Retirement Account and Health Savings Accounts, moving expenses, forfeited interest penalty for premature withdrawal of time deposits, the capital loss deduction, and others.[4] Deductions *for* AGI are sometimes known as *above-the-line* deductions because on the tax return they are taken before the "line" designating AGI. The principal deductions *for* AGI are discussed in Chapters 6, 7, 8, 9, and 11.

Adjusted Gross Income (AGI). AGI is an important subtotal that serves as the basis for computing percentage limitations on certain itemized deductions, such as medical expenses, charitable contributions, and certain casualty losses. For example, medical expenses are deductible only to the extent they exceed 7.5 percent of

---

[3]Beth must include $43,900 in computing taxable income ($30,000 salary + $900 interest + $1,000 lottery prize + $12,000 alimony). She can exclude $41,000 ($10,000 gift from aunt + $6,000 child support + $25,000 damages). The unrealized gain on the stock held for investment also is not included in gross income. Such gain will be included in gross income only when it is realized upon disposition of the stock.

[4]§ 62.

AGI, and charitable contribution deductions may not exceed 50 percent of AGI. These limitations might be described as a 7.5 percent *floor* under the medical expense deduction and a 50 percent *ceiling* on the charitable contribution deduction.

EXAMPLE 3

Keith earned a salary of $65,000 in the current tax year. He contributed $4,000 to his traditional Individual Retirement Account (IRA) and sustained a $1,000 capital loss on the sale of Wren Corporation stock. His AGI is computed as follows:

Gross income		
Salary		$65,000
Less: Deductions *for* AGI		
IRA contribution	$4,000	
Capital loss	1,000	(5,000)
AGI		$60,000

EXAMPLE 4

Assume the same facts as in Example 3, and that Keith also had medical expenses of $5,800. Medical expenses may be included in itemized deductions to the extent they exceed 7.5% of AGI. In computing his itemized deductions, Keith may include medical expenses of $1,300 [$5,800 medical expenses − $4,500 (7.5% × $60,000 AGI)]. ∎

Itemized Deductions. As a general rule, personal expenditures are disallowed as deductions in arriving at taxable income. However, Congress has chosen to allow specified personal expenses as **itemized deductions.** Such expenditures include medical expenses, certain taxes and interest, and charitable contributions.

In addition to these personal expenses, taxpayers are allowed itemized deductions for expenses related to (1) the production or collection of income and (2) the management of property held for the production of income.[5] These expenses, sometimes referred to as *nonbusiness expenses,* differ from trade or business expenses (discussed previously). Trade or business expenses, which are deductions *for* AGI, must be incurred in connection with a trade or business. Nonbusiness expenses, on the other hand, are expenses incurred in connection with an income-producing activity that does not qualify as a trade or business. Such expenses are itemized deductions.

EXAMPLE 5

Leo is the owner and operator of a video game arcade. All allowable expenses he incurs in connection with the arcade business are deductions *for* AGI. In addition, Leo has an extensive portfolio of stocks and bonds. Leo's investment activity is not treated as a trade or business. All allowable expenses that Leo incurs in connection with these investments are itemized deductions. ∎

Itemized deductions include, but are not limited to, the expenses listed in Exhibit 3–3. See Chapter 10 for a detailed discussion of itemized deductions.

Standard Deduction. The **standard deduction,** which is set by Congress, is a specified amount that depends on the filing status of the taxpayer. The effect of the standard deduction is to exempt a taxpayer's income, up to the specified amount, from Federal income tax liability. In the past, Congress has attempted to set the tax-free amount represented by the standard deduction approximately equal to an estimated poverty level,[6] but it has not always been consistent in doing so.

---

[5]§ 212.
[6]S.Rep. No. 92–437, 92nd Cong., 1st Sess., 1971, p. 54. Another purpose of the standard deduction was discussed in Chapter 1 under Influence of the Internal Revenue Service—Administrative Feasibility. The size of the standard deduction has a direct bearing on the number of taxpayers who are in a position to itemize deductions. Reducing the number of taxpayers who itemize also reduces the audit effort required from the IRS.

| **EXHIBIT 3–3** | **Partial List of Itemized Deductions** |

Medical expenses in excess of 7.5% of AGI
State and local income or sales taxes
Real estate taxes
Personal property taxes
Interest on home mortgage
Investment interest (to a limited extent)
Charitable contributions (within specified percentage limitations)
Casualty and theft losses in excess of 10% of AGI
Miscellaneous expenses (to the extent such expenses exceed 2% of AGI)
    Union dues
    Professional dues and subscriptions
    Certain educational expenses
    Tax return preparation fee
    Investment counsel fees
    Unreimbursed employee business expenses (after a percentage reduction for
       meals and entertainment)

The standard deduction is the sum of two components: the *basic* standard deduction and the *additional* standard deduction.[7] Table 3–1 lists the basic standard deduction allowed for taxpayers in each filing status. All taxpayers allowed a *full* standard deduction are entitled to the applicable amount listed in Table 3–1. The standard deduction amounts are subject to adjustment for inflation each year.

Certain taxpayers are not allowed to claim *any* standard deduction, and the standard deduction is *limited* for others. These provisions are discussed later in the chapter.

A taxpayer who is age 65 or over *or* blind qualifies for an *additional standard deduction* of $1,000 or $1,250, depending on filing status (see amounts in Table 3–2). Two additional standard deductions are allowed for a taxpayer who is age 65 or over *and*

| **TABLE 3–1** | **Basic Standard Deduction Amounts** |

	Standard Deduction Amount	
Filing Status	**2005**	**2006**
Single	$ 5,000	$ 5,150
Married, filing jointly	10,000	10,300
Surviving spouse	10,000	10,300
Head of household	7,300	7,550
Married, filing separately	5,000	5,150

[7]§ 63(c)(1).

TABLE 3–2	Amount of Each Additional Standard Deduction		
Filing Status		**2005**	**2006**
Single		$1,250	$1,250
Married, filing jointly		1,000	1,000
Surviving spouse		1,000	1,000
Head of household		1,250	1,250
Married, filing separately		1,000	1,000

blind. The additional standard deduction provisions also apply for a qualifying spouse who is age 65 or over or blind, but a taxpayer may not claim an additional standard deduction for a dependent.

To determine whether to itemize, the taxpayer compares the *total* standard deduction (the sum of the basic standard deduction and any additional standard deductions) with total itemized deductions. Taxpayers are allowed to deduct the *greater* of itemized deductions or the standard deduction. Taxpayers whose itemized deductions are less than the standard deduction compute their taxable income using the standard deduction rather than itemizing. Approximately 70 percent of individual taxpayers choose the standard deduction option.

EXAMPLE 6

Sara, who is single, is 66 years old. She had total itemized deductions of $5,900 during 2006. Her total standard deduction is $6,400 ($5,150 basic standard deduction plus $1,250 additional standard deduction). Sara should compute her taxable income for 2006 using the standard deduction ($6,400), since it exceeds her itemized deductions ($5,900). ■

Personal and Dependency Exemptions. Exemptions are allowed for the taxpayer, for the taxpayer's spouse, and for each dependent of the taxpayer. The exemption amount is $3,200 in 2005 and $3,300 in 2006.

Application of the Tax Formula

The tax formula shown in Figure 3–1 is illustrated in Example 7.

EXAMPLE 7

Grace, age 25, is single and has no dependents. She is a high school teacher and earned a $40,000 salary in 2006. Her other income consisted of a $1,000 prize won in a sweepstakes contest and $500 interest on municipal bonds that she had received as a graduation gift in 2003. During 2006, she sustained a deductible capital loss of $1,000. Her itemized deductions are $5,400. Grace's taxable income for the year is computed as follows:

Income (broadly conceived)	
Salary	$40,000
Prize	1,000
Interest on municipal bonds	500
	$41,500
Less: Exclusion—	
Interest on municipal bonds	(500)
Gross income	$41,000
Less: Deduction *for* adjusted gross income—	
Capital loss	(1,000)
Adjusted gross income	$40,000

Less: The greater of total itemized deductions ($5,400) *or*	
the standard deduction ($5,150)	(5,400)
Personal and dependency exemptions	
(1 × $3,300)	(3,300)
Taxable income	$31,300

The structure of the individual income tax return (Form 1040, 1040A, or 1040EZ) differs somewhat from the tax formula in Figure 3–1. On the tax return, gross income generally is the starting point in computing taxable income. With few exceptions, exclusions are not reported on the tax return.

Individuals Not Eligible for the Standard Deduction

The following individual taxpayers are ineligible to use the standard deduction and must therefore itemize:[8]

- A married individual filing a separate return where either spouse itemizes deductions.
- A nonresident alien.
- An individual filing a return for a period of less than 12 months because of a change in the annual accounting period.

Special Limitations for Individuals Who Can Be Claimed as Dependents

Special rules apply to the standard deduction and personal exemption of an individual who can be claimed as a dependent on another person's tax return.

When filing his or her own tax return, a *dependent's* basic standard deduction in 2006 is limited to the greater of $850 or the sum of the individual's earned income for the year plus $300.[9] However, if the sum of the individual's earned income plus $300 exceeds the normal standard deduction, the standard deduction is limited to the appropriate amount shown in Table 3–1. These limitations apply only to the basic standard deduction. A dependent who is 65 or over or blind or both is also allowed the additional standard deduction amount on his or her own return (refer to Table 3–2). These provisions are illustrated in Examples 8 through 11.

Handwritten margin note:
Dependent's SDA
(Larger of $850
  (Earned Inc +
   300
Less
(Indiv SDA ($5150)

EXAMPLE 8

Susan, who is 17 years old and single, is claimed as a dependent on her parents' tax return. During 2006, she received $1,200 interest (unearned income) on a savings account. She also earned $400 from a part-time job. When Susan files her own tax return, her standard deduction is $850 (the greater of $850 or the sum of earned income of $400 plus $300). ∎

EXAMPLE 9

Assume the same facts as in Example 8, except that Susan is 67 years old and is claimed as a dependent on her son's tax return. In this case, when Susan files her own tax return, her standard deduction is $2,100 [$850 (the greater of $850 or the sum of earned income of $400 plus $300) + $1,250 (the additional standard deduction allowed because Susan is 65 or over)]. ∎

EXAMPLE 10

Peggy, who is 16 years old and single, earned $600 from a summer job and had no unearned income during 2006. She is claimed as a dependent on her parents' tax return. Her standard deduction is $900 (the greater of $850 or the sum of $600 earned income plus $300). ∎

---

[8] § 63(c)(6).
[9] § 63(c)(5). Both the $850 amount and the $300 amount are subject to adjustment for inflation each year. The amounts were $800 and $250, respectively, for 2005.

EXAMPLE 11

Jack, who is a 20-year-old, single, full-time college student, is claimed as a dependent on his parents' tax return. He worked as a musician during the summer of 2006, earning $5,900. Jack's standard deduction is $5,150 (the greater of $850 or the sum of $5,900 earned income plus $300, but limited to the $5,150 standard deduction for a single taxpayer). ∎

LO.2

Apply the rules for arriving at personal exemptions.

Personal Exemptions

The use of exemptions in the tax system is based in part on the idea that a taxpayer with a small amount of income should be exempt from income taxation. An exemption frees a specified amount of income from tax ($3,200 in 2005 and $3,300 in 2006). The exemption amount is indexed (adjusted) annually for inflation.

Exemptions that are allowed for the taxpayer and spouse are designated as **personal exemptions**. Those exemptions allowed for the care and maintenance of other persons are called dependency exemptions and are discussed in the next section.

An individual cannot claim a personal exemption if he or she is claimed as a dependent by another.

EXAMPLE 12

Assume the same facts as in Example 11. On his own income tax return,[10] Jack's taxable income is determined as follows:

Gross income	$ 5,900
Less: Standard deduction	(5,150)
Personal exemption	(–0–)
Taxable income	$ 750

Note that Jack is not allowed a personal exemption because he is claimed as a dependent by his parents. ∎

When a husband and wife file a joint return, they may claim two personal exemptions. However, when separate returns are filed, a married taxpayer cannot claim an exemption for his or her spouse *unless* the spouse has no gross income and is not claimed as the dependent of another taxpayer.[11]

The determination of marital status generally is made at the end of the taxable year, except when a spouse dies during the year. Spouses who enter into a legal separation under a decree of divorce or separate maintenance before the end of the year are considered to be unmarried at the end of the taxable year. Table 3–3 illustrates the effect of death or divorce upon marital status.

TABLE 3–3	**Marital Status for Exemption Purposes**

	Marital Status for 2006
• Walt is the widower of Helen who died on January 3, 2006.	Walt and Helen are considered to be married for purposes of filing the 2006 return.
• Bill and Jane entered into a divorce decree that is effective on December 31, 2006.	Bill and Jane are considered to be unmarried for purposes of filing the 2006 return.

---

[10]As noted in Table 3–6, Jack's situation is such that he will be required to file an income tax return.   [11]§ 151(b).

For *Federal* tax purposes, the law does not recognize same-sex marriages. By virtue of the Defense of Marriage Act (Pub. L. No. 104–199), a marriage means a legal union only between a man and a woman as husband and wife.

The amount of the exemption is not reduced due to the taxpayer's death. For example, refer to the case of Helen in Table 3–3. Although she lived for only three days in 2006, the full personal exemption of $3,300 is allowed for the tax year. The same rule applies to dependency exemptions. As long as an individual qualified as a dependent at the time of death, the full amount of the exemption can be claimed.

Dependency Exemptions

LO.3

Apply the rules for determining dependency exemptions.

As is the case with personal exemptions, a taxpayer is permitted to claim an exemption of $3,300 in 2006 ($3,200 in 2005) for each person who qualifies as a dependent. A **dependency exemption** is available for either a qualifying child or a qualifying relative and must not run afoul of certain other rules (i.e., joint return, nonresident alien prohibitions).

Qualifying Child

One of the objectives of the Working Families Tax Relief Act of 2004 was to establish a uniform definition of qualifying child. Aside from minor modifications, the qualifying child definition applies to the following tax benefits:

- Dependency exemption.
- Head-of-household filing status.
- Earned income tax credit.
- Child tax credit.
- Credit for child and dependent care expenses.

A **qualifying child** must meet the relationship, abode, age, and support tests.[12]

Relationship Test. The relationship test includes a taxpayer's child (son, daughter), adopted child, stepchild, eligible foster child, brother, sister, half brother, half sister, stepbrother, stepsister, or a *descendant* of any of these parties (e.g., grandchild, nephew, niece). Note that *ancestors* of any of these parties (e.g., uncles and aunts) and in-laws (e.g., son-in-law, brother-in-law) *are not included.*

An adopted child includes a child lawfully placed with the taxpayer for legal adoption even though the adoption is not final. An eligible foster child is one who is placed with the taxpayer by an authorized placement agency or by a judgment decree or other order of any court of competent jurisdiction.

EXAMPLE 13

Maureen's household includes her mother, grandson, stepbrother, stepbrother's daughter, uncle, and sister. All meet the relationship test for a qualifying child except the mother and uncle. ∎

Abode Test. A qualifying child must live with the taxpayer for more than half of the year. For this purpose, temporary absences (e.g., school, vacation, medical care, military service, detention in a juvenile facility) are disregarded. Special rules apply in the case of certain kidnapped children.[13]

Age Test. A qualifying child must be under age 19 or under age 24 in the case of a student. A student is a child who, during any part of five months of the year, is

---

[12]§ 152(c).
[13]§ 152(f)(6).

TABLE 3–4	Tiebreaker Rules for Claiming Qualified Child

Persons Eligible to Claim Exemption	Person Prevailing
One of the persons is the parent.	Parent
Both persons are the parents, and the child lives longer with one parent.	Parent with the longer period of residence
Both persons are the parents, and the child lives with each the same period of time.	Parent with the higher adjusted gross income (AGI)
None of the persons is the parent.	Person with highest AGI

enrolled full time at a school or government-sponsored on-farm training course.[14] The age test does not apply to a child who is disabled during any part of the year.[15]

Support Test. In order to be a qualifying child, the individual must not be self-supporting (i.e., provide more than one-half of his or her own support). In the case of a child who is a full-time student, scholarships are not considered to be support.[16]

EXAMPLE 14

Shawn, age 23, is a full-time student and lives with his parents and an older cousin. During 2006, Shawn receives his support from the following sources: 30% from a part-time job, 30% from a scholarship, 20% from his parents, and 20% from the cousin. Shawn is not self-supporting and can be claimed by his parents as a dependent. (Note: Shawn cannot be a qualifying child as to his cousin due to the relationship test.) ■

Tiebreaker Rules. In some situations, a child may be a qualifying child to more than one person. In this event, the tax law specifies which person has priority in claiming the dependency exemption.[17] Called "tiebreaker rules," these rules are summarized in Table 3–4 and are illustrated in the examples that follow.

EXAMPLE 15

Tim, age 15, lives in the same household with his mother and grandmother. As the parent (see Table 3–4), the mother has priority as to the dependency exemption. ■

EXAMPLE 16

Jennifer, age 17, lives in the same household with her parents during the entire year. If her parents file separate returns, the one with the higher AGI has priority as to the dependency exemption. ■

EXAMPLE 17

Assume the same facts as in Example 16, except that the father moves into an apartment in November (Jennifer remains with her mother). The mother has priority as to the dependency exemption. ■

EXAMPLE 18

Carlos, age 12, lives in the same household with his two aunts. The aunt with the higher AGI has priority as to the dependency exemption. ■

---

[14]§ 152(f)(2).

[15]Within the meaning of § 22(e)(3). See the discussion of the credit for elderly and disabled in Chapter 13.

[16]§ 152(f)(5).

[17]§ 152(c)(4).

Resorting to the tiebreaker rules in Table 3–4 is not necessary if the person who would prevail does not claim the exemption. Thus, in Example 15, the mother can allow the grandmother to claim Tim as a dependent by not claiming him on her own return.

Qualifying Relative

Besides establishing the concept of a qualifying child, the Working Families Tax Relief Act of 2004 also provided for a second category of dependency exemption designated as the **qualifying relative**. The rules involved largely carried over then-existing law to post-2004 years.

A qualifying relative must meet the relationship, gross income, and support tests.[18] As in the case of the qualifying child category, qualifying relative status also requires that the joint return and nonresident alien restrictions be avoided (see Other Rules for Dependency Exemptions below).

Relationship Test. The relationship test for a qualifying relative is more expansive than for a qualifying child. Also included are the following relatives:

- Lineal ascendants (e.g., parents, grandparents).
- Collateral ascendants (e.g., uncles, aunts).
- Certain in-laws (e.g., son-, daughter-, father-, mother-, brother-, and sister-in-law).[19]

Children who do not satisfy the qualifying child definition may meet the qualifying relative criteria.

EXAMPLE 19

Inez provides more than half of the support of her son, age 20, who is neither disabled nor a full-time student. The son is not a qualifying child due to the age test but would be a qualifying relative (if the gross income test is met). Consequently, Inez may claim a dependency exemption for her son. ■

The relationship test also includes unrelated parties who live with the taxpayer (i.e., are members of the household). Member-of-the-household status is not available for anyone whose relationship with the taxpayer violates local law or anyone who was a spouse during any part of the year.[20] However, an ex-spouse can qualify as a member of the household in a year following that of the divorce.

As the relationship test indicates, the category designation of "qualifying relative" is somewhat misleading. As just noted, persons other than relatives can qualify as dependents. Furthermore, not all relatives will qualify—notice the absence of the "cousin" grouping.

EXAMPLE 20

Charles provides more than half of the support of a family friend who lives with him and a cousin who lives in another city. Presuming the gross income test is met, the family friend is a qualifying relative, but the cousin is not. ■

Gross Income Test. A dependent's gross income must be *less* than the exemption amount—$3,200 in 2005 and $3,300 in 2006. Gross income is determined by the income that is taxable. In the case of scholarships, for example, include the taxable portion (e.g., amounts received for room and board) and exclude the nontaxable portion (e.g., amounts received for books and tuition).

---

[18]§ 152(d).

[19]Once established by marriage, in-law status continues to exist and survives divorce.

[20]§§ 152(d)(2)(H) and (f)(3).

EXAMPLE 21	Elsie provides more than half of the support of her son, Tom, who does not live with her. Tom, age 26, is a full-time student in medical school, earns $3,000 from a part-time job, and receives a $12,000 scholarship covering his tuition. Elsie may claim Tom as a dependent since he meets the gross income test and is a qualifying relative. (Note: Tom is not a qualifying child due to either the abode or the age test.) ■

EXAMPLE 22	Aaron provides more than half of the support of his widowed aunt, Myrtle, who does not live with him. Myrtle's income for the year is as follows: dividend income of $1,100; earnings from pet sitting of $1,200; Social Security benefits of $6,000; and interest from City of Milwaukee bonds of $8,000. Since Myrtle's gross income is only $2,300 ($1,100 + $1,200), she meets the gross income test and can be claimed as Aaron's dependent. ■

In contrast, the qualifying child category of dependency exemptions does not contain a gross income test. Consequently, it is no longer necessary to have a special exception to the gross income test for a child of the taxpayer who is under age 19 or under age 24 and a full-time student.

Support Test. Over one-half of the support of the qualifying relative must be furnished by the taxpayer. Support includes food, shelter, clothing, toys, medical and dental care, education, and the like. However, a scholarship (both taxable and nontaxable portions) received by a student is not included for purposes of computing whether the taxpayer furnished more than half of the child's support.

EXAMPLE 23	Hal contributed $3,400 (consisting of food, clothing, and medical care) toward the support of his nephew, Sam, who lives with him. Sam earned $1,500 from a part-time job and received a $2,000 scholarship to attend a local university. Assuming that the other dependency tests are met, Hal can claim Sam as a dependent since he has contributed more than half of Sam's support. The $2,000 scholarship is not included as support for purposes of this test. ■

If the individual does not spend funds that have been received from any source, the unexpended amounts are not counted for purposes of the support test.

EXAMPLE 24	Emily contributed $3,000 to her father's support during the year. In addition, her father received $2,400 in Social Security benefits, $200 of interest, and wages of $600. Her father deposited the Social Security benefits, interest, and wages in his own savings account and did not use any of the funds for his support. Thus, the Social Security benefits, interest, and wages are not considered as support provided by Emily's father. Emily may claim her father as a dependent if the other tests are met. ■

Capital expenditures for items such as furniture, appliances, and automobiles are included in total support if the item does, in fact, constitute support.

EXAMPLE 25	Norm purchased a television set costing $650 and gave it to his mother who lives with him. The television set was placed in the mother's bedroom and was used exclusively by her. Norm should include the cost of the television set in determining the support of his mother. ■

An exception to the support test involves a **multiple support agreement**. A multiple support agreement permits one of a group of taxpayers who furnish support for a qualifying relative to claim a dependency exemption for that individual even if no one person provides more than 50 percent of the support.[21] The group together must provide more than 50 percent of the support. Any person who contributed *more than 10 percent* of the support is entitled to claim the exemption if

[21]§ 152(d)(3).

each person in the group who contributed more than 10 percent files a written consent. This provision frequently enables one of the children of aged dependent parents to claim an exemption when none of the children meets the 50 percent support test.

Each person who is a party to the multiple support agreement must meet all other requirements (except the support requirement) for claiming the exemption. A person who does not meet the relationship or member-of-the-household requirement, for instance, cannot claim the dependency exemption under a multiple support agreement. It does not matter if he or she contributes more than 10 percent of the individual's support.

EXAMPLE 26

Wanda, who resides with her son, Adam, received $12,000 from various sources during the year. This constituted her entire support for the year. She received support from the following:

	Amount	Percentage of Total
Adam, a son	$ 5,760	48
Bob, a son	1,200	10
Carol, a daughter	3,600	30
Diane, a friend	1,440	12
	$12,000	100

If Adam and Carol file a multiple support agreement, either may claim the dependency exemption for Wanda. Bob may not claim Wanda because he did not contribute more than 10% of her support. Bob's consent is not required in order for Adam and Carol to file a multiple support agreement. Diane does not meet the relationship or member-of-the-household test and cannot be a party to the agreement. The decision as to who claims Wanda rests with Adam and Carol. It is possible for Carol to claim Wanda, even though Adam furnished more of Wanda's support. ■

ETHICAL *Considerations*   **DISCOVERING LOST DEPENDENCY EXEMPTIONS**

For the six years prior to his death in late 2006, Jesse lived with his daughter, Hannah. Because he had no source of income, Jesse was supported by equal contributions from Hannah and his two sons, Bill and Bob. At Jesse's funeral, his surviving children are amazed to discover that none of them has been claiming Jesse as a dependent. Upon the advice of the director of the funeral home, they decide to divide, among themselves, the dependency exemptions for the past six years. Multiple Forms 2120 are executed, and each of the three children files amended returns for different past years. As Jesse died before the end of the current year, no deduction is planned for 2006.

Comment on the tax expectations of the parties involved.

Each person who qualifies under the more-than-10 percent rule (except for the person claiming the exemption) must complete Form 2120 (Multiple Support Declaration) waiving the exemption. The person claiming the exemption must attach all Forms 2120 to his or her own return.

Another exception to the support test applies when parents with children are divorced or separated under a decree of separate maintenance. For unmarried parents, living apart (for the last six months of the year) will suffice. A special rule applies if the parents meet the following conditions:

- Provide more than half of the support (either jointly or singly) of the child (or children).
- Have custody (either jointly or singly) of the child (or children) for more than half of the year.

The special rule grants the dependency exemption(s) to the noncustodial parent if the divorce (or separate maintenance) decree so specifies *or* the custodial parent issues a waiver.[22]

The waiver, Form 8332 (Release of Claim to Exemption of Child of Divorced or Separated Parents), can apply to a single year, a number of specified years, or all future years. The noncustodial parent must attach a copy of Form 8332 to his or her return.

If the special rule does not apply (i.e., the divorce decree is silent or the custodial parent does not sign Form 8332), the dependency exemption(s) for the child (children) will be awarded in accordance with the qualifying child or qualifying relative rules.[23] The special rule will not apply if a multiple support agreement is in effect.

When the special rule does not apply and support may have to be determined, the following rules as to source govern:

- Alimony received by the custodial parent does not count as support by the payor parent.
- If a parent has remarried, amounts received from the parent's spouse are considered to be provided by that parent.[24]

Other Rules for Dependency Exemptions

In addition to fitting into either the qualifying child or the qualifying relative category, a dependent must meet the joint return and the citizenship or residency tests.

Joint Return Test. If a dependent is married, the supporting taxpayer (e.g., the parent of a married child) generally is not permitted a dependency exemption if the married individual files a joint return with his or her spouse.[25] The joint return rule does not apply, however, if the following conditions are met:

- The reason for filing is to claim a refund for tax withheld.
- No tax liability would exist for either spouse on separate returns.
- Neither spouse is required to file a return.

See Table 3–6 later in the chapter and the related discussion concerning income level requirements for filing a return.

EXAMPLE 27

Paul provides over half of the support of his son Quinn. He also provides over half of the support of Vera, who is Quinn's wife. During the year, both Quinn and Vera had part-time jobs. In order to recover the taxes withheld, they file a joint return. If Quinn and Vera are not required to file a return, Paul is allowed to claim both as dependents. ∎

Citizenship or Residency Test. To be a dependent, the individual must be either a U.S. citizen, a U.S. resident, or a resident of Canada or Mexico for some part of the calendar year in which the taxpayer's tax year begins.[26]

---

[22]§ 152(e).

[23]The qualifying child category predominates over the qualifying relative. § 152(d)(1)(D).

[24]§ 152(d)(5).

[25]§ 152(b)(2).

[26]§ 152(b)(3).

ETHICAL *Considerations*   **A CHANGE OF RESIDENCE CAN BE REWARDING**

Linda is a citizen of Honduras and a resident of Chicago. For many years she has supported her parents and grandparents, who were citizens and residents of Honduras. In 2006, Linda convinces her relatives to relocate and become residents of Mexico. For tax purposes, what is Linda trying to accomplish? Is this an appropriate thing for Linda to do?

Under an exception, an adopted child need not be a citizen or resident of the United States (or a contiguous country) as long as his or her principal abode is with a U.S. citizen.

EXAMPLE 28

Esther is a U.S. citizen who lives and works in Spain. She has adopted Benito, a four-year-old Italian national, who lives with her and is a member of her household. Although Benito does not meet the usual citizenship or residency test, he is covered by the exception. Benito is a qualifying child, and Esther can claim him as a dependent. ■

Comparison of Categories for Dependency Exemptions

Concept Summary 3–1 sets forth the tests for the two categories of dependency exemptions. In contrasting the two categories, the following observations are in order:

- As to the relationship tests, the qualifying relative category is considerably more expansive. Besides including those prescribed under the qualifying child grouping, other relatives are added. Nonrelated persons who are members of the household are also included.
- The support tests are entirely different. In the case of a qualifying child, support is not necessary. What is required is that the child not be self-supporting.
- The qualifying child category has no gross income limitation, whereas the qualifying relative category has no age restriction.

Phaseout of Exemptions

Several provisions of the tax law are intended to increase the tax liability of more affluent taxpayers who might otherwise enjoy some benefit from having some of their taxable income subject to the lower income tax brackets (e.g., 10 percent, 15 percent, 25 percent). One such provision phases out certain itemized deductions and is discussed in Chapter 10. Another provision phases out personal and dependency exemptions and is considered below.[27] In 2001, however, Congress decided that both of these provisions imposed an unfair burden on high-income individual taxpayers and decided on their repeal. To avoid an immediate revenue loss, the repeal was postponed until 2006. Furthermore, to spread the impact of the revenue loss, the repeal is taking place in two stages and will not be complete until 2010. The personal and dependency exemption phaseout remains at two-thirds for 2006 and 2007 and at one-third for 2008 and 2009.

The phaseout of exemptions occurs as AGI exceeds specified threshold amounts (indexed annually for inflation). For 2005 and 2006, the phaseout *begins* when AGI exceeds the following:

---

[27]§ 151(d)(3).

CONCEPT SUMMARY 3–1

Tests for Dependency Exemption after 2004

	Category	
Qualifying Child		**Qualifying Relative[1]**
Relationship[2]		Support
Abode[3]		Relationship[4] or member of household[3]
Age		Gross income
Support		
Joint return[5]		Joint return[5]
Citizenship or residency[6]		Citizenship or residency[6]

[1] These rules are largely the same as those applicable to pre-2005 years.

[2] Children and their descendants, and siblings and stepsiblings and their descendants.

[3] The rules for abode are the same as for member of the household.

[4] Children and their descendants, siblings and their children, parents and their ascendants, uncles and aunts, stepparents and stepsiblings, and certain in-laws.

[5] The joint return rules are the same for each category.

[6] The citizenship or residency rules are the same for each category.

	2005	2006
Joint returns/surviving spouse	$218,950	$225,750
Head of household	182,450	188,150
Single	145,950	150,500
Married, filing separately	109,475	112,875

Exemptions are phased out by 2 percent for each $2,500 (or fraction thereof) by which the taxpayer's AGI exceeds the threshold amounts. For a married taxpayer filing separately, the phaseout is 2 percent for each $1,250 or fraction thereof. Then, the amount of the phased-out exemptions is multiplied by $2/3$ (the reduction-of-phaseout fraction) for tax years 2006 and 2007.

The allowable exemption amount can be determined with the following steps:

1. AGI − threshold amount = excess amount
2. Excess amount ÷ $2,500 = reduction factor [rounded up to the next whole increment (e.g., 18.1 = 19)] × 2 = phaseout percentage
3. Phaseout percentage (from step 2) × exemption amount = amount of exemptions phased out
4. Amount of exemptions phased out × reduction-of-phaseout fraction = phaseout amount
5. Exemption amount − phaseout amount = allowable exemption deduction

EXAMPLE 29

Frederico is married but files a separate return in 2006. His AGI is $132,875. He is entitled to one personal exemption.

1. $132,875 − $112,875 = $20,000 excess amount
2. [($20,000 ÷ $1,250) × 2] = 32% (phaseout percentage)
3. 32% × $3,300 = $1,056 amount of exemption phased out

TAX *in the News*   **HOW TO SUBTLY PLUCK THE CHICKEN**

No government likes to admit that it is enacting new taxes or even raising the rates on existing taxes. Needless to say, this is particularly true of the U.S. Congress. But there are more subtle ways to raise revenue (or to curtail revenue loss). The most popular way is to use a so-called *stealth tax*. A stealth tax is not really a tax at all. Instead, it is a means of depriving higher-income taxpayers of the benefits of certain tax provisions thought to be available to all.

The heart and soul of the stealth tax is the phaseout approach. Thus, as income increases, the tax benefit thought to be derived from a particular relief provision decreases.

Since the phaseout is gradual and not drastic, many affected taxpayers are unaware of what has happened. Although the tax law is rampant with phaseouts, the two most flagrant limit the deductibility of personal and dependency exemptions and itemized deductions. (The itemized deduction phaseout is discussed in Chapter 10.)

As noted in the text, however, Congress has had some misgivings about the stealth tax imposed on personal and dependency exemptions. These misgivings cannot be too severe since scheduled relief does not *start* until year 2006 and is not *completed* until year 2010!

4. $1,056 \times \frac{2}{3} = \$704$ phaseout amount
5. $3,300 - \$704 = \$2,596$ allowable exemption deduction ■

The elimination of the phaseout of exemptions, as well as the phaseout of certain itemized deductions, will ultimately add much needed simplicity to the tax law. Unfortunately, reaching this objective by means of a gradual reduction of the phaseout (i.e., a phaseout of a phaseout) unduly adds further complexity to the existing rules.

Child Tax Credit

In addition to providing a dependency exemption, a child of the taxpayer may also generate a tax credit. Called the **child tax credit,** the amount allowed is $1,000 through 2009 for each dependent child (including stepchildren and eligible foster children) under the age of 17.[28] For a more complete discussion of the child tax credit, see Chapter 13.

Tax Determination

Tax Table Method

LO.4

Use the proper method for determining the tax liability.

The tax liability is computed using either the Tax Table method or the Tax Rate Schedule method. Most taxpayers compute their tax using the **Tax Table.** Eligible taxpayers compute taxable income (as shown in Figure 3–1) and *must* determine their tax by reference to the Tax Table. The following taxpayers, however, may not use the Tax Table method:

* An individual who files a short period return (see Chapter 18).
* Individuals whose taxable income exceeds the maximum (ceiling) amount in the Tax Table. The 2005 Tax Table applies to taxable income below $100,000 for Form 1040.
* An estate or trust.

The IRS does not release the Tax Tables until late in the year to which they apply. The Tax Rate Schedules, however, are released at the end of the year

---

[28]§ 24(a). The credit was scheduled to be reduced to $700 in 2005, but the reduction was canceled by the Working Families Tax Relief Act of 2004 and remains at $1,000.

TABLE 3–5   2006 Tax Rate Schedule for Single Taxpayers

| If Taxable Income Is | | | Of the |
Over	But Not Over	The Tax Is:	Amount Over
$ –0–	$ 7,550	10%	$ –0–
7,550	30,650	$ 755.00 + 15%	7,550
30,650	74,200	4,220.00 + 25%	30,650
74,200	154,800	15,107.50 + 28%	74,200
154,800	336,550	37,675.50 + 33%	154,800
336,550		97,653.00 + 35%	336,550

preceding their applicability. To illustrate, the Tax Table for 2006 will be available at the end of 2006. The Tax Rate Schedules for 2006, however, were released at the end of 2005.[29] For purposes of estimating tax liability and making quarterly prepayments, the Tax Rate Schedules will usually need to be consulted. Based on its availability, the 2005 Tax Table will be used to illustrate the tax computation using the Tax Table method.

Although the Tax Table is derived by using the Tax Rate Schedules (discussed below), the tax calculated using the two methods may vary slightly. This variation occurs because the tax for a particular income range in the Tax Table is based on the midpoint amount.

EXAMPLE 30

Linda is single and has taxable income of $30,000 for calendar year 2005. To determine Linda's tax using the Tax Table (see Appendix A), find the $30,000 to $30,050 income line. The tax of $4,171 is actually the tax the Tax Rate Schedule would yield on taxable income of $30,025 (i.e., the midpoint amount between $30,000 and $30,050). ■

Tax Rate Schedule Method

Prior to 2001 tax legislation, the **Tax Rate Schedules** contained rates of 15, 28, 31, 36, and 39.6 percent. These rates were scheduled to be reduced to 10, 15, 25, 28, 33, and 35 percent by year 2006. JGTRRA of 2003, however, accelerated the phase-in and made the new rates effective as of January 1, 2003.[30] A sunset provision reinstates the original rates (pre-2001) after 2010.

The 2006 rate schedule for single taxpayers is reproduced in Table 3–5. This schedule is used to illustrate the tax computations in Examples 31, 32, and 33.

EXAMPLE 31

Pat is single and had $5,870 of taxable income in 2006. His tax is $587 ($5,870 × 10%). ■

Several terms are used to describe tax rates. The rates in the Tax Rate Schedules are often referred to as *statutory* (or nominal) rates. The *marginal* rate is the highest rate that is applied in the tax computation for a particular taxpayer. In Example 31, the statutory rate and the marginal rate are both 10 percent.

EXAMPLE 32

Chris is single and had taxable income of $50,000 in 2006. Her tax is $9,057.50 [$4,220 + 25%($50,000 − $30,650)]. ■

[29]The 2006 Tax Table was not available from the IRS at the date of publication of this text. The Tax Table for 2005 and the Tax Rate Schedules for 2005 and 2006 are reproduced in Appendix A. For quick reference, the 2005 and 2006 Tax Rate Schedules are also reproduced inside the front cover of this text.
[30]§ 1(i).

The *average* rate is equal to the tax liability divided by taxable income. In Example 32, Chris has statutory rates of 10 percent, 15 percent, and 25 percent, and a marginal rate of 25 percent. Chris's average rate is 18.12 percent ($9,057.50 tax liability ÷ $50,000 taxable income).

Note that $4,220, which is the starting point in the tax computation in Example 32, is 10 percent of the $7,550 taxable income in the first bracket + 15 percent of the $23,100 ($30,650 − $7,550) taxable income in the second bracket. Chris's income in excess of $30,650 is taxed at a 25 percent rate. This reflects the *progressive* (or graduated) rate structure on which the U.S. income tax system is based. A tax is progressive if a higher rate of tax applies as the tax base increases.

EXAMPLE 33

Carl is single and had taxable income of $80,000 in 2006. His tax is $16,731.50 [$15,107.50 + 28%($80,000 − $74,200)]. Note that the effect of this computation is to tax part of Carl's income at 10%, part at 15%, part at 25%, and part at 28%. An alternative computational method provides a clearer illustration of the progressive rate structure:

Tax on $7,550 at 10%	$ 755.00
Tax on $30,650 − $7,550 at 15%	3,465.00
Tax on $74,200 − $30,650 at 25%	10,887.50
Tax on $80,000 − $74,200 at 28%	1,624.00
Total	$16,731.50

■

A special computation limits the effective tax rate on qualified dividends (see Chapter 4) and net long-term capital gain (see Chapter 16).

Computation of Net Taxes Payable or Refund Due

The pay-as-you-go feature of the Federal income tax system requires payment of all or part of the taxpayer's income tax liability during the year. These payments take the form of Federal income tax withheld by employers or estimated tax paid by the taxpayer or both.[31] The payments are applied against the tax from the Tax Table or Tax Rate Schedules to determine whether the taxpayer will get a refund or pay additional tax.

Employers are required to withhold income tax on compensation paid to their employees and to pay this tax over to the government. The employer notifies the employee of the amount of income tax withheld on Form W–2 (Wage and Tax Statement). The employee should receive this form by January 31 after the year in which the income tax is withheld.

If taxpayers receive income that is not subject to withholding or income from which not enough tax is withheld, they must pay estimated tax. These individuals must file Form 1040–ES (Estimated Tax for Individuals) and pay in quarterly installments the income tax and self-employment tax estimated to be due (see Chapter 13 for a thorough discussion).

The income tax from the Tax Table or the Tax Rate Schedules is reduced first by the individual's tax credits. There is an important distinction between tax credits and tax deductions. Tax credits reduce the tax liability dollar-for-dollar. Tax deductions reduce taxable income on which the tax liability is based.

EXAMPLE 34

Gail is a taxpayer in the 25% tax bracket. As a result of incurring $1,000 in child care expenses (see Chapter 13 for details), she is entitled to a $200 child care credit ($1,000 child care expenses × 20% credit rate). She also contributed $1,000 to the American Cancer Society and included this amount in her itemized deductions. The child care credit results in a $200 reduction of Gail's tax liability for the year. The contribution to the American Cancer

---

[31]§ 3402 for withholding; § 6654 for estimated payments.

Society reduces taxable income by $1,000 and results in a $250 reduction in Gail's tax liability ($1,000 reduction in taxable income × 25% tax rate). ∎

Tax credits are discussed in Chapter 13. The following are several of the more common credits:

- Earned income credit.
- Credit for child and dependent care expenses.
- Credit for the elderly.
- Foreign tax credit.
- Child tax credit.

EXAMPLE 35

Kelly, age 30, is a head of household with a disabled and dependent mother living with him. During 2006, Kelly had the following: taxable income, $30,000; income tax withheld, $3,250; estimated tax payments, $600; and credit for dependent care expenses, $200. Kelly's net tax payable is computed as follows:

Income tax (from 2006 Tax Rate Schedule, Appendix A)		$ 3,963
Less: Tax credits and prepayments—		
Credit for dependent care expenses	$ 200	
Income tax withheld	3,250	
Estimated tax payments	600	(4,050)
Net taxes payable or (refund due if negative)		$ (87)	∎

LO.5

Identify and work with kiddie tax situations.

Unearned Income of Children under Age 14 Taxed at Parents' Rate

At one time, a dependent child could claim an exemption on his or her own return even if claimed as a dependent by the parents. This enabled a parent to shift investment income (such as interest and dividends) to a child by transferring ownership of the assets producing the income. The child would pay no tax on the income to the extent that it was sheltered by the child's exemption.

Also, an additional tax motivation existed for shifting income from parents to children. Although a child's unearned income in excess of the exemption amount was subject to tax, it was taxed at the child's rate, rather than the parents' rate.

To reduce the tax savings that result from shifting income from parents to children, the net **unearned income** (commonly called investment income) of certain minor children is taxed as if it were the parents' income.[32] Unearned income includes such income as taxable interest, dividends, capital gains, rents, royalties, pension and annuity income, and income (other than earned income) received as the beneficiary of a trust. This provision, commonly referred to as the **kiddie tax,** applies to any child for any taxable year if the child has not reached age 14 by the close of the taxable year, has at least one living parent, and has unearned income of more than $1,700. The *kiddie tax* provision does not apply to a child age 14 or older. However, the limitation on the use of the standard deduction and the unavailability of the personal exemption do apply to such a child as long as he or she is eligible to be claimed as a dependent by a parent.

Net Unearned Income. Net unearned income of a dependent child is computed as follows:

Unearned income

Less: $850

Less: The greater of
- $850 of the standard deduction *or*
- The amount of allowable itemized deductions directly connected with the production of the unearned income

Equals: Net unearned income

If net unearned income is zero (or negative), the child's tax is computed without using the parents' rate. If the amount of net unearned income (regardless of source) is positive, the net unearned income is taxed at the parents' rate. The $850 amounts in the preceding formula are subject to adjustment for inflation each year (refer to footnote 9).

Tax Determination. If a child under age 14 has net unearned income, there are two options for computing the tax on the income. A separate return may be filed for the child, or the parents may elect to report the child's income on their own return. If a separate return is filed for the child, the tax on net unearned income (referred to as the *allocable parental tax*) is computed as though the income had been included on the parents' return. Form 8615 is used to compute the tax. The steps required in this computation are illustrated below.

EXAMPLE 36

Olaf and Olga have a child, Hans (age 10). In 2006, Hans received $2,900 of interest income and paid investment-related fees of $200. Olaf and Olga had $70,000 of taxable income, not including their child's investment income. The parents have no qualified dividends or capital gains. Olaf and Olga do not make the parental election.

1. **Determine Hans's net unearned income**

Gross income (unearned)	$ 2,900
Less: $850	(850)
Less: The greater of	
• $850 or	
• Investment expense ($200)	(850)
Equals: Net unearned income	$ 1,200

---

[32]§ 1(g).

2. Determine allocable parental tax

Parents' taxable income	$ 70,000
Plus: Hans's net unearned income	1,200
Equals: Revised taxable income	$ 71,200
Tax on revised taxable income	$ 10,915
Less: Tax on parents' taxable income	(10,615)
Allocable parental tax ($1,200 × 25%)	$ 300

(handwritten: ← at parents' rate; Calculated; Calculated; ← tax on 1200)

3. Determine Hans's nonparental source tax

Hans's AGI	$ 2,900
Less: Standard deduction	(850)
Less: Personal exemption	(–0–)
Equals: Taxable income	$ 2,050
Less: Net unearned income	(1,200)
Nonparental source taxable income	$ 850
Equals: Tax ($850 × 10% rate)	$ 85

4. Determine Hans's total tax liability

Nonparental source tax (step 3)	$ 85
Allocable parental tax (step 2)	300
Total tax	$ 385

Election to Claim Certain Unearned Income on Parent's Return. If a child under age 14 is required to file a tax return and meets all of the following requirements, the parent may elect to report the child's unearned income that exceeds $1,700 on the parent's own tax return:

- Gross income is from interest and dividends only.
- Gross income is more than $850 but less than $8,500.
- No estimated tax has been paid in the name and Social Security number of the child, and the child is not subject to backup withholding (see Chapter 13).

If the parental election is made, the child is treated as having no gross income and then is not required to file a tax return.

The parent(s) must also pay an additional tax equal to the smaller of $85 or 10 percent of the child's gross income over $850. Parents who have substantial itemized deductions based on AGI (see Chapter 10) may find that making the parental election increases total taxes for the family unit. Taxes should be calculated both with the parental election and without it to determine the appropriate choice.

Other Provisions. If parents have more than one child subject to the tax on net unearned income, the tax for the children is computed as shown in Example 36 and then allocated to the children based on their relative amounts of income. For children of divorced parents, the taxable income of the custodial parent is used to determine the allocable parental tax. This parent is the one who may elect to report the child's unearned income. For married individuals filing separate returns, the individual with the greater taxable income is the applicable parent.

LO.6

Recognize the filing requirements and the proper filing status.

Filing Considerations

Under the category of filing considerations, the following questions need to be resolved:

- Is the taxpayer required to file an income tax return?
- If so, which form should be used?

- When and how should the return be filed?
- In computing the tax liability, which column of the Tax Table or which Tax Rate Schedule should be used?

The first three questions are discussed under Filing Requirements, and the last is treated under Filing Status.

Filing Requirements

General Rules. An individual must file a tax return if certain minimum amounts of gross income have been received. The general rule is that a tax return is required for every individual who has gross income that equals or exceeds the sum of the exemption amount plus the applicable standard deduction.[33] For example, a single taxpayer under age 65 must file a tax return in 2006 if gross income equals or exceeds $8,450 ($3,300 exemption plus $5,150 standard deduction). Table 3–6 lists the income levels[34] that require tax returns under the general rule and under certain special rules.

The additional standard deduction for being age 65 or older is considered in determining the gross income filing requirements. For example, note in Table 3–6 that the 2006 filing requirement for a single taxpayer age 65 or older is $9,700 ($5,150 basic standard deduction + $1,250 additional standard deduction + $3,300 exemption). However, the additional standard deduction for blindness is not taken into account. The 2006 filing requirement for a single taxpayer under age 65 and blind is $8,450 ($5,150 basic standard deduction + $3,300 exemption).

TABLE 3–6	Filing Levels		
Filing Status		**2005 Gross Income**	**2006 Gross Income**
Single			
Under 65 and not blind		$ 8,200	$ 8,450
Under 65 and blind		8,200	8,450
65 or older		9,450	9,700
Married, filing joint return			
Both spouses under 65 and neither blind		$16,400	$16,900
Both spouses under 65 and one or both spouses blind		16,400	16,900
One spouse 65 or older		17,400	17,900
Both spouses 65 or older		18,400	18,900
Married, filing separate return			
All—whether 65 or older or blind		$ 3,200	$ 3,300
Head of household			
Under 65 and not blind		$10,500	$10,850
Under 65 and blind		10,500	10,850
65 or older		11,750	12,100
Qualifying widow(er)			
Under 65 and not blind		$13,200	$13,600
Under 65 and blind		13,200	13,600
65 or older		14,200	14,600

---

[33]The gross income amounts for determining whether a tax return must be filed are adjusted for inflation each year.

[34]§ 6012(a)(1).

A self-employed individual with net earnings of $400 or more from a business or profession must file a tax return regardless of the amount of gross income.

Even though an individual has gross income below the filing level amounts and therefore does not owe any tax, he or she must file a return to obtain a tax refund of amounts withheld. A return is also necessary to obtain the benefits of the earned income credit allowed to taxpayers with little or no tax liability. Chapter 13 discusses the earned income credit.

Filing Requirements for Dependents. Computation of the gross income filing requirement for an individual who can be claimed as a dependent on another person's tax return is subject to more complex rules. Such an individual must file a return if he or she has *any* of the following:

- Earned income only and gross income that is more than the total standard deduction (including any additional standard deduction) that the individual is allowed for the year.
- Unearned income only and gross income of more than $850 plus any additional standard deduction that the individual is allowed for the year.
- Both earned and unearned income and gross income of more than the larger of $850 or the sum of earned income plus $300 (but limited to the applicable basic standard deduction), plus any additional standard deduction that the individual is allowed for the year.

Thus, the filing requirement for a dependent who has no unearned income is the total of the *basic* standard deduction plus any *additional* standard deduction, which includes both the additional deduction for blindness and the deduction for being age 65 or older. For example, the 2006 filing requirement for a single dependent who is under age 65 and not blind is $5,150, the amount of the basic standard deduction for 2006. The filing requirement for a single dependent under age 65 and blind is $6,400 ($5,150 basic standard deduction + $1,250 additional standard deduction).

Selecting the Proper Form. The 2006 tax forms had not been released at the date of publication of this text. The following comments apply to the 2005 forms. It is possible that some provisions will change for the 2006 forms.

Although a variety of forms are available to individual taxpayers, the use of some of these forms is restricted. For example, Form 1040EZ cannot be used if:

- Taxpayer claims any dependents;
- Taxpayer (or spouse) is 65 or older or blind; or
- Taxable income is $100,000 or more.

Taxpayers who desire to itemize deductions *from* AGI cannot use Form 1040A, but must file Form 1040 (the long form).

The E-File Approach. In addition to traditional paper returns, the **e-file** program is an increasingly popular alternative. Here, the required tax information is transmitted to the IRS electronically either directly from the taxpayer (i.e., an "e-file online return") or indirectly through an electronic return originator (ERO). EROs are tax professionals who have been accepted into the electronic filing program by the IRS. Such parties hold themselves out to the general public as "authorized IRS e-file providers." Providers often are also the preparers of the return.

For direct online e-filing, a taxpayer must have a personal computer and tax preparation software with the capability of conveying the information via modem to an electronic return transmitter. Otherwise a taxpayer must use an authorized provider who makes the e-file transmission. In most cases the provider charges a fee for the services rendered.

TAX *in the News*   **SPECIAL RULES FOR CERTAIN MILITARY PERSONNEL**

The Military Family Tax Relief Act of 2003 allows certain members of the military more time to file their Federal income tax return. If they are outside the United States and Puerto Rico *but not* in a combat zone, the filing date is extended to June 15. If additional taxes are due, however, interest still begins to accrue after April 15. For those deployed in a designated combat zone, the filing date is postponed until 180 days after the last day of combat service. Furthermore, in such cases, interest *does not* accrue during the deferral period. These filing dates are equally applicable when the military person is married and files a joint return.

All taxpayers and tax return preparers must attest to the returns they file. For most taxpayers, this attesting can be done through an electronic return signature using a personal identification number (a Self-Select PIN). Information on establishing a Self-Select PIN can be found in the instructions to Form 1040, Form 1040A, or Form 1040EZ, or at **http://www.irs.gov/efile**. If certain paper documents must be submitted, a one-page form must be completed and filed when the return is e-filed. Form 8453 (U.S. Individual Income Tax Declaration for an IRS *e-file* Return) is the version required when a provider is used. A direct e-file online return requires the use of Form 8453–OL, which must be signed and filed by the taxpayer after the e-file return is accepted by the IRS.

The e-file approach has two major advantages. First, compliance with the format required by the IRS eliminates many errors that would otherwise occur. Second, the time required for processing a refund usually is reduced to three weeks or less.

When and Where to File. Tax returns of individuals are due on or before the fifteenth day of the fourth month following the close of the tax year. For the calendar year taxpayer, the usual filing date is on or before April 15 of the following year.[35] When the due date falls on a Saturday, Sunday, or legal holiday, the last day for filing falls on the next business day. If the return is mailed to the proper address with sufficient postage and is postmarked on or before the due date, it is deemed timely filed. The Code enables the IRS to prescribe rules governing the filing of returns using various private parcel delivery services (e.g., DHL, FedEx, UPS).[36]

If a taxpayer is unable to file the return by the specified due date, a six-month extension of time can be obtained by filing Form 4868 (Application for Automatic Extension of Time to File U.S. Individual Income Tax Return).[37]

Although obtaining an extension excuses a taxpayer from a penalty for failure to file, it does not insulate against the penalty for failure to pay. If more tax is owed, the filing of Form 4868 should be accompanied by an additional remittance to cover the balance due. The failure to file and failure to pay penalties are discussed in Chapter 1.

The return should be sent or delivered to the Regional Service Center listed in the instructions for each type of return or contained in software applications.[38] Because of an IRS reorganization that began in October 2000 and is still ongoing, some taxpayers may be required to file at a different Service Center than in the past. Eventually, 8 of the 10 Service Centers will process all individual returns, and 2 will handle all business returns.

---

[35]§ 6072(a).
[36]§ 7502(f).
[37]Reg. § 1.6081–4.

[38]The Regional Service Centers and the geographic area each covers can also be found at **http://www.irs.gov/file** or in tax forms packages.

If an individual taxpayer needs to file an amended return (e.g., because of a failure to report income or to claim a deduction or tax credit), Form 1040X is filed. The form generally must be filed within three years of the filing date of the original return or within two years from the time the tax was paid, whichever is later.

Mode of Payment. Usually, payment is made by check. In that event, the check should be made out to "United States Treasury."

The IRS has approved the use of MasterCard, American Express, Discover, and Visa to pay Federal taxes. The use of a credit card to pay taxes will result in a charge against the cardholder by the credit card company.

Filing Status

The amount of tax will vary considerably depending on which Tax Rate Schedule is used. This is illustrated in the following example.

EXAMPLE 37

The following amounts of tax are computed using the 2006 Tax Rate Schedules for a taxpayer (or taxpayers in the case of a joint return) with $40,000 of taxable income (see Appendix A).

Filing Status	Amount of Tax
Single	$6,557.50
Married, filing joint return	5,245.00
Married, filing separate return	6,557.50
Head of household	5,462.50

Rates for Single Taxpayers. A taxpayer who is unmarried or separated from his or her spouse by a decree of divorce or separate maintenance and does not qualify for another filing status must use the rates for single taxpayers. Marital status is determined as of the last day of the tax year, except when a spouse dies during the year. In that case, marital status is determined as of the date of death. State law governs whether a taxpayer is considered married, divorced, or legally separated.

Under a special relief provision, however, married persons who live apart may be able to qualify as single. Married taxpayers who are considered single under the *abandoned spouse rules* are allowed to use the head-of-household rates. See the discussion of this filing status under Abandoned Spouse Rules later in the chapter.

Rates for Married Individuals. The joint return [Tax Rate Schedule Y, Code § 1(a)] was originally enacted in 1948 to establish equity between married taxpayers in common law states and those in community property states. Before the joint

FILING A JOINT RETURN

John Garth is a U.S. citizen and resident, but he spends a lot of time in London where his employer sends him on frequent assignments. John is married to Victoria, a citizen and resident of the United Kingdom.

Can John and Victoria file a joint return for U.S. Federal income tax purposes? Although § 6013(a)(1) specifically precludes the filing of a joint return if one spouse is a nonresident alien, another Code provision permits an exception. Under § 6013(g), the parties can elect to treat the nonqualifying spouse as a "resident" of the United States. This election would allow John and Victoria to file jointly.

But should John and Victoria make this election? If Victoria has considerable income of her own (from non-U.S. sources), the election could be ill-advised. As a nonresident alien, Victoria's non-U.S. source income *would not* be subject to the U.S. income tax. If she is treated as a U.S. resident, however, her non-U.S. source income *will be subject to U.S. tax.* Under the U.S. global approach to taxation, all income (regardless of where earned) of anyone who is a *resident* or *citizen* of the United States is subject to tax.

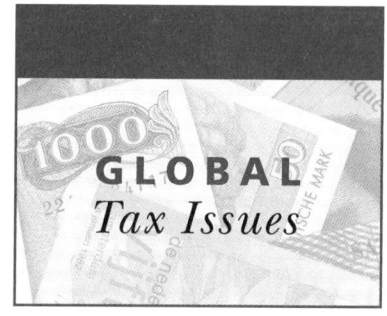

GLOBAL
Tax Issues

return rates were enacted, taxpayers in community property states were in an advantageous position relative to taxpayers in common law states because they could split their income. For instance, if one spouse earned $100,000 and the other spouse was not employed, each spouse could report $50,000 of income. Splitting the income in this manner caused the total income to be subject to lower marginal tax rates. Each spouse would start at the bottom of the rate structure.

Taxpayers in common law states did not have this income-splitting option, so their taxable income was subject to higher marginal rates. This inconsistency in treatment was remedied by the joint return provisions. The progressive rates in the joint return Tax Rate Schedule are constructed based on the assumption that income is earned equally by the two spouses.

If married individuals elect to file separate returns, each reports only his or her own income, exemptions, deductions, and credits, and each must use the Tax Rate Schedule applicable to married taxpayers filing separately. It is generally advantageous for married individuals to file a joint return, since the combined amount of tax is lower. However, special circumstances (e.g., significant medical expenses incurred by one spouse subject to the 7.5 percent limitation) may warrant the election to file separate returns. It may be necessary to compute the tax under both assumptions to determine the most advantageous filing status.

When Congress enacted the rate structure available to those filing joint returns, it intended to favor married taxpayers. In certain situations, however, the parties would incur less tax if they were not married and filed separate returns. The additional tax that a joint return caused, commonly called the **marriage penalty,** usually developed when *both* spouses had large taxable incomes. Long aware of the inequity of the marriage penalty, Congress reduced the effect of the problem in JGTRRA of 2003. Beginning in 2003, the standard deduction available to married filers increased to 200 percent of that applicable to single persons. Furthermore and also beginning in 2003, the 15 percent bracket for joint filers increased to 200 percent of the size of that applicable to single filers.

Although changes in the tax rates and the standard deduction have reduced the marriage penalty, the Code places some limitations on married persons who file separate returns. Some examples of these limitations are listed below.

- If either spouse itemizes deductions, the other spouse must also itemize.
- The earned income credit and the credit for child and dependent care expenses cannot be claimed (see Chapter 13).

- No deduction is allowed for interest paid on qualified education loans (see Chapter 10).
- Only $1,500 of excess capital losses can be claimed (see Chapter 16).

In such cases, being single would be preferable to being married and filing separately.

The joint return rates also apply for two years following the death of one spouse, if the surviving spouse maintains a household for a dependent child. The child must be a son, stepson, daughter, or stepdaughter who qualifies as a dependent of the taxpayer. This is referred to as **surviving spouse** status.[39]

EXAMPLE 38

Fred dies in 2005 leaving Ethel with a dependent child. For the year of Fred's death (2005), Ethel files a joint return with Fred (presuming the consent of Fred's executor is obtained). For the next two years (2006 and 2007), Ethel, as a surviving spouse, may use the joint return rates. In subsequent years, Ethel may use the head-of-household rates if she continues to maintain a household as her home that is the domicile of the child. ■

Keep in mind, however, that for the year of death, the surviving spouse is treated as being married. Thus, a joint return can be filed if the deceased spouse's executor agrees. If not, the surviving spouse is forced into the status of married filing separately.

Rates for Heads of Household.

Unmarried individuals who maintain a household for a dependent (or dependents) are entitled to use the **head-of-household** rates.[40] The tax liability using the head-of-household rates falls between the liability using the joint return Tax Rate Schedule and the liability using the Tax Rate Schedule for single taxpayers.

To qualify for head-of-household rates, a taxpayer must pay more than half the cost of maintaining a household as his or her home. The household must also be the principal home of a dependent. Except for temporary absences (e.g., school, hospitalization), the dependent must live in the taxpayer's household for over half the year.

A dependent must satisfy either the qualifying child or the qualifying relative criteria. For head-of-household purposes, a qualifying relative must also meet the relationship test.[41]

EXAMPLE 39

Dylan is single and maintains a household in which he and his cousin live. Even though the cousin may qualify as a dependent (under the member-of-the-household test), Dylan cannot claim head-of-household filing status. A cousin does not meet the relationship test. ■

EXAMPLE 40

Emma, a widow, maintains a household in which she and her aunt live. If the aunt qualifies as a dependent, Emma may file as head of household. Note that an aunt meets the relationship test. ■

EXAMPLE 41

Nancy maintains a household in which she and her daughter, Bernice, live. Bernice, age 27, is single and earns $9,000 from a part-time job. Nancy does not qualify for head-of-household filing status as she cannot claim Bernice as a dependent (due to the gross income test).[42] ■

---

[39]§ 2(a). The IRS label for surviving spouse status is "Qualifying Widow(er) with Dependent Child."
[40]§ 2(b).
[41]§ 2(b)(3)(B).

[42]Can Bernice be a dependent under the qualifying child rules? Even though the gross income test is inapplicable for a qualifying child, Bernice does not meet the age test.

A special rule allows taxpayers to avoid having to live with their parents. Head-of-household status still may be claimed if the taxpayer maintains a *separate home* for his or her *parent or parents* if at least one parent qualifies as a dependent of the taxpayer.[43]

EXAMPLE 42

Rick, an unmarried individual, lives in New York City and maintains a household in Detroit for his dependent parents. Rick may use the head-of-household rates even though his parents do not reside in his New York home. ∎

Head-of-household status is not changed during the year by the death of the dependent. As long as the taxpayer provided more than half of the cost of maintaining the household prior to the dependent's death, head-of-household status is preserved.

ETHICAL *Considerations*   **THE HIDDEN BENEFITS OF TAKING CARE OF A RELATIVE**

For several years, Chester, a widower, has maintained a household in which he and his aunt, Heloise, live. As the aunt has no income, Chester claims her as his dependent. In early June 2005, Heloise is admitted to a medical facility for treatment of a mental disorder. In January 2006, Heloise unexpectedly dies while still at the facility.

In completing his Federal income tax return for both 2005 and 2006, Chester intends to file as head of household and to claim Heloise as his dependent. Comment on the propriety of what Chester plans to do.

Abandoned Spouse Rules. When married persons file separate returns, several unfavorable tax consequences result. For example, the taxpayer must use the Tax Rate Schedule for married taxpayers filing separately. To mitigate such harsh treatment, Congress enacted provisions commonly referred to as the **abandoned spouse** rules. These rules allow a married taxpayer to file as a head of household if all of the following conditions are satisfied:[44]

- The taxpayer does not file a joint return.
- The taxpayer paid more than one-half the cost of maintaining his or her home for the tax year.
- The taxpayer's spouse did not live in the home during the last six months of the tax year.
- The home was the principal residence of the taxpayer's son, daughter, stepson, stepdaughter, foster child, or adopted child for more than half the year, and the child can be claimed as a dependent.[45]

Gains and Losses from Property Transactions—In General

LO.7

Possess an overview of property transactions.

Gains and losses from property transactions are discussed in detail in Chapters 14 through 17. Because of their importance in the tax system, however, they are introduced briefly at this point.

When property is sold or otherwise disposed of, gain or loss may result. Such gain or loss has an effect on the income tax position of the party making the sale or

---

[43] § 2(b)(1)(B).
[44] § 7703(b).
[45] § 152(f)(1). The dependency requirement does not apply, however, if the taxpayer could have claimed a dependency exemption except for the fact that the exemption was claimed by the noncustodial parent under a written agreement.

other disposition when the *realized* gain or loss is *recognized* for tax purposes. Without realized gain or loss, there generally can be no recognized gain or loss. The concept of realized gain or loss is expressed as follows:

$$\text{Amount realized} \atop \text{from the sale} - {\text{Adjusted basis of} \atop \text{the property}} = {\text{Realized gain} \atop \text{(or loss)}}$$

The amount realized is the selling price of the property less any costs of disposition (e.g., brokerage commissions) incurred by the seller. The adjusted basis of the property is determined as follows:

Cost (or other original basis) at date of acquisition[46]

Add: Capital additions

Subtract: Depreciation (if appropriate) and other capital recoveries
            (see Chapter 8)

Equals: Adjusted basis at date of sale or other disposition

All realized gains are recognized (taxable) unless some specific part of the tax law provides otherwise (see Chapter 15 dealing with certain nontaxable exchanges). Realized losses may or may not be recognized (deductible) for tax purposes, depending on the circumstances involved. Generally, losses realized from the disposition of personal use property (property neither held for investment nor used in a trade or business) are not recognized.

EXAMPLE 43

During the current year, Ted sells his sailboat (adjusted basis of $4,000) for $5,500. Ted also sells one of his personal automobiles (adjusted basis of $8,000) for $5,000. Ted's realized gain of $1,500 from the sale of the sailboat is recognized. On the other hand, the $3,000 realized loss on the sale of the automobile is not recognized and will not provide Ted with any deductible tax benefit. ■

Once it has been determined that the disposition of property results in a recognized gain or loss, the next step is to classify the gain or loss as capital or ordinary. Although ordinary gain is fully taxable and ordinary loss is fully deductible, the same may not hold true for capital gains and capital losses.

Gains and Losses from Property Transactions—Capital Gains and Losses

To obtain a good perspective on how the Federal income tax functions, some overview of property transactions is needed. This is particularly the case with capital gains and losses, which can generate unique tax consequences. For in-depth treatment of property transactions (including capital gains and losses), refer to Chapters 14 through 17. For now, the overview appearing below should suffice.

Definition of a Capital Asset

Capital assets are defined in the Code as any property held by the taxpayer *other than* property listed in § 1221. The list in § 1221 includes inventory, accounts receivable, and depreciable property or real estate used in a business. Thus, the sale or exchange of assets in these categories usually results in ordinary income or loss treatment (see Chapter 17).

---

[46]Cost usually means purchase price plus expenses related to the acquisition of the property and incurred by the purchaser (e.g., brokerage commissions). For the basis of property acquired by gift or inheritance and other basis rules, see Chapter 14.

EXAMPLE 44

Kelly owns a pizza parlor. During the current year, he sells two automobiles. The first automobile, which had been used as a pizza delivery car for three years, was sold at a loss of $1,000. Because this automobile is an asset used in his business, Kelly has an ordinary loss deduction of $1,000, rather than a capital loss deduction. The second automobile, which Kelly had owned for two years, was his personal use car. It was sold for a gain of $800. The personal use car is a capital asset. Therefore, Kelly has a capital gain of $800. ∎

The principal capital assets held by an individual taxpayer include assets held for personal (rather than business) use, such as a personal residence or an automobile, and assets held for investment purposes (e.g., corporate securities and land). Capital assets generally include collectibles, which are subject to somewhat unique tax treatment. **Collectibles** include art, antiques, gems, metals, stamps, some coins and bullion, and alcoholic beverages that are held as investments.

Taxation of Net Capital Gain

In 2006, net capital gains are classified and taxed as follows:

Classification	Maximum Rate
Short-term gains (held for one year or less)	35%
Long-term gains (held for more than one year)—	
Collectibles	28%
Certain depreciable property used in a trade or business (known as unrecaptured § 1250 gain and discussed in Chapter 17)	25%
All other long-term capital gains	15% or 5%

The special tax rate applicable to long-term capital gains is called the alternative tax computation. It is to be used only if the taxpayer's regular tax rate *exceeds* the applicable alternative tax rate. In the case of the 15 percent classification (see above), the applicable alternative tax rate is 5 percent if the taxpayer's regular tax bracket is 15 percent or less.[47]

EXAMPLE 45

During the year, Polly is in the 15% tax bracket and has the following capital gains for the year:

Robin Corporation stock (held for 6 months)	$1,000	
Crow Corporation stock (held for 13 months)	1,000	

Polly's tax on these transactions is $150 ($1,000 × 15%) as to Robin and $50 ($1,000 × 5%) as to Crow. ∎

EXAMPLE 46

Assume the same facts as in Example 45, except that Polly's regular tax bracket for the year is 28% (not 15%). Polly's tax on these transactions now becomes $280 ($1,000 × 28%) as to Robin and $150 ($1,000 × 15%) as to Crow. ∎

Determination of Net Capital Gain

In order to arrive at a net capital gain, capital losses must be taken into account. The capital losses are aggregated by holding period (short term and long term) and applied against the gains in that category. If excess losses result, they are then

---

[47]§ 1(h)(1) as amended by JGTRRA of 2003. For recognized gains prior to May 6, 2003, the maximum rates were 20% and 10%.

shifted to the category carrying the *highest* tax rate. A *net capital gain* will occur if the net long-term capital gain (NLTCG) exceeds the net short-term capital loss (NSTCL).

EXAMPLE 47

In the current year, Colin is in the 35% tax bracket and has the following capital transactions:

Penguin Corporation stock (held for 8 months)	$ 1,000
Owl Corporation stock (held for 10 months)	(3,000)
Stamp collection (held for 5 years)	2,000
Land (held as an investment for 3 years)	4,000

The Penguin Corporation short-term capital gain (STCG) of $1,000 is offset by the Owl Corporation short-term capital loss (STCL) of $3,000. The net STCL of $2,000 is then applied against the collectible gain of $2,000. The end result is a net long-term capital gain of $4,000 from the land sale. Colin's net capital gain is taxed at a 15% rate. Note that the stamp collection gain would have been taxed at a higher 28% rate had it not been offset by the excess short-term capital loss. ■

Treatment of Net Capital Loss

For individual taxpayers, net capital loss can be used to offset ordinary income of up to $3,000 ($1,500 for married persons filing separate returns). If a taxpayer has both short- and long-term capital losses, the short-term category is used first to arrive at the $3,000. Any remaining net capital loss is carried over indefinitely until exhausted. When carried over, the excess capital loss retains its classification as short or long term.

EXAMPLE 48

In 2006, Tina has a short-term capital loss of $2,000, a long-term capital loss of $2,500, and no capital gains. She can deduct $3,000 ($2,000 short-term + $1,000 long-term) of this amount as an ordinary loss. The remaining $1,500 is carried over to 2007 as a long-term capital loss. ■

LO.8

Identify tax planning opportunities associated with the individual tax formula.

TAX PLANNING *Considerations*

Maximizing the Use of the Standard Deduction

In most cases, the choice between using the standard deduction and itemizing deductions *from* AGI is a simple matter—pick whichever yields the larger tax benefit. Families in the initial stages of home ownership, for example, will invariably make the itemization choice due to the substantial mortgage interest and property tax payments involved. Older taxpayers, however, have paid for their homes and are enjoying senior citizen property tax exemptions. For them, the more attractive benefit is the additional standard deduction that can accompany the standard deduction choice.

In some cases, the difference between the standard deduction and itemizing may not be a significant amount. Here, taxes might be saved by alternating between the two options. The taxpayer does this by using the cash method to concentrate multiple years' deductions in a single year. Then, the standard deduction is used in alternate years.

EXAMPLE 49

The Chengs, ages 59 and 60, are married and file a joint return. Their usual AGI is $90,000, and their itemized annual expenses approximate $9,800 comprised as follows: $4,000 (state income tax), $3,600 (property taxes on personal residence), and $2,200 (yearly church pledge). For tax years 2005 and 2006, the Chengs make no changes and follow their usual payment procedure. As a result, they claim the standard deduction for each year for a total deduction of $20,300 ($10,000 for 2005 + $10,300 for 2006). ■

EXAMPLE 50

Assume the same facts as in Example 49, except that in January 2006 the Chengs pay their property taxes and church pledges for both 2005 and 2006.[48] Now they will claim a standard deduction of $10,000 for 2005 and itemized deductions of $15,600 ($4,000 + $3,600 + $3,600 + $2,200 + $2,200) for 2006. The total deduction for both years becomes $25,600 ($10,000 for 2005 + $15,600 for 2006). Comparing this amount with that reached in Example 49 reflects a difference of $5,300 ($25,600 − $20,300). Presuming a tax bracket of 25%, the procedure followed in Example 50 saves the Chengs $1,325 ($5,300 × 25%) in taxes. ■

The shifting of deductions between years through the timing of payments can be effective with certain other itemized deductions besides property taxes and charitable contributions. For a further discussion of this possibility, see Chapter 10.

Dependency Exemptions

The Joint Return Test. A married person can be claimed as a dependent only if that individual does not file a joint return with his or her spouse. If a joint return has been filed, the damage may be undone if separate returns are substituted on a timely basis (on or before the due date of the return).

EXAMPLE 51

While preparing a client's 2005 income tax return on April 7, 2006, the tax practitioner discovered that the client's daughter filed a joint return with her husband in late January of 2006. Presuming the daughter otherwise qualifies as the client's dependent, the exemption is not lost if she and her husband file separate returns on or before April 17, 2006. ■

An initial election to file a joint return must be considered carefully in any situation in which the taxpayers might later decide to amend their return and file separately. As indicated above, separate returns may be substituted for a joint return only if the amended returns are filed on or before the normal due date of the return. If the taxpayers in Example 51 attempt to file separate returns after April 17, 2006, the returns will not be accepted, and the joint return election is binding.[49]

Keep in mind that the filing of a joint return is not fatal to the dependency exemption if the parties are filing solely to recover all income tax withholdings, they are not required to file a return, and no tax liability would exist on separate returns.

Support Considerations. The support of a qualifying child becomes relevant only if the child is self-supporting. In cases where the child has an independent source of funds, planning could help prevent an undesirable result. When a qualifying relative is involved, meeting the support test is essential, as the dependency exemption is not otherwise available.

EXAMPLE 52

In 2006, Imogene maintains a household that she shares with her son and mother. The son, Barry, is 23 years of age and a full-time student in law school. The mother, Gladys, is 68 years of age and active in charitable causes. Barry works part-time for a local law firm, while Gladys has income from investments. In resolving the support issue (or self-support in the case of Barry), compare Imogene's contribution with that made by Barry and Gladys.[50] In this connection, what Barry and Gladys do with their funds becomes crucial. The funds that are used for nonsupport purposes (e.g., purchase of investments) or not used at all (e.g., deposited in a bank) should not be considered. To the extent possible, control how much Barry and Gladys contribute to their own support. Records should be maintained showing the amount of support and its source. ■

---

[48]In some taxing jurisdictions, it may be impossible to delay payment on ad valorem property taxes without incurring some penalty. If the delay is minimal, however, the penalty is apt to be mild.

[49]Reg. § 1.6013–1(a)(1).

[50]As part of her support contribution to Barry and Gladys, Imogene can count the fair market value of the meals and lodging she provides.

Example 52 does not mention the possible application of the gross income test. Presuming Barry is a qualifying child, the amount he earns does not matter, as the gross income test does not apply. Gladys, however, comes under the qualifying relative category, where the gross income test applies. Therefore, for her to be claimed as a dependent, her income that is taxable will have to be less than $3,300.

Community Property Ramifications. In certain cases, state law can have an effect on the availability of a dependency exemption.

E X A M P L E   53

In 2006, Mitch provides more than half of the support of his son, Ross, and daughter-in-law, Connie, who live with him. Ross, age 22, is a full-time student, while Connie earns $4,000 from a part-time job. Ross and Connie do not file a joint return. All parties live in New York, a common law state. Mitch can claim Ross as a dependent, as he is a qualifying child. Connie is not a dependent because she does not meet the gross income test under the qualifying relative category. ■

E X A M P L E   54

Assume the same facts as in Example 53, except that all parties live in Arizona, a community property state. Now, Connie also qualifies as a dependent. Since Connie's gross income is only $2,000 (one-half of the community income), she satisfies the gross income test. ■

Relationship to the Deduction for Medical Expenses. Generally, medical expenses are deductible only if they are paid on behalf of the taxpayer, his or her spouse, and their dependents. Since deductibility may rest on dependency status, planning is important in arranging multiple support agreements.

E X A M P L E   55

During the year, Zelda will be supported by her two sons (Vern and Vito) and her daughter (Maria). Each will furnish approximately one-third of the required support. If the parties decide that the dependency exemption should be claimed by the daughter under a multiple support agreement, any medical expenses incurred by Zelda should be paid by Maria. ■

In planning a multiple support agreement, take into account which of the parties is most likely to exceed the 7.5 percent limitation (see Chapter 10). In Example 55, for instance, Maria might be a poor choice if she and her family do not expect to incur many medical and drug expenses of their own.

One exception permits the deduction of medical expenses paid on behalf of someone who is not a spouse or a dependent. If the person could be claimed as a dependent *except* for the gross income or joint return test, the medical expenses are, nevertheless, deductible. For additional discussion, see Chapter 10.

ETHICAL
Considerations   **NONDEPENDENTS CAN PROVIDE TAX BENEFITS**

For tax year 2006, Alexis provided more than half of the support of her parents who do not live with her. She cannot claim them as her dependents because they have too much gross income and file a joint return. Nevertheless, she pays $15,000 for her father's dental implants and $18,000 for her mother's hip replacement. From a tax standpoint, has Alexis acted wisely? Explain.

Taking Advantage of Tax Rate Differentials

It is natural for taxpayers to be concerned about the tax rates they are paying. How does a tax practitioner communicate information about rates to clients? There are several possibilities.

The marginal rate (refer to Examples 31 through 33) provides information that can help a taxpayer evaluate a particular course of action or structure a transaction in the most advantageous manner. For example, a taxpayer who is in the 15 percent bracket this year and expects to be in the 28 percent bracket next year should, if possible, defer payment of deductible expenses until next year to maximize the tax benefit of the deduction.

A note of caution is in order with respect to shifting income and expenses between years. Congress has recognized the tax planning possibilities of such shifting and has enacted many provisions to limit a taxpayer's ability to do so. Some of these limitations on the shifting of income are discussed in Chapters 4, 5, and 18. Limitations that affect a taxpayer's ability to shift deductions are discussed in Chapters 6 through 11 and in Chapter 18.

A taxpayer's *effective rate* can be an informative measure of the effectiveness of tax planning. The effective rate is computed by dividing the taxpayer's tax liability by the total amount of income. A low effective rate can be considered an indication of effective tax planning.

One way of lowering the effective rate is to exclude income from the tax base. For example, a taxpayer might consider investing in tax-free municipal bonds rather than taxable corporate bonds. Although pre-tax income from corporate bonds is usually higher, after-tax income may be higher if the taxpayer invests in tax-free municipals.

Another way of lowering the effective rate is to make sure that the taxpayer's expenses and losses are deductible. For example, losses on investments in passive activities may not be deductible (see Chapter 11). Therefore, a taxpayer who plans to invest in an activity that will produce a loss in the early years should take steps to ensure that the business is treated as active rather than passive. Active losses are deductible while passive losses are not.

Income of Minor Children

Taxpayers can use several strategies to avoid or minimize the effect of the rules that tax the unearned income of certain minor children at the parents' rate. The kiddie tax rules do not apply once a child reaches age 14. Parents should consider giving a younger child assets that defer taxable income until the child reaches age 14. For example, U.S. government Series EE savings bonds can be used to defer income until the bonds are cashed in (see Chapter 4).

Growth stocks typically pay little in the way of dividends. However, the profit on an astute investment may more than offset the lack of dividends. The child can hold the stock until he or she reaches age 14. If the stock is sold then at a profit, the profit is taxed at the child's low rates.

Taxpayers in a position to do so can employ their children in their business and pay them a reasonable wage for the work they actually perform (e.g., light office help, such as filing). The child's earned income is sheltered by the standard deduction, and the parents' business is allowed a deduction for the wages. The kiddie tax rules have no effect on earned income, even if it is earned from the parents' business.

KEY TERMS

Abandoned spouse, 3–31	Itemized deductions, 3–6	Qualifying relative, 3–13
Child tax credit, 3–19	Kiddie tax, 3–23	Standard deduction, 3–6
Collectibles, 3–33	Marriage penalty, 3–29	Surviving spouse, 3–30
Dependency exemptions, 3–11	Multiple support agreement, 3–14	Tax Rate Schedules, 3–20
e-file, 3–26	Personal exemptions, 3–10	Tax Table, 3–19
Head-of-household, 3–30	Qualifying child, 3–11	Unearned income, 3–23

PROBLEM MATERIALS

DISCUSSION QUESTIONS

1. Rearrange the following items to show the correct formula for arriving at *taxable income* of individuals under the Federal income tax:

   8 a. Taxable income.

   1 b. Income (broadly conceived).

   5 c. Adjusted gross income.

   4 d. Deductions *for* AGI.

   9 e. Child tax credit.

   6 f. The greater of the standard deduction or itemized deductions.

   7 g. Personal and dependency exemptions.

   3 h. Gross income.

   2 i. Exclusions.

2. During the year, a taxpayer had the following transactions: borrowed money from a bank, received repayment of a loan made to a relative several years ago, recovered a rent deposit made on an apartment recently vacated, and sold a personal automobile for a loss. Discuss the income tax ramifications of each of these transactions.

3. Which of the following are *exclusions* from gross income?
   a. Interest received from City of Seattle bonds.
   b. Workers' compensation benefits received due to job injury.
   c. Alimony received from ex-spouse.
   d. Reward received for furnishing information that led to the arrest of an arsonist.
   e. "Gift" received by justice of the peace for dismissing a traffic violation. *(payment)*
   f. Inheritance received upon death of uncle.

4. Which of the following items are *inclusions* in gross income?
   a. Child support received from ex-spouse.
   b. Interest received from General Electric bonds.
   c. Damages awarded due to personal injury resulting from an automobile accident.
   d. Plasma TV set received for being the tenth caller in a contest sponsored by a local radio station.
   e. Value of meals and lodging received by an employee while working on an oil rig in the Gulf of Mexico.
   f. A cash honorarium received by a former U.S. senator for giving a college commencement address.

5. Does a U.S. citizen who works abroad run the risk of "double taxation"? Why or why not?

Decision Making

6. In late 2006, the Polks come to you for tax advice. They are considering selling some stock investments for a loss and making a contribution to a traditional IRA. In reviewing their situation, you note that they have large medical expenses and a casualty loss, with neither being covered by insurance. What advice would you give to the Polks?
   - Sell the gain to offset loss.
   - Still to IRA for future.

7. The Andersons retain you to compute their tax liability for 2006. They are expecting to pay less tax than usual for several reasons. First, both became 65 during the year. Second, they paid significant medical and dental bills that were not covered by insurance. Are the Andersons' expectations correct? Explain.

   Issue ID

   [handwritten: ASD — Jopposit (itemized vs BSD) Yes]

8. Mel, age 76 and a widower, is being claimed as a dependent by his daughter. How does this situation affect the following?
   a. Mel's own individual filing requirement. *[handwritten: Can't use personal exemption]*
   b. Mel's personal exemption. *[handwritten: No more]*
   c. The standard deduction allowed to Mel. *[handwritten: OK but {850 or (earned inc + 300)} < 5150]*
   d. The availability of any additional standard deduction. *[handwritten: OK]*

9. Harriet, age 80, is claimed as a dependent by Amy. Harriet and Amy are related to each other, and Amy does not furnish more than half of Harriet's support. Explain how this tax result can occur. *[handwritten: Total of multiple supporting parties > 50% & Amy > 10%]*

   Issue ID

10. Under what circumstances might the son of a taxpayer be claimed as a dependent under the qualifying relative category and not be eligible as a qualifying child? *[handwritten: >50% support]*

11. As to the dependency exemption rules, contrast the following for the qualifying child and qualifying relative categories:
    a. Relationship test. *[handwritten: QC (son, sister...), QR (parent, aunt, uncle...) broader]*
    b. Gross income test. *[handwritten: No limit of QC]*
    c. Joint return test. *[handwritten: The same, not allow in both]*
    d. Support test. *[handwritten: >50% on QR, and not on QC if child is not self-supporting]*
    e. Age test. *[handwritten: QC: 19/24 student, QR: no limit]*
    f. Abode test. *[handwritten: QC: >1/2 yr living in, QR: only if needed for part of HH (1 yr.)]*

12. For years 2006 and 2007, Trevor provides more than half of the support of his ex-wife, Carrie, her mother, Adriana, and his brother-in-law, Hector. Trevor and Carrie were divorced in 2006, but for financial reasons, they continue to share the same house. Adriana lives with Hector in another city.
    a. How many dependency exemptions may Trevor claim for 2006? *[handwritten: A & H]*
    b. How many dependency exemptions may Trevor claim for 2007? *[handwritten: C, A & H]*
    c. If your answers in (a) and (b) are different, explain why. *[handwritten: Ex-spouse can't be claimed as dep. on yr of divorce]*
    d. What circumstances might change your answer to (b)?

    Issue ID

13. Roberto, who is single, is a U.S. citizen and resident. He provides almost all of the support of his parents and two aunts, who are citizens and residents of Guatemala. Roberto's parents and aunts are seriously considering moving to and becoming residents of Mexico. Would such a move have any impact on Roberto? Why or why not? *[handwritten: Yes, they can be claimed as his dep.]*

    Issue ID

14. Margo and her two brothers equally provide more than half of their parents' support. Margo tells her brothers to decide which one of them will claim the parents as dependents because the exemptions will not save her any income taxes.
    a. What is Margo's reason for her position?
    b. Can the brothers divide the exemptions between them, or must one of them claim *both* parents?

    Issue ID

15. In determining his income tax liability for the year, Aaron finds that he would pay slightly less using the Tax Rate Schedules than under the Tax Tables.
    a. Why could this be the case?
    b. Does Aaron have freedom of choice in this matter? Explain.

16. In connection with the kiddie tax, comment on the following:
    a. Justification for the tax.
    b. Earned income versus unearned income.
    c. Age of minor.
    d. Effect of parental election.

17. Marianne is age 70 and widowed. In terms of gross income, what is her filing requirement for 2006?
    a. How is the amount of the filing requirement determined?
    b. Would your answer change if Marianne also is blind? Explain.

18. In 2006, Ginger's husband dies. Ginger plans to file as a surviving spouse for tax years 2006 through 2008. Ginger's only dependent is her mother, who lives with her. Comment on any misconceptions Ginger may have regarding the tax law.

19. Comment on the availability of head-of-household filing status for 2006 in each of the following situations:
    a. Taxpayer lives alone but maintains the household of his parents, only one of whom qualifies as his dependent. *OK*
    b. Taxpayer, a single parent, maintains a home in which she and her unmarried son live. The son, age 18, earns $4,000 from a part-time job. *OK*
    c. Assume the same facts as in (b) except that the son is age 20, not 18. *Not HH*
    d. Taxpayer lives alone but maintains the household where her dependent daughter lives. *No since daughter is not considered part of HH.*

20. Florence's husband died in 2003. During 2006, Florence maintains a household in which she and her son, Derrick, live. Determine Florence's filing status for 2006 based on the following independent variables:
    a. Derrick is single and does not qualify as Florence's dependent. *Not HHH*
    b. Derrick is married and does not qualify as Florence's dependent. *Not*
    c. Derrick is married and does qualify as Florence's dependent. *AB Is HHH*
    d. Would any of the previous answers change if Florence's husband died in 2004 (not 2003)? Explain. *(C) will be Jointly (surving spouse*

21. Several years ago, after a particularly fierce argument, Fran's husband moved out and has not been heard from or seen since. Because Fran cannot locate her husband, she has been using "married, filing separate" status when filing her income tax return. Comment on Fran's status. *Abandoned spouse ⇒ HHH*

22. During the year, Milton sold the following items: a recreational vehicle (RV) for a $6,000 loss; unimproved land for a $10,000 gain; and a sailboat for a $1,000 gain. The RV and sailboat were personal use assets, while the land was held as an investment. How are these transactions handled for income tax purposes?

23. As soon as Kaitlyn learned about the lower rates applicable to capital gains, she sold her stamp collection for a $15,000 gain. Comment on Kaitlyn's tax situation if she is in the:
    a. 33% tax bracket.
    b. 15% tax bracket.

24. For 2006, Arlene's only capital transactions are a short-term loss of $2,000 and a long-term loss of $2,000. How are these losses handled for tax purposes?

25. What are collectibles?
    a. How is the sale of collectibles handled for tax purposes?
    b. In connection with (a), would it matter if the collectible had been held for more than one year? For one year or less?

Issue ID

26. Marcie is divorced, and her married son, Jamie (age 25), and his wife, Audry (age 18), live with her. During 2006, Jamie earned $3,500 from a part-time job and filed a joint return with Audry to recover his withholdings. Audry has no income. Marcie can prove that she provided more than 50% of Jamie and Audry's support. Marcie does not plan to claim Jamie as a dependent because he has too much gross income. She does not plan to claim Audry as a dependent because Audry signed the joint return with Jamie. In fact, Marcie plans to use single filing status as none of the persons living in her household qualifies as her dependent. Comment on Marcie's intentions based on the following assumptions:
    a. All parties live in Indiana (a common law state).
    b. All parties live in California (a community property state).

Decision Making

27. Erica and her two brothers equally furnish all of the support of their mother. Erica is married and has four children. Her brothers are single and claim the standard deduction. Erica's mother is not in good health. What suggestions can you make regarding the tax position of the parties?

PROBLEMS

28. Compute the taxable income for 2006 in each of the following independent situations:
    a. Sidney and Cora, ages 39 and 37, are married and file a joint return. In addition to two dependent children, they have AGI of $55,000 and itemized deductions of $8,300.
    b. Kay, age 66, is unmarried and supports her two dependent parents who live in their own home. She has AGI of $70,000 and itemized deductions of $8,100.
    c. Colin, age 60, is an abandoned spouse. The household he maintains includes two unmarried stepdaughters, ages 16 and 17, who qualify as his dependents. He has AGI of $81,000 and itemized deductions of $7,900.
    d. Angel, age 33, is a surviving spouse and maintains a household for her four dependent children. She has AGI of $48,000 and itemized deductions of $8,200.
    e. Dale, age 42, is divorced but maintains the home in which he and his daughter, Jill, live. Jill is single and qualifies as Dale's dependent. Dale has AGI of $54,000 and itemized deductions of $6,900.

    Note: Problems 29 and 30 can be solved by referring to Figure 3–1, Exhibits 3–1 through 3–3, Tables 3–1 and 3–2, and the discussion under Deductions for Adjusted Gross Income in this chapter.

29. Compute the taxable income for 2006 for Quincy on the basis of the following information. His filing status is head of household.

Salary	$40,000
Interest income from bonds issued by General Motors Corporation	1,200
Child support payments made	3,600
Alimony payments made	2,400
Contribution to traditional IRA	4,000
Gift from grandparents	30,000
Capital loss from stock investment	4,000
Amount won in football office pool (sports gambling is against the law where Quincy lives)	3,200
Number of dependents (parents, ages 66 and 68)	2
Age	40

30. Compute the taxable income for 2006 for Marjory on the basis of the following information. Marjory is married but has not seen or heard from her husband since 2004.

Salary	$ 60,000
Interest on bonds issued by the City of Independence (MO)	2,000
Interest on CD issued by Hibernia National Bank	1,800
Cash dividend received on GE common stock	2,300
Life insurance proceeds paid on death of aunt (Marjory was the designated beneficiary of the policy)	50,000
Inheritance received on death of aunt	110,000
Carlton (a cousin) repaid a loan Marjory made to him in 2003 (no interest was provided for)	5,000
Itemized deductions (state income tax, property taxes on residence, interest on home mortgage, charitable contributions)	7,200
Number of dependents (children, ages 13 and 15)	2
Age	40

31. Determine the amount of the standard deduction allowed for 2006 in the following independent situations. In each case, assume the taxpayer is claimed as another person's dependent.
    a. Hollis, age 17, has income as follows: $500 interest from a certificate of deposit and $4,900 from repairing cars.

b. Sheila, age 18, has income as follows: $400 cash dividends from a stock investment and $3,400 from handling a paper route.

c. Trent, age 15, has income as follows: $1,200 interest on a bank savings account and $400 for painting a neighbor's fence.

d. Susan, age 15, has income as follows: $300 cash dividends from a stock investment and $600 from grooming pets.

e. Molly, age 66 and a widow, has income as follows: $1,100 from a bank savings account and $1,900 from baby-sitting.

32. Using the legend provided below, classify each statement as to the taxpayer for dependency exemption purposes.

Legend

QC = Could be a qualifying child

QR = Could be a qualifying relative

B = Could satisfy the definition of both a qualifying child and a qualifying relative

N = Could not satisfy the definition of *either* a qualifying child or a qualifying relative

---

a. Taxpayer's son has gross income of $6,000.

b. Taxpayer's niece has gross income of $6,000.

c. Taxpayer's mother lives with him.

d. Taxpayer's daughter is age 25 and not disabled.

e. Taxpayer's daughter is age 18 but does not live with him.

f. Taxpayer's cousin does not live with her.

g. Taxpayer's brother lives with her.

h. Taxpayer's sister does not live with him.

i. Taxpayer's nephew is age 20 and a full-time student.

j. Taxpayer's grandson does not live with her and has gross income of $7,000.

33. For tax year 2006, determine the number of personal and dependency exemptions in each of the following independent situations:

a. Leo and Amanda (ages 48 and 46) are husband and wife and furnish more than 50% of the support of their two children, Elton (age 18) and Trista (age 24). During the year, Elton earns $4,500 providing transportation for elderly persons with disabilities, and Trista receives a $5,000 scholarship for tuition at the law school she attends.

b. Audry (age 65) is divorced and lives alone. She maintains a household in which her ex-husband, Clint, and his mother, Olive, live and furnishes more than 50% of their support. Olive is age 82 and blind.

c. Jacque (age 52) furnishes more than 50% of the support of his married daughter, Carin, and her husband, Pierce, who live with him. Both Carin and Pierce are age 18. During the year, Pierce earned $4,000 from a part-time job. All parties live in New York (a common law state).

d. Assume the same facts as in (c), except that all parties live in Nevada (a community property state).

34. Compute the number of personal and dependency exemptions in each of the following independent situations:

a. Alberto, a U.S. citizen and resident, contributes 100% of the support of his parents who are citizens of Mexico and live there.

b. Pablo, a U.S. citizen and resident, contributes 100% of the support of his parents who are citizens of Guatemala. Pablo's father is a resident of Guatemala, and his mother is a legal resident of the United States.

c. Marlena, a U.S. citizen and resident, contributes 100% of the support of her parents who are also U.S. citizens but are residents of Germany.

d. Elena is a U.S. citizen and a resident of Italy. Her household includes Mario, a four-year-old adopted son who is a citizen of Spain.

35. Determine how many dependency exemptions would be available in each of the following independent situations. Specify whether any such exemptions would come under the qualifying child or the qualifying relative category.
    a. Richard maintains a household that includes a cousin (age 12), a niece (age 18), and a son (age 20). The cousin and niece are full-time students, and the son is unemployed. Richard furnishes all of their support.
    b. Minerva provides all of the support of a family friend's son (age 18) who lives with her. She also furnishes most of the support of her stepmother who does not live with her.
    c. Raul, a U.S. citizen, lives in Costa Rica. Raul's household includes an adopted daughter, Helena, who is age 9 and a citizen of Costa Rica. Raul provides all of Helena's support.
    d. Maxine maintains a household that includes her ex-husband, her mother-in-law, and her brother-in-law (age 23 and a full-time student). Maxine provides more than half of all of their support. Maxine is single and was divorced several years ago.

36. In 2006, Tommy, age 8, lives in a household with his mother, uncle, and grandfather. The household is maintained by the grandfather. The parties, all of whom file separate returns, have AGI as follows: $18,000 (mother), $50,000 (uncle), and $40,000 (grandfather).
    a. Who is eligible to claim Tommy as a dependent?
    b. Who has preference as to the exemption?

37. Determine the number of personal and dependency exemptions for 2006 in each of the following independent situations:
    a. Marcus (age 68) and Alice (age 65 and blind) file a joint return. They furnish more than 50% of the support of a cousin, Ann, who lives with them. Ann (age 20) is a full-time student and earns $4,000 during the year tutoring special needs children.
    b. Penny (age 45) is single and maintains a household in which she and her nephew, Kurt, live. Kurt (age 18) earns $3,900 from doing yard work, but receives more than 50% of his support from Penny.
    c. Trent (age 38) is single and lives alone. He provides more than 50% of the support of his parents (ages 69 and 70) who are in a nursing home.
    d. Jack and Carol were divorced in 2005, and Carol has custody of their three children (ages 5, 7, and 9). Although Carol furnished more than half of their support, the divorce decree awards the dependency exemptions to Jack. Carol does not sign a Form 8332.

38. Buddy and Heloise (ages 86 and 85) live in an assisted care facility and for years 2005 and 2006 received their support from the following sources:

	Percentage of Support
Social Security benefits	17%
Son	10
Daughter	27
Cousin	11
Brother	24
Family friend (not related)	11

    a. Which persons are eligible to claim the dependency exemptions under a multiple support agreement?
    b. Must Buddy and Heloise be claimed by the same person(s) for both 2005 and 2006?
    c. Who, if anyone, can claim their medical expenses?

39. Dudley and Lisa Berg are married and file a joint return. Their four children and Dudley's parents qualify as their dependents. If the Bergs have AGI of $250,000, what is their allowable deduction for personal and dependency exemptions for 2006?

40. Kevin, age 12, is a full-time student supported by his parents who claim him on their tax return for 2006. Kevin's parents present you with the following information and ask that you prepare Kevin's Federal income tax return for the year:

Wages from summer job	$2,500
Interest on savings account at First National Bank	1,400
Interest on City of Detroit bonds Kevin received as an inheritance from his grandfather two years ago	900

a. What is Kevin's taxable income for 2006?

b. Kevin's parents file a joint return for 2006 on which they report taxable income of $86,000 (no qualified dividends or capital gains). Compute Kevin's 2006 tax liability.

Issue ID

Decision Making

41. Walter and Nancy provide 60% of the support of their daughter (age 18) and son-in-law (age 22). The son-in-law (John) is a full-time student at a local university, while the daughter (Irene) holds various part-time jobs from which she earns $11,000. Walter and Nancy engage you to prepare their tax return for 2006. During a meeting with them in late March of 2007, you learn that John and Irene have filed a joint return. What tax advice would you give based on the following assumptions:

a. All parties live in Louisiana (a community property state).

b. All parties live in New Jersey (a common law state).

42. Using the Tax Rate Schedules, compute the 2006 tax liability for each taxpayer:

a. Hector (age 42) is a surviving spouse and provides all of the support of his three minor children who live with him. He also maintains the household in which his parents live and furnished 60% of their support. Besides interest on City of Flint bonds in the amount of $1,200, Hector's father received $2,400 from a part-time job. Hector has a salary of $70,000, a short-term capital loss of $4,000, a cash prize of $2,000 from a church raffle, and itemized deductions of $9,500.

b. Penny (age 45) is single and provides more than 50% of the support of Rosalyn (a family friend), Flo (a niece, age 18), and Jerold (a nephew, age 18). Both Rosalyn and Flo live with Penny, but Jerold (a French citizen) lives in Canada. Penny earns a salary of $80,000, contributes $4,000 to a traditional IRA, and receives sales proceeds of $15,000 for an RV that cost $40,000 and was used for vacations. She has $8,000 in itemized deductions.

43. Keri, age 12, is claimed as a dependent on her parents' 2006 return, on which they report taxable income of $90,000 (no qualified dividends or capital gains). Keri earned $2,300 pet sitting and $1,900 in interest on a savings account. What are Keri's taxable income and tax liability for 2006?

44. Rhett, age 13, is claimed as a dependent on his parents' 2006 return. During the year, Rhett earned $3,200 in interest income and $1,400 from part-time jobs.

a. What is Rhett's taxable income?

b. How much of Rhett's income is taxed at his rate? At his parents' rate?

c. Can the parental election be made? Why or why not?

45. Which of the following individuals are required to file a tax return for 2006? Should any of these individuals file a return even if filing is not required? Why?

a. Sam is married and files a joint return with his spouse, Lana. Both Sam and Lana are 67 years old. Their combined gross income was $18,500.

b. Ronald is a dependent child under age 19 who received $5,100 in wages from a part-time job.

c. Mike is single and is 67 years old. His gross income from wages was $9,900.

d. Patricia, age 19, is a self-employed single individual with gross income of $4,500 from an unincorporated business. Business expenses amounted to $4,000.

46. Which of the following taxpayers must file a Federal income tax return for 2006?

a. Ben, age 19, is a full-time college student. He is claimed as a dependent by his parents. He earned $5,200 wages during the year.

b. Anita, age 12, is claimed as a dependent by her parents. She earned interest income of $1,200 during the year.

c. Earl, age 16, is claimed as a dependent by his parents. He earned wages of $2,700 and interest of $1,100 during the year.

d. Karen, age 16 and blind, is claimed as a dependent by her parents. She earned wages of $2,600 and interest of $1,200 during the year.

e. Pat, age 17, is claimed as a dependent by her parents. She earned interest of $300 during the year. In addition, she earned $550 during the summer operating her own business at the beach, where she painted caricatures of her customers.

47. In each of the following *independent* situations, determine Bianca's filing status for 2006.

a. Bianca's husband died in December 2006, and she is the executor of his estate. Her late husband had no income for 2006.

b. Same as (a), except the husband died in 2005 (not 2006). Bianca maintains a household that includes her sister who qualifies as a dependent.

c. Same as (b). Bianca's household also includes Perry, her husband's 14-year-old son by a prior marriage. Perry qualifies as Bianca's dependent.

d. Bianca was abandoned by her husband in 2004. She maintains a household that includes two daughters (ages 12 and 13) who qualify as her dependents.

48. In each of the following *independent* situations, determine Winston's filing status for 2006. Winston is not married.

a. Winston maintains a household in which he and his unmarried son, Ward, live. Ward does not qualify as Winston's dependent.

b. Same as (a), except that Ward is married.

c. Winston lives alone, but he maintains a household in which his parents live. The mother qualifies as Winston's dependent, but the father does not.

d. Winston lives alone but maintains a household in which his married daughter, Karin, lives. Both Karin and her husband (Winston's son-in-law) qualify as Winston's dependents.

49. Nadia died in 2005 and is survived by her husband, Jerold, and her 18-year-old daughter, Macy. Jerold is the executor of Nadia's estate. Jerold maintains the household in which he and Macy live and furnishes more than 50% of her support. Macy had earnings from part-time employment as follows: $4,000 in 2005; $5,000 in 2006; and $6,000 in 2007. She is a full-time student for 2007 (but not for 2005 and 2006). What is Jerold's filing status for:

a. 2005?

b. 2006?

c. 2007?

50. Miles died in 2005 and is survived by his wife, Rosalyn (age 39), his married daughter, Sue (age 18), and his son-in-law, Peyton (age 22). Rosalyn is the executor of her husband's estate. She also maintains the household where she, Sue, and Peyton live and furnishes more than 50% of their support. During 2005 and 2006, Peyton is a full-time student, while Sue earns $16,000 ($8,000 each year) conducting aerobics classes. Sue and Peyton do not file joint returns. For years 2005 and 2006, what is Rosalyn's filing status, and how many exemptions can she claim based on each of the following assumptions?

a. All parties live in Pennsylvania (a common law state).

b. All parties live in Texas (a community property state).

51. During 2006, Reed had the following transactions involving capital assets:

Gain on the sale of customized ice-fishing cabin (held for 11 months and used for recreational purposes)	$ 8,000
Loss from garage sale (personal clothing, furniture, appliances held for more than a year)	(6,000)
Loss on the sale of GMC stock (held as an investment for 10 months)	(1,000)
Gain on the sale of a city lot (held as an investment for 3 years)	3,000

a. If Reed is in the 28% tax bracket, how much income tax results?

b. If Reed is in the 15% bracket?

52. During 2006, Valerie had the following gains and losses from the sale of capital assets:

Loss on the sale of GE stock (held for 5 months)	($2,000)
Gain on the sale of a coin collection (held for 3 years as an investment)	3,000
Gain on the sale of undeveloped land (held for 5 years as an investment)	2,000

a. If Valerie is in the 33% tax bracket, how much income tax results?

b. If Valerie is in the 15% tax bracket?

53. Each year, the Hundleys normally have itemized deductions of $9,500, including a $3,600 pledge payment to their church. Upon the advice of a friend, they do the following: in early January 2006, they pay their pledge for 2005; during 2006, they pay the pledge for 2006; and in late December 2006, they prepay their pledge for 2007.

Decision Making

    a. Explain what the Hundleys are trying to accomplish.

    b. What will be the tax saving if their marginal tax bracket is 25% for all three years? (Assume the standard deduction amounts for 2006 and 2007 are the same.)

CUMULATIVE PROBLEMS

Tax Return Problem

Decision Making

Communications

54. Horace Fern, age 43, lives at 321 Grant Avenue, Cheyenne, WY 82002. Horace's mother, Kate (age 65), lived with him until her death in August 2005. Up to the time of her death, Kate qualified as Horace's dependent. Horace maintained the household where he and his mother lived.

    Horace is a manager for Bison Lumber Company at a yearly salary of $72,000. Because his job duties will be expanded, Bison plans to increase Horace's salary by 10% starting in 2006.

    During 2005, Horace paid $3,300 ($300 each month) in alimony to Janet, his ex-wife. As Janet was remarried in late November, Horace's alimony obligation has terminated.

    Besides his salary, Horace received interest income of $6,700 from Western Bank and $7,300 from First Savings Bank on $400,000 in certificates of deposit (CDs) he owns. Horace received the CDs as a gift from his mother several years ago.

    Except as otherwise noted, Horace's expenditures for 2005 are summarized below:

Interest on home mortgage	$3,300
Property taxes on home	1,200
Sales taxes (actual amount paid)	1,600
Charitable contributions	600

Relevant Social Security numbers are as follows:

Horace Fern	111–20–4444
Kate Fern	333–55–1111
Janet Fern	520–33–4432

Federal income taxes withheld from Horace's salary amounted to $13,000. FICA taxes withheld by his employer were $5,508 [($72,000 × 6.2% for Social Security) + ($72,000 × 1.45% for Medicare)].

Part 1—Tax Computation

Compute Horace's net tax payable or refund due for 2005. Horace does not wish to contribute to the Presidential Election Campaign Fund. If he has overpaid, he wants the amount refunded. If you use tax forms for your computations, you will need Form 1040 and Schedules A and B. Suggested software: TurboTax.

Part 2—Tax Planning

In addition to preparing the return for 2005, Horace has asked you to advise him regarding his tax situation for 2006. He is particularly concerned about the tax effects of the following:

- The death of Kate.
- The cessation of alimony payments due to Janet's remarriage.
- The salary increase.
- Interest income on the CDs.

Write a letter to Horace in which you summarize (in approximate amounts) how much more (or less) he will owe in income taxes for 2006. Also include recommendations on what can be done to mitigate the tax consequences resulting from the investment in CDs. Assume that Horace's itemized deductions will remain constant in 2006.

Tax Return Problem

55. Bob and Melissa Rand are married and live at 2460 Westpark Drive, Sutter, CA 91330. Bob is an electrician and is employed by a local home builder, while Melissa is a part-time receptionist for a law firm.

The Rands have the following receipts for 2006:

Salaries ($72,000 + $22,000)		$94,000
Interest income—		
City of Sutter bonds	$ 800	
Boeing Corporation bonds	1,100	
Bank of America CD	1,300	3,200
Gift from Melissa's parents		4,000
Garden City settlement		20,000
Property transactions—		
Camper sale	$ 5,200	
Hardy Street lot sale	11,000	
Garage sale	4,100	20,300

In early 2006, while she was shopping at Garden City, Melissa was injured by the collapse of carelessly displayed merchandise. To keep her from filing a lawsuit, Garden City paid Melissa $20,000 to sign a release from liability. The camper was built by Bob in his spare time from materials costing $2,200. The Hardy Street lot was purchased by the Rands as an investment in March 2002 for $15,000. Unfortunately, the lot declined in value due to a general deterioration of the neighborhood. The garage sale involved personal items (household effects such as clothing and furniture, with an estimated original cost of $12,000).

The Rands have the following expenditures for 2006:

Contribution to traditional IRA	$4,000
Itemized deductions—	
Medical expenses (including insurance premiums) net of reimbursements	3,800
State income taxes (including amounts withheld)	7,200
Property taxes on personal residence	3,600
Interest on home mortgage	4,100
Charitable contributions (supported by receipts)	1,300

The Rands support two daughters, Heather (age 17) and Robyn (age 18), who live with them. Bob and his two brothers contribute equally toward the support of their parents (Wesley and Mrytle Rand) who lived in their own home until Myrtle died in February 2006. Wesley has since moved to a nursing home. The brothers, John and Alan Rand, have sent Bob a Form 2120 giving him the right to claim whatever dependency exemptions are available for their parents.

a. Compute the Rands' taxable income for 2006.

b. If the Rands had $7,600 of Federal income tax withheld during 2006, compute their net tax payable (or refund due) for the year.

RESEARCH PROBLEMS

Note: Solutions to Research Problems can be prepared by using the **RIA Checkpoint**® **Student Edition** online research product, which is available to accompany this text. It is also possible to prepare solutions to the Research Problems by using tax research materials found in a standard tax library.

Research Problem 1. Jeff and Suzy are the biological parents of Monique, born in 1993. The parents never married, and shortly after the birth, Suzy left the household and took Monique with her. In 1994, Jeff had Suzy sign a Form 8332 in which she waived the dependency exemption as to Monique for 1994 "and all years thereafter." Although Jeff contributes nothing toward the support of Monique, he has been claiming her as a dependent every year since 1994. Starting in 2003, Suzy has also been claiming Monique as a dependent.

Needless to say, the IRS is not likely to permit a dependent to be claimed twice! In the event of audit, should Jeff or Suzy be allowed the deduction for Monique? Why?

Partial list of research aids:
§§ 151(e)(1) and (2).
Jeffrey R. King, 121 T.C. 245 (2003).

Communications

Research Problem 2. John and Marge Hudgens were married 26 years ago and have one child, Monica. Sometime in January 2005 after a particularly fierce argument, John packed his clothes and left for parts unknown. Marge has neither seen nor heard from him since.

Marge is employed and maintains the house where she and Monica live. Monica is a full-time student and will graduate from law school on May 9, 2006. During 2005 and 2006, Monica (age 22) earned over $9,000 each year from part-time jobs. She deposited part of her earnings in a savings account under her name and used the rest for her support. The remainder of Monica's support was provided by Marge.

Marge contacts you in March of 2006 regarding tax advice. Specifically, she is interested in the answers to the following questions for 2005 and 2006:

- What is her filing status?
- Can she claim Monica as a dependent?

a. Write a letter to Marge addressing her concerns. Marge lives at 1349 Center Street, Warrensburg, MO 64093.
b. Also prepare a memo for your firm's client files.

Research Problem 3. Bart and Arlene Keating are husband and wife and live in Mineola, Oregon. They have been married for 18 years and have four children, all of whom are teenagers. After the birth of her last child, Arlene took a job as a city clerk and, over the years, has become city treasurer. Since graduating from high school, Bart has worked as a dispatcher for the city fire and ambulance departments. As Arlene has some college training in finance and accounting, she handles the family's financial affairs, including reconciling the bank account, paying bills, and preparing all tax returns. She also takes care of major purchases (e.g., autos, furniture) and servicing of debt (e.g., home mortgage, auto loans, charge accounts).

The Keatings themselves maintain a modest lifestyle, but Arlene is quite generous with the children. All are well-dressed, attend summer camp, and have their own cars. Bart believes Arlene obtains any additional funds for the children's support through credit card financing and bank loans.

The Keatings filed joint returns for 2002 and 2003 that reflected their salary income. Arlene prepared the returns, and Bart signed them without reviewing them first. The returns did not show the $90,000 Arlene had embezzled from her employer over this two-year period.

The City of Mineola discovers the theft, and Arlene is tried and convicted of grand larceny. Due to the adverse publicity generated by these events, the Keatings are divorced, and Arlene moves to another state.

In 2006, the IRS assesses a deficiency against Bart for the income taxes that would have resulted if the embezzled amounts had been reported as income.

What are the rights of the parties?

Partial list of research aids:
§§ 6013(d)(3) and 6015.
Kathryn Cheshire, 115 T.C. 183 (2000).
Evelyn M. Martin, 80 TCM 665, T.C.Memo. 2000–346.

Internet *Activity*

Use the tax resources of the Internet to address the following questions. Do not restrict your search to the World Wide Web, but include a review of newsgroups and general reference materials, practitioner sites and resources, primary sources of the tax law, chat rooms and discussion groups, and other opportunities.

Research Problem 4. Find and print a Form 2120, Multiple Support Declaration. Fill in the form and use it to illustrate one of your recommendations for Discussion Question 27.

Research Problem 5. In terms of electronic filing, what guidance, if any, does the IRS provide when a taxpayer uses a computer? What if a tax preparer is involved?

Research Problem 6. A nonresident alien earns money in the United States that is subject to Federal income tax. What guidance does the IRS provide on what tax form needs to be used and on when it should be filed? In terms of the proper filing date, does it matter whether the earnings were subject to income tax withholding?

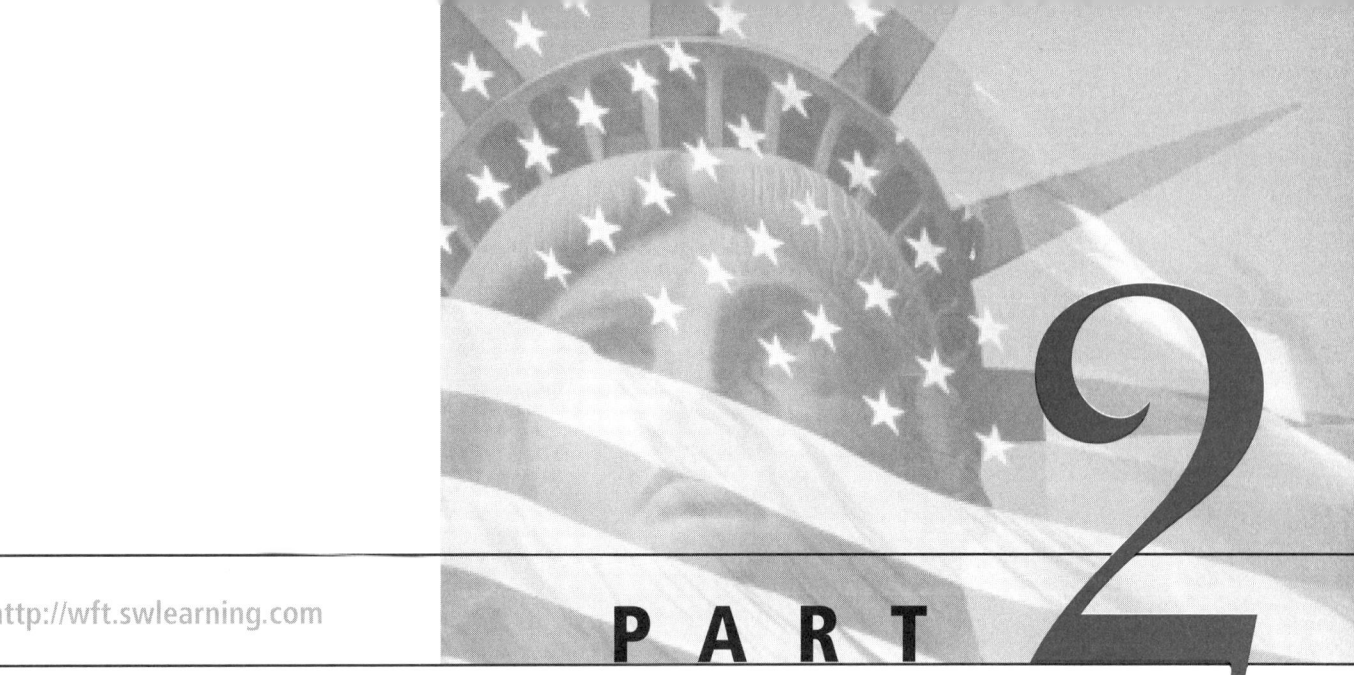

http://wft.swlearning.com

PART 2

Gross Income

Part II presents the income component of the basic tax model. Included in this presentation are the determination of what is income and the statutory exclusions that are permitted in calculating gross income. Because the taxpayer's accounting method and accounting period affect when income is reported, an introductory discussion of these topics is also included.

CHAPTER 4
Gross Income: Concepts and Inclusions

CHAPTER 5
Gross Income: Exclusions

CHAPTER 4

Gross Income: Concepts and Inclusions

LEARNING OBJECTIVES

After completing Chapter 4, you should be able to:

LO.1

Explain the concepts of gross income and realization and distinguish between the economic, accounting, and tax concepts of gross income.

LO.2

Describe the cash and accrual methods of accounting and the related effects of the choice of taxable year.

LO.3

Identify who should pay the tax on a particular item of income in various situations.

LO.4

Apply the Internal Revenue Code provisions on alimony, loans made at below-market interest rates, annuities, prizes and awards, group term life insurance, unemployment compensation, and Social Security benefits.

LO.5

Identify tax planning strategies for minimizing gross income.

Mr. Zarin lost over $2.5 million of his own money gambling. The casino then allowed him to gamble on credit. After several months, his liability to the casino totaled more than $3.4 million. Following protracted negotiations, the casino agreed to settle its claim against Mr. Zarin for a mere $500,000. Although Mr. Zarin had paid for gambling losses of $3 million, the IRS had the audacity to ask him to pay tax on $2.9 million, that is, the amount the casino marked down his account.[1] Mr. Zarin undoubtedly had difficulty understanding how he could be deemed to have income in this situation.

Given an understanding of the income tax formula, though, one can see how the "free" gambling Mr. Zarin enjoyed could constitute income. The starting point in the formula is the determination of gross income rather than "net income." Once gross income is determined, the next step is to determine the allowable deductions. In Mr. Zarin's way of thinking, these steps were collapsed.

This chapter is concerned with the first step in the computation of taxable income—the determination of gross income. Questions that are addressed include the following:

- What: What is income?
- When: In which tax period is the income recognized?
- Who: Who must include the item of income in gross income?

The Code provides an all-inclusive definition of gross income in § 61. Chapter 5 presents items of income that are specifically excluded from gross income (exclusions).

LO.1

Explain the concepts of gross income and realization and distinguish between the economic, accounting, and tax concepts of gross income.

Gross Income—What Is It?

Definition

Section 61(a) of the Internal Revenue Code defines the term **gross income** as follows:

> Except as otherwise provided in this subtitle, gross income means all income from whatever source derived.

[1] *Zarin v. Comm.*, 90–2 USTC ¶50,530, 66 AFTR2d 90–5679, 916 F.2d 110 (CA–3, 1990).

FROM "ALL SOURCES" IS A BROAD DEFINITION

When § 61 refers to "income from whatever source derived," the taxing authorities are reaching far beyond the borders of the United States. Although one interpretation of "source" in this context is type of income (wages, interest, etc.), a broader interpretation revolves around the place where the income is generated. In this context, citizens and residents of the United States are subject to taxation on income earned from sources both inside and outside the country. This "worldwide income" tax base can cause potential double taxation problems, with other countries also taxing income earned within their borders, but mechanisms such as the foreign tax credit can alleviate these tax burdens.

Recently, some U.S. corporations have relocated to other countries to avoid the higher U.S. tax rates on income earned abroad. Congress is considering ways of stopping this "flight of capital." The American Jobs Creation Act of 2004 (AJCA) provided an incentive for companies to bring profits back into the United States. Some economists and politicians, however, have questioned how well this incentive has worked and how many jobs it has created.

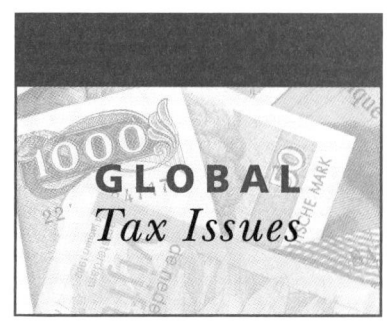

GLOBAL *Tax Issues*

This definition is derived from the language of the Sixteenth Amendment to the Constitution.

Supreme Court decisions have made it clear that all sources of income are subject to tax unless Congress specifically excludes the type of income received:

> The starting point in all cases dealing with the question of the scope of what is included in "gross income" begins with the basic premise that the purpose of Congress was to use the full measure of its taxing power.[2]

Although at this point we know that *income* is to be broadly construed, we still do not have a satisfactory definition of the term *income*. Congress left it to the judicial and administrative branches to thrash out the meaning of income. Early in the development of the income tax law, a choice was made between two competing models: economic income and accounting income.

Economic and Accounting Concepts

The term **income** is used in the Code but is not separately defined. Thus, early in the history of our tax laws, the courts were required to interpret "the commonly understood meaning of the term which must have been in the minds of the people when they adopted the Sixteenth Amendment to the Constitution."[3] In determining the definition of income, the Supreme Court rejected the economic concept of income.

Economists measure income (**economic income**) by first determining the fair market value of the individual's net assets at the beginning and end of the year (change in net worth). Then, to arrive at economic income, this change in net worth is added to the goods and services that person actually consumed during the period. Economic income also includes imputed values for such items as the rental value of an owner-occupied home and the value of food a taxpayer might grow for personal consumption.[4]

---

[2]*James v. U.S.*, 61–1 USTC ¶9449, 7 AFTR2d 1361, 81 S.Ct. 1052 (USSC, 1961).
[3]*Merchants Loan and Trust Co. v. Smietanka*, 1 USTC ¶42, 3 AFTR 3102, 41 S.Ct. 386 (USSC, 1921).

[4]See Henry C. Simons, *Personal Income Taxation* (Chicago: University of Chicago Press, 1933), Chapters 2–3.

EXAMPLE 1

Helen's economic income is calculated as follows:

Fair market value of Helen's assets on December 31, 2006	$220,000	
Less liabilities on December 31, 2006	(40,000)	
Net worth on December 31, 2006		$ 180,000
Fair market value of Helen's assets on January 1, 2006	$200,000	
Less liabilities on January 1, 2006	(80,000)	
Net worth on January 1, 2006		(120,000)
Increase in net worth		$ 60,000
Consumption		
Food, clothing, and other personal expenditures		25,000
Imputed rental value of the home Helen owns and occupies		12,000
Economic income		$ 97,000 ■

The need to value assets annually would make compliance with the tax law burdensome and would cause numerous controversies between the taxpayer and the IRS over valuation. In addition, using market values to determine income for tax purposes could result in liquidity problems. The taxpayer's assets may increase in value even though they are not readily convertible into the cash needed to pay the tax (e.g., commercial real estate). Thus, the IRS, Congress, and the courts have rejected the economic concept of income as impractical.

In contrast, the accounting concept of income is founded on the realization principle.[5] According to this principle, income (**accounting income**) is not recognized until it is realized. For realization to occur, (1) an exchange of goods or services must take place between the accounting entity and some independent, external group, and (2) in the exchange the accounting entity must receive assets that are capable of being objectively valued. Thus, the mere appreciation in the market value of assets before a sale or other disposition is not sufficient to warrant income recognition. In addition, the imputed savings that arise when individuals create assets for their own use (e.g., feed grown for a farmer's own livestock) are not income because no exchange has occurred. The courts and the IRS have ruled, however, that embezzlement proceeds and buried treasures found satisfy the realization requirement and, therefore, must be recognized as income.[6]

The Supreme Court expressed an inclination toward the accounting concept of income when it adopted the realization requirement in *Eisner v. Macomber*:

> Income may be defined as the gain derived from capital, from labor, or from both combined, provided it is understood to include profit gained through a sale or conversion of capital assets. . . . Here we have the essential matter: not a gain accruing to capital; not a *growth* or *increment* of value *in* investment; but a gain, a profit, something of exchangeable value, *proceeding from* the property, *severed from* the capital however invested or employed, and *coming in*, being "*derived*"—that is, *received* or *drawn by* the recipient for his separate use, benefit and disposal—*that is*, income derived from the property.[7]

In summary, *income* represents an increase in wealth recognized for tax purposes only upon realization.

---

[5]See the American Accounting Association Committee Report on the "Realization Concept," *The Accounting Review* (April 1965): 312–322.
[6]*Rutkin v. U.S.*, 52–1 USTC ¶9260, 41 AFTR2d 596, 72 S.Ct. 571 (USSC, 1952); Rev.Rul. 61, 1953–1 C.B. 17.

[7]1 USTC ¶32, 3 AFTR 3020, 40 S.Ct. 189 (USSC, 1920).

TAX *in the News*   **IF FREE IS TAXED, IT'S NOT FREE**

Major League Baseball teams provide complimentary tickets to any of their players who ask for them. The tickets are given to family members, friends, or even the parking attendant in the stadium parking lot. The players have been happy to oblige because the tickets haven't cost them anything.

Now, however, the free tickets are disappearing. The reason is that "free is no longer free." Starting in 2005, the IRS is including the value of the tickets in the player's gross income. Jimmy Banks, the traveling secretary for the Chicago Cubs, says he saw a tremendous decline in player requests for tickets this past season.

Now a computer system in the Chicago Cubs clubhouse keeps track of the tickets that players request on their laptops. The key to inclusion in gross income is the player's request for tickets rather than whether the tickets are picked up at the stadium ticket office.

As one Cubs player says, "We get paid well. But under this new system, I have to shake my head and tell lots of people . . . I just can't do anything for you."

Source: *Adapted from Joseph A. Reaves, "IRS Stems Flow of Free Tickets," USA Today, September 20, 2005, p. 5C.*

Comparison of the Accounting and Tax Concepts of Income

Although income tax rules frequently parallel financial accounting measurement concepts, differences do exist. Of major significance, for example, is the fact that unearned (prepaid) income received by an accrual basis taxpayer often is taxed in the year of receipt. For financial accounting purposes, such prepayments are not treated as income until earned.[8] Because of this and other differences, many corporations report financial accounting income that is substantially different from the amounts reported for tax purposes (see Reconciliation of Corporate Taxable Income and Accounting Income in Chapter 20).

The Supreme Court provided an explanation for some of the variations between accounting and taxable income in a decision involving inventory and bad debt adjustments:

> The primary goal of financial accounting is to provide useful information to management, shareholders, creditors, and others properly interested; the major responsibility of the accountant is to protect these parties from being misled. The primary goal of the income tax system, in contrast, is the equitable collection of revenue. . . . Consistently with its goals and responsibilities, financial accounting has as its foundation the principle of conservatism, with its corollary that 'possible errors in measurement [should] be in the direction of understatement rather than overstatement of net income and net assets.' In view of the Treasury's markedly different goals and responsibilities, understatement of income is not destined to be its guiding light.
>
> . . . Financial accounting, in short, is hospitable to estimates, probabilities, and reasonable certainties; the tax law, with its mandate to preserve the revenue, can give no quarter to uncertainty.[9]

Form of Receipt

Gross income is not limited to cash received. "It includes income realized in any form, whether in money, property, or services. Income may be realized [and recognized], therefore, in the form of services, meals, accommodations, stock or other property, as well as in cash."[10]

---

[8]Similar differences exist in the deduction area.

[9]*Thor Power Tool Co. v. Comm.*, 79–1 USTC ¶9139, 43 AFTR2d 79–362, 99 S.Ct. 773 (USSC, 1979).

[10]Reg. § 1.61–1(a).

EXAMPLE 2

Ostrich Corporation allows Bill, an employee, to use a company car for his vacation. Bill realizes income equal to the rental value of the car for the time and mileage. ∎

EXAMPLE 3

Terry owes $10,000 on a mortgage. The creditor accepts $8,000 in full satisfaction of the debt. Terry realizes income of $2,000 from retiring the debt.[11] ∎

EXAMPLE 4

Martha is an attorney. She agrees to draft a will for Tom, a neighbor, who is a carpenter. In exchange, Tom repairs her back porch. Martha and Tom both have gross income equal to the fair market value of the services they provide. ∎

Recovery of Capital Doctrine

The Constitution grants Congress the power to tax income but does not define the term. Because the Constitution does not define income, it would seem that Congress could simply tax gross receipts. Although Congress does allow certain deductions, none are constitutionally required. However, the Supreme Court has held that there is no income subject to tax until the taxpayer has recovered the capital invested.[12] This concept is known as the **recovery of capital doctrine**.

In its simplest application, this doctrine means that sellers can reduce their gross receipts (selling price) by the adjusted basis of the property sold.[13] This net amount, in the language of the Code, is gross income.

EXAMPLE 5

Dave sold common stock for $15,000. He had purchased the stock for $12,000. Dave's gross receipts are $15,000. This amount consists of a $12,000 recovery of capital and $3,000 of gross income. ∎

Collections on annuity contracts and installment payments received from sales of property must be allocated between recovery of capital and income. Annuities are discussed in this chapter, and installment sales are discussed in Chapter 18.

LO.2

Describe the cash and accrual methods of accounting and the related effects of the choice of taxable year.

Year of Inclusion

Taxable Year

The annual accounting period or **taxable year** is a basic component of our tax system.[14] Generally, an entity must use the *calendar year* to report its income. However, a *fiscal year* (a period of 12 months ending on the last day of any month other than December) can be elected if the taxpayer maintains adequate books and records. This fiscal year option generally is not available to partnerships, S corporations, and personal service corporations, as discussed in Chapter 18.[15]

Determining the particular year in which the income will be taxed is important for determining when the tax must be paid. But the year each item of income is subject to tax can also affect the total tax liability over the entity's lifetime. This is true for the following reasons:

- With a progressive rate system, a taxpayer's marginal tax rate can change from year to year.
- Congress may change the tax rates.

[11]Reg. § 1.61–12. See *U.S. v. Kirby Lumber Co.*, 2 USTC ¶814, 10 AFTR 458, 52 S.Ct. 4 (USSC, 1931). Exceptions to this general rule are discussed in Chapter 5.
[12]*Doyle v. Mitchell Bros. Co.*, 1 USTC ¶17, 3 AFTR 2979, 38 S.Ct. 467 (USSC, 1916).
[13]For a definition of "adjusted basis," see the Glossary of Tax Terms in Appendix C.
[14]See Accounting Periods in Chapter 18.
[15]§§ 441(a) and (d).

- The relevant rates may change because of a change in the entity's status (e.g., a person may marry or a business may be incorporated).
- Several provisions in the Code are dependent on the taxpayer's gross income for the year (e.g., whether the person can be claimed as a dependent, as discussed in Chapter 3).

Accounting Methods

The year an item of income is subject to tax often depends upon which acceptable **accounting method** the taxpayer regularly employs.[16] The three primary methods of accounting are (1) the cash receipts and disbursements method, (2) the accrual method, and (3) the hybrid method. Most individuals use the cash receipts and disbursements method of accounting, whereas most corporations use the accrual method. The Regulations require the accrual method for determining purchases and sales when inventory is an income-producing factor.[17] Some businesses employ a hybrid method that is a combination of the cash and accrual methods of accounting.

In addition to these overall accounting methods, a taxpayer may choose to spread the gain from an installment sale of property over the collection periods by using the *installment method* of income recognition. Contractors may either spread profits from contracts over the periods in which the work is done (the *percentage of completion method*) or defer all profit until the year in which the project is completed (the *completed contract method*, which can be used only in limited circumstances).[18]

The IRS has the power to prescribe the accounting method to be used by the taxpayer. Section 446(b) grants the IRS broad powers to determine if the accounting method used *clearly reflects income*:

> If no method of accounting has been regularly used by the taxpayer, or *if the method used does not clearly reflect income, the computation of taxable income shall be made under such method as, in the opinion of the Secretary . . . does clearly reflect income.*

A change in the method of accounting requires the consent of the IRS.[19]

Cash Receipts Method. Under the **cash receipts method**, property or services received are included in the taxpayer's gross income in the year of actual or constructive receipt by the taxpayer or agent, regardless of whether the income was earned in that year.[20] The income received need not be reduced to cash in the same year. All that is necessary for income recognition is that property or services received have a fair market value—a cash equivalent.[21] Thus, a cash basis taxpayer who receives a note in payment for services has income in the year of receipt equal to the fair market value of the note. However, a creditor's mere promise to pay (e.g., an account receivable), with no supporting note, usually is not considered to have a fair market value.[22] Thus, the cash basis taxpayer defers income recognition until the account receivable is collected.

E X A M P L E   6

Dana, an accountant, reports her income by the cash method. In 2006, she performed an audit for Orange Corporation and billed the client for $5,000, which was collected in 2007. In 2006, Dana also performed an audit for Blue Corporation. Because of Blue's precarious financial position, Dana required Blue to issue an $8,000 secured negotiable note in

---

[16]See Accounting Methods in Chapter 18.

[17]Reg. § 1.446–1(c)(2)(i). Other circumstances in which the accrual method must be used are presented in Chapter 18. For the small business exception to the inventory requirement, see Rev.Proc. 2002–28, 2002–1 C.B. 815.

[18]§§ 453 and 460. See Chapter 18 for limitations on the use of the installment method and the completed contract method.

[19]§ 446(e). See Chapter 18.

[20]*Julia A. Strauss*, 2 B.T.A. 598 (1925). See the Glossary of Tax Terms in Appendix C for a discussion of the terms "cash equivalent doctrine" and "constructive receipt."

[21]Reg. §§ 1.446–1(a)(3) and (c)(1)(i).

[22]*Bedell v. Comm.*, 1 USTC ¶359, 7 AFTR 8469, 30 F.2d 622 (CA–2, 1929).

payment of the fee. The note had a fair market value of $6,000. Dana collected $8,000 on the note in 2007. Dana's gross income for the two years is as follows:

	2006	2007
Fair market value of note received from Blue	$6,000	
Cash received		
From Orange on account receivable		$ 5,000
From Blue on note receivable		8,000
Less: Recovery of capital		(6,000)
Total gross income	$6,000	$ 7,000

Generally, a check received is considered a cash equivalent. Thus, a cash basis taxpayer must recognize the income when the check is received. This is true even if the taxpayer receives the check after banking hours.[23]

Accrual Method. Under the **accrual method**, an item is generally included in the gross income for the year in which it is earned, regardless of when the income is collected. The income is earned when (1) all the events have occurred that fix the right to receive such income and (2) the amount to be received can be determined with reasonable accuracy.[24]

Generally, the taxpayer's rights to the income accrue when title to property passes to the buyer or the services are performed for the customer or client.[25] If the rights to the income have accrued but are subject to a potential refund claim (e.g., under a product warranty), the income is reported in the year of sale, and a deduction is allowed in subsequent years when actual claims accrue.[26]

Where the taxpayer's rights to the income are being contested (e.g., when a contractor fails to meet specifications), the year in which the income is subject to tax depends upon whether payment has been received. If payment has not been received, no income is recognized until the claim is settled. Only then is the right to the income established.[27] However, if the payment is received before the dispute is settled, the court-made **claim of right doctrine** requires the taxpayer to recognize the income in the year of receipt.[28]

EXAMPLE 7

A contractor completed a building in 2006 and presented a bill to the customer. The customer refused to pay the bill and claimed that the contractor had not met specifications. A settlement with the customer was not reached until 2007. No income accrues to the contractor until 2007. If the customer paid for the work and then filed suit for damages, the contractor cannot defer the income (the income is taxable in 2006). ∎

The measure of accrual basis income is generally the amount the taxpayer has a right to receive. Unlike the cash basis, the fair market value of the customer's obligation is irrelevant in measuring accrual basis income.

EXAMPLE 8

Assume the same facts as in Example 6, except that Dana is an accrual basis taxpayer. Dana must recognize $13,000 ($8,000 + $5,000) gross income in 2006, the year her rights to the income accrued. ∎

---

[23]*Charles F. Kahler*, 18 T.C. 31 (1952).
[24]Reg. § 1.451–1(a).
[25]*Lucas v. North Texas Lumber Co.*, 2 USTC ¶484, 8 AFTR 10276, 50 S.Ct. 184 (USSC, 1930).
[26]*Brown v. Helvering*, 4 USTC ¶1222, 13 AFTR 851, 54 S.Ct. 356 (USSC, 1933).

[27]*Burnet v. Sanford and Brooks*, 2 USTC ¶636, 9 AFTR 603, 51 S.Ct. 150 (USSC, 1931).
[28]*North American Oil Consolidated Co. v. Burnet*, 3 USTC ¶943, 11 AFTR 16, 52 S.Ct. 613 (USSC, 1932).

Hybrid Method. The **hybrid method** is a combination of the accrual method and the cash method. Generally, when the hybrid method is used, inventory is an income-producing factor. Therefore, the Regulations require that the accrual method be used for determining sales and cost of goods sold. In this circumstance, to simplify record keeping, the taxpayer accounts for inventory using the accrual method and uses the cash method for all other income and expense items (e.g., dividend and interest income). The hybrid method is primarily used by small businesses.

Exceptions Applicable to Cash Basis Taxpayers

Constructive Receipt. Income that has not actually been received by the taxpayer is taxed as though it had been received—the income is constructively received—under the following conditions:

- The amount is made readily available to the taxpayer.
- The taxpayer's actual receipt is not subject to substantial limitations or restrictions.[29]

The rationale for the **constructive receipt** doctrine is that if the income is available, the taxpayer should not be allowed to postpone the income recognition. For instance, a taxpayer is not permitted to defer income for December services by refusing to accept payment until January. However, determining whether the income is *readily available* and whether *substantial limitations or restrictions exist* necessitates a factual inquiry that leads to a judgment call.[30] The following are some examples of the application of the constructive receipt doctrine.

EXAMPLE 9

Ted is a member of a barter club. In 2006, Ted performed services for other club members and earned 1,000 points. Each point entitles him to $1 in goods and services sold by other members of the club; the points can be used at any time. In 2007, Ted exchanged his points for a new high-definition TV. Ted must recognize $1,000 gross income in 2006 when the 1,000 points were credited to his account.[31] ■

EXAMPLE 10

On December 31, an employer issued a bonus check to an employee but asked her to hold it for a few days until the company could make deposits to cover the check. The income was not constructively received on December 31 since the issuer did not have sufficient funds in its account to pay the debt.[32] ■

EXAMPLE 11

Rick owns interest coupons that mature on December 31. The coupons can be converted to cash at any bank at maturity. Thus, the income is constructively received by Rick on December 31, even though Rick failed to cash in the coupons until the following year.[33] Dove Company mails a dividend check to Rick on December 31, 2006. Rick does not receive the check until January 2007. Rick does not realize gross income until 2007.[34] ■

The constructive receipt doctrine does not reach income that the taxpayer is not yet entitled to receive even though the taxpayer could have contracted to receive the income at an earlier date.

---

[29]Reg. § 1.451–2(a).

[30]*Baxter v. Comm.*, 87–1 USTC ¶9315, 59 AFTR2d 87–1068, 816 F.2d 493 (CA–9, 1987).

[31]Rev.Rul. 80–52, 1980–1 C.B. 100.

[32]*L. M. Fischer*, 14 T.C. 792 (1950).

[33]Reg. § 1.451–2(b).

[34]Reg. § 1.451–2(b).

EXAMPLE 12

Sara offers to pay Ivan $100,000 for land in December 2006. Ivan refuses but offers to sell the land to Sara on January 1, 2007, when he will be in a lower tax bracket. If Sara accepts Ivan's offer, the gain is taxed to Ivan in 2007 when the sale is completed.[35] ■

Income set apart or made available is not constructively received if its actual receipt is subject to *substantial restrictions.* The life insurance industry has used substantial restrictions as a cornerstone for designing life insurance contracts with favorable tax features. Ordinary life insurance policies provide (1) current protection—an amount payable in the event of death—and (2) a savings feature—a cash surrender value payable to the policyholder if the policy is terminated during the policyholder's life. The annual increase in cash surrender value is not taxable because the policyholder must cancel the policy to actually receive the increase in value. Because the cancellation requirement is a substantial restriction, the policyholder does not constructively receive the annual increase in cash surrender value.[36] Employees often receive from their employers property subject to substantial restrictions. Generally, no income is recognized until the restrictions lapse.[37]

EXAMPLE 13

Carlos is a key employee of Red, Inc. The corporation gives stock with a value of $10,000 to Carlos. The stock cannot be sold, however, for five years. Carlos is not required to recognize income until the restrictions lapse at the end of five years. ■

ETHICAL *Considerations*   CHOOSING WHEN TO FILE INSURANCE CLAIMS

Dr. Randolph, a cash basis taxpayer, knows that he will be in a lower marginal tax bracket in 2007 than in 2006. To take advantage of the expected decrease in his tax rate, Dr. Randolph instructs his office manager to delay filing the medical insurance claims for services performed in November and December until January 2007. This will assure that the receipts will not be included in his 2006 gross income. Is Dr. Randolph abusing the cash method of accounting rules?

Original Issue Discount. Lenders frequently make loans that require a payment at maturity of more than the amount of the original loan. The difference between the amount due at maturity and the amount of the original loan is actually interest but is referred to as **original issue discount**. Under the general rules of tax accounting, the cash basis lender would not report the original issue discount as interest income until the year the amount is collected, although an accrual basis borrower would deduct the interest as it is earned. However, the Code puts the lender and borrower on parity by requiring that the original issue discount be reported when it is earned, regardless of the taxpayer's accounting method.[38] The interest "earned" is calculated by the effective interest rate method.

EXAMPLE 14

On January 1, 2006, Mark, a cash basis taxpayer, pays $82,645 for a 24-month certificate. The certificate is priced to yield 10% (the effective interest rate) with interest compounded annually. No interest is paid until maturity, when Mark receives $100,000. Thus, Mark's gross

---

[35]*Cowden v. Comm.,* 61–1 USTC ¶9382, 7 AFTR2d 1160, 289 F.2d 20 (CA–5, 1961).
[36]*Theodore H. Cohen,* 39 T.C. 1055 (1963).
[37]§ 83(a). See also the discussion of Restricted Property Plans in Chapter 19.
[38]§§ 1272(a)(3) and 1273(a).

income from the certificate is $17,355 ($100,000 − $82,645). Mark's income earned each year is calculated as follows:

2006 (.10 × $82,645) =	$ 8,264
2007 [.10 × ($82,645 + $8,264)] =	9,091
	$17,355

∎

The original issue discount rules do not apply to U.S. savings bonds (discussed in the following paragraphs) or to obligations with a maturity date of one year or less from the date of issue.[39] See Chapter 16 for additional discussion of the tax treatment of original issue discount.

Series E and Series EE Bonds.

Certain U.S. government savings bonds (Series E before 1980 and Series EE after 1979) are issued at a discount and are redeemable for fixed amounts that increase at stated intervals. No interest payments are actually made. The difference between the purchase price and the amount received on redemption is the bondholder's interest income from the investment.

The income from these savings bonds is generally deferred until the bonds are redeemed or mature. Furthermore, Series E bonds previously could be exchanged within one year of their maturity date for Series HH bonds, and the interest on the Series E bonds could be further deferred until maturity of the Series HH bonds.[40] Thus, U.S. savings bonds have attractive income deferral features not available with corporate bonds and certificates of deposit issued by financial institutions.

Of course, the deferral feature of government bonds issued at a discount is not an advantage if the investor has insufficient income to be subject to tax as the income accrues. In fact, the deferral may work to the investor's disadvantage if the investor has other income in the year the bonds mature or the bunching of the bond interest into one tax year creates a tax liability. Fortunately, U.S. government bonds have a provision for these investors. A cash basis taxpayer can elect to include in gross income the annual increment in redemption value.[41]

EXAMPLE 15

Kate purchases Series EE U.S. savings bonds for $500 (face value of $1,000) on January 2 of the current year. If the bonds are redeemed during the first six months, no interest is paid. At December 31, the redemption value is $519.60.

If Kate elects to report the interest income annually, she must report interest income of $19.60 for the current year. If she does not make the election, she will report no interest income for the current year. ∎

When a taxpayer elects to report the income from the bonds on an annual basis, the election applies to all such bonds the taxpayer owns at the time of the election and to all such securities acquired subsequent to the election. A change in the method of reporting the income from the bonds requires permission from the IRS.

Amounts Received under an Obligation to Repay.

The receipt of funds with an obligation to repay that amount in the future is the essence of borrowing. Because the taxpayer's assets and liabilities increase by the same amount, no income is realized when the borrowed funds are received. Because amounts paid to the taxpayer by mistake and customer deposits are often classified as borrowed funds, receipt of these funds is not a taxable event.

---

[39]§ 1272(a)(2).

[40]Treas. Dept. Circulars No. 1–80 and No. 2–80, 1980–1 C.B. 714, 715. Note that interest is paid at semiannual intervals on the Series HH bonds and must be included in income as received. Refer to Chapter 5 for a discussion

of the savings bond interest exclusion. This exchange opportunity applied through August 31, 2004.

[41]§ 454(a).

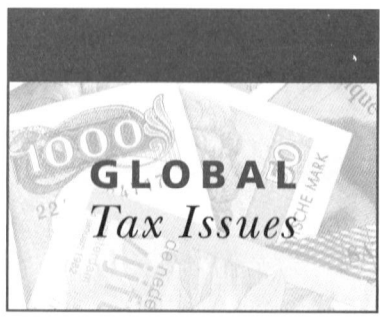

TAX CREDIT NEUTRALIZES FOREIGN INCOME TAXES

When a U.S. taxpayer invests in a foreign country, that investment income is subject to tax in the United States and may also be subject to tax in the foreign country. However, the taxpayer is allowed a credit on his or her U.S. Federal income tax return for income taxes paid to the foreign country. The credit system allows the taxpayer to treat the taxes paid to the foreign country as though they were paid to the United States. If the foreign taxes paid are less than the U.S. tax on the income, the foreign taxes have cost the taxpayer nothing. On the other hand, if the foreign taxes are greater than the U.S. tax on the income, the credit is limited to the amount of the U.S. tax on the income. In this case, the taxes paid by the taxpayer will exceed what they would have been if the income had been earned in the United States.

EXAMPLE 16

A landlord receives a damage deposit from a tenant. The landlord does not recognize income until the deposit is forfeited because the landlord has an obligation to repay the deposit if no damage occurs.[42] However, if the deposit is in fact a prepayment of rent, it is taxed in the year of receipt. ∎

Exceptions Applicable to Accrual Basis Taxpayers

Prepaid Income. For financial reporting purposes, advance payments received from customers are reflected as prepaid income and as a liability of the seller. However, for tax purposes, the prepaid income often is taxed in the year of receipt.

EXAMPLE 17

In December 2006, a tenant pays his January 2007 rent of $1,000. The accrual basis landlord must include the $1,000 in her 2006 gross income for tax purposes, although the unearned rent income is reported as a liability on the landlord's December 31, 2006 balance sheet. ∎

Taxpayers have repeatedly argued that deferral of income until it is actually earned properly matches revenues and expenses. Moreover, a proper matching of income with the expenses of earning the income is necessary to clearly reflect income, as required by the Code. The IRS responds that § 446(b) grants it broad powers to determine whether an accounting method clearly reflects income. The IRS further argues that generally accepted financial accounting principles should not dictate tax accounting for prepaid income because of the practical problems of collecting Federal revenues. Collection of the tax is simplest in the year the taxpayer receives the cash from the customer or client.

After a number of years of continual disputes between the IRS and taxpayers, in 1971 the IRS relented and modified its rules on the prepaid income issue in some situations, as explained below.

Deferral of Advance Payments for Goods. Generally, a taxpayer can elect to defer recognition of income from *advance payments for goods* if the method of accounting for the sale is the same for tax and financial reporting purposes.[43]

EXAMPLE 18

Brown Company will ship goods only after payment for the goods has been received. In December 2006, Brown received $10,000 for goods that were not shipped until January 2007.

---

[42]*John Mantell,* 17 T.C. 1143 (1952).

[43]Reg. § 1.451–5(b). See Reg. § 1.451–5(c) for exceptions to this deferral opportunity. The financial accounting conformity requirement is not applicable to contractors who use the completed contract method.

Brown can elect to report the income for tax purposes in 2007, assuming the company reports the income in 2007 for financial reporting purposes. ■

(handwritten: — Year of receipt: proportionally calculated.)

Deferral of Advance Payments for Services.

Revenue Procedure 2004–34[44] permits an accrual basis taxpayer to defer recognition of income for *advance payments for services* to be performed after the end of the tax year of receipt. The portion of the advance payment that relates to services performed in the tax year of receipt is included in gross income in the tax year of receipt. The portion of the advance payment that relates to services to be performed after the tax year of receipt is included in gross income in the tax year following the tax year of receipt of the advance payment.

(handwritten: — Year after receipt: remaining amt of advance payment.)

Yellow Corporation, an accrual basis calendar year taxpayer, sells its services under 12-month, 24-month, and 36-month contracts. The corporation provides services to each customer every month. On May 1, 2006, Yellow Corporation sold the following customer contracts:

(handwritten: 8 months of 2006.)

Length of Contract	Total Proceeds
12 months	$3,000
24 months	4,800
36 months	7,200

Yellow may defer until 2007 all of the income that will be earned after 2006.

Length of Contract	Income Recorded in 2006	Income Recorded in 2007
12 months	$2,000 ($3,000 × 8/12)	$1,000 ($3,000 × 4/12)
24 months	1,600 ($4,800 × 8/24)	3,200 ($4,800 × 16/24)
36 months	1,600 ($7,200 × 8/36)	5,600 ($7,200 × 28/36) ■

(margin: EXAMPLE 19)

Revenue Procedure 2004–34 does not apply to prepaid rent or prepaid interest. These items are always taxed in the year of receipt.

Income Sources

Personal Services

It is a well-established principle of taxation that income from personal services must be included in the gross income of the person who performs the services. This principle was first established in a Supreme Court decision, *Lucas v. Earl.*[45] Mr. Earl entered into a binding agreement with his wife under which Mrs. Earl was to receive one-half of Mr. Earl's salary. Justice Holmes used the celebrated **fruit and tree metaphor** to explain that the fruit (income) must be attributed to the tree from which it came (Mr. Earl's services). A mere **assignment of income** does not shift the liability for the tax.

Services of an Employee.

Services performed by an employee for the employer's customers are considered performed by the employer. Thus, the employer is taxed on the income from the services provided to the customer, and the employee is taxed on any compensation received from the employer.[46]

(margin box:)

LO.3

Identify who should pay the tax on a particular item of income in various situations.

---

[44]2004–1 C.B. 991.

[45]2 USTC ¶496, 8 AFTR 10287, 50 S.Ct. 241 (USSC, 1930).

[46]*Sargent v. Comm.*, 91–1 USTC ¶50,168, 67 AFTR2d 91–718, 929 F.2d 1252 (CA–8, 1991).

EXAMPLE 20

Dr. Shontelle incorporates her medical practice and enters into a contract to work for the corporation for a salary. All patients contract to receive their services from the corporation, and those services are provided through the corporation's employee, Dr. Shontelle. The corporation must include the patients' fees in its gross income. Dr. Shontelle must include her salary in her gross income. The corporation is allowed a deduction for the reasonable salary paid to Dr. Shontelle (see the discussion of unreasonable compensation in Chapter 6). ■

Services of a Child. In the case of a child, the Code specifically provides that amounts earned from personal services must be included in the child's gross income. This result applies even though the income is paid to other persons (e.g., the parents).[47]

Income from Property

Income from property (interest, dividends, rent) must be included in the gross income of the *owner* of the property. If a father clips interest coupons from bonds shortly before the interest payment date and gives the coupons to his son, the interest will still be taxed to the father. A father who assigns rents from rental property to his daughter will be taxed on the rent since he retains ownership of the property.[48]

Often income-producing property is transferred after income from the property has accrued, but before the income is recognized under the transferor's method of accounting. The IRS and the courts have developed rules to allocate the income between the transferor and the transferee.

Interest. According to the IRS, interest accrues daily. Therefore, the interest for the period that includes the date of the transfer is allocated between the transferor and transferee based on the number of days during the period that each owned the property.

EXAMPLE 21

Floyd, a cash basis taxpayer, gave his son, Seth, bonds with a face amount of $10,000 and an 8% stated annual interest rate. The gift was made on January 31, 2006, and the interest was paid on December 31, 2006. Floyd must recognize $68 in interest income (8% × $10,000 × $31/365$). Seth will recognize $732 in interest income ($800 − $68). ■

When the transferor must recognize the income from the property depends upon the method of accounting and the manner in which the property was transferred. In the case of a gift of income-producing property, the donor must recognize his or her share of the accrued income at the time it would have been recognized had the donor continued to own the property.[49] However, if the transfer is a sale, the transferor must recognize the accrued income at the time of the sale. This results because the accrued interest will be included in the sales proceeds.

EXAMPLE 22

Assume the same facts as in Example 21, except that the interest that was payable as of December 31 was not actually or constructively received by the bondholders until January 3, 2007. As a cash basis taxpayer, Floyd generally does not recognize interest income until it is received. If Floyd had continued to own the bonds, the interest would have been included in his 2007 gross income, the year it would have been received. Therefore, Floyd must include the $68 accrued income in his gross income as of January 3, 2007.

---

[47]§ 73. For circumstances in which the child's unearned income is taxed at the parents' rate, see Unearned Income of Children under Age 14 Taxed at Parents' Rate in Chapter 3.

[48]*Galt v. Comm.*, 54–2 USTC ¶9457, 46 AFTR 633, 216 F.2d 41 (CA–7, 1954); *Helvering v. Horst*, 40–2 USTC ¶9787, 24 AFTR 1058, 61 S.Ct. 144 (USSC, 1940).
[49]Rev.Rul. 72–312, 1972–1 C.B. 22.

Further assume that Floyd sold identical bonds on the date of the gift. The bonds sold for $9,900, including accrued interest. On January 31, 2006, Floyd must recognize the accrued interest of $68 on the bonds sold. Thus, the selling price of the bonds is $9,832 ($9,900 − $68). ■

Dividends. A corporation is taxed on its earnings, and the shareholders are taxed on the dividends paid to them from the corporation's after-tax earnings. The dividend can take the form of an actual dividend or a constructive dividend (e.g., shareholder use of corporate assets).

Partial relief from the double taxation of dividends has been provided in the Jobs and Growth Tax Relief Reconciliation Act of 2003. Generally, dividends received in taxable years beginning after 2002 are taxed at the same marginal rate that is applicable to a net capital gain.[50] Thus, individuals otherwise subject to the 10 or 15 percent marginal tax rate pay only a 5 percent tax on qualified dividends received. Individuals subject to the 25, 28, 33, or 35 percent marginal tax rate pay a 15 percent tax on qualified dividends received. Thus, dividends receive favorable treatment as compared to interest income.

Note that qualified dividends are not treated as capital gains in the gains and losses netting process; thus, they are *not* reduced by capital losses. Qualified dividend income is merely taxed at the rates that would apply to the taxpayer if he or she had an excess of net long-term capital gain over net short-term capital loss.

Because the beneficial tax rate is intended to mitigate double taxation, only certain dividends are eligible for the beneficial treatment. Excluded are certain dividends from foreign corporations, dividends from tax-exempt entities, and dividends that do not satisfy the holding period requirement.

A dividend from a foreign corporation is eligible for qualified dividend status only if one of the following requirements is met: (1) the foreign corporation's stock is traded on an established U.S. securities market, or (2) the foreign corporation is eligible for the benefits of a comprehensive income tax treaty between its country of incorporation and the United States.

To satisfy the holding period requirement, the stock on which the dividend is paid must have been held for more than 60 days during the 120-day period beginning 60 days before the ex-dividend date.[51] The purpose of this requirement is to prevent the taxpayer from buying the stock shortly before the dividend is paid, receiving the dividend, and then selling the stock at a loss (a capital loss) after the stock goes ex-dividend. A stock's price often declines after the stock goes ex-dividend.

EXAMPLE 23

In June 2006, Green Corporation pays a dividend of $1.50 on each share of its common stock. Madison and Daniel, two unrelated shareholders, each own 1,000 shares of the stock. Consequently, each receives $1,500 (1,000 shares × $1.50). Assume Daniel satisfies the 60/120-day holding period rule, but Madison does not. The $1,500 Daniel receives is subject to preferential 15%/5% treatment. The $1,500 Madison receives, however, is not. Because Madison did not comply with the holding period rule, her dividend is not a *qualified dividend* and is taxed at ordinary income rates. ■

EXAMPLE 24

Assume that both Madison and Daniel in Example 23 are in the 35% tax bracket. Consequently, Madison pays a tax of $525 (35% × $1,500) on her dividend, while Daniel pays a tax of $225 (15% × $1,500) on his. The $300 saving that Daniel enjoys underscores the advantages of a qualified dividend. ■

---

[50]§ 1(h)(11).

[51]The ex-dividend date is the date following the record date on which the corporation finalizes the list of shareholders who will receive the dividends.

Unlike interest, dividends do not accrue on a daily basis because the declaration of a dividend is at the discretion of the corporation's board of directors. Generally, dividends are taxed to the person who is entitled to receive them—the shareholder of record as of the corporation's record date.[52] Thus, if a taxpayer sells stock after a dividend has been declared but before the record date, the dividend generally will be taxed to the purchaser.

If a donor makes a gift of stock to someone (e.g., a family member) after the declaration date but before the record date, the Tax Court has held that the donor does not shift the dividend income to the donee. The *fruit* has sufficiently ripened as of the declaration date to tax the dividend income to the donor of the stock.[53] In a similar set of facts, the Fifth Circuit Court of Appeals concluded that the dividend income should be included in the gross income of the donee (the owner at the record date). In this case, the taxpayer gave stock to a qualified charity (a charitable contribution) after the declaration date and before the record date.[54]

EXAMPLE 25

On June 20, the board of directors of Black Corporation declares a $10 per share dividend. The dividend is payable on June 30, to shareholders of record on June 25. As of June 20, Maria owned 200 shares of Black Corporation's stock. On June 21, Maria sold 100 of the shares to Norm for their fair market value and gave 100 of the shares to Sam (her son). Both Norm and Sam are shareholders of record as of June 25. Norm (the purchaser) will be taxed on $1,000 since he is entitled to receive the dividend. However, Maria (the donor) will be taxed on the $1,000 received by Sam (the donee) because the gift was made after the declaration date of the dividend. ■

ETHICAL *Considerations* ENHANCING LOTTERY WINNINGS

Some family members have net losses from gambling, which can be used only to reduce gambling gains. Another family member has a substantial gain from winning the lottery.

Suppose that the winner gives the winning ticket to the family members with gambling losses, thereby creating what is tantamount to tax-exempt income. Evaluate this proposal.

Income Received by an Agent

Income received by the taxpayer's agent is considered to be received by the taxpayer. A cash basis principal must recognize the income at the time it is received by the agent.[55]

EXAMPLE 26

Jack, a cash basis taxpayer, delivered cattle to the auction barn in late December. The auctioneer, acting as the farmer's agent, sold the cattle and collected the proceeds in December. The auctioneer did not pay Jack until the following January. Jack must include the sales proceeds in his gross income for the year the auctioneer received the funds. ■

Income from Partnerships, S Corporations, Trusts, and Estates

A **partnership** is not a separate taxable entity. Rather, the partnership merely files an information return (Form 1065), which serves to provide the data necessary for determining the character and amount of each partner's distributive share of the

---

[52]Reg. § 1.61–9(c). The record date is the cutoff for determining the shareholders who are entitled to receive the dividend.
[53]*M. G. Anton*, 34 T.C. 842 (1960).
[54]*Caruth Corp. v. U.S.*, 89–1 USTC ¶9172, 63 AFTR2d 89–716, 865 F.2d 644 (CA–5, 1989).
[55]Rev.Rul. 79–379, 1979–2 C.B. 204.

Mr. Banks sued his employer for employment discrimination and received a settlement. Banks's attorney received approximately one-third of the settlement, and Banks reasoned that he should include only the remaining amount in his gross income.

The U.S. Supreme Court disagreed. The Court applied "assignment of income" and "principal-agent" reasoning to conclude that Banks was required to include the entire settlement amount in his gross income. The Court considered the lawsuit a property interest. Banks controlled the lawsuit and diverted some of the proceeds to the attorney; that is, Banks assigned a portion of his income to the attorney. The Court rejected Banks's argument that he and the attorney were partners pursuing the lawsuit. Instead, the Court concluded that Banks and his attorney maintained a "quintessential principal-agent relationship," with the attorney-agent pursuing the rights of his principal, Banks. Under well-settled principles of tax law, the amount received as a result of the agent's efforts nevertheless belonged to Banks, the principal. According to the Court, the tax treatment of the amount due the attorney would have to be addressed through the tax deduction rules. For Mr. Banks, this deduction was classified as a miscellaneous itemized deduction subject to the 2 percent floor under § 67. After the Supreme Court decision, Congress modified § 67 to allow the deduction as a deduction *for* AGI.

Source: *Comm. v. Banks*, 2005–1 USTC ¶50,155, 95 AFTR2d 2005–659, 125 S.Ct. 826 (USSC, 2005).

partnership's income and deductions. Each partner must then report his or her distributive share of the partnership's income and deductions for the partnership's tax year ending within or with the partner's tax year. The income must be reported by each partner in the year it is earned, even if such amounts are not actually distributed to the partners. Because a partner pays tax on income as the partnership earns it, a distribution by the partnership to the partner is treated under the recovery of capital rules.[56]

EXAMPLE 27

Tara owns a one-half interest in the capital and profits of T & S Company (a calendar year partnership). For tax year 2006, the partnership earned revenue of $150,000 and had operating expenses of $80,000. During the year, Tara withdrew from her capital account $2,500 per month (for a total of $30,000). For 2006, Tara must report $35,000 as her share of the partnership's profits [½ × ($150,000 − $80,000)] even though she received distributions of only $30,000. ∎

Contrary to the general provision that a corporation must pay tax on its income, a *small business corporation* may elect to be taxed similarly to a partnership. Thus, the shareholders, rather than the corporation, pay the tax on the corporation's income.[57] The electing corporation is referred to as an **S corporation**. Generally, the shareholders report their proportionate shares of the corporation's income and deductions for the year, whether or not the corporation actually makes any distributions to the shareholders.

The *beneficiaries of estates and trusts* generally are taxed on the income earned by the estates or trusts that is actually distributed or required to be distributed to them.[58] Any income not taxed to the beneficiaries is taxable to the estate or trust.

Income in Community Property States

General. State law in Louisiana, Texas, New Mexico, Arizona, California, Washington, Idaho, Nevada, and Wisconsin is based upon a community property system. In Alaska, spouses can choose to have the community property rules apply. All other states have a common law property system. The basic difference between

[56]§ 706(a) and Reg. § 1.706–1(a)(1). For further discussion, see Chapter 20.
[57]§§ 1361(a) and 1366. For further discussion, see Chapter 20.
[58]§§ 652(a) and 662(a). For further discussion of the taxation of income from partnerships, S corporations, trusts, and estates, see *West Federal Taxation: Corporations, Partnerships, Estates, and Trusts*, Chapters 10, 11, 12, and 19.

TAX *in the News*   TRUST SPLITS INCOME FROM LOTTERY

The WLT Trust won the Pennsylvania Powerball Lottery in December 2004 and received $93.4 million. The trust had three related beneficiaries. Assuming all of the income was distributed, the income was split among three income tax returns and three tax rate schedules in 2004—the schedules of the three beneficiaries. The total income tax on the lottery winnings was less than if there had been only one winner.

Undoubtedly, the creator of the trust had such income splitting in mind when the trust was created, and the trust agreement provided a means for identifying which lottery tickets purchased by the relatives would be considered purchased by the trust.

Source: *Adapted from "Family Members Share Second-Largest Prize in PA Lottery History,"* **http://www.palottery.state.pa.us/lottery/cwp/view.asp?A=11&Q=479428**.

common law and community property systems centers around the property rights of married persons. Questions about community property income most frequently arise when the husband and wife file separate returns.

Under a **community property** system, all property is deemed either to be separately owned by the spouse or to belong to the marital community. Property may be held separately by a spouse if it was acquired before marriage or received by gift or inheritance following marriage. Otherwise, any property is deemed to be community property. For Federal tax purposes, each spouse is taxed on one-half of the income from property belonging to the community.

The laws of Texas, Louisiana, Wisconsin, and Idaho distinguish between separate property and the income it produces. In these states, the income from separate property belongs to the community. Accordingly, for Federal income tax purposes, each spouse is taxed on one-half of the income. In the remaining community property states, separate property produces separate income that the owner-spouse must report on his or her Federal income tax return.

What appears to be income, however, may really represent a recovery of capital. A recovery of capital and gain realized on separate property retain their identity as separate property. Items such as nontaxable stock dividends, royalties from mineral interests, and gains and losses from the sale of property take on the same classification as the assets to which they relate.

EXAMPLE 28

Bob and Jane are husband and wife and reside in California. Among other transactions during the year, the following occurred:

- Nontaxable stock dividend received by Jane on stock that was given to her after her marriage by her mother.
- Gain of $10,000 on the sale of unimproved land purchased by Bob before his marriage.
- Oil royalties of $15,000 from a lease Jane acquired after marriage with her separate funds.

Since the stock dividend was distributed on stock held by Jane as separate property, it also is her separate property. The same result occurs for the oil royalties Jane receives. All of the proceeds from the sale of the unimproved land (including the gain of $10,000) are Bob's separate property. ∎

In all community property states, income from personal services (e.g., salaries, wages, income from a professional partnership) is generally treated as if one-half is earned by each spouse.

EXAMPLE 29

Fred and Wilma are married but file separate returns. Fred received $25,000 salary and $300 taxable interest on a savings account he established in his name. The deposits to the savings account were made from Fred's salary that he earned since the marriage. Wilma collected

$2,000 taxable dividends on stock she inherited from her father. Wilma's gross income is computed as follows under three assumptions as to the state of residency of the couple:

	California	Texas	Common Law States
Dividends	$ 2,000	$ 1,000	$2,000
Salary	12,500	12,500	–0–
Interest	150	150	–0–
	$14,650	$13,650	$2,000

Community Property Spouses Living Apart. The general rules for taxing the income from services performed by residents of community property states can create complications and even inequities for spouses who are living apart.

Cole and Debra were married but living apart for the first nine months of 2006 and were divorced as of October 1, 2006. In December 2006, Cole married Emily, who was married but living apart from Frank before their divorce in June 2006. Cole and Frank had no income from personal services in 2006.

Cole brought into his marriage to Emily a tax liability on one-half of Debra's earnings for the first nine months of the year. However, Emily left with Frank a tax liability on one-half of her earnings for the first six months of 2006. ■

Congress has developed a simple solution to the many tax problems of community property spouses living apart. A spouse (or former spouse) is taxed only on his or her actual earnings from personal services if the following conditions are met:[59]

• The individuals live apart for the entire year.
• They do not file a joint return with each other.
• No portion of the earned income is transferred between the individuals.

Jim and Lori reside in a community property state, and both are gainfully employed. On July 1, 2006, they separated, and on June 30, 2007, they were divorced. Assuming their only source of income is wages, one-half of such income for each year is earned by June 30, and they did not file a joint return for 2006, each should report the following gross income:

	Jim's Separate Return	Lori's Separate Return
2006	One-half of Jim's wages	One-half of Jim's wages
	One-half of Lori's wages	One-half of Lori's wages
2007	All of Jim's wages	All of Lori's wages

The results would be the same if Jim or Lori married another person in 2007, except that the newlyweds would probably file a joint return. ■

The IRS may absolve from liability an *innocent spouse* who does not live apart for the entire year and files a separate return but omits his or her share of the community income received by the other spouse. To qualify for the innocent spouse relief, the taxpayer must not know or must have no reason to know of the omitted community income. Even if all of these requirements cannot be satisfied, the IRS has additional statutory authority to absolve the innocent spouse from tax liability. If, under the facts and circumstances, it is inequitable to hold the spouse liable for any unpaid tax, the IRS can absolve the spouse from tax liability.

[59]§ 66.

Items Specifically Included in Gross Income

The general principles of gross income determination (discussed in the previous sections) as applied by the IRS and the courts have on occasion yielded results Congress found unacceptable. Consequently, Congress has provided more specific rules for determining the gross income from certain sources. Some of these special rules appear in §§ 71–90 of the Code.

Alimony and Separate Maintenance Payments

When a married couple divorce or become legally separated, state law generally requires a division of the property accumulated during the marriage. In addition, one spouse may have a legal obligation to support the other spouse. The Code distinguishes between the support payments (alimony or separate maintenance) and the property division in terms of the tax consequences.

Alimony and separate maintenance payments are *deductible* by the party making the payments and are *includible* in the gross income of the party receiving the payments.[60] Thus, income is shifted from the income earner to the income beneficiary, who is better able to pay the tax on the amount received.

EXAMPLE 32

Pete and Tina are divorced, and Pete is required to pay Tina $15,000 of alimony each year. Pete earns $31,000 a year. The tax law presumes that because Tina receives the $15,000, she is better able than Pete to pay the tax on that amount. Therefore, Tina must include the $15,000 in her gross income, and Pete is allowed to deduct $15,000 from his gross income. ■

A transfer of property *other than cash* to a former spouse under a divorce decree or agreement is not a taxable event. The transferor is not entitled to a deduction and does not recognize gain or loss on the transfer. The transferee does not recognize income and has a cost basis equal to the transferor's basis.[61]

EXAMPLE 33

Paul transfers stock to Rosa as part of a 2006 divorce settlement. The cost of the stock to Paul is $12,000, and the stock's value at the time of the transfer is $15,000. Rosa later sells the stock for $16,000. Paul is not required to recognize gain from the transfer of the stock to Rosa, and Rosa has a realized and recognized gain of $4,000 ($16,000 − $12,000) when she sells the stock. ■

In the case of *cash payments*, however, it is often difficult to distinguish payments under a support obligation (alimony) and payments for the other spouse's property (property settlement). In 1984, Congress developed objective rules to classify the payments.

Post-1984 Agreements and Decrees. Payments made under post-1984 agreements and decrees are *classified as alimony* only if the following conditions are satisfied:

1. The payments are in cash.
2. The agreement or decree does not specify that the payments are not alimony.
3. The payor and payee are not members of the same household at the time the payments are made.
4. There is no liability to make the payments for any period after the death of the payee.[62]

---

[60]§§ 71 and 215.

[61]§ 1041, added to the Code in 1984 to repeal the rule of *U.S. v. Davis*, 62–2 USTC ¶9509, 9 AFTR2d 1625, 82 S.Ct. 1190 (USSC, 1962). Under the *Davis* rule, which applied to pre-1985 divorces, a property transfer incident to divorce was a taxable event.

[62]§ 71(b)(1). This set of alimony rules can also apply to pre-1985 agreements and decrees if both parties agree in writing. The rules applicable to pre-1985 agreements and decrees are not discussed in this text.

Tax Treatment of Payments and Transfers Pursuant to Post-1984 Divorce Agreements and Decrees

	Payor	Recipient
Alimony	Deduction from gross income.	Included in gross income.
Alimony recapture	Included in gross income of the third year.	Deducted from gross income of the third year.
Child support	Not deductible.	Not includible in gross income.
Property settlement	No income or deduction.	No income or deduction; basis for the property is the same as the transferor's basis.

Requirement 1 simplifies the law by clearly distinguishing alimony from a property division; that is, if the payment is not in cash, it must be a property division. Requirement 2 allows the parties to determine by agreement whether or not the payments will be alimony. The prohibition on cohabitation—requirement 3—is aimed at assuring the alimony payments are associated with duplicative living expenses (maintaining two households).[63] Requirement 4 is an attempt to prevent alimony treatment from being applied to what is, in fact, a payment for property rather than a support obligation. That is, a seller's estate generally will receive payments for property due after the seller's death. Such payments after the death of the payee could not be for the payee's support.

Front-Loading. As a further safeguard against a property settlement being disguised as alimony, special rules apply to post-1986 agreements if payments in the first or second year exceed $15,000. If the change in the amount of the payments exceeds statutory limits, **alimony recapture** results to the extent of the excess alimony payments. In the *third* year, the payor must include the excess alimony payments for the first and second years in gross income, and the payee is allowed a deduction for these excess alimony payments. The recaptured amount is computed as follows:[64]

$$R = D + E$$

$$D = B - (C + \$15,000)$$

$$E = A - \left(\frac{B - D + C}{2} + \$15,000 \right)$$

R = amount recaptured in Year 3 tax return
D = recapture from Year 2
E = recapture from Year 1
A, B, C = payments in the first (A), second (B), and third (C) calendar years of the agreement or decree, where $D \geq 0$, $E \geq 0$

The recapture formula provides an objective technique for determining alimony recapture. Thus, at the time of the divorce, the taxpayers can ascertain the tax consequences. The general concept is that if the alimony payments decrease by more than $15,000 between years in the first three years, there will be alimony recapture with respect to the decrease in excess of $15,000 each year. This rule is applied for the change between Year 2 and Year 3 (D in the above formula). However, rather than making the same calculation for Year 2 payments versus Year 1 payments, the Code requires that the *average* of the payments in Years 2 and 3 be compared with the Year 1

[63]*Alexander Washington*, 77 T.C. 601 (1981) at 604.　　[64]§ 71(f).

payments (E in the above formula). For this purpose, revised alimony for Year 2 (alimony deducted for Year 2 minus the alimony recapture for Year 2) is used.

EXAMPLE 34

Wes and Rita are divorced in 2006. Under the agreement, Rita is to receive $50,000 in 2006, $20,000 in 2007, and nothing thereafter. The payments are to cease upon Rita's death or remarriage. In 2008, Wes must include an additional $32,500 in gross income for alimony recapture, and Rita is allowed a deduction for the same amount.

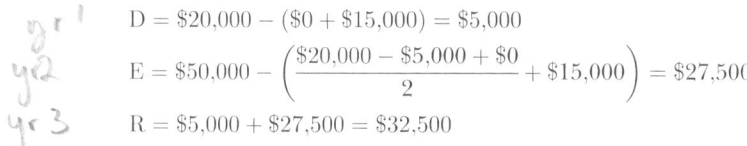

$$D = \$20,000 - (\$0 + \$15,000) = \$5,000$$

$$E = \$50,000 - \left(\frac{\$20,000 - \$5,000 + \$0}{2} + \$15,000\right) = \$27,500$$

$$R = \$5,000 + \$27,500 = \$32,500$$

Note that for 2006 Wes deducts alimony of $50,000, and Rita includes $50,000 in her gross income. For 2007, the amount of the alimony deduction for Wes is $20,000, and Rita's gross income from the alimony is $20,000.

If instead Wes paid $50,000 of alimony in 2006 and nothing for the following years, $35,000 would be recaptured in 2008.

$$D = \$0 - (\$0 + \$15,000) = -\$15,000, \text{ but D must be } \geq \$0$$

$$E = \$50,000 - \left(\frac{\$0 - \$0 + \$0}{2} + \$15,000\right) = \$35,000$$

$$R = \$0 + \$35,000 = \$35,000$$ ■

Alimony recapture does not apply if the decrease in payments is due to the death of either spouse or the remarriage of the payee.[65] Recapture is not applicable because these events typically terminate alimony under state laws. In addition, the recapture rules do not apply to payments where the amount is contingent (e.g., a percentage of income from certain property or a percentage of the payor spouse's compensation), the payments are to be made over a period of three years or longer (unless death, remarriage, or other contingency occurs), and the contingencies are beyond the payor's control.[66]

EXAMPLE 35

Under a 2006 divorce agreement, Ed is to receive an amount equal to one-half of Nina's income from certain rental properties for 2006–2009. Payments are to cease upon the death of Ed or Nina or upon the remarriage of Ed. Ed receives $50,000 in 2006 and $50,000 in 2007; in 2008, however, the property is vacant, and Ed receives nothing. Nina, who deducted alimony in 2006 and 2007, is not required to recapture any alimony in 2008 because the payments were contingent. ■

ETHICAL *Considerations*   AVOIDING FRONT-LOADING WITH EQUAL PAYMENTS

Ike and Tina accumulated substantial assets during their marriage. In the divorce negotiations, Tina is willing to allow Ike to take title to some of the jointly owned assets, but she expects a cash payment in exchange. Ike is concerned that under the front-loading rules for alimony, a lump-sum cash payment will result in gross income to him in the third year. He proposes to make equal annual cash payments over the next four years to Tina, rather than a lump-sum payment

now. However, Tina does not want the amount she is entitled to receive to be subject to the risk that Ike will not be able to make future payments. Therefore, Ike proposes that he will place the lump-sum amount in an escrow account to be held by his attorney, and Tina will be permitted to withdraw an equal amount each year for the next four years (plus interest). Will Ike's plan achieve the tax avoidance he desires? Is the plan ethical?

---

[65]§ 71(f)(5)(A).   [66]§ 71(f)(5)(C).

Child Support. A taxpayer does not realize income from the receipt of child support payments made by his or her former spouse. This result occurs because the money is received subject to the duty to use the money for the child's benefit. The payor is not allowed to deduct the child support payments because the payments are made to satisfy the payor's legal obligation to support the child.

In many cases, it is difficult to determine whether an amount received is alimony or child support. If the amount of the payments would be reduced upon the happening of a contingency related to a child (e.g., the child attains age 21 or dies), the amount of the future reduction in the payment is deemed child support.[67]

E X A M P L E   3 6

A divorce agreement provides that Matt is required to make periodic alimony payments of $500 per month to Grace. However, when Matt and Grace's child reaches age 21, marries, or dies (whichever occurs first), the payments will be reduced to $300 per month. Grace has custody of the child. Since the required contingency is the cause for the reduction in the payments, from $500 to $300, child support payments are $200 per month, and alimony is $300 per month. ■

Imputed Interest on Below-Market Loans

As discussed earlier in the chapter, generally no income is recognized unless it is realized. Realization generally occurs when the taxpayer performs services or sells goods and thus becomes entitled to a payment from the other party. It follows that no income is realized if the goods or services are provided at no charge. Under this interpretation of the realization requirement, before 1984, interest-free loans were used to shift income between taxpayers.

E X A M P L E   3 7

Veneia (daughter) is in the 20% (combined Federal and state rates) tax bracket and has no investment income. Kareem (father) is in the 50% (combined Federal and state rates) tax bracket and has $200,000 in a money market account earning 10% interest. Kareem would like Veneia to receive and pay tax on the income earned on the $200,000. Because Kareem would also like to have access to the $200,000 should he need the money, he does not want to make an outright gift of the money, nor does he want to commit the money to a trust.

Before 1984, Kareem could achieve his goals as follows. He could transfer the money market account to Veneia in exchange for her $200,000 non-interest-bearing note, payable on Kareem's demand. As a result, Veneia would receive the income, and the family's taxes would be decreased by $6,000.

Decrease in Kareem's tax—	
(.10 × $200,000).50 =	($10,000)
Increase in Veneia's tax—	
(.10 × $200,000).20 =	4,000
Decrease in the family's taxes	($ 6,000) ■

Under the 1984 amendments to the Code, Kareem in Example 37 is required to recognize **imputed interest** income.[68] Veneia is deemed to have incurred interest expense equal to Kareem's imputed interest income. Veneia's interest may be deductible on her return as investment interest if she itemizes deductions (see Chapter 10). To complete the fictitious series of transactions, Kareem is then deemed to have given Veneia the amount of the imputed interest she did not pay. The gift received by Veneia is not subject to income tax (see Chapter 5), although Kareem may be subject to the gift tax (unified transfer tax) on the amount deemed given to Veneia (refer to Chapter 1).

---

[67]§ 71(c)(2).   [68]§ 7872(a)(1).

Imputed interest is calculated using the rate the Federal government pays on new borrowings and is compounded semiannually. This Federal rate is adjusted monthly and is published by the IRS.[69] Actually, there are three Federal rates: short-term (not over three years and including demand loans), mid-term (over three years but not over nine years), and long-term (over nine years).[70]

EXAMPLE 38

Assume the Federal rate applicable to the loan in Example 37 is 7% through June 30 and 8% from July 1 through December 31. Kareem made the loan on January 1, and the loan is still outstanding on December 31. Kareem must recognize interest income of $15,280, and Veneia has interest expense of $15,280. Kareem is deemed to have made a gift of $15,280 to Veneia.

[handwritten: Kareen's income : +15,280]
[handwritten: V's income : −15,280]

Interest calculations:	
January 1–June 30—	
.07($200,000) (½ year)	$ 7,000
July 1–December 31—	
.08($200,000 + $7,000) (½ year)	8,280
	$15,280

If interest is charged on the loan but is less than the Federal rate, the imputed interest is the difference between the amount that would have been charged at the Federal rate and the amount actually charged.

EXAMPLE 39

Assume the same facts as in Example 38, except that Kareem charged 6% interest, compounded annually.

[handwritten: If Kareem chrg V 6% loan]
[handwritten: ⇒ K : +3,280]
[handwritten: V = −3280]

Interest at the Federal rate	$ 15,280
Less interest charged (.06 × $200,000)	(12,000)
Imputed interest	$ 3,280

The imputed interest rules apply to the following *types* of below-market loans:[71]

1. Gift loans (made out of love, affection, or generosity, as in Example 37).
2. Compensation-related loans (employer loans to employees).
3. Corporation-shareholder loans (a corporation's loans to its shareholders).
4. Tax avoidance loans and other loans that significantly affect the borrower's or lender's Federal tax liability (discussed in the following paragraphs).

The effects of the first three types of loans on the borrower and lender are summarized in Concept Summary 4–2.

Tax Avoidance and Other Below-Market Loans. In addition to the three specific types of loans that are subject to the imputed interest rules, the Code includes a catchall provision for *tax avoidance loans* and other arrangements that have a significant effect on the tax liability of the borrower or lender. The Conference Report provides the following example of an arrangement that might be subject to the imputed interest rules.[72]

EXAMPLE 40

Annual dues for the Good Health Club are $400. In lieu of paying dues, a member can make a $4,000 deposit, refundable at the end of one year. The club can earn $400 interest on the deposit.

---

[69] §§ 7872(b)(2) and (f)(2).
[70] § 1274(d).
[71] § 7872(c).
[72] H. Rep. No. 98–861, 98th Cong., 2d Sess., 1984, p. 1023.

CONCEPT SUMMARY 4–2

Effect of Certain Below-Market Loans on the Lender and Borrower

Type of Loan		Lender	Borrower
Gift	Step 1	Interest income	Interest expense
	Step 2	Gift made	Gift received
Compensation-related	Step 1	Interest income	Interest expense
	Step 2	Compensation expense	Compensation income
Corporation to shareholder	Step 1	Interest income	Interest expense
	Step 2	Dividend paid	Dividend income

If interest were not imputed, an individual with $4,000 could, in effect, earn tax-exempt income on the deposit. That is, rather than invest the $4,000, earn $400 in interest, pay tax on the interest, and then pay $400 in dues, the individual could avoid tax on the interest by making the deposit. Thus, income and expenses are imputed as follows: interest income and nondeductible health club fees for the club member; income from fees and interest expense for the club. ∎

Many commercially motivated transactions could be swept into this other below-market loans category. However, the Temporary Regulations have carved out a frequently encountered exception for customer prepayments. If the prepayments are included in the recipient's income under the recipient's method of accounting, the payments are not considered loans and, thus, are not subject to the imputed interest rules.[73]

Exceptions and Limitations. No interest is imputed on total outstanding *gift loans* of $10,000 or less between individuals, unless the loan proceeds are used to purchase income-producing property.[74] This exemption eliminates from these complex provisions immaterial amounts that do not result in apparent shifts of income. However, if the proceeds of such a loan are used to purchase income-producing property, the limitations discussed in the following paragraphs apply instead.

On loans of $100,000 or less between individuals, the imputed interest cannot exceed the borrower's net investment income for the year (gross income from all investments less the related expenses).[75] As discussed above, one of the purposes of the imputed interest rules is to prevent high-income taxpayers from shifting income to relatives in a lower marginal bracket. This shifting of investment income is considered to occur only to the extent the borrower has net investment income. Thus, the income imputed to the lender is limited to the borrower's net investment income. As a further limitation, or exemption, if the borrower's net investment income for the year does not exceed $1,000, no interest is imputed on loans of $100,000 or less. However, these limitations for loans of $100,000 or less do not apply if a principal purpose of a loan is tax avoidance. In such a case, interest is imputed, and the imputed interest is not limited to the borrower's net investment income.[76]

[73]Prop.Reg. § 1.7872–2(b)(1)(i).
[74]§ 7872(c)(2).
[75]§ 7872(d).

[76]*Deficit Reduction Tax Bill of 1984: Explanation of the Senate Finance Committee* (April 2, 1984), p. 484.

TAX *in the News* — LOANS TO EXECUTIVES PROHIBITED

Interest-free loans have become a popular form of compensation for executives. Several examples of multimillion-dollar loans have come to light as a result of recent bankruptcies by large corporations. The board of directors often justifies the loans as necessary to enable the executive to purchase a residence or to buy stock in the company.

Loans by publicly held corporations to their executives are now generally prohibited by Federal law. The Sarbanes-Oxley Act of 2002 (Public Law No. 107–294) places a general prohibition on loans by corporations to their executives. However, an exception permits corporate loans to finance the acquisition of a personal residence for an executive.

EXAMPLE 41

Vicki made interest-free gift loans as follows:

Borrower	Amount	Borrower's Net Investment Income	Purpose
Susan	$ 8,000	$ –0–	Education
Dan	9,000	500	Purchase of stock
Bonnie	25,000	–0–	Purchase of a business
Megan	90,000	15,000	Purchase of a residence
Olaf	120,000	–0–	Purchase of a residence

Assume that tax avoidance is not a principal purpose of any of the loans. The loan to Susan is not subject to the imputed interest rules because the $10,000 exception applies. The $10,000 exception does not apply to the loan to Dan because the proceeds were used to purchase income-producing assets. However, under the $100,000 exception, the imputed interest is limited to Dan's investment income ($500). Since the $1,000 exception also applies to this loan, no interest is imputed.

No interest is imputed on the loan to Bonnie because the $100,000 exception applies. Interest is imputed on the loan to Megan based on the lesser of (1) the borrower's $15,000 net investment income or (2) the interest as calculated by applying the Federal rate to the outstanding loan. None of the exceptions apply to the loan to Olaf because the loan was for more than $100,000.

Assume the relevant Federal rate is 10% and the loans were outstanding for the entire year. Vicki would recognize interest income, compounded semiannually, as follows:

Loan to Megan:	
First 6 months (.10 × $90,000 × ½ year)	$ 4,500
Second 6 months (.10 × $94,500 × ½ year)	4,725
	$ 9,225

Loan to Olaf:	
First 6 months (.10 × $120,000 × ½ year)	$ 6,000
Second 6 months (.10 × $126,000 × ½ year)	6,300
	$12,300

| Total imputed interest ($9,225 + $12,300) | $21,525 |

As with gift loans, there is a $10,000 exemption for *compensation-related loans* and *corporation-shareholder loans*. However, the $10,000 exception does not apply if tax avoidance is one of the principal purposes of a loan.[77] This vague tax avoidance standard makes practically all compensation-related and corporation-shareholder

[77]§ 7872(c)(3).

CONCEPT SUMMARY 4-3

Exceptions to the Imputed Interest Rules for Below-Market Loans

Exception	Eligible Loans	Ineligible Loans and Limitations
De minimis—aggregate loans of $10,000 or less	Gift loans	Proceeds used to purchase income-producing assets.
	Employer-employee	Principal purpose is tax avoidance.
	Corporation-shareholder	Principal purpose is tax avoidance.
Aggregate loans of $100,000 or less	Between individuals	Principal purpose is tax avoidance. For all other loans, interest is imputed to the extent of the borrower's net investment income if that income exceeds $1,000.

loans suspect. Nevertheless, the $10,000 exception should apply when an employee's borrowing was necessitated by personal needs (e.g., to meet unexpected expenses) rather than tax considerations.

These exceptions to the imputed interest rules are summarized in Concept Summary 4–3.

Income from Annuities

Annuity contracts generally require the purchaser (the annuitant) to pay a fixed amount for the right to receive a future stream of payments. Typically, the issuer of the contract is an insurance company and will pay the annuitant a cash value if the annuitant cancels the contract. The insurance company invests the amounts received from the annuitant, and the income earned serves to increase the cash value of the policy. No income is recognized by the annuitant at the time the cash value of the annuity increases because the taxpayer has not actually received any income. The income is not constructively received because, generally, the taxpayer must cancel the policy to receive the increase in value (the increase in value is subject to substantial restrictions).

EXAMPLE 42

Jean, age 50, pays $30,000 for an annuity contract that is to pay her $500 per month beginning when she reaches age 65 and continuing until her death. If Jean should cancel the policy after one year, she would receive $30,200. The $200 increase in value is not includible in Jean's gross income as long as she does not actually receive the $200. ■

The tax accounting problem associated with receiving payments under an annuity contract is one of apportioning the amounts received between recovery of capital and income.

EXAMPLE 43

In 2006, Tom purchased for $15,000 an annuity intended as a source of retirement income. In 2008, when the cash value of the annuity is $17,000, Tom collects $1,000 on the contract. Is the $1,000 gross income, recovery of capital, or a combination of recovery of capital and income? ■

The statutory solution to this problem depends upon whether the payments began before or after the annuity starting date and upon when the policy was acquired.

Collections before the Annuity Starting Date. Generally, an annuity contract specifies a date on which monthly or annual payments will begin—the annuity starting date. Often the contract will also allow the annuitant to collect a limited amount before the starting date. The amount collected may be characterized as either an actual withdrawal of the increase in cash value or a loan on the policy. In 1982, Congress changed the rules applicable to these withdrawals and loans.

Collections (including loans) equal to or less than the post-August 13, 1982 increases in cash value must be included in gross income. Amounts received in excess of post-August 13, 1982 increases in cash value are treated as a recovery of capital until the taxpayer's cost has been entirely recovered. Additional amounts are included in gross income.[78]

The taxpayer may also be subject to a penalty on early distributions of 10 percent of the income recognized. The penalty generally applies if the amount is received before the taxpayer reaches age 59½ or is disabled.[79] The early distribution penalty is deemed necessary to prevent taxpayers from using annuities as a way of avoiding the original issue discount rules. That is, the investment in the annuity earns a return that is not taxed until it is collected under the annuity rules, whereas the interest on a certificate of deposit is taxed each year as the income accrues. Thus, the annuity offers a tax advantage (deferral of income) that Congress does not want exploited.

EXAMPLE 44

Jack, age 50, purchased an annuity policy for $30,000 in 2004. In 2006, when the cash value of the policy has increased to $33,000, Jack withdraws $4,000. He must recognize $3,000 of income ($33,000 cash value − $30,000 cost) and must pay a penalty of $300 ($3,000 × 10%). The remaining $1,000 is a recovery of capital and reduces Jack's basis in the annuity policy. ■

Collections on and after the Annuity Starting Date. The annuitant can exclude from income (as a recovery of capital) the proportion of each payment that the investment in the contract bears to the expected return under the contract. The *exclusion amount* is calculated as follows:

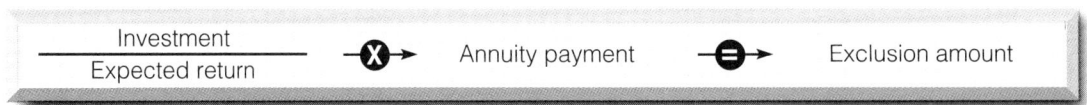

$$\frac{\text{Investment}}{\text{Expected return}} \quad \bigotimes \longrightarrow \quad \text{Annuity payment} \quad \bigominus \longrightarrow \quad \text{Exclusion amount}$$

The *expected return* is the annual amount to be paid to the annuitant multiplied by the number of years the payments will be received. The payment period may be fixed (a *term certain*) or for the life of one or more individuals. When payments are for life, the taxpayer generally must use the annuity table published by the IRS to determine the expected return (see Table 4–1). This is an actuarial table that contains life expectancies.[80] The expected return is calculated by multiplying the appropriate multiple (life expectancy) by the annual payment.

EXAMPLE 45

The taxpayer, age 54, purchases an annuity from an insurance company for $90,000. She is to receive $500 per month for life. Her life expectancy (from Table 4–1) is 29.5 years from the annuity starting date. Thus, her expected return is $500 × 12 × 29.5 = $177,000, and the exclusion amount is $3,051 [($90,000 investment/$177,000 expected return) × $6,000

---

[78]§ 72(e)(3); Reg. § 1.72–9.

[79]§ 72(q).

[80]The life expectancies in Table 4–1 apply for annuity investments made on or after July 1, 1986. See *General Rules for Pensions and Annuities*, IRS Publication

939 (Rev. April 2003), p. 25. See also *Pension and Annuity Income*, IRS Publication 575 (Rev. Feb. 2004).

TABLE 4–1	Ordinary Life Annuities: One Life—Expected Return Multiples				

Age	Multiple	Age	Multiple	Age	Multiple
5	76.6	42	40.6	79	10.0
6	75.6	43	39.6	80	9.5
7	74.7	44	38.7	81	8.9
8	73.7	45	37.7	82	8.4
9	72.7	46	36.8	83	7.9
10	71.7	47	35.9	84	7.4
11	70.7	48	34.9	85	6.9
12	69.7	49	34.0	86	6.5
13	68.8	50	33.1	87	6.1
14	67.8	51	32.2	88	5.7
15	66.8	52	31.3	89	5.3
16	65.8	53	30.4	90	5.0
17	64.8	54	29.5	91	4.7
18	63.9	55	28.6	92	4.4
19	62.9	56	27.7	93	4.1
20	61.9	57	26.8	94	3.9
21	60.9	58	25.9	95	3.7
22	59.9	59	25.0	96	3.4
23	59.0	60	24.2	97	3.2
24	58.0	61	23.3	98	3.0
25	57.0	62	22.5	99	2.8
26	56.0	63	21.6	100	2.7
27	55.1	64	20.8	101	2.5
28	54.1	65	20.0	102	2.3
29	53.1	66	19.2	103	2.1
30	52.2	67	18.4	104	1.9
31	51.2	68	17.6	105	1.8
32	50.2	69	16.8	106	1.6
33	49.3	70	16.0	107	1.4
34	48.3	71	15.3	108	1.3
35	47.3	72	14.6	109	1.1
36	46.4	73	13.9	110	1.0
37	45.4	74	13.2	111	.9
38	44.4	75	12.5	112	.8
39	43.5	76	11.9	113	.7
40	42.5	77	11.2	114	.6
41	41.5	78	10.6	115	.5

annual payment]. The $3,051 is a nontaxable return of capital, and $2,949 is included in gross income. ∎

The *exclusion ratio* (investment ÷ expected return) applies until the annuitant has recovered his or her investment in the contract. Once the investment is recovered, the entire amount of subsequent payments is taxable. If the annuitant dies

TABLE 4-2	Number of Anticipated Monthly Annuity Payments under the Simplified Method

Age	Number of Anticipated Monthly Payments
55 and under	360
56–60	310
61–65	260
66–70	210
71 and over	160

before recovering the investment, the unrecovered cost (adjusted basis) is deductible in the year the payments cease (usually the year of death).[81]

EXAMPLE 46

Assume the taxpayer in Example 45 receives annuity payments for 30.5 years (366 months). For the last 12 months [366 − (12 × 29.5) = 12], the taxpayer will include $500 each month in gross income. If instead the taxpayer dies after 36 months, she is eligible for an $80,847 deduction on her final tax return.

Cost of the contract	$90,000
Cost previously recovered	
$90,000/$177,000 × 36($500) =	(9,153)
Deduction	$80,847

Simplified Method for Annuity Distributions from Qualified Retirement Plans. A simplified method is required for allocating basis to the annuity payments received under a qualified retirement plan. The portion of each annuity payment that is excluded as a return of capital is the employee's investment in the contract divided by the number of anticipated monthly payments determined in accordance with Table 4–2.[82]

EXAMPLE 47

Andrea, age 62, receives an annuity distribution of $500 per month for life from her qualified retirement plan beginning in January 2006. Her investment in the contract is $100,100. The excludible amount of each payment is $385 ($100,100 investment/260 monthly payments). Thus, $115 ($500 − $385) of each annuity payment is included in Andrea's gross income. ∎

The rules for annuity payments received after the basis has been recovered by the annuitant and for the annuitant who dies before the basis is recovered are the same as under the exclusion ratio method discussed earlier.

Prizes and Awards

The fair market value of prizes and awards (other than scholarships exempted under § 117, to be discussed subsequently) must be included in gross income.[83] Therefore, TV giveaway prizes, magazine publisher prizes, door prizes, and awards from an employer to an employee in recognition of performance are fully taxable to the recipient.

[81]§ 72(b).
[82]§ 72(d).
[83]§ 74.

TAX *in the News*	***SURVIVOR* WINNER DID NOT SURVIVE IRS AUDIT**

Richard Hatch received $1 million as the winner of CBS's first *Survivor* contest. However, he failed to include the prize in his gross income for the year it was received, although it was clearly an increase in wealth realized. He has been charged with tax evasion and has entered a plea of "not guilty." His defense is that CBS was responsible for paying the tax. According to CBS, Hatch knew that it was his responsibility to pay the income tax on the money.

Source: *Adapted from* ***http://www.thesmokinggun.com/archive/0118051hatch1.html*** *and "Survivor Champion Pleads Not Guilty to Tax, Fraud Charges,"* Wall Street Journal, *September 20, 2005, p. D2.*

A narrow exception permits a prize or award to be excluded from gross income if *all* of the following requirements are satisfied:

- The prize or award is received in recognition of religious, charitable, scientific, educational, artistic, literary, or civic achievement (e.g., Nobel Prize, Pulitzer Prize).
- The recipient transfers the prize or award to a qualified governmental unit or nonprofit organization.
- The recipient was selected without any action on his or her part to enter the contest or proceeding.
- The recipient is not required to render substantial future services as a condition for receiving the prize or award.[84]

Because the transfer of the property to a qualified governmental unit or nonprofit organization ordinarily would be a charitable contribution (an itemized deduction as presented in Chapter 10), the exclusion produces beneficial tax consequences in the following situations:

- The taxpayer does not itemize deductions and thus would receive no tax benefit from the charitable contribution.
- The taxpayer's charitable contributions exceed the annual statutory ceiling on the deduction.
- Including the prize or award in gross income would reduce the amount of deductions the taxpayer otherwise would qualify for because of gross income limitations (e.g., the gross income test for a dependency exemption, the adjusted gross income limitation in calculating the medical expense deduction).

Another exception is provided for certain *employee achievement awards* in the form of tangible personal property (e.g., a gold watch). The awards must be made in recognition of length of service or safety achievement. Generally, the ceiling on the excludible amount for an employee is $400 per taxable year. However, if the award is a qualified plan award, the ceiling on the exclusion is $1,600 per taxable year.[85]

Group Term Life Insurance

For many years, the IRS did not attempt to tax the value of life insurance protection provided to an employee by the employer. Some companies took undue advantage of the exclusion by providing large amounts of insurance protection for executives. Therefore, Congress enacted § 79, which created a limited exclusion for **group term life insurance**. The premiums on the first $50,000 of group term life insurance protection are excludible from the employee's gross income.

---

[84]§ 74(b).   [85]§§ 74(c) and 274(j).

TABLE 4–3	Uniform Premiums for $1,000 of Group Term Life Insurance Protection

Attained Age on Last Day of Employee's Tax Year	Cost per $1,000 of Protection for One-Month Period*
Under 25	$ .05
25–29	.06
30–34	.08
35–39	.09
40–44	.10
45–49	.15
50–54	.23
55–59	.43
60–64	.66
65–69	1.27
70 and above	2.06

*Reg. § 1.79–3, effective for coverage after June 30, 1999.

The benefits of this exclusion are available only to employees. Proprietors and partners are not considered employees. The Regulations generally require broad-scale coverage of employees to satisfy the *group* requirement (e.g., shareholder-employees would not constitute a qualified group). The exclusion applies only to term insurance (protection for a period of time but with no cash surrender value) and not to ordinary life insurance (lifetime protection plus a cash surrender value that can be drawn upon before death).

As mentioned, the exclusion applies to the first $50,000 of group term life insurance protection. For each $1,000 of coverage in excess of $50,000, the employee must include the amounts indicated in Table 4–3 in gross income.[86]

EXAMPLE 48

Finch Corporation has a group term life insurance policy with coverage equal to the employee's annual salary. Keith, age 52, is president of the corporation and receives an annual salary of $75,000. Keith must include $69 in gross income from the insurance protection for the year.

$$\frac{\$75,000 - \$50,000}{\$1,000} \times .23 \times 12 \text{ months} = \$69$$

Generally, the amount that must be included in gross income, computed from Table 4–3, is much less than the price an individual would pay an insurance company for the same amount of protection. Thus, even the excess coverage provides some tax-favored income for employees when group term life insurance coverage in excess of $50,000 is desirable.

If the plan discriminates in favor of certain key employees (e.g., officers), the key employees are not eligible for the exclusion. In such a case, the key employees must include in gross income the *greater* of actual premiums paid by the employer or the amount calculated from the Uniform Premiums in Table 4–3. The other employees are still eligible for the $50,000 exclusion and continue to use the Uniform Premiums table to compute the income from excess insurance protection.[87]

[86]Reg. § 1.79–3(d)(2).   [87]§ 79(d).

Unemployment Compensation

The unemployment compensation program is sponsored and operated by the states and Federal government to provide a source of income for people who have been employed and are temporarily (hopefully) out of work. In a series of rulings over a period of 40 years, the IRS exempted unemployment benefits from tax. These payments were considered social benefit programs for the promotion of the general welfare. After experiencing dissatisfaction with the IRS's treatment of unemployment compensation, Congress amended the Code to provide that the benefits are taxable.[88]

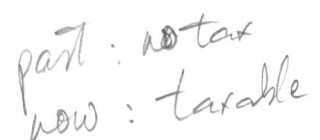

Social Security Benefits

If a taxpayer's income exceeds a specified base amount, as much as 85 percent of Social Security retirement benefits must be included in gross income. The taxable amount of benefits is determined through the application of one of two formulas that utilize a unique measure of income—*modified adjusted gross income (MAGI)*.[89] MAGI is, generally, the taxpayer's adjusted gross income from all sources (other than Social Security) plus the foreign earned income exclusion and any tax-exempt interest income.

In the formulas, two sets of base amounts are established. The first set is as follows:

- $32,000 for married taxpayers who file a joint return.
- $0 for married taxpayers who do not live apart for the entire year but file separate returns.
- $25,000 for all other taxpayers.

The second set of base amounts is as follows:

- $44,000 for married taxpayers who file a joint return.
- $0 for married taxpayers who do not live apart for the entire year but file separate returns.
- $34,000 for all other taxpayers.

If MAGI plus one-half of Social Security benefits exceeds the first set of base amounts, but not the second set, the taxable amount of Social Security benefits is the *lesser* of the following:

- .50(Social Security benefits).
- .50[MAGI + .50(Social Security benefits) − first base amount].

---

[88]§ 85.

[89]§ 86. The rationale for taxing 85% of the Social Security benefits is as follows: For the average Social Security recipient, 15% of the amount received is a recovery of amounts that the individual paid into the program, and the remainder of the benefits is financed by the employer's contribution and interest earned by the Social Security fund.

EXAMPLE 49

A married couple with adjusted gross income of $30,000, no tax-exempt interest, and $11,000 of Social Security benefits who file jointly must include $1,750 of the benefits in gross income. This works out as the lesser of the following:

1. .50($11,000) = $5,500.
2. .50[$30,000 + .50($11,000) − $32,000] = .50($3,500) = $1,750.

If instead the couple had adjusted gross income of $15,000 and their Social Security benefits totaled $5,000, none of the benefits would be taxable, since .50[$15,000 + .50($5,000) − $32,000] is not a positive number. ■

If MAGI plus one-half of Social Security benefits exceeds the second set of base amounts, the taxable amount of Social Security benefits is the *lesser* of 1 or 2 below:

1. .85(Social Security benefits).
2. Sum of:
   a. .85[MAGI + .50(Social Security benefits) − second base amount], and
   b. Lesser of:
      • Amount included through application of the first formula.
      • $4,500 ($6,000 for married filing jointly).

EXAMPLE 50

A married couple who file jointly have adjusted gross income of $72,000, no tax-exempt interest, and $12,000 of Social Security benefits. Their includible Social Security benefits will be $10,200.

Include the lesser of the following:

1. .85($12,000) = $10,200.
2. Sum of:
   a. .85[$72,000 + .50($12,000) − $44,000] = $28,900, and
   b. Lesser of:
      • Amount calculated by the first formula, which is the lesser of:
         • .50($12,000) = $6,000.
         • .50[$72,000 + .50($12,000) − $32,000] = $23,000.
      • $6,000.

The sum equals $34,900 ($28,900 + $6,000). Since 85% of the Social Security benefits received is less than this amount, $10,200 is included in the couple's gross income. ■

LO.5

Identify tax planning strategies for minimizing gross income.

The materials in this chapter have focused on the following questions:

• What is income?
• When is the income recognized?
• Who is the taxpayer?

TAX PLANNING
Considerations

Planning strategies suggested by these materials include the following:

• Maximize economic benefits that are not included in gross income.
• Defer the recognition of income.
• Shift income to taxpayers who are in a lower marginal tax bracket.

Some specific techniques for accomplishing these strategies are discussed in the following paragraphs.

Nontaxable Economic Benefits

Home ownership is the prime example of economic income from capital that is not subject to tax. If the taxpayer uses his or her capital to purchase investments, but pays rent on a personal residence, the taxpayer would pay the rent from after-tax income. However, if the taxpayer purchases a personal residence instead of the investments, he or she would give up gross income from the forgone investments in exchange for the rent savings. The savings in rent enjoyed as a result of owning the home are not subject to tax. Thus, the homeowner will have substituted nontaxable for taxable income.

Tax Deferral

General. Since deferred taxes are tantamount to interest-free loans from the government, the deferral of taxes is a worthy goal of the tax planner. However, the tax planner must also consider the tax rates for the years the income is shifted from and to. For example, a one-year deferral of income from a year in which the taxpayer's tax rate was 28 percent to a year in which the tax rate will be 35 percent would not be advisable if the taxpayer expects to earn less than a 7 percent after-tax return on the deferred tax dollars.

The taxpayer can often defer the recognition of income from appreciated property by postponing the event triggering realization (the final closing on a sale or exchange of property). If the taxpayer needs cash, obtaining a loan by using the appreciated property as collateral may be the least costly alternative. When the taxpayer anticipates reinvesting the proceeds, a sale may be inadvisable.

EXAMPLE 51

Ira owns 100 shares of Pigeon Company common stock with a cost of $20,000 and a fair market value of $50,000. Although the stock's value has increased substantially in the past three years, Ira thinks the growth days are over. If he sells the Pigeon stock, Ira will invest the proceeds from the sale in other common stock. Assuming Ira's marginal tax rate on the sale is 15%, he will have only $45,500 [$50,000 − .15($50,000 − $20,000)] to reinvest. The alternative investment must substantially outperform Pigeon in the future in order for the sale to be beneficial. ∎

Selection of Investments. Because no tax is due until a gain has been recognized, the law favors investments that yield appreciation rather than annual income.

EXAMPLE 52

Vera can buy a corporate bond or an acre of land for $10,000. The bond pays $1,000 of interest (10%) each year, and Vera expects the land to increase in value 10% each year for the next 10 years. She is in the 40% (combined Federal and state) tax bracket for ordinary income and 26% for qualifying capital gains. Assuming the bond would mature or the land would be sold in 10 years and Vera would reinvest the interest at a 10% before-tax return, she would accumulate the following amount at the end of 10 years.

		Bond	Land
Original investment		$10,000	$10,000
Annual income	$ 1,000		
Less tax	(400)		
	$ 600		
Compound amount reinvested for 10 years at 6% after-tax	×13.18	7,908	
		$17,908	
Compound amount, 10 years at 10%			× 2.59
			$25,900
Less tax on sale:			
26%($25,900 − $10,000)			(4,134)
			$21,766

Therefore, the value of the deferral that results from investing in the land rather than in the bond is $3,858 ($21,766 − $17,908). ∎

Series EE bonds can also be purchased for long-term deferrals of income. In situations where the taxpayer's goal is merely to shift income one year into the future, bank certificates of deposit are useful tools. If the maturity period is one year or less, all interest is reported in the year of maturity. Time certificates are especially useful for a taxpayer who realizes an unusually large gain from the sale of property in one year (and thus is in a high tax bracket) but expects his or her gross income to be less the following year.

Cash Basis. The timing of income from services can often be controlled through the use of the cash method of accounting. Although taxpayers are somewhat constrained by the constructive receipt doctrine (they cannot turn their backs on income), seldom will customers and clients offer to pay before they are asked. The usual lag between billings and collections (e.g., December's billings collected in January) will result in a continuous deferring of some income until the last year of operations. A salaried individual approaching retirement may contract with the employer before the services are rendered to receive a portion of compensation in the lower tax bracket retirement years.

Prepaid Income. For the accrual basis taxpayer who receives advance payments from customers, the transactions should be structured to avoid payment of tax on income before the time the income is actually earned. Revenue Procedure 2004–34 provides the guidelines for deferring the tax on prepayments for services, and Regulation § 1.451–5 provides the guidelines for deferrals on sales of goods. In addition, both cash and accrual basis taxpayers can sometimes defer income by stipulating that the payments are deposits rather than prepaid income. For example, a landlord should require an equivalent damage deposit rather than prepayment of the last month's rent under the lease.

Shifting Income to Relatives

The tax liability of a family can be minimized by shifting income from higher- to lower-bracket family members. This can be accomplished through gifts of income-producing property. Furthermore, in many cases, income can be shifted with no negative effect on the family's investment plans.

EXAMPLE 53

Adam, who is in the 28% tax bracket, would like to save for his children's education. All of the children are under 14 years of age. Adam could transfer income-producing properties to the children, and the children could each receive up to $850 of income each year (refer to Chapter 3) with no tax liability. The next $850 would be taxed at the child's tax rate. After a child has more than $1,700 income, there is no tax advantage to shifting more income to the child (because the income will be taxed at the parents' rate) until the child is 14 years old (when all income will be taxed according to the child's tax rate). ■

The Uniform Gifts to Minors Act, a model law adopted by all states (but with some variations among the states), facilitates income shifting. Under the Act, a gift of intangibles (e.g., bank accounts, stocks, bonds, life insurance contracts) can be made to a minor but with an adult serving as custodian. Usually, a parent who makes the gift is also named as custodian. The state laws allow the custodian to sell or redeem and reinvest the principal and to accumulate or distribute the income, practically at the custodian's discretion provided there is no commingling of the child's income with the parent's property. Thus, the parent can give appreciated securities to the child, and the donor custodian can then sell the securities and reinvest the proceeds, thereby shifting both the gain and the annual income to the child. Such planning is limited by the tax liability calculation provision for a child under the age of 14 (refer to Chapter 3).

U.S. government bonds (Series EE) can be purchased by parents for their children. When this is done, the children generally should file a return and elect to report the income on the accrual basis.

Abby pays $7,500 for Series EE bonds in 2006 and immediately gives them to Wade (her son), who will enter college the year of original maturity of the bonds. The bonds have a maturity value of $10,000. Wade elects to report the annual increment in redemption value as income for each year the bonds are held. The first year the increase is $250, and Wade includes that amount in his gross income. If Wade has no other income, no tax will be due on the $250 bond interest, since such an amount will be more than offset by his available standard deduction. The following year, the increment is $260, and Wade includes this amount in income. Thus, over the life of the bonds, Wade will include $2,500 in income ($10,000 − $7,500), none of which will result in a tax liability, assuming he has no other income. However, if the election had not been made, Wade would be required to include $2,500 in income on the bonds in the year of original maturity, if they were redeemed as planned. This amount of income might result in a tax liability. ■

In some cases, it may be advantageous for the child not to make the accrual election. For example, a child under age 14 with investment income of more than $1,700 each year and parents in the 25, 28, 33, or 35 percent tax bracket would probably benefit from deferring the tax on the savings bond interest. The child would also benefit from the use of the usually lower tax rate (rather than subjecting the income to the parents' tax rate) if the bonds mature after the child is age 14 or older.

Accounting for Community Property

The classification of income as community or separate property becomes important when either of two events occurs:

- Husband and wife, married taxpayers, file separate income tax returns for the year.
- Husband and wife obtain a divorce and therefore have to file separate returns for the year (refer to Chapter 3).

For planning purposes, it behooves married persons to keep track of the source of income (community or separate). To be in a position to do this effectively when income-producing assets are involved, it may be necessary to distinguish between separate and community property.[90]

Alimony

The person making the alimony payments favors a divorce settlement that includes a provision for deductible alimony payments. On the other hand, the recipient prefers that the payments do not qualify as alimony. If the payor is in a higher tax bracket than the recipient, both parties may benefit by increasing the payments and structuring them so that they qualify as alimony.

Carl and Polly are negotiating a divorce settlement. Carl has offered to pay Polly $10,000 each year for 10 years, but payments would cease upon Polly's death. Polly is willing to accept the offer, if the agreement will specify that the cash payments are not alimony. Carl is in the 35% tax bracket, and Polly's marginal rate is 15%.

---

[90]Being able to distinguish between separate and community property is crucial to the determination of a property settlement incident to a divorce. It also is vital in the estate tax area (refer to Chapter 1) since the surviving wife's or husband's share of the community property is not included in the gross estate of the deceased spouse.

If Carl and Polly agree that Carl will pay Polly $12,000 of alimony each year, both will have improved after-tax cash flows.

| | Annual Cash Flows | |
	Carl	Polly
Nonalimony payments	($10,000)	$10,000
Alimony payments	($12,000)	$12,000
Tax effects		
.35($12,000)	4,200	
.15($12,000)		(1,800)
After-tax cash flows	($ 7,800)	$10,200
Benefit of alimony option	$ 2,200	$ 200

Both parties benefit at the government's expense if the $12,000 alimony option is used. ■

KEY TERMS

Accounting income, 4–4

Accounting method, 4–7

Accrual method, 4–8

Alimony and separate maintenance payments, 4–20

Alimony recapture, 4–21

Annuity, 4–27

Assignment of income, 4–13

Cash receipts method, 4–7

Claim of right doctrine, 4–8

Community property, 4–18

Constructive receipt, 4–9

Economic income, 4–3

Fruit and tree metaphor, 4–13

Gross income, 4–2

Group term life insurance, 4–31

Hybrid method, 4–9

Imputed interest, 4–23

Income, 4–3

Original issue discount, 4–10

Partnership, 4–16

Recovery of capital doctrine, 4–6

S corporation, 4–17

Taxable year, 4–6

PROBLEM MATERIALS

DISCUSSION QUESTIONS

1. The conservatism principle has been found useful for financial accounting purposes. Why have the IRS and the courts chosen not to adopt this principle for tax accounting purposes?

2. In each of the following, determine the taxpayer's "income" for the current year as computed by an economist and as computed for tax purposes. Explain any differences.
   a. A cash basis taxpayer overcharged a customer by billing her twice for the same item in 2005. The taxpayer notified the customer of the mistake in December 2005 and refunded the overcharge in January 2006.
   b. In the previous year, the taxpayer purchased stock for $4,000. By the end of the year, the stock had declined in value to $3,000. In the current year, the taxpayer sold the stock for $6,500.
   c. The taxpayer, a carpenter, purchased a house for investment for $100,000. He renovated the house. The taxpayer spent $14,000 on materials, and he estimates that the value of his time spent on the work (what he would have charged a customer for the same work) was $20,000. He sold the property the following year for $140,000.

d.   The sole shareholder in a corporation purchased property from the corporation for $10,000. The fair market value of the property was $15,000.

3. Charley visits Reno, Nevada, once each year to gamble. This year his gambling loss was $15,000. He commented to you, "At least I didn't have to pay for my airfare and hotel room. The casino paid that because I am such a good customer. That was worth at least $2,500." What are the relevant tax issues for Charley?

Issue ID

4. Tom's job requires 40 hours of work each week, and he is never required to work overtime. He gets one month of vacation each year. Tom uses his weekends and two weeks of his vacation to make repairs and improvements to his personal residence. Ed's job requires considerable overtime, and he has only two weeks of vacation each year. Because his job demands so much of his time, Ed is required to pay others to make repairs and improvements to his personal residence. Under these circumstances, does the tax law favor Tom or Ed?

5. Cecil buys wrecked cars and stores them on his property. Recently, he purchased a 1990 Ford Taurus for $250. If he can sell all of the usable parts, his total proceeds from the Taurus would be over $2,000. As of the end of the year, he has sold only the radio for $50, and he does not know how many, if any, of the remaining parts will ever be sold. What are Cecil's income recognition issues?

Issue ID

6. An employee receives a $3,000 payment from a customer in late 2006 and submits the payment to the employer in early 2007. When is the cash basis employer required to include the $3,000 in gross income?

7. Jared, a self-employed insect exterminator, uses the cash method of accounting to report his income. In December 2006, Jared received a check for $400 from a client. Jared deposited the check near the end of December. In early January 2007, the bank notified him that the check did not clear because of insufficient funds in the customer's account. The bank sent the check through a second time, and it cleared in January 2007. Jared computes his income using his deposit records. Therefore, he included the $400 in his 2006 gross income.
   a.   In what year should Jared report the $400 of income?
   b.   Why does it matter to Jared whether he reports the income in 2006 or 2007, as long as he actually reports it?

8. In 2006, Albert found dinosaur bones on a tract of land that he had owned for several years. When Albert bought the property, he was unaware that the bones were there. An appraiser told him the bones were worth $25,000. In 2007, Albert sold the bones to a museum for $26,000.
   a.   What is Albert's gross income in 2006 from the discovery of the bones?
   b.   What is Albert's gross income in 2007 from the sale of the bones?

9. Allyson, a cash basis taxpayer, pays $889 for a 4% certificate of deposit (CD) that is to pay her $1,000 at maturity. She purchases the certificate on July 1, 2006, and it will mature on June 30, 2009. Allyson holds the CD until maturity.
   a.   Under the original issue discount (OID) rules, for which years does the CD affect Allyson's gross income?
   b.   Do you think that the OID rules were enacted for equitable reasons, out of concern for the taxpayer's burden in complying with the law, or for other reasons?

10. What tax advantage does a Series EE U.S. government savings bond due in three years have over a bank CD due in three years that does not pay interest until the maturity date?

11. Coal, Inc., an accrual basis taxpayer, sells goods under terms that allow a customer who is not completely satisfied to return the goods within 30 days of receipt and receive a refund of the purchase price. On December 15, 2006, a customer purchased a product for $500. Coal's cost was $400. The customer returned the product on January 5, 2007, and received a refund of $500. How do these transactions affect Coal's gross income for:
   a.   2006?
   b.   2007?

12. Rex paid $4,000 for an automobile that needed substantial repairs. He worked nights and weekends to restore the car and spent $1,200 on parts for it. He knows he can sell

[handwritten margin note: Give: tax on her bracket. Same amt of tax inc.]

the car for $9,000. His daughter's college tuition is due in a few days. Would it matter, after taxes, whether Rex sells the car and pays the tuition, or whether he gives the car to his daughter and she sells it for $9,000 and pays her tuition?

13. Sarah, a cash basis taxpayer, sued her former employer for wage discrimination. Her attorney agreed to pursue the case on a contingent fee basis—the attorney would receive one-third of any settlement or court award. The parties reached a settlement, and the attorney for Sarah's former employer wrote a check payable to Sarah for $200,000 and a check payable to her attorney for $100,000. Sarah reasons that she and the attorney were partners in the lawsuit who shared profits two-thirds and one-third. Therefore, she includes $200,000 in her gross income. Is Sarah's analysis correct? Explain.

14. Who pays the tax on (a) the income of an S corporation and (b) the income of a partnership?

Issue ID

15. Mike and Debbie were residents of California. In 2006, Debbie left Mike, and he has been unable to find her even though he hired a private investigator to do so. Mike and Debbie are still married at year-end. Both Debbie and Mike were employed, and each had substantial investments. They did not have any children. How will Debbie's absence complicate Mike's 2006 income tax return?

16. Why do the alimony rules require alimony recapture when certain large cash payments are made in the first three years after a divorce?

Decision Making

[handwritten margin note: Security]

17. Sam and Jean are negotiating their divorce agreement, which requires the division of their jointly owned property. Sam has proposed that he receive the couple's house (basis of $60,000 and fair market value of $100,000) while Jean would receive (a) securities (basis of $115,000 and fair market value of $100,000) or (b) five annual payments of $23,739 each, which is equivalent to a $100,000 loan at 6% interest. Jean will probably sell the securities if she receives them. Jean has too many unhappy memories about the house and does not want to live in it or own it. Which option should she accept?

Issue ID

18. William and Abigail, who live in San Francisco, have been experiencing problems with their marriage. They have a three-year-old daughter, April, who stays with William's parents during the day since both William and Abigail are employed. Abigail worked to support William while he attended medical school, and now she has been accepted by a medical school in Mexico. Abigail has decided to divorce William and attend medical school. April will stay in San Francisco because of her strong attachment to her grandparents and because they can provide her with excellent day care. Abigail knows that William will expect her to contribute to the cost of raising April. Abigail also feels that, to finance her education, she must receive cash for her share of the property they accumulated during their marriage. In addition, she feels she should receive some reimbursement for her contribution to William's support while he was in medical school. She expects the divorce proceedings will take several months. Identify the relevant tax issues for Abigail.

Decision Making

[handwritten margin note: - Basis of sec. - Alimony or not.]

19. Bob and Mary are planning to divorce. Bob has offered to pay Mary $12,000 each year for 10 years or to transfer to her common stock he owns with a fair market value of $100,000 in satisfaction of Mary's share of the marital property. What factors should Mary consider in deciding between these two options?

20. In the case of a below-market loan between relatives, why does the borrower not recognize income from the transaction?

21. Rose Corporation made a $1 million interest-free loan to its new chief executive officer on July 1, 2006, so that he could acquire a personal residence. The Federal rate is 6%. What are the tax consequences of the loan to the CEO and to Rose?

Issue ID

22. Brad is the president of the Yellow Corporation. He and other members of his family control the corporation. Brad has a temporary need for $50,000, and the corporation has excess cash. He could borrow the money from a bank at 9%, and Yellow is earning 6% on its temporary investments. Yellow has made loans to other employees on several occasions. Therefore, Brad is considering borrowing $50,000 from the corporation. He will repay the loan principal in two years plus interest at 5%. Identify the relevant tax issues for Brad and the Yellow Corporation.

23. When Betty was 78 years old, she purchased an annuity contract for $75,600. The contract was to pay her $8,900 per year over her remaining life. How much of the annuity payment for the twelfth year would Betty be required to include in her gross income if she actually lived for 13 years after the annuity payments began?

24. Given the broad concept of gross income contained in the Internal Revenue Code, does § 79 applicable to group term life insurance assure that some premiums can be excluded from gross income, or does it assure that some of the premiums in certain circumstances will be included in gross income?

25. Evelyn is 66 years old and unmarried. She receives $12,000 a year in Social Security benefits and a taxable pension of $15,000 from her employer's retirement plan. According to the tax rate schedule, she is in the 15% marginal tax bracket on her Federal income tax return and the 5% marginal tax bracket (the top tax rate) on her state income tax return. The state bases her state taxable income on her Federal taxable income. She claims the standard deduction on both her Federal and state returns. If Evelyn earns an additional $3,000 of income from a part-time job, what would her marginal tax rate for Federal and state income tax be on that income? How much would her after-tax earnings be from the part-time job?

PROBLEMS

26. Compute the taxpayer's current-year (1) economic income and (2) gross income for tax purposes from the following events:

    a. A college football coach received $450,000 to terminate his long-term employment contract.

    b. A high school student received $800 for mowing his neighbor's lawn during the summer.

    c. The taxpayer sold securities for $12,000. The securities cost $5,000 four years ago. The fair market value of the securities at the beginning of the year was $10,000.

    d. The taxpayer owned land that increased in value by $200,000 when a major retailer announced plans to build a store on adjoining property.

    e. The taxpayer raises cattle. He began the year with no cattle. During the year, he spent $23,000 to purchase cattle and to feed them. His receipts from the sale of the cattle were $45,000. He and his family consumed cattle he raised with a value of $1,000, and there were no cattle on hand at the end of the year.

    f. The taxpayer's employer allowed her to use a company automobile on her vacation. The rental value of the automobile for the vacation period was $1,000.

N/A   450 K

800   800

21K   7K

200 K   ∅

23K   22.5K

27. Amos recently completed medical school and is beginning his medical practice. Most of his patients are covered by health insurance with a co-pay requirement (e.g., the patient pays $10, and the insurance company is billed for the remainder). It takes approximately two months to collect from the health insurance plan. What advice can you provide Amos regarding the selection of a tax accounting method?

Issue ID

Cash method.

28. Which of the following investments of $10,000 each will yield the greater after-tax value assuming the taxpayer is in the 35% tax bracket for ordinary income and 15% for qualifying capital gains and dividends in all years and the investments will be liquidated at the end of five years?

    a. Land that will increase in value by 6% each year.

    b. A taxable bond yielding 6% before tax, and the interest can be reinvested at 6% before tax.

    c. Common stock paying a 5% dividend each year that can be reinvested in common stock paying a 5% dividend each year. The value of the stock will not change.

    Prepare a brief speech for your tax class in which you explain why the future value of the land will exceed the future value of the taxable bond. Also explain why the after-tax return on the stock will exceed the after-tax return earned on the bond.

Decision Making

Communications

Given: Compound amount of $1 and compound value of annuity payments at the end of five years:

Interest Rate	$1 Compounded for 5 Years	$1 Annuity Compounded for 5 Years
6%	$1.34	$5.64
3.90%	1.20	5.39
4.25%	1.23	5.44

29. Determine the taxpayer's gross income for tax purposes in each of the following situations:
    a. Olga, a cash basis taxpayer, sold a corporate bond with accrued interest of $200 for $10,500. Olga's cost of the bond was $10,000.
    b. Olga needed $10,000 to make a down payment on her house. She instructed her broker to sell some stock to raise the $10,000. Olga's cost of the stock was $3,000. Based on her broker's advice, instead of selling the stock, she borrowed the $10,000 using the stock as collateral for the debt.
    c. Olga owned a vacant lot that was zoned for residential housing. She spent $900 in attorney fees to get the property rezoned as commercial. The property's value increased by $10,000 as a result of the rezoning.

30. Determine Amos Seagull's gross income in each of the following cases:
    a. In the current year, Seagull Corporation purchased an automobile for $25,000. The company was to receive a $1,500 rebate from the manufacturer. However, the corporation directed that the rebate be paid to Amos, the corporation's sole shareholder.
    b. Amos sold his corporation. In addition to the selling price of the stock, he received $50,000 for a covenant not to compete—an agreement that he will not compete with his former business for five years.
    c. Amos and his neighbor got into an argument over Amos's dog. The neighbor built a fence to keep the dog out of his yard. The fence added $1,500 to the value of Amos's property.

Decision Making

31. Al is an attorney who conducts his practice as a sole proprietor. During 2006, he received cash of $150,000 for legal services. Of the amount collected, $25,000 was for services provided in 2005. At the end of 2006, Al had accounts receivable of $45,000, all for services rendered in 2006. At the end of the year, Al received $5,000 as a deposit on property a client was in the process of selling. Compute Al's gross income for 2006:
    a. Using the cash basis of accounting.
    b. Using the accrual basis of accounting.
    c. Advise Al on which method of accounting he should use.

32. Selma opened a farm implements store in 2006. The only accounting records she maintains are her cash receipts and disbursements for the business. Cash receipts for 2006 total $500,000, and cash disbursements (for inventory) total $350,000. The cash receipts include the $50,000 Selma originally invested in the business and a $5,000 customer deposit on a new tractor that is to be delivered by the factory in January 2007. You determine that there were no accounts receivable at the beginning of the year. At the end of the year, accounts receivable total $15,000. The inventory on hand at the end of the year is $75,000, and $40,000 is owed to vendors for inventory purchases received before year-end. Determine the gross income for the store for 2006 for tax purposes.

Decision Making

Communications

33. Your client is a new partnership, Aspen Associates, which is an engineering consulting firm. Generally, Aspen bills clients for services at the end of each month. Client billings are about $50,000 each month. On average, it takes 45 days to collect the receivables. Aspen's expenses are primarily for salary and rent. Salaries are paid on the last day of each month, and rent is paid on the first day of each month. The partnership has a line of credit with a bank, which requires monthly financial statements. These must be prepared using the accrual method. Aspen's managing partner, Amanda Sims, has suggested that the firm should also use the accrual method for tax purposes and thus reduce accounting fees by $600. Assume the partners are in the 35% (combined Federal and state) marginal tax bracket. Write a letter to your client explaining why you believe

it would be worthwhile for Aspen to file its tax return on the cash basis even though its financial statements are prepared on the accrual basis. Aspen's address is 100 James Tower, Denver, CO 80208.

34. Color Paint Shop, Inc. (459 Ellis Avenue, Harrisburg, PA 17111), is an accrual basis taxpayer that paints automobiles. During the year, the company painted Samuel's car and was to receive a $1,000 payment from his insurance company. Samuel was not satisfied with the work, however, and the insurance company refused to pay. In December 2006, Color and Samuel agreed that Color would receive $800 for the work, subject to final approval by the insurance company. In the past, Color had come to terms with customers only to have the insurance company negotiate an even lesser amount. In May 2007, the insurance company reviewed the claim and paid the $800 to Color. An IRS agent thinks that Color, as an accrual basis taxpayer, should report $1,000 of income in 2006, when the work was done, and then deduct a $200 loss in 2007. Prepare a memo to Susan Apple, a tax partner for whom you are working, with the recommended treatment for the disputed income.

Communications

35. Determine the effect of the following on a cash basis taxpayer's gross income for 2005 and 2006:
    a. In December 2005, the taxpayer negotiated his employment contract for 2006. The employer offered to pay the taxpayer $10,000 in December 2005 as a signing bonus and a $100,000 salary to be paid in 2006. The taxpayer rejected that offer but agreed to receive the $100,000 salary in 2006, and $15,000 to be received in four years.
    b. In addition to a signing bonus of $10,000 to be paid in December 2005, the taxpayer was to receive $10,000 on the last day of each month in 2006. On December 31, 2006, the taxpayer told his employer to pay the December salary on January 1, 2007.
    c. The taxpayer charges $100 per hour for his services. On December 31, 2006, the taxpayer worked eight hours for a client. The client told the taxpayer that his wife had the checkbook, but if the taxpayer would wait until the wife returned, the client would pay the $800. The taxpayer had another appointment, however, and told the client to mail him a check instead. The taxpayer received the check on January 2, 2007.

36. Morris is not one to take a lot of risks. All of his investments are in Series EE U.S. government savings bonds and bank CDs. Determine the tax consequences from his investments for 2006.
    a. On June 30, 2006, he cashed in Series EE bonds that he had purchased in 1996. His cost of the bonds was $6,139, and the maturity value was $10,000. This is an effective before-tax yield of 5% per year. Morris did not elect to take the annual increments in value into income each year.
    b. On September 30, 2006, Morris redeemed a two-year CD, interest rate of 4%, that he had purchased from the local bank on October 1, 2004. He paid $9,244 for the CD and received $10,000 at maturity. He immediately invested the $10,000 in a one-year CD, interest rate of 5%, with a maturity value of $10,500.

37. Swan Appliance Company, an accrual basis taxpayer, sells home appliances and service contracts. Determine the effect of each of the following transactions on the company's 2006 gross income assuming that the company uses any available options to defer its taxes.
    a. In December 2005, the company received a $1,200 advance payment from a customer for an appliance that Swan special ordered from the manufacturer. The appliance did not arrive from the manufacturer until January 2006, and Swan immediately delivered it to the customer. The sale was reported in 2006 for financial accounting purposes.
    b. In June 2006, the company sold a 12-month service contract for $240. The company also sold a 24-month service contract for $480 in December 2006.
    c. On December 31, 2006, the company sold an appliance for $1,200. The company received $500 cash and a note from the customer for $700 and $260 interest, to be paid at the rate of $40 a month for 24 months. Because of the customer's poor credit record, the fair market value of the note was only $600. The cost of the appliance was $750.

38. Freda is a cash basis taxpayer. In 2006, she negotiated her salary for 2007. Her employer offered to pay her $20,000 each month—a total of $240,000 for the year. Freda countered that she would accept $20,000 each month for the first nine months of the

year and the remaining $60,000 in January 2008. The employer accepted Freda's terms for 2007 and 2008.

    a. Did Freda actually or constructively receive $240,000 in 2007?

    b. What could explain Freda's willingness to spread her salary over a longer period of time?

Decision Making

39. The Bonhaus Apartments is a new development and is in the process of structuring its lease agreements. The company would like to set the damage deposits high enough that tenants will keep the apartments in good condition. The company is actually more concerned about damage than about tenants not paying their rent.

    a. Discuss the tax effects of the following alternatives:
- $400 damage deposit and $400 rent for the final month of the lease.
- $800 rent for the final two months of the lease and no damage deposit.
- $800 damage deposit with no rent prepayment.

    b. Which option do you recommend?

40. Gus was unable to pay his bills as they came due. One of his creditors got a court order to garnish Gus's royalty receipts from a book contract. In addition, his royalties were garnished for child support. His earnings statement from the publishing company for the year reflected the following:

Royalties	$125,000
Payments to creditors	(20,000)
Child support payments	(12,000)
Received by Gus	$ 93,000

    a. Gus reasons that he received a benefit of only $93,000 and, therefore, that is what he should include in his gross income. Is Gus correct?

    b. Gus also owns all of the stock of a corporation that owns an apartment building. Gus put the apartment building in the corporation to limit his legal liability. He collects all of the rent and pays all of the expenses. Rent received is $48,000, and expenses are $30,000. Gus included $18,000 in his gross income. Is this correct?

    c. Same as (b) except the corporation made an S election.

41. Tracy, a cash basis taxpayer, is employed by Eagle Corporation, also a cash basis taxpayer. Tracy is a full-time employee of the corporation and receives a salary of $60,000 per year. He also receives a bonus equal to 10% of all collections from clients he serviced during the year. Determine the tax consequences of the following events to the corporation and to Tracy:

    a. On December 31, 2006, Tracy was visiting a customer. The customer gave Tracy a $3,000 check payable to the corporation for appraisal services Tracy performed during 2006. Tracy did not deliver the check to the corporation until January 2007.

    b. The facts are the same as in (a), except that the corporation is an accrual basis taxpayer and Tracy deposited the check on December 31, but the bank did not add the deposit to the corporation's account until January 2007.

    c. The facts are the same as in (a), except that the customer told Tracy to hold the check until January when the customer could make a bank deposit that would cover the check.

42. Fran, Gary, and Heidi each have a one-third interest in the capital and profits of the FGH Partnership. Each partner had a capital account of $50,000 at the beginning of the tax year. The partnership profits for the tax year were $180,000. Changes in their capital accounts during the tax year were as follows:

	Fran	Gary	Heidi	Total
Beginning balance	$ 50,000	$ 50,000	$ 50,000	$150,000
Withdrawals	(20,000)	(25,000)	(10,000)	(55,000)
Additional contributions	–0–	–0–	5,000	5,000
Allocation of profits	60,000	60,000	60,000	180,000
Ending balance	$ 90,000	$ 85,000	$105,000	$280,000

In arriving at the $180,000 of partnership profits, the partnership deducted $1,800 ($600 for each partner) in premiums paid for group term life insurance on the partners. Fran and Gary are 39 years old, and Heidi is 35 years old. Other employees are also eligible for group term life insurance equal to their annual salary. These premiums of $10,000 have been deducted in calculating the partnership profits of $180,000. Compute each partner's gross income from the partnership for the tax year.

43. In 2006, Alva received dividends on her stocks as follows:

Amur Corporation (a French corporation whose stock is traded on an established U.S. securities market)	$55,000
Blaze, Inc., a Delaware corporation	25,000
Grape, Inc., a Virginia corporation	12,000

a. Alva purchased the Grape stock four years ago, and she purchased the Amur stock two years ago. She purchased the Blaze stock 15 days before it went ex-dividend and sold it 20 days later at a $22,000 loss. Alva had no other capital gains and losses for the year. She is in the 35% marginal tax bracket. Compute Alva's tax on her dividend income for 2006.
b. Alva's daughter, who is not Alva's dependent, had taxable income of $6,000, which included $1,000 of dividends on Grape, Inc. stock. The daughter had purchased the stock two years ago. Compute the daughter's tax liability on the dividends.
c. Alva can earn 5% before-tax interest on a corporate bond or a 4% dividend on a preferred stock. Assuming the appreciation in value is the same, which investment produces the greater after-tax income?
d. Same as part (c), except Alva's daughter is to make the investment.

44. Liz and Doug were divorced on July 1 of the current year after 10 years of marriage. Their current year's income received before the divorce was as follows:

Doug's salary	$41,000
Liz's salary	55,000
Rent on apartments purchased by Liz 15 years ago	6,000
Dividends on stock Doug inherited from his mother 4 years ago	1,900
Interest on a savings account in Liz's name funded with her salary	1,800

Allocate the income to Liz and Doug assuming they live in:
a. California.
b. Texas.

45. Nell and Kirby are in the process of negotiating their divorce agreement. What would be the tax consequences to Nell and Kirby if the following, considered individually, became part of the agreement?
a. Nell and Kirby will continue as joint owners of the personal residence. Nell can continue to occupy the residence as long as she so desires. If she ever sells the residence, however, Kirby will receive one-half the proceeds. The fair rental value of the residence is $2,000 per month.
b. Nell will receive $1,000 per month for 100 months, and Kirby will receive the $180,000 in securities (adjusted basis is $100,000) that were formerly owned jointly by the couple. If Nell dies before she receives all of the payments, Kirby is not required to continue the payments.
c. Nell is to have custody of their 12-year-old son and is to receive $600 per month until (1) the child dies or (2) attains age 21 (whichever occurs first).

46. Karen and Al are in the process of negotiating a divorce agreement. Al believes that Karen should pay him at least $30,000 per year, but he would like to get as much in the first two years in cash as the tax law will permit to be treated as alimony. He is willing to surrender his one-half interest in some stock in exchange for more cash. Karen and Al own stock worth $120,000 that originally cost $80,000. Al is aware that Karen is very concerned about the tax consequences of the divorce agreement. What would be the tax consequences of the following alternative agreements?
a. Al receives $30,000 per year for life and one-half of the jointly owned stock.
b. Al receives $50,000 per year in Years 1, 2, and 3 and $30,000 per year for the remainder of his life. He does not receive any of the stock.
c. Al receives $80,000 in Year 1 and $30,000 per year for the remainder of his life.

47. Under the terms of their divorce agreement, Barry is to transfer common stock (cost of $25,000, market value of $60,000) to Sandra. Barry and Sandra have a 14-year-old child. Sandra will have custody of the child, and Barry is to pay $300 per month as child support. In addition, Sandra is to receive $1,000 per month for 10 years, or until her death if earlier. However, the payments will be reduced to $750 per month when their child reaches age 21. In the first year under the agreement, Sandra receives the common stock and the correct cash payments for six months. How will the terms of the agreement affect Sandra's gross income?

Decision Making

48. Roy decides to buy a personal residence and goes to the bank for a $150,000 loan. The bank tells him he can borrow the funds at 7% if his father will guarantee the debt. Roy's father, Hal, owns CDs currently yielding 6%. The Federal rate is 5%. Hal is willing to do either of the following:

    • Cash in the CDs and lend Roy the funds at 6% interest.
    • Guarantee the loan for Roy.

    Hal will consider lending the funds to Roy at an even lower interest rate, depending on the tax consequences. Hal is in the 35% marginal tax bracket. Roy, whose only source of income is his salary, is in the 15% marginal tax bracket. The interest Roy pays on the mortgage will be deductible by him. Considering only the tax consequences, which option will maximize the family's after-tax wealth?

49. On June 30, 2006, Ridge borrowed $62,000 from his employer. On July 1, 2006, Ridge used the money as follows:

Interest-free loan to Ridge's controlled corporation (operated by Ridge on a part-time basis)	$31,000
Interest-free loan to Tab (Ridge's son)	11,000
National Bank of Grundy 6% CD ($14,840 due at maturity, June 30, 2007)	14,000
National Bank of Grundy 6.25% CD ($6,773 due at maturity, June 30, 2008)	6,000
	$62,000

    Ridge's employer did not charge him interest. The applicable Federal rate was 7% throughout the relevant period. Tab had investment income of $800 for the year, and he used the loan proceeds to pay medical school tuition. There were no other outstanding loans between Ridge and Tab. What are the effects of the preceding transactions on Ridge's taxable income for 2006?

50. Indicate whether the imputed interest rules should apply in the following situations. Assume all the loans were made at the beginning of the tax year.
    a. Mike loaned his sister $80,000 to buy a new home. Mike did not charge interest on the loan. The Federal rate was 4.5%. Mike's sister had $900 of investment income for the year.
    b. Sam's employer maintains an emergency loan fund for its employees. During the year, Sam's wife was very ill, and he incurred unusually large medical expenses. He borrowed $9,000 from his employer's emergency loan fund for six months. The Federal rate was 5.5%. Sam and his wife had no investment income for the year.
    c. Jody borrowed $15,000 from her controlled corporation for six months. She used the funds to pay her daughter's college tuition. The corporation charged Jody 4% interest. The Federal rate was 4.5%. Jody had $3,500 of investment income for the year.

51. Vito is the sole shareholder of Vito, Inc. He is also employed by the corporation. On June 30, 2006, Vito borrowed $8,000 from Vito, Inc., and on July 1, 2007, he borrowed an additional $4,000. Both loans were due on demand. No interest was charged on the loans, and the Federal rate was 8% for all relevant dates. Vito used the money to purchase a boat, and he had $1,100 of investment income. Determine the tax consequences to Vito and Vito, Inc. in each of the following situations:
    a. The loans are considered employer-employee loans.
    b. The loans are considered corporation-shareholder loans.

52. Thelma retires after 30 years of service with her employer. She is 66 years old and has contributed $20,000 to her employer's qualified pension fund. She elects to receive her retirement benefits as an annuity of $2,000 per month for the remainder of her life.
    a. Assume that Thelma retires in June 2006 and collects six annuity payments this year. What is her gross income from the annuity payments in the first year?
    b. Assume that Thelma lives 30 years after retiring. What is her gross income from the annuity payments in the twenty-ninth year?
    c. Assume that Thelma dies after collecting 180 payments. She collected six payments in the year of her death. What are Thelma's gross income and deductions from the annuity contract in the year of her death?

53. For each of the following, determine the amount that should be included in gross income:
    a. Joe was selected as the most valuable player in the Super Bowl. In recognition of this, he was awarded a sports car worth $60,000 and $150,000 in cash.
    b. Wanda won the Mrs. America beauty contest. She received various prizes valued at $100,000. None of the $100,000 was for a scholarship or travel expenses.
    c. George was awarded the Nobel Peace Prize. He donated the $900,000 check he received to State University, his alma mater.

54. The LMN Partnership has a group term life insurance plan. Each partner has $150,000 protection, and each employee has protection equal to twice his or her annual salary. Employee Alice (age 36) has $85,000 of insurance under the plan, and partner Kay (age 54) has $150,000 of coverage. Because the plan is a "group plan," it is impossible to determine the cost of coverage for an individual employee or partner.
    a. Assuming the plan is nondiscriminatory, how much must Alice and Kay each include in gross income as a result of the partnership paying the insurance premiums?
    b. Assume that the partnership is incorporated. Kay becomes a shareholder and an employee who receives a $75,000 annual salary. The corporation provides Kay with $150,000 of group term life insurance coverage under a nondiscriminatory plan. What is Kay's gross income as a result of the corporation paying the insurance premiums?

55. Herbert was employed for the first six months of the year and earned $90,000 in salary. During the next six months, he collected $6,800 of unemployment compensation, borrowed $12,000 (using his personal residence as collateral), and withdrew $2,000 from his savings account (including $60 interest). He received dividends of $550. His luck was not all bad, for in December he won $1,500 in the lottery on a $5 ticket. Calculate Herbert's gross income.

56. Linda and Don are married and file a joint return. In 2006, they received $9,000 in Social Security benefits and $35,000 in taxable pension benefits and interest.

    Decision Making

    a. Compute the couple's adjusted gross income on a joint return.
    b. Don would like to know whether they should sell for $100,000 (at no gain or loss) a corporate bond that pays 8% in interest each year and use the proceeds to buy a $100,000 nontaxable State of Virginia bond that will pay $6,000 in interest each year.
    c. If Linda in (a) works part-time and earns $30,000, how much would Linda and Don's adjusted gross income increase?

57. Melissa and Jim are married and file a joint return. Jim is 62 years old, and his employer has offered a buyout program under which Jim could retire and receive additional retirement pay. If he retires, he would receive $60,000 a year as retirement pay and approximately $12,000 a year in interest. His Social Security benefits would be $15,000 per year. Melissa is 55 years old and is not employed. Their itemized deductions and personal exemption deductions total $18,000 a year. If Jim continues to work, he will receive a salary of approximately $80,000 per year, interest of $12,000 per year, and no Social Security benefits.
    a. Melissa and Jim would like you to compute their taxable income for 2006. First assume Jim does not retire. Then assume he does retire. Assume that, based on their gross income, 85% of the Social Security benefits are included in gross income.
    b. Assume Melissa and Jim will be in the 30% bracket (combined Federal and state rates). Compute the change in their after-tax cash flow following Jim's retirement.

58. Donna does not think she has an income tax problem but would like to discuss her situation with you just to make sure she will not get hit with an unexpected tax liability. Base your suggestions on the following relevant financial information:
   a. Donna's share of the SAT Partnership income is $70,000, but none of the income can be distributed because the partnership needs the cash for operations.
   b. Donna's Social Security benefits totaled $8,400, but Donna loaned the cash received to her nephew.
   c. Donna assigned to a creditor the right to collect $1,200 interest on some bonds she owned.
   d. Donna and her husband lived together in California until September, when they separated. Donna has heard rumors that her husband had substantial gambling winnings since they separated.

CUMULATIVE PROBLEMS

Tax Return Problem

Decision Making

Communications

59. Daniel B. Butler and Freida C. Butler, husband and wife, file a joint return. The Butlers live at 625 Oak Street in Corbin, KY 27521. Dan's Social Security number is 482–61–1231, and Freida's is 162–79–1245. Dan was born on January 15, 1960, and Freida was born on August 20, 1960.

   During 2005, Dan and Freida furnished over half of the total support of each of the following individuals, all of whom still live at home:
   a. Gina, their daughter, age 22, a full-time student, who married on December 21, 2005, has no income of her own, and for 2005 did not file a joint return with her husband, Casey, who earned $10,600 during 2005. Gina's Social Security number is 336–62–3760.
   b. Sam, their son, age 20, who had gross income of $6,300 in 2005. Sam dropped out of college in October 2005. He had graduated from high school in May 2005. Sam's Social Security number is 223–33–8906.
   c. Ben, their oldest son, age 27, who is a full-time graduate student with gross income of $5,200. Ben's Social Security number is 905–19–1760.

   Dan was employed as a manager by WJJJ, Inc. (employer identification number 38–7766723, 604 Franklin Street, Corbin, KY 27521), and Freida was employed as a salesperson for Corbin Realty, Inc. (employer identification number 38–8455227, 899 Central Street, Corbin, Ky 27521). Information from the W–2 Forms provided by the employers is presented below. Dan and Freida use the cash method.

Line	Description	Dan	Freida
1	Wages, tips, other compensation	$86,000	$38,000
2	Federal income tax withheld	$12,000	$7,500
3	Social Security wages	$86,000	$38,000
4	Social Security tax withheld	$5,332	$2,356
5	Medicare wages and tips	$86,000	$38,000
6	Medicare tax withheld	$1,247	$551
15	State	Kentucky	Kentucky
16	State wages, tips, etc.	$86,000	$38,000
17	State income tax withheld	$2,700	$1,800

Freida sold a house on December 30, 2005, and will be paid a commission of $2,000 (not included in the $38,000 reported on the W–2) on the January 10, 2006 closing date.

Other income (as reported on 1099 Forms) for 2005 consisted of the following:

Dividends on CSX stock (qualified)	$2,900
Interest on savings at Second Bank	1,300
Interest on City of Corbin bonds	900
Interest on First Bank CD	383

The $383 from First Bank was original issue discount. Dan and Freida collected $15,000 on the First Bank CD that matured on September 30, 2005. The CD was purchased on October 1, 2003, for $14,000, and the yield to maturity was 3.5%.

Dan received a Schedule K–1 from the Falcon Partnership which showed his distributive share as $11,000. In addition to the above information, Dan and Freida's itemized deductions included the following:

Paid on 2004 Kentucky income tax	$ 300
Personal property tax paid	600
Real estate taxes paid	1,800
Interest on home mortgage (Corbin S&L)	4,900
Cash contributions to the Boy Scouts	975

Sales tax from the sales tax table is $1,198. Dan and Freida made Federal estimated tax payments of $4,000.

Part 1—Tax Computation
Compute Dan and Freida's 2005 Federal income tax payable (or refund due). If you use tax forms for your computations, you will need Form 1040 and Schedules A, B, and E. Suggested software: TurboTax.

Part 2—Tax Planning
Dan plans to reduce his work schedule and work only halftime for WJJJ in 2006. He has been writing songs for several years and wants to devote more time to developing a career as a songwriter. Because of the uncertainty in the music business, however, he would like you to make all computations assuming he will have no income from songwriting in 2006. To make up for the loss of income, Freida plans to increase the amount of time she spends selling real estate. She estimates she will be able to earn $70,000 in 2006. Assume all other income and expense items will be approximately the same as they were in 2005. Assume Sam will be enrolled in college as a full-time student for the summer and fall semesters. Will the Butlers have more or less disposable income (after Federal income tax) in 2006? Write a letter to the Butlers that contains your advice and prepare a memo for the tax files.

60. Cecil C. Seymour is a 66-year-old widower. He had income for 2006 as follows:

Tax Return Problem

Pension from former employer	$29,500
Interest income from Alto National Bank	5,500
Interest income on City of Alto bonds	2,700
Dividends received from IBM	2,000
Collections on annuity contract he purchased from Great Life Insurance	4,800
Social Security benefits	12,000
Rent income on townhouse	7,600

The cost of the annuity was $52,800, and Cecil was expected to receive a total of 240 monthly payments of $400. Cecil has received 22 payments through 2006.

Cecil's 40-year-old daughter, Sarah C. Seymour, borrowed $40,000 from Cecil on January 2, 2006. She used the money to start a new business. Cecil does not charge her interest because she could not afford to pay it, but he does expect to eventually collect the principal. Sarah is living with Cecil until the business becomes profitable. Except for housing, Sarah provides her own support from her business and $1,600 in dividends on stocks that she inherited from her mother.

Other relevant information is presented below:
- Cecil's Social Security number: 259–83–4444
- Address: 3840 Springfield Blvd., Alto, GA 30754
- Sarah's Social Security number: 257–49–8862
- Expenses on rental townhouse:

Utilities	$1,500
Maintenance	1,000
Depreciation	2,000
Real estate taxes	750
Insurance	500

- State income taxes paid: $3,300
- County personal property taxes paid: $2,100
- Payments on estimated 2006 Federal income tax: $5,900
- Charitable contributions of cash to Alto Baptist Church: $6,400
- Federal interest rate: 6%
- Sales taxes paid: $912

Compute Cecil's 2006 Federal income tax payable (or refund due).

RESEARCH PROBLEMS

Communications

Note: Solutions to Research Problems can be prepared by using the **RIA Checkpoint**® **Student Edition** online research product, which is available to accompany this text. It is also possible to prepare solutions to the Research Problems by using tax research materials found in a standard tax library.

Research Problem 1.   Tranquility Funeral Home, Inc., your client, is an accrual basis taxpayer that sells pre-need funeral contracts. Under these contracts, the customer pays in advance for goods and services to be provided at the contract beneficiary's death. These payments are refundable at the contract purchaser's request, pursuant to state law, at any time until the goods and services are furnished. Tranquility, consistent with its financial accounting reporting, includes the payments in income for the year the funeral service is provided. The IRS agent insists that the payments are prepaid income subject to tax in the year of receipt. Your client believes the amounts involved are customer deposits. Write a letter to Tranquility that contains your advice about how the issue should be resolved. The client's address is 400 Rock Street, Memphis, TN 38152.

Research Problem 2.   Paul is an insurance agent who receives a commission on each policy he sells. During the year, he purchased a policy on his own life, naming his wife as the beneficiary. He did not report the commission on the policy as gross income because he considered the commission a reduction in his cost for the life insurance. An IRS agent has challenged the exclusion. Who is correct?

Research Problem 3.   The Cheyenne Golf and Tennis Club requires its members to purchase stock in the corporation and to make a deposit of $10,000. The deposit is to be repaid in 30 years, and no interest is charged. Is the deposit subject to the imputed interest rules for below-market loans?

Partial list of research aids:
TAM 9735002.

Research Problem 4.   The taxpayer is an employee of a consulting firm and had over 50,000 miles of air travel in the current year. Her employer reimbursed all of the taxpayer's transportation expenses, but allows the taxpayer to retain the frequent-flyer miles. During the year, the taxpayer used the accumulated miles to purchase an airline ticket for her vacation. Without the frequent-flyer miles, the taxpayer would have been required to pay $1,200 for the ticket. Is the taxpayer required to recognize gross income from the receipt and use of the frequent-flyer miles?

Internet *Activity*

Use the tax resources of the Internet to address the following questions. Do not restrict your search to the World Wide Web, but include a review of newsgroups and general reference materials, practitioner sites and resources, primary sources of the tax law, chat rooms and discussion groups, and other opportunities.

Research Problem 5.   Determine the applicable Federal rate for purposes of below-market loans. Use this figure to complete Problem 49 for this chapter.

Communications

Research Problem 6.   Go to the Web page of a consulting firm that offers counseling services to individuals as they negotiate the terms of a divorce. What specific tax-related services do these firms offer? Send an e-mail message to one of these firms suggesting that it add a specific service or revise its Web page to emphasize other tax-related services for its clients.

CHAPTER 5

Gross Income: Exclusions

LEARNING OBJECTIVES

After completing Chapter 5, you should be able to:

LO.1
Understand that statutory authority is required to exclude an item from gross income.

LO.2
Identify the circumstances under which various items are excludible from gross income.

LO.3
Determine the extent to which receipts can be excluded under the tax benefit rule.

LO.4
Describe the circumstances under which income must be reported from the discharge of indebtedness.

LO.5
Identify tax planning strategies for obtaining the maximum benefit from allowable exclusions.

Items Specifically Excluded from Gross Income

Chapter 4 discussed the concepts and judicial doctrines that affect the determination of gross income. If an income item is within the all-inclusive definition of gross income, the item can be excluded only if the taxpayer can locate specific authority for doing so. Chapter 5 focuses on the exclusions Congress has authorized. These exclusions are listed in Exhibit 5–1.

Tax advisers spend countless hours trying to develop techniques to achieve tax-exempt status for income. Employee benefits planning is greatly influenced by the availability of certain types of exclusions. Taxes play an important role in employee benefits, as well as in other situations, because attaining an exclusion is another means of enhancing after-tax income. For example, for a person whose combined Federal and state marginal tax rate is 40 percent, $1.00 of tax-exempt income is equivalent to $1.67 [$1 ÷ (1 − .4)] in income subject to taxation. The tax adviser's ideal is to attach the right labels or provide the right wording to render income nontaxable without affecting the economics of the transaction.

Consider the case of an employee who is in the 28 percent marginal tax bracket and is paying $3,000 a year for health insurance. If the employer provided this protection in a manner that qualified for exclusion treatment but reduced the employee's salary by $3,000, the employee's after-tax and after-insurance income would increase at no additional cost to the employer.

EXHIBIT 5–1	**Summary of Principal Exclusions from Gross Income**

1. Donative items
   Gifts, bequests, and inheritances (§ 102)
   Life insurance proceeds paid by reason of death (§ 101)
   Accelerated death benefits [§ 101(g)]
   Survivor benefits for public safety officer killed in the line of duty [§ 101(h)]
   Scholarships (§ 117)
2. Personal and welfare items
   Injury or sickness payments (§ 104)
   Public assistance payments (Rev.Rul. 71–425, 1971–2 C.B. 76)
   Amounts received under insurance contracts for certain living expenses (§ 123)
   Reimbursement for the costs of caring for a foster child (§ 131)
   Disaster relief payments (§ 139)
3. Wage and salary supplements
   a. Fringe benefits
      Accident and health benefits (§§ 105 and 106)
      Health Savings Accounts [§ 106(d)]
      Lodging and meals furnished for the convenience of the employer (§ 119)
      Rental value of parsonages (§ 107)
      Employee achievement awards [§ 74(c)]
      Employer contributions to employee group term life insurance (§ 79)
      Cafeteria plans (§ 125)
      Educational assistance payments (§ 127)
      Child or dependent care (§ 129)
      Services provided to employees at no additional cost to the employer (§ 132)
      Employee discounts (§ 132)
      Working condition and de minimis fringes (§ 132)
      Athletic facilities provided to employees (§ 132)
      Qualified transportation fringe (§ 132)
      Qualified moving expense reimbursement (§ 132)
      Qualified retirement planning services (§ 132)
      Tuition reductions granted to employees of educational institutions (§ 117)
      Child adoption expenses (§ 137)
      Long-term care insurance (§ 7702B)
   b. Military benefits
      Combat pay (§ 112)
      Housing, uniforms, and other benefits (§ 134)
   c. Foreign earned income (§ 911)
4. Investor items
   Interest on state and local government obligations (§ 103)
   Improvements by tenant to landlord's property (§ 109)
   Fifty percent exclusion for gain from sale of certain small business stock (§ 1202)
5. Benefits for the elderly
   Social Security benefits (except in the case of certain higher-income taxpayers) (§ 86)
6. Other benefits
   Income from discharge of indebtedness (§ 108)
   Recovery of a prior year's deduction that yielded no tax benefit (§ 111)
   Gain from the sale of personal residence (§ 121)
   Educational savings bonds (§ 135)
   Qualified tuition program (§ 529)
   Coverdell Education Savings Account (§ 530)
   Lessee construction allowances for short-term leases (§ 110)

| **TAX** *in the News* | **AVOIDING A NATURAL DISASTER CAN CREATE A TAX BURDEN** |

In a recent letter ruling, the IRS apologetically explained why payments received from the Federal Emergency Management Agency (FEMA) to be used to prevent flooding must be included in the recipient's gross income. The payments were taxable because the IRS could not find a specific provision in the Internal Revenue Code to justify excluding them from gross income. The IRS explained that it has requested specific authority for such an exclusion, but so far Congress has not responded.

Salary received to use to purchase health insurance	$ 3,000
Less: Taxes ($3,000 × 28%)	(840)
Cash available to purchase health insurance	$ 2,160
Less: Cost of health insurance	(3,000)
Excess of cost of health insurance over cash available	$ 840

Thus, the employee in this case is $840 better off with a salary reduction of $3,000 and employer-provided health insurance. The employee may still decide that the $3,000 salary is preferable if, for example, the employee feels that health insurance is no longer needed. Understanding the tax influence, however, does enable the employee to make a more informed choice.

LO.1

Understand that statutory authority is required to exclude an item from gross income.

Statutory Authority

Sections 101 through 150 provide the authority for excluding specific items from gross income. In addition, other exclusions are scattered throughout the Code. Each exclusion has its own legislative history and reason for enactment. Certain exclusions are intended as a form of indirect welfare payments. Other exclusions prevent double taxation of income or provide incentives for socially desirable activities (e.g., nontaxable interest on certain U.S. government bonds where the owner uses the funds for educational expenses).

In some cases, Congress has enacted exclusions to rectify the effects of judicial decisions. For example, the Supreme Court held that the fair market value of improvements (not made in lieu of rent) made by a tenant to the landlord's property should be included in the landlord's gross income upon termination of the lease.[1] The landlord was required to include the value of the improvements in gross income even though the property had not been sold or otherwise disposed of. Congress provided relief in this situation by enacting § 109, which defers taxing the value of the improvements until the property is sold.[2]

At times Congress responds to specific events. For example, in 2001 Congress enacted § 139 to ensure that victims of a *qualified disaster* (disaster resulting from a terrorist attack, presidentially declared disaster, common carrier accident of a catastrophic nature) would not be required to include payments received for living expenses, funeral expenses, and property damage resulting from the disaster in gross income.

LO.2

Identify the circumstances under which various items are excludible from gross income.

Gifts and Inheritances

General

Beginning with the Income Tax Act of 1913 and continuing to the present, Congress has allowed the recipient of a gift to exclude the value of the property from

[1]*Helvering v. Bruun*, 40–1 USTC ¶9337, 24 AFTR 652, 60 S.Ct. 631 (USSC, 1940).

[2]If the tenant made the improvements in lieu of rent, the value of the improvements is not eligible for exclusion.

TAX *in the News*	**BEGGING AS A TAX-DISFAVORED OCCUPATION**

In five recent decisions, the Tax Court ruled that amounts received from begging are nontaxable gifts. In a reversal of the normal roles, the beggars contended that the amounts received were earned income while the IRS argued that the taxpayers had merely received gifts. The beggars wanted the fruit of their efforts to be treated as earned income in order to qualify them for the earned income credit.

gross income. The exclusion applies to gifts made during the life of the donor (*inter vivos* gifts) and transfers that take effect upon the death of the donor (bequests and inheritances).[3] However, as discussed in Chapter 4, the recipient of a gift of income-producing property is subject to tax on the income subsequently earned from the property. Also, as discussed in Chapter 1, the donor or the decedent's estate may be subject to gift or estate taxes on the transfer.

In numerous cases, gifts are made in a business setting. For example, a salesperson gives a purchasing agent free samples; an employee receives cash from his or her employer on retirement; a corporation makes payments to employees who were victims of a natural disaster; a corporation makes a cash payment to a deceased employee's spouse. In these and similar instances, it is frequently unclear whether the payment was a gift or whether it represents compensation for past, present, or future services.

The courts have defined a **gift** as "a voluntary transfer of property by one to another without adequate [valuable] consideration or compensation therefrom."[4] If the payment is intended to be for services rendered, it is not a gift, even though the payment is made without legal or moral obligation and the payor receives no economic benefit from the transfer. To qualify as a gift, the payment must be made "out of affection, respect, admiration, charity or like impulses."[5] Thus, the cases on this issue have been decided on the basis of the donor's intent.

In a landmark case, *Comm. v. Duberstein*,[6] the taxpayer (Duberstein) received a Cadillac from a business acquaintance. Duberstein had supplied the businessman with the names of potential customers with no expectation of compensation. The Supreme Court concluded:

> . . . despite the characterization of the transfer of the Cadillac by the parties [as a gift] and the absence of any obligation, even of a moral nature, to make it, it was at the bottom a recompense for Duberstein's past service, or an inducement for him to be of further service in the future.

Duberstein was therefore required to include the fair market value of the automobile in gross income.

Gifts to Employees

In the case of cash or other property *received by an employee* from his or her employer, Congress has eliminated any ambiguity. Transfers from an employer to an employee cannot be excluded as a gift.[7] However, victims of a qualified disaster who are reimbursed by their employers for living expenses, funeral expenses, and property damage can exclude the payments from gross income under § 139, as previously discussed.

---

[3]§ 102.

[4]*Estate of D. R. Daly*, 3 B.T.A. 1042 (1926).

[5]*Robertson v. U.S.*, 52–1 USTC ¶9343, 41 AFTR 1053, 72 S.Ct. 994 (USSC, 1952).

[6]60–2 USTC ¶9515, 5 AFTR2d 1626, 80 S.Ct. 1190 (USSC, 1960).

[7]§ 102(c).

TAX *in the News*	FREQUENT-FLYER MILES WILL NOT BE TAXED

IRS officials believe that when a taxpayer receives frequent-flyer miles in connection with business travel, the taxpayer has received income. This is clearly true if the taxpayer has deducted the cost of the airline ticket. Under the tax benefit rule, the frequent-flyer miles should be included in gross income as a recovery of a prior deduction. If the employer pays for the business travel but the employee is awarded the frequent-flyer miles, the employee has obviously received additional compensation.

Nevertheless, the IRS has announced (Announcement 2002–18) that it will not attempt to tax frequent-flyer miles. The major consideration in creating this nonstatutory exemption was the complexity that would result from attempting to tax the miles. Distinguishing the miles awarded for personal travel (nontaxable reduction in the cost of ticket) from the business miles would be difficult. Furthermore, the valuation issues would be horrendous.

Employee Death Benefits

Frequently, an employer makes payments (**death benefits**) to a deceased employee's surviving spouse, children, or other beneficiaries. If the decedent had a nonforfeitable right to the payments (e.g., the decedent's accrued salary), the amounts are generally taxable to the recipient just the same as if the employee had lived and collected the payments. But when the employer makes voluntary payments, the gift issue arises. Generally, the IRS considers such payments to be compensation for prior services rendered by the deceased employee.[8] However, some courts have held that payments to an employee's surviving spouse or other beneficiaries are gifts if the following are true:[9]

- The payments were made to the surviving spouse and children rather than to the employee's estate.
- The employer derived no benefit from the payments.
- The surviving spouse and children performed no services for the employer.
- The decedent had been fully compensated for services rendered.
- Payments were made pursuant to a board of directors' resolution that followed a general company policy of providing payments for families of deceased employees (but not exclusively for families of shareholder-employees).

When all of the above conditions are satisfied, the payment is presumed to have been made *as an act of affection or charity*. When one or more of these conditions is not satisfied, the surviving spouse and children may still be deemed the recipients of a gift if the payment is made in light of the survivors' financial needs.[10]

Life Insurance Proceeds

General Rule

Life insurance proceeds paid to the beneficiary because of the death of the insured are exempt from income tax.[11]

EXAMPLE 1

Mark purchases an insurance policy on his life and names his wife, Linda, as the beneficiary. Mark pays $45,000 in premiums. When he dies, Linda collects the insurance proceeds of $200,000. The $200,000 is exempt from Federal income tax. ∎

---

[8]Rev.Rul. 62–102, 1962–2 C.B. 37.

[9]*Estate of Sydney J. Carter v. Comm.*, 72–1 USTC ¶9129, 29 AFTR2d 332, 453 F.2d 61 (CA–2, 1972), and the cases cited there.

[10]*Simpson v. U.S.*, 58–2 USTC ¶9923, 2 AFTR2d 6036, 261 F.2d 497 (CA–7, 1958), *cert. denied* 79 S.Ct. 724 (USSC, 1958).

[11]§ 101(a).

Congress chose to exempt life insurance proceeds for the following reasons:

- For family members, life insurance proceeds serve much the same purpose as a nontaxable inheritance.
- In a business context (as well as in a family situation), life insurance proceeds replace an economic loss suffered by the beneficiary.

E X A M P L E   2

Gold Corporation purchases a life insurance policy to cover its key employee. If the proceeds were taxable, the corporation would require more insurance coverage to pay the tax as well as to cover the economic loss of the employee. ■

Thus, in general, Congress concluded that making life insurance proceeds exempt from income tax was a good policy.

Accelerated Death Benefits

Generally, if the owner of a life insurance policy cancels the policy and receives the cash surrender value, the taxpayer must recognize gain equal to the excess of the amount received over premiums paid on the policy (a loss is not deductible). The gain is recognized because the general exclusion provision for life insurance proceeds applies only to life insurance proceeds paid upon the death of the insured. If the taxpayer cancels the policy and receives the cash surrender value, the life insurance policy is treated as an investment by the insured.

In a limited circumstance, however, the insured is permitted to receive the benefits of the life insurance contract without having to include the gain in gross income. Under the **accelerated death benefits** provisions, exclusion treatment is available for insured taxpayers who are either terminally ill or chronically ill.[12] A terminally ill taxpayer can collect the cash surrender value of the policy from the insurance company or assign the policy proceeds to a qualified third party. The resultant gain, if any, is excluded from the insured's gross income. A *terminally ill* individual is one whom a medical doctor certifies as having an illness that is reasonably expected to cause death within 24 months.

In the case of a chronically ill patient, no gain is recognized if the proceeds of the policy are used for the long-term care of the insured. A person is *chronically ill* if he or she is certified as being unable to perform without assistance certain activities

---

[12]§ 101(g).

of daily living. These exclusions for the terminally ill and the chronically ill are available only to the insured. Thus, a person who purchases a life insurance policy from the insured does not qualify.

EXAMPLE 3

Tom owned a term life insurance policy at the time he was diagnosed as having a terminal illness. After paying $5,200 in premiums, he sold the policy to Amber Benefits, Inc., a company that is authorized by the State of Virginia to purchase such policies. Amber paid Tom $50,000. When Tom died six months later, Amber collected the face amount of the policy, $75,000. Tom is not required to include the $44,800 gain ($50,000 − $5,200) on the sale of the policy in his gross income. Assume Amber pays additional premiums of $4,000 during the six-month period. When Amber collects the life insurance proceeds of $75,000, it must include the $21,000 gain ($75,000 proceeds − $50,000 cost − $4,000 additional premiums paid) in gross income. ∎

ETHICAL *Considerations* **SHOULD THE TERMINALLY ILL PAY SOCIAL SECURITY TAXES?**

The rationale for excluding accelerated death benefits from the gross income of the terminally ill is that they often use the funds to pay medical expenses and other costs associated with dying and do not have the ability to pay tax on the gain from the accelerated receipt of the life insurance proceeds. Yet the wages of a terminally ill person who is employed (or profits of a self-employed person) are subject to Social Security taxes. The Social Security taxes are intended to pay for retirement benefits, but a terminally ill person is unlikely to collect any Social Security benefits.

Several bills have been introduced in Congress to exempt the terminally ill from the Social Security tax. Evaluate the equity of the current tax treatment versus that in the proposed legislation.

Transfer for Valuable Consideration

A life insurance policy (other than one associated with accelerated death benefits) may be transferred after it is issued by the insurance company. If the policy is *transferred for valuable consideration*, the insurance proceeds are includible in the gross income of the transferee to the extent the proceeds received exceed the amount paid for the policy by the transferee plus any subsequent premiums paid.

EXAMPLE 4

Adam pays premiums of $4,000 for an insurance policy in the face amount of $10,000 upon the life of Beth and subsequently transfers the policy to Carol for $6,000. On Beth's death, Carol receives the proceeds of $10,000. The amount that Carol can exclude from gross income is limited to $6,000 plus any premiums she paid subsequent to the transfer. ∎

The Code, however, provides four exceptions to the rule illustrated in the preceding example. These exceptions permit exclusion treatment for transfers to the following:

1. A partner of the insured.
2. A partnership in which the insured is a partner.
3. A corporation in which the insured is an officer or shareholder.
4. A transferee whose basis in the policy is determined by reference to the transferor's basis.

The first three exceptions facilitate the use of insurance contracts to fund buy-sell agreements.

EXAMPLE 5

Rick and Sam are equal partners who have an agreement that allows either partner to purchase the interest of a deceased partner for $50,000. Neither partner has sufficient cash to actually buy the other partner's interest, but each has a life insurance policy on his own life in the amount of $50,000. Rick and Sam could exchange their policies (usually at little or no taxable gain), and upon the death of either partner, the surviving partner could collect tax-free insurance proceeds. The proceeds could then be used to purchase the decedent's interest in the partnership. ■

The fourth exception applies to policies that were transferred pursuant to a tax-free exchange or were received by gift.[13]

Investment earnings arising from the reinvestment of life insurance proceeds are generally subject to income tax. Often the beneficiary will elect to collect the insurance proceeds in installments. The annuity rules (discussed in Chapter 4) are used to apportion the installment payment between the principal element (excludible) and the interest element (includible).[14]

Scholarships

General Information

Payments or benefits received by a student at an educational institution may be (1) compensation for services, (2) a gift, or (3) a scholarship. If the payments or benefits are received as compensation for services (past or present), the fact that the recipient is a student generally does not render the amounts received nontaxable.[15]

EXAMPLE 6

State University waives tuition for all graduate teaching assistants. The tuition waived is intended as compensation for services and is therefore included in the graduate assistant's gross income. ■

As discussed earlier, gifts are not includible in gross income.

The **scholarship** rules are intended to provide exclusion treatment for education-related benefits that cannot qualify as gifts but are not compensation for services. According to the Regulations, "a scholarship is an amount paid or allowed to, or for the benefit of, an individual to aid such individual in the pursuit of study or research."[16] The recipient must be a candidate for a degree at an educational institution.[17]

EXAMPLE 7

Terry enters a contest sponsored by a local newspaper. Each contestant is required to submit an essay on local environmental issues. The prize is one year's tuition at State University. Terry wins the contest. The newspaper has a legal obligation to Terry (as contest winner). Thus, the benefits are not a gift. However, since the tuition payment aids Terry in pursuing her studies, the payment is a scholarship. ■

A scholarship recipient may exclude from gross income the amount used for tuition and related expenses (fees, books, supplies, and equipment required for courses), provided the conditions of the grant do not require that the funds be used for other purposes.[18] Amounts received for room and board are *not* excludible

---

[13]See the discussion of gifts in Chapter 14 and tax-free exchanges in Chapters 15 and 20.

[14]Reg. §§ 1.72–7(c)(1) and 1.101–7T.

[15]Reg. § 1.117–2(a). See *C. P. Bhalla*, 35 T.C. 13 (1960), for a discussion of the distinction between a scholarship and compensation. See also *Bingler v. Johnson*, 69–1 USTC ¶9348, 23 AFTR2d 1212, 89 S.Ct. 1439 (USSC, 1969).

For potential exclusion treatment, see the subsequent discussion of qualified tuition reductions.

[16]Prop.Reg. § 1.117–6(c)(3)(i).

[17]§ 117(a).

[18]§ 117(b).

and are treated as earned income for purposes of calculating the standard deduction for a taxpayer who is another taxpayer's dependent.[19]

EXAMPLE 8

Kelly receives a scholarship of $9,500 from State University to be used to pursue a bachelor's degree. She spends $4,000 on tuition, $3,000 on books and supplies, and $2,500 for room and board. Kelly may exclude $7,000 ($4,000 + $3,000) from gross income. The $2,500 spent for room and board is includible in Kelly's gross income.

The scholarship is Kelly's only source of income. Her parents provide more than 50% of Kelly's support and claim her as a dependent. Kelly's standard deduction of $2,800 ($2,500 + $300) exceeds her $2,500 gross income. Thus, she has no taxable income. ∎

Timing Issues

Frequently, the scholarship recipient is a cash basis taxpayer who receives the money in one tax year but pays the educational expenses in a subsequent year. The amount eligible for exclusion may not be known at the time the money is received. In that case, the transaction is held *open* until the educational expenses are paid.[20]

EXAMPLE 9

In August 2006, Sanjay received $10,000 as a scholarship for the academic year 2006–2007. Sanjay's expenditures for tuition, books, and supplies were as follows:

August–December 2006	$3,000
January–May 2007	4,500
	$7,500

Sanjay's gross income for 2007 includes $2,500 ($10,000 − $7,500) that is not excludible as a scholarship. None of the scholarship is included in his gross income in 2006. ∎

Disguised Compensation

Some employers make scholarships available solely to the children of key employees. The tax objective of these plans is to provide a nontaxable fringe benefit to the executives by making the payment to the child in the form of an excludible scholarship. However, the IRS has ruled that the payments are generally includible in the gross income of the parent-employee.[21]

Qualified Tuition Reduction Plans

Employees (including retired and disabled former employees) of nonprofit educational institutions are allowed to exclude a tuition waiver from gross income, if the waiver is pursuant to a **qualified tuition reduction plan**.[22] The plan may not discriminate in favor of highly compensated employees. The exclusion applies to the employee, the employee's spouse, and the employee's dependent children. The exclusion also extends to tuition reductions granted by any nonprofit educational institution to employees of any other nonprofit educational institution (reciprocal agreements).

EXAMPLE 10

ABC University allows the dependent children of XYZ University employees to attend ABC University with no tuition charge. XYZ University grants reciprocal benefits to the children of ABC University employees. The dependent children can also attend tuition-free the university where their parents are employed. Employees who take advantage of these benefits are not required to recognize gross income. ∎

[19]Prop.Reg. § 1.117–6(h).
[20]Prop.Reg. § 1.117–6(b)(2).
[21]Rev.Rul. 75–448, 1975–2 C.B. 55. *Richard T. Armantrout*, 67 T.C. 996 (1977).
[22]§ 117(d).

Generally, the exclusion is limited to _undergraduate_ tuition waivers. However, in the case of teaching or research assistants, graduate tuition waivers may also qualify for exclusion treatment. According to the Proposed Regulations, the exclusion is limited to the value of the benefit in excess of the employee's reasonable compensation.[23] Thus, a tuition reduction that is a substitute for cash compensation cannot be excluded.

Susan is a graduate research assistant. She receives a $5,000 salary for 500 hours of service over a nine-month period. This pay, $10 per hour, is reasonable compensation for Susan's services. In addition, Susan receives a waiver of $6,000 for tuition. Susan may exclude the tuition waiver from gross income. ■

Compensation for Injuries and Sickness

Damages

A person who suffers harm caused by another is often entitled to compensatory damages. The tax consequences of the receipt of damages depend on the type of harm the taxpayer has experienced. The taxpayer may seek recovery for (1) a loss of income, (2) expenses incurred, (3) property destroyed, or (4) personal injury.

Generally, reimbursement for a loss of income is taxed the same as the income replaced (see the exception under Personal Injury below). The recovery of an expense is not income, unless the expense was deducted. Damages that are a recovery of the taxpayer's previously deducted expenses are generally taxable under the tax benefit rule, discussed later in this chapter.

A payment for damaged or destroyed property is treated as an amount received in a sale or exchange of the property. Thus, the taxpayer has a realized gain if the damage payments received exceed the property's basis. Damages for personal injuries receive special treatment under the Code.

Personal Injury. The legal theory of personal injury damages is that the amount received is intended "to make the plaintiff [the injured party] whole as before the injury."[24] It follows that if the damage payments received were subject to tax, the after-tax amount received would be less than the actual damages incurred and the injured party would not be "whole as before the injury."

In terms of personal injury damages, a distinction is made between compensatory damages and punitive damages. Under specified circumstances, compensatory damages may be excluded from gross income. Under no circumstances may punitive damages be excluded from gross income.

Compensatory damages are intended to compensate the taxpayer for the damages incurred. Only those compensatory damages received on account of _physical personal injury or physical sickness_ can be excluded from gross income.[25] Such exclusion treatment includes amounts received for loss of income associated with the physical personal injury or physical sickness. Compensatory damages awarded on account of emotional distress are not received on account of physical injury or physical sickness and thus cannot be excluded (except to the extent of any amount received for medical care) from gross income. Likewise, any amounts received for age discrimination or injury to one's reputation cannot be excluded.

Punitive damages are amounts the person who caused the harm must pay to the victim as punishment for outrageous conduct. Punitive damages are not intended to compensate the victim, but rather to punish the party who caused the harm. Thus, it follows that amounts received as punitive damages may actually place

[handwritten margin notes: — Amt rec. to restore as whole is excludible. — Emotional distress comp is NOT excludible. Punishment payment is NOT excludible]

---

[23]Prop.Reg. § 1.117–6(d).

[24]_C. A. Hawkins_, 6 B.T.A. 1023 (1928).

[25]§ 104(a)(2).

CONCEPT SUMMARY 5–1

Taxation of Damages

Type of Claim	Taxation of Award or Settlement
Breach of contract (generally loss of income)	Taxable.
Property damages	Recovery of cost; gain to the extent of the excess over basis. A loss is deductible for business property and investment property to the extent of basis over the amount realized. A loss may be deductible for personal use property (see discussion of casualty losses in Chapter 7).
Personal injury	
Physical	All compensatory amounts are excluded unless previously deducted (e.g., medical expenses). Amounts received as punitive damages are included in gross income.
Nonphysical	Compensatory damages and punitive damages are included in gross income.

the victim in a better economic position than before the harm was experienced. Logically, punitive damages are thus included in gross income.

EXAMPLE 12

Tom, a television announcer, was dissatisfied with the manner in which Ron, an attorney, was defending the television station in a libel case. Tom stated on the air that Ron was botching the case. Ron sued Tom for slander, claiming damages for loss of income from clients and potential clients who heard Tom's statement. Ron's claim is for damages to his business reputation, and the amounts received are taxable.

Ron collected on the suit against Tom and was on his way to a party to celebrate his victory when a negligent driver, Norm, drove a truck into Ron's automobile, injuring Ron. Ron filed suit for the physical personal injuries and claimed as damages the loss of income for the period he was unable to work as a result of the injuries. Ron also collected punitive damages that were awarded because of Norm's extremely negligent behavior. Ron's wife also collected damages for the emotional distress she experienced as a result of the accident. Ron may exclude the amounts he received for damages, except the punitive damages. Ron's wife must include the amounts she received for damages in gross income because the amounts were not received because of physical personal injuries or sickness. ■

Workers' Compensation

State workers' compensation laws require the employer to pay fixed amounts for specific job-related injuries. The state laws were enacted so that the employee will not have to go through the ordeal of a lawsuit (and possibly not collect damages because of some defense available to the employer) to recover the damages. Although the payments are intended, in part, to compensate for a loss of future income, Congress has specifically exempted workers' compensation benefits from inclusion in gross income.[26]

Accident and Health Insurance Benefits

The income tax treatment of accident and health insurance benefits depends on whether the policy providing the benefits was purchased by the taxpayer or the

[26]§ 104(a)(1).

TAX *in the News*	ABANDONING PARENT GETS AN "UNDESERVED" BENEFIT TAX-FREE

A father who abandoned his son in infancy and refused to support him financially or emotionally was awarded half of the workers' compensation death benefit when the son was killed in the September 11, 2001 terrorist attacks. The court concluded that the Workers' Compensation Law defines *parent* in strictly biological terms and therefore the father was entitled to the benefit.

Furthermore, under IRS Regulation § 1.101–1(a)(1), the death benefit is excluded from the father's gross income because the benefit has the characteristics of life insurance proceeds payable by reason of the death of the son.

taxpayer's employer. Benefits collected under an accident and health insurance policy *purchased by the taxpayer* are excludible. In this case, benefits collected under the taxpayer's insurance policy are excluded even though the payments are a substitute for income.[27]

> **EXAMPLE 13**
>
> Bonnie purchases a medical and disability insurance policy. The insurance company pays Bonnie $1,000 per week to replace wages she loses while in the hospital. Although the payments serve as a substitute for income, the amounts received are tax-exempt benefits collected under Bonnie's insurance policy. ∎

> **EXAMPLE 14**
>
> Joe's injury results in a partial paralysis of his left foot. He receives $20,000 for the injury from his accident insurance company under a policy he had purchased. The $20,000 accident insurance proceeds are tax-exempt. ∎

A different set of rules applies if the accident and health insurance protection was *purchased by the individual's employer*, as discussed in the following section.

Employer-Sponsored Accident and Health Plans

Congress encourages employers to provide employees, retired former employees, and their dependents with **accident and health benefits**, disability insurance, and long-term care plans. The *premiums* are deductible by the employer and excluded from the employee's income.[28] Although § 105(a) provides the general rule that the employee has includible income when he or she collects the insurance *benefits*, two exceptions are provided.

Section 105(b) generally excludes payments received for medical care of the employee, spouse, and dependents. However, if the payments are for expenses that do not meet the Code's definition of medical care,[29] the amount received must be included in gross income. In addition, the taxpayer must include in gross income any amounts received for medical expenses that were deducted by the taxpayer on a prior return.

> **EXAMPLE 15**
>
> In 2006, Tab's employer-sponsored health insurance plan pays $4,000 for hair transplants that do not meet the Code's definition of medical care. Tab must include the $4,000 in his gross income for 2006. ∎

---

[27]§ 104(a)(3).

[28]§ 106, Reg. § 1.106–1, and Rev.Rul. 82–196, 1982–1 C.B. 106.

[29]See the discussion of medical care in Chapter 10.

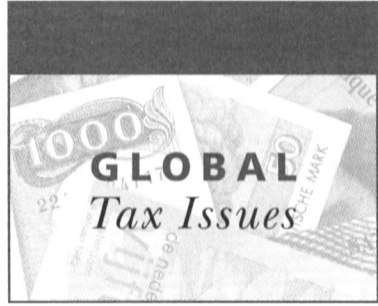
GLOBAL
Tax Issues

Section 105(c) excludes payments for the permanent loss or the loss of the use of a member or function of the body or the permanent disfigurement of the employee, spouse, or a dependent. Payments that are a substitute for salary (e.g., related to the period of time absent) are includible.

EXAMPLE 16

Jill loses an eye in an automobile accident unrelated to her work. As a result of the accident, Jill incurs $2,000 of medical expenses, which she deducts on her return. She collects $10,000 from an accident insurance policy carried by her employer. The benefits are paid according to a schedule of amounts that vary with the part of the body injured (e.g., $10,000 for loss of an eye, $20,000 for loss of a hand). Because the payment is for loss of a *member or function of the body*, the $10,000 is excluded from gross income. Jill is absent from work for a week as a result of the accident. Her employer provides her with insurance for the loss of income due to illness or injury. Jill collects $500, which is includible in gross income. ■

Medical Reimbursement Plans

In lieu of providing the employee with insurance coverage for hospital and medical expenses, the employer may agree to reimburse the employee for these expenses. The amounts received through the insurance coverage (insured plan benefits) are excluded from income under § 105 (as previously discussed). Unfortunately in terms of cost considerations, the insurance companies that issue this type of policy usually require a broad coverage of employees. An alternative is to have a plan that is not funded with insurance (a self-insured arrangement). The benefits received under a self-insured plan can be excluded from the employee's income, if the plan does not discriminate in favor of highly compensated employees.[30]

Legislation enacted in 2003 provides an alternative means of accomplishing a medical reimbursement plan. The employer can purchase a medical insurance plan with a high deductible (e.g., the employee is responsible for the first $2,100 of medical expenses) and then make contributions to the employee's **Health Savings Account (HSA)**.[31] The employer can make contributions each month up to the maximum contribution of 100 percent of the deductible amount. The monthly deductible amount is limited to the *lesser* of one-twelfth of the annual deductible under a high-deductible plan or $2,700 for self-only coverage. An individual who has family coverage is limited to the *lesser* of one-twelfth of the annual deductible under a high-deductible plan or $5,450. Withdrawals from the HSA must be used to reimburse the employee for the medical expenses paid by the employee that are not covered under the high-deductible plan. The employee is not taxed on the employer's contributions to the HSA, the earnings on the funds in the account, or the withdrawals made for medical expenses.[32]

Long-Term Care Insurance Benefits

Generally, **long-term care insurance**, which covers expenses such as the cost of care in a nursing home, is treated the same as accident and health insurance benefits. Thus, the employee does not recognize income when the employer pays the premiums. When benefits are received from the policy, whether the employer or the individual purchased the policy, the exclusion from gross income is limited to the greater of the following amounts:

- $250 in 2006 (indexed amount for 2005 is $240) for each day the patient receives the long-term care.
- The actual cost of the care.

The above amount is reduced by any amounts received from other third parties (e.g., damages received).[33]

EXAMPLE 17

Hazel, who suffers from Alzheimer's disease, is a patient in a nursing home for the last 30 days of 2006. While in the nursing home, she incurs total costs of $7,600. Medicare pays $3,200 of the costs. Hazel receives $4,500 from her long-term care insurance policy (which pays $150 per day while she is in the facility).

The amount that Hazel may exclude is calculated as follows:

Greater of:		
Daily statutory amount of $250 ($250 × 30 days)	$7,500	
Actual cost of the care	7,600	$ 7,600
Less: Amount received from Medicare		(3,200)
Amount of exclusion		$ 4,400

Therefore, Hazel must include $100 ($4,500 − $4,400) of the long-term care benefits received in her gross income. ∎

The exclusion for long-term care insurance is not available if it is provided as part of a cafeteria plan or a flexible spending plan.

Meals and Lodging

Furnished for the Convenience of the Employer

As discussed in Chapter 4, income can take any form, including meals and lodging. However, § 119 excludes from income the value of meals and lodging provided to

---

[32]§§ 106(d), 223(b), and 223(d). The amounts for 2005 are $2,650 and $5,250.

[33]§ 7702B. See § 213(d)(10) for the limitations on the amount of the employee's exclusion for premiums paid by the employer.

the employee and the employee's spouse and dependents under the following conditions:[34]

- The meals and/or lodging are *furnished* by the employer, on the employer's *business premises*, for the *convenience of the employer*.
- In the case of lodging, the *employee is required* to accept the lodging as a condition of employment.

The courts have construed both of these requirements strictly.

Furnished by the Employer. The following two questions have been raised with regard to the *furnished by the employer* requirement:

- Who is considered an *employee*?
- What is meant by *furnished*?

The IRS and some courts have reasoned that because a partner is not an employee, the exclusion does not apply to a partner. However, the Tax Court and the Fifth Circuit Court of Appeals have ruled in favor of the taxpayer on this issue.[35]

The Supreme Court held that a cash meal allowance was ineligible for the exclusion because the employer did not actually furnish the meals.[36] Similarly, one court denied the exclusion where the employer paid for the food and supplied the cooking facilities but the employee prepared the meal.[37]

On the Employer's Business Premises. The *on the employer's business premises* requirement, applicable to both meals and lodging, has resulted in much litigation. The Regulations define business premises as simply "the place of employment of the employee."[38] Thus, the Sixth Circuit Court of Appeals held that a residence, owned by the employer and occupied by an employee, two blocks from the motel that the employee managed was not part of the business premises.[39] However, the Tax Court considered an employer-owned house across the street from the hotel that was managed by the taxpayer to be on the business premises of the employer.[40] Apparently, the closer the lodging to the business operations, the more likely the convenience of the employer is served.

For the Convenience of the Employer. The *convenience of the employer* test is intended to focus on the employer's motivation for furnishing the meals and lodging rather than on the benefits received by the employee. If the employer furnishes the meals and lodging primarily to enable the employee to perform his or her duties properly, it does not matter that the employee considers these benefits to be a part of his or her compensation.

The Regulations give the following examples in which the tests for excluding meals are satisfied:[41]

- A restaurant requires its service staff to eat their meals on the premises during the busy lunch and breakfast hours.
- A bank furnishes meals on the premises for its tellers to limit the time the employees are away from their booths during the busy hours.

---

[34]§ 119(a). The meals and lodging are also excluded from FICA and FUTA tax. *Rowan Companies, Inc. v. U.S.*, 81–1 USTC ¶9479, 48 AFTR2d 81–5115, 101 S.Ct. 2288 (USSC, 1981).

[35]Rev.Rul. 80, 1953–1 C.B. 62; *Comm. v. Doak*, 56–2 USTC ¶9708, 49 AFTR 1491, 234 F.2d 704 (CA–4, 1956); but see *G. A. Papineau*, 16 T.C. 130 (1951); *Armstrong v. Phinney*, 68–1 USTC ¶9355, 21 AFTR2d 1260, 394 F.2d 661 (CA–5, 1968).

[36]*Comm. v. Kowalski*, 77–2 USTC ¶9748, 40 AFTR2d 6128, 98 S.Ct. 315 (USSC, 1977).

[37]*Tougher v. Comm.*, 71–1 USTC ¶9398, 27 AFTR2d 1301, 441 F.2d 1148 (CA–9, 1971).

[38]Reg. § 1.119–1(c)(1).

[39]*Comm. v. Anderson*, 67–1 USTC ¶9136, 19 AFTR2d 318, 371 F.2d 59 (CA–6, 1966).

[40]*J. B. Lindeman*, 60 T.C. 609 (1973).

[41]Reg. § 1.119–1(f).

- A worker is employed at a construction site in a remote part of Alaska. The employer must furnish meals and lodging due to the inaccessibility of other facilities.

If more than half of the employees to whom meals are furnished receive their meals for the convenience of the employer, then all such employee meals are treated as provided for the convenience of the employer.[42] Thus, in this situation, all employees are treated the same (either all of the employees are allowed exclusion treatment, or none of the employees can exclude the meals from gross income).

EXAMPLE 18

Allison's Restaurant has a restaurant area and a bar. Nine employees work in the restaurant and three work in the bar. All of the employees are provided one meal per day. In the case of the restaurant workers, the meals are provided for the convenience of the employer. The meals provided to the bar employees do not satisfy the convenience of the employer requirement. Because more than half of the employees receive their meal for the convenience of the employer, all 12 employees qualify for exclusion treatment. ■

Required as a Condition of Employment.

The *employee is required to accept* test applies only to lodging. If the employee's use of the housing would serve the convenience of the employer, but the employee is not required to use the housing, the exclusion is not available.

EXAMPLE 19

VEP, a utilities company, has all of its service personnel on 24-hour call for emergencies. The company encourages its employees to live near the plant so that the employees can respond quickly to emergency calls. Company-owned housing is available rent-free. Only 10 of the employees live in the company housing because it is not suitable for families.

Although the company-provided housing serves the convenience of the employer, it is not required. Therefore, the employees who live in the company housing cannot exclude its value from gross income. ■

In addition, if the employee has the *option* of cash or lodging, the *required* test is not satisfied.

EXAMPLE 20

Khalid is the manager of a large apartment complex. The employer gives Khalid the option of rent-free housing (value of $6,000 per year) or an additional $5,000 per year. Khalid selects the housing option. Therefore, he must include $6,000 in gross income. ■

Other Housing Exclusions

Employees of Educational Institutions.

An employee of an educational institution may be able to exclude the value of campus housing provided by the employer. Generally, the employee does not recognize income if he or she pays annual rents equal to or greater than 5 percent of the appraised value of the facility. If the rent payments are less than 5 percent of the value of the facility, the deficiency must be included in gross income.[43]

EXAMPLE 21

Swan University provides on-campus housing for its full-time faculty during the first three years of employment. The housing is not provided for the convenience of the employer. Professor Edith pays $3,000 annual rent for the use of a residence with an appraised value of $100,000 and an annual rental value of $12,000. Edith must recognize $2,000 gross income [.05($100,000) − $3,000 = $2,000] for the value of the housing provided to her. ■

---

[42]§ 119(b)(4).   [43]§ 119(d).

Ministers of the Gospel. Ministers of the gospel can exclude (1) the rental value of a home furnished as compensation; (2) a rental allowance paid to them as compensation, to the extent the allowance is used to rent or provide a home; or (3) the rental value of a home owned by the minister.[44] The housing or housing allowance must be provided as compensation for the conduct of religious worship, the administration and maintenance of religious organizations, or the performance of teaching and administrative duties at theological seminaries.

EXAMPLE 22

Pastor Bill is allowed to live rent-free in a house owned by the congregation. The annual rental value of the house is $6,000 and is provided as part of the pastor's compensation for ministerial services. Assistant Pastor Olga is paid a $4,500 cash housing allowance. She uses the $4,500 to pay rent and utilities on a home she and her family occupy. Neither Pastor Bill nor Assistant Pastor Olga is required to recognize gross income associated with the housing or housing allowance. ■

Military Personnel. Military personnel are allowed housing exclusions under various circumstances. Authority for these exclusions generally is found in Federal laws that are not part of the Internal Revenue Code.[45]

Other Employee Fringe Benefits

Specific Benefits

Congress has enacted exclusions to encourage employers to (1) finance and make available child care facilities, (2) provide athletic facilities for employees, (3) finance certain employees' education, and (4) pay or reimburse child adoption expenses. These provisions are summarized as follows:

- The employee does not have to include in gross income the value of child and dependent care services paid for by the employer and incurred to enable the employee to work. The exclusion cannot exceed $5,000 per year ($2,500 if married and filing separately). For a married couple, the annual exclusion cannot exceed the earned income of the spouse who has the lesser amount of earned income. For an unmarried taxpayer, the exclusion cannot exceed the taxpayer's earned income.[46]
- The value of the use of a gymnasium or other athletic facilities by employees, their spouses, and their dependent children may be excluded from an employee's gross income. The facilities must be on the employer's premises, and substantially all of the use of the facilities must be by employees and their family members.[47]
- Qualified employer-provided educational assistance (tuition, fees, books, and supplies) at the undergraduate and graduate level is excludible from gross income. The exclusion is subject to an annual employee statutory ceiling of $5,250.[48]
- The employee can exclude from gross income up to $10,960 of expenses incurred to adopt a child where the adoption expenses are paid or reimbursed by the employer under a qualified adoption assistance program.[49] The limit on the exclusion is the same even if the child has special needs (is not physically or mentally capable of caring for himself or herself). However, for a child with special needs, the $10,960 exclusion from gross income applies even if

[44]§ 107 and Reg. § 1.107–1.
[45]H. Rep. No. 99–841, 99th Cong., 2d Sess., p. 548 (1986). See also § 134.
[46]§ 129. The exclusion applies to the same types of expenses that, if they were paid by the employee (and not reimbursed by the employer), would be eligible for the credit for child and dependent care expense discussed in Chapter 13.
[47]§ 132(j)(4).
[48]§ 127.
[49]§ 137.

the actual adoption expenses are less than that amount. The exclusion is phased out as adjusted gross income increases from $164,410 to $204,410.

Cafeteria Plans *(select benefit options)*

+ Any non-cash is excluded.

+ Any cash rec. is taxable.

Generally, if an employee is offered a choice between cash and some other form of compensation, the employee is deemed to have constructively received the cash even when the noncash option is elected. Thus, the employee has gross income regardless of the option chosen.

An exception to this constructive receipt treatment is provided under the **cafeteria plan** rules. Under such a plan, the employee is permitted to choose between cash and nontaxable benefits (e.g., group term life insurance, health and accident protection, and child care). If the employee chooses the otherwise nontaxable benefits, the cafeteria plan rules enable the benefits to remain nontaxable.[50] Cafeteria plans provide tremendous flexibility in tailoring the employee pay package to fit individual needs. Some employees (usually the younger group) prefer cash, while others (usually the older group) will opt for the fringe benefit program. However, Congress excluded long-term care insurance from the excludible benefits that can be provided under a cafeteria plan.[51] Thus, the employer must provide these benefits separate from the cafeteria plan.

EXAMPLE 23

Hawk Corporation offers its employees (on a nondiscriminatory basis) a choice of any one or all of the following benefits:

Benefit	Cost
Group term life insurance	$ 200
Hospitalization insurance for family members	2,400
Child care payments	1,800
	$4,400

If a benefit is not selected, the employee receives cash equal to the cost of the benefit. Kay, an employee, has a spouse who works for another employer that provides hospitalization insurance but no child care payments. Kay elects to receive the group term life insurance, the child care payments, and $2,400 of cash. Only the $2,400 must be included in Kay's gross income. ∎

Flexible Spending Plans

Flexible spending plans (often referred to as flexible benefit plans) operate much like cafeteria plans. Under these plans, the employee accepts lower cash compensation in return for the employer agreeing to pay certain costs that the employer can pay without the employee recognizing gross income. For example, assume the employer's health insurance policy does not cover dental expenses. The employee could estimate his or her dental expenses for the upcoming year and agree to a salary reduction equal to the estimated dental expenses. The employer then pays or reimburses the employee for the actual dental expenses incurred, with a ceiling of the amount of the salary reduction. If the employee's actual dental expenses are less than the reduction in cash compensation, the employee cannot recover the difference. Hence, these plans are often referred to as *use or lose* plans. As is the case for cafeteria plans, flexible spending plans cannot be used to pay long-term care insurance premiums.

---

[50]§ 125.   [51]§ 125(f).

TAX *in the News*	**TAXPAYERS HAVE LONGER TO USE BEFORE THEY LOSE PLAN BENEFITS**

Under a flexible spending plan, an employee's salary reduction goes into an account that can be used for various fringe benefits. Most commonly, the account is used to pay the employee's medical expenses and dental expenses that are not covered by insurance and child care expenses. If the amount set aside is not actually spent for the designated purpose, however, the employee cannot recover the unused balance. Consequently, each year millions of dollars that are set aside in such accounts are forfeited by employees.

In a recent Notice, the IRS announced that employers can now amend their plans to allow employees a grace period of two and one-half months. That is, the amount set aside in a calendar year plan can be used until March 15 of the following year. Employers will generally amend the plans to provide that payments made before March 15 of the current year be taken first from the beginning-of-the-year balance in the account.

General Classes of Excluded Benefits

An employer can confer numerous forms and types of economic benefits on employees. Under the all-inclusive concept of income, the benefits are taxable unless one of the provisions previously discussed specifically excludes the item from gross income. The amount of the income is the fair market value of the benefit. This reasoning can lead to results that Congress considers unacceptable, as illustrated in the following example.

EXAMPLE 24

Vern is employed in New York as a ticket clerk for Trans National Airlines. He has a sick mother in Miami, Florida, but has no money for plane tickets. Trans National has daily flights from New York to Miami that often leave with empty seats. The cost of a round-trip ticket is $400, and Vern is in the 25% tax bracket. If Trans National allows Vern to fly without charge to Miami, under the general gross income rules, Vern has income equal to the value of a ticket. Therefore, Vern must pay $100 tax (.25 × $400) on a trip to Miami. Because Vern does not have $100, he cannot visit his mother, and the airplane flies with another empty seat. ■

If Trans National in Example 24 will allow employees to use resources that would otherwise be wasted, why should the tax laws interfere with the employee's decision to take advantage of the available benefit? Thus, to avoid the undesirable results that occur in Example 24 and in similar situations, as well as to create uniform rules for fringe benefits, Congress established seven broad classes of nontaxable employee benefits:[52]

- No-additional-cost services.
- Qualified employee discounts.
- Working condition fringes.
- *De minimis* fringes.
- Qualified transportation fringes.
- Qualified moving expense reimbursements.
- Qualified retirement planning services.

No-Additional-Cost Services. Example 24 illustrates the **no-additional-cost service** type of fringe benefit. The services will be nontaxable if all of the following conditions are satisfied:

- The employee receives services, as opposed to property.
- The employer does not incur substantial additional cost, including forgone revenue, in providing the services to the employee.

---

[52]See, generally, § 132.

- The services are offered to customers in the ordinary course of the business in which the employee works.[53]

Assume that Vern in Example 24 can fly without charge only if the airline cannot fill the seats with paying customers. That is, Vern must fly on standby. Although the airplane may burn slightly more fuel because Vern is on the airplane and Vern may receive the same meal as paying customers, the additional costs would not be substantial. Thus, the trip could qualify as a no-additional-cost service.

On the other hand, assume that Vern is given a reserved seat on a flight that is frequently full. The employer would be forgoing revenue to allow Vern to fly. This forgone revenue would be a substantial additional cost, and thus the benefit would be taxable. ∎

Note that if Vern were employed in a hotel owned by Trans National, the receipt of the airline ticket would be taxable because Vern did not work in that line of business. However, the Code allows the exclusion for reciprocal benefits offered by employers in the same line of business.

Grace is employed as a desk clerk for Plush Hotels, Inc. The company and Chain Hotels, Inc., have an agreement that allows any of their employees to stay without charge in either company's resort hotels during the off-season. If Grace takes advantage of the plan by staying in a Chain Hotel, she is not required to recognize income. ∎

The no-additional-cost exclusion extends to the employee's spouse and dependent children and to retired and disabled former employees. In the Regulations, the IRS has conceded that partners who perform services for the partnership are employees for purposes of the exclusion.[54] (As discussed earlier in the chapter, the IRS's position is that partners are not employees for purposes of the § 119 meals and lodging exclusion.) However, the exclusion is not allowed to highly compensated employees unless the benefit is available on a nondiscriminatory basis.

Qualified Employee Discounts.
When the employer sells goods or services (other than no-additional-cost benefits just discussed) to the employee for a price that is less than the price charged regular customers, the employee realizes income equal to the discount. However, the discount, referred to as a **qualified employee discount**, can be excluded from the gross income of the employee, subject to the following conditions and limitations:

- The exclusion is not available for real property (e.g., a house) or for personal property of the type commonly held for investment (e.g., common stocks).
- The property or services must be from the same line of business in which the employee works.
- In the case of *property*, the exclusion is limited to the *gross profit component* of the price to customers.
- In the case of *services*, the exclusion is limited to 20 percent of the customer price.[55]

Silver Corporation, which operates a department store, sells a television set to a store employee for $300. The regular customer price is $500, and the gross profit rate is 25%. The corporation also sells the employee a service contract for $120. The regular customer price for the contract is $150. The employee must include $75 in gross income.

---

[53]Reg. § 1.132–2.
[54]Reg. § 1.132–1(b).

[55]§ 132(c).

Customer price for property	$ 500
Less: Gross profit (25%)	(125)
	$ 375
Employee price	(300)
Income	$ 75
Customer price for service	$ 150
Less: 20 percent	(30)
	$ 120
Employee price	(120)
Income	$ –0–

■

EXAMPLE 28

Assume the same facts as in Example 27, except that the employee is a clerk in a hotel operated by Silver Corporation. Because the line of business requirement is not met, the employee must recognize $200 income ($500 − $300) from the purchase of the television and $30 income ($150 − $120) from the service contract. ■

As in the case of no-additional-cost benefits, the exclusion applies to employees (including service partners), employees' spouses and dependent children, and retired and disabled former employees. However, the exclusion does not apply to highly compensated individuals unless the discount is available on a nondiscriminatory basis.

Working Condition Fringes. Generally, an employee is not required to include in gross income the cost of property or services provided by the employer if the employee could deduct the cost of those items if he or she had actually paid for them.[56] These benefits are called **working condition fringes.**

EXAMPLE 29

Mitch is a CPA employed by an accounting firm. The employer pays Mitch's annual dues to professional organizations. Mitch is not required to include the payment of the dues in gross income because if he had paid the dues, he would have been allowed to deduct the amount as an employee business expense (as discussed in Chapter 9). ■

In many cases, this exclusion merely avoids reporting income and an offsetting deduction. However, in two specific situations, the working condition fringe benefit rules allow an exclusion where the expense would not be deductible if paid by the employee:

- Automobile salespeople are allowed to exclude the value of certain personal use of company demonstrators (e.g., commuting to and from work).[57]
- The employee business expense would be eliminated by the 2 percent floor on miscellaneous deductions under § 67 (see Chapter 10).

Unlike the other fringe benefits discussed previously, working condition fringes can be made available on a discriminatory basis and still qualify for the exclusion.

***De Minimis* Fringes.** As the term suggests, *de minimis* fringe benefits are so small that accounting for them is impractical.[58] The House Report contains the following examples of *de minimis* fringes:

- The typing of a personal letter by a company secretary, occasional personal use of a company copying machine, occasional company cocktail parties or

---

[56]§ 132(d).
[57]§ 132(j)(3).

[58]§ 132(e).

picnics for employees, occasional supper money or taxi fare for employees because of overtime work, and certain holiday gifts of property with a low fair market value are excluded.

- Subsidized eating facilities (e.g., an employees' cafeteria) operated by the employer are excluded if located on or near the employer's business premises, if revenue equals or exceeds direct operating costs, and if nondiscrimination requirements are met.

When taxpayers venture beyond the specific examples contained in the House Report and the Regulations, there is obviously much room for disagreement as to what is *de minimis.* However, note that except in the case of subsidized eating facilities, the *de minimis* fringe benefits can be granted in a manner that favors highly compensated employees.

Qualified Transportation Fringes.
The intent of the exclusion for **qualified transportation fringes** is to encourage the use of mass transit for commuting to and from work. Qualified transportation fringes encompass the following transportation benefits provided by the employer to the employee:[59]

1. Transportation in a commuter highway vehicle between the employee's residence and the place of employment.
2. A transit pass.
3. Qualified parking.

Statutory dollar limits are placed on the amount of the exclusion. Categories (1) and (2) above are combined for purposes of applying the limit. In this case, the limit on the exclusion for 2006 is $105 per month. Category (3) has a separate limit. For qualified parking, the limit on the exclusion for 2006 is $205 per month. Both of these dollar limits are indexed annually for inflation.

A *commuter highway vehicle* is any highway vehicle with a seating capacity of at least six adults (excluding the driver). In addition, at least 80 percent of the vehicle's use must be for transporting employees between their residences and place of employment.

Qualified parking includes the following:

- Parking provided to an employee on or near the employer's business premises.
- Parking provided to an employee on or near a location from which the employee commutes to work via mass transit, in a commuter highway vehicle, or in a carpool.

Qualified transportation fringes may be provided directly by the employer or may be in the form of cash reimbursements.

EXAMPLE 30

Gray Corporation's offices are located in the center of a large city. The company pays for parking spaces to be used by the company officers. Steve, a vice president, receives $250 of such benefits each month. The parking space rental qualifies as a qualified transportation fringe. Of the $250 benefit received each month by Steve, $205 is excludible from gross income. The balance of $45 is included in his gross income. The same result would occur if Steve paid for the parking and was reimbursed by his employer. ■

Qualified Moving Expense Reimbursements.
Qualified moving expenses that are reimbursed or paid by the employer are excludible from gross income. A qualified moving expense is one that would be deductible under § 217. See the discussion of moving expenses in Chapter 9.

---

[59]§ 132(f).

Qualified Retirement Planning Services. Qualified retirement planning services include any retirement planning advice or information that an employer who maintains a qualified retirement plan provides to an employee or the employee's spouse.[60] Congress decided to exclude the value of such services from gross income because they are a key part of retirement income planning. Such an exclusion should motivate more employers to provide retirement planning services to their employees.

Nondiscrimination Provisions. For no-additional-cost services, qualified employee discounts, and qualified retirement planning services, if the plan is discriminatory in favor of highly compensated employees, these key employees are denied exclusion treatment. However, the non-highly compensated employees who receive benefits from the plan can still enjoy exclusion treatment for the no-additional-cost services, qualified employee discounts, and qualified retirement planning services.[61]

EXAMPLE 31

Dove Company's officers are allowed to purchase goods from the company at a 25% discount. Other employees are allowed only a 15% discount. The company's gross profit margin on these goods is 30%.

Peggy, an officer in the company, purchased goods from the company for $750 when the price charged to customers was $1,000. Peggy must include $250 in gross income because the plan is discriminatory.

Leo, an employee of the company who is not an officer, purchased goods for $850 when the customer price was $1,000. Leo is not required to recognize income because he received a qualified employee discount. ∎

De minimis (except in the case of subsidized eating facilities) and working condition fringe benefits can be provided on a discriminatory basis. The *de minimis* benefits are not subject to tax because the accounting problems that would be created are out of proportion to the amount of additional tax that would result. A nondiscrimination test would simply add to the compliance problems. In the case of working condition fringes, the types of services required vary with the job. Therefore, a nondiscrimination test probably could not be satisfied, although usually there is no deliberate plan to benefit a chosen few. Likewise, the qualified transportation fringe and the qualified moving expense reimbursement can be provided on a discriminatory basis.

Taxable Fringe Benefits

If the fringe benefits cannot qualify for any of the specific exclusions or do not fit into any of the general classes of excluded benefits, the taxpayer must recognize gross income equal to the fair market value of the benefits. Obviously, problems are frequently encountered in determining values. The IRS has issued extensive Regulations addressing the valuation of personal use of an employer's automobiles and meals provided at an employer-operated eating facility.[62]

If a fringe benefit plan discriminates in favor of highly compensated employees, generally those employees are not allowed to exclude the benefits they receive that other employees do not enjoy. However, the highly compensated employees, as well as the other employees, are generally allowed to exclude the nondiscriminatory benefits.[63]

---

[60]§§ 132(a)(7) and (m).

[61]§§ 132(j)(1) and 132(m)(2).

[62]Reg. § 1.61–21(d). Generally, the income from the personal use of the employer's automobile is based on the lease value of the automobile (what it would have cost the employee to lease the automobile). Meals are valued at

150% of the employer's direct costs (e.g., food and labor) of preparing the meals.

[63]§§ 79(d), 105(h), 127(b)(2), and 132(j)(1). See the discussion of the term "highly compensated employee" in Chapter 19.

CONCEPT SUMMARY 5–2

General Classes of Excluded Benefits

Benefit	Description and Examples	Coverage Allowed	Effect of Discrimination
1. No-additional-cost services	The employee takes advantage of the employer's excess capacity (e.g., free passes for airline employees).	Current, retired, and disabled employees; their spouses and dependent children; spouses of deceased employees. Partners are treated as employees.	No exclusion for highly compensated employees.
2. Qualified discounts on goods	The employee is allowed to purchase the employer's merchandise at a price that is not less than the employer's cost.	Same as (1) above.	Same as (1) above.
3. Qualified discounts on services	The employee is allowed a discount (maximum of 20%) on services the employer offers to customers.	Same as (1) above.	Same as (1) above.
4. Working condition fringes	Expenses paid by the employer that would be deductible if paid by the employee (e.g., a mechanic's tools). Also, includes auto salesperson's use of a car held for sale.	Current employees, partners, directors, and independent contractors.	No effect.
5. *De minimis* items	Expenses so immaterial that accounting for them is not warranted (e.g., occasional supper money, personal use of the copy machine).	*Any recipient* of a fringe benefit.	No effect.
6. Qualified transportation fringes	Transportation benefits provided by the employer to employees including commuting in a commuter highway vehicle, a transit pass, and qualified parking.	Current employees.	No effect.
7. Qualified moving expense reimbursements	Qualified moving expenses that are paid or reimbursed by the employer. A qualified moving expense is one that would be deductible under § 217.	Current employees.	No effect.
8. Qualified retirement planning services	Qualified retirement planning services that are provided by the employer.	Current employees and spouses.	Same as (1) above.

MED Company has a medical reimbursement plan that reimburses officers for 100% of their medical expenses, but reimburses all other employees for only 80% of their medical expenses. Cliff, the president of the company, was reimbursed $1,000 during the year for medical expenses. Cliff must include $200 in gross income [(1 − .80) × $1,000 = $200].

E X A M P L E   32

Mike, an employee who is not an officer, received $800 (80% of his actual medical expenses) under the medical reimbursement plan. None of the $800 is includible in his gross income. ■

Foreign Earned Income

A U.S. citizen is generally subject to U.S. tax on his or her income regardless of the income's geographic origin. The income may also be subject to tax in the foreign country, and thus the taxpayer must carry a double tax burden. Out of a sense of fairness and to encourage U.S. citizens to work abroad (so that exports might be increased), Congress has provided alternative forms of relief from taxes on foreign earned income. The taxpayer can elect *either* (1) to include the foreign income in his or her taxable income and then claim a credit for foreign taxes paid or (2) to exclude the foreign earnings from his or her U.S. gross income (the **foreign earned income exclusion**).[64] The foreign tax credit option is discussed in Chapter 13, but as is apparent from the following discussion, most taxpayers will choose the exclusion.

Foreign earned income consists of the earnings from the individual's personal services rendered in a foreign country (other than as an employee of the U.S. government). To qualify for the exclusion, the taxpayer must be either of the following:

* A bona fide resident of the foreign country (or countries).
* Present in a foreign country (or countries) for at least 330 days during any 12 consecutive months.[65]

EXAMPLE 33

Sandra's trips to and from a foreign country in connection with her work were as follows:

Arrived in Foreign Country	Arrived in United States
March 10, 2005	February 1, 2006
March 7, 2006	June 1, 2006

During the 12 consecutive months ending on March 10, 2006, Sandra was present in the foreign country for at least 330 days (365 days less 28 days in February and 7 days in March 2006). Therefore, all income earned in the foreign country through March 10, 2006, is eligible for the exclusion. The income earned from March 11, 2006, through May 31, 2006, is also eligible for the exclusion because Sandra was present in the foreign country for 330 days during the 12 consecutive months ending on May 31, 2006. ■

The exclusion is *limited* to $80,000. For married persons, both of whom have foreign earned income, the exclusion is computed separately for each spouse. Community property rules do not apply (the community property spouse is not deemed to have earned one-half of the other spouse's foreign earned income). If all the days in the tax year are not qualifying days, then the taxpayer must compute the maximum exclusion on a daily basis ($80,000 divided by the number of days in the entire year and multiplied by the number of qualifying days).

EXAMPLE 34

Keith qualifies for the foreign earned income exclusion. He was present in France for all of 2006. Keith's salary for 2006 is $90,000. Since all of the days in 2006 are qualifying days, Keith can exclude $80,000 of his $90,000 salary.

[64]§ 911(a).
[65]§ 911(d). For the definition of resident, see Reg. § 1.871–2(b). Under the Regulations, a taxpayer is not a resident if he or she is there for a definite period (e.g., until completion of a construction contract).

Assume instead that only 335 days were qualifying days. Then, Keith's exclusion is limited to $73,425, computed as follows:

$$\$80{,}000 \times \frac{335 \text{ days in foreign country}}{365 \text{ days in the year}} = \$73{,}425 \quad \blacksquare$$

ETHICAL *Considerations* | **WHO SHOULD BENEFIT FROM THE FOREIGN EARNED INCOME EXCLUSION?**

Perhaps the tax law should be changed so that when an employer transfers an employee to a foreign country for a period sufficient to qualify for the foreign earned income exclusion, the benefits of the exclusion could be allocated to the employee, the employer, or both. The purpose of the tax law in this area is to increase exports; therefore, a case can be made that all of the tax benefits should be assigned to the employer. One way of accomplishing this would be to ensure that the employer's after-tax cost for compensation paid to an employee is the same whether the employee works in the United States or in a foreign country. However, employees may not be willing to work abroad unless they receive some of the tax benefit. Evaluate the equity of a change in the tax law that would assign some or all of the tax benefit to the employer.

In addition to the exclusion for foreign earnings, the *reasonable housing costs* incurred by the taxpayer and the taxpayer's family in a foreign country in excess of a base amount may be excluded from gross income. The base amount is 16 percent of the U.S. government pay scale for a GS–14 (Step 1) employee, which varies from year to year.[66]

As previously mentioned, the taxpayer may elect to include the foreign earned income in gross income and claim a credit (an offset against U.S. tax) for the foreign tax paid. The credit alternative may be advantageous if the individual's foreign earned income far exceeds the excludible amount so that the foreign taxes paid exceed the U.S. tax on the amount excluded. However, once an election is made, it applies to all subsequent years unless affirmatively revoked. A revocation is effective for the year of the change and the four subsequent years.

Interest on Certain State and Local Government Obligations

At the time the Sixteenth Amendment was ratified by the states, there was some question as to whether the Federal government possessed the constitutional authority to tax interest on state and local government obligations. Taxing such interest was thought to violate the doctrine of intergovernmental immunity in that the tax would impair the state and local governments' ability to finance their operations.[67] Thus, interest on state and local government obligations was specifically exempted from Federal income taxation.[68] However, the Supreme Court has concluded that there is no constitutional prohibition against levying a nondiscriminatory Federal income tax on state and local government obligations.[69] Nevertheless, currently the statutory exclusion still exists.

Obviously, the exclusion of the interest reduces the cost of borrowing for state and local governments. A taxpayer in the 35 percent tax bracket requires only a 5.2 percent yield on a tax-exempt bond to obtain the same after-tax income as a taxable bond paying 8 percent interest [$5.2\% \div (1 - .35) = 8\%$].

---

[66]§ 911(c).
[67]*Pollock v. Farmer's Loan & Trust Co.*, 3 AFTR 2602, 15 S.Ct. 912 (USSC, 1895).
[68]§ 103(a).

[69]*South Carolina v. Baker III*, 88–1 USTC ¶9284, 61 AFTR2d 88–995, 108 S.Ct. 1355 (USSC, 1988).

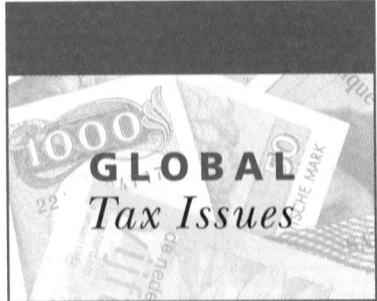

The current exempt status applies solely to state and local government bonds. Thus, income received from the accrual of interest on a condemnation award or an overpayment of state income tax is fully taxable.[70] Nor does the exemption apply to gains on the sale of tax-exempt securities.

EXAMPLE 35

Megan purchases State of Virginia bonds for $10,000 on July 1, 2005. The bonds pay $400 interest each June 30th and December 31st. On March 31, 2006, Megan sells the bonds for $10,500 plus $200 accrued interest. Megan must recognize a $500 gain ($10,500 − $10,000), but the $200 accrued interest is exempt from taxation. ∎

State and local governments have developed sophisticated financial schemes to attract new industry. For example, local municipalities have issued bonds to finance the construction of plants to be leased to private enterprise. By arranging the financing with low-interest municipal obligations, the plants could be leased at a lower cost than the private business could otherwise obtain. However, Congress has placed limitations on the use of tax-exempt securities to finance private business.[71]

Dividends

General Information

A *dividend* is a payment to a shareholder with respect to his or her stock (see Chapter 4). Dividends to shareholders are taxable only to the extent the payments are made from *either* the corporation's *current earnings and profits* (similar to net income per books) or its *accumulated earnings and profits* (similar to retained earnings per books).[72] Distributions that exceed earnings and profits are treated as a nontaxable recovery of capital and reduce the shareholder's basis in the stock. Once the shareholder's basis is reduced to zero, any subsequent distributions are taxed as capital gains (see Chapter 14).[73]

Some payments are frequently referred to as dividends but are not considered dividends for tax purposes:

- Dividends received on deposits with savings and loan associations, credit unions, and banks are actually interest (a contractual rate paid for the use of money).
- Patronage dividends paid by cooperatives (e.g., for farmers) are rebates made to the users and are considered reductions in the cost of items purchased from the association. The rebates are usually made after year-end (after the cooperative has determined whether it has met its expenses) and are apportioned among members on the basis of their purchases.

[70]*Kieselbach v. Comm.*, 43–1 USTC ¶9220, 30 AFTR 370, 63 S.Ct. 303 (USSC, 1943); *U.S. Trust Co. of New York v. Anderson*, 3 USTC ¶1125, 12 AFTR 836, 65 F.2d 575 (CA–2, 1933).
[71]See § 103(b).

[72]§ 316(a). Refer to the discussion of the beneficial tax rates for qualified dividends in Chapter 4.
[73]§ 301(c). See Chapter 5, *West Federal Taxation: Corporations, Partnerships, Estates, and Trusts,* for a detailed discussion of corporate distributions.

- Mutual insurance companies pay dividends on unmatured life insurance policies that are considered rebates of premiums.
- Shareholders in a mutual investment fund are allowed to report as capital gains their proportionate share of the fund's gains realized and distributed. The capital gain and ordinary income portions are reported on the Form 1099 that the fund supplies its shareholders each year.

ETHICAL *Considerations* | **BENEFICIARIES AND VICTIMS OF CHANGES IN DIVIDEND TAXATION**

Beginning in 2003, the tax rate on dividends was reduced to the rate applied to long-term capital gains. Such a rate reduction should have caused the market prices of dividend-paying stocks to increase and the market prices of bonds to decrease as funds were diverted to investments in stock. Thus, taxpayers who were heavily invested in dividend-paying stocks at the time of the rate reduction were beneficiaries of the change while those individuals who were primarily invested in bonds were victims. When Congress enacts new laws, should it consider the economic consequences of the change on taxpayers who made investment decisions under a prior law? Would a "grandfather" provision help?

Stock Dividends

When a corporation issues a simple stock dividend (e.g., common stock issued to common shareholders), the shareholder has merely received additional shares that represent the same total investment. Thus, the shareholder does not realize income.[74] However, if the shareholder has the *option* of receiving either cash or stock in the corporation, the individual realizes gross income whether he or she receives stock or cash.[75] A taxpayer who elects to receive the stock could be deemed to be in constructive receipt of the cash he or she has rejected.[76] However, the amount of the income in this case is the value of the stock received, rather than the cash the shareholder has rejected. See Chapter 14 for a detailed discussion of stock dividends.

Educational Savings Bonds

The cost of a college education has risen dramatically during the past 15 years. The U.S. Department of Education estimates that by the year 2007, the cost of attending a publicly supported university for four years will exceed $60,000. For a private university, the cost is expected to exceed $200,000. Consequently, Congress has attempted to assist low- to middle-income parents in saving for their children's college education.

The assistance is in the form of an interest income exclusion on **educational savings bonds**.[77] The interest on Series EE U.S. government savings bonds may be excluded from gross income if the bond proceeds are used to pay qualified higher education expenses. The exclusion applies only if both of the following requirements are satisfied:

- The savings bonds are issued after December 31, 1989.
- The savings bonds are issued to an individual who is at least 24 years old at the time of issuance.

The exclusion is not available for a married couple who file separate returns.

---

[74]*Eisner v. Macomber*, 1 USTC ¶32, 3 AFTR 3020, 40 S.Ct. 189 (USSC, 1920); § 305(a).

[75]§ 305(b).

[76]Refer to the discussion of constructive receipt in Chapter 4.

[77]§ 135.

The redemption proceeds must be used to pay qualified higher education expenses. *Qualified higher education expenses* consist of tuition and fees paid to an eligible educational institution for the taxpayer, spouse, or dependent. In calculating qualified higher education expenses, the tuition and fees paid are reduced by excludible scholarships and veterans' benefits received. If the redemption proceeds (both principal and interest) exceed the qualified higher education expenses, only a pro rata portion of the interest will qualify for exclusion treatment.

EXAMPLE 36

Tracy's redemption proceeds from qualified savings bonds during the taxable year are $6,000 (principal of $4,000 and interest of $2,000). Tracy's qualified higher education expenses are $5,000. Since the redemption proceeds exceed the qualified higher education expenses, only $1,667 [($5,000/$6,000) × $2,000] of the interest is excludible. ■

The exclusion is limited by the application of the wherewithal to pay concept. That is, once the modified adjusted gross income exceeds a threshold amount, the phaseout of the exclusion begins. *Modified adjusted gross income* (*MAGI*) is adjusted gross income prior to the § 911 foreign earned income exclusion and the educational savings bond exclusion. The threshold amounts are adjusted for inflation each year. For 2006, the phaseout begins at $63,100 ($94,700 on a joint return).[78] The phaseout is completed when MAGI exceeds the threshold amount by more than $15,000 ($30,000 on a joint return). The otherwise excludible interest is reduced by the amount calculated as follows:

$$\frac{\text{MAGI} - \$63,100}{\$15,000} \times \frac{\text{Excludible interest}}{\text{before phaseout}} = \frac{\text{Reduction in}}{\text{excludible interest}}$$

On a joint return, $94,700 is substituted for $63,100 (in 2006), and $30,000 is substituted for $15,000.

EXAMPLE 37

Assume the same facts as in Example 36, except that Tracy's MAGI for 2006 is $70,000. The phaseout results in Tracy's interest exclusion being reduced by $767 { [($70,000 − $63,100)/$15,000] × $1,667 }. Therefore, Tracy's exclusion is $900 ($1,667 − $767). ■

Qualified Tuition Programs

Nearly all, if not all, states have created programs whereby parents can in effect prepay their child's college tuition. The prepayment serves as a hedge against future increases in tuition. Generally, if the child does not attend college, the parents are refunded their payments plus interest. Upon first impression, these prepaid tuition programs resemble the below-market loans discussed in Chapter 4. That is, assuming the tuition increases, the parent receives a reduction in the child's tuition in exchange for the use of the funds. However, Congress has created an exclusion provision for these programs.[79]

Under a **qualified tuition program**, the amounts contributed must be used for qualified higher education expenses. These expenses include tuition, fees, books, supplies, room and board, and equipment required for enrollment or attendance at a college, university, or certain vocational schools. Qualified higher education expenses also include the expenses for special needs services that are incurred in connection with the enrollment and attendance of special needs students.

The earnings of the contributed funds, including the discount on tuition charged to participants, are not included in gross income provided that the contributions and earnings are used for qualified higher education expenses.

---

[78]The indexed amounts for 2005 are $61,200 and $91,850.

[79]§ 529. For another way to beneficially fund educational costs, see the discussion of Coverdell Education Savings Accounts (CESAs) in Chapter 19 (§ 530).

E X A M P L E   3 8

Agnes paid $20,000 into a qualified tuition program to be used for her son's college tuition. When her son graduated from high school, the fund balance had increased to $30,000 as a result of interest credited to the account. The interest was not included in Agnes's gross income. During the current year, $7,500 of the balance in the fund was used to pay the son's tuition and fees. None of this amount is included in either Agnes's or the son's gross income. ■

If the parent receives a refund (e.g., child does not attend college), the excess of the amount refunded over the amount contributed by the parent is included in the parent's gross income.

Qualified tuition programs have been expanded to apply to private educational institutions as well as public educational institutions. Distributions made after December 31, 2003, from such a plan maintained by an entity other than the state for qualified higher education expenses are eligible for exclusion from gross income.

Tax Benefit Rule

Generally, if a taxpayer obtains a deduction for an item in one year and in a later year recovers all or a portion of the prior deduction, the recovery is included in gross income in the year received.[80]

E X A M P L E   3 9

A taxpayer deducted as a loss a $1,000 receivable from a customer when it appeared the amount would never be collected. The following year, the customer paid $800 on the receivable. The taxpayer must report the $800 as gross income in the year it is received. ■

However, the § 111 **tax benefit rule** provides that no income is recognized upon the recovery of a deduction, or the portion of a deduction, that did not yield a tax benefit in the year it was taken. If the taxpayer in Example 39 had no tax liability in the year of the deduction (e.g., itemized deductions and personal exemptions exceeded adjusted gross income), the recovery would be partially or totally excluded from gross income in the year of the recovery.[81]

E X A M P L E   4 0

Before deducting a $1,000 loss from an uncollectible business receivable, Ali had taxable income of $200, computed as follows:

Adjusted gross income	$ 13,300
Itemized deductions and personal exemptions	(13,100)
Taxable income	$ 200

The business bad debt deduction yields only a $200 tax benefit. That is, taxable income is reduced by only $200 (to zero) as a result of the bad debt deduction. Therefore, if the customer makes a payment on the previously deducted receivable in a subsequent year, only the first $200 is a recovery of a prior deduction and thus is taxable. Any additional amount collected is nontaxable because only $200 of the loss yielded a reduction in taxable income. ■

Income from Discharge of Indebtedness

A transfer of appreciated property (fair market value is greater than adjusted basis) in satisfaction of a debt is an event that triggers the realization of income. The transaction is treated as a sale of the appreciated property followed by payment of the debt.[82] Foreclosure by a creditor is also treated as a sale or exchange of the property.[83]

---

[80]§ 111(a).
[81]Itemized deductions are discussed in Chapter 10.

[82]Reg. § 1.1001–2(a).
[83]*Estate of Delman v. Comm.*, 73 T.C. 15 (1979).

EXAMPLE 41

Juan owes State Bank $100,000 on an unsecured note. He satisfies the note by transferring to the bank common stock with a basis of $60,000 and a fair market value of $100,000. Juan must recognize a $40,000 gain on the transfer. Juan also owes the bank $50,000 on a note secured by land. When Juan's basis in the land is $20,000 and the land's fair market value is $50,000, the bank forecloses on the loan and takes title to the land. Juan must recognize a $30,000 gain on the foreclosure. ■

In some cases, creditors will not exercise their right of foreclosure and will even forgive a portion of the debt to assure the vitality of the debtor. In such cases, the debtor realizes income from discharge of indebtedness.

EXAMPLE 42

Brown Corporation is unable to meet the mortgage payments on its factory building. Both the corporation and the mortgage holder are aware of the depressed market for industrial property in the area. Foreclosure would only result in the creditor's obtaining unsalable property. To improve Brown Corporation's financial position and thus improve Brown's chances of obtaining the additional credit necessary for survival from other lenders, the creditor agrees to forgive all amounts past due and to reduce the principal amount of the mortgage. ■

Generally, the income realized by the debtor from the forgiveness of a debt is taxable.[84] A similar debt discharge (produced by a different creditor motivation) associated with personal use property is illustrated in Example 43.

EXAMPLE 43

In 2001, Joyce borrowed $60,000 from National Bank to purchase her personal residence. Joyce agreed to make monthly principal and interest payments for 15 years. The interest rate on the note was 7%. In 2006, when the balance on the note has been reduced through monthly payments to $48,000, the bank offers to accept $45,000 in full settlement of the note. The bank makes the offer because interest rates have increased to 11%. Joyce accepts the bank's offer. As a result, Joyce must recognize $3,000 ($48,000 − $45,000) of gross income.[85] ■

The following discharge of indebtedness situations are subject to special treatment:[86]

1. Creditors' gifts.
2. Discharges under Federal bankruptcy law.
3. Discharges that occur when the debtor is insolvent.
4. Discharge of the farm debt of a solvent taxpayer.
5. Discharge of **qualified real property business indebtedness**.
6. A seller's cancellation of the buyer's indebtedness.
7. A shareholder's cancellation of the corporation's indebtedness.
8. Forgiveness of certain loans to students.

If the creditor reduces the debt as an act of *love, affection,* or *generosity,* the debtor has simply received a nontaxable gift (situation 1). Rarely will a gift be found to have occurred in a business context. A businessperson may settle a debt for less than the amount due, but as a matter of business expediency (e.g., high collection costs or disputes as to contract terms) rather than generosity.[87]

In situations 2, 3, 4, and 5, the Code allows the debtor to reduce his or her basis in the assets by the realized gain from the discharge.[88] Thus, the realized gain is merely deferred until the assets are sold (or depreciated). Similarly, in situation 6 (a price reduction), the debtor reduces the basis in the specific assets financed by the seller.[89]

[84] *U.S. v. Kirby Lumber Co.,* 2 USTC ¶814, 10 AFTR 458, 52 S.Ct. 4 (USSC, 1931), codified in § 61(a)(12).
[85] Rev.Rul. 82–202, 1982–1 C.B. 35.
[86] §§ 108 and 1017.
[87] *Comm. v. Jacobson,* 49–1 USTC ¶9133, 37 AFTR 516, 69 S.Ct. 358 (USSC, 1949).
[88] §§ 108(a), (c), (e), and (g). Note that § 108(b) provides that other tax attributes (e.g., net operating loss) will be reduced by the realized gain from the debt discharge prior to the basis adjustment unless the taxpayer elects to apply the basis adjustment first.
[89] § 108(e)(5).

A shareholder's cancellation of the corporation's indebtedness to him or her (situation 7) usually is considered a contribution of capital to the corporation by the shareholder. Thus, the corporation's paid-in capital is increased, and its liabilities are decreased by the same amount.[90]

Many states make loans to students on the condition that the loan will be forgiven if the student practices a profession in the state upon completing his or her studies. The amount of the loan that is forgiven (situation 8) is excluded from gross income.[91]

The present law excludes certain types of economic gains from taxation. Therefore, taxpayers may find tax planning techniques helpful in obtaining the maximum benefits from the exclusion of such gains. Following are some of the tax planning opportunities made available by the exclusions described in this chapter.

> **LO.5**
>
> Identify tax planning strategies for obtaining the maximum benefit from allowable exclusions.

TAX PLANNING
Considerations

Life Insurance

Life insurance offers several favorable tax attributes. As discussed in Chapter 4, the annual increase in the cash surrender value of the policy is not taxable (because no income has been actually or constructively received). By borrowing on the policy's cash surrender value, the owner can actually receive the policy's increase in value in cash but without recognizing income.

Employee Benefits

Generally, employees view accident and health insurance, as well as life insurance, as necessities. Employees can obtain group coverage at much lower rates than individuals would have to pay for the same protection. Premiums paid by the employer can be excluded from the employees' gross income. Because of the exclusion, employees will have a greater after-tax and after-insurance income if the employer pays a lower salary but also pays the insurance premiums.

EXAMPLE 44

Pat receives a salary of $30,000. The company has group insurance benefits, but Pat is required to pay his own premiums as follows:

Hospitalization and medical insurance	$1,400
Term life insurance ($30,000 coverage)	200
Disability insurance	400
	$2,000

To simplify the analysis, assume Pat's tax rate on income is 25%. After paying taxes of $7,500 (.25 × $30,000) and $2,000 for insurance, Pat has $20,500 ($30,000 − $7,500 − $2,000) for his other living needs.

If Pat's employer reduced Pat's salary by $2,000 (to $28,000) but paid his insurance premiums, Pat's tax liability would be only $7,000 ($28,000 × .25). Thus, Pat would have $21,000 ($28,000 − $7,000) to meet his other living needs. The change in the compensation plan would save Pat $500 ($21,000 − $20,500). ∎

Similarly, employees must often incur expenses for child care and parking. The employee can have more income for other uses if the employer pays these costs for the employee but reduces the employee's salary by the cost of the benefits.

The use of cafeteria plans has increased dramatically in recent years. These plans allow employees to tailor their benefits to meet their individual situations. Thus, where both spouses in a married couple are working, duplications of benefits can be avoided, and other needed benefits can often be added. If less than all of the employee's allowance is spent, the employee can receive cash.

---

[90]§ 108(e)(6).   [91]§ 108(f).

The meals and lodging exclusion enables employees to receive from their employer what they ordinarily must purchase with after-tax dollars. Although the requirements that the employee live and take his or her meals on the employer's premises limit the tax planning opportunities, the exclusion is an important factor in the employee's compensation in certain situations (e.g., hotels, motels, restaurants, farms, and ranches).

The employees' discount provision is especially important for manufacturers and wholesalers. Employees of manufacturers can avoid tax on the manufacturer's, wholesaler's, and retailer's markups. The wholesaler's employees can avoid tax on an amount equal to the wholesale and retail markups.

It should be recognized that the exclusion of benefits is generally available only to employees. Proprietors and partners must pay tax on the same benefits their employees receive tax-free. By incorporating and becoming an employee of the corporation, the former proprietor or partner can also receive these tax-exempt benefits. Thus, the availability of employee benefits is a consideration in the decision to incorporate.

Investment Income

Tax-exempt state and local government bonds are almost irresistible investments for many high-income taxpayers. To realize the maximum benefit from the exemption, the investor can purchase zero-coupon bonds. Like Series EE U.S. government savings bonds, these investments pay interest only at maturity. The advantage of the zero-coupon feature for a tax-exempt bond is that the investor can earn tax-exempt interest on the accumulated principal and interest. If the investor purchases a bond that pays the interest each year, the interest received may be such a small amount that an additional tax-exempt investment cannot be made. In addition, reinvesting the interest may entail transaction costs (broker's fees). The zero-coupon feature avoids these problems.

Series EE U.S. government savings bonds can earn tax-exempt interest if the bond proceeds are used for qualified higher education expenses. Many taxpayers can foresee these expenditures being made for their children's educations. In deciding whether to invest in the bonds, however, the investor must take into account the income limitations for excluding the interest from gross income.

KEY TERMS

Accelerated death benefits, 5-7

Accident and health benefits, 5-13

Cafeteria plan, 5-19

Compensatory damages, 5-11

De minimis fringes, 5-22

Death benefits, 5-6

Educational savings bonds, 5-29

Flexible spending plans, 5-19

Foreign earned income exclusion, 5-26

Gift, 5-5

Health Savings Account (HSA), 5-14

Life insurance proceeds, 5-6

Long-term care insurance, 5-15

No-additional-cost service, 5-20

Punitive damages, 5-11

Qualified employee discount, 5-21

Qualified real property business indebtedness, 5-32

Qualified transportation fringes, 5-23

Qualified tuition program, 5-30

Qualified tuition reduction plan, 5-10

Scholarship, 5-9

Tax benefit rule, 5-31

Working condition fringes, 5-22

P R O B L E M   M A T E R I A L S

DISCUSSION QUESTIONS

1. Uncle John promised Tom, "Come and take care of me and I will leave you the farm when I die." Tom took care of Uncle John for the five years preceding his death. When Uncle John died, in accordance with his will, Tom received the farm. Can Tom exclude the value of the farm from his gross income as a gift or inheritance, or has he received compensation income?

2. A few years prior to her death Hattie gave Albert, her nephew, a bond with a cost and face amount of $10,000. The bond paid $400 of interest each year. Albert collected interest on the bond for five years and then collected the face amount of the bond. The beneficiary of Hattie's life insurance policy was her niece, Samantha. Hattie had paid $6,000 in premiums, and the face amount of the policy was $10,000. When Hattie died, Samantha elected to collect the life insurance proceeds in $2,400 installments each year for five years. How much should Albert and Samantha include in their gross incomes from the bond and life insurance?

[handwritten: 400/yr for each.]

3. Pearl Lumber Company is located in an isolated area that is sometimes referred to as "Tornado Alley." Most of the people who live in the area are employed by Pearl. The company created a nonprofit foundation to assist tornado victims. The majority of the beneficiaries are Pearl's employees. What are the relevant issues regarding the payments made by the nonprofit foundation to tornado victims?

Issue ID

4. Hannah was a cash basis taxpayer. She died during the year, and her husband, Wade, and her son, Jim, were the beneficiaries of her estate. Wade received Hannah's accrued salary and commissions, $10,000 at the time of her death. Jim received $10,000 as the beneficiary of Hannah's group term life insurance policy. The insurance premiums had been paid by the employer. What are the effects of the above on Wade's and Jim's gross income?

5. Matt's truck was stalled on the side of the road. Abby stopped to help and called Al, who agreed to repair the truck for $75. Matt paid Al $75 and Abby $25. The payment to Al was made because of a contractual obligation and therefore is not a gift. The payment to Abby was not made because of a contractual obligation. Does this mean that the payment Abby received is a gift?

[handwritten: No. Still a compensation for service.]

6. When Ted was age 92 and suffering from a terminal illness, he sold his life insurance policy to the Violet Capital Fund for $80,000. Ted had paid $30,000 of premiums on the policy. Later that same year Ted died, and Violet Capital collected the face amount of the policy of $100,000. Determine the effect of these transactions on Ted's gross income and on Violet Capital's gross income.

7. Amber Finance Company requires its customers to purchase a credit life insurance policy. Amber is the beneficiary of the policy to the extent of the remaining balance on the loan at the time of the customer's death. In 2004, Amber wrote off as uncollectible a $5,000 account receivable from Aly. When Aly died in 2006, the life insurance policy was still in force, and Amber received $5,000. Is the $5,000 of life insurance proceeds received by Amber included in its gross income?

8. Ed paid $39,000 of life insurance premiums before cashing in his life insurance policy for the $45,000 cash surrender value. He decided he could invest the money and earn a higher rate of return. Sarah, who has a terminal illness, cashed in her life insurance policy (cost of $39,000 and proceeds of $45,000) to go on an around-the-world cruise. Determine the amounts that Ed and Sarah should include in their gross income.

[handwritten: 0 on Sara's / 6K on Ed's]

9. José is an undergraduate student and receives a scholarship that pays $10,000 for tuition, $6,000 for room and meals, and $1,000 for books. How much is José required to include in gross income?

10. Sarah's automobile was struck by a corporate truck that was driven by a drunk employee of the corporation. The company has admitted liability, and Sarah is negotiating a

Decision Making

settlement. Sarah has asked for $100,000 for the loss of income she suffered from the injury, $50,000 in medical bills (which she has not deducted), and $80,000 in punitive damages. The company has made the following counteroffer: it will pay her $50,000 for medical expenses and $160,000 for lost wages, but no punitive damages because punitive damages create complications with its insurance company. Assuming that Sarah is in the 33% marginal tax bracket, should she accept the company's offer?

11. Sara was a victim of assault and battery. She sued the assailant and was awarded $120,000 of actual damages and $240,000 in punitive damages. How much of the award of $360,000 should Sara include in her gross income?

12. Wes was a major league baseball pitcher before a career-ending injury caused by a negligent driver. Wes sued the driver and collected $15 million as compensation for lost estimated future income as a pitcher and $10 million as punitive damages. Sam was also a major league baseball pitcher and earned $25 million for pitching. Do the amounts that Wes and Sam receive have the same effect on their gross income? Explain.

13. Holly was injured while working in a factory and received $12,000 as workers' compensation while she was unable to work because of the injury. Jill was laid off by the same factory and collected $12,000 in unemployment compensation. Since neither Holly nor Jill actually worked for the amounts received, should they each include the $12,000 in gross income?

14. How are Health Savings Accounts (HSAs) used as an employee fringe benefit? How does an HSA differ from traditional health insurance?

15. Paul is in the 15% marginal tax bracket, and Betty is in the 35% marginal tax bracket. They each pay $6,300 in health insurance premiums for themselves and their families. Their employer has offered to provide group health insurance, but each employee would have to forgo a $7,000 salary increase. How would the change in compensation affect Paul, Betty, and the employer?

16. What is the difference between a "cafeteria plan" and an employee "flexible spending plan"?

17. Ted works for Sage Motors, an automobile dealership. All employees can buy a car at the company's cost plus 2%. The company does not charge employees the $175 transfer service fee that nonemployees must pay. Ted purchased an automobile for $24,480 ($24,000 + $480). The company's cost was $24,000. The price for a nonemployee would have been $27,775 ($27,600 + $175 transfer service fee). What is Ted's gross income from the purchase of the automobile?

18. Zack works at the Silver Life Country Club. All employees, their spouses, and children are allowed to use the club's golf and swimming facilities the same as club members. The annual membership dues are $4,000 for a family. A major consideration in Zack's accepting the job was that his son, a possible future golf professional, would be allowed to play golf each day. Is Zack required to include any of the $4,000 in gross income?

19. Eagle Life Insurance Company pays its employees $.30 per mile for driving their personal automobiles to and from work. The company reimburses each employee who rides the bus $100 a month for the cost of a pass. Tom collected $100 for his automobile mileage, and Ted received $100 as reimbursement for the cost of a bus pass.
    a. What are the effects of the above on Tom's and Ted's gross income?
    b. Assume that Tom and Ted are in the 28% marginal tax bracket and the actual before-tax cost for Tom to drive to and from work is $.30 per mile. What are Tom's and Ted's after-tax costs of commuting to and from work?

Issue ID

20. Several of Egret Company's employees have asked the company to create a hiking trail that employees could use during their lunch hours. The company owns vacant land that is being held for future expansion, but would have to spend approximately $50,000 if it were to make a trail. Nonemployees would be allowed to use the facility as part of the company's effort to build strong community support. What are the relevant tax issues for the employees?

21. Marla, a U.S. citizen, has been working on a construction project in a foreign country for the past nine months. The project will be completed in a few weeks. She has an offer to work on another three-month project in that same foreign country. Alternatively, she could return to the United States and seek employment. How does the tax law affect Marla's decision?

22. Tedra is in the 35% marginal tax bracket. She is very risk averse and is considering purchasing U.S. government bonds due in 10 years that yield 5.6% before tax. Triple A rated State of Virginia bonds due in 10 years yield 4%. Which is the better alternative, assuming the bonds are of equal risk?

Decision Making

23. Maria is a cash basis farmer and a member of a farmers' cooperative. During 2005, she purchased $100,000 in feed, seeds, and fertilizer from the cooperative, all of which was deducted. She had a $20,000 loss from the farming operations and $75,000 in gross income from other sources. In 2006, she received a $1,000 patronage dividend from the cooperative as a rebate on her 2005 purchases. What effect does the patronage dividend have on Maria's 2005 and 2006 gross income?

24. Arthur paid $50,000 to the Virginia Qualified Tuition Program: $25,000 for his son, Robert, and $25,000 for his daughter, Peggy. Only Peggy went to college. The $25,000 in the account for her was accepted in full payment of four years of tuition, which otherwise would have been $40,000. Since Robert did not attend college, $31,100 ($25,000 plus $6,100 interest) was refunded to Arthur. What are the tax consequences to Arthur, to Peggy, and to Robert?

25. Mary is a cash basis taxpayer. In 2006, she earned only $5,400, which was less than her standard deduction and personal exemption. In January 2007, Mary's employer determined that he had miscalculated her December 2006 bonus and that she should have received an additional $1,000 of compensation in 2006. The employer paid Mary the $1,000 in 2007. If Mary had received the $1,000 in 2006, it would not have resulted in any tax liability because her gross income would still have been less than her standard deduction and personal exemption. In 2007, Mary had over $30,000 in taxable income. Does the tax benefit rule apply to Mary's situation? Explain.

26. Ida purchased a ranch. She gave the seller $50,000 cash and a 7% note for $450,000. When the principal on the note had been reduced to $420,000, the seller agreed to accept $350,000 in retirement of the debt. The creditor made the offer because interest rates had increased substantially. Ida was not undergoing bankruptcy and was not insolvent.
    a. Did Ida realize income from retiring the debt, and, if so, is she required to include the amount in her gross income?
    b. What if the creditor was a bank rather than the party who sold the ranch to Ida?

27. Harry has experienced financial difficulties as a result of his struggling business. He has been behind on his mortgage payments for the last six months. The mortgage holder, who is a friend of Harry's, has offered to accept $80,000 in full payment of the $100,000 owed on the mortgage and payable over the next 10 years. The interest rate of the mortgage is 7%, and the market rate is now 8%. What tax issues are raised by the creditor's offer?

Issue ID

PROBLEMS

28. During the year, Wilbur received the following in connection with his father's estate:

    • His father's will named Wilbur as the executor of the estate. He received $7,500 for serving as executor.
    • Wilbur was also a beneficiary of his father's estate and received real estate that was included in the estate at a value of $100,000 that his father had purchased for $30,000.
    • Wilbur was the beneficiary of one of his father's life insurance policies. He elected to collect the proceeds of the $100,000 policy in four installments of $30,000 each. Each $30,000 payment consists of principal and interest. He collected $30,000 this year.

    Determine the effect on Wilbur's gross income.

29. Determine the gross income to the beneficiaries in each of the following cases:
    a. When José died, his daughter collected $2,500 in accrued vacation pay from his employer.
    b. Josh was unable to work for several months because of an illness. His employer made Josh's car payments of $1,500 while Josh was ill.
    c. Jay died after purchasing a $50,000 life insurance policy that was pledged to pay the $40,000 mortgage on his home, with the remaining proceeds of $10,000 paid to his wife.
    d. Lavender, Inc., was the beneficiary of a $100,000 life insurance policy it had purchased on the life of its chief executive officer who died during the year.

30. Laura was recently diagnosed with cancer and has begun chemotherapy treatments. She has incurred a lot of medical and other general living expenses and is in need of cash. Therefore, she is considering cashing in her life insurance policy. She has paid $15,000 in premiums. The policy has a face amount of $50,000, and the Viatical Benefits Company has offered to pay her $35,000 and to pay subsequent premiums.
    a. What will be the tax consequences to Laura of assigning the benefits to Viatical, assuming she has been diagnosed by a cancer specialist as having less than one year to live?
    b. Same as in (a), except that the physician has opined that Laura will live for several years, but will be unable to perform the normal functions of daily living without the assistance of a practical nurse.

31. Determine whether the taxpayer has gross income in each of the following situations:

    a. Jim is a waiter in a restaurant. The rule of thumb is that a customer should leave the waiter a tip equal to 15% of the bill. Jim has a charming personality, provides exceptionally good service, and has developed an almost personal relationship with many of his repeat customers. As a result, Jim generally receives a 20% tip. In the current year, he received $36,000 in tips. The standard 15% rate would have yielded $27,000 in tips.
    b. Tara works at a grocery store, bagging groceries and carrying them to the customers' automobiles. Her employer posts a sign saying that the employees are paid by the hour and that customers are not expected to tip them. Tara received $1,800 in tips from customers.
    c. Sheila worked at a hotel. Her home was damaged by a fire. Sheila's employer allowed her to stay at the hotel for no charge until she could return to her home. The normal charge for the room Sheila occupied during this period was $500, and the hotel had several vacant rooms.
    d. Kara's home was damaged by a fire that had spread from a fire in a national forest. The President of the United States declared the county where she lived a "qualified disaster area." The Federal government paid her $1,500 for living expenses while her home was being repaired. How does the payment for living expenses affect Kara's gross income?

32. Donald was killed in an accident while he was on the job. His employer provided him with group term life insurance of $150,000 (twice his annual salary), which was payable to his widow, Darlene. Premiums on this policy totaling $1,500 have been included in Donald's gross income under § 79. Darlene also received $80,000 under workers' compensation associated with the accident. In addition, Donald had purchased a $100,000 life insurance policy that paid $200,000 in the case of an accidental death. The proceeds were payable to Darlene, who elected to receive payments of $25,000 each year for a 10-year period. What is Darlene's gross income from the above in 2006?

33. Fay and Edward are partners in an accounting firm. The partners have entered into an arm's length agreement requiring Fay to purchase Edward's partnership interest from Edward's estate if he dies before Fay. The price is set at 150% of the book value of Edward's partnership interest at the time of his death. Fay purchased an insurance policy on Edward's life to fund this agreement. After Fay had paid $40,000 in premiums, Edward was killed in an automobile accident, and Fay collected $1.5 million of life insurance proceeds. Fay used the life insurance proceeds to purchase Edward's partnership interest.

    a.   What amount should Fay include in her gross income from receiving the life insurance proceeds?

    b.   The insurance company paid Fay $15,000 interest on the life insurance proceeds during the period Edward's estate was in administration. During this period, Fay had left the insurance proceeds with the insurance company. Is this interest taxable?

    c.   When Fay paid $1.5 million for Edward's partnership interest, priced as specified in the agreement, the fair market value of Edward's interest was $2 million. How much should Fay include in her gross income from this bargain purchase?

34. Sarah was an all-state soccer player during her junior and senior years in high school. She accepted an athletic scholarship from State University. The scholarship provided the following:

Tuition and fees	$8,000
Housing and meals	7,500
Books and supplies	1,000

    a.   Determine the effect of the scholarship on Sarah's gross income. *7500*

    b.   Sarah's brother, Walt, was not a gifted athlete, but he received $8,000 from their father's employer as a scholarship during the year. The employer grants the children of all executives a scholarship equal to annual tuition and fees. Determine the effect of the scholarship on Walt's and his father's gross income. *all b/c it's compensation to only Executives.*

35. Alejandro was awarded an academic scholarship to State University for the 2006–2007 academic year. He received $5,000 in August and $6,000 in December 2006. Alejandro had enough personal savings to pay all expenses as they came due. Alejandro's expenditures for the relevant period were as follows:

Tuition, August 2006	$3,300
Tuition, December 2006	3,400
Room and board	
August–December 2006	3,000
January–May 2007	2,400
Books and educational supplies	
August–December 2006	1,000
January–May 2007	1,200

Determine the effect on Alejandro's gross income for 2006 and 2007.

36. Liz sued an overzealous bill collector and received the following settlement:

Damage to her automobile the collector attempted to repossess	$ 1,000
Physical damage to her arm caused by the collector	8,000
Loss of income while her arm was healing	6,000
Punitive damages	30,000

    a.   What effect does the settlement have on Liz's gross income?

    b.   Assume Liz also collected $40,000 of damages for slander to her personal reputation caused by the bill collector misrepresenting the facts to Liz's employer and other creditors. Is this $40,000 included in Liz's gross income?

37. Determine the effect on gross income in each of the following cases:

    a.   Eloise received $150,000 in settlement of a sex discrimination case against her former employer.

    b.   Nell received $10,000 for damages to her personal reputation. She also received $40,000 punitive damages.

    c.   Orange Corporation, an accrual basis taxpayer, received $50,000 from a lawsuit filed against its auditor who overcharged for services rendered in a previous year.

    d.   Beth received $10,000 compensatory damages and $30,000 punitive damages in a lawsuit she filed against a tanning parlor for severe burns she received from using its tanning equipment.

    e.   Joanne received compensatory damages of $75,000 and punitive damages of $300,000 from a cosmetic surgeon who botched her nose job.

38. Rex, age 45, is an officer of Blue Company, which provides him with the following nondiscriminatory fringe benefits in 2006:

    • Hospitalization insurance premiums for Rex and his dependents. The cost of the coverage for Rex is $2,700 per year, and the additional cost for his dependents is $3,600 per year. The plan has a $2,000 deductible, but his employer contributed $1,500 to Rex's Health Savings Account. Rex withdrew only $800 from the HSA, and the account earned $50 interest during the year.
    • Long-term care insurance premiums for Rex, at a cost of $3,600 per year.
    • Insurance premiums of $840 for salary continuation payments. Under the plan, Rex will receive his regular salary in the event he is unable to work due to illness. Rex collected $4,500 on the policy to replace lost wages while he was ill during the year.
    • Rex is a part-time student working on his bachelor's degree in engineering. His employer reimbursed his $5,200 tuition under a plan available to all full-time employees.

    Determine the amount Rex must include in gross income.

Communications

39. The UVW Union and HON Corporation are negotiating contract terms. Assume the union members are in the 28% marginal tax bracket and all benefits are provided on a nondiscriminatory basis. Write a letter to the UVW Union members explaining the tax consequences of the options discussed below. The union's address is 905 Spruce Street, Washington, D.C. 20227.
    a. The company would impose a $100 deductible on medical insurance benefits. Most employees incur more than $100 each year in medical expenses.
    b. Employees would get an additional paid holiday with the same annual income (the same pay but less work).
    c. An employee who did not need health insurance (because the employee's spouse works and receives family coverage) would be allowed to receive the cash value of the coverage.

Decision Making

40. Mauve Corporation has a group hospitalization insurance plan that has a $200 deductible amount for hospital visits and a $15 deductible for doctor visits and prescriptions. The deductible portion paid by employees who have children has become substantial for some employees. The company is considering adopting a medical reimbursement plan or a flexible benefits plan to cover the deductible amounts. Either of these plans can be tailored to meet the needs of the employees. What are the cost considerations to the employer that should be considered in choosing between these plans?

41. Bertha spent the last 60 days of 2006 in a nursing home. The cost of the services provided to her was $12,000. Medicare paid $7,100 toward the cost of her stay. Bertha also received $8,000 of benefits under a long-term care insurance policy she purchased. What is the effect on Bertha's gross income?

42. Tim is the vice president of western operations for Maroon Oil Company and is stationed in San Francisco. He is required to live in an employer-owned home, which is three blocks from his company office. The company-provided home is equipped with high-speed Internet access and several telephone lines. Tim receives telephone calls and e-mails that require immediate attention any time of day or night because the company's business is spread all over the world. A full-time administrative assistant resides in the house to assist Tim with the urgent business matters. Tim often uses the home for entertaining customers, suppliers, and employees. The fair market value of comparable housing is $8,500 per month. Tim is also provided with free parking at his company's office. The value of the parking is $325 per month. Calculate the amount associated with the company-provided housing and free parking that Tim must include in his gross income.

43. Does the taxpayer recognize gross income in the following situations?

    a. Ann is a registered nurse working in a community hospital. She is not required to take her lunch on the hospital premises, but she can eat in the cafeteria at no charge. The hospital adopted this policy to encourage employees to stay on the premises and be available in case of emergencies. During the year, Ann ate most of her meals on the premises. The total value of those meals was $750.

b.   Ira is the manager of a hotel. His employer allows him to live in one of the rooms rent-free or to receive a $600 per month cash allowance for rent. Ira has elected to live in the hotel.

c.   Seth is a forest ranger and lives in his employer's cabin in the forest. He is required to live there, and because there are no restaurants nearby, the employer supplies Seth with groceries that he cooks and eats on the premises.

d.   Rocky is a partner in the BAR Ranch (a partnership). He is the full-time manager of the ranch. BAR has a business purpose for Rocky's living on the ranch.

600

∅

∅ possible, but may have to include b/c he's partner.

Decision Making

44. Betty is considering taking an early retirement offered by her employer. She would receive $2,000 per month, indexed for inflation. However, she would no longer be able to use the company's health facilities, and she would be required to pay her hospitalization insurance of $7,800 each year. Betty and her husband will file a joint return and take the standard deduction. She currently receives a salary of $40,000 a year, and her employer pays for all of her hospitalization insurance. If she retires, Betty would not be able to use her former employer's exercise facilities because of the commuting distance. She would like to continue to exercise, however, and will therefore join a health club at a cost of $50 per month. Betty and her husband have other sources of income and are in and will remain in the 25% marginal tax bracket. She currently pays Social Security taxes of 7.65% on her salary, but her retirement pay would not be subject to this tax. She will earn about $11,000 a year from a part-time job. Betty would like to know whether she should accept the early retirement offer.

Communications

45. Finch Construction Company provides the carpenters it employs with all of the required tools. However, the company believes that this practice has led to some employees not taking care of the tools and to the mysterious disappearance of some tools. The company is considering requiring all of its employees to provide their own tools. Each employee's salary would be increased by $1,500 to compensate for the additional cost. Write a letter to Finch's management explaining the tax consequences of this plan to the carpenters. Finch's address is 300 Harbor Drive, Vermillion, SD 57069.

46. Redbird, Inc., does not provide its employees with any tax-exempt fringe benefits. The company is considering adopting a hospital and medical benefits insurance plan that will cost approximately $7,000 per employee. In order to adopt this plan, the company may have to reduce salaries and/or lower future salary increases. Redbird is in the 35% (combined Federal and state rates) bracket. Redbird is also responsible for matching the Social Security and Medicare taxes withheld on employees' salaries. The benefits insurance plan will not be subject to the Social Security and Medicare taxes. The employees generally fall into three marginal tax rate groups:

Income Tax	Social Security and Medicare Tax	Total
.15	.0765	.2265
.25	.0765	.3265
.35	.0145	.3645

The company has asked you to assist in its financial planning for the benefits insurance plan by computing the following:

a.   How much taxable compensation is the equivalent of $7,000 exempt compensation for each of the three classes of employees?

b.   What is the company's after-tax cost of the taxable compensation computed in (a) above?

c.   What is the company's after-tax cost of the exempt compensation?

d.   Briefly explain your conclusions from the above analysis.

Decision Making

47. Rosa's employer has instituted a flexible benefits program. Rosa is allowed to select from a variety of benefits, but the total cost cannot exceed $3,000. The company's medical insurance plan does not cover dental expenses. Rosa's daughter needs approximately $3,000 worth of dental work. Rosa decides to set aside the maximum amount of her salary in the flexible benefits plan for the reimbursement of dental expenses. Rosa is in the 25% marginal tax bracket.

a. Rosa uses the entire $3,000 for the reimbursement of her daughter's dental expenses. How much has Rosa decreased her tax liability? What is the after-tax cost of the dental expenses?

b. Before Rosa uses any of the available $3,000, her daughter gets married. Therefore, the daughter's dental expenses are no longer covered by the plan. Since Rosa will not need to use the $3,000, can she receive the $3,000 unused balance in the plan? If so, what are the tax consequences to Rosa?

c. Should Rosa automatically set aside the maximum amount so that she will maximize her salary deferral under the plan?

48. Canary Corporation would like you to review its employee fringe benefits program with regard to the tax consequences of the plan for the company's president (Polly), who is also the majority shareholder:

a. The company has a qualified retirement plan. The company pays the cost of employees attending a retirement planning seminar. The employee must be within 10 years of retirement, and the cost of the seminar is $1,500 per attendee.

b. The company owns a parking garage that is used by customers, employees, and the general public. Only the general public is required to pay for parking. The charge to the general public for Polly's parking for the year would have been $2,700 (a $225 monthly rate).

c. All employees are allowed to use the company's fixed charge long-distance telephone services, as long as the privilege is not abused. Although no one has kept track of the actual calls, Polly's use of the telephone had a value (what she would have paid on her personal telephone) of approximately $600.

d. The company owns a condominium at the beach, which it uses to entertain customers. Employees are allowed to use the facility without charge when the company has no scheduled events. Polly used the facility 10 days during the year. Her use had a rental value of $1,000.

e. The company is in the household moving business. Employees are allowed to ship goods without charge whenever there is excess space on a truck. Polly purchased a dining room suite for her daughter. Company trucks delivered the furniture to the daughter. Normal freight charges would have been $750.

f. The company has a storage facility for household goods. Officers are allowed a 20% discount on charges for storing their goods. All other employees are allowed a 10% discount. Polly's discounts for the year totaled $900.

49. George is a U.S. citizen who is employed by Hawk Enterprises, a global company. Beginning on July 1, 2006, George began working in London. He worked there until January 31, 2007, when he transferred to Paris. He worked in Paris the remainder of 2007. His salary for the first six months of 2006 was $95,000, and it was earned in the United States. His salary for the remainder of 2006 was $135,000, and it was earned in London. George's 2007 salary from Hawk was $275,000, with part being earned in London and part being earned in Paris. What is George's gross income in 2006 and 2007?

50. Determine Hazel's gross income from the following receipts for the year:

Gain on sale of Augusta County bonds	$ 600
Interest on U.S. government savings bonds	300
Interest on state income tax refund	150
Interest on Augusta County bonds	900
Patronage dividend from Potato Growers Cooperative	1,600

The patronage dividend was received in March of the current year for amounts paid and deducted in the previous year as expenses of Hazel's profitable cash basis farming business.

51. Ezra purchased 1,000 shares of Golden Gate Utility Fund for $15,000 in 2006. At the end of 2006, he received an additional 50 fund shares in lieu of receiving $700 in cash dividends. At the end of the year, the value of Ezra's Golden Gate Utility Fund shares was $14,500.

a. What is Ezra's 2006 gross income from the Golden Gate Utility Fund shares?

b. Ezra also received 100 shares of Giant, Inc. stock when the company declared a two-for-one stock dividend. At the time of the stock dividend, the shares were trading for $90 a share. Ezra did not have the option of receiving cash in lieu of the Giant stock. What are the tax consequences of Ezra's receipt of the additional shares of Giant stock?

52. Tonya purchased State of Virginia bonds in 2000 for $10,000. The bonds pay $600 interest each year. At the time she purchased the bonds, the yield on comparable taxable securities was 10%. She was in the 39.6% marginal tax bracket. Tonya's income in the current year is approximately the same as in 2000. However, Congress has lowered the tax rates, so her marginal rate is only 35%.
    a. What should be the effect of the change in the tax rates on the market value of Tonya's bonds?
    b. Assume that after she purchased the bonds, Tonya's state of residence changed its income tax law to make the Virginia bonds exempt from that state's income tax. What should be the effect of the change in the state law on the market value of Tonya's bonds?

53. Lynn Swartz's husband died three years ago. Her parents have an income of over $200,000 a year and want to assure that funds will be available for the education of Lynn's 8-year-old son, Eric. Lynn is currently earning $45,000 a year. Lynn's parents have suggested that they start a savings account for Eric. They have calculated that if they invest $4,000 a year for the next 8 years, at the end of 10 years sufficient funds will be available for Eric's college expenses. Lynn realizes that the tax treatment of the investments could significantly affect the amount of funds available for Eric's education. She asked you to write a letter to her advising her about options available to her parents and to her for Eric's college education. Lynn's address is 100 Myrtle Cove, Fairfield, CT 06432.

Decision Making

Communications

54. Starting in 1997, Chuck and Luane have been purchasing Series EE bonds in their name to use for the higher education of their daughter (Susie who currently is age 18). During the year, they cash in $12,000 of the bonds to use for freshman year tuition, fees, and room and board. Of this amount, $5,000 represents interest. Of the $12,000, $8,000 is used for tuition and fees, and $4,000 is used for room and board. Their AGI, before the educational savings bond exclusion, is $97,000.
    a. Determine the tax consequences for Chuck and Luane, who will file a joint return, and for Susie.
    b. Assume that Chuck and Luane purchased the bonds in Susie's name. Determine the tax consequences for Chuck and Luane and for Susie.
    c. How would your answer for (a) change if Chuck and Luane file separate returns?

55. Carlos is considering investing $4,000 in a qualified tuition program for the benefit of his son. He estimates that in eight years, when his son enters college, the cost of tuition will have increased by 50%. His son will go to school full-time and should be in the 15% marginal tax bracket as a result of his part-time work. Alternatively, Carlos can invest the $4,000 in a corporate bond fund, which is expected to yield 7% each year. Carlos expects to be in the 33% marginal tax bracket in all relevant years. Which alternative appears preferable? The compound amount of $1 at 4.69% in eight years is 1.44.

56. How does the tax benefit rule apply in the following cases?
    a. In December 2005, Wilma purchased a new automobile for her personal use. Early in January 2006, she received a $1,500 rebate from the manufacturer.
    b. Wilma's accountant was negligent in computing the Virginia income tax liability due on her personal return for 2001. As a result, she paid $5,000 more state income tax than she was required to pay. The error was not discovered until after the statute of limitations had run; thus, it was too late to correct the error. She had claimed the Virginia income tax paid as an itemized deduction on her Federal income tax return. The accountant paid Wilma $5,000 as compensation for his negligence.
    c. In 2006, Wilma received $400 of patronage dividends from an agricultural cooperative. The dividends were paid for $10,000 in purchases of cattle feed and $2,500 in household item purchases. She uses the cash method for her farming business.

57. Fran, who is in the 35% tax bracket, recently collected $100,000 on a life insurance policy she carried on her father. She currently owes $120,000 on her personal residence and $120,000 on business property. National Bank holds the mortgage on both pieces of property and has agreed to accept $100,000 in complete satisfaction of either

Decision Making

mortgage. The interest rate on the mortgages is 8%, and both mortgages are payable over 10 years. What would be the tax consequences of each of the following alternatives, assuming Fran currently deducts the mortgage interest on her tax return?

    a.   Retire the mortgage on the residence.

    b.   Retire the mortgage on the business property.

Which alternative should Fran select?

58. Robin, who was experiencing financial difficulties, was able to adjust his debts as follows:

    a.   His father agreed to cancel a $10,000 debt to help him out in his time of need. Robin's father told him, "I am not going to treat you any better than I treat your brothers and sister; therefore, the $10,000 is coming out of your inheritance from me."

    b.   Robin's controlled corporation canceled a $6,000 debt he owed to the company.

    c.   The Trust Land Company, which had sold Robin land, reduced the mortgage on the land by $12,000 and forgave him from paying $4,000 in accrued interest. Robin had deducted the interest on the previous year's tax return.

CUMULATIVE PROBLEMS

Tax Return Problem

59. Alfred E. Old and Beulah Crane, each age 42, married on September 7, 2005. Alfred and Beulah will file a joint return for 2005. Alfred's Social Security number is 262–60–3815. Beulah's Social Security number is 259–68–4285, and she will adopt "Old" as her married name. They live at 211 Brickstone Drive, Atlanta, GA 30304.

Alfred was divorced from Sarah Old in March 2004. Under the divorce agreement, Alfred is to pay Sarah $900 per month for the next 10 years or until Sarah's death, whichever occurs first. Alfred pays Sarah $10,800 in 2005. In addition, in January 2005, Alfred pays Sarah $50,000, which is designated as being for her share of the marital property. Also, Alfred is responsible for all prior years' income taxes. Sarah's Social Security number is 444–10–2211.

Alfred's salary for 2005 is $70,000, and his employer, Cherry, Inc. (Federal I.D. No. 59–7766723), provides him with group term life insurance equal to twice his annual salary. His employer withheld $10,900 for Federal income taxes and $3,400 for state income taxes. The following amounts were withheld for FICA taxes: $4,340 ($70,000 × 6.2%) for Social Security and $1,015 ($70,000 × 1.45%) for Medicare.

Beulah recently graduated from law school and is employed by Legal Aid Society, Inc. (Federal I.D. No. 59–9472635), as a public defender. She receives a salary of $38,000 in 2005. Her employer withheld $4,900 for Federal income taxes and $2,300 for state income taxes. The following amounts were withheld for FICA taxes: $2,356 ($38,000 × 6.2%) for Social Security and $551 ($38,000 × 1.45%) for Medicare.

Beulah has $1,500 in dividends on Yellow Corporation stock she inherited. Beulah receives a $850 refund of 2004 state income taxes. She used the standard deduction on her 2004 Federal income tax return. Alfred receives a $1,200 refund on his 2004 state income taxes. He itemized deductions on his 2004 Federal income tax return. Alfred and Beulah pay $4,300 interest and $1,450 property taxes on their personal residence in 2005. Their charitable contributions total $1,000 (all to their church). They paid sales taxes of $1,400 for which they maintain the receipts.

Compute the Olds' net tax payable (or refund due) for 2005. If you use tax forms for your solution, you will need Form 1040 and Schedules A and B. Suggested software: TurboTax.

Tax Return Problem

Communications

60. Martin S. Albert (Social Security number 363–22–1141) is 39 years old and is married to Michele R. Albert (Social Security number 259–05–8242). The Alberts live at 512 Ferry Road, Newport News, VA 23100. They file a joint return and have two dependent children (Charlene, age 17, and Jordan, age 18). Charlene's Social Security number is 260–12–1234, and Jordan's Social Security number is 263–23–4321. In 2006, Martin and Michele had the following transactions:

    a.   Martin received $108,000 in salary from Red Steel Corporation, where he is a construction engineer. Withholding for Federal income tax was $9,500. The amounts withheld for FICA tax were as follows: $5,840 ($94,200 × 6.2%) for Social Security and $1,420 ($97,918 × 1.45%) for Medicare. Martin worked in Mexico from January 1, 2005, until February 15, 2006. His $108,000 salary for 2006 includes $16,000 he earned for January and one-half of February 2006 while working in Mexico.

b. Martin and Michele received $800 in dividends on Green, Inc. stock and $400 interest on Montgomery County (Virginia) school bonds.

c. Martin received $300 interest from a Bahamian bank account.

d. Michele received 50 shares of Applegate Corporation common stock as a stock dividend. The shares had a fair market value of $2,000 at the time Michele received them, and she did not have the option of receiving cash.

e. Martin and Michele received a $900 refund on their 2005 Virginia income taxes. Their itemized deductions in 2005 totaled $11,600.

f. Martin paid $6,000 alimony to his former wife, Rose T. Morgan (Social Security number 262–55–4813).

g. Martin and Michele kept the receipts for their sales taxes paid of $1,100.

h. Martin and Michele's itemized deductions were as follows:

- State income tax paid and withheld totaled $5,100.
- Real estate taxes on their principal residence were $3,400.
- Mortgage interest on their principal residence was $4,500.
- Cash contributions to the church totaled $2,800.

Part 1—Tax Computation
Compute the Alberts' net tax payable (or refund due) for 2006.

Part 2—Tax Planning
The Alberts are considering buying another house. Their house mortgage payments would increase by $500 (to $1,500) per month, which includes a $250 increase in interest and a $100 increase in property tax. The Alberts would like to know how much the mortgage payments would increase net of any change in their income tax. Write a letter to the Alberts that contains your advice.

RESEARCH PROBLEMS

Note: Solutions to Research Problems can be prepared by using the **RIA Checkpoint**® **Student Edition** online research product, which is available to accompany this text. It is also possible to prepare solutions to the Research Problems by using tax research materials found in a standard tax library.

Communications

Research Problem 1. David Hobson is the minister at the First Baptist Church. As part of his compensation, David receives an $800 per month housing allowance. David is purchasing his residence, and he uses the $800 each month to make mortgage and property tax payments. The mortgage interest and property taxes are deducted (as itemized deductions) on David's tax return. The examining IRS agent thinks David would be enjoying a double benefit if the housing allowance is excluded and the itemized deductions are allowed. In addition, the agent contends that the housing allowance exclusion should apply only where the church provides the residence or the minister uses the funds to pay rent. Therefore, the agent maintains that David should include in gross income the $800 received each month. David has asked your assistance in this matter. Write a letter to David that contains your advice and prepare a memo for the tax files. David's address is 982 Richmond Drive, Hollis, OK 73550.

Research Problem 2. Sam received a MegaBank credit card in 2000 and charged items costing over $3,000. He moved to a new location, misplaced the card, and forgot that he owed the money. In 2004, MegaBank decided that Sam's account would never be collected. MegaBank sent him a Form 1099–C, indicating that he had $3,000 of income from discharge of the debt in 2004. The IRS is trying to collect tax on the $3,000. Sam contends that he still owes the money to MegaBank, that he intends to repay it, and that he informed MegaBank of this after the IRS informed him that he had income from the discharge of the debt. Sam is neither bankrupt nor insolvent. Is Sam required to recognize income in 2004 from the discharge of the indebtedness?

Research Problem 3.   Sales personnel employed by Ivory Sales, Inc., accumulate substantial frequent-flyer miles traveling for the company. Since Ivory Sales reimburses its employees for travel expenses incurred, the company, rather than the employee, is entitled to the frequent-flyer miles. The company is considering a change in policy that would permit the employees to retain the miles for their personal use. Ivory Sales would like to know the income tax implications to the employees of the proposed change in policy.

Research Problem 4.   Melissa and Aubry Brown were divorced in Florida, the state where they were married and now reside. Under the divorce agreement, Aubry was to pay Melissa $1,000 per month. The agreement further stated that "the provisions of this agreement shall apply to and bind the heirs of the agreement." An IRS agent interprets the agreement as meaning that Aubry is required to continue the payments as long as he lives and that if Melissa should die first, the payments would continue to her estate. Therefore, the agent argues that the agreement violates the alimony definition in § 71 that prohibits any liability for payments after the death of the payee spouse. Is the IRS agent correct?

Partial list of research aids:
Johnny Desauguste, T.C. Summary Opinion, 2005–60.

Internet *Activity*

Communications

Use the tax resources of the Internet to address the following questions. Do not restrict your search to the World Wide Web, but include a review of newsgroups and general reference materials, practitioner sites and resources, primary sources of the tax law, chat rooms and discussion groups, and other opportunities.

Research Problem 5.   Go to the IRS site on the Internet and download instructions and regulations relative to educational savings bonds and qualified tuition programs. Summarize one of the key provisions in these materials in outline format.

Research Problem 6.   Employers often use the Internet as a means of attracting applications from potential employees. Locate an Internet site offering employment opportunities, ideally one provided by a well-known corporation. How does the employer promote its fringe benefit and cafeteria plan packages? Contrast several such sites.

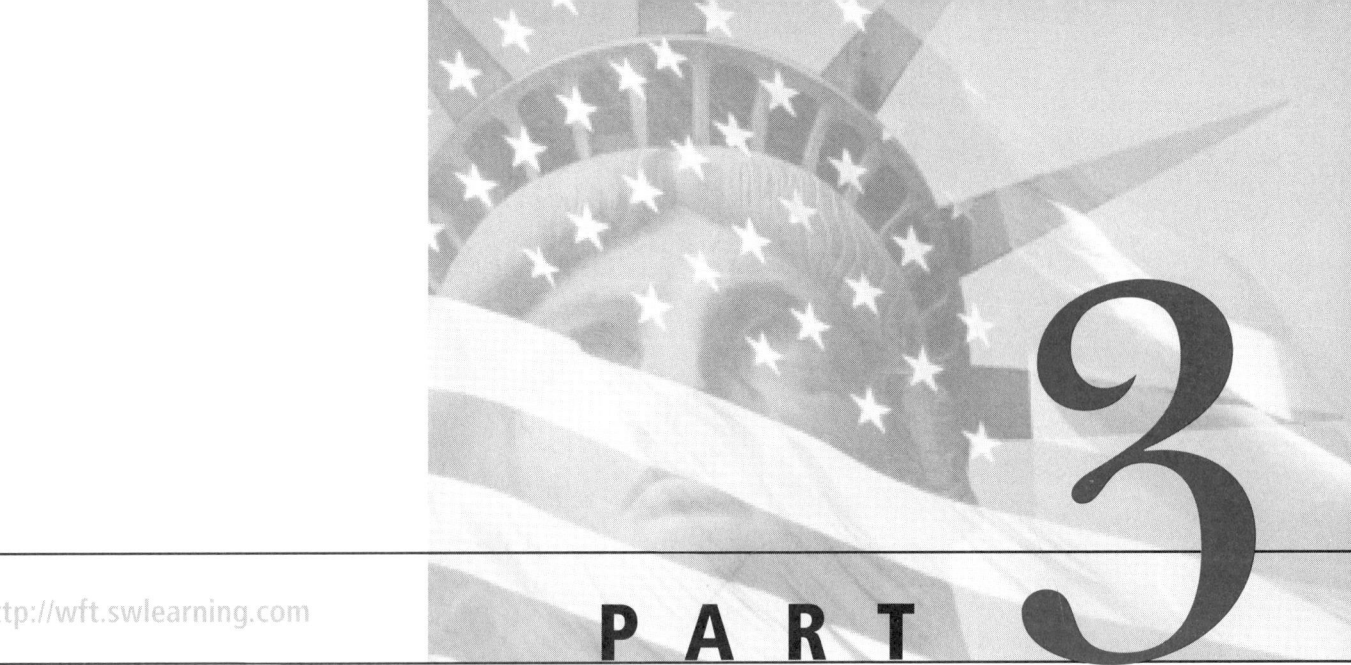

PART 3

Deductions

Part III presents the deduction component of the basic tax model. Deductions are classified as business versus nonbusiness, "for" versus "from," employee versus employer, active versus passive, and reimbursed versus unreimbursed. The effect of each of these classifications is analyzed. The presentation includes not only the deductions that are permitted, but also limitations and disallowances associated with deductions. Because deductions can exceed gross income, the treatment of losses is also included.

CHAPTER

6

Deductions and Losses: In General

LEARNING OBJECTIVES

After completing Chapter 6, you should be able to:

LO.1

Differentiate between deductions *for* and *from* adjusted gross income and understand the relevance of the differentiation.

LO.2

Describe the cash and accrual methods of accounting.

LO.3

Apply the Internal Revenue Code deduction disallowance provisions associated with the following: public policy limitations, political activities,

excessive executive compensation, investigation of business opportunities, hobby losses, vacation home rentals, payment of others' expenses, personal expenditures, capital expenditures, related-party transactions, and expenses related to tax-exempt income.

LO.4

Identify tax planning opportunities for maximizing deductions and minimizing the disallowance of deductions.

OUTLINE

LO.1

Differentiate between deductions *for* and *from* adjusted gross income and understand the relevance of the differentiation.

Classification of Deductible Expenses

The tax law has an all-inclusive definition of income; that is, income from whatever source derived is includible in gross income. Income cannot be excluded unless there is a specific statement to that effect in the Internal Revenue Code.

Similarly, deductions are disallowed unless a specific provision in the tax law permits them. The inclusive definition of income and the exclusive definition of deductions may not seem fair to taxpayers, but it is the structure of the tax law.

The courts have held that whether and to what extent deductions are allowed depends on legislative grace.[1] In other words, any exclusions from income and all deductions are gifts from Congress!

It is important to classify deductible expenses as **deductions for adjusted gross income** (AGI) or **deductions from adjusted gross income.** Deductions *for* AGI can be claimed whether or not the taxpayer itemizes. Deductions *from* AGI result in a tax benefit only if they exceed the taxpayer's standard deduction. If itemized deductions (*from* AGI) are less than the standard deduction, they provide no tax benefit.

EXAMPLE 1

Steve is a self-employed CPA. Ralph is one of Steve's employees. During the year, Steve and Ralph incur the following expenses:

	Steve	Ralph
Dues to American Institute of CPAs and State Society of CPAs	$ 400	$ 300
Subscriptions to professional journals	500	200
Registration fees for tax conferences	800	800
	$1,700	$1,300

[1] *New Colonial Ice Co. v. Helvering*, 4 USTC ¶1292, 13 AFTR 1180, 54 S.Ct. 788 (USSC, 1934).

TAX *in the News* | **PROPER TREATMENT OF YOUR VOICE**

Almost all people use their voice in their work. What do you do if it does not function the way that you want it to? An increasing number of people are deciding that their voice is too high pitched, too monotone, too nasal, or too much like the opposite sex. Women are often concerned that they sound too shrill, too Valley girl, or too faint, whereas men worry about being too gravelly or too weak.

Help in achieving the desired vocal results, often referred to as cosmetic voice changing, is available from personal voice trainers. Such treatments are not cheap. Sandra McKnight, a voice coach in Santa Fe who offers voice training over the phone, charges $640 for a typical treatment program consisting of four 75-minute sessions. In-person sessions with a speech pathologist can cost much more.

Are such treatments deductible for tax purposes? One possible approach might be to deduct the cost as a medical expense (assuming the reasons for the treatment are not merely cosmetic). The disadvantage here is the 7.5 percent floor on medical expenses. Another possibility might be to deduct the cost as a § 162 trade or business expense. Unfortunately, such an approach is more likely to be successful for an entertainer than for a business executive.

Source: *Adapted from Jennifer Saranow, "A Personal Trainer for Your Voice,"* Wall Street Journal, *February 17, 2005, p. D1.*

Steve does not reimburse any of his employees for dues, subscriptions, or educational programs.

Steve's expenses are classified as a deduction *for* AGI. Therefore, he can deduct the $1,700 on his Federal income tax return. Ralph's expenses are classified as deductions *from* AGI. Ralph will be able to benefit from the $1,300 of expenses on his Federal income tax return only if he itemizes deductions. If he takes the standard deduction instead, the $1,300 of expenses will have no effect on the calculation of his taxable income. Even if Ralph does itemize deductions, he must reduce the $1,300 of expenses, which are classified as miscellaneous itemized deductions, by 2% of his AGI. As this example illustrates, whether a deduction is classified as *for* AGI or *from* AGI can affect the benefit the taxpayer receives from the deduction. ∎

Deductions *for* AGI are also important in determining the *amount* of itemized deductions because many itemized deductions are limited to amounts in excess of specified percentages of AGI. Examples of itemized deductions that are limited by AGI are medical expenses and personal casualty losses. Itemized deductions that are deductible only to the extent that they exceed a specified percentage of AGI are increased when AGI is decreased. Likewise, when AGI is increased, these itemized deductions are decreased.

EXAMPLE 2

Tina earns a salary of $20,000 and has no other income. She itemizes deductions during the current year. Medical expenses for the year are $1,800. Since medical expenses are deductible only to the extent they exceed 7.5% of AGI, Tina's medical expense deduction is $300 [$1,800 − (7.5% × $20,000)]. If Tina had a $2,000 deduction *for* AGI, her medical expense deduction would be $450 [$1,800 − (7.5% × $18,000)], or $150 more. If the $2,000 deduction was *from* AGI, her medical expense deduction would remain $300 since AGI is unchanged. ∎

Deductions for Adjusted Gross Income

To understand how deductions of individual taxpayers are classified, it is necessary to examine the role of § 62. The purpose of § 62 is to classify various deductions as deductions *for* AGI. It does not provide the statutory authority for taking the deduction. For example, § 212 allows individuals to deduct expenses attributable to income-producing property. Section 212 expenses that are attributable to rents or royalties are classified as deductions *for* AGI. Likewise, a deduction for trade or business expenses is allowed by § 162. These expenses are classified as deductions *for* AGI.

If a deduction is not listed in § 62, it is an itemized deduction, not a deduction *for* AGI. Following is a *partial* list of the items classified as deductions *for* AGI by § 62:

- Expenses attributable to a trade or business carried on by the taxpayer. A trade or business does not include the performance of services by the taxpayer as an employee.
- Expenses incurred by a taxpayer in connection with the performance of services as an employee if the expenses are reimbursed and other conditions are satisfied.
- Deductions that result from losses on the sale or exchange of property by the taxpayer.
- Deductions attributable to property held for the production of rents and royalties.
- The deduction for payment of alimony.
- The deduction for one-half of the self-employment tax paid by a self-employed taxpayer.
- The deduction for the medical insurance premiums paid by a self-employed taxpayer for coverage of the taxpayer, spouse, and any dependents.
- Certain contributions to pension, profit sharing, and annuity plans of self-employed individuals.
- The deduction for certain retirement savings allowed by § 219 (e.g., traditional IRAs).
- The penalty imposed on premature withdrawal of funds from time savings accounts or deposits.
- The deduction for moving expenses.
- The deduction for interest paid on student loans.
- The deduction for qualified tuition and related expenses under § 222 (refer to Chapter 9).
- The deduction for up to $250 for teacher supplies for elementary and secondary school teachers (refer to Chapter 9).

These items are covered in detail in various chapters in the text.

Itemized Deductions

The Code defines itemized deductions as the deductions allowed other than "the deductions allowable in arriving at adjusted gross income."[2] Thus, if a deduction is not properly classified as a deduction *for* AGI, then it is classified as an itemized deduction.

Section 212 Expenses. Section 212 allows deductions for ordinary and necessary expenses paid or incurred for the following:

- The production or collection of income.
- The management, conservation, or maintenance of property held for the production of income.
- Expenses paid in connection with the determination, collection, or refund of any tax.

Section 212 expenses related to rent and royalty income are deductions *for* AGI.[3] Expenses paid in connection with the determination, collection, or refund of taxes related to the income of sole proprietorships, rents and royalties, or farming operations are deductions *for* AGI. All other § 212 expenses are itemized deductions (deductions *from* AGI). For example, investment-related expenses (e.g., safe deposit box rentals) are deductible as itemized deductions attributable to the production of investment income.[4]

[2]§ 63(d).
[3]§ 62(a)(4).
[4]Reg. § 1.212–1(g).

Deductible Personal Expenses. Taxpayers are allowed to deduct certain expenses that are primarily personal in nature. These expenses, which generally are not related to the production of income, are deductions *from* AGI (itemized deductions). Some of the more frequently encountered deductions in this category include the following:

- Contributions to qualified charitable organizations (not to exceed a specified percentage of AGI).
- Medical expenses (in excess of 7.5 percent of AGI).
- Certain state and local taxes (e.g., real estate taxes and state and local income or sales taxes).
- Personal casualty losses (in excess of an aggregate floor of 10 percent of AGI and a $100 floor per casualty).
- Certain personal interest (e.g., mortgage interest on a personal residence).

Itemized deductions are discussed in detail in Chapter 10.

Trade or Business Expenses and Production of Income Expenses

Section 162(a) permits a deduction for all ordinary and necessary expenses paid or incurred in carrying on a trade or business. These include reasonable salaries paid for services, expenses for the use of business property, and one-half of self-employment taxes paid (see Chapter 13). Such expenses are deducted *for* AGI.

It is sometimes difficult to determine whether an expenditure is deductible as a trade or business expense. The term "trade or business" is not defined in the Code or Regulations, and the courts have not provided a satisfactory definition. It is usually necessary to ask one or more of the following questions to determine whether an item qualifies as a trade or business expense:

- Was the use of the particular item related to a business activity? For example, if funds are borrowed for use in a business, the interest is deductible as a business expense.
- Was the expenditure incurred with the intent to realize a profit or to produce income? For example, expenses in excess of the income from raising horses are not deductible if the activity is classified as a personal hobby rather than a trade or business.
- Were the taxpayer's operation and management activities extensive enough to indicate the carrying on of a trade or business?

Section 162 *excludes* the following items from classification as trade or business expenses:

- Charitable contributions or gifts.
- Illegal bribes and kickbacks and certain treble damage payments.
- Fines and penalties.

A bribe paid to a domestic official is not deductible if it is illegal under the laws of the United States. Foreign bribes are deductible unless they are unlawful under the Foreign Corrupt Practices Act of 1977.[5]

Ordinary and Necessary Requirement. The terms **ordinary and necessary** are found in both §§ 162 and 212. To be deductible, any trade or business expense must be "ordinary and necessary." In addition, compensation for services must be "reasonable" in amount.

Many expenses that are necessary are *not* ordinary. Neither "ordinary" nor "necessary" is defined in the Code or Regulations. The courts have held that

---

[5]§ 162(c)(1).

TAX *in the News*   **PENALTY OR RESTITUTION: THE TAX CONSEQUENCES**

Penalties and fines are not deductible for Federal income tax purposes. To allow a deduction would be contrary to public policy.

Recently, a major financial service company settled charges brought by New York state regulators (office of New York Attorney General Eliot Spitzer and the New York Insurance Department). The company was accused of rigging bids for large corporate insurance contracts and steering the business to insurers that paid it sizable so-called commissions. While not admitting any wrongdoing, the company agreed to pay $850 million in restitution (i.e., "disgorgement of profits") to be spread among its clients.

Note, however, that the parties were careful not to designate the settlement as a penalty or a fine. Instead, it was labeled as restitution to clients. Therefore, according to several tax experts, it appears that the settlement can be classified as a business expense under § 162. If the settlement is fully deductible, the company can reduce its out-of-pocket cost by as much as $297.5 million ($850 million × 35%).

Should the choice of words in a settlement ("penalty" versus "restitution") be the determinant as to whether a payment is deductible or not?

Source: *Adapted from Ian McDonald, "Marsh's Settlement Looks Like Eligible for a Tax Deduction,"* Wall Street Journal, *February 7, 2005, p. C1.*

an expense is *necessary* if a prudent businessperson would incur the same expense and the expense is expected to be appropriate and helpful in the taxpayer's business.[6]

EXAMPLE 3

Pat purchased a manufacturing concern that had just been adjudged bankrupt. Because the business had a poor financial rating, Pat satisfied some of the obligations to employees and outside salespeople incurred by the former owners. Pat had no legal obligation to pay these debts, but felt this was the only way to keep salespeople and employees. The Second Circuit Court of Appeals found that the payments were necessary in that they were both appropriate and helpful.[7] However, the court held that the payments were *not* ordinary but were in the nature of capital expenditures to build a reputation. Therefore, no deduction was allowed. ∎

An expense is *ordinary* if it is normal, usual, or customary in the type of business conducted by the taxpayer and is not capital in nature.[8] However, an expense need not be recurring to be deductible as ordinary.

EXAMPLE 4

Albert engaged in a mail-order business. The post office judged that his advertisements were false and misleading. Under a fraud order, the post office stamped "fraudulent" on all letters addressed to Albert's business and returned them to the senders. Albert spent $30,000 on legal fees in an unsuccessful attempt to force the post office to stop. The legal fees (though not recurring) were ordinary business expenses because they were normal, usual, or customary in the circumstances.[9] ∎

For § 212 deductions, the law requires that expenses bear a reasonable and proximate relationship to (1) the production or collection of income or to (2) the management, conservation, or maintenance of property held for the production of income.[10]

---

[6] *Welch v. Helvering,* 3 USTC ¶1164, 12 AFTR 1456, 54 S.Ct. 8 (USSC, 1933).
[7] *Dunn and McCarthy, Inc. v. Comm.,* 43–2 USTC ¶9688, 31 AFTR 1043, 139 F.2d 242 (CA–2, 1943).
[8] *Deputy v. DuPont,* 40–1 USTC ¶9161, 23 AFTR 808, 60 S.Ct. 363 (USSC, 1940).
[9] *Comm. v. Heininger,* 44–1 USTC ¶9109, 31 AFTR 783, 64 S.Ct. 249 (USSC, 1943).
[10] Reg. § 1.212–1(d).

EXAMPLE 5

Wendy owns a small portfolio of investments, including 10 shares of Hawk, Inc. common stock worth $1,000. She incurred $350 in travel expenses to attend the annual shareholders' meeting where she voted her 10 shares against the current management group. No deduction is permitted because a 10-share investment is insignificant in value in relation to the travel expenses incurred.[11] ■

Reasonableness Requirement. The Code refers to **reasonableness** solely with respect to salaries and other compensation for services.[12] But the courts have held that for any business expense to be ordinary and necessary, it must also be reasonable in amount.[13]

What constitutes reasonableness is a question of fact. If an expense is unreasonable, the excess amount is not allowed as a deduction. The question of reasonableness generally arises with respect to closely held corporations where there is no separation of ownership and management.

Transactions between the shareholders and the closely held company may result in the disallowance of deductions for excessive salaries and rent expense paid by the corporation to the shareholders. The courts will view an unusually large salary in light of all relevant circumstances and may find that the salary is reasonable despite its size.[14] If excessive payments for salaries and rents are closely related to the percentage of stock owned by the recipients, the payments are generally treated as dividends.[15] Since dividends are not deductible by the corporation, the disallowance results in an increase in the corporate taxable income. Deductions for reasonable salaries will not be disallowed *solely* because the corporation has paid insubstantial portions of its earnings as dividends to its shareholders.

EXAMPLE 6

Sparrow Corporation, a closely held corporation, is owned equally by Lupe, Carlos, and Ramon. The company has been highly profitable for several years and has not paid dividends. Lupe, Carlos, and Ramon are key officers of the company, and each receives a salary of $200,000. Salaries for similar positions in comparable companies average only $100,000. Amounts paid the owners in excess of $100,000 may be deemed unreasonable, and, if so, a total of $300,000 in salary deductions by Sparrow is disallowed. The disallowed amounts are treated as dividends rather than salary income to Lupe, Carlos, and Ramon because the payments are proportional to stock ownership. Salaries are deductible by the corporation, but dividends are not. ■

Business and Nonbusiness Losses

Section 165 provides for a deduction for losses not compensated for by insurance. As a general rule, deductible losses of individual taxpayers are limited to those incurred in a trade or business or in a transaction entered into for profit. Individuals are also allowed to deduct losses that are the result of a casualty. Casualty losses include, but are not limited to, fire, storm, shipwreck, and theft. See Chapter 7 for a further discussion of this topic. Deductible personal casualty losses are reduced by $100 per casualty, and the aggregate of all personal casualty losses is reduced by 10 percent of AGI. A personal casualty loss is an itemized deduction. See Concept Summary 6–3 near the end of the chapter for the classification of expenses.

---

[11]*J. Raymond Dyer*, 36 T.C. 456 (1961).

[12]§ 162(a)(1).

[13]*Comm. v. Lincoln Electric Co.*, 49–2 USTC ¶9388, 38 AFTR 411, 176 F.2d 815 (CA–6, 1949).

[14]*Kennedy, Jr. v. Comm.*, 82–1 USTC ¶9186, 49 AFTR2d 82–628, 671 F.2d 167 (CA–6, 1982), *rev'g* 72 T.C. 793 (1979).

[15]Reg. § 1.162–8.

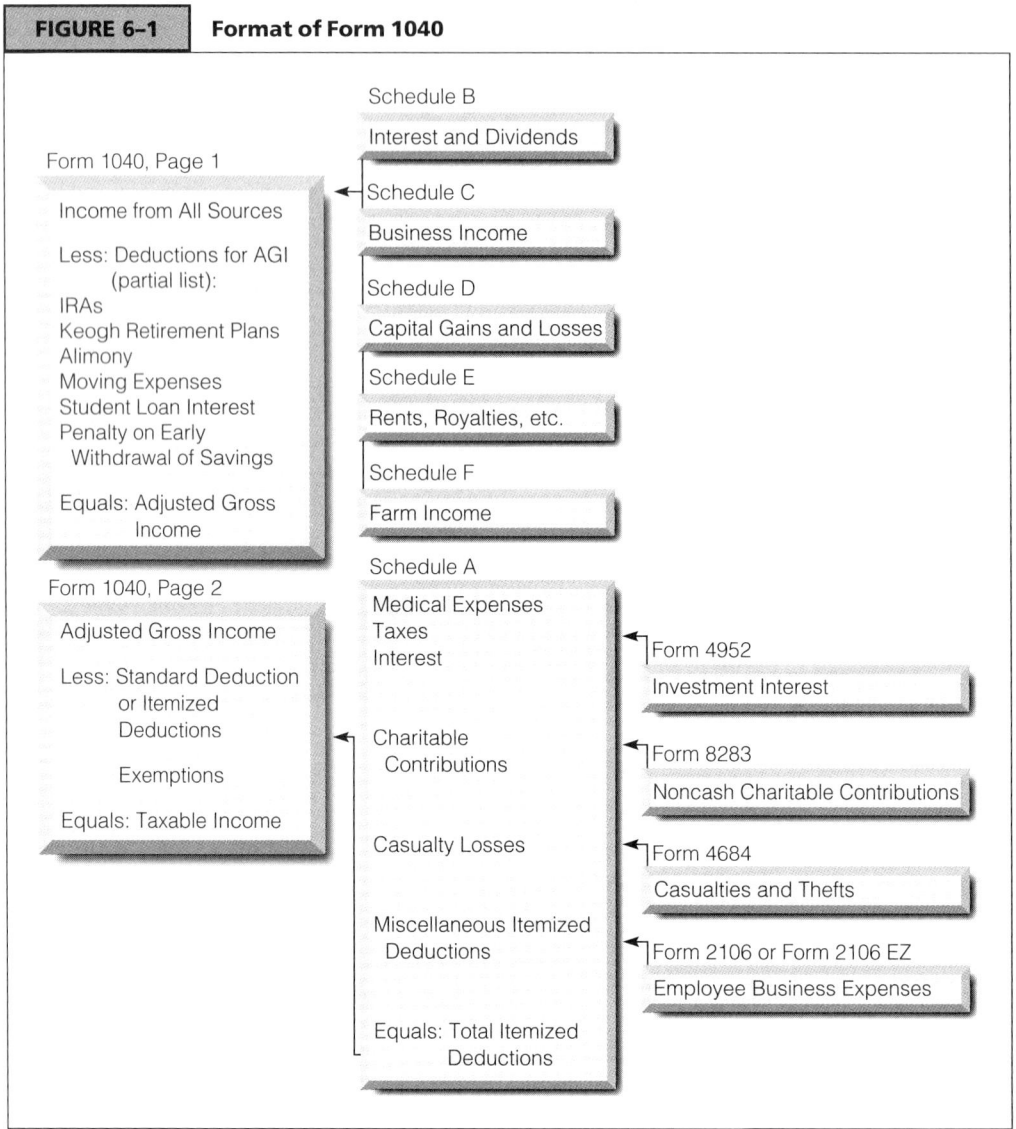

FIGURE 6–1   Format of Form 1040

Reporting Procedures

All deductions *for* and *from* AGI wind up on pages 1 and 2 of Form 1040. All deductions *for* AGI are reported on page 1. The last line on page 1 is adjusted gross income.

The first item on page 2 is also adjusted gross income. Itemized deductions are entered next, followed by the deduction for personal and dependency exemptions. The result is taxable income.

Most of the deductions *for* AGI on page 1 originate on supporting schedules. Examples include business expenses (Schedule C) and rent, royalty, partnership, and fiduciary deductions (Schedule E). Other deductions *for* AGI, such as traditional IRAs, Keogh retirement plans, and alimony, are entered directly on page 1 of Form 1040.

All itemized deductions on page 2 are carried over from Schedule A. Some Schedule A deductions originate on other forms. Examples include investment interest, noncash charitable contributions in excess of $500, casualty losses, and unreimbursed employee expenses.

Form 1040 becomes a summary of the detailed information entered on the other schedules and forms. See Figure 6–1.

Deductions and Losses—Timing of Expense Recognition

LO.2

Describe the cash and accrual methods of accounting.

Importance of Taxpayer's Method of Accounting

A taxpayer's **accounting method** is a major factor in determining taxable income. The method used determines when an item is includible in income and when an item is deductible on the tax return. Usually, the taxpayer's regular method of record keeping is used for income tax purposes.[16] The taxing authorities do not require uniformity among all taxpayers. They do require that the method used clearly reflect income and that items be handled consistently.[17] The most common methods of accounting are the cash method and the accrual method.

Throughout the portions of the Code dealing with deductions, the phrase "paid or incurred" is used. *Paid* refers to the cash basis taxpayer who gets a deduction only in the year of payment. *Incurred* concerns the accrual basis taxpayer who obtains the deduction in the year in which the liability for the expense becomes certain (refer to Chapter 4).

Cash Method Requirements

The expenses of cash basis taxpayers are deductible only when they are actually paid with cash or other property. Promising to pay or issuing a note does not satisfy the actually paid requirement.[18] However, the payment can be made with borrowed funds. At the time taxpayers charge expenses on their credit cards, they are allowed to claim the deduction. They are deemed to have simultaneously borrowed money from the credit card issuer and constructively paid the expenses.[19]

Although the cash basis taxpayer must have actually or constructively paid the expense, payment does not assure a current deduction. Cash basis and accrual basis taxpayers cannot take a current deduction for capital expenditures except through amortization, depletion, or depreciation over the life (actual or statutory) of the asset. The Regulations set forth the general rule that an expenditure that creates an asset having a useful life that extends substantially beyond the end of the tax year must be capitalized.[20]

John, a calendar year and cash basis taxpayer, rents property from Carl. On July 1, 2006, John pays $24,000 rent for the 24 months ending June 30, 2008. The prepaid rent extends 18 months after the close of the tax year—substantially beyond the year of payment. Therefore, John must capitalize the prepaid rent and amortize the expense on a monthly basis. His deduction for 2006 is $6,000. ■

EXAMPLE 7

The Tax Court and the IRS took the position that an asset that will expire or be consumed by the end of the tax year following the year of payment must be prorated. The Ninth Circuit Court of Appeals held that such expenditures are currently deductible, however, and the Supreme Court apparently concurs (the one-year rule for prepaid expenses).[21]

Assume the same facts as in Example 7 except that John is required to pay only 12 months' rent in 2006. He pays $12,000 on July 1, 2006. The entire $12,000 is deductible in 2006. ■

EXAMPLE 8

---

[16]§ 446(a).

[17]§§ 446(b) and (e); Reg. § 1.446–1(a)(2).

[18]*Page v. Rhode Island Trust Co., Exr.*, 37–1 USTC ¶9138, 19 AFTR 105, 88 F.2d 192 (CA–1, 1937).

[19]Rev.Rul. 78–39, 1978–1 C.B. 73. See also Rev.Rul. 80–335, 1980–2 C.B. 170, which applies to pay-by-phone arrangements.

[20]Reg. § 1.461–1(a).

[21]*Zaninovich v. Comm.*, 80–1 USTC ¶9342, 45 AFTR2d 80–1442, 616 F.2d 429 (CA–9, 1980), *rev'g* 69 T.C. 605 (1978). Cited by the Supreme Court in *Hillsboro National Bank v. Comm.*, 83–1 USTC ¶9229, 51 AFTR2d 83–874, 103 S.Ct. 1134 (USSC, 1983).

The payment must be required, not a voluntary prepayment, to obtain the current deduction under the one-year rule.[22] The taxpayer must also demonstrate that allowing the current deduction will not result in a material distortion of income. Generally, the deduction will be allowed if the item is recurring or was made for a business purpose rather than to manipulate income.[23]

As Chapter 18 explains, not all taxpayers are allowed to use the cash method.[24] For example, in most cases the taxpayer is required to use the accrual method for sales and cost of goods sold if inventories are an income-producing factor of the business.

Accrual Method Requirements

The period in which an accrual basis taxpayer can deduct an expense is determined by applying the *all events test* and the *economic performance test.* A deduction cannot be claimed until (1) all the events have occurred to create the taxpayer's liability and (2) the amount of the liability can be determined with reasonable accuracy. Once these requirements are satisfied, the deduction is permitted only if economic performance has occurred. The economic performance test is met only when the service, property, or use of property giving rise to the liability is actually performed for, provided to, or used by the taxpayer.[25]

EXAMPLE 9

On December 22, 2006, Chris's entertainment business sponsored a jazz festival in a rented auditorium at a local college. His business is responsible for cleaning up the auditorium after the festival and for reinstalling seats that were removed so more people could attend the festival. Since the college is closed over the Christmas holidays, the company hired by Chris to perform the work did not begin these activities until January 2, 2007. The cost to Chris is $1,200. Chris cannot deduct the $1,200 until 2007, when the services are performed. ■

An exception to the economic performance requirements allows certain *recurring items* to be deducted if the following conditions are met:

- The item is recurring in nature and is treated consistently by the taxpayer.
- Either the accrued item is not material, or accruing it results in better matching of income and expenses.
- All the events have occurred that determine the fact of the liability, and the amount of the liability can be determined with reasonable accuracy.
- Economic performance occurs within a reasonable period (but not later than 8½ months after the close of the taxable year).[26]

EXAMPLE 10

Rick, an accrual basis, calendar year taxpayer, entered into a monthly maintenance contract during the year. He makes a monthly accrual at the end of every month for this service and pays the fee sometime between the first and fifteenth of the following month when services are performed. The amount involved is immaterial, and all the other tests are met. The December 2006 accrual is deductible in 2006 even though the service is performed on January 12, 2007. ■

EXAMPLE 11

Rita, an accrual basis, calendar year taxpayer, shipped merchandise sold on December 30, 2006, via Greyhound Van Lines on January 2, 2007, and paid the freight charges at that time. Since Rita reported the sale of the merchandise in 2006, the shipping charge should also be deductible in 2006. This procedure results in a better matching of income and expenses. ■

---

[22]*Bonaire Development Co. v. Comm.,* 82–2 USTC ¶9428, 50 AFTR2d 82–5167, 679 F.2d 159 (CA–9, 1982).

[23]*Keller v. Comm.,* 84–1 USTC ¶9194, 53 AFTR2d 84–663, 725 F.2d 1173 (CA–8, 1984), *aff'g* 79 T.C. 7 (1982).

[24]§ 448.

[25]§ 461(h).

[26]§ 461(h)(3)(A).

Reserves for estimated expenses (frequently employed for financial accounting purposes) generally are not allowed for tax purposes because the economic performance test cannot be satisfied.

Blackbird Airlines is required by Federal law to test its engines after 3,000 flying hours. Aircraft cannot return to flight until the tests have been conducted. An unrelated aircraft maintenance company does all of the company's tests for $1,500 per engine. For financial reporting purposes, the company accrues an expense based upon $.50 per hour of flight and credits an allowance account. The actual amounts paid for maintenance are offset against the allowance account. For tax purposes, the economic performance test is not satisfied until the work has been done. Therefore, the reserve method cannot be used for tax purposes. ∎

EXAMPLE 12

Disallowance Possibilities

The tax law provides for the disallowance of certain types of expenses. Without specific restrictions in the tax law, taxpayers might attempt to deduct certain items that in reality are personal expenditures. For example, specific tax rules are provided to determine whether an expenditure is for trade or business purposes or related to a personal hobby.

Certain disallowance provisions are a codification or extension of prior court decisions. After the courts denied deductions for payments considered to be in violation of public policy, the tax law was changed to provide specific authority for the disallowance of these deductions. Discussions of specific disallowance provisions in the tax law follow.

> **LO.3**
>
> Apply the Internal Revenue Code deduction disallowance provisions associated with the following: public policy limitations, political activities, excessive executive compensation, investigation of business opportunities, hobby losses, vacation home rentals, payment of others' expenses, personal expenditures, capital expenditures, related-party transactions, and expenses related to tax-exempt income.

Public Policy Limitation

Justification for Denying Deductions.
The courts developed the principle that a payment that is in violation of public policy is not a necessary expense and is not deductible.[27] Although a bribe or fine may be appropriate, helpful, and even contribute to the profitability of an activity, the courts held that to allow such expenses would frustrate clearly defined public policy. A deduction would dilute the effect of the penalty since the government would be indirectly subsidizing a taxpayer's wrongdoing.

Accordingly, the IRS was free to restrict deductions if, in its view, the expenses were contrary to public policy. But since the law did not explain which actions violated public policy, taxpayers often had to go to court to determine whether or not their expense fell into this category.

Furthermore, the public policy doctrine could be arbitrarily applied in cases where no clear definition had emerged. To solve these problems, Congress enacted legislation that attempts to limit the use of the doctrine. Under the legislation, deductions are disallowed for certain specific types of expenditures that are considered contrary to public policy:

- Bribes and kickbacks including those associated with Medicare or Medicaid (in the case of foreign bribes and kickbacks, only if the payments violate the U.S. Foreign Corrupt Practices Act of 1977).
- Fines and penalties paid to a government for violation of law.

Brown Corporation, a moving company, consistently loads its trucks with weights in excess of the limits allowed by state law. The additional revenue more than offsets the fines levied. The fines are for a violation of public policy and are not deductible. ∎

EXAMPLE 13

---

[27] *Tank Truck Rentals, Inc. v. Comm.*, 58–1 USTC ¶9366, 1 AFTR2d 1154, 78 S.Ct. 507 (USSC, 1958).

• Two-thirds of the treble damage payments made to claimants resulting from violation of the antitrust law.[28]

To be disallowed, the bribe or kickback must be illegal under either Federal or state law and must also subject the payer to a criminal penalty or the loss of a license or privilege to engage in a trade or business. For a bribe or kickback that is illegal under state law, a deduction is denied only if the state law is generally enforced.

EXAMPLE 14

During the year, Keith, an insurance salesman, paid $5,000 to Karen, a real estate broker. The payment represented 20% of the commissions Keith earned from customers referred by Karen. Under state law, the splitting of commissions by an insurance salesperson is an act of misconduct that could warrant a revocation of the salesperson's license. Keith's $5,000 payments to Karen are not deductible provided the state law is generally enforced. ∎

Legal Expenses Incurred in Defense of Civil or Criminal Penalties. To deduct legal expenses, the taxpayer must be able to show that the origin and character of the claim are directly related to a trade or business, an income-producing activity, or the determination, collection, or refund of a tax. Personal legal expenses are not deductible. Thus, legal fees incurred in connection with a criminal defense are deductible only if the crime is associated with the taxpayer's trade or business or income-producing activity.[29]

EXAMPLE 15

Debra, a financial officer of Blue Corporation, incurs legal expenses in connection with her defense in a criminal indictment for evasion of Blue's income taxes. Debra may deduct her legal expenses because she is deemed to be in the trade or business of being an executive. The legal action impairs her ability to conduct this business activity.[30] ∎

Deductible legal expenses associated with the following are deductible *for* AGI:

• Ordinary and necessary expenses incurred in connection with a trade or business.
• Ordinary and necessary expenses incurred in conjunction with rental or royalty property held for the production of income.

All other deductible legal expenses are deductible *from* AGI. For example, legal expenses generally are deductible *from* AGI if they are for fees for tax advice relative to the preparation of an individual's income tax return. Contrast this with the deduction *for* classification of legal fees for tax advice relative to the preparation of the portion of the tax return for a sole proprietor's trade or business (Schedule C) or an individual's rental or royalty income (Schedule E).

Expenses Relating to an Illegal Business. The usual expenses of operating an illegal business (e.g., a numbers racket) are deductible.[31] However, § 162 disallows a deduction for fines, bribes to public officials, illegal kickbacks, and other illegal payments.

EXAMPLE 16

Sam owns and operates an illegal gambling establishment. In connection with this activity, he has the following expenses during the year:

---

[28]§§ 162(c), (f), and (g).
[29]*Comm. v. Tellier*, 66–1 USTC ¶9319, 17 AFTR2d 633, 86 S.Ct. 1118 (USSC, 1966).
[30]Rev.Rul. 68–662, 1968–2 C.B. 69.
[31]*Comm. v. Sullivan*, 58–1 USTC ¶9368, 1 AFTR2d 1158, 78 S.Ct. 512 (USSC, 1958).

Rent	$ 60,000
Payoffs to the police	40,000
Depreciation on equipment	100,000
Wages	140,000
Interest	30,000
Criminal fines	50,000
Illegal kickbacks	10,000
Total	$430,000

All of the usual expenses (rent, depreciation, wages, and interest) are deductible; payoffs, fines, and kickbacks are not deductible. Of the $430,000 spent, $330,000 is deductible and $100,000 is not. ■

An exception applies to expenses incurred in illegal trafficking in drugs.[32] *Drug dealers* are not allowed a deduction for ordinary and necessary business expenses incurred in their business. In arriving at gross income from the business, however, dealers may reduce total sales by the cost of goods sold.[33] In this regard, no distinction is made between legal and illegal businesses in calculating gross income. Treating cost of goods sold as a negative income item rather than as a deduction item produces the unseemly result that a drug dealer's taxable income is reduced by cost of goods sold.

Political Contributions and Lobbying Activities

Political Contributions. Generally, no business deduction is permitted for direct or indirect payments for political purposes.[34] Historically, the government has been reluctant to accord favorable tax treatment to business expenditures for political purposes. Allowing deductions might encourage abuses and enable businesses to have undue influence upon the political process.

Lobbying Expenditures. Lobbying expenses incurred in attempting to influence state or Federal legislation or the actions of certain high-ranking public officials (e.g., the President, Vice President, cabinet-level officials, and the two most senior officials in each agency of the executive branch) are not deductible.[35] The disallowance also applies to a pro rata portion of the membership dues of trade associations and other groups that are used for lobbying activities.

E X A M P L E   1 7

Egret Company pays a $10,000 annual membership fee to the Free Trade Group, a trade association for plumbing wholesalers. The trade association estimates that 70% of its dues are allocated to lobbying activities. Thus, Egret Company's deduction is limited to $3,000 ($10,000 × 30%). ■

There are three exceptions to the disallowance of lobbying expenses. An exception is provided for influencing local legislation (e.g., city and county governments). Second, the disallowance provision does not apply to activities devoted solely to monitoring legislation. Third, a *de minimis* exception is provided for annual in-house expenditures (lobbying expenses other than those paid to professional lobbyists or any portion of dues used by associations for lobbying) if such expenditures do not exceed $2,000. If the in-house expenditures exceed $2,000, none of the in-house expenditures can be deducted.

---

[32]§ 280E.
[33]Reg. § 1.61–3(a). Gross income is defined as sales minus cost of goods sold. Thus, while § 280E prohibits any deductions for drug dealers, it does not modify the normal definition of gross income.

[34]§ 276.
[35]§ 162(e).

Excessive Executive Compensation

The deduction of executive compensation is subject to two limitations. As discussed earlier in this chapter, the compensation of shareholder-employees of closely held corporations is subject to the reasonableness requirement. The second limitation, the so-called millionaires' provision, applies to publicly held corporations (a corporation that has at least one class of stock registered under the Securities Act of 1934).[36]

The millionaires' provision does not limit the amount of compensation that can be paid to an employee. Instead, it limits the amount the employer can deduct for the compensation of a covered executive to $1 million annually. Covered employees include the chief executive officer and the four other most highly compensated officers.

Employee compensation *excludes* the following:

- Commissions based on individual performance.
- Certain performance-based compensation based on company performance according to a formula approved by a board of directors compensation committee (comprised solely of two or more outside directors) and by shareholder vote. The performance attainment must be certified by this compensation committee.
- Payments to tax-qualified retirement plans.
- Payments that are excludible from the employee's gross income (e.g., certain fringe benefits).

Investigation of a Business

Investigation expenses are expenses paid or incurred to determine the feasibility of entering a new business or expanding an existing business. They include such costs as travel, engineering and architectural surveys, marketing reports, and various legal and accounting services. How such expenses are treated for tax purposes depends on a number of variables, including the following:

- The current business, if any, of the taxpayer.
- The nature of the business being investigated.
- The extent to which the investigation has proceeded.
- Whether or not the acquisition actually takes place.

If the taxpayer is in a business the *same as or similar to* that being investigated, all investigation expenses are deductible in the year paid or incurred. The tax result is the same whether or not the taxpayer acquires the business being investigated.[37]

EXAMPLE 18

Terry, an accrual basis sole proprietor, owns and operates three motels in Georgia. In the current year, Terry incurs expenses of $8,500 in investigating the possibility of acquiring several additional motels located in South Carolina. The $8,500 is deductible in the current year whether or not Terry acquires the motels in South Carolina. ∎

When the taxpayer is *not* in a business that is the same as or similar to the one being investigated, the tax result depends on whether the new business is acquired. If the business is not acquired, all investigation expenses generally are nondeductible.[38]

---

[36]§ 162(m).

[37]§ 195. *York v. Comm.*, 58–2 USTC ¶9952, 2 AFTR2d 6178, 261 F.2d 421 (CA–4, 1958).

[38]Rev.Rul. 57–418, 1957–2 C.B. 143; *Morton Frank*, 20 T.C. 511 (1953); and *Dwight A. Ward*, 20 T.C. 332 (1953).

CONCEPT SUMMARY 6–1

Costs of Investigating a Business

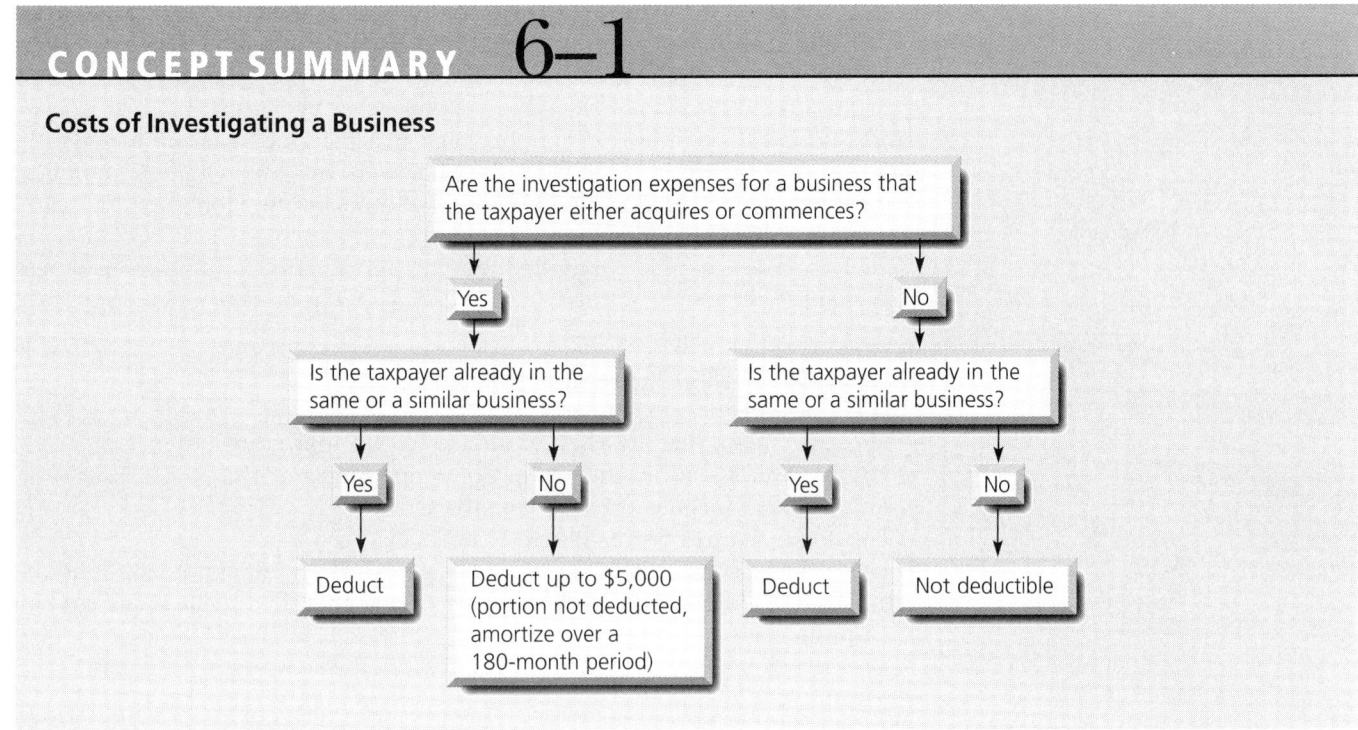

Lynn, a retired merchant, incurs expenses in traveling from Rochester, New York, to California to investigate the feasibility of acquiring several auto care centers. If no acquisition takes place, none of the expenses are deductible. ∎

EXAMPLE 19

If the taxpayer is *not* in a business that is the same as or similar to the one being investigated and actually acquires the new business, the expenses must be capitalized as start-up expenses. At the election of the taxpayer, the first $5,000 of the expenses can be immediately deducted. Any excess expenses can be amortized over a period of 180 months (15 years). In arriving at the $5,000 immediate deduction allowed, a dollar-for-dollar reduction must be made for those expenses in excess of $50,000.[39]

Tina owns and operates 10 restaurants located in various cities throughout the Southeast. She travels to Atlanta to discuss the acquisition of an auto dealership. In addition, she incurs legal and accounting costs associated with the potential acquisition. After incurring total investigation costs of $52,000, she acquires the auto dealership on October 1, 2006.

Tina may immediately deduct $3,000 [$5,000 − ($52,000 − $50,000)] and amortize the balance of $49,000 ($52,000 − $3,000) over a period of 180 months. For calendar year 2006, therefore, Tina can deduct $3,817 [$3,000 + ($49,000 × 3/180)]. ∎

EXAMPLE 20

Hobby Losses

Business or investment expenses are deductible only if the taxpayer can show that the activity was entered into for the purpose of making a profit. Certain activities may have either profit-seeking or personal attributes, depending upon individual circumstances. Examples include raising horses and operating a farm used as a

---

[39]§ 195(b). Prior to October 22, 2004 (the effective date of the American Jobs Creation Act), no immediate deduction was available, but the amortization period was not less than 60 months.

weekend residence. While personal losses are not deductible, losses attributable to profit-seeking activities may be deducted and used to offset a taxpayer's other income. For this reason, the tax law limits the deductibility of **hobby losses.**

General Rules. If an individual can show that an activity has been conducted with the intent to earn a profit, losses from the activity are fully deductible. The hobby loss rules apply only if the activity is not engaged in for profit. Hobby expenses are deductible only to the extent of hobby income.[40]

The Regulations stipulate that the following nine factors should be considered in determining whether an activity is profit seeking or a hobby:[41]

- Whether the activity is conducted in a businesslike manner.
- The expertise of the taxpayers or their advisers.
- The time and effort expended.
- The expectation that the assets of the activity will appreciate in value.
- The taxpayer's previous success in conducting similar activities.
- The history of income or losses from the activity.
- The relationship of profits earned to losses incurred.
- The financial status of the taxpayer (e.g., if the taxpayer does not have substantial amounts of other income, this may indicate that the activity is engaged in for profit).
- Elements of personal pleasure or recreation in the activity.

The presence or absence of a factor is not by itself determinative of whether the activity is profit seeking or a hobby. Rather, the decision is a subjective one that is based on an analysis of the facts and circumstances.

ETHICAL *Considerations* **WHEN IS A DAIRY FARM A TRADE OR BUSINESS?**

Wes has been an orthopedic surgeon in Atlanta for 15 years. He would like to devote less time to his medical practice, spend more time with his family, and pay less income tax. His net income from his medical practice has been about $500,000 per year for the past five years.

Wes grew up on a dairy farm in southeastern Georgia. He has many fond memories of his childhood and believes a farm would be an excellent environment for his three children.

Wes purchases a dairy farm about 30 miles from Atlanta. He hires two full-time employees to handle the milking operations and other part-time employees as needed. In addition, Wes and his family participate in performing various activities on the farm.

Wes commutes to Atlanta four days a week to continue his medical practice. Because he is devoting less time to the practice, his net income decreases to $400,000. Wes has a loss of $75,000 for the dairy farm that he attributes to depressed milk prices and his inexperience at running the farm. He considers the medical practice and the dairy farm to be separate trades or businesses. Therefore, on the Federal income tax return, the $75,000 net loss is offset against the $400,000 net income. Assume that the net income and net loss from the medical practice and the dairy farm, respectively, remain approximately the same for the next four years.

Is the position adopted by Wes defensible? Discuss.

Presumptive Rule of § 183. The Code provides a rebuttable presumption that an activity is profit seeking if the activity shows a profit in at least three of any five prior consecutive years.[42] If the activity involves horses, a profit in at least two of seven consecutive years meets the presumptive rule. If these profitability tests are met, the activity is presumed to be a trade or business rather than a personal hobby. In this situation, the IRS bears the burden of proving that the activity is personal rather than trade or business related.

---

[40]§ 183(b)(2).
[41]Reg. §§ 1.183–2(b)(1) through (9).

[42]§ 183(d).

Camille, an executive for a large corporation, is paid a salary of $200,000. Her husband is a collector of antiques. Several years ago, he opened an antique shop in a local shopping center and spends most of his time buying and selling antiques. He occasionally earns a small profit from this activity but more frequently incurs substantial losses. If the losses are business related, they are fully deductible against Camille's salary income on a joint return. In resolving this issue, consider the following:

- Initially determine whether the antique activity has met the three-out-of-five years profit test.
- If the presumption is not met, the activity may nevertheless qualify as a business if the taxpayer can show that the intent is to engage in a profit-seeking activity. It is not necessary to show actual profits.
- Attempt to fit the operation within the nine criteria prescribed in the Regulations and listed above. These criteria are the factors considered in trying to rebut the § 183 presumption. ∎

Determining the Amount of the Deduction. If an activity is deemed to be a hobby, the expenses are deductible only to the extent of the gross income from the hobby. These expenses must be deducted in the following order:

- Amounts deductible under other Code sections without regard to the nature of the activity, such as property taxes and home mortgage interest.
- Amounts deductible under other Code sections if the activity had been engaged in for profit, but only if those amounts do not affect adjusted basis. Examples include maintenance, utilities, and supplies.
- Amounts that affect adjusted basis and would be deductible under other Code sections if the activity had been engaged in for profit.[43] Examples include depreciation, amortization, and depletion.

These deductions are deductible *from* AGI as itemized deductions to the extent they exceed 2 percent of AGI.[44] If the taxpayer uses the standard deduction rather than itemizing, all hobby loss deductions are wasted.

Jim, the vice president of an oil company, has AGI of $80,000. He decides to pursue painting in his spare time. He uses a home studio, comprising 10% of the home's square footage. During the current year, Jim incurs the following expenses:

Frames	$ 350
Art supplies	300
Fees paid to models	1,000
Home studio expenses:	
Total property taxes	900
Total home mortgage interest	10,000
Depreciation on 10% of home	500
Total home maintenance and utilities	3,600

During the year, Jim sold paintings for a total of $3,200. If the activity is held to be a hobby, Jim is allowed deductions as follows:

Gross income	$ 3,200
Deduct: Taxes and interest (10% of $10,900)	(1,090)
Remainder	$ 2,110

---

[43]Reg. § 1.183–1(b)(1).   [44]Reg. § 1.67–1T(a)(1)(iv) and Rev.Rul. 75–14, 1975–1 C.B. 90.

Deduct: Frames	$ 350	
Art supplies	300	
Models' fees	1,000	
Maintenance and utilities (10%)	360	(2,010)
Remainder		$ 100
Depreciation ($500, but limited to $100)		(100)
Net income		$ –0–

Ded : Cost → 10% AGI (handwritten annotation)

Jim includes the $3,200 of income in AGI, making his AGI $83,200. The taxes and interest are itemized deductions, deductible in full. The remaining $2,110 of expenses are reduced by 2% of his AGI ($1,664), so the net deduction is $446. Since the property taxes and home mortgage interest are deductible anyway, the net effect is a $2,754 ($3,200 less $446) increase in taxable income. ■

EXAMPLE 23

Assume that Jim's activity in Example 22 is held to be a business. The business is located in a small office building he owns. Expenses are property taxes of $90, mortgage interest of $1,000, frames of $350, art supplies of $300, models' fees of $1,000, maintenance and utilities of $360, and depreciation of $500. Under these circumstances, Jim could deduct expenses totaling $3,600. All these expenses would be trade or business expenses deductible *for* AGI. His reduction in AGI would be as follows:

Gross income		$ 3,200
Less: Taxes and interest	$1,090	
Other business expenses	2,010	
Depreciation	500	(3,600)
Reduction in AGI		($ 400)

■

Rental of Vacation Homes

Restrictions on the deductions allowed for part-year rentals of personal **vacation homes** were written into the law to prevent taxpayers from deducting essentially personal expenses as rental losses. Many taxpayers who owned vacation homes had formerly treated the homes as rental property and generated rental losses as deductions *for* AGI. For example, a summer cabin would be rented for 2 months per year, used for vacationing for 1 month, and left vacant the rest of the year. The taxpayer would then deduct 11 months' depreciation, utilities, maintenance, etc., as rental expenses, resulting in a rental loss. Section 280A eliminates this treatment by allowing deductions on residences used primarily for personal purposes only to the extent of the income generated. Only a break-even situation is allowed; no losses can be deducted.

There are three possible tax treatments for residences used for both personal and rental purposes. The treatment depends upon the *relative time* the residence is used for personal purposes versus rental use.

Primarily Personal Use. If the residence is *rented* for *fewer than 15 days* in a year, it is treated as a personal residence. The rent income is excluded from gross income, and mortgage interest and real estate taxes are allowed as itemized deductions, as with any personal residence.[45] No other expenses (e.g., depreciation, utilities, maintenance) are deductible. Although this provision exists primarily for administrative convenience, several bills have been introduced in Congress that would have repealed this exclusion from gross income.

EXAMPLE 24

Dixie owns a vacation cottage on the lake. During the current year, she rented it for $1,600 for two weeks, lived in it two months, and left it vacant the remainder of the year. The year's

---

[45] § 280A(g).

TAX *in the News*   **MAKING MONEY AT THE MASTERS, BUT NOT AS A GOLFER**

On the second weekend in April, one group comes to Augusta to make money, and another group leaves town also to make money. Of course, those coming to Augusta are the PGA Tour golfers participating in the Masters Golf Tournament. They have the opportunity to make money, both from the tournament purse and from future endorsements. Both the tournament purse money and the endorsement money are included in gross income.

Those leaving town are Augusta homeowners. If you own a residence in Augusta and are not a golf fan, you have an opportunity to "get out of town" for the week and get paid for leaving. Typical rents paid for the tournament week in 2005 were as follows:

Size of House	Distance from Augusta National	Amount of Rent
1,700 square feet	1 mile	$ 3,000
3,800 square feet	2 miles	6,800
4,500 square feet	2 miles	15,000

The best part is that the homeowners can enjoy their vacation even more knowing that the rent income received is excluded from gross income.

Source: *Adapted from "Money's Worth,"* Wall Street Journal, *February 16, 2005, p. D3.*

---

expenses amounted to $6,000 mortgage interest expense, $500 property taxes, $1,500 utilities and maintenance, and $2,400 depreciation. Since the property was not rented for at least 15 days, the income is excluded, the mortgage interest and property tax expenses are itemized deductions, and the remaining expenses are nondeductible personal expenses. ∎

Primarily Rental Use. If the residence is *rented* for 15 days or more in a year and is *not used* for personal purposes for more than the greater of (1) 14 days or (2) 10 percent of the total days rented, the residence is treated as rental property.[46] The expenses must be allocated between personal and rental days if there are any personal use days during the year. The deduction of the expenses allocated to rental days can exceed rent income and result in a rental loss. The loss may be deductible under the passive activity loss rules (discussed in Chapter 11).

EXAMPLE 25

Assume instead that Dixie in Example 24 used the cottage for 12 days and rented it for 48 days for $4,800. Since she rented the cottage for 15 days or more but did not use it for more than 14 days, the cottage is treated as rental property. The expenses must be allocated between personal and rental days.

	Percentage of Use	
	Rental 80%	Personal 20%
Income	$ 4,800	$ –0–
Expenses		
Mortgage interest ($6,000)	($ 4,800)	($1,200)
Property taxes ($500)	(400)	(100)
Utilities and maintenance ($1,500)	(1,200)	(300)
Depreciation ($2,400)	(1,920)	(480)
Total expenses	($ 8,320)	($2,080)
Rental loss	($ 3,520)	$ –0–

Dixie deducts the $3,520 rental loss *for* AGI (assuming she meets the passive activity loss rules, discussed in Chapter 11). She also has an itemized deduction for property taxes of $100 associated with the personal use. The mortgage interest of $1,200 associated with the

---

[46]§ 280A(d) and Prop.Reg. § 1.280A–3(c).

personal use is not deductible as an itemized deduction because the cottage is not a qualified residence (qualified residence interest) for this purpose (see Chapter 10). The portion of utilities and maintenance and depreciation attributable to personal use is not deductible. ■

EXAMPLE 26

Assume instead that Dixie in Example 24 rented the cottage for 200 days and lived in it for 19 days. The cottage is primarily rental use since she rented it for 15 days or more and did not use it for personal purposes for more than 20 days (10% of the rental days). The expenses must be allocated between personal and rental days as illustrated in Example 25. ■

Personal/Rental Use. If the residence is rented for 15 days or more in a year *and* is used for personal purposes for more than the greater of (1) 14 days or (2) 10 percent of the total days rented, it is treated as a personal/rental use residence. The expenses must be allocated between personal days and rental days. Expenses are allowed only to the extent of rent income.

EXAMPLE 27

Assume instead that Dixie in Example 24 rented the property for 30 days and lived in it for 30 days. The residence is classified as personal/rental use property since she used it more than 14 days and rented it for 15 days or more. The expenses must be allocated between rental use and personal use, and the rental expenses are allowed only to the extent of rent income. ■

If a residence is classified as personal/rental use property, the expenses that are deductible anyway (e.g., real estate taxes and mortgage interest) must be deducted first. If a positive net income results, otherwise nondeductible expenses that do not affect adjusted basis (e.g., maintenance, utilities, insurance) are allowed next. Finally, if any positive balance remains, depreciation is allowed. Any disallowed expenses allocable to rental use are carried forward and used in future years subject to the same limitations.

Expenses must be allocated between personal and rental days before the limits are applied. The courts have held that real estate taxes and mortgage interest, which accrue ratably over the year, are allocated on the basis of 365 days.[47] The IRS, however, disagrees and allocates real estate taxes and mortgage interest on the basis of total days of use.[48] Other expenses (utilities, maintenance, depreciation, etc.) are allocated on the basis of total days used.

EXAMPLE 28

Jason rents his vacation home for 60 days and lives in the home for 30 days. The limitations on personal/rental use residences apply. Jason's gross rent income is $10,000. For the entire year (not a leap year), the real estate taxes are $2,190; his mortgage interest expense is $10,220; utilities and maintenance expense equals $2,400; and depreciation is $9,000. Using the IRS approach, these amounts are deductible in this specific order:

Gross income	$10,000
Deduct: Taxes and interest ($^{60}/_{90} \times $12,410$)	(8,273)
Remainder to apply to rental operating expenses and depreciation	$ 1,727
Deduct: Utilities and maintenance ($^{60}/_{90} \times $2,400$)	(1,600)
Balance	$ 127
Deduct: Depreciation ($^{60}/_{90} \times $9,000 = $6,000$ but limited to above balance)	(127)
Net rent income	$ –0–

The nonrental use portion of real estate taxes and mortgage interest ($4,137 in this case) is deductible if the taxpayer elects to itemize (see Chapter 10). The personal use

[47]*Bolton v. Comm.*, 82–2 USTC ¶9699, 51 AFTR2d 83–305, 694 F.2d 556 (CA–9, 1982).   [48]Prop.Reg. § 1.280A–3(d)(4).

portion of utilities, maintenance, and depreciation is not deductible in any case. Jason has a carryover of $5,873 ($6,000 − $127) of the unused depreciation. Also note that the basis of the property is not reduced by the $5,873 depreciation not allowed because of the above limitation. (See Chapter 14 for a discussion of the reduction in basis for depreciation allowed or allowable.) ■

EXAMPLE 29

Using the court's approach in allocating real estate taxes and mortgage interest, Jason, in Example 28, would have this result:

Gross income	$10,000
Deduct: Taxes and interest ($^{60}/_{365}$ × $12,410)	(2,040)
Remainder to apply to rental operating expenses and depreciation	$ 7,960
Deduct: Utilities and maintenance ($^{60}/_{90}$ × $2,400)	(1,600)
Balance	$ 6,360
Deduct: Depreciation ($^{60}/_{90}$ × $9,000, but limited to $6,360)	(6,000)
Net rent income	$ 360

Jason can deduct $10,370 ($12,410 paid − $2,040 deducted as expense in computing net rent income) of personal use mortgage interest and real estate taxes as itemized deductions. ■

Note the contrasting results in Examples 28 and 29. The IRS's approach (Example 28) results in no rental gain or loss and an itemized deduction for real estate taxes and mortgage interest of $4,137. In Example 29, Jason has net rent income of $360 and $10,370 of itemized deductions. The court's approach decreases his taxable income by $10,010 ($10,370 itemized deductions less $360 net rent income). The IRS's approach reduces his taxable income by only $4,137.

EXAMPLE 30

Assume instead that Jason in Example 28 had not lived in the home at all during the year. The house is rental property. The rental loss is calculated as follows:

Gross income		$10,000
Expenses		
Taxes and interest	($12,410)	
Utilities and maintenance	(2,400)	
Depreciation	(9,000)	
Total expenses		($23,810)
Rental loss		($13,810)

Whether any of the rental loss would be deductible depends upon whether Jason actively participated in the rental activity and met the other requirements for passive activity losses (discussed in Chapter 11). ■

Conversion to Rental Property. A related issue is whether or not a taxpayer's *primary residence* is subject to the preceding rules if it is converted to rental property. If the vacation home rules apply, a taxpayer who converts a personal residence to rental property during the tax year, without any tax avoidance motive, could have the allowable deductions limited to the rent income. This would occur if the personal use exceeded the greater of 14 days or 10 percent of rental days test (a likely situation). The Code, however, provides that during a *qualified rental period*, any personal use days are not counted as personal use days in terms of classifying the use of the residence as *personal/rental use* rather than as *primarily rental use*.[49] In effect, the

---

[49]§ 280A(d).

CONCEPT SUMMARY 6–2

Vacation/Rental Home

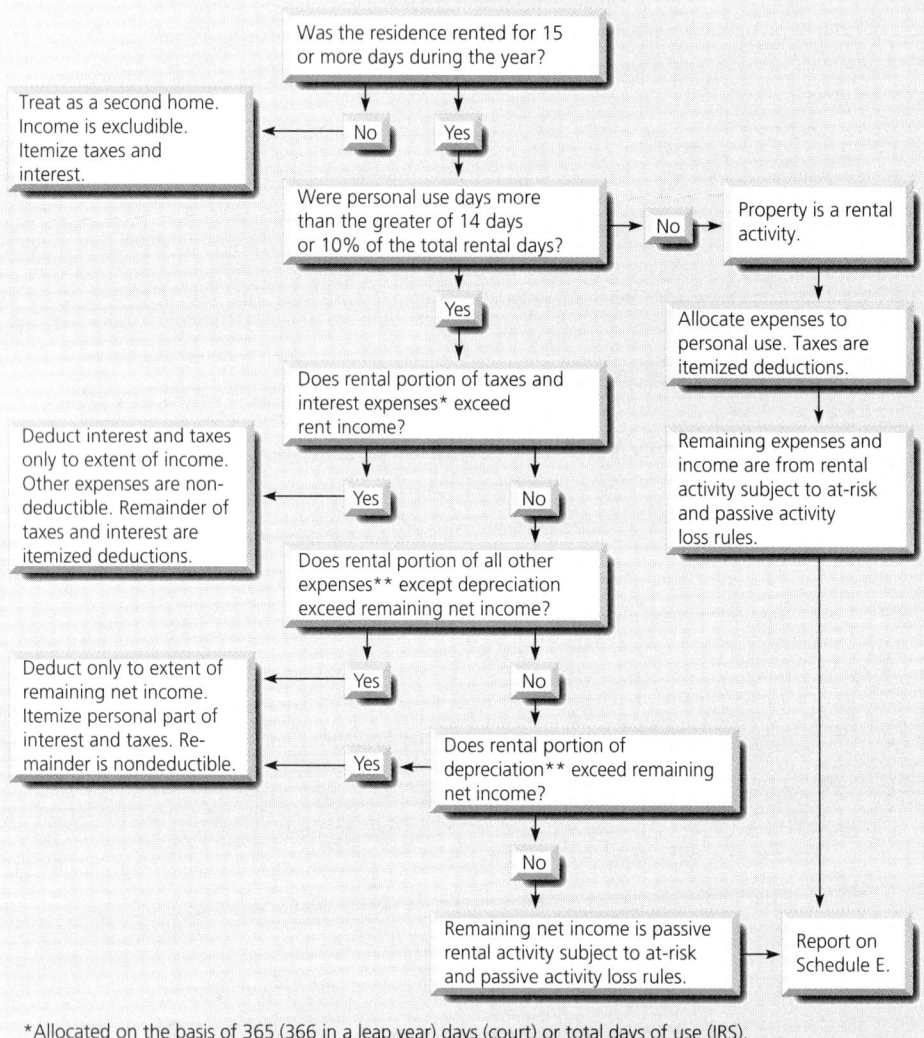

*Allocated on the basis of 365 (366 in a leap year) days (court) or total days of use (IRS).
**Allocated on the basis of total days of use.

deduction for expenses of the property incurred during a qualified rental period is not subject to the personal use test of the vacation home rules. A qualified rental period is a consecutive period of 12 or more months. The period begins or ends in the taxable year in which the residence is rented or held for rental at a fair price. The residence must not be rented to a related party. If the property is sold before the 12-month period expires, the qualified rental period is the actual time rented.

EXAMPLE 31

Rhonda converts her residence to rental property on May 1 and rents it for the remainder of 2006 for $5,600 and for all of 2007 for $8,400. The house would be classified as personal/rental use property (personal use days during 2006 are greater than both 14 days and 10% of rental days) except that this is a qualified rental period. Therefore, Rhonda's deduction for rental expenses is not limited to the gross income of $5,600 in 2006. ■

See Concept Summary 6–2 for a summary of the vacation home rules.

Expenditures Incurred for Taxpayer's Benefit or Taxpayer's Obligation

An expense must be incurred for the taxpayer's benefit or arise from the taxpayer's obligation. An individual cannot claim a tax deduction for the payment of the expenses of another individual.

EXAMPLE 32

During the current year, Fred pays the property taxes on his son Vern's home. Neither Fred nor Vern can take a deduction for the amount paid for Vern's property taxes. Fred is not entitled to a deduction because the property taxes are not his obligation. Vern cannot claim a deduction because he did not pay the property taxes. The tax result would have been more favorable had Fred made a cash gift to Vern and let him pay the property taxes. Then Vern could have deducted the property taxes. Fred likely would not be liable for any gift taxes depending upon the amount involved due to the annual exclusion (see Chapter 1). A deduction would have been created with no cash difference to the family. ■

One exception to this disallowance rule is the payment of medical expenses for a dependent. Such expenses are deductible by the payer subject to the normal rules that limit the deductibility of medical expenses (see Chapter 10).[50]

ETHICAL *Considerations*   **HOW THE PAYMENT IS MADE**

Dan and Jeff both have sons who graduated from college recently and are employed by the same company in a rural community where rental housing is not readily available. Each father lends his son $10,000; the sons combine their resources and use the $20,000 as a down payment on a house they buy together.

During 2006, the sons make all the mortgage payments on their house until December when they are furloughed from their jobs. Dan gives his son $900 to use to pay his share of the mortgage payment, and Jeff pays $900 directly to the mortgage company for his son. In each of these $900 amounts, $800 represents interest on the mortgage.

Over lunch recently, Dan and Jeff were discussing their sons' real estate investment and the $900 mortgage pay-

ment each father had funded. Jeff indicated that since he had paid the mortgage payment directly, he was going to deduct the $800 of interest on Schedule A of his Form 1040. After this conversation, Dan concludes that, in substance, he and Jeff have done the same thing. Accordingly, Dan calls his son and tells him that he wants to deduct the $800 on his tax return. Though Dan's son is not pleased, he agrees to permit his father to take the deduction and says he will not deduct the mortgage interest on his own return.

Evaluate the propriety of the position taken by Dan. What if Dan's son takes a more aggressive position and deducts the entire $900 payment rather than agreeing to his father's proposal?

Disallowance of Personal Expenditures

Section 262 states that "except as otherwise expressly provided in this chapter, no deduction shall be allowed for personal, living, or family expenses." To justify a deduction, an individual must be able to identify a particular section of the Code that sanctions the deduction (e.g., charitable contributions, medical expenses). Sometimes the character of a particular expenditure is not easily determined.

EXAMPLE 33

During the current year, Howard pays $2,500 in legal fees and court costs to obtain a divorce from his wife, Vera. Included in the divorce action is a property settlement concerning the disposition of income-producing property owned by Howard. In a similar situation, the Tax

---

[50]§ 213(a).

Court held that the taxpayer could not deduct any such costs.[51] "Although fees primarily related to property division concerning his income-producing property, they weren't ordinary and necessary expenses paid for conservation or maintenance of property held for production of income. Legal fees incurred in defending against claims that arise from a taxpayer's marital relationship aren't deductible expenses regardless of possible consequences on taxpayer's income-producing property." ∎

The IRS has clarified the issue of the deduction of legal fees incurred in connection with a divorce.[52] To be deductible, an expense must relate solely to tax advice in a divorce proceeding. For example, legal fees attributable to the determination of dependency exemptions of children are deductible if the fees are distinguishable from the general legal fees incurred in obtaining a divorce. Other examples are the costs of creating a trust to make periodic alimony payments and the determination of the tax consequences of a property settlement. Therefore, it is advisable to request an itemization of attorney's fees to substantiate a deduction for the tax-related amounts.

Disallowance of Deductions for Capital Expenditures

The Code specifically disallows a deduction for "any amount paid out for new buildings or for permanent improvements or betterments made to increase the value of any property or estate."[53] The Regulations further define capital expenditures to include those expenditures that add to the value or prolong the life of property or adapt the property to a new or different use.[54] Incidental repairs and maintenance of the property are not capital expenditures and can be deducted as ordinary and necessary business expenses. Repairing a roof is a deductible expense, but replacing a roof is a capital expenditure subject to depreciation deductions over its useful life. The tune-up of a delivery truck is an expense; a complete overhaul probably is a capital expenditure.

Capitalization versus Expense. When an expenditure is capitalized rather than expensed, the deduction is at best deferred and at worst lost forever. Although an immediate tax benefit for a large cash expenditure is lost, the cost may be deductible in increments over a longer period of time.

If the expenditure is for a tangible asset that has an ascertainable life, it is capitalized and may be deducted as depreciation (or cost recovery) over the life of the asset (for depreciation) or over a statutory period (for cost recovery under either ACRS or MACRS).[55] Land is not subject to depreciation (or cost recovery) since it does not have an ascertainable life.

EXAMPLE 34

Stan purchased a prime piece of land located in an apartment-zoned area. Stan paid $500,000 for the property, which had an old but usable apartment building on it. He immediately had the building demolished at a cost of $100,000. The $500,000 purchase price and the $100,000 demolition costs must be capitalized, and the basis of the land is $600,000. Since land is a nondepreciable asset, no deduction is allowed. More favorable tax treatment might result if Stan rented the apartments in the old building for a period of time to attempt to establish that there was no intent to demolish the building. If Stan's attempt is successful, it might be possible to allocate a substantial portion of the original purchase price of the property to the building (a depreciable asset). When the building is later demolished, any remaining adjusted basis can be deducted as an ordinary (§ 1231) loss. (See Chapter 17 for a discussion of the treatment of § 1231 assets.) ∎

---

[51] *Harry H. Goldberg*, 29 TCM 74, T.C.Memo. 1970–27.
[52] Rev.Rul. 72–545, 1972–2 C.B. 179.
[53] § 263(a)(1).

[54] Reg. § 1.263(a)–1(b).
[55] See Chapter 8 for the discussion of depreciation and cost recovery.

If the expenditure is for an intangible asset (e.g., copyright, patent, covenant not to compete, goodwill), the capitalized expenditure can be amortized, regardless of whether or not the intangible asset has an ascertainable life. Intangible assets, referred to as § 197 intangibles, are amortized over a 15-year statutory period using the straight-line method. See Chapter 8 for additional discussion of the amortization of intangibles.

Transactions between Related Parties

The Code places restrictions on the recognition of gains and losses from **related-party transactions.** Without these restrictions, relationships created by birth, marriage, and business would provide endless possibilities for engaging in financial transactions that produce tax savings with no real economic substance or change. For example, to create an artificial loss, a wife could sell investment property to her husband at a loss and deduct the loss on their joint return. Her husband could then hold the asset indefinitely, and the family would sustain no real economic loss. A complex set of laws has been designed to eliminate such possibilities.

Losses. The Code provides for the disallowance of any "losses from sales or exchanges of property . . . directly or indirectly" between related parties.[56] When the property is subsequently sold to a nonrelated party, any gain recognized is reduced by the loss previously disallowed. Any disallowed loss not used by the related-party buyer to offset the recognized gain on a subsequent sale or exchange to an unrelated party is permanently lost.

E X A M P L E   35

Freida sells common stock with a basis of $1,000 to her son, Bill, for $800. Bill sells the stock several years later for $1,100. Freida's $200 loss is disallowed upon the sale to Bill, and only $100 of gain ($1,100 selling price − $800 basis − $200 disallowed loss) is taxable to him upon the subsequent sale. ■

E X A M P L E   36

George sells common stock with a basis of $1,050 to his son, Ray, for $800. Ray sells the stock eight months later to an unrelated party for $900. Ray's gain of $100 ($900 selling price − $800 basis) is not recognized because of George's previously disallowed loss of $250. Note that the offset may result in only partial tax benefit upon the subsequent sale (as in this case). If the property had not been transferred to Ray, George could have recognized a $150 loss upon the subsequent sale to the unrelated party ($1,050 basis − $900 selling price). ■

E X A M P L E   37

Pete sells common stock with a basis of $1,000 to an unrelated third party for $800. Pete's son repurchased the same stock in the market on the same day for $800. The $200 loss is not allowed because the transaction is an indirect sale between related parties.[57] ■

Unpaid Expenses and Interest. The law prevents related taxpayers from engaging in tax avoidance schemes where one related taxpayer uses the accrual method of accounting and the other uses the cash basis. An accrual basis, closely held corporation, for example, could borrow funds from a cash basis individual shareholder. At the end of the year, the corporation would accrue and deduct the interest, but the cash basis lender would not recognize interest income since no interest had been paid. Section 267 specifically defers the deduction of the accruing taxpayer until the recipient taxpayer must include it in income; that is, when it is actually paid to the cash basis taxpayer. This *matching* provision applies to interest as well as other expenses, such as salaries and bonuses.

---

[56]§ 267(a)(1).
[57]*McWilliams v. Comm.*, 47–1 USTC ¶9289, 35 AFTR 1184, 67 S.Ct. 1477 (USSC, 1947).

This deduction deferral provision does not apply if both of the related taxpayers use the accrual method or both use the cash method. Likewise, it does not apply if the related party reporting income uses the accrual method and the related party taking the deduction uses the cash method.

Relationships and Constructive Ownership. Section 267 operates to disallow losses and defer deductions only between related parties. Losses or deductions generated by similar transactions with an unrelated party are allowed. *Related parties* include the following:

- Brothers and sisters (whether whole, half, or adopted), spouse, ancestors (parents, grandparents), and lineal descendants (children, grandchildren) of the taxpayer.
- A corporation owned more than 50 percent (directly or indirectly) by the taxpayer.
- Two corporations that are members of a controlled group.
- A series of other complex relationships between trusts, corporations, and individual taxpayers.

Constructive ownership provisions are applied to determine whether the taxpayers are related. Under these provisions, stock owned by certain relatives or related entities is *deemed* to be owned by the taxpayer for purposes of applying the loss and expense deduction disallowance provisions. A taxpayer is deemed to own not only his or her stock but also the stock owned by lineal descendants, ancestors, brothers and sisters or half-brothers and half-sisters, and spouse. The taxpayer is also deemed to own his or her proportionate share of stock owned by any partnership, corporation, estate, or trust of which the taxpayer is a member. An individual is deemed to own any stock owned, directly or indirectly, by his or her partner. However, constructive ownership by an individual of the partnership's and the other partner's shares does not extend to the individual's spouse or other relatives (no double attribution).

EXAMPLE 38

The stock of Sparrow Corporation is owned 20% by Ted, 30% by Ted's father, 30% by Ted's mother, and 20% by Ted's sister. On July 1 of the current year, Ted loaned $10,000 to Sparrow Corporation at 8% annual interest, principal and interest payable on demand. For tax purposes, Sparrow uses the accrual basis, and Ted uses the cash basis. Both are on a calendar year. Since Ted is deemed to own the 80% owned by his parents and sister, he constructively owns 100% of Sparrow Corporation. If the corporation accrues the interest within the taxable year, no deduction can be taken until payment is made to Ted. ■

Substantiation Requirements

The tax law is built on a voluntary system. Taxpayers file their tax returns, report income and take deductions to which they are entitled, and pay their taxes through withholding or estimated tax payments during the year. The taxpayer has the burden of proof for substantiating expenses deducted on the returns and must retain adequate records. Upon audit, the IRS will disallow any undocumented or unsubstantiated deductions. These requirements have resulted in numerous conflicts between taxpayers and the IRS.

Some events throughout the year should be documented as they occur. For example, it is generally advisable to receive a pledge payment statement from one's church, in addition to a canceled check (if available) for proper documentation of a charitable contribution.[58] In addition, for charitable contributions, a donor must

[58]Rev.Proc. 92–71, 1992–2 C.B. 437, addresses circumstances where checks are not returned by a financial institution or where electronic transfers are made.

obtain a receipt from the donee for contributions of $250 or more. Other types of deductible expenditures may require receipts or some other type of support.

Specific and *more stringent* rules for deducting travel, entertainment, and gift expenses are discussed in Chapter 9. Certain mixed-use (both personal and business use) and listed property are also subject to the adequate records requirement (discussed in Chapter 8).

Expenses and Interest Relating to Tax-Exempt Income

Certain income, such as interest on municipal bonds, is tax-exempt.[59] The law also allows the taxpayer to deduct expenses incurred for the production of income.[60] Deduction disallowance provisions, however, make it impossible to make money at the expense of the government by excluding interest income and deducting interest expense.[61]

EXAMPLE 39

Sandy, a taxpayer in the 35% bracket, purchased $100,000 of 6% municipal bonds. At the same time, she used the bonds as collateral on a bank loan of $100,000 at 8% interest. A positive cash flow would result from the tax benefit as follows:

Cash paid out on loan	($8,000)
Cash received from bonds	6,000
Tax savings from deducting interest expense (35% of $8,000 interest expense)	2,800
Net positive cash flow	$ 800

■

To eliminate the possibility illustrated in Example 39, the Code specifically disallows as a deduction the expenses of producing tax-exempt income. Interest on any indebtedness incurred or continued to purchase or carry tax-exempt obligations also is disallowed.

Judicial Interpretations. It is often difficult to show a direct relationship between borrowings and investment in tax-exempt securities. Suppose, for example, that a taxpayer borrows money, adds it to existing funds, buys inventory and stocks, then later sells the inventory and buys municipal bonds. A series of transactions such as these can completely obscure any connection between the loan and the tax-exempt investment. One solution would be to disallow interest on any debt to the extent that the taxpayer holds any tax-exempt securities. This approach would preclude individuals from deducting part of their home mortgage interest if they owned any municipal bonds. The law was not intended to go to such extremes. As a result, judicial interpretations have tried to be reasonable in disallowing interest deductions.

In one case, a company used municipal bonds as collateral on short-term loans to meet seasonal liquidity needs.[62] The court disallowed the interest deduction on the grounds that the company could predict its seasonal liquidity needs. The company could anticipate the need to borrow the money to continue to carry the tax-exempt securities. The same company *was* allowed an interest deduction on a building mortgage, even though tax-exempt securities it owned could have been sold to pay off the mortgage. The court reasoned that short-term liquidity needs would have been impaired if the tax-exempt securities were sold. Furthermore, the

---

[59]§ 103.

[60]§ 212.

[61]§ 265.

[62]*The Wisconsin Cheeseman, Inc. v. U.S.*, 68–1 USTC ¶9145, 21 AFTR2d 383, 388 F.2d 420 (CA–7, 1968).

court ruled that carrying the tax-exempt securities bore no relationship to the long-term financing of a construction project.

EXAMPLE 40

In January of the current year, Alan borrowed $100,000 at 8% interest. He used the loan proceeds to purchase 5,000 shares of stock in White Corporation. In July, he sold the stock for $120,000 and reinvested the proceeds in City of Denver bonds, the income from which is tax-exempt. Assuming the $100,000 loan remained outstanding throughout the entire year, Alan cannot deduct the interest attributable to the period in which he held the bonds. ■

LO.4

Identify tax planning opportunities for maximizing deductions and minimizing the disallowance of deductions.

TAX PLANNING
Considerations

Time Value of Tax Deductions

Cash basis taxpayers often have the ability to make early payments for their expenses at the end of the tax year. This may permit the payments to be deducted currently instead of in the following tax year. In view of the time value of money, a tax deduction this year may be worth more than the same deduction next year. Before employing this strategy, the taxpayer must consider next year's expected income and tax rates and whether a cash-flow problem may develop from early payments. Thus, the time value of money as well as tax rate changes must be considered when an expense can be paid and deducted in either of two years.

EXAMPLE 41

Jena pledged $5,000 to her church's special building fund. She can make the contribution in December 2006 or January 2007. Jena is in the 35% tax bracket in 2006, and in the 28% bracket in 2007. She itemizes in both years. Assume Jena's discount rate is 8%. If she takes the deduction in 2006, she saves $454 ($1,750 − $1,296), due to the decrease in the tax rates and the time value of money.

	2006	2007
Contribution	$5,000	$5,000
Tax bracket	.35	.28
Tax savings	$1,750	$1,400
Discounted @ 8%	1.0	.926
Savings in present value	$1,750	$1,296

■

Unreasonable Compensation

In substantiating the reasonableness of a shareholder-employee's compensation, an internal comparison test is sometimes useful. If it can be shown that nonshareholder-employees and shareholder-employees in comparable positions receive comparable compensation, it is indicative that compensation is not unreasonable.

Another possibility is to demonstrate that the shareholder-employee has been underpaid in prior years. For example, the shareholder-employee may have agreed to take a less-than-adequate salary during the unprofitable formative years of the business. The expectation is that the "postponed" compensation would be paid in later, more profitable years. The agreement should be documented, if possible, in the corporate minutes.

Keep in mind that in testing for reasonableness, the *total* pay package must be considered. Look at all fringe benefits or perquisites, such as contributions by the corporation to a qualified pension plan. Even though those amounts are not immediately available to the covered shareholder-employee, they must be taken into account.

CONCEPT SUMMARY 6–3

Classification of Expenses

Expense Item	Deductible For AGI	Deductible From AGI	Not Deductible	Applicable Code §
Investment expenses				
Rent and royalty	X			§ 62(a)(4)
All other investments		X[4]		§ 212
Employee expenses				
Commuting expenses			X	§ 262
Travel and transportation[1]		X[4,5]		§ 162(a)(2)
Reimbursed expenses[1]	X			§ 62(a)(2)(A)
Moving expenses	X			§ 62(a)(15)
Entertainment[1]		X[4,5]		§ 162(a)
Teacher supplies	X[11]	X[4]		§ 62(a)(2)(D)
All other employee expenses[1]		X[4,5]		§ 162(a)
Certain expenses of performing artists	X			§ 62(a)(2)(B)
Trade or business expenses	X			§§ 162 and 62(a)(1)
Casualty losses				
Business	X			§ 165(c)(1)
Personal		X[6]		§ 165(c)(3)
Tax determination				
Collection or refund expenses	X[8]	X		§§ 212 and 62(a)(1) or (4)
Bad debts	X			§§ 166 and 62(a)(1) or (3)
Medical expenses		X[7]		§ 213
Charitable contributions		X		§ 170
Taxes				
Trade or business	X			§§ 162 and 62(a)(1)
Personal taxes				
Real property		X		§ 164(a)(1)
Personal property		X		§ 164(a)(2)
State and local income *or* sales		X		§§ 164(a)(3) and (b)(5)
Investigation of a business[2]	X			§§ 162 and 62(a)(1)
Interest				
Business	X			§§ 162 and 62(a)(1)
Personal	X[9]	X[3]	X[10]	§§ 163(a), (d), and (h)
Qualified tuition and related expenses	X			§§ 62(a)(18) and 222
All other personal expenses			X	§ 262

[1] Deduction for AGI if reimbursed, an adequate accounting is made, and employee is required to repay excess reimbursements.

[2] Provided certain criteria are met.

[3] Subject to the excess investment interest and the qualified residence interest provisions.

[4] Subject (in the aggregate) to a 2%-of-AGI floor imposed by § 67.

[5] Only 50% of meals and entertainment are deductible.

[6] Subject to a $100 floor per event and a 10%-of-AGI floor per tax year.

[7] Subject to a 7.5%-of-AGI floor.

[8] Only the portion relating to business, rental, or royalty income or losses.

[9] Only the portion relating to student loans.

[10] Other personal interest is disallowed.

[11] Subject to a statutory limit of $250.

Excessive Executive Compensation

With the $1 million limit on the deduction of compensation of covered employees, many corporations and their executives must engage in additional tax planning. Previously, concerns over the deductibility of compensation related primarily to closely held corporations. The $1 million limit applies specifically to publicly held corporations. In many instances, it is now necessary for these corporations to restructure the compensation packages of their top executives in order to deduct payments in excess of $1 million. Opportunities include compensation payable on a commission basis, certain other performance-based compensation, payments to qualified retirement plans, and payments that are excludible fringe benefits.

Shifting Deductions

Taxpayers should manage their obligations to avoid the loss of a deduction. Deductions can be shifted among family members, depending upon which member makes the payment. For example, a father buys a condo for his daughter and puts the title in both names. The taxpayer who makes the payment gets the deduction for the property taxes. If the condo is owned by the daughter only and her father makes the payment, neither is entitled to a deduction. In this case, the father should make a cash gift to the daughter who then makes the payment to the taxing authority.

Hobby Losses

To demonstrate that an activity has been entered into for the purpose of making a profit, a taxpayer should treat the activity as a business. The business should engage in advertising, use business letterhead stationery, and maintain a business phone.

If a taxpayer's activity earns a profit in three out of five consecutive years, the presumption is that the activity is engaged in for profit. It may be possible for a cash basis taxpayer to meet these requirements by timing the payment of expenses or the receipt of revenues. The payment of certain expenses incurred before the end of the year might be made in the following year. The billing of year-end sales might be delayed so that collections are received in the following year.

Keep in mind that the three-out-of-five-years rule under § 183 is not absolute. All it does is shift the presumption. If a profit is not made in three out of five years, the losses may still be allowed if the taxpayer can show that they are due to the nature of the business. For example, success in artistic or literary endeavors can take a long time. Also, depending on the state of the economy, even full-time farmers and ranchers are often unable to show a profit. How can one expect a part-time farmer or rancher to do so?

Merely satisfying the three-out-of-five-years rule does not guarantee that a taxpayer is automatically home free. If the three years of profits are insignificant relative to the losses of other years, or if the profits are not from the ordinary operation of the business, the taxpayer is vulnerable. The IRS may still be able to establish that the taxpayer is not engaged in an activity for profit.

| EXAMPLE 42 | Ashley had the following gains and losses in an artistic endeavor: |

2002	($50,000)
2003	(65,000)
2004	400
2005	200
2006	125

Under these circumstances, the IRS might try to overcome the presumption. ∎

If Ashley in Example 42 could show conformity with the factors enumerated in the Regulations or could show evidence of business hardships (e.g., injury, death, or illness), the government cannot override the presumption.[63]

Capital Expenditures

On the sale of a sole proprietorship where the sales price exceeds the fair market value of the tangible assets and stated intangible assets, a planning opportunity may exist for both the seller and the buyer. The seller's preference is for the excess amount to be allocated to goodwill. Goodwill is a capital asset whereas a covenant not to compete produces ordinary income treatment (see Chapter 16).

Because both a covenant and goodwill are amortized over a statutory 15-year period, the tax results of a covenant and goodwill are the same for the buyer. However, the buyer should recognize that an allocation to goodwill rather than a covenant may provide a tax benefit to the seller. Therefore, the seller and buyer, in negotiating the sales price, should factor in the tax benefit to the seller of having the excess amount labeled goodwill rather than a covenant not to compete. Of course, if the noncompetition aspects of a covenant are important to the buyer, part of the excess amount can be assigned to a covenant.

KEY TERMS

Accounting method, 6–9	Deductions from adjusted gross income, 6–2	Reasonableness, 6–7
Deductions for adjusted gross income, 6–2	Hobby losses, 6–16	Related-party transactions, 6–25
	Ordinary and necessary, 6–5	Vacation homes, 6–18

PROBLEM MATERIALS

DISCUSSION QUESTIONS

1. "All income must be reported and all deductions are allowed unless specifically disallowed in the Code." Discuss.

2. Discuss the difference in the tax treatment of deductions *for* and deductions *from* AGI.

[handwritten: Above / Below the line (Itemized)]

3. Does an expenditure that is classified as a deduction *from* AGI produce the same tax benefit as an expenditure that is classified as a deduction *for* AGI? Explain.

4. Classify each of the following expenditures as a deduction *for* AGI, a deduction *from* AGI, or not deductible:
   a. Pete gives $1,000 to his mother for her birthday. *[handwritten: None]*
   b. Janet gives $1,000 to the First Baptist Church. *[handwritten: From]*
   c. Alex pays Dr. Dafashy $1,000 for medical services rendered. *[handwritten: None or from AGI if > 7.5% floor.]*
   d. Susan pays alimony of $1,000 to Herman. *[handwritten: For]*
   e. Rex, who is self-employed, contributes $1,000 to his pension plan. *[handwritten: For]*
   f. April pays expenses of $500 associated with her rental property. *[handwritten: For]*

5. Classify each of the following expenditures as a deduction *for* AGI, a deduction *from* AGI, or not deductible:
   a. Amos contributes $500 to his H.R. 10 plan (i.e., a retirement plan for a self-employed individual). *[handwritten: For]*

---

[63]*Faulconer, Sr. v. Comm.*, 84–2 USTC ¶9955, 55 AFTR2d 85–302, 748 F.2d 890 (CA–4, 1984), *rev'g* 45 TCM 1084, T.C.Memo. 1983–165.

b. Keith pays $500 of child support to his former wife, Renee, for the support of their son, Chris. *None*

c. Judy pays $500 for professional dues that are reimbursed by her employer. *For*

d. Ted pays $500 as the monthly mortgage payment on his personal residence. Of this amount, $100 represents a payment on principal, and $400 represents an interest payment. *$400 from*

e. Lynn pays $500 to a moving company for moving her household goods to Detroit where she is starting a new job. She is not reimbursed by her employer. *For*

f. Ralph pays property taxes of $1,500 on his personal residence. *From*

If Susan is self-employed or rental/royalty investment

Yes

6. Larry and Susan each invest $10,000 in separate investment activities. They each incur deductible expenses of $800 associated with their respective investments. Explain why Larry's expenses are properly classified as deductions *from* AGI (itemized deductions) and Susan's expenses are appropriately classified as deductions *for* AGI.

7. Must an expense be both ordinary and necessary in order to be deducted as a trade or business expense under § 162?

750 excludible

1500 >> 100 shares ⇒ not expense.

8. Mabel, a machinist employed by Silver Airlines, owns 100 shares of Silver Airlines stock. Silver has 900,000 shares of stock outstanding. Mabel spends $1,500 to travel to Denver for Silver's annual meeting. Her expenses would have been $750 more, but she was permitted to fly free on Silver. She attended both days of the shareholders' meeting and actively participated. What are the tax consequences of the trip for Mabel?

9. Sid and Vienne are the owners of a corporation. To reduce the corporation's taxable income, they pay a $3,000 salary each month to their eight-year-old daughter, Paula. Why is this salary disallowed as a deduction?

10. Which of the following losses are deductible?
    a. Loss on the sale of a factory building used in a trade or business.
    b. Loss on the sale of a truck held for personal use.
    c. Loss from the destruction by a tornado of a warehouse used in a trade or business.
    d. Loss on the destruction by fire of the taxpayer's residence.
    e. Loss on the sale of Lavender Corporation stock held as an investment.

10,000 Sched. E
6000 1040.

11. Mary Kate owns a building that she leases to an individual who operates a grocery store. Rent income is $10,000 and rental expenses are $6,000. On what Form 1040 schedule or schedules are the income and expenses reported?

12. Distinguish between the timing for the recording of a deduction under the cash method versus the accrual method. Discuss any exceptions.

13. What is the "actually paid" requirement for the deduction of an expense by a cash basis taxpayer? Does actual payment ensure a deduction?

14. What is the significance of the all events and economic performance tests?

15. Pelican, an accrual method taxpayer, provides a one-year warranty on the vacuum cleaners it manufactures. Claims under the warranty typically amount to 2% of sales. Can Pelican use the reserve method to account for the warranty expense?

16. Clear, Inc., is a bottled water distributor. Clear's delivery trucks frequently are required to park in "No Parking" zones in order to make their deliveries. If the trucks are occasionally ticketed, can Clear deduct the fines it pays?

Issue ID

To foreign country ⇒ not against law ⇒ deductible

17. Ted is an agent for an airline manufacturer and is negotiating a sale with a representative of the U.S. government and with a representative of a developing country. Ted's company has sufficient capacity to handle only one of the orders. Both orders will have the same contract price. Ted believes that if his employer will authorize a $500,000 payment to the representative of the foreign country, he can guarantee the sale. He is not sure that he can obtain the same result with the U.S. government. Identify the relevant tax issues for Ted.

18. Stuart, an insurance salesman, is arrested for allegedly robbing a convenience store. He hires an attorney who is successful in getting the charges dropped. Is the attorney's fee deductible?

19. Linda operates a drug-running operation. Which of the following expenses she incurs can reduce taxable income?
    a. Bribes paid to border guards. ✗
    b. Salaries to employees. ✓
    c. Price paid for drugs purchased for resale. ✓
    d. Kickbacks to police. ✗
    e. Rent on an office. ✗
    f. Depreciation on office furniture and equipment. ✗
    g. Tenant's casualty insurance. ✗

20. Gordon anticipates that being positively perceived by the individual who is elected mayor will be beneficial for his business. Therefore, he contributes to the campaigns of both the Democratic and the Republican candidates. The Republican candidate is elected mayor. Can Gordon deduct any of the political contributions he made?

21. Melissa, the owner of a sole proprietorship, does not provide health insurance for her 20 employees. She plans to spend $1,500 lobbying in opposition to legislation that would require her to provide health insurance for her employees. Discuss the tax advantages and disadvantages of paying the $1,500 to a professional lobbyist rather than spending the $1,500 on in-house lobbying expenditures.

22. What limits exist on the deductibility of executive compensation? Do the limits apply to all types of business entities? Are there any exceptions to the limitations?

23. Paul operates a restaurant in Cleveland. He travels to Columbus to investigate acquiring a business. He incurs expenses as follows: $1,500 for travel, $2,000 for legal advice, and $3,500 for market analysis. Based on the different tax consequences listed below, describe the circumstances that were involved in Paul's investigation of the business.
    a. Paul deducts the $7,000 of expenses incurred.
    b. Paul cannot deduct any of the $7,000 of expenses incurred.
    c. Paul deducts $5,000 of the expenses incurred and amortizes the $2,000 balance over a period of 180 months.

24. Hector conducts a business with the following results for the year:

Revenue	$22,000
Depreciation on car	2,960
Operating expenses of car	2,100
Rent	650
Wages	8,200
Amortization of intangibles	680

    Hector estimates that due to a depressed real estate market, the value of land owned by the business declined by $5,200. Calculate the effect of Hector's business on his AGI.

25. Sarah owns a vacation home in the Tennessee mountains. Without considering the vacation home, she has gross income of $65,000. During the year, she rented the cabin for two weeks to a friend for $2,500. Sarah herself used the cabin during four weeks of the year. The total expenses for the year consisted of $10,000 mortgage interest, $1,500 property tax, $2,000 utilities and maintenance, and $3,200 depreciation.
    a. What effect does the rental of the vacation cabin have on Sarah's AGI?
    b. What expenses can Sarah deduct? Which are deductible *for* AGI, and which are deductible *from* AGI?

26. Contrast the differing results obtained by using the IRS's approach and the court's approach to allocating property taxes and mortgage interest in a personal/rental situation. Which method would the taxpayer prefer?

27. Karen and Andy own a beach house. They have an agreement with a rental agent to rent it up to 200 days per year. For the past three years, the agent has been successful in renting it for 200 days. Karen and Andy use the beach house for one week during the summer and one week during Thanksgiving. Their daughter, Sarah, a college student, has asked if she and some friends can use the beach house for the week of spring break. Advise Karen and Andy how they should respond and identify any relevant tax issues.

Issue ID

28. Hank was transferred from Phoenix to North Dakota on March 1 of the current year. He immediately put his home in Phoenix up for rent. The home was rented May 1 to November 30 and was vacant during the month of December. It was rented again on January 1 for six months. What expenses, if any, can Hank deduct on his return? Which deductions are *for* AGI and which ones are *from* AGI?

Decision Making

Add her names to title ⇒ get ded.
or gift to H & J.

29. Erika would like to help Hillary and James, her daughter and son-in-law, with their short-term financial problems. To help them avoid foreclosure, she proposes to make the monthly mortgage payments on their home for the past six months. Erika's preference is to make the payments directly to the mortgage company. However, she is willing to give the money to Hillary and James who would then make the payments. Advise Erika on which option, if either, offers preferential tax treatment to her.

30. Isiah repaired the roof on his apartment building at a cost of $9,200. During the same year, Rachel replaced the roof on her rental house for $9,200. Both taxpayers are on the cash basis. Are their expenditures treated the same on their tax returns? Why or why not?

Issue ID

31. a. Which of the following are related parties under § 267?

   - Mother
   - Sister
   - Nephew
   - Aunt
   - Cousin
   - Granddaughter
   - Corporation and a shareholder who owns 45% of the stock

   b. What negative tax consequences can result from being classified as a related party?

32. Jake owns City of Charleston bonds with an adjusted basis of $100,000. During the year, he receives interest payments of $4,000. Jake partially financed the purchase of the bonds by borrowing $70,000 at 6% interest. Jake's interest payments on the loan this year are $4,100, and his principal payments are $1,000.
   a. Should Jake report any interest income this year?
   b. Can Jake deduct any interest expense this year?

PROBLEMS

33. Sandra is an attorney. She incurs the following expenses when she and her employee, Fred, attend the American Bar Association convention in San Francisco:

Conference registration:	
Sandra	$800
Fred	800
Airline tickets from Pittsburgh to San Francisco:	
Sandra	900
Fred	400
Lodging in San Francisco:	
Sandra	650
Fred	350
Rental car in San Francisco:	
Sandra	325
Fred	–0–

Calculate the effect of these expenses on Sandra's AGI.

34. Carlton received the following income and incurred and paid the following expenses during the current year:

Decision Making

Salary income	$79,000
Dividend income	4,000
Interest income	3,000
Contributions to First Church	2,900
Real estate taxes on personal residence	1,900
Alimony paid to former spouse	12,000
Contribution to traditional IRA	4,000
Mortgage interest on personal residence	6,000
State income taxes	3,500
Loss on the sale of stock	900
State sales tax	1,150

Carlton is not yet eligible to participate in his employer's retirement plan.
a.   Calculate Carlton's AGI.
b.   Should Carlton itemize deductions *from* AGI or take the standard deduction?

35. Julie is a student and earns $13,200 working part-time at the college ice cream shop. She has no other income. Her medical expenses for the year totaled $3,200. During the year, she suffered a casualty loss of $3,600 when her apartment burned. Julie contributed $1,500 to her church. Upon the advice of her parents, Julie is trying to decide whether to contribute $4,000 to the traditional IRA her parents have set up for her. What effect would the IRA contribution have on Julie's itemized deductions?

36. Drew and his wife Cassie own all of the stock of Thrush. Cassie is the president and Drew is the vice president. Cassie and Drew are paid salaries of $400,000 and $300,000, respectively, each year. They consider the salaries to be reasonable based on a comparison with salaries paid for comparable positions in comparable companies. They project Thrush's taxable income for next year, before their salaries, to be $800,000. They decide to place their four teenage children on the payroll and to pay them total salaries of $100,000. The children will each work about five hours per week for Thrush.
a.   What are Drew and Cassie trying to achieve by hiring the children?
b.   Calculate the tax consequences of hiring the children on Thrush, and on Drew and Cassie's family.

37. Audra incurs the following losses during the current tax year from the sale of:

Brown, Inc. stock	$ 1,100
Audra's personal use car	11,000
Audra's personal residence	12,000
City of Newburyport bonds	900

She also had a theft loss on her uninsured business use car of $1,500. Calculate Audra's deductible losses.

38. Falcon, Inc., paid salaries of $500,000 to its employees during its first year of operations. At the end of the year, Falcon had unpaid salaries of $45,000.
a.   Calculate the salary deduction if Falcon is a cash basis taxpayer.
b.   Calculate the salary deduction if Falcon is an accrual basis taxpayer.

39. Doris, a calendar year taxpayer, is the owner of a sole proprietorship that uses the cash method. She leases an office building for $72,000 for an 18-month period on August 1, 2006. In order to obtain this favorable lease rate, she pays the $72,000 at the inception of the lease. How much rent expense may Doris deduct on her 2006 tax return?

40. Duck, an accrual basis corporation, sponsored a rock concert on December 29, 2006. Gross receipts were $300,000. The following expenses were incurred and paid as indicated:

Expense		Payment Date
Rental of coliseum	$ 25,000	December 21, 2006
Cost of goods sold:		
Food	30,000	December 30, 2006
Souvenirs	60,000	December 30, 2006
Performers	100,000	January 5, 2007
Cleaning of coliseum	10,000	February 1, 2007

Since the coliseum was not scheduled to be used again until January 15, the company with which Duck had contracted did not actually perform the cleanup until January 8–10, 2007.

Calculate Duck's net income from the concert for tax purposes for 2006.

41. Mercedes, an attorney with a leading Miami law firm, is convicted of failing to file Federal income tax returns for 2001–2003. Her justification for failing to do so was the pressures of her profession (80- to 90-hour workweeks). She is assessed taxes, interest, and penalties of $112,000 by the IRS. In addition, she incurs related legal fees of $75,000. Determine the amount that Mercedes can deduct, and classify it as a deduction *for* or a deduction *from* AGI.

42. Darby runs an illegal numbers racket. His gross revenues are $550,000, and he incurs the following expenses:

Illegal kickbacks	$20,000
Salaries	80,000
Rent	24,000
Utilities and telephone	9,000
Bribes to police	25,000
Interest	6,000
Medical insurance premiums for employees	4,000
Depreciation on equipment	12,000

   a. What is Darby's net income from this business that is includible in taxable income?

   b. If the business was an illegal drug operation and cost of goods sold was $100,000, how would your answer differ?

43. Polly made the following political contributions:

To national Republican Party	$1,000
To national Democratic Party	1,000
To local candidate for mayor	700
To candidate for state senate	200
To candidate for school board	250

How much can Polly deduct?

Decision Making

Communications

44. Amber, a publicly held corporation, currently pays its president an annual salary of $900,000. In addition, it contributes $20,000 annually to a defined contribution pension plan for him. As a means of increasing company profitability, the board of directors decides to increase the president's compensation. Two proposals are being considered. Under the first proposal, the salary and pension contribution for the president would be increased by 30%. Under the second proposal, Amber would implement a performance-based compensation program that is projected to provide about the same amount of additional compensation and pension contribution for the president.

a. Evaluate the alternatives from the perspective of Amber, Inc.

b. Prepare a letter to Amber's board of directors that contains your recommendations. Address the letter to the board chairperson, Agnes Riddle, whose address is 100 James Tower, Cleveland, OH 44106.

 45. Vermillion, Inc., a publicly held corporation, pays the following salaries to its executives:

	Salary	Bonus	Retirement Plan Contribution
CEO	$2,000,000	$100,000	$80,000
Executive vice president	1,800,000	90,000	72,000
Treasurer	1,600,000	–0–	64,000
Marketing vice president	1,500,000	75,000	60,000
Operations vice president	1,400,000	70,000	56,000
Distribution vice president	1,200,000	60,000	48,000
Research vice president	1,100,000	–0–	44,000
Controller	800,000	–0–	32,000

Vermillion normally does not pay bonuses, but after reviewing the results of operations for the year, the board of directors decided to pay a 5% bonus to selected executives. What is the amount of these payments that Vermillion may deduct?

46. Jenny, the owner of a very successful restaurant chain, is exploring the possibility of expanding the chain into a city in the neighboring state. She incurs $25,000 of expenses associated with this investigation. Based on the regulatory environment for restaurants in the city, she decides not to do so. During the year, she also investigates opening a hotel that will be part of a national hotel chain. Her expenses for this are $51,000. The hotel begins operations on November 1. Determine the amount that Jenny can deduct in the current year for investigating these two businesses.

47. Tim traveled to a neighboring state to investigate the purchase of two restaurants. His expenses included travel, legal, accounting, and miscellaneous expenses. The total was $30,000. He incurred the expenses in June and July 2006.

a. What can Tim deduct in 2006 if he was in the restaurant business and did not acquire the two restaurants?

b. What can Tim deduct in 2006 if he was in the restaurant business and acquired the two restaurants and began operating them on October 1, 2006?

c. What can Tim deduct in 2006 if he did not acquire the two restaurants and was not in the restaurant business?

d. What can he deduct in 2006 if he acquired the two restaurants, but was not in the restaurant business when he acquired them? Operations began on September 1, 2006.

48. Alex, who is single, conducts an activity that is appropriately classified as a hobby. The activity produces the following revenues and expenses:

Revenue	$18,000
Property taxes	3,000
Materials and supplies	4,500
Utilities	2,000
Advertising	5,000
Insurance	750
Depreciation	4,000

Without regard to this activity, Alex's AGI is $42,000. Determine how much income Alex must report, the amount of the expenses he is permitted to deduct, and his taxable income.

49. Samantha is an executive with an AGI of $100,000 before considering income or loss from her miniature horse business. Her income comes from prizes for winning horse shows, stud fees, and sales of yearlings. Samantha's home is on 20 acres; she uses 10 of these 20 acres for the horses and has erected stables, paddocks, fences, tack houses, and other related improvements there.

Samantha uses an office in her home that is 10% of the square footage of the house. She uses the office exclusively for maintaining files of breeding lines, histories, and show and veterinary records. Her books show the following income and expenses for the current year:

Income from fees, prizes, and sales	$22,000
Expenses	
Entry fees	1,000
Feed and veterinary bills	4,000
Supplies	900
Publications and dues	500
Travel to horse shows (no meals)	2,300
Salaries and wages of employees	8,000
Depreciation on horse equipment	3,000
Depreciation on horse farm improvements	7,000
Depreciation on 10% of home	1,000
Total home mortgage interest	24,000
Total property taxes on home	2,200
Total property taxes on horse farm improvements	800

The mortgage interest is only on her home. The horse farm improvements are not mortgaged.

a.   How must Samantha treat the income and expenses of the operation if the miniature horse activity is held to be a hobby?

b.   How would your answer in part (a) differ if the horse operation is held to be a business?

50.   Adelene, who lives in a winter resort area, rented her personal residence for 14 days while she was visiting Brussels. Rent income was $5,000. Related expenses for the year were as follows:

Real property taxes	$ 3,800
Mortgage interest	7,500
Utilities	3,700
Insurance	2,500
Repairs	2,100
Depreciation	15,000

Determine the effect on Adelene's AGI.

51.   During the year (not a leap year), Anna rented her vacation home for 45 days, used it personally for 20 days, and left it vacant for 300 days. She had the following income and expenses:

Rent income	$ 7,000
Expenses	
Real estate taxes	2,500
Interest on mortgage	9,000
Utilities	2,400
Repairs	1,000
Roof replacement (a capital expenditure)	12,000
Depreciation	7,000

a.   Compute Anna's net rent income or loss and the amounts she can itemize on her tax return, using the court's approach to allocating property taxes and interest.

b.   How would your answer in part (a) differ using the IRS's method of allocating property taxes and interest?

52.   How would your answer in Problem 51 differ if Anna had rented the house for 87 days and had used it personally for 13 days?

53. Chee, single, age 40, had the following income and expenses during the year (not a leap year):

Income

Salary	$43,000
Rental of vacation home (rented 60 days, used personally 60 days, vacant 245 days)	4,000
Municipal bond interest	2,000
Dividend from General Electric	400

Expenses

Interest

On home mortgage	8,400
On vacation home	4,758
On loan used to buy municipal bonds	3,100

Taxes

Property tax on home	2,200
Property tax on vacation home	1,098
State income tax	3,300
State sales tax	900
Charitable contributions	1,100
Tax return preparation fee	300
Utilities and maintenance on vacation home	2,600
Depreciation on rental 50% of vacation home	3,500

Calculate Chee's taxable income for the year before personal exemptions.

54. Velma and Clyde operate a retail sports memorabilia shop. For the current year, sales revenue is $50,000 and expenses are as follows:

Decision Making

Cost of goods sold	$19,000
Advertising	1,000
Utilities	2,000
Rent	4,000
Insurance	1,500
Wages to Boyd	7,000

Velma and Clyde pay $7,000 in wages to Boyd, a part-time employee. Since this amount is $1,000 below the minimum wage, Boyd threatens to file a complaint with the appropriate Federal agency. Although Velma and Clyde pay no attention to Boyd's threat, Chelsie (Velma's mother) gives Boyd a check for $1,000 for the disputed wages. Both Velma and Clyde ridicule Chelsie for wasting money when they learn what she has done. The retail shop is the only source of income for Velma and Clyde.
   a.   Calculate Velma and Clyde's AGI.
   b.   Can Chelsie deduct the $1,000 payment on her tax return?
   c.   How could the tax position of the parties be improved?

55. Terry is purchasing a business from Anne. The amount being paid exceeds the fair market value of the identifiable assets of the business by $400,000. Advise Terry on the tax consequences of the $400,000 being allocated to goodwill versus it being allocated to a 10-year covenant not to compete.

56. Jay's sole proprietorship has the following assets:

Decision Making

	Basis	Fair Market Value
Cash	$ 10,000	$ 10,000
Accounts receivable	18,000	18,000
Inventory	25,000	30,000
Patent	22,000	40,000
Land	50,000	75,000
	$125,000	$173,000

The building in which Jay's business is located is leased. The lease expires at the end of the year.

Jay is age 70 and would like to retire. He expects to be in the 35% tax bracket. Jay is negotiating the sale of the business with Lois, a key employee. They have agreed on the fair market value of the assets, as indicated above, and agree the total purchase price should be about $200,000.

a.   Advise Jay regarding how the sale should be structured.

b.   Advise Lois regarding how the purchase should be structured.

c.   What might they do to achieve an acceptable compromise?

Decision Making

Communications

57.   Eleanor Saxon sold stock (basis of $68,000) to her brother, Ridge, for $55,000, the fair market value.

a.   What are the tax consequences to Eleanor?

b.   What are the tax consequences to Ridge if he later sells the stock for $90,000? For $49,000? For $66,000?

c.   Write a letter to Eleanor in which you inform her of the tax consequences if she sells the stock to Ridge for $55,000 and explain how a sales transaction could be structured that would produce better tax consequences for her. Eleanor's address is 32 Country Lane, Lawrence, KS 66045.

58.   The Robin Corporation is owned as follows:

Irene	29%
Paul, Irene's husband	16%
Sylvia, Irene's mother	15%
Ron, Irene's father	25%
Quinn, an unrelated party	15%

Robin is on the accrual basis, and Irene and Paul are on the cash basis. Irene and Paul each loaned the Robin Corporation $40,000 out of their separate funds. On December 31, 2006, Robin accrued interest at 8% on both loans. The interest was paid on February 4, 2007. What is the tax treatment of this interest expense/income to Irene, Paul, and Robin?

59.   What is Karla's constructive ownership of Wren Corporation, given the following information?

Shares owned by Karla	900
Shares owned by Sam, Karla's uncle	600
Shares owned by Barbara, Karla's partner	30
Shares owned by Vera, Karla's granddaughter	670
Shares owned by unrelated parties	800

60.   Chris has a brokerage account and buys on the margin, which resulted in an interest expense of $15,000 during the year. Income generated through the brokerage account was as follows:

Municipal interest	$ 40,000
Taxable dividends and interest	160,000

How much investment interest can Chris deduct?

Decision Making

 61.   During the current year, Robert pays the following amounts associated with his own residence and that of his daughter, Anne:

Property taxes:	
On home owned by Robert	$3,000
On home owned by Anne	1,500
Mortgage interest:	
Associated with Robert's home	8,000
Associated with Anne's home	4,500

Repairs to:

Robert's home	$1,200
Anne's home	700

Utilities:

Robert's home	2,700
Anne's home	1,600

Replacement of roof:

Robert's home	4,000

a. Which of these expenses can Robert deduct?
b. Which of these expenses can Anne deduct?
c. Are the deductions *for* AGI or *from* AGI (itemized)?
d. How could the tax consequences be improved?

CUMULATIVE PROBLEMS

62. Helen Archer, age 38, is single and lives at 120 Sanborne Avenue, Springfield, IL 60740. Her Social Security number is 648–11–9981. Helen has been divorced from her former husband, Albert, for three years. She has a son, Jason, who is age 17. His Social Security number is 648–98–3471. Helen does not wish to contribute $3 to the Presidential Election Campaign Fund.

Tax Return Problem

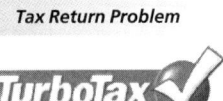

Helen, an advertising executive, earned a salary of $69,000 in 2005. Her employer withheld $7,800 in Federal income tax, $3,100 in state income tax, and the appropriate amount of FICA tax: $4,278 for Social Security tax and $1,001 for Medicare tax.

Helen has legal custody of Jason. Jason lives with his father during summer vacation. Albert indicates that his expenses for Jason are $11,000. Helen can document that she spent $5,500 for Jason's support during 2005. In prior years, Helen gave a signed Form 8332 to Albert regarding Jason. For 2005, she has decided not to do so.

Helen's mother died on January 7, 2005. Helen inherited assets worth $400,000 from her mother. As the sole beneficiary of her mother's life insurance policy, Helen received insurance proceeds of $150,000. Her mother's cost basis for the life insurance policy was $70,000. Helen's favorite aunt gave her $10,000 for her birthday in October.

On November 8, 2005, Helen sells for $19,000 Amber stock that she had purchased for $20,000 from her first cousin, Walt, on December 5, 2000. Walt's cost basis for the stock was $22,000, and the stock was worth $20,000 on December 5, 2000. On December 1, 2005, Helen sold Falcon stock for $12,000. She had acquired the stock on July 2, 2005, for $9,000.

An examination of Helen's records reveals the following information:

- Received interest income of $2,800 from First Savings Bank.
- Received groceries valued at $1,000 from a local grocery store for being the 100,000th customer.
- Received qualified dividend income of $900 from Amber.
- Received $2,500 of interest income on City of Springfield school bonds.
- Received alimony of $12,000 from Albert.
- Received a distribution of $4,500 from ST Partnership. Her distributive share of the partnership passive taxable income was $4,900.

From her checkbook records, she determines that she made the following payments during 2005:

- Charitable contributions of $2,000 to First Presbyterian Church and $1,000 to the American Red Cross (proper receipts obtained).
- Mortgage interest on her residence of $6,700.
- Property taxes of $3,100 on her residence and $800 on her car.
- Estimated Federal income taxes of $7,000 and estimated state income taxes of $1,000.

- Medical expenses of $5,000 for her and $800 for Jason. In December her medical insurance policy reimbursed $1,200 of her medical expenses.
- A $500 ticket for parking in a handicapped space.
- Attorney's fees of $250 associated with unsuccessfully contesting the parking ticket.
- Contribution of $100 to the campaign of a candidate for governor.
- Since she did not maintain records of the sales tax she paid, she calculates the amount from the sales tax table to be $1,197.

Calculate Helen's net tax payable or refund due for 2005. If you use tax forms, you will need Form 1040 and Schedules A, B, D, and E. Suggested software: TurboTax.

Tax Return Problem

Decision Making

Communications

63. John and Mary Jane Sanders are married, filing jointly. Their address is 204 Shoe Lane, Blacksburg, VA 24061. They are expecting their first two children (twins) in early 2007. John's salary in 2006 was $91,000, from which $12,400 of Federal income tax and $4,500 of state income tax were withheld. Mary Jane made $47,000 and had $3,100 of Federal income tax and $2,050 of state income tax withheld. The appropriate amount of FICA tax was withheld for John and for Mary Jane: for John, Social Security tax of $5,642 and Medicare tax of $1,320; for Mary Jane, Social Security tax of $2,914 and Medicare tax of $682. John's Social Security number is 648–11–8899, and Mary Jane's Social Security number is 648–22–7788.

John and Mary Jane are both covered by their employer's medical insurance policies with three-fourths of the premiums being paid by the employers. The total premiums were $4,500 for John and $3,300 for Mary Jane. Mary Jane received medical benefits of $6,200 under the plan. John was not ill during 2006.

John makes alimony payments of $30,000 per year to June, his former wife. He also makes child support payments of $12,000 for his son, Rod, who lives with June except for two months in the summer when he visits John and Mary Jane. At the time of the divorce, John worked for a Fortune 500 company and received a salary of $250,000. As a result of corporate downsizing, he lost his job.

Mary Jane's father lived with them until his death in November. His only sources of income were salary of $1,900, unemployment compensation benefits of $3,500, and Social Security benefits of $3,200. Of this amount, he deposited $5,000 in a savings account. The remainder of his support of $7,500, which included funeral expenses of $5,100, was provided by John and Mary Jane.

Other income received by the Sanderses was as follows:

Interest on certificates of deposit	$5,000
Share of S corporation taxable income (distributions from the S corporation to Mary Jane were $350)	600
Award received by Mary Jane from employer for outstanding suggestion for cutting costs	2,000

John has always wanted to operate his own business. In October 2006, he incurred expenses of $8,000 in investigating the establishment of a retail computer franchise. With the birth of the twins expected next year, however, he decides to forgo self-employment for at least a couple of years.

John and Mary Jane made charitable contributions of $3,600 during the year and paid an additional $1,200 in state income taxes in 2006 upon filing their 2005 state income tax return. Their deductible home mortgage interest was $9,000, and their property taxes came to $3,500. They paid sales taxes of $1,700 for which they have receipts.

Part 1—Tax Computation

Calculate John and Mary Jane's tax (or refund) due for 2006.

Part 2—Tax Planning

Assume that the Sanderses come to you for advice in December 2006. John has learned that he will receive a $30,000 bonus. He wants to know if he should take it in December 2006 or in January 2007. Mary Jane will quit work on December 31 to stay home with the twins. Their itemized deductions will decrease by $2,050 because Mary Jane will not have state income taxes withheld. Mary Jane will not receive the employee award in 2007. She expects the medical benefits received to be $5,000. The Sanderses expect all of their other income items to remain the same in 2007. Write a letter to John and Mary Jane that contains your advice and prepare a memo for the tax files.

RESEARCH PROBLEMS

Note: Solutions to Research Problems can be prepared by using the **RIA Checkpoint**® **Student Edition** online research product, which is available to accompany this text. It is also possible to prepare solutions to the Research Problems by using tax research materials found in a standard tax library.

Research Problem 1.   Green Motor Transportation Corporation is a nationwide long-haul freight concern that owns and operates approximately 15,000 trucks. For tax purposes, Green uses a calendar year and the accrual method of accounting.

Every year, Green is required to pay for a large number of fees, licenses, insurance, and permits (designated as FLIP expenses) in order to legally operate its fleet of vehicles in the large number of states in which it does business. Although the FLIP expenses are accrued for financial accounting purposes, they are expensed for tax purposes. None of the FLIP expenses covers a period of more than one year in duration. This practice has been followed consistently by Green for many years and, until recently, has never been questioned by the IRS.

Upon audit of Green's tax return, the IRS disallowed approximately 55% of the FLIP expenses that had been claimed as a deduction. Although the disallowed expenses were paid in 2003, the IRS held that they were applicable to year 2004. Because Green used the accrual method both for accounting and for tax purposes, the IRS found that a prorating of these expenses was necessary. Green disputed the proration based on the notion that the expenses did not provide a "substantial" benefit to future years. Under an informal policy followed by the IRS, prepaid expenses of less than a year can be expensed in the year paid if certain conditions are met. Green contended that these conditions were met as the FLIP expenses were routine in nature, did not distort income, and were not designed to be manipulative.

The IRS disputed the existence of any such "one-year rule" being available to preclude deducting prepaid expenses. But regardless of whether the rule existed, it would, in any event, not apply to accrual basis taxpayers.

Who is right? Can Green Motor Transportation Corporation deduct all of the FLIP expenses paid in 2003, or must 55% of this amount be deferred to 2004?

Research Problem 2.   Gray Chemical Company manufactured pesticides that were toxic. Over the course of several years, the toxic waste contaminated the air and water around the company's plant. Several employees suffered toxic poisoning, and the Environmental Protection Agency cited the company for violations. In court, the judge found Gray guilty and imposed fines of $15 million. The company voluntarily set up a charitable fund for the purpose of bettering the environment and funded it with $8 million. The company incurred legal expenses in setting up the foundation and defending itself in court. The court reduced the fine from $15 million to $7 million.

Communications

Gray Chemical Company deducted the $8 million paid to the foundation and the legal expenses incurred. The IRS disallowed both deductions on the grounds that the payment was, in fact, a fine and in violation of public policy.

Gray's president, Ted Jones, has contacted you regarding the deductibility of the $7 million fine, the $8 million payment to the foundation, and the legal fees. Write a letter to Mr. Jones that contains your advice and prepare a memo for the tax files. Gray's address is 200 Lincoln Center, Omaha, NE 68182.

Partial list of research aids:
§§ 162(a) and (f).
Reg. § 1.162–21(b).

Research Problem 3.   Rex and Agnes Harrell purchased a beach house at Duck, North Carolina, in early 2004. Although they intended to use the beach house occasionally for recreational purposes, they also planned to rent it through the realty agency that had handled the purchase in order to help pay the mortgage payments, property taxes, and maintenance costs. Rex is a surgeon, and Agnes is a counselor.

The beach house was in need of substantial repairs. Rather than hiring a contractor, Rex and Agnes decided they would make the repairs themselves. During both high school and college, Rex had worked summers in construction. In addition, he had taken an advanced course in woodworking and related subjects from a local community college several years ago.

During 2004, according to a log maintained by the Harrells, they occupied the beach house 38 days and rented it 49 days. The log also indicated that on 24 of the 38 days that they occupied the beach house, one or both of them were engaged in work on the beach house. Their two teenage children were with them on all of these days, but did not help with the work being done. On their 2004 income tax return, Rex and Agnes, who filed a joint return, treated the beach house as a rental property and deducted a pro rata share of the property taxes, mortgage interest, utilities, maintenance and repairs, and depreciation in determining their net loss from the beach home. An IRS agent has limited the deductions to the rent income. He contends that the 14-day personal use provision was exceeded and that many of the alleged repairs were capital expenditures. Advise the Harrells on how they should respond to the IRS.

Research Problem 4. Sam Adams is a CPA who is also an aspiring actor. In 2005, his AGI (before any deductions for performing arts expenses) was $42,000 and was from the following sources:

CPA practice	$30,000
Acting jobs (4 employers)	12,000

Expenses associated with his acting career were $9,000. Sam deducted these expenses under § 162 and classified them as deductions *for* AGI under § 62(a)(2)(B).

The IRS contends that the expenses are not eligible for treatment under § 62(a)(2)(B) and should be classified as miscellaneous itemized deductions (subject to the 2%-of-AGI floor). According to the IRS, § 62(a)(2)(B) is not available because Sam has exceeded the AGI ceiling under § 62(b)(1)(C). Advise Sam on the appropriate tax treatment.

Research Problem 5. Professor Shelia Crane is a drama professor at Municipal University with an annual salary of $75,000. In addition, Professor Crane is a playwright. She normally writes two plays each year. Her revenues and expenses from the playwright activity are as follows:

	Revenues	Expenses
2001	$ –0–	$ 9,000
2002	–0–	7,000
2003	500	10,000
2004	2,000	8,500
2005	–0–	6,000

Professor Crane works diligently to get her plays produced. One of her plays has been read at Lincoln Center, and two have been performed by local theater groups. In 2001, she was awarded a sabbatical, and in 2004, she received a $10,000 summer research grant from the university.

The IRS audited Professor Crane's 2003 return and classified her playwright activity as a hobby. Professor Crane comes to you for advice.

Use the tax resources of the Internet to address the following questions. Do not restrict your search to the World Wide Web, but include a review of newsgroups and general reference materials, practitioner sites and resources, primary sources of the tax law, chat rooms and discussion groups, and other opportunities.

Internet
Activity

Research Problem 6.   Locate and read a recent judicial or administrative ruling regarding the deductibility of hobby losses. Look for rulings that deal with horse breeding, professional sports teams, or art collecting activities. Which criteria did the ruling emphasize in upholding or reversing the taxpayer's deduction for such losses?

Research Problem 7.   The $1 million maximum compensation deduction does not seem to have deterred large corporations from remunerating their executives at very high levels. What techniques are being used to work around the millionaires' provision? Are executives taking pay cuts, or are their salaries being deferred or changed in nature due to § 162(m)?

CHAPTER 7

Deductions and Losses: Certain Business Expenses and Losses

LEARNING OBJECTIVES

After completing Chapter 7, you should be able to:

LO.1
Determine the amount, classification, and timing of the bad debt deduction.

LO.2
Understand the tax treatment of worthless securities including § 1244 stock.

LO.3
Distinguish between deductible and nondeductible losses of individuals.

LO.4
Identify a casualty and determine the amount, classification, and timing of casualty and theft losses.

LO.5
Recognize and apply the alternative tax treatments for research and experimental expenditures.

LO.6
Calculate the domestic production activities deduction.

LO.7
Determine the amount of the net operating loss and recognize the impact of the carryback and carryover provisions.

LO.8
Identify tax planning opportunities in deducting certain business expenses, business losses, and personal losses.

Working with the tax formula for individuals requires the proper classification of items that are deductible *for* adjusted gross income (AGI) and items that are deductions *from* AGI (itemized deductions). Business expenses and losses, discussed in this chapter, are reductions of gross income to arrive at the taxpayer's AGI. Expenses and losses incurred in connection with a transaction entered into for profit and attributable to rents and royalties are deducted *for* AGI. All other expenses and losses incurred in connection with a transaction entered into for profit are deducted *from* AGI.

The situation of Robert P. Groetzinger provides an interesting insight into the importance of the proper classification for the individual taxpayer. Groetzinger terminated his employment with a private company and devoted virtually all of his working time to pari-mutuel wagering on dog races. He had no other profession or employment, and his only sources of income, apart from his gambling winnings, were interest, dividends, and sales from investments. During the tax year in question, he went to the track six days a week and devoted 60 to 80 hours per week to preparing and making wagers on his own account.

The tax question that this case presents is whether Groetzinger's gambling activities constitute a trade or business. If the gambling is a trade or business, his gambling losses are deductions *for* AGI. If the gambling activity is not a trade or business, the losses are itemized deductions, and Groetzinger's taxes increase by $2,142.[1]

Deductible losses on personal use property are deducted as an itemized deduction. Itemized deductions are deductions *from* AGI. While the general coverage of itemized deductions is in Chapter 10, casualty and theft losses on personal use property are discussed in this chapter.

In determining the amount and timing of the deduction for bad debts, proper classification is again important. A business bad debt is classified as a deduction *for* AGI, and a nonbusiness bad debt is classified as a short-term capital loss.

Other topics discussed in Chapter 7 are research and experimental expenditures, the production activities deduction, and the net operating loss deduction.

---

[1] *Groetzinger v. Comm.*, 85–2 USTC ¶9622, 56 AFTR2d 85–5683, 771 F.2d 269 (CA–7, 1985).

Bad Debts

LO.1

Determine the amount, classification, and timing of the bad debt deduction.

If a taxpayer sells goods or provides services on credit and the account receivable subsequently becomes worthless, a **bad debt** deduction is permitted only if income arising from the creation of the account receivable was previously included in income.[2] No deduction is allowed, for example, for a bad debt arising from the sale of a product or service when the taxpayer is on the cash basis because no income is reported until the cash has been collected. Permitting a bad debt deduction for a cash basis taxpayer would amount to a double deduction because the expenses of the product or service rendered are deducted when payments are made to suppliers and to employees, or at the time of the sale.

EXAMPLE 1

Tracy, an individual engaged in the practice of accounting, performed accounting services for Pat for which she charged $8,000. Pat never paid the bill, and his whereabouts are unknown.

If Tracy is an accrual basis taxpayer, she includes the $8,000 in income when the services are performed. When she determines that Pat's account will not be collected, she deducts the $8,000 as a bad debt expense.

If Tracy is a cash basis taxpayer, she does not include the $8,000 in income until payment is received. When she determines that Pat's account will not be collected, she cannot deduct the $8,000 as a bad debt expense because it was never recognized as income. ∎

A bad debt can also result from the nonrepayment of a loan made by the taxpayer or from purchased debt instruments.

Specific Charge-Off Method

Taxpayers (other than certain financial institutions) may use only the **specific charge-off method** in accounting for bad debts. Certain financial institutions are allowed to use the **reserve method** for computing deductions for bad debts.

A taxpayer using the specific charge-off method may claim a deduction when a specific business debt becomes either partially or wholly worthless or when a specific nonbusiness debt becomes wholly worthless.[3] For the business debt, the taxpayer must satisfy the IRS that the debt is partially worthless and must demonstrate the amount of worthlessness.

If a business debt previously deducted as partially worthless becomes totally worthless in a future year, only the remainder not previously deducted can be deducted in the future year.

In the case of total worthlessness, a deduction is allowed for the entire amount in the year the debt becomes worthless. The amount of the deduction depends on the taxpayer's basis in the bad debt. If the debt arose from the sale of services or products and the face amount was previously included in income, that amount is deductible. If the taxpayer purchased the debt, the deduction is equal to the amount the taxpayer paid for the debt instrument.

One of the more difficult tasks is determining if and when a bad debt is worthless. The loss is deductible only in the year of partial or total worthlessness for business debts and only in the year of total worthlessness for nonbusiness debts. Legal proceedings need not be initiated against the debtor when the surrounding facts indicate that such action will not result in collection.

EXAMPLE 2

In 2004, Ross loaned $1,000 to Kay, who agreed to repay the loan in two years. In 2006, Kay disappeared after the note became delinquent. If a reasonable investigation by Ross indicates that he cannot find Kay or that a suit against Kay would not result in collection, Ross can deduct the $1,000 in 2006. ∎

---

[2]Reg. § 1.166–1(e).   [3]§ 166(a) and Reg. § 1.166.

CONCEPT SUMMARY 7–1

Specific Charge-Off Method

Expense deduction and account write-off	The expense arises and the write-off takes place when a specific business account becomes either partially or wholly worthless or when a specific nonbusiness account becomes wholly worthless.
Recovery of accounts previously written off	If the account recovered was written off during the current taxable year, the write-off entry is reversed. If the account recovered was written off during a previous taxable year, income is created subject to the tax benefit rule.

Bankruptcy is generally an indication of at least partial worthlessness of a debt. Bankruptcy may create worthlessness before the settlement date. If this is the case, the deduction may be taken in the year of worthlessness.

EXAMPLE 3

In Example 2, assume that Kay filed for personal bankruptcy in 2005 and that the debt is a business debt. At that time, Ross learned that unsecured creditors (including Ross) were ultimately expected to receive 20 cents on the dollar. In 2006, settlement is made and Ross receives only $150. He should deduct $800 ($1,000 loan − $200 expected settlement) in 2005 and $50 in 2006 ($200 balance − $150 proceeds). ■

If a receivable has been written off as uncollectible during the current tax year and is subsequently collected during the current tax year, the write-off entry is reversed. If a receivable has been written off as uncollectible, the collection of the receivable in a later tax year may result in income being recognized. Income will result if the deduction yielded a tax benefit in the year it was taken. See Examples 39 and 40 in Chapter 5.

Business versus Nonbusiness Bad Debts

A **nonbusiness bad debt** is a debt unrelated to the taxpayer's trade or business either when it was created or when it became worthless. The nature of a debt depends on whether the lender was engaged in the business of lending money or whether there is a proximate relationship between the creation of the debt and the lender's trade or business. The use to which the borrowed funds are put by the debtor is of no consequence. Loans to relatives or friends are the most common type of nonbusiness bad debt.

EXAMPLE 4

Jamil loaned his friend, Esther, $1,500. Esther used the money to start a business, which subsequently failed. Even though the proceeds of the loan were used in a business, the loan is a nonbusiness bad debt because the business was Esther's, not Jamil's. ■

The distinction between a business bad debt and a nonbusiness bad debt is important. A **business bad debt** is deductible as an ordinary loss in the year incurred, whereas a nonbusiness bad debt is always treated as a short-term capital loss. Thus, regardless of the age of a nonbusiness bad debt, the deduction may be of limited benefit due to the capital loss limitations on deductibility in any one year. The maximum amount of a net short-term capital loss that an individual can deduct against ordinary income in any one year is $3,000 (see Chapter 16 for a detailed discussion). Although no deduction is allowed when a nonbusiness bad

---

WRITING OFF BAD DEBTS IN AUSTRALIA

In Australia, a small business must identify bad debts and physically write them off by June 30, or the business will not be allowed a deduction. Even if the debts have been referred to a collection agency, they must be physically written off the books. To claim a bad debt under Australian law, the business must be on the accrual basis, there must be little possibility of the debt being paid, and the debt must be written off before June 30.

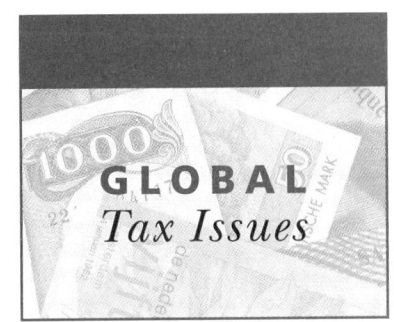

GLOBAL Tax Issues

---

debt is partially worthless, the taxpayer is entitled to deduct the net amount of the loss upon final settlement.

The following example is an illustration of business bad debts adapted from the Regulations.[4]

EXAMPLE 5

In 2005, Leif sold his business but retained a claim (note or account receivable) against Bob. The claim became worthless in 2006. Leif's loss is treated as a business bad debt because the debt was created in the conduct of his former trade or business. Leif is accorded business bad debt treatment even though he was holding the note as an investor and was no longer in a trade or business when the claim became worthless. ∎

The nonbusiness bad debt provisions are *not* applicable to corporations. It is assumed that any loans made by a corporation are related to its trade or business. Therefore, any bad debts of a corporation are business bad debts.

Loans between Related Parties

Loans between related parties (especially family members) raise the issue of whether the transaction was a *bona fide* loan or a gift. The Regulations state that a bona fide debt arises from a debtor-creditor relationship based on a valid and enforceable obligation to pay a fixed or determinable sum of money. Thus, individual circumstances must be examined to determine whether advances between related parties are gifts or loans. Some considerations are these:

- Was a note properly executed?
- Was there a reasonable rate of interest?
- Was collateral provided?
- What collection efforts were made?
- What was the intent of the parties?

EXAMPLE 6

Lana loans $2,000 to her widowed mother for an operation. Lana's mother owns no property and is not employed, and her only income consists of Social Security benefits. No note is issued for the loan, no provision for interest is made, and no repayment date is mentioned. In the current year, Lana's mother dies leaving no estate. Assuming the loan is not repaid, Lana cannot take a deduction for a nonbusiness bad debt because the facts indicate that no debtor-creditor relationship existed. ∎

Worthless Securities

A loss is allowed for securities that become *completely* worthless during the year (**worthless securities**).[5] Such securities are shares of stock, bonds, notes, or other evidence of indebtedness issued by a corporation or government. The losses generated are treated as capital losses deemed to have occurred on the *last day* of the

LO.2

Understand the tax treatment of worthless securities including § 1244 stock.

---

[4]Reg. § 1.166–5(d).   [5]§ 165(g).

CONCEPT SUMMARY 7–2

Bad Debt Deductions

taxable year. By treating the loss as having occurred on the last day of the taxable year, a loss that would otherwise have been classified as short term (if the date of worthlessness was used) may be classified as a long-term capital loss. Capital losses may be of limited benefit due to the $3,000 capital loss limitation.[6]

EXAMPLE 7

Ali, a calendar year taxpayer, owns stock in Owl Corporation (a publicly held company). The stock was acquired as an investment on May 31, 2005, at a cost of $5,000. On April 1, 2006, the stock became worthless. Since the stock is deemed to have become worthless as of December 31, 2006, Ali has a capital loss from an asset held for 19 months (a long-term capital loss). ■

Small Business Stock

The general rule is that shareholders receive capital gain or loss treatment upon the sale or exchange of stock. However, it is possible to receive an ordinary loss deduction if the loss is sustained on **small business stock (§ 1244 stock)**. This loss

[6]§ 1211(b).

could arise from a sale of the stock or from the stock becoming worthless. Only *individuals*[7] who acquired the stock *from* the corporation are eligible to receive ordinary loss treatment under § 1244. The ordinary loss treatment is limited to $50,000 ($100,000 for married individuals filing jointly) per year. Losses on § 1244 stock in excess of the statutory limits receive capital loss treatment.

The corporation must meet certain requirements for the loss on § 1244 stock to be treated as an *ordinary*—rather than a capital—loss. The major requirement is that the total amount of money and other property received by the corporation for stock as a contribution to capital (or paid-in surplus) does not exceed $1 million. The $1 million test is made at the time the stock is issued. Section 1244 stock can be common or preferred stock. Section 1244 applies only to losses. If § 1244 stock is sold at a gain, the Section is not applicable, and the gain is capital gain.

EXAMPLE 8

On July 1, 2004, Iris, a single individual, purchased 100 shares of Eagle Corporation common stock for $100,000. The Eagle stock qualifies as § 1244 stock. On June 20, 2006, Iris sells all of the Eagle stock for $20,000. Because the Eagle stock is § 1244 stock, Iris has $50,000 of ordinary loss and $30,000 of long-term capital loss. ■

Losses of Individuals

LO.3

Distinguish between deductible and nondeductible losses of individuals.

An individual may deduct the following losses under § 165(c):

- Losses incurred in a trade or business.
- Losses incurred in a transaction entered into for profit.
- Losses caused by fire, storm, shipwreck, or other casualty or by theft.

An individual taxpayer may deduct losses to property used in the taxpayer's trade or business or losses to property used in a transaction entered into for profit. Examples include a loss on property used in a proprietorship, a loss on property held for rent, or a loss on stolen bearer bonds. Note that an individual's losses on property used in a trade or business or on transactions entered into for profit are not limited to losses caused by fire, storm, shipwreck, or other casualty or by theft.

An individual taxpayer suffering losses from damage to nonbusiness property can deduct only those losses attributable to fire, storm, shipwreck, or other casualty or theft. Although the meaning of the terms *fire, storm, shipwreck,* and *theft* is relatively free from dispute, the term *other casualty* needs further clarification. It means casualties analogous to fire, storm, or shipwreck. The term also includes accidental loss of property provided the loss qualifies under the same rules as any other casualty. These rules are that the loss must result from an event that is (1) identifiable; (2) damaging to property; and (3) sudden, unexpected, and unusual in nature.

A *sudden event* is one that is swift and precipitous and not gradual or progressive. An *unexpected event* is an event that is ordinarily unanticipated and occurs without the intent of the individual who suffers the loss. An *unusual event* is one that is extraordinary and nonrecurring and does not commonly occur during the activity in which the taxpayer was engaged when the destruction occurred.[8] Examples include hurricanes, tornadoes, floods, storms, shipwrecks, fires, auto accidents, mine cave-ins, sonic booms, and vandalism. Weather that causes damage (drought, for example) must be unusual and severe for the particular region. Damage must be to the taxpayer's property to qualify as a **casualty loss.**

A taxpayer can take a deduction for a casualty loss from an automobile accident only if the damage was not caused by the taxpayer's willful act or willful negligence.

---

[7]The term "individuals" for this purpose includes a partnership but not a trust or an estate.

[8]Rev.Rul. 72–592, 1972–2 C.B. 101.

TAX *in the News*   **A CASUALTY LOSS DEDUCTION?**

The Alabama Department of Revenue is pushing a bill that will allow the department to stop unscrupulous tax preparers.

Source: *Adapted from "Bill to Put Fraudulent Tax Preparers Out of Business Passes Committee,"* The Associated Press State & Local Wire, *May 4, 2005.*

One of the schemes used by the preparers is to claim casualty losses on property not even owned by the taxpayer.

EXAMPLE 9

Ted parks his car on a hill and fails to set the brake properly and to curb the wheels. As a result of Ted's negligence, the car rolls down the hill and is damaged. The repairs to Ted's car should qualify for casualty loss treatment since Ted's act of negligence appears to be simple rather than willful. ■

ETHICAL *Considerations*   **WHAT IS A CASUALTY LOSS?**

Casualty loss deductions are limited when the losses involve property not connected with a trade or business or a transaction entered into for profit. To be eligible for deduction, such losses must arise from fire, storm, shipwreck, or other casualty or from theft.

Joe is a member of a labor union that recently negotiated a new collective bargaining agreement with his employer.

Under the agreement, Joe forfeited rights worth $10,000. Joe believes that his forfeited rights constitute property worth $10,000 and, hence, he is entitled to a casualty loss deduction on his current-year Federal tax return.

Evaluate Joe's plan.

LO.4

Identify a casualty and determine the amount, classification, and timing of casualty and theft losses.

Events That Are Not Casualties

Not all acts of God are treated as casualty losses for income tax purposes. Because a casualty must be sudden, unexpected, and unusual, progressive deterioration (such as erosion due to wind or rain) is not a casualty because it does not meet the suddenness test.

Examples of nonsudden events that generally do not qualify as casualties include disease and insect damage. When the damage was caused by termites over a period of several years, some courts have disallowed a casualty loss deduction.[9] On the other hand, some courts have held that termite damage over periods of up to 15 months after infestation constituted a sudden event and was, therefore, deductible as a casualty loss.[10] Despite the existence of some judicial support for the deductibility of termite damage as a casualty loss, the current position of the IRS is that termite damage is not deductible.[11]

Other examples of events that are not casualties are losses resulting from a decline in value rather than an actual loss of the property. No loss was allowed where the taxpayer's home declined in value as a result of a landslide that destroyed neighboring homes but did no actual damage to the taxpayer's home.[12] Similarly, a taxpayer was allowed a loss for the actual flood damage to his property but not for the decline in market value due to the property's being flood-prone.[13]

---

[9]*Fay v. Helvering,* 41–2 USTC ¶9494, 27 AFTR 432, 120 F.2d 253 (CA–2, 1941); *U.S. v. Rogers,* 41–1 USTC ¶9442, 27 AFTR 423, 120 F.2d 244 (CA–9, 1941).
[10]*Rosenberg v. Comm.,* 52–2 USTC ¶9377, 42 AFTR 303, 198 F.2d 46 (CA–8, 1952); *Shopmaker v. U.S.,* 54–1 USTC ¶9195, 45 AFTR 758, 119 F.Supp. 705 (D.Ct. Mo., 1953).

[11]Rev.Rul. 63–232, 1963–2 C.B. 97.
[12]*H. Pulvers v. Comm.,* 69–1 USTC ¶9222, 23 AFTR2d 69–678, 407 F.2d 838 (CA–9, 1969).
[13]*S. L. Solomon,* 39 TCM 1282, T.C.Memo. 1980–87.

Theft Losses

Theft includes, but is not necessarily limited to, larceny, embezzlement, and robbery.[14] Theft does not include misplaced items.[15]

Theft losses are computed like other casualty losses (discussed in the following section), but the *timing* for recognition of the loss differs. A theft loss is deducted in the year of discovery, not the year of the theft (unless, of course, the discovery occurs in the same year as the theft). If, in the year of the discovery, a claim exists (e.g., against an insurance company) and there is a reasonable expectation of recovering the adjusted basis of the asset from the insurance company, no deduction is permitted.[16] If, in the year of settlement, the recovery is less than the asset's adjusted basis, a partial deduction may be available. If the recovery is greater than the asset's adjusted basis, gain may be recognized.

EXAMPLE 10

Keith's new sailboat, which he uses for personal purposes, was stolen from the storage marina in December 2005. He discovered the loss on June 3, 2006, and filed a claim with his insurance company that was settled on January 30, 2007. Assuming there is a reasonable expectation of full recovery, no deduction is allowed in 2006. A partial deduction may be available in 2007 if the actual insurance proceeds are less than the lower of the fair market value or the adjusted basis of the asset. (Loss measurement rules are discussed later in this chapter.) ∎

When to Deduct Casualty Losses

General Rule. Generally, a casualty loss is deducted in the year the loss occurs. However, no casualty loss is permitted if a reimbursement claim with a *reasonable prospect of full recovery* exists.[17] If the taxpayer has a partial claim, only part of the loss can be claimed in the year of the casualty, and the remainder is deducted in the year the claim is settled.

EXAMPLE 11

Brian's new sailboat was completely destroyed by fire in 2006. Its cost and fair market value were $10,000. Brian's only claim against the insurance company was on a $7,000 policy and was not settled by year-end. The following year, 2007, Brian settled with the insurance company for $6,000. He is entitled to a $3,000 deduction in 2006 and a $1,000 deduction in 2007. If Brian held the sailboat for personal use, the $3,000 deduction in 2006 is reduced first by $100 and then by 10% of his 2006 AGI. The $1,000 deduction in 2007 is reduced by 10% of his 2007 AGI (see the following discussion on the $100 and 10% floors). ∎

If a taxpayer receives reimbursement for a casualty loss sustained and deducted in a previous year, an amended return is not filed for that year. Instead, the taxpayer must include the reimbursement in gross income on the return for the year in which it is received to the extent that the previous deduction resulted in a tax benefit.

EXAMPLE 12

Fran had a deductible casualty loss of $5,000 on her 2005 tax return. Fran's taxable income for 2005 was $60,000. In June 2006, Fran is reimbursed $3,000 for the prior year's casualty loss. Fran includes the entire $3,000 in gross income for 2006 because the deduction in 2005 produced a tax benefit. ∎

Disaster Area Losses. An exception to the general rule for the time of deduction is allowed for **disaster area losses**, which are casualties sustained in an area designated as a disaster area by the President of the United States.[18] In such cases, the taxpayer may *elect* to treat the loss as having occurred in the taxable year immediately

---

[14]Reg. § 1.165–8(d).

[15]*Mary Francis Allen*, 16 T.C. 163 (1951).

[16]Reg. §§ 1.165–1(d)(2) and 1.165–8(a)(2).

[17]Reg. § 1.165–1(d)(2)(i).

[18]§ 165(h).

preceding the taxable year in which the disaster actually occurred. The rationale for this exception is to provide immediate relief to disaster victims in the form of accelerated tax benefits.

If the due date, plus extensions, for the prior year's return has not passed, a taxpayer makes the election to claim the disaster area loss on the prior year's tax return. If the disaster occurs after the prior year's return has been filed, it is necessary to file either an amended return or a refund claim. In any case, the taxpayer must show clearly that such an election is being made.

Disaster loss treatment also applies in the case of a personal residence that has been rendered unsafe for use as a residence because of a disaster. This provision applies when, within 120 days after the President designates the area as a disaster area, the state or local government where the residence is located orders the taxpayer to demolish or relocate the residence.[19]

EXAMPLE 13

Janice owns a personal residence in Louisiana. On September 28, 2006, a hurricane severely damaged Janice's home. The amount of her uninsured loss was $50,000. Because of the extent of the damage in the area, the President of the United States designated the area a disaster area. Because Janice's loss is a disaster area loss, she may elect to file an amended return for 2005 and take the loss in that year. If Janice elects this course of action, the amount of the loss will be reduced first by $100 and then by 10% of her 2005 AGI. If Janice forgoes the election, she may take the loss on her 2006 income tax return. The amount of the loss will be reduced first by $100 and then by 10% of her 2006 AGI. ■

Measuring the Amount of Loss

Amount of Loss. The rules for determining the amount of a loss depend in part on whether business use, income-producing use, or personal use property was involved. Another factor that must be considered is whether the property was partially or completely destroyed.

If business property or property held for the production of income (e.g., rental property) is *completely destroyed*, the loss is equal to the adjusted basis of the property at the time of destruction.

EXAMPLE 14

Vicki's automobile, which was used only for business purposes, was destroyed by fire. Vicki had unintentionally allowed her insurance coverage to expire. The fair market value of the automobile was $9,000 at the time of the fire, and its adjusted basis was $10,000. Vicki is allowed a loss deduction of $10,000 (the basis of the automobile). The $10,000 loss is a deduction *for* AGI. ■

A different measurement rule applies for *partial destruction* of business property and income-producing property and for *partial* or *complete destruction* of personal use property. In these situations, the loss is the *lesser* of the following:

- The adjusted basis of the property.
- The difference between the fair market value of the property before the event and the fair market value immediately after the event.

EXAMPLE 15

Kelly's uninsured automobile, which was used only for business purposes, was damaged in an accident. At the date of the accident, the fair market value of the automobile was $12,000, and its adjusted basis was $9,000. After the accident, the automobile was appraised at $4,000. Kelly's loss deduction is $8,000 (the lesser of the adjusted basis or the decrease in fair market value). The $8,000 loss is a deduction *for* AGI. ■

[19]§ 165(k).

The deduction for the loss of property that is part business and part personal must be computed separately for the business portion and the personal portion.

Any insurance recovery reduces the loss for business, production of income, and personal use losses. In fact, a taxpayer may realize a gain if the insurance proceeds exceed the amount of the loss. Chapter 17 discusses the treatment of net gains and losses on business property and income-producing property.

A taxpayer is not permitted to deduct a casualty loss for damage to insured personal use property unless a *timely insurance claim* is filed with respect to the damage to the property. This rule applies to the extent that any insurance policy provides for full or partial reimbursement for the loss.[20]

Generally, an appraisal before and after the casualty is needed to measure the amount of the loss. However, the *cost of repairs* to the damaged property is acceptable as a method of establishing the loss in value provided the following criteria are met:

- The repairs are necessary to restore the property to its condition immediately before the casualty.
- The amount spent for such repairs is not excessive.
- The repairs do not extend beyond the damage suffered.
- The value of the property after the repairs does not, as a result of the repairs, exceed the value of the property immediately before the casualty.[21]

Reduction for $100 and 10 Percent-of-AGI Floors.

The amount of the loss for personal use property must be further reduced by a $100 *per event* floor and a 10 percent-of-AGI *aggregate* floor.[22] The $100 floor applies separately to each casualty and applies to the entire loss from each casualty (e.g., if a storm damages both a taxpayer's residence and automobile, only $100 is subtracted from the total amount of the loss). The losses are then added together, and the total is reduced by 10 percent of the taxpayer's AGI. The resulting loss is the taxpayer's itemized deduction for casualty and theft losses.

[handwritten margin note: –$100 each casualty 10% AGI to total.]

EXAMPLE 16

Rocky, who had AGI of $30,000, was involved in a motorcycle accident. His motorcycle, which was used only for personal use and had a fair market value of $12,000 and an adjusted basis of $9,000, was completely destroyed. He received $5,000 from his insurance company. Rocky's casualty loss deduction is $900 [$9,000 basis − $5,000 insurance − $100 floor − $3,000 (.10 × $30,000 AGI)]. The $900 casualty loss is an itemized deduction (*from* AGI). ■

When a nonbusiness casualty loss is spread between two taxable years because of the *reasonable prospect of recovery* doctrine, the loss in the second year is not reduced by the $100 floor. This result occurs because this floor is imposed per event and has already reduced the amount of the loss in the first year. However, the loss in the second year is still subject to the 10 percent floor based on the taxpayer's second-year AGI (refer to Example 11).

Taxpayers who suffer qualified disaster area losses can elect to deduct the losses in the year preceding the year of occurrence. The disaster loss is treated as having occurred in the preceding taxable year. Hence, the 10 percent-of-AGI floor is determined by using the AGI of the year for which the deduction is claimed.[23]

Multiple Losses.

The rules for computing loss deductions where multiple losses have occurred are explained in Examples 17 and 18.

---

[20]§ 165(h)(4)(E).
[21]Reg. § 1.165–7(a)(2)(ii).

[22]§ 165(c)(3).
[23]§ 165(i).

EXAMPLE 17

During the year, Tim had the following casualty losses:

		Fair Market Value of Asset		
Asset	Adjusted Basis	Before the Casualty	After the Casualty	Insurance Recovery
A	$900	$600	$–0–	$400
B	300	800	250	100

(handwritten margin notes: "Business Casualty", "Not reduced by $1,000 & or 10% =) for AGI")

(handwritten to right of table: = 500, = 200)

Assets A and B were used in Tim's business at the time of the casualty. The following losses are allowed:

Asset A: $500. The complete destruction of a business asset results in a deduction of the adjusted basis of the property (reduced by any insurance recovery) regardless of the asset's fair market value.

Asset B: $200. The partial destruction of a business (or personal use) asset results in a deduction equal to the lesser of the adjusted basis ($300) or the decline in value ($550), reduced by any insurance recovery ($100).

Both the Asset A and Asset B losses are deductions *for* AGI. The $100 floor and the 10%-of-AGI floor do not apply because the assets are business assets. ■

EXAMPLE 18

During the year, Emily had AGI of $20,000 and the following casualty losses:

(handwritten: "complete loss")

		Fair Market Value of Asset		
Asset	Adjusted Basis	Before the Casualty	After the Casualty	Insurance Recovery
A	$ 900	$ 600	$ –0–	$200
B	2,500	4,000	1,000	–0–
C	800	400	100	250

(handwritten margin note: "Personal casualty")

(handwritten to right of table: = 400 –100, = 2500 –100, = 50 : –100)

Assets A, B, and C were held for personal use, and the losses to these three assets are from three different casualties. The loss for each asset is computed as follows:

(handwritten margin: "complete 100%", "partial", "partial")

Asset A: $300. The lesser of the adjusted basis of $900 or the $600 decline in value, reduced by the insurance recovery of $200, minus the $100 floor.

Asset B: $2,400. The lesser of the adjusted basis of $2,500 or the $3,000 decline in value, minus the $100 floor.

Asset C: $0. The lesser of the adjusted basis of $800 or the $300 decline in value, reduced by the insurance recovery of $250, minus the $100 floor.

Emily's itemized casualty loss deduction for the year is $700:

Asset A loss	$ 300
Asset B loss	2,400
Asset C loss	–0–
Total loss	$ 2,700
Less: 10% of AGI (10% × $20,000)	(2,000)
Itemized casualty loss deduction	$ 700

■

Statutory Framework for Deducting Losses of Individuals

Casualty and theft losses incurred by an individual in connection with a trade or business are deductible *for* AGI.[24] These losses are not subject to the $100 per event and the 10 percent-of-AGI limitations.

Casualty and theft losses incurred by an individual in a transaction entered into for profit are not subject to the $100 per event and the 10 percent-of-AGI limitations. If these losses are attributable to rents or royalties, the deduction is *for* AGI.[25] However, if these losses are not connected with property held for the production of rents and royalties, they are deductions *from* AGI. More specifically, these losses are classified as other miscellaneous itemized deductions. An example of this type of loss would be the theft of a security. However, theft losses of investment property are not subject to the 2 percent-of-AGI floor on certain miscellaneous itemized deductions (explained in Chapter 9).

Casualty and theft losses attributable to personal use property are subject to the $100 per event and the 10 percent-of-AGI limitations. These losses are itemized deductions, but they are not subject to the 2 percent-of-AGI floor.[26]

Personal Casualty Gains and Losses

If a taxpayer has personal casualty and theft gains as well as losses, a special set of rules applies for determining the tax consequences. A **personal casualty gain** is the recognized gain from a casualty or theft of personal use property. A **personal casualty loss** for this purpose is a casualty or theft loss of personal use property after the application of the $100 floor. A taxpayer who has both gains and losses for the taxable year must first net (offset) the personal casualty gains and personal casualty losses. If the gains exceed the losses, the gains and losses are treated as gains and losses from the sale of capital assets. The capital gains and losses are short term or long term, depending on the period the taxpayer held each of the assets. In the netting process, personal casualty and theft gains and losses are not netted with the gains and losses on business and income-producing property.

EXAMPLE 19

During the year, Cliff had the following personal casualty gains and losses (after deducting the $100 floor):

Asset	Holding Period	Gain or (Loss)
A	Three months	($ 300)
B	Three years	(2,400)
C	Two years	3,200

Cliff computes the tax consequences as follows:

Personal casualty gain	$ 3,200
Personal casualty loss ($300 + $2,400)	(2,700)
Net personal casualty gain	$ 500

Cliff treats all of the gains and losses as capital gains and losses and has the following:

Short-term capital loss (Asset A)	$ 300
Long-term capital loss (Asset B)	2,400
Long-term capital gain (Asset C)	3,200

---

[24]§ 62(a)(1).
[25]§ 62(a)(4).
[26]§ 67(b)(3).

CONCEPT SUMMARY   7–3

Casualty Gains and Losses

	Business Use or Income-Producing Property	Personal Use Property
Event creating the loss	Any event.	Casualty or theft.
Amount	The lesser of the decline in fair market value or the adjusted basis, but always the adjusted basis if the property is totally destroyed.	The lesser of the decline in fair market value or the adjusted basis.
Insurance	Insurance proceeds received reduce the amount of the loss.	Insurance proceeds received (or for which there is an unfiled claim) reduce the amount of the loss.
$100 floor	Not applicable.	Applicable per event.
Gains and losses	Gains and losses are netted (see detailed discussion in Chapter 17).	Personal casualty and theft gains and losses are netted.
Gains exceeding losses		The gains and losses are treated as gains and losses from the sale of capital assets.
Losses exceeding gains		The gains—and the losses to the extent of gains—are treated as ordinary items in computing AGI. The losses in excess of gains, to the extent they exceed 10% of AGI, are itemized deductions.

If personal casualty losses exceed personal casualty gains, all gains and losses are treated as ordinary items. The gains—and the losses to the extent of gains—are treated as ordinary income and ordinary loss in computing AGI. Losses in excess of gains are deducted as itemized deductions to the extent the losses exceed 10 percent of AGI.[27]

EXAMPLE 20

During the year, Hazel had AGI of $20,000 and the following personal casualty gain and loss (after deducting the $100 floor):

Asset	Holding Period	Gain or (Loss)
A	Three years	($2,700)
B	Four months	200

Hazel computes the tax consequences as follows:

Personal casualty loss	($2,700)
Personal casualty gain	200
Net personal casualty loss	($2,500)

Hazel treats the gain and the loss as ordinary items. The $200 gain and $200 of the loss are included in computing AGI. Hazel's itemized deduction for casualty losses is computed as follows:

Casualty loss in excess of gain ($2,700 − $200)	$ 2,500
Less: 10% of AGI (10% × $20,000)	(2,000)
Itemized deduction	$ 500

∎

ETHICAL Considerations — THE AMOUNT OF A CASUALTY LOSS

In the case of a casualty loss to personal use property, the loss is allowed only to the extent that it exceeds $100 and the net casualty loss for the tax year exceeds 10 percent of AGI. The amount of the loss allowed is the lesser of (1) the decline in the fair market value of the property as a result of the casualty or (2) the adjusted basis of the property.

Milt and his family sold their home, put their belongings in storage units, and rented a smaller residence. Abnormally wet weather during the year caused the storage units to leak badly. Among the items in storage was a large personal library that Milt's wife had inherited from her father many years ago. The collection included books that were leather bound, antebellum, and signed editions. Most of the books suffered water damage and were destroyed beyond repair. Following the damage, Milt had the books appraised. The appraiser calculated a replacement value of $35,000 for the books. Milt is considering claiming a loss deduction of $35,000 for the damage to the books. Evaluate Milt's plan.

Research and Experimental Expenditures

LO.5

Recognize and apply the alternative tax treatments for research and experimental expenditures.

Section 174 covers the treatment of research and experimental expenditures. The Regulations define **research and experimental expenditures** as follows:

> all such costs incident to the development of an experimental or pilot model, a plant process, a product, a formula, an invention, or similar property, and the improvement of already existing property of the type mentioned. The term does not include expenditures such as those for the ordinary testing or inspection of materials or products for quality control or those for efficiency surveys, management studies, consumer surveys, advertising, or promotions.[28]

Expenses in connection with the acquisition or improvement of land or depreciable property are not research and experimental expenditures. Rather, they increase the basis of the land or depreciable property. However, depreciation on a building used for research may be a research and experimental expense. Only the depreciation that is a research and experimental expense (not the cost of the asset) is subject to the three alternatives discussed below.

The law permits the following *three alternatives* for the handling of research and experimental expenditures:

- Expensed in the year paid or incurred.
- Deferred and amortized.
- Capitalized.

If the costs are capitalized, a deduction is not available until the research project is abandoned or is deemed worthless. Since many products resulting from research projects do not have a definite and limited useful life, a taxpayer should ordinarily elect to write off the expenditures immediately or to defer and amortize them. It is generally preferable to elect an immediate write-off of the research expenditures because of the time value of the tax deduction.

The law also provides for a research activities credit. The credit amounts to 20 percent of certain research and experimental expenditures.[29] (The credit is discussed more fully in Chapter 13.)

Expense Method

A taxpayer can elect to expense all of the research and experimental expenditures incurred in the current year and all subsequent years. The consent of the IRS is not

---

[28]Reg. § 1.174–2(a)(1).

[29]§ 41. See the information in Chapter 13 on the termination date for the research activities credit.

---

required if the method is adopted for the first taxable year in which such expenditures were paid or incurred. Once the election is made, the taxpayer must continue to expense all qualifying expenditures unless a request for a change is made to, and approved by, the IRS. In certain instances, a taxpayer may incur research and experimental expenditures before actually engaging in any trade or business activity. In such instances, the Supreme Court has applied a liberal standard of deductibility and permitted a deduction in the year of incurrence.[30]

Deferral and Amortization Method

Alternatively, research and experimental expenditures may be deferred and amortized if the taxpayer makes an election.[31] Under the election, research and experimental expenditures are amortized ratably over a period of not less than 60 months. A deduction is allowed beginning with the month in which the taxpayer first realizes benefits from the experimental expenditure. The election is binding, and a change requires permission from the IRS.

EXAMPLE 21

Gold Corporation decides to develop a new line of adhesives. The project begins in 2006. Gold incurs the following expenses in 2006 in connection with the project:

Salaries	$25,000
Materials	8,000
Depreciation on machinery	6,500

Gold incurs the following expenses in 2007 in connection with the project:

Salaries	$18,000
Materials	2,000
Depreciation on machinery	5,700

The benefits from the project will be realized starting in March 2008. If Gold Corporation elects a 60-month deferral and amortization period, there is no deduction prior to March 2008, the month benefits from the project begin to be realized. The deduction for 2008 is $10,867, computed as follows:

Salaries ($25,000 + $18,000)	$43,000
Materials ($8,000 + $2,000)	10,000
Depreciation ($6,500 + $5,700)	12,200
Total	$65,200
$65,200 × (10 months/60 months) =	$10,867

■

---

[30] *Snow v. Comm.*, 74–1 USTC ¶9432, 33 AFTR2d 74–1251, 94 S.Ct. 1876 (USSC, 1974).

[31] § 174(b)(2).

The option to treat research and experimental expenditures as deferred expense is usually employed when a company does not have sufficient income to offset the research and experimental expenses. Rather than create net operating loss carryovers that might not be utilized because of the 20-year limitation on such carryovers, the deferral and amortization method may be used. The deferral of research and experimental expenditures should also be considered if the taxpayer expects higher tax rates in the future.

Domestic Production Activities Deduction X

> **LO.6**
>
> Calculate the domestic production activities deduction.

The American Jobs Creation Act of 2004 was enacted to replace certain tax provisions that our world trading partners regarded as allowing unfair advantage to U.S. exports. Among other changes, the Act created a new deduction based on the income from manufacturing activities (designated as *production activities*).[32] The new **production activities deduction (PAD)** is contained in § 199.

Operational Rules

Calculation of the Production Activities Deduction. For tax years beginning in 2005 or 2006, the PAD is based on the following formula:[33]

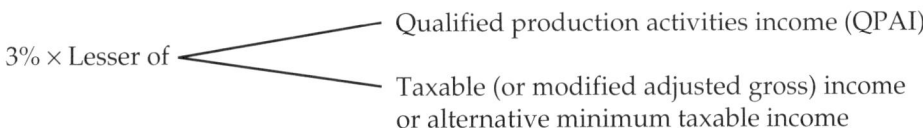

$3\% \times$ Lesser of

Qualified production activities income (QPAI)

Taxable (or modified adjusted gross) income or alternative minimum taxable income

For tax years beginning in 2007 to 2009, the 3 percent factor is increased to 6 percent. For tax years beginning in 2010 and thereafter, the factor is increased to 9 percent.

Taxable income is determined without regard to the PAD. In the case of an individual (a sole proprietorship or an owner of a flow-through entity), **modified adjusted gross income** is substituted for taxable income.[34]

The taxable income limitation is determined after the application of any net operating loss (NOL) deduction for the tax year (NOLs are explained in detail later in the chapter). Thus, a company with an NOL carryforward for a tax year is ineligible for the PAD if the carryforward eliminates current taxable income. Further, a taxpayer that has an NOL carryback may lose part or all of the PAD benefit for that year. As taxable income is reduced by the NOL carryback, there is a corresponding reduction in the PAD. If qualified production activities income (QPAI) cannot be used in a particular year due to the taxable income limitation (see the above formula), it is lost forever. (The calculation of QPAI is explained in the next section.)

EXAMPLE 22

Opal, Inc., manufactures and sells costume jewelry. It also sells costume jewelry purchased from other manufacturers. During 2006, Opal had a *profit* of $200,000 (QPAI) from the sale of its own manufactured jewelry and a *loss* of $50,000 from the sale of the purchased jewelry. Based on this information, Opal's QPAI is $200,000, and its taxable income is $150,000 ($200,000 − $50,000). Opal's PAD becomes $4,500 [3% of the lesser of $200,000 (QPAI) or $150,000 (taxable income)]. ∎

---

[32]Section 101 of the *American Jobs Creation Act of 2004*, Public Law No. 108-357 (October 22, 2004).

[33]§ 199(a).

[34]§ 199(d)(2). Generally, modified AGI is AGI prior to the effect of § 199.

EXAMPLE 23

Assume the same facts as in Example 22, except that Opal also has an NOL carryover from 2005 of $300,000. As taxable income for 2006 is zero ($200,000 − $50,000 − $300,000), there is no PAD. ■

Another important limitation is that the amount of the PAD cannot exceed 50 percent of **W–2 wages** paid by the taxpayer during the tax year.[35] The purpose of this limitation is to preserve U.S. manufacturing jobs and to discourage their outsourcing. An employer's W–2 wages include the sum of the aggregate amount of wages and elective deferrals required to be included on the W–2 wage statements for employees during the employer's taxable year. Elective deferrals include those amounts deferred under § 457 plans and Roth contributions (see Chapter 19). An employer includes wages paid to all workers during a tax year and not just the wages of the employees engaged in qualified production activities.

EXAMPLE 24

In 2006, Red, Inc., has QPAI of $2 million and taxable income of $2.1 million. Since Red outsources much of its work to independent contractors, its W–2 wage base, which for Red is related entirely to production activities, is $80,000. Although Red's PAD normally would be $60,000 [3% of the lesser of $2 million (QPAI) or $2.1 million (taxable income)], it is limited to $40,000 [50% of $80,000 (W–2 wages)]. ■

EXAMPLE 25

Assume the same facts as in Example 24, except that Red also pays salaries of $50,000 related to its *nonproduction* activities. As the wage limitation now becomes $65,000 [50% of $130,000 ($80,000 + $50,000)], the usual PAD amount of $60,000 can be claimed. ■

Calculation of Qualified Production Activities Income. Qualified production activities income (**QPAI**) is the excess of domestic production gross receipts (**DPGR**) over the sum of:[36]

• The cost of goods sold allocated to such receipts.
• Other deductions, expenses, or losses directly allocated to such receipts.
• The ratable portion of deductions, expenses, and losses not directly allocable to such receipts or another class of income.

QPAI is determined on an item-by-item basis—not on a division-by-division or transaction-by-transaction basis. Because all items must be netted in the calculation, the final QPAI amount can be either positive or negative. The effect of the netting rule is to preclude taxpayers from selecting only profitable product lines or profitable transactions when calculating QPAI.

EXAMPLE 26

A taxpayer manufactures pants and shirts with the following QPAI results: $5 for one pair of pants and a negative $2 for one shirt. Because the two items are netted, the QPAI amount that controls is $3 ($5 − $2). ■

Five specific categories of DPGR qualify for the PAD:[37]

• The lease, license, sale, exchange, or other disposition of qualified production property (QPP) that was manufactured, produced, grown, or extracted (MPGE) in the United States.
• Qualified films largely created in the United States.
• The production of electricity, natural gas, or potable water.
• Construction (but not self-construction) performed in the United States.
• Engineering and architectural services for domestic construction.

[35]§ 199(b).
[36]§ 199(c).
[37]§ 199(c)(4).

The sale of food and beverages prepared by a taxpayer at a retail establishment and the transmission or distribution of electricity, natural gas, or potable water are specifically excluded from the definition of DPGR.

Eligible Taxpayers

The deduction is available to a variety of taxpayers including individuals, partnerships, S corporations, C corporations, cooperatives, estates, and trusts. For a pass-through entity (e.g., partnerships, S corporations), the deduction flows through to the individual owners. In the case of a sole proprietor, a deduction *for* AGI results and is claimed on Form 1040, line 35 on page 1. A Form 8903 must be attached to support the deduction.

For additional information on the domestic production activities deduction, see Chapter 3 in *West Federal Taxation: Corporations, Partnerships, Estates, and Trusts.*

Net Operating Losses

The requirement that every taxpayer file an annual income tax return (whether on a calendar year or a fiscal year) may result in certain inequities for taxpayers who experience cyclical patterns of income or expense. Inequities result from the application of a progressive rate structure to taxable income determined on an annual basis. A **net operating loss (NOL)** in a particular tax year would produce no tax benefit if the Code did not provide for the carryback and carryforward of such losses to profitable years.

<table>
<tr><td>

LO.7

Determine the amount of the net operating loss and recognize the impact of the carryback and carryover provisions.

</td></tr>
</table>

EXAMPLE 27

Juanita has a business and realizes the following taxable income or loss over a five-year period: Year 1, $50,000; Year 2, ($30,000); Year 3, $100,000; Year 4, ($200,000); and Year 5, $380,000. She is married and files a joint return. Hubert also has a business and has a taxable income pattern of $60,000 every year. He, too, is married and files a joint return. Note that both Juanita and Hubert have total taxable income of $300,000 over the five-year period. Assume there is no provision for carryback or carryover of NOLs. Juanita and Hubert would have the following five-year tax bills:

Year	Juanita's Tax	Hubert's Tax
1	$ 6,745	$ 8,245
2	–0–	8,245
3	18,115	8,245
4	–0–	8,245
5	106,251	8,245
	$131,111	$41,225

The computation of tax is made without regard to any NOL benefit.
Rates applicable to 2006 are used to compute the tax.

Even though Juanita and Hubert realized the same total taxable income ($300,000) over the five-year period, Juanita had to pay taxes of $131,111, while Hubert paid taxes of only $41,225. ■

To provide partial relief from this inequitable tax treatment, a deduction is allowed for NOLs.[38] This provision permits NOLs for any one year to be offset against taxable income of other years. The NOL provision is intended as a form of relief for business income and losses. Thus, only losses from the operation of a trade or business (or profession), casualty and theft losses, or losses from the confiscation of a business by a foreign government can create an NOL. In other words, a salaried

---

[38]§ 172.

individual with itemized deductions and personal exemptions in excess of gross income is not permitted to deduct the excess amounts as an NOL. On the other hand, a personal casualty loss is treated as a business loss and can therefore create (or increase) an NOL for an individual.

Carryback and Carryover Periods

General Rules. An NOL must be applied initially to the two taxable years preceding the year of the loss (unless an election is made not to carry the loss back at all). It is carried first to the second prior year, and then to the immediately preceding tax year (or until used up). If the loss is not fully used in the carryback period, it must be carried forward to the first year after the loss year, and then forward to the second, third, etc., year after the loss year. The carryover period is 20 years. A loss sustained in 2006 is used in this order: 2004, 2005, 2007 through 2026.

A three-year carryback period is available for any portion of an individual's NOL resulting from a casualty or theft loss. The three-year carryback rule also applies to NOLs that are attributable to presidentially declared disasters that are incurred by a small business or a taxpayer engaged in farming. A small business is one whose average annual gross receipts for a three-year period are $5 million or less.

If the loss is being carried to a preceding year, an amended return is filed on Form 1040X, or a quick refund claim is filed on Form 1045. In either case, a refund of taxes previously paid is requested. Form 1045 is an application for a tentative refund. The IRS normally will process Form 1045 and pay the refund within 90 days of the date it is filed. When the loss is carried forward, the current return shows an NOL deduction for the prior year's loss.

Sequence of Use of NOLs. When the taxpayer has NOLs in two or more years, the rule is always to use the earliest year's loss first until it is completely absorbed. The later years' losses can then be used until they also are absorbed or lost. Thus, one year's return could show NOL carryovers from two or more years. Each loss is computed and applied separately.

Election to Forgo Carryback. A taxpayer can *irrevocably elect* not to carry back an NOL to any of the prior years. In that case, the loss is available as a carryover for 20 years. The election is made if it is to the taxpayer's tax advantage. For example, a taxpayer might be in a low marginal tax bracket in the carryback years but expect to be in a high marginal tax bracket in future years. Therefore, it would be to the taxpayer's advantage to use the NOL to offset income in years when the tax rate is high rather than use it when the tax rate is relatively low.

EXAMPLE 28

For 2006, taxpayer and spouse have an NOL of $10,000. The NOL may be carried back and applied against taxable income first in 2004 and then in 2005. Any remaining NOL is carried forward to years 2007 through 2026. If, however, the taxpayer and spouse elect to forgo the carryback period, the NOL initially is carried to 2007 and then to years 2008 through 2026. ∎

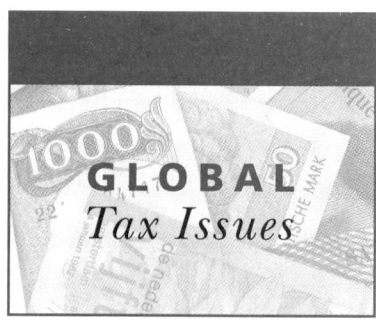

TAX PERKS

President Gloria Arroyo of the Philippines recently approved the Investment Priorities Plan for 2005. The plan lists priority activities whose development is to be encouraged through the use of tax incentives. The tax incentives include income tax holidays, NOL carryovers, and accelerated depreciation of plant, machinery, and equipment.

Source: *Adapted from Judy T. Gulane, "Palace Okays Priority List of Businesses with Perks,"* Business World (Philippines), *May 26, 2005.*

GLOBAL
Tax Issues

Computation of the Net Operating Loss

Since the NOL provisions apply solely to business-related losses, certain adjustments must be made so that the loss more closely resembles the taxpayer's *economic* loss. The required adjustments for corporate taxpayers are usually insignificant because a corporation's tax loss is generally similar to its economic loss. However, in computing taxable income, individual taxpayers are allowed deductions for such items as personal and dependency exemptions and itemized deductions that do not reflect actual business-related economic losses.

To arrive at the NOL for an individual, taxable income must be adjusted by adding back the following items:[39]

1. No deduction is allowed for personal and dependency exemptions. These amounts do not reflect economic, or business, outlays and hence must be added back.

2. The NOL carryover or carryback from another year is not allowed in the computation of the current year's NOL.

3. Capital losses and nonbusiness deductions are limited in determining the current year's NOL. These limits are as follows:

   a. The excess of nonbusiness capital losses over nonbusiness capital gains must be added back.

   b. The excess of nonbusiness deductions over the sum of nonbusiness income and *net* nonbusiness capital gains must be added back. *Net nonbusiness capital gains* are the excess of nonbusiness capital gains over nonbusiness capital losses. *Nonbusiness income* includes such passive items as dividends and interest. It does not include such items as salaries, alimony, rents, and gains and losses on the sale or exchange of business assets. *Nonbusiness deductions* are total itemized deductions less personal casualty and theft losses and losses incurred in a transaction entered into for profit.

      A taxpayer who does not itemize deductions computes the excess of nonbusiness deductions over nonbusiness income by substituting the standard deduction for total itemized deductions.

   c. The excess of business capital losses over the sum of business capital gains and the excess of nonbusiness income and net nonbusiness capital gains over nonbusiness deductions must be added back.

   d. The add-back for net nonbusiness capital losses and excess business capital losses does not include net capital losses not included in the current-year computation of taxable income because of the capital loss limitation provisions (discussed in Chapter 16).

---

[39]§ 172(d); Reg. § 1.172–3(a).

The capital loss and nonbusiness deduction limits are illustrated in Examples 29 through 32.

EXAMPLE 29

For 2006, taxpayer and spouse have $6,000 of nonbusiness capital losses and $4,000 of nonbusiness capital gains. They must add back $2,000 ($6,000 − $4,000) in determining the excess of nonbusiness capital losses over nonbusiness capital gains. ∎

EXAMPLE 30

For 2006, taxpayer and spouse have $2,000 of nonbusiness capital gains, $1,000 of nonbusiness capital losses, $2,000 of interest income, and no itemized deductions. They must add back $7,300 {$10,300 standard deduction − [$2,000 interest income + $1,000 ($2,000 − $1,000) net nonbusiness capital gains]}. Note that, in this example, there is no excess of nonbusiness capital losses over nonbusiness capital gains. ∎

EXAMPLE 31

For 2006, taxpayer and spouse have $2,000 of nonbusiness capital gains, $1,000 of nonbusiness capital losses, $10,000 of interest income, $10,500 of itemized deductions (none of which are personal casualty and theft losses), $4,000 of business capital losses, and $1,000 of business capital gains. They must add back $2,500 {$4,000 business capital losses − [$1,000 business capital gains + ($10,000 nonbusiness income + $1,000 net nonbusiness capital gains − $10,500 nonbusiness deductions)]}. Note that, in this example, there is no excess of nonbusiness capital losses over nonbusiness capital gains, nor is there an excess of nonbusiness deductions over the sum of nonbusiness income and net nonbusiness capital gains. ∎

EXAMPLE 32

For 2006, taxpayer and spouse have $2,000 of nonbusiness capital gains, $3,000 of nonbusiness capital losses, $9,000 of interest income, $11,000 of itemized deductions (none of which are personal casualty and theft losses), $8,000 of business capital losses, and $4,000 of business capital gains. They must add back $2,000 ($11,000 − $9,000), the excess of nonbusiness deductions over nonbusiness income, and $3,000, the excess of combined capital losses. Because of the capital loss limitations, only $3,000 of the loss would have been used in computing taxable income for the year. ∎

Example 33 illustrates the computation of an NOL.

EXAMPLE 33

James opened a retail store in 2005 and experienced an NOL of $185 for that year. James had no taxable income for 2003 or 2004. James is married, has no dependents, and files a joint return. For 2006, James and his wife have the following taxable income:

Gross income from the business	$ 67,000	
Less: Business expenses	(71,000)	($ 4,000)
Salary from a part-time job		875
Interest on savings account		525
Nonbusiness long-term capital gain		1,000
NOL carryover from 2005		(185)
Net loss on rental property		(100)
Adjusted gross income		($ 1,885)
Less: Itemized deductions		
Interest expense	$ 3,000	
Taxes	5,300	
Casualty loss	2,000	
Total itemized deductions		(10,300)
Exemptions (2 × $3,300)		(6,600)
Taxable income		($18,785)

James's NOL is computed as follows:

Taxable income				($18,785)
Add:				
Net operating loss from 2005			$ 185	
Personal exemptions (2)			6,600	
Excess of nonbusiness deductions over nonbusiness income				
Total itemized deductions		$ 10,300		
Less: Casualty loss		(2,000)		
		$ 8,300		
Less: Interest	$ 525			
Less: Long-term capital gain	1,000	(1,525)	6,775	13,560
Net operating loss				($ 5,225)

The NOL can be thought of as follows:

Business loss	($ 4,000)
Rental loss	(100)
Casualty loss	(2,000)
Salary income	875
Net operating loss	($ 5,225)

Recomputation of Tax Liability for Year to Which Net Operating Loss Is Carried

When an NOL is carried back to a nonloss year, the taxable income and income tax for the carryback year must be recomputed by including the NOL as a deduction *for* AGI. Several deductions (such as medical expenses and charitable contributions) are based on the amount of AGI. When an NOL is carried back, all such deductions *except* the charitable contributions deduction must be recomputed on the basis of the new AGI after the NOL has been applied. The deduction for charitable contributions is determined without regard to any NOL carryback but with regard to any other modification affecting AGI. Furthermore, any tax credits limited by or based upon the tax must be recomputed, based on the recomputed tax.

E X A M P L E 34

Peggy sustains an NOL of $11,000 in 2006. Because Peggy had no taxable income in 2004, the loss is carried back to 2005. For 2005, the joint income tax return of Peggy and her husband was as follows:

Salary income		$ 13,000
Dividends (not qualified dividends)		4,000
Net short-term capital gain		1,400
Adjusted gross income		$ 18,400
Itemized deductions		
Charitable contributions	$3,700	
Medical [$1,400 − ($18,400 × 7.5%)]	20	
Interest	5,700	
Taxes	1,420	(10,840)
Exemptions (2 × $3,200)		(6,400)
Taxable income		$ 1,160
Tax (married filing jointly)		$ 116

Peggy's new tax liability for the carryback year is computed as follows:

Adjusted gross income		$ 18,400
Less: Net operating loss		(11,000)
Recomputed adjusted gross income		$ 7,400
Itemized deductions		
Charitable contributions	$3,700	
Medical [$1,400 − ($7,400 × 7.5%)]	845	
Interest	5,700	
Taxes	1,420	(11,665)
Exemptions (2 × $3,200)		(6,400)
Recomputed taxable income		($ 10,665)
Tax		$ –0–
Tax originally paid and refund claim		$ 116

Calculation of the Remaining Net Operating Loss

After computing the amount of the refund claim for the initial carryback year, it is then necessary to determine the extent to which any NOL remains to carry over to future years. The amount of this carryover loss is the excess of the NOL over the taxable income of the year to which the loss is being applied. However, the taxable income of the year to which the loss is being applied must be determined with the following *modifications*:

- No deduction is allowed for excess capital losses over capital gains.
- No deduction is allowed for the NOL that is being carried back. However, deductions are allowed for NOLs occurring before the loss year.
- Any deductions claimed that are based on or limited by AGI must be determined after making the preceding adjustments. However, charitable contributions do not take into account any NOL carryback.
- No deduction is allowed for personal and dependency exemptions.

EXAMPLE 35

Referring to the facts in Example 34, the NOL carryover from 2005 available for future years is ($3,440), computed as follows:

Salary income		$ 13,000
Dividends (not qualified dividends)		4,000
Net short-term capital gain		1,400
Adjusted gross income		$ 18,400
Itemized deductions		
Charitable contributions	$3,700	
Medical [$1,400 − ($18,400 × 7.5%)]	20	
Interest	5,700	
Taxes	1,420	(10,840)
Exemptions (not allowed)		–0–
Modified taxable income		$ 7,560
Net operating loss		($ 11,000)
Modified taxable income		7,560
Net operating loss to carry forward		($ 3,440)

CONCEPT SUMMARY 7–4

Computation of Net Operating Loss

Taxable income shown on the return
Add back:

1. Personal and dependency exemptions.
2. Net operating loss carryover or carryback from another year.
3. The excess of nonbusiness capital losses over nonbusiness capital gains.
4. The excess of nonbusiness deductions over the sum of nonbusiness income plus *net* nonbusiness capital gains.
5. The excess of business capital losses over the sum of business capital gains plus the excess of nonbusiness income and *net* nonbusiness capital gains over nonbusiness deductions. The add-back from the total of items 3 and 5 will not exceed $3,000 because of the capital loss limitation rules.

Equals the net operating loss

Since the ending figure is negative, it represents the NOL remaining to carry over to 2007 or later years. ■

Tax Consequences of the *Groetzinger* Case

In the *Groetzinger* case discussed earlier in the chapter, the court established that the appropriate tests for determining if gambling is a trade or business are whether an individual engages in gambling full-time in good faith, with regularity, and for the production of income as a livelihood, and not as a mere hobby. The court held that Robert Groetzinger satisfied the tests because of his constant and large-scale effort. Skill was required and was applied. He did what he did for a livelihood, though with less than successful results. His gambling was not a hobby, a passing fancy, or an occasional bet for amusement. Therefore, his gambling was a trade or business, and hence, he was able to deduct his gambling losses *for* AGI. If the court had ruled that Groetzinger's gambling was not a trade or business, his gambling losses would have been limited to his gambling winnings and would have been classified as itemized deductions.

Documentation of Related-Taxpayer Loans, Casualty Losses, and Theft Losses

Since non-bona fide loans between related taxpayers may be treated as gifts, adequate documentation is needed to substantiate a bad debt deduction if the loan subsequently becomes worthless. Documentation should include proper execution of the note (legal form) and the establishment of a bona fide purpose for the loan. In addition, it is desirable to stipulate a reasonable rate of interest and a fixed maturity date.

Since a theft loss is not permitted for misplaced items, a loss should be documented by a police report and evidence of the value of the property (e.g., appraisals, pictures of the property, newspaper clippings). Similar documentation of the value of property should be provided to support a casualty loss deduction because the amount of loss is measured, in part, by the decline in fair market value of the property.

Casualty loss deductions must be reported on Form 4684.

LO.8

Identify tax planning opportunities in deducting certain business expenses, business losses, and personal losses.

TAX PLANNING *Considerations*

Small Business Stock

Because § 1244 limits the amount of loss classified as ordinary loss on a yearly basis, a taxpayer might maximize the benefits of § 1244 by selling the stock in more than one taxable year. The result could be that the losses in any one taxable year would not exceed the § 1244 limits on ordinary loss.

E X A M P L E   36

Mitch, a single individual, purchased small business stock in 2004 for $150,000 (150 shares at $1,000 per share). On December 20, 2006, the stock is worth $60,000 (150 shares at $400 per share). Mitch wants to sell the stock at this time. Mitch earns a salary of $80,000 a year, has no other capital transactions, and does not expect any in the future. If Mitch sells all of the small business stock in 2006, his recognized loss will be $90,000 ($60,000 − $150,000). The loss will be characterized as a $50,000 ordinary loss and a $40,000 long-term capital loss. In computing taxable income for 2006, Mitch could deduct the $50,000 ordinary loss but could deduct only $3,000 of the capital loss. The remainder of the capital loss could be carried over and used in future years subject to the $3,000 limitation if Mitch has no capital gains. If Mitch sells 82 shares in 2006, he will recognize an ordinary loss of $49,200 [82 × ($1,000 − $400)]. If Mitch then sells the remainder of the shares in 2007, he will recognize an ordinary loss of $40,800 [68 × ($1,000 − $400)]. Mitch could deduct the $49,200 ordinary loss in computing 2006 taxable income and the $40,800 ordinary loss in computing 2007 taxable income. ■

Casualty Losses

A special election is available for taxpayers who sustain casualty losses in an area designated by the President as a disaster area. This election affects only the timing, not the calculation, of the deduction. The deduction can be taken in the year before the year in which the loss occurred. Thus, for a loss occurring between January 1 and December 31, 2006, an individual can take the deduction on the 2005 return. The benefit, of course, is a faster refund (or reduction in tax). It will also be advantageous to carry the loss back if the taxpayer's tax rate in the carryback year is higher than the tax rate in the year of the loss.

To find out if an event qualifies as a disaster area loss, one can look in any of the major tax services, the Weekly Compilation of Presidential Documents, or the *Internal Revenue Bulletin.*

Net Operating Losses

In certain instances, it may be advisable for a taxpayer to elect not to carry back an NOL. For an individual, the benefits from the loss carryback could be scaled down or lost due to the economic adjustments that must be made to taxable income for the year to which the loss is carried. For example, a taxpayer should attempt to minimize the number of taxable years to which an NOL is carried. The more years to which the NOL is applied, the more benefits are lost from adjustments for items such as personal and dependency exemptions.

The election not to carry back the loss might also be advantageous if there is a disparity in marginal tax rates applicable to different tax years.

E X A M P L E   37

Abby sustained an NOL of $10,000 in Year 3. Her marginal tax bracket in Year 1 was 15%. In Year 4, however, she expects her bracket to be 35% due to a large profit she will make on a business deal. If Abby carries her loss back, her refund will be $1,500 (15% × $10,000). If she elects not to carry it back to Year 1 but chooses, instead, to carry it forward, her savings will be $3,500 (35% × $10,000). Even considering the time value of an immediate tax refund, Abby appears to be better off using the carryover approach. ■

KEY TERMS

Bad debt, 7–3

Business bad debt, 7–4

Casualty loss, 7–7

Disaster area losses, 7–9

Domestic production gross receipts (DPGR), 7–18

Modified adjusted gross income, 7–17

Net operating loss (NOL), 7–19

Nonbusiness bad debt, 7–4

Personal casualty gain, 7–13

Personal casualty loss, 7–13

Production activities deduction (PAD), 7–17

Qualified production activities income (QPAI), 7–18

Research and experimental expenditures, 7–15

Reserve method, 7–3

Section 1244 stock, 7–6

Small business stock, 7–6

Specific charge-off method, 7–3

Theft losses, 7–9

Worthless securities, 7–5

W–2 wages, 7–18

PROBLEM MATERIALS

DISCUSSION QUESTIONS

1. Discuss whether a cash basis taxpayer can take a bad debt deduction.

2. Ron sells his business accounts receivable of $100,000 to Mike for $80,000 (80% of the actual accounts receivable). Mike later determines that he will be able to collect only $9,000 of a $10,000 receivable. Discuss the amount and classification of Mike's bad debt deduction.

3. Discuss whether legal proceedings are necessary to show that a debt is worthless.

4. Discuss the tax treatment for the recovery of an account receivable previously written off as uncollectible.

5. Discuss the application of the nonbusiness bad debt provisions to an individual taxpayer.

6. Discuss whether a bona fide loan can exist between related parties.

7. John was the sole shareholder of Blonde, Inc. The corporation had 26 salaried employees, which included John. Several years ago Blonde began experiencing financial difficulties. As a result, John made several loans to the corporation in an attempt to continue business operations and pay employee salaries. The corporation eventually filed for bankruptcy under Chapter 7 of the bankruptcy code. Upon the final discharge of the corporation's debts, John's loans remained unpaid and were worthless. Identify the relevant tax issues for John with respect to his loans to Blonde, Inc.

Issue ID

8. Mary is in the business of buying and selling stocks and bonds. She has a bond of Velvet Corporation for which she paid $15,000. If the bond becomes worthless, what are the tax consequences of the bond being characterized as a worthless security? As a bad debt?

9. Discuss the ordinary loss limitations on the sale of § 1244 stock and the advantages of such a characterization.

10. Jim discovers that one of his business warehouses has extensive termite damage. Discuss whether he may take a deduction for the damage to the building.

11. Janice was involved in an automobile accident, and the police cited her for driving under the influence of alcohol. Discuss whether Janice may claim a casualty loss deduction for the damage to her car.

12. Discuss the tax treatment when a taxpayer has a partial claim for a personal casualty loss in 2005 and an additional loss in 2006 when the claim is settled.

13. Discuss the treatment for a reimbursement received for a casualty loss sustained and deducted in a previous tax year.

14. Discuss the measurement rule for partial or complete destruction of personal use property.

15. Discuss the tax consequences of not making an insurance claim when insured personal use property is subject to a loss.

16. Discuss the circumstances under which the cost of repairs to the damaged property can be used to measure the amount of a casualty loss.

17. Discuss the treatment of casualty losses associated with rental property.

18. Ben sustained a loss on the theft of bearer bonds that he owned. Discuss the tax treatment of the loss on Ben's individual tax return.

19. When casualty losses exceed casualty gains, only the amount of the casualty loss in excess of casualty gains is subject to the 10%-of-AGI floor. Discuss the significance of netting losses against gains in this manner rather than having the entire casualty loss be subject to the 10%-of-AGI floor.

Issue ID

20. Kelly decided to invest in Lime, Inc. common stock after reviewing Lime's public disclosures, including recent financial statements and a number of press releases issued by Lime. On August 7, 2004, Kelly purchased 60,000 shares of Lime for $210,000. In May 2005, Lime entered into a joint venture with Cherry, Inc. In November 2005, the joint venture failed, and Lime's stock began to decline in value. In December 2005, Cherry filed a lawsuit against Lime for theft of corporate opportunity and breach of fiduciary responsibility. In February 2006, Lime filed a countersuit against Cherry for fraud and misappropriation of funds. At the end of December 2006, Kelly's stock in Lime was worth $15,000. Identify the relevant tax issues for Kelly.

Issue ID

21. Henry owned 1,000 acres of unimproved farmland. During the spring of the current year, shortly after Henry had tilled the ground, a storm blew away four inches of topsoil from 60% of his acreage. Identify the relevant tax issues for Henry.

22. Discuss whether depreciation can qualify as a research and experimental expenditure.

23. Discuss the alternatives for the tax treatment of research and experimental expenditures.

Issue ID

24. Power and Light, a public utility company, planned a research and development project. To obtain a construction permit to expand its facilities, the company filed an application with state regulatory agencies and conducted various studies to support its application as required by the agencies. Because the taxpayer's expansion involved both the construction of a nuclear power plant and the installation of an ultrahigh voltage electric transmission line, the agencies required that the company conduct several types of environmental impact studies for site selection. The studies measured specific site conditions and the resulting environmental impact of the construction and operation of the project. The company conducted part of the studies directly and used a research organization to conduct the remainder of the studies on its behalf. Identify the relevant tax issues for Power and Light.

25. The PAD is unlike other deductions and is designed to provide a tax benefit in a somewhat unique manner. Explain this statement.

26. Jack and Kathleen are equal partners in the Red Partnership. For the year, they receive a pass-through of the same amount of QPAI and W–2 wages from Red. Nevertheless, Jack is able to claim a larger PAD on his income tax return than Kathleen. Why?

27. Discuss whether a salaried individual with only itemized deductions and personal exemptions in excess of gross income can claim an NOL.

28. Discuss the periods to which an individual taxpayer's 2006 NOL may be carried.

29. Discuss whether an NOL carryover from a prior year can create an NOL for the current year.

30. Discuss the recomputation of the tax liability for the year to which an NOL is carried.

31. Thomas believes that he has an NOL for the current year and wants to carry it back to a previous year and receive a tax refund. In determining his NOL, Thomas offset his business income by alimony payments he made to his ex-wife, contributions he made to his traditional Individual Retirement Account (IRA), and moving expenses he incurred. His reason for using these items in the NOL computation is that each item is a deduction *for* AGI. Identify the relevant tax issues for Thomas.

Issue ID

PROBLEMS

32. Several years ago John Johnson, who is not in the lending business, loaned Sara $30,000 to purchase an automobile to be used for personal purposes. In August of the current year, Sara filed for bankruptcy, and John was notified that he could not expect to receive more than $4,000. As of the end of the current year, John has received $1,000. John has contacted you about the possibility of taking a bad debt deduction for the current year.

    Write a letter to John that contains your advice as to whether he can claim a bad debt deduction for the current year. Also, prepare a memo for the tax files. John's address is 100 Tyler Lane, Erie, PA 16563.

Communications

33. Sue loaned her sister Janice $10,000 three years ago. Janice has never made any payments to Sue, and Sue has never tried to collect from Janice. This year, Janice filed for bankruptcy and told Sue that she would not be able to repay any of the $10,000 loan. Determine Sue's tax treatment for the loan for the current year.

34. Ron is in the business of purchasing accounts receivable. Last year, Ron purchased an account receivable with a face value of $100,000 for $72,000. During the current year, Ron was notified that he could not expect to collect more than 80 cents on the dollar with respect to the receivable. Determine the maximum amount of the bad debt deduction for Ron for the current year.

35. Mable and Jack file a joint return. For the current year, they had the following items:

Salaries	$180,000
Loss on sale of § 1244 stock acquired two years ago	95,000
Gain on sale of § 1244 stock acquired six months ago	12,000
Nonbusiness bad debt	16,000

Determine their AGI for the current year.

36. Mary, a single taxpayer, purchased 10,000 shares of § 1244 stock several years ago at a cost of $20 per share. In November of the current year, Mary received an offer to sell the stock for $12 per share. She has the option of either selling all of the stock now or selling half of the stock now and half of the stock in January of next year. Mary will receive a salary of $80,000 for the current year and $90,000 next year. Mary will have long-term capital gains of $8,000 for the current year and $10,000 next year. If Mary's goal is to minimize her AGI for the two years, determine whether she should sell all of her stock this year or half of her stock this year and half next year.

Decision Making

37. During the current year, Jacob's personal residence and some of the contents were damaged by a fire. Information with respect to the home and contents is as follows:

Asset	Adjusted Basis	FMV Before	FMV After	Insurance Recovery
Home	$200,000	$600,000	$300,000	$150,000
Contents	100,000	80,000	50,000	10,000

In a separate incident, Jacob had a car accident. The car had originally cost Jacob $25,000. At the time of the accident, the car was worth $50,000. After the accident, the car was worth only $5,000. Because the car was a collector's item, Jacob paid $40,000 to have it restored. The car was not insured at the time of the accident.

If Jacob's AGI is $90,000 before considering the above events, determine the amount of his deductible loss.

Decision Making

38. Olaf owns a 500-acre farm in Minnesota. A tornado hit the area and destroyed a farm building and some farm equipment and damaged a barn. Fortunately for Olaf, the tornado occurred after he had harvested his corn crop. Applicable information is as follows:

Item	Adjusted Basis	FMV Before	FMV After	Insurance Proceeds
Building	$90,000	$ 70,000	$ –0–	$70,000
Equipment	40,000	50,000	–0–	25,000
Barn	90,000	120,000	70,000	25,000

Because of the extensive damage caused by the tornado, the President designated the area as a disaster area.

Olaf, who files a joint return with his wife, Anna, had $174,000 of taxable income last year. Their taxable income for the current year, excluding the loss from the tornado, is $250,000.

Determine the amount of Olaf and Anna's loss and the year in which they should take the loss.

39. Heather owns a two-story building. The first floor houses her business, and the second floor is her personal residence. During the current year, a fire caused major damage to the building and its contents. Heather purchased the building for $800,000 and has taken depreciation of $150,000 on the business portion. At the time of the fire, the building had a fair market value of $900,000. Immediately after the fire, the fair market value was $200,000. The insurance recovery on the building was $600,000. The contents of the building were insured for any loss at fair market value. The first-floor assets had an adjusted basis of $220,000 and a fair market value of $175,000. These assets were totally destroyed. The second-floor assets had an adjusted basis of $50,000 and a fair market value of $65,000. These assets were also totally destroyed. If Heather's AGI is $100,000 before considering the effects of the fire, determine her itemized deduction as a result of the fire. Also determine Heather's AGI.

Decision Making

Communications

40. On July 24 of the current year, Sam Smith was involved in an accident with his business use automobile. Sam had purchased the car for $30,000. The automobile had a fair market value of $20,000 before the accident and $8,000 immediately after the accident. Sam has taken $20,000 of depreciation on the car. The car is insured for the fair market value of any loss. Because of Sam's history, he is afraid that if he submits a claim, his policy will be canceled. Therefore, he is considering not filing a claim. Sam believes that the tax loss deduction will help mitigate the loss of the insurance reimbursement. Sam's current marginal tax rate is 35%.

Write a letter to Sam that contains your advice with respect to the tax and cash-flow consequences of filing versus not filing a claim for the insurance reimbursement for the damage to his car. Also, prepare a memo for the tax files. Sam's address is 450 Colonel's Way, Warrensburg, MO 64093.

41. Blue Corporation, a manufacturing company, decided to develop a new line of merchandise. The project began in 2006. Blue had the following expenses in connection with the project:

	2006	2007
Salaries	$300,000	$400,000
Materials	80,000	70,000
Insurance	10,000	15,000
Utilities	7,000	8,000
Cost of inspection of materials for quality control	4,000	4,000
Promotion expenses	10,000	7,000

	2006	2007
Advertising	$ –0–	$ 30,000
✗ Equipment depreciation	10,000	12,000
Cost of market survey	8,000	–0–

The new product will be introduced for sale beginning in July 2008. Determine the amount of the deduction for research and experimental expenditures for 2006, 2007, and 2008 if:

a. Blue Corporation elects to expense the research and experimental expenditures.

b. Blue Corporation elects to amortize the research and experimental expenditures over 60 months.

42. In 2006, Purple, Inc., a C corporation, has QPAI of $100,000 and a marginal tax rate of 35%. Calculate the tax savings resulting from the PAD.

43. Barbara, a calendar year taxpayer, owns and operates a company that manufactures toys. For 2006, she has modified AGI of $420,000 and QPAI of $390,000. Ignoring the W–2 wage limitation, calculate Barbara's PAD.

44. Tan, Inc., has QPAI of $400,000 but has an overall NOL of $15,000 for the tax year. Calculate Tan's PAD, if any, for 2006.

45. Green, Inc., manufactures skirts and blouses in the United States. The QPAI derived from the manufacture of one skirt is $7, and the QPAI from one blouse is a negative $3. What amount of QPAI is available to Green for calculating the PAD?

46. In 2006, Rose, Inc., has QPAI of $2 million and taxable income of $1 million. Since Rose outsources much of its work to independent contractors, its W–2 wage base is only $600,000. Calculate any PAD for this company. What suggestions might you make to enable Rose to increase its PAD?

Decision Making

47. Sam and Sally, his spouse, file a joint return. They have five dependent children. For 2006, they have the following items:

Salaries	$60,000
Interest income	5,000
Casualty loss (after $100 reduction)	70,000
Other itemized deductions	21,000

a. Determine Sam and Sally's taxable income for 2006.

b. Determine Sam and Sally's NOL for 2006.

48. Mary, a single taxpayer with two dependent children, has the following items of income and expense during 2006:

Gross receipts from business	$144,000
Business expenses	180,000
Alimony received	22,000
Interest income	40,000
Itemized deductions (no casualty or theft)	28,000

a. Determine Mary's taxable income for 2006.

b. Determine Mary's NOL for 2006.

49. Gus, who is married and files a joint return, owns a grocery store. In 2006, his gross sales were $276,000, and operating expenses were $320,000. Other items on his 2006 return were as follows:

Nonbusiness capital gains (short term)	$20,000
Nonbusiness capital losses (long term)	9,000
Itemized deductions (no casualty or theft)	18,000
Ordinary nonbusiness income	8,000
Salary from part-time job	10,000

During the year 2004, Gus had no taxable income. In 2005, Gus had taxable income of $22,700 computed as follows:

Net business income	$ 60,000
Interest income	2,000
Adjusted gross income	$ 62,000
Less: Itemized deductions	
Charitable contributions of $40,000, limited to 50% of AGI	$31,000
Medical expenses of $6,550, limited to the amount in excess of 7.5% of AGI ($6,550 − $4,650)	1,900
Total itemized deductions	(32,900)
Exemptions (2 × $3,200)	(6,400)
Taxable income	$ 22,700

a. What is Gus's 2006 NOL?
b. Determine Gus's recomputed taxable income for 2005.
c. Determine the amount of Gus's 2006 NOL to be carried forward to 2007.

50. During 2006, Rick and his wife, Sara, had the following items of income and expense to report:

Gross receipts from business	$400,000
Business expenses	525,000
Interest income from bank savings accounts	8,000
Sara's salary	50,000
Long-term capital gain on stock held as an investment	4,000
Itemized deductions (no casualty or theft)	15,000

a. Assuming Rick and Sara file a joint return, what is their taxable income for 2006?
b. What is the amount of Rick and Sara's NOL for 2006?

51. Assume that in addition to the information in Problem 50, Rick and Sara had no taxable income for the year 2004 and $5,300 of taxable income for 2005 computed as follows:

Salary	$ 25,000
Capital loss	(1,000)
Adjusted gross income	$ 24,000
Less: Itemized deductions	
Charitable contributions of $20,000, limited to 50% of AGI	$12,000
Medical expenses of $2,100, limited to the amount in excess of 7.5% of AGI ($2,100 − $1,800)	300
Total itemized deductions	(12,300)
Exemptions (2 × $3,200)	(6,400)
Taxable income	$ 5,300

a. Determine Rick and Sara's recomputed taxable income for 2005.
b. Determine the amount of Rick and Sara's 2006 NOL to be carried forward to 2007.

52. Robert and Susan Reid had an NOL of $30,000 in 2006. They had no taxable income for the year 2004 and $15,850 of taxable income for 2005 computed as follows:

Communications

Salary	$ 50,000
Capital loss	(4,000)
Adjusted gross income	$ 46,000
Less: Itemized deductions	
Charitable contributions of $24,000, limited to 50% of AGI	$23,000
Medical expenses of $4,200, limited to the amount in excess of 7.5% of AGI ($4,200 − $3,450)	750
Total itemized deductions	(23,750)
Exemptions (2 × $3,200)	(6,400)
Taxable income	$ 15,850

Write a letter to Robert and Susan informing them of the amount of the remaining NOL to be carried forward if the loss is applied against the 2005 taxable income. Also, prepare a memo for the tax files. Their address is 201 Jerdone Avenue, Conway, SC 29526.

53. Pete and Polly are married and file a joint return. They had the following income and deductions for 2006:

Salary	$50,000
Interest from savings account	5,000
Itemized deductions	8,000
2005 NOL carried to 2006	60,000

   a. What is Pete and Polly's taxable income for 2006?
   b. What is Pete and Polly's NOL for 2006?
   c. What is Pete and Polly's NOL to be carried to 2007?

54. Soong, single and age 32, had the following items for the tax year 2006:

   • Salary of $30,000.
   • Interest income from U.S. government bonds of $2,000.
   • Dividends from a foreign corporation of $500.
   • Sale of small business § 1244 stock on October 20, 2006, for $20,000. The stock had been acquired two years earlier for $65,000.
   • Business bad debt of $4,000.
   • Nonbusiness bad debt of $5,000.
   • Sale of small business § 1244 stock on November 12, 2006, for $4,000. The stock had been acquired on June 5, 2006, for $800.
   • Sale of preferred stock on December 4, 2006, for $40,000. The stock was acquired four years ago for $18,000.
   • Total itemized deductions of $20,000 (no casualty or theft).

   a. Determine Soong's NOL for 2006.
   b. Assuming Soong has had taxable income for each of the last five years, determine the carryback year to which the 2006 NOL should be applied.

55. Nell, single and age 38, had the following income and expense items in 2006:

Nonbusiness bad debt	$ 6,000
Business bad debt	2,000
Nonbusiness long-term capital gain	4,000
Nonbusiness short-term capital loss	3,000
Salary	40,000
Interest income	1,000

   Determine Nell's AGI for 2006.

56. Assume that in addition to the information in Problem 55, Nell had the following items in 2006:

Personal casualty gain on an asset held for four months	$10,000
Personal casualty loss on an asset held for two years	1,000

   Determine Nell's AGI for 2006.

57. Assume that in addition to the information in Problems 55 and 56, Nell had the following items in 2006:

Personal casualty loss on an asset held for five years	$60,000
Interest expense on home mortgage	5,000

   Determine Nell's taxable income and NOL for 2006.

58. Jed, age 55, is married with no children. During 2006, Jed had the following income and expense items:
   a. Three years ago, Jed loaned a friend $10,000 to help him purchase a new car. In June of the current year, Jed learned that his friend had been declared bankrupt

and had left the country. There is no possibility that Jed will ever collect any of the $10,000.

b. In April of last year, Jed purchased some stock for $5,000. In March of the current year, the company was declared bankrupt, and Jed was notified that his shares of stock were worthless.

c. Several years ago, Jed purchased some § 1244 stock for $120,000. This year, he sold the stock for $30,000.

d. In July of this year, Jed sold some land that he had held for two years for $60,000. He had originally paid $42,000 for the land.

e. Jed received $40,000 of interest income from State of Minnesota bonds.

f. In September, Jed's home was damaged by an earthquake. Jed's basis in his home was $430,000. The value of the home immediately before the quake was $610,000. After the quake, the home was worth $540,000. Because earthquake damage was an exclusion on Jed's homeowner's insurance policy, he received no insurance recovery.

g. Jed received a salary of $80,000.

h. Jed made a charitable contribution of $4,000.

If Jed files a joint return for 2006, determine his NOL for the year.

CUMULATIVE PROBLEMS

Tax Return Problem

Decision Making

Communications

TurboTax ✓

59. Jane Smith, age 40, is single and has no dependents. She is employed as a legal secretary by Legal Services, Inc. She owns and operates Typing Services located near the campus of Florida Atlantic University at 1986 Campus Drive. Jane is a material participant in the business. She is a cash basis taxpayer. Jane lives at 2020 Oakcrest Road, Boca Raton, FL 33431. Jane's Social Security number is 123–89–6666. Jane indicates that she wishes to designate $3 to the Presidential Election Campaign Fund. During 2005, Jane had the following income and expense items:

a. $50,000 salary from Legal Services, Inc.

b. $20,000 gross receipts from her typing services business.

c. $700 interest income from Acme National Bank.

d. $1,000 Christmas bonus from Legal Services, Inc.

e. $60,000 life insurance proceeds on the death of her sister.

f. $5,000 check given to her by her wealthy aunt.

g. $100 won in a bingo game.

h. Expenses connected with the typing service:

Office rent	$7,000
Supplies	4,400
Utilities and telephone	4,680
Wages to part-time typists	5,000
Payroll taxes	500
Equipment rentals	3,000

i. $8,346 interest expense on a home mortgage (paid to San Jose Savings and Loan).

j. $5,000 fair market value of silverware stolen from her home by a burglar on October 12, 2005. Jane had paid $4,000 for the silverware on July 1, 1996. She was reimbursed $1,500 by her insurance company.

k. Jane had loaned $2,100 to a friend, Joan Jensen, on June 3, 2002. Joan declared bankruptcy on August 14, 2005, and was unable to repay the loan. Assume the loan is a bona fide debt.

l. Legal Services, Inc., withheld Federal income tax of $7,500 and FICA tax of $3,551 {Social Security tax of $2,878 [($51,000 − $4,580) × 6.2%] + Medicare tax of $673 [($51,000 − $4,580) × 1.45%]}.

m. Alimony of $10,000 received from her former husband, Ted Smith.

n. Interest income of $800 on City of Boca Raton bonds.

o. Jane made estimated Federal tax payments of $1,000.

p. Sales taxes from the sales tax table of $654.

q. Charitable contributions of $2,500.

Part 1—Tax Computation

Compute Jane Smith's 2005 Federal income tax payable (or refund due). If you use tax forms for your computations, you will need Forms 1040 and 4684 and Schedules A, C, and D. Suggested software: TurboTax.

Part 2—Tax Planning

In 2006, Jane plans to continue her job with Legal Services, Inc. Therefore, items a, d, and l will recur in 2006. Jane plans to continue her typing services business (refer to item b) and expects gross receipts of $26,000. She projects that all business expenses (refer to item h) will increase by 10%, except for office rent, which, under the terms of her lease, will remain the same as in 2005. Items e, f, g, j, and k will not recur in 2006. Items c, i, m, n, p, and q will be approximately the same as in 2005.

Jane would like you to compute the minimum amount of estimated tax she will have to pay for 2006 so that she will not have to pay any additional tax upon filing her 2006 Federal income tax return. Write a letter to Jane that contains your advice and prepare a memo for the tax files.

60. Alan Rice, age 45, and his wife, Ruth, live at 230 Wood Lane, Salt Lake City, UT 84201. Alan's Social Security number is 885–33–3774. Ruth's Social Security number is 885–33–4985. Alan and Ruth had the following items for the year 2006:

Tax Return Problem

- Salary of $70,000.
- Nonbusiness bad debt of $10,000.
- Sale of § 1244 stock resulting in a gain of $25,000. The stock was acquired nine months earlier.
- Rental income of $35,000.
- Rental expenses of $31,000.
- Casualty loss on rental property of $8,000.
- Personal casualty loss (from one event) of $23,000.
- Other itemized deductions of $15,000.
- NOL carryover from 2005 of $18,000.
- Federal income tax withheld of $3,600.

Compute Alan and Ruth's 2006 Federal income tax payable (or refund due).

RESEARCH PROBLEMS

Note: Solutions to Research Problems can be prepared by using the **RIA Checkpoint®** **Student Edition** online research product, which is available to accompany this text. It is also possible to prepare solutions to the Research Problems by using tax research materials found in a standard tax library.

THOMSON
RIA ™

Research Problem 1. During 2006, John was the chief executive officer and a shareholder of Maze, Inc. He owned 60% of the outstanding stock of Maze. In 2003, John and Maze, as co-borrowers, obtained a $100,000 loan from United National Bank. This loan was secured by John's personal residence. Though Maze was listed as a co-borrower, John repaid the loan in full in 2006. On Maze's Form 1120 tax returns, no loans from shareholders were reported. Discuss whether John is entitled to a bad debt deduction for the amount of the payment on the loan.

Partial list of research aids:
U.S. v. Generes, 405 U.S. 93 (1972).
Dale H. Sundby, T.C.Memo. 2003–204.
Arrigoni v. Comm., 73 T.C. 792 (1980).
Estate of Herbert M. Rapoport, T.C.Memo. 1982–584.
Clifford L. Brody and Barbara J. DeClerk, T.C. Summary Opinion, 2004–149.

Research Problem 2. Jed Johnson is the owner and president of Teal Bank. One day last year, he was having lunch with Hal Smith, a customer of the bank. During the conversation, Jed learned that Hal was interested in trying to acquire a particular line of business. Jed knew of such a business and shared this information with Hal. Hal contacted the owners of the business and eventually acquired the company. Early this year, Hal sent Jed a check for $25,000 as a "finder's fee" for helping him locate the company that he acquired.

For the current year, Jed has a business loss of $40,000 that he wants to carry back and apply against previous years' income. He also has itemized deductions, none arising from casualty or theft losses, of $20,000. Discuss how the "finder's fee" should be treated and what effect it will have on any potential NOL carryback.

Communications

Research Problem 3.   Jeb Simmons operated an illegal gambling business out of his home. While executing a search warrant, the local sheriff seized gambling paraphernalia and $200,000 in cash. Subsequently, Jeb voluntarily consented to forfeit to the state the cash that had been seized in connection with the execution of the search warrant. Write a letter to Jeb advising him as to whether he can claim a loss under § 165 for the seized cash. Also, prepare a memo for the tax files. Jeb's address is 100 Honey Lane, Macon, GA 62108.

Research Problem 4.   James Morgan invested $40,000 in a company that issued him a short-term promissory note bearing an interest rate of 28%. Unbeknownst to James, the company was part of a pyramid scheme. During the current year, James was notified that he had lost his entire investment. Evaluate the possibility of James claiming a theft loss on his current year's tax return.

Research Problem 5.   Rocky Sole, Inc., is in the business of designing, developing, manufacturing, and selling hiking boots. The company's design department activities relate to the design, development, modification, and improvement of Rocky Sole's hiking boots. The department produces drawings containing ideas for new products or improvements on existing products. When agreement is reached on a new design, the department evaluates the appropriate manufacturing process. The design department does no internal testing to determine how the hiking boots will perform. Evaluate the possibility of Rocky Sole, Inc., claiming all of the costs incurred by the design department as research and experimental expenditures under § 174.

 Internet *Activity*

Use the tax resources of the Internet to address the following questions. Do not restrict your search to the World Wide Web, but include a review of newsgroups and general reference materials, practitioner sites and resources, primary sources of the tax law, chat rooms and discussion groups, and other opportunities.

Research Problem 6.   Find a newspaper article that discusses tax planning for casualty losses when a disaster area designation is made. Does the article convey the pertinent tax rules correctly? Then list all of the locations identified by the President as Federal disaster areas in the last two years.

Communications

Research Problem 7.   Scan several publications that are read by owners of small businesses. Some of the articles in these publications address tax-related issues such as how to structure a new business. Do these articles do an adequate job of conveying the benefits of issuing § 1244 small business stock? Prepare a short memo explaining the use of § 1244 stock and post it to a newsgroup that is frequented by inventors, engineers, and others involved in startup corporations.

http://wft.swlearning.com

CHAPTER 8

Depreciation, Cost Recovery, Amortization, and Depletion

LEARNING OBJECTIVES

After completing Chapter 8, you should be able to:

LO.1
Understand the rationale for the cost consumption concept and identify the relevant time periods for depreciation, ACRS, and MACRS.

LO.2
Determine the amount of cost recovery under MACRS.

LO.3
Recognize when and how to make the § 179 expensing election, calculate the amount of the deduction, and apply the effect of the election in making the MACRS calculation.

LO.4
Identify listed property and apply the deduction limitations on listed property and on luxury automobiles.

LO.5
Determine when and how to use the alternative depreciation system (ADS).

LO.6
Be aware of the major characteristics of ACRS.

LO.7
Identify intangible assets that are eligible for amortization and calculate the amount of the deduction.

LO.8
Determine the amount of depletion expense including being able to apply the alternative tax treatments for intangible drilling and development costs.

LO.9
Perform the reporting procedures for cost recovery.

LO.10
Identify tax planning opportunities for cost recovery, amortization, and depletion.

OUTLINE

LO.1

Understand the rationale for the cost consumption concept and identify the relevant time periods for depreciation, ACRS, and MACRS.

Overview

General

The Internal Revenue Code provides for a deduction for the consumption of the cost of an asset through depreciation, cost recovery, amortization, or depletion. These deductions are applications of the recovery of capital doctrine (discussed in Chapter 4). The concept of depreciation is based on the premise that the asset acquired (or improvement made) benefits more than one accounting period. Otherwise, the expenditure is deducted in the year incurred—see Chapter 6 and the discussion of capitalization versus expense.

Congress completely overhauled the **depreciation** rules in 1981 tax legislation by creating the accelerated **cost recovery** system (ACRS). Substantial modifications were made to ACRS in 1986 tax legislation (MACRS). These changes to the depreciation rules and the time frames involved are noted in Concept Summary 8–1. A knowledge of all of the depreciation and cost recovery rules may be needed as Example 1 illustrates for cost recovery.

EXAMPLE 1

The Brown Company owns a building purchased in 1986 that has a 19-year cost recovery life. In 2005, the business purchased a computer. To compute the cost recovery for 2005, Brown used the ACRS rules for the building and the MACRS rules for the computer. For 2006, there would be no additional cost recovery for the building because the basis of the building at the beginning of 2006 would be $0. ∎

The statutory changes that have taken place since 1980 have widened the gap that exists between the accounting and tax versions of depreciation. The tax rules that existed prior to 1981 were much more compatible with generally accepted accounting principles.

This chapter initially focuses on the MACRS rules.[1] Because they cover more recent property acquisitions (i.e., after 1986), their use is more widespread. The ACRS rules, however, are reviewed in Concept Summary 8–5 and briefly discussed on page 8–18. The pre-1981 rules are covered in Appendix H. The chapter concludes with a discussion of the amortization of intangible property and startup expenditures and the depletion of natural resources.

Taxpayers may write off the cost of certain assets that are used in a trade or business or held for the production of income. A write-off may take the form of

---

[1]§ 168. The terms "depreciation" and "cost recovery" are used interchangeably in the text and in § 168.

CONCEPT SUMMARY 8–1

Depreciation and Cost Recovery: Relevant Time Periods

System	Date Property Is Placed in Service
Pre-1981 depreciation	Before January 1, 1981, and *certain* property placed in service after December 31, 1980.
Original accelerated cost recovery system (ACRS)	After December 31, 1980, and before January 1, 1987.
Modified accelerated cost recovery system (MACRS)	After December 31, 1986.

depreciation (or cost recovery), depletion, or amortization. Tangible assets, other than natural resources, are *depreciated*. Natural resources, such as oil, gas, coal, and timber, are *depleted*. Intangible assets, such as copyrights and patents, are *amortized*. Generally, no write-off is allowed for an asset that does not have a determinable useful life.

Concepts Relating to Depreciation

Nature of Property. Property includes both realty (real property) and personalty (personal property). Realty generally includes land and buildings permanently affixed to the land. Personalty is defined as any asset that is not realty.[2] Personalty includes furniture, machinery, equipment, and many other types of assets. Do not confuse personalty (or personal property) with *personal use* property. Personal use property is any property (realty or personalty) that is held for personal use rather than for use in a trade or business or an income-producing activity. Write-offs are not allowed for personal use assets.

[handwritten margin note: personalty ≠ personal use property]

In summary, both realty and personalty can be either business use/income-producing property or personal use property. Examples include a residence (realty that is personal use), an office building (realty that is business use), a dump truck (personalty that is business use), and regular wearing apparel (personalty that is personal use). It is imperative that this distinction between the *classification* of an asset (realty or personalty) and the *use* to which the asset is put (business or personal) be understood.

Assets used in a trade or business or for the production of income are eligible for cost recovery if they are subject to wear and tear, decay or decline from natural causes, or obsolescence. Assets that do not decline in value on a predictable basis or that do not have a determinable useful life (e.g., land, stock, antiques) are not eligible for cost recovery.

Placed in Service Requirement. The key date for the commencement of depreciation is the date an asset is placed in service. This date, and not the purchase date of an asset, is the relevant date. This distinction is particularly important for an asset that is purchased near the end of the tax year, but not placed in service until after the beginning of the following tax year.

Cost Recovery Allowed or Allowable. The basis of cost recovery property must be reduced by the cost recovery allowed and by not less than the allowable amount. The *allowed* cost recovery is the cost recovery actually taken, whereas the *allowable* cost recovery is the amount that could have been taken under the

---

[2]Refer to Chapter 1 for a further discussion.

applicable cost recovery method. If the taxpayer does not claim any cost recovery on property during a particular year, the basis of the property must still be reduced by the amount of cost recovery that should have been deducted (the allowable cost recovery).

EXAMPLE 2

On March 15, Jack paid $10,000 for a copier to be used in his business. The copier is five-year property. Jack elected to use the straight-line method of cost recovery, but did not take cost recovery in years 3 or 4. Therefore, the allowed cost recovery (cost recovery actually deducted) and the allowable cost recovery are as follows:

	Cost Recovery Allowed	Cost Recovery Allowable
Year 1	$1,000	$1,000
Year 2	2,000	2,000
Year 3	–0–	2,000
Year 4	–0–	2,000
Year 5	2,000	2,000
Year 6	1,000	1,000

If Jack sold the copier for $800 in year 7, he would recognize an $800 gain ($800 amount realized – $0 adjusted basis) because the adjusted basis of the copier is zero. ■

Cost Recovery Basis for Personal Use Assets Converted to Business or Income-Producing Use.
If personal use assets are converted to business or income-producing use, the basis for cost recovery and for loss is the _lower_ of the adjusted basis or the fair market value at the time the property was converted. As a result of this lower-of-basis rule, losses that occurred while the property was personal use property will not be recognized for tax purposes through the cost recovery of the property.

EXAMPLE 3

Hans acquires a personal residence for $120,000. Four years later, when the fair market value is only $100,000, he converts the property to rental use. The basis for cost recovery is $100,000, since the fair market value is less than the adjusted basis. The $20,000 decline in value is deemed to be personal (since it occurred while the property was held for personal use) and therefore nondeductible. ■

LO.2

Determine the amount of cost recovery under MACRS.

Modified Accelerated Cost Recovery System (MACRS)

Under the **modified accelerated cost recovery system (MACRS)**, the cost of an asset is recovered over a predetermined period that is generally shorter than the useful life of the asset or the period the asset is used to produce income. The MACRS rules were designed to encourage investment, improve productivity, and simplify the law and its administration.

MACRS provides separate cost recovery tables for realty (real property) and personalty (personal property). Write-offs are not available for land because it does not have a determinable useful life. Cost recovery allowances for real property, other than land, are based on recovery lives specified in the law. The IRS provides tables that specify cost recovery allowances for personalty and for realty.

TAX INCENTIVES FOR THE TEXTILE INDUSTRY IN INDIA

The Indian Finance Ministry announced that it will retain the special depreciation benefits for textile machinery installed under the Technology Upgradation Fund Scheme (TUFS). The intent is to build the capacity of the textile industry. The incentive allows 50 percent depreciation in the first year the machinery is in service.

Source: *Adapted from "Depreciation Benefits under TUFS to Continue for Textile Sector,"* The Indian Express Online Media Ltd., *March 31, 2005.*

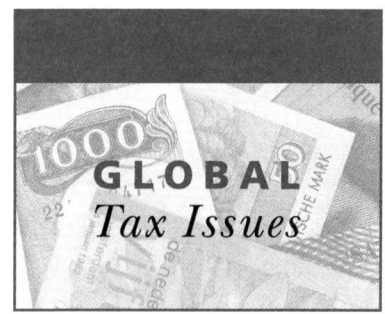

GLOBAL
Tax Issues

Personalty: Recovery Periods and Methods

Classification of Property. The general effect of TRA of 1986 was to lengthen asset lives compared to those used under ACRS. MACRS provides that the cost recovery basis of eligible personalty (and certain realty) is recovered over 3, 5, 7, 10, 15, or 20 years. Property is classified by recovery period under MACRS as follows (see Exhibit 8–1 for examples):[3]

3-year 200% class ...... ADR midpoints of 4 years and less.[4] Excludes automobiles and light trucks. Includes racehorses more than 2 years old and other horses more than 12 years old.

5-year 200% class ...... ADR midpoints of more than 4 years and less than 10 years, adding automobiles, light trucks, qualified technological equipment, renewable energy and biomass properties that are small power production facilities, research and experimentation property, semiconductor manufacturing equipment, and computer-based central office switching equipment.

7-year 200% class ...... ADR midpoints of 10 years and more and less than 16 years, adding property with no ADR midpoint not classified elsewhere. Includes railroad track and office furniture, fixtures, and equipment.

10-year 200% class ..... ADR midpoints of 16 years and more and less than 20 years, adding single-purpose agricultural or horticultural structures, any tree or vine bearing fruits or nuts.

15-year 150% class ..... ADR midpoints of 20 years and more and less than 25 years, including sewage treatment plants, and telephone distribution plants and comparable equipment used for the two-way exchange of voice and data communications.

20-year 150% class ..... ADR midpoints of 25 years and more, other than real property with an ADR midpoint of 27.5 years and more, and including sewer pipes.

---

[3]§ 168(e).   [4]Rev.Proc. 87–56, 1987–2 C.B. 674 is the source for the ADR midpoint lives.

EXHIBIT 8–1	Cost Recovery Periods: MACRS Personalty

Class of Property	Examples
3-year	Tractor units for use over-the-road.
	Any horse that is not a racehorse and is more than 12 years old at the time it is placed in service.
	Any racehorse that is more than 2 years old at the time it is placed in service.
	Breeding hogs.
	Special tools used in the manufacturing of motor vehicles such as dies, fixtures, molds, and patterns.
5-year	Automobiles and taxis.
	Light and heavy general-purpose trucks.
	Buses.
	Trailers and trailer-mounted containers.
	Typewriters, calculators, and copiers.
	Computers and peripheral equipment.
	Breeding and dairy cattle.
	Rental appliances, furniture, carpets, etc.
7-year	Office furniture, fixtures, and equipment.
	Breeding and work horses.
	Agricultural machinery and equipment.
	Railroad track.
10-year	Vessels, barges, tugs, and similar water transportation equipment.
	Assets used for petroleum refining or for the manufacture of grain and grain mill products, sugar and sugar products, or vegetable oils and vegetable oil products.
	Single-purpose agricultural or horticultural structures.
15-year	Land improvements.
	Assets used for industrial steam and electric generation and/or distribution systems.
	Assets used in the manufacture of cement.
	Assets used in pipeline transportation.
	Electric utility nuclear production plant.
	Municipal wastewater treatment plant.
20-year	Farm buildings except single-purpose agricultural and horticultural structures.
	Gas utility distribution facilities.
	Water utilities.
	Municipal sewer.

Accelerated depreciation is allowed for these six MACRS classes of property. Two hundred percent declining-balance is used for the 3-, 5-, 7-, and 10-year classes, with a switchover to straight-line depreciation when it yields a larger amount. One hundred and fifty percent declining-balance is allowed for the 15- and 20-year classes, with an appropriate straight-line switchover.[5] The appropriate computation methods and conventions are built into the tables, so it is not necessary to calculate the appropriate percentages. To determine the amount of the cost recovery allowances, simply identify the asset by class and go to the appropriate table for the percentage. The MACRS percentages for personalty appear in Table 8–1 (*all tables are located at the end of the chapter prior to the Problem Materials*).

Taxpayers may *elect* the straight-line method to compute cost recovery allowances for each of these classes of property. Certain property is not eligible for accelerated cost recovery and must be depreciated under an alternative depreciation system (ADS). Both the straight-line election and ADS are discussed later in the chapter.

MACRS views property as placed in service in the middle of the first year (the **half-year convention**).[6] Thus, for example, the statutory recovery period for three-year property begins in the middle of the year an asset is placed in service and ends three years later. In practical terms, this means that taxpayers must wait an extra year to recover the cost of depreciable assets. That is, the actual write-off periods are 4, 6, 8, 11, 16, and 21 years. MACRS also allows for a half-year of cost recovery in the year of disposition or retirement.

EXAMPLE 4

Kareem acquires a five-year class asset on April 10, 2006, for $30,000. Kareem's cost recovery deduction for 2006 is $6,000, computed as follows:

MACRS cost recovery
  [$30,000 × .20 (Table 8–1)] $6,000   ∎

EXAMPLE 5

Assume the same facts as in Example 4 and that Kareem disposes of the asset on March 5, 2008. Kareem's cost recovery deduction for 2008 is $2,880 [$30,000 × ½ × .192 (Table 8–1)]. ∎

Disposed year
⇒ ½ of year
⇒ × ½

Mid-Quarter Convention. If more than 40 percent of the value of property other than eligible real estate (see Realty: Recovery Periods and Methods for a discussion of eligible real estate) is placed in service during the last quarter of the year, a **mid-quarter convention** applies.[7] Under this convention, property acquisitions are grouped by the quarter they were acquired for cost recovery purposes. Acquisitions during the first quarter are allowed 10.5 months of cost recovery; the second quarter, 7.5 months; the third quarter, 4.5 months; and the fourth quarter, 1.5 months. The percentages are shown in Table 8–2.

---

[5]§ 168(b).
[6]§ 168(d)(4)(A).

[7]§ 168(d)(3).

EXAMPLE 6

Silver Corporation acquires the following five-year class property in 2006:

Property Acquisition Dates	Cost
February 15	$ 200,000
July 10	400,000
December 5	600,000
Total	$1,200,000

If Silver Corporation uses the statutory percentage method, the cost recovery allowances for the first two years are computed as indicated below. Since more than 40% ($600,000/$1,200,000 = 50%) of the acquisitions are in the last quarter, the mid-quarter convention applies.

2006

	Mid-Quarter Convention Depreciation	Total Depreciation
February 15	$200,000 × .35 (Table 8–2)	$ 70,000
July 10	$400,000 × .15	60,000
December 5	$600,000 × .05	30,000
		$160,000

2007

	Mid-Quarter Convention Depreciation	Total Depreciation
February 15	$200,000 × .26 (Table 8–2)	$ 52,000
July 10	$400,000 × .34	136,000
December 5	$600,000 × .38	228,000
		$416,000

When property to which the mid-quarter convention applies is disposed of, the property is treated as though it were disposed of at the midpoint of the quarter. Hence, in the quarter of disposition, cost recovery is allowed for one-half of the quarter.

EXAMPLE 7

Assume the same facts as in Example 6, except that Silver Corporation sells the $400,000 asset on November 30 of 2007. The cost recovery allowance for 2007 is computed as follows:

February 15	$200,000 × .26 (Table 8–2)	$ 52,000
July 10	$400,000 × .34 × (3.5/4)	119,000
December 5	$600,000 × .38	228,000
Total		$399,000

Realty: Recovery Periods and Methods

Under MACRS, the cost recovery period for residential rental real estate is 27.5 years, and the straight-line method is used for computing the cost recovery allowance. **Residential rental real estate** includes property where 80 percent or more of the gross rental revenues are from nontransient dwelling units (e.g., an apartment building).

CONCEPT SUMMARY **8–2**

Statutory Percentage Method under MACRS

	Personal Property	Real Property*
Convention	Half-year or mid-quarter	Mid-month
Cost recovery deduction in the year of disposition	Half-year for year of disposition or half-quarter for quarter of disposition	Half-month for month of disposition

*Straight-line method must be used.

Hotels, motels, and similar establishments are not residential rental property. Low-income housing is classified as residential rental real estate. Nonresidential real estate has a recovery period of 39 years (31.5 years for such property placed in service before May 13, 1993) and is also depreciated using the straight-line method.[8]

Some items of real property are not treated as real estate for purposes of MACRS. For example, single-purpose agricultural structures are in the 10-year MACRS class. Land improvements are in the 15-year MACRS class.

All eligible real estate is depreciated using the **mid-month convention**. Regardless of when during the month the property is placed in service, it is deemed to have been placed in service at the middle of the month. This allows for one-half month's cost recovery for the month the property is placed in service. If the property is disposed of before the end of the recovery period, one-half month's cost recovery is permitted for the month of disposition regardless of the specific date of disposition.

Cost recovery is computed by multiplying the applicable rate (Table 8–6) by the cost recovery basis.

[handwritten: 93 → '06 = 13 yrs]

[handwritten: non residential]

Alec acquired a building on April 1, 1993, for $800,000. If the building is classified as residential rental real estate, the cost recovery allowance for 2006 is $29,088 (.03636 × $800,000). If the building is classified as nonresidential real estate, the 2006 cost recovery allowance is $25,400 (.03175 × $800,000). (See Table 8–6 for percentages.) ∎

EXAMPLE 8

[handwritten: why not 3.175 b/t 1986 & 5/93 ?]

Assume the same facts as in Example 8, except that Alec acquired the nonresidential building on November 19, 2006. The 2006 cost recovery allowance is $2,568 [$800,000 × .00321 (Table 8–6)]. ∎

EXAMPLE 9

ETHICAL *Considerations*   **PROPER CLASSIFICATION OF REAL PROPERTY**

Joan owns an apartment building containing eight essentially identical apartment units. Joan lives in one of the apartments and leases the other seven to tenants who use the apartments as dwelling units. The apartment that Joan occupies has 1,200 square feet of space. Joan uses 200 square feet of the apartment for a home office for her business. Joan satisfies the requirements of § 280A for deduction of the expenses of a home office including expenses for deprecia-

tion. Joan understands that a home office usually has a cost recovery period of 39 years because a home is not classified as residential rental property. However, she reasons that because her apartment building meets the 80 percent gross rental income test, she is entitled to compute the cost recovery on her home office using a cost recovery period of 27.5 years. Evaluate Joan's plan.

---

[8]§§ 168(b), (c), and (e).

Straight-Line Election

Although MACRS requires straight-line depreciation for all eligible real estate as previously discussed, the taxpayer may *elect* to use the straight-line method for personal property.[9] The property is depreciated using the class life (recovery period) of the asset with a half-year convention or a mid-quarter convention, whichever is applicable. The election is available on a class-by-class and year-by-year basis. The percentages for the straight-line election with a half-year convention appear in Table 8–3.

EXAMPLE 10

Terry acquires a 10-year class asset on August 4, 2006, for $100,000. He elects the straight-line method of cost recovery. Terry's cost recovery deduction for 2006 is $5,000 ($100,000 × .050). His cost recovery deduction for 2007 is $10,000 ($100,000 × .100). (See Table 8–3 for percentages.) ■

LO.3

Recognize when and how to make the § 179 expensing election, calculate the amount of the deduction, and apply the effect of the election in making the MACRS calculation.

Election to Expense Assets

Section 179 (Election to Expense Certain Depreciable Business Assets) permits the taxpayer to elect to write off up to $108,000 in 2006 ($105,000 in 2005) of the acquisition cost of *tangible personal property* used in a trade or business. Amounts that are expensed under § 179 may not be capitalized and depreciated. The **§ 179 expensing** election is an annual election and applies to the acquisition cost of property placed in service that year. The immediate expense election is not available for real property or for property used for the production of income.[10] The base for calculating the standard MACRS deduction is net of the § 179 expense.

EXAMPLE 11

Kelly acquires machinery (five-year class asset) on February 1, 2006, at a cost of $152,000 and elects to expense $108,000 under § 179. Kelly also takes the statutory percentage cost recovery (see Table 8–1 for percentage) for 2006. As a result, the total deduction for the year is calculated as follows:

§ 179 expense	$108,000
Standard MACRS calculation	
[($152,000 − $108,000) × .20]	8,800
	$116,800

■

Annual Limitations. Two additional limitations apply to the amount deductible under § 179. First, the ceiling amount on the deduction is reduced dollar-for-dollar when property (other than eligible real estate) placed in service during the taxable year exceeds $430,000 in 2006 ($420,000 in 2005). Second, the amount expensed under § 179 cannot exceed the aggregate amount of taxable income derived from the conduct of any trade or business by the taxpayer. Taxable income of a trade or business is computed without regard to the amount expensed under § 179. Any § 179 expensed amount in excess of taxable income is carried forward to future taxable years and added to other amounts eligible for expensing. The § 179 amount eligible for expensing in a carryforward year is limited to the *lesser* of (1) the statutory dollar amount ($108,000 in 2006) reduced by the cost of § 179 property placed in service in excess of $430,000 in the carryforward year or (2) the business income limitation in the carryforward year.

---

[9]§ 168(b)(5).

[10]§§ 179(b) and (d). The § 179 amount allowed is per taxpayer, per year. On a joint return, the statutory amount applies to the couple. If the taxpayers are married and file separate returns, each spouse is eligible for 50% of the statutory amount.

CONCEPT SUMMARY $8\text{-}3$

Straight-Line Election under MACRS

	Personal Property	Real Property*
Convention	Half-year or mid-quarter	Mid-month
Cost recovery deduction in the year of disposition	Half-year for year of disposition or half-quarter for quarter of disposition	Half-month for month of disposition
Elective or mandatory	Elective	Mandatory
Breadth of election	Class by class	

*Straight-line method must be used.

EXAMPLE 12

Jill owns a computer service and operates it as a sole proprietorship. In 2006, she will net $11,000 before considering any § 179 deduction. If Jill spends $491,000 on new equipment, her § 179 expense deduction is computed as follows:

§ 179 deduction before adjustment	$108,000
Less: Dollar limitation reduction ($491,000 − $430,000)	(61,000)
Remaining § 179 deduction	$ 47,000
Business income limitation	$ 11,000
§ 179 deduction allowed	$ 11,000
§ 179 deduction carryforward ($47,000 − $11,000)	$ 36,000	■

Effect on Basis. The basis of the property for cost recovery purposes is reduced by the § 179 amount after it is adjusted for property placed in service in excess of $430,000. This adjusted amount does not reflect any business income limitation.

EXAMPLE 13

Assume the same facts as in Example 12 and that the new equipment is five-year class property. After considering the § 179 deduction, Jill's cost recovery deduction for 2006 (see Table 8–1 for percentage) is calculated as follows:

Standard MACRS calculation
   [($491,000 − $47,000) × 20] $88,800   ■

Conversion to Personal Use. Conversion of the expensed property to personal use at any time results in recapture income (see Chapter 17). A property is converted to personal use if it is not used predominantly in a trade or business. Regulations provide for the mechanics of the recapture.[11]

Business and Personal Use of Automobiles and Other Listed Property

> **LO.4**
>
> Identify listed property and apply the deduction limitations on listed property and on luxury automobiles.

Limits exist on MACRS deductions for automobiles and other listed property that are used for both personal and business purposes.[12] If the listed property is *predominantly used* for business, the taxpayer is allowed to use the *statutory percentage method*

---

[11]Reg. § 1.179–1(e).   [12]§ 280F.

to recover the cost. In cases where the property is *not predominantly used* for business, the cost is recovered using the *straight-line method.*

Listed property includes the following:

- Any passenger automobile.
- Any other property used as a means of transportation.
- Any property of a type generally used for purposes of entertainment, recreation, or amusement.
- Any computer or peripheral equipment, with the exception of equipment used exclusively at a regular business establishment, including a qualifying home office.
- Any cellular telephone or other similar telecommunications equipment.
- Any other property specified in the Regulations.

Automobiles and Other Listed Property Used Predominantly in Business. For listed property to be considered as *predominantly used in business*, its *business usage* must exceed 50 percent.[13] The use of listed property for production of income does not qualify as business use for purposes of the more-than-50 percent test. However, both production of income and business use percentages are used to compute the cost recovery deduction.

EXAMPLE 14

On September 1, 2006, Emma places in service listed five-year recovery property. The property cost $10,000. If Emma uses the property 40% for business and 25% for the production of income, the property is not considered as predominantly used for business. The cost is recovered using straight-line cost recovery. Emma's cost recovery allowance for the year is $650 ($10,000 × 10% × 65%). If, however, Emma uses the property 60% for business and 25% for the production of income, the property is considered as used predominantly for business. Therefore, she may use the statutory percentage method. Emma's cost recovery allowance for the year is $1,700 ($10,000 × .200 × 85%). ■

The method for determining the percentage of business usage for listed property is specified in the Regulations. The Regulations provide that for automobiles a mileage-based percentage is to be used. Other listed property is to use the most appropriate unit of time (e.g., hours) the property is actually used (rather than available for use).[14]

Limits on Cost Recovery for Automobiles. The law places special limitations on the cost recovery deduction for passenger automobiles. These statutory dollar limits were imposed on passenger automobiles because of the belief that the tax system was being used to underwrite automobiles whose cost and luxury far exceeded what was needed for their business use.

---

[13]§ 280F(b)(3).   [14]Reg. § 1.280F–6T(e).

A *passenger automobile* is any four-wheeled vehicle manufactured for use on public streets, roads, and highways with an unloaded gross vehicle weight (GVW) rating of 6,000 pounds or less.[15] This definition specifically excludes vehicles used directly in the business of transporting people or property for compensation such as taxicabs, ambulances, hearses, and trucks and vans as prescribed by the Regulations.

The following limits apply to the cost recovery deductions for passenger automobiles for 2005:[16]

Year	Recovery Limitation*
1	$2,960
2	4,700
3	2,850
Succeeding years until the cost is recovered	1,675

*The indexed amounts for 2006 were not available at the time of this writing.

For an automobile placed in service in 2005, the limitation for subsequent years' cost recovery will be based on the limits for the year the automobile was placed in service. Hence, the limit for the third year's cost recovery for an automobile placed in service in 2005 is $2,850 and not a limit published in 2007.[17]

There are also separate cost recovery limitations for trucks and vans and for electric automobiles. Because these limitations are applied in the same manner as those imposed on passenger automobiles, these additional limitations are not discussed further in this chapter.

The limits are imposed before any percentage reduction for personal use. In addition, the limitation in the first year includes any amount the taxpayer elects to expense under § 179.[18] If the passenger automobile is used partly for personal use, the personal use percentage is ignored for the purpose of determining the unrecovered cost available for deduction in later years.

EXAMPLE 15

On July 1, 2006, Dan places in service a new automobile that cost $40,000. He does not elect § 179 expensing. The car is always used 80% for business and 20% for personal. Dan chooses the MACRS 200% declining-balance method of cost recovery (see the 5-year column in Table 8–1). The depreciation computation for 2006–2011 is summarized below:

Year	MACRS Amount	Recovery Limitation	Depreciation Allowed
2006	$6,400	$2,368	$2,368
	($40,000 × 20% × 80%)	($2,960 × 80%)	
2007	$10,240	$3,760	$3,760
	($40,000 × 32% × 80%)	($4,700 × 80%)	
2008	$6,144	$2,280	$2,280
	($40,000 × 19.2% × 80%)	($2,850 × 80%)	
2009	$3,686	$1,340	$1,340
	($40,000 × 11.52% × 80%)	($1,675 × 80%)	
2010	$3,686	$1,340	$1,340
	($40,000 × 11.52% × 80%)	($1,675 × 80%)	
2011	$1,843	$1,340	$1,340
	($40,000 × 5.76% × 80%)	($1,675 × 80%)	

[15]§ 280F(d)(5).

[16]§ 280F(a)(1). Since the 2006 indexed amounts were not available at the time of this writing, the 2005 amounts are used in the Examples and in the Problem Materials.

[17]Cost recovery limitations for prior years can be found in IRS Publication 463.

[18]§ 280F(d)(1).

The cost recovery allowed is the lesser of the MACRS amount or the recovery limitation. If Dan continues to use the car after 2011, his cost recovery is limited to the lesser of the recoverable basis or the recovery limitation (i.e., $1,675 × business use percentage). For this purpose, the recoverable basis is computed as if the full recovery limitation was allowed even if it was not. Thus, the recoverable basis as of January 1, 2012, is $24,465 ($40,000 − $2,960 − $4,700 − $2,850 − $1,675 − $1,675 − $1,675). ∎

The cost recovery limitations are maximum amounts. If the regular calculation produces a lesser amount of cost recovery, the lesser amount is used.

EXAMPLE 16

On April 2, 2006, Gail places in service a used automobile that cost $10,000. The car is always used 70% for business and 30% for personal use. Therefore, the cost recovery allowance for 2006 is $1,400 ($10,000 × 20% × 70%), which is less than $2,072 ($2,960 × 70%). ∎

Note that the cost recovery limitations apply *only* to passenger automobiles and not to other listed property.

Special Limitation. The American Jobs Creation Act of 2004 (AJCA) placed a limit on the § 179 deduction for certain vehicles not subject to the statutory dollar limits on cost recovery deductions that are imposed on passenger automobiles. This new limit is $25,000. The limit applies to sport utility vehicles with an unloaded GVW rating of more than 6,000 pounds and not more than 14,000 pounds.[19]

EXAMPLE 17

During 2006, Jay acquires and places in service a sport utility vehicle that cost $70,000 and has a GVW of 8,000 pounds. Jay uses the vehicle 100% of the time for business use. The total deduction for 2006 with respect to the SUV is $34,000, computed as follows:

§ 179 expense	$25,000
Standard MACRS calculation	
[($70,000 − $25,000) × .20 (Table 8–1)]	9,000
	$34,000

∎

Automobiles and Other Listed Property Not Used Predominantly in Business. The cost of listed property that does not pass the more-than-50 percent business usage test in the year the property is placed in service must be recovered using the straight-line method.[20] The straight-line method to be used is that required under the alternative depreciation system (explained later in the chapter). This system requires a straight-line recovery period of five years for automobiles. However, even though the straight-line method is used, the cost recovery allowance for passenger automobiles cannot exceed the dollar limitations.

Straight-line recovery is still under dollar limitations.

EXAMPLE 18

On July 27, 2006, Fred places in service an automobile that cost $20,000. The auto is used 40% for business and 60% for personal use. The cost recovery allowance for 2006 is $800 [$20,000 × 10% (Table 8–5) × 40%]. ∎

EXAMPLE 19

Assume the same facts as in Example 18, except that the automobile cost $50,000. The cost recovery allowance for 2006 is $1,184 [$50,000 × 10% (Table 8–5) = $5,000 (limited to $2,960) × 40%]. ∎ *limitation b/f ratable calc.*

If the listed property fails the more-than-50 percent business usage test, the straight-line method must be used for the remainder of the property's life. This

---

[19]§ 179(b)(6).   [20]§ 280F(b)(1).

applies even if at some later date the business usage of the property increases to more than 50 percent. Even though the straight-line method must continue to be used, however, the amount of cost recovery will reflect the increase in business usage.

EXAMPLE 20

Assume the same facts as in Example 19, except that in 2007, Fred uses the automobile 70% for business and 30% for personal use. Fred's cost recovery allowance for 2007 is $2,800 [$20,000 × 20% (Table 8–5) × 70%], which is less than 70% of the second-year limit. ∎

Change from Predominantly Business Use.

If the business use percentage of listed property falls to 50 percent or lower after the year the property is placed in service, the property is subject to *cost recovery recapture.* The amount required to be recaptured and included in the taxpayer's return as ordinary income is the excess cost recovery.

Excess cost recovery is the excess of the cost recovery deduction taken in prior years using the statutory percentage method over the amount that would have been allowed if the straight-line method had been used since the property was placed in service.[21]

EXAMPLE 21

Seth purchased a car on January 22, 2006, at a cost of $20,000. Business usage was 80% in 2006, 70% in 2007, 40% in 2008, and 60% in 2009. Seth's excess cost recovery to be recaptured as ordinary income in 2008 is computed as follows:

2006	
MACRS [($20,000 × .20 × .80) (limited to $2,960) × .80]	$ 2,368
Straight-line [($20,000 × .10 × .80) (limited to $2,960) × .80]	(1,600)
Excess	$ 768
2007	
MACRS [($10,000 × .32 × .70) (limited to $4,700) × .70]	$ 3,290
Straight-line [($20,000 × .20 × .70) (limited to $4,700) × .70]	(2,800)
Excess	$ 490
2008	
2006 excess	$ 768
2007 excess	490
Ordinary income recapture	$ 1,258

∎

After the business usage of the listed property drops below the more-than-50 percent level, the straight-line method must be used for the remaining life of the property.

EXAMPLE 22

Assume the same facts as in Example 21. Seth's cost recovery allowance for the years 2008 and 2009 would be $1,140 and $1,005, computed as follows:

2008—$1,140   [($20,000 × 20% × .40) limited to $2,850 × 40%]
2009—$1,005   [($20,000 × 20% × .60) limited to $1,675 × 60%]

∎

---

[21]§ 280F(b)(2).

Leased Automobiles. A taxpayer who leases a passenger automobile must report an *inclusion amount* in gross income. The inclusion amount is computed from an IRS table for each taxable year for which the taxpayer leases the automobile. The purpose of this provision is to prevent taxpayers from circumventing the cost recovery dollar limitations by leasing, instead of purchasing, an automobile.

The dollar amount of the inclusion is based on the fair market value of the automobile and is prorated for the number of days the auto is used during the taxable year. The prorated dollar amount is then multiplied by the business and income-producing usage percentage to determine the amount to be included in gross income.[22] The taxpayer deducts the lease payments, multiplied by the business and income-producing usage percentage. The net effect is that the annual deduction for the lease payment is reduced by the inclusion amount.

EXAMPLE 23

On April 1, 2006, Jim leases and places in service a passenger automobile worth $40,000. The lease is to be for a period of five years. During the taxable years 2006 and 2007, Jim uses the automobile 70% for business and 30% for personal use. Assuming the dollar amounts from the IRS table for 2006 and 2007 are $83 and $184, Jim must include $44 in gross income for 2006 and $129 for 2007, computed as follows:

2006	$83 × (275/365) × 70% = $44
2007	$184 × (365/365) × 70% = $129

In addition, Jim can deduct 70% of the lease payments each year because this is the business use percentage. ∎

Substantiation Requirements. Listed property is now subject to the substantiation requirements of § 274. This means that the taxpayer must prove the business usage as to the amount of expense or use, the time and place of use, the business purpose for the use, and the business relationship to the taxpayer of persons using the property. Substantiation requires adequate records or sufficient evidence corroborating the taxpayer's statement. However, these substantiation requirements do not apply to vehicles that, by reason of their nature, are not likely to be used more than a *de minimis* amount for personal purposes.[23]

---

[22]Reg. § 1.280F–7(a).   [23]§§ 274(d) and (i).

Alternative Depreciation System (ADS)

LO.5

Determine when and how to use the alternative depreciation system (ADS).

The alternative depreciation system (ADS) must be used for the following:[24]

- To calculate the portion of depreciation treated as an alternative minimum tax (AMT) adjustment for purposes of the corporate and individual AMT (see Chapters 12 and 20).[25]
- To compute depreciation allowances for property for which any of the following is true:
  - Used predominantly outside the United States.
  - Leased or otherwise used by a tax-exempt entity.
  - Financed with the proceeds of tax-exempt bonds.
  - Imported from foreign countries that maintain discriminatory trade practices or otherwise engage in discriminatory acts.
- To compute depreciation allowances for earnings and profits purposes (see Chapter 20).

In general, ADS depreciation is computed using straight-line recovery without regard to salvage value. However, for purposes of the AMT, depreciation of personal property is computed using the 150 percent declining-balance method with an appropriate switch to the straight-line method.

The taxpayer must use the half-year or the mid-quarter convention, whichever is applicable, for all property other than eligible real estate. The mid-month convention is used for eligible real estate. The applicable ADS rates are found in Table 8–4, 8–5, and 8–7.

The recovery periods under ADS are as follows:[26]

- The ADR midpoint life for property that does not fall into any of the following listed categories.
- Five years for qualified technological equipment, automobiles, and light-duty trucks.
- Twelve years for personal property with no class life.
- Forty years for all residential rental property and all nonresidential real property.

Taxpayers may *elect* to use the 150 percent declining-balance method to compute the regular income tax rather than the 200 percent declining-balance method that is available for personal property. Hence, if the election is made, there will be no difference between the cost recovery for computing the regular income tax and the AMT.[27]

EXAMPLE 24

On March 1, 2006, Abby purchases computer-based telephone central office switching equipment for $80,000. If Abby uses statutory percentage cost recovery (assuming no § 179 election), the cost recovery allowance for 2006 is $16,000 [$80,000 × 20% (Table 8–1, five-year class property)]. If Abby elects to use ADS 150% declining-balance cost recovery for the regular income tax (assuming no § 179 election), the cost recovery allowance for 2006 is $12,000 [$80,000 × 15% (Table 8–4, five-year class property)]. ∎

In lieu of depreciation under the regular MACRS method, taxpayers may *elect* straight-line under ADS for property that qualifies for the regular MACRS method.

---

[24]§ 168(g).

[25]This AMT adjustment applies for real and personal property placed in service before January 1, 1999. However, it will continue to apply for personal property placed in service after December 31, 1998, if the taxpayer uses the 200% declining-balance method for regular income tax purposes. See Chapter 12.

[26]The class life for certain properties described in § 168(e)(3) is specially determined under § 168(g)(3)(B).

[27]For personal property placed in service before January 1, 1999, taxpayers making the election are required to use the ADS recovery periods in computing cost recovery for the regular income tax. The ADS recovery periods generally are longer than the regular recovery periods under MACRS.

CONCEPT SUMMARY   8–4

Listed Property Cost Recovery

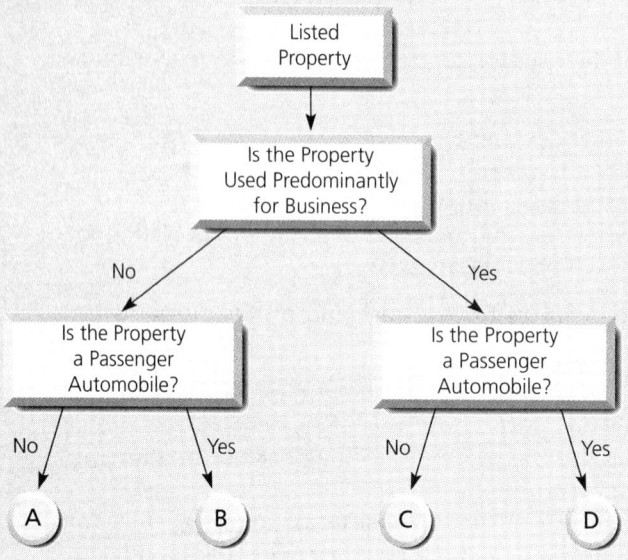

Legend to Tax Treatment

A Straight-line cost recovery reduced by the personal use percentage.
B Straight-line cost recovery subject to the recovery limitations ($2,960, $4,700, $2,850, $1,675) and reduced by the personal use percentage.
C Statutory percentage cost recovery reduced by the personal use percentage.
D Statutory percentage cost recovery subject to the recovery limitations ($2,960, $4,700, $2,850, $1,675) and reduced by the personal use percentage.

The election is available on a class-by-class and year-by-year basis for property other than eligible real estate. The election for eligible real estate is on a property-by-property basis. One reason for making this election is to avoid a difference between deductible depreciation and earnings and profits depreciation.

EXAMPLE 25

Polly acquires an apartment building on March 17, 2006, for $700,000. She takes the maximum cost recovery allowance for determining taxable income. Polly's cost recovery allowance for computing 2006 taxable income is $20,153 [$700,000 × .02879 (Table 8–6)]. However, Polly's cost recovery for computing her earnings and profits is only $13,853 [$700,000 × .01979 (Table 8–7)]. ∎

LO.6

Be aware of the major characteristics of ACRS.

Accelerated Cost Recovery System (ACRS)

The major characteristics of the **accelerated cost recovery system (ACRS)** are listed in Concept Summary 8–5. Note that for personalty, except for 20-year property, the recovery period expired (all of the cost recovery basis has been recovered) prior to 2005. For 20-year property, the recovery period expired during 2005. For realty, the recovery period also expired during 2005.

CONCEPT SUMMARY 8–5

Characteristics of ACRS

Property	Accounting Convention	Life	Method
Personalty	Half-year or mid-quarter	3, 5, 7, 10, 15, or 20 years	Accelerated or straight-line
Realty	Mid-month	15, 18, or 19 years	Accelerated or straight-line

Amortization

Taxpayers can claim an **amortization** deduction on intangible assets called "amortizable § 197 intangibles." The amount of the deduction is determined by amortizing the adjusted basis of such intangibles ratably over a 15-year period beginning in the month in which the intangible is acquired.[28]

An *amortizable § 197 intangible* is any § 197 intangible acquired after August 10, 1993, and held in connection with the conduct of a trade or business or for the production of income. Section 197 intangibles include goodwill and going-concern value, franchises, trademarks, and trade names. Covenants not to compete, copyrights, and patents are also included if they are acquired in connection with the acquisition of a business. Generally, self-created intangibles are not § 197 intangibles. The 15-year amortization period applies regardless of the actual useful life of an amortizable § 197 intangible. No other depreciation or amortization deduction is permitted with respect to any amortizable § 197 intangible except those permitted under the 15-year amortization rules.

> **LO.7**
>
> Identify intangible assets that are eligible for amortization and calculate the amount of the deduction.

Always 15 yrs.

EXAMPLE 26

On June 1, 2006, Neil purchased and began operating the Falcon Café. Of the purchase price, $90,000 is correctly allocated to goodwill. The deduction for amortization for 2006 is $3,500 [($90,000/15) × (7/12)]. ∎

ETHICAL *Considerations* **COMPUTING § 197 AMORTIZATION**

Lime Motors entered into an agreement to buy out Clarissa's interest in Lime Motors. Part of the agreement calls for Lime Motors to pay Clarissa $300,000 for a covenant not to compete for a period of three years. Under the agreement, Clarissa will be paid $5,000 per month plus interest for 60 months. Oscar, the accountant for Lime Motors, intends to expense the payments of $5,000 plus interest because they are to be made over a 60-month period (rather than over the three-year period). Evaluate the appropriateness of Oscar's plan.

Startup expenditures are also partially amortizable under § 195. This treatment is available only by election.[29] A taxpayer must make this election no later than the time prescribed by law for filing the return for the taxable year in which the trade or business begins.[30] If no election is made, the startup expenditures must be capitalized.[31]

(1) Start up
(2) 5000 − (n − 50K)

The elective treatment for startup expenditures allows the taxpayer to deduct the lesser of (1) the amount of startup expenditures with respect to the trade or business or (2) $5,000, reduced, but not below zero, by the amount by which the startup expenditures exceed $50,000. Any startup expenditures not deducted may

---

[28]§ 197(a).
[29]§ 195(b).
[30]§ 195(d).
[31]§ 195(a).

be amortized ratably over a 180-month period beginning in the month in which the trade or business begins.[32]

EXAMPLE 27

Green Corporation begins business on August 1, 2006. The corporation has startup expenditures of $47,000. If Green Corporation elects § 195, the total amount of startup expenditures that Green Corporation may deduct in 2006 is $6,167, computed as follows:

Deductible amount	$5,000
Amortizable amount {[($47,000 − $5,000)/180] × 5 months}	1,167
Total deduction	$6,167

EXAMPLE 28

Assume the same facts as in Example 27, except that the startup expenditures are $53,000. The total deduction for the year 2006 is $3,417, computed as follows:

Deductible amount [$5,000 − ($53,000 − $50,000)]	$2,000
Amortizable amount {[($53,000 − $2,000)/180] × 5 months}	1,417
Total deduction	$3,417

Expenditures that are subject to capitalization and elective amortization under § 195 as startup expenditures generally must satisfy two requirements.[33] First, the expenditures must be paid or incurred in connection with any one of the following:

- The creation of an active trade or business.
- The investigation of the creation or acquisition of an active trade or business.
- Any activity engaged in for profit in anticipation of such activity becoming an active trade or business.

Second, such costs must be the kinds of costs that would be currently deductible if paid or incurred in connection with the operation of an existing trade or business in the same field as that entered into by the taxpayer.

The costs of creating a new active trade or business could include advertising; salaries and wages; travel and other expenses incurred in lining up prospective distributors, suppliers, or customers; and salaries and fees for executives, consultants, and professional services. Costs that relate to either created or acquired businesses could include expenses incurred for the analysis or survey of potential markets, products, labor supply, transportation facilities, and the like. Startup expenditures do not include any amount with respect to which a deduction is allowable under § 163(a) (interest), § 164 (taxes), and § 174 (research and experimental expenditures).[34]

Other assets that could be subject to amortization include research and experimental expenditures under § 174 (see Chapter 7) and organization expenses under § 248 (see Chapter 20).

LO.8

Determine the amount of depletion expense including being able to apply the alternative tax treatments for intangible drilling and development costs.

Depletion

Natural resources (e.g., oil, gas, coal, gravel, timber) are subject to **depletion**, which is simply a form of depreciation applicable to natural resources. Land generally cannot be depleted.

The owner of an interest in the natural resource is entitled to deduct depletion. An owner is one who has an economic interest in the property.[35] An economic interest requires the acquisition of an interest in the resource in place and the receipt of income from the extraction or severance of that resource. Like depreciation, depletion is a deduction *for* adjusted gross income.

---

[32]§ 195(b)(1)(A) and (B).
[33]§ 195(c)(1)(A) and (B).

[34]§ 195(c).
[35]Reg. § 1.611–1(b).

Although all natural resources are subject to depletion, oil and gas wells are used as an example in the following paragraphs to illustrate the related costs and issues.

In developing an oil or gas well, the producer must make four types of expenditures:

- Natural resource costs. *→ depletion*
- Intangible drilling and development costs. *→ below*
- Tangible asset costs. *→ depreciation*
- Operating costs. *→ ordinary ded for AGI*

Natural resources are physically limited, and the costs to acquire them (e.g., oil under the ground) are, therefore, recovered through depletion. Costs incurred in making the property ready for drilling such as the cost of labor in clearing the property, erecting derricks, and drilling the hole are **intangible drilling and development costs (IDC)**. These costs generally have no salvage value and are a lost cost if the well is dry. Costs for tangible assets such as tools, pipes, and engines are capital in nature. These costs must be capitalized and recovered through depreciation (cost recovery). Costs incurred after the well is producing are operating costs. These costs would include expenditures for such items as labor, fuel, and supplies. Operating costs are deductible when incurred (on the accrual basis) or when paid (on the cash basis).

The expenditures for depreciable assets and operating costs pose no unusual problems for producers of natural resources. The tax treatment of depletable costs and intangible drilling and development costs is quite a different matter.

Intangible Drilling and Development Costs (IDC)

Intangible drilling and development costs can be handled in one of two ways at the option of the taxpayer. They can be *either* charged off as an expense in the year in which they are incurred *or* capitalized and written off through depletion. The taxpayer makes the election in the first year such expenditures are incurred either by taking a deduction on the return or by adding them to the depletable basis. No formal statement of intent is required. Once made, the election is binding on both the taxpayer and the IRS for all such expenditures in the future. If the taxpayer fails to make the election to expense IDC on the original timely filed return the first year such expenditures are incurred, an automatic election to capitalize them has been made and is irrevocable.

(1) Expense in the yr.
(2) Capitalized → depletion.

As a general rule, it is more advantageous to expense IDC. The obvious benefit of an immediate write-off (as opposed to a deferred write-off through depletion) is not the only advantage. Since a taxpayer can use percentage depletion, which is calculated without reference to basis (see Example 32), the IDC may be completely lost as a deduction if they are capitalized.

Depletion Methods

There are two methods of calculating depletion: cost and percentage. Cost depletion can be used on any wasting asset (and is the only method allowed for timber). Percentage depletion is subject to a number of limitations, particularly for oil and gas deposits. Depletion should be calculated both ways, and generally the method that results in the *larger* deduction is used. The choice between cost and percentage depletion is an annual election.

Cost Depletion. Cost depletion is determined by using the adjusted basis of the asset.[36] The basis is divided by the estimated recoverable units of the asset (e.g., barrels, tons) to arrive at the depletion per unit. The depletion per unit then is multiplied by the number of units sold (*not* the units produced) during the year to arrive at the cost depletion allowed. Cost depletion, therefore, resembles the units-of-production method of calculating depreciation.

[36]§ 612.

EXHIBIT 8–2	Sample of Percentage Depletion Rates

22% Depletion

Cobalt	Sulfur
Lead	Tin
Nickel	Uranium
Platinum	Zinc

15% Depletion

Copper	Oil and gas
Gold	Oil shale
Iron	Silver

14% Depletion

Borax	Magnesium carbonates
Calcium carbonates	Marble
Granite	Potash
Limestone	Slate

10% Depletion

Coal	Perlite
Lignite	Sodium chloride

5% Depletion

Gravel	Pumice
Peat	Sand

EXAMPLE 29

On January 1, 2006, Pablo purchases the rights to a mineral interest for $1 million. At that time, the remaining recoverable units in the mineral interest are estimated to be 200,000. The depletion per unit is $5 [$1,000,000 (adjusted basis) ÷ 200,000 (estimated recoverable units)]. If during the year 60,000 units are mined and 25,000 are sold, the cost depletion is $125,000 [$5 (depletion per unit) × 25,000 (units sold)]. ∎

If the taxpayer later discovers that the original estimate was incorrect, the depletion per unit for future calculations must be redetermined based on the revised estimate.[37]

EXAMPLE 30

Assume the same facts as in Example 29. In 2007, Pablo realizes that an incorrect estimate was made. The remaining recoverable units now are determined to be 400,000. Based on this new information, the revised depletion per unit is $2.1875 [$875,000 (adjusted basis) ÷ 400,000 (estimated recoverable units)]. Note that the adjusted basis is the original cost ($1,000,000) reduced by the depletion claimed in 2006 ($125,000). If 30,000 units are sold in 2007, the depletion for the year is $65,625 [$2.1875 (depletion per unit) × 30,000 (units sold)]. ∎

Percentage Depletion. Percentage depletion (also referred to as statutory depletion) is a specified percentage provided for in the Code. The percentage varies according to the type of mineral interest involved. A sample of these percentages is shown in Exhibit 8–2. The rate is applied to the gross income from the property, but

[37]§ 611(a).

$< 50 \%$

in no event may percentage depletion exceed 50 percent of the taxable income from the property before the allowance for depletion.[38]

EXAMPLE 31

Assuming gross income of $100,000, a depletion rate of 22%, and other expenses relating to the property of $60,000, the depletion allowance is determined as follows:

Gross income	$100,000
Less: Other expenses	(60,000)
Taxable income before depletion	$ 40,000
Depletion allowance [the lesser of $22,000 (22% × $100,000) or $20,000 (50% × $40,000)]	(20,000)
Taxable income after depletion	$ 20,000

The adjusted basis of the property is reduced by $20,000, the depletion allowed. If the other expenses had been only $55,000, the full $22,000 could have been deducted, and the adjusted basis would have been reduced by $22,000. ∎

Note that percentage depletion is based on a percentage of the gross income from the property and makes no reference to cost. Thus, when percentage depletion is used, it is possible to deduct more than the original cost of the property. If percentage depletion is used, however, the adjusted basis of the property (for computing cost depletion) must be reduced by the amount of percentage depletion taken until the adjusted basis reaches zero.

Effect of Intangible Drilling Costs on Depletion.
The treatment of IDC has an effect on the depletion deduction in two ways. If the costs are capitalized, the basis for cost depletion is increased. As a consequence, the cost depletion is increased. If IDC are expensed, they reduce the taxable income from the property. This reduction may result in application of the provision that limits depletion to 50 percent (100 percent for certain oil and gas wells) of taxable income before deducting depletion.

EXAMPLE 32

Iris purchased the rights to an oil interest for $1 million. The recoverable barrels were estimated to be 200,000. During the year, 50,000 barrels were sold for $2 million. Regular expenses amounted to $800,000, and IDC were $650,000. If the IDC are capitalized, the depletion per unit is $8.25 ($1,000,000 + $650,000 ÷ 200,000 barrels), and the following taxable income results:

Depletion amt = 1.65 M

Gross income	$2,000,000
Less: Expenses	(800,000) ✓
Taxable income before depletion	$1,200,000 ✓
Cost depletion ($8.25 × 50,000) = $412,500	
Percentage depletion (15% × $2,000,000) = $300,000	
Greater of cost or percentage depletion	(412,500)
Taxable income	$ 787,500

greater one

If the IDC are expensed, the taxable income is $250,000, calculated as follows:

Depletion amt = 1 M

Gross income	$ 2,000,000
Less: Expenses, including IDC	(1,450,000)
Taxable income before depletion	$ 550,000

800 + 650

---

[38]§ 613(a). Special rules apply for certain oil and gas wells under § 613A (e.g., the 50% ceiling is replaced with a 100% ceiling, and the percentage depletion may not exceed 65% of the taxpayer's taxable income from all sources before the allowance for depletion).

Cost depletion [($1,000,000 ÷ 200,000 barrels) × 50,000 barrels]
   = $250,000
Percentage depletion (15% of $2,000,000 = $300,000, limited
   to 100% of $550,000 taxable income before depletion) =
   $300,000

Greater of cost or percentage depletion	(300,000)
Taxable income	$ 250,000

For further restrictions on the use or availability of the percentage depletion method, see § 613.

Reporting Procedures

L0.9

Perform the reporting procedures for cost recovery.

Sole proprietors engaged in a business should file a Schedule C, Profit or Loss from Business, to accompany Form 1040. Schedule C for 2005 is presented because the 2006 form was not yet available.

The top part of page 1 requests certain key information about the taxpayer (e.g., name, address, Social Security number, principal business activity, and the accounting method used). Part I provides for the reporting of items of income. If the business requires the use of inventories and the computation of cost of goods sold (see Chapter 18 for when this is necessary), Part III must be completed and the cost of goods sold amount transferred to line 4 of Part I.

Part II allows for the reporting of deductions. Some of the deductions discussed in this chapter and their location on the form are depletion (line 12) and depreciation (line 13). Other expenses (line 27) include those items not already covered (see lines 8–26). An example would be research and experimental expenditures.

If depreciation is claimed, it should be supported by completing Form 4562. Form 4562 for 2005 is presented because the 2006 form was not yet available. The amount listed on line 22 of Form 4562 is then transferred to line 13 of Part II of Schedule C.

EXAMPLE 33

Thomas Andrews, Social Security number 123–45–6789, was employed as an accountant until May 2005, when he opened his own practice. His address is 279 Mountain View, Ogden, UT 84201. Andrews keeps his books on the cash basis and had the following revenue and business expenses in 2005:

a. Revenue from accounting practice, $192,000.
b. Insurance, $5,000.
c. Office supplies, $4,000.
d. Office rent, $16,000.
e. Copier lease payments, $3,000.
f. Licenses, $2,000.
g. New furniture and fixtures were acquired on May 10, for $142,000. Thomas elects § 179 expensing and uses the statutory percentage cost recovery method.

Andrews would report the above information on Schedule C and Form 4562 as illustrated on the following pages. ■

TAX PLANNING *Considerations*

Cost Recovery

Cost recovery schedules should be reviewed annually for possible retirements, abandonments, and obsolescence.

EXAMPLE 34

An examination of the cost recovery schedule of Eagle Company reveals the following:

- Asset A was abandoned when it was discovered that the cost of repairs would be in excess of the cost of replacement. Asset A had an adjusted basis of $3,000.
- Asset J became obsolete this year, at which point, its adjusted basis was $8,000.

Assets A and J should be written off for an additional expense of $11,000 ($3,000 + $8,000). ■

Form **4562** (Rev. January 2006) Department of the Treasury Internal Revenue Service	**Depreciation and Amortization** (Including Information on Listed Property) ▶ See separate instructions. ▶ Attach to your tax return.	OMB No. 1545-0172 **2005** Attachment Sequence No. **67**
Name(s) shown on return *Thomas Andrews*	Business or activity to which this form relates *Accounting services*	Identifying number *123 45 6789*

Part I Election To Expense Certain Property Under Section 179
Note: *If you have any listed property, complete Part V before you complete Part I.*

1 Maximum amount. See the instructions for a higher limit for certain businesses	**1**	$105,000
2 Total cost of section 179 property placed in service (see instructions)	**2**	142,000
3 Threshold cost of section 179 property before reduction in limitation	**3**	$420,000
4 Reduction in limitation. Subtract line 3 from line 2. If zero or less, enter -0-	**4**	-0-
5 Dollar limitation for tax year. Subtract line 4 from line 1. If zero or less, enter -0-. If married filing separately, see instructions	**5**	105,000

(a) Description of property	(b) Cost (business use only)	(c) Elected cost
6 *Furniture and Fixtures*	*142,000*	*105,000*

7 Listed property. Enter the amount from line 29 . . . **7**		
8 Total elected cost of section 179 property. Add amounts in column (c), lines 6 and 7	**8**	105,000
9 Tentative deduction. Enter the **smaller** of line 5 or line 8.	**9**	105,000
10 Carryover of disallowed deduction from line 13 of your 2004 Form 4562	**10**	-0-
11 Business income limitation. Enter the smaller of business income (not less than zero) or line 5 (see instructions)	**11**	105,000
12 Section 179 expense deduction. Add lines 9 and 10, but do not enter more than line 11	**12**	105,000
13 Carryover of disallowed deduction to 2006. Add lines 9 and 10, less line 12 ▶ **13**		

Note: *Do not use Part II or Part III below for listed property. Instead, use Part V.*

Part II Special Depreciation Allowance and Other Depreciation (Do not include listed property.) (See instructions.)

14 Special allowance for certain aircraft, certain property with a long production period, and qualified NYL or GO Zone property (other than listed property) placed in service during the tax year (see instructions)	**14**	
15 Property subject to section 168(f)(1) election	**15**	
16 Other depreciation (including ACRS)	**16**	

Part III MACRS Depreciation (Do not include listed property.) (See instructions.)

Section A

17 MACRS deductions for assets placed in service in tax years beginning before 2005	**17**	
18 If you are electing to group any assets placed in service during the tax year into one or more general asset accounts, check here ▶ ☐		

Section B—Assets Placed in Service During 2005 Tax Year Using the General Depreciation System

(a) Classification of property	(b) Month and year placed in service	(c) Basis for depreciation (business/investment use only—see instructions)	(d) Recovery period	(e) Convention	(f) Method	(g) Depreciation deduction
19a 3-year property						
b 5-year property						
c 7-year property		*37,000*	*7- year*	*HY*	*200DB*	*5,287*
d 10-year property						
e 15-year property						
f 20-year property						
g 25-year property			25 yrs.		S/L	
h Residential rental property			27.5 yrs.	MM	S/L	
			27.5 yrs.	MM	S/L	
i Nonresidential real property			39 yrs.	MM	S/L	
				MM	S/L	

Section C—Assets Placed in Service During 2005 Tax Year Using the Alternative Depreciation System

20a Class life					S/L	
b 12-year			12 yrs.		S/L	
c 40-year			40 yrs.	MM	S/L	

Part IV Summary (see instructions)

21 Listed property. Enter amount from line 28	**21**	
22 **Total.** Add amounts from line 12, lines 14 through 17, lines 19 and 20 in column (g), and line 21. Enter here and on the appropriate lines of your return. Partnerships and S corporations—see instr.	**22**	*110,287*
23 For assets shown above and placed in service during the current year, enter the portion of the basis attributable to section 263A costs . . **23**		

For Paperwork Reduction Act Notice, see separate instructions. Cat. No. 12906N Form **4562** (2005) (Rev. 1-2006)

SCHEDULE C (Form 1040)	**Profit or Loss From Business**	OMB No. 1545-0074

SCHEDULE C
(Form 1040)

Department of the Treasury
Internal Revenue Service   (99)

Profit or Loss From Business
(Sole Proprietorship)
▶ **Partnerships, joint ventures, etc., must file Form 1065 or 1065-B.**
▶ **Attach to Form 1040 or 1041.**   ▶ **See Instructions for Schedule C (Form 1040).**

OMB No. 1545-0074

20**05**

Attachment
Sequence No. **09**

Name of proprietor
Thomas Andrews

Social security number (SSN)
123 45 6789

A Principal business or profession, including product or service (see page C-2 of the instructions)
Accounting Services

B Enter code from pages C-8, 9, & 10
▶

C Business name. If no separate business name, leave blank.
Andrews Accounting Services

D Employer ID number (EIN), if any

E Business address (including suite or room no.) ▶ *279 Mountain View*
City, town or post office, state, and ZIP code   *Ogden, UT 84201*

F Accounting method: **(1)** ☒ Cash   **(2)** ☐ Accrual   **(3)** ☐ Other (specify) ▶

G Did you "materially participate" in the operation of this business during 2005? If "No," see page C-3 for limit on losses   ☒ Yes ☐ No

H If you started or acquired this business during 2005, check here . . . . ▶ ☐

Part I   Income

1	Gross receipts or sales. **Caution.** If this income was reported to you on Form W-2 and the "Statutory employee" box on that form was checked, see page C-3 and check here . . . . . ▶ ☐	1	*192,000*
2	Returns and allowances	2	
3	Subtract line 2 from line 1	3	*192,000*
4	Cost of goods sold (from line 42 on page 2)	4	
5	**Gross profit.** Subtract line 4 from line 3.	5	*192,000*
6	Other income, including Federal and state gasoline or fuel tax credit or refund (see page C-3) . . .	6	
7	**Gross income.** Add lines 5 and 6 . . . . ▶	7	*192,000*

Part II   Expenses. Enter expenses for business use of your home **only** on line 30.

8	Advertising	8		18	Office expense . . .	18	*4,000*
9	Car and truck expenses (see page C-3).	9		19	Pension and profit-sharing plans	19	
10	Commissions and fees . .	10		20	Rent or lease (see page C-5):		
11	Contract labor (see page C-4)	11			**a** Vehicles, machinery, and equipment .	20a	*3,000*
12	Depletion	12			**b** Other business property. . .	20b	*16,000*
13	Depreciation and section 179 expense deduction (not included in Part III) (see page C-4)	13	*110,287*	21	Repairs and maintenance . .	21	
				22	Supplies (not included in Part III)	22	
				23	Taxes and licenses	23	*2,000*
				24	Travel, meals, and entertainment:		
					a Travel	24a	
14	Employee benefit programs (other than on line 19). .	14			**b** Deductible meals and entertainment (see page C-5)	24b	
15	Insurance (other than health) .	15	*5,000*	25	Utilities	25	
16	Interest:			26	Wages (less employment credits) .	26	
	a Mortgage (paid to banks, etc.) .	16a		27	Other expenses (from line 48 on page 2)	27	
	b Other	16b					
17	Legal and professional services	17					

28	**Total expenses** before expenses for business use of home. Add lines 8 through 27 in columns . . ▶	28	*140,287*
29	Tentative profit (loss). Subtract line 28 from line 7	29	*51,713*
30	Expenses for business use of your home. Attach **Form 8829**	30	
31	**Net profit or (loss).** Subtract line 30 from line 29. • If a profit, enter on **Form 1040, line 12,** and **also** on **Schedule SE, line 2** (statutory employees, see page C-6). Estates and trusts, enter on Form 1041, line 3. • If a loss, you **must** go to line 32.	31	*51,713*

32 If you have a loss, check the box that describes your investment in this activity (see page C-6).
• If you checked 32a, enter the loss on **Form 1040, line 12,** and **also** on **Schedule SE, line 2** (statutory employees, see page C-6). Estates and trusts, enter on Form 1041, line 3.
• If you checked 32b, you **must** attach **Form 6198.** Your loss may be limited.

32a ☐ All investment is at risk.
32b ☐ Some investment is not at risk.

For Paperwork Reduction Act Notice, see page C-7 of the instructions.   Cat. No. 11334P   Schedule C (Form 1040) 2005

Because of the deductions for cost recovery, interest, and ad valorem property taxes, investments in real estate can be highly attractive. In figuring the economics of such investments, one should be sure to take into account any tax savings that result.

E X A M P L E   35

In early January 2005, Vern purchased residential rental property for $170,000 (of which $20,000 was allocated to the land and $150,000 to the building). Vern made a down payment of $25,000 and assumed the seller's mortgage for the balance. Under the mortgage agreement, monthly payments of $1,000 are required and are applied toward interest, taxes, insurance, and principal. Since the property was already occupied, Vern continued to receive rent of $1,200 per month from the tenant. Vern actively participates in this activity and hence comes under the special rule for a rental real estate activity with respect to the limitation on passive activity losses (refer to Chapter 11). Vern is in the 33% tax bracket.

During 2006, Vern's expenses were as follows:

Interest	$10,000
Taxes	800
Insurance	1,000
Repairs and maintenance	2,200
Depreciation ($150,000 × .03636)	5,454
Total	$19,454

The deductible loss from the rental property is computed as follows:

Rent income ($1,200 × 12 months)	$ 14,400
Less expenses (see above)	(19,454)
Net loss	($ 5,054)

But what is Vern's overall position for the year when the tax benefit of the loss is taken into account? Considering just the cash intake and outlay, it is summarized below:

Intake—		
Rent income	$14,400	
Tax savings [33% (income tax bracket) × $5,054		
(loss from the property)]	1,668	$ 16,068
Outlay—		
Mortgage payments ($1,000 × 12 months)	$12,000	
Repairs and maintenance	2,200	(14,200)
Net cash benefit		$ 1,868 ■

It should be noted, however, that should Vern cease being an active participant in the rental activity, the passive activity loss rules would apply, and Vern could lose the current period benefit of the loss.

Another consideration when making decisions with respect to cost recovery is whether fast or slow cost recovery will be more beneficial for the taxpayer. If the taxpayer's goal is to recover the cost of fixed assets as quickly as possible, the following strategies should be used:

• When constructing a facility, try to avoid "fixture" classification. Refer to the discussion in Chapter 1 on page 1–6.
• When electing § 179 expensing, choose assets with longer lives.
• Choose accelerated cost recovery methods where available.

If a taxpayer has a new business with little income or a business with a net operating loss carryover, the taxpayer's goal may be to slow down cost recovery. In such a situation, the taxpayer should:

- Choose the straight-line cost recovery method.
- Make no election under § 179.
- Defer placing assets in service in the current tax year or postpone capital outlays until future tax years.

Amortization

When a business is purchased, goodwill and covenants not to compete are both subject to a statutory amortization period of 15 years. Therefore, the purchaser does not derive any tax benefits when part of the purchase price is assigned to a covenant rather than to goodwill.

Thus, from the purchaser's perspective, bargaining for a covenant should be based on legal rather than tax reasons. Note, however, that from the seller's perspective, goodwill is a capital asset and the covenant is an ordinary income asset.

Since the amortization period for both goodwill and a covenant is 15 years, the purchaser may want to attempt to minimize these amounts if the purchase price can be assigned to assets with shorter lives (e.g., inventory, receivables, and personalty). Conversely, the purchaser may want to attempt to maximize these amounts if part of the purchase price will otherwise be assigned to assets with longer recovery periods (e.g., realty) or to assets not eligible for cost recovery (e.g., land).

Depletion

Since the election to use the cost or percentage depletion method is an annual election, a taxpayer can use cost depletion (if higher) until the basis is exhausted and then switch to percentage depletion in the following years.

EXAMPLE 36

Assume the following facts for Melissa:

Remaining depletable basis	$ 11,000
Gross income (10,000 units)	100,000
Expenses (other than depletion)	30,000

Since cost depletion is limited to the basis of $11,000 and if the percentage depletion is $22,000 (assume a 22% rate), Melissa would choose the latter. Her basis is then reduced to zero. In future years, however, she can continue to take percentage depletion since percentage depletion is taken without reference to the remaining basis. ∎

The election to expense intangible drilling and development costs is a onetime election. Once the election is made to either expense or capitalize the IDC, it is binding on all future expenditures. The permanent nature of the election makes it extremely important for the taxpayer to determine which treatment will provide the greater tax advantage. (Refer to Example 32 for an illustration of the effect of using the two different alternatives for a given set of facts.)

Cost Recovery Tables

Summary of Tables

Table 8–1	Modified ACRS statutory percentage table for personalty.
	Applicable depreciation methods: 200 or 150 percent declining-balance switching to straight-line.
	Applicable recovery periods: 3, 5, 7, 10, 15, 20 years.
	Applicable convention: half-year.
Table 8–2	Modified ACRS statutory percentage table for personalty.
	Applicable depreciation method: 200 percent declining-balance switching to straight-line.
	Applicable recovery periods: 3, 5, 7 years.
	Applicable convention: mid-quarter.
Table 8–3	Modified ACRS optional straight-line table for personalty.
	Applicable depreciation method: straight-line.
	Applicable recovery periods: 3, 5, 7, 10, 15, 20 years.
	Applicable convention: half-year.
Table 8–4	Alternative minimum tax declining-balance table for personalty.
	Applicable depreciation method: 150 percent declining-balance switching to straight-line.
	Applicable recovery periods: 3, 5, 7, 9.5, 10, 12 years.
	Applicable convention: half-year.
Table 8–5	Alternative depreciation system straight-line table for personalty.
	Applicable depreciation method: straight-line.
	Applicable recovery periods: 5, 9.5, 12 years.
	Applicable convention: half-year.
Table 8–6	Modified ACRS straight-line table for realty.
	Applicable depreciation method: straight-line.
	Applicable recovery periods: 27.5, 31.5, 39 years.
	Applicable convention: mid-month.
Table 8–7	Alternative depreciation system straight-line table for realty.
	Applicable depreciation method: straight-line.
	Applicable recovery period: 40 years.
	Applicable convention: mid-month.

Assume every asset purchased in middle of yr :: 3-yr has 4.

DB: Decline Balance

If sell on 3rd yr (1/2)
⇒ 14.81% × cost
② "sell in middle" of year

TABLE 8–1	MACRS Accelerated Depreciation for Personal Property Assuming Half-Year Convention

For Property Placed in Service after December 31, 1986

Recovery Year	3-Year (200% DB)	5-Year (200% DB)	7-Year (200% DB)	10-Year (200% DB)	15-Year (150% DB)	20-Year (150% DB)
1	33.33	20.00	14.29	10.00	5.00	3.750
2	44.45	32.00	24.49	18.00	9.50	7.219
3	14.81*	19.20	17.49	14.40	8.55	6.677
4	7.41	11.52*	12.49	11.52	7.70	6.177
5		11.52	8.93*	9.22	6.93	5.713
6		5.76	8.92	7.37	6.23	5.285
7			8.93	6.55*	5.90*	4.888
8			4.46	6.55	5.90	4.522
9				6.56	5.91	4.462*
10				6.55	5.90	4.461
11				3.28	5.91	4.462
12					5.90	4.461
13					5.91	4.462
14					5.90	4.461
15					5.91	4.462
16					2.95	4.461
17						4.462
18						4.461
19						4.462
20						4.461
21						2.231

*Switchover to straight-line depreciation.

quarter of taxable yr

TABLE 8–2	MACRS Accelerated Depreciation for Personal Property Assuming Mid-Quarter Convention

For Property Placed in Service after December 31, 1986 (Partial Table*)

Recovery Year	First Quarter	3-Year Second Quarter	Third Quarter	Fourth Quarter
1	58.33	41.67	25.00	8.33
2	27.78	38.89	50.00	61.11

Recovery Year	First Quarter	5-Year Second Quarter	Third Quarter	Fourth Quarter
1	35.00	25.00	15.00	5.00
2	26.00	30.00	34.00	38.00

Recovery Year	First Quarter	7-Year Second Quarter	Third Quarter	Fourth Quarter
1	25.00	17.85	10.71	3.57
2	21.43	23.47	25.51	27.55

*The figures in this table are taken from the official tables that appear in Rev.Proc. 87–57, 1987–2 C.B. 687. Because of their length, the complete tables are not presented.

| **TABLE 8–3** | **MACRS Straight-Line Depreciation for Personal Property Assuming Half-Year Convention*** |

For Property Placed in Service after December 31, 1986

MACRS Class	% First Recovery Year	Other Recovery Years Years	Other Recovery Years %	Last Recovery Year Year	Last Recovery Year %
3-year	16.67	2–3	33.33	4	16.67
5-year	10.00	2–5	20.00	6	10.00
7-year	7.14	2–7	14.29	8	7.14
10-year	5.00	2–10	10.00	11	5.00
15-year	3.33	2–15	6.67	16	3.33
20-year	2.50	2–20	5.00	21	2.50

*The official table contains a separate row for each year. For ease of presentation, certain years are grouped in this table. In some instances, this will produce a difference of .01 for the last digit when compared with the official table.

| **TABLE 8–4** | **Alternative Minimum Tax: 150% Declining-Balance Assuming Half-Year Convention** |

For Property Placed in Service after December 31, 1986 (Partial Table*)

Recovery Year	3-Year 150%	5-Year 150%	7-Year 150%	9.5-Year 150%	10-Year 150%	12-Year 150%
1	25.00	15.00	10.71	7.89	7.50	6.25
2	37.50	25.50	19.13	14.54	13.88	11.72
3	25.00**	17.85	15.03	12.25	11.79	10.25
4	12.50	16.66**	12.25**	10.31	10.02	8.97
5		16.66	12.25	9.17**	8.74**	7.85
6		8.33	12.25	9.17	8.74	7.33**
7			12.25	9.17	8.74	7.33
8			6.13	9.17	8.74	7.33
9				9.17	8.74	7.33
10				9.16	8.74	7.33
11					4.37	7.32
12						7.33
13						3.66

*The figures in this table are taken from the official table that appears in Rev.Proc. 87–57, 1987–2 C.B. 687. Because of its length, the complete table is not presented.
**Switchover to straight-line depreciation.

TABLE 8–5	ADS Straight-Line for Personal Property Assuming Half-Year Convention

For Property Placed in Service after December 31, 1986 (Partial Table)*

Recovery Year	5-Year Class	9.5-Year Class	12-Year Class
1	10.00	5.26	4.17
2	20.00	10.53	8.33
3	20.00	10.53	8.33
4	20.00	10.53	8.33
5	20.00	10.52	8.33
6	10.00	10.53	8.33
7		10.52	8.34
8		10.53	8.33
9		10.52	8.34
10		10.53	8.33
11			8.34
12			8.33
13			4.17

*The figures in this table are taken from the official table that appears in Rev.Proc. 87–57, 1987–2 C.B. 687. Because of its length, the complete table is not presented. The tables for the mid-quarter convention also appear in Rev.Proc. 87–57.

TABLE 8–6	MACRS Straight-Line Depreciation for Real Property Assuming Mid-Month Convention*

For Property Placed in Service after December 31, 1986: 27.5-Year Residential Real Property

| Recovery Year(s) | The Applicable Percentage Is (Use the Column for the Month in the First Year the Property Is Placed in Service): | | | | | | | | | | | |
	1	2	3	4	5	6	7	8	9	10	11	12
1	3.485	3.182	2.879	2.576	2.273	1.970	1.667	1.364	1.061	0.758	0.455	0.152
2–18	3.636	3.636	3.636	3.636	3.636	3.636	3.636	3.636	3.636	3.636	3.636	3.636
19–27	3.637	3.637	3.637	3.637	3.637	3.637	3.637	3.637	3.637	3.637	3.637	3.637
28	1.970	2.273	2.576	2.879	3.182	3.485	3.636	3.636	3.636	3.636	3.636	3.636
29	0.000	0.000	0.000	0.000	0.000	0.000	0.152	0.455	0.758	1.061	1.364	1.667

For Property Placed in Service after December 31, 1986, and before May 13, 1993: 31.5-Year Nonresidential Real Property

| Recovery Year(s) | The Applicable Percentage Is (Use the Column for the Month in the First Year the Property Is Placed in Service): | | | | | | | | | | | |
	1	2	3	4	5	6	7	8	9	10	11	12
1	3.042	2.778	2.513	2.249	1.984	1.720	1.455	1.190	0.926	0.661	0.397	0.132
2–19	3.175	3.175	3.175	3.175	3.175	3.175	3.175	3.175	3.175	3.175	3.175	3.175
20–31	3.174	3.174	3.174	3.174	3.174	3.174	3.174	3.174	3.174	3.174	3.174	3.174
32	1.720	1.984	2.249	2.513	2.778	3.042	3.175	3.175	3.175	3.175	3.175	3.175
33	0.000	0.000	0.000	0.000	0.000	0.000	0.132	0.397	0.661	0.926	1.190	1.455

For Property Placed in Service after May 12, 1993: 39-Year Nonresidential Real Property

| Recovery Year(s) | The Applicable Percentage Is (Use the Column for the Month in the First Year the Property Is Placed in Service): | | | | | | | | | | | |
	1	2	3	4	5	6	7	8	9	10	11	12
1	2.461	2.247	2.033	1.819	1.605	1.391	1.177	0.963	0.749	0.535	0.321	0.107
2–39	2.564	2.564	2.564	2.564	2.564	2.564	2.564	2.564	2.564	2.564	2.564	2.564
40	0.107	0.321	0.535	0.749	0.963	1.177	1.391	1.605	1.819	2.033	2.247	2.461

*The official tables contain a separate row for each year. For ease of presentation, certain years are grouped in these tables. In some instances, this will produce a difference of .001 for the last digit when compared with the official tables.

Use for AMT w/ properties b/t 1988 - 1998.

TABLE 8–7	ADS Straight-Line for Real Property Assuming Mid-Month Convention

For Property Placed in Service after December 31, 1986

Recovery Year	Month Placed in Service											
	1	2	3	4	5	6	7	8	9	10	11	12
1	2.396	2.188	1.979	1.771	1.563	1.354	1.146	0.938	0.729	0.521	0.313	0.104
2–40	2.500	2.500	2.500	2.500	2.500	2.500	2.500	2.500	2.500	2.500	2.500	2.500
41	0.104	0.312	0.521	0.729	0.937	1.146	1.354	1.562	1.771	1.979	2.187	2.396

KEY TERMS

Accelerated cost recovery system (ACRS), 8–18

Alternative depreciation system (ADS), 8–17

Amortization, 8–19

Cost depletion, 8–21

Cost recovery, 8–2

Depletion, 8–20

Depreciation, 8–2

Half-year convention, 8–7

Intangible drilling and development costs (IDC), 8–21

Listed property, 8–12

Mid-month convention, 8–9

Mid-quarter convention, 8–7

Modified accelerated cost recovery system (MACRS), 8–4

Percentage depletion, 8–22

Residential rental real estate, 8–8

Section 179 expensing, 8–10

Startup expenditures, 8–19

P R O B L E M   M A T E R I A L S

DISCUSSION QUESTIONS

1. Discuss whether property that is classified as personalty is subject to cost recovery.

2. If a taxpayer does not take any cost recovery on an asset during the year, what will be the impact on the basis of the asset?

3. Discuss whether landscaping costs are eligible for cost recovery.

4. At the beginning of the current year, Henry purchased a ski resort for $10 million. Henry does not own the land on which the resort is located. The Federal government owns the land, and Henry has the right to operate the resort on the land pursuant to Special Use Permits, which are terminable at will by the Federal government, and Term Special Use Permits, which allow the land to be used for a fixed number of years. In preparing the income tax return for the current year, Henry properly allocated $2 million of the purchase price to the costs of constructing mountain roads, slopes, and trails. Since the acquisition, Henry has spent an additional $1 million on maintaining the mountain roads, slopes, and trails. Identify the relevant tax issues for Henry.

Issue ID

5. During the taxable year, Pale, an electric utility company, constructed a hydroelectric dam and placed it in service. In connection with the dam, Pale was required under a Federal Power Commission license to construct and maintain various facilities for the preservation of fish and for public recreation. The fish preservation facilities constructed below the dam consisted of an entrance pool, a fish ladder, and a holding pool. The recreational facilities located above the dam included access roads, fixed wharves, landings, and other facilities. All of these facilities are tangible properties, some of which are inextricably associated with the land. Identify the relevant tax issues for Pale.

Issue ID

6. Discuss the computation of cost recovery in the year an asset is placed in service when the half-year convention is used.

7. Discuss the computation of cost recovery in the year of sale of an asset when the half-year convention is being used.

8. Discuss whether the acquisition of real property affects the 40% test to determine whether the mid-quarter convention must be used.

9. Discuss the computation of cost recovery in the year of sale of an asset when the mid-quarter convention is being used.

10. Discuss the mid-month convention.

11. Discuss whether an election may be made to use MACRS straight-line cost recovery on only a portion of the personalty placed in service during the tax year.

12. Discuss whether the mid-quarter convention applies if a taxpayer makes a straight-line election under MACRS.

13. Discuss whether § 179 expensing may be taken on an asset that a taxpayer acquires to help with her personal investments.

14. Explain how the § 179 limited expensing deduction affects the computation of MACRS cost recovery.

15. Discuss the treatment of a § 179 expensing carryforward.

16. Discuss the definition of *taxable income* as it is used in limiting the § 179 expensing amount.

Issue ID

17. Ana owns a motor home sales and rental business. During the current year, her rental fleet had a total of 33 motor homes, including a new Gulfstream Motor Home. The Gulfstream was purchased for $80,000 in July of the current year. The usual terms of the motor home rentals are much like those for car rentals—a daily or weekly fee, a daily mileage allowance of 100 miles, and a mileage charge of $.50 for each additional mile. Most renters use the motor homes for fewer than 30 days. Although the motor homes are rented out, they are also listed for sale. As such, any motor home can be sold at any time. Identify the relevant tax issues for Ana with respect to the new Gulfstream Motor Home.

18. Discuss the implications of an automobile used in a trade or business having a gross vehicle weight (GVW) exceeding 6,000 pounds.

19. Discuss whether an automobile is subject to the statutory dollar limits on cost recovery if the automobile fails the more-than-50% business use test for listed property.

20. Discuss the purpose of the lease inclusion amount and explain how it is determined with respect to leased passenger automobiles.

21. Explain the amortization period of a § 197 intangible if the actual useful life is less than 15 years.

Issue ID

22. Harold and Bart own 75% of the stock of Orange Motors. The other 25% of the stock is owned by Jeb. Orange Motors entered into an agreement with Harold and Bart to acquire all of their stock in Orange Motors. In addition, Harold and Bart signed a noncompete agreement with Orange Motors. Under the terms of the noncompete agreement, Orange will pay Harold and Bart $15,000 each per year for four years. Identify the relevant tax issues for Orange Motors.

23. Discuss the amortization of startup expenditures.

Issue ID

24. In May 2006, George began searching for a trade or business to acquire. In anticipation of finding a suitable aquisition, George hired an investment banker to evaluate three potential businesses. He also hired a law firm to begin drafting regulatory approval documents for a target company. Eventually, George decided to purchase all the assets of Blue Corporation. Blue Corporation and George entered into an acquisition agreement on December 1, 2006. Identify the relevant tax issues for George.

25. Briefly discuss how cost depletion is computed for a particular tax year.

PROBLEMS

26. On November 4, 2004, Blue Company acquired an asset (27.5-year residential real property) for $100,000 for use in its business. In 2004 and 2005, respectively, Blue took $321 and $2,564 of cost recovery. These amounts were incorrect because Blue applied the wrong percentages (i.e., those for 39-year rather than 27.5-year). Blue should have taken $455 and $3,636 cost recovery in 2004 and 2005. On January 1, 2006, the asset was sold for $98,000. Calculate the gain or loss on the sale of the asset in 2006.

27. José purchased a house for $175,000 in 2003. He used the house as his personal residence. In March 2006, when the fair market value of the house was $210,000, he converted the house to rental property. What is José's cost recovery for 2006?

28. Blue Corporation acquired a new tractor on August 15, 2006, for $150,000. Blue did not elect immediate expensing under § 179. Determine Blue's cost recovery for 2006.

29. Walt acquires a new 10-year class asset on June 17, 2006, for $220,000. This is the only asset acquired by Walt during the year. He does not elect immediate expensing under § 179. Compute Walt's cost recovery for 2006.

30. Juan acquires a new five-year class asset on March 14, 2006, for $200,000. This is the only asset acquired by Juan during the year. He does not elect immediate expensing under § 179. On July 15, 2007, Juan sells the asset.
    a. Determine Juan's cost recovery for 2006.
    b. Determine Juan's cost recovery for 2007.

31. Debra acquired the following new assets during the current year:

Date	Asset	Cost
April 11	Furniture	$50,000
July 28	Trucks	30,000
November 3	Computers	60,000

    Determine the cost recovery for the current year. Debra does not elect immediate expensing under § 179.

32. On July 10, 1997, Wade purchased and placed in service a warehouse. The warehouse cost $850,000. On May 7, 2006, Wade sold the warehouse.
    a. Determine Wade's cost recovery for 1997.
    b. Determine Wade's cost recovery for 2006.

33. On April 3, 2006, Terry purchased and placed in service a building. The building cost $2 million. An appraisal determined that 25% of the total cost was attributed to the value of the land. The bottom floor of the building is leased to a retail business for $32,000. The other floors of the building are rental apartments with an annual rent of $160,000. Determine Terry's cost recovery for 2006.

34. On November 5, 2006, Chris acquires land with a warehouse on it for $3 million. The land was valued at $1 million. On January 10, 2017, Chris sells the land and warehouse for $4.5 million. Calculate Chris's cost recovery for 2006. For 2017.

35. Janice acquired an apartment building on June 4, 2006, for $1.4 million. The value of the land is $200,000. Janice sold the apartment building on November 29, 2012.
    a. Determine Janice's cost recovery for 2006.
    b. Determine Janice's cost recovery for 2012.

36. Lori, who is single, purchased a new copier (five-year class property) for $30,000 and new furniture (seven-year class property) for $112,000 on May 20, 2006. Lori expects the taxable income derived from her business (without regard to the amount expensed under § 179) to be about $200,000. Lori wants to elect immediate § 179 expensing, but she doesn't know which asset she should expense under § 179.

Decision Making

    a.   Determine Lori's total deduction if the § 179 expense is first taken with respect to the copier.

    b.   Determine Lori's total deduction if the § 179 expense is first taken with respect to the furniture.

    c.   What is your advice to Lori?

37.   Jack owns a small business that he operates as a sole proprietor. In 2006, Jack will net $80,000 of business income before consideration of any § 179 deduction. Jack spends $432,000 on new equipment in 2006. If Jack also has $4,000 of § 179 deduction carryforwards from 2005, determine his § 179 expense deduction for 2006 and the amount of any carryforward.

38.   Olga is the proprietor of a small business. In 2006, the business income, before consideration of any cost recovery or § 179 deduction, is $180,000. Olga spends $132,000 for new furniture and elects to take the § 179 deduction on the furniture. Olga's cost recovery deduction for 2006, except for the cost recovery deduction with respect to the furniture, is $86,000. Determine Olga's total cost recovery for 2006 with respect to the furniture and the amount of any § 179 carryforward.

Decision Making

39.   On March 10, 2006, Yoon purchased three-year class property for $20,000. On December 15, 2006, Yoon purchased five-year class property for $127,000. He has net business income of $140,000 before consideration of any § 179 deduction.

    a.   Calculate Yoon's cost recovery for 2006, assuming he does not make the § 179 election or use straight-line cost recovery.

    b.   Calculate Yoon's cost recovery for 2006, assuming he does elect to use § 179 and does not elect to use straight-line cost recovery.

    c.   Assuming Yoon's marginal tax rate is 33%, determine his tax benefit from electing § 179.

40.   Martha owns a business that she operates as a sole proprietor. In 2006, she will have net income of $22,000 before regular MACRS and the § 179 expense are deducted. Martha spent $40,000 on a new five-year class asset in June 2006. She also has $5,000 of § 179 carryforwards from prior years. Determine Martha's § 179 deduction for 2006 and any § 179 carryforward.

Communications

41.   John Johnson is considering acquiring an automobile at the beginning of 2006 that he will use 100% of the time as a taxi. The purchase price of the automobile is $35,000. John has heard of cost recovery limits on automobiles and wants to know how much of the $35,000 he can deduct in the first year. Write a letter to John in which you present your calculations. Also, prepare a memo for the tax files. John's address is 100 Morningside, Clinton, MS 39058.

42.   On October 15, 2006, Jon purchased and placed in service a new car. The purchase price was $30,000. This was the only business use asset Jon acquired in 2006. He used the car 80% of the time for business and 20% for personal use. Jon used the statutory percentage method of cost recovery. Calculate the total deduction Jon may take for 2006 with respect to the car.

43.   On June 5, 2006, Leo purchased and placed in service a new car that cost $18,000. The business use percentage for the car is always 100%. Compute Leo's cost recovery deduction in 2006 and 2007.

44.   On March 15, 2006, Helen purchased and placed in service a new Ford Excursion. The purchase price was $60,000, and the vehicle had a rating of 6,500 GVW. The vehicle was used 100% for business. Calculate the maximum total deduction Helen may take with respect to the vehicle in 2006.

45.   On May 28, 2006, Mary purchased and placed in service a new $20,000 car. The car was used 60% for business, 20% for production of income, and 20% for personal use. In 2007, the usage changed to 40% for business, 30% for production of income, and 30% for personal use. Mary did not elect immediate expensing under § 179. Compute the cost recovery and any cost recovery recapture in 2007.

Decision Making

46.   Sally purchased a new computer (five-year property) on June 1, 2006, for $4,000. Sally could use the computer 100% of the time in her business, or she could allow her family to also use the computer. Sally estimates that if her family uses the

computer, the business use will be 45% and the personal use will be 55%. Determine the tax cost to Sally, in the year of acquisition, of allowing her family to use the computer. Assume that Sally would not elect § 179 limited expensing and that her marginal tax rate is 28%.

47. At the beginning of the current year, Abdel purchased a new computer (five-year class property) for $8,000. During the year, Abdel used the computer 80% of the time for his personal investments and 20% of the time for personal use. Calculate the maximum total deduction Abdel can take with respect to the computer for the current tax year.

48. Midway through 2006, Abdel leases and places in service a passenger automobile. The lease will run for five years, and the payments are $700 per month. During 2006, Abdel uses the car 65% for business use and 35% for personal use. Assuming the inclusion dollar amount from the IRS table is $85, determine the tax consequences to Abdel from the lease for the year 2006.

49. Dennis Harding is considering acquiring a new automobile that he will use 100% for business. The purchase price of the automobile would be $35,000. If Dennis leased the car for five years, the lease payments would be $375 per month. Dennis will acquire the car on January 1, 2006. The inclusion dollar amounts from the IRS table for the next five years are $95, $209, $309, $372, and $430. Dennis desires to know the effect on his adjusted gross income of purchasing versus leasing the car for the next five years. Write a letter to Dennis and present your calculations. Also, prepare a memo for the tax files. His address is 150 Avenue I, Memphis, TN 38112.

Decision Making

Communications

50. On March 5, 2006, Nell purchased new equipment for $90,000. The equipment has an ADS midpoint of 9.5 years. Determine Nell's cost recovery deduction for computing 2006 taxable income using the straight-line method under ADS and assuming she does not make a § 179 election.

51. In 2006, Muhammad purchased a new computer for $14,000. The computer is used 100% for business. Muhammad did not make a § 179 election with respect to the computer. If Muhammad uses the statutory percentage method, determine his cost recovery deduction for 2006 for computing taxable income and for computing his alternative minimum tax.

52. Jamie purchased $100,000 of new office furniture for her business in June of the current year. Jamie understands that if she elects to use ADS to compute her regular income tax, there will be no difference between the cost recovery for computing the regular income tax and the AMT. Jamie wants to know the *regular* income tax cost, after three years, of using ADS rather than MACRS. Assume that Jamie does not elect § 179 limited expensing and that her marginal tax rate is 28%.

Decision Making

53. Mike Saxon is negotiating the purchase of a business. The final purchase price has been agreed upon, but the allocation of the purchase price to the assets is still being discussed. Appraisals on a warehouse range from $1.2 million to $1.5 million. If a value of $1.2 million is used for the warehouse, the remainder of the purchase price, $800,000, will be allocated to goodwill. If $1.5 million is allocated to the warehouse, goodwill will be $500,000. Mike wants to know what effect each alternative will have on cost recovery and amortization during the first year. Under the agreement, Mike will take over the business on January 1 of next year. Write a letter to Mike in which you present your calculations and recommendation. Also, prepare a memo for the tax files. Mike's address is 200 Rolling Hills Drive, Shavertown, PA 18708.

Decision Making

Communications

54. Oleander Corporation, a calendar year entity, begins business on March 1, 2006. The corporation has startup expenditures of $58,000. If Oleander elects § 195 treatment, determine the total amount of startup expenditures that it may deduct in 2006.

55. Mary is considering acquiring an active business. During her preliminary investigations, she incurs startup expenditures of $45,000. She ultimately acquires the business and begins operations on May 2 of the current year. If Mary elects § 195 treatment, determine her startup expenditure deduction for the current year.

56. Wes acquired a mineral interest during the year for $10 million. A geological survey estimated that 250,000 tons of the mineral remained in the deposit. During the year, 80,000 tons were mined, and 45,000 tons were sold for $12 million. Other expenses

amounted to $5 million. Assuming the mineral depletion rate is 22%, calculate Wes's lowest taxable income.

Decision Making

57. Chris purchased an oil interest for $2 million. Recoverable barrels were estimated to be 500,000. During the year, 120,000 barrels were sold for $3.84 million, regular expenses (including cost recovery) were $1.24 million, and IDC were $1 million. Calculate Chris's taxable income under the expensing and capitalization methods of handling IDC.

CUMULATIVE PROBLEMS

Tax Return Problem

TurboTax ✓

58. Janice Morgan, age 32, is single and has no dependents. She is a freelance writer. In January 2005, Janice opened her own office located at 2751 Waldham Road, Pleasantville, NM 17196. She called her business Writers Anonymous. Janice is a cash basis taxpayer. She lives at 132 Stone Avenue, Pleasantville, NM 17196. Her Social Security number is 189–57–6691. Janice desires to contribute to the Presidential Election Campaign Fund.

During 2005, Janice had the following income and expense items connected with her business:

Income from sale of articles	$115,000
Rent	16,500
Utilities	7,900
Supplies	1,800
Insurance	5,000
Travel (including meals of $1,200)	3,500

Janice purchased and placed in service the following fixed assets for her business:

- Furniture and fixtures (new) costing $19,000 on January 10, 2005.
- Computer equipment (new) costing $40,000 on July 28, 2005.

Janice would like to deduct these costs as soon as possible.

Janice's itemized deductions are as follows:

State income tax	$2,000
Home mortgage interest paid to First Bank	6,000
Property taxes on home	1,500
Charitable contributions	1,200

Janice did not keep a record of the sales tax she paid. The amount from the sales tax table is $437.

Janice has interest income of $4,000 on certificates of deposit at Second Bank. Janice makes estimated tax payments of $5,000 for 2005.

Compute Janice Morgan's 2005 Federal income tax payable (or refund due). If you use tax forms for your computations, you will need Form(s) 1040 and 4562 and Schedules A, B, C, and SE. Suggested software: TurboTax.

Tax Return Problem

Decision Making

Communications

59. John Smith, age 31, is single and has no dependents. At the beginning of 2006, John started his own excavation business and named it Earth Movers. John lives at 1045 Center Street, Lindon, UT, and his business is located at 381 State Street, Lindon, UT. The zip code for both addresses is 84059. John's Social Security number is 321–09–6456, and the business identification number is 98–1234567. John is a cash basis taxpayer. During 2006, John had the following items in connection with his business:

Fees for services	$512,000
Building rental expense	36,000
Office furniture and equipment rental expense	9,000
Office supplies	2,500
Utilities	4,000
Salary for secretary	34,000

Salary for equipment operators	$ 42,000
Payroll taxes	7,000
Fuel and oil for the equipment	21,000
Purchase of three new front-end loaders on January 15, 2006, for $390,000. John made the election under § 179.	390,000
Purchase of a new dump truck on January 18, 2006	45,000

During 2006, John had the following additional items:

Interest income from First National Bank	$ 10,000
Dividends from ExxonMobil	9,500
Quarterly estimated tax payments	11,500

On October 8, 2006, John inherited IBM stock from his Aunt Mildred. John had been her favorite nephew. According to the data provided by the executor of Aunt Mildred's estate, the stock was valued for estate tax purposes at $110,000. John is considering selling the IBM stock for $115,000 on December 29, 2006, and using $75,000 of the proceeds to purchase an Acura NSX. He would use the car 100% for business. John wants to know what effect these transactions would have on his 2006 adjusted gross income.

Write a letter to John in which you present your calculations. Also, prepare a memo for the tax files.

RESEARCH PROBLEMS

Note: Solutions to Research Problems can be prepared by using the **RIA Checkpoint®** **Student Edition** online research product, which is available to accompany this text. It is also possible to prepare solutions to the Research Problems by using tax research materials found in a standard tax library.

Communications

Research Problem 1. Harry Pickart, one of your clients, operates a business that rents aircraft parts to motion picture studios for use in film production. Harry purchased most of the aircraft parts at auctions held throughout the United States. At those auctions, Harry usually acquired the parts in large quantities because he speculated that he would be able to use at least some of them in his rental business. After the conclusion of a film production, the movie studio returns the aircraft parts it rented from Harry. The parts are often returned in damaged condition or with pieces missing. Harry sometimes attempts to repair a damaged part so that it can be rented again. After being subjected to wear and tear from use, however, a part deteriorates over time, which varies depending on the particular part and its treatment by the studios during rental. Harry believes that all of the aircraft parts have a useful life of less than four years and, therefore, are entitled to be classed as three-year property. Write a letter to Harry that contains your advice on whether the aircraft parts can be depreciated over three years. Also, prepare a memo for the tax files. Harry's mailing address is P.O. Box 100, Sun River, OR 97600.

Research Problem 2. United Bank is a federally chartered banking institution engaged in the business of issuing credit cards to customers. United also regularly purchases credit card receivables and/or cardholders' accounts from other financial institutions. Thereafter, United may or may not extend additional credit to the customers on these accounts. In connection with its credit card business, United derives interest income, fees, and interchange income. United wants to know whether costs incurred in connection with the acquisition of credit card receivables must be capitalized under § 263 or whether they can be amortized under § 195.

Research Problem 3. Keith has just finished building a new golf course. He would like to know whether he can take a cost recovery deduction with respect to the golf course greens.

Research Problem 4. Juan owns a business that acquires exotic automobiles that are high-technology, state-of-the-art vehicles with unique design features or equipment. The exotic automobiles are not licensed or set up to be used on the road. Rather, the cars are used exclusively for car shows or related promotional photography. Juan would like to know whether he can take a cost recovery deduction with respect to the exotic automobiles on his Federal income tax return.

Partial list of research aids:
Bruce Selig, 70 TCM 1125, T.C.Memo. 1995–519.

Research Problem 5. Bud purchased farmland from Enos. Bud paid Enos $400,000 for the land. Bud also paid Enos $100,000 for the peanut base acres and payment yield assigned to the land. Bud would like to know whether he can take cost recovery or amortization on the $100,000 payment.

 Internet *Activity*

Use the tax resources of the Internet to address the following questions. Do not restrict your search to the World Wide Web, but include a review of newsgroups and general reference materials, practitioner sites and resources, primary sources of the tax law, chat rooms and discussion groups, and other opportunities.

Research Problem 6. Locate a financial calculator program that assesses the wisdom of buying versus leasing a new car. Install the program on your computer and become familiar with it. Use the program to work through Problem 49 in this chapter.

Research Problem 7. Changes to depreciation systems often are discussed by policy makers and observers of the tax system. Outline the terms and policy objectives of one of the changes currently proposed by the Treasury, a member of Congress, or a tax policy think tank.

CHAPTER 9

Deductions: Employee and Self-Employed-Related Expenses

LEARNING OBJECTIVES

After completing Chapter 9, you should be able to:

LO.1
Distinguish between employee and self-employed status.

LO.2
Recognize deductible transportation expenses.

LO.3
Know how travel expenses are treated.

LO.4
Determine the moving expense deduction.

LO.5
Differentiate between deductible and nondeductible education expenses.

LO.6
Understand how entertainment expenses are treated.

LO.7
Identify other employee expenses.

LO.8
Become familiar with various deductions for contributions to retirement accounts.

LO.9
Appreciate the difference between accountable and nonaccountable employee plans.

LO.10
Work with the limitations on miscellaneous itemized deductions.

LO.11
Develop tax planning ideas related to employee business expenses.

OUTLINE

Considering the large number of taxpayers affected, the tax treatment of job-related expenses is unusually complex. To resolve this matter in a systematic fashion, a number of key questions must be asked:

- Is the taxpayer an *employee* or *self-employed?*
- If an employee, what expenses *qualify* as deductions?
- How are the expenses that qualify *classified* for tax purposes?
- To the extent the expenses are classified as deductions *from* AGI, are they subject to any *limitation?*

Once these questions have been posed and answered, the chapter considers various planning procedures available to maximize the deductibility of employee expenses.

LO.1

Distinguish between employee and self-employed status.

Employee versus Self-Employed

When one person performs services for another, the person performing the service is either an employee or self-employed (an **independent contractor**). Failure to recognize employee status can have serious consequences. Not only can interest and penalties result, but negative media coverage can impair career opportunities (see the *Tax in the News* on the following page).

The problem is likely to intensify since businesses are increasingly relying on the services of self-employed persons for numerous reasons. Unlike employees, self-employed persons do not have to be included in various fringe benefit programs (e.g., group term life insurance) and retirement plans. Since they are not covered by FICA and FUTA (see Chapter 1), these payroll costs are avoided. The IRS is very much aware of the tendency of businesses to wrongly classify workers as self-employed rather than as employees.

TAX *in the News*   NANNYGATE REVISITED

For those who remember the nomination fiascoes during the Clinton administration involving Zoe Baird (Attorney General, 1993) and Bobby Ray Inman (Secretary of Defense, 1994), and President Bush's nomination of Linda Chavez (Secretary of Labor, 2001), the Bernard Kerik incident in December 2004 must have been a touch of déjà vu. Nominated by President Bush to be head of Homeland Security, Kerik felt compelled to withdraw when it came to light that he had employed an illegal immigrant as a nanny. Ironically, as Secretary of Homeland Security, he would have overseen the enforcement of the nation's immigration laws. Furthermore, Kerik had compounded the wrongdoing by not paying any employment taxes on the wages earned by the nanny.

The moral of the story? If you aspire to a high-profile government appointment, avoid the nannygate trap!

In terms of tax consequences, employment status also makes a great deal of difference to the persons who perform the services. Expenses of self-employed taxpayers, to the extent allowable, are classified as deductions *for* AGI and are reported on Schedule C (Profit or Loss From Business) of Form 1040.[1] With the exception of reimbursement under an accountable plan (see later in the chapter), expenses of employees are deductions *from* AGI. They are reported on Form 2106 (Employee Business Expenses) and Schedule A (Itemized Deductions) of Form 1040.[2]

But when does an employer-employee relationship exist? Such a relationship exists when the employer has the right to specify the end result and the ways and means by which that result is to be attained.[3] An employee is subject to the will and control of the employer with respect not only to what shall be done but also to how it shall be done. If the individual is subject to the direction or control of another only to the extent of the end result but not as to the means of accomplishment, an employer-employee relationship does not exist. An example is the preparation of a taxpayer's return by an independent CPA.

Certain factors indicate an employer-employee relationship. They include (1) the right to discharge without legal liability the person performing the service, (2) the furnishing of tools or a place to work, and (3) payment based on time spent rather than the task performed. Each case is tested on its own merits, and the right to control the means and methods of accomplishment is the definitive test. Generally, physicians, lawyers, dentists, contractors, subcontractors, and others who offer services to the public are not classified as employees.

Arnold is a lawyer whose major client accounts for 60% of his billings. He does the routine legal work and income tax returns at the client's request. He is paid a monthly retainer in addition to amounts charged for extra work. Arnold is a self-employed individual. Even though most of his income comes from one client, he still has the right to determine how the end result of his work is attained. ■

EXAMPLE 1

Ellen is a lawyer hired by Arnold to assist him in the performance of services for the client mentioned in Example 1. Ellen is under Arnold's supervision; he reviews her work and pays her an hourly fee. Ellen is an employee of Arnold. ■

EXAMPLE 2

Frank is a licensed practical nurse who works as a private-duty nurse. He is under the supervision of the patient's doctor and is paid by the patient. Frank is not an employee of either the patient (who pays him) or the doctor (who supervises him). The ways and means of attaining the end result (care of the patient) are under his control. ■

EXAMPLE 3

---

[1] §§ 62(a)(1) and 162(a). See Appendix B for a reproduction of Schedule C.
[2] See Appendix B for a reproduction of Schedule A.

[3] Reg. § 31.3401(c)-(1)(b).

Employees in a special category are also allowed to file Schedule C to report income and deduct expenses *for* AGI. These employees are called **statutory employees** because they are not common law employees under the rules explained above. The wages or commissions paid to statutory employees are not subject to Federal income tax withholding but are subject to Social Security tax.[4]

Employee Expenses—In General

Once the employment relationship is established, employee expenses fall into one of the following categories:

- Transportation.
- Travel.
- Moving.
- Education.
- Entertainment.
- Other.

These expenses are discussed below in the order presented.

Keep in mind, however, that these expenses are not necessarily limited to employees. A deduction for business transportation, for example, is equally available to taxpayers who are self-employed.

LO.2

Recognize deductible transportation expenses.

Transportation Expenses

Qualified Expenditures

An employee may deduct unreimbursed employment-related transportation expenses as an itemized deduction *from* AGI. **Transportation expenses** include only the cost of transporting the employee from one place to another in the course of employment when the employee is *not* away from home *in travel status*. Such costs include taxi fares, automobile expenses, tolls, and parking.

Commuting Expenses. Commuting between home and one's place of employment is a personal, nondeductible expense. The fact that one employee drives 30 miles to work and another employee walks six blocks is of no significance.[5]

EXAMPLE 4

Geraldo is employed by Sparrow Corporation. He drives 22 miles each way to work. The 44 miles he drives each workday are nondeductible commuting expenses. ∎

The rule that disallows a deduction for commuting expenses has several exceptions. An employee who uses an automobile to transport heavy tools to work and who otherwise would not drive to work is allowed a deduction, but only for the additional costs incurred to transport the work implements. Additional costs are those exceeding the cost of commuting by the same mode of transportation without the tools. For example, the rental of a trailer for transporting tools is deductible, but the expenses of operating the automobile generally are not deductible.[6] The Supreme Court has held that a deduction is permitted only when the taxpayer can show that the automobile would not have been used without the necessity to transport tools or equipment.[7]

---

[4]See Circular E, *Employer's Tax Guide* (IRS Publication 15), for further discussion of statutory employees.
[5]*Tauferner v. U.S.*, 69–1 USTC ¶9241, 23 AFTR2d 69–1025, 407 F.2d 243 (CA–10, 1969).

[6]Rev.Rul. 75–380, 1975–2 C.B. 59.
[7]*Fausner v. Comm.*, 73–2 USTC ¶9515, 32 AFTR2d 73–5202, 93 S.Ct. 2820 (USSC, 1973).

Another exception is provided for an employee who has a second job. The expenses of getting from one job to another are deductible. If the employee goes home between jobs, the deduction is based on the distance between jobs.

In the current year, Cynthia holds two jobs, a full-time job with Blue Corporation and a part-time job with Wren Corporation. During the 250 days that she works (adjusted for weekends, vacation, and holidays), Cynthia customarily leaves home at 7:30 A.M. and drives 30 miles to the Blue Corporation plant, where she works until 5:00 P.M. After dinner at a nearby café, Cynthia drives 20 miles to Wren Corporation and works from 7:00 to 11:00 P.M. The distance from the second job to Cynthia's home is 40 miles. Her deduction is based on 20 miles (the distance between jobs). ■

EXAMPLE 5

If the taxpayer is required to incur a transportation expense to travel between work stations, that expense is deductible.

Norman is the local manager for a national chain of fast-food outlets. Each workday he drives from his home to his office to handle administrative matters. Most of his day, however, is then spent making the rounds of the retail outlets, after which he drives home. The costs incurred in driving to his office and driving home from the last outlet are nondeductible commuting expenses. The other transportation costs are deductible. ■

EXAMPLE 6

Likewise, the commuting costs from home to a temporary work station and from the temporary work station to home are deductible.

Vivian works for a firm in downtown Denver and commutes to work. She occasionally works in a customer's office. On one such occasion, Vivian drove directly to the customer's office, a round-trip distance from her home of 40 miles. She did not go into her office, which is a 52-mile round-trip. Her mileage for going to and from the temporary work station is deductible. ■

EXAMPLE 7

Also deductible is the reasonable travel cost between the general working area and a temporary work station outside that area.[8]

Sam, a building inspector in Minneapolis, regularly inspects buildings for building code violations for his employer, a general contractor. During one busy season, the St. Paul inspector became ill, and Sam was required to inspect several buildings in St. Paul. The expenses for transportation for the trips to St. Paul are deductible. ■

EXAMPLE 8

What constitutes the general working area depends on the facts and circumstances of each situation. Furthermore, if an employee customarily works on several temporary assignments in a localized area, that localized area becomes the regular place of employment. Transportation from home to these locations becomes a personal, nondeductible commuting expense.

Computation of Automobile Expenses

A taxpayer has two choices in determining automobile expenses: the automatic mileage method and the actual cost method. If a mixed-use automobile is involved, only the expenses attributable to the business use are deductible. The percentage of business use is usually arrived at by comparing the business mileage with total mileage—both business and personal.

Automatic Mileage Method. Also called the standard mileage method, the **automatic mileage method** is convenient in that it simplifies record keeping.

[8]Rev.Rul. 90–23, 1990–1 C.B. 28 and Rev.Rul. 190, 1953–2 C.B. 303, as amplified by Rev.Rul. 94–47, 1994–2 C.B. 18.

The rate allowed per mile takes into account average operating expenses (such as gas and oil, repairs, and depreciation). Consequently, the taxpayer only has to multiply the automatic mileage rate by the miles driven to compute the deduction for business transportation.

For 2006, the deduction is based on 44.5 cents per mile for business miles.[9] The mileage rate for 2005 was split as follows: 40.5 cents for January–August and 48.5 cents for September–December. The late-year increase of eight cents was due to the sudden rise in the cost of gasoline triggered by Hurricanes Katrina and Rita. Parking fees and tolls are allowed in addition to expenses computed using the automatic mileage method.

Generally, a taxpayer may elect either method for any particular year. However, the following restrictions apply:

- The vehicle must be owned or leased by the taxpayer.
- The vehicle is not used for hire (e.g., taxicab).
- If five or more vehicles are in use (for business purposes) at the *same* time (not alternately), a taxpayer may not use the automatic mileage method.
- A basis adjustment is required if the taxpayer changes from the automatic mileage method to the actual operating cost method. Depreciation is considered allowed for the business miles in accordance with the following schedule for the most recent five years:

Year	Rate per Mile
2006	17 cents
2005	17 cents
2004	16 cents
2003	16 cents
2002	15 cents

EXAMPLE 9

Tim purchased his automobile in 2003 for $36,000. It is used 90% for business purposes. Tim drove the automobile for 10,000 business miles in 2005; 8,500 business miles in 2004; and 6,000 business miles in 2003. At the beginning of 2006, the basis of the business portion is $28,380.

Depreciable basis ($36,000 × 90%)	$32,400
Less depreciation:	
2005 (10,000 miles × 17 cents)	(1,700)
2004 (8,500 miles × 16 cents)	(1,360)
2003 (6,000 miles × 16 cents)	(960)
Adjusted business basis 1/1/2006	$28,380

- Use of the automatic mileage method in the first year the auto is placed in service is considered an election to exclude the auto from the MACRS method of depreciation (discussed in Chapter 8).
- A taxpayer may not switch to the automatic mileage method if the MACRS statutory percentage method or the election to expense under § 179 has been used.

Actual Cost Method. Under this method, the actual cost of operating the automobile is used to compute the deduction. Actual costs include the following expenses:

- Gas and oil, lubrication.
- Depreciation (or lease payments).

[9]Rev.Proc. 2005–78, I.R.B. No. 51, 1177.

- Insurance.
- Dues to auto clubs.
- Repairs.
- Tires and other parts.
- Licenses and registration fees.
- Parking and tolls.

As noted in Chapter 8, the allowance for depreciation (or lease payments) is subject to limitations when mixed-use vehicles are involved (see Example 15 on page 8–13). Interest on car loans is not deductible if the taxpayer is an employee, but it can qualify as a business expense if the taxpayer is self-employed.[10] Sales taxes paid on the purchase of a car are added to the cost of the car and recovered by means of the depreciation deduction. In mixed-use situations, the portion of the sales tax attributable to personal use may, in some cases, be claimed as a deduction *from* AGI (see Chapter 10 and the choice required between state and local income and sales taxes).

Except for parking and tolls, none of the expenses noted above can be separately claimed under the automatic mileage method. A deduction for parking tickets and other traffic violations is not allowed under either method due to the public policy limitation (see Chapter 6).

Travel Expenses

LO.3

Know how travel expenses are treated.

Definition of Travel Expenses

An itemized deduction is allowed for unreimbursed travel expenses related to a taxpayer's employment. **Travel expenses** are more broadly defined in the Code than are transportation expenses. Travel expenses include transportation expenses and meals and lodging while away from home in the pursuit of a trade or business. Meals cannot be lavish or extravagant under the circumstances. Transportation expenses (as previously discussed) are deductible even though the taxpayer is not away from home. A deduction for travel expenses is available only if the taxpayer is away from his or her tax home. Travel expenses also include reasonable laundry and incidental expenses.

Away-from-Home Requirement

The crucial test for the deductibility of travel expenses is whether the employee is away from home overnight. "Overnight" need not be a 24-hour period, but it must be a period substantially longer than an ordinary day's work and must require rest, sleep, or a relief-from-work period.[11] A one-day business trip is not travel status, and meals and lodging for such a trip are not deductible.

overnight is ded.

Temporary Assignments.
The employee must be away from home for a temporary period. If the taxpayer-employee is reassigned to a new post for an indefinite period of time, that new post becomes his or her tax home. *Temporary* indicates that the assignment's termination is expected within a reasonably short period of time. The position of the IRS is that the tax home is the business location, post, or station of the taxpayer. Thus, travel expenses are not deductible if a taxpayer is reassigned for an indefinite period and does not move his or her place of residence to the new location.

---

[10]An interest deduction could be available if the purchase of the auto was financed with a home equity loan. See the discussion of itemized deductions in Chapter 10.

[11]*U.S. v. Correll,* 68–1 USTC ¶9101, 20 AFTR2d 5845, 88 S.Ct. 445 (USSC, 1967); Rev.Rul. 75–168, 1975–1 C.B. 58.

EXAMPLE 10	Malcolm's employer opened a branch office in San Diego. Malcolm was assigned to the new office for three months to train a new manager and to assist in setting up the new office. He tried commuting from his home in Los Angeles for a week and decided that he could not continue driving several hours a day. He rented an apartment in San Diego, where he lived during the week. He spent weekends with his wife and children at their home in Los Angeles. Malcolm's rent, meals, laundry, incidentals, and automobile expenses in San Diego are deductible. To the extent that Malcolm's transportation expense related to his weekend trips home exceeds what his cost of meals and lodging would have been, the excess is personal and nondeductible. ∎
EXAMPLE 11	Assume that Malcolm in Example 10 was transferred to the new location to become the new manager permanently. His wife and children continued to live in Los Angeles until the end of the school year. Malcolm is no longer "away from home" because the assignment is not temporary. His travel expenses are not deductible. ∎

To curtail controversy in this area, the Code specifies that a taxpayer "*shall not* be treated as *temporarily* away from home during any period of employment if such period exceeds 1 year."[12]

Determining the Tax Home. Under ordinary circumstances, determining the location of a taxpayer's tax home does not present a problem. The tax home is the area in which the taxpayer derives his or her principal source of income. When the taxpayer has more than one place of employment, the tax home is based on the amount of time spent in each area.

It is possible for a taxpayer never to be away from his or her tax home. In other words, the tax home follows the taxpayer. Thus, all meals and lodging remain personal and are not deductible. The reason for this result is that there is no duplication of expenses.[13]

EXAMPLE 12	Jim is single and lives with his parents. Although he is employed full-time as a long-haul truck driver, he contributes nothing toward the cost of maintaining his parents' household. The meals and lodging expenses Jim incurs while on the road are not deductible. ∎

Restrictions on Travel Expenses

The possibility always exists that taxpayers will attempt to treat vacation or pleasure travel as deductible business travel. To prevent such practices, the law contains restrictions on certain travel expenses.

Conventions. For travel expenses to be deductible, a convention must be directly related to the taxpayer's trade or business.[14]

EXAMPLE 13	Dr. Hill, a pathologist who works for a hospital in Ohio, travels to Las Vegas to attend a two-day session on recent developments in estate planning. No deduction is allowed for Dr. Hill's travel expenses. ∎
EXAMPLE 14	Assume the same facts as in Example 13, except that the convention deals entirely with recent developments in forensic medicine. Under these circumstances, a travel deduction is allowed. ∎

[12]§ 162(a).

[13]Rev.Rul. 73–539, 1973–2 C.B. 37 and *James O. Henderson*, 70 TCM 1407, T.C.Memo. 1995–559, *aff'd* by 98–1 USTC ¶50,375, 81 AFTR2d 98–1748, 143 F.3d 497 (CA–9, 1998).

[14]§ 274(h)(1).

If the proceedings of the convention are videotaped, the taxpayer must attend convention sessions to view the videotaped materials along with other participants. This requirement does not disallow deductions for costs (other than travel, meals, and entertainment) of renting or using videotaped materials related to business.

EXAMPLE 15

A CPA is unable to attend a convention at which current developments in taxation are discussed. She pays $200 for videotapes of the lectures and views them at home later. The $200 is an itemized deduction if the CPA is an employee. If she is self-employed, the $200 is a deduction *for* AGI. ▪

The Code places stringent restrictions on the deductibility of travel expenses of the taxpayer's spouse or dependent.[15] Generally, the accompaniment by the spouse or dependent must serve a bona fide business purpose, and the expenses must be otherwise deductible.

EXAMPLE 16

Assume the same facts as in Example 14 with the additional fact that Dr. Hill is accompanied by Mrs. Hill. Mrs. Hill is not employed, but possesses secretarial skills and takes notes during the proceedings. No deduction is allowed for Mrs. Hill's travel expenses. ▪

EXAMPLE 17

Modify the facts in Example 16 to make Mrs. Hill a nurse trained in pathology, who is employed by Dr. Hill as his assistant. Now, Mrs. Hill's travel expenses qualify as deductions. ▪

Travel to learn culture...

Education. Travel as a form of education is not deductible.[16] If, however, the education qualifies as a deduction, the travel involved is allowed.

EXAMPLE 18

Greta, a German teacher, travels to Germany to maintain general familiarity with the language and culture. No travel expense deduction is allowed. ▪

EXAMPLE 19

Jean-Claude, a scholar of French literature, travels to Paris to do specific library research that cannot be done elsewhere and to take courses that are offered only at the Sorbonne. The travel costs are deductible, assuming that the other requirements for deducting education expenses (discussed later in the chapter) are met. ▪

Combined Business and Pleasure Travel

To be deductible, travel expenses need not be incurred in the performance of specific job functions. Travel expenses incurred in attending a professional convention are deductible by an employee if attendance is connected with services as an employee. For example, an employee of a law firm can deduct travel expenses incurred in attending a meeting of the American Bar Association.

Domestic Travel. Travel deductions have been used in the past by persons who claimed a tax deduction for what was essentially a personal vacation. As a result, several provisions have been enacted to govern deductions associated with combined business and pleasure trips. If the business/pleasure trip is from one point in the United States to another point in the United States, the transportation expenses are deductible only if the trip is *primarily for business*.[17] If the trip is primarily for pleasure, no transportation expenses qualify as a deduction. Meals, lodging, and other expenses are allocated between business and personal days.

US Travel

Primarily for Business?

Y   N

Tickets (ded)   No

Lodging, meals, other

Allocated b/t Bus & Personal

---

[15]§ 274(m)(3).
[16]§ 274(m)(2).

[17]Reg. § 1.162–2(b)(1).

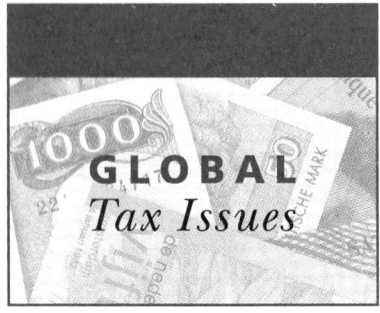

GLOBAL *Tax Issues*

CONVENTIONS IN FARAWAY LANDS

Certain restrictions are imposed on the deductibility of expenses paid or incurred to attend conventions located outside the North American area. The expenses are disallowed unless it is established that the meeting is directly related to a trade or business of the taxpayer. Disallowance also occurs unless the taxpayer shows that it is as reasonable for the meeting to be held in a foreign location as within the North American area.

The foreign convention rules do not operate to bar a deduction to an employer if the expense is compensatory in nature. For example, a trip to Rome won by a top salesperson is included in the gross income of the employee and is fully deductible by the employer.

EXAMPLE 20

In the current year, Hana travels from Seattle to New York primarily for business. She spends five days conducting business and three days sightseeing and attending shows. Her plane and taxi fare amounts to $560. Her meals amount to $100 per day, and lodging and incidental expenses are $150 per day. She can deduct the transportation charges of $560, since the trip is primarily for business (five days of business versus three days of sightseeing). Meals are limited to five days and are subject to the 50% cutback (discussed later in the chapter) for a total of $250 [5 days × ($100 × 50%)], and other expenses are limited to $750 (5 days × $150). If Hana is an employee, the unreimbursed travel expenses are miscellaneous itemized deductions. ∎

EXAMPLE 21

Assume Hana goes to New York for a two-week vacation. While there, she spends several hours renewing acquaintances with people in her company's New York office. Her transportation expenses are not deductible. ∎

Foreign Travel. When the trip is *outside the United States*, special rules apply. Transportation expenses must be allocated between business and personal unless (1) the taxpayer is away from home for seven days or less *or* (2) less than 25 percent of the time was for personal purposes. No allocation is required if the taxpayer has no substantial control over arrangements for the trip or the desire for a vacation is not a major factor in taking the trip. If the trip is primarily for pleasure, no transportation charges are deductible. Days devoted to travel are considered business days. Weekends, legal holidays, and intervening days are considered business days, provided that both the preceding and succeeding days were business days.[18]

EXAMPLE 22

In the current year, Robert takes a trip from New York to Japan primarily for business purposes. He is away from home from June 10 through June 19. He spends three days vacationing and seven days conducting business (including two travel days). His airfare is $2,500, his meals amount to $100 per day, and lodging and incidental expenses are $160 per day. Since Robert is away from home for more than seven days and more than 25% of his time is devoted to personal purposes, only 70% (7 days business/10 days total) of the transportation is deductible. His deductions are as follows:

Transportation (70% × $2,500)		$1,750
Lodging ($160 × 7)		1,120
Meals ($100 × 7)	$ 700	
Less: 50% cutback (discussed later)	(350)	350
Total		$3,220

∎

[18]§ 274(c) and Reg. § 1.274–4. For purposes of the seven-days-or-less exception, the departure travel day is not counted.

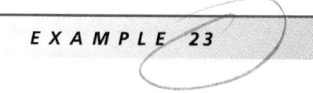

Assume the same facts as in Example 22. Robert is gone the same period of time, but spends only two days (rather than three) vacationing. Now no allocation of transportation is required. Since the pleasure portion of the trip is less than 25% of the total, all of the airfare qualifies for the travel deduction. ∎

E X A M P L E   23

Moving Expenses

Moving expenses are deductible for moves in connection with the commencement of work at a new principal place of work.[19] Both employees and self-employed individuals can deduct these expenses. To be eligible for a moving expense deduction, a taxpayer must meet two basic tests: distance and time.

LO.4

Determine the moving expense deduction.

Distance Test

To meet the distance test, the taxpayer's new job location must be at least 50 miles farther from the taxpayer's old residence than the old residence was from the former place of employment. In this regard, the location of the new residence is not relevant. This eliminates a moving deduction for taxpayers who purchase a new home in the same general area without changing their place of employment. Those who accept a new job in the same general area as the old job location are also eliminated.

Harry is permanently transferred to a new job location. The distance from Harry's former home to his new job (80 miles) exceeds the distance from his former home to his old job (30 miles) by at least 50 miles. Harry has met the distance test for a moving expense deduction. (See the following diagram.)

E X A M P L E   24

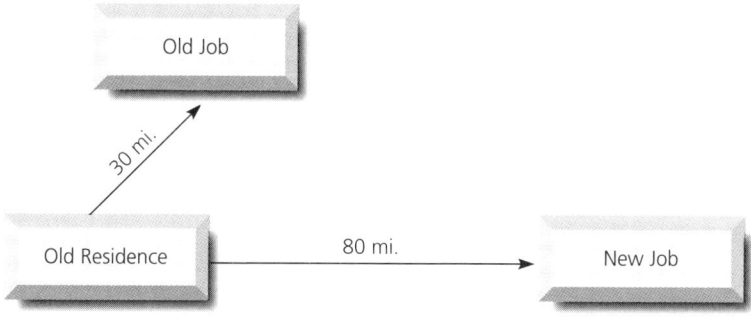

If Harry is not employed before the move, his new job must be at least 50 miles from his former residence. In this instance, Harry has met the distance test if he was not previously employed. ∎

Time Test

To meet the time test, an employee must be employed on a full-time basis at the new location for 39 weeks in the 12-month period following the move. If the taxpayer is a self-employed individual, he or she must work in the new location for 78 weeks during the next two years. The first 39 weeks must be in the first 12 months. The time test is suspended if the taxpayer dies, becomes disabled, or is discharged or transferred by the new employer through no fault of the employee.

A taxpayer might not be able to meet the 39-week test by the due date of the tax return for the year of the move. For this reason, two alternatives are allowed. The taxpayer can take the deduction in the year the expenses are incurred, even though

---

[19]§ 217(a).

the 39-week test has not been met. If the taxpayer later fails to meet the test, either (1) the income of the following year is increased by an amount equal to the deduction previously claimed for moving expenses, or (2) an amended return is filed for the year of the move. The second alternative is to wait until the test is met and then file an amended tax return for the year of the move.

Treatment of Moving Expenses

What Is Included. "Qualified" moving expenses include *reasonable* expenses of:

- Moving household goods and personal effects.
- Traveling from the former residence to the new place of residence.

For this purpose, *traveling* includes lodging, but not meals, for the taxpayer and members of the household.[20] The taxpayer can elect to use actual auto expenses (no depreciation is allowed) or the automatic mileage method. In this case, moving expense mileage is limited in 2006 to 18 cents per mile for each car. The automatic mileage rate for 2005 depended on when the move was made—15 cents per mile for January through August and 22 cents per mile for September through December. These expenses are also limited by the reasonableness standard. For example, if one moves from Texas to Florida via Maine and takes six weeks to do so, the transportation and lodging must be allocated between personal and moving expenses.

EXAMPLE 25

Jill is transferred by her employer from the Atlanta office to the San Francisco office. In this connection, she spends the following amounts:

Cost of moving furniture	$2,800
Transportation	700
Meals	200
Lodging	300

Jill's total qualified moving expense is $3,800 ($2,800 + $700 + $300). ■

The moving expense deduction is allowed regardless of whether the employee is transferred by the existing employer or is employed by a new employer. It is allowed if the employee moves to a new area and obtains employment or switches from self-employed status to employee status (and vice versa). The moving expense deduction is also allowed if an individual is unemployed before obtaining employment in a new area.

What Is Not Included. In addition to meals while en route, the moving expense deduction does *not* include the following costs:

- New car tags and driver's licenses.
- Loss on the sale of a residence or penalty for breaking a lease.
- Forfeiture of security deposits and loss from disposing of club memberships.
- Pre-move house-hunting expenses.
- Temporary living expenses.

Also not deductible are the costs of moving servants and others who are not members of the household.

How Treated. Qualified moving expenses that are paid (or reimbursed) by the employer are not reported as part of the gross income of the employee.[21] Moving expenses that are paid (or reimbursed) by the employer and are not qualified moving expenses are included in the employee's gross income and are not deductible.

reimbursed moving exp → ∅
reimbursed non-qualified moving exp → income.

[20]§ 217(b).

[21]§§ 132(a)(6) and (g).

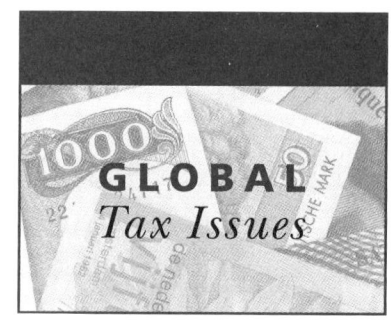

EXPATRIATES AND THE MOVING EXPENSE DEDUCTION

GLOBAL Tax Issues

Expatriates, U.S. persons who accept work assignments overseas, enjoy several favorable tax advantages regarding foreign moves. First, the cost of storing household goods qualifies as a moving expense. This could lead to a major tax saving since expatriates do not ship most of their household effects to the foreign location. Furthermore, the cost of storage, particularly in a climate-controlled facility, is not insignificant.

The second advantage expatriates could enjoy is an exemption from the time test. Those who return to the United States to retire are absolved from the 39-week or 78-week work requirement. Thus, the return home expenses are treated as qualified moving expenses.

The employer is responsible for allocating the reimbursement between the qualified and nonqualified moving expenses. Reimbursed qualified moving expenses are separately stated on the Form W–2 given to the employee for the year involved. Qualified moving expenses that are not reimbursed and those of self-employed taxpayers are deductions *for* AGI.[22]

Form 3903 is used to report the details of the moving expense deduction if the employee is not reimbursed or a self-employed person is involved.

ETHICAL *Considerations* | **MANIPULATING THE REAL ESTATE MARKET**

Ingrid is a key employee of Robin Corporation, an auto parts manufacturer located in Detroit. Robin would like to establish a presence in Tennessee and wants Ingrid to be in charge of the regional operation. Ingrid is reluctant to make the move because she fears that she will have to sell her residence in Detroit at a loss. Robin buys the house from Ingrid for $620,000, its cost to her. One year later, Robin sells the property for $550,000. Nothing regarding the sale of the residence is ever reflected on Ingrid's income tax return. Robin Corporation pays for all of Ingrid's other moving expenses. Do you have any qualms as to the way these matters have been handled for income tax purposes?

Education Expenses

General Requirements

LO.5
Differentiate between deductible and nondeductible education expenses.

An employee can deduct expenses incurred for education (**education expenses**) as ordinary and necessary business expenses provided the expenses are incurred for either of two reasons:

- To maintain or improve existing skills required in the present job.
- To meet the express requirements of the employer or the requirements imposed by law to retain his or her employment status. *Allowed*

Education expenses are *not* deductible if the education is for either of the following purposes (except as discussed below under A Limited Deduction Approach):

- To meet the minimum educational standards for qualification in the taxpayer's existing job.
- To qualify the taxpayer for a new trade or business.[23] *Not Allowed*

---

[22]§ 62(a)(15). [23]Reg. §§ 1.162–5(b)(2) and (3).

Fees incurred for professional qualification exams (the bar exam, for example) and fees for review courses (such as a CPA review course) are not deductible.[24] If the education incidentally results in a promotion or raise, the deduction still can be taken as long as the education maintained and improved existing skills and did not qualify a person for a new trade or business. A change in duties is not always fatal to the deduction if the new duties involve the same general work. For example, the IRS has ruled that a practicing dentist's education expenses incurred to become an orthodontist are deductible.[25]

Requirements Imposed by Law or by the Employer for Retention of Employment

Taxpayers are permitted to deduct education expenses if additional courses are required by the employer or are imposed by law. Many states require a minimum of a bachelor's degree and a specified number of additional courses to retain a teaching job. In addition, some public school systems have imposed a master's degree requirement and require teachers to make satisfactory progress toward a master's degree in order to keep their positions. If the required education is the minimum degree required for the job, no deduction is allowed.

A taxpayer classified as a staff accountant who went back to school to obtain a bachelor's degree in accounting was not allowed to deduct the expenses. Although some courses tended to maintain and improve his existing skills in his entry-level position, the degree was the minimum requirement for his job.[26]

Expenses incurred for education required by law for various professions will also qualify for deduction.

EXAMPLE 26

In order to satisfy the State Board of Public Accountancy rules for maintaining her CPA license, Nancy takes an auditing course sponsored by a local college. The cost of the education is deductible. ∎

Maintaining or Improving Existing Skills

The "maintaining or improving existing skills" requirement in the Code has been difficult for both taxpayers and the courts to interpret. For example, a business executive may be permitted to deduct the costs of obtaining an MBA on the grounds that the advanced management education is undertaken to maintain and improve existing management skills. The executive is eligible to deduct the costs of specialized, nondegree management courses that are taken for continuing education or to maintain or improve existing skills. Expenses incurred by the executive to obtain a law degree are not deductible, however, because the education constitutes training for a new trade or business. The Regulations deny a self-employed accountant a deduction for expenses relating to law school.[27]

Classification of Specific Items

Education expenses include books, tuition, typing, and transportation (e.g., from the office to night school) and travel (e.g., meals and lodging while away from home at summer school).

---

[24]Reg. § 1.212–1(f) and Rev.Rul. 69–292, 1969–1 C.B. 84.

[25]Rev.Rul. 74–78, 1974–1 C.B. 44.

[26]Reg. § 1.162–5(b)(2)(iii) Example (2); *Collin J. Davidson*, 43 TCM 743, T.C.Memo. 1982–119. But see the subsequent discussion of § 222 (i.e., the deduction for higher education qualified tuition and related expenses).

[27]Reg. § 1.162–5(b)(3)(ii) Example (1).

TAX *in the News* | IS AN MBA DEGREE DEDUCTIBLE?

Education that maintains or improves existing skills is deductible, but education that qualifies a taxpayer for a new field is not. But how do these basic rules apply to a conventional (i.e., nonspecialized) MBA degree? Does being a manager or a consultant require an MBA degree? Generally, the answer has always been that it does not. In this regard, therefore, the education does not create a new skill, so its cost should be deductible.

Several recent holdings, however, have found that an MBA degree can lead to qualifying for a new trade or business.

But these holdings involved situations where the education resulted in a job change and satisfied different minimum requirements set by the employer. In one case, for example, the taxpayer moved from the position of investment analyst to become an investment banker, and the latter position required an MBA degree. Under these circumstances, the cost of the education was held to be nondeductible.

But barring a change to a job where the degree is required, the cost of an MBA degree should be deductible as merely improving existing managerial skills.

EXAMPLE 27

Bill, who holds a bachelor of education degree, is a secondary education teacher in the Los Angeles school system. The school board recently raised its minimum education requirement for new teachers from four years of college training to five. A grandfather clause allows teachers with only four years of college to continue to qualify if they show satisfactory progress toward a graduate degree. Bill enrolls at the University of California and takes three graduate courses. His unreimbursed expenses for this purpose are as follows:

Books and tuition	$2,600
Lodging while in travel status (June–August)	1,150
Meals while in travel status	800
Laundry while in travel status	220
Transportation	600

Bill has an itemized deduction as follows:

Books and tuition	$2,600
Lodging	1,150
Meals less 50% cutback (see below)	400
Laundry	220
Transportation	600
	$4,970

■

A Limited Deduction Approach

One of the major shortcomings of the education deduction, previously discussed, is that it is unavailable for taxpayers obtaining a basic skill. Thus, a taxpayer working for an accounting firm cannot deduct the cost of earning a bachelor's degree in accounting. Under 2001 tax legislation, this shortcoming has been partly resolved with the **deduction for qualified tuition and related expenses.**

A deduction *for* AGI is allowed for qualified tuition and related expenses involving higher education (i.e., postsecondary). The maximum amount of the deduction varies depending on the year involved. Further, the deduction is unavailable if the taxpayer's AGI exceeds a prescribed amount.[28] The phase-ins and limitations are summarized in Table 9–1.

---

[28]The dollar caps, AGI limitations, and phase-ins are contained in § 222(b). Though this provision is scheduled to expire at the end of 2005, Congress is likely to extend it.

TABLE 9–1	Phase-in Rules for Qualified Tuition Deduction		
Tax Years Involved	Filing Status	AGI Limit	Maximum Deduction Allowed
2002–2003	Single	$ 65,000*	} $3,000
	Married	130,000*	
2004–2005	Single	65,000	} 4,000
	Married	130,000	
	Single	65,001 to 80,000*	} 2,000
	Married	130,001 to 160,000*	} 2,000

*No deduction at all is available if AGI exceeds this amount.

Various aspects of the higher education tuition deduction are summarized below:

- Qualified tuition and related expenses include whatever is required for enrollment at the institution. Usually, student activity fees, books, and room and board are not included.[29]
- The expense need not be employment related, although it can be.
- The deduction is available for a taxpayer's spouse or anyone who can be claimed as a dependent and is an eligible student.
- The deduction is not available for married persons who file separate returns.[30]
- To avoid a "double benefit," the deduction must be coordinated with other education provisions (i.e., HOPE and lifetime learning credits). Along this same line, no deduction is allowed for a taxpayer who qualifies as another's dependent.[31]
- The deduction *for* AGI classification avoids the 2 percent-of-AGI floor on miscellaneous itemized deductions. As noted later in the chapter, this is the fate suffered by other education-related employee expenses.

EXAMPLE 28

§222 amount is ded
Exceed amt is from AGI
and is under qualification
rules.

Tina is single and a full-time employee of a CPA firm. During 2005, she attends law school at night and incurs the following expenses: $4,200 for tuition and $340 for books and supplies. Presuming she satisfies the AGI limitation (see Table 9–1), she can claim $4,000 as a deduction *for* AGI. If she itemizes her deductions for the year, can she claim the $540 not allowed under § 222 ($200 tuition in excess of $4,000 + $340 for books and supplies) as an education expense eligible for itemized deduction treatment? No, because obtaining a law degree leads to a new trade or business.[32] ■

Other Provisions Dealing with Education

The focus of this chapter is on the deduction aspects of certain items.[33] For education, however, two important provisions involve the income aspects. One deals with the exclusion of certain scholarships from gross income.[34] The other deals with the

[29]Section 222(d) refers to § 25A(f), which deals with the HOPE and lifetime learning credits (see Chapter 13). Student activity fees and prescribed course-related books could be allowed if they are a condition for enrollment.
[30]§ 222(d)(4).
[31]§ 222(c).

[32]*Steven Galligan*, 83 TCM 1859, T.C.Memo. 2002–150.
[33]Another deduction item relating to education is the deduction of interest on education loans, which is covered in § 221 and discussed in Chapter 10.
[34]§ 117.

exclusion from gross income of amounts provided by the employer under certain educational assistance programs.[35] Both of these provisions are discussed in Chapter 5.

Closely tied to the income aspects is the Coverdell Education Savings Account (discussed in Chapter 19). Although contributions to this type of savings account are not deductible, payouts of benefits can qualify as exclusions from gross income.[36]

Further favorable tax treatment of education occurs in the form of credits. Both the HOPE and the lifetime learning credits are discussed in Chapter 13.[37]

Entertainment Expenses

LO.6

Understand how entertainment expenses are treated.

Many taxpayers attempt to deduct personal entertainment expenses as business expenses. For this reason, the tax law restricts the deductibility of entertainment expenses. The Code contains strict record-keeping requirements and provides restrictive tests for the deduction of certain types of **entertainment expenses**.

Cutback Adjustment

During the administration of Jimmy Carter, considerable controversy arose regarding the "three martini" business lunch. By virtue of allowing a tax deduction, should the tax law be subsidizing a practice that contained a significant element of personal pleasure? One possible remedy for the situation was to disallow any deduction for business entertainment, but this option was regarded as being too harsh. Instead the *cutback* rule was instituted. Rather than disallowing *all* of the deduction, allow only a certain percentage, and the rest of the expenditure would be cut back. Currently, only 50 percent of meal and entertainment expenses are allowed as a deduction.[38] The limitation applies in the context of both employment and self-employment status. Although the 50 percent cutback can apply to either the employer or the employee, it will not apply twice. The cutback applies to the one who really pays (economically) for the meals or entertainment.

EXAMPLE 29

Jane, an employee of Pato Corporation, entertains one of her clients. If Pato Corporation does not reimburse Jane, she is subject to the cutback adjustment. If, however, Pato Corporation reimburses Jane (or pays for the entertainment directly), Pato suffers the cutback. ∎

In certain situations, however, a full 50 percent cutback seems unfair. If, for example, the hours of service are regulated (by the U.S. Department of Transportation) and away-from-home meals are frequent and necessary, the "three martini" business lunch type of abuse is unlikely. Consequently, the cutback rule is mitigated for the following types of employees:

- Certain air transportation employees, such as flight crews, dispatchers, mechanics, and control tower operators.
- Interstate truck and bus drivers.
- Certain railroad employees, such as train crews and dispatchers.
- Certain merchant mariners.

Starting in 1998, the cutback for these types of employees is reduced by 5 percent at two-year intervals until it reaches 20 percent in year 2008 and thereafter. Thus, 80 percent of the cost of meals will eventually be allowed as a deduction. For 2006–2007, 75 percent is allowed (for 2004–2005, 70 percent was allowed).

[handwritten: 98 → add 5% each year.]

---

[35]§ 127.
[36]§ 530.
[37]§ 25A.
[38]§ 274(n).

All related to meals & entertainment.

What Is Covered. Transportation expenses are not affected by the cutback rule—only meals and entertainment. The cutback also applies to taxes and tips relating to meals and entertainment. Cover charges, parking fees at an entertainment location, and room rental fees for a meal or cocktail party are also subject to the 50 percent rule.

EXAMPLE 30

Joe pays a $30 cab fare to meet his client for dinner. The meal costs $120, and Joe leaves a $20 tip. His deduction is $100 [($120 + $20) × 50% + $30 cab fare]. ■

What Is Not Covered. The cutback rule has a number of exceptions. One exception covers the case where the full value of the meals or entertainment is included in the compensation of the employee (or independent contractor).

EXAMPLE 31

Myrtle wins an all-expense-paid trip to Europe for selling the most insurance for her company during the year. Her employer treats this trip as additional compensation to Myrtle. The cutback adjustment does not apply to the employer. ■

Another exception applies to meals and entertainment in a subsidized eating facility or where the *de minimis* fringe benefit rule is met (see Chapter 5).[39]

EXAMPLE 32

General Hospital has an employee cafeteria on the premises for its doctors, nurses, and other employees. The cafeteria operates at cost. The cutback rule does not apply to General Hospital. ■

EXAMPLE 33

Canary Corporation gives a ham, a fruitcake, and a bottle of wine to each employee at year-end. Since the *de minimis* fringe benefit exclusion applies to business gifts of packaged foods and beverages, their *full* cost is deductible by Canary. ■

A similar exception applies to employer-paid recreational activities for employees (e.g., the annual Christmas party or spring picnic).[40]

Classification of Expenses

Entertainment expenses are categorized as follows: those *directly related* to business and those *associated with* business.[41] Directly related expenses are related to an actual business meeting or discussion. These expenses are distinguished from entertainment expenses that are incurred to promote goodwill, such as maintaining existing customer relations. To obtain a deduction for directly related entertainment, it is not necessary to show that actual benefit resulted from the expenditure as long as there was a reasonable expectation of benefit. To qualify as directly related, the expense should be incurred in a clear business setting. If there is little possibility of engaging in the active conduct of a trade or business due to the nature of the social facility, it is difficult to qualify the expenditure as directly related to business.

Expenses associated with, rather than directly related to, business entertainment must serve a specific business purpose, such as obtaining new business or continuing existing business. These expenditures qualify only if the expenses directly precede or follow a bona fide business discussion. Entertainment occurring on the same day as the business discussion meets the test.

---

[39]§ 274(n)(2).
[40]§ 274(e)(4).
[41]§ 274(a)(1)(A).

Restrictions upon Deductibility

Business Meals. Any business meal is deductible only if the following are true:[42]

- The meal is directly related to or associated with the active conduct of a trade or business.
- The expense is not lavish or extravagant under the circumstances.
- The taxpayer (or an employee) is present at the meal.

A business meal with a business associate or customer is not deductible unless business is discussed before, during, or after the meal. This requirement is not intended to disallow the deduction for a meal consumed while away from home on business.

EXAMPLE 34

Lacy travels to San Francisco for a business convention. She pays for dinner with three colleagues and is not reimbursed by her employer. They do not discuss business. She can deduct 50% of the cost of her meal. However, she cannot deduct the cost of her colleagues' meals. ■

The *clear business purpose* test requires that meals be directly related to or associated with the active conduct of a business. A meal is not deductible if it serves no business purpose.

The taxpayer or an employee must be present at the business meal for the meal to be deductible. An independent contractor who renders significant services to the taxpayer is treated as an employee.

EXAMPLE 35

Lance, a party to a contract negotiation, buys dinner for other parties to the negotiation but does not attend the dinner. No deduction is allowed. ■

No ded.

Club Dues. The Code provides: "No deduction shall be allowed ... for amounts paid or incurred for membership in any club organized for business, pleasure, recreation, or other social purpose."[43] Although this prohibition seems quite broad, the IRS does allow a deduction for dues to clubs whose primary purpose is public service and community volunteerism (e.g., Kiwanis, Lions, Rotary).

Even though dues are not deductible, actual entertainment at a club may qualify.

EXAMPLE 36

During the current year, Vincent spent $1,400 on business lunches at the Lakeside Country Club. The annual membership fee was $6,000, and Vincent used the facility 60% of the time for business. Presuming the lunches meet the business meal test, Vincent may claim $700 (50% × $1,400) as a deduction. None of the club dues are deductible. ■

Ticket : Yes

Ticket Purchases for Entertainment. A deduction for the cost of a ticket for an entertainment activity is limited to the face value of the ticket.[44] This limitation is applied before the 50 percent rule. The face value of a ticket includes any tax. Under this rule, the excess payment to a scalper for a ticket is not deductible. Similarly, the fee to a ticket agency for the purchase of a ticket is not deductible.

Expenditures for the rental or use of a luxury skybox at a sports arena in excess of the face value of regular tickets are disallowed as deductions. If a luxury skybox is used for entertainment that is directly related to or associated with business, the deduction is limited to the face value of nonluxury box seats. All seats in the luxury skybox are counted, even when some seats are unoccupied.

luxury → non-luxury ded.

---

[42]§ 274(k).
[43]§ 274(a)(3).
[44]§ 274(l).

The taxpayer may also deduct stated charges for food and beverages under the general rules for business entertainment. The deduction for skybox seats, food, and beverages is limited to 50 percent of cost.

EXAMPLE 37

In the current year, Jay Company pays $12,000 to rent a 10-seat skybox at City Stadium for three football games. Nonluxury box seats at each event range in cost from $55 to $95 a seat. In March, a Jay representative and five clients use the skybox for the first game. The entertainment follows a bona fide business discussion, and Jay spends $290 for food and beverages during the game. The deduction for the first sports event is as follows:

Food and beverages	$ 290
Deduction for seats ($95 × 10 seats)	950
Total entertainment expense	$1,240
50% limitation	× .50
Deduction	$ 620

Business Gifts. Business gifts are deductible to the extent of $25 per donee per year.[45] An exception is made for gifts costing $4 or less (e.g., pens with the employee's or company's name on them) or promotional materials. Such items are not treated as business gifts subject to the $25 limitation. In addition, incidental costs such as engraving of jewelry and nominal charges for gift-wrapping, mailing, and delivery are not included in the cost of the gift in applying the limitation. Gifts to superiors and employers are not deductible.

The $25 limitation on business gifts cannot be circumvented by having the donor's spouse join in the gift or by making multiple gifts that include the customer's family.

Records must be maintained to substantiate business gifts.

LO.7

Identify other employee expenses.

Other Employee Expenses

Office in the Home

Employees and self-employed individuals are not allowed a deduction for **office in the home expenses** unless a portion of the residence is used *exclusively* on a *regular basis* as either of the following:

- The principal place of business for any trade or business of the taxpayer.
- A place of business used by clients, patients, or customers.

Employees must meet an additional test: The use must be for the *convenience of the employer* rather than merely being "appropriate and helpful."[46]

The precise meaning of "principal place of business" has been the subject of considerable controversy.[47] Congress ultimately resolved the controversy by amending the Code.[48] The term "principal place of business" now includes a place of business that satisfies the following requirements:

- The office is used by the taxpayer to conduct administrative or management activities of a trade or business.
- There is no other fixed location of the trade or business where the taxpayer conducts these activities.

---

[45]§ 274(b)(1).
[46]§ 280A(c)(1).
[47]See the restrictive interpretation arrived at in *Comm. v. Soliman*, 93–1 USTC ¶50,014, 71 AFTR2d 93–463, 113 S.Ct. 701 (USSC, 1993).
[48]§ 280A(c)(1) as modified by the Tax Reform Act of 1997.

Dr. Smith is a self-employed anesthesiologist. During the year, he spends 30 to 35 hours per week administering anesthesia and postoperative care to patients in three hospitals, none of which provides him with an office. He also spends two or three hours per day in a room in his home that he uses exclusively as an office. He does not meet patients there, but he performs a variety of tasks related to his medical practice (e.g., contacting surgeons, bookkeeping, reading medical journals). A deduction will be allowed since Dr. Smith uses the office in the home to conduct administrative or management activities of his trade or business, and there is no other fixed location where these activities can be carried out. ∎

The exclusive use requirement means that a specific part of the home must be used *solely* for business purposes. A deduction, if permitted, requires an allocation of total expenses of operating the home between business and personal use based on floor space or number of rooms.

Even if the taxpayer meets the above requirements, the allowable home office expenses cannot exceed the gross income from the business less all other business expenses attributable to the activity. Furthermore, the home office expenses that are allowed as itemized deductions anyway (e.g., mortgage interest and real estate taxes) must be deducted first. All home office expenses of an employee are miscellaneous itemized deductions, except those (such as interest and taxes) that qualify as other personal itemized deductions. Home office expenses of a self-employed individual are trade or business expenses and are deductible *for* AGI.

Any disallowed home office expenses are *carried forward* and used in future years subject to the same limitations.

Rick is a certified public accountant employed by a regional CPA firm as a tax manager. He operates a separate business in which he refinishes furniture in his home. For this business, he uses two rooms in the basement of his home exclusively and regularly. The floor space of the two rooms constitutes 10% of the floor space of his residence. Gross income from the business totals $8,000. Expenses of the business (other than home office expenses) are $6,500. Rick incurs the following home office expenses:

Real property taxes on residence	$ 4,000
Interest expense on residence	7,500
Operating expenses of residence	2,000
Depreciation on residence (based on 10% business use)	250

Rick's deductions are determined as follows:

Business income		$ 8,000
Less: Other business expenses		(6,500)
		$ 1,500
Less: Allocable taxes ($4,000 × 10%)	$400	
Allocable interest ($7,500 × 10%)	750	(1,150)
		$ 350
Allocable operating expenses of the residence ($2,000 × 10%)		(200)
		$ 150
Allocable depreciation ($250, limited to remaining income)		(150)
		$ –0–

Rick has a carryover of $100 (the unused excess depreciation). Because he is self-employed, the allocable taxes and interest ($1,150), the other deductible office expenses ($200 + $150), and $6,500 of other business expenses are deductible *for* AGI. ∎

Form 8829 (Expenses for Business Use of Your Home) is available from the IRS for computation of the office in the home deduction.

The home office limitation cannot be circumvented by leasing part of one's home to an employer, using it as a home office, and deducting the expenses as a rental expense under § 212.

Miscellaneous Employee Expenses

Miscellaneous employee expenses include those costs that are job related and are not otherwise covered elsewhere. As the focus here is on their deductibility, this discussion presumes that such expenses have not been reimbursed by the employer under an accountable plan arrangement (discussed later in the chapter).

Expenses related to maintaining job status make up a significant category of miscellaneous expenses. They include such costs as union dues, membership dues to professional organizations, subscriptions to trade publications and professional journals, and various license fees paid to government agencies and other regulatory bodies.

Special Clothing. To be deductible, special clothing must be both specifically required as a condition of employment and not adaptable for regular wear. For example, a police officer's uniform must be worn when "on duty" but is not suitable for "off-duty" activities. Its cost, therefore, is deductible. When special clothing qualifies for deductibility, so does the cost of its maintenance (i.e., alterations, laundry, dry cleaning).

Whether the out-of-pocket cost of military uniforms is deductible depends on the duty status of the taxpayer. If a member of the National Guard (or reserves) is not on active duty, then the cost of the uniform qualifies for deductibility. For those on active duty, the cost of regular uniforms does not qualify because the uniforms are suitable for ordinary street wear. Even for those on active duty, some apparel, such as ceremonial attire (dress blues) or combat gear, will qualify because it is not adaptable for regular wear.

The cost of clothing possessing *safety* features to prevent workplace injuries will qualify. This includes such items as safety glasses, shoes (e.g., "steel-toed"), special gloves, lab coats, and "hard hats." The tolerance of the IRS in the area of safety clothing is partially attributable to its lack of suitability for personal use.

Job Hunting. The expenses incurred in seeking employment can be deductible under certain conditions. The search must involve the same trade or business as the taxpayer's current position. No deduction is allowed for the cost of obtaining the first job. An unemployed person, however, can qualify for the deduction if there has not been a significant time lapse since the last job. In terms of deductibility, it does not matter whether the job search is successful. Nor does a change in jobs have to result. Costs that qualify include job counseling, compilation and distribution of biographical data (such as work history), and unreimbursed travel for job interviews.

Educator Expenses. The Job Creation and Worker Assistance Act of 2002, as amended by the Working Families Tax Relief Act of 2004, provides limited relief for elementary and secondary school teachers. For taxable years beginning during 2002, 2003, 2004, or 2005, eligible educators can claim up to $250 for school supplies as a deduction *for* AGI.[49] Eligible educators must work at least 900 hours during a school year as a teacher, instructor, counselor, principal, or aide at either public or private elementary and secondary schools. Covered costs include unreimbursed expenses for books, supplies, computer and other equipment, and supplementary materials used in the classroom.

EXAMPLE 40

Hortense is a full-time teacher at Hoover Elementary. During 2005, she spends $1,200 for school supplies for her fourth grade class. Under an accountable plan (see later in the chapter), Hoover reimburses her for $400 of these supplies. As to the $800 balance, Hortense may claim $250 as a deduction *for* AGI and $550 as a miscellaneous itemized deduction (subject to the 2%-of-AGI floor). ■

Although the educator expense provision expires at the end of 2005, there is good reason to believe that Congress will extend it. When such an extension occurs, it probably will be made retroactive in application.

Contributions to Retirement Accounts

Pension considerations are an essential feature of any compensation arrangement. As noted in Chapter 1, providing retirement security for employees can be justified on both economic and social grounds. Because the public sector (i.e., Social Security) will not provide sufficient retirement security for recipients, the private sector must fill the need. Congress has given the private sector the necessary incentive by enacting various measures that provide significant tax advantages for retirement plans. These plans fall into two major classifications: those available to employees and those available to self-employed persons.

Employee IRAs

Pension plans covering employees follow one of two income tax approaches. Most plans allow an *exclusion* for the contributions the employee makes to the plan. The employee's income tax return shows nothing regarding the contribution—no income, exclusion, or deduction. This is the case even if the contribution is funded entirely (or partially) by means of a salary reduction.[50]

The other income tax approach is followed by the **traditional IRA.** Here, the contributing employee is allowed a deduction *for* AGI. The amount, a maximum of $4,000 for 2006, is reported as a deduction on Form 1040.[51] As with the exclusion

---

[49]§ 62(a)(2)(D).
[50]See, for example, §§ 401(k), 403(b), and 457.
[51]§§ 219 and 408.

variety of pension plan, nothing is taxed to the employee-participant until distributions from the traditional IRA occur. Consequently, all of these types of retirement plans carry the advantage of deferring the taxation of income. As described in Chapter 19, all retirement plans are subject to various rules regarding coverage requirements, degree of vesting, excessive contributions, and premature distributions. Generally, these rules are less stringent for traditional IRAs.

The traditional IRA is to be distinguished from the **Roth IRA**, which takes a radically different tax approach. No tax benefit (i.e., exclusion or deduction) results from the initial contribution to a Roth IRA. Instead, later distributions (including postcontribution earnings) are recovered tax-free.[52]

Self-Employed Keogh (H.R. 10) Plans

Self-employed taxpayers can also participate in retirement plans with tax-favored benefits. Known as Keogh (or H.R. 10) plans, these arrangements follow the deduction approach of traditional IRAs.[53] The amount contributed under a plan is a deduction *for* AGI and is reported as a deduction on Form 1040. The plan established by a self-employed taxpayer who has employees must meet stringent requirements to ensure that it provides similar retirement benefits for the group. The law is structured to ensure that employees share an owner-employer's ability to defer taxes.

The operational rules governing Keogh (H.R. 10) plans are covered in Chapter 19.

Classification of Employee Expenses

LO.9

Appreciate the difference between accountable and nonaccountable employee plans.

The classification of employee expenses depends on whether they are reimbursed by the employer under an accountable plan. If so, then they are not reported by the employee at all. In effect, therefore, this result is equivalent to treating the expenses as deductions *for* AGI.[54] If the expenses are reimbursed under a nonaccountable plan or are not reimbursed at all, then they are classified as deductions *from* AGI and can be claimed only if the employee-taxpayer itemizes. An exception is made for moving expenses and the employment-related expenses of a qualified performing artist.[55] Here, deduction *for* AGI classification is allowed.

For classification purposes, therefore, the difference between accountable and nonaccountable plans is significant.

Accountable Plans

In General. An **accountable plan** requires the employee to satisfy these two requirements:

- Adequately account for (substantiate) the expenses. An employee renders an *adequate accounting* by submitting a record, with receipts and other substantiation, to the employer.[56]
- Return any excess reimbursement or allowance. An "excess reimbursement or allowance" is any amount that the employee does not adequately account for as an ordinary and necessary business expense.

Substantiation. The law provides that no deduction is allowed for any travel, entertainment, business gift, or listed property (automobiles, computers) expenditure

---

[52]§ 408A.
[53]§ 401(c).
[54]§ 62(a)(2).

[55]As defined in § 62(b).
[56]Reg. § 1.162–17(b)(4).

unless properly substantiated by adequate records. The records should contain the following information:[57]

- The amount of the expense.
- The time and place of travel or entertainment (or date of gift).
- The business purpose of the expense.
- The business relationship of the taxpayer to the person entertained (or receiving the gift).

} record

This means the taxpayer must maintain an account book or diary in which the above information is recorded at the time of the expenditure. Documentary evidence, such as itemized receipts, is required to support any expenditure for lodging while traveling away from home and for any other expenditure of $75 or more. If a taxpayer fails to keep adequate records, each expense must be established by a written or oral statement of the exact details of the expense and by other corroborating evidence.[58]

Must record for > $75 expense

EXAMPLE 41

Bertha has travel expenses substantiated only by canceled checks. The checks establish the date, place, and amount of the expenditure. Because neither the business relationship nor the business purpose is established, the deduction is disallowed.[59] ∎

EXAMPLE 42

Dwight has travel and entertainment expenses substantiated by a diary showing the time, place, and amount of the expenditure. His oral testimony provides the business relationship and business purpose. However, since he has no receipts, any expenditures of $75 or more are disallowed.[60] ∎

Deemed Substantiation. In lieu of reimbursing actual expenses for travel away from home, many employers reduce their paperwork by adopting a policy of reimbursing employees with a *per diem* allowance, a flat dollar amount per day of business travel. Of the substantiation requirements listed above, the *amount* of the expense is proved, or *deemed substantiated*, by using such a per diem allowance or reimbursement procedure. The amount of expenses that is deemed substantiated is equal to the lesser of the per diem allowance or the amount of the Federal per diem rate.

The regular Federal per diem rate is the highest amount that the Federal government will pay to its employees for lodging, meals, and incidental expenses[61] while in travel status away from home in a particular area. The rates are different for different locations.[62]

The use of the standard Federal per diem rates for meals and incidental expenses constitutes an adequate accounting. Employees and self-employed persons can use these standard allowances instead of deducting the actual cost of daily meals and incidental expenses, even if not reimbursed. There is no standard lodging allowance, however.

Only the amount of the expense is considered substantiated under the deemed substantiated method. The other substantiation requirements must be provided: place, date, business purpose of the expense, and the business relationship of the parties involved.

---

[57]§ 274(d).
[58]Reg. § 1.274–5T(c)(3).
[59]*William T. Whitaker*, 56 TCM 47, T.C.Memo. 1988–418.
[60]*W. David Tyler*, 43 TCM 927, T.C.Memo. 1982–160.
[61]Incidental expenses include tips and fees to porters, bellhops, hotel maids, etc. For travel away from home after 2002, the term does *not* include

expenses for laundry and dry cleaning of clothing, lodging taxes, and telephone calls.
[62]*Per Diem Rates* (IRS Publication 1542) contains the list and amounts for the year. This publication is available only on the Internet at **http://www.irs.gov.** A print edition is no longer published. Links to per diem rates can also be found at **http://www.gsa.gov.**

Nonaccountable Plans

deductible (handwritten)

A **nonaccountable plan** is one in which an adequate accounting or return of excess amounts, or both, is not required. All reimbursements of expenses are reported in full as wages on the employee's Form W–2. Any allowable expenses are deductible in the same manner as are unreimbursed expenses.

2% floor (handwritten)

Unreimbursed Employee Expenses. Unreimbursed employee expenses are treated in a straightforward manner. Meals and entertainment expenses are subject to the 50 percent limit. Total unreimbursed employee business expenses are usually reported as miscellaneous itemized deductions subject to the 2 percent-of-AGI floor (see below). If the employee could have received, but did not seek, reimbursement for whatever reason, none of the employment-related expenses are deductible.

Failure to Comply with Accountable Plan Requirements. An employer may have an accountable plan and require employees to return excess reimbursements or allowances, but an employee may fail to follow the rules of the plan. In that case, the expenses and reimbursements are subject to nonaccountable plan treatment.

Reporting Procedures

The reporting requirements range from no reporting at all (accountable plans when all requirements are met) to the use of some or all of the following forms: Form W–2 (Wage and Tax Statement), Form 2106 (Employee Business Expenses) or Form 2106–EZ (Unreimbursed Employee Business Expenses), and Schedule A (Itemized Deductions) for nonaccountable plans and unreimbursed employee expenses.

Reimbursed employee expenses that are adequately accounted for under an accountable plan are deductible *for* AGI on Form 2106. Allowed excess expenses, expenses reimbursed under a nonaccountable plan, and unreimbursed expenses are deductible *from* AGI on Schedule A, subject to the 2 percent-of-AGI floor.

When a reimbursement under an accountable plan is paid in separate amounts relating to designated expenses such as meals or entertainment, no problem arises. The reimbursements and expenses are reported as such on the appropriate forms. If the reimbursement is made in a single amount, an allocation must be made to determine the appropriate portion of the reimbursement that applies to meals and entertainment and to other employee expenses.

EXAMPLE 43

Elizabeth, who is employed by Green Company, had AGI of $42,000. During the year, she incurred $2,000 of transportation and lodging expense and $1,000 of meals and entertainment expense, all fully substantiated. Elizabeth received $1,800 reimbursement under an accountable plan. The reimbursement rate that applies to meals and entertainment is 33.33% ($1,000 meals and entertainment expense/$3,000 total expenses). Thus, $600 ($1,800 × 33.33%) of the reimbursement applies to meals and entertainment, and $1,200 ($1,800 − $600) applies to transportation and lodging. Elizabeth's itemized deduction consists of the $800 ($2,000 total − $1,200 reimbursement) of unreimbursed transportation and lodging expenses and $400 ($1,000 − $600) of unreimbursed meal and entertainment expenses as follows:

Transportation and lodging	$ 800
Meals and entertainment ($400 × 50%)	200
Total (reported on Form 2106)	$1,000
Less: 2% of $42,000 AGI (see limitation discussed below)	(840)
Deduction (reported on Schedule A)	$ 160

In summary, Elizabeth reports $3,000 of expenses and the $1,800 reimbursement on Form 2106 and $160 as a miscellaneous itemized deduction on Schedule A. ∎

ETHICAL *Considerations* | **A CUSTOMIZED REIMBURSEMENT AGREEMENT**

In connection with his job at Yellow Corporation, Brayden incurs certain employment-related expenses. Brayden renders an adequate accounting to Yellow and is reimbursed for 50 percent of his expenditures. Under an agreement he has with Yellow, the reimbursement specifically covers the meals and entertainment portion of the employee expenses.

What tax benefit is Brayden trying to obtain as a result of the reimbursement agreement with Yellow? Will he succeed? Should employers and employees enter into such agreements?

Limitations on Itemized Deductions

LO.10

Work with the limitations on miscellaneous itemized deductions.

Many itemized deductions, such as medical expenses and charitable contributions, are subject to limitations expressed as a percentage of AGI. These limitations may be expressed as floors or ceilings and are discussed in Chapter 10.

Miscellaneous Itemized Deductions Subject to the 2 Percent Floor

Certain miscellaneous itemized deductions, including most *unreimbursed employee business expenses*, are aggregated and then reduced by 2 percent of AGI.[63] Expenses subject to the 2 percent floor include the following:

- All § 212 expenses, except expenses of producing rent and royalty income (refer to Chapter 6).
- All unreimbursed employee expenses (after the 50 percent reduction, if applicable) except moving.
- Professional dues and subscriptions.
- Union dues and work uniforms.
- Employment-related education expenses (except for § 222 qualified tuition and related expenses).
- Malpractice insurance premiums.
- Expenses of job hunting (including employment agency fees and résumé-writing expenses).
- Home office expenses of an employee or outside salesperson.
- Legal, accounting, and tax return preparation fees.
- Hobby expenses (up to hobby income).
- Investment expenses, including investment counsel fees, subscriptions, and safe deposit box rental.
- Custodial fees relating to income-producing property or a traditional IRA or a Keogh plan.
- Any fees paid to collect interest or dividends.
- Appraisal fees establishing a casualty loss or charitable contribution.

---

[63]§ 67.

WILL SEPARATE RETURNS BY MARRIED PERSONS SAVE TAXES?

Andy and Nancy are married and live in Connecticut. Both are employed and work at home. Nancy's employer pays for her employment-related expenses. Unfortunately, Andy's employee expenses, although considerable in amount, are not reimbursed. Every year Andy and Nancy file separate Federal income tax returns, and each itemizes. On his return, Andy also claims the expenses relating to the office in the home they share and deducts the fees he pays for the preparation of their tax returns.

How is the procedure Andy and Nancy are following saving them income taxes? Evaluate the appropriateness of the procedure.

Miscellaneous Itemized Deductions Not Subject to the 2 Percent Floor

Certain miscellaneous itemized deductions, including the following, are not subject to the 2 percent floor:

- Impairment-related work expenses of handicapped individuals.
- Gambling losses to the extent of gambling winnings.
- Certain terminated annuity payments.

EXAMPLE 44

Ted, who has AGI of $20,000, has the following miscellaneous itemized deductions:

Gambling losses (to extent of gains)	$1,200
Tax return preparation fees	300
Unreimbursed employee transportation	200
Professional dues and subscriptions	260
Safe deposit box rental	30

Ted's itemized deductions are as follows:

Deduction not subject to 2% floor (gambling losses)		$1,200
Deductions subject to 2% floor ($300 + $200 + $260 + $30)	$ 790	
Less 2% of AGI	(400)	390
Total miscellaneous itemized deductions		$1,590

If instead Ted's AGI is $40,000, the floor is $800 (2% of $40,000), and he cannot deduct any expenses subject to the 2% floor. ■

LO.11

Develop tax planning ideas related to employee business expenses.

TAX PLANNING
Considerations

Self-Employed Individuals

Some taxpayers have the flexibility to be classified as either employees or self-employed individuals. Examples include real estate agents and direct sellers. These taxpayers should carefully consider all factors and not automatically assume that self-employed status is preferable.

It is advantageous to deduct one's business expenses *for* AGI and avoid the 2 percent floor. However, a self-employed individual may have higher expenses, such as local gross receipts taxes, license fees, franchise fees, personal property taxes, and occupation taxes. In addition, the record-keeping and filing requirements can be quite burdensome.

TAX *in the News* — **RELIEF FOR MEMBERS OF THE ARMED FORCES RESERVES**

In the Military Family Tax Relief Act of 2003, Congress provided various tax benefits for reservists, one of which deals with the classification of travel expenses. Members of the Reserves or National Guard who travel to drills and other service-related activities may claim the expenses as deductions *for* AGI. Previously, the expenses were not deductible unless the taxpayer itemized. (As miscellaneous itemized deductions, they were subject to the 2 percent-of-AGI floor.) To qualify for the deduction *for* AGI classification, the trip must be more than 100 miles from home and include an overnight stay. Any deduction is limited to the Federal per diem rates applicable to the area involved.

One of the most expensive considerations is the Social Security tax versus the self-employment tax. For an employee in 2006, for example, the Social Security tax applies at a rate of 6.2 percent on a base amount of wages of $94,200, and the Medicare tax applies at a rate of 1.45 percent with no limit on the base amount. For self-employed persons, the rate, but not the base amount, for each tax doubles. Even though a deduction *for* AGI is allowed for one-half of the self-employment tax paid, an employee and a self-employed individual are not in the same tax position on equal amounts of earnings. The self-employment tax is explained in Chapter 13. For the applicability of these taxes to employees, see Chapter 1.

After analyzing all these factors, a taxpayer may decide that employee status is preferable to self-employed status.

Shifting Deductions between Employer and Employee

An employee can avoid the 2 percent floor for employee business expenses. Typically, an employee incurs travel and entertainment expenses in the course of employment. The employer gets the deduction if it reimburses the employee, and the employee gets the deduction *for* AGI. An adequate accounting must be made, and excess reimbursements cannot be kept by the employee.

Transportation and Travel Expenses

Adequate detailed records of all transportation and travel expenses should be kept. Since the regular mileage allowance often is modest in amount, a new, expensive automobile used primarily for business may generate a higher expense based on actual cost. In using the actual cost method, include the business portion of depreciation, repairs and maintenance, automobile club dues, insurance, gasoline and oil, and other related costs. The cost of gasoline, when coupled with the poor mileage performance of some vehicles, can be a significant factor. If the taxpayer is located in a metropolitan area, automobile insurance is more expensive. For the self-employed taxpayer, the business portion of finance charges (i.e., interest on car loans) can be included.

Once a method is chosen, a later change may be possible. Conversion from the automatic mileage method to the actual cost method is allowed if a basis adjustment is made for depreciation deemed taken (see Example 9). Conversion from the actual cost method to the automatic mileage method is possible only if the taxpayer has not used the MACRS statutory percentage method or claimed § 179 limited expensing.

If a taxpayer wishes to sightsee or vacation on a business trip, it would be beneficial to schedule business on both a Friday and a Monday to turn the weekend into business days for allocation purposes. It is especially crucial to schedule appropriate business days when foreign travel is involved.

Moving Expenses

Persons who retire and move to a new location incur personal nondeductible moving expenses. If the retired person accepts a full-time job in the new location, the moving expenses are deductible.

EXAMPLE 45

At the time of his retirement from the national office of a major accounting firm, Gordon had an annual salary of $420,000. He moves from New York City to Seattle to retire. To qualify for the moving expense deduction, Gordon accepts a full-time teaching position at a Seattle junior college at an annual salary of $15,000. If Gordon satisfies the 39-week test, his moving expenses are deductible. The disparity between the two salaries (previous and current) is of no consequence. ■

Education Expenses

Education expenses are treated as nondeductible personal items unless the individual is employed or is engaged in a trade or business. A temporary leave of absence for further education is one way to reasonably assure that the taxpayer is still qualified, even if a full-time student. An individual was permitted to deduct education expenses even though he resigned from his job, returned to school full-time for two years, and accepted another job in the same field upon graduation. The court held that the student had merely suspended active participation in his field.[64]

If the time out of the field is too long, educational expense deductions will be disallowed. For example, a teacher who left the field for four years to raise her child and curtailed her employment searches and writing activities was denied a deduction. She was not actively engaged in the trade or business of being an educator.[65]

To secure the deduction, an individual should arrange his or her work situation to preserve employee or business status.

The deduction for qualified tuition and related expenses provides some relief from the current restrictions on the deduction of education expenses by employees. First, the education expense does not have to be work related. Second, it is a deduction *for* (not *from*) AGI. Unfortunately, the deduction possesses severe shortcomings: not only is the annual amount allowed quite modest, but it may be unavailable to certain taxpayers. It is not available, for example, to those who exceed an AGI ceiling or to someone who can be claimed as a dependent of another.

Entertainment Expenses

Proper documentation of expenditures is essential because of the strict record-keeping requirements and the restrictive tests that must be met. For example, documentation that consists solely of credit card receipts and canceled checks may be inadequate to substantiate the business purpose and business relationship.[66] Taxpayers should maintain detailed records of amounts, time, place, business purpose, and business relationships. A credit card receipt details the place, date, and amount of the expense. A notation made on the receipt of the names of the person(s) attending, the business relationship, and the topic of discussion should constitute proper documentation.

Associated with or goodwill entertainment is not deductible unless a business discussion is conducted immediately before or after the entertainment. Furthermore, a business purpose must exist for the entertainment. Taxpayers should arrange for a business discussion before or after such entertainment. They must provide documentation of the business purpose, such as obtaining new business from a prospective customer.

---

[64]*Stephen G. Sherman*, 36 TCM 1191, T.C.Memo. 1977–301.

[65]*Brian C. Mulherin*, 42 TCM 834, T.C.Memo. 1981–454; *George A. Baist*, 56 TCM 778, T.C.Memo. 1988–554.

[66]*Kenneth W. Guenther*, 54 TCM 382, T.C.Memo. 1987–440.

Unreimbursed meals and entertainment are subject to the 50 percent cutback rule in addition to the 2 percent floor. Consequently, the procedure of negotiating a salary reduction, as discussed in the next section, is even more valuable to the taxpayer.

Unreimbursed Employee Business Expenses

The 2 percent floor for unreimbursed employee business expenses offers a tax planning opportunity for married couples. If one spouse has high miscellaneous expenses subject to the floor, it may be beneficial for the couple to file separate returns. If they file jointly, the 2 percent floor is based on the incomes of both. Filing separately lowers the reduction to 2 percent of only one spouse's income.

Other provisions of the law should be considered, however. For example, filing separately could cost a couple losses of up to $25,000 from self-managed rental units under the passive activity loss rules (discussed in Chapter 11).

Another possibility is to negotiate a salary reduction with one's employer in exchange for the 100 percent reimbursement of employee expenses. The employee is better off because the 2 percent floor does not apply. The employer is better off because certain expense reimbursements are not subject to Social Security and other payroll taxes.

KEY TERMS

Accountable plan, 9–24	Entertainment expenses, 9–17	Office in the home expenses, 9–20
Automatic mileage method, 9–5	Independent contractor, 9–2	Roth IRAs, 9–24
Deduction for qualified tuition and related expenses, 9–15	IRAs (traditional), 9–23	Statutory employees, 9–4
Education expenses, 9–13	Moving expenses, 9–11	Transportation expenses, 9–4
	Nonaccountable plan, 9–26	Travel expenses, 9–7

PROBLEM MATERIALS

DISCUSSION QUESTIONS

1. Lyle and Joan are married and file a joint return for the year. Both incur work-related expenses that are not reimbursed. If Lyle is employed and Joan is self-employed, how should the expenses be handled for tax purposes?

2. Bernard operates a hair styling salon as a sole proprietor. Because his shop has several extra work stations that are not being used, he is considering renting these to other stylists, but he wants to avoid any employer-employee relationship with them. Advise Bernard on the type of working arrangement he should set up to ensure that any new stylists will be classified as independent contractors and not as employees.

   Decision Making

3. Alexis is a CPA employed by the Tampa office of a national accounting firm. Although she usually commutes daily to the downtown office, on occasion she goes from her home directly to a client's business location. Also, on weekends she drives to a local university to attend classes leading toward a master's degree in accounting. If Alexis uses her personal automobile in these activities, what mileage can qualify as deductible?

4. Andy has just purchased a new automobile that he plans to use about 80% of the time for business. As he tries to decide between the actual cost method and the automatic mileage method, advise Andy on the tax treatment of the following items:
   a. State and local sales tax on the purchase of the auto.
   b. Business parking.

   Decision Making

c.   Interest on auto loan.
d.   Depreciation.
e.   Auto insurance and automobile club dues.

Issue ID

5.   In 2004, Emma purchased an automobile, which she uses for both business and personal purposes. Although Emma does not keep records as to operating expenses (e.g., gas, oil, repairs), she can prove the percentage of business use and the miles driven each year. In March 2006, Emma seeks your advice as to what income tax benefit, if any, she can derive from the use of her automobile. What would you suggest?

6.   Tyler, a member of a St. Louis law firm, travels to Chicago for business conferences on Friday and Monday. During the intervening weekend, he attends a Cubs baseball game and visits various museums. Discuss the deductibility of Tyler's expenses for the trip.

Issue ID

7.   Dr. Werner is a full-time professor of accounting at Pelican University. During the year, he teaches continuing education programs for CPA groups in several cities. He also serves as an expert witness in numerous lawsuits involving accounting fraud. Comment on the possible tax treatment of Dr. Werner's job-related expenses.

8.   What tax effect, if any, does an employee's temporary assignment to another job site have? Does the employee's tax home change?

9.   a.   Under what circumstances might a taxpayer never be away from home for income tax purposes?
b.   What are the tax consequences of such a status?
c.   What is the principal consideration in avoiding this result?

10.   Dr. and Mrs. Hampton attend a two-day seminar in Baltimore on current developments in orthopedic surgery. Dr. Hampton owns and operates a bone and joint clinic in Charleston, West Virginia. Mrs. Hampton is the office manager and accountant for the clinic and also schedules all the surgeries performed. Comment on the deductibility of the Hamptons' expenses in attending the seminar.

11.   Dr. Mendoza is a professor of Romance languages at State University. In order to prepare a paper to be delivered at an academic symposium, he travels to Spain to conduct research on the life of Cervantes. Comment on the tax treatment of Dr. Mendoza's trip expenses based on the following assumptions:
a.   He spends two days doing research and three days sightseeing.
b.   He spends three weeks doing research and two weeks sightseeing.
c.   He spends four weeks doing research and one week sightseeing.

Decision Making

12.   Marge is scheduled to go to Paris on business. While there, she would like to do some sightseeing. When she mentions this to a friend, the friend suggests that she plan her weekends wisely. What does the friend's suggestion mean from a tax perspective?

13.   In November 2006, Quincy moves from Minneapolis to Baltimore to accept a new job. On his 2006 timely filed income tax return, Quincy deducts the qualified moving expenses involved. In June 2007, Quincy becomes unhappy with his work situation, quits the job, and moves back to Minneapolis. Comment on Quincy's income tax problem.

14.   For the convenience of her employer, Ashley is transferred from the Manhattan office to the Los Angeles office. In addition to the usual moving expenses, she incurs the following costs: penalty for breaking the old apartment lease and a pre-move trip to find a new apartment. Comment on the tax treatment of Ashley's moving expenses based on the following assumptions:
a.   The employer reimburses Ashley for *all* expenses.
b.   The employer pays for *all* expenses directly.

Issue ID

15.   During 2006, Kaitlyn incurs both deductible and nondeductible education expenses. Some of the deductible expenses are deductions *for* AGI, while the rest are deductions *from* AGI. Provide examples of Kaitlyn's expenses that could be:
a.   Nondeductible.
b.   Deductible as deductions *for* AGI.
c.   Deductible as deductions *from* AGI.

16. In connection with § 222 (deduction for qualified tuition and related expenses), comment on the relevance of the following:
    a. The education involved must be employment related.
    b. The deduction avoids the 2%-of-AGI floor.
    c. The deduction is subject to an AGI limitation.
    d. The taxpayers are married persons who file separate returns.
    e. The expenses involved the taxpayer's son who is a qualifying child.
    f. The expenses are paid by a daughter who is claimed by her father as a dependent.

17. What was the original justification for the cutback adjustment?
    a. Does the cutback adjustment completely solve the problem it was intended to correct?
    b. Are any exceptions made to the cutback adjustment? Why?

18. In each of the following situations, indicate whether there is a cutback adjustment and, if so, to whom it applies (i.e., employer or employee):
    a. The employer expects certain employees to entertain their key customers. The employer does not reimburse the employees for these costs.
    b. Same as (a) except that the employees are reimbursed for these costs.
    c. Each year the employer awards its top salesperson an expense-paid trip to the Cayman Islands.
    d. The employer has a cafeteria for its employees where meals are furnished at cost.
    e. The employer sponsors an annual Fourth of July picnic for its employees.
    f. Every Christmas, the employer gives each employee a turkey.

19. For tax purposes, what difference does it make whether entertainment is *directly related to* or *associated with* a trade or business?

20. At the last minute, a law firm purchases 10 tickets to the Super Bowl in order to entertain certain key clients. Comment on some possible tax ramifications of this situation.

Issue ID

21. In connection with the office in the home deduction, comment on the following factors:
    a. Taxpayer claims the standard deduction.
    b. The office is also used to pay personal bills.
    c. The expenses exceed the income from the business.
    d. Taxpayer rents, rather than owns, the home.

22. In 2005, Myrna, a full-time fifth grade teacher, spent $1,400 on supplies for her classes. The school district, upon the rendition of an adequate accounting, reimbursed her for $400 of these expenses. How should Myrna handle this matter for income tax purposes?

23. Trent, a resident of Florida, attends Vanderbilt University. After graduation, he moves to Dallas where he begins a job search. Shortly thereafter, he accepts a position with a local radio station as an announcer. Trent's college degree is in management. Presuming no reimbursement, what employment-related expenses might Trent be eligible to deduct?

Issue ID

24. How do traditional IRAs and Roth IRAs differ? Do these types of retirement plans possess any similarities? Explain.

25. In terms of travel expenses, what is deemed substantiation?
    a. How does it simplify accounting procedures?
    b. Under what circumstances may it be used?
    c. What expenses does it cover? Not cover?

26. What tax return reporting procedures must be followed by an employee under the following circumstances?
    a. Expenses and reimbursements are equal under an accountable plan.
    b. Reimbursements at the appropriate Federal per diem rate exceed expenses, and an adequate accounting is made to the employer.
    c. Expenses exceed reimbursements under a nonaccountable plan.

27. Olivia, a recent graduate from law school, is employed by a law firm as an attorney. In order to specialize, she would like to continue her education and earn a graduate

Issue ID

degree in tax law. She is hesitant to quit her job and go back to school full-time, however, as that might jeopardize her deduction for education expenses. Furthermore, she is concerned that developing a tax specialty could be treated as acquiring skills for a new trade or business. Comment on Olivia's concerns and provide constructive planning advice.

Decision Making

28. Kim has just graduated from college and is interviewing for a position in marketing. Crane Corporation has offered her a job as a sales representative that will require extensive travel and entertainment but provide valuable experience. Under the offer, she has two options: a salary of $48,000 and she absorbs all expenses; a salary of $35,000 and Crane reimburses for all expenses. Crane assures Kim that the $13,000 difference in the two options will be adequate to cover the expenses incurred. What issues should have an impact on Kim's choice?

Issue ID

Decision Making

29. Harriet plans to retire and move to Arizona. In connection with the move, she will incur considerable expense. Do you have any tax advice for Harriet?

30. Comment on the deductibility of each of the following items:
    a. Expenses incurred by taxpayer, a member of the New Mexico National Guard, to participate in a three-day training session conducted in Texas.
    b. Dues to a teamster's union paid by a truck driver.
    c. Computer supplies purchased by a college professor for use in the graduate seminars she teaches.
    d. Fee paid to take the state bar exam. Taxpayer is employed as a paralegal by a law firm.
    e. Cost of business suits taxpayer is required to wear at work. Taxpayer, a staff accountant, otherwise dresses casually.
    f. Annual membership fee to Palm Harbor Country Club. Taxpayer uses the facility 60% of the time for business.
    g. Cost of safety work shoes. Taxpayer is a self-employed stonemason.

PROBLEMS

31. During the year, Marlon holds two jobs. After an eight-hour day at his first job, he works three hours at the second job. On Mondays and Fridays of each week, he returns home for dinner before going to the second job. On the midweek days (Tuesday through Thursday), he goes directly from the first job to the second job, stopping along the way for a meal. The mileage involved is as follows:

Home to first job	20
First job to second job	25
Home to second job	30

   a. Assuming Marlon works 50 weeks during the year, how much of his mileage is deductible?
   b. Can Marlon deduct the midweek meals he purchased? Why or why not?

32. Jenny is the regional sales manager for a bagel retail chain. She starts her working day by driving from home to the regional office, works there for several hours, and then visits the three sales outlets in her region. Relevant mileage is as follows:

Home to regional office	15
Regional office to sales outlet #1	10
Sales outlet #1 to sales outlet #2	8
Sales outlet #2 to sales outlet #3	12
Sales outlet #3 to home	18

   If Jenny uses the automatic mileage method and works on 240 days in 2006, what is her deduction for the year?

33. On July 1, 2004, Nelson purchased a new automobile for $38,000. Miles driven are as follows: 15,000 in 2004; 20,000 in 2005; and 18,000 in 2006. If Nelson uses the auto 90%

for business and 10% for personal use, determine its basis as of January 1, 2007, based on the following assumptions:

a.   Nelson uses the automatic mileage method.

b.   Nelson uses the actual cost method. (Assume that *no* § 179 expensing is claimed and that 200% declining-balance with the half-year convention is used—see Chapter 8.)

34. Maureen went from Portland to Naples (Florida) on business. Her time was spent as follows:

Tuesday	Travel
Wednesday	Business
Thursday	Sightseeing
Friday	Business
Saturday and Sunday	Sightseeing
Monday	Business
Tuesday	Travel

Maureen's expenses are summarized below:

Airfare	$2,300
Lodging (Tuesday through Monday at $160 per day)	1,120
Meals (Wednesday through Monday at $140 per day)	840

Maureen is a self-employed real estate consultant who specializes in assisted-living housing projects.

a.   How much can Maureen deduct for the trip?

b.   Assume instead that the destination of Maureen's business trip is Naples, Italy (not Naples, Florida). How much can she deduct?

c.   How will any deductions in (a) and (b) be classified?

35. Graham, the regional manager for a national retail drug chain, is based in Denver, Colorado. During March and April of this year, he has to replace temporarily the district manager in Cheyenne, Wyoming. During this period, Graham flies to Cheyenne on Sunday night, spends the week at the district office, and returns home to Denver on Friday afternoon. The cost of returning home is $360, while the cost of spending the weekend in Cheyenne would have been $320.

a.   Presuming no reimbursement by his employer, how much, if any, of these weekend expenses may Graham deduct?

b.   Would your answer in (a) change if the amounts involved are reversed (i.e., the trip home cost $320; staying in Cheyenne would have been $360)?

36. In June of this year, Dr. and Mrs. Alvin Lord traveled to Memphis to attend a three-day conference sponsored by the American Society of Implant Dentistry. Alvin, a practicing oral surgeon, participated in scheduled technical sessions dealing with the latest developments in surgical procedures. On two days, Mrs. Lord attended group meetings where various aspects of family tax planning were discussed. On the other day, she went sightseeing. Mrs. Lord does not work for her husband, but she does their tax returns and handles the family investments. Expenses incurred in connection with the conference are summarized below:

Airfare (two tickets)	$1,040
Lodging (single and double occupancy are the same rate—$220 each day)	660
Meals ($200 × 3 days)*	600
Conference registration fee (includes $120 for Family Tax Planning sessions)	520
Car rental	240

* Split equally between Dr. and Mrs. Lord.

How much, if any, of these expenses can the Lords deduct?

37. On Thursday, Justin flies from Baltimore (his home office) to Cadiz (Spain). He conducts business on Friday and Tuesday; vacations on Saturday, Sunday, and Monday (a legal holiday in Spain); and returns to Baltimore on Thursday. Justin was scheduled to return home on Wednesday, but all flights were canceled due to bad weather. Therefore, he spent Wednesday watching floor shows at a local casino.
    a. For tax purposes, what portion of Justin's trip is regarded as being for business?
    b. Suppose Monday had not been a legal holiday. Would this change your answer in (a)?
    c. Under either (a) or (b), how much of Justin's airfare qualifies as a deductible business expense?

Decision Making

38. Monica travels from her office in Boston to Lisbon, Portugal, on business. Her absence of 13 days was spent as follows:

Thursday	Depart for and arrive at Lisbon
Friday	Business transacted
Saturday and Sunday	Vacationing
Monday through Friday	Business transacted
Saturday and Sunday	Vacationing
Monday	Business transacted
Tuesday	Depart Lisbon and return to office in Boston

    a. For tax purposes, how many days has Monica spent on business?
    b. What difference does it make?
    c. Could Monica have spent more time than she did vacationing on the trip without loss of existing tax benefits? Explain.

39. Doyle, a CPA, is a manager with a national accounting firm in Atlanta, Georgia. In 2006, he decides to quit his job and set up a private practice of public accounting in Santa Fe, New Mexico. In connection with the move, Doyle incurs the following expenses:

Penalty for breaking lease on Atlanta apartment	$3,200
Lodging during move	480
Meals during move	390
Packing and moving household goods	2,400
Mileage for personal autos	2,800 miles

    How much, if any, of these expenses can Doyle deduct?

40. Marvin is employed as a full-time high school teacher. The school district where he works recently instituted a policy requiring all of its teachers to start working on a master's degree. Pursuant to this new rule, Marvin spent most of the summer of 2005 taking graduate courses at an out-of-town university. His expenses are as follows:

Tuition	$4,300
Books and course materials	650
Lodging	1,200
Meals	1,600
Laundry and dry cleaning	220
Campus parking	300

    In addition, Marvin drove his personal automobile 1,500 miles in connection with the education. He uses the automatic mileage method.
    a. How much, if any, of these expenses might qualify as deductions *for* AGI?
    b. How much, if any, of these expenses might qualify as deductions *from* AGI?

41. In each of the following independent situations, determine how much, if any, qualifies as a deduction *for* AGI under § 222 (qualified tuition and related expenses):
    a. Ruby is single and is employed as a nurse practitioner. During 2005, she spends $4,200 in tuition to attend law school at night. Her AGI is $64,000.
    b. Jacque is single and is employed as a pharmacist. During 2005, he spends $2,100 ($1,900 for tuition and $200 for books) to take a course in herbal supplements at a local university. His AGI is $70,000.
    c. How much, if any, of the above amounts *not allowed under* § 222 might otherwise qualify as a deduction *from* AGI?

42. Britney is a licensed commercial pilot who works for Gull Charter Jet Service. Typically, Britney, who lives near the airport, flies a charter out of Tupelo, Mississippi, to either Las Vegas or Reno, spends several nights there, and then returns home with the same group. Gull provides Britney with a travel allowance of $1,600 per month but requires no accountability. For calendar year 2006, Britney had the following job-related expenses:

Meals	$ 7,100
Lodging	11,400
Transportation (taxis, limos)	580
Uniforms	1,720
Dry cleaning of uniforms	340
Annual physical exam	610

The uniforms are required to be worn on the job. The Federal Aviation Administration requires the annual physical exam for the maintenance of a commercial pilot's license. How may Britney treat these expenses for Federal income tax purposes?

43. Grebe Associates paid $40,000 for a 20-seat skybox at Municipal Stadium for eight professional football games. Regular seats to these games range from $50 to $70 each. At one game, an employee of Grebe entertained 19 clients. Grebe furnished food and beverages for the event at a cost of $450. The game was preceded by a bona fide business discussion, and all expenses are adequately substantiated.
    a. How much may Grebe deduct for this event?
    b. Would your answer in (a) change if only 15 (not 19) clients participated—four of the seats were not occupied?

44. During the current year, Kevin, the assistant manager of a truck leasing firm, made gifts that cost the following amounts:

To Darlene (Kevin's secretary) for Christmas ($2 was for gift wrapping)	$32
To George (Kevin's boss) on his birthday	31
To Susan (a key client) for Christmas	20
To John (a key client) for Christmas	28

Kevin also took Darlene to lunch (cost of $88) on her birthday. Presuming Kevin has adequate substantiation and is not reimbursed, how much can he deduct?

45. Felicia is employed full-time as an accountant for a national grocery chain. She also has a private consulting practice, which provides tax advice and financial planning to the general public. For this purpose, she maintains an office in her home. Expenses relating to the office are as follows:

Real property taxes	$4,800
Interest on home mortgage	4,200
Operating expenses of home	600
Depreciation allocated to 25% business use	1,800

Felicia's income from consulting is $18,000, and the related expenses are $6,000.
    a. What is Felicia's office in the home deduction?
    b. Suppose Felicia's income from the consulting is only $8,000 (not $18,000). How does this change the answer to part (a)?

46. Victor has AGI of $94,000 during the year and the following expenses related to his employment:

Lodging while in travel status	$3,400
Meals during travel	3,200
Business transportation	5,200
Entertainment of clients	2,200
Professional dues and subscriptions	900

Victor is reimbursed $10,000 under his employer's accountable plan. What are Victor's deductions *for* and *from* AGI?

Decision Making

47. During the year, Angelina had the following expenses related to her employment:

Airfare	$9,000
Meals	3,800
Lodging	4,700
Transportation while in travel status (taxis, limos)	920
Entertainment of clients	7,200

Although Angelina renders an adequate accounting to her employer, she is reimbursed for only $11,000 of the above expenses. What are Angelina's tax consequences based on the following assumptions?
a. The $11,000 reimbursement does not designate which expenses are covered.
b. The reimbursement specifically covers *only* the meals and entertainment expenses.
c. The reimbursement covers any of the expenses *other than* meals and entertainment.
d. If Angelina has a choice of reimbursement procedures [parts (a), (b), or (c) above], which should she select and why?

48. Audry, age 38 and single, earned a salary of $59,000. She had interest income of $1,600 and had a $2,000 long-term capital loss from the sale of a stock investment. Audry incurred the following employment-related expenses during the year:

Transportation	$5,500
Meals	2,800
Lodging	4,200
Entertaining clients	2,200
Professional dues and subscriptions	300

Under an accountable plan, Audry receives reimbursements of $4,500 from her employer. Calculate her AGI and itemized employee business expenses.

49. B. J. and Carolyn Grace are full-time employees. B. J. is a junior college teacher, and Carolyn is a registered nurse at a hospital. During 2006, they incur the following employment-related expenses:

School supplies for use in the classroom	$1,400
Emergency room uniforms	800
Union dues (teachers association)	200
Job hunting expenses (Carolyn obtained another nursing position but decided not to change jobs)	1,300
Continuing education correspondence courses (required to maintain nursing license)	380
Professional dues and subscriptions	1,100

None of these expenses are reimbursed by the employers.

For the year, the Graces file a joint return reflecting AGI of $94,000. They have other itemized deductions (i.e., interest on home mortgage, property taxes on personal residence, state income taxes, charitable contributions) of $14,500. Determine the total amount of itemized deductions allowed to the Graces for tax year 2006.

CUMULATIVE PROBLEMS

Tax Return Problem

Decision Making

Communications

50. George M. and Martha J. Jordan have no dependents and are both under age 65. George is a statutory employee of Consolidated Jobbers, a wholesaler of commercial equipment (business code is 421400), and his Social Security number is 582–99–4444. Martha is an executive with General Corporation, and her Social Security number is 241–88–6642. The Jordans live at 321 Oak Street, Lincoln, NV 89553. They both want to contribute to the Presidential Election Campaign Fund.

In 2005, George earned $49,200 in commissions. His employer withheld FICA taxes of $3,764 [($49,200 × 6.2%) + ($49,200 × 1.45%)] but does not withhold Federal income taxes. George paid $3,000 in estimated taxes. Martha earned $61,900, from which her employer withheld $6,250 for Federal income taxes and $4,735 [($61,900 × 6.2%) + ($61,900 × 1.45%)] for FICA taxes. Neither George nor Martha received any expense reimbursements.

George uses his automobile in his employment, and during 2005, his business mileage is 24,900 miles (allocable ratably throughout the year). Parking and tolls in connection with business use are $340 and $280, respectively. Fines paid for traffic violations (during business use) total $420. In deducting business use of his automobile, George always uses the automatic mileage method. His other employment-related expenses for the year are as follows:

Airfare	$1,820
Meals	2,600
Lodging	1,700
Entertainment	1,400
Business gifts	1,320

The business gifts consist of 30 fruit baskets George sent to key customers during the Christmas season. Each basket cost $40 (not including $4 for wrapping and shipping).

During the year, Martha enrolled in a weekend MBA program at a local university. In this regard, she spent the following amounts: $2,800 (tuition), $360 (books and computer supplies), $190 (meals while on campus), and $120 (bus fare to and from campus). Martha took her secretary to lunch on two occasions ($68 and $74) and her boss on one occasion ($120). She spent $140 on professional dues and $220 on trade journals.

Neither George nor Martha is covered under an employer-sponsored retirement plan. However, each contributes $4,000 (for a total of $8,000) to a traditional IRA.

In addition to their salaries, the Jordans received the amounts listed below during the year:

Interest on certificate of deposit issued by Reno State Bank	$ 1,500
Gifts from Martha's parents ($25,000 apiece to Martha and George)	50,000
Distribution from Pyramid Life	100,600

The distribution from Pyramid Life represents the maturity value ($100,000) plus interest ($600) of an insurance policy on Harvey Jordan's life. Harvey was George's uncle and had designated George as the beneficiary of the policy. Because Harvey died overseas, the insurance company had delayed in making the distribution to George. The gifts from Martha's parents are belated wedding presents and are not expected to occur again.

The Jordans had other expenditures as follows:

Charitable contributions (cash)	$2,100
Medical and dental expenses	7,800
Real property taxes on residence	3,200
Sales taxes—actual amount (receipts available)	2,000
Home mortgage interest	7,000
Tax return preparation fee	300

Part 1—Tax Computation
Compute the Jordans' Federal income tax payable or refund due, assuming they file a joint income tax return, for 2005. If they have overpaid, they want the amount refunded. You will need Form 1040 and Schedules A, B, and C. Suggested software: TurboTax.

Part 2—Tax Planning
Martha and George request your help in deciding where to invest the extra $150,000 (life insurance and gift proceeds) they received in 2005. They are considering two alternatives:

- Municipal bonds that yield 4.5%.
- Common stock that regularly pays cash dividends of 6%.

a. Calculate the better alternative for next year. Assume that Martha and George will have the same income and deductions in 2006, except for the income from the investment they choose. In computing the tax, use the tax rate schedules for 2006.

b. What other factors should the Jordans take into account?

c. Write a memo to the Jordans, explaining their alternatives.

51. John R. Dorsey is single, age 36, and lives at 6240 Pinerock, Seattle, WA 98122. He is employed as a sales and claims agent for the commercial vehicle division of Hawk Corporation, a casualty insurance company. John's annual salary of $80,000 does not include a performance bonus. The bonus is announced in December of each year but is not paid until the following January. John received a bonus of $12,000 for 2005 (paid in 2006) and a bonus of $15,000 for 2006 (paid in 2007). Hawk withheld $15,000 for Federal income tax and $7,232 [($94,200 × 6.2%) + ($96,000 × 1.45%)] for FICA in 2006. Hawk *also* provides John with a modest expense account allowance of $4,000 but requires no accounting to be rendered as to how the amount is spent. John's Social Security number is 531–60–1890.

- John uses his personal automobile in his work and claims the automatic mileage method as to qualified business use. Typically, his work assignments follow one of three patterns. First, he may spend the entire day at the office where he meets with current and prospective policyholders and handles other business-related matters. Second, he goes to the office for a while and then visits various sites to assess the damage to clients' vehicles. Third, he goes directly from home to the claim sites. Mileage for 2006 is as follows: 3,200 for home to office; 4,000 for office to claim sites; and 3,300 for home to claim sites.

- John's other employment-related expenses are summarized below:

Business lunches for employees on special occasions (e.g., birthdays)	$ 610
Lunches, dinners, and other entertainment (e.g., nightclubs, sporting events) of clients	3,800
Christmas gifts for 24 key clients (e.g., managers of fleet car operations) consisting of a cheese tray ($25 cost + $4 shipping)	696
Dues to professional organizations and subscriptions to trade journals	520
Cost of attending three-day conference sponsored by an insurance trade group [$1,100 (airfare) + $390 (lodging) + $410 (meals) + $350 (registration) + $180 (car rental and parking)]	2,430
Job search expenses	1,200
Online continuing education program	800

In connection with the job search expenses, John heard that a competing insurance company had a vacancy in a comparable position that paid a larger salary. Through a recruiting firm, he applied for the job but was turned down. The continuing education program dealt with procedures for maintaining and improving client relations.

- Besides the items already noted, John's receipts for 2006 are as follows:

Qualified dividends from GE common stock		$ 980
Interest income—		
City of Seattle bonds	$1,700	
Boeing Corporation bonds	1,100	
Wells Fargo Bank CD	1,300	4,100
Repayment of loan by Cindy Dorsey		4,200
City of Seattle medical reimbursement		7,800
Life insurance proceeds		50,000
Jury duty fees		180
Gambling winnings		900

Six months ago, John loaned his sister, Cindy, $4,000 to help her purchase a car. No note was signed, and no interest was provided for. When she repaid the loan in 2006, Cindy insisted on adding $200 in gratitude for the favor.

In 2005, John was hospitalized because of an injury caused by the operator of a public works vehicle. Since the city was at fault, it reimbursed John for the medical expenses caused by the accident [Note: John received no tax benefit from the $7,800 he paid in 2005.].

As a result of the death of their grandmother in early 2006, John and his brothers and sisters each received varying amounts as the beneficiaries of several life insurance policies she owned. John is paid his distribution of $50,000 in August of 2006.

• In addition to those already noted, John's expenditures for 2006 are as follows:

Medical—		
Insurance premiums	$3,600	
Medical and dental (including prescriptions) not covered by insurance	2,900	$ 6,500
Taxes—		
State and local sales taxes	$2,400	
Property taxes on residence	4,200	6,600
Interest on home mortgage		4,800
Charitable contributions		1,200
Purchase of SeaRay cabin cruiser		13,500
Jury duty expenses		210
Gambling losses		800

John keeps track of the sales taxes paid during the year and can substantiate the $2,400 listed. The state of Washington does not impose an income tax.

John acquired the cabin cruiser from a former classmate at a bargain price of $13,500—it had an appraised value of $18,000. Because the classmate was going through the financial throes of a divorce, he was in dire need of liquid assets. However, two days after the October purchase and before John could obtain any insurance coverage, the boat was stolen. The storage facility where the boat was kept limits its theft liability to $500 per item, and John was paid this amount in March 2007. As boats that are stolen are often taken to Canada and sold, John does not expect to recover his property.

Expenses related to the jury duty consisted of parking and meals and, as is frequently the case, exceeded what he was paid for serving on the jury.

As is true with all of his expenses, John can substantiate the gambling losses.

Based on the information given, determine John's income tax payable or refund due for 2006.

RESEARCH PROBLEMS

Note: Solutions to Research Problems can be prepared by using the **RIA Checkpoint®** **Student Edition** online research product, which is available to accompany this text. It is also possible to prepare solutions to the Research Problems by using tax research materials found in a standard tax library.

Research Problem 1. Richard Harding is the sheriff of Howard County, Indiana. In addition to the usual law enforcement duties, the sheriff has the responsibility of maintaining the detention facility (i.e., county jail). Further, he must furnish meals for all prisoners in accordance with certain nutritional standards prescribed by the state. Although the sheriff must absorb the cost of the meals, the county provides a personal allowance.

During the year, Sheriff Harding received a salary of $35,000 (as reported on a Form W–2 issued by Howard County). He spent $90,000 on prisoner meals and received meal allowances of $110,000. On his income tax return, he reported the salary as employee income, but listed the allowances and meals on a Schedule C. Thus, he treated himself as self-employed by claiming the cost of the meals as a deduction *for* AGI.

Upon audit, the IRS determined that the Schedule C treatment was improper. Harding was not in a separate trade or business of providing meals, but was merely carrying out his employment-related duties. The costs of the meals are employee business expenses deductible only as miscellaneous itemized deductions on Schedule A. As such, they are subject to the 2%-of-AGI floor.

Is Sheriff Harding or the IRS correct? Why?

Research Problem 2. Al Hardee has been employed as a salesman by Robin Chevrolet at its Milwaukee dealership. In early May, Al and the general manager of the office had a serious dispute over job procedures. When it became clear that the two could no longer work together amicably, Al contacted Robin's CEO regarding a possible solution. As the general manager planned to retire in five months, it was decided that Al would spend this period working at the Green Bay branch. After the manager's retirement, Al was to rejoin the Milwaukee office.

Al's residence is only a few blocks from the Milwaukee office, but it is 96 miles (one-way) from the Green Bay worksite. During the next five months (i.e., May to October), Al made 120 trips driving from his home in Milwaukee to the Green Bay job. His only records of his trips are a wall calendar with the workdays circled and the credit card receipts he received from gasoline purchases. The employee records of the Green Bay dealership can, however, support Al's on-the-job presence.

Upon termination of the five-month assignment and after the retirement of the general manager, Al requested a transfer back to the Milwaukee office. The CEO turned down the request on the grounds that Al was no longer needed in Milwaukee. During his absence and unknown to Al, his job position in Milwaukee had been eliminated. However, the CEO offered to make the Green Bay assignment permanent. Hurt and disgusted, Al quit and took a job with a competing Milwaukee car dealership.

On his Federal income tax return, Al claimed a deduction for employee transportation expenses, computed as follows: 120 (number of trips) × 192 (round-trip mileage) × automatic mileage rate for the year. The IRS disallowed the deduction on two grounds. First, Al's job status in Green Bay was *permanent*, not *temporary*. Thus, his tax home had changed from Milwaukee to Green Bay. This, in turn, made his transportation expenses nondeductible commuting expenses. Second, even if the transportation was warranted, the expenses were not properly substantiated. Consequently, the lack of substantiation precludes any deduction.

Should Al be allowed a deduction for his transportation expenses? Explain.

Partial list of research aids:
Reg. § 1.162–2(e).
Reg. § 1.274–5T(c)(3).
Rev.Rul. 99–7, 1999–1 C.B. 363.
Teresita T. Diaz, 84 TCM 148, T.C.Memo. 2002–192.
Richard M. Brockman, 85 TCM 733, T.C.Memo. 2003–3.

Research Problem 3. Carrie Hopkins is a qualified teacher in the San Francisco Unified School District. Currently, she teaches at North Lincoln High School where she is also head of the English Department. North Lincoln is a culturally diverse school with a predominantly Asian student population. As a department head, Carrie has considerable input on the curriculum content of the courses offered by her school.

During the summer, Carrie enrolled in a course sponsored by the University of California, Berkeley Extension Program. The course, entitled "Southeast Asia: Sacred Places," was conducted in Thailand, Cambodia, and Indonesia and dealt with the effect of religious traditions on the culture of Southeast Asia. The course was taught by university staff, and successful completion by a student qualified for undergraduate college credit. The course is conducted overseas to enhance the significance of the subject matter covered. Although Carrie's employer approved of her academic endeavors, it did not require her to take the course. Further, it did not reimburse her for any of the expenses involved. Except for several minor sightseeing trips, Carrie devoted most of her time during the course to the materials assigned and covered.

As a result of what she learned from the course she took, Carrie made various improvements to the content of her department's curriculum. She also feels that the course increased her ability to understand and communicate with the Asian students in her classes.

On her Federal income tax return, Carrie deducted all of the expenses incurred in connection with the extension course. Upon audit by the IRS, the deduction is disallowed. Who should prevail?

Partial list of research aids:
§§ 162(a), 262(a), and 274(m)(2).
Reg. § 1.162–5(e).
Harry H. Takahashi, 87 T.C. 126 (1986).
Ann Jorgensen, 79 TCM 1926, T.C.Memo. 2000–138.

Research Problem 4. Rick Beam has been an independent sales representative for various   **Communications**
textile manufacturers for many years. His products consist of soft goods, such as
tablecloths, curtains, and drapes. Rick's customers are clothing store chains, department
stores, and smaller specialty stores. The employees of these companies who are
responsible for purchasing merchandise are known as buyers. These companies generally
prohibit their buyers from accepting gifts from manufacturers' sales representatives.

Each year Rick gives cash gifts (never more than $25) to most of the buyers who are
his customers. Generally, he cashes a large check in November and gives the money
personally to the buyers around Christmas. Rick says, "This is one of the ways that I
maintain my relationship with my buyers." He maintains adequate substantiation of all
the gifts.

Rick's deductions for these gifts have been disallowed by the IRS, based on
§ 162(c)(2). Rick is confused and comes to you, a CPA, for advice.
a. Write a letter to Rick concerning his tax position on this issue. Rick's address is 948
Octavia Street, Baton Rouge, LA 70821.
b. Prepare a memo for your files supporting the advice you have given.

Use the tax resources of the Internet to address the following questions. Do not restrict   **Internet**
your search to the World Wide Web, but include a review of newsgroups and general   *Activity*
reference materials, practitioner sites and resources, primary sources of the tax law,
chat rooms and discussion groups, and other opportunities.

Research Problem 5. What are the guidelines regarding the deductibility of conventions
held outside the North American area? Refer to Chapter 1 of IRS Publication No. 463.

Research Problem 6. In reporting employee business expenses, when can Form 2106–EZ
be used instead of Form 2106?

Research Problem 7. Determine whether your city qualifies for the "high-cost" travel per
diem allowances provided by the IRS.

Research Problem 8. Examine Form 8829 and the instructions for its use and answer the
following questions:
a. The difference between *direct* and *indirect* expenses (lines 9 through 21).
b. The purpose served by lines 23 and 41.

CHAPTER 10

Deductions and Losses: Certain Itemized Deductions

LEARNING OBJECTIVES

After completing Chapter 10, you should be able to:

LO.1
Distinguish between deductible and nondeductible personal expenses.

LO.2
Define medical expenses and compute the medical expense deduction.

LO.3
Contrast deductible taxes and nondeductible fees, licenses, etc.

LO.4
Understand the Federal income tax treatment of state and local income taxes and sales taxes.

LO.5
Distinguish between deductible and nondeductible interest and apply the appropriate limitations to deductible interest.

LO.6
Understand charitable contributions and their related measurement problems and percentage limitations.

LO.7
List the business and personal expenditures that are deductible either as miscellaneous itemized deductions or as other itemized deductions.

LO.8
Recognize the limitation on certain itemized deductions applicable to high-income taxpayers.

LO.9
Identify tax planning procedures that can maximize the benefit of itemized deductions.

OUTLINE

LO.1

Distinguish between deductible and nondeductible personal expenses.

General Classification of Expenses

As a general rule, the deduction of personal expenditures is disallowed by § 262 of the Code. However, Congress has chosen to allow certain personal expenditures to be deducted as itemized deductions. Personal expenditures that are deductible as itemized deductions include medical expenses, certain taxes, mortgage interest, investment interest, and charitable contributions. These expenditures and other personal expenditures that are allowed as itemized deductions are covered in this chapter. Any personal expenditures not specifically allowed as itemized deductions by the tax law are nondeductible.

Allowable itemized deductions are deductible *from* AGI in arriving at taxable income if the taxpayer elects to itemize. The election to itemize is appropriate when total itemized deductions exceed the standard deduction based on the taxpayer's filing status (refer to Chapter 3).[1]

LO.2

Define medical expenses and compute the medical expense deduction.

Medical Expenses

General Requirements

Medical expenses paid for the care of the taxpayer, spouse, and dependents are allowed as an itemized deduction to the extent the expenses are not reimbursed. The **medical expense** deduction is limited to the amount by which such expenses *exceed* 7.5 percent of the taxpayer's AGI.

EXAMPLE 1

During the year, Iris had medical expenses of $4,800, of which $1,000 was reimbursed by her insurance company. If her AGI for the year is $40,000, the itemized deduction for medical expenses is limited to $800 [$4,800 − $1,000 = $3,800 − (7.5% × $40,000)]. ∎

---

[1]The total standard deduction is the sum of the basic standard deduction and the additional standard deduction (refer to Chapter 3).

<table>
<tr><td colspan="2">TAX in the News</td><td colspan="2">**THE PRESIDENT AND VICE PRESIDENT ITEMIZE**</td></tr>
</table>

Approximately two-thirds of all individual taxpayers take the standard deduction each year rather than itemize. President George W. Bush and Vice President Richard B. Cheney are among the one-third who itemize. The President, who files a joint return with his wife, released his 2004 tax return to the public. The itemized deductions, along with certain other information from the Bush tax return, are shown in the column to the right.

Vice President Cheney, who did not release Schedule A–Itemized Deductions, reported gross income of $1,747,794 and itemized deductions of $405,695.

Gross income	$784,219
Adjusted gross income	$784,219
Itemized deductions:	
Medical expenses	$ –0–
Taxes	24,344
Interest	–0–
Charitable contributions	77,785
Job expenses and other miscellaneous deductions	28,548
Total itemized deductions	$130,677

Medical Expenses Defined

The term *medical care* includes expenditures incurred for the "diagnosis, cure, mitigation, treatment, or prevention of disease, or for the purpose of affecting any structure or function of the body."[2] A *partial* list of deductible and nondeductible medical items appears in Exhibit 10–1.

A medical expense does not have to relate to a particular ailment to be deductible. Since the definition of medical care is broad enough to cover preventive measures, the cost of periodic physical and dental exams qualifies even for a taxpayer in good health.

Amounts paid for unnecessary *cosmetic surgery* are not deductible medical expenses. However, if cosmetic surgery is deemed necessary, it is deductible as a medical expense. Cosmetic surgery is necessary when it ameliorates (1) a deformity arising from a congenital abnormality, (2) a personal injury, or (3) a disfiguring disease.

Art, a calendar year taxpayer, paid $11,000 to a plastic surgeon for a face lift. Art, age 75, merely wanted to improve his appearance. The $11,000 does not qualify as a medical expense since the surgery was unnecessary. ∎

EXAMPLE 2

As a result of a serious automobile accident, Marge's face is disfigured. The cost of restorative cosmetic surgery is deductible as a medical expense. ∎

EXAMPLE 3

The cost of care in a *nursing home or home for the aged,* including meals and lodging, can be included in deductible medical expenses if the primary reason for being in the home is to get medical care. If the primary reason for being there is personal, any costs for medical or nursing care can be included in deductible medical expenses, but the cost of meals and lodging must be excluded.[3]

Norman has a chronic heart ailment. In October, his family decides to place Norman in a nursing home equipped to provide medical and nursing care facilities. Total nursing home expenses amount to $15,000 during the year. Of this amount, $4,500 is directly attributable to medical and nursing care. Since Norman is in need of significant medical and nursing care and is placed in the facility primarily for this purpose, all $15,000 of the nursing home costs are deductible (subject to the 7.5% floor). ∎

EXAMPLE 4

---

[2]§ 213(d)(1)(A).   [3]Reg. § 1.213–1(e)(1)(v).

EXHIBIT 10–1	Examples of Deductible and Nondeductible Medical Expenses

Deductible	Nondeductible
Medical (including dental, mental, and hospital) care	Funeral, burial, or cremation expenses
Prescription drugs	Nonprescription drugs (except insulin)
Special equipment	Bottled water
Wheelchairs	Toiletries, cosmetics
Crutches	Diaper service, maternity clothes
Artificial limbs	Programs for the *general* improvement of health
Eyeglasses (including contact lenses)	Weight reduction
Hearing aids	Health spas
Transportation for medical care	Social activities (e.g., dancing and swimming lessons)
Medical and hospital insurance premiums	Unnecessary cosmetic surgery
Long-term care insurance premiums (subject to limitations)	
Cost of alcohol and drug rehabilitation	
Certain costs to stop smoking	
Weight reduction programs related to obesity	

Special child needed care (handwritten margin note)

Tuition expenses of a dependent at a special school may be deductible as a medical expense. The cost of medical care can include the expenses of a special school for a mentally or physically handicapped individual. The deduction is allowed if a principal reason for sending the individual to the school is the school's special resources for alleviating the infirmities. In this case, the cost of meals and lodging, in addition to the tuition, is a proper medical expense deduction.[4]

EXAMPLE 5

Jason's daughter Marcia attended public school through the seventh grade. Because Marcia was a poor student, she was examined by a psychiatrist who diagnosed an organic problem that created a learning disability. Upon the recommendation of the psychiatrist, Marcia is enrolled in a private school so that she can receive individual attention. The school has no special program for students with learning disabilities and does not provide special medical treatment. The expense related to Marcia's attendance is not deductible as a medical expense. The cost of any psychiatric care, however, qualifies as a medical expense. ■

Example 5 shows that the recommendation of a physician does not automatically make the expenditure deductible.

Capital Expenditures for Medical Purposes

Some examples of *capital expenditures* for medical purposes are swimming pools if the taxpayer does not have access to a neighborhood pool and air conditioners if they do not become permanent improvements (e.g., window units).[5] Other

---

[4]*Donald R. Pfeifer*, 37 TCM 816, T.C.Memo. 1978–189. Also see Rev.Rul. 78–340, 1978–2 C.B. 124.

[5]Rev.Rul. 55–261, 1955–1 C.B. 307, modified by Rev.Rul. 68–212, 1968–1 C.B. 91.

examples include dust elimination systems,[6] elevators,[7] and a room built to house an iron lung. These expenditures are medical in nature if they are incurred as a medical necessity upon the advice of a physician, the facility is used primarily by the patient alone, and the expense is reasonable.

Capital expenditures normally are adjustments to basis and are not deductible. However, both a capital expenditure for a permanent improvement and expenditures made for the operation or maintenance of the improvement may qualify as medical expenses. If a capital expenditure qualifies as a medical expense, the allowable cost is deductible in the year incurred. Although depreciation is required for most other capital expenditures, it is not required for capital expenditures for medical purposes.

A capital improvement that ordinarily would not have a medical purpose qualifies as a medical expense if it is directly related to prescribed medical care and is deductible to the extent that the expenditure *exceeds* the increase in value of the related property. Appraisal costs related to capital improvements are also deductible, but not as medical expenses. These costs are expenses incurred in the determination of the taxpayer's tax liability.[8]

Building rooms... for med reason. => all are ded on the same year (no need to depreciate)

Fred is afflicted with heart disease. His physician advises him to install an elevator in his residence so he will not be required to climb the stairs. The cost of installing the elevator is $3,000, and the increase in the value of the residence is determined to be only $1,700. Therefore, $1,300 ($3,000 − $1,700) is deductible as a medical expense. Additional utility costs to operate the elevator and maintenance costs are deductible as medical expenses as long as the medical reason for the capital expenditure continues to exist. ■	*EXAMPLE 6*

The full cost of certain home-related capital expenditures incurred to enable a *physically handicapped* individual to live independently and productively qualifies as a medical expense. Qualifying costs include expenditures for constructing entrance and exit ramps to the residence, widening hallways and doorways to accommodate wheelchairs, installing support bars and railings in bathrooms and other rooms, and adjusting electrical outlets and fixtures.[9] These expenditures are subject to the 7.5 percent floor only, and the increase in the home's value is deemed to be zero.

ramps, entrance for handicapped are ded.

Medical Expenses Incurred for Spouse and Dependents

In computing the medical expense deduction, a taxpayer may include medical expenses for a spouse and for a person who was a dependent at the time the expenses were paid or incurred. Of the requirements that normally apply in determining dependency status,[10] neither the gross income nor the joint return test applies in determining dependency status for medical expense deduction purposes.

Ernie (age 22) is married and a full-time student at a university. During the year, Ernie incurred medical expenses that were paid by Matilda (Ernie's mother). She provided more than half of Ernie's support for the year. Even if Ernie files a joint return with his wife, Matilda may claim the medical expenses she paid for him. Matilda would combine Ernie's expenses with her own before applying the 7.5% floor. ■	*EXAMPLE 7*

For *divorced persons* with children, a special rule applies to the noncustodial parent. The noncustodial parent may claim any medical expenses he or she pays even though the custodial parent claims the children as dependents. This rule applies if the dependency exemptions could have been shifted to the noncustodial parent by the custodial parent's waiver (refer to Chapter 3).

---

[6]*F. S. Delp*, 30 T.C. 1230 (1958).

[7]*Riach v. Frank*, 62–1 USTC ¶9419, 9 AFTR2d 1263, 302 F.2d 374 (CA–9, 1962).

[8]§ 212(3).

[9]For a complete list of the items that qualify, see Rev.Rul. 87–106, 1987–2 C.B. 67.

[10]Refer to Chapter 3 for discussion of these requirements.

EXAMPLE 8

Irv and Joan are divorced in 2005, and Joan is awarded custody of their child, Keith. During 2006, Irv makes the following payments to Joan: $3,600 for child support and $2,500 for Keith's medical bills. Together, Irv and Joan provide more than half of Keith's support. Even though Joan claims Keith as a dependent, Irv can combine the $2,500 of medical expenses that he pays for Keith with his own when calculating his medical expense deduction. ■

Transportation, Meal, and Lodging Expenses for Medical Treatment

Payments for transportation to and from a point of treatment for medical care are deductible as medical expenses (subject to the 7.5 percent floor). Transportation expenses for medical care include bus, taxi, train, or plane fare, charges for ambulance service, and out-of-pocket expenses for the use of an automobile. A mileage allowance of 18 cents per mile[11] may be used instead of actual out-of-pocket automobile expenses. Whether the taxpayer chooses to claim out-of-pocket automobile expenses or the 18 cents per mile automatic mileage option, related parking fees and tolls can also be deducted. The cost of meals while en route to obtain medical care is not deductible.

A deduction is also allowed for the transportation expenses of a parent who must accompany a child who is receiving medical care or for a nurse or other person giving assistance to a person who is traveling to get medical care and cannot travel alone.

A deduction is allowed for lodging while away from home for medical expenses if the following requirements are met:[12]

- The lodging is primarily for and essential to medical care.
- Medical care is provided by a doctor in a licensed hospital or a similar medical facility (e.g., a clinic).
- The lodging is not lavish or extravagant under the circumstances.
- There is no significant element of personal pleasure, recreation, or vacation in the travel away from home.

The deduction for lodging expenses included as medical expenses cannot exceed $50 *per* night for *each* person. The deduction is allowed not only for the patient but also for a person who must travel with the patient (e.g., a parent traveling with a child who is receiving medical care).

EXAMPLE 9

Herman, a resident of Winchester, Kentucky, is advised by his family physician that Martha, Herman's dependent and disabled mother, needs specialized treatment for her heart condition. Consequently, Herman and Martha fly to Cleveland, Ohio, where Martha receives the therapy at a heart clinic on an out-patient basis. Expenses in connection with the trip are as follows:

Round trip airfare ($250 each)	$500
Lodging in Cleveland for two nights ($60 each per night)	240

Herman's medical expense deduction for transportation is $500, and his medical expense deduction for lodging is $200 ($50 per night per person). Because Martha is disabled, it is assumed that his accompanying her is justified. ■

No deduction is allowed for the cost of meals unless they are part of the medical care and are furnished at a medical facility. When allowable, such meals are not subject to the 50 percent limit applicable to business meals.

---

[11]This amount is adjusted periodically. The allowance was 15 cents from January 1 to August 31, 2005. The allowance was increased to 22 cents for the period September 1 through December 31, 2005.

[12]§ 213(d)(2).

ETHICAL Considerations — TRAVEL EXPENSES: MEDICAL OR PERSONAL?

Ron, who lives in Phoenix, has a chronic heart problem. He flies to Rochester, Minnesota, several times each year for checkups and treatment at the Mayo Clinic, which has one of the most highly rated heart treatment programs in the United States. On each trip, he visits his two children, who live in Rochester with his ex-wife. Is Ron justified in deducting the cost of his airline tickets and his lodging in Rochester as a medical expense?

Amounts Paid for Medical Insurance Premiums

Medical insurance premiums are included with other medical expenses subject to the 7.5 percent floor. Premiums paid by the taxpayer under a group plan or an individual plan are included as medical expenses. If an employer pays all or part of the taxpayer's medical insurance premiums, the amount paid by the employer is not included in gross income by the employee. Likewise, the premium is not included in the employee's medical expenses.

[handwritten: Indiv's ins. premium included as med. expense.]

If a taxpayer is *self-employed*, insurance premiums paid for medical coverage are deductible as a *business* expense (*for* AGI).[13] The deduction *for* AGI is allowed for premiums paid on behalf of the taxpayer, the taxpayer's spouse, and dependents of the taxpayer. The deduction is not allowed to any taxpayer who is eligible to participate in a subsidized health plan maintained by any employer of the taxpayer or of the taxpayer's spouse. Premiums paid for medical insurance coverage of *employees* are deductible as business expenses.

[handwritten: Self. emp's ins. premium is business expense (FOR AGI)]

Ellen, a sole proprietor of a restaurant, has two dependent children. During the year, she paid health insurance premiums of $1,800 for her own coverage and $1,000 for coverage of her two children. Ellen can deduct $2,800 as a business deduction (for AGI) in computing her taxable income. ∎

EXAMPLE 10

Taxpayers may also include premiums paid on qualified long-term care insurance contracts in medical expenses, subject to limitations based on the age of the insured. For 2006, the per-person limits range from $280 for taxpayers age 40 and under to $3,530 for taxpayers over age 70. See IRS Publication 502 for details relating to requirements for qualified long-term care insurance contracts.

[handwritten: Limits on premium On LT-care ins]

Year of Deduction

Regardless of a taxpayer's method of accounting, medical expenses are deductible only in the year *paid*. In effect, this places all individual taxpayers on a cash basis as far as the medical expense deduction is concerned. One exception, however, is allowed for deceased taxpayers. If the medical expenses are paid within one year from the day following the day of death, they can be treated as being paid at the time they were *incurred*. Thus, such expenses may be reported on the final income tax return of the decedent or on earlier returns if incurred before the year of death.

[handwritten: All are "cash-basis" for med-exp.]

No current deduction is allowed for payment for medical care to be rendered in the future unless the taxpayer is under an obligation to make the payment.[14] Whether an obligation to make the payment exists depends upon the policy of the physician or the institution furnishing the medical care.

[handwritten: Future service ⇒ future ded except freq. pre-paid.]

---

[13]§ 162(l).

[14]*Robert S. Basset*, 26 T.C. 619 (1956).

EXAMPLE 11

Upon the recommendation of his regular dentist, in late December 2006 Gary consults Dr. Smith, a prosthodontist, who specializes in crown and bridge work. Dr. Smith tells Gary that he can do the restorative work for $12,000. To cover his lab bill, however, Dr. Smith requires that 40% of this amount be prepaid. Accordingly, Gary pays $4,800 in December 2006. The balance of $7,200 is paid when the work is completed in July 2007. Under these circumstances, the qualifying medical expenses are $4,800 for 2006 and $7,200 in 2007. The result would be the same even if Gary prepaid the full $12,000 in 2006. ■

Reimbursements

[handwritten note in margin: If itemized ded, # reimb must be GI next yr (yr rec)]

If medical expenses are reimbursed in the same year as paid, no problem arises. The reimbursement merely reduces the amount that would otherwise qualify for the medical expense deduction. But what happens if the reimbursement occurs in a later year than the expenditure? In computing casualty losses, any reasonable prospect of recovery must be considered (refer to Chapter 7). For medical expenses, however, any expected reimbursement is disregarded in measuring the amount of the deduction. Instead, the reimbursement is accounted for separately in the year in which it occurs.

Under the *tax benefit rule*, a taxpayer who receives an insurance reimbursement for medical expenses deducted in a previous year might have to include the reimbursement in gross income in the year of receipt. However, a taxpayer who did not itemize deductions in the year the expenses were paid did not receive a tax benefit and is *not* required to include a reimbursement in gross income.

The tax benefit rule applies to reimbursements if the taxpayer itemized deductions in the previous year. In this case, the taxpayer may be required to report some or all of the medical expense reimbursement in income in the year the reimbursement is received. Under the tax benefit rule, the taxpayer must include the reimbursement in income up to the amount of the deductions that decreased taxable income in the earlier year.

EXAMPLE 12

Homer had AGI of $20,000 for 2006. He was injured in a car accident and paid $1,300 for hospital expenses and $700 for doctor bills. Homer also incurred medical expenses of $600 for his dependent child. In 2007, Homer was reimbursed $650 by his insurance company for the medical expenses attributable to the car accident. His deduction for medical expenses in 2006 is computed as follows:

Hospitalization	$ 1,300
Bills for doctor's services	700
Medical expenses for dependent	600
Total	$ 2,600
Less: 7.5% of $20,000	(1,500)
Medical expense deduction (assuming Homer itemizes his deductions)	$ 1,100

Assume that Homer would have elected to itemize his deductions even if he had no medical expenses in 2006. If the reimbursement for medical care had occurred in 2006, the medical expense deduction would have been only $450 [$2,600 (total medical expenses) − $650 (reimbursement) − $1,500 (floor)], and Homer would have paid more income tax.

Since the reimbursement was made in a subsequent year, Homer will include $650 in gross income for 2007. If Homer had not itemized in 2006, he would not include the $650 reimbursement in 2007 gross income because he would have received no tax benefit in 2006. ■

Health Savings Accounts

Qualifying individuals may make deductible contributions to a **Health Savings Account (HSA)**. An HSA is a qualified trust or custodial account administered by a qualified HSA trustee, which can be a bank, insurance company, or other IRS-approved trustee. The HSA funds are used to pay for the individual's medical expenses in excess of the deductible amount under a high-deductible policy.[15]

A taxpayer can use an HSA in conjunction with a high-deductible medical insurance policy to help reduce the overall cost of medical coverage. Converting from a low-deductible to a high-deductible plan can generally save an individual 20 to 40 percent in premiums. The high-deductible policy provides coverage for extraordinary medical expenses (in excess of the deductible), and expenses not covered by the policy can be paid with funds withdrawn from the HSA.

EXAMPLE 13

Sanchez, who is married and has three dependent children, carries a high-deductible medical insurance policy with a deductible of $4,400. He establishes an HSA and contributes the maximum allowable amount to the HSA in 2006. During 2006, the Sanchez family incurs medical expenses of $7,000. The high-deductible policy covers $2,600 of the expenses ($7,000 expenses − $4,400 deductible). Sanchez may withdraw $4,400 from the HSA to pay the medical expenses not covered by the high-deductible policy. ■

High-Deductible Plans.
High-deductible policies are less expensive than low-deductible policies, so taxpayers with low medical costs can benefit from the lower premiums and use funds from the HSA to pay costs not covered by the high-deductible policy. A plan must meet two requirements to qualify as a high-deductible plan.[16]

1. The annual deductible is not less than $1,050 for self-only coverage ($2,100 for family coverage).
2. The sum of the annual deductible and other out-of-pocket costs (excluding premiums) under the plan does not exceed $5,250 for self-only coverage ($10,500 for family coverage).

Tax Treatment of HSA Contributions and Distributions.
To establish an HSA, a taxpayer contributes funds to a tax-exempt trust.[17] As illustrated in the preceding example, funds can be withdrawn from an HSA to pay medical expenses that are not covered by the high-deductible policy. The following general tax rules apply to HSAs:

1. Contributions made by the taxpayer to an HSA are deductible from gross income to arrive at AGI (deduction *for* AGI). Thus, the taxpayer does not need to itemize in order to take the deduction.
2. Earnings on HSAs are not subject to taxation unless distributed, in which case taxability depends on the way the funds are used.[18]

   • Distributions from HSAs are excluded from gross income if they are used to pay for medical expenses not covered by the high-deductible policy.
   • Distributions that are not used to pay for medical expenses are included in gross income and are subject to an additional 10 percent penalty if made before age 65, death, or disability. Such distributions made by reason of death or disability and distributions made after the HSA beneficiary becomes eligible for Medicare are taxed but not penalized.

HSAs have at least two other attractive features. First, an HSA is portable. Taxpayers who switch jobs can take their HSAs with them. Second, coverage is more widely available under the HSA rules than under the previous Archer MSA rules.

---

[15]§ 223. In December 2003, President Bush signed legislation creating HSAs as a replacement for Archer Medical Savings Accounts (MSAs). The HSA legislation was part of the Medicare reform law. The HSA has been described as a new and improved Archer MSA.

[16]§ 223(c)(2).
[17]§ 223(d).
[18]§ 223(f).

Generally, anyone under age 65 who has a high-deductible plan and is not covered by another policy that is not a high-deductible plan can establish an HSA.

Deductible Amount. The annual deduction for contributions to an HSA is limited to the sum of the monthly limitations. The monthly limitation is calculated for each month that the individual is an eligible individual. The monthly deduction is not allowed after the individual becomes eligible for Medicare coverage.

The amount of the monthly limitation for an individual who has self-only coverage in 2006 is the *lesser* of one-twelfth of the annual deductible under the high-deductible plan or $2,700. An individual who has family coverage in 2006 is limited to the *lesser* of one-twelfth of the annual deductible under the high-deductible plan or $5,450.[19] For an eligible taxpayer who has attained age 55 by the end of the tax year, the limit on annual contributions in 2006 is increased by $600. This additional amount is referred to as a *catchup* contribution. These amounts are subject to annual cost-of-living adjustments.

EXAMPLE 14

Liu, who is married and self-employed, carries a high-deductible medical insurance policy with an annual deductible of $4,000. In addition, he has established an HSA. Liu's maximum annual contribution to the HSA is $4,000 (the lesser of $5,450 or the annual deductible). ■

EXAMPLE 15

During 2006, Adam, who is self-employed, made 12 monthly payments of $700 for an HSA contract that provides medical insurance coverage with a $3,600 deductible. The plan covers Adam, his wife, and two children. Of the $700 monthly fee, $400 was for the high-deductible policy and $300 was deposited into an HSA. The deductible monthly contribution to the HSA is calculated as follows:

Amount of the annual deductible under the plan	$3,600
Maximum annual deduction for family coverage	$5,450
Monthly limitation (1/12 of $3,600)	$ 300

Because Adam is self-employed, he can deduct $4,800 of the amount paid for the high-deductible policy ($400 per month × 12 months) as a deduction *for* AGI (refer to Example 10). In addition, he can deduct the $3,600 ($300 × 12) paid to the HSA as a deduction *for* AGI. ■

LO.3

Contrast deductible taxes and nondeductible fees, licenses, etc.

Taxes

A deduction is allowed for certain state and local taxes paid or accrued by a taxpayer.[20] The deduction was created to relieve the burden of multiple taxes upon the same source of revenue.

Deductibility as a Tax

A distinction must be made between a tax and a fee, since fees are not deductible unless incurred as an ordinary and necessary business expense or as an expense in the production of income. The IRS has defined a tax as follows:

A tax is an enforced contribution exacted pursuant to legislative authority in the exercise of taxing power, and imposed and collected for the purpose of raising revenue to be used for public or governmental purposes, and not as payment for some special privilege granted or service rendered. Taxes are, therefore, distinguished from various other contributions and charges imposed for particular purposes under particular powers or

[19]§ 223(b)(2). The limits were $2,650 and $5,250 in 2005.
[20]Most deductible taxes are listed in § 164, while nondeductible items are included in § 275.

| **EXHIBIT 10–2** | **Deductible and Nondeductible Taxes** |

Deductible	Nondeductible
State, local, and foreign real property taxes	Federal income taxes
	FICA taxes imposed on employees
State and local personal property taxes	Employer FICA taxes paid on domestic household workers
State and local income taxes *or* sales/use taxes	Estate, inheritance, and gift taxes
Foreign income taxes	Federal, state, and local excise taxes (e.g., gasoline, tobacco, spirits)
The environmental tax	Foreign income taxes if the taxpayer chooses the foreign tax credit option
	Taxes on real property to the extent such taxes are to be apportioned and treated as imposed on another taxpayer

functions of the government. In view of such distinctions, the question whether a particular contribution or charge is to be regarded as a tax depends upon its real nature.[21]

Accordingly, fees for dog licenses, automobile inspection, automobile titles and registration, hunting and fishing licenses, bridge and highway tolls, drivers' licenses, parking meter deposits, postage, etc., are not deductible if personal in nature. These items, however, could be deductible if incurred as a business expense or for the production of income. Deductible and nondeductible taxes are summarized in Exhibit 10–2.

Property Taxes

State, local, and foreign taxes on real property are generally deductible only by the person upon whom the tax is imposed. Deductible personal property taxes must be *ad valorem* (assessed in relation to the value of the property). Therefore, a motor vehicle tax based on weight, model, year, and horsepower is not an ad valorem tax. However, a tax based on value and other criteria may qualify in part.

A state imposes a motor vehicle registration tax on 4% of the value of the vehicle plus 40 cents per hundredweight. Belle, a resident of the state, owns a car having a value of $4,000 and weighing 3,000 pounds. Belle pays an annual registration fee of $172. Of this amount, $160 (4% of $4,000) is deductible as a personal property tax. The remaining $12, based on the weight of the car, is not deductible. ∎

E X A M P L E   16

Assessments for Local Benefits. As a general rule, real property taxes do not include taxes assessed for local benefits since such assessments tend to increase the value of the property (e.g., special assessments for streets, sidewalks, curbing, and other similar improvements). A taxpayer was denied a deduction for the cost of a new sidewalk (relative to a personal residence), even though the construction was required by the city and the sidewalk may have provided an incidental benefit to the public welfare.[22] Such assessments are added to the adjusted basis of the taxpayer's property.

---

[21]Rev.Rul. 57–345, 1957–2 C.B. 132, and Rev.Rul. 70–622, 1970–2 C.B. 41.   [22]*Erie H. Rose*, 31 TCM 142, T.C.Memo. 1972–39; Reg. § 1.164–4(a).

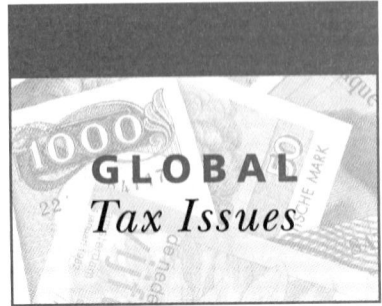

GLOBAL Tax Issues

DEDUCTIBILITY OF FOREIGN TAXES

Josef, a citizen of the United States who works primarily in New York, also works several months each year in Austria. He owns a residence in Austria and pays income taxes to Austria on the income he earns there. Both the property tax he pays on his Austrian residence and the income tax he pays on his Austrian income are deductible in computing U.S. taxable income.

Apportionment of Real Property Taxes between Seller and Purchaser.

Real estate taxes for the entire year are apportioned between the buyer and seller on the basis of the number of days the property was held by each during the real property tax year. This apportionment is required whether the tax is paid by the buyer or the seller or is prorated according to the purchase agreement. It is the apportionment that determines who is entitled to deduct the real estate taxes in the year of sale. The required apportionment prevents the shifting of the deduction for real estate taxes from the buyer to the seller, or vice versa.

In making the apportionment, the assessment date and the lien date are disregarded. The date of sale counts as a day the property is owned by the buyer. In leap years, the taxes are prorated over 366 days.[23]

EXAMPLE 17

A county's real property tax year runs from April 1 to March 31. Susan, the owner on April 1, 2006, of real property located in the county, sells the real property to Bob on June 30, 2006. Bob owns the real property from June 30, 2006, through March 31, 2007. The tax for the real property tax year April 1, 2006, through March 31, 2007, is $3,650. The portion of the real property tax treated as imposed upon Susan, the seller, is $900 [(90/365) × $3,650, April 1 through June 29, 2006], and $2,750 [(275/365) × $3,650, June 30, 2006 through March 31, 2007] of the tax is treated as imposed upon Bob, the purchaser. ■

If the actual real estate taxes are not prorated between the buyer and seller as part of the purchase agreement, adjustments are required. The adjustments are necessary to determine the amount realized by the seller and the adjusted basis of the property to the buyer. If the buyer pays the entire amount of the tax, he or she has, in effect, paid the seller's portion of the real estate tax and has therefore paid more for the property than the actual purchase price. Thus, the amount of real estate tax that is apportioned to the seller (for Federal income tax purposes) and paid by the buyer is added to the buyer's adjusted basis. The seller must increase the amount realized on the sale by the same amount.

EXAMPLE 18

Seth sells real estate on October 3, 2007, for $100,000. The buyer, Wilma, pays the real estate taxes of $3,650 for the 2007 calendar year, which is the real estate property tax year. Of the real estate taxes, $2,750 (for 275 days) is apportioned to and is deductible by the seller, Seth, and $900 (for 90 days) of the taxes is deductible by Wilma. The buyer has, in effect, paid Seth's real estate taxes of $2,750 and has therefore paid $102,750 for the property. Wilma's basis is increased to $102,750, and the amount realized by Seth from the sale is increased to $102,750. ■

The opposite result occurs if the seller (rather than the buyer) pays the real estate taxes. In this case, the seller reduces the amount realized from the sale by the amount that has been apportioned to the buyer. The buyer is required to reduce his or her adjusted basis by a corresponding amount.

[23]A year is a leap year if its number is divisible by 4.

Ruth sells real estate to Butch for $50,000 on October 3, 2007. While Ruth held the property, she paid the real estate taxes of $1,095 for the calendar year, which is the real estate property tax year. Although Ruth paid the entire $1,095 of real estate taxes, $270 of that amount is apportioned to Butch, based on the number of days he owned the property, and is therefore deductible by him. The effect is that the buyer, Butch, has paid only $49,730 ($50,000 − $270) for the property. The amount realized by Ruth, the seller, is reduced by $270, and Butch reduces his basis in the property to $49,730. ∎

EXAMPLE 19

State and Local Income Taxes and Sales Taxes

The position of the IRS is that state and local income taxes imposed upon an individual are deductible only as itemized deductions, even if the taxpayer's sole source of income is from a business, rents, or royalties.

Cash basis taxpayers are entitled to deduct state income taxes withheld by the employer in the year the taxes are withheld. In addition, estimated state income tax payments are deductible in the year the payment is made by cash basis taxpayers even if the payments relate to a prior or subsequent year.[24] If the taxpayer overpays state income taxes because of excessive withholdings or estimated tax payments, the refund received is included in gross income of the following year to the extent that the deduction reduced taxable income in the prior year.

LO.4

Understand the Federal income tax treatment of state and local income taxes and sales taxes.

Leona, a cash basis, unmarried taxpayer, had $800 of state income tax withheld during 2006. Additionally in 2006, Leona paid $100 that was due when she filed her 2005 state income tax return and made estimated payments of $300 on her 2006 state income tax. When Leona files her 2006 Federal income tax return in April 2007, she elects to itemize deductions, which amount to $5,500, including the $1,200 of state income tax payments and withholdings, all of which reduce her taxable income.

As a result of overpaying her 2006 state income tax, Leona receives a refund of $200 early in 2007. She will include this amount in her 2007 gross income in computing her Federal income tax. It does not matter whether Leona received a check from the state for $200 or applied the $200 toward her 2007 state income tax. ∎

EXAMPLE 20

Itemized Deduction for Sales Taxes Paid. Individuals can elect to deduct either their state and local income taxes *or* their sales/use taxes paid as an itemized deduction on Schedule A of Form 1040. This American Jobs Creation Act provision was effective beginning with 2004 returns. The annual election can reflect actual sales/use tax payments *or* an amount from an IRS table (see Appendix A). The amount from the table may be increased by sales tax paid on the purchase of motor vehicles, boats, and other specified items. Most likely, the sales tax deduction will be elected by those living in states with no individual income tax (e.g., Texas and Washington).

Interest

A deduction for interest has been allowed since the income tax law was enacted in 1913. Despite its long history of congressional acceptance, the interest deduction has been one of the most controversial areas in the tax law. The controversy centered around the propriety of allowing the deduction of interest charges for the purchase of consumer goods and services and interest on borrowings used to acquire investments (investment interest). Personal (consumer) interest is not deductible. This includes credit card interest, interest on car loans, and any other interest that is not interest on qualified education loans, **investment interest**, home

LO.5

Distinguish between deductible and nondeductible interest and apply the appropriate limitations to deductible interest.

[24]Rev.Rul. 71–190, 1971–1 C.B. 70. See also Rev.Rul. 82–208, 1982–2 C.B. 58, where a deduction is not allowed when the taxpayer cannot, in good faith, reasonably determine that there is additional state income tax liability.

mortgage interest, or business interest. Interest on qualified education loans, investment interest, and qualified residence (home mortgage) interest continue to be deductible, subject to limits discussed on the following pages.

Allowed and Disallowed Items

The Supreme Court has defined *interest* as compensation for the use or forbearance of money.[25] The general rule permits a deduction for interest paid or accrued within the taxable year on indebtedness.

Interest on Qualified Education Loans.
Taxpayers who pay interest on a qualified education loan may deduct the interest as a deduction *for* AGI. A qualified education loan does not include indebtedness to certain related parties. For 2006, the maximum deduction is $2,500. The deduction is phased out for taxpayers with modified AGI (MAGI) between $50,000 and $65,000 ($105,000 and $135,000 on joint returns). The deduction is not allowed for taxpayers who are claimed as dependents or for married taxpayers filing separately.[26]

Investment Interest.
Taxpayers frequently borrow funds that they use to acquire investment assets. When the interest expense is large relative to the income from the investments, substantial tax benefits could result. Congress has therefore limited the deductibility of interest on funds borrowed for the purpose of purchasing or continuing to hold investment property. Investment interest expense is *now* limited to net investment income for the year.

Investment income is gross income from interest, dividends (see below), annuities, and royalties not derived in the ordinary course of a trade or business. Income from a passive activity and income from a real estate activity in which the taxpayer actively participates are not included in investment income (see Chapter 11).

The following types of income are not included in investment income unless the taxpayer *elects* to do so.

- Net capital gain attributable to the disposition of (1) property producing the types of income just enumerated or (2) property held for investment purposes.

[25] *Old Colony Railroad Co. v. Comm.*, 3 USTC ¶880, 10 AFTR 786, 52 S.Ct. 211 (USSC, 1932).

[26] § 221. See § 221(b)(2)(c) for the definition of MAGI. The phaseout amounts are subject to adjustments for inflation. The $2,500 limitation and the phase-out amounts apply to tax returns for 2006. For 2005, the amounts were the same.

- Qualified dividends that are taxed at the same marginal rate that is applicable to a net capital gain.

A taxpayer may include net capital gain and qualifying dividends as investment income by electing to do so on Form 4952. The election is available only if the taxpayer agrees to reduce amounts qualifying for the 15 percent (5 percent for low-income taxpayers) rates that otherwise apply to net capital gain (see Chapter 16) and qualifying dividends (refer to Chapter 4) by an equivalent amount.

EXAMPLE 21

Terry incurred $13,000 of interest expense related to her investments during the year. Her investment income included $4,000 of interest, $2,000 of qualifying dividends, and a $5,000 net capital gain on the sale of investment securities. If Terry does not make the election to include the net capital gain and qualified dividends in investment income, her investment income for purposes of computing the investment income limitation is $4,000 (interest income). If she does make the election, her investment income is $11,000 ($4,000 interest + $2,000 qualifying dividends + $5,000 net capital gain). ∎

Net investment income is the excess of investment income over investment expenses. Investment expenses are those deductible expenses directly connected with the production of investment income. Investment expenses *do not* include interest expense. When investment expenses fall into the category of miscellaneous itemized deductions that are subject to the 2 percent-of-AGI floor, some may not enter into the calculation of net investment income because of the floor.

EXAMPLE 22

Gina has AGI of $80,000, which includes qualified dividends of $15,000 and interest income of $3,000. Besides investment interest expense, she paid $3,000 of city ad valorem property tax on stocks and bonds and had the following miscellaneous itemized expenses:

Safe deposit box rental (to hold investment securities)	$ 120
Investment counsel fee	1,200
Unreimbursed business travel	850
Uniforms	600

Before Gina can determine her investment expenses for purposes of calculating net investment income, those miscellaneous expenses that are not investment expenses are disallowed before any investment expenses are disallowed under the 2%-of-AGI floor. This is accomplished by selecting the *lesser* of the following:

1. The amount of investment expenses included in the total of miscellaneous itemized deductions subject to the 2%-of-AGI floor.
2. The amount of miscellaneous expenses deductible after the 2%-of-AGI rule is applied.

The amount under item 1 is $1,320 [$120 (safe deposit box rental) + $1,200 (investment counsel fee)]. The item 2 amount is $1,170 [$2,770 (total of miscellaneous expenses) − $1,600 (2% of $80,000 AGI)].

Then, Gina's investment expenses are calculated as follows:

Deductible miscellaneous deductions investment expense (the lesser of item 1 or item 2)	$1,170
Plus: Ad valorem tax on investment property	3,000
Total investment expenses	$4,170

Gina elects to include the qualified dividends in investment income. Gina's net investment income is $13,830 ($18,000 investment income − $4,170 investment expenses). ∎

After net investment income is determined, deductible investment interest expense can be calculated.

EXAMPLE 23

Adam is a single person employed by a law firm. His investment activities for the year are as follows:

Net investment income	$30,000
Investment interest expense	44,000

Adam's investment interest deduction is $30,000. ■

The amount of investment interest disallowed is carried over to future years. In Example 23, therefore, the amount that is carried over to the following year is $14,000 ($44,000 investment interest expense − $30,000 allowed). No limit is placed on the length of the carryover period. The investment interest expense deduction is determined by completing Form 4952.

Qualified Residence Interest. *Qualified residence interest* is interest paid or accrued during the taxable year on indebtedness (subject to limitations) *secured* by any property that is a qualified residence of the taxpayer. Qualified residence interest falls into two categories: (1) interest on acquisition indebtedness and (2) interest on home equity loans. Before discussing each of these categories, however, the term qualified residence must be defined.

A *qualified residence* includes the taxpayer's principal residence and one other residence of the taxpayer or spouse. The *principal residence* is one that meets the requirement for nonrecognition of gain upon sale under § 121 (see Chapter 15). The *one other residence,* or second residence, refers to one that is used as a residence if not rented or, if rented, meets the requirements for a personal residence under the rental of vacation home rules (refer to Chapter 6). A taxpayer who has more than one second residence can make the selection each year of which one is the qualified second residence. A residence includes, in addition to a house in the ordinary sense, cooperative apartments, condominiums, and mobile homes and boats that have living quarters (sleeping accommodations and toilet and cooking facilities).

Although in most cases interest paid on a home mortgage is fully deductible, there are limitations.[27] Interest paid or accrued during the tax year on aggregate **acquisition indebtedness** of $1 million or less ($500,000 for married persons filing separate returns) is deductible as qualified residence interest. *Acquisition indebtedness* refers to amounts incurred in acquiring, constructing, or substantially improving a qualified residence of the taxpayer.

Qualified residence interest also includes interest on **home equity loans**. These loans utilize the personal residence of the taxpayer as security. Because the funds from home equity loans can be used for personal purposes (e.g., auto purchases, medical expenses), what would otherwise have been nondeductible consumer interest becomes deductible qualified residence interest.

However, interest is deductible only on the portion of a home equity loan that does not exceed the *lesser of:*

- The fair market value of the residence, reduced by the acquisition indebtedness, *or*
- $100,000 ($50,000 for married persons filing separate returns).

EXAMPLE 24

Larry owns a personal residence with a fair market value of $150,000 and an outstanding first mortgage of $120,000. Therefore, his equity in his home is $30,000 ($150,000 − $120,000). Larry issues a lien on the residence and in return borrows $15,000 to purchase a new family automobile. All interest on the $135,000 of debt is treated as qualified residence interest. ■

EXAMPLE 25

Leon and Pearl, married taxpayers, took out a mortgage on their home for $290,000 in 1990. In March of the current year, when the home has a fair market value of $400,000 and they

[27]§ 163(h)(3).

TAX *in the News*	**A RECOMMENDATION TO LIMIT THE MORTGAGE INTEREST DEDUCTION**

In January 2005, President George W. Bush established the President's Advisory Panel on Federal Tax Reform to provide advice on reforming the Internal Revenue Code. The Panel was charged with considering options to accomplish the following objectives:

- Simplify Federal tax laws to reduce the costs and administrative burdens of compliance with such laws.
- Share the burdens and benefits of the Federal tax structure in an appropriately progressive manner while recognizing the importance of homeownership and charity in American society.
- Promote long-run economic growth and job creation, and better encourage work effort, saving, and investment, so as to strengthen the competitiveness of the United States in the global marketplace.

The Panel's Final Report contains the following controversial recommendations relative to the tax treatment of mortgage interest:

- The deduction for mortgage interest should be replaced with a Home Credit equal to 15 percent of interest paid on a *principal residence*. The Home Credit would be available to all homeowners, whether they itemize or take the standard deduction. The principal residence requirement eliminates tax benefits for interest paid on a second home.
- Limit the mortgage interest base for the Home Credit to a specified maximum principal amount. The principal amount would be based on average regional housing costs. Based on current prices, the limits would range between approximately $227,000 and $412,000. This recommendation would reduce the tax benefits currently available to owners of expensive homes with large mortgages.

Source: ***http://www.taxreformpanel.gov/final-report/TaxReform_Ch5.pdf*** and ***http://www.taxreformpanel.gov/final-report/ TaxReform_App.pdf***.

owe $195,000 on the mortgage, Leon and Pearl take out a home equity loan for $120,000. They use the funds to purchase a boat to be used for recreational purposes. The boat, which does not have living quarters, does not qualify as a personal residence. On a joint return, Leon and Pearl can deduct all of the interest on the first mortgage since it is acquisition indebtedness. Of the $120,000 home equity loan, only the interest on the first $100,000 is deductible. The interest on the remaining $20,000 is not deductible because it exceeds the statutory ceiling of $100,000. ■

Interest Paid for Services. Mortgage loan companies commonly charge a fee for finding, placing, or processing a mortgage loan. Such fees are often called **points** and are expressed as a percentage of the loan amount. Borrowers often have to pay points to obtain the necessary financing. To qualify as deductible interest, the points must be considered compensation to a lender solely for the use or forbearance of money. The points cannot be a form of service charge or payment for specific services if they are to qualify as deductible interest.[28]

Points must be capitalized and are amortized and deductible ratably over the life of the loan. A special exception permits the purchaser of a personal residence to deduct qualifying points in the year of payment.[29] The exception also covers points paid to obtain funds for home improvements.

During 2006, Thelma purchases a new residence for $130,000 and pays points of $2,600 to obtain mortgage financing. At Thelma's election, the $2,600 can be claimed as an interest deduction for tax year 2006. ■

EXAMPLE 26

Points paid to *refinance* an existing home mortgage cannot be immediately expensed, but must be capitalized and amortized as interest expense over the life of the new loan.[30]

---

[28]Rev.Rul. 67–297, 1967–2 C.B. 87.
[29]§ 461(g)(2).

[30]Rev.Rul. 87–22, 1987–1 C.B. 146.

EXAMPLE 27

Sandra purchased her residence several years ago, obtaining a 30-year mortgage at an annual interest rate of 9%. In the current year, Sandra refinances the mortgage in order to reduce the interest rate to 6%. To obtain the refinancing, she has to pay points of $2,600. The $2,600 paid comes under the usual rule applicable to points. The $2,600 must be capitalized and amortized over the life of the mortgage. ∎

Points paid by the seller for a buyer are, in effect, treated as an adjustment to the price of the residence, and the buyer is treated as having used cash to pay the points that were paid by the seller. A buyer may deduct seller-paid points in the tax year in which they are paid if several conditions are met. Refer to Revenue Procedure 94–27 for a complete list of these conditions.[31]

Prepayment Penalty. When a mortgage or loan is paid off in full in a lump sum before its term (early), the lending institution may require an additional payment of a certain percentage applied to the unpaid amount at the time of prepayment. This is known as a prepayment penalty and is considered to be interest (e.g., personal, qualified residence, investment) in the year paid. The general rules for deductibility of interest also apply to prepayment penalties.

Interest Paid to Related Parties. Nothing prevents the deduction of interest paid to a related party as long as the payment actually took place and the interest meets the requirements for deductibility. Recall from Chapter 6 that a special rule for related taxpayers applies when the debtor uses the accrual basis and the related creditor is on the cash basis. If this rule is applicable, interest that has been accrued but not paid at the end of the debtor's tax year is not deductible until payment is made and the income is reportable by the cash basis recipient.

Tax-Exempt Securities. The tax law provides that no deduction is allowed for interest on debt incurred to purchase or carry tax-exempt securities.[32] A major problem for the courts has been to determine what is meant by the words *to purchase or carry*. Refer to Chapter 6 for a detailed discussion of these issues.

Restrictions on Deductibility and Timing Considerations

Taxpayer's Obligation. Allowed interest is deductible if the related debt represents a bona fide obligation for which the taxpayer is liable.[33] Thus, a taxpayer may not deduct interest paid on behalf of another individual. For interest to be deductible, both the debtor and the creditor must intend for the loan to be repaid. Intent of the parties can be especially crucial between related parties such as a shareholder and a closely held corporation. A shareholder may not deduct interest paid by the corporation on his or her behalf.[34] Likewise, a husband may not deduct interest paid on his wife's property if he files a separate return, except in the case of qualified residence interest. If both husband and wife consent in writing, either the husband or the wife may deduct the allowed interest on the principal residence and one other residence.

Time of Deduction. Generally, interest must be paid to secure a deduction unless the taxpayer uses the accrual method of accounting. Under the accrual method, interest is deductible ratably over the life of the loan.

[31]Rev.Proc. 94–27, 1994–1 C.B. 613.
[32]§ 265(a)(2).
[33]*Arcade Realty Co.*, 35 T.C. 256 (1960).
[34]*Continental Trust Co.*, 7 B.T.A. 539 (1927).

CONCEPT SUMMARY 10–1

Deductibility of Personal, Education, Investment, and Mortgage Interest

Type	Deductible	Comments
Personal (consumer) interest	No	Includes any interest that is not home mortgage interest, qualified education loan interest, investment interest, or business interest. Examples include car loans, credit cards, etc.
Qualified education interest	Yes	Deduction *for* AGI; subject to limitations.
Investment interest (*not* related to rental or royalty property)	Yes	Itemized deduction; limited to net investment income for the year; disallowed interest can be carried over to future years.
Investment interest (related to rental or royalty property)	Yes	Deduction *for* AGI; limited to net investment income for the year; disallowed interest can be carried over to future years.
Qualified residence interest on acquisition indebtedness	Yes	Deductible as an itemized deduction; limited to indebtedness of $1 million.
Qualified residence interest on home equity indebtedness	Yes	Deductible as an itemized deduction; limited to indebtedness equal to lesser of $100,000 or FMV of residence minus acquisition indebtedness.

EXAMPLE 28

On November 1, 2006, Ramon borrows $1,000 to purchase appliances for a rental house. The loan is payable in 90 days at 12% interest. On the due date in January 2007, Ramon pays the $1,000 note and interest amounting to $30. Ramon can deduct the accrued portion ($^{2}/_{3} \times$ $30 = $20) of the interest in 2006 only if he is an accrual basis taxpayer. Otherwise, the entire amount of interest ($30) is deductible in 2007. ■

Prepaid Interest. Accrual method reporting is imposed on cash basis taxpayers for interest prepayments that extend beyond the end of the taxable year.[35] Such payments must be allocated to the tax years to which the interest payments relate. These provisions are intended to prevent cash basis taxpayers from *manufacturing* tax deductions before the end of the year by prepaying interest.

Classification of Interest Expense

Whether interest is deductible *for* AGI or as an itemized deduction (*from*) depends on whether the indebtedness has a business, investment, or personal purpose. If the indebtedness is incurred in relation to a business (other than performing services as an employee) or for the production of rent or royalty income, the interest is deductible *for* AGI. If the indebtedness is incurred for personal use, such as qualified residence interest, any deduction allowed is reported on Schedule A of Form 1040 if the taxpayer elects to itemize. If the taxpayer is an employee who incurs debt in relation to his or her employment, the interest is considered to be personal, or consumer, interest. Business expenses appear on Schedule C of Form 1040, and expenses related to rents or royalties are reported on Schedule E.

If a taxpayer deposits money in a certificate of deposit (CD) that has a term of one year or less and the interest cannot be withdrawn without penalty, the full amount of the interest must still be included in income, even though part of the interest is forfeited due to an early withdrawal. However, the taxpayer will be allowed a deduction *for* AGI as to the forfeited amount.

---

[35]§ 461(g)(1).

LO.6

Understand charitable contributions and their related measurement problems and percentage limitations.

Charitable Contributions

Individuals and corporations are allowed to deduct contributions made to qualified *domestic* organizations.[36] Contributions to qualified charitable organizations serve certain social welfare needs and thus relieve the government of the cost of providing these needed services to the community.

The **charitable contribution** provisions are among the most complex in the tax law. To determine the amount deductible as a charitable contribution, several important questions must be answered:

- What constitutes a charitable contribution?
- Was the contribution made to a qualified organization?
- When is the contribution deductible?
- What record-keeping and reporting requirements apply to charitable contributions?
- How is the value of donated property determined?
- What special rules apply to contributions of property that has increased in value?
- What percentage limitations apply to the charitable contribution deduction?
- What rules apply to amounts in excess of percentage limitations (carryovers)?

These questions are addressed in the sections that follow.

Criteria for a Gift

A *charitable contribution* is defined as a gift made to a qualified organization.[37] The major elements needed to qualify a contribution as a gift are a donative intent, the absence of consideration, and acceptance by the donee. Consequently, the taxpayer has the burden of establishing that the transfer was made from motives of *disinterested generosity* as established by the courts.[38] This test is quite subjective and has led to problems of interpretation (refer to the discussion of gifts in Chapter 5).

Benefit Received Rule. When a donor derives a tangible benefit from a contribution, he or she cannot deduct the value of the benefit.

EXAMPLE 29

Ralph purchases a ticket at $100 for a special performance of the local symphony (a qualified charity). If the price of a ticket to a symphony concert is normally $35, Ralph is allowed only $65 as a charitable contribution. ■

An exception to this benefit rule provides for the deduction of an automatic percentage of the amount paid for the right to purchase athletic tickets from colleges and universities.[39] Under this exception, 80 percent of the amount paid to or for the benefit of the institution qualifies as a charitable contribution deduction.

[handwritten: 80% rule on ticket guarantee donation]

EXAMPLE 30

Janet donates $500 to State University's athletic department. The payment guarantees that she will have preferred seating on the 50-yard line. Subsequently, Janet buys four $35 game tickets. Under the exception to the benefit rule, she is allowed a $400 (80% of $500) charitable contribution deduction for the taxable year.

If, however, Janet's $500 donation includes four $35 tickets, that portion [$140 ($35 × 4)] and the remaining portion of $360 ($500 − $140) are treated as separate amounts. Thus, Janet is allowed a charitable contribution deduction of $288 (80% of $360). ■

---

[36]§ 170.
[37]§ 170(c).
[38]*Comm. v. Duberstein,* 60–2 USTC ¶9515, 5 AFTR2d 1626, 80 S.Ct. 1190 (USSC, 1960).
[39]§ 170(l).

Contribution of Services.

No deduction is allowed for a contribution of one's services to a qualified charitable organization. However, unreimbursed expenses related to the services rendered may be deductible. For example, the cost of a uniform (without general utility) that is required to be worn while performing services may be deductible, as are certain out-of-pocket transportation costs incurred for the benefit of the charity. In lieu of these out-of-pocket costs for an automobile, a standard mileage rate of 14 cents per mile is allowed.[40] Deductions are permitted for transportation, reasonable expenses for lodging, and the cost of meals while away from home incurred in performing the donated services. The travel expenses are not deductible if the travel involves a significant element of personal pleasure, recreation, or vacation.[41]

Grace, a delegate representing her church in Miami, Florida, travels to a two-day national meeting in Denver, Colorado, in February. After the meeting, Grace spends two weeks at a nearby ski resort. Under these circumstances, none of the transportation, meals, or lodging is deductible because the travel involved a significant element of personal pleasure, recreation, or vacation. ■

EXAMPLE 31

Nondeductible Items.

In addition to the benefit received rule and the restrictions placed on contribution of services, the following items may *not* be deducted as charitable contributions:

- Dues, fees, or bills paid to country clubs, lodges, fraternal orders, or similar groups.
- Cost of raffle, bingo, or lottery tickets.
- Cost of tuition.
- Value of blood given to a blood bank.
- Donations to homeowners associations.
- Gifts to individuals.
- Rental value of property used by a qualified charity.

Qualified Organizations

To be deductible, a contribution must be made to one of the following organizations:[42]

- A state or possession of the United States or any subdivisions thereof.
- A corporation, trust, community chest, fund, or foundation that is situated in the United States and is organized and operated exclusively for religious, charitable, scientific, literary, or educational purposes or for the prevention of cruelty to children or animals.
- A veterans' organization.
- A fraternal organization operating under the lodge system.
- A cemetery company.

The IRS publishes a list of organizations that have applied for and received tax-exempt status under § 501 of the Code.[43] This publication is updated frequently and may be helpful in determining if a gift has been made to a qualifying charitable organization.

Because gifts made to needy individuals are not deductible, a deduction will not be permitted if a gift is received by a donee in an individual capacity rather than as a representative of a qualifying organization.

---

[40]§ 170(i).
[41]§ 170(j).
[42]§ 170(c).
[43]Although this *Cumulative List of Organizations*, IRS Publication 78 (available by purchase from the Superintendent of Documents, U.S. Government Printing Office, Washington, DC 20402), may be helpful, qualified organizations are not required to be listed. Not all organizations that qualify are listed in this publication. The list is also available on the Web at **http://www.irs.gov**.

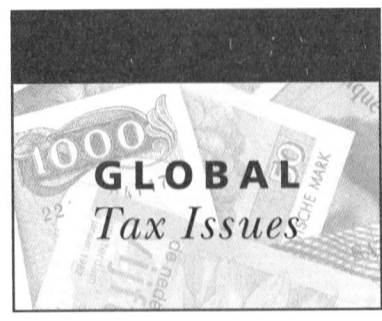

CHOOSE THE CHARITY WISELY

Ibrahim, a U.S. citizen of Turkish descent, was distressed by the damage caused by a major earthquake in Turkey. He donated $100,000 to the Earthquake Victims' Relief Fund, a Turkish charitable organization that was set up to help victims of the earthquake. Ahmed, also a U.S. citizen of Turkish descent, donated $200,000 to help with the relief effort. However, Ahmed's contribution went to his mosque, which sent the proceeds of a fund drive to the Earthquake Victims' Relief Fund in Turkey. Ibrahim's contribution is not deductible, but Ahmed's is. Why? Contributions to charitable organizations are not deductible unless the organization is a U.S. charity.

Time of Deduction

A charitable contribution generally is deducted in the year the payment is made. This rule applies to both cash and accrual basis individuals. A contribution is ordinarily deemed to have been made on the delivery of the property to the donee. For example, if a gift of securities (properly endorsed) is made to a qualified charitable organization, the gift is considered complete on the day of delivery or mailing. However, if the donor delivers the certificate to his or her bank or broker or to the issuing corporation, the gift is considered complete on the date the stock is transferred on the books of the corporation.

A contribution made by check is considered delivered on the date of mailing. Thus, a check mailed on December 31, 2006, is deductible on the taxpayer's 2006 tax return. If the contribution is charged on a bank credit card, the date the charge is made determines the year of deduction.

Record-Keeping and Valuation Requirements

Record-Keeping Requirements. No deduction is allowed for contributions of $250 or more unless the taxpayer obtains *written substantiation* of the contribution from the charitable organization. The substantiation must specify the amount of cash and a description (but not value) of any property other than cash contributed. The substantiation must be obtained before the earlier of (1) the due date (including extensions) of the return for the year the contribution is claimed or (2) the date such return is filed.

Additional information is required if the value of the donated property is over $500 but not over $5,000. Also, the taxpayer must file Section A of Form 8283 (Noncash Charitable Contributions) for such contributions.

For noncash contributions with a claimed value in excess of $5,000 ($10,000 in the case of nonpublicly traded stock), the taxpayer must obtain a qualified appraisal and must file Section B of Form 8283. This schedule must show a summary of the appraisal and must be attached to the taxpayer's return. Failure to comply with these reporting rules may result in disallowance of the charitable contribution deduction. Additionally, significant overvaluation exposes the taxpayer to rather stringent penalties.[44]

Valuation Requirements. Property donated to a charity is generally valued at fair market value at the time the gift is made. The Code and Regulations give very little guidance on the measurement of the fair market value except to say, "The fair market value is the price at which the property would change hands between a

[44]The amounts discussed in this section ($250, $500, $5,000, and $10,000) apply to 2005 tax returns. Amounts for 2006 had not been announced at the date of this writing.

willing buyer and a willing seller, neither being under any compulsion to buy or sell and both having reasonable knowledge of relevant facts."

Generally, charitable organizations do not attest to the fair market value of the donated property. Nevertheless, the taxpayer must maintain reliable written evidence of the following information concerning the donation:

- The fair market value of the property and how that value was determined.
- The amount of the reduction in the value of the property (if required) for certain appreciated property and how that reduction was determined.
- Terms of any agreement with the charitable organization dealing with the use of the property and potential sale or other disposition of the property by the organization.
- A signed copy of the appraisal if the value of the property was determined by appraisal. Only for a contribution of art with an aggregate value of $20,000 or more must the appraisal be attached to the taxpayer's return.

Limitations on Charitable Contribution Deduction

In General. The potential charitable contribution deduction is the total of all donations, both money and property, that qualify for the deduction. After this determination is made, the actual amount of the charitable contribution deduction that is allowed for individuals for the tax year is limited as follows:

- If the qualifying contributions for the year total 20 percent or less of AGI, they are fully deductible.
- If the qualifying contributions are more than 20 percent of AGI, the deductible amount may be limited to either 20 percent, 30 percent, or 50 percent of AGI, depending on the type of property given and the type of organization to which the donation is made.
- In any case, the maximum charitable contribution deduction may not exceed 50 percent of AGI for the tax year.

To understand the complex rules for computing the amount of a charitable contribution, it is necessary to understand the distinction between capital gain property and ordinary income property. In addition, it is necessary to understand when the 50 percent, 30 percent, and 20 percent limitations apply. If a taxpayer's contributions for the year exceed the applicable percentage limitations, the excess contributions may be carried forward and deducted during a five-year carryover period. These topics are discussed in the sections that follow.

Ordinary Income Property. **Ordinary income property** is any property that, if sold, will result in the recognition of ordinary income. The term includes inventory for sale in the taxpayer's trade or business, a work of art created by the donor, and a manuscript prepared by the donor. It also includes, *for purposes of the charitable contribution calculation*, a capital asset held by the donor for less than the required holding period for long-term capital gain treatment (long term is a period longer than one year). To the extent that disposition of property results in the recognition of ordinary income due to the recapture of depreciation, it is ordinary income property.[45]

If ordinary income property is contributed, the deduction is equal to the fair market value of the property less the amount of ordinary income that would have been reported if the property were sold. In most instances, the deduction is limited to the adjusted basis of the property to the donor.

---

[45]For a more complete discussion of the difference between ordinary income and capital gain property, see Chapter 16.

EXAMPLE 32

Tim donates stock in White Corporation to a university on May 1, 2006. Tim had purchased the stock for $2,500 on March 3, 2006, and the stock had a value of $3,600 when he made the donation. Since he had not held the property long enough to meet the long-term capital gain requirement, Tim would have recognized a short-term capital gain of $1,100 if he had sold the property. Since short-term capital gain property is treated as ordinary income property for charitable contribution purposes, Tim's charitable contribution deduction is limited to the property's adjusted basis of $2,500 ($3,600 − $1,100 = $2,500). ■

In Example 32, suppose the stock had a fair market value of $2,300 (rather than $3,600) when it was donated to charity. Because the fair market value now is less than the adjusted basis, the charitable contribution deduction is $2,300.

Capital Gain Property. Capital gain property is any property that would have resulted in the recognition of long-term capital gain or § 1231 gain if the property had been sold by the donor.[46] As a general rule, the deduction for a contribution of capital gain property is equal to the fair market value of the property.

Two major exceptions disallow the deductibility of the appreciation on long-term capital gain property. One exception concerns certain private foundations. Private foundations are organizations that traditionally do not receive their funding from the general public (e.g., the Ford Foundation). Generally, foundations fall into two categories: operating and nonoperating. A private *operating* foundation is one that spends substantially all of its income in the active conduct of the charitable undertaking for which it was established. Other private foundations are *nonoperating* foundations. However, if a private nonoperating foundation distributes the contributions it receives according to special rules within two and one-half months following the year of the contribution, the organization is treated the same as public charities and private operating foundations. Often, only the private foundation knows its status (operating or nonoperating) for sure, and the status can change from year to year.

If capital gain property is contributed to a private nonoperating foundation, the taxpayer must reduce the contribution by the long-term capital gain that would have been recognized if the property had been sold at its fair market value. The effect of this provision is to limit the deduction to the property's adjusted basis.[47]

EXAMPLE 33

Walter purchases land for $8,000 on January 1, 1986, and donates it to a private nonoperating foundation on June 21, 2006, when it is worth $20,000. Walter's charitable contribution is $8,000 ($20,000 − $12,000), the land's basis. ■

If, in Example 33, Walter had donated the land to either a public charity or a private operating foundation, his charitable contribution would be $20,000, the fair market value of the land.

A second exception applying to capital gain property relates to *tangible personalty*. Tangible personalty is all property that is not realty (land and buildings) and does not include intangible property such as stock or securities. If tangible personalty is contributed to a public charity such as a museum, church, or university, the charitable deduction may have to be reduced. The amount of the reduction is the long-term capital gain that would have been recognized if the property had been sold for its fair market value. The reduction is required *if* the property is put to an unrelated use. The term *unrelated use* means a use that is unrelated to the exempt purpose or function of the charitable organization.

---

[46]See General Scheme of Taxation in Chapter 16 for a discussion of holding periods.

[47]§ 170(e)(5). Taxpayers who donate *qualified appreciated stock* to private nonoperating foundations may deduct the fair market value of the stock. Qualified appreciated stock is stock for which market quotations are readily available on an established securities market.

A taxpayer in this instance must establish that the property is not in fact being put to an unrelated use by the donee. The taxpayer must also establish that at the time of the contribution it was reasonable to anticipate that the property would not be put to an unrelated use. For a contribution of personalty to a museum, if the work of art is the kind of art normally retained by the museum, it is reasonable for a donor to anticipate that the work of art will not be put to an unrelated use. This is the case even if the object is later sold or exchanged by the museum.[48]

EXAMPLE 34

donation for display, unrelated use = sale.

Myrtle contributes a Picasso painting, for which she paid $20,000, to a local museum. She had owned the painting for four years. It had a value of $30,000 at the time of the donation. The museum displays the painting for two years and subsequently sells it for $50,000. The charitable contribution is $30,000. It is not reduced by the unrealized appreciation since the painting is put to a related use even though it is later sold by the museum. ■

Fifty Percent Ceiling. Contributions made to public charities may not exceed 50 percent of an individual's AGI for the year. Excess contributions may be carried over to the next five years. The 50 percent ceiling on contributions applies to the following types of public charities:

- A church or a convention or association of churches.
- An educational organization that maintains a regular faculty and curriculum.
- A hospital or medical school.
- An organization supported by the government that holds property or investments for the benefit of a college or university.
- A Federal, state, or local governmental unit.
- An organization normally receiving a substantial part of its support from the public or a governmental unit.

In the remaining discussion of charitable contributions, public charities and private foundations (both operating and nonoperating) that qualify for the 50 percent ceiling will be referred to as *50 percent organizations*.

The 50 percent ceiling also applies to contributions to the following organizations:

- All private operating foundations.
- Certain private nonoperating foundations that distribute the contributions they receive to public charities and private operating foundations within two and one-half months following the year they receive the contribution.
- Certain private nonoperating foundations in which the contributions are pooled in a common fund and the income and principal sum are paid to public charities.

Thirty Percent Ceiling. A 30 percent ceiling applies to contributions of cash and ordinary income property to private nonoperating foundations that are not 50 percent organizations. The 30 percent ceiling also applies to contributions of appreciated capital gain property to 50 percent organizations unless the taxpayer makes a special election (see below).

Donations:
(1) to 30% org.
(2) Appreciated capital gain properties.

In the event the contributions for any one tax year involve both 50 percent and 30 percent property, the allowable deduction comes first from the 50 percent property.

EXAMPLE 35

During the year, Lisa makes the following donations to her church: cash of $2,000 and unimproved land worth $30,000. Lisa had purchased the land four years ago for $22,000 and held it as an investment. Therefore, it is long-term capital gain property. Lisa's AGI for the year is $60,000. Disregarding percentage limitations, Lisa's potential deduction is $32,000 [$2,000 (cash) + $30,000 (fair market value of land)].

---

[48]Reg. § 1.170A–4(b)(3)(ii)(b).

CONCEPT SUMMARY 10–2

Determining the Deduction for Contributions of Appreciated Property by Individuals

If the Type of Property Contributed Is:	And the Property Is Contributed to:	The Contribution Is Measured by:	But the Deduction Is Limited to:
1. Capital gain property	A 50% organization	Fair market value of the property	30% of AGI
2. Ordinary income property	A 50% organization	The basis of the property*	50% of AGI
3. Capital gain property (and the property is tangible personal property put to an unrelated use by the donee)	A 50% organization	The basis of the property*	50% of AGI
4. Capital gain property (and the reduced deduction is elected)	A 50% organization	The basis of the property	50% of AGI
5. Capital gain property	A private nonoperating foundation that is not a 50% organization	The basis of the property*	The lesser of: 1. 20% of AGI 2. 50% of AGI minus other contributions to 50% organizations

*If the fair market value of the property is less than the adjusted basis (i.e., the property has declined in value instead of appreciating), the fair market value is used.

In applying the percentage limitations, however, the *current* deduction for the land is limited to $18,000 [30% (limitation applicable to long-term capital gain property) × $60,000 (AGI)]. Thus, the total deduction is $20,000 ($2,000 cash + $18,000 land). Note that the total deduction does not exceed $30,000, which is 50% of Lisa's AGI. ∎

[handwritten: Forego appreciation ⇒ 50%]

Under a special election, a taxpayer may choose to forgo a deduction of the appreciation on capital gain property. Referred to as the *reduced deduction election*, this enables the taxpayer to move from the 30 percent limitation to the 50 percent limitation.

EXAMPLE 36

Assume the same facts as in Example 35, except that Lisa makes the reduced deduction election. Now the deduction becomes $24,000 [$2,000 (cash) + $22,000 (basis in land)] because both donations fall under the 50% limitation. Thus, by making the election, Lisa has increased her charitable contribution deduction by $4,000 [$24,000 − $20,000 (Example 35)]. ∎

Although the reduced deduction election appears attractive, it should be considered carefully. The election sacrifices a deduction for the appreciation on long-term capital gain property that might eventually be allowed. Note that in Example 35, the potential deduction was $32,000, yet in Example 36 only $24,000 is allowed. The reason the potential deduction is decreased by $8,000 ($32,000 − $24,000) is that no carryover is allowed for the amount sacrificed by the election.

Twenty Percent Ceiling. A 20 percent ceiling applies to contributions of appreciated long-term capital gain property to private nonoperating foundations that are not 50 percent organizations.

Contribution Carryovers. Contributions that exceed the percentage limitations for the current year can be carried over for five years. In the carryover process, such contributions do not lose their identity for limitation purposes. Thus, if the contribution originally involved 30 percent property, the carryover will continue to be classified as 30 percent property in the carryover year.

Assume the same facts as in Example 35. Because only $18,000 of the $30,000 value of the land is deducted in the current year, the balance of $12,000 may be carried over to the following year. But the carryover will still be treated as long-term capital gain property and is subject to the 30%-of-AGI limitation. ■

EXAMPLE 37

In applying the percentage limitations, current charitable contributions must be claimed first before any carryovers can be considered. If carryovers involve more than one year, they are utilized in a first-in, first-out order.

Miscellaneous Itemized Deductions

No deduction is allowed for personal, living, or family expenses.[49] However, a taxpayer may incur a number of expenditures related to employment. If an employee or outside salesperson incurs unreimbursed business expenses or expenses that are reimbursed under a nonaccountable plan, including travel and transportation, the expenses are deductible as **miscellaneous itemized deductions**.[50] Certain other expenses also fall into the special category of miscellaneous itemized deductions. Some are deductible only if, in total, they exceed 2 percent of the taxpayer's AGI. These miscellaneous itemized deductions include (but are not limited to) the following:

LO.7

List the business and personal expenditures that are deductible either as miscellaneous itemized deductions or as other itemized deductions.

- Professional dues to membership organizations.
- Uniforms or other clothing that cannot be used for normal wear.
- Fees incurred for the preparation of one's tax return or fees incurred for tax litigation before the IRS or the courts.
- Job-hunting costs.
- Fee paid for a safe deposit box used to store papers and documents relating to taxable income-producing investments.
- Investment expenses that are deductible under § 212 as discussed in Chapter 6.
- Appraisal fees to determine the amount of a casualty loss or the fair market value of donated property.
- Hobby losses up to the amount of hobby income (see Chapter 6).
- Unreimbursed employee expenses (see Chapter 9).

Certain employee business expenses that are reimbursed are not itemized deductions, but are deducted *for* AGI. Employee business expenses are discussed in depth in Chapter 9.

ETHICAL *Considerations*   JOB HUNTING IN SKI COUNTRY: A DEDUCTIBLE EXPENSE?

George, an avid skier, manages the ski department of a sporting goods store in St. Louis. He has been taking ski vacations in Lake Tahoe for several years and is considering finding a job in Lake Tahoe and moving there. George recently learned that he can deduct job-hunting expenses on his Federal income tax return. One of his customers,

---

[49]§ 262.

[50]Actors and performing artists who meet certain requirements are not subject to this rule.

who is a CPA, told George that transportation costs can be deducted if the primary purpose of the trip is to hunt for a job. According to the CPA, other travel costs must be allocated between job-hunting days and personal days. George plans to fly to Reno on Sunday, have job interviews each morning from Monday through Thursday, and ski each afternoon after the job interviews are concluded. He plans to ski all day Friday and Saturday and fly back to St. Louis on Saturday night. Is George justified in taking a deduction for job-hunting expenses this year? Will he be justified in taking future deductions if he is unable to find a job this year and continues his job-hunting trips each year for the next several years?

Other Miscellaneous Deductions

Certain expenses and losses do not fall into any category of itemized deductions already discussed but are nonetheless deductible. The following expenses and losses are deductible on line 27 of Schedule A as Other Miscellaneous Deductions.

* Gambling losses up to the amount of gambling winnings.
* Impairment-related work expenses of a handicapped person.
* Federal estate tax on income in respect of a decedent.
* Deduction for repayment of amounts under a claim of right if more than $3,000 (discussed in Chapter 18).
* The unrecovered investment in an annuity contract when the annuity ceases by reason of death, discussed in Chapter 4.

Unlike the expenses and losses discussed previously under Miscellaneous Itemized Deductions, the above expenses and losses are not subject to the 2 percent-of-AGI floor.

Comprehensive Example of Schedule A

Harry and Jean Brown, married filing jointly, had the following transactions for 2005:

Medicines that required a prescription	$ 430
Doctor and dentist bills paid and not reimbursed	2,120
Medical insurance premium payments	1,200
Contact lenses	175
Transportation for medical purposes (280 miles × 15 cents/mile* + $1.00 parking)	43
State income tax withheld	620
Real estate taxes	1,580
Interest paid on qualified residence mortgage	2,840
Charitable contributions in cash	860
Transportation in performing charitable services (800 miles × 14 cents/mile + $7.00 parking and tolls)	119
Unreimbursed employee expenses (from Form 2106)	870
Tax return preparation	150
Safe deposit box (used for keeping investment documents and tax records)	170

*All the mileage was prior to September 1.

The Browns' AGI is $40,000. Their completed 2005 Schedule A on the following page reports itemized deductions totaling $7,377. Schedule A for 2005 is presented because the 2006 form was not available at the date of this printing.

SCHEDULES A&B	Schedule A—Itemized Deductions	OMB No. 1545-0074
(Form 1040)	(Schedule B is on back)	20**05**
Department of the Treasury Internal Revenue Service (99)	▶ **Attach to Form 1040.** ▶ **See Instructions for Schedules A&B (Form 1040).**	Attachment Sequence No. **07**

Name(s) shown on Form 1040	Your social security number
Harry and Jean Brown	*371 30 3987*

Medical and Dental Expenses		**Caution.** Do not include expenses reimbursed or paid by others.			
	1	Medical and dental expenses (see page A-2) . . .	1	*3,968*	
	2	Enter amount from Form 1040, line 38 | 2 | *40,000*			
	3	Multiply line 2 by 7.5% (.075).	3	*3,000*	
	4	Subtract line 3 from line 1. If line 3 is more than line 1, enter -0-	4		*968*
Taxes You Paid (See page A-2.)	5	State and local **(check only one box):** a ☒ Income taxes, **or** b ☐ General sales taxes (see page A-3) . . .	5	*620*	
	6	Real estate taxes (see page A-5)	6	*1,580*	
	7	Personal property taxes	7		
	8	Other taxes. List type and amount ▶ ------------------	8		
	9	Add lines 5 through 8	9		*2,200*
Interest You Paid (See page A-5.)	10	Home mortgage interest and points reported to you on Form 1098	10	*2,840*	
	11	Home mortgage interest not reported to you on Form 1098. If paid to the person from whom you bought the home, see page A-6 and show that person's name, identifying no., and address ▶	11		
Note. Personal interest is not deductible.	12	Points not reported to you on Form 1098. See page A-6 for special rules	12		
	13	Investment interest. Attach Form 4952 if required. (See page A-6.)	13		
	14	Add lines 10 through 13	14		*2,840*
Gifts to Charity	15a	Total gifts by cash or check. If you made any gift of $250 or more, see page A-7	15a	*860*	
If you made a gift and got a benefit for it, see page A-7.	b	Gifts by cash or check after August 27, 2005, that you elect to treat as qualified contributions (see page A-7) | 15b |			
	16	Other than by cash or check. If any gift of $250 or more, see page A-7. You **must** attach Form 8283 if over $500	16	*119*	
	17	Carryover from prior year	17		
	18	Add lines 15a, 16, and 17	18		*979*
Casualty and Theft Losses	19	Casualty or theft loss(es). Attach Form 4684. (See page A-8.)	19		
Job Expenses and Certain Miscellaneous Deductions (See page A-8.)	20	Unreimbursed employee expenses—job travel, union dues, job education, etc. Attach Form 2106 or 2106-EZ if required. (See page A-8.) ▶ ------------------	20	*870*	
	21	Tax preparation fees.	21	*150*	
	22	Other expenses—investment, safe deposit box, etc. List type and amount ▶ ------------------	22	*170*	
	23	Add lines 20 through 22	23	*1,190*	
	24	Enter amount from Form 1040, line 38 | 24 | *40,000*			
	25	Multiply line 24 by 2% (.02)	25	*800*	
	26	Subtract line 25 from line 23. If line 25 is more than line 23, enter -0-	26		*390*
Other Miscellaneous Deductions	27	Other—from list on page A-9. List type and amount ▶ ------------------	27		
Total Itemized Deductions	28	Is Form 1040, line 38, over $145,950 (over $72,975 if married filing separately)? ☒ **No.** Your deduction is not limited. Add the amounts in the far right column for lines 4 through 27. Also, enter this amount on Form 1040, line 40. ☐ **Yes.** Your deduction may be limited. See page A-9 for the amount to enter. ⎬ ▶	28		*7,377*
	29	If you elect to itemize deductions even though they are less than your standard deduction, check here ▶ ☐			

For Paperwork Reduction Act Notice, see Form 1040 instructions.   Cat. No. 11330X   **Schedule A (Form 1040) 2005**

LO.8

Recognize the limitation on certain itemized deductions applicable to high-income taxpayers.

Overall Limitation on Certain Itemized Deductions

Congress has enacted several provisions limiting tax benefits for high-income taxpayers. These limitations include the exemption phaseout (refer to Chapter 3) and a phaseout of itemized deductions. For 2006, the phaseout of itemized deductions (also referred to as a *cutback adjustment*) applies to taxpayers whose AGI exceeds $150,500 ($75,250 for married taxpayers filing separately).[51] The limitation applies to the following frequently encountered itemized deductions:[52]

- Taxes.
- Home mortgage interest, including points.
- Charitable contributions.
- Unreimbursed employee expenses subject to the 2 percent-of-AGI floor.
- All other expenses subject to the 2 percent-of-AGI floor.

The following deductions are *not* subject to the limitation on itemized deductions:

- Medical and dental expenses.
- Investment interest expense.
- Nonbusiness casualty and theft losses.
- Gambling losses.

The overall limitation applicable to itemized deductions is being phased out over a four-year period, beginning in 2006. Therefore, taxpayers subject to the limitation must use a two-step computation to determine the reduction required by the overall limitation.

Step 1

Calculate the lesser of :

- 3 percent of the amount by which AGI exceeds $150,500 ($75,250 if married filing separately).
- 80 percent of itemized deductions that are affected by the limit.

Step 2

Multiply the amount computed in Step 1 by the fraction that applies to the tax year involved. For 2006 and 2007, the phaseout is equal to two-thirds of the Step 1 amount. For 2008 and 2009, the phaseout is equal to one-third of the Step 1 amount. The overall limitation will no longer exist for taxable years beginning after 2009.

The overall limitation is applied after applying all other limitations to itemized deductions that are affected by the overall limitation. Other limitations apply to charitable contributions, certain meals and entertainment expenses, and certain miscellaneous itemized deductions.

EXAMPLE 38

Herman, who is single, had AGI of $200,000 for 2006. He incurred the following expenses and losses during the year:

Medical expenses before 7.5%-of-AGI limitation	$16,000
State and local income taxes	3,200
Real estate taxes	2,800

---

[51]For 2005, the limitation applied if AGI exceeded $145,950 ($72,975 for married taxpayers filing separately).

[52]Other deductions subject to the limitation include Federal estate tax on income in respect of a decedent, certain amortizable bond premiums, the deduction for repayment of certain amounts, certain unrecovered investments in an annuity, and impairment-related work expenses.

TAX *in the News*   **THE FIRST FAMILY AND ITEMIZED DEDUCTION PHASEOUTS**

President George W. and Laura Bush itemized deductions on their 2004 tax return (refer to Tax in the News, page 10–3). Because of their income level, their itemized deductions were reduced, as shown in the column to the right.

The top marginal rate of 35 percent applied to President and Mrs. Bush's taxable income in 2004. Therefore, the phaseout of itemized deductions cost them $6,736 in additional Federal income tax ($19,246 reduction × 35% marginal tax rate).

Itemized Deductions	
Medical expenses	$ –0–
Taxes	24,344
Interest	–0–
Charitable contributions	77,785
Job expenses and most other miscellaneous deductions	28,548
Total itemized deductions	$130,677
Reduction due to phaseout [($784,219 AGI − $142,700) × .03]	(19,246)
Itemized deductions allowed	$111,431

Home mortgage interest	$ 7,200
Charitable contributions	2,000
Casualty loss before 10% limitation (after $100 floor)	21,500
Unreimbursed employee expenses subject to 2%-of-AGI limitation	4,300
Gambling losses (Herman had $3,000 gambling income)	7,000

Herman's itemized deductions *before* the overall limitation are computed as follows:

Medical expenses [$16,000 − (7.5% × $200,000)]	$ 1,000
State and local income taxes	3,200
Real estate taxes	2,800
Home mortgage interest	7,200
Charitable contributions	2,000
Casualty loss [$21,500 − (10% × $200,000)]	1,500
Unreimbursed employee expenses [$4,300 − (2% × $200,000)]	300
Gambling losses ($7,000 loss limited to $3,000 of gambling income)	3,000
Total itemized deductions before overall limitation	$21,000

Herman's itemized deductions subject to the overall limitation are as follows:

State and local income taxes	$ 3,200
Real estate taxes	2,800
Home mortgage interest	7,200
Charitable contributions	2,000
Unreimbursed employee expenses	300
Total	$15,500

Step 1

Calculate the lesser of :

• 3% ($200,000 AGI − $150,500)	$ 1,485
• 80% of itemized deductions subject to limitation ($15,500 × .80)	12,400

Robert Ryan, a candidate for governor, has released his tax return to the public. As Ryan's former tax adviser, you examine the return closely and realize that a considerable amount of his income was not reported on the return. You confide to a friend in the tabloid newspaper business that you are aware that a candidate for a high public office has filed a fraudulent tax return. Your friend assures you that you will

be able to sell your story for at least $25,000 to a tabloid and still remain anonymous. Another friend, a CPA, argues that you should inform Ryan and give him an opportunity to correct the problem. You tell your friend that you are concerned that Ryan will be very vindictive if you approach him about the issue. Which course of action will you choose?

Step 2

Multiply the Step 1 amount by two-thirds ($1,485 × 2/3)	$990

Therefore, the amount of the reduction is $990, and Herman has $20,010 of deductible itemized deductions, computed as follows:

Deductible itemized deductions subject to overall limitation ($15,500 − $990)	$14,510
Itemized deductions not subject to overall limitation:	
Medical expenses	1,000
Casualty loss	1,500
Gambling losses	3,000
Deductible itemized deductions	$20,010 ∎

LO.9

Identify tax planning procedures that can maximize the benefit of itemized deductions.

TAX PLANNING *Considerations*

Effective Utilization of Itemized Deductions

Since an individual may use the standard deduction in one year and itemize deductions in another year, it is frequently possible to obtain maximum benefit by shifting itemized deductions from one year to another. For example, if a taxpayer's itemized deductions and the standard deduction are approximately the same for each year of a two-year period, the taxpayer should use the standard deduction in one year and shift itemized deductions (to the extent permitted by law) to the other year. The individual could, for example, prepay a church pledge for a particular year to shift the deduction to the current year or avoid paying end-of-the-year medical expenses to shift the deduction to the following year.

Utilization of Medical Deductions

When a taxpayer anticipates that medical expenses will approximate the percentage floor, much might be done to generate a deductible excess. Any of the following procedures can help build a deduction by the end of the year:

- Incur the obligation for needed dental work or have needed work carried out.[53] Orthodontic treatment, for example, may have been recommended for a member of the taxpayer's family.
- Have elective remedial surgery that may have been postponed from prior years (e.g., tonsillectomies, vasectomies, correction of hernias, hysterectomies).

[53]Prepayment of medical expenses does not generate a current deduction unless the taxpayer is under an obligation to make the payment.

- Incur the obligation for capital improvements to the taxpayer's personal residence recommended by a physician (e.g., an air filtration system to alleviate a respiratory disorder).

As an aid to taxpayers who may experience temporary cash-flow problems at the end of the year, the use of bank credit cards is deemed to be payment for purposes of timing the deductibility of charitable and medical expenses.

EXAMPLE 39

On December 13, 2006, Marge (a calendar year taxpayer) purchases two pairs of prescription contact lenses and one pair of prescribed orthopedic shoes for a total of $305. These purchases are separately charged to Marge's bank credit card. On January 6, 2007, Marge receives her statement containing these charges and makes payment shortly thereafter. The purchases are deductible as medical expenses in the year charged (2006) and not in the year the account is settled (2007). ∎

Recognizing which expenditures qualify for the medical deduction also may be crucial to exceeding the percentage limitations.

EXAMPLE 40

Mortimer employs Lana (an unrelated party) to care for his incapacitated and dependent mother. Lana is not a trained nurse but spends approximately one-half of the time performing nursing duties (e.g., administering injections and providing physical therapy) and the rest of the time doing household chores. An allocable portion of Lana's wages that Mortimer pays (including the employer's portion of FICA taxes) qualifies as a medical expense. ∎

Timing the Payment of Deductible Taxes

It is sometimes possible to defer or accelerate the payment of certain deductible taxes, such as state income tax, real property tax, and personal property tax. For instance, the final installment of estimated state income tax is generally due after the end of a given tax year. Accelerating the payment of the final installment could result in larger itemized deductions for the current year.

EXAMPLE 41

Jenny, who is single, expects to have itemized deductions of $4,800 in 2006 and $2,500 in 2007. She plans to pay $900 as the final installment on her 2006 estimated state income tax, which is due on January 15, 2007. The standard deduction for 2006 is $5,150 for single taxpayers. If Jenny does not pay the final installment until 2007, she will not itemize in either 2006 or 2007. However, if she pays the final installment in December 2006, her itemized deductions will be $5,700 ($4,800 + $900) in 2006, and she will benefit from itemizing. ∎

Protecting the Interest Deduction

Although the deductibility of prepaid interest by a cash basis taxpayer has been severely restricted, a notable exception allows a deduction for points paid by the buyer to obtain financing for the purchase or improvement of a principal residence in the year of payment. However, such points must actually be paid by the taxpayer obtaining the loan and must represent a charge for the use of money. It has been held that points paid from the mortgage proceeds do not satisfy the payment requirement.[54] Also, the portion of the points attributable to service charges does not represent deductible interest.[55] Taxpayers financing home purchases or improvements usually should direct their planning toward avoiding these two hurdles to immediate deductibility.

---

[54]*Alan A. Rubnitz,* 67 T.C. 621 (1977). Seller-paid points may also be deductible by the buyer under the provisions of Rev.Proc. 94–27, cited in footnote 31.

[55]*Donald L. Wilkerson,* 70 T.C. 240 (1978).

In rare instances, a taxpayer may find it desirable to forgo the immediate expensing of points in the year paid. Instead, it could prove beneficial to capitalize the points and write them off as interest expense over the life of the mortgage.

EXAMPLE 42

Gerald purchases a home on December 15, 2006, for $380,000 with $120,000 cash and a 15-year mortgage of $260,000 financed by the Greater Metropolis National Bank. Gerald pays two points in addition to interest allocated to the period from December 15 until December 31, 2006, at an annual rate of 6%. Since Gerald does not have enough itemized deductions to exceed the standard deduction for 2006, he should elect to capitalize the interest expense and amortize the points over 15 years. In this instance, Gerald would deduct $346.67 for 2007, as part of his qualified residence interest expense [$5,200 (two points) divided by 15 years], if he elects to itemize that year. ■

Because personal (consumer) interest is not deductible, taxpayers should consider making use of home equity loans. Recall that these loans utilize the personal residence of the taxpayer as security. The funds from these loans can be used for personal purposes (e.g., auto loans, vacations). By making use of home equity loans, therefore, what would have been nondeductible consumer interest becomes deductible qualified residence interest.

Assuring the Charitable Contribution Deduction

For a charitable contribution deduction to be available, the recipient must be a qualified charitable organization. Sometimes the mechanics of how the contribution is carried out can determine whether or not a deduction results.

EXAMPLE 43

Fumiko wants to donate $5,000 to her church's mission in Kobe, Japan. In this regard, she considers three alternatives:

1. Send the money directly to the mission.
2. Give the money to her church with the understanding that it is to be passed on to the mission.
3. Give the money directly to the missionary in charge of the mission who is currently in the United States on a fund-raising trip.

If Fumiko wants to obtain a deduction for the contribution, she should choose alternative 2. A direct donation to the mission (alternative 1) is not deductible because the mission is a foreign charity. A direct gift to the missionary (alternative 3) does not comply since an individual cannot be a qualified charity for income tax purposes.[56] ■

When making noncash donations, the type of property chosen can have decided implications in determining the amount, if any, of the deduction.

EXAMPLE 44

Sam wants to give $60,000 in value to his church in some form other than cash. In this connection, he considers four alternatives:

1. Stock held for two years as an investment with a basis of $100,000 and a fair market value of $60,000.
2. Stock held for five years as an investment with a basis of $10,000 and a fair market value of $60,000.
3. The rent-free use for a year of a building that normally leases for $5,000 a month.
4. A valuable stamp collection held as an investment and owned for 10 years with a basis of $10,000 and a fair market value of $60,000. The church plans to sell the collection if and when it is donated.

[56]*Thomas E. Lesslie*, 36 TCM 495, T.C.Memo. 1977–111.

Alternative 1 is ill-advised as the subject of the gift. Even though Sam would obtain a deduction of $60,000, he would forgo the potential loss of $40,000 that would be recognized if the property were sold.[57] Alternative 2 makes good sense since the deduction still is $60,000 and none of the $50,000 of appreciation that has occurred must be recognized as income. Alternative 3 yields no deduction at all and is not a wise choice. Alternative 4 involves tangible personalty that the recipient does not plan to use. As a result, the amount of the deduction is limited to $10,000, the stamp collection's basis.[58] ■

For property transfers (particularly real estate), the ceiling limitations on the amount of the deduction allowed in any one year (50 percent, 30 percent, or 20 percent of AGI, as the case may be) could be a factor to take into account. With proper planning, donations can be controlled to stay within the limitations and therefore avoid the need for a carryover of unused charitable contributions.

EXAMPLE 45

Andrew wants to donate a tract of unimproved land held as an investment to the University of Maryland (a qualified charitable organization). The land has been held for six years and has a current fair market value of $300,000 and a basis to Andrew of $50,000. Andrew's AGI for the current year is estimated to be $200,000, and he expects much the same for the next few years. In the current year, he deeds (transfers) an undivided one-fifth interest in the real estate to the university. ■

What has Andrew in Example 45 accomplished for income tax purposes? In the current year, he will be allowed a charitable contribution deduction of $60,000 ($1/5 \times$ $300,000), which will be within the applicable limitation of AGI (30% $\times$ $200,000). Presuming no other charitable contributions for the year, Andrew has avoided the possibility of a carryover. In future years, Andrew can arrange donations of undivided interests in the real estate to stay within the bounds of the percentage limitations. The only difficulty with this approach is the need to revalue the real estate each year before the donation, since the amount of the deduction is based on the fair market value of the interest contributed at the time of the contribution.

EXAMPLE 46

Tiffany dies in October 2006. In completing her final income tax return for 2006, Tiffany's executor determines the following information: AGI of $104,000 and a donation by Tiffany to her church of stock worth $60,000. Tiffany had purchased the stock two years ago for $50,000 and held it as an investment. Tiffany's executor makes the reduced deduction election and, as a consequence, claims a charitable contribution deduction of $50,000. With the election, the potential charitable contribution deduction of $50,000 ($60,000 − $10,000) is less than the 50% ceiling of $52,000 ($104,000 × 50%). If the executor had not made the election, the potential charitable contribution deduction of $60,000 would have been reduced by the 30% ceiling to $31,200 ($104,000 × 30%). No carryover of the $28,800 ($60,000 − $31,200) would have been available. ■

KEY TERMS

Acquisition indebtedness, 10–16	Home equity loans, 10–16	Net investment income, 10–15
Capital gain property, 10–24	Investment income, 10–14	Ordinary income property, 10–23
Charitable contribution, 10–20	Investment interest, 10–13	Points, 10–17
Health Savings Account (HSA), 10–8	Medical expense, 10–2	Qualified residence interest, 10–14
	Miscellaneous itemized deductions, 10–27	

---

[57]*LaVar M. Withers*, 69 T.C. 900 (1978).

[58]No reduction of appreciation is necessary in alternative 2 since stock is intangible property and not tangible personalty.

DISCUSSION QUESTIONS

1. Erin, who prepared her own income tax return for the current year, failed to claim a deduction for her contribution to a traditional Individual Retirement Account (IRA). Her AGI, as reported on the incorrect return, was $100,000, and her medical expenses were $10,000.
   a. Will the correction of this omission affect the amount of medical expenses Erin can deduct? Explain.
   b. Will Erin's medical expense deduction increase or decrease when she corrects her return?

2. Roberta incurred expenses for the following items during the year:

   - Medical insurance premiums.
   - Life insurance premiums.
   - Nonprescription calcium supplements to prevent osteoporosis.
   - Fees for an alcohol rehabilitation program.
   - Contact lenses.
   - Travel expenses to obtain treatment at the Mayo Clinic in Minnesota.

   Which of these expenses can Roberta include as medical expenses for purposes of computing her medical expense deduction?

3. Joe was in an accident and required cosmetic surgery for injuries to his nose. He also had the doctor do additional surgery to reshape his chin, which had not been injured. Will the cosmetic surgery to Joe's nose qualify as a medical expense? Will the cosmetic surgery to Joe's chin qualify as a medical expense? Explain.

Decision Making

4. Frank, a widower, had a serious stroke and is no longer capable of caring for himself. He has three sons, all of whom live in different states. Because they are unable to care for Frank in their homes, his sons have placed him in a nursing home equipped to provide medical and nursing care. Total nursing home expenses amount to $36,000 per year. Of this amount, $15,000 is directly attributable to medical and nursing care. Frank's Social Security benefits are used to pay for $10,000 of the nursing home charges. He has no other income. His sons plan to split the remaining medical expenses equally.
   a. What portion of the nursing home charges is potentially deductible as a medical expense?
   b. Can you provide Frank's sons with a tax planning idea for maximizing the deduction for his medical expenses?

5. Nathan, a physically handicapped individual, paid $10,000 for the installation of wheelchair ramps, support bars, and railings in his personal residence. These improvements increased the value of his personal residence by $2,500. How much of Nathan's expenditure qualifies as a medical expense deduction (subject to the 7.5% floor)? Explain.

6. Bob and June were divorced in 2004. In July of 2006, their daughter, Harriet, broke her leg while playing soccer. Harriet lives with June, and June claims her as a dependent. Bob pays for the medical expenses related to Harriet's injury. Can Bob claim the medical expenses he pays for Harriet on his tax return?

7. In 2006, David, a sole proprietor of a bookstore, pays a $7,500 premium for medical insurance for himself and his family. Joan, an employee of a small firm that doesn't provide her with medical insurance, pays medical insurance premiums of $8,000 for herself. How does the tax treatment differ for David and Joan?

8. Arturo, a calendar year taxpayer, paid $16,000 in medical expenses and sustained a $20,000 casualty loss in 2006. He expects $12,000 of the medical expenses and $14,000 of the casualty loss to be reimbursed by insurance companies in 2007. Before

considering any limitations on these deductions, how much can Arturo include in determining his itemized deductions for 2006?

9. Hubert, a self-employed taxpayer, is married and has two children. He has asked you to explain the tax and nontax advantages of establishing a Health Savings Account (HSA) for himself and his family.

10. A local ophthalmologist's advertising campaign included a certificate for a free radial keratotomy for the lucky winner of a drawing. Ahmad held the winning ticket, which was drawn in December 2005. Ahmad had no vision problems and was uncertain what he should do with the prize. In February 2006, Ahmad's daughter, who lives with his former wife, was diagnosed with a vision problem that could be treated with either prescription glasses or a radial keratotomy. The divorce decree requires that Ahmad pay for all medical expenses incurred for his daughter. Identify the relevant tax issues for Ahmad.

Issue ID

11. Theodore sold his personal residence to Colleen and paid real estate taxes of $9,450 for the year, $3,250 of which was apportioned to Colleen based on the period she owned the property during the year. What are the income tax consequences to each party?

12. Julia owns a principal residence in California, a condo in New York City, and a houseboat in Florida. All of the properties have mortgages on which Julia pays interest. What are the limitations on Julia's mortgage interest deduction? What strategy should Julia consider to maximize her mortgage interest deduction?

Decision Making

13. Jimmy Wolf's car was destroyed by a tornado. Unfortunately, his insurance had lapsed two days before he incurred the loss. Jimmy uses his car for both business and personal use. Jimmy, who is self-employed, does not have adequate savings to replace the car and must borrow money to purchase a new car. He is considering taking out a home equity loan, at a 4% interest rate, to obtain funds for the purchase. Sherry, his wife, would prefer not to do so because they paid off their mortgage recently and she does not want to incur any obligations related to their home. She would prefer to sell some of their stock in Bluebird, Inc., to raise funds to purchase the new car. Jimmy does not want to sell the stock because it has declined in value since they purchased it and he is convinced that its price will increase within the next two years. Jimmy has suggested that they obtain conventional financing for the purchase from their bank, which charges 7% interest on car loans. Identify the tax issues related to each of the three alternatives Jimmy and Sherry are considering.

Issue ID

14. Jerry purchased a personal residence from Kim. In order to sell the residence, Kim agreed to pay $3,000 in points related to Jerry's mortgage. Discuss the deductibility of the points.

15. Ellen borrowed $50,000 from her parents for a down payment on a condominium. She paid interest of $3,200 in 2004, $0 in 2005, and $9,000 in 2006. The IRS disallowed the deduction. Can you offer any explanation for the disallowance?

16. To dissuade his pastor from resigning and taking a position with a larger church, Michael, an ardent leader of the congregation, gives the pastor a new car. Is the cost of the car deductible by Michael as a charitable contribution? Explain.

17. Paula contributed Orange Corporation common stock to the United Way. In addition, she contributed tables and chairs from her proprietorship's inventory to the high school in her city. Should Paula's charitable contribution deduction for these contributions be determined by the basis or fair market value of the contributed items?

18. Nancy, who is a professor at State University, does some of her writing and class preparation at home at night. Her department provides faculty members with a $1,500 allowance for a desktop computer for use at school, but does not ordinarily provide computers for use at home. In order to have a computer for use at school and at home, Nancy has asked the department to provide her with a notebook computer that costs $2,500. The head of her department is willing to provide the standard $1,500 allowance and will permit Nancy to purchase the $2,500 notebook computer if she makes a donation of $1,000 to the department. If she acquires the notebook computer, Nancy's home use of the computer will be approximately 60% for business and 40% for personal

Issue ID

use not related to her job. Discuss the tax issues that Nancy should consider in deciding whether to acquire the notebook computer under these conditions.

Issue ID

19. Harry, whose combined Federal and state income tax rates total 40% in 2006, expects to retire in 2007 and have a combined tax rate of 30%. He plans to donate $100,000 to his church. Because he will not have the cash available until 2007, Harry donates land (long-term capital gain property) with a basis of $20,000 and fair market value of $100,000 to the church in December 2006. He reacquires the land from the church for $100,000 in February 2007. Discuss Harry's tax objectives and all tax issues related to his actions.

Issue ID

20. Zina decided to have a garage sale to get rid of a number of items that she no longer needed, including books, old stereo equipment, clothing, bicycles, and furniture. She scheduled the sale for Friday and Saturday, but was forced to close at noon Friday because of a torrential downpour. She had collected $500 for the items she sold before closing. The heavy rains continued through the weekend, and Zina was unable to continue the sale. She had not enjoyed dealing with the people who came to the sale on Friday morning, so she donated the remaining items to several local organizations. Zina has asked your advice on how she should treat these events on her tax return. List some of the tax issues you would discuss with her.

Issue ID

21. William, a high school teacher, earns about $40,000 each year. In December 2006, he won $1 million in the state lottery. William plans to donate $100,000 to his church. He has asked you, his tax adviser, whether he should donate the $100,000 in 2006 or 2007. Identify the tax issues related to William's decision.

Issue ID

22. The Skins Game, which involves four of the top golfers on the PGA Tours, is held each year on the weekend after Thanksgiving. Total prize money amounts to $1 million, and the leading money winner also receives an automobile as a prize. Twenty percent of the money won by each player goes to charity. In addition, on the par three holes, the winner of the hole receives the keys to an automobile, which goes to the player's favorite charity. Identify the relevant tax issues for the players. Consider the following possibilities with respect to the car won by the leading money winner: (1) keep the car for personal use and sell his or her present car; (2) sell the new car; (3) give the car to a friend or relative; (4) donate the car to charity; or (5) give the car to his or her caddy.

Decision Making

23. Colin had AGI of $180,000 in 2006. He contributed stock in White, Inc. (a publicly traded corporation), to the United Way, a qualified charitable organization. The stock was worth $105,000 on the date it was contributed. Colin had acquired it as an investment two years ago at a cost of $84,000.
    a. What is the total amount that Colin can deduct as a charitable contribution, assuming he carries over any disallowed contribution from 2006 to future years?
    b. What is the maximum amount that Colin can deduct as a charitable contribution in 2006?
    c. What factors should Colin consider in deciding how to treat the contribution for Federal income tax purposes?
    d. Assume Colin dies in December 2006. What advice would you give the executor of his estate with regard to possible elections that can be made relative to the contribution?

PROBLEMS

24. Doug and Karen are married and together have AGI of $80,000 in 2006. They have two dependents and file a joint return. They pay $3,000 for a high-deductible health insurance policy and contribute $2,400 to a qualified Health Savings Account. During the year, they paid the following amounts for medical care: $7,500 in doctor and dentist bills and hospital expenses, and $1,700 for prescribed medicine and drugs. In November 2006, they received an insurance reimbursement of $2,100 for hospitalization. They expect to receive an additional reimbursement of $1,000 in January 2007. Determine the maximum deduction allowable for medical expenses in 2006.

25. Andy had AGI of $80,000 for 2006. He was injured in a rock climbing accident and paid $5,200 for hospital expenses and $2,800 for doctor bills. Andy also incurred medical

expenses of $2,400 for his child, Jodi, who lives with his former wife, Pearl, and is claimed as a dependent by her. In 2007, Andy was reimbursed $2,600 by his insurance company for the medical expenses attributable to the rock climbing accident.

a. Compute Andy's deduction for medical expenses in 2006.

b. Assume that Andy would have elected to itemize his deductions even if he had no medical expenses in 2006. How much, if any, of the $2,600 reimbursement must be included in gross income in 2007?

c. Assume that Andy's other itemized deductions in 2006 were $5,300 and that he filed as a head of household. How much of the $2,600 reimbursement must he include in gross income in 2007?

26. Juan suffers from emphysema and severe allergies and, upon the recommendation of his physician, has a dust elimination system installed in his personal residence. In connection with the system, Juan incurs and pays the following amounts during the current year:

Dust elimination system	$7,500
Increase in utility bills due to the system	400
Cost of certified appraisal	300

The system has an estimated useful life of 10 years. The appraisal was to determine the value of Juan's residence with and without the system. The appraisal states that the system increased the value of Juan's residence by $1,500. How much of these expenditures qualifies for the medical expense deduction in the current year?

27. For calendar year 2006, Jean was a self-employed consultant with no employees. She had $80,000 net profit from consulting and paid $7,000 in medical insurance premiums on a policy covering 2006. How much of these premiums may Jean deduct as a deduction *for* AGI, and how much may she deduct as an itemized deduction (subject to the 7.5% floor)?

28. During the current year, Susan incurred and paid the following expenses for Beth (her daughter), Ed (her father), and herself:

Surgery for Beth	$4,500
Red River Academy charges for Beth:	
Tuition	5,100
Room, board, and other expenses	4,800
Psychiatric treatment	5,100
Doctor bills for Ed	2,200
Prescription drugs for Susan, Beth, and Ed	780
Insulin for Ed	540
Nonprescription drugs for Susan, Beth, and Ed	570
Charges at Heartland Nursing Home for Ed:	
Medical care	5,000
Lodging	2,700
Meals	2,650

Beth qualifies as Susan's dependent, and Ed would also qualify except that he receives $7,400 of taxable retirement benefits from his former employer. Beth's psychiatrist recommended Red River Academy because of its small classes and specialized psychiatric treatment program that is needed to treat Beth's illness. Ed is a paraplegic and diabetic, and Heartland offers the type of care that he requires.

Upon the recommendation of a physician, Susan has an air filtration system installed in her personal residence. She suffers from severe allergies. In connection with this equipment, Susan incurs and pays the following amounts during the year:

Filtration system and cost of installation	$6,500
Increase in utility bills due to the system	700
Cost of certified appraisal	360

The system has an estimated useful life of 10 years. The appraisal was to determine the value of Susan's residence with and without the system. The appraisal states that the system increased the value of Susan's residence by $2,200. Ignoring the 7.5% floor, what is the total of Susan's expenses that qualify for the medical expense deduction?

Issue ID

29. In May, Rebecca's daughter, Susan, sustained a serious injury that made it impossible for her to continue living alone. Susan, who is a novelist, moved back into Rebecca's home after the accident. Susan has begun writing a new novel based on her recent experiences. To accommodate Susan, Rebecca incurred significant remodeling expenses (widening hallways, building a separate bedroom and bathroom, making kitchen appliances accessible to Susan). In addition, Rebecca had an indoor swimming pool constructed so Susan could do rehabilitation exercises prescribed by her physician.

    In September, Susan underwent major reconstructive surgery in Denver. The surgery was performed by Dr. Rama Patel, who specializes in treating injuries of the type sustained by Susan. Rebecca drove Susan from Champaign, Illinois, to Denver, a total of 1,100 miles, in Susan's specially equipped van. They left Champaign on Tuesday morning and arrived in Denver on Thursday afternoon. Rebecca incurred expenses for gasoline, highway tolls, meals, and lodging while traveling to Denver. Rebecca stayed in a motel near the clinic for eight days while Susan was hospitalized. Identify the relevant tax issues based on this information and prepare a list of questions that you would need to ask Rebecca and Susan in order to advise them as to the resolution of any issues you have identified.

30. During 2006, Shauna, who is self-employed, paid $550 per month for an HSA contract that provides medical insurance coverage with a $4,200 deductible. The plan covers Shauna, her husband, and their two children. Of the $550 monthly fee, $175 was for the high-deductible policy, and $375 was deposited into an HSA. How much of the amount paid for the high-deductible policy can Shauna deduct as a deduction *for* AGI?

Communications

31. In 1999, Angela purchased a personal residence from Victor. She paid $300,000 for the residence. Victor paid real estate taxes of $9,125 for the real estate property tax year, of which $5,500 was allocable to the portion of the year that Angela owned the residence. Angela sold the residence to Earl for $350,000 on December 8, 2006. Earl paid real estate taxes of $10,220 for the real estate property tax year, of which $9,576 was allocable to the portion of the year that Angela owned the residence. Angela has provided you with the above information and asked that you determine her basis in the residence at the date of sale, the amount realized for the residence, her gain on the sale, and her property tax deduction for 2006. Write a letter to Angela Henson, who lives at 17250 Calistoga Drive, El Dorado, KS 67042, to communicate your answers.

32. Dylan is a self-employed, calendar year taxpayer. He reports on the cash basis. Dylan made the following estimated state income tax payments:

Date	Amount
January 15, 2006	$1,800 (4th payment for 2005)
April 15, 2006	2,250 (1st payment for 2006)
June 15, 2006	2,250 (2nd payment for 2006)
September 15, 2006	2,250 (3rd payment for 2006)
January 15, 2007	2,250 (4th payment for 2006)

    Dylan had a tax overpayment of $1,200 on his 2005 state income tax return and, rather than requesting a refund, had the overpayment applied to his 2006 state income taxes. What is the amount of Dylan's state income tax itemized deduction for his 2006 Federal income tax return?

Decision Making

Communications

33. Carol Sharp incurred $29,250 of interest expense related to her investments in 2006. Her investment income included $7,000 of interest, $5,500 of qualified dividends, and a $12,750 net capital gain on the sale of securities. Carol has asked you to compute the amount of her deduction for investment interest, taking into consideration any options she might have. In addition, she has asked for your suggestions as to any tax planning alternatives that might be available. Write a letter to her that contains your advice. Carol lives at 208 Lone Tree Circle, Napa, CA 94558.

34. Justine borrowed $100,000 to acquire a parcel of land to be held for investment purposes. During 2006, she paid interest of $11,000 on the loan. She had AGI of $75,000 for the year. Other items related to Justine's investments include the following:

Investment income	$10,000
Long-term capital gain on sale of stock	7,500
Investment counsel fees	2,000

Justine is unmarried and elects to itemize her deductions. She has no miscellaneous itemized deductions other than the investment counsel fees.
   a. Determine Justine's investment interest deduction for 2006, assuming she does not make any special election regarding the computation of investment income.
   b. Discuss the treatment of Justine's investment interest that is disallowed in 2006.
   c. What election could Justine make to increase the amount of her investment interest deduction for 2006?

35. In 1997, Roland, who is single, purchased a personal residence for $340,000 and took out a mortgage of $200,000 on the property. In May of the current year, when the residence had a fair market value of $440,000 and Roland owed $140,000 on the mortgage, he took out a home equity loan for $220,000. He used the funds to purchase a recreational vehicle, which he uses 100% for personal use. What is the maximum amount on which Roland can deduct home equity interest?

36. Ron and Tom are equal owners in Robin Corporation. On July 1, 2006, each lends the corporation $30,000 at an annual interest rate of 10%. Ron and Tom are brothers. Both shareholders are on the cash method of accounting, and Robin Corporation is on the accrual method. All parties use the calendar year for tax purposes. On June 30, 2007, Robin repays the loans of $60,000 together with the specified interest of $6,000.
   a. How much of the interest can Robin Corporation deduct in 2006? In 2007?
   b. When is the interest included in Ron and Tom's gross income?

37. Nadia donates $4,000 to Eastern University's athletic department. The payment guarantees that Nadia will have preferred seating near the 50-yard line.
   a. Assume Nadia subsequently buys four $100 game tickets. How much can she deduct as a charitable contribution to the university's athletic department?
   b. Assume that Nadia's $4,000 donation includes four $100 tickets. How much can she deduct as a charitable contribution to the university's athletic department?

38. Becky had AGI of $100,000 in 2006. She donated Amber Corporation stock with a basis of $11,000 to a qualified charitable organization on July 5, 2006.
   a. What is the amount of Becky's deduction, assuming that she purchased the stock on December 4, 2005, and the stock had a fair market value of $19,000 when she made the donation?
   b. Assume the same facts as in (a), except that Becky purchased the stock on July 1, 2003.
   c. Assume the same facts as in (a), except that the stock had a fair market value of $7,000 (rather than $19,000) when Becky donated it to the charity.

39. Pedro contributes a painting to an art museum in 2006. He has owned the painting for 12 years, and it is worth $130,000 at the time of the donation. Pedro's adjusted basis for the painting is $90,000, and his AGI for 2006 is $250,000. Pedro has asked you whether he should make the reduced deduction election for this contribution. Write a letter to Pedro Valdez at 1289 Greenway Avenue, Foster City, CA 94404 and advise him on this matter.

Decision Making

Communications

40. During the year, Carl made the following contributions to a qualified public charity:

Cash	$220,000
Stock in Goldfinch, Inc. (a publicly traded corporation)	280,000

Carl acquired the stock in Goldfinch, Inc., as an investment five years ago at a cost of $120,000. Carl's AGI is $840,000.
   a. What is Carl's charitable contribution deduction?
   b. How are excess amounts, if any, treated?

Decision Making

41. Ramon had AGI of $180,000 in 2006. He contributed stock in Charlton, Inc. (a publicly traded corporation), to the American Heart Association, a qualified charitable organization. The stock was worth $105,000 on the date it was contributed. Ramon had acquired it as an investment two years ago at a cost of $84,000.
    a. What is the total amount that Ramon can deduct as a charitable contribution, assuming he carries over any disallowed contribution from 2006 to future years?
    b. What is the maximum amount that Ramon can deduct as a charitable contribution in 2006?
    c. What factors should Ramon consider in deciding how to treat the contribution for Federal income tax purposes?
    d. Assume Ramon dies in December 2006. What advice would you give the executor of his estate with regard to possible elections that can be made relative to the contribution?

42. On December 30, 2006, Roberta purchased four tickets to a charity ball sponsored by the city of San Diego for the benefit of underprivileged children. Each ticket cost $200 and had a fair market value of $35. On the same day as the purchase, Roberta gave the tickets to the minister of her church for personal use by his family. At the time of the gift of the tickets, Roberta pledged $4,000 to the building fund of her church. The pledge was satisfied by a check dated December 31, 2006, but not mailed until January 3, 2007.
    a. Presuming Roberta is a cash basis and calendar year taxpayer, how much can she deduct as a charitable contribution for 2006?
    b. Would the amount of the deduction be any different if Roberta is an accrual basis taxpayer? Explain.

Decision Making

Communications

43. In December each year, Alice Young contributes 10% of her gross income to the United Way (a 50% organization). Alice, who is in the 35% marginal tax bracket, is considering the following alternatives as charitable contributions in December 2006:

	Fair Market Value
(1) Cash donation	$21,000
(2) Unimproved land held for six years ($3,000 basis)	21,000
(3) Blue Corporation stock held for eight months ($3,000 basis)	21,000
(4) Gold Corporation stock held for two years ($26,000 basis)	21,000

Alice has asked you to help her decide which of the potential contributions listed above will be most advantageous taxwise. Evaluate the four alternatives and write a letter to Alice to communicate your advice to her. Her address is 2622 Bayshore Drive, Berkeley, CA 94709.

Decision Making

Communications

44. Manuel and Rosa Garcia, both age 45, are married and have no dependents. They have asked you to advise them whether they should file jointly or separately in 2005. They present you with the following information:

	Manuel	Rosa	Joint
Salary	$40,000		
Business net income		$100,000	
Interest income	400	1,200	$2,200
Deductions *for* AGI	2,000	13,000	
Medical expenses	9,500	600	
State income tax	800	2,000	
Real estate tax			3,400
Mortgage interest			5,200
Unreimbursed employee expenses	1,100		

If they file separately, Manuel and Rosa will split the real estate tax and mortgage interest deductions equally. Write Manuel and Rosa a letter in which you make and explain a recommendation on filing status for 2005. Manuel and Rosa reside at 5904 Stevens Avenue, Durham, NC 27707.

45. Kelsey, who is a head of household with one dependent, had AGI of $315,500 for 2006. He incurred the following expenses and losses during the year:

Medical expenses before 7.5%-of-AGI limitation	$25,000
State and local income taxes	4,300
State sales tax	1,205
Real estate taxes	3,705
Home mortgage interest	4,400
Credit card interest	820
Charitable contribution	3,800
Casualty loss before 10% limitation (after $100 floor)	38,000
Unreimbursed employee expenses subject to 2%-of-AGI limitation	7,100

Calculate Kelsey's allowable itemized deductions for the year.

46. Matt and Gail Mann are married, have two dependents, and file a joint return for 2006. Information for the year includes the following:

AGI	$279,900
State and local income taxes	6,200
Real estate taxes	8,500
Home mortgage interest	8,600
Charitable contributions	9,100
Gambling losses (gambling income of $4,800 was included in AGI)	6,700

Compute the allowable itemized deductions for 2006 for the Manns.

47. Eldrick, who is single, had AGI of $350,000 during 2006. He incurred the following expenses and losses during the year:

Medical expenses before 7.5%-of-AGI limitation	$36,000
State and local income taxes	5,700
State sales tax	780
Real estate taxes	4,900
Home mortgage interest	5,900
Charitable contributions	5,200
Casualty loss before 10% limitation (after $100 floor)	44,000
Unreimbursed employee expenses subject to 2%-of-AGI limitation	8,200
Gambling losses (Eldrick had $6,800 of gambling income)	9,200

Compute Eldrick's itemized deductions before and after the overall limitation.

48. For calendar year 2006, Stuart and Pamela Gibson file a joint return reflecting AGI of $264,000. Their itemized deductions are as follows:

Medical expenses	$25,300
Casualty loss (not covered by insurance)	28,600
Interest on home mortgage	11,000
Interest on credit cards	800
Property taxes on home	14,300
Charitable contributions	18,700
State income tax	16,500
Tax return filing fees	1,200

After all necessary adjustments are made, what is the amount of itemized deductions the Gibsons may claim?

CUMULATIVE PROBLEMS

Tax Return Problem

Decision Making

49. Alice J. and Bruce M. Byrd are married taxpayers who file a joint return. Their Social Security numbers are 034–48–4382 and 016–50–9556, respectively. Alice's birthday is September 21, 1959, and Bruce's is June 27, 1958. They live at 473 Revere Avenue, Ames, MA 01850. Alice is the office manager for Ames Dental Clinic, 433 Broad Street, Ames, MA 01850 (employer identification number 37-4000456). Bruce is the manager of a Super Burgers fast-food outlet owned and operated by Plymouth Corporation, 1247 Central Avenue, Hauppauge, NY 11788 (employer identification number 37–6000987).

The following information is shown on their Wage and Tax Statements (Form W–2) for 2005.

Line	Description	Alice	Bruce
1	Wages, tips, other compensation	$52,600	$61,500
2	Federal income tax withheld	4,180	5,990
3	Social Security wages	52,600	61,500
4	Social Security tax withheld	3,261	3,813
5	Medicare wages and tips	52,600	61,500
6	Medicare tax withheld	763	892
15	State	Massachusetts	Massachusetts
16	State wages, tips, etc.	52,600	61,500
17	State income tax withheld	2,280	2,990

The Byrds provide over half of the support of their two children, Cynthia (born January 25, 1981, Social Security number 017–44–9126) and John (born February 7, 1983, Social Security number 017–27–4148), who live with them. Both children are full-time students and live with the Byrds except when they are away at college. Cynthia earned $3,700 from a summer internship in 2005, and John earned $3,400 from a part-time job.

During 2005, the Byrds furnished 60% of the total support of Bruce's widower father, Sam Byrd (born March 6, 1930, Social Security number 034–82–8583). Sam lived alone and covered the rest of his support with his Social Security benefits. Sam died in November, and Bruce, the beneficiary of a policy on Sam's life, received life insurance proceeds of $600,000 on December 28.

The Byrds had the following expenses relating to their personal residence during 2005:

Property taxes	$4,720
Interest on home mortgage	9,130
Repairs to roof	4,780
Utilities	3,810
Fire and theft insurance	2,290

The following facts relate to medical expenses for 2005:

Medical insurance premiums	$4,380
Doctor bill for Sam incurred in 2004 and not paid until 2005	7,760
Operation for Sam	7,310
Prescription medicines for Sam	860
Hospital expenses for Sam	2,850
Reimbursement from insurance company, received in 2005	3,000

The medical expenses for Sam represent most of the 60% Bruce contributed toward his father's support.

Other relevant information follows:

- When they filed their 2004 state return in 2005, the Byrds paid additional state income tax of $950.
- During 2005, Alice and Bruce attended a dinner dance sponsored by the Ames Police Disability Association (a qualified charitable organization). The Byrds paid $400 for the tickets. The cost of comparable entertainment would normally be $160.
- The Byrds contributed $4,800 to Ames Assembly Church and gave used clothing (cost of $1,100 and fair market value of $450) to the Salvation Army. All donations are supported by receipts.
- In 2005, the Byrds received interest income of $2,695, which was reported on a Form 1099–INT from Second National Bank.
- Alice's employer requires that all employees wear uniforms to work. During 2005, Alice spent $482 on new uniforms and $211 on laundry charges.
- Bruce paid $320 for an annual subscription to the *Journal of Franchise Management.*
- Neither Alice's nor Bruce's employer reimburses for employee expenses.
- The Byrds do not keep the receipts for the sales taxes they paid and had no major purchases subject to sales tax.
- Alice and Bruce paid no estimated Federal income tax. Neither Alice nor Bruce wishes to designate $3 to the Presidential Election Campaign Fund.

Part 1—Tax Computation
Compute net tax payable or refund due for Alice and Bruce Byrd for 2005. If they have overpaid, they want the amount to be refunded to them. If you use tax forms for your computations, you will need Form 1040 and Schedules A and B. Suggested software: TurboTax.

Part 2—Tax Planning
Alice and Bruce are planning some significant changes for 2006. They have provided you with the following information and asked you to project their taxable income and tax liability for 2006.

The Byrds will invest the $600,000 of life insurance proceeds in short-term certificates of deposit (CDs) and use the interest for living expenses during 2006. They expect to earn total interest of $21,000 on the CDs.

Bruce has been promoted to regional manager, and his salary for 2006 will be $85,000. He estimates that state income tax withheld will increase by $4,000.

Alice, who has been diagnosed with a serious illness, will take a leave of absence from work during 2006. The estimated cost for her medical treatment is $14,500, of which $5,500 will be reimbursed by their insurance company in 2006.

John will graduate from college in December 2005 and will take a job in New York City in January 2006. His starting salary will be $37,500.

Assume all the information reported in 2005 will be the same in 2006 unless other information has been presented above.

50. Paul and Donna Decker are married taxpayers, ages 44 and 42, who file a joint return for 2006. The Deckers live at 1121 College Avenue, Carmel, IN 46032. Paul is an assistant manager at Carmel Motor Inn, and Donna is a teacher at Carmel Elementary School. They present you with W–2 forms that reflect the following information:

Tax Return Problem

	Paul	Donna
Salary	$58,000	$56,000
Federal tax withheld	10,300	9,700
State income tax withheld	900	800
FICA (Social Security and Medicare) withheld	4,437	4,284
Social Security numbers	222–11–4567	333–11–9872

Donna is the custodial parent of two children from a previous marriage who reside with the Deckers through the school year. The children, Larry and Jane Parker, reside with their father, Bob, during the summer. Relevant information for the children follows:

	Larry	Jane
Age	17	18
Social Security numbers	305–11–4567	303–11–9872
Months spent with Deckers	9	9

Under the divorce decree, Bob pays child support of $150 per month per child during the nine months the children live with the Deckers. Bob says he spends $200 per month per child during the three summer months they reside with him. Donna and Paul can document that they provide $2,000 support per child per year. The divorce decree is silent as to which parent can claim the exemption for the children.

In August, Paul and Donna added a suite to their home to provide more comfortable accommodations for Hannah Snyder (263–33–4738), Donna's mother, who had moved in with them in February 2005 after the death of Donna's father. Not wanting to borrow money for this addition, Paul sold 300 shares of Acme Corporation stock for $50 per share on May 3, 2006, and used the proceeds of $15,000 to cover construction costs. The Deckers had purchased the stock on April 29, 2002, for $25 per share. They received dividends of $750 on the jointly owned stock a month before the sale.

Hannah, who is 66 years old, received $7,500 in Social Security benefits during the year, of which she gave the Deckers $2,000 to use toward household expenses and deposited the remainder in her personal savings account. The Deckers determine that they have spent $2,500 of their own money for food, clothing, medical expenses, and other items for Hannah. They do not know what the rental value of Hannah's suite would be, but they estimate it would be at least $300 per month.

Interest paid during the year included the following:

Home mortgage interest (paid to Carmel Federal Savings & Loan)	$7,890
Interest on an automobile loan (paid to Carmel National Bank)	1,490
Interest on Citibank Visa card	870

In July, Paul hit a submerged rock while boating. Fortunately, he was thrown from the boat, landed in deep water, and was uninjured. However, the boat, which was uninsured, was destroyed. Paul had paid $25,000 for the boat in June 2005, and its value was appraised at $18,000 on the date of the accident.

The Deckers paid doctor and hospital bills of $8,700 and were reimbursed $2,000 by their insurance company. They spent $640 for prescription drugs and medicines and $2,810 for premiums on their health insurance policy. They have filed additional claims of $1,200 with their insurance company and have been told they will receive payment for that amount in January 2007. Included in the amounts paid for doctor and hospital bills were payments of $380 for Hannah and $850 for the children.

Additional information of potential tax consequence follows:

Real estate taxes paid	$3,700
Sales taxes paid (per table)	1,379
Cash contributions to church	2,100
Appraised value of books donated to public library	740
Paul's unreimbursed employee expenses to attend hotel management convention:	
Airfare	340
Hotel	170
Meals	95
Registration fee	340
Refund of state income tax for 2005 (the Deckers itemized on their 2005 Federal tax return)	1,520

Compute net tax payable or refund due for the Deckers for 2006. Ignore the child tax credit in your computations. If they have overpaid, the amount is to be credited toward their taxes for 2007.

RESEARCH PROBLEMS

Note: Solutions to Research Problems can be prepared by using the **RIA Checkpoint**® **Student Edition** online research product, which is available to accompany this text. It is also possible to prepare solutions to the Research Problems by using tax research materials found in a standard tax library.

THOMSON
★
RIA

Research Problem 1.   After several years of a difficult marriage, Donald and Marla agreed to a divorce. As part of the property settlement, Marla transferred to Donald corporate stock, a commercial building, and a personal residence. Donald transferred other property to Marla, but the fair market value of the property was $600,000 less than the fair market value of the property Marla had transferred to him. To make the settlement equal, Donald agreed to pay Marla $600,000, payable over 10 years at 8% interest. For several years, Donald deducted the interest on his Federal income tax return as investment interest. Upon audit, the IRS disallowed the interest deduction, classifying it as nondeductible personal interest. Donald believes the interest is deductible and has asked you to find support for the deduction. Write a letter indicating your findings to Donald Jansen, 104 South Fourth Street, Dalton, GA 30720.

Communications

Partial list of research aids:
Gilmore v. U.S., 63–1 USTC ¶9285, 11 AFTR2d 758, 83 S.Ct. 623 (USSC, 1963).
John L. Seymour, 109 T.C. 279 (1997).

Research Problem 2.   Josef Abrams, an attorney, paid $30,000 during the year for his children to attend Jewish schools. On his tax return, Abrams deducted $18,000, based on the argument that 60% of his children's instruction was religious and that payments related to that type of instruction constituted contributions to the temple for conducting its religious functions. He did not attempt to deduct the 40% of tuition that was related to secular education. Further, Abrams argued that the IRS had allowed members of the Church of Scientology to deduct the portion of fees paid to the church that were related to religious education, and that disallowance of his deduction would constitute unequal application of the law. Write a letter to Mr. Abrams explaining whether the $18,000 is deductible or nondeductible. He lives at 122 Southmoor, Stamford, CT 00902.

Communications

Research Problem 3.   In January, Ron, a fireman, was injured in the line of duty as a result of interference by a homeowner. He incurred medical expenses of $6,500 related to his injuries. Ron sued the homeowner and was awarded damages of $26,500 in December. The court indicated that $6,500 of the award was for payment of Ron's medical expenses and $20,000 was for punitive damages. Ron has prepared his return for the year and has asked you to review it. You notice that Ron has not reported any part of the award as income and has included the medical expense in computing his itemized deductions. Write a brief summary of the advice you should give Ron.

Communications

Research Problem 4.   Tom and Mary Smith, whose son was found murdered in a parking garage, offered a $100,000 reward for the city police to use to obtain information leading to the arrest and conviction of the murderer. As a result of the reward, a person who had overheard the murderer telling a friend about the crime reported the conversation to the police. The murderer was arrested and convicted, and the Smiths contributed the money to the police department, which gave the reward to the informant. Can the Smiths treat the payment as an itemized deduction?

Research Problem 5.   Marcia, a shareholder in a corporation with stores in five states, donated stock with a basis of $10,000 to a qualified charitable organization in 2005. Although the stock of the corporation was not traded on a public stock exchange, many shares had been sold over the last three years. Based on the average selling price for the stock in 2005, Marcia deducted $95,000 on her 2005 tax return. Marcia received a notice from the IRS that the $95,000 deduction had been reduced to $10,000 because she had not obtained a qualified appraisal or attached a summary of her appraisal to her tax return. Marcia has asked you to advise her on this matter. Write a letter containing your conclusions to Ms. Marcia Meyer, 1311 Santos Court, San Bruno, CA 94066.

Communications

Partial list of research aids:
Reg. § 1.170A–13(c)(2).

Internet
Activity

Use the tax resources of the Internet to address the following questions. Do not restrict your search to the World Wide Web, but include a review of newsgroups and general reference materials, practitioner sites and resources, primary sources of the tax law, chat rooms and discussion groups, and other opportunities.

Research Problem 6.   Find the IRS Web site and print a copy of Schedule A. If the 2006 Schedule A is available, compare it with the 2005 Schedule A in the text (page 10–29) and discuss any changes.

Research Problem 7.   Search the Internet for stories about major charitable contributions by individuals, including Bill Gates, Ted Turner, and at least one other individual. Briefly discuss any tax issues that are related to the contributions.

CHAPTER

11

Passive Activity Losses

LEARNING OBJECTIVES

After completing Chapter 11, you should be able to:

LO.1

Discuss tax shelters and the reasons for at-risk and passive loss limitations.

LO.2

Explain the at-risk limitation.

LO.3

Describe how the passive loss rules limit deductions for losses, and identify the taxpayers subject to these restrictions.

LO.4

Discuss the definition of passive activities and the rules for identifying an activity.

LO.5

Analyze and apply the tests for material participation.

LO.6

Understand the nature of rental activities under the passive loss rules.

LO.7

Recognize the relationship between the at-risk and passive activity limitations.

LO.8

Discuss the special treatment available to real estate activities.

LO.9

Determine the proper tax treatment upon the disposition of a passive activity.

LO.10

Suggest tax planning strategies to minimize the effect of the passive loss limitations.

L0.1

Discuss tax shelters and the reasons for at-risk and passive loss limitations.

The Tax Shelter Problem

Before Congress enacted legislation to reduce or eliminate their effectiveness, **tax shelters** were popular investments for tax avoidance purposes because they could generate deductions and other benefits that could be used to offset income from other sources. Because of the tax avoidance potential of many tax shelters, they were attractive to wealthy taxpayers in high income tax brackets. Many tax shelters merely provided an opportunity for "investors" to buy deductions and credits in ventures that were not expected to generate a profit, even in the long run.

Although it may seem odd that a taxpayer would intentionally invest in an activity that was designed to produce losses, there is a logical explanation. The typical tax shelter operated as a partnership and relied heavily on nonrecourse financing.[1] Accelerated depreciation and interest expense deductions generated large losses in the early years of the activity. At the very least, the tax shelter deductions deferred the recognition of any net income from the venture until the activity was sold. In the best of situations, the investor could realize additional tax savings by offsetting other income (e.g., salary, interest, and dividends) with deductions flowing from the tax shelter. Ultimately, the sale of the investment would result in capital gain. The following examples illustrate what was possible *before* Congress enacted legislation to curb tax shelter abuses.

EXAMPLE 1

Bob, who earned a salary of $400,000 as a business executive and dividend income of $15,000, invested $20,000 for a 10% interest in a cattle-breeding tax shelter. Through the use of $800,000 of nonrecourse financing and available cash of $200,000, the partnership acquired a herd of an exotic breed of cattle costing $1 million. Depreciation, interest, and other deductions related to the activity resulted in a loss of $400,000, of which Bob's share was $40,000. Bob was allowed to deduct the $40,000 loss, even though he had invested and stood to lose only $20,000 if the investment became worthless. The net effect of the $40,000 deduction from the partnership was that a portion of Bob's salary and dividend income was "sheltered," and as a result, he was required to calculate his tax liability on only $375,000 of income [$415,000 (salary and dividends) − $40,000 (deduction)] rather than $415,000. If this deduction were available under current law and if Bob was in a combined Federal and state income tax bracket of 40%, this deduction would generate a tax savings of $16,000 ($40,000 × 40%) in the first year alone! ∎

A review of Example 1 shows that the taxpayer took a *two-for-one* write-off ($40,000 deduction, $20,000 investment). In the heyday of tax shelters, promoters often promised *multiple* write-offs for the investor.

---

[1]Nonrecourse debt is an obligation for which the borrower is not personally liable. An example of nonrecourse debt is a liability on real estate acquired by a partnership without the partnership or any of the partners assuming any liability for the mortgage. The acquired property generally is pledged as collateral for the loan.

The first major provision aimed at tax shelters was the **at-risk limitation.** Its objective is to limit a taxpayer's deductions to the amount "at risk," which is the amount the taxpayer stands to lose if the investment turns out to be a financial disaster.

EXAMPLE 2

Returning to the facts of Example 1, under the current at-risk rules Bob would be allowed to deduct $20,000 (i.e., the amount that he could lose if the business failed). This deduction would reduce his other income, and as a result, Bob would have to report only $395,000 of income ($415,000 − $20,000). The remaining nondeductible $20,000 loss and any future losses flowing from the partnership would be suspended under the at-risk rules and would be deductible in the future only as his at-risk amount increased. ■

The second major attack on tax shelters came with the passage of the passive activity loss rules. These rules are intended to halt an investor's ability to benefit from the mismatching of an entity's expenses and income that often occurs in the early years of the business. Congress observed that despite the at-risk limitations, investors could still deduct losses flowing from an entity and thereby defer their tax liability on other income. In effect, passive activity rules have, to a great degree, made the term *tax shelter* obsolete. Now such ventures where investors are not involved in the day-to-day operations of the business are generally referred to as passive investments, or *passive activities*, rather than tax shelters.

The **passive loss** rules require the taxpayer to segregate all income and losses into three categories: active, passive, and portfolio. In general, the passive loss limits disallow the deduction of passive losses against active or portfolio income, even when the taxpayer is at risk to the extent of the loss. In general, passive losses can only offset passive income.

EXAMPLE 3

Returning to the facts of Example 1, the passive activity loss rules further restrict Bob's ability to claim the $20,000 tax deduction shown in Example 2. Because Bob is a passive investor and does not materially participate in any meaningful way in the activities of the cattle-breeding operation, the $20,000 loss allowed under the at-risk rules is disallowed under the passive loss rules. The passive loss is disallowed because Bob does not generate any passive income that could absorb his passive loss. Further, his salary (active income) and dividends (portfolio income) cannot be used to absorb any of the passive loss. Consequently, Bob's current-year taxable income must reflect his nonpassive income of $415,000, and he receives no current benefit from his share of the partnership loss. However, all is not lost because Bob's share of the entity's loss is *suspended*; it is carried forward and can be deducted in the future when he has passive income or sells his interest in the activity. ■

This chapter explores the nature of the at-risk limits and passive activity loss rules and their impact on investors. An interesting consequence of these rules is that now investors evaluating potential investments must consider mainly the economics of the venture instead of the tax benefits or tax avoidance possibilities that an investment may generate.

At-Risk Limits

> **LO.2**
>
> Explain the at-risk limitation.

The at-risk provisions limit the deductibility of losses from business and income-producing activities. These provisions, which apply to individuals and closely held corporations, are designed to prevent taxpayers from deducting losses in excess of their actual economic investment in an activity. In the case of an S corporation or a partnership, the at-risk limits apply at the owner level. Under the at-risk rules, a taxpayer's deductible loss from an activity for any taxable year is limited to the amount the taxpayer has at risk at the end of the taxable year (the amount the taxpayer could actually lose in the activity).

TAX *in the News*	WITH TAX SHELTERS IN THE SPOTLIGHT, TAXPAYERS SHOULD BE CAUTIOUS!

Over the years, the at-risk and passive loss rules have gone a long way toward curbing abusive tax shelters. To the IRS's chagrin, however, some tax shelters are not restricted by these rules and continue to be a problem, as many reports in the media have shown. In response, the IRS has launched a major assault on tax shelters marketed to wealthy individuals. Already, the IRS has collected over $3.2 billion from taxpayers involved in the "Son of Boss" tax shelter. With other tax shelters also under attack, taxpayers who entered transactions that sounded too good to be true should be concerned.

Meanwhile, the publicity surrounding the IRS's efforts has driven a wedge between shelter marketers and their clients. As a consequence, many clients have sought damages from the accounting and law firms that developed the questionable shelters. Those firms and executives whose shelters are under scrutiny by the IRS are at risk of losing enormous amounts of money as well as their reputations.

While the amount at risk generally vacillates over time, the initial amount considered at risk consists of the following:[2]

- The amount of cash and the adjusted basis of property contributed to the activity by the taxpayer.
- Amounts borrowed for use in the activity for which the taxpayer is personally liable or has pledged as security property not used in the activity.

This amount generally is increased each year by the taxpayer's share of income and is decreased by the taxpayer's share of losses and withdrawals from the activity. In addition, because general partners are jointly and severally liable for recourse debts of the partnership, their at-risk amounts are increased when the partnership increases its debt and are decreased when the partnership reduces its debt. However, a taxpayer generally is not considered at risk with respect to borrowed amounts if either of the following is true:

- The taxpayer is not personally liable for repayment of the debt (e.g., nonrecourse debt).
- The lender has an interest (other than as a creditor) in the activity.

An important exception provides that in the case of an activity involving the holding of real property, a taxpayer is considered at risk for his or her share of any *qualified nonrecourse financing* that is secured by real property used in the activity.[3]

Subject to the passive activity rules discussed later in the chapter, a taxpayer may deduct a loss as long as the at-risk amount is positive. However, once the at-risk amount is exhausted, any remaining loss cannot be deducted until a later year. Any losses disallowed for any given taxable year by the at-risk rules may be deducted in the first succeeding year in which the rules do not prevent the deduction—that is, when there is, and to the extent of, a positive at-risk amount.

EXAMPLE 4

In 2006, Sue invests $40,000 in an oil partnership that, by the use of nonrecourse loans, spends $60,000 on deductible intangible drilling costs applicable to her interest. Assume Sue's interest in the partnership is subject to the at-risk limits but is not subject to the passive loss limits. Since Sue has only $40,000 of capital at risk, she cannot deduct more than $40,000 against her other income and must reduce her at-risk amount to zero ($40,000 at-risk amount − $40,000 loss deducted). The nondeductible loss of $20,000 ($60,000 loss generated − $40,000 loss allowed) can be carried over to 2007. ■

---

[2]§ 465(b)(1).

[3]Section 465(b)(6) defines qualified nonrecourse financing.

CONCEPT SUMMARY 11–1

Calculation of At-Risk Amount

Increases to a taxpayer's at-risk amount:

- Cash and the adjusted basis of property contributed to the activity.
- Amounts borrowed for use in the activity for which the taxpayer is personally liable or has pledged as security property not used in the activity.
- Taxpayer's share of amounts borrowed for use in the activity that are qualified nonrecourse financing.
- Taxpayer's share of the activity's income.

Decreases to a taxpayer's at-risk amount:

- Withdrawals from the activity.
- Taxpayer's share of the activity's loss.
- Taxpayer's share of any reductions of debt for which recourse against the taxpayer exists or reductions of qualified nonrecourse debt.

EXAMPLE 5

In 2007, Sue has taxable income of $15,000 from the oil partnership and invests an additional $10,000 in the venture. Her at-risk amount is now $25,000 ($0 beginning balance + $15,000 taxable income + $10,000 additional investment). This enables Sue to deduct the carryover loss and requires her to reduce her at-risk amount to $5,000 ($25,000 at-risk amount − $20,000 carryover loss allowed). ∎

An additional complicating factor is that previously allowed losses must be recaptured to the extent the at-risk amount is reduced below zero.[4] That is, previous losses that were allowed must be offset by the recognition of enough income to bring the at-risk amount up to zero. This rule applies in such situations as when the amount at risk is reduced below zero by distributions to the taxpayer or when the status of indebtedness changes from recourse to nonrecourse.

Passive Loss Limits

Classification and Impact of Passive Income and Losses

Classification. The passive loss rules require income and losses to be classified into one of three categories: active, passive, or portfolio. **Active income** includes the following:

- Wages, salary, commissions, bonuses, and other payments for services rendered by the taxpayer.
- Profit from a trade or business in which the taxpayer is a material participant.
- Gain on the sale or other disposition of assets used in an active trade or business.
- Income from intangible property if the taxpayer's personal efforts significantly contributed to the creation of the property.

Portfolio income includes the following:

- Interest, dividends, annuities, and royalties not derived in the ordinary course of a trade or business.

LO.3

Describe how the passive loss rules limit deductions for losses, and identify the taxpayers subject to these restrictions.

[4]§ 465(e).

- Gain or loss from the disposition of property that produces portfolio income or is held for investment purposes.

Section 469 provides that income or loss from the following activities is treated as *passive*:

- Any trade or business or income-producing activity in which the taxpayer does not materially participate.
- Subject to certain exceptions, all rental activities, whether the taxpayer materially participates or not.

Although the Code defines rental activities as passive activities, several exceptions allow losses from certain real estate rental activities to offset nonpassive (active or portfolio) income. The exceptions are discussed under Special Passive Activity Rules for Real Estate Activities later in the chapter.

General Impact. Losses or expenses generated by passive activities can be deducted only to the extent of income from all of the taxpayer's passive activities. Any excess may not be used to offset income from active sources or portfolio income. Instead, any unused passive losses are suspended and carried forward to future years to offset passive income generated in those years. Otherwise, suspended losses may be used only when a taxpayer disposes of his or her entire interest in an activity. In that event, all current and suspended losses related to the activity may offset active and portfolio income.

EXAMPLE 6

Kim, a physician, earns $150,000 from her full-time practice. She also receives $10,000 in dividends and interest from various portfolio investments, and her share of a passive loss from a tax shelter not limited by the at-risk rules is $60,000. Because the loss is a passive loss, it is not deductible against her other income. The loss is suspended and is carried over to the future. If Kim has passive income from this investment or from other passive investments in the future, she can offset the suspended loss against that passive income. If she does not have passive income to offset this suspended loss in the future, she will be allowed to offset the loss against other types of income when she eventually disposes of the passive activity. ∎

Impact of Suspended Losses. When a taxpayer disposes of his or her entire interest in a passive activity, the actual economic gain or loss from the investment, including any suspended losses, can finally be determined. As a result, under the passive loss rules, upon a fully taxable disposition, any overall loss realized from the activity by the taxpayer is recognized and can be offset against any income.

A fully taxable disposition generally involves a sale of the property to a third party at arm's length and thus, presumably, for a price equal to the property's fair market value. Gain recognized upon a transfer of an interest in a passive activity generally is treated as passive and is first offset by the suspended losses from that activity.

EXAMPLE 7

Rex sells an apartment building, a passive activity, with an adjusted basis of $100,000 for $180,000. In addition, he has suspended losses of $60,000 associated with the building. His total gain, $80,000, and his taxable gain, $20,000, are calculated as follows:

Net sales price	$ 180,000
Less: Adjusted basis	(100,000)
Total gain	$ 80,000
Less: Suspended losses	(60,000)
Taxable gain (passive)	$ 20,000

∎

If current and suspended losses of the passive activity exceed the gain realized or if the sale results in a realized loss, the amount of

- any loss from the activity for the tax year (including losses suspended in the activity disposed of)

in excess of

- net income or gain for the tax year from all passive activities (without regard to the activity disposed of)

is treated as a loss that is not from a passive activity. In computing the loss from the activity for the year of disposition, any gain or loss recognized is included.

EXAMPLE 8

Dean sells an apartment building, a passive activity, with an adjusted basis of $100,000 for $150,000. In addition, he has current and suspended losses of $60,000 associated with the building and has no other passive activities. His total gain of $50,000 and his deductible loss of $10,000 are calculated as follows:

Net sales price	$ 150,000
Less: Adjusted basis	(100,000)
Total gain	$ 50,000
Less: Suspended losses	(60,000)
Deductible loss (not passive)	($ 10,000)

The $10,000 deductible loss is offset against Dean's active and portfolio income. ■

Carryovers of Suspended Losses.

In the above examples, it was assumed that the taxpayer had an interest in only one passive activity, and as a result, the suspended loss was related exclusively to the activity that was disposed of. Taxpayers often own interests in more than one activity, however, and in that case, any suspended losses must be allocated among the activities in which the taxpayer has an interest. The allocation to an activity is made by multiplying the disallowed passive activity loss from all activities by the following fraction:

$$\frac{\text{Loss from activity}}{\text{Sum of losses for taxable year from all activities having losses}}$$

EXAMPLE 9

Diego has investments in three passive activities with the following income and losses for 2005:

Activity A	($ 30,000)
Activity B	(20,000)
Activity C	25,000
Net passive loss	($ 25,000)
Net passive loss allocated to:	
Activity A ($25,000 × $30,000/$50,000)	($ 15,000)
Activity B ($25,000 × $20,000/$50,000)	(10,000)
Total suspended losses	($ 25,000)

[handwritten: all 3 in 1 group]

■

Suspended losses are carried over indefinitely and are offset in the future against any passive income from the activities to which they relate.[5]

---

[5]§ 469(b).

E X A M P L E   1 0

Assume the same facts as in Example 9 and that Activity A produces $10,000 of income in 2006. Of the suspended loss of $15,000 from 2005 for Activity A, $10,000 is offset against the income from this activity. If Diego sells Activity A in early 2007, then the remaining $5,000 suspended loss is used in determining his taxable gain or loss. ■

Passive Credits. Credits arising from passive activities are limited in much the same way as passive losses. Passive credits can be utilized only against regular tax attributable to passive income,[6] which is calculated by comparing the tax on all income (including passive income) with the tax on income excluding passive income.

E X A M P L E   1 1

Sam owes $50,000 of tax, disregarding net passive income, and $80,000 of tax, considering both net passive and other taxable income (disregarding the credits in both cases). The amount of tax attributable to the passive income is $30,000. ■

Sam in the preceding example can claim a maximum of $30,000 of passive activity credits; the excess credits are carried over. These passive activity credits (such as the low-income housing credit and rehabilitation credit—discussed in Chapter 13) can be used only against the *regular* tax attributable to passive income. If a taxpayer has a net loss from passive activities during a given year, no credits can be used.

Carryovers of Passive Credits. Tax credits attributable to passive activities can be carried forward indefinitely much like suspended passive losses. Unlike passive losses, however, passive credits are lost forever when the activity is disposed of in a taxable transaction where loss is recognized. Credits are allowed on dispositions only when there is sufficient tax on passive income to absorb them.

E X A M P L E   1 2

Alicia sells a passive activity for a gain of $10,000. The activity had suspended losses of $40,000 and suspended credits of $15,000. The $10,000 gain is offset by $10,000 of the suspended losses, and the remaining $30,000 of suspended losses is deductible against Alicia's active and portfolio income. The suspended credits are lost forever because the sale of the activity did not generate any tax. This is true even if Alicia has positive taxable income or is subject to the alternative minimum tax (discussed in Chapter 12). ■

E X A M P L E   1 3

If Alicia in Example 12 had realized a $100,000 gain on the sale of the passive activity, the suspended credits could have been used to the extent of regular tax attributable to the net passive income.

Gain on sale	$100,000
Less: Suspended losses	(40,000)
Taxable gain	$ 60,000

If the tax attributable to the taxable gain of $60,000 is $15,000 or more, the entire $15,000 of suspended credits can be used. If the tax attributable to the gain is less than $15,000, the excess of the suspended credits over the tax attributable to the gain is lost forever. ■

When a taxpayer has an adequate regular tax liability from passive activities to trigger the use of suspended credits, the credits lose their character as passive credits. They are reclassified as regular tax credits and made subject to the same limits as other credits (discussed in Chapter 13).

[6]§ 469(d)(2).

Passive Activity Changes to Active. If a formerly passive activity becomes an active one, suspended losses are allowed to the extent of income from the now active business.[7] If any of the suspended loss remains, it continues to be treated as a loss from a passive activity. The excess suspended loss can be deducted from passive income or carried over to the next tax year and deducted to the extent of income from the now active business in the succeeding year(s). The activity must continue to be the same activity.

Taxpayers Subject to the Passive Loss Rules

The passive loss rules apply to individuals, estates, trusts, personal service corporations, and closely held C corporations.[8] Passive income or loss from investments in S corporations or partnerships (see Chapter 20) flows through to the owners, and the passive loss rules are applied at the owner level.

Personal Service Corporations. Application of the passive loss limitations to **personal service corporations** is intended to prevent taxpayers from sheltering personal service income by creating personal service corporations and acquiring passive activities at the corporate level.

<table><tr><td>Five tax accountants, who earn a total of $1 million a year in their individual practices, agree to work together in a newly formed personal service corporation. Shortly after its formation, the corporation invests in a passive activity that produces a $200,000 loss during the year. Because the passive loss rules apply to personal service corporations, the corporation may not deduct the $200,000 loss against the $1 million of active income. ■</td><td>*EXAMPLE 14*</td></tr></table>

Determination of whether a corporation is a *personal service corporation* is based on rather broad definitions. A personal service corporation is a corporation that meets *both* of the following conditions:

- The principal activity is the performance of personal services.
- Such services are substantially performed by employee-owners.

Generally, personal service corporations include those in the fields of health, law, engineering, architecture, accounting, actuarial science, performing arts, and consulting.[9] A corporation is treated as a personal service corporation if more than 10 percent of the stock (by value) is held by employee-owners.[10] An employee is treated as an employee-owner if he or she owns stock on *any day* during the taxable year.[11] For these purposes, shareholder status and employee status do not even have to occur on the same day.

Closely Held C Corporations. Application of the passive loss rules to closely held (non-personal service) C corporations is also intended to prevent individuals from incorporating to avoid the passive loss limitations. A corporation is classified as a **closely held corporation** if at any time during the taxable year more than 50 percent of the value of its outstanding stock is owned, directly or indirectly, by or for five or fewer individuals. Closely held C corporations (other than personal service corporations) may use passive losses to offset *active* income, but not portfolio income.

[7]§ 469(f).
[8]§ 469(a).
[9]§ 448(d)(2)(A).
[10]§ 469(j)(2).
[11]§ 269A(b)(2).

EXAMPLE 15

Silver Corporation, a closely held (non-personal service) C corporation, has $500,000 of passive losses from a rental activity, $400,000 of active income, and $100,000 of portfolio income. The corporation may offset $400,000 of the $500,000 passive loss against the $400,000 of active business income, but may not offset the remainder against the $100,000 of portfolio income. Thus, $100,000 of the passive loss is suspended ($500,000 passive loss − $400,000 offset against active income). ■

Application of the passive loss limitations to closely held C corporations prevents taxpayers from transferring their portfolio investments to such corporations in order to offset passive losses against portfolio income.

LO.4

Discuss the definition of passive activities and the rules for identifying an activity.

Passive Activities Defined

Section 469 specifies that the following types of activities are to be treated as passive:

- Any trade or business or income-producing activity in which the taxpayer does not materially participate.
- Subject to certain exceptions, all rental activities.

To understand the meaning of the term *passive activity* and the impact of the rules, one must address the following issues, each of which is the subject of statutory or administrative guidance:

- What constitutes an activity?
- What is meant by material participation?
- When is an activity a rental activity?

Even though guidance is available to help the taxpayer deal with these issues, their resolution is anything but simple.

Identification of an Activity. Identifying what constitutes an activity is a necessary first step in applying the passive loss limitations. Taxpayers who are involved in complex business operations need to determine whether a given segment of their overall business operations constitutes a separate activity or is to be treated as part of a single activity. Proper treatment is necessary in order to determine whether income or loss from an activity is active or passive.

EXAMPLE 16

Ben owns a business with two separate departments. Department A generates net income of $120,000, and Department B generates a net loss of $95,000. Ben participates for 700 hours in the operations of Department A and for 100 hours in Department B. If Ben is allowed to treat the departments as components of a single activity, he can offset the $95,000 loss from Department B against the $120,000 of income from Department A. ■

EXAMPLE 17

Assume the same facts as in the previous example. If Ben is required to treat each department as a separate activity, the tax result is not as favorable. Because he is a material participant in Department A (having devoted 700 hours to it), the $120,000 profit is active income. However, he is not considered a material participant in Department B (100 hours), and the $95,000 loss is a passive loss. Therefore, Ben cannot offset the $95,000 passive loss from Department B against the $120,000 of active income from Department A. (A complete discussion of the material participation rules follows.) ■

Recall that on the disposition of a passive activity, a taxpayer is allowed to offset suspended losses from the activity against other types of income. Therefore, identifying what constitutes an activity is of crucial importance for this purpose too.

EXAMPLE 18

Linda owns a business with two departments. Department A has a net loss of $125,000 in the current year, and Department B has a $70,000 net loss. She disposes of Department B at the end of the year. Assuming Linda is allowed to treat the two departments as separate passive activities, she can offset the passive loss from Department B against other types of income in the following order: gain from disposition of the passive activity, other passive income, and nonpassive income. This treatment leaves her with a suspended loss of $125,000 from Department A. If Departments A and B are treated as components of the same activity, however, on the disposal of Department B, its $70,000 net loss would be suspended along with the other $125,000 of suspended loss of the activity. ■

The current rules used to delineate what constitutes an activity for purposes of the passive loss limitations are provided in the Regulations.[12] These guidelines state that, in general, a taxpayer can treat one or more trade or business activities or rental activities as a single activity if those activities form an *appropriate economic unit* for measuring gain or loss. To determine what ventures form an appropriate economic unit, all of the relevant facts and circumstances must be considered. Taxpayers may use any reasonable method in applying the facts and circumstances. The following example, adapted from the Regulations, illustrates the application of the general rules for grouping activities.[13]

EXAMPLE 19

George owns a men's clothing store and a video game parlor in Chicago. He also owns a men's clothing store and a video game parlor in Milwaukee. Reasonable methods of applying the facts and circumstances test may result in any of the following groupings:

- All four activities may be grouped into a single activity because of common ownership and control.
- The clothing stores may be grouped into an activity, and the video game parlors may be grouped into a separate activity.
- The Chicago activities may be grouped into an activity, and the Milwaukee activities may be grouped into a separate activity.
- Each of the four activities may be treated as a separate activity. ■

Regrouping of Activities. Taxpayers should carefully consider all tax factors in deciding how to group their activities. Once activities have been grouped, they cannot be regrouped unless the original grouping was clearly inappropriate or there has been a material change in the facts and circumstances. The Regulations also grant the IRS the right to regroup activities when both of the following conditions exist:[14]

- The taxpayer's grouping fails to reflect one or more appropriate economic units.
- One of the primary purposes of the taxpayer's grouping is to avoid the passive loss limitations.

Special Grouping Rules for Rental Activities. Two rules deal specifically with the grouping of rental activities. These provisions are designed to prevent taxpayers from grouping rental activities, which are generally passive, with other businesses in a way that would result in a tax advantage.

First, a rental activity may be grouped with a trade or business activity only if one activity is insubstantial in relation to the other. That is, the rental activity must be insubstantial in relation to the trade or business activity, or the trade or business activity must be insubstantial in relation to the rental activity. The Regulations provide no clear guidelines as to the meaning of "insubstantial."[15]

---

[12]Reg. § 1.469–4.

[13]Reg. § 1.469–4(c)(3).

[14]Reg. § 1.469–4(f).

[15]Reg. § 1.469–4(d).

EXAMPLE 20

Schemers, a firm of CPAs, owns a building in downtown Washington, D.C., in which they conduct their public accounting practice. The firm also rents space on the street level of the building to several retail establishments. Of the total revenue generated by the firm, 95% is associated with the public accounting practice, and 5% is related to the rental operation. It is likely that the rental activity would be considered insubstantial relative to the accounting practice and the two ventures could be grouped as one nonrental activity. This grouping could be advantageous to the firm, particularly if the rental operation generates a loss! Alternatively, treating the rental operation as a *separate* activity may be advantageous if this operation produces (passive) income. The passive income could then be used to absorb otherwise nondeductible passive losses. ∎

Second, taxpayers generally may not treat an activity involving the rental of real property and an activity involving the rental of personal property as a single activity.

LO.5

Analyze and apply the tests for material participation.

Material Participation. If an individual taxpayer materially participates in a nonrental trade or business activity, any loss from that activity is treated as an active loss that can offset active or portfolio income. If a taxpayer does not materially participate, however, the loss is treated as a passive loss, which can only offset passive income. Therefore, controlling whether a particular activity is treated as active or passive is an important part of the tax strategy of a taxpayer who owns an interest in one or more businesses. Consider the following examples.

EXAMPLE 21

Dewayne, a corporate executive, earns a salary of $600,000 per year. In addition, he owns a separate business in which he participates. The business produces a loss of $100,000 during the year. If Dewayne materially participates in the business, the $100,000 loss is an active loss that may offset his active income from his corporate employer. If he does not materially participate, the loss is passive and is suspended. Dewayne may use the suspended loss in the future only when he has passive income or disposes of the activity. ∎

EXAMPLE 22

Kay, an attorney, earns $350,000 a year in her law practice. She owns interests in two activities, A and B, in which she participates. Activity A, in which she does *not* materially participate, produces a loss of $50,000. Kay has not yet met the material participation standard for Activity B, which produces income of $80,000. However, she can meet the material participation standard if she spends an additional 50 hours in Activity B during the year. Should Kay attempt to meet the material participation standard for Activity B? If she continues working in Activity B and becomes a material participant, the $80,000 of income from the activity is *active*, and the $50,000 passive loss from Activity A must be suspended. A more favorable tax strategy is for Kay to *not meet* the material participation standard for Activity B, thus making the income from that activity passive. This enables her to offset the $50,000 passive loss from Activity A against the passive income from Activity B. ∎

It is possible to devise numerous scenarios in which the taxpayer could control the tax outcome by increasing or decreasing his or her participation in different activities. Examples 21 and 22 demonstrate some of the possibilities. The conclusion reached in most analyses of this type is that taxpayers will benefit by having profitable activities classified as passive so that any passive losses can be used to offset that passive income. If the activity produces a loss, however, the taxpayer will benefit if it is classified as active so that the loss is not subject to the passive loss limitations.

As discussed previously, a nonrental trade or business in which a taxpayer owns an interest must be treated as a passive activity unless the taxpayer materially participates. As the Staff of the Joint Committee on Taxation explained, a material participant is one who has "a significant nontax economic profit motive" for taking on activities and selects them for their economic value. In contrast, a passive investor mainly seeks a return from a capital investment (including a possible reduction in taxes) as a supplement to an ongoing source of livelihood.[16] Even if the concept or the implication of being a material participant is clear, the precise meaning of the term **material participation** can be vague. As enacted, § 469 requires a taxpayer to participate on a *regular, continuous, and substantial* basis in order to be a material participant. In many situations, however, it is difficult or impossible to gain any assurance that this nebulous standard is met.

In response to this dilemma, Temporary Regulations[17] provide seven tests that are intended to help taxpayers cope with these issues. Material participation is achieved by meeting any *one of* the tests. These tests can be divided into three categories:

- Tests based on current participation.
- Tests based on prior participation.
- Test based on facts and circumstances.

Tests Based on Current Participation. The first four tests are quantitative tests that require measurement, in hours, of the taxpayer's participation in the activity during the year.

1. *Does the individual participate in the activity for more than 500 hours during the year?*

The purpose of the 500-hour requirement is to restrict deductions from the types of trade or business activities Congress intended to treat as passive activities. The 500-hour standard for material participation was adopted for the following reasons:[18]

- Few investors in traditional tax shelters devote more than 500 hours a year to such an investment.
- The IRS believes that income from an activity in which the taxpayer participates for more than 500 hours a year should not be treated as passive.

2. *Does the individual's participation in the activity for the taxable year constitute substantially all of the participation in the activity of all individuals (including nonowner employees) for the year?*

EXAMPLE 23

Ned, a physician, operates a separate business in which he participates for 80 hours during the year. He is the only participant and has no employees in the separate business. Ned meets the material participation standard of Test 2. If he had employees, it could be difficult to apply Test 2, because the Temporary Regulations do not define the term *substantially all*. ■

3. *Does the individual participate in the activity for more than 100 hours during the year, and is the individual's participation in the activity for the year not less than the participation of any other individual (including nonowner employees) for the year?*

EXAMPLE 24

Adam, a college professor, owns a separate business in which he participates 110 hours during the year. He has an employee who works 90 hours during the year. Adam meets the material participation standard under Test 3, but probably does not meet it under Test 2 because his participation is only 55% of the total participation. It is unlikely that 55% would meet the *substantially all* requirement of Test 2. ■

---

[16]*General Explanation of the Tax Reform Act of 1986* ("Blue Book"), prepared by The Staff of the Joint Committee on Taxation, May 4, 1987, H.R. 3838, 99th Cong., p. 212.

[17]Temp.Reg. § 1.469–5T(a). The Temporary Regulations are also Proposed Regulations. Temporary Regulations have the same effect as final Regu-

lations. Refer to Chapter 2 for a discussion of the different categories of Regulations.

[18]T.D. 8175, 1988–1 C.B. 191.

Tests 2 and 3 are included because the IRS recognizes that the operation of some activities does not require more than 500 hours of participation during the year.

4. *Is the activity a significant participation activity for the taxable year, and does the individual's aggregate participation in all significant participation activities during the year exceed 500 hours?*

A **significant participation activity** is a trade or business in which the individual's participation exceeds 100 hours during the year. This test treats taxpayers as material participants if their aggregate participation in several significant participation activities exceeds 500 hours. Test 4 thus accords the same treatment to an individual who devotes an aggregate of more than 500 hours to several significant participation activities as to an individual who devotes more than 500 hours to a single activity.

EXAMPLE 25

Mike owns five different businesses. He participates in each activity during the year as follows:

Activity	Hours of Participation
A	110
B	140
C	120
D	150
E	100

Activities A, B, C, and D are significant participation activities, and Mike's aggregate participation in those activities is 520 hours. Therefore, Activities A, B, C, and D are not treated as passive activities. Activity E is not a significant participation activity (not more than 100 hours), so it is not included in applying the 500-hour test. Activity E is treated as a passive activity, unless Mike meets one of the other material participation tests for that activity. ■

EXAMPLE 26

Assume the same facts as in the previous example, except that Activity A does not exist. All of the activities are now treated as passive. Activity E is not counted in applying the more-than-500-hour test, so Mike's aggregate participation in significant participation activities is 410 hours (140 in Activity B + 120 in Activity C + 150 in Activity D). He could meet the significant participation test for Activity E by participating for one more hour in the activity. This would cause Activities B, C, D, and E to be treated as nonpassive activities. However, before deciding whether to participate for at least one more hour in Activity E, Mike should assess how the participation would affect his overall tax liability. ■

Tests Based on Prior Participation. Tests 5 and 6 are based on material participation in prior years. Under these tests, a taxpayer who is no longer a participant in an activity can continue to be *classified* as a material participant. The IRS takes the position that material participation in a trade or business for a long period of time is likely to indicate that the activity represents the individual's principal livelihood, rather than a passive investment. Consequently, withdrawal from the activity, or reduction of participation to the point where it is not material, does not change the classification of the activity from active to passive.

5. *Did the individual materially participate in the activity for any 5 taxable years (whether consecutive or not) during the 10 taxable years that immediately precede the taxable year?*

EXAMPLE 27

Dawn, who owns a 50% interest in a restaurant, was a material participant in the operations of the restaurant from 2000 through 2004. She retired at the end of 2004 and is no longer involved in the restaurant except as an investor. Dawn will be treated as a material participant in the restaurant in 2005. Even if she does not become involved in the restaurant as a material participant again, she will continue to be treated as a material participant in 2006, 2007, 2008, and 2009. In 2010 and later years, Dawn's share of income or loss from the restaurant will be classified as passive unless she materially participates in those years. ∎

For withdrawals

6. *Is the activity a personal service activity, and did the individual materially participate in the activity for any three preceding taxable years (whether consecutive or not)?*

As indicated above, the material participation standards differ for personal service activities and other businesses. An individual who was a material participant in a personal service activity for *any three years* prior to the taxable year continues to be treated as a material participant after withdrawal from the activity.

EXAMPLE 28

Evan, a CPA, retires from the EFG Partnership after working full-time in the partnership for 30 years. As a retired partner, he will continue to receive a share of the profits of the firm for the next 10 years, even though he will not participate in the firm's operations. Evan also owns an interest in a passive activity that produces a loss for the year. Because he continues to be treated as a material participant in the EFG Partnership, his income from the partnership is active income. Therefore, he is not allowed to offset the loss from his passive investment against the income from the EFG Partnership. ∎

Test Based on Facts and Circumstances. Test 7 assesses the facts and circumstances to determine whether the taxpayer has materially participated.

7. *Based on all the facts and circumstances, did the individual participate in the activity on a regular, continuous, and substantial basis during the year?*

Unfortunately, the Temporary Regulations provide little guidance as to the meaning of regular, continuous, and substantial participation.[19] However, a part of the Temporary Regulations has been reserved for further development of this test. For the time being, taxpayers should rely on Tests 1 through 6 in determining whether the material participation standards have been met.

Participation Defined. Participation generally includes any work done by an individual in an activity that he or she owns. Participation does not include work if it is of a type not customarily done by owners *and* if one of its principal purposes is to avoid the disallowance of passive losses or credits. Also, work done in an individual's capacity as an investor (e.g., reviewing financial reports in a nonmanagerial capacity) is not counted in applying the material participation tests. However, participation by an owner's spouse counts as participation by the owner.[20]

EXAMPLE 29

Tom, who is a partner in a CPA firm, owns a computer store that has operated at a loss during the year. In order to offset this loss against the income from his CPA practice, Tom would like to avoid having the computer business classified as a passive activity. Through December 15, he has worked 400 hours in the business in management and selling activities. During the last two weeks of December, he works 80 hours in management and selling activities and 30 hours doing janitorial chores. Also during the last two weeks in December, Tom's wife participates 40 hours as a salesperson. She has worked as a salesperson in the computer store in prior years, but has not done so during the current year. If any of Tom's work is of a type not customarily done by owners *and* if one of its principal purposes is to avoid the disallowance of passive losses or credits, it is not counted in applying the material participation tests. It is likely that Tom's 480 hours of participation in management and selling activities will count as participation, but the 30 hours spent doing janitorial chores will not. However, the 40 hours of participation by his wife will count, and as a result, Tom will qualify as a material participant under the more-than-500-hour rule (480 + 40 = 520). ∎

---

[19]Temp.Reg. § 1.469–5T(b)(2).　　　　　　[20]Temp.Reg. § 1.469–5T(f)(3).

Limited Partners. A *limited* partner is one whose liability to third-party creditors of the partnership is limited to the amount the partner has invested in the partnership. Such a partnership must have at least one *general* partner, who is fully liable in an individual capacity for the debts of the partnership to third parties. Generally, a *limited partner* is not considered a material participant unless he or she qualifies under Test 1, 5, or 6 in the above list. However, a *general partner* may qualify as a material participant by meeting any of the seven tests. If a general partner also owns a limited interest in the same limited partnership, all interests are treated as a general interest.[21]

ETHICAL *Considerations*　　**A LOVERS' TRIANGLE AND THE PASSIVE LOSS RULES**

The troubled marriage of John and Eleanor finally reached an impasse, and they mutually agreed to divorce. Shortly after the divorce was finalized, John married Kristen. The three have known each other for years from working together to harvest the grapes of a vineyard owned by John. Prior to the divorce, each had worked 200 hours in the vineyard in the current year. The investment generates a loss for the current year, and John wants to classify the loss as active rather than passive. In order for the loss to be classified as active, the participation of John

and his spouse together must exceed 500 hours. John claims that meeting that threshold is not a problem. He worked 200 hours, and Eleanor, who was his wife when the work was done, worked 200 hours. Kristen, who files a joint return with John, also worked 200 hours. John feels it is proper to aggregate Eleanor and Kristen's participation with his own. This approach makes the loss deductible in full. "Besides," says John, "there is nothing in the law that says I can't do this." As John's tax return preparer, how do you react?

LO.6

Understand the nature of rental activities under the passive loss rules.

Rental Activities Defined. The Code specifies that, subject to certain exceptions, all rental activities are to be treated as passive activities.[22] A **rental activity** is defined as any activity where payments are received principally for the use of tangible (real or personal) property.[23] Importantly, an activity that is classified as a rental activity is subject to the passive activity loss rules, even if the taxpayer involved is a material participant.

EXAMPLE 30

Sarah owns an apartment building and spends an average of 60 hours a week in its operation. Assuming that the apartment building operation is classified as a rental activity, it is automatically subject to the passive activity rules, even though Sarah spends more than 500 hours a year in its operation. ■

Temporary Regulations, however, provide exceptions for certain situations where activities involving rentals of real and personal property are *not* to be *treated* as rental activities.[24]

EXAMPLE 31

Dan owns a DVD rental business. Because the average period of customer use is seven days or less, Dan's DVD business is not treated as a rental activity. ■

The fact that Dan's DVD business in the previous example is not treated as a rental activity does not necessarily mean that it is classified as a nonpassive activity. Instead, the DVD business is treated as a trade or business activity subject to the material participation standards. If Dan is a material participant, the business is treated as active. If he is not a material participant, it is treated as a passive activity.

Thus, activities covered by any of the following six exceptions provided by the Temporary Regulations are not *automatically* treated as nonpassive activities merely because they would not be classified as rental activities. Instead, the activities are subject to the material participation tests.

---

[21]Temp.Reg. § 1.469–5T(e)(3)(ii).
[22]§ 469(c)(2).

[23]§ 469(j)(8).
[24]Temp.Reg. § 1.469–1T(e)(3)(ii).

1. *The average period of customer use of the property is seven days or less.*   *any rental*

Under this exception, activities involving the short-term use of tangible property such as automobiles, DVDs, tuxedos, tools, and other such property are not treated as rental activities. The provision also applies to short-term rentals of hotel or motel rooms.

This exception is based on the presumption that a person who rents property for seven days or less is generally required to provide *significant services* to the customer. Providing such services supports a conclusion that the person is engaged in a service business rather than a rental business.

2. *The average period of customer use of the property is 30 days or less, and the owner of the property provides significant personal services.*   *property rental Bed & Breakfast*

For longer-term rentals, the presumption that significant services are provided is not automatic, as it is in the case of the seven-day exception. Instead, the taxpayer must be able to *prove* that significant personal services are rendered in connection with the activity. Relevant facts and circumstances include the frequency with which such services are provided, the type and amount of labor required to perform the services, and the value of the services relative to the amount charged for the use of the property. Significant personal services include only services provided by *individuals.*[25]

3. *The owner of the property provides extraordinary personal services. The average period of customer use is of no consequence in applying this test.*   *proper + service*

Extraordinary personal services are services provided by individuals where the customers' use of the property is incidental to their receipt of the services. For example, a patient's use of a hospital bed is incidental to his or her receipt of medical services. Another example is the use of a boarding school's dormitory, which is incidental to the scholastic services received.

4. *The rental of the property is treated as incidental to a nonrental activity of the taxpayer.*

Rentals of real property incidental to a nonrental activity are not considered a passive activity. The Temporary Regulations provide that the following rentals are not passive activities:[26]

- *Property held primarily for investment.* This occurs where the principal purpose for holding the property is the expectation of gain from the appreciation of the property and the gross rent income is less than 2 percent of the lesser of (1) the unadjusted basis or (2) the fair market value of the property.

EXAMPLE 32

Ramon invests in vacant land for the purpose of realizing a profit on its appreciation. He leases the land during the period it is held. The land's unadjusted basis is $250,000, and the fair market value is $350,000. The lease payments are $4,000 per year. Because gross rent income is less than 2% of $250,000, the activity is not a rental activity. ∎

- *Property used in a trade or business.* This occurs where the property is owned by a taxpayer who is an owner of the trade or business using the rental property. The property must also have been used in the trade or business during the year or during at least two of the five preceding taxable years. The 2 percent test above also applies in this situation.

EXAMPLE 33

A farmer owns land with an unadjusted basis of $250,000 and a fair market value of $350,000. He used it for farming purposes in 2004 and 2005. In 2006, he leases the land to another farmer for $4,000. The activity is not a rental activity. ∎

---

[25]Temp.Reg. § 1.469–1T(e)(3)(iv).   [26]Temp.Regs. §§ 1.469–1T(e)(3)(vi)(B) through (D).

- *Lodging rented for the convenience of an employer.* If an employer provides lodging for an employee incidental to the employee's performance of services in the employer's trade or business, no rental activity exists.

These rules were written to prevent taxpayers from converting active or portfolio income into passive income for the purpose of offsetting other passive losses.

5. *The taxpayer customarily makes the property available during defined business hours for nonexclusive use by various customers.*

EXAMPLE 34

Pat is the owner-operator of a public golf course. Some customers pay daily greens fees each time they use the course, while others purchase weekly, monthly, or annual passes. The golf course is open every day from sunrise to sunset, except on certain holidays and on days when the course is closed due to inclement weather conditions. Pat is not engaged in a rental activity, regardless of the average period customers use the course. ∎

6. *The property is provided for use in an activity conducted by a partnership, S corporation, or joint venture in which the taxpayer owns an interest.*

EXAMPLE 35

Joe, a partner in the Skyview Partnership, contributes the use of a building to the partnership. The partnership has net income of $30,000 during the year, of which Joe's share is $10,000. Unless the partnership is engaged in a rental activity, none of Joe's income from the partnership is income from a rental activity. ∎

LO.7   Interaction of the At-Risk and Passive Activity Limits

Recognize the relationship between the at-risk and passive activity limitations.

The determination of whether a loss is suspended under the passive loss rules is made *after* application of the at-risk rules, as well as other provisions relating to the measurement of taxable income. A loss that is not allowed for the year because the taxpayer is not at risk with respect to it is suspended under the at-risk provision and not under the passive loss rules. Further, a taxpayer's basis is reduced by deductions (e.g., depreciation) even if the deductions are not currently usable because of the passive loss rules.

EXAMPLE 36

Jack's adjusted basis in a passive activity is $10,000 at the beginning of 2005. His loss from the activity in 2005 is $4,000. Since Jack has no passive activity income, the $4,000 cannot be deducted. At year-end, Jack has an adjusted basis and an at-risk amount of $6,000 in the activity and a suspended passive loss of $4,000. ∎

EXAMPLE 37

Jack in Example 36 has a loss of $9,000 in the activity in 2006. Since the $9,000 exceeds his at-risk amount ($6,000) by $3,000, that $3,000 loss is disallowed by the at-risk rules. If Jack has no passive activity income, the remaining $6,000 is suspended under the passive activity rules. At year-end, he has:

- A $3,000 loss suspended under the at-risk rules.
- $10,000 of suspended passive losses.
- An adjusted basis and an at-risk amount in the activity of zero. ∎

EXAMPLE 38

Jack in Example 37 realizes $1,000 of passive income from the activity in 2007. Because the $1,000 increases his at-risk amount, $1,000 of the $3,000 unused loss is reclassified as a passive loss. If he has no other passive income, the $1,000 income is offset by $1,000 of suspended passive losses. At the end of 2007, Jack has:

- No taxable passive income.
- $2,000 ($3,000 − $1,000) of unused losses under the at-risk rules.

- $10,000 of (reclassified) suspended passive losses ($10,000 + $1,000 of reclassified unused at-risk losses − $1,000 of passive losses offset against passive income).
- An adjusted basis and an at-risk amount in the activity of zero. ∎

EXAMPLE 39

In 2008, Jack has no gain or loss from the activity in Example 38. He contributes $5,000 more to the passive activity. Because the $5,000 increases his at-risk amount, the $2,000 of losses suspended under the at-risk rules is reclassified as passive. Jack gets no passive loss deduction in 2008. At year-end, he has:

- No suspended losses under the at-risk rules.
- $12,000 of suspended passive losses ($10,000 + $2,000 of reclassified suspended at-risk losses).
- An adjusted basis and an at-risk amount of $3,000 ($5,000 additional investment − $2,000 of reclassified losses). ∎

Special Passive Activity Rules for Real Estate Activities

LO.8

Discuss the special treatment available to real estate activities.

The passive loss limits contain two exceptions related to real estate activities. These exceptions allow all or part of real estate rental losses to offset active or portfolio income, even though the activity otherwise is defined as a passive activity.

Material Participation in a Real Property Trade or Business. Losses from real estate rental activities are *not* treated as passive losses for certain real estate professionals.[27] To qualify for nonpassive treatment, a taxpayer must satisfy both of the following requirements:

- More than half of the personal services that the taxpayer performs in trades or businesses are performed in real property trades or businesses in which the taxpayer materially participates.
- The taxpayer performs more than 750 hours of services in these real property trades or businesses as a material participant.

Taxpayers who do not satisfy the above requirements must continue to treat losses from real estate rental activities as passive losses.

---

[27]§ 469(c)(7).

EXAMPLE 40

During the current year, Della performs personal service activities as follows: 900 hours as a personal financial planner, 550 hours in a real estate development business, and 600 hours in a real estate rental activity. Any loss Della incurs in the real estate rental activity will *not* be subject to the passive loss rules, since more than 50% of her personal services are devoted to real property trades or businesses, and her material participation in those real estate activities exceeds 750 hours. Thus, any loss from the real estate rental activity can offset active and portfolio sources of income. ■

As discussed earlier, a spouse's work is taken into consideration in satisfying the material participation requirement. However, the hours worked by a spouse are *not* taken into account when ascertaining whether a taxpayer has worked for more than 750 hours in real property trades or businesses during a year.[28] Services performed by an employee are not treated as being related to a real estate trade or business unless the employee performing the services owns more than a 5 percent interest in the employer. Additionally, a closely held C corporation may also qualify for the passive loss relief if more than 50 percent of its gross receipts for the year are derived from real property trades or businesses in which it materially participates.

Real Estate Rental Activities. The second exception is more significant in that it is not restricted to real estate professionals. This exception allows individuals to deduct up to $25,000 of losses from real estate rental activities against active and portfolio income.[29] The potential annual $25,000 deduction is reduced by 50 percent of the taxpayer's AGI in excess of $100,000. Thus, the entire deduction is phased out at $150,000 of AGI. If married individuals file separately, the $25,000 deduction is reduced to zero unless they lived apart for the entire year. If they lived apart for the entire year, the loss amount is $12,500 each, and the phaseout begins at $50,000. AGI for purposes of the phaseout is calculated without regard to IRA deductions, Social Security benefits, interest deductions on education loans, and net losses from passive activities.

To qualify for the $25,000 exception, a taxpayer must meet the following requirements:[30]

- Actively participate in the real estate rental activity.
- Own 10 percent or more (in value) of all interests in the activity during the entire taxable year (or shorter period during which the taxpayer held an interest in the activity).

[28]§ 469(c)(7)(B) and Reg. § 1.469–9.
[29]§ 469(i).
[30]§ 469(i)(6).

The difference between *active participation* and *material participation* is that the former can be satisfied without regular, continuous, and substantial involvement in operations as long as the taxpayer participates in making management decisions in a significant and bona fide sense. In this context, relevant management decisions include such decisions as approving new tenants, deciding on rental terms, and approving capital or repair expenditures.

The $25,000 allowance is available after all active participation rental losses and gains are netted and applied to other passive income. If a taxpayer has a real estate rental loss in excess of the amount that can be deducted under the real estate rental exception, that excess is treated as a passive loss.

EXAMPLE 41

Brad, who has $90,000 of AGI before considering rental activities, has $85,000 of losses from a real estate rental activity in which he actively participates. He also actively participates in another real estate rental activity from which he has $25,000 of income. He has other passive income of $36,000. Of the net rental loss of $60,000, $36,000 is absorbed by the $36,000 of passive income, leaving $24,000 that can be deducted against active or portfolio income because of the availability of the $25,000 allowance. ■

The $25,000 offset allowance is an aggregate of both deductions and credits in deduction equivalents. The deduction equivalent of a passive activity credit is the amount of deductions that reduces the tax liability for the taxable year by an amount equal to the credit.[31] A taxpayer with $5,000 of credits and a tax bracket of 25 percent would have a deduction equivalent of $20,000 ($5,000 ÷ 25%).

If the total deduction and deduction equivalent exceed $25,000, the taxpayer must allocate the allowance on a pro rata basis, first among the losses (including real estate rental activity losses suspended in prior years) and then to credits in the following order: (1) credits other than rehabilitation and low-income housing credits, (2) rehabilitation credits, and (3) low-income housing credits.

EXAMPLE 42

Kevin is an active participant in a real estate rental activity that produces $8,000 of income, $26,000 of deductions, and $1,500 of credits. Kevin, who is in the 25% tax bracket, may deduct the net passive loss of $18,000 ($8,000 − $26,000). After deducting the loss, he has an available deduction equivalent of $7,000 ($25,000 − $18,000 passive loss). Therefore, the maximum amount of credits that he may claim is $1,750 ($7,000 × 25%). Since the actual credits are less than this amount, Kevin may claim the entire $1,500 credit. ■

EXAMPLE 43

Kelly, who is in the 25% tax bracket, is an active participant in three separate real estate rental activities. The relevant tax results for each activity are as follows:

- Activity A: $20,000 of losses.
- Activity B: $10,000 of losses.
- Activity C: $4,200 of credits.

Kelly's deduction equivalent from the credits is $16,800 ($4,200 ÷ 25%). Therefore, the total passive deductions and deduction equivalents are $46,800 ($20,000 + $10,000 + $16,800), which exceeds the maximum allowable amount of $25,000. Consequently, Kelly must allocate pro rata first from among losses and then from among credits. Deductions from losses are limited as follows:

- Activity A {$25,000 × [$20,000 ÷ ($20,000 + $10,000)]} = $16,667.
- Activity B {$25,000 × [$10,000 ÷ ($20,000 + $10,000)]} = $8,333.

Since the amount of passive deductions exceeds the $25,000 maximum, the deduction balance of $5,000 and passive credits of $4,200 must be carried forward. Kelly's suspended losses and credits by activity are as follows:

---

[31]§ 469(j)(5).

	Total	Activity		
		A	B	C
Allocated losses	$ 30,000	$ 20,000	$10,000	$ –0–
Allocated credits	4,200	–0–	–0–	4,200
Utilized losses	(25,000)	(16,667)	(8,333)	–0–
Suspended losses	5,000	3,333	1,667	–0–
Suspended credits	4,200	–0–	–0–	4,200

■

ETHICAL *Considerations*   **HOW ACTIVE IS ACTIVE?**

Last year, George and Louise purchased several rental units near the university hoping to benefit from their expected appreciation and cash flow. Because George and Louise both have full-time jobs, they are unable to spend time managing the facilities. Consequently, they contracted with a well-regarded property manager to attract renters, collect the rents, and respond to service calls. After the close of the year, the property manager provided George and Louise with an accounting of the revenues and expenses related to the operation of the units. Though the results showed a positive cash flow, the impact of depreciation and mortgage interest expenses produced a net tax loss.

Not wanting to forgo claiming a loss on their income tax return, they chose to claim the loss under the real estate rental activity exception. Have George and Louise acted properly? *No*

LO.9

Determine the proper tax treatment upon the disposition of a passive activity.

Dispositions of Passive Interests

Recall from an earlier discussion that if a taxpayer disposes of an entire interest in a passive activity, any suspended losses (and in certain cases, suspended credits) may be utilized when calculating the final economic gain or loss on the investment. In addition, if a loss ultimately results, that loss can offset other types of income. However, the consequences may differ if the activity is disposed of in a transaction that is other than a fully taxable transaction. The following discusses the treatment of suspended passive losses in other types of dispositions.

Disposition of a Passive Activity at Death. A transfer of a taxpayer's interest in an activity by reason of the taxpayer's death results in suspended losses being allowed (to the decedent) to the extent they exceed the amount, if any, of the step-up in basis allowed.[32] Suspended losses are lost to the extent of the amount of the basis increase. The losses allowed generally are reported on the final return of the deceased taxpayer.

EXAMPLE 44

A taxpayer dies with passive activity property having an adjusted basis of $40,000, suspended losses of $10,000, and a fair market value at the date of the decedent's death of $75,000. The increase (i.e., step-up) in basis (see Chapter 14) is $35,000 (fair market value at date of death in excess of adjusted basis). None of the $10,000 suspended loss is deductible by either the decedent or the beneficiary. The suspended losses ($10,000) are lost because they do not exceed the step-up in basis ($35,000). ■

EXAMPLE 45

A taxpayer dies with passive activity property having an adjusted basis of $40,000, suspended losses of $10,000, and a fair market value at the date of the decedent's death of $47,000. Since

---

[32]§ 469(g)(2).

the step-up in basis is only $7,000 ($47,000 − $40,000), the suspended losses allowed are limited to $3,000 ($10,000 suspended loss at time of death − $7,000 increase in basis). The $3,000 loss available to the decedent is reported on the decedent's final income tax return. ■

Disposition of a Passive Activity by Gift.
In a disposition of a taxpayer's interest in a passive activity by gift, the suspended losses are added to the basis of the property.[33]

EXAMPLE 46

A taxpayer makes a gift of passive activity property having an adjusted basis of $40,000, suspended losses of $10,000, and a fair market value at the date of the gift of $100,000. The taxpayer cannot deduct the suspended losses in the year of the disposition. However, the suspended losses transfer with the property and are added to the adjusted basis of the property in the hands of the donee. ■

Installment Sale of a Passive Activity.
An installment sale of a taxpayer's entire interest in a passive activity triggers the recognition of the suspended losses.[34] The losses are allowed in each year of the installment obligation in the ratio that the gain recognized in each year bears to the total gain on the sale.

EXAMPLE 47

Stan sells his entire interest in a passive activity for $100,000. His adjusted basis in the property is $60,000. If he uses the installment method, his gross profit ratio is 40% ($40,000/$100,000). If Stan receives a $20,000 down payment, he will recognize a gain of $8,000 (40% of $20,000). If the activity has a suspended loss of $25,000, Stan will deduct $5,000 [($8,000 ÷ $40,000) × $25,000] of the suspended loss in the first year. ■

Nontaxable Exchange of a Passive Activity.
In a nontaxable exchange of a passive investment, the taxpayer keeps the suspended losses, which generally become deductible when the acquired property is sold. If the activity of the old and the new property is the same, suspended losses can be used before the activity's disposition.

EXAMPLE 48

A taxpayer exchanges a duplex for a limited partnership interest in a § 721 nonrecognition transaction (see Chapter 20 for details). The suspended losses from the duplex are not deductible until the limited partnership interest is sold. Two different activities exist: a real estate rental activity and a limited partnership activity. If the taxpayer had continued to own the duplex and the duplex had future taxable income, the suspended losses would have become deductible before the time of disposition. ■

EXAMPLE 49

In a § 1031 nontaxable exchange (see Chapter 15 for details), a taxpayer exchanges a duplex for an apartment building. The suspended losses from the duplex are deductible against future taxable income of the apartment building, because the same activity exists. ■

Utilizing Passive Losses

Perhaps the biggest challenge individuals face with the passive loss rules is to recognize the potential impact of the rules and then to structure their affairs to minimize this impact. Taxpayers who have passive activity losses (PALs) should adopt a strategy of generating passive activity income that can be sheltered by existing passive losses. One approach is to buy an interest in a passive activity that is generating income (referred to as passive income generators, or PIGs). Then the PAL can offset income from the PIG. From a tax perspective, it would be foolish to buy a

> **LO.10**
> Suggest tax planning strategies to minimize the effect of the passive loss limitations.

TAX PLANNING
Considerations

---

[33]§ 469(j)(6).   [34]§ 469(g)(3).

loss-generating passive activity unless one has other passive income to shelter or the activity is rental real estate that can qualify for the $25,000 exception or the exception available to real estate professionals.

If a taxpayer does invest in an activity that produces losses subject to the passive loss rules, the following strategies may help to minimize the loss of current deductions:

- If money is borrowed to finance the purchase of a passive activity, the associated interest expense is generally treated as part of any passive loss. Consequently, by increasing the amount of cash used to purchase the passive investment, the investor will need less debt and will incur less interest expense. By incurring less interest expense, a possible suspended passive loss deduction is reduced.

- If the investor does not have sufficient cash readily available for the larger down payment, it can be obtained by borrowing against the equity in his or her personal residence. The interest expense on such debt will be deductible under the qualified residence interest provisions (see Chapter 10) and will not be subject to the passive loss limitations. Thus, the taxpayer avoids the passive loss limitation and secures a currently deductible interest expense.

Often unusable passive losses accumulate and provide no current tax benefit because the taxpayer has no passive income. When the taxpayer disposes of the entire interest in a passive activity, however, any suspended losses from that activity are used to reduce the taxable gain. If any taxable gain still remains, it can be offset by losses from other passive activities. As a result, the taxpayer should carefully select the year in which a passive activity is disposed of. It is to the taxpayer's advantage to wait until sufficient passive losses have accumulated to offset any gain recognized on the asset's disposition.

EXAMPLE 50

Bill, a calendar year taxpayer, owns interests in two passive activities: Activity A, which he plans to sell in December of this year at a gain of $100,000; and Activity B, which he plans to keep indefinitely. Current and suspended losses associated with Activity B total $60,000, and Bill expects losses from the activity to be $40,000 next year. If Bill sells Activity A this year, the $100,000 gain can be offset by the current and suspended losses of $60,000 from Activity B, producing a net taxable gain of $40,000. However, if Bill delays the sale of Activity A until January of next year, the $100,000 gain will be fully offset by the $100,000 of losses generated by Activity B ($60,000 current and prior losses + $40,000 next year's loss). Consequently, by postponing the sale by one month, he could avoid recognizing $40,000 of gain that would otherwise result. ■

Taxpayers with passive losses should consider the level of their involvement in all other trades or businesses in which they have an interest. If they show that they do not materially participate in a profitable activity, the activity becomes a passive activity. Any income generated by the profitable business then could be sheltered by current and suspended passive losses. Family partnerships in which certain members do not materially participate would qualify. The silent partner in any general partnership engaged in a trade or business would also qualify.

EXAMPLE 51

Gail has an investment in a limited partnership that produces annual passive losses of approximately $25,000. She also owns a newly acquired interest in a convenience store where she works. Her share of the store's income is $35,000. If she works enough to be classified as a material participant, her $35,000 share of income is treated as active income. This results in $35,000 being subject to tax every year, while her $25,000 loss is suspended. However, if Gail reduces her involvement at the store so that she is not a material participant, the $35,000 of income receives passive treatment. Consequently, the $35,000 of income can be offset by the $25,000 passive loss, resulting in only $10,000 being subject to tax. Thus, by reducing her involvement, Gail ensures that the income from the profitable trade or

CONCEPT SUMMARY 11–2

Passive Activity Loss Rules: General Concepts

What is the fundamental passive activity rule?	Passive activity losses may be deducted only against passive activity income and gains. Losses not allowed are suspended and used in future years.
Who is subject to the passive activity rules?	Individuals. Estates. Trusts. Personal service corporations. Closely held C corporations.
What is a passive activity?	Trade or business or income-producing activity in which the taxpayer does not materially participate during the year, or rental activities, subject to certain exceptions, regardless of the taxpayer's level of participation.
What is an activity?	One or more trade or business or rental activities that comprise an appropriate economic unit.
How is an appropriate economic unit determined?	Based on a reasonable application of the relevant facts and circumstances.
What is material participation?	In general, the taxpayer participates in a regular, continuous, and substantial basis. More specifically, when the taxpayer meets the conditions of one of the seven tests provided in the Regulations.
What is a rental activity?	In general, an activity where payments are received for the use of tangible property. More specifically, a rental activity that does *not* meet one of the six exceptions provided in the Regulations. Special rules apply to rental real estate.

business receives passive treatment and can then be used to absorb passive losses from other passive activities. ■

As this chapter has shown, the passive loss rules can have a dramatic effect on a taxpayer's ability to claim passive losses currently. As a result, it is important to keep accurate records of all sources of income and losses, particularly any suspended passive losses and credits and the activities to which they relate, so that their potential tax benefit will not be lost.

Finally, because of the restrictive nature of the passive activity loss rules, it may be advantageous for a taxpayer to use a vacation home enough to convert it to a second residence. This would enable all of the qualified interest and real estate taxes to be deducted without limitation. However, this strategy would lead to the loss of other deductions, such as repairs, maintenance, and insurance.

KEY TERMS

Active income, 11–5	Material participation, 11–13	Rental activity, 11–16
At-risk limitation, 11–3	Passive loss, 11–3	Significant participation activity, 11–14
Closely held corporation, 11–9	Personal service corporations, 11–9	Tax shelters, 11–2
Extraordinary personal services, 11–17	Portfolio income, 11–5	

P R O B L E M   M A T E R I A L S

D I S C U S S I O N   Q U E S T I O N S

1. Congress has passed two major provisions to limit a taxpayer's ability to use tax shelters to reduce or defer Federal income tax. What are these provisions?

2. Alice invested $100,000 for a 25% interest in a partnership in which she is not a material participant. The partnership borrowed $200,000 from a bank and used the proceeds to acquire a building. What is Alice's at-risk amount if the $200,000 was borrowed on a recourse loan?

3. List some events that increase and decrease an investor's at-risk amount. What are some strategies that a taxpayer can employ to increase the at-risk amount in order to claim a higher deduction for losses?

4. James invested $10,000 in a cattle-feeding operation that used nonrecourse notes to purchase $100,000 in feed, which was fed to the cattle and expensed. His share of the expense was $18,000. How much can James deduct?

5. Explain the meaning of the terms *active income*, *portfolio income*, and *passive income.*

6. Manuel owns an interest in an activity that produces a $100,000 loss during the year. Would he generally prefer to have the activity classified as active or passive? Discuss.

7. Kim owns an interest in an activity that produces $100,000 of income during the year. Would Kim prefer to have the activity classified as active or passive? Discuss.

8. What is a suspended passive loss? Why is it important to allocate suspended losses in cases where a taxpayer has interests in more than one passive activity?

9. Upon a taxable disposition of a passive activity, the taxpayer can utilize any suspended losses and credits related to that activity. Do you agree? Explain.

10. Discuss whether the passive loss rules apply to the following: individuals, closely held C corporations, S corporations, partnerships, and personal service corporations.

11. New-Tech Services, Inc., is owned by four engineers, all of whom work full-time for the corporation. The corporation has eight other full-time employees, all on the clerical staff. New-Tech provides consulting services to inventors. The corporation has invested in a passive activity that produces a $60,000 loss this year. Can New-Tech deduct the loss in the current year? Explain.

12. Gray Corporation has $100,000 of active income and a $55,000 passive loss. Under what circumstances is Gray prohibited from deducting the loss? Allowed to deduct the loss?

13. Discuss what constitutes a passive activity.

14. The Regulations prohibit grouping rental activities in certain circumstances. Discuss these rules.

15. What is the significance of the term *material participation?* Why is the extent of a taxpayer's participation in an activity important in determining whether a loss from the activity is deductible or nondeductible?

16. Why did the IRS adopt the more-than-500-hour standard for material participation?

17. Keith, a physician, operates a separate business that he acquired nine years ago. If he participates 90 hours in the business and it incurs a loss of $20,000, under what circumstances can Keith claim an active loss?

Decision Making 18. Suzanne owns interests in a bagel shop, a lawn and garden store, and a convenience store. Several full-time employees work at each of the enterprises. As of the end of November of the current year, Suzanne has worked 150 hours in the bagel shop, 250 hours at the lawn and garden store, and 70 hours at the convenience store. In reviewing her financial records, you learn that she has no passive investments that are generating income and that she expects these three ventures collectively to produce a loss. What recommendation would you offer Suzanne as she plans her activities for the remainder of the year?

19. Rene retired from public accounting after a long and successful career of 45 years. As part of her retirement package, she continues to share in the profits and losses of the firm, albeit at a lower rate than when she was working full-time. Because Rene wants to stay busy during her retirement years, she has invested and works in a local hardware business, operated as a partnership. Unfortunately, the business has recently gone through a slump and has not been generating profits. Identify relevant tax issues for Rene.

    Issue ID

20. Some types of work are counted in applying the material participation standards, and some types are not counted. Discuss and give examples of each type.

21. Even though Sylvia is a full-time employee at a major software developer, she has never given up her love for pottery. For many years, she has spent evenings and weekends working to develop a profitable pottery business by making original pieces to sell to the general public. How should Sylvia treat the income or loss generated by her pottery venture? What are the tax issues?

    Issue ID

22. Kevin, a limited partner in Zelcova Gardens, is informed that his portion of the entity's current loss is $10,000. As a limited partner, can Kevin assume that his share of the partnership loss is a passive loss?

23. In general, the definition of a passive activity includes rental activities. However, certain activities involving rentals of real and personal property are not *treated* as rental activities. Explain.

24. How is *passive activity* defined in the Code, and what aspects of the definition have been clarified by final or Temporary Regulations?

25. Laura owns an apartment building and a videocassette and DVD rental business. She participates for more than 500 hours in the operations of each activity. Are the businesses active or passive?

26. Hilda incurs a loss of $60,000 on a real estate rental activity during the current year. Under what circumstances can Hilda treat the entire loss as nonpassive?

27. Since his college days, Charles has developed an entrepreneurial streak. After working in his family's grocery business, he has decided to start several ventures on his own. Even though Charles is independently wealthy, he is looking forward to working in each of the ventures. He plans to "drop in" on the businesses from time to time between personal trips to Europe, the Caribbean, and the South Pacific. As of the end of the year, he has established computer software stores in Dayton, Austin, and Seattle; bagel bakeries in Albany, Athens (Georgia), and Tallahassee; and mountain bike and ski rental shops in small towns in Vermont, West Virginia, Colorado, and California. Identify the tax issues facing Charles.

    Issue ID

28. Rick, a full-time real estate professional, earns $5,000 for development services rendered to an S corporation that owns and manages apartment units held for rent. He also owns an interest in the entity. His share of the S corporation's rental losses for the year totals $5,000. Identify the issues that are relevant in determining how Rick treats the items of income and loss for tax purposes.

    Issue ID

29. Elizabeth owns an interest in a dress shop that has three full-time employees; during the year, she works 450 hours in the shop. Elizabeth also owns an apartment building with no employees in which she works 1,200 hours. Is either activity a passive activity? Explain.

30. Matt owns a small apartment building that generates a loss during the year. Under what circumstances can Matt deduct a loss from the rental activity, and what limitations apply?

31. What are the differences between material participation and active participation under the passive loss rules?

32. Robert owns rental property that generally produces positive taxable income and cash flow. This year, however, Robert's current loss is $5,000. Before considering the effect of the depreciation deduction, however, the property would have generated a $1,500 profit. Robert's AGI for the year is $170,000. He asks you about the treatment of his loss for the current year. Robert also mentions that he has been considering either selling the property (within the next five years) or exchanging it for other rental property. Identify the tax issues.

PROBLEMS

33. In the current year, Lionel invests $20,000 for an interest in a partnership engaged in the wholesale distribution of plumbing supplies. Lionel is a material participant, and his share of the partnership loss is $25,000. Discuss the tax treatment of Lionel's share of the loss, and compute his at-risk amount.

34. In the current year, Bill Parker (54 Oak Drive, St. Paul, MN 55162) is considering making an investment of $60,000 in Best Choice Partnership. The prospectus provided by Bill's broker indicates that the partnership investment is not a passive activity and that Bill's share of the entity's loss in the current year will likely be $40,000, while his share of the partnership loss next year will probably be $25,000. Write a letter to Bill in which you indicate how the losses would be treated for tax purposes in the current and next years.

35. Amanda wishes to invest $40,000 in a relatively safe venture and has discovered two alternatives that would produce the following reportable ordinary income and loss over the next three years:

Year	Alternative 1 Income (Loss)	Alternative 2 Income (Loss)
1	($ 24,000)	($48,000)
2	(24,000)	32,000
3	72,000	40,000

She is interested in the after-tax effects of these alternatives over a three-year horizon. Assume that Amanda's investment portfolio produces sufficient passive income to offset any potential passive loss that may arise from these alternatives, that her cost of capital is 8% (the present value factors are 0.92593, 0.85734, and 0.79383), that she is in the 25% tax bracket, that each investment alternative possesses equal growth potential, and that each alternative exposes her to comparable financial risk. In addition, assume that in the loss years for each alternative, there is no cash flow from or to the investment (i.e., the loss is due to depreciation), while in those years when the income is positive, cash flows to Amanda equal the amount of the income. Based on these facts, compute the present value of these two investment alternatives and determine which option Amanda should choose.

36. Dorothy acquired passive Activity A in January 2001 and Activity B in September 2002. Through 2004, Activity A was profitable, but it produced losses of $200,000 in 2005 and $100,000 in 2006. Dorothy has passive income from Activity B of $20,000 in 2005 and $40,000 in 2006. After offsetting passive income, how much of the net losses may she deduct?

37. Hazel has investments in two nonrental passive activities: Activity A, acquired seven years ago and profitable until the current year, and Activity B, acquired this year. Currently, Hazel's shares of the activities' losses are $10,000 from Activity A and $6,000 from Activity B. What is the total of Hazel's suspended losses from these activities?

38. Bob, an attorney, earns $200,000 from his law practice in the current year. He receives $45,000 in dividends and interest during the year. In addition, he incurs a loss of $50,000 from an investment in a passive activity acquired three years ago. What is Bob's net income for the current year after considering the passive investment?

Decision Making

39. Emily has $100,000 that she wishes to invest and is considering the following two options:

    - Option A: Investment in Redbird Mutual Fund, which is expected to produce interest income of $8,000 per year.
    - Option B: Investment in Cardinal Limited Partnership (buys, sells, and operates wine vineyards). Emily's share of the partnership's ordinary income and loss over the next three years would be:

Year	Income (Loss)
1	($ 8,000)
2	(2,000)
3	34,000

    Emily is interested in the after-tax effects of these alternatives over a three-year horizon. Assume that Emily's investment portfolio produces ample passive income to offset any passive losses that may be generated. Her cost of capital is 8% (the present value factors are 0.92593, 0.85734, and 0.79383), and she is in the 28% tax bracket. The two investment alternatives possess equal growth potential and comparable financial risk. Based on these facts, compute the present value of these two investment alternatives and determine which option Emily should choose.

40. Ray acquired an activity several years ago, and in the current year, it generated a loss of $50,000. Ray has AGI of $140,000 before considering the loss from the activity. If the activity is a bakery and Ray is not a material participant, what is his AGI?

Decision Making

41. Wade owns two passive investments, Activity A and Activity B. He plans to dispose of Activity A, either in the current year or next year. Celene has offered to buy Activity A this year for an amount that would produce a taxable passive gain to Wade of $100,000. However, if the sale, for whatever reason, is not made to Celene, Wade feels that he could find a buyer who would pay about $5,000 less than Celene. Passive losses and gains generated (and expected to be generated) by Activity B follow:

Two years ago	($35,000)
Last year	(35,000)
This year	(5,000)
Next year	(20,000)
Future years	Minimal profits

    All of Activity B's losses are suspended. Should Wade close the sale of Activity A with Celene this year, or should he wait until next year and sell to another buyer? Wade is in the 35% tax bracket.

42. Saundra has investments in four passive activity partnerships purchased several years ago. Last year, the income and losses were as follows:

Activity	Income (Loss)
A	$ 10,000
B	(5,000)
C	(25,000)
D	(20,000)

    In the current year, she sold her interest in Activity D for a $19,000 gain. Activity D, which had been profitable until last year, had a current loss of $1,000. How will the sale of Activity D affect Saundra's taxable income in the current year?

43. Leon sells his interest in a passive activity for $100,000. Determine the tax effect of the sale based on each of the following independent facts:
    a. Adjusted basis in this investment is $35,000. Losses from prior years that were not deductible due to the passive loss restrictions total $40,000.

b.   Adjusted basis in this investment is $75,000. Losses from prior years that were not deductible due to the passive loss restrictions total $40,000.

c.   Adjusted basis in this investment is $75,000. Losses from prior years that were not deductible due to the passive loss restrictions total $40,000. In addition, suspended credits total $10,000.

44. Orange, Inc., a closely held personal service corporation, has $100,000 of passive losses. In addition, Orange has $80,000 of active business income and $20,000 of portfolio income. How much of the passive loss may Orange use to offset the other types of income?

45. White, Inc., earns $400,000 from operations in the current year. White also receives $36,000 in dividends and interest on various portfolio investments. During the year, White pays $150,000 to acquire a 20% interest in a passive activity that produces a $200,000 loss. How will these facts affect White's taxable income, assuming the corporation is:
a.   A personal service corporation?
b.   A closely held (non-personal service) C corporation?

Decision Making
Communications

46. Kristin Graf (123 Baskerville Mill Road, Jamison, PA 18929) is trying to decide how to invest a $10,000 inheritance. One option is to make an additional investment in Rocky Road Adventures in which she has an at-risk basis of $0, suspended losses under the at-risk rules of $7,000, and suspended passive losses of $1,000. If Kristin makes this investment, her share of the expected profits this year would be $8,000. If her investment stays the same, her share of profits from Rocky Road Adventures would be $1,000. Another option is to invest $10,000 as a limited partner in the Ragged Mountain Winery; this investment would produce passive income of $9,000. Write a letter to Kristin to review the tax consequences of each alternative. Kristin is in the 28% tax bracket.

Decision Making

47. Last year, Juan, a real estate developer, purchased 25 acres of farmland on the outskirts of town for $100,000. He expects that the land's value will appreciate rapidly as the town expands in that direction. Since the property was recently reappraised at $115,000, some of the appreciation has already taken place. To enhance his return from the investment, Juan decides he will begin renting the land to a local farmer. He has determined that a fair rent would be at least $1,500 but no more than $3,500 per year. Juan also has an interest in a passive activity that generates a $2,800 loss annually. How do the passive loss rules affect Juan's decision on how much rent to charge for the farmland?

Decision Making

48. The end of the year is approaching, and Maxine has begun to focus on ways of minimizing her income tax liability. Several years ago, she purchased an investment in Teal Limited Partnership, which is subject to both the at-risk and the passive activity loss rules. (Last year, Maxine sold a different investment that was subject to these rules but produced passive income.) She believes that her investment in Teal has good long-term economic prospects. However, it has been generating tax losses for several years in a row. In fact, when she was discussing last year's income tax return with her tax accountant, he said that unless "things change" with respect to her investments, she would not be able to deduct losses this year.
a.   What was the accountant referring to in his comment?
b.   You learn that Maxine's current at-risk basis in her investment is $1,000 and her share of the current loss is expected to be $13,000. Based on these facts, how will her loss be treated?
c.   After reviewing her situation, Maxine's financial adviser suggests that she invest at least an additional $12,000 in Teal in order to ensure a full loss deduction in the current year. How do you react to his suggestion?
d.   What would you suggest Maxine consider as she attempts to maximize her current-year deductible loss?

49. A number of years ago, Lee acquired a 20% interest in the BlueSky Partnership for $60,000. The partnership was profitable through 2005, and Lee's amount at risk in the partnership interest was $120,000 at the beginning of 2006. BlueSky incurred a loss of $400,000 in 2006 and reported income of $200,000 in 2007. Assuming Lee is not a

material participant, how much of his loss from BlueSky Partnership is deductible in 2006 and 2007?

50. Last year, Fran invested $40,000 for an interest in a partnership in which she is a material participant. Her share of the partnership's loss for the year was $50,000. In the current year, Fran's share of the partnership's income is $30,000. What is the effect on her taxable income for the current year?

51. Jonathan, a physician, earns $200,000 from his practice. He also receives $18,000 in dividends and interest on various portfolio investments. During the year, he pays $45,000 to acquire a 20% interest in a partnership that produces a $300,000 loss.
    a. Compute Jonathan's AGI, assuming he does not participate in the operations of the partnership.
    b. Compute Jonathan's AGI, assuming he is a material participant in the operations of the partnership.

52. Five years ago, Gerald invested $150,000 in a passive activity, his sole investment venture. On January 1, 2005, his amount at risk in the activity was $30,000. His shares of the income and losses were as follows:

Year	Income (Loss)
2005	($ 40,000)
2006	(30,000)
2007	50,000

How much can Gerald deduct in 2005 and 2006? What is his taxable income from the activity in 2007? Consider the at-risk rules as well as the passive loss rules.

53. Beth acquired an activity four years ago. The loss from the activity is $35,000 in the current year. She has AGI of $120,000 before considering the loss from the activity. The activity is an apartment building, and Beth is not an active participant. What is her AGI after considering the activity?

54. During the current year, Maria Gonzales works 1,200 hours as a computer consultant, 320 hours in a real estate development business, and 400 hours in real estate rental activities. Jorge, her husband, works 250 hours in the real estate development business and 180 hours in the real estate rental business. Maria earns $60,000 as a computer consultant, while she and Jorge lost $18,000 in the real estate development business and $26,000 in the real estate rental business. How should they treat the losses?

55. Bonnie and Adam are married with no dependents and live in New Hampshire (not a community property state). Since Adam has large medical expenses, they seek your advice about filing separately to save taxes. Their income and expenses for 2006 are as follows:

Decision Making

Bonnie's salary	$ 40,000
Adam's salary	25,000
Interest income (joint)	1,800
Rental loss from actively managed rental property	(22,000)
Adam's unreimbursed medical expenses	8,000
All other itemized deductions:*	
Bonnie	9,000
Adam	3,000

*None subject to limitations

Determine whether Bonnie and Adam should file jointly or separately for 2006.

56. Mary and Charles have owned a beach cottage on the New Jersey shore for several years and have always used it as a family retreat. When they acquired the property, they had no intentions of renting it. Because family circumstances have changed, they are considering using the cottage for only two weeks a year and renting it for the remainder

Decision Making

of the year. Their AGI approximates $80,000 per year, and they are in the 30% tax bracket (combined Federal and state). Interest and real estate taxes total $8,000 per year and are expected to continue at this level in the foreseeable future. If Mary and Charles rent the property, their *incremental* revenue and expenses are projected to be:

Rent income	$ 20,000
Rental commissions	(3,000)
Maintenance expenses	(8,000)
Depreciation expense	(10,000)

If the cottage is converted to rental property, they plan to be actively involved in key rental and maintenance decisions. Given the tax effects of converting the property to rental use, would the cash flow from renting the property be enough to meet the $12,000 annual mortgage payment?

57. During the current year, Gene performs services as follows: 1,800 hours as a CPA in his tax practice and 50 hours in an apartment leasing operation in which he has a 15% interest. Because of his oversight duties, Gene is considered to be an active participant. He expects that his share of the loss realized from the apartment leasing operation will be $30,000 while his tax practice will show a profit of approximately $80,000. Gene is single and has no other income besides that stated above. Discuss the character of the income and losses generated by these activities.

58. Ida, who has AGI of $80,000 before considering rental activities, is active in three separate real estate rental activities and is in the 28% tax bracket. She has $12,000 of losses from Activity A, $18,000 of losses from Activity B, and income of $10,000 from Activity C. She also has $2,100 of tax credits from Activity A. Calculate her deductions and credits allowed and the suspended losses and credits.

59. Ella has $105,000 of losses from a real estate rental activity in which she actively participates. She has other rental income of $25,000 and other passive income of $32,000. How much rental loss can Ella deduct against active and portfolio income (ignoring the at-risk rules)? Does she have any suspended losses to carry over?

60. Faye dies owning an interest in a passive activity property with an adjusted basis of $240,000, suspended losses of $42,000, and a fair market value of $270,000. What can be deducted on her final income tax return?

61. In 2005, Nina gave her son a passive activity (adjusted basis of $100,000, fair market value of $180,000, and $25,000 of suspended losses). In 2006, the son realizes income of $12,000 from the passive activity. What are the tax effects to Nina and her son in 2005 and 2006?

62. Tonya sells a passive activity in the current year for $150,000. Her adjusted basis in the activity is $50,000, and she uses the installment method of reporting the gain. The activity has suspended losses of $12,000. Tonya receives $60,000 in the year of sale. What is her gain? How much of the suspended losses can she deduct?

RESEARCH PROBLEMS

Note: Solutions to Research Problems can be prepared by using the **RIA Checkpoint®
Student Edition** online research product, which is available to accompany this text. It is also possible to prepare solutions to the Research Problems by using tax research materials found in a standard tax library.

Research Problem 1. George and Judy Cash own a 30-foot yacht that is moored at Oregon Inlet on the Outer Banks of North Carolina. The yacht is offered for rent to tourists during March through November every year. George and Judy live too far away to be involved in the yacht's routine operation and maintenance. They are, however, able to perform certain periodic tasks, such as cleaning and winterizing it. Routine daily management, operating, and chartering responsibilities have been contracted to

"Captain Mac." George and Judy are able to document spending 120 hours on the yacht chartering activities during the year. Determine how any losses resulting from the activity are treated under the passive activity loss rules.

Research Problem 2. Lane Mitchell (77 Lakeview Drive, Salt Lake City, UT 84109) is a married individual who files a separate return for the taxable year. He is employed full-time as an accountant and also owns an interest in a minor league baseball team. He does no work in connection with the activity and anticipates that the activity will produce a loss. He pays his wife to work as an office receptionist in connection with the activity. Her work requires an average of 20 hours a week. Write a letter to Lane and explain whether he will be allowed to deduct his share of the loss from the activity.

Communications

Research Problem 3. David Drayer (2632 Holkham Drive, Lewisburg, PA 17837) is the lead partner in a local accounting firm whose practice consists of tax consulting and compliance. The firm also serves clients by providing write-up and payroll processing services. As his firm has grown, David has developed various ways to build its business prospects.

Communications

David and his wife, Judy, created DJ Partnership to purchase an office building where David moved his practice. Because the building is larger than the practice currently needs, space is rented to other tax practitioners. In addition to providing office space, the partnership offers professional and administrative services on an exclusive basis to the tenants. These services include secretarial support, telephone answering service, tax professionals available for special projects, access to a tax research library, computer hardware technology, and miscellaneous administrative support. DJ Partnership considers its primary activity to be providing professional and administrative services to its tenants rather than being a lessor.

Because of the attractiveness of the services offered to its tenants, the building is fully leased. In the first year, Judy works full-time at the partnership, and David commits about 550 hours to its affairs. For the first year, the partnership incurs a tax loss of $60,000. Without considering the impact of the loss, David and Judy's AGI is $175,000. Write a letter to David in which you provide advice on the deductibility of the $60,000 loss for Federal income tax purposes. Because David is a professional, feel free to make use of technical language in your letter.

Partial list of research aids:
Reg. § 1.469–1T(e)(3)(ii).

Use the tax resources of the Internet to address the following questions. Do not restrict your search to the World Wide Web, but include a review of newsgroups and general reference materials, practitioner sites and resources, primary sources of the tax law, chat rooms and discussion groups, and other opportunities.

Internet
Activity

Research Problem 4. Scan the materials offered in several newsgroups frequented by tax advisers and consultants. Summarize the government's current strategies for identifying and sanctioning taxpayers and entities benefiting from and promoting abusive tax shelters.

Research Problem 5. Download and print a copy of Form 6198 and its instructions. Use these materials to complete the requirements of Problem 33.

Research Problem 6. Code § 199 (i.e., the new production activities deduction) makes reference to § 469. In what context?

PART 4

Special Tax Computation Methods, Payment Procedures, and Tax Credits

Part IV presents several topics that relate to the theme of tax liability determination. The taxpayer must calculate the tax liability in accordance with the basic tax formula and also in accordance with the tax formula for the alternative minimum tax (AMT). The basic tax formula was presented in Part I, and the AMT formula is covered in Part IV. Tax credits reduce the amount of the calculated tax liability. The specific procedures for the timing of the payment of the tax liability are also discussed.

CHAPTER 12
Alternative Minimum Tax

CHAPTER 13
Tax Credits and Payment Procedures

Alternative Minimum Tax

LEARNING OBJECTIVES

After completing Chapter 12, you should be able to:

LO.1
Explain the rationale for the alternative minimum tax (AMT).

LO.2
Understand the formula for computing the AMT for individuals.

LO.3
Identify the adjustments made in calculating the AMT.

LO.4
Identify the tax preferences that are included in calculating the AMT.

LO.5
Apply the formula for computing the AMT and illustrate Form 6251.

LO.6
Describe the role of the AMT credit in the alternative minimum tax structure.

LO.7
Understand the basic features of the corporate AMT.

LO.8
Identify tax planning opportunities to minimize the AMT.

LO.1

Explain the rationale for the alternative minimum tax (AMT).

Bob and Carol are unmarried individuals who work for the same employer and have the same amount of gross income and the same amount of deductions. Bob's tax return is prepared by Adam, and Carol's tax return is prepared by Eve. While discussing their tax liability one day at lunch, Carol is dismayed to learn that she paid $15,000 more in Federal income taxes than Bob did for the tax year. Carol meets with Eve that evening. Eve reviews Carol's tax return and assures her that her tax liability was properly calculated.

The above events raise a number of interesting questions for Bob and Carol that can be answered after completing this chapter. Why didn't Bob and Carol have the same tax liability? Were both tax returns properly prepared? Should Carol consider replacing her tax return preparer Eve with Adam? Is it possible and/or desirable for Carol to file an amended return? Should Bob do anything?

The tax law contains many incentives that are intended to influence the economic and social behavior of taxpayers (refer to Chapter 1). Some taxpayers have been able to take advantage of enough of these incentives to avoid or minimize any liability for Federal income tax. Although these taxpayers were reducing taxes legally, Congress became concerned about the inequity that results when taxpayers with substantial economic incomes can avoid paying any income tax. Such inequity undermines respect for the entire tax system.[1] To attempt to alleviate this inequity, the **alternative minimum tax (AMT)** was enacted as a backup to the regular income tax.

The individual AMT is discussed in the first part of this chapter. The corporate AMT is similar to the individual AMT, but differs in several important ways. Details of the corporate AMT are presented in the last part of the chapter.

LO.2

Understand the formula for computing the AMT for individuals.

Individual Alternative Minimum Tax

AMT Formula for Alternative Minimum Taxable Income (AMTI)

The AMT is separate from, but parallel to, the regular income tax system.[2] Most income and expense items are treated the same way for both regular income tax and AMT purposes. For example, a taxpayer's salary is included in computing taxable income and is also included in alternative minimum taxable income (AMTI). Alimony paid is allowed as a deduction *for* AGI for both regular income tax and AMT purposes. Certain itemized deductions, such as charitable contributions and gambling losses, are allowed for both regular income tax and AMT purposes.

---

[1] *General Explanation of the Tax Reform Act of 1986 ("Blue Book")*, prepared by The Staff of the Joint Committee on Taxation, May 4, 1987, H.R. 3838, 99th Cong., pp. 432–433.

[2] § 55.

TAX *in the News*   **THE AMT: FROM 155 TO 33 MILLION**

Often the tax law is changed to prevent or reduce certain perceived abuses. Such was the case when the AMT was enacted in 1969. The identifiable perceived abuse was that 155 individual taxpayers had zero Federal income tax liability despite having incomes in excess of $200,000.

Thus, the original idea behind the AMT was one of fairness, based on the premise that taxpayers with significant economic income should pay at least a minimum amount of tax.

Although this idea has not changed, the tax is fast becoming anything but fair, according to most observers. The problem is that because Congress has not significantly updated the provisions of the AMT to account for inflation, more and more taxpayers are becoming subject to the tax—an estimated 33 million taxpayers in 2010 if the law is not changed. Thus, a tax that was perceived as fair when it affected only a "few" now is perceived as unfair because it affects "many."

On the other hand, some income and expense items are treated differently for regular income tax and AMT purposes. For example, interest income on bonds issued by state, county, or local governments is *excluded* in computing taxable income. However, interest on such bonds is *included* in computing AMTI if the bonds are private activity bonds. The deduction for personal and dependency exemptions is *allowed* for regular income tax purposes, but is *disallowed* for AMT purposes.

Private Activity Bonds:
— Build Stadium.

In other cases, certain items are considered in both the regular income tax and AMT computations, but the amounts are different. For example, the completed contract method can be used to report income from some long-term contracts for regular income tax purposes, but the percentage of completion method is required for AMT purposes. Thus, the amount of income included in taxable income will differ from the amount included in AMTI. Depreciation is allowed as a deduction for both regular income tax and AMT purposes, but the *amount* of the regular income tax deduction may be different from the amount of the AMT deduction. Medical expenses are deductible in calculating both taxable income and AMTI, but the floor on the deduction is different.

Med expense floor is diff.

The parallel but separate nature of the AMT means that AMTI will differ from taxable income. It is possible to compute AMTI by direct application of the AMT provisions, using the following formula:

> Gross income computed by applying the AMT rules
> **Minus:** Deductions computed by applying the AMT rules
> **Equals:** AMTI before tax preferences
> **Plus:** Tax preferences
> **Equals:** Alternative minimum taxable income

While the direct approach for computing AMTI appears quite logical, both the tax law and the tax forms provide a very different approach. Both of these use taxable income (for Form 6251, taxable income *before* the deduction for personal exemptions and dependency deductions) as the starting point for computing AMTI, as shown in Figure 12–1. This indirect approach for computing AMTI is analogous to the indirect approach used in calculating a net operating loss.

The purpose of the AMT formula is to *reconcile* taxable income to AMTI. This reconciliation is similar to a bank reconciliation, which reconciles a checkbook balance to a bank balance by considering differences between the depositor's records and the bank's records. The reconciliation of taxable income to AMTI is accomplished by entering reconciling items to account for differences between regular income tax provisions and AMT provisions. These reconciling items are referred to as **AMT adjustments** or **tax preferences**. *Adjustments* can be either positive or negative, as shown in the formula in Figure 12–1. Tax preferences are always positive.

Adjustments. Most adjustments relate to *timing differences* that arise because of *separate* regular income tax and AMT treatments. Adjustments that are caused by

FIGURE 12–1	Alternative Minimum Taxable Income (AMTI) Formula

Taxable income
Plus: Positive AMT adjustments
Minus: Negative AMT adjustments
Equals: Taxable income after AMT adjustments
Plus: Tax preferences
Equals: Alternative minimum taxable income

timing differences will eventually *reverse;* that is, positive adjustments will be offset by negative adjustments in the future, and vice versa.[3]

For example, **circulation expenditures** can give rise to a timing difference that requires an AMT adjustment. For regular income tax purposes, circulation expenditures can be deducted in the year incurred. For AMT purposes, however, circulation expenditures must be deducted over a three-year period. This difference in treatment will be used to illustrate the role of adjustments in the formula for computing AMTI.

EXAMPLE 1

Bob had taxable income of $100,000 in 2006. In computing taxable income, he deducted $30,000 of circulation expenditures incurred in 2006. Bob's allowable deduction for AMT purposes was only $10,000. Therefore, an AMT adjustment was required in 2006 as follows:

Taxable income		$100,000
+AMT adjustment:		
Circulation expenditures deducted for regular		
income tax purposes	$ 30,000	
Circulation expenditures allowed for AMT purposes	(10,000)	
Positive adjustment		20,000
=AMTI before tax preferences		$120,000
+Tax preferences		–0–
AMTI		$120,000

Analysis of this computation shows that the allowable AMT deduction is $20,000 less than the allowable regular income tax deduction. Therefore, AMTI is $20,000 greater than taxable income. This is accomplished by entering a positive AMT adjustment of $20,000. ∎

EXAMPLE 2

Assume that Bob from Example 1 has taxable income of $95,000 in 2007. He is allowed to deduct $10,000 of circulation expenditures for AMT purposes, but is not allowed a deduction for regular income tax purposes because all $30,000 was deducted in 2006. Therefore, a *negative* AMT adjustment is required.

Taxable income		$ 95,000
–AMT adjustment:		
Circulation expenditures deducted for regular		
income tax purposes	$ –0–	
Circulation expenditures allowed for AMT purposes	(10,000)	
Negative adjustment		(10,000)
=AMTI before tax preferences		$ 85,000
+Tax preferences		–0–
AMTI		$ 85,000

[3]§ 56.

Analysis of this computation shows that the allowable AMT deduction is $10,000 more than the allowable regular income tax deduction. Therefore, AMTI is $10,000 less than taxable income. This is accomplished by entering a negative AMT adjustment of $10,000. ∎

As noted previously, timing differences eventually reverse. Therefore, total positive adjustments will be offset by total negative adjustments with respect to a particular item.

EXAMPLE 3

Refer to Examples 1 and 2. The difference in regular income tax and AMT treatments of circulation expenditures will result in AMT adjustments over a three-year period.

Year	Regular Income Tax Deduction	AMT Deduction	AMT Adjustment
2006	$30,000	$10,000	+$20,000
2007	–0–	10,000	–10,000
2008	–0–	10,000	–10,000
Total	$30,000	$30,000	$ –0–

As the last column illustrates, if positive and negative AMT adjustments with respect to a particular item are caused by a timing difference, they will eventually net to zero. ∎

The adjustments for circulation expenditures and other items are discussed in detail under AMT Adjustments.

Although most adjustments relate to timing differences, there are exceptions. See the subsequent discussion of such items under Itemized Deductions. Adjustments that do not relate to timing differences result in a permanent difference between taxable income and AMTI.

Tax Preferences. Some deductions and exclusions allowed to taxpayers for regular income tax purposes provide extraordinary tax savings. Congress has chosen to single out these items, which are referred to as tax preferences.[4] The AMT is designed to take back all or part of the tax benefits derived through the use of preferences in the computation of taxable income for regular income tax purposes. This is why taxable income, which is the starting point in computing AMTI, is increased by tax preference items. The effect of adding these preference items is to disallow for *AMT purposes* those preferences that were allowed in the regular income tax computation. Tax preferences include the following items, which are discussed in detail under AMT Preferences:

- Percentage depletion in excess of the property's adjusted basis.
- Excess intangible drilling costs reduced by 65 percent of the net income from oil, gas, and geothermal properties.
- Interest on certain private activity bonds.
- Excess of accelerated over straight-line depreciation on real property placed in service before 1987.
- Excess of accelerated over straight-line depreciation on *leased* personal property placed in service before 1987.
- Excess of amortization allowance over depreciation on pre-1987 certified pollution control facilities.
- Seven percent of the exclusion from gross income associated with gains on the sale of certain small business stock under § 1202.

---

[4]§ 57.

FIGURE 12–2	Alternative Minimum Tax Formula

Regular taxable income
Plus or minus: Adjustments
Equals: Taxable income after AMT adjustments
Plus: Tax preferences
Equals: Alternative minimum taxable income
Minus: Exemption
Equals: Alternative minimum tax base
Times: 26% or 28% rate
Equals: Tentative minimum tax before foreign tax credit
Minus: Alternative minimum tax foreign tax credit
Equals: Tentative minimum tax
Minus: Regular tax liability*
Equals: Alternative minimum tax (if amount is positive)

*This is the regular tax liability for the year reduced by any allowable foreign tax credit.

AMT Formula: Other Components

To convert AMTI to AMT, other formula components including the exemption, rates, credit, and regular tax liability must be considered. The impact of each of these components is depicted in the AMT formula in Figure 12–2.

The relationship between the regular tax liability and the tentative AMT is key to the AMT formula. If the regular tax liability exceeds tentative AMT, then the AMT is zero. If the tentative AMT exceeds the regular tax liability, the amount of the excess is the AMT. In essence, the taxpayer will pay whichever tax liability is greater—that calculated using the regular income tax rules or that calculated using the AMT rules. However, both the tax law and Form 6251 adopt this excess approach with the taxpayer paying the regular tax liability plus any AMT.

EXAMPLE 4

Anna, an unmarried individual, has regular taxable income of $100,000. She has positive adjustments of $40,000 and tax preferences of $25,000. Calculate her AMT for 2006. Anna's regular tax liability is $22,332. Her AMT is calculated as follows:

Taxable income (TI)	$100,000
Plus: Adjustments	40,000
Equals: TI after AMT adjustments	$140,000
Plus: Tax preferences	25,000
Equals: AMTI	$165,000
Minus: AMT exemption ($40,250 − $13,125)	(27,125)*
Equals: AMT base	$137,875
Times: AMT rate	× 26%
Equals: Tentative AMT	$ 35,848
Minus: Regular tax liability	(22,332)
Equals: AMT	$ 13,516

*Discussed below under Exemption Amount.

Anna will pay the IRS a total of $35,848, consisting of her regular tax liability of $22,332 plus her AMT of $13,516. ■

Exemption Amount. The exemption amount can be thought of as a materiality provision. As such, it enables a taxpayer with a small amount of positive adjustments and tax preferences to avoid being subject to the burden of the AMT.

The *initial* exemption amount in 2006 is $58,000 for married taxpayers filing joint returns, $40,250 for single taxpayers, and $29,000 for married taxpayers filing separate returns.[5] However, the exemption is *phased out* at a rate of 25 cents on the dollar when AMTI exceeds these levels:

- $112,500 for single taxpayers.
- $150,000 for married taxpayers filing jointly.
- $75,000 for married taxpayers filing separately.

The phaseout of the exemption amount is an application of the wherewithal to pay concept. As the income level increases, so does the taxpayer's ability to pay income taxes.

The following example explains the calculation of the phaseout of the AMT exemption.

Hugh, who is single, has AMTI of $192,500 for the year. His $40,250 initial exemption amount is reduced by $20,000 [($192,500 − $112,500) × 25% phaseout rate]. Hugh's AMT exemption is $20,250 ($40,250 exemption − $20,000 reduction). ∎

The following table shows the beginning and end of the AMT exemption phaseout range for each filing status.

Status	Exemption	Phaseout Begins at	Phaseout Ends at
Married, joint	$58,000*	$150,000	$382,000
Single or head of household	40,250*	112,500	273,500
Married, separate	29,000*	75,000	191,000

*See footnote 5.

EXAMPLE 5

AMT Rate Schedule. A graduated, two-tier AMT rate schedule applies to non-corporate taxpayers. A 26 percent rate applies to the first $175,000 of the AMT base ($87,500 for married, filing separately), and a 28 percent rate applies to the AMT base in excess of $175,000 ($87,500 for married, filing separately).[6] Any net capital gain and qualified dividend income included in the AMT base are taxed at the favorable alternative tax rates for capital gains (15 percent or 5 percent) rather than at the AMT statutory rates. See the discussion of the alternative tax on capital gains in Chapter 16.

Regular Tax Liability. The AMT is equal to the tentative minimum tax minus the *regular tax liability*. In most cases, the regular tax liability is equal to the amount of tax from the Tax Table or Tax Rate Schedules decreased by any foreign tax credit allowable for regular income tax purposes. The foreign tax credit is allowed as a reduction of the tentative minimum tax.

In an AMT year, the taxpayer's total tax liability is equal to the tentative minimum tax (refer to Figure 12–2). The tentative minimum tax consists of two potential components: the regular tax liability and the AMT. The disallowance of credits does not affect a taxpayer's total liability in an AMT year. However, it does decrease

---

[5]§ 55(d). For tax years beginning in 2006 and thereafter, the exemption amount is scheduled to be reduced to $45,000 for married taxpayers filing jointly, $33,750 for single taxpayers, and $22,500 for married taxpayers filing separately. However, the general consensus is that Congress is highly likely to extend the increased exemption amounts for 2006. Thus, these increased amounts are used in all AMT calculations in this chapter.

[6]§ 55(b)(1).

the amount of the AMT and, as a consequence, reduces the minimum tax credit (discussed subsequently) available to be carried forward.

It is also possible that taxpayers who have adjustments and preferences but *do not pay* AMT will lose the benefit of some or all of their nonrefundable credits. This result occurs because a taxpayer may claim many nonrefundable credits only to the extent that his or her regular tax liability exceeds the tentative minimum tax.

EXAMPLE 6

Vern has total nonrefundable *business* credits of $10,000, regular tax liability of $33,000, and tentative minimum tax of $25,000. He can claim only $8,000 of the nonrefundable credits in the current year ($33,000 − $8,000 = $25,000). The disallowed $2,000 credit is eligible for carryback and carryover. ■

For tax years 2000–2005, all nonrefundable personal credits can offset both the regular income tax (less foreign tax credit) and AMT. For tax years after 2005, only *certain* nonrefundable personal tax credits (i.e., child tax credit, adoption expenses credit, and credit for elective deferrals and IRA contributions) can offset both the regular income tax (less any foreign tax credit) and the AMT in full after all other nonrefundable personal tax credits have been utilized.[7]

AMT Adjustments

LO.3

Identify the adjustments made in calculating the AMT.

Direction of Adjustments. It is necessary to determine not only the amount of an adjustment, but also whether the adjustment is positive or negative. Careful study of Example 3 reveals the following pattern with regard to *deductions:*

- If the deduction allowed for regular income tax purposes exceeds the deduction allowed for AMT purposes, the difference is a positive adjustment.
- If the deduction allowed for AMT purposes exceeds the deduction allowed for regular income tax purposes, the difference is a negative adjustment.

Conversely, the direction of an adjustment attributable to an *income* item can be determined as follows:

- If the income reported for regular income tax purposes exceeds the income reported for AMT purposes, the difference is a negative adjustment.
- If the income reported for AMT purposes exceeds the income reported for regular income tax purposes, the difference is a positive adjustment.

Circulation Expenditures. For regular income tax purposes, circulation expenditures, other than those the taxpayer elects to charge to a capital account, may be expensed in the year incurred.[8] These expenditures include expenses incurred to establish, maintain, or increase the circulation of a newspaper, magazine, or other periodical.

Circulation expenditures are not deductible in the year incurred for AMT purposes. In computing AMTI, these expenditures must be capitalized and amortized ratably over the three-year period beginning with the year in which the expenditures were made.[9]

The AMT adjustment for circulation expenditures is the amount expensed for regular income tax purposes minus the amount that can be amortized for AMT purposes. The adjustment can be either positive or negative (refer to Examples 1, 2, and 3). A taxpayer can avoid the AMT adjustments for circulation expenditures by electing to write off the expenditures over a three-year period for regular income tax purposes.[10]

---

[7]§ 26(a)(2) as amended by the Working Families Tax Relief Act of 2004.

[8]§ 173(a).

[9]§ 56(b)(2)(A)(i).

[10]§ 59(e)(2)(A).

Depreciation of Post-1986 Real Property. The AMT depreciation adjustment for real property applies only to real property placed in service before January 1, 1999. Real property placed in service after December 31, 1998, uses the same MACRS recovery periods (see Table 8–6) for calculating the AMT as for calculating the regular income tax. Therefore, for such property, the AMT conforms to the regular income tax.

For real property placed in service after 1986 (MACRS property) and before January 1, 1999, AMT depreciation is computed under the alternative depreciation system (ADS), which uses the straight-line method over a 40-year life. The depreciation lives for regular income tax purposes are 27.5 years for residential rental property and 39 years for all other real property.[11] The difference between AMT depreciation and regular income tax depreciation is treated as an adjustment in computing the AMT. The differences will be positive during the regular income tax life of the asset because the cost is written off over a shorter period for regular income tax purposes. For example, during the 27.5-year income tax life of residential real property, the regular income tax depreciation will exceed the AMT depreciation because AMT depreciation is computed over a 40-year period.

Table 8–6 is used to compute regular income tax depreciation on real property placed in service after 1986. For AMT purposes, depreciation on real property placed in service after 1986 and before January 1, 1999, is computed under the ADS (refer to Table 8–7).

In January 1998, Sara placed in service a residential building that cost $100,000. Regular income tax depreciation, AMT depreciation, and the AMT adjustment are as follows:

EXAMPLE 7

	Depreciation		
Year	Regular Income Tax	AMT	AMT Adjustment
1998	$3,485[a]	$2,396[b]	$1,089
1999	3,636[c]	2,500[d]	1,136
2000	3,636	2,500	1,136
2001	3,636	2,500	1,136
2002	3,636	2,500	1,136
2003	3,636	2,500	1,136
2004	3,636	2,500	1,136
2005	3,636	2,500	1,136
2006	3,636	2,500	1,136

[a]$100,000 cost × 3.485% (Table 8–6) = $3,485.
[b]$100,000 cost × 2.396% (Table 8–7) = $2,396.
[c]$100,000 cost × 3.636% (Table 8–6) = $3,636.
[d]$100,000 cost × 2.500% (Table 8–7) = $2,500.

Note that if the building had been placed in service in 1999 or thereafter, there would have been no AMT depreciation adjustment for the tax year it was placed in service or for subsequent years. The depreciation for the tax year the building was placed in service would have been $3,485 ($100,000 × 3.485%) for both regular income tax purposes and AMT purposes. ∎

After real property placed in service before January 1, 1999, has been held for the entire depreciation period for regular income tax purposes, the asset will be fully depreciated. However, the depreciation period under the ADS is 41 years due to application of the half-year convention, so depreciation will continue for AMT

---

[11]The 39-year life generally applies to nonresidential real property placed in service on or after May 13, 1993.

purposes. This causes negative adjustments after the property has been fully depreciated for regular income tax purposes.

EXAMPLE 8

Handwritten note: "Abg adj AMTY ⇒ reduce"

Assume the same facts as in the previous example for the building placed in service in 1998, and compute the AMT adjustment for 2026 (the twenty-ninth year of the asset's life). Regular income tax depreciation is zero (refer to Table 8–6). AMT depreciation is $2,500 ($100,000 cost × 2.500% from Table 8–7). Therefore, Sara has a negative AMT adjustment of $2,500 ($0 regular income tax depreciation − $2,500 AMT depreciation). ■

Handwritten note: "At the end: AMT = Reg. depr."

After real property is fully depreciated for both regular income tax and AMT purposes, the positive and negative adjustments that have been made for AMT purposes will net to zero.

Depreciation of Post-1986 Personal Property.

For most personal property placed in service after 1986 (MACRS property), the MACRS deduction for regular income tax purposes is based on the 200 percent declining-balance method with a switch to straight-line when that method produces a larger depreciation deduction for the asset. Refer to Table 8–1 for computing regular income tax depreciation.

Handwritten note: "AMT : Table 8.4"

For AMT purposes, the taxpayer must use the ADS for such property placed in service before January 1, 1999. This method is based on the 150 percent declining-balance method with a similar switch to straight-line for all personal property.[12] Refer to Table 8–4 for percentages to be used in computing AMT depreciation.

All personal property placed in service after 1986 may be taken into consideration in computing one net adjustment. Using this netting process, the AMT adjustment for a tax year is the difference between the total MACRS depreciation for all personal property computed for regular income tax purposes and the total ADS depreciation computed for AMT purposes. When the total of MACRS deductions exceeds the total of ADS deductions, the amount of the adjustment is positive. When the total of ADS deductions exceeds the total of MACRS deductions, the adjustment for AMTI is negative.

Handwritten note: "MACRS − ADS"

The MACRS deduction for personal property is larger than the ADS deduction in the early years of an asset's life. However, the ADS deduction is larger in the later years. This is so because ADS lives (based on class life) are longer than MACRS lives (based on recovery period).[13] Over the ADS life of the asset, the same amount of depreciation is deducted for both regular income tax and AMT purposes. In the same manner as other timing adjustments, the AMT adjustments for depreciation will net to zero over the ADS life of the asset.

The taxpayer may elect to use the ADS for regular income tax purposes. If this election is made, no AMT adjustment is required because the depreciation deduction is the same for regular income tax and for the AMT. The election eliminates the burden of maintaining two sets of tax depreciation records.

Handwritten note: "Personal Property after 1/1/1999: no need to adj."

Tax legislation enacted in 1997 either reduced or eliminated the AMT adjustment for the depreciation of personal property. Prior to the effective date of this legislation, the difference between regular income tax depreciation and AMT depreciation was caused by longer recovery periods for the AMT (class life versus MACRS recovery periods) and more accelerated depreciation methods for the regular income tax (200 percent declining balance rather than 150 percent declining balance). The statute now provides that the MACRS recovery periods are to be used in calculating AMT depreciation. Thus, if the taxpayer elects to use the 150 percent declining-balance method for regular income tax purposes, there are no AMT adjustments. Conversely, if the taxpayer uses the 200 percent declining-balance method for regular income tax purposes, there is an AMT adjustment for depreciation. Note,

---

[12]§ 56(a)(1).

[13]Class lives and recovery periods are established for all assets in Rev.Proc. 87–56, 1987–2 C.B. 674.

however, that this AMT recovery period conformity provision applies only to property placed in service after December 31, 1998. Thus, the adjustment continues to apply for personal property placed in service before January 1, 1999.

Pollution Control Facilities.
For regular income tax purposes, the cost of certified pollution control facilities may be amortized over a period of 60 months. For AMT purposes, the cost of these facilities placed in service after 1986 and before January 1, 1999, must be depreciated under the ADS over the appropriate class life, determined as explained above for depreciation of post-1986 property.[14] The required adjustment for AMTI is equal to the difference between the amortization deduction allowed for regular income tax purposes and the depreciation deduction computed under the ADS. The adjustment may be positive or negative.

Tax legislation enacted in 1997 reduced the AMT adjustment for pollution control facilities for property placed in service after December 31, 1998. This reduction is achieved by providing conformity in the recovery periods used for regular income tax purposes and AMT purposes (MACRS recovery periods).

Expenditures Requiring 10-Year Write-off for AMT Purposes.
Certain expenditures that may be deducted in the year incurred for regular income tax purposes must be written off over a 10-year period for AMT purposes. These rules apply to (1) mining exploration and development costs and (2) research and experimental expenditures.

In computing taxable income, taxpayers are allowed to deduct certain mining exploration and development expenditures. The deduction is allowed for expenditures paid or incurred during the taxable year for exploration (ascertaining the existence, location, extent, or quality of a deposit or mineral) and for development of a mine or other natural deposit, other than an oil or gas well.[15] Mining development expenditures are expenses paid or incurred after the existence of ores and minerals in commercially marketable quantities has been disclosed.

For AMT purposes, however, mining exploration and development costs must be capitalized and amortized ratably over a 10-year period.[16] The AMT adjustment for mining exploration and development costs that are expensed is equal to the amount expensed minus the allowable expense if the costs had been capitalized and amortized ratably over a 10-year period. This provision does not apply to costs relating to an oil or gas well.

EXAMPLE 9

In 2006, Audrey incurs $150,000 of mining exploration expenditures and deducts this amount for regular income tax purposes. For AMT purposes, these mining exploration expenditures must be amortized over a 10-year period. Audrey must make a positive adjustment for AMTI of $135,000 ($150,000 allowed for regular income tax − $15,000 for AMT) for 2006, the first year. In each of the next nine years for AMT purposes, Audrey is required to make a negative adjustment of $15,000 ($0 allowed for regular income tax − $15,000 for AMT). ∎

To avoid the AMT adjustments for mining exploration and development costs, a taxpayer may elect to write off the expenditures over a 10-year period for regular income tax purposes.[17]

Similar rules apply to the computation of the adjustment for research and experimental expenditures.

Use of Completed Contract Method of Accounting.
For a long-term contract, taxpayers are required to use the percentage of completion method for AMT

---

[14]§ 56(a)(5).
[15]§§ 617(a) and 616(a).
[16]§ 56(a)(2).

[17]§§ 59(e)(2)(D) and (E).

purposes.[18] However, in limited circumstances, taxpayers can use the completed contract method for regular income tax purposes.[19] Thus, a taxpayer recognizes a different amount of income for regular income tax purposes than for AMT purposes. The resulting AMT adjustment is equal to the difference between income reported under the percentage of completion method and the amount reported using the completed contract method. The adjustment can be either positive or negative, depending on the amount of income recognized under the different methods.

A taxpayer can avoid an AMT adjustment on long-term contracts by using the percentage of completion method for regular income tax purposes rather than the completed contract method.

Incentive Stock Options. Incentive stock options (ISOs) are granted by employers to help attract new personnel and retain those already employed. At the time an ISO is granted, the employer corporation sets an option price for the corporate stock. If the value of the stock increases during the option period, the employee can obtain stock at a favorable price by exercising the option. Employees are generally restricted as to when they can dispose of stock acquired under an ISO (e.g., a certain length of employment may be required). Therefore, the stock may not be freely transferable until some specified period has passed. See Chapter 19 for details regarding ISOs.

The exercise of an ISO does not increase regular taxable income.[20] However, for AMT purposes, the excess of the fair market value of the stock over the exercise price (the *spread*) is treated as an adjustment in the first taxable year in which the rights in the stock are freely transferable or are not subject to a substantial risk of forfeiture.[21]

EXAMPLE 10

In 2004, Manuel exercised an ISO that had been granted by his employer, Gold Corporation. Manuel acquired 1,000 shares of Gold stock for the option price of $20 per share. The stock became freely transferable in 2006. The fair market value of the stock at the date of exercise was $50 per share. For AMT purposes, Manuel has a positive adjustment of $30,000 ($50,000 fair market value – $20,000 option price) for 2006. The transaction does not affect regular taxable income in 2004 or 2006. ∎

No adjustment is required if the taxpayer exercises the option and disposes of the stock in the same tax year because the bargain element gain is reported for both regular income tax and AMT purposes in the same tax year.

The regular income tax basis of stock acquired through exercise of ISOs is different from the AMT basis. The regular income tax basis of the stock is equal to its cost, whereas the AMT basis is equal to the fair market value on the date the options are exercised. Consequently, the gain or loss upon disposition of the stock is different for regular income tax purposes and AMT purposes.

EXAMPLE 11

Assume the same facts as in the previous example and that Manuel sells the stock for $60,000 in 2008. His gain for regular income tax purposes is $40,000 ($60,000 amount realized – $20,000 regular income tax basis). For AMT purposes, the gain is $10,000 ($60,000 amount realized – $50,000 AMT basis). Therefore, Manuel has a $30,000 negative adjustment in computing AMT in 2008 ($40,000 regular income tax gain – $10,000 AMT gain). Note that the $30,000 negative adjustment upon disposition in 2008 offsets the $30,000 positive adjustment when the stock became freely transferable in 2006. ∎

Adjusted Gain or Loss. When property is sold during the year or a casualty occurs to business or income-producing property, gain or loss reported for regular income

---

[18]§ 56(a)(3).

[19]See Chapter 18 for a detailed discussion of the completed contract and percentage of completion methods of accounting.

[20]§ 421(a).

[21]§ 56(b)(3).

tax may be different than gain or loss determined for the AMT. This difference occurs because the adjusted basis of the property for AMT purposes must reflect any current and prior AMT adjustments for the following:[22]

- Depreciation.
- Circulation expenditures.
- Research and experimental expenditures.
- Mining exploration and development costs.
- Amortization of certified pollution control facilities.

A negative gain or loss adjustment is required if:

- the gain for AMT purposes is less than the gain for regular income tax purposes;
- the loss for AMT purposes is more than the loss for regular income tax purposes; or
- a loss is computed for AMT purposes and a gain is computed for regular income tax purposes.

Otherwise, the AMT gain or loss adjustment is positive.

EXAMPLE 12

In January 1998, Kate paid $100,000 for a duplex acquired for rental purposes. Regular income tax depreciation, AMT depreciation, and the AMT adjustment are as follows:

	Depreciation		
Year	Regular Income Tax	AMT	AMT Adjustment
1998	$3,485[a]	$2,396[b]	$1,089
1999	3,636[c]	2,500[d]	1,136
2000	3,636	2,500	1,136
2001	3,636	2,500	1,136
2002	3,636	2,500	1,136
2003	3,636	2,500	1,136
2004	3,636	2,500	1,136
2005	3,636	2,500	1,136

[a]$100,000 cost × 3.485% (Table 8–6) = $3,485.
[b]$100,000 cost × 2.396% (Table 8–7) = $2,396.
[c]$100,000 cost × 3.636% (Table 8–6) = $3,636.
[d]$100,000 cost × 2.500% (Table 8–7) = $2,500. ∎

EXAMPLE 13

Kate sold the duplex on December 20, 2006, for $105,000. Regular income tax depreciation for 2006 is $3,485 [($100,000 cost × 3.636% from Table 8–6) × (11.5/12)]. AMT depreciation for 2006 is $2,396 [($100,000 cost × 2.500% from Table 8–7) × (11.5/12)]. Kate's positive AMT adjustment for 2006 is $1,089 ($3,485 regular income tax depreciation − $2,396 AMT depreciation). ∎

Because depreciation on the duplex differs for regular income tax and AMT purposes, the adjusted basis is different for regular income tax and AMT purposes. Consequently, the gain or loss on disposition of the duplex is different for regular income tax and AMT purposes.

[22]§ 56(a)(6).

EXAMPLE 14

The adjusted basis of Kate's duplex is $67,578 for regular income tax purposes and $77,708 for AMT purposes.

	Regular Income Tax	AMT
Cost	$100,000	$100,000
Depreciation		
1998	(3,485)	(2,396)
1999	(3,636)	(2,500)
2000	(3,636)	(2,500)
2001	(3,636)	(2,500)
2002	(3,636)	(2,500)
2003	(3,636)	(2,500)
2004	(3,636)	(2,500)
2005	(3,636)	(2,500)
2006	(3,485)	(2,396)
Adjusted basis	$ 67,578	$ 77,708

The regular income tax gain is $37,422, and the AMT gain is $27,292.

	Regular Income Tax	AMT
Amount realized	$105,000	$105,000
Adjusted basis	(67,578)	(77,708)
Recognized gain	$ 37,422	$ 27,292

Because the regular income tax and AMT gain on the sale of the duplex differ, Kate must make a negative AMT adjustment of $10,130 ($37,422 regular income tax gain − $27,292 AMT gain). Note that this negative adjustment offsets the $10,130 total of the nine positive adjustments for depreciation ($1,089 in 1998 + $1,136 in 1999 + $1,136 in 2000 + $1,136 in 2001 + $1,136 in 2002 + $1,136 in 2003 + $1,136 in 2004 + $1,136 in 2005 + $1,089 in 2006). ■

Passive Activity Losses. Losses on passive activities are not deductible in computing either the regular income tax or the AMT. This does not, however, eliminate the possibility of adjustments attributable to passive activities.

The rules for computing taxable income differ from the rules for computing AMTI. It follows, then, that the rules for computing a loss for regular income tax purposes differ from the AMT rules for computing a loss. Therefore, any *passive loss* computed for regular income tax purposes may differ from the passive loss computed for AMT purposes.[23]

EXAMPLE 15

Soong acquired two passive activities in 2006. He received net passive income of $10,000 from Activity A and had no AMT adjustments or preferences in connection with the activity. Activity B had gross income of $27,000 and operating expenses (not affected by AMT adjustments or preferences) of $19,000. Soong claimed MACRS depreciation of $20,000 for Activity B; depreciation under the ADS would have been $15,000. In addition, Soong deducted $10,000 of percentage depletion in excess of basis. The following comparison illustrates the differences in the computation of the passive loss for regular income tax and AMT purposes for Activity B.

---

[23]See Chapter 11.

	Regular Income Tax	AMT
Gross income	$ 27,000	$ 27,000
Deductions:		
Operating expenses	($ 19,000)	($ 19,000)
Depreciation	(20,000)	(15,000)
Depletion	(10,000)	–0–
Total deductions	($ 49,000)	($ 34,000)
Passive loss	($ 22,000)	($ 7,000)

Because the adjustment for depreciation ($5,000) applies and the preference for depletion ($10,000) is not taken into account in computing AMTI, the regular income tax passive activity loss of $22,000 for Activity B is reduced by these amounts, resulting in a passive activity loss of $7,000 for AMT purposes. ■

For regular income tax purposes, Soong would offset the $10,000 of net passive income from Activity A with $10,000 of the passive loss from Activity B. For AMT purposes, he would offset the $10,000 of net passive income from Activity A with the $7,000 passive activity loss allowed from Activity B, resulting in passive activity income of $3,000. Thus, in computing AMTI, Soong makes a positive passive loss adjustment of $3,000 [$10,000 (passive activity loss allowed for regular income tax) − $7,000 (passive activity loss allowed for the AMT)]. To avoid duplication, the AMT adjustment for depreciation and the preference for depletion are *not* reported separately. They are accounted for in determining the AMT passive loss adjustment.

EXAMPLE 16

Assume the same facts as in the previous example. For regular income tax purposes, Soong has a suspended passive loss of $12,000 [$22,000 (amount of loss) − $10,000 (used in 2006)]. This suspended passive loss can offset passive income in the future or can offset active or portfolio income when Soong disposes of the loss activity (refer to Chapter 11). For AMT purposes, Soong's suspended passive loss is $0 [$7,000 (amount of loss) − $7,000 (amount used in 2006)]. ■

Alternative Tax Net Operating Loss Deduction. In computing taxable income, taxpayers are allowed to deduct net operating loss (NOL) carryovers and carrybacks (refer to Chapter 7). The regular income tax NOL must be modified, however, in computing AMTI. The starting point in computing the **alternative tax NOL deduction (ATNOLD)** is the NOL computed for regular income tax purposes. The regular income tax NOL is then modified for AMT adjustments and tax preferences with the result being the ATNOLD. Thus, preferences and adjustment items that have benefited the taxpayer in computing the regular income tax NOL are added back, thereby reducing or eliminating the ATNOLD.[24]

EXAMPLE 17

In 2006, Max incurred an NOL of $100,000. Max had no AMT adjustments, but his deductions included tax preferences of $18,000. His ATNOLD carryback to 2004 is $82,000 ($100,000 regular income tax NOL − $18,000 tax preferences deducted in computing the NOL). ■

In Example 17, if the adjustment was not made to the regular income tax NOL, the $18,000 in tax preference items deducted in 2006 would have the effect of reducing AMTI in the year (or years) the 2006 NOL is utilized. This would weaken the entire concept of the AMT.

A ceiling exists on the amount of the ATNOLD that can be deducted in the carryback or carryforward year. The deduction is limited to 90 percent of AMTI (before the ATNOLD) for the carryback or carryforward year.

---

[24]§ 56(a)(4).

EXAMPLE 18

Assume the same facts as in the previous example. Max's AMTI (before the ATNOLD) in 2004 is $90,000. Therefore, of the $82,000 ATNOLD carried back to 2004 from 2006, only $81,000 ($90,000 × 90%) can be used in recalculating the 2004 AMT. The unused $1,000 of 2006 ATNOLD is now carried to 2005 for use in recalculating the 2005 AMT. ■

A taxpayer who has an ATNOLD that is carried back or over to another year must use the ATNOLD against AMTI in the carryback or carryforward year even if the regular income tax, rather than the AMT, applies.

EXAMPLE 19

Emily's ATNOLD for 2007 (carried over from 2006) is $10,000. AMTI before considering the ATNOLD is $25,000. If Emily's regular income tax exceeds the AMT, the AMT does not apply. Nevertheless, Emily's ATNOLD of $10,000 is "used up" in 2007 and is not available for carryover to a later year. ■

For regular income tax purposes, the NOL generally can be carried back 2 years and forward 20 years. However, the taxpayer may elect to forgo the 2-year carryback. These rules generally apply to the ATNOLD as well, except that the election to forgo the 2-year carryback is available for the ATNOLD only if the taxpayer elected it for the regular income tax NOL.

Itemized Deductions. Most of the itemized deductions that are allowed for regular income tax purposes are allowed for AMT purposes. Itemized deductions that are allowed for AMT purposes include the following:

- Casualty losses.
- Gambling losses.
- Charitable contributions.
- Medical expenses in excess of 10 percent of AGI.
- Estate tax on income in respect of a decedent.
- Qualified interest.

Taxes (state, local, and foreign income taxes, sales taxes, and property taxes) and miscellaneous itemized deductions that are subject to the 2 percent-of-AGI floor are not allowed in computing AMT.[25] A positive AMT adjustment in the total amount of the regular income tax deduction for each is required.

If the taxpayer's gross income includes the recovery of any tax deducted as an itemized deduction for regular income tax purposes, a negative AMT adjustment in the amount of the recovery is allowed for AMTI purposes.[26] For example, state, local, and foreign income taxes can be deducted for regular income tax purposes, but cannot be deducted in computing AMTI. Because of this, any refund of such taxes from a prior year is not included in AMTI. Therefore, in calculating AMTI, the taxpayer must make a negative adjustment for an income tax refund that has been included in computing regular taxable income. Under the tax benefit rule, a tax refund is included in regular taxable income to the extent that the taxpayer obtained a tax benefit by deducting the tax in a prior year.

Cutback Adjustment. The 3 percent cutback adjustment that applies to regular income tax itemized deductions of certain high-income taxpayers (refer to Chapter 10) does not apply in computing AMT.[27] The effect of the 3 percent cutback adjustment is to disallow a portion of the taxpayer's itemized deductions for regular income tax purposes. Because this cutback adjustment does not apply for AMT purposes, taxable income, which is the starting point for computing AMTI, must be reduced by the amount of the disallowed deductions. This reduction is a negative AMT adjustment.

[25]§ 56(b)(1)(A).
[26]§ 56(b)(1)(D).

[27]§ 56(b)(1)(F).

Medical Expenses. The rules for determining the AMT deductions for medical expenses are sufficiently complex to require further explanation. For regular income tax purposes, medical expenses are deductible to the extent they exceed 7.5 percent of AGI. However, for AMT purposes, medical expenses are deductible only to the extent they exceed 10 percent of AGI.[28]

EXAMPLE 20

Joann incurred medical expenses of $16,000 in 2006. She had AGI of $100,000 for the year. Her AMT adjustment for medical expenses is computed as follows:

	Regular Income Tax	AMT
Medical expenses incurred	$16,000	$ 16,000
Less reduction:		
$100,000 AGI × 7.5%	(7,500)	
$100,000 AGI × 10%		(10,000)
Medical expense deduction	$ 8,500	$ 6,000

Joann's AMT adjustment for medical expenses is $2,500 ($8,500 regular income tax deduction − $6,000 AMT deduction). ∎

Interest in General. The AMT itemized deduction allowed for interest expense includes only qualified housing interest and investment interest to the extent of net investment income that is included in the determination of AMTI.[29] Any interest that is deducted in calculating the regular income tax that is not permitted in calculating the AMT is treated as a positive adjustment.

In computing regular taxable income, taxpayers who itemize can deduct the following types of interest (refer to Chapter 10):

* Qualified residence interest.
* Investment interest, subject to the investment interest limitations (discussed under Investment Interest below).
* Qualified interest on student loans.

Housing Interest. Under current regular income tax rules, taxpayers who itemize can deduct *qualified residence interest* on up to two residences. The deduction is limited to interest on acquisition indebtedness up to $1 million and home equity indebtedness up to $100,000. Acquisition indebtedness is debt that is incurred in acquiring, constructing, or substantially improving a qualified residence of the taxpayer and is secured by the residence. Home equity indebtedness is indebtedness secured by a qualified residence of the taxpayer, but does not include acquisition indebtedness.

EXAMPLE 21

Gail, who used the proceeds of a mortgage to acquire a personal residence, paid mortgage interest of $112,000 in 2006. Of this amount, $14,000 is attributable to acquisition indebtedness in excess of $1 million. For regular income tax purposes, Gail may deduct mortgage interest of $98,000 ($112,000 total − $14,000 disallowed). ∎

The mortgage interest deduction for AMT purposes is limited to *qualified housing interest*, rather than *qualified residence interest*. Qualified housing interest includes only interest incurred to acquire, construct, or substantially improve the taxpayer's principal residence and such interest on one other qualified dwelling used for personal purposes. A home equity loan qualifies only if it meets the definition of qualified housing interest, which frequently is not the case. When additional mortgage

[28]§ 56(b)(1)(B).   [29]§ 56(b)(1)(C).

interest is incurred (e.g., a mortgage refinancing), interest paid is deductible as qualified housing interest for AMT purposes only if:

- The proceeds are used to acquire or substantially improve a qualified residence.
- Interest on the prior loan was qualified housing interest.
- The amount of the loan was not increased.

A positive AMT adjustment is required in the amount of the difference between qualified *residence* interest allowed as an itemized deduction for regular income tax purposes and qualified *housing* interest allowed in the determination of AMTI.

Investment Interest. Investment interest is deductible for regular income tax purposes and for AMT purposes to the extent of qualified net investment income.

EXAMPLE 22

For the year, Dan had net investment income of $16,000 before deducting investment interest. He incurred investment interest expense of $30,000 during the year. His investment interest deduction is $16,000. ■

Even though investment interest is deductible for both regular income tax and AMT purposes, an adjustment is required if the amount of investment interest deductible for regular income tax purposes differs from the amount deductible for AMT purposes. For example, an adjustment will arise if proceeds from a home equity loan are used to purchase investments. Interest on a home equity loan is deductible as qualified residence interest for regular income tax purposes, but is not deductible for AMT purposes unless the proceeds are used to acquire or substantially improve a qualified residence. For AMT purposes, however, interest on a home equity loan is deductible as investment interest expense if proceeds from the loan are used for investment purposes.

To determine the AMT adjustment for investment interest expense, it is necessary to compute the investment interest deduction for both regular income tax and AMT purposes. This computation is illustrated in the following example.

EXAMPLE 23

Tom had $20,000 interest income from corporate bonds and $5,000 dividends from preferred stock. He reported the following amounts of investment income for regular income tax and AMT purposes:

	Regular Income Tax	AMT
Corporate bond interest	$20,000	$20,000
Preferred stock dividends	5,000	5,000
Net investment income	$25,000	$25,000

Tom incurred investment interest expense of $10,000 related to the corporate bonds. He also incurred $4,000 interest on a home equity loan and used the proceeds of the loan to purchase preferred stock. For regular income tax purposes, this $4,000 is deductible as qualified residence interest. His *investment* interest expense for regular income tax and AMT purposes is computed below:

	Regular Income Tax	AMT
To carry corporate bonds	$10,000	$10,000
On home equity loan to carry preferred stock	–0–	4,000
Total investment interest expense	$10,000	$14,000

Investment interest expense is deductible to the extent of net investment income. Because the amount deductible for regular income tax purposes ($10,000) differs from the amount deductible for AMT purposes ($14,000), an AMT adjustment is required. The adjustment is computed as follows:

AMT deduction for investment interest expense	$ 14,000
Regular income tax deduction for investment interest expense	(10,000)
Negative AMT adjustment	$ 4,000 ■

As discussed subsequently under AMT Preferences, the interest on private activity bonds is a tax preference for AMT purposes. Such interest can also affect the calculation of the AMT investment interest deduction in that it is included in the calculation of net investment income.

Other Adjustments. The standard deduction and the personal and dependency exemption also give rise to AMT adjustments.[30] The standard deduction is not allowed as a deduction in computing AMTI. Although a person who does not itemize is rarely subject to the AMT, it is possible. In such a case, the taxpayer is required to enter a positive adjustment for the standard deduction in computing the AMT.

The personal and dependency exemption amount deducted for regular income tax purposes is not allowed in computing AMT. Therefore, taxpayers must enter a positive AMT adjustment for the personal and dependency exemption amount claimed in computing the regular income tax. A separate exemption (see Exemption Amount) is allowed for AMT purposes. To allow both the regular income tax exemption amount and the AMT exemption amount would result in extra benefits for taxpayers.

EXAMPLE 24

Eli, who is single, has no dependents and does not itemize deductions. He earned a salary of $108,450 in 2006. Based on this information, Eli's taxable income for 2006 is $100,000 ($108,450 − $5,150 standard deduction − $3,300 exemption). ■

EXAMPLE 25

Assume the same facts as in Example 24. In addition, assume Eli's tax preferences for the year totaled $150,000. Eli's AMTI is $258,450 ($100,000 taxable income + $5,150 adjustment for standard deduction + $3,300 adjustment for exemption + $150,000 tax preferences). ■

AMT Preferences

LO.4

Identify the tax preferences that are included in calculating the AMT.

Percentage Depletion. Congress originally enacted the percentage depletion rules to provide taxpayers with incentives to invest in the development of specified natural resources. Percentage depletion is computed by multiplying a rate specified in the Code times the gross income from the property (refer to Chapter 8).[31] The percentage rate is based on the type of mineral involved. The basis of the property is reduced by the amount of depletion taken until the basis reaches zero. However, once the basis of the property reaches zero, taxpayers are allowed to continue taking percentage depletion deductions. Thus, over the life of the property, depletion deductions may greatly exceed the cost of the property.

The percentage depletion preference is equal to the excess of the regular income tax deduction for percentage depletion over the adjusted basis of the property at the end of the taxable year.[32] Basis is determined without regard to the depletion deduction for the taxable year. This preference item is figured separately for each piece of property for which the taxpayer is claiming depletion.

---

[30]§ 56(b)(1)(E).

[31]§ 613(a).

[32]§ 57(a)(1). Note that the preference label does not apply to percentage depletion on oil and gas wells for independent producers and royalty owners as defined in § 613A(c).

TAX *in the News*   BEING TREATED LIKE THE RICH

The United States is frequently described as the land of opportunity, where an individual can come from humble beginnings and end up very wealthy. Needless to say, being rich is perceived as superior to being poor.

Of course, there are some negatives associated with being rich. As income grows, so does the percentage paid in Federal income tax (i.e., progressive tax rates ranging from 10 percent to 35 percent). Also, as a rich person, you are likely to be subject to the alternative minimum tax (AMT).

Historically, the above statement regarding the AMT was true. It was supposed to apply only to upper-income taxpayers who were otherwise not paying their fair share of Federal income tax. However, as the data in the table indicate, the AMT has been creeping up on a growing number of taxpayers, many of whom do not consider themselves to be rich and are better described as middle class.

Factors likely to trigger the AMT for the middle class include large itemized deductions for state income and property taxes, high medical expenses, home equity debt not used for acquiring or improving a residence, and a large number of personal and dependency exemptions.

Although Congress has modified the AMT on several occasions (sometimes with the objective of restricting its scope), the number of taxpayers covered continues to grow.

According to projections, the 10 million taxpayer mark may be reached in 2005.

Year	Number of Form 1040s Filed with AMT Imposed
1990	100,000
1991	200,000
1992	300,000
1993	300,000
1994	400,000
1995	400,000
1996	500,000
1997	600,000
1998	900,000
1999	1,000,000
2000	1,300,000
2001	1,100,000
2002	1,900,000
2003	2,400,000

Source: *Adapted from "Class War Revelation,"* Wall Street Journal, *April 15, 2005, p. A10.*

EXAMPLE 26

Depletion = $22K
Basis = $10K
AMT + $12K

Kim owns a mineral property that qualifies for a 22% depletion rate. The basis of the property at the beginning of the year is $10,000. Gross income from the property for the year is $100,000. For regular income tax purposes, Kim's percentage depletion deduction (assume it is not limited by taxable income from the property) is $22,000. For AMT purposes, Kim has a tax preference of $12,000 ($22,000 − $10,000). ■

Intangible Drilling Costs. In computing the regular income tax, taxpayers are allowed to deduct certain intangible drilling and development costs in the year incurred, although such costs are normally capital in nature (refer to Chapter 8). The deduction is allowed for costs incurred in connection with oil and gas wells and geothermal wells.

For AMT purposes, excess intangible drilling costs (IDC) for the year are treated as a preference.[33] The preference for excess IDC is computed as follows:

> **IDC expensed in the year incurred**
> **Minus:** Deduction if IDC were capitalized and amortized over 10 years
> **Equals:** Excess of IDC expense over amortization
> **Minus:** 65% of net oil and gas and geothermal income
> **Equals:** Tax preference item

---

[33]§ 57(a)(2).

Intang. Drilling Cost

Ben, who incurred IDC of $50,000 during the year, elected to expense that amount. His net oil and gas income for the year was $60,000. Ben's tax preference for IDC is $6,000 [($50,000 IDC − $5,000 amortization) −(65% × $60,000 income)]. ∎

EXAMPLE 27

IDC expense $50K
10/yr amort.   ($5K)
                   ─────
                   $45K
65% of $60K   ($39K)
                   ─────
AMT Pref. =   6K

A taxpayer can avoid the preference for IDC by electing to write off the expenditures over a 10-year period for regular income tax purposes.

Interest on Private Activity Bonds. Income from private activity bonds is not included in taxable income, and expenses related to carrying such bonds are not deductible for regular income tax purposes. However, interest on private activity bonds is included as a preference in computing AMTI. Therefore, expenses incurred in carrying the bonds are offset against the interest income in computing the tax preference.[34]

The Code contains a lengthy, complex definition of private activity bonds.[35] In general, private activity bonds are bonds issued by states or municipalities with more than 10 percent of the proceeds being used for private business use. For example, a bond issued by a city whose proceeds are used to construct a factory that is leased to a private business at a favorable rate is a private activity bond.

ETHICAL *Considerations*   TAX-EXEMPT BONDS AND THE AMT

Glenn, who is age 32, single, and in the 25 percent tax bracket, recently inherited $1 million of municipal bonds from his mother. Rather than change investments, Glenn decides to keep the bonds for the time being.

The information he received from the municipality shortly after the end of the year has confused Glenn about the tax treatment of the bond interest. He had thought that interest on all municipal bonds is tax-exempt, but he recently read an article that explained that interest from bonds classified as private activity bonds is excludible from income for regular income tax purposes but is a tax preference for the AMT. Glenn has asked the municipality for clarification on the

status of the bonds, but he has received no answer. A review of his mother's tax returns for the past three years reveals that none included any income from the bonds.

Since he wants to file his return this week, Glenn has to decide what to do about the bond interest. He is considering not treating the bonds as private activity bonds based on what his mother did. His justification for this position is that his mother was an astute businesswoman and would have used the proper treatment. Furthermore, if Glenn does not treat the bonds as private activity bonds, the interest will not be subject to either the regular income tax or the AMT. Evaluate Glenn's proposal.

Depreciation. For real property and leased personal property placed in service before 1987, there is an AMT preference for the excess of accelerated depreciation over straight-line depreciation.[36] However, examination of the cost recovery tables for pre-1987 real property (refer to Chapter 8) reveals that from the eighth year on, accelerated depreciation will not exceed straight-line depreciation. Consequently, taxpayers no longer have preferences attributable to pre-1987 real property.

Accelerated depreciation on pre-1987 leased personal property was computed using specified ACRS percentages. AMT depreciation was based on the straight-line method, which was computed using the half-year convention, no salvage value, and a longer recovery period.[37] As a result, in the early years of the life of the asset, the cost recovery allowance used in computing the regular income tax was greater than the straight-line depreciation deduction allowed in computing AMT. The excess depreciation was treated as a tax preference item. For all leased personal property placed in service before 1987 (3-year, 5-year, 10-year, and 15-year public utility

---

[34]§ 57(a)(5).
[35]§ 141.
[36]§ 57(a)(6).

[37]The specified lives for AMT purposes are 5 years for 3-year property, 8 years for 5-year property, 15 years for 10-year property, and 22 years for 15-year property.

TAX *in the News*	DISTINGUISHING BETWEEN TAXABLE AND EXEMPT BONDS FOR AMT PURPOSES

Interest on state and local bonds generally is exempt from the regular income tax, but it may be subject to the AMT.

If the state or local bond is a private activity bond, then the interest is a tax preference for AMT purposes. According to the Bond Market Association, interest from almost 8.7 percent of the $1.9 trillion municipal bond market is subject to the AMT. The association's Web site (**http://www.investinginbonds.com**) provides a primer on the AMT's effect on municipal bonds and explains how to determine if the related interest is subject to the AMT.

property), the cost recovery period has expired. Since there is no excess depreciation, there is no tax preference for AMT purposes.

The preference item for excess depreciation on leased personal property is figured separately for each piece of property. No preference is reported in the year the taxpayer disposes of the property.

Fifty Percent Exclusion for Certain Small Business Stock. Fifty percent of the gain on the sale of certain small business stock is excludible from gross income for regular income tax purposes. Seven percent of the excluded amount is a tax preference for AMT purposes.[38]

LO.5

Apply the formula for computing the AMT and illustrate Form 6251.

Illustration of the AMT Computation

The computation of the AMT is illustrated in the following example.

EXAMPLE 28

Hans Sims, who is single, had taxable income for 2006 as follows:

Salary		$ 92,000
Interest		8,000
Adjusted gross income		$100,000
Less itemized deductions:		
Medical expenses ($17,500 − 7.5% of $100,000 AGI)[a]	$10,000	
State income taxes	4,000	
Interest[b]		
Home mortgage (for qualified housing)	20,000*	
Investment interest	3,300*	
Contributions (cash)	5,000*	
Casualty losses ($14,000 − 10% of $100,000 AGI)	4,000*	(46,300)
		$ 53,700
Less personal exemption		(3,300)
Taxable income		$ 50,400

[a] Total medical expenses were $17,500, reduced by 7.5% of AGI, resulting in an itemized deduction of $10,000. However, for AMT purposes, the reduction is 10%, which leaves an AMT itemized deduction of $7,500 ($17,500 − 10% of $100,000 AGI). Therefore, an adjustment of $2,500 ($10,000 − $7,500) is required for medical expenses disallowed for AMT purposes.

[b] In this illustration, all interest is deductible in computing AMTI. Qualified housing interest is deductible. Investment interest ($3,300) is deductible to the extent of net investment income included in the minimum tax base. For this purpose, the $8,000 of interest income is treated as net investment income.

[38] § 57(a)(7).

Deductions marked by an asterisk are allowed as *alternative minimum tax itemized deductions*, and AMT adjustments are required for the other itemized deductions. Thus, adjustments are required for state income taxes and for medical expenses to the extent the medical expenses deductible for regular income tax purposes are not deductible in computing AMT (see note [a] above). In addition to the items that affected taxable income, Hans had $35,000 interest on private activity bonds (an exclusion tax preference). AMTI is computed as follows:

Taxable income	$ 50,400
Plus: Adjustments	
State income taxes	4,000
Medical expenses (see note [a] above)	2,500
Personal exemption	3,300
Plus: Tax preference (interest on private activity bonds)	35,000
Equals: AMTI	$ 95,200
Minus: AMT exemption	(40,250)
Equals: Minimum tax base	$ 54,950
Times: AMT rate	× 26%
Equals: Tentative AMT	$ 14,287
Minus: Regular income tax on taxable income	(9,158)
Equals: AMT	$ 5,129

The solution to Example 28 is also presented on Form 6251. Though this example is for 2006, 2005 tax forms are used because the 2006 tax forms were not available at the time of this writing.

Note that the $3,300 personal exemption amount is a positive adjustment in the Example 28 solution, but does not appear as an adjustment in Form 6251. This difference occurs because line 1 of Form 6251 includes the amount from line 41 of Form 1040. Line 41 of Form 1040 is taxable income before the deduction for personal and dependency exemptions.

AMT Credit

As discussed previously, timing differences give rise to adjustments to the minimum tax base. In later years, the timing differences reverse, as was illustrated in several of the preceding examples. To provide equity for the taxpayer when timing differences reverse, the regular income tax liability may be reduced by a tax credit for prior years' minimum tax liability attributable to timing differences. The **alternative minimum tax credit may be carried over indefinitely.** Therefore, there is no need to keep track of when the minimum tax credit arose.[39]

> **LO.6**
>
> Describe the role of the AMT credit in the alternative minimum tax structure.

EXAMPLE 29

Assume the same facts as in Example 3. Also assume that in 2006, Bob paid AMT as a result of the $20,000 positive adjustment arising from the circulation expenditures. In 2007, $10,000 of the timing difference reverses, resulting in regular taxable income that is $10,000 greater than AMTI. Because Bob has already paid AMT as a result of the write-off of circulation expenditures, he is allowed an AMT credit in 2007. The AMT credit can offset Bob's regular income tax liability in 2007 to the extent that his regular income tax liability exceeds his tentative AMT. ■

[39]§ 53.

Form **6251**	**Alternative Minimum Tax—Individuals**	OMB No. 1545-0074
Department of the Treasury Internal Revenue Service (99)	▶ See separate instructions. ▶ Attach to Form 1040 or Form 1040NR.	20**05** Attachment Sequence No. **32**

Name(s) shown on Form 1040   *Hans Sims*

Your social security number

Part I   Alternative Minimum Taxable Income (See instructions for how to complete each line.)

1	If filing Schedule A (Form 1040), enter the amount from Form 1040, line 41 (minus any amount on Form 8914, line 2), and go to line 2. Otherwise, enter the amount from Form 1040, line 38 (minus any amount on Form 8914, line 2), and go to line 7. (If less than zero, enter as a negative amount)	**1**	*53,700*
2	Medical and dental. Enter the **smaller** of Schedule A (Form 1040), line 4, **or** 2½% of Form 1040, line 38 .	**2**	*2,500*
3	Taxes from Schedule A (Form 1040), line 9	**3**	*4,000*
4	Enter the home mortgage interest adjustment, if any, from line 6 of the worksheet on page 2 of the instructions	**4**	
5	Miscellaneous deductions from Schedule A (Form 1040), line 26	**5**	
6	If Form 1040, line 38, is over $145,950 (over $72,975 if married filing separately), enter the amount from line 9 of the **Itemized Deductions Worksheet** on page A-9 of the Instructions for Schedules A & B (Form 1040)	**6** (	)
7	Tax refund from Form 1040, line 10 or line 21	**7** (	)
8	Investment interest expense (difference between regular tax and AMT)	**8**	
9	Depletion (difference between regular tax and AMT)	**9**	
10	Net operating loss deduction from Form 1040, line 21. Enter as a positive amount	**10**	
11	Interest from specified private activity bonds exempt from the regular tax	**11**	*35,000*
12	Qualified small business stock (7% of gain excluded under section 1202)	**12**	
13	Exercise of incentive stock options (excess of AMT income over regular tax income)	**13**	
14	Estates and trusts (amount from Schedule K-1 (Form 1041), box 12, code A)	**14**	
15	Electing large partnerships (amount from Schedule K-1 (Form 1065-B), box 6)	**15**	
16	Disposition of property (difference between AMT and regular tax gain or loss)	**16**	
17	Depreciation on assets placed in service after 1986 (difference between regular tax and AMT) . . .	**17**	
18	Passive activities (difference between AMT and regular tax income or loss)	**18**	
19	Loss limitations (difference between AMT and regular tax income or loss)	**19**	
20	Circulation costs (difference between regular tax and AMT)	**20**	
21	Long-term contracts (difference between AMT and regular tax income)	**21**	
22	Mining costs (difference between regular tax and AMT)	**22**	
23	Research and experimental costs (difference between regular tax and AMT)	**23**	
24	Income from certain installment sales before January 1, 1987	**24** (	)
25	Intangible drilling costs preference	**25**	
26	Other adjustments, including income-based related adjustments	**26**	
27	Alternative tax net operating loss deduction	**27** (	)
28	**Alternative minimum taxable income.** Combine lines 1 through 27. (If married filing separately and line 28 is more than $191,000, see page 7 of the instructions.)	**28**	*95,200*

Part II   Alternative Minimum Tax

29	Exemption. (If this form is for a child under age 14, see page 7 of the instructions.)		

IF your filing status is . . .	AND line 28 is not over . . .	THEN enter on line 29 . . .		
Single or head of household	$112,500	$40,250		
Married filing jointly or qualifying widow(er) . .	150,000	58,000	**29**	*40,250*
Married filing separately	75,000	29,000		

If line 28 is **over** the amount shown above for your filing status, see page 7 of the instructions.

30	Subtract line 29 from line 28. If zero or less, enter -0- here and on lines 33 and 35 and stop here .	**30**	*54,950*
31	• If you reported capital gain distributions directly on Form 1040, line 13; you reported qualified dividends on Form 1040, line 9b; **or** you had a gain on both lines 15 and 16 of Schedule D (Form 1040) (as refigured for the AMT, if necessary), complete Part III on the back and enter the amount from line 55 here. • **All others:** If line 30 is $175,000 or less ($87,500 or less if married filing separately), multiply line 30 by 26% (.26). Otherwise, multiply line 30 by 28% (.28) and subtract $3,500 ($1,750 if married filing separately) from the result.	**31**	*14,287*
32	Alternative minimum tax foreign tax credit (see page 7 of the instructions)	**32**	
33	Tentative minimum tax. Subtract line 32 from line 31	**33**	*14,287*
34	Tax from Form 1040, line 44 (minus any tax from Form 4972 and any foreign tax credit from Form 1040, line 47). If you used Schedule J to figure your tax, the amount for line 44 of Form 1040 must be refigured without using Schedule J (see page 9 of the instructions)	**34**	*9,158*
35	**Alternative minimum tax.** Subtract line 34 from line 33. If zero or less, enter -0-. Enter here and on Form 1040, line 45	**35**	*5,129*

For Paperwork Reduction Act Notice, see page 9 of the instructions.   Cat. No. 13600G   Form **6251** (2005)

CONCEPT SUMMARY 12–1

AMT Adjustments and Preferences for Individuals

Adjustments	Positive	Negative	Both*
Circulation expenditures			X
Depreciation of post-1986 real property			X
Depreciation of post-1986 personal property			X
Pollution control facilities			X
Mining exploration and development costs			X
Research and experimental expenditures			X
Completed contract method			X
Incentive stock options	X**		
Adjusted gain or loss			X
Passive activity losses			X
Alternative tax NOL deduction			X
Itemized deductions:			
Medical expenses	X		
State income tax or sales tax	X		
Property tax on realty	X		
Property tax on personalty	X		
Miscellaneous itemized deductions	X		
Tax benefit rule for state income tax refund		X	
Cutback adjustment		X	
Qualified interest on student loans	X		
Qualified residence interest that is not qualified housing interest	X		
Qualified residence interest that is AMT investment interest	X	X	
Private activity bond interest that is AMT investment interest		X	
Standard deduction	X		
Personal exemptions and dependency deductions	X		

Preferences

	Positive		
Percentage depletion in excess of adjusted basis	X		
Intangible drilling costs	X		
Private activity bond interest income	X		
Depreciation on pre-1987 leased personal property	X		
§ 1202 exclusion for certain small business stock	X		

*Timing differences.

**While the adjustment is a positive adjustment, the AMT basis for the stock is increased by the amount of the positive adjustment.

The AMT credit is applicable only for the AMT that results from timing differences. It is not available in connection with **AMT exclusions**, which represent permanent differences rather than timing differences between the regular income tax liability and the AMT. These AMT exclusions include the following:

- The standard deduction.
- Personal exemptions.
- Medical expenses, to the extent deductible for regular income tax purposes but not deductible in computing AMT.
- Other itemized deductions not allowable for AMT purposes, including miscellaneous itemized deductions, taxes, and interest expense.
- Excess percentage depletion.
- Tax-exempt interest on specified private activity bonds.

EXAMPLE 30

Don, who is single, has zero taxable income for 2006. He also has positive timing adjustments of $300,000 and AMT exclusions of $100,000. His AMT base is $400,000 because his AMT exemption is phased out completely due to the level of AMTI. Don's tentative AMT is $108,500 [($175,000 × 26% AMT rate) + ($225,000 × 28% AMT rate)]. ∎

To determine the amount of AMT credit to carry over, the AMT must be recomputed reflecting only the AMT exclusions and the AMT exemption amount.

EXAMPLE 31

Assume the same facts as in the previous example. If there had been no positive timing adjustments for the year, Don's tentative AMT would have been $15,535 [($100,000 AMT exclusions − $40,250 exemption) × 26% AMT rate]. Don may carry over an AMT credit of $92,965 ($108,500 AMT − $15,535 related to AMT exclusions) to 2007 and subsequent years. ∎

LO.7

Understand the basic features of the corporate AMT.

Corporate Alternative Minimum Tax

The AMT applicable to corporations is similar to that applicable to noncorporate taxpayers. However, there are several important differences:

- The corporate AMT rate is 20 percent versus a top rate of 28 percent for noncorporate taxpayers.[40]
- The AMT exemption for corporations is $40,000 reduced by 25 percent of the amount by which AMTI exceeds $150,000.[41]
- Tax preferences applicable to noncorporate taxpayers are also applicable to corporate taxpayers, but some adjustments differ (shown later in the chapter).

Although there are computational differences, the corporate AMT and the noncorporate AMT have the identical objective: to force taxpayers who are more profitable than their taxable income reflects to pay additional tax. The formula for determining the corporate AMT appears in Figure 12–3.

Repeal of AMT for Small Corporations

Tax legislation enacted in 1997 repealed the AMT for small corporations for tax years beginning after December 31, 1997. For this purpose, a corporation is classified as a small corporation if it had average annual gross receipts of not more than $5 million for the three-year period beginning after December 1993. A corporation will continue to be classified as a small corporation if its average annual gross receipts for the three-year period preceding the current tax year and any intervening three-year periods do not exceed $7.5 million. However, if a corporation ever

---

[40]§ 55(b)(1)(B).   [41]§§ 55(d)(2) and (3).

FIGURE 12–3	**AMT Formula for Corporations**

Taxable income
Plus: Income tax NOL deduction
Plus or minus: AMT adjustments
Plus: Tax preferences
Equals: AMTI before ATNOLD
Minus: ATNOLD (limited to 90% of AMTI before ATNOLD)
Equals: AMTI
Minus: Exemption
Equals: AMT base
Times: 20% rate
Equals: Tentative minimum tax before AMT foreign tax credit
Minus: AMT foreign tax credit
Equals: Tentative minimum tax
Minus: Regular tax liability before credits minus regular foreign tax credit
Equals: AMT if positive

fails the gross receipts test, it is ineligible for small corporation classification in future tax years.[42]

Tax legislation enacted in 1998 provided an additional opportunity for a corporation to be classified as a small corporation. A corporation will automatically be classified as a small corporation in the first tax year of existence.[43]

ETHICAL *Considerations*   AMT AND SMALL CORPORATIONS

Abigail is the controller of a medium-size company specializing in the construction of single-family homes. As such, she prepares the corporate tax return.

The corporation expects its gross revenues in each of its first three years of operations to be about $12 million and to increase thereafter at an annual 15 percent rate. Abigail is aware that the corporation is eligible for the small corporation exception to the AMT in its first year but will not be thereafter.

The corporation uses the completed contract method of accounting for 2006. After 2006, however, Abigail has the corporation switch from the completed contract method to the percentage of completion method.

Evaluate what Abigail has done.

AMT Adjustments

Adjustments Applicable to Individuals and Corporations. The following adjustments that were discussed in connection with the individual AMT also apply to the corporate AMT:

- Excess of MACRS over ADS depreciation on real and personal property placed in service after 1986.
- Pollution control facilities placed in service after 1986 (AMT requires ADS depreciation over the asset's ADR life if placed in service before January 1,

---

[42]§§ 55(e)(1)(A) and (B). An estimated 3 million corporations (95% of incorporated businesses) qualify for this exemption.

[43]§ 55(e)(1)(C).

1999, and over the MACRS recovery period if placed in service after December 31, 1998; 60-month amortization is allowed for regular income tax purposes).

- Mining and exploration expenditures (AMT requires amortization over 10 years versus immediate expensing allowed for regular income tax purposes).
- Income on long-term contracts (AMT requires percentage of completion method; completed contract method is allowed in limited circumstances for regular income tax purposes).
- Dispositions of assets (if gain or loss for AMT purposes differs from gain or loss for regular income tax purposes).
- Allowable ATNOLD (which cannot exceed 90 percent of AMTI before deduction for ATNOLD).

Adjustment Applicable Only to Corporations. An AMT adjustment applicable only to corporations is the adjusted current earnings (ACE) adjustment.[44] The **ACE adjustment** generally applies to all corporations[45] and has a significant impact on both tax and financial accounting.

Corporations are subject to an AMT adjustment equal to 75 percent of the excess of ACE over AMTI before the ACE adjustment.[46] Historically, the government has not required conformity between tax accounting and financial accounting. For many years, the only *direct* conformity requirement was that a corporation that used the LIFO method for tax accounting also had to use LIFO for financial accounting.[47] Through the ACE adjustment, Congress is *indirectly* imposing a conformity requirement on corporations. Though a corporation may still choose to use different methods for tax and financial accounting purposes, it may no longer be able to do so without incurring AMT as a result of the ACE adjustment. Thus, a corporation may incur AMT not only because of specifically targeted adjustments and preferences, but also as a result of any methods that cause ACE to exceed AMTI before the ACE adjustment.

The ACE adjustment can be either a positive or a negative amount. AMTI is increased by 75 percent of the excess of ACE over unadjusted AMTI. Or AMTI is reduced by 75 percent of the excess of unadjusted AMTI over ACE. The negative adjustment is limited to the aggregate of the positive adjustments under ACE for prior years, reduced by the previously claimed negative adjustments. See Concept Summary 12–2. Thus, the ordering of the timing differences is crucial because any lost negative adjustment is permanent. Unadjusted AMTI is AMTI without the ACE adjustment or the ATNOLD.[48]

EXAMPLE 32

A calendar year corporation has the following data:

	2005	2006	2007
Pre-adjusted AMTI	$3,000	$3,000	$3,100
Adjusted current earnings	4,000	3,000	2,000

In 2005, because ACE exceeds unadjusted AMTI by $1,000, $750 (75% × $1,000) is included as a positive adjustment to AMTI. No adjustment is necessary for 2006. As unadjusted AMTI exceeds ACE by $1,100 in 2007, there is a potential negative adjustment to AMTI of $825 ($1,100 × 75%). Since the total increases to AMTI for prior years equal $750 and there are no previously claimed negative adjustments, only $750 of the potential negative adjustment reduces AMTI for 2007. Further, $75 of the negative amount is lost forever.

---

[44]§ 56(c).
[45]The ACE adjustment does not apply to S corporations. § 56(g)(6).
[46]§ 56(g).

[47]§ 472(c).
[48]§§ 56(g)(1) and (2).

CONCEPT SUMMARY 12–2

Determining the ACE Adjustment*

```
                    ┌─────────────────────────┐
                    │ Calculate Taxable Income │
                    └─────────────────────────┘
                                 │
                    ┌─────────────────────────┐
                    │ Calculate AMTI by adjusting Taxable │
                    │ Income as required by § 56 and § 58 │
                    │ and increasing Taxable Income by    │
                    │ § 57 tax preference items           │
                    └─────────────────────────┘
                                 │
                    ┌─────────────────────────┐
                    │ Calculate Adjusted Current Earnings │
                    │ by adjusting AMTI as required (many │
                    │ of the adjustments based on earnings│
                    │ and profits adjustments)            │
                    └─────────────────────────┘
                                 │
                            ◇ Is
                        Adjusted Current
                          Earnings
            Yes ─────  greater than pre-  ───── No
                          adjustment
                            AMTI? ◇
             │                                      │
 ┌──────────────────────────┐      ┌──────────────────────────┐
 │ Increase AMTI by 75% of   │      │ Decrease AMTI by 75% of the│
 │ the excess of Adjusted    │      │ excess of AMTI             │
 │ Current Earnings over AMTI│      │ (pre-adjustment) over      │
 │ (pre-adjustment)          │      │ Adjusted Current Earnings  │
 │                           │      │ to extent of net previous  │
 │                           │      │ increases                  │
 └──────────────────────────┘      └──────────────────────────┘
```

*Reprinted with permission from *Oil and Gas Tax Quarterly*. Copyright 1989 Matthew Bender & Company, Inc., a member of the LexisNexis Group. All Rights Reserved.

ACE should not be confused with current earnings and profits. Although many items are treated in the same manner, certain variations exist. For example, Federal income taxes, deductible in computing earnings and profits, are not deductible in determining ACE.

The starting point for computing ACE is AMTI, which is defined as regular taxable income after AMT adjustments (other than the ATNOLD and ACE adjustments) and tax preferences. The resulting figure is adjusted for several items in order to arrive at ACE.

Tax Preferences

AMTI includes designated tax preference items. In some cases, this has the effect of subjecting nontaxable income to the AMT. Tax preference items that apply to individuals also apply to corporations.

EXAMPLE 33

The following information applies to Brown Corporation (a calendar year taxpayer) for 2006:

Taxable income	$4,000,000
Mining exploration costs	500,000
Percentage depletion claimed (the property has a zero adjusted basis)	1,700,000
Interest on City of Elmira (Michigan) private activity bonds	900,000

Brown Corporation's AMTI for 2006 is determined as follows:

Taxable income		$4,000,000
Adjustments:		
Excess mining exploration costs [$500,000 (amount expensed) − $50,000 (amount allowed over a 10-year amortization period)]		450,000
Tax preferences:		
Excess depletion	$1,700,000	
Interest on private activity bonds	900,000	2,600,000
AMTI		$7,050,000 ■

Exemption Amount

The tentative AMT is 20 percent of AMTI that exceeds the corporation's exemption amount. The exemption amount for a corporation is $40,000 reduced by 25 percent of the amount by which AMTI exceeds $150,000.

EXAMPLE 34

Blue Corporation has AMTI of $180,000. The exemption amount is reduced by $7,500 [25% × ($180,000 − $150,000)], and the amount remaining is $32,500 ($40,000 − $7,500). Thus, Blue Corporation's AMT base (refer to Figure 12–3) is $147,500 ($180,000 − $32,500). ■

Note that the exemption amount phases out entirely when AMTI reaches $310,000.

Other Aspects of the AMT

All of a corporation's AMT is available for carryover as a minimum tax credit. This is so regardless of whether the adjustments and preferences originate from timing differences or AMT exclusions.

EXAMPLE 35

In Example 33, the AMTI exceeds $310,000, so no exemption is allowed. The tentative minimum tax is $1,410,000 (20% of $7,050,000). Assume the regular income tax liability is $1,360,000, and the AMT liability is $50,000 ($1,410,000 − $1,360,000). The amount of the minimum tax credit carryover is $50,000, which is all of the current year's AMT. ■

LO.8

Identify tax planning opportunities to minimize the AMT.

TAX PLANNING
Considerations

Responding to Bob and Carol

The chapter began with a set of circumstances involving Bob and Carol that raised a number of interesting questions. By now, the student should have arrived at a logical reason for the difference in Bob and Carol's tax liabilities and expect the following to happen to Bob.

Bob contacts Adam, his tax return preparer, and explains in an excited voice that he has received a bill from the IRS for $15,000 plus interest associated with the underpayment of his tax liability. Adam has Bob fax him a copy of the IRS deficiency notice. He checks Bob's tax file and then calls Bob to explain that Bob does owe the IRS the $15,000 plus interest. Somehow Bob's tax return was prepared without including a Form 6251 (the alternative minimum tax). Adam suggests that Bob stop by his office later that afternoon to discuss the disposition of the matter further.

Avoiding Preferences and Adjustments

Several strategies and elections are available to help taxpayers avoid having preferences and adjustments.

- A taxpayer who is in danger of incurring AMT liability should not invest in tax-exempt private activity bonds unless doing so makes good investment sense. Any AMT triggered by interest on private activity bonds reduces the yield on an investment in the bonds. Other tax-exempt bonds or taxable corporate bonds might yield a better after-tax return.
- A taxpayer may elect to expense certain costs in the year incurred or to capitalize and amortize the costs over some specified period. The decision should be based on the present discounted value of after-tax cash flows under the available alternatives. Costs subject to elective treatment include circulation expenditures, mining exploration and development costs, and research and experimental expenditures.

Controlling the Timing of Preferences and Adjustments

The AMT exemption often keeps items of tax preference from being subject to the AMT. To use the AMT exemption effectively, taxpayers should avoid bunching preferences and positive adjustments in any one year. To avoid this bunching, taxpayers should attempt to control the timing of such items when possible.

Taking Advantage of the AMT/Regular Tax Rate Differential

A taxpayer who cannot avoid triggering the AMT in a given year can usually save taxes by taking advantage of the rate differential between the AMT and the regular income tax.

Peter, a real estate dealer who expects to be in the 35% regular income tax bracket in 2007, is subject to the AMT in 2006 at the 26% rate. He is considering the sale of a parcel of land (inventory) at a gain of $100,000. If he sells the land in 2007, he will have to pay tax of $35,000 ($100,000 gain × 35% regular income tax rate). However, if he sells the land in 2006, he will pay tax of $26,000 ($100,000 gain × 26% AMT rate). Thus, accelerating the sale into 2006 will save Peter $9,000 ($35,000 − $26,000) in tax. ■

EXAMPLE 36

Cora, who expects to be in the 35% tax bracket in 2007, is subject to the AMT in 2006 at the 26% rate. She is going to contribute $10,000 in cash to her alma mater, State University. If Cora makes the contribution in 2007, she will save tax of $3,500 ($10,000 contribution × 35% regular income tax rate). However, if she makes the contribution in 2006, she will save tax of $2,600 ($10,000 contribution × 26% AMT rate). Thus, deferring the contribution until 2007 will save Cora $900 ($3,500 − $2,600) in tax. ■

EXAMPLE 37

This deferral/acceleration strategy should be considered for any income or expenses where the taxpayer can control the timing. This strategy applies to corporations as well as to individuals.

KEY TERMS

ACE adjustment, 12–28	Alternative tax NOL deduction (ATNOLD), 12–15	Incentive stock options (ISOs), 12–12
Alternative minimum tax (AMT), 12–2	AMT adjustments, 12–3	Private activity bonds, 12–21
Alternative minimum tax credit, 12–23	AMT exclusions, 12–26	Tax preferences, 12–3
	Circulation expenditures, 12–4	

P R O B L E M   M A T E R I A L S

D I S C U S S I O N   Q U E S T I O N S

1. Since there is a regular income tax, why is there a need for an AMT?

2. How can the AMT be calculated without using taxable income (as determined for purposes of the regular income tax) as a starting point?

3. What is the difference between AMT adjustments and tax preferences?

4. Identify which of the following are tax preferences:
   a. Seven percent of the exclusion associated with gains on the sale of certain small business stock.
   b. Exclusion on the receipt of property by gift or by inheritance.
   c. Exclusion associated with payment of premiums by the employer on group term life insurance for coverage not in excess of $50,000.
   d. Percentage depletion in excess of the property's adjusted basis.
   e. Tax-exempt interest on certain private activity bonds.
   f. Exclusion of life insurance proceeds received as the result of death.

5. Identify which of the following are tax preferences:
   a. Exclusion on the receipt of property by inheritance.
   b. Exclusion to employee on the employer's contribution to the employee's pension plan.
   c. Excess of deduction for circulation expenditures for regular income tax purposes over the deduction for AMT purposes.
   d. Excess of amortization allowance over depreciation on pre-1987 certified pollution control facilities.
   e. Excess of accelerated over straight-line depreciation on real property placed in service before 1987.

6. Describe the tax formula for the AMT.

7. If the regular income tax liability is greater than the tentative AMT, there is no AMT liability, and the total income tax liability is equal to the regular income tax liability. Evaluate the correctness of this statement.

8. For the exemption amount, indicate the following:
   a. Purpose of the exemption.
   b. Amount of the exemption in 2006.
   c. Reason for the phaseout of the exemption.
   d. Amount at which the phaseout of the exemption is complete.

9. What are the AMT rates for an individual taxpayer? To what levels of income do the rates apply?

10. How do nonrefundable tax credits affect the calculation of the AMT?

11. Tad, who owns and operates a business, acquired machinery and placed it in service in June 1998. The machinery is 10-year property. Does Tad need to make an AMT adjustment in 1998 and in 2006 for the depreciation on the machinery? Explain.

12. How can an individual taxpayer avoid having an AMT adjustment for mining exploration and development costs?

Issue ID

13. Rick, who is single, incurs mining exploration and development costs associated with his energy company. He would expense the costs in the current year in order to reduce his regular income tax, but is aware that this would create a positive adjustment for AMT purposes. His AGI is large enough to reduce the AMT exemption amount to zero. Therefore, he is considering electing to amortize the mining exploration and development costs over 10 years to avoid having to pay any AMT. Advise Rick.

14. Certain taxpayers have the option of using either the percentage of completion method or the completed contract method for reporting profit on long-term contracts. What impact could the AMT have on this decision?

15. If the stock received under an incentive stock option (ISO) is sold in the year of exercise, there is no AMT adjustment. If the stock is sold in a later year, there will be an AMT adjustment. Evaluate the validity of these statements.

16. In 1998, Desiree purchased a building for $500,000 to be used in her business. She sells the building in the current tax year. Explain why her recognized gain or loss for regular income tax purposes will be different from her recognized gain or loss for AMT purposes.

17. Celine is going to be subject to the AMT in 2006. She owns an investment building and *Issue ID* is considering disposing of it and investing in other realty. Based on an appraisal of the building's value, the realized gain would be $85,000. Ed has offered to purchase the building from Celine with the closing date being December 29, 2006. Ed wants to close the transaction in 2006 because certain beneficial tax consequences will result only if the transaction is closed prior to the beginning of 2007. Abby has offered to purchase the building with the closing date being January 2, 2007. The building has a $95,000 greater AMT adjusted basis. For regular income tax purposes, Celine expects to be in the 25% tax bracket in 2006 and the 28% tax bracket in 2007. What are the relevant tax issues that Celine faces in making her decision?

18. Passive activity losses are not deductible in computing either taxable income or AMTI. Explain why an adjustment for passive activity losses may be required for AMT purposes.

19. What effect do adjustments and preferences have on the calculation of the ATNOLD?

20. The following itemized deductions are allowed for regular income tax purposes: medical expenses, state and local income taxes or sales tax, real estate taxes, personal property taxes, home mortgage interest, investment interest, charitable contributions of cash, charitable contributions of property, casualty and theft losses, unreimbursed employee business expenses, and gambling losses. Which of these itemized deductions can result in an AMT adjustment?

21. Matt, who is single, has always elected to itemize deductions rather than take the *Issue ID* standard deduction. In prior years, his itemized deductions always exceeded the standard deduction by a substantial amount. As a result of paying off the mortgage on his residence, he projects that his itemized deductions for 2006 will exceed the standard deduction by only $500. Matt anticipates that the amount of his itemized deductions will remain about the same in the foreseeable future. Matt's AGI is $150,000. He is investing the amount of his former mortgage payment each month in tax-exempt bonds. A friend recommends that Matt buy a beach house in order to increase his itemized deductions with the mortgage interest deduction. What are the relevant tax issues for Matt?

22. Warren's 3% cutback adjustment for regular income tax purposes reduces his itemized deductions from $25,000 to $21,000. What effect will this have in calculating Warren's AMTI?

23. In computing the AMT itemized deduction for interest, it is possible that some interest allowed for regular income tax purposes will not be allowed. Explain.

24. Could computation of the AMT ever require an adjustment for the standard deduction or personal and dependency exemptions? Explain.

25. Alvin owns a mineral deposit that qualifies for the 15% percentage depletion rate. Under what circumstances will the depletion deduction for regular income tax purposes and AMT purposes not be the same?

26. Ian received a gift of $250,000 from his Aunt Nell. He is going to invest the proceeds in *Issue ID* either taxable bonds earning interest at a 7% rate or tax-exempt bonds earning interest at a 5% rate. What are the relevant tax issues for Ian?

27. What is the purpose of the AMT credit? Briefly describe how the credit is computed.

28. What requirements must be satisfied for a corporation to be exempt from the AMT?

29. What is the ACE adjustment? Does it apply to both individual and corporate taxpayers?

30. Rose, Inc.'s regular income tax liability is $114,000, and its tentative AMT is $120,000. Are there any circumstances in which Rose would desire to accelerate $20,000 of income to the current year rather than delaying it until next year?

PROBLEMS

31. Use the following data to calculate Reba's AMT base in 2006:

Taxable income	$210,000
Positive AMT adjustments	72,000
Negative AMT adjustments	62,000
AMT preferences	30,000

Reba will file as a head of household.

Communications

32. Arthur East, an unmarried individual who is age 66, has taxable income of $145,000. He has AMT positive adjustments of $62,000 and tax preferences of $50,000.
    a. What is Arthur's AMT?
    b. What is the total amount of Arthur's tax liability?
    c. Draft a letter to Arthur explaining why he must pay more than the regular income tax liability. Arthur's address is 100 Colonel's Way, Conway, SC 29526.

33. Calculate the AMT for the following cases in 2006. The taxpayer has regular taxable income of $525,000 and does not have any credits.

	Tentative AMT	
Filing Status	Case 1	Case 2
Single	$194,000	$175,000
Married, filing jointly	194,000	175,000

34. Calculate the exemption amount for the following cases in 2006 for a single taxpayer, a married taxpayer filing jointly, and a married taxpayer filing separately.

Case	AMTI
1	$160,000
2	250,000
3	450,000

35. Leona has nonrefundable credits of $65,000 for 2006. None of these nonrefundable credits are personal credits that qualify for special treatment. Her regular income tax liability before credits is $135,000, and her tentative AMT is $78,000.
    a. What is the amount of Leona's AMT?
    b. What is the amount of Leona's regular income tax liability after credits?

Decision Making

36. Angela, who is single, incurs circulation expenditures of $153,000 during 2006. She is in the process of deciding whether to expense the $153,000 or to capitalize it and elect to deduct it over a three-year period. Angela already knows that she will be subject to the AMT for 2006 at both the 26% and the 28% rates. Angela is in the 28% bracket for regular income tax purposes this year (has regular taxable income of $153,000 before considering the circulation expenses) and expects to be in the 28% bracket in 2007 and 2008. Advise Angela on whether she should elect the three-year write-off rather than expensing the $153,000 in 2006.

37. Vito owns and operates a news agency (as a sole proprietorship). During 2006, he incurred expenses of $150,000 to increase circulation of newspapers and magazines that his agency distributes. For regular income tax purposes, he elected to expense the $150,000 in 2006. In addition, he incurred $90,000 in circulation expenditures in 2007 and again elected expense treatment. What AMT adjustments will be required in 2006 and 2007 as a result of the circulation expenditures?

38. Ted acquires an apartment building for $900,000 in March with $750,000 being allocated to the building and $150,000 to the land. Determine the amount of the AMT cost recovery adjustment for 2006 if the apartment building is purchased and placed in service in:
    a. 1998.
    b. 2006.

39. In March 2006, Helen Carlon acquired used equipment for her business at a cost of $300,000. The equipment is 5-year class property for regular income tax purposes and for AMT purposes.

    Decision Making

    Communications

    a. If Helen depreciates the equipment using the method that will produce the greatest deduction for 2006 for regular income tax purposes, what is the amount of the AMT adjustment? Helen does not elect § 179 limited expensing.
    b. How can Helen reduce the AMT adjustment to $0? What circumstances would motivate her to do so?
    c. Draft a letter to Helen regarding the choice of depreciation methods. Helen's address is 500 Monticello Avenue, Glendale, AZ 85306.

40. In 2006, Gary incurred $600,000 of mining and exploration expenditures. He elects to deduct the expenditures as quickly as the tax law allows for regular income tax purposes.

    Decision Making

    a. How will Gary's treatment of mining and exploration expenditures affect his regular income tax and AMT computations for 2006?
    b. How can Gary avoid having AMT adjustments related to the mining and exploration expenditures?
    c. What factors should Gary consider in deciding whether to deduct the expenditures in the year incurred?

41. Rust Company is a real estate construction business with average annual gross receipts of $3 million. Rust uses the completed contract method on a contract that requires 16 months to complete. The contract is for $500,000 with estimated costs of $300,000. At the end of 2006, $180,000 of costs had been incurred. The contract is completed in 2007 with the total cost being $295,000. Determine the amount of adjustments for AMT purposes for 2006 and 2007.

42. Burt, the CFO of Amber, Inc., is granted stock options in 2006 that qualify as incentive stock options. In 2011, the rights in the stock become freely transferable and not subject to a substantial risk of forfeiture. Burt exercises the stock options in 2010 when the option price is $70,000 and the fair market value of the stock is $100,000. He sells the stock in 2014 for $150,000. What are the regular income tax consequences and the AMT consequences for Burt in:
    a. 2006?
    b. 2010?
    c. 2011?
    d. 2014?

43. In 2006, Lori exercised an incentive stock option that had been granted by her employer, Black Corporation. Lori acquired 100 shares of Black stock for the option price of $175 per share. The rights in the stock become freely transferable and not subject to a substantial risk of forfeiture in 2006. The fair market value of the stock at the date of exercise was $210 per share. Lori sells the stock for $320 per share later in 2006.
    a. What is the amount of Lori's AMT adjustment in 2006, and what is her recognized gain on the sale for regular income tax purposes and AMT purposes?
    b. How would your answers in (a) change if Lori had sold the stock in 2007 rather than in 2006?

44. Buford sells an apartment building for $720,000. His adjusted basis is $406,000 for regular income tax purposes and $450,000 for AMT purposes. Calculate Buford's:
    a. Gain for regular income tax purposes.
    b. Gain for AMT purposes.
    c. AMT adjustment, if any.

45. Freda acquired a passive activity in 2006 for $870,000. Gross income from operations of the activity was $160,000. Operating expenses, not including depreciation, were $122,000. Regular income tax depreciation of $49,750 was computed under MACRS. AMT depreciation, computed under ADS, was $41,000. Compute Freda's passive loss deduction and passive loss suspended for regular income tax purposes and for AMT purposes.

46. Wally and Gloria incur and pay medical expenses in excess of insurance reimbursements during the year as follows:

For Wally	$11,000
For Gloria (spouse)	4,000
For Chuck (son)	1,500
For Carter (Gloria's father)	13,000

Wally and Gloria's AGI is $200,000. They file a joint return. Chuck and Carter are Wally and Gloria's dependents.
    a. What is Wally and Gloria's medical expense deduction for regular income tax purposes?
    b. What is Wally and Gloria's medical expense deduction for AMT purposes?
    c. What is the amount of the AMT adjustment for medical expenses?

47. Wolfgang's AGI is $140,000. He has the following itemized deductions for 2006:

Medical expenses [$12,000 − (7.5% × $140,000)]	$ 1,500
State income taxes	4,200
Charitable contributions	5,000
Home mortgage interest on his personal residence	6,500
Casualty loss (after $100 and 10% reductions)	1,800
Miscellaneous itemized deductions	
[$3,500 − 2%($140,000)]	700
	$19,700

    a. Calculate Wolfgang's itemized deductions for AMT purposes.
    b. What is the amount of the AMT adjustment?

48. Tom, who is single, owns a personal residence in the city. He also owns a cabin near a ski resort in the mountains. He uses the cabin as a vacation home. In February 2006, he borrowed $75,000 on a home equity loan and used the proceeds to reduce credit card obligations and other debt. During 2006, he paid the following amounts of interest:

On his personal residence	$12,000
On the cabin	6,000
On the home equity loan	4,500
On credit card obligations	1,200

What amount, if any, must Tom recognize as an AMT adjustment in 2006?

49. During the current year, Yoon earned $10,000 in dividends on corporate stock and incurred $13,000 of investment interest expense related to the stock holdings. Yoon also earned $5,000 interest on private activity bonds and incurred interest expense of $3,500 in connection with the bonds.
    a. How much investment interest expense can Yoon deduct for regular income tax and AMT purposes for the year?
    b. What is the amount of the adjustment for AMT purposes?

50. Walter and Edith, who are married with two dependents, had AGI of $110,000 in 2006. Their AGI included net investment income of $10,000 and gambling income of $2,500.

They incurred the following expenses during the year (all of which resulted in itemized deductions for regular income tax purposes):

Medical expenses (before 7.5%-of-AGI floor)	$9,500
State income taxes (exceed sales taxes)	2,800
Personal property tax	900
Real estate tax	9,100
Interest on personal residence	8,600
Interest on home equity loan (proceeds were used to buy a new fishing boat)	1,800
Investment interest expense	2,600
Charitable contribution (cash)	4,200
Unreimbursed employee expenses (before 2%-of-AGI floor)	3,800

a. What is the amount of Walter and Edith's AMT adjustment for itemized deductions in 2006? Is it positive or negative?

b. Assume the same facts as above and that Walter and Edith also earned interest of $5,000 on private activity bonds. They borrowed money to buy these bonds and paid interest of $3,900 on the loan. Determine the effect on AMTI.

51. Chuck is single, has no dependents, and does not itemize deductions. In 2006, he claims a personal exemption of $3,300 and has taxable income of $112,000. His tax preferences total $109,000. What is Chuck's AMTI for 2006?

52. Emily owns a coal mine (basis of $12,000 at the beginning of the year) that qualifies for a 15% depletion rate. Gross income from the property was $140,000, and net income before the percentage depletion deduction was $60,000. What is Emily's tax preference for excess depletion?

53. Amos incurred and expensed intangible drilling costs (IDC) of $70,000. His net oil and gas income was $60,000. What is the amount of Amos's tax preference item for IDC?

54. Jack, who is single with no dependents and does not itemize, provides you with the following information for 2006:

Short-term capital loss	$ 5,000
Long-term capital gain	25,000
Municipal bond interest received on private activity bonds acquired in 1996	9,000
Dividends from Citigroup	1,500
Excess of FMV over cost of ISOs (the rights became freely transferable and not subject to a substantial risk of forfeiture in 2006)	35,000

What is the total amount of Jack's tax preference items and AMT adjustments for 2006?

55. Pat, who is single with no dependents, received a salary of $90,000 in 2006. She had interest income of $1,000, dividend income of $5,000, gambling income of $4,000, and interest income from private activity bonds of $40,000. The dividends are not qualified dividends. The following additional information is relevant:

Medical expenses (before 7.5%-of-AGI floor)	$12,000
State income taxes	4,100
Real estate taxes	2,800
Mortgage interest on residence	3,100
Investment interest expense	1,800
Gambling losses	5,100

Compute Pat's tentative minimum tax for 2006.

56. Renee and Sanjeev, who are married, had taxable income of $273,000 for 2006. They had positive AMT adjustments of $38,000, negative AMT adjustments of $14,000, and tax preference items of $67,500.

a. Compute their AMTI.

b. Compute their tentative minimum tax.

57. Farr, who is single, has no dependents and does not itemize. She has the following items relative to her tax return for 2006:

Bargain element from the exercise of an ISO (no restrictions apply to the stock)	$ 45,000
MACRS depreciation on shopping mall building acquired after 1986 and before 1999 (ADS depreciation would have yielded $26,000)	49,000
Percentage depletion in excess of property's adjusted basis	50,000
Taxable income for regular income tax purposes	121,000

a. Determine Farr's AMT adjustments and preferences for 2006.
b. Calculate the AMT (if any) for 2006.

58. Lynn is single and has no dependents. Based on the financial information presented below, compute Lynn's AMT for 2006.

Income:	
Salary	$33,000
Taxable interest on corporate bonds	1,800
Dividend income	1,900
Business income	64,000
Expenditures:	
Medical expenses	12,000
State income taxes	6,000
Real estate taxes	8,500
Mortgage (qualified housing) interest	9,200
Investment interest	5,500
Cash contributions to various charities	2,900

Additional information:

- The $64,000 business income is from Apex Office Supplies Company, a sole proprietorship Lynn owns and operates. Apex claimed MACRS depreciation of $3,175 on real and personal property used in the business. ADS depreciation on the property would have been $2,500.
- Lynn received interest of $30,000 on City of Pensacola private activity bonds.

59. Bonnie, who is single, has taxable income of $0 in 2006. She has positive timing adjustments of $200,000 and AMT exclusion items of $100,000 for the year. What is the amount of Bonnie's AMT credit for carryover to 2007?

60. Aqua, Inc., a calendar year corporation, has the following gross receipts and taxable income for 1993–2006:

Year	Gross Receipts	Taxable Income
1993	$11,000,000	$3,000,000
1994	4,800,000	900,000
1995	5,300,000	1,500,000
1996	4,600,000	700,000
1997	8,200,000	1,200,000
1998	8,500,000	1,900,000
1999	5,200,000	1,300,000
2000	8,000,000	1,500,000
2001	6,000,000	1,450,000
2002	6,200,000	1,375,000
2003	6,100,000	1,425,000
2004	8,000,000	1,400,000
2005	7,000,000	1,312,000
2006	7,500,000	985,000

a.   When is Aqua first exempt from the AMT as a small corporation?

b.   Is Aqua subject to the AMT for 2006?

61. Gray Corporation (a calendar year corporation) reports the following information for the years listed below:

	2005	2006	2007
Unadjusted AMTI	$3,000	$2,000	$5,000
Adjusted current earnings	4,000	3,000	2,000

Compute the ACE adjustment for each year.

62. In each of the following independent situations, determine the tentative AMT:

	AMTI (Before the Exemption Amount)
Quincy Corporation	$150,000
Redland Corporation	160,000
Tanzen Corporation	320,000

63. Brown Corporation (a calendar year taxpayer) had the following transactions:

Taxable income	$2,600,000
Depreciation for regular income tax purposes on realty in excess of ADS (placed in service in 1996)	550,000
Excess amortization of certified pollution control facilities	450,000
Tax-exempt interest on private activity bonds	1,030,000
Percentage depletion in excess of the property's adjusted basis	60,000

a.   Calculate Brown's regular income tax liability.

b.   Calculate Brown's tentative AMT.

c.   Calculate Brown's AMT.

CUMULATIVE PROBLEMS

64. Robert M. and Jane R. Armstrong live at 1802 College Avenue, Carmel, IN 46302. They are married and file a joint return for 2005. The Armstrongs have two dependent children, Ellen J. and Sean M., who are 10-year-old twins. Ellen's Social Security number is 333–42–3368, and Sean's is 333–42–3369. Robert pays child support of $12,000 for Amy, his 17-year-old daughter from his previous marriage. Amy's Social Security number is 111–22–4300. According to the divorce decree, Margaret, Robert's former wife, has legal custody of Amy. Margaret provides the balance of Amy's support (about $6,000).

    Robert (224–36–9987) is a factory foreman, and Jane (443–56–3421) is a computer systems analyst. The Armstrongs' W–2 Forms for 2005 reflect the following information:

Tax Return Problem

Communications

	Robert	Jane
Salary (Indiana Foundry, Inc.)	$91,000	
Salary (Carmel Computer Associates)		$104,000
Federal income tax withheld	22,750	26,000
Social Security wages	90,000	90,000
Social Security withheld	5,580	5,580
Medicare wages	91,000	104,000
Medicare tax withheld	1,320	1,508
State wages	91,000	104,000
State income tax withheld	3,970	4,710

In addition to their salaries, the Armstrongs had the following income items in 2005:

Interest income (Carmel Sanitation District Bonds)	$20,500
Interest income (Carmel National Bank)	3,100
Qualified dividend income (Able Computer Corporation)	4,000
Gambling income	4,200
Gift from Uncle Raymond to Robert	5,000

Jane inherited $600,000 from her grandfather in January and invested the money in the Carmel Sanitation District Bonds, which are private activity bonds. Jane was selected as the "Citizen of the Year" and received an award of $6,000. She used the $6,000 to pay credit card debt.

The Armstrongs incurred the following expenses during 2005:

Medical expenses (doctor and hospital bills)	$16,800
Real property tax on personal residence	4,900
Mortgage interest on personal residence (reported on Form 1098)	6,400
Investment interest expense	2,300
Contributions	9,000
Gambling losses	4,800
Sales taxes (from sales tax table)	1,913

On March 1, Robert and Jane contributed Ace stock to the Carmel Salvation Army, a public charity. They had acquired the stock on February 9, 1994, for $5,200. The stock was listed on the New York Stock Exchange at a value of $6,500 on the date of the contribution. In addition, Robert and Jane contributed $2,500 during the year to Second Church.

Robert sold five acres of land to a real estate developer on October 12, 2005, for $85,000. He had acquired the land on May 15, 2001, for $77,000.

Use Forms 1040, 4952, 6251, and 8283 and Schedules A, B, and D to compute the tax liability (including AMT) for Robert and Jane Armstrong for 2005. Suggested software: TurboTax. Write a letter to the Armstrongs indicating whether they have a refund or balance due for 2005, and suggest possible tax planning strategies for 2006.

Tax Return Problem   65. Ron T. Freeman, age 38, is divorced and has no dependents. He pays alimony of $18,000 per year to his former wife, Kate. Kate's husband was killed in a hunting accident in 2006. At the time of the accident, their baby was only six weeks old. Ron decided to invest $10,000 each year in a mutual fund in Kate's baby's name to be used as a college fund. He made the initial $10,000 investment in 2006. Ron's Social Security number is 444–11–2222, and Kate's is 555–67–2222. Ron's address is 201 Front Street, Missoula, MT 59812. He is independently wealthy as a result of having inherited sizable holdings in real estate and corporate stocks and bonds. Ron is a minister at First Methodist Church, but he accepts no salary from the church. However, he does reside in the church's parsonage free of charge. The fair rental value of the parsonage is $2,000 a month. The church also provides him a cash grocery allowance of $200 a week. Examination of Ron's financial records provides the following information for 2006:

a. On January 16, 2006, Ron sold 2,000 shares of stock for a gain of $44,000. The stock was acquired nine months ago.

b. He received $49,000 of interest on private activity bonds.

c. He received gross rent income of $190,000 from an apartment complex he owns. He qualifies as an active participant.

d. Expenses related to the apartment complex, which he acquired in 1986, were $245,000.

e. Ron's interest income (on CDs) totaled $12,000. Since he invests only in growth stocks, he has no dividend income.

f. He won $9,000 on the lottery.

g. On October 9, 2003, Ron exercised his rights under Egret Corporation's incentive stock option plan. For an option price of $20,000, he acquired stock worth $68,000. The stock became freely transferable in 2006. At the date the stocks became freely transferable, the fair market value was $82,000.

h. Ron was the beneficiary of a $750,000 life insurance policy on his Uncle Jake. He received the proceeds in October.

i. Ron had the following potential itemized deductions *from* AGI:

- $1,600 fair market value of stock contributed to Methodist Church (basis of stock was $1,400). He had owned the stock for two years.
- $3,500 interest on consumer purchases.
- $3,600 state and local income tax.
- $4,500 medical expenses (before 7.5% floor) for himself and $8,500 of hospital expenses associated with Kate's deceased husband.
- $200 for a safe deposit box that is used to store investments and related legal documents.
- $8,000 paid for lottery tickets associated with playing the state lottery. Ron contributed his net winnings of $1,000 to the church.
- $3,000 contribution to his traditional IRA.
- Since Ron lived in Montana, he had no sales tax.

Compute Ron's tax liability, including AMT if applicable, before prepayments or credits, for 2006.

RESEARCH PROBLEMS

Note: Solutions to Research Problems can be prepared by using the **RIA Checkpoint®** **Student Edition** online research product, which is available to accompany this text. It is also possible to prepare solutions to the Research Problems by using tax research materials found in a standard tax library.

Research Problem 1. Gretchen is the owner of a housing unit in a cooperative housing corporation. As a tenant-stockholder, she deducts $4,800 of real estate taxes (i.e., her proportionate share of the property taxes paid by the cooperative) as an itemized deduction. She claims the $4,800 under § 216(a)(1), rather than under § 164(a)(1), because she does not have direct ownership of the housing unit.

Gretchen is aware that § 56(b)(1)(A)(ii) disallows the deduction for real estate property taxes in calculating the AMT. In calculating her AMT, Gretchen deducts the $4,800 (i.e., does not treat it as a positive adjustment) in converting regular taxable income to AMTI. Her justification for this treatment is the statutory language of § 56(b)(1)(A)(ii), which refers only to taxes deducted under § 164(a).

The IRS disagrees with Gretchen's interpretation and assesses a tax deficiency. In its opinion, the disallowance of the deduction in calculating the AMT applies to real estate taxes deducted under either § 164(a)(1) or § 216(a)(1).

Who is right?

Research Problem 2. In filing his tax return for 2005, Rayford Giles includes a Form 6251 for the AMT. In making the AMT calculation, he included itemized deductions that were allowable for AMT purposes of $20,000. In calculating his regular income tax liability, he used the standard deduction of $5,000 because his itemized deductions were completely phased out under § 68. By using the itemized deductions in calculating his AMT, Rayford was able to reduce his AMT liability. As support for his position, Rayford cites § 56(b)(1)(F), which provides that the itemized deduction phaseout (applicable in calculating the regular income tax) does not apply in calculating the AMT.

Will Rayford's position withstand IRS scrutiny?

Research Problem 3. Stuart is a journalist for a metropolitan newspaper. He has a degree in journalism from a major midwestern university.

For the past 10 years, Stuart has prepared his own income tax return. He finds doing so to be challenging and stimulating and believes that he pays lower taxes than he would if he hired a tax return preparer.

His 2004 return is audited. Although it included an AMT form (Form 6251), Stuart had not prepared it properly. Data from his Form 1040 were transferred to the wrong line in several places. In other cases, positive adjustments were not included because Stuart had failed to calculate them (e.g., did not recalculate itemized deductions for AMT purposes and did not have a positive adjustment for the personal exemption). Based on the IRS's calculation, a deficiency of $3,000 was assessed. Stuart's response to the IRS is that Form 6251 is ambiguous and misleading and, therefore, he should not be liable for the AMT. Evaluate Stuart's argument.

Partial list of research aids:
William M. Christine, 66 TCM 1025, T.C.Memo. 1993–473.

Research Problem 4.   On his 2005 Federal income tax return, Walter deducted state income taxes of $8,000 for amounts withheld and estimated tax payments made in 2005. When he filed his 2005 state income tax return in April 2006, he discovered that he had overpaid his state income taxes by $1,500. Rather than having the $1,500 refunded to him, he treated it as a 2006 estimated tax payment. The year 2005 was not an AMT year for Walter.

   In preparing his 2006 Federal income tax return, Walter is confused about how he should treat the $1,500 in calculating his Federal income tax liability. He knows that under the § 111 tax benefit rule, he should include the $1,500 in gross income in calculating his regular taxable income. However, since he is going to be subject to the AMT, he is uncertain as to how he should treat the $1,500 in calculating AMT. He thinks that the amount could be treated as a negative adjustment in converting taxable income to AMTI if 2005 had been an AMT year. Since it was not, Walter is unsure of the treatment.

   Advise Walter on the appropriate treatment of the $1,500 in calculating his 2006 Federal income tax liability.

 Internet *Activity*

Use the tax resources of the Internet to address the following questions. Do not restrict your search to the World Wide Web, but include a review of newsgroups and general reference materials, practitioner sites and resources, primary sources of the tax law, chat rooms and discussion groups, and other opportunities.

Research Problem 5.   Locate a current proposal to modify the structure or scope of the AMT for individuals. Describe the proposal, the entity making the proposal, and potential motivations for submitting the modification to Congress.

Communications

Research Problem 6.   Go to one of the tax newsgroups and post a short note on one of the following items relative to individuals who are subject to the AMT:
a.   Interest deductions on vacation homes.
b.   Charitable contributions of appreciated securities.
c.   Tax preparation fees.
d.   Adequacy of the exemption amount.
e.   Indexing of AMT rates.

CHAPTER 13

Tax Credits and Payment Procedures

LEARNING OBJECTIVES

After completing Chapter 13, you should be able to:

LO.1
Explain how tax credits are used as a tool of Federal tax policy.

LO.2
Distinguish between refundable and nonrefundable credits and understand the order in which they can be used by taxpayers.

LO.3
Describe various business-related tax credits.

LO.4
Describe various tax credits that are available primarily to individual taxpayers.

LO.5
Understand the tax withholding and payment procedures applicable to employers.

LO.6
Understand the payment procedures applicable to self-employed persons.

LO.7
Identify tax planning opportunities related to tax credits and payment procedures.

OUTLINE

As explained in Chapter 1, Federal tax law often serves other purposes besides merely raising revenue for the government. Evidence of equity, social, and economic considerations, among others, is found throughout the tax law. These considerations also bear heavily in the area of **tax credits**. Consider the following examples:

EXAMPLE 1

Paul and Peggy, husband and wife, are both employed outside the home. Their combined salaries are $50,000. However, after paying for child care expenses of $2,000 on behalf of their daughter, Polly, the net economic benefit from both spouses working is $48,000. The child care expenses are, in a sense, business related since they would not have been incurred if both spouses did not work outside the home. If no tax benefits are associated with the child care expenditures, $50,000 is subject to tax.

Another couple, Alicia and Diego, also have a child, John. Diego stays at home to care for John (the value of those services is $2,000) while Alicia earns a $48,000 salary. Because the value of Diego's services rendered is not subject to tax, only Alicia's earnings of $48,000 are subject to tax. ■

The credit for child and dependent care expenses mitigates the inequity felt by working taxpayers who must pay for child care services in order to work outside the home.

EXAMPLE 2

Graham, age 66, is a retired taxpayer who receives $14,000 of Social Security benefits as his only source of income in 2006. His Social Security benefits are excluded from gross income. Therefore, Graham's income tax is $0. In 2006, Olga, a single taxpayer 66 years of age, has, as her sole source of income, $14,000 from a pension plan funded by her former employer. Assuming Olga has no itemized deductions or deductions *for* AGI, her income tax for 2006 (before credits) is $430, based on the following computation:

Pension plan benefits	$14,000
Less: Basic standard deduction	(5,150)
Additional standard deduction	(1,250)
Personal exemption	(3,300)
Taxable income	$ 4,300
Income tax (at 10%)	$ 430

■

The tax credit for elderly or disabled taxpayers was enacted to mitigate this inequity.

EXAMPLE 3

Jane is a single parent who depends on the government's "safety net" for survival—she receives benefits under the Temporary Assistance to Needy Families program in the amount of $15,000 per year. However, she very much wishes to work. Jane has located a job that will pay $15,500 per year and has found an individual to care for her child at no cost. But, with the $1,185.75 ($15,500 × 7.65%) withholding for Social Security and Medicare taxes, the economic benefit from working is less than remaining reliant on the government ($14,314.25 as compared to $15,000). ∎

To help offset the effect of Social Security and Medicare taxes on wages of the working poor and to provide an incentive to work, the earned income credit is used to increase the after-tax earnings of qualified individuals. In addition, the earned income credit helps offset the regressive nature of certain taxes, such as the Social Security and Medicare taxes, which impose a relatively larger burden on low-income taxpayers than on more affluent taxpayers.

These three tax credits and many of the other important tax credits available to individuals and other types of taxpayers are a major focus of this chapter. The chapter begins by discussing important tax policy considerations relevant to tax credits. Tax credits are categorized as being either refundable or nonrefundable. The distinction between refundable and nonrefundable credits is important because it may affect the taxpayer's ability to enjoy a tax benefit from a particular credit.

Next an overview of the priority of tax credits is presented. The credit portion of the chapter continues with a discussion of the credits available to businesses and to individual taxpayers and the ways in which credits enter into the calculation of the tax liability.

The Federal tax system has long been based on the pay-as-you-go concept. That is, taxpayers or their employers are required to make regular deposits with the Federal government during the year as payment toward the tax liability that will be determined at the end of the tax year. These deposits are in effect refundable credits. The chapter concludes with a discussion of procedures used in calculating tax deposits, special problems encountered by self-employed persons when estimating their tax payments, and penalties imposed on underpayments.

Tax Policy Considerations

Congress has generally used tax credits to achieve social or economic objectives or to promote equity among different types of taxpayers. For example, the disabled access credit was enacted to accomplish a social objective: to encourage taxpayers to renovate older buildings so they would be in compliance with the Americans with Disabilities Act. This Act requires businesses and institutions to make their facilities more accessible to persons with various types of disabilities. As another example, the foreign tax credit, which has been a part of the law for decades, has as its purpose the economic and equity objectives of mitigating the burden of multiple taxation on a single stream of income.

A tax credit should not be confused with an income tax deduction. Certain expenditures of individuals (e.g., business expenses) are permitted as deductions from gross income in arriving at adjusted gross income (AGI). Additionally, individuals are allowed to deduct certain nonbusiness and investment-related expenses *from* AGI. While the tax benefit received from a tax deduction depends on the tax rate, a tax credit is not affected by the tax rate of the taxpayer.

> **LO.1**
> Explain how tax credits are used as a tool of Federal tax policy.

EXAMPLE 4

Assume Congress wishes to encourage a certain type of expenditure. One way to accomplish this objective is to allow a tax credit of 25% for such expenditures. Another way is to allow an itemized deduction for the expenditures. Assume that Abby's tax rate is 15%, while Bill's tax rate is 35%, and that each itemizes deductions. In addition, assume that Carmen does not incur enough qualifying expenditures to itemize deductions. The following tax benefits are available to each taxpayer for a $1,000 expenditure:

	Abby	Bill	Carmen
Tax benefit if a 25% credit is allowed	$250	$250	$250
Tax benefit if an itemized deduction is allowed	150	350	–0–

As these results indicate, tax credits provide benefits on a more equitable basis than do tax deductions. Equally apparent is that the deduction approach in this case benefits only taxpayers who itemize deductions, while the credit approach benefits all taxpayers who make the specified expenditure. ■

For many years, Congress has used the tax credit provisions of the Code liberally in implementing tax policy. Although budget constraints and economic considerations often have dictated the repeal of some credits, other credits, such as those applicable to expenses incurred for child and dependent care, have been kept to respond to important social policy considerations. Still other credits, such as the one available to low-income workers, have been retained based on economic and equity considerations. Finally, as the myriad of tax proposals so frequently pending before Congress makes clear, the use of tax credits as a tax policy tool continues to evolve as economic and political circumstances change.

LO.2

Distinguish between refundable and nonrefundable credits and understand the order in which they can be used by taxpayers.

Overview and Priority of Credits

Refundable versus Nonrefundable Credits

As illustrated in Exhibit 13–1, certain credits are refundable while others are nonrefundable. **Refundable credits** are paid to the taxpayer even if the amount of the credit (or credits) exceeds the taxpayer's tax liability.

EXHIBIT 13–1	**Partial Listing of Refundable and Nonrefundable Credits**

Refundable Credits

Taxes withheld on wages

Earned income credit

Nonrefundable Credits

Credit for child and dependent care expenses

Credit for elderly or disabled

Adoption expenses credit

Child tax credit*

Education tax credits

Credit for certain retirement plan contributions

Foreign tax credit

General business credit, which includes the following:
- Tax credit for rehabilitation expenditures
- Work opportunity tax credit
- Welfare-to-work credit
- Research activities credit
- Low-income housing credit
- Disabled access credit
- Credit for small employer pension plan startup costs
- Credit for employer-provided child care

*The credit is refundable to the extent of 15 percent of the taxpayer's earned income in excess of $11,300 for 2006 (indexed for inflation). Parents with three or more qualifying children may compute the refundable portion using an alternative method.

EXAMPLE 5

Ted, who is single, had taxable income of $21,000 in 2006. His income tax from the 2006 Tax Rate Schedule is $2,773. During 2006, Ted's employer withheld income tax of $3,200. Ted is entitled to a refund of $427 because the credit for tax withheld on wages is a refundable credit. ∎

Nonrefundable credits are not paid if they exceed the taxpayer's tax liability.

EXAMPLE 6

Tina is single, age 67, and retired. Her taxable income for 2006 is $1,320, and the tax on this amount is $132. Tina's tax credit for the elderly is $225. This credit can be used to reduce her net tax liability to zero, but it will not result in a refund, even though the credit ($225) exceeds Tina's tax liability ($132). This result occurs because the tax credit for the elderly is a nonrefundable credit. ∎

Some nonrefundable credits, such as the foreign tax credit, are subject to carryover provisions if they exceed the amount allowable as a credit in a given year. Other nonrefundable credits, such as the tax credit for the elderly (refer to Example 6), are not subject to carryover provisions and are lost if they exceed the limitations. Because some credits are refundable and others are not and because some credits are subject to carryover provisions while others are not, the order in which credits are offset against the tax liability can be important.[1]

[1]With the passage of the Tax Relief Reconciliation Act of 2001, the ordering rules and limitations applied when offsetting tax credits against both the regular income tax liability and the alternative minimum tax liability have become increasingly complex. In addition, different variations of these rules will apply over time as this legislation is fully implemented. Further discussion of the intricacies of these rules is beyond the scope of this chapter.

General Business Credit

As shown in Exhibit 13–1, the **general business credit** is composed of a number of other credits, each of which is computed separately under its own set of rules. The general business credit combines these credits into one amount to limit the amount of business credits that can be used to offset a taxpayer's income tax liability. The idea behind combining the credits is to prevent a taxpayer from completely avoiding an income tax liability in any one year by offsetting it with business credits that would otherwise be available.

Two special rules apply to the general business credit. First, any unused credit must be carried back 1 year, then forward 20 years. Second, for any tax year, the general business credit is limited to the taxpayer's *net income tax* reduced by the greater of:[2]

- The *tentative minimum tax*.
- 25 percent of *net regular tax liability* that exceeds $25,000.[3]

In order to understand the general business credit limitation, several terms need defining:

- *Net income tax* is the sum of the regular tax liability and the alternative minimum tax reduced by certain nonrefundable tax credits.
- *Tentative minimum tax* for this purpose is reduced by the foreign tax credit allowed.
- *Regular tax liability* is determined from the appropriate tax table or tax rate schedule, based on taxable income. However, the regular tax liability does not include certain taxes (e.g., alternative minimum tax).
- *Net regular tax liability* is the regular tax liability reduced by certain nonrefundable credits (e.g., credit for child and dependent care expenses, foreign tax credit).

E X A M P L E   7

Floyd's general business credit for the current year is $70,000. His net income tax is $150,000, tentative minimum tax is $130,000, and net regular tax liability is $150,000. He has no other tax credits. Floyd's general business credit allowed for the tax year is computed as follows:

Net income tax	$ 150,000
Less: The greater of	
• $130,000 (tentative minimum tax)	
• $31,250 [25% × ($150,000 − $25,000)]	(130,000)
Amount of general business credit allowed for tax year	$ 20,000

Floyd then has $50,000 ($70,000 − $20,000) of unused general business credits that may be carried back or forward as discussed below. ■

Treatment of Unused General Business Credits

Unused general business credits are initially carried back one year and are applied to reduce the tax liability during that year. Thus, the taxpayer may receive a tax refund as a result of the carryback. Any remaining unused credits are then carried forward 20 years.[4]

A FIFO method is applied to the carrybacks, carryovers, and utilization of credits earned during a particular year. The oldest credits are used first in determining

---

[2]§ 38(c).
[3]This amount is $12,500 for married taxpayers filing separately unless one of the spouses is not entitled to the general business credit.

[4]§ 39(a)(1).

the amount of the general business credit. The FIFO method minimizes the potential for loss of a general business credit benefit due to the expiration of credit carryovers, since the earliest years are used before the current credit for the taxable year.

EXAMPLE 8

This example illustrates the use of general business credit carryovers.

General business credit carryovers		
2003	$ 4,000	
2004	6,000	
2005	2,000	
Total carryovers	$12,000	
2006 general business credit		$ 40,000
Total credit allowed in 2006 (based on tax liability)	$50,000	
Less: Utilization of carryovers		
2003	(4,000)	
2004	(6,000)	
2005	(2,000)	
Remaining credit allowed in 2006	$38,000	
Applied against		
2006 general business credit		(38,000)
2006 unused amount carried forward to 2007		$ 2,000 ∎

Specific Business-Related Tax Credit Provisions

Each component of the general business credit is determined separately under its own set of rules. Some of the more important credits that make up the general business credit are explained here in the order listed in Exhibit 13–1.

Tax Credit for Rehabilitation Expenditures

Taxpayers are allowed a tax credit for expenditures incurred to rehabilitate industrial and commercial buildings and certified historic structures. The **rehabilitation expenditures credit** is intended to discourage businesses from moving from older, economically distressed areas (e.g., inner cities) to newer locations and to encourage the preservation of historic structures. The current operating features of this credit follow:[5]

Rate of the Credit for Rehabilitation Expenses	Nature of the Property
10%	Nonresidential buildings and residential rental property, other than certified historic structures, originally placed in service before 1936
20%	Nonresidential and residential certified historic structures

---

[5]§ 47.

TABLE 13–1	Recapture Calculation for Rehabilitation Expenditures Credit
If the Property Is Held for	**The Recapture Percentage Is**
Less than 1 year	100
One year or more but less than 2 years	80
Two years or more but less than 3 years	60
Three years or more but less than 4 years	40
Four years or more but less than 5 years	20
Five years or more	0

When taking the credit, the basis of a rehabilitated building must be reduced by the full rehabilitation credit allowed.[6]

EXAMPLE 9

Juan spent $60,000 to rehabilitate a building (adjusted basis of $40,000) that had originally been placed in service in 1932. He is allowed a $6,000 (10% × $60,000) credit for rehabilitation expenditures. Juan then increases the basis of the building by $54,000 [$60,000 (rehabilitation expenditures) − $6,000 (credit allowed)]. If the building were an historic structure, the credit allowed would be $12,000 (20% × $60,000), and the building's depreciable basis would increase by $48,000 [$60,000 (rehabilitation expenditures) − $12,000 (credit allowed)]. ∎

To qualify for the credit, buildings must be substantially rehabilitated. A building has been *substantially rehabilitated* if qualified rehabilitation expenditures exceed the greater of:

- The adjusted basis of the property before the rehabilitation expenditures, or
- $5,000.

Qualified rehabilitation expenditures do not include the cost of acquiring a building, the cost of facilities related to a building (such as a parking lot), and the cost of enlarging an existing building.

Recapture of Tax Credit for Rehabilitation Expenditures. The rehabilitation credit taken must be recaptured if the rehabilitated property is disposed of prematurely or if it ceases to be qualifying property. The **rehabilitation expenditures credit recapture** is based on a holding period requirement of five years and is added to the taxpayer's regular tax liability in the recapture year. The recapture amount is also *added* to the adjusted basis of the rehabilitation expenditures for purposes of determining the amount of gain or loss realized on the property's disposition.

The portion of the credit recaptured is a specified percentage of the credit that was taken by the taxpayer. This percentage is based on the period the property was held by the taxpayer, as shown in Table 13–1.

EXAMPLE 10

On March 15, 2003, Rashad placed in service $30,000 of rehabilitation expenditures on a building qualifying for the 10% credit. A credit of $3,000 ($30,000 × 10%) was allowed, and the basis of the building was increased by $27,000 ($30,000 − $3,000). The building was sold on December 15, 2006. Rashad must recapture a portion of the rehabilitation credit based on the schedule in Table 13–1. Because he held the rehabilitated property for more than three years but less than four, 40% of the credit, or $1,200, is added to his 2006 tax liability. Also, the adjusted basis of the rehabilitation expenditures is increased by the $1,200 recapture amount. ∎

---

[6]§ 50(c).

Work Opportunity Tax Credit

The **work opportunity tax credit** was enacted to encourage employers to hire individuals from one or more of a number of targeted and economically disadvantaged groups.[7] Examples of such targeted persons include qualified ex-felons, high-risk youths, food stamp recipients, veterans, summer youth employees, and persons receiving certain welfare benefits.

Computation of the Work Opportunity Tax Credit: General.
The credit generally is equal to 40 percent of the first $6,000 of wages (per eligible employee) for the first 12 months of employment. Thus, the credit is not available for any wages paid to an employee after the *first year* of employment. If the employee's first year overlaps two of the employer's tax years, however, the employer may take the credit over two tax years. If the credit is elected, the employer's tax deduction for wages is reduced by the amount of the credit.

For an employer to qualify for the 40 percent credit, the employee must (1) be certified by a designated local agency as being a member of one of the targeted groups and (2) have completed at least 400 hours of service to the employer. If an employee meets the first condition but not the second, the credit rate is reduced to 25 percent provided the employee has completed a minimum of 120 hours of service to the employer.

EXAMPLE 11

In January 2006, Green Company hires four individuals who are certified to be members of a qualifying targeted group. Each employee works 800 hours and is paid wages of $8,000 during the year. Green Company's work opportunity credit is $9,600 [($6,000 × 40%) × 4 employees]. If the tax credit is taken, Green must reduce its deduction for wages paid by $9,600. No credit is available for wages paid to these employees after their first year of employment. ∎

EXAMPLE 12

On June 1, 2006, Maria, a calendar year taxpayer, hires Joe, a member of a targeted group, and obtains the required certification. During the last seven months of 2006, Joe is paid $3,500 for 500 hours of work. Maria is allowed a credit of $1,400 ($3,500 × 40%) for 2006. Joe continues to work for Maria in 2007 and is paid $7,000 through May 31, 2007. Because up to $6,000 of first-year wages are eligible for the credit, Maria is allowed a 40% credit on $2,500 [$6,000 − $3,500 (wages paid in 2006)] of wages paid in 2007, or $1,000 ($2,500 × 40%). None of Joe's wages paid after May 31, the end of the first year of employment, is eligible for the credit. ∎

Computation of the Work Opportunity Tax Credit: Qualified Summer Youth Employees.
The credit for qualified summer youth employees is allowed on wages for services during any 90-day period between May 1 and September 15. The maximum wages eligible for the credit are $3,000 per summer youth employee. The credit rate is the same as that under the general provision for the work opportunity tax credit. If the employee continues employment after the 90-day period as a member of another targeted group, the amount of the wages eligible for the general work opportunity tax credit as a member of the new target group is reduced by the wages paid to the employee as a qualified summer youth employee.

A *qualified summer youth employee* must be age 16 or 17 on the hiring date. An additional requirement for qualifying is that the individual's principal place of abode must be within an empowerment zone, enterprise community, or renewal community.

---

[7]§ 51. At the time of this writing, the credit is available only if qualifying employees start work by December 31, 2005. However, the general consensus is that Congress will extend this provision for 2006. Therefore, Chapter 13 examples and problems assume its continuing availability for qualifying employees who start work by December 31, 2006.

Welfare-to-Work Credit

The **welfare-to-work credit**[8] is available to employers hiring individuals who have been long-term recipients of family assistance welfare benefits. In general, *long-term recipients* are those individuals who are certified by a designated local agency as being a member of a family receiving assistance under a public aid program for at least an 18-month period ending on the hiring date. Unlike the work opportunity credit, which applies only to first-year wages paid to qualified individuals, the welfare-to-work credit is available for qualified wages paid in the *first two years* of employment. If an employee's first and second work years overlap two or more of the employer's tax years, the employer may take the credit during the applicable tax years. If the welfare-to-work credit is taken, the employer's tax deduction for wages is reduced by the amount of the credit.

An employer is prohibited from taking both the work opportunity credit and the welfare-to-work credit for wages paid to a qualified employee in a given tax year.

Maximum Credit. The credit is equal to 35 percent of the first $10,000 of qualified wages paid to an employee in the first year of employment, plus 50 percent of the first $10,000 of qualified wages paid in the second year of employment, resulting in a maximum credit per qualified employee of $8,500 [$3,500 (year 1) + $5,000 (year 2)]. The credit rate is higher for second-year wages to encourage employers to retain qualified individuals, thereby promoting the overall welfare-to-work goal.

EXAMPLE 13

In April 2006, Blue Company hired three individuals who are certified as long-term family assistance recipients. Each employee is paid $12,000 during 2006. Two of the three individuals continue to work for Blue Company in 2007, earning $9,000 each during the year. Blue Company's welfare-to-work credit is $10,500 [(35% × $10,000) × 3 employees] for 2006 and $9,000 [(50% × $9,000) × 2 employees] for 2007. ■

Research Activities Credit

To encourage research and experimentation, usually described as research and development (R & D), a credit is allowed for certain qualifying expenditures paid or incurred by a taxpayer. The **research activities credit** is the *sum* of two components: an incremental research activities credit and a basic research credit.[9]

Incremental Research Activities Credit. The incremental research activities credit is equal to 20 percent of the *excess* of qualified research expenses for the taxable year over the base amount.

In general, *research expenditures* qualify if the research relates to discovering technological information that is intended for use in the development of a new or improved business component of the taxpayer. Such expenses qualify fully if the research is performed in-house (by the taxpayer or employees). If the research is conducted by persons outside the taxpayer's business (under contract), only 65 percent of the amount paid qualifies for the credit.[10]

---

[8]§ 51A. At the time of this writing, the credit is available only if qualifying employees start work by December 31, 2005. However, the general consensus is that Congress will extend this provision for 2006. Therefore, Chapter 13 examples and problems assume its continuing availability for qualifying employees who start work by December 31, 2006.

[9]§ 41. At the time of this writing, both components of the research credit are available only if qualifying expenditures are paid or incurred by December

31, 2005. However, the general consensus is that Congress will extend this provision for 2006. Therefore, Chapter 13 examples and problems assume its continuing availability in 2006.

[10]In the case of payments to a qualified research consortium, § 41(b)(3)(A) provides that 75% of the amount paid qualifies for the credit. For amounts paid to an energy research consortium, § 41(b)(3)(D) allows the full amount to qualify for the credit.

EXAMPLE 14

George incurs the following research expenditures:

| In-house wages, supplies, computer time | $50,000 |
| Paid to Cutting Edge Scientific Foundation for research | 30,000 |

George's qualified research expenditures are $69,500 [$50,000 + ($30,000 × 65%)]. ∎

Beyond the general guidelines described above, the Code does not give specific examples of qualifying research. However, the credit is *not* allowed for research that falls into certain categories, including the following:[11]

- Research conducted after the beginning of commercial production of the business component.
- Surveys and studies such as market research, testing, and routine data collection.
- Research conducted *outside* the United States (other than research undertaken in Puerto Rico and possessions of the United States).
- Research in the social sciences, arts, or humanities.

Determining the *base amount* involves a relatively complex series of computations, meant to approximate recent historical levels of research activity by the taxpayer. Thus, the credit is allowed only for increases in research expenses. A discussion of these computations is beyond the scope of this presentation.

EXAMPLE 15

Jack, a calendar year taxpayer, incurs qualifying research expenditures of $200,000 at the beginning of the year. Assuming the base amount is $100,000, the incremental research activities credit is $20,000 [($200,000 − $100,000) × 20%]. ∎

Qualified research and experimentation expenditures are not only eligible for the 20 percent credit, but can also be *expensed* in the year incurred.[12] In this regard, a taxpayer has two choices:[13]

- Use the full credit and reduce the expense deduction for research expenses by 100 percent of the credit.
- Retain the full expense deduction and reduce the credit by the product of 100 percent of the credit times the maximum corporate tax rate (35 percent).

As an alternative to the expense deduction, the taxpayer may *capitalize* the research expenses and *amortize* them over 60 months or more. In this case, the amount capitalized and subject to amortization is reduced by the full amount of the credit *only* if the credit exceeds the amount allowable as a deduction.

EXAMPLE 16

Assume the same facts as in Example 15, which shows that the potential incremental research activities credit is $20,000. The expense that the taxpayer can deduct and the credit amount are as follows:

	Credit Amount	Deduction Amount
• Full credit and reduced deduction		
$20,000 − $0	$20,000	
$200,000 − $20,000		$180,000

---

[11]§ 41(d). See also Reg. §§ 1.41–1 through 1.41–7.
[12]§ 174. Also refer to the discussion of rules for deducting research and experimental expenditures in Chapter 7.
[13]§ 280C(c).

	Credit Amount	Deduction Amount
• Reduced credit and full deduction		
$20,000 − [(1.00 × $20,000) × .35]	$13,000	
$200,000 − $0		$200,000
• Full credit and capitalize and elect to amortize costs over 60 months		
$20,000 − $0	20,000	
($200,000/60) × 12		40,000

Basic Research Credit. Corporations (other than S corporations or personal service corporations) are allowed an additional 20 percent credit for basic research payments made in *excess* of a base amount. This credit is not available to individual taxpayers. *Basic research payments* are defined as amounts paid in cash to a qualified basic research organization, such as a college or university or a tax-exempt organization operated primarily to conduct scientific research.

Basic research is defined generally as any original investigation for the advancement of scientific knowledge not having a specific commercial objective. The definition excludes basic research conducted outside the United States and basic research in the social sciences, arts, or humanities. This reflects the intent of Congress to encourage high-tech research in the United States.

The calculation of this additional credit for basic research expenditures is complex and is based on expenditures in excess of a specially defined base amount.[14] The portion of the basic research expenditures not in excess of the base amount is treated as a part of the qualifying expenditures for purposes of the regular credit for incremental research activities.

EXAMPLE 17

Orange Corporation, a qualifying corporation, pays $75,000 to a university for basic research. Assume that Orange's base amount for the basic research credit is $50,000. The basic research activities credit allowed is $5,000 [($75,000 − $50,000) × 20%]. The $50,000 of basic research expenditures that equal the base amount are treated as research expenses for purposes of the regular incremental research activities credit. ■

Low-Income Housing Credit

To encourage building owners to make affordable housing available for low-income individuals, Congress has made a credit available to owners of qualified low-income housing projects.[15]

More than any other, the **low-income housing credit** is influenced by nontax factors. For example, certification of the property by the appropriate state or local agency authorized to provide low-income housing credits is required. These credits are issued based on a nationwide allocation.

The amount of the credit is based on the qualified basis of the property. The qualified basis depends on the number of units rented to low-income tenants. Tenants are low-income tenants if their income does not exceed a specified percentage of the area median gross income. The amount of the credit is determined by multiplying the qualified basis by the applicable percentage. The credit is allowed over a 10-year period if the property continues to meet the required conditions.

[14]§ 41(e).

[15]§ 42.

EXAMPLE 18

Sarah spends $1 million to build a qualified low-income housing project completed January 1 of the current year. The entire project is rented to low-income families. Assume the credit rate for property placed in service during January is 8.08%.[16] Sarah may claim a credit of $80,800 ($1,000,000 × 8.08%) in the current year and in each of the following nine years. Generally, first-year credits are prorated based on the date the project is placed in service. A full year's credit is taken in each of the next nine years, and any remaining first-year credit is claimed in the eleventh year. ■

Recapture of a portion of the credit may be required if the number of units set aside for low-income tenants falls below a minimum threshold, if the taxpayer disposes of the property or the interest in it, or if the taxpayer's amount at risk decreases.

ETHICAL *Considerations* **A WIN-WIN SITUATION OR AN INCALCULABLE LOSS?**

John and Susie rent a unit at an apartment complex owned by Mitch Brown, who has been Susie's friend since they attended business school together. One day Mitch told Susie about the thousands of tax dollars that he has saved by claiming the low-income housing credit for his investment in the apartment complex. Susie was pleased that Mitch had reduced his tax burden because she believes that the government rarely uses its resources wisely. Inadvertently, though, Mitch let the fact slip that the apartment complex "qualifies" for the credit only because he overstates the percentage of low-income tenants living in the facility. Mitch admitted that by claiming that John and Susie are low-income tenants (even though they aren't), the percentage of low-income tenants is just enough for Mitch to "qualify" for the credit. Mitch said that because John and Susie were his friends, he was passing along some of his tax savings to them in the form of lower rent.

John and Susie know that if they report Mitch to the IRS, he will not only lose the economic benefits of the credit, but will also have legal troubles. Further, if Mitch were to be sentenced to prison for the tax fraud, his children would probably become wards of the state. In addition, John and Susie would have to pay higher rent. What course of action would you recommend to John and Susie?

Disabled Access Credit

The **disabled access credit** is designed to encourage small businesses to make their facilities more accessible to disabled individuals. The credit is available for any eligible access expenditures paid or incurred by an eligible small business. The credit is calculated at the rate of 50 percent of the eligible expenditures that exceed $250 but do not exceed $10,250. Thus, the maximum amount for the credit is $5,000 ($10,000 × 50%).[17]

An *eligible small business* is one that during the previous year either had gross receipts of $1 million or less or had no more than 30 full-time employees. An eligible business can include a sole proprietorship, partnership, regular corporation, or S corporation.

Eligible access expenditures are generally any reasonable and necessary amounts that are paid or incurred to make certain changes to facilities. These changes must involve the removal of architectural, communication, physical, or transportation barriers that would otherwise make a business inaccessible to disabled and handicapped individuals. Examples of qualifying projects include installing ramps, widening doorways, and adding raised markings on elevator control buttons. However, eligible expenditures do *not* include amounts that are paid or incurred in connection with any facility that has been placed in service after the enactment of the credit (i.e., November 5, 1990).

---

[16]The rate is subject to adjustment every month by the IRS.   [17]§ 44.

To the extent a disabled access credit is available, no deduction or credit is allowed under any other provision of the tax law. The adjusted basis for depreciation is reduced by the amount of the credit.

E X A M P L E 19	This year Red, Inc., an eligible business, makes $11,000 of capital improvements to business realty that had been placed in service in June 1990. The expenditures are intended to make Red's business more accessible to the disabled and are considered eligible expenditures for purposes of the disabled access credit. The amount of the credit is $5,000 [($10,250 − $250) × 50%]. Although $11,000 of eligible expenditures are incurred, only the excess of $10,250 over $250 qualifies for the credit. Further, the depreciable basis of the capital improvement is $6,000 because the basis must be reduced by the amount of the credit [$11,000 (cost) − $5,000 (amount of the credit)]. ∎

Credit for Small Employer Pension Plan Startup Costs

Small businesses are entitled to a nonrefundable credit for administrative costs associated with establishing and maintaining certain qualified retirement plans.[18] While such costs (e.g., payroll system changes, consulting fees) generally are deductible as ordinary and necessary business expenses, the credit is intended to lower the after-tax cost of establishing a qualified retirement program and thereby to encourage qualifying businesses to offer retirement plans for their employees. The **credit for small employer pension plan startup costs** is available for eligible employers at the rate of 50 percent of qualified startup costs. An eligible employer is one with fewer than 100 employees who have earned at least $5,000 of compensation. Qualified startup costs include ordinary and necessary expenses incurred in connection with establishing or maintaining an employer pension plan and retirement-related education costs.[19] The maximum credit is $500 (based on a maximum $1,000 of qualifying expenses), and the deduction for the startup costs incurred is reduced by the amount of the credit. The credit can be claimed for qualifying costs incurred in each of the three years beginning with the tax year in which the retirement plan becomes effective (maximum total credit over three years of $1,500).

E X A M P L E 20	Maple Company decides to establish a qualified retirement plan for its employees. In the process, it pays consulting fees of $1,200 to a firm that will provide educational seminars to Maple's employees and will assist the payroll department in making necessary changes to the payroll system. Maple may claim a credit for the pension plan startup costs of $500 ($1,200 of qualifying costs, limited to $1,000 × 50%), and its deduction for these expenses is reduced to $700 ($1,200 − $500). ∎

Credit for Employer-Provided Child Care

The scope of § 162 trade or business expenses includes an employer's expenditures incurred to provide for the care of children of employees as ordinary and necessary business expenses. Another option now available permits employers to claim a credit for qualifying expenditures incurred while providing child care facilities to their employees during normal working hours.[20] The **credit for employer-provided child care,** limited annually to $150,000, is composed of the aggregate of two components: 25 percent of qualified child care expenses and 10 percent of qualified child care resource and referral services. *Qualified child care expenses* include the costs of acquiring, constructing, rehabilitating, expanding, and operating a child care facility. *Child care resource and referral services* include amounts paid or incurred under a contract to provide child care resource and referral services to an

---

[18]§ 45E. Currently, this credit is scheduled to expire for years after December 31, 2010.

[19]§§ 45E(c)(1) and (d)(1).

[20]§ 45F. Currently, this credit is scheduled to expire for years after December 31, 2010.

employee. To prevent an employer from obtaining a double benefit by claiming a credit and the associated deductions on the same expenditures, any qualifying expenses otherwise deductible by the taxpayer must be reduced by the amount of the credit. In addition, the taxpayer's basis for any property acquired or constructed and used for qualifying purposes is reduced by the amount of the credit. If within 10 years of being placed in service, a child care facility ceases to be used for a qualified use, the taxpayer will be required to recapture a portion of the credit previously claimed.[21]

EXAMPLE 21

During the year, Tan Company constructed a child care facility for $400,000 to be used by its employees who have preschool-aged children in need of child care services while their parents are at work. In addition, Tan incurred salaries for child care workers and other administrative costs associated with the facility of $100,000 during the year. As a result, Tan's credit for employer-provided child care is $125,000 [($400,000 + $100,000) × 25%]. Correspondingly, the basis of the facility is reduced to $300,000 ($400,000 − $100,000), and the deduction for salaries and administrative costs is reduced to $75,000 ($100,000 − $25,000). ∎

Other Tax Credits

Earned Income Credit

LO.4

Describe various tax credits that are available primarily to individual taxpayers.

The **earned income credit,** which has been a part of the law for many years, consistently has been justified as a means of providing tax equity to the working poor. In addition, the credit has been designed to help offset regressive taxes that are a part of our tax system, such as the gasoline and Social Security taxes. Further, the credit is intended to encourage economically disadvantaged individuals to become contributing members of the workforce.[22]

In 2006, the earned income credit is determined by multiplying a maximum amount of earned income by the appropriate credit percentage (see Table 13–2). Generally, earned income includes employee compensation and net earnings from self-employment but excludes items such as interest, dividends, pension benefits, nontaxable employee compensation, and alimony. If a taxpayer has children, the credit percentage used in the calculation depends on the number of qualifying children. Thus, in 2006, the maximum earned income credit for a taxpayer with one qualifying child is $2,747 ($8,080 × 34%) and $4,536 ($11,340 × 40%) for a taxpayer with two or more qualifying children. However, the maximum earned income credit is phased out completely if the taxpayer's earned income or AGI exceeds certain thresholds as shown in Table 13–2.[23] To the extent that the greater of earned income or AGI exceeds $16,810 in 2006 for married taxpayers filing a joint return ($14,810 for other taxpayers), the difference, multiplied by the appropriate phaseout percentage, is subtracted from the maximum earned income credit.

EXAMPLE 22

In 2006, Grace Brown, who is married, files a joint return and otherwise qualifies for the earned income credit. Grace receives wages of $25,000, and she and her husband have no other income. The Browns have one qualifying child. The current earned income credit is $2,747 ($8,080 × 34%) reduced by $1,309 [($25,000 − $16,810) × 15.98%]. Thus, the earned income credit is $1,438. If the Browns have two or more qualifying children, the calculation produces a credit of $4,536 ($11,340 × 40%) reduced by $1,725 [($25,000 − $16,810) × 21.06%]. Thus, the Brown's earned income credit is $2,811 if they have two or more children. ∎

---

[21]§ 45F(d).

[22]§ 32. The earned income credit is not available if the taxpayer's unearned
  income (e.g., interest, dividends) exceeds $2,800 in 2006 ($2,700 in 2005).
  See § 32(i).

[23]§ 32(a)(2)(B).

| TABLE 13–2 | **Earned Income Credit and Phaseout Percentages** |

Tax Year	Number of Qualifying Children	Maximum Earned Income	Credit Percentage	Phaseout Begins	Phaseout Percentage	Phaseout Ends
2006	*Married, Filing Joint:*					
	One child	$ 8,080	34.00	$16,810	15.98	$34,001
	Two or more children	11,340	40.00	16,810	21.06	38,348
	No qualifying children	5,380	7.65	8,740	7.65	14,120
	Other Taxpayers:					
	One child	$ 8,080	34.00	$14,810	15.98	$32,001
	Two or more children	11,340	40.00	14,810	21.06	36,348
	No qualifying children	5,380	7.65	6,740	7.65	12,120
2005	*Married, Filing Joint:*					
	One child	$ 7,830	34.00	$16,370	15.98	$33,030
	Two or more children	11,000	40.00	16,370	21.06	37,263
	No qualifying children	5,220	7.65	8,530	7.65	13,750
	Other Taxpayers:					
	One child	$ 7,830	34.00	$14,370	15.98	$31,030
	Two or more children	11,000	40.00	14,370	21.06	35,263
	No qualifying children	5,220	7.65	6,530	7.65	11,750

Earned Income Credit Table. It is not necessary to compute the credit as shown in Example 22. To simplify the compliance process, the IRS issues an Earned Income Credit Table for the determination of the appropriate amount of the credit. This table and a worksheet are included in the instructions available to individual taxpayers.

Eligibility Requirements. Eligibility for the credit may depend not only on the taxpayer meeting the earned income and AGI thresholds, but also on whether he or she has a qualifying child. The term *qualifying child* generally has the same meaning here as it does for purposes of determining who qualifies as a dependent (see Chapter 3).

In addition to being available for taxpayers with qualifying children, the earned income credit is also available to certain *workers without children*. However, this provision is available only to taxpayers aged 25 through 64 who cannot be claimed as a dependent on another taxpayer's return. As shown in Table 13–2, the credit for 2006 is calculated on a maximum earned income of $5,380 times 7.65 percent and reduced by 7.65 percent of earned income over $8,740 for married taxpayers filing a joint return ($6,740 for other taxpayers).

EXAMPLE 23

Walt, who is single, 28 years of age, and is not claimed as a dependent on anyone else's return, earns $7,000 during 2006. Even though he does not have any qualifying children, he qualifies for the earned income credit. His credit is $412 ($5,380 × 7.65%) reduced by $20 [($7,000 − $6,740) × 7.65%]. Thus, Walt's earned income credit is $392. If, instead, Walt's earned income is $6,000, his earned income credit is $412. In this situation, there is no phaseout of the maximum credit because his earned income is not in excess of $6,740. ■

Advance Payment. The earned income credit is a form of negative income tax (a refundable credit for taxpayers who do not have a tax liability). An eligible individual may elect to receive advance payments of the earned income credit from his or her employer (rather than receiving the credit from the IRS upon filing the tax

TAX *in the News*	THE EARNED INCOME CREDIT: A BOOST TO THE WORKING POOR AND MERCHANTS, TOO!

Since 1975, the earned income credit has helped keep millions of Americans from falling below the poverty line. The tax benefits that go to over 20 million families represent one of the nation's biggest antipoverty efforts. However, these benefits don't come without problems: fraudulent claims are believed to be common (the IRS estimates that over 30 percent of the benefits are paid in error), and compliance requirements are dauntingly complex (the IRS instructions exceed 50 pages).

The benefits from the earned income credit that flow to the working poor have also led to another problem. Some merchants are targeting this group of taxpayers—and their refunds. Pawn shops, jewelers, and auto dealerships in poor neighborhoods often offer to prepare tax returns, hoping to benefit in three ways: they collect fees for preparing the returns, they offer bridge loans at exorbitant interest rates before a tax refund arrives, and they sell high-priced goods to individuals expecting a windfall from their tax refunds. Needless to say, some of these merchants provide fair and valuable assistance to many needy taxpayers; however, many other merchants are in this niche for the sole purpose of lining their own pockets. The caveat "buyer beware" could never be more appropriate.

return). The amount that can be received in advance is limited to 60 percent of the credit that is available to a taxpayer with only one qualifying child. If this election is made, the taxpayer must file a certificate of eligibility (Form W–5) with his or her employer and *must* file a tax return for the year the income is earned.[24]

Tax Credit for Elderly or Disabled Taxpayers

The credit for the elderly was originally enacted to provide tax relief on retirement income for individuals who were not receiving substantial benefits from tax-free Social Security payments.[25] Currently, the **tax credit for the elderly or disabled** applies to the following:

- Taxpayers age 65 or older.
- Taxpayers under age 65 who are retired with a **permanent and total disability** and who have disability income from a public or private employer on account of the disability. A person generally is considered permanently and totally disabled if he or she is unable to engage in any substantial gainful activity due to a physical or mental impairment for a period of at least 12 months (or lesser period if the disability results in death).

The *maximum* allowable credit is $1,125 (15% × $7,500 of qualifying income), but the credit will be less for a taxpayer who receives Social Security benefits or has AGI exceeding specified amounts. Under these circumstances, the base used in the credit computation is reduced. Many taxpayers receive Social Security benefits or have AGI high enough to reduce the base for the credit to zero. In addition, because the credit is nonrefundable, the allowable credit cannot exceed the taxpayer's tax liablity.

The eligibility requirements and the tax computation are somewhat complicated. Consequently, an individual may elect to have the IRS compute his or her tax and the amount of the tax credit.

The credit generally is based on an initial amount (referred to as the *base amount*) and the filing status of the taxpayer in accordance with Table 13–3. To qualify for the credit, married taxpayers who live together must file a joint return. For taxpayers under age 65 who are retired on permanent and total disability, the base amounts could be less than those shown in Table 13–3 because these amounts are limited to taxable disability income.

---

[24]§ 3507.

[25]§ 22. This credit is not subject to indexation.

| TABLE 13–3 | Base and Threshold Amounts for Tax Credit for Elderly or Disabled Taxpayers |

Status	Base Amount	Threshold Amount
Single, head of household, or surviving spouse	$5,000	$ 7,500
Married, joint return, only one spouse qualifies	5,000	10,000
Married, joint return, both spouses qualify	7,500	10,000
Married, separate returns, spouses live apart the entire year (amount for each spouse)	3,750	5,000

This initial base amount is *reduced* by (1) Social Security, Railroad Retirement, and certain excluded pension benefits and (2) one-half of the taxpayer's AGI in excess of a threshold amount (see Table 13–3), which is a function of the taxpayer's filing status. The credit may be calculated using the procedure presented in the following example.

EXAMPLE 24

Paul and Peggy, husband and wife, are both over age 65 and receive Social Security benefits of $1,000 in the current year. On a joint return, they report AGI of $21,000.

Base amount (from Table 13–3)		$ 7,500
Less: Qualifying nontaxable benefits	$1,000	
One-half of excess of AGI over threshold amount from Table 13–3 $[(\$21,000 - \$10,000) \times \frac{1}{2}]$	5,500	
Total reductions		(6,500)
Balance subject to credit		$ 1,000
Multiply balance subject to credit by 15%—this is the tax credit allowed, subject to tax liability limitation		$ 150

Schedule R of Form 1040 is used to calculate and report the credit.

Foreign Tax Credit

Both individual taxpayers and corporations may claim a tax credit for foreign income tax paid on income earned and subject to tax in another country or a U.S. possession.[26] As an alternative, a taxpayer may claim a deduction instead of a credit.[27] In most instances, the **foreign tax credit (FTC)** is advantageous since it provides a direct offset against the tax liability.

The purpose of the FTC is to mitigate double taxation since income earned in a foreign country is subject to both U.S. and foreign taxes. However, the ceiling limitation formula may result in some form of double taxation or taxation at rates in excess of U.S. rates when the foreign tax rates are higher than the U.S. rates. This is a distinct possibility because U.S. tax rates are often lower than those of many foreign countries.

Other special tax treatments applicable to taxpayers working outside the United States include the foreign earned income exclusion (refer to Chapter 5) and limitations on deducting expenses of employees working outside the United

---

[26]Section 27 provides for the credit, but the qualifications and calculation procedure for the credit are contained in §§ 901–908.   [27]§ 164.

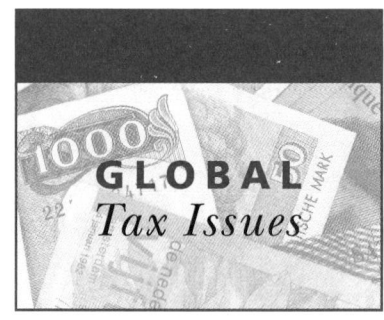

SOURCING INCOME IN CYBERSPACE—GETTING IT RIGHT WHEN CALCULATING THE FOREIGN TAX CREDIT

The overall limitation on the foreign tax credit (FTC) plays a critical role in restricting the amount of the credit available to a taxpayer. In the overall limitation formula, the taxpayer must characterize the year's taxable income as either earned (or sourced) inside the United States or earned from sources outside the United States. As a general rule, a relatively greater percentage of foreign-source income in the formula will lead to a larger FTC. Therefore, determining the source of various types of income is critical in the proper calculation of the credit. However, classifying income as either foreign or U.S. source is not always a simple matter.

For example, consumers and businesses are using the Internet to conduct more and more commerce involving both products and services. The problem is that the existing income-sourcing rules were developed long before the existence of the Internet, and taxing authorities are finding it challenging to apply these rules to Internet transactions. Where does a sale take place when the Web server is in Scotland, the seller is in India, and the customer is in Illinois? Where is a service performed when all activities take place over the Net? These questions and more will have to be answered by the United States and its trading partners as the Internet economy grows in size and importance.

States (refer to Chapter 9). Recall from the earlier discussion that a taxpayer may not take advantage of *both* the FTC and the foreign earned income exclusion.

Computation. Taxpayers are required to compute the FTC based upon an overall limitation.[28] The FTC allowed is the *lesser* of the foreign taxes imposed or the *overall limitation* determined according to the following formula:

$$\frac{\text{Foreign-source taxable income}}{\text{Worldwide taxable income}} \times \text{U.S. tax before FTC}$$

For individual taxpayers, worldwide taxable income in the overall limitation formula is determined *before* personal and dependency exemptions are deducted.

EXAMPLE 25

In 2006, Carlos, a calendar year taxpayer, has $10,000 of income from Country Y, which imposes a 15% tax, and $20,000 from Country Z, which imposes a 50% tax. He has taxable income of $56,800 from within the United States, is married filing a joint return, and claims two dependency exemptions. Thus, although Carlos's taxable income for purposes of determining U.S. tax is $86,800, taxable income amounts used in the limitation formula are not reduced by personal and dependency exemptions. Thus, for this purpose, taxable income is $100,000 [$86,800 + (4 × $3,300)]. Assume that Carlos's U.S. tax before the credit is $14,815. Overall limitation:

$$\frac{\text{Foreign-source taxable income}}{\text{Worldwide taxable income}} = \frac{\$30,000}{\$100,000} \times \$14,815 = \$4,445$$

In this case, $4,445 is allowed as the FTC because this amount is less than the $11,500 of foreign taxes imposed [$1,500 (Country Y) + $10,000 (Country Z)]. ∎

Thus, the overall limitation may result in some of the foreign income being subjected to double taxation. Unused FTCs [e.g., the $7,055 ($11,500 − $4,445) from Example 25] can be carried back 1 year and forward 10 years.[29]

---

[28]§ 904.

[29]§ 904(c) and Reg. § 1.904–2(g), Example 1. This treatment of unused FTCs applies to tax years ending after October 22, 2004. Prior law provided a two-year carryback and a five-year carryforward.

Only foreign income taxes, war profits taxes, and excess profits taxes (or taxes paid in lieu of such taxes) qualify for the credit.[30] In determining whether or not a tax is an income tax, U.S. criteria are applied. Thus, value added taxes (VAT), severance taxes, property taxes, and sales taxes do not qualify because they are not regarded as taxes on income. Such taxes may be deductible, however.

Adoption Expenses Credit

Adoption expenses paid or incurred by a taxpayer may give rise to the **adoption expenses credit**.[31] The provision is intended to assist taxpayers who incur nonrecurring costs directly associated with the adoption process, such as adoption fees, attorney fees, court costs, social service review costs, and transportation costs.

In 2006, up to $10,960 of costs incurred to adopt an eligible child qualify for the credit.[32] An eligible child is one who is:

- under 18 years of age at the time of the adoption or
- physically or mentally incapable of taking care of himself or herself.

A taxpayer may claim the credit in the year qualifying expenses were paid or incurred if they were paid or incurred *during or after* the tax year in which the adoption was finalized. For qualifying expenses paid or incurred in a tax year *prior* to the year when the adoption was finalized, the credit must be claimed in the tax year following the tax year during which the expenses are paid or incurred. A married couple must file a joint return.

EXAMPLE 26

In late 2005, Sam and Martha pay $4,000 in legal fees, adoption fees, and other expenses directly related to the adoption of an infant daughter, Susan. In 2006, the year in which the adoption becomes final, they pay an additional $8,000. Sam and Martha are eligible for a $10,960 credit in 2006 (for expenses, limited by the $10,960 ceiling, paid in 2005 and 2006). ∎

The amount of the credit that is otherwise available is phased out for taxpayers whose AGI (modified for this purpose) exceeds $164,410 in 2006, and the credit is completely eliminated when the AGI reaches $204,410. The resulting credit is calculated by reducing the allowable credit (determined without this reduction) by the allowable credit multiplied by the ratio of the excess of the taxpayer's AGI over $164,410 to $40,000.[33]

EXAMPLE 27

Assume the same facts as in the previous example, except that Sam and Martha's AGI is $189,410 in 2006. As a result, their available credit in 2006 is reduced from $10,960 to $4,110 {$10,960 − [$10,960 ($25,000/$40,000)]}. ∎

The credit is nonrefundable and is available to taxpayers only in a year in which this credit and the other nonrefundable credits do not exceed the taxpayer's tax liability. However, any unused adoption expenses credit may be carried over for up to five years, being utilized on a first-in, first-out basis.

Child Tax Credit

The **child tax credit** provisions allow individual taxpayers to take a tax credit based solely on the *number* of their qualifying children. This credit is one of several "family-friendly" provisions that currently are part of our tax law. To be eligible for the

---

[30]Reg. § 1.901–1(a)(3)(i).

[31]§ 23.

[32]§ 23(b)(1). In 2005, the maximum amount of eligible costs was $10,630. This ceiling is adjusted for inflation annually. Special rules are used in calculating the credit when adopting "a child with special needs." See § 23(d)(3).

[33]§ 23(b)(2). The AGI threshold amount is indexed for inflation. In 2005, the phaseout of the credit began when AGI exceeded $159,450.

credit, the child must be under age 17, a U.S. citizen, and claimed as a dependent on the taxpayer's return.

Maximum Credit and Phaseouts. Under current law, the maximum credit available is $1,000 per child.[34] The available credit is phased out for higher-income taxpayers beginning when AGI reaches $110,000 for joint filers ($55,000 for married taxpayers filing separately) and $75,000 for single taxpayers. The credit is phased out by $50 for each $1,000 (or part thereof) of AGI above the threshold amounts.[35] Since the maximum credit amount available to taxpayers depends on the number of qualifying children, the income level at which the credit is phased out completely also depends on the number of children qualifying for the credit.

E X A M P L E   **28**

Juanita and Alberto are married and file a joint tax return claiming their two children, ages six and eight, as dependents. Their AGI is $122,400. Juanita and Alberto's available child tax credit is $1,350, computed as their maximum credit of $2,000 ($1,000 × 2 children) reduced by a $650 phaseout. Since Juanita and Alberto's AGI is in excess of the $110,000 threshold, the maximum credit must be reduced by $50 for every $1,000 (or part thereof) above the threshold amount {$50 × [($122,400 − $110,000)/$1,000]}. Thus, the credit reduction equals $650 [$50 × 13 (rounded from 12.4)]. Therefore, Juanita and Alberto's child tax credit is $1,350. ■

Credit for Child and Dependent Care Expenses

A credit is allowed to taxpayers who incur employment-related expenses for child or dependent care.[36] The **credit for child and dependent care expenses** is a specified percentage of expenses incurred to enable the taxpayer to work or to seek employment. Expenses on which the credit for child and dependent care expenses is based are subject to limitations.

Eligibility. To be eligible for the credit, an individual must have either of the following:

* A dependent under age 13.
* A dependent or spouse who is physically or mentally incapacitated and who lives with the taxpayer for more than one-half of the year.

Generally, married taxpayers must file a joint return to obtain the credit.

Eligible Employment-Related Expenses. Eligible expenses include amounts paid for household services and care of a qualifying individual that are incurred to enable the taxpayer to be employed. Child and dependent care expenses include expenses incurred in the home, such as payments for a housekeeper. Out-of-the-home expenses incurred for the care of a dependent under the age of 13 also qualify for the credit. In addition, out-of-the-home expenses incurred for an older dependent or spouse who is physically or mentally incapacitated qualify for the credit if that person regularly spends at least eight hours each day in the taxpayer's household. This makes the credit available to taxpayers who keep handicapped older children and elderly relatives in the home instead of institutionalizing them. Out-of-the-home expenses incurred for services provided by a dependent care center will qualify only if the center complies with all applicable laws and regulations of a state or unit of local government.

    Child care payments to a relative are eligible for the credit unless the relative is a child (under age 19) of the taxpayer.

---

[34]§ 24. The maximum credit per child is scheduled to remain at $1,000 through 2010.

[35]AGI is modified for purposes of this calculation. The threshold amounts are *not* indexed for inflation. See §§ 24(a) and (b).

[36]§ 21.

EXAMPLE 29

Wilma is an employed mother of an eight-year-old child. She pays her mother, Rita, $1,500 per year to care for the child after school. Wilma pays her daughter Eleanor, age 17, $900 for the child's care during the summer. Of these amounts, only the $1,500 paid to Rita qualifies as employment-related child care expenses. ■

Earned Income Ceiling. The total for qualifying employment-related expenses is limited to an individual's earned income. For married taxpayers, this limitation applies to the spouse with the *lesser* amount of earned income. Special rules are provided for taxpayers with nonworking spouses who are disabled or are full-time students. If a nonworking spouse is physically or mentally disabled or is a full-time student, he or she is *deemed* to have earned income for purposes of this limitation. The deemed amount is $250 per month if there is one qualifying individual in the household or $500 per month if there are two or more qualifying individuals in the household. In the case of a student-spouse, the student's income is *deemed* to be earned only for the months that the student is enrolled on a full-time basis at an educational institution.[37]

Calculation of the Credit. In general, the credit is equal to a percentage of *unreimbursed* employment-related expenses up to $3,000 for one qualifying individual and $6,000 for two or more individuals. The credit rate varies between 20 percent and 35 percent, depending on the taxpayer's AGI. The following chart shows the applicable percentage for taxpayers as AGI increases:

Adjusted Gross Income		Applicable Rate of Credit
Over	But Not Over	
$ 0	$15,000	35%
15,000	17,000	34%
17,000	19,000	33%
19,000	21,000	32%
21,000	23,000	31%
23,000	25,000	30%
25,000	27,000	29%
27,000	29,000	28%
29,000	31,000	27%
31,000	33,000	26%
33,000	35,000	25%
35,000	37,000	24%
37,000	39,000	23%
39,000	41,000	22%
41,000	43,000	21%
43,000	No limit	20%

EXAMPLE 30

Nancy, who has two children under age 13, worked full-time while her spouse, Ron, was attending college for 10 months during the year. Nancy earned $22,000 and incurred $6,200 of child care expenses. Ron is *deemed* to be fully employed and to have earned $500 for each of the 10 months (or a total of $5,000). Since Nancy and Ron have AGI of $22,000, they are allowed a credit rate of 31%. Nancy and Ron are limited to $5,000 in qualified child care

[37]§ 21(d).

expenses (the lesser of $6,000 or $5,000). Therefore, they are entitled to a tax credit of $1,550 (31% × $5,000) for the year. ■

ETHICAL *Considerations*   USING THE CREDIT FOR CHILD AND DEPENDENT CARE EXPENSES

Your friends, Bob and Carol, have hired a child care provider to come into their home for three hours a day to care for their child while they both are at work. The child care provider, Delores, charges $2,400 for her services for the year. Bob and Carol have learned that up to $3,000 of qualifying expenditures will generate a credit for child and dependent care expenses and that qualifying expenditures can include payments for housecleaning services. As a result, they ask Delores whether she would be interested in working several hours more per week, after Bob returns from work, for the sole purpose of cleaning the house. Bob offers to pay Delores $600 for the additional work, and she seems interested. For Bob and Carol, the net cost of the additional services would be $480 [$600 – ($600 × 20%)] due to the availability of the credit for child and dependent care expenses.

You learn of Bob and Carol's opportunity, but think it is unfair. If you hired Delores to perform similar housecleaning services, your net cost would be $600, and not $480, because you do not qualify for the credit. You are not sure that Bob and Carol should "take advantage" of the system in this way. How do you suppose Bob and Carol will feel, or should feel, about this "abuse" if you approach them?

Dependent Care Assistance Program. Recall from Chapter 5 that a taxpayer is allowed an exclusion from gross income for a limited amount reimbursed for child or dependent care expenses. However, the taxpayer is not allowed both an exclusion from gross income and a child and dependent care credit on the same amount. The $3,000 and $6,000 ceilings for allowable child and dependent care expenses are reduced dollar for dollar by the amount of reimbursement.[38]

Assume the same facts as in Example 30, except that of the $6,200 paid for child care, Nancy was reimbursed $2,500 by her employer under a qualified dependent care assistance program. Under the employer's plan, the reimbursement reduces Nancy's taxable wages. Thus, Nancy and Ron have AGI of $19,500 ($22,000 – $2,500). The maximum amount of child care expenses for two or more dependents of $6,000 is reduced by the $2,500 reimbursement, resulting in a tax credit of $1,120 [32% × ($6,000 – $2,500)]. ■

E X A M P L E   31

Reporting Requirements. The credit is claimed by completing and filing Form 2441, Credit for Child and Dependent Care Expenses.

Education Tax Credits

Two credits, the **HOPE scholarship credit** and the **lifetime learning credit,**[39] are available to help qualifying low- and middle-income individuals defray the cost of higher education. The credits, both of which are nonrefundable, are available for qualifying tuition and related expenses incurred by students pursuing undergraduate or graduate degrees or vocational training. Room, board, and book costs are ineligible for the credits.

Maximum Credit. The HOPE scholarship credit permits a maximum credit of $1,650 per year (100 percent of the first $1,100 of tuition expenses plus 50 percent of the next $1,100 of tuition expenses) for the *first two years* of postsecondary education.[40]

---

[38]§ 21(c).

[39]§ 25A.

[40]The $1,100 qualifying expense base for the HOPE scholarship credit is subject to inflation adjustment. The base was $1,000 for years prior to 2006, and the maximum credit was $1,500.

The lifetime learning credit permits a credit of 20 percent of qualifying expenses (up to $10,000 per year) incurred in a year in which the HOPE scholarship credit is not claimed with respect to a given student. Generally, the lifetime learning credit is used for individuals who are beyond the first two years of postsecondary education.

Eligible Individuals. Both education credits are available for qualified expenses incurred by a taxpayer, taxpayer's spouse, or taxpayer's dependent. The HOPE scholarship credit is available per eligible student, while the lifetime learning credit is calculated per taxpayer. To be eligible for the HOPE credit, a student must take at least one-half the full-time course load for at least one academic term at a qualifying educational institution. No comparable requirement exists for the lifetime learning credit. Therefore, taxpayers who are seeking new job skills or maintaining existing skills through graduate training or continuing education are eligible for the lifetime learning credit. Taxpayers who are married must file joint returns in order to claim either education credit.

Income Limitations. Both education credits are subject to income limitations and are combined for purposes of the limitation calculation. The allowable credit amount is phased out, beginning when the taxpayer's AGI (modified for this purpose) reaches $45,000 ($90,000 for married taxpayers filing jointly).[41] The reduction in 2006 is equal to the extent to which AGI exceeds $45,000 ($90,000 for married filing jointly) as a percentage of the $10,000 ($20,000 for married filing jointly) phaseout range. The credits are completely eliminated when AGI reaches $55,000 ($110,000 for married filing jointly).

EXAMPLE 32

Dean and Audry are married, file a joint tax return, have modified AGI under $90,000, and have two children, Raymond and Kelsey. During fall 2006, Raymond is beginning his freshman year at State University, and Kelsey is beginning her senior year. During the prior semester, Kelsey completed her junior year. Both Raymond and Kelsey are full-time students and may be claimed as dependents on their parents' tax return. Raymond's qualifying expenses total $4,300 for the fall semester while Kelsey's qualifying expenses total $10,200 for the prior and current semesters. For 2006, Dean and Audry may claim a $1,650 HOPE scholarship credit [(100% × $1,100) + (50% × $1,100)] relating to Raymond's expenses and a $2,000 lifetime learning credit (20% × $10,000) relating to Kelsey's expenses. Kelsey's tuition expenses are ineligible for the HOPE scholarship credit because she is beyond the first two years of postsecondary education. ∎

EXAMPLE 33

Assume the same facts as in Example 32, except that Dean and Audry's modified AGI for 2006 is $102,000. Dean and Audry are eligible to claim $1,460 in total education credits for 2006. Their available credits totaling $3,650 ($1,650 HOPE scholarship credit + $2,000 lifetime learning credit) must be reduced because their AGI exceeds the $90,000 limit for married taxpayers. The percentage reduction is computed as the amount by which modified AGI exceeds the limit, expressed as a percentage of the phaseout range, or [($102,000 − $90,000)/$20,000)], resulting in a 60% reduction. Therefore, the maximum available credit for 2006 is $1,460 ($3,650 × 40% allowable portion). ∎

Restrictions on Double Tax Benefit. Taxpayers are prohibited from receiving a double tax benefit associated with qualifying educational expenses. Therefore, taxpayers who claim an education credit may not deduct the expenses, nor may they claim the credit for amounts that are otherwise excluded from gross income (e.g., scholarships, employer-paid educational assistance). However, a taxpayer may claim an education tax credit and exclude from gross income amounts distributed from a

---

[41] § 25A(d). For 2005, the AGI bases were $43,000 and $87,000. § 25A(h)(2)(A).

| TABLE 13–4 | "Saver's" Credit Rate and AGI Thresholds |

Joint Return		Head of Household		All Other Cases		Applicable Percentage
Over	Not Over	Over	Not Over	Over	Not Over	
$ 0	$30,000	$ 0	$22,500	$ 0	$15,000	50%
30,000	32,500	22,500	24,375	15,000	16,250	20%
32,500	50,000	24,375	37,500	16,250	25,000	10%
50,000		37,500		25,000		0%

Coverdell Education Savings Account as long as the distribution is not used for the same expenses for which the credit is claimed.

Credit for Certain Retirement Plan Contributions

Taxpayers may claim a nonrefundable **credit for certain retirement plan contributions** based on eligible contributions of up to $2,000 to certain qualified retirement plans established after 2001, such as traditional and Roth IRAs and § 401(k) plans.[42] This credit, sometimes referred to as the "saver's credit," was enacted to encourage lower- and middle-income taxpayers to contribute to qualified retirement plans. The benefit provided by this credit is in addition to any deduction or exclusion that otherwise is available due to the qualifying contribution. In calculating the credit, the qualifying contributions are reduced by taxable distributions from any of the qualifying plans received by the taxpayer and spouse during the tax year and the two previous tax years and during the period prior to the due date of the return.

The credit rate applied to the eligible expenses depends on the taxpayer's AGI[43] and filing status as shown in Table 13–4. However, the maximum credit allowed to an individual is $1,000 ($2,000 × 50%). As the taxpayer's AGI increases, the rate applied to contributions in calculating the credit is reduced, and once AGI exceeds the upper end of the applicable range, no credit is available. To qualify for the credit, the taxpayer must be at least 18 years of age and cannot be a dependent of another taxpayer or a full-time student.

Earl and Josephine, married taxpayers, each contribute $2,500 to their respective § 401(k) plans offered through their employers. The AGI reported on their joint return is $45,000. The maximum amount of contributions that may be taken into account in calculating the credit is limited to $2,000 for Earl and $2,000 for Josephine. As a result, they may claim a credit for their retirement plan contributions of $400 [($2,000 × 2) × 10%]. They would not qualify for the credit if their AGI had exceeded $50,000. ■

E X A M P L E   34

Payment Procedures

The tax law contains elaborate rules that require the prepayment of various Federal taxes. Consistent with the pay-as-you-go approach to the collection of taxes, these rules carry penalties for lack of compliance.[44] Prepayment procedures fall into two major categories: those applicable to employers and those applicable to self-employed persons. For employers, both payroll taxes (FICA and FUTA) and

LO.5

Understand the tax withholding and payment procedures applicable to employers.

---

[42]§ 25B. This credit is scheduled to expire for tax years beginning after December 31, 2006. The maximum credit allowed is not indexed for inflation.

[43]For purposes of this credit, the AGI thresholds are modified to include certain excluded income items. See § 25B(e).

[44]See, for example, § 3403 (employer liable for any taxes withheld and not paid over to the IRS), § 6656 (penalty on amounts withheld and not paid over), and § 6654 (penalty for failure by an individual to pay estimated income taxes).

CONCEPT SUMMARY   13–1

Tax Credits

Credit	Computation	Comments
Tax withheld on wages (§ 31)	Amount is reported to employee on Form W–2.	Refundable credit.
Earned income (§ 32)	Amount is determined by reference to Earned Income Credit Table published by IRS. Computations of underlying amounts in Earned Income Credit Table are illustrated in Example 22.	Refundable credit. A form of negative income tax to assist low-income taxpayers. Earned income and AGI must be less than certain threshold amounts. Generally, one or more qualifying children must reside with the taxpayer.
Child and dependent care (§ 21)	Rate ranges from 20% to 35% depending on AGI. Maximum base for credit is $3,000 for one qualifying individual, $6,000 for two or more.	Nonrefundable personal credit. No carryback or carryforward. Benefits taxpayers who incur employment-related child or dependent care expenses in order to work or seek employment. Eligible taxpayers must have a dependent under age 13 or a dependent (any age) or spouse who is physically or mentally incapacitated.
Elderly or disabled (§ 22)	15% of sum of base amount minus reductions for (1) Social Security and other nontaxable benefits and (2) excess AGI. Base amount is fixed by law (e.g., $5,000 for a single taxpayer).	Nonrefundable personal credit. No carryback or carryforward. Provides relief for taxpayers not receiving substantial tax-free retirement benefits.
Adoption expenses (§ 23)	Up to $10,960 of costs incurred to adopt an eligible child qualify for the credit. Taxpayer claims the credit in the year qualified expenses were paid or incurred if they were paid or incurred during or after year in which adoption was finalized. For expenses paid or incurred in a year prior to when adoption was finalized, credit must be claimed in tax year following the tax year during which the expenses are paid or incurred.	Nonrefundable credit. Unused credit may be carried forward five years. Purpose is to assist taxpayers who incur nonrecurring costs associated with the adoption process.
Child (§ 24)	Credit is based on *number* of qualifying children under age 17. Maximum credit is $1,000 per child. Credit is phased out for higher-income taxpayers.	Generally a nonrefundable credit. Refundable in certain cases. Purpose is to provide tax relief for low- to moderate-income families with children.
Education (§ 25A)	HOPE scholarship credit is available for qualifying education expenses of students in first two years of postsecondary education. Maximum credit is $1,650 per year per eligible student. Credit is phased out for higher-income taxpayers.	Nonrefundable credit. Credit is designed to help defray costs of first two years of higher education for low- to middle-income families.
	Lifetime learning credit permits a credit of 20% of qualifying expenses (up to $10,000 per year) provided HOPE scholarship credit is not claimed with respect to those expenses. Credit is calculated per taxpayer, not per student, and is phased out for higher-income taxpayers.	Nonrefundable credit. Credit is designed to help defray costs of higher education beyond first two years, and for costs incurred in maintaining or improving existing job skills, for low- to middle-income taxpayers.

Tax Credits—Continued

Credit	Computation	Comments
Credit for certain retirement plan contributions (§ 25B)	Calculation is based on amount of contribution multiplied by a percentage that depends on the taxpayer's filing status and AGI.	Nonrefundable credit. Purpose is to encourage contributions to qualified retirement plans by low- and middle-income taxpayers.
Foreign tax (§ 27)	Foreign taxable income/total worldwide taxable income × U.S. tax = overall limitation. Lesser of foreign taxes imposed or overall limitation.	Nonrefundable credit. Unused credits may be carried back 1 year and forward 10 years. Purpose is to prevent double taxation of foreign income.
General business (§ 38)	May not exceed net income tax minus the greater of tentative minimum tax or 25% of net regular tax liability that exceeds $25,000.	Nonrefundable credit. Components include tax credit for rehabilitation expenditures, work opportunity tax credit, welfare-to-work credit, research activities credit, low-income housing credit, disabled access credit, credit for small employer pension plan startup costs, and credit for employer-provided child care. Unused credit may be carried back 1 year and forward 20 years. FIFO method applies to carrybacks, carryovers, and credits earned during current year.
Rehabilitation expenditures (§ 47)	Qualifying investment times rehabilitation percentage, depending on type of property. Regular rehabilitation rate is 10%; rate for certified historic structures is 20%.	Nonrefundable credit. Part of general business credit and therefore subject to same carryback, carryover, and FIFO rules. Purpose is to discourage businesses from moving from economically distressed areas to newer locations.
Research activities (§ 41)	Incremental credit is 20% of excess of computation year expenditures over the base amount. Basic research credit is allowed to certain corporations for 20% of cash payments to qualified organizations that exceed a specially calculated base amount.	Nonrefundable credit. Part of general business credit and therefore subject to same carryback, carryover, and FIFO rules. Purpose is to encourage high-tech research in the United States.
Low-income housing (§ 42)	Appropriate rate times eligible basis (portion of project attributable to low-income units). Credit is available each year for 10 years. Recapture may apply.	Nonrefundable credit. Part of general business credit and therefore subject to same carryback, carryover, and FIFO rules. Purpose is to encourage construction of housing for low-income individuals.
Disabled access (§ 44)	Credit is 50% of eligible access expenditures that exceed $250, but do not exceed $10,250. Maximum credit is $5,000. Available only to eligible small businesses.	Nonrefundable credit. Part of general business credit and therefore subject to same carryback, carryover, and FIFO rules. Purpose is to encourage small businesses to become more accessible to disabled individuals.
Credit for small employer pension plan startup costs (§ 45E)	Credit equals 50% of qualified startup costs incurred by eligible employers. Maximum annual credit is $500. Deduction for related expenses is reduced by the amount of the credit.	Nonrefundable credit. Part of general business credit and therefore subject to same carryback, carryover, and FIFO rules. Purpose is to encourage small employers to establish qualified retirement plans for their employees.

Tax Credits—Continued

Credit	Computation	Comments
Credit for employer-provided child care (§ 45F)	Credit is equal to 25% of qualified child care expenses plus 10% of qualified expenses for child care resource and referral services. Maximum credit is $150,000. Deduction for related expenses or basis must be reduced by the amount of the credit.	Nonrefundable credit. Part of general business credit and therefore subject to same carryback, carryover, and FIFO rules. Purpose is to encourage employers to provide child care for their employees' children during normal working hours.
Work opportunity (§ 51)	Credit is limited to 40% of the first $6,000 of wages paid to each eligible employee.	Nonrefundable credit. Part of the general business credit and therefore subject to the same carryback, carryover, and FIFO rules. Purpose is to encourage employment of individuals in specified groups.
Welfare-to-work (§ 51A)	Credit is limited to 35% of first $10,000 of wages paid to each eligible employee in first year of employment, plus 50% of first $10,000 of wages paid to each eligible employee in second year of employment.	Nonrefundable credit. Part of general business credit and therefore subject to same carryback, carryover, and FIFO rules. Purpose is to encourage employment of long-term recipients of family assistance welfare benefits.

income taxes may be involved. With self-employed taxpayers, the focus is on the income tax and the self-employment tax.

Procedures Applicable to Employers

Employment taxes include FICA (Federal Insurance Contributions Act) and FUTA (Federal Unemployment Tax Act). The employer usually is responsible for withholding the employee's share of FICA (commonly referred to as Social Security tax) and appropriate amounts for income taxes. In addition, the employer must match the FICA portion withheld and fully absorb the cost of FUTA. The sum of the employment taxes and the income tax withholdings must be paid to the IRS at specified intervals.

The key to employer compliance in this area involves the resolution of the following points:

- Ascertaining which employees and wages are covered by employment taxes and are subject to withholding for income taxes.
- Arriving at the amount to be paid and/or withheld.
- Reporting and paying employment taxes and income taxes withheld to the IRS on a timely basis through the use of proper forms and procedures.

Coverage Requirements. Circular E, Employer's Tax Guide (Publication 15), issued by the IRS, contains a listing of which employees and which wages require withholdings for income taxes and employment taxes. Excerpts from Circular E appear in Exhibit 13–2. In working with Exhibit 13–2, consider the following observations:

- The designation "Exempt" in the income tax withholding column does not mean that the amount paid is nontaxable to the employee. It merely relieves the employer from having to withhold.

EXHIBIT 13–2	Withholding Classifications

Special Classes of Employment and Special Types of Payments	Treatment under Employment Taxes		
	Income Tax Withholding	Social Security and Medicare	Federal Unemployment
Employee business expense reimbursement:			
1. Accountable plan.			
a. Amounts not exceeding specified government rate for per diem or standard mileage.	Exempt	Exempt	Exempt
b. Amounts in excess of specified government rate for per diem or standard mileage.	Withhold	Taxable	Taxable
2. Nonaccountable plan.	Withhold	Taxable	Taxable
Family employees:			
1. Child employed by parent (or partnership in which each partner is a parent of the child).	Withhold	Exempt until age 18; age 21 for domestic service.	Exempt until age 21
2. Parent employed by child.	Withhold	Taxable if in course of the son's or daughter's business.	Exempt
3. Spouse employed by spouse.	Withhold	Taxable if in course of spouse's business.	Exempt
Household employees: Domestic service in private homes. Farmers see Publication 51 (Circular A).	Exempt (withhold if both employer and employee agree).	Taxable if paid $1,500 or more in cash in 2006. Exempt if performed by an individual under age 18 during any portion of the calendar year and is not the principal occupation of the employee.	Taxable if employer paid total cash wages of $1,000 or more in any quarter in the current or preceding calendar year.
Interns working in hospitals.	Withhold	Taxable	Exempt
Newspaper carriers under age 18.	Exempt (withhold if both employer and employee agree).	Exempt	Exempt
Salespersons:			
1. Common law employees.	Withhold	Taxable	Taxable
2. Statutory employees.	Exempt	Taxable	Taxable, except for full-time life insurance sales agents.
Scholarships and fellowship grants: [includible in income under § 117(c)].	Withhold	Taxability depends on the nature of the employment and the status of the organization.	Taxability depends on the nature of the employment and the status of the organization.
Severance or dismissal pay.	Withhold	Taxable	Taxable
Tips, if less than $20 in a month.	Exempt	Exempt	Exempt
Worker's compensation.	Exempt	Exempt	Exempt

TABLE 13–5	**FICA Rates and Base**

	Social Security Tax			Medicare Tax			
	Percent	×	Base Amount	+	Percent	×	Base Amount	=	Maximum Tax
1991	6.20%	×	$53,400	+	1.45%	×	$125,000	=	$5,123.30
1992	6.20%	×	55,500	+	1.45%	×	130,200	=	5,328.90
1993	6.20%	×	57,600	+	1.45%	×	135,000	=	5,528.70
1994	6.20%	×	60,600	+	1.45%	×	Unlimited	=	Unlimited
1995	6.20%	×	61,200	+	1.45%	×	Unlimited	=	Unlimited
1996	6.20%	×	62,700	+	1.45%	×	Unlimited	=	Unlimited
1997	6.20%	×	65,400	+	1.45%	×	Unlimited	=	Unlimited
1998	6.20%	×	68,400	+	1.45%	×	Unlimited	=	Unlimited
1999	6.20%	×	72,600	+	1.45%	×	Unlimited	=	Unlimited
2000	6.20%	×	76,200	+	1.45%	×	Unlimited	=	Unlimited
2001	6.20%	×	80,400	+	1.45%	×	Unlimited	=	Unlimited
2002	6.20%	×	84,900	+	1.45%	×	Unlimited	=	Unlimited
2003	6.20%	×	87,000	+	1.45%	×	Unlimited	=	Unlimited
2004	6.20%	×	87,900	+	1.45%	×	Unlimited	=	Unlimited
2005	6.20%	×	90,000	+	1.45%	×	Unlimited	=	Unlimited
2006	6.20%	×	94,200	+	1.45%	×	Unlimited	=	Unlimited
2007 on	6.20%	×	*	+	1.45%	×	Unlimited	=	Unlimited

*Not yet determined.

E X A M P L E   35

Lee works for Yellow Corporation and has the type of job where tips are not common but do occur. If Lee's total tips amount to less than $20 per month, Yellow Corporation need not withhold Federal income taxes on the tips. Nevertheless, Lee must include the tips in his gross income. ■

- In some cases, income tax withholding is not required but is voluntary. This is designated "Exempt (withhold if both employer and employee agree)."

E X A M P L E   36

Pat is employed as a gardener by a wealthy family. In the past, he has encountered difficulty in managing his finances so as to be in a position to pay the income tax due every April 15. To ease the cash-flow problem that develops in April, Pat asks his employer to withhold income taxes from his wages. ■

- The Social Security and Medicare (FICA) column refers to the employer's share. The same is true of the Federal Unemployment (FUTA) column since the employee does not contribute to this tax.

Amount of FICA Taxes. The FICA tax has two components: Social Security tax (old age, survivors, and disability insurance) *and* Medicare tax (hospital insurance). The tax rates and wage base under FICA have increased both frequently and substantially over the years. There appears to be every reason to predict that the rates and/or base amount will continue to rise in the future. As Table 13–5 shows, the top base amount differs for the Medicare portion (now unlimited) and for the Social Security portion. Also note that Table 13–5 represents the employee's share of the tax. The employer must match the employee's portion.

Withholdings from employees must continue until the maximum base amount is reached. In 2006, for example, FICA withholding ceases for the Social Security portion (6.2 percent) once the employee has earned wages subject to FICA in the

---

TAX *in the News*   **WILL SOCIAL SECURITY BE THERE FOR YOU WHEN YOU NEED IT?**

With an estimated 77 million baby boomers becoming eligible for Social Security over the next decade or so, and with fewer employees paying into the system, a logical question for younger Americans who are just now entering the workforce is whether the Social Security system will be solvent when they reach their retirement years. This question often arose during the 2004 presidential campaign. Moreover, it continues to be discussed in the news media as well as in hearings in Congress. Reality seems to suggest that with a burgeoning number of retirees drawing Social Security for a longer period of time because their life expectancies are increasing, the assets accumulated in the Social Security trust fund will be strained at some point in the future.

Things seem to be fine now, but beginning in about 2018, the Social Security Administration expects to be paying out more in benefits than it collects from the payroll tax. Interest income on the trust fund assets will help balance the books until about 2028 when the trust fund assets are expected to begin falling. Some suggest that by as early as 2042, the Social Security trust fund could run dry.

So, do we have a crisis on our hands? Will benefits be cut or will payroll taxes be increased? Will a "means test" be applied before retirees can receive their monthly checks? Will part or all of the Social Security contributions be "privatized"? The answers to these questions and the integrity of the system are issues that undoubtedly will take years to resolve.

---

amount of $94,200. For the Medicare portion (1.45 percent), however, the employer is required to withhold on all wages without limit. This contrasts with years prior to 1994 when a maximum base existed for the Medicare portion also.

EXAMPLE 37

In 2006, Keshia earned a salary of $140,000 from her employer. Therefore, FICA taxes withheld from her salary are $5,840 ($94,200 × 6.2%) plus $2,030 ($140,000 × 1.45%) for a total of $7,870. In addition to paying the amount withheld from Keshia's salary to the government, her employer also has to pay $7,870. ∎

In at least two situations, it is possible for an employee to have paid excess FICA taxes.

EXAMPLE 38

During 2006, Kevin changed employers in the middle of the year and earned $50,000 (all of which was subject to FICA) from each job. As a result, each employer withheld $3,825 [(6.2% × $50,000) + (1.45% × $50,000)] for a total of $7,650. Although each employer acted properly, Kevin's total FICA tax liability for the year is only $7,290 [(6.2% × $94,200) + (1.45% × $100,000)]. Thus, Kevin has overpaid his share of FICA taxes by $360 [$7,650 (amount paid) − $7,290 (amount of correct liability)]. He should claim this amount as a tax credit when filing his income tax return for 2006. The tax credit will reduce any income tax Kevin might owe or, possibly, generate a tax refund. ∎

EXAMPLE 39

During 2006, Lori earned $73,000 from her regular job and $27,000 from a part-time job (all of which was subject to FICA). As a result, one employer withheld $5,585 [(6.2% × $73,000) + (1.45% × $73,000)] while the other employer withheld $2,065 [(6.2% × $27,000) + (1.45% × $27,000)] for a total of $7,650. Lori's total FICA tax liability for the year is only $7,290 [(6.2% × $94,200) + (1.45% × $100,000)]. Thus, Lori has overpaid her share of FICA taxes by $360 [$7,650 (amount paid) − $7,290 (amount of correct liability)]. She should claim this amount as a tax credit when filing her income tax return for 2006. ∎

In Examples 38 and 39, the employee is subject to overwithholding. In both cases, however, the employee was able to obtain a credit for the excess withheld. The same result does not materialize for the portion paid by the employer. Since this amount is not refundable, in some situations employers may pay more FICA taxes than the covered employees.

The mere fact that a husband and wife are both employed does not, by itself, result in overwithholding of FICA taxes.

EXAMPLE 40

During 2006, Jim and Betty (husband and wife) are both employed, and each earns wages subject to FICA of $50,000. Accordingly, each has $3,825 FICA withheld [(6.2% × $50,000) + (1.45% × $50,000)] for a total of $7,650. Since neither spouse paid FICA tax on wages in excess of $94,200 (Social Security tax) [see Table 13–5], there is no overwithholding. ∎

A spouse employed by another spouse is subject to FICA. However, children under the age of 18 who are employed in a parent's trade or business are exempted.

Amount of Income Tax Withholding. Arriving at the amount to be withheld for income tax purposes is not so simple. It involves three basic steps:[45]

- Have the employee complete Form W–4, Employee's Withholding Allowance Certificate.
- Determine the employee's payroll period.
- Compute the amount to be withheld, usually using either the wage-bracket tables or the percentage method.

Form W–4 reflects the employee's marital status and **withholding allowances**. Generally, it need not be filed with the IRS and is retained by the employer as part of the payroll records.

The employer need not verify the number of exemptions claimed. Any misinformation on the form will be attributed to the employee. However, if the employer has reason to believe that the employee made a false statement, the IRS should be notified. In the meantime, the Form W–4 should be honored. Employees are subject to both civil and criminal penalties for filing false withholding statements.

On the current Form W–4, an employee may claim *withholding allowances* for the following: personal exemptions for self and spouse and dependency exemptions. One *special withholding allowance* may be claimed if the employee is single and has only one job, if the employee is married and has only one job and the spouse is not employed, or if wages from a second job or a spouse's wages (or both) are $1,000 or less. An additional allowance is available if the employee expects to file using the head-of-household status or if the employee expects to claim a credit for child and dependent care expenses on qualifying expenditures of at least $1,500. A taxpayer qualifying for the child tax credit may claim one or two additional allowances for each eligible child. An employee who plans to itemize deductions or claim adjustments to income (e.g., alimony, deductible IRA contributions) should use the worksheet provided on Form W–4 to determine the correct number of additional allowances.

To avoid having too little tax withheld, some employees may find it necessary to reduce their withholding allowances. This might be the case for an employee who has more than one job or who has other sources of income that are not subject to adequate withholding. Likewise, a married employee who has a working spouse or more than one job might wish to claim fewer allowances.

If both spouses of a married couple are employed, they may allocate their total allowances between themselves as they see fit. The same allocation procedure is required if a taxpayer has more than one job. In no event should the same allowance be claimed more than once at the same time. It is permissible to declare *fewer* allowances than the taxpayer is entitled to in order to increase the amount of withholding. Doing so, however, does not affect the number of personal and dependency exemptions allowable on the employee's income tax return. An employee is also permitted to have the employer withhold a certain dollar amount in addition to the required amount. This additional dollar amount can be arbitrary or calculated in accordance with a worksheet on Form W–4.

---

[45]The withholding provisions are contained in §§ 3401 and 3402. These Sections will not be referenced specifically in the discussion that follows.

EXAMPLE 41

Carl, who earns $75,000, is married to Carol, who earns $85,000. They have three dependent children and will claim the standard deduction. Assume they do not qualify to claim the child tax credit. Together they should be entitled to five allowances [2 (for personal exemptions) + 3 (for dependency exemptions)]. The special withholding allowance is not available since both spouses earn more than $1,000. If Carl is the spouse first employed and his Form W–4 reflects five allowances, Carol's Form W–4 should report none. They could, however, reallocate their allowances between them as long as the total claimed does not exceed five. ∎

The period of service for which an employee is paid is known as the *payroll period*. Daily, weekly, biweekly, semimonthly, and monthly periods are the most common arrangements. If an employee has no regular payroll period, he or she is considered to be paid on a daily basis.

Once the allowances are known (as reflected on Form W–4) and the payroll period determined, the amount to be withheld for Federal income taxes can be computed. The computation usually is made by using the wage-bracket tables or the percentage method.

Wage-bracket tables are available for daily, weekly, biweekly, semimonthly, and monthly payroll periods for single (including heads of household) and married taxpayers. An extract of the tables dealing with married persons on a monthly payroll period is reproduced in Table 13–6. The data in Table 13–6 are for wages paid in 2006. Example 42 illustrates the use of withholding tables.

EXAMPLE 42

Tom is married and has three dependent children and no additional withholding allowances are available. In his job with Pink Corporation, he earns $4,500 in May 2006. Assuming Tom's wife has a part-time job for which she earns $5,000 for the year and all available allowances are claimed on his Form W–4, Pink should withhold $307 a month from his wages. This amount is taken from the five allowances column in the $4,480–$4,520 wage bracket. The five allowances result from personal exemptions (two) plus dependency exemptions (three). Note that an additional withholding allowance is not available for Tom's wife because she has a job for which she earned more than $1,000. ∎

Although the wage-bracket table requires few, if any, calculations, the percentage method is equally acceptable. Its use may be necessary for payroll periods where no wage-bracket tables are available (quarterly, semiannual, and annual payroll periods) and where wages paid exceed the amount allowed for use of the wage-bracket tables. The percentage method is particularly useful when payroll computations are computerized. This method, however, requires the use of a conversion chart based on one withholding allowance. That is, the amount of one allowance is equal to the personal and dependency exemption amount divided by the number of payroll periods in a year. For example, the amount of one allowance for a taxpayer who is paid weekly is $63.46 ($3,300/52 payroll periods)—see Table 13–7.

To use the percentage method, proceed as follows:

Step 1. Multiply the amount of one allowance (as specified in the conversion chart in Table 13–7) by the employee's total allowances (taken from Form W–4).

Step 2. Subtract the product reached in step 1 from the employee's wages. The remainder is called "amount of wages."

Step 3. Using the result derived in step 2, compute the income tax withholding under the proper percentage-method table.

The table used in applying the percentage method for those with monthly payroll periods is reproduced in Table 13–8. An illustration of the percentage method follows.

TABLE 13–6	Wage-Bracket Withholding Table

MARRIED Persons—MONTHLY Payroll Period
(For Wages Paid in 2006)

If the wages are—		And the number of withholding allowances claimed is—										
At least	But less than	0	1	2	3	4	5	6	7	8	9	10
		The amount of income tax to be withheld is—										
$3,240	$3,280	$327	$286	$244	$203	$162	$122	$94	$67	$39	$12	$0
3,280	3,320	333	292	250	209	168	127	98	71	43	16	0
3,320	3,360	339	298	256	215	174	133	102	75	47	20	0
3,360	3,400	345	304	262	221	180	139	106	79	51	24	0
3,400	3,440	351	310	268	227	186	145	110	83	55	28	0
3,440	3,480	357	316	274	233	192	151	114	87	59	32	4
3,480	3,520	363	322	280	239	198	157	118	91	63	36	8
3,520	3,560	369	328	286	245	204	163	122	95	67	40	12
3,560	3,600	375	334	292	251	210	169	127	99	71	44	16
3,600	3,640	381	340	298	257	216	175	133	103	75	48	20
3,640	3,680	387	346	304	263	222	181	139	107	79	52	24
3,680	3,720	393	352	310	269	228	187	145	111	83	56	28
3,720	3,760	399	358	316	275	234	193	151	115	87	60	32
3,760	3,800	405	364	322	281	240	199	157	119	91	64	36
3,800	3,840	411	370	328	287	246	205	163	123	95	68	40
3,840	3,880	417	376	334	293	252	211	169	128	99	72	44
3,880	3,920	423	382	340	299	258	217	175	134	103	76	48
3,920	3,960	429	388	346	305	264	223	181	140	107	80	52
3,960	4,000	435	394	352	311	270	229	187	146	111	84	56
4,000	4,040	441	400	358	317	276	235	193	152	115	88	60
4,040	4,080	447	406	364	323	282	241	199	158	119	92	64
4,080	4,120	453	412	370	329	288	247	205	164	123	96	68
4,120	4,160	459	418	376	335	294	253	211	170	129	100	72
4,160	4,200	465	424	382	341	300	259	217	176	135	104	76
4,200	4,240	471	430	388	347	306	265	223	182	141	108	80
4,240	4,280	477	436	394	353	312	271	229	188	147	112	84
4,280	4,320	483	442	400	359	318	277	235	194	153	116	88
4,320	4,360	489	448	406	365	324	283	241	200	159	120	92
4,360	4,400	495	454	412	371	330	289	247	206	165	124	96
4,400	4,440	501	460	418	377	336	295	253	212	171	130	100
4,440	4,480	507	466	424	383	342	301	259	218	177	136	104
4,480	4,520	513	472	430	389	348	307	265	224	183	142	108
4,520	4,560	519	478	436	395	354	313	271	230	189	148	112
4,560	4,600	525	484	442	401	360	319	277	236	195	154	116
4,600	4,640	531	490	448	407	366	325	283	242	201	160	120
4,640	4,680	537	496	454	413	372	331	289	248	207	166	124
4,680	4,720	543	502	460	419	378	337	295	254	213	172	130
4,720	4,760	549	508	466	425	384	343	301	260	219	178	136
4,760	4,800	555	514	472	431	390	349	307	266	225	184	142
4,800	4,840	561	520	478	437	396	355	313	272	231	190	148
4,840	4,880	567	526	484	443	402	361	319	278	237	196	154
4,880	4,920	573	532	490	449	408	367	325	284	243	202	160
4,920	4,960	579	538	496	455	414	373	331	290	249	208	166
4,960	5,000	585	544	502	461	420	379	337	296	255	214	172
5,000	5,040	591	550	508	467	426	385	343	302	261	220	178
5,040	5,080	597	556	514	473	432	391	349	308	267	226	184
5,080	5,120	603	562	520	479	438	397	355	314	273	232	190
5,120	5,160	609	568	526	485	444	403	361	320	279	238	196
5,160	5,200	615	574	532	491	450	409	367	326	285	244	202
5,200	5,240	621	580	538	497	456	415	373	332	291	250	208
5,240	5,280	627	586	544	503	462	421	379	338	297	256	214
5,280	5,320	633	592	550	509	468	427	385	344	303	262	220
5,320	5,360	639	598	556	515	474	433	391	350	309	268	226
5,360	5,400	645	604	562	521	480	439	397	356	315	274	232
5,400	5,440	651	610	568	527	486	445	403	362	321	280	238
5,440	5,480	657	616	574	533	492	451	409	368	327	286	244
5,480	5,520	663	622	580	539	498	457	415	374	333	292	250
5,520	5,560	669	628	586	545	504	463	421	380	339	298	256
5,560	5,600	675	634	592	551	510	469	427	386	345	304	262
5,600	5,640	681	640	598	557	516	475	433	392	351	310	268
5,640	5,680	687	646	604	563	522	481	439	398	357	316	274
5,680	5,720	696	652	610	569	528	487	445	404	363	322	280
5,720	5,760	706	658	616	575	534	493	451	410	369	328	286
5,760	5,800	716	664	622	581	540	499	457	416	375	334	292
5,800	5,840	726	670	628	587	546	505	463	422	381	340	298
5,840	5,880	736	676	634	593	552	511	469	428	387	346	304

TABLE 13–7	Conversion Chart for 2006

Payroll Period	Amount of One Allowance
Daily	$ 12.69
Weekly	63.46
Biweekly	126.92
Semimonthly	137.50
Monthly	275.00
Quarterly	825.00
Semiannual	1,650.00
Annual	3,300.00

TABLE 13–8	Table for Percentage Method of Withholding for Wages Paid through 2006

TABLE 4—MONTHLY Payroll Period

(a) SINGLE person (including head of household)—

If the amount of wages (after subtracting withholding allowances) is:	The amount of income tax to withhold is:
Not over $221	$0

Over—	But not over—		of excess over—
$221	—$833 . .	10%	—$221
$833	—$2,687 . .	$61.20 plus 15%	—$833
$2,687	—$6,104 . .	$339.30 plus 25%	—$2,687
$6,104	—$13,054 . .	$1,193.55 plus 28%	—$6,104
$13,054	—$28,200 . .	$3,139.55 plus 33%	—$13,054
$28,200	. . . . . .	$8,137.73 plus 35%	—$28,200

(b) MARRIED person—

If the amount of wages (after subtracting withholding allowances) is:	The amount of income tax to withhold is:
Not over $667	$0

Over—	But not over—		of excess over—
$667	—$1,908 . .	10%	—$667
$1,908	—$5,670 . .	$124.10 plus 15%	—$1,908
$5,670	—$10,575 . .	$688.40 plus 25%	—$5,670
$10,575	—$16,288 . .	$1,914.65 plus 28%	—$10,575
$16,288	—$28,629 . .	$3,514.29 plus 33%	—$16,288
$28,629	. . . . . .	$7,586.82 plus 35%	—$28,629

E X A M P L E   43

Assume the same facts as in Example 42, except that Tom's income tax withholding is determined using the percentage method.

Step 1. $275 (amount of one allowance for a monthly payroll period) × 5 (total allowances) = $1,375.

Step 2. $4,500 (monthly salary) − $1,375 (step 1) = $3,125 (amount of wages).

Step 3. Referring to Table 13–8: $124.10 + 15% ($3,125 − $1,908) = $306.65.   ■

Note that the wage-bracket tables yield an amount for income tax withholding of $307 (refer to Example 42) while the percentage method results in $306.65 (refer to Example 43). The difference occurs because the wage-bracket table amounts are derived by computing the withholding on the median wage within each bracket and rounded to the nearest dollar.

Reporting and Payment Procedures.   Proper handling of employment taxes and income tax withholdings requires considerable compliance effort on the part of the employer. Among the Federal forms that have to be filed are the following:

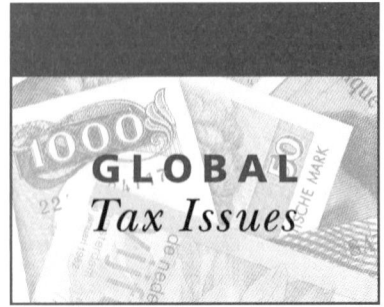

FOREIGN "WITHHOLDING TAX" PERFORMS AN IMPORTANT ROLE

Taxpayers in the United States are accustomed to having their employer withhold a portion of their salary or wages and then forward the amounts to the government in payment of their income tax liabilities. As a rule, other types of income, such as dividends, interest, and annuities, are not subject to withholding because the IRS has adequate mechanisms in place to assure a high level of tax compliance. But for payments of U.S.-source income to foreign taxpayers, the IRS would not be as confident that it is getting its due were it not for the so-called withholding tax.

To ensure the collection of the income tax on amounts paid to nonresident aliens and foreign corporations, the person *paying* the income, rather than the recipient, is required to withhold and forward the appropriate payment to the government. Although the withholding rate is typically 30 percent, the rate can vary in certain situations. In some situations, this withholding mechanism will also prevent the taxpayer from having to file an income tax return with the U.S. government.

Form Designation	Title
SS–4	Application for Employer Identification Number
W–2	Wage and Tax Statement
W–3	Transmittal of Wage and Tax Statements
940 or 940 EZ	Employer's Annual Federal Unemployment (FUTA) Tax Return
941	Employer's Quarterly Federal Tax Return

Form SS–4 is the starting point since it provides the employer with an identification number that must be used on all of the other forms filed with the IRS and the Social Security Administration. The number issued consists of nine digits and is hyphenated between the second and third digits (e.g., 72–1987316).

Form W–2 furnishes essential information to employees concerning wages paid, FICA, and income tax withholdings. Copies of Form W–2 are distributed to several parties for various purposes: to enable the employee to complete his or her income tax return, to inform the Social Security Administration of the amount of FICA wages earned by the employee, and to serve as a permanent record for the employer and employee of the payroll information contained on the form. Form W–2 must be furnished to an employee not later than January 31 of the following year. If an employee leaves a place of employment before the end of the year, Form W–2 can be given to him or her at any time after employment ends but no later than the following January 31. However, if the terminated employee asks for Form W–2, it must be given to him or her within 30 days after the request or the final wage payment, whichever is later.

Form W–3 must accompany the copies of Forms W–2 filed by the employer with the Social Security Administration. Its basic purpose is to summarize and reconcile the amounts withheld for FICA and income taxes from *all* employees.

Form 940 (or Form 940 EZ) constitutes the employer's annual accounting for FUTA purposes. Generally, it must be filed on or before January 31 of the following year and must be accompanied by the payment of any undeposited FUTA due the Federal government.

Whether or not deposits[46] are required, most employers must settle their employment taxes every quarter. To do this, Form 941 must be filed on or before the last day of the month following the end of each calendar quarter.

---

[46]Deposit requirements are specified in each current issue of Circular E, Employer's Tax Guide, IRS Publication 15. Under current rules, employers must make deposits on either a monthly or a semiweekly basis.

Backup Withholding. Some types of payments made to individuals by banks or businesses are subject to backup withholding under certain conditions. Backup withholding is designed to ensure that income tax is collected on interest and other payments reported on a Form 1099. If backup withholding applies in 2006, the payer must withhold 28 percent of the gross amount. Backup withholding applies when the taxpayer does not give the business or bank his or her identification number in the required manner and in certain other situations.[47]

Procedures Applicable to Self-Employed Persons

Although the following discussion largely centers on self-employed taxpayers, some of the procedures may be applicable to employed persons. In many cases, for example, employed persons may be required to pay estimated tax if they have income other than wages that is not subject to withholding. An employee may conduct a second trade or business in a self-employment capacity. Depending on the circumstances, the second job may require the payment of a self-employment tax. In addition, taxpayers whose income consists primarily of rentals, dividends, or interest (this list is not all-inclusive) may be required to pay estimated tax.

Estimated Tax for Individuals. **Estimated tax** is the amount of tax (including alternative minimum tax and self-employment tax) an individual expects to owe for the year after subtracting tax credits and income tax withheld. Any individual who has estimated tax for the year of $1,000 or more *and* whose withholding does not equal or exceed the required annual payment (discussed below) must make quarterly payments.[48] Otherwise, a penalty may be assessed. No quarterly payments are required (and no penalty will apply on an underpayment) if the taxpayer's estimated tax is under $1,000. No penalty will apply if the taxpayer had no tax liability for the preceding tax year *and* the preceding tax year was a taxable year of 12 months *and* the taxpayer was a citizen or resident for the entire preceding tax year. In this regard, having no tax liability is not the same as having no additional tax to pay.

The required annual payment must first be computed. This is the *smaller* of the following amounts:

- Ninety percent of the tax shown on the current year's return.
- One hundred percent of the tax shown on the preceding year's return (the return must cover the full 12 months of the preceding year). If the AGI on the preceding year's return exceeds $150,000 ($75,000 if married filing separately), the 100 percent requirement is increased to 110 percent.

In general, one-fourth of this required annual payment is due on April 15, June 15, and September 15 of the tax year and January 15 of the following year.

An equal part of withholding is deemed paid on each due date. Thus, the quarterly installment of the required annual payment reduced by the applicable withholding is the estimated tax to be paid. Payments are to be accompanied by the payment voucher for the appropriate date from Form 1040–ES.

Married taxpayers may make joint estimated tax payments even though a joint income tax return is not subsequently filed. In such event, the estimated tax payments may be applied against the separate return liability of the spouses as they see fit. If a husband and wife cannot agree on a division of the estimated tax payments, the Regulations provide that the payments are to be allocated in proportion to the tax liability on the separate returns.

---

[47]§ 3406(a). The backup withholding rate is equal to the fourth lowest tax rate for single filers.

[48]§§ 6654(c)(1) and 6654(e)(1).

Penalty on Underpayments. A nondeductible penalty is imposed on the amount of underpayment of estimated tax. The rate for this penalty is adjusted quarterly to reflect changes in the average prime rate.

An *underpayment* occurs when any installment (the sum of estimated tax paid and income tax withheld) is less than 25 percent of the required annual payment. The penalty is applied to the amount of the underpayment for the period of the underpayment.[49]

EXAMPLE 44

Marta made the following payments of estimated tax for 2006 and had no income tax withheld:

April 17, 2006	$1,400
June 15, 2006	2,300
September 15, 2006	1,500
January 15, 2007	1,800

Marta's actual tax for 2006 is $8,000, and her tax in 2005 was $10,000. Therefore, each installment should have been at least $1,800 [($8,000 × 90%) × 25%]. Of the payment on June 15, $400 will be credited to the unpaid balance of the first quarterly installment due on April 17,[50] thereby effectively stopping the underpayment penalty for the first quarterly period. Of the remaining $1,900 payment on June 15, $100 is credited to the September 15 payment, resulting in this third quarterly payment being $200 short. Then $200 of the January 15 payment is credited to the September 15 shortfall, ending the period of underpayment for that portion due. The January 15, 2007 installment is now underpaid by $200, and a penalty will apply from January 15, 2007, to April 16, 2007 (unless paid sooner). Marta's underpayments for the periods of underpayment are as follows:

1st installment due:	$400 from April 17 to June 15
2nd installment due:	Paid in full
3rd installment due:	$200 from September 15, 2006 to January 15, 2007
4th installment due:	$200 from January 15 to April 16, 2007
■

If a possible underpayment of estimated tax is indicated, Form 2210 should be filed to compute the penalty due or to justify that no penalty applies.

Self-Employment Tax. The tax on self-employment income is levied to provide Social Security and Medicare benefits (old age, survivors, and disability insurance and hospital insurance) for self-employed individuals. Individuals with net earnings of $400 or more from self-employment are subject to the **self-employment tax.**[51] For 2006, the self-employment tax is 15.3 percent of self-employment income up to $94,200 and 2.9 percent of self-employment income in excess of $94,200. In other words, for 2006 the self-employment tax is 12.4 percent of self-employment earnings up to $94,200 (for the Social Security portion) *plus* 2.9 percent of the total amount of self-employment earnings (for the Medicare portion)—see Table 13–9.

Currently, self-employed taxpayers are allowed a deduction from net earnings from self-employment, at one-half of the self-employment rate, for purposes of determining self-employment tax[52] *and* an income tax deduction for one-half the amount of self-employment tax paid.[53]

Determining the amount of self-employment tax to be paid for 2006 involves completing the steps in Figure 13–1. The result of step 3 or 4 is the amount of self-employment tax to be paid. For *income tax purposes*, the amount to be reported is net earnings from self-employment before the deduction for one-half of the

[49]§ 6654(b)(2).
[50]Payments are credited to unpaid installments in the order in which the installments are required to be paid. § 6654(b)(3).
[51]§ 6017.
[52]§ 1402(a)(12).
[53]§ 164(f).

TABLE 13–9	Self-Employment Tax: Social Security and Medicare Portions		

Year		Tax Rate	Ceiling Amount
2006	Social Security portion	12.4%	$94,200
	Medicare portion	2.9%	Unlimited
	Aggregate rate	15.3%	
2005	Social Security portion	12.4%	$90,000
	Medicare portion	2.9%	Unlimited
	Aggregate rate	15.3%	

FIGURE 13–1	2006 Self-Employment Tax Worksheet

1. Net earnings from self-employment. _____
2. Multiply line 1 by 92.35%. _____
3. If the amount on line 2 is $94,200 or less, multiply the line 2 amount by 15.3%. This is the self-employment tax. _____
4. If the amount on line 2 is more than $94,200, multiply the excess of line 2 over $94,200 by 2.9% and add $14,412.60. This is the self-employment tax. _____

self-employment tax. Then the taxpayer is allowed a deduction *for* AGI of one-half of the self-employment tax.

EXAMPLE 45

Using the format in Figure 13–1, the self-employment tax is determined for two taxpayers with net earnings from self-employment for 2006 as follows: Ned, $55,000 and Terry, $120,000.

Ned's Self-Employment Tax Worksheet

1. Net earnings from self-employment. $ 55,000.00
2. Multiply line 1 by 92.35%. $ 50,792.50
3. If the amount on line 2 is $94,200 or less, multiply the line 2 amount by 15.3%. This is the self-employment tax. $ 7,771.25
4. If the amount on line 2 is more than $94,200, multiply the excess of line 2 over $94,200 by 2.9% and add $14,412.60. This is the self-employment tax. _____

Terry's Self-Employment Tax Worksheet

1. Net earnings from self-employment. $120,000.00
2. Multiply line 1 by 92.35%. $110,820.00
3. If the amount on line 2 is $94,200 or less, multiply the line 2 amount by 15.3%. This is the self-employment tax. _____
4. If the amount on line 2 is more than $94,200, multiply the excess of line 2 over $94,200 by 2.9% and add $14,412.60. This is the self-employment tax. $ 14,894.58

| FIGURE 13–2 | 2005 Self-Employment Tax Worksheet |

1. Net earnings from self-employment. _____
2. Multiply line 1 by 92.35%. _____
3. If the amount on line 2 is $90,000 or less, multiply the line 2 amount by 15.3%. This is the self-employment tax. _____
4. If the amount on line 2 is more than $90,000, multiply the excess of line 2 over $90,000 by 2.9% and add $13,770. This is the self-employment tax. _____

For income tax purposes, Ned has net earnings from self-employment of $55,000 and a deduction *for* AGI of $3,885.63 (one-half of $7,771.25). Terry has net earnings from self-employment of $120,000 and a deduction *for* AGI of $7,447.29 (one-half of $14,894.58). Both taxpayers benefit from the deduction for one-half of the self-employment tax paid. ∎

For 2005, the self-employment tax computations are similar to those for 2006. The only difference is that the tax base was lower for 2005 than it is for 2006 (see Table 13–9 and Figure 13–2).

If an individual also receives wages subject to FICA tax, the ceiling amount of the Social Security portion on which the self-employment tax is computed is reduced. Thus, the self-employment tax may be reduced if a self-employed individual also receives FICA wages in excess of the ceiling amount.

EXAMPLE 46

In 2006, Kelly had $65,000 of net earnings from the conduct of a bookkeeping service (trade or business activity). She also received wages as an employee amounting to $40,000 during the year. The amount of Kelly's self-employment income subject to the Social Security portion (12.4%) is $54,200 ($94,200 − $40,000), producing a tax of $6,721 ($54,200 × 12.4%). All of Kelly's net self-employment earnings are subject to the Medicare portion of the self-employment tax of 2.9%. Therefore, the self-employment tax on this portion is $1,740.81 ($60,028 × 2.9%).

	Social Security Portion
Ceiling amount	$ 94,200
Less: FICA wages	(40,000)
Net ceiling	$ 54,200
Net self-employment income ($65,000 × 92.35%)	$ 60,028
Lesser of net ceiling or net self-employment income	$ 54,200

∎

Net earnings from self-employment include gross income from a trade or business less allowable trade or business deductions, the distributive share of any partnership income or loss derived from a trade or business activity, and net income from rendering personal services as an independent contractor. Gain or loss from the disposition of property (including involuntary conversions) is excluded from the computation of self-employment income unless the property involved is inventory.

Foreign Tax Credit

A U.S. citizen or resident working abroad (commonly referred to as an *expatriate*) may elect to take either a foreign tax credit or the foreign earned income exclusion. In cases where the income tax of a foreign country is higher than the U.S. income tax, the credit choice usually is preferable. If the reverse is true, electing the foreign earned income exclusion probably reduces the overall tax burden.

TAX PLANNING
Considerations

Unfortunately, the choice between the credit and the earned income exclusion is not without some limitations. The election of the foreign earned income exclusion, once made, can be revoked for a later year. However, once revoked, the earned income exclusion will not be available for a period of five years unless the IRS consents to an earlier date. This will create a dilemma for expatriates whose job assignments over several years shift between low- and high-bracket countries.

EXAMPLE 47

In 2005, Ira, a calendar year taxpayer, is sent by his employer to Saudi Arabia (a low-tax country). For 2005, therefore, Ira elects the foreign earned income exclusion. In 2006, Ira's employer transfers him to France (a high-tax country). Accordingly, he revokes the foreign earned income exclusion election for 2006 and chooses instead to use the foreign tax credit. If Ira is transferred back to Saudi Arabia (or any other low-tax country) within five years, he may not utilize the foreign earned income exclusion. ■

Credit for Child and Dependent Care Expenses

A taxpayer may incur employment-related expenses that also qualify as medical expenses (e.g., a nurse is hired to provide in-the-home care for an ill and incapacitated dependent parent). Such expenses may be either deducted as medical expenses (subject to the 7.5 percent limitation) or utilized in determining the credit for child and dependent care expenses. If the credit for child and dependent care expenses is chosen and the employment-related expenses exceed the limitation ($3,000, $6,000, or earned income, as the case may be), the excess may be considered a medical expense. If, however, the taxpayer chooses to deduct qualified employment-related expenses as medical expenses, any portion that is not deductible because of the 7.5 percent limitation may not be used in computing the credit for child and dependent care expenses.

EXAMPLE 48

Alicia has the following tax position for 2006:

Adjusted gross income		$30,000
Potential itemized deductions *from* AGI—		
Other than medical expenses	$3,500	
Medical expenses	6,600	$10,100

All of Alicia's medical expenses were incurred to provide nursing care for her disabled father while she was working. The father lives with Alicia and qualifies as her dependent. ■

What should Alicia do in this situation? One approach would be to use $3,000 of the nursing care expenses to obtain the maximum credit for child and dependent care expenses allowed of $810 (27% × $3,000). The balance of these expenses should be claimed as medical expenses. After a reduction of 7.5 percent of AGI, this would produce a medical expense deduction of $1,350 [$3,600 (remaining medical expenses) − (7.5% × $30,000)].

Another approach would be to claim the full $6,600 as a medical expense and forgo the credit for child and dependent care expenses. After the 7.5 percent adjustment of $2,250 (7.5% × $30,000), a deduction of $4,350 remains.

The choice, then, is between a credit of $810 plus a deduction of $1,350 or a credit of $0 plus a deduction of $4,350. Which is better, of course, depends on the relative tax savings involved, which in turn are dependent on the taxpayer's marginal tax bracket.

One of the traditional goals of *family tax planning* is to minimize the total tax burden within the family unit. With proper planning and implementation, the credit for child and dependent care expenses can be used to help achieve this goal. For example, payments to certain relatives for the care of qualifying dependents and children qualify for the credit if the care provider is *not* a child (under age 19) of the taxpayer. Thus, if the care provider is in a lower tax bracket than the taxpayer, the following benefits result:

- Income is shifted to a lower-bracket family member.
- The taxpayer qualifies for the credit for child and dependent care expenses.

In addition, the goal of minimizing the family income tax liability can be enhanced in some other situations, but only if the credit's limitations are recognized and avoided. For example, tax savings may still be enjoyed even if the qualifying expenditures incurred by a cash basis taxpayer have already reached the annual ceiling ($3,000 or $6,000). To the extent that any additional payments can be shifted into future tax years, the benefit from the credit may be preserved on these excess expenditures.

EXAMPLE 49

Andre, a calendar year and cash basis taxpayer, has spent $3,000 by December 1 on qualifying child care expenditures for his dependent 11-year-old son. The $250 that is due the care provider for child care services rendered in December does not generate a tax credit benefit if the amount is paid in the current year because the $3,000 ceiling has been reached. However, if the payment can be delayed until the next year, the total credit over the two-year period for which Andre is eligible may be increased. ∎

A similar shifting of expenditures to a subsequent year may be wise if the potential credit otherwise generated would exceed the tax liability available to absorb the credit.

Adjustments to Increase Withholding

The penalty for underpayment of estimated tax by individuals is computed for each quarter of the tax year. A taxpayer can play *catch-up* to a certain extent. Each quarterly payment is credited to the unpaid portion of any previous required installment. Thus, the penalty stops on that portion of the underpayment for the previous quarter. However, since income tax withheld is assumed to have been paid evenly throughout the year and is allocated equally among the four installments in computing any penalty, a taxpayer who would otherwise be subject to a penalty for underpayment should increase withholdings late in the year. This can be done by changing the number of allowances claimed on Form W–4 or by special arrangement with the employer to increase the amount withheld.

A similar way to avoid (or reduce) a penalty for underpayment is to have the employer continue Social Security withholding beyond the base amount.

EXAMPLE 50

Rose, a calendar year taxpayer, earns $125,000 from her job. In late October 2006, she realizes that she will be subject to a penalty for underpayment of estimated tax due to income from outside sources. Consequently, she instructs her employer to continue FICA withholdings for the rest of 2006. If this is done, an extra $30,800 [$125,000 (annual salary) − $94,200 (base amount of the Social Security portion for 2006)] will be subject to the 6.2% Social Security portion of the FICA tax [7.65% (total FICA rate) − 1.45% (Medicare portion of the FICA rate)]. Thus, Rose generates an additional $1,910 (6.2% × $30,800) that will be deemed withheld ratably during 2006. ∎

Adjustments to Avoid Overwithholding

Publication 505, Tax Withholding and Estimated Tax, contains worksheets that tax-payers may use to take advantage of special provisions for avoiding overwithhold-ing. Extra exemptions for withholding purposes are allowed if the taxpayer has unusually large itemized deductions, deductions *for* AGI, or tax credits. Net losses from Schedules C, D, E, and F may be considered in computing the number of extra withholding exemptions. Net operating loss carryovers may also be consid-ered in the computation. A taxpayer who is entitled to extra withholding exemp-tions for any of these reasons should file a new Form W–4, Employee's Withholding Allowance Certificate, with his or her employer.

KEY TERMS

Adoption expenses credit, 13–20

Child tax credit, 13–20

Credit for certain retirement plan contributions, 13–25

Credit for child and dependent care expenses, 13–21

Credit for employer-provided child care, 13–14

Credit for small employer pension plan startup costs, 13–14

Disabled access credit, 13–13

Earned income credit, 13–15

Employment taxes, 13–28

Estimated tax, 13–37

Foreign tax credit (FTC), 13–18

General business credit, 13–6

HOPE scholarship credit, 13–23

Lifetime learning credit, 13–23

Low-income housing credit, 13–12

Nonrefundable credits, 13–5

Permanent and total disability, 13–17

Refundable credits, 13–4

Rehabilitation expenditures credit, 13–7

Rehabilitation expenditures credit recapture, 13–8

Research activities credit, 13–10

Self-employment tax, 13–38

Tax credits, 13–2

Tax credit for the elderly or disabled, 13–17

Welfare-to-work credit, 13–10

Withholding allowances, 13–32

Work opportunity tax credit, 13–9

PROBLEM MATERIALS

DISCUSSION QUESTIONS

1. Would an individual taxpayer receive greater benefit from deducting an expenditure or from taking a credit equal to 25% of the expenditure? How would your response change if the item would only be deductible *from* AGI?

2. What is a refundable credit? Give examples. What is a nonrefundable credit? Give examples.

3. In determining the maximum amount of the general business credit allowed an individual taxpayer for a tax year, *net income tax, tentative minimum tax, regular tax liability,* and *net regular tax liability* are important concepts.
   a. Define each term.
   b. Using these terms, state the general business credit limitation for an individual tax-payer for the current year.

4. Discuss the treatment of unused general business credits.

5. Clint, a self-employed engineering consultant, is contemplating purchasing an old building for renovation. After the work is completed, Clint plans to rent out two-thirds of the floor space to businesses and to live and work in the remaining portion. Identify the relevant tax issues for Clint.   *Issue ID*

6. If property on which the tax credit for rehabilitation expenditures was claimed is prematurely disposed of or ceases to be qualified property, how is the tax liability affected in the year of the disposition or disqualification?

7. Discuss the purpose of the work opportunity tax credit. Who receives the tax benefits from the credit? Give examples of the types of individuals who, if hired, give rise to the credit.

8. Explain the purpose and calculation procedure of the welfare-to-work credit.

9. Explain the alternatives a taxpayer has in claiming the deduction and credit for research and experimentation expenditures.

10. Explain the purpose of the disabled access credit and describe the general characteristics of its computation.

11. Is the earned income credit a form of negative income tax? Why or why not?

12. Briefly discuss the requirements that must be satisfied for a taxpayer to qualify for the earned income credit.

13. Individuals who receive substantial Social Security benefits are usually not eligible for the tax credit for the elderly or disabled because these benefits effectively eliminate the base upon which the credit is computed. Explain.

14. In general, when would an individual taxpayer find it more beneficial to use the foreign earned income exclusion rather than the foreign tax credit in computing his or her income tax liability?

Issue ID

15. Tara was recently called into the partner's office and offered a one-year assignment in her public accounting firm's London office. Realizing that Tara will face incremental expenses while in London, such as for foreign income taxes and rent, the firm will try to make her "whole" from a financial perspective by increasing her salary to help offset the expenses she will incur while living overseas. If Tara takes the assignment, she will likely rent her personal residence and sell several major tangible assets such as her personal automobile. Identify the relevant tax issues.

16. Discuss, in general, the calculation of the adoption expenses credit.

17. Distinguish between the child tax credit and the credit for child and dependent care expenses.

18. Peter is not concerned about the credit for child and dependent care expenses because his AGI in 2006 is considerably in excess of $40,000. Is Peter under a misconception regarding the tax law? Explain.

Decision Making

19. Polly and her spouse, Leo, file a joint return and expect to report AGI of $70,000 in 2006. Polly's employer offers a child and dependent care reimbursement plan that allows up to $3,500 of qualifying expenses to be reimbursed in exchange for a $3,500 reduction in the employee's salary. Because Polly and Leo have one minor child requiring child care that costs $3,500 each year, she is wondering if she should sign up for the program instead of taking advantage of the credit for child and dependent care expenses. Assuming Polly and Leo are in the 25% tax bracket, analyze the effect of the two alternatives. How would your answer differ if Polly and Leo's AGI was $14,000 instead of $70,000? Assume in this case that their marginal tax rate is 10%.

20. Camilla, a college freshman, was pleased to read that the tax law provides education tax credits. However, she is confused as to the applicability of the different credits. Briefly explain (1) who is eligible and (2) what the maximum credit amount is for the HOPE scholarship credit and the lifetime learning credit.

21. Identify two tax credits enacted by Congress that are designed to encourage the establishment of or contributions to qualified retirement plans.

22. Discuss the rationale underlying the enactment of the following tax credits:
    a. Rehabilitation expenditures credit.
    b. Low-income housing credit.
    c. Research activities credit.

d. Earned income credit.
e. Foreign tax credit.

23. Elaborate rules exist that require employers to prepay various types of Federal taxes. Summarize the major issues that an employer must resolve if it is to comply with the requirements.

Issue ID

24. If an employer is not required to withhold income taxes on an item of income paid to an employee, does this mean that the item is nontaxable? Explain.

25. Keith, a sole proprietor, owns and operates a grocery store. Keith's wife and his 17-year-old son work in the business and are paid wages. Will the wife and son be subject to FICA? Explain.

26. Although Vicki is entitled to four withholding allowances, she claimed just one on her Form W–4.
a. Why would Vicki claim fewer allowances than she is entitled to?
b. Is this procedure permissible?
c. Will this affect the number of personal and dependency exemptions Vicki can claim on her Federal income tax return?

27. You read that self-employed taxpayers get a double deduction for one-half of the self-employment tax—a deduction in computing the self-employment tax and a deduction *for* AGI in calculating taxable income. Is this true? Explain.

PROBLEMS

28. Carol has a tentative general business credit of $110,000 for the current year. Her net regular tax liability before the general business credit is $125,000, and her tentative minimum tax is $100,000. Compute Carol's allowable general business credit for the year.

29. Oak Corporation has the following general business credit carryovers:

2002	$ 20,000
2003	60,000
2004	20,000
2005	80,000
Total carryovers	$180,000

If the general business credit generated by activities during 2006 equals $170,000 and the total credit allowed during the current year is $320,000 (based on tax liability), what amounts of the current general business credit and carryovers are utilized against the 2006 income tax liability? What is the amount of unused credit carried forward to 2007?

30. In January 2004, William purchased and placed into service a pre-1936 building that houses retail businesses. The cost was $240,000, of which $25,000 applied to the land. In modernizing the facility, William incurred $280,000 of renovation costs of the type that qualify for the tax credit for rehabilitation expenditures. These improvements were placed in service in October 2006.
a. Compute William's tax credit for rehabilitation expenditures for 2006.
b. Calculate the cost recovery deductions for the building and the renovation costs for 2006.

31. Red Company hires six individuals on January 15, 2006, qualifying Red for the work opportunity tax credit. Three of these individuals receive wages of $7,000 each during 2006, with each working more than 400 hours during the year. The other three receive wages of $4,000 each in 2006, with each working 300 hours during the year.
a. Calculate the amount of Red's work opportunity tax credit for 2006.
b. Assume Red pays total wages of $120,000 to its employees during the year. How much of this amount is deductible in 2006 if the work opportunity tax credit is taken?

32. In March 2006, Wren Corporation hired three individuals, Trent, Bernice, and Benita, all of whom are certified as long-term family assistance recipients. Each employee is paid $11,000 during 2006. Only Bernice continued to work for Wren in 2007, earning $13,500. Wren does not claim the work opportunity credit with respect to any of the employees hired in 2006.
    a. Compute Wren Corporation's welfare-to-work credit for 2006 and 2007.
    b. Assume Wren Corporation pays total wages of $325,000 to its employees during 2006 and $342,000 during 2007. How much may Wren claim as a wage deduction for 2006 and 2007 if the welfare-to-work credit is claimed in both years?

Decision Making

33. Michael, a calendar year taxpayer, informs you that during June 2006, he incurs expenditures of $50,000 that qualify for the incremental research activities credit. In addition, it is determined that his base amount for the year is $35,000.
    a. Determine Michael's incremental research activities credit for the year.
    b. Michael is in the 25% tax bracket. Determine which approach to the research expenditures and the research activities credit (other than capitalization and subsequent amortization) would provide the greater tax benefit to Michael.

Communications

34. Ahmed Zinna (16 Southside Drive, Charlotte, NC 28204), one of your clients, owns two restaurants in downtown Charlotte and has come to you seeking advice concerning the tax consequences of complying with the Americans with Disabilities Act. He understands that he needs to install various features at his businesses (e.g., ramps, doorways, and restrooms that are handicapped accessible) to make them more accessible to disabled individuals. He asks whether any tax credits will be available to help offset the cost of the necessary changes. He estimates the cost of the planned changes to his facilities as follows:

Location	Projected Cost
Calvin Street	$22,000
Stowe Avenue	8,500

He reminds you that the Calvin Street restaurant was constructed in 2001 while the Stowe Avenue restaurant is in a building that was constructed in 1986. Ahmed operates his business as a sole proprietorship and has approximately eight employees at each location. Write a letter to Ahmed in which you summarize your conclusions concerning the tax consequences of his proposed capital improvements.

35. Which of the following individuals qualify for the earned income credit for 2006?
    a. Eduardo is single, 19 years of age, and has no qualifying children. His income consists of $8,000 in wages.
    b. Kate maintains a household for a dependent 12-year-old son and is eligible for head-of-household tax rates. Her income consists of $13,500 of salary and $300 of taxable interest.
    c. Keith and Susan are married and file a joint return. Keith and Susan have no dependents. Their combined income consists of $28,500 of salary and $100 of taxable interest. Adjusted gross income is $28,600.
    d. George is a 26-year-old, self-supporting, single taxpayer. He has no qualifying children and generates earnings of $9,000.

36. Alma and George are married and live in an apartment with their three minor children (ages 6, 8, and 9) whom they support. Alma and George earned $26,500 during 2006. George contributed $500 to a traditional IRA, and they use the standard deduction on their joint return. Calculate the amount, if any, of Alma and George's earned income credit.

Decision Making

37. Joyce, a widow, lives in an apartment with her two minor children (ages 8 and 10) whom she supports. Joyce earns $32,000 during 2006. She uses the standard deduction.
    a. Calculate the amount, if any, of Joyce's earned income credit.
    b. During the year, Joyce is offered a new job that has greater future potential than her current job. If she accepts the job offer, her earnings for the year would be $36,500; however, she will not qualify for the earned income credit. Using after-tax cash-flow calculations, determine whether Joyce should accept the new job offer.

38. Joe, age 68, is a single retiree who receives the following income and retirement benefits during the current year:

Fully taxable pension from Joe's former employer	$ 9,750
Dividends and interest income	500
Social Security benefits	1,750
Total	$12,000

Assume Joe has no deductions *for* AGI and does not itemize his deductions. Is he eligible for the tax credit for the elderly? If so, calculate the amount of the credit.

39. Kim, a U.S. citizen and resident, owns and operates a novelty goods business. During 2006, Kim has taxable income of $100,000, made up as follows: $50,000 from foreign sources and $50,000 from U.S. sources. In calculating taxable income, the standard deduction is used. The income from foreign sources is subject to foreign income taxes of $26,000. For 2006, Kim files a joint return claiming his three children as dependents.

Decision Making

   a. Assuming Kim chooses to claim the foreign taxes as an income tax credit, what is his income tax liability for 2006?
   b. Recently, Kim has become disenchanted with the location of his business and is considering moving his foreign operation to a different country. Based on his research, if he moves his business to his country of choice, all relevant revenues and costs would remain approximately the same except that the income taxes payable to that country would be only $8,000. Given that all of the foreign income taxes paid are available to offset the U.S. tax liability (whether he operates in a high-tax or a low-tax foreign jurisdiction), what impact will this have on his decision regarding the potential move?

40. Zinnia Corporation is an international wholesaler headquartered in the United States. Of its worldwide taxable income of $3 billion, $1.25 billion is foreign sourced. Before any credits, Zinnia's U.S. income tax liability is $1.05 billion. If income taxes paid to foreign countries total $600 million, what is Zinnia's U.S. income tax liability after benefiting from the foreign tax credit?

41. Ann and Bill were on the list of a local adoption agency for several years seeking to adopt a child. Finally, in 2005, good news comes their way and an adoption seems imminent. They pay qualified adoption expenses of $4,000 in 2005 and $11,000 in 2006. Assume the adoption becomes final in 2006. Ann and Bill always file a joint income tax return.
   a. Determine the amount of the adoption expenses credit available to Ann and Bill assuming their combined annual income is $90,000. What year(s) will they benefit from the credit?
   b. Assuming Ann and Bill's modified AGI in 2005 and 2006 is $175,000, calculate the amount of the adoption expenses credit.

42. Durell and Earline are married, file a joint return, and claim dependency exemptions for their two children, ages 5 years and 6 months. They also claim Earline's son from a previous marriage, age 18, as a dependent. Durell and Earline's combined AGI is $56,000.
   a. Compute Durell and Earline's child tax credit.
   b. Assume the same facts, except that Durell and Earline's combined AGI is $119,000. Compute their child tax credit.

43. Kevin and Jane are husband and wife and have one dependent child, age 9. Kevin is a full-time student for all of the current year, while Jane earns $36,000 as a nurse's aide. To provide care for their child while Kevin attends classes and Jane works, they pay Sara (Jane's 17-year-old sister) $2,900. Sara is not a dependent of Kevin and Jane. Assuming Kevin and Jane file a joint return, what, if any, is their credit for child and dependent care expenses?

44. Ralph and Jill are husband and wife and have two dependent children under the age of 13. They both are gainfully employed and during the current year earn salaries as follows: $22,500 (Ralph) and $5,000 (Jill). To care for their children while they work,

they pay Megan (Ralph's mother) $5,600. Assuming Ralph and Jill file a joint return, what, if any, is their credit for child and dependent care expenses?

Communications

45. Bernadette, a longtime client of yours, is an architect and president of the local Rotary chapter. To keep up-to-date with the latest developments in her profession, she attends continuing education seminars offered by the architecture school at State University. During 2006, Bernadette spends $2,000 on course tuition to attend such seminars. She also spends another $400 on architecture books during the year. Bernadette's son is a senior majoring in engineering at the University of the Midwest. During the 2006 calendar year, Bernadette's son incurs the following expenses: $8,200 for tuition ($4,100 per semester) and $750 for books and supplies. Bernadette's son, whom she claims as a dependent, lives at home while attending school full-time. Bernadette is married, files a joint return, and has a combined AGI with her husband of $95,000.
    a. Calculate Bernadette's education tax credit for 2006.
    b. In her capacity as president of the local Rotary chapter, Bernadette has asked you to make a 30–45 minute speech outlining the different ways the tax law helps defray (1) the cost of higher education and (2) the cost of continuing education once someone is in the workforce. Prepare an outline of possible topics for presentation. A tentative title for your presentation is "How Can the Tax Law Help Pay for College and Continuing Professional Education?"

46. Kathleen and Glenn decide that this is the year to begin getting serious about saving for their retirement by participating in their employers' § 401(k) plans. As a result, they each have $3,000 of their salary set aside in their qualified plans.
    a. Calculate the credit for certain retirement plan contributions available to Kathleen and Glenn if the AGI on their joint return is $32,000.
    b. Kathleen and Glenn persuade their dependent 15-year-old son, Joel, to put $500 of his part-time earnings into a Roth IRA during the year. What is the credit for certain retirement plan contributions available to Joel? His AGI is $7,000.

47. In each of the following independent situations, determine the amount of FICA that should be withheld from the employee's 2006 salary by the employer.
    a. Harry earns a $50,000 salary, files a joint return, and claims four withholding allowances.
    b. Hazel earns a $100,000 salary, files a joint return, and claims four withholding allowances.
    c. Tracy earns a $180,000 salary, files a joint return, and claims four withholding allowances.
    d. Alicia's 17-year-old son, Carlos, earns $10,000 at the family business.

Communications

48. During 2006, Greg Cruz (1401 Orangedale Road, Troy, MI 48084) works for Maple Corporation and Gray Company. He earns $60,000 at Maple Corporation where he is a full-time employee. Greg also works part-time for Gray Company for wages of $45,000.
    a. Did Greg experience an overwithholding of FICA taxes? Write a letter to Greg and a memo for the tax files in which you explain your conclusion.
    b. Did Maple Corporation and Gray Company overpay the employer's portion of FICA? Explain.

49. In each of the following independent situations, determine the maximum withholding allowances permitted Eli (an employee) on Form W–4.
    a. Eli is single with no dependents.
    b. Eli is married to a nonemployed spouse, and they have no dependents.
    c. Eli is married to Vera, an employed spouse who earns $25,000, and they have three dependent children. Eli and Vera do not qualify for the child tax credit. On the Form W–4 that she filed with the employer, Vera claimed zero allowances.
    d. Assume the same facts as in (c), except that Eli and Vera fully support Eli's mother, who lives with them. The mother (age 70 and blind) qualifies as their dependent. (Refer to Chapter 3.)
    e. Eli is single with no dependents but works for two employers, one on a full-time basis and the other on a part-time basis. The Form W–4 filed with the first employer (the full-time job) reflects two withholding exemptions. The wages from each job exceed $1,000.
    f. Assume the same facts as in (e), except that Eli is married to a nonemployed spouse.

50. Jane, who is expecting to finish college in May 2006, is fortunate to have already arranged full-time employment for after graduation. She will begin work on July 1, 2006, as a staff accountant at a nearby professional services firm with a starting salary of $45,000 per year. Jane is married to Craig, who plans to be a full-time student throughout the year. They anticipate generating no income for the year other than the salary from her new position.

    Decision Making

   a. How many withholding allowances would you expect Jane to claim on her Form W–4?

   b. Assuming Jane receives her salary on a monthly basis, what amount will be withheld if her employer uses the wage-bracket tables to calculate withholdings?

   c. Assuming Jane receives her salary on a monthly basis, what amount will be withheld if her employer uses the percentage method to calculate withholdings?

   d. Assuming Jane and Craig use the standard deduction, calculate the Federal income tax liability on their projected taxable income for 2006. What changes would you recommend Jane make to her W–4 to correct any over- or under-withholding for the current year?

   e. What further changes should she make to her W–4 at the beginning of 2007?

51. Norm is married to a nonemployed spouse and has four dependents. He is employed by Beige Corporation and is paid a monthly salary of $4,245 ($50,940 per year). Using these facts, determine the amount to be withheld by Beige Corporation for Federal income tax purposes under the wage-bracket tables and under the percentage method for 2006.

52. Julie, being self-employed, is required to make estimated payments of her tax liability for the year. Her tax liability for 2005 was $25,000, and her AGI was less than $150,000. For 2006, Julie ultimately determines that her income tax liability is $18,000. During the year, however, she made the following payments, totaling $13,000:

April 17, 2006	$ 4,500
June 15, 2006	2,800
September 15, 2006	4,100
January 15, 2007	1,600
	$13,000

   Because she prepaid so little of her ultimate income tax liability, she now realizes that she may be subject to the penalty for underpayment of estimated tax.

   a. Determine Julie's exposure to the penalty for underpayment of estimated tax.

   b. The same as (a) except that Julie's tax liability for 2005 was $15,960.

53. During 2006, Helen, the owner of a store, has the following income and expenses:

Gross profit on sales	$73,000
Income from part-time job (subject to FICA)	50,000
Business expenses (related to store)	15,000
Fire loss on store building	2,200
Dividend income	200
Long-term capital gain on the sale of a stock investment	2,000

   Using the format illustrated in the text, compute Helen's self-employment tax and allowable income tax deduction for the self-employment tax paid.

CUMULATIVE PROBLEMS

54. Beth R. Jordan lives at 2322 Skyview Road, Mesa, AZ 85202. She is a tax accountant with Mesa Manufacturing Company, 1203 Western Avenue, Mesa, AZ 85201 (employer identification number 38–7788214). She also writes computer software programs for tax practitioners and has a part-time tax practice. Beth is single and has no dependents. Beth's birthday is July 4, 1971, and her Social Security number is 111–35–2222. She wants to contribute $3 to the Presidential Election Campaign Fund.

    Tax Return Problem

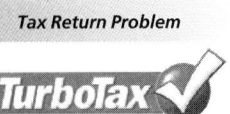

The following information is shown on Beth's Wage and Tax Statement (Form W–2) for 2005.

Line	Description	Amount
1	Wages, tips, other compensation	$63,000.00
2	Federal income tax withheld	11,000.00
3	Social Security wages	63,000.00
4	Social Security tax withheld	3,906.00
5	Medicare wages and tips	63,000.00
6	Medicare tax withheld	913.50
15	State	Arizona
16	State wages, tips, etc.	63,000.00
17	State income tax withheld	1,650.00

During 2005, Beth received interest of $1,300 from Home Federal Savings and Loan and $400 from Home State Bank. Each financial institution reported the interest income on a Form 1099–INT. She received qualified dividends of $500 from Gray Corporation, $400 from Blue Corporation, and $1,200 from Orange Corporation. Each corporation reported Beth's dividend payments on a Form 1099–DIV.

Beth received a $1,600 income tax refund from the state of Arizona on May 12, 2005. On her 2004 Federal income tax return, she reported total itemized deductions of $7,700, which included $2,400 of state income tax withheld by her employer.

Fees earned from her part-time tax practice in 2005 totaled $3,800. She paid $600 to have the tax returns processed by a computerized tax return service.

On February 1, 2005, Beth bought 500 shares of Gray Corporation common stock for $17.60 a share. On July 16, Beth sold the stock for $14 a share.

Beth bought a used sports utility vehicle for $3,000 on June 5, 2005. She purchased the vehicle from her brother-in-law, who was unemployed and was in need of cash. On November 2, 2005, she sold the vehicle to a friend for $3,400.

On January 2, 2005, Beth acquired 100 shares of Blue Corporation common stock for $30 a share. She sold the stock on December 19, 2005, for $55 a share.

During 2005, Beth received royalties of $16,000 on a software program she had written. Beth incurred the following expenditures in connection with her software-writing activities:

Cost of personal computer (100% business use)	$7,000
Cost of printer (100% business use)	2,000
Furniture	3,000
Supplies	650
Fee paid to computer consultant	3,500

Beth elected to expense the maximum portion of the cost of the computer, printer, and furniture allowed under the provisions of § 179. This equipment and furniture were placed in service on January 15, 2005.

Although her employer suggested that Beth attend a convention on current developments in corporate taxation, Beth was not reimbursed for the travel expenses of $1,420 she incurred in attending the convention. The $1,420 included $200 for the cost of meals.

During 2005, Beth paid $300 for prescription medicines and $2,875 in doctor bills, hospital bills, and medical insurance premiums. Beth paid real property taxes of $1,766 on her home. Interest on her home mortgage was $3,845, and interest to credit card companies was $320. Beth contributed $30 each week to her church and $10 each week to the United Way. Professional dues and subscriptions totaled $350. Beth maintained her sales tax receipts. The total is $1,954.

Beth paid estimated taxes of $1,000.

Part 1—Tax Computation

Compute the net tax payable or refund due for Beth R. Jordan for 2005. If you use tax forms for your solution, you will need Forms 1040, 2106–EZ, and 4562 and Schedules A, B, C, D, and SE. Suggested software: TurboTax.

Part 2—Tax Planning

Beth is anticipating significant changes in her life in 2006, and she has asked you to estimate her taxable income and tax liability for 2006. She just received word that she has been qualified to adopt a two-year-old daughter. Beth expects the adoption will be finalized in 2006 and that she will incur approximately $2,000 of adoption expenses. In addition, she expects to incur approximately $3,500 of child and dependent care expenses relating to the care of her new daughter, which will enable her to keep her job at Mesa Manufacturing Company. However, with the additional demands on her time because of her daughter, she has decided to discontinue her two part-time jobs (i.e., the part-time tax practice and her software business) and she will cease making estimated income tax payments. In your computations, assume all other income and expenditures will remain at approximately the same levels as in 2005.

55. Wade and Jane Lawrence are married and file a joint return. Wade's Social Security number is 222–33–1111, and Jane's Social Security number is 111–22–5555. They reside at 100 Olive Lane, Covington, LA 70400. They have two dependent children, Sean and Debra, ages 12 and 16, respectively. Wade is a self-employed businessman (sole proprietor of an unincorporated business), and Jane is a corporate executive. Wade has the following income and expenses from his business:

Tax Return Problem

Gross income	$280,000
Business expenses	200,000

Records related to Jane's employment provide the following information:

Salary	$160,000
Unreimbursed travel expenses (including $200 of meals)	1,000
Unreimbursed entertainment expenses	600

Other pertinent information relating to 2006 follows:

Proceeds from sale of stock acquired on July 15, 2006 (cost of $10,000), and sold on August 1, 2006	$ 8,000
Proceeds from sale of stock acquired on September 18, 2005 (cost of $6,000), and sold on October 5, 2006	4,800
Wages paid to full-time domestic worker for housekeeping and child supervision	10,000
Interest income received	8,000
Total itemized deductions (not including any potential deductions above)	26,900
Federal income tax withheld	29,000
Estimated payments of Federal income tax	30,000

Compute the net tax payable or refund due for Wade and Jane Lawrence for 2006.

RESEARCH PROBLEMS

Note: Solutions to Research Problems can be prepared by using the **RIA Checkpoint®** **Student Edition** online research product, which is available to accompany this text. It is also possible to prepare solutions to the Research Problems by using tax research materials found in a standard tax library.

THOMSON
™
RIA

Research Problem 1.   Ashby and Curtis, a young professional couple, have a two-year-old son, Jason. Curtis works full-time as an electrical engineer, but Ashby has not worked outside the home since Jason was born. As Jason is getting older, Ashby feels that he would benefit from attending nursery school several times a week, which would give her an opportunity to reinvigorate her love of painting at a nearby art studio. Ashby thinks that if she is lucky, the proceeds from the sale of her paintings will pay for the nursery school tuition. But, in addition, she is planning to claim the credit for child and dependent care expenses because the care provided Jason at the nursery school is required for her to pursue her art. Can Ashby and Curtis claim the credit for child and dependent care expenses for the nursery school expenditure?

Communications

Research Problem 2. Your ophthalmologist, Dr. Hunter Francis (55 Wheatland Drive, Hampton, CT 06247), has been very pleased with the growth of his practice in the 15 years he has been in business. This growth has resulted, at least in part, because he has aggressively marketed his services and tried to accommodate clients with various needs. This year Dr. Francis purchased a sophisticated piece of equipment that enables him to diagnose persons with mental handicaps, hearing impairments, and physical disabilities without having to go through a series of questions. In addition, he can treat his patients who are not disabled much more accurately and efficiently by using this equipment.

Since purchasing the machine this year for $9,500, Dr. Francis has used it on many occasions. Unfortunately, he has not been able to attract any disabled patients, even though previously he referred such people to other ophthalmologists who owned the necessary equipment. Therefore, the primary purpose for acquiring the equipment (i.e., to attract disabled patients) has not been realized, but he has put it to good use in treating other patients. Write a letter to Dr. Francis explaining whether he may claim the disabled access credit for this acquisition.

Research Problem 3. You recently read an article in your school newspaper about Professor Rodney Taylor, one of your favorite professors in the religious studies department. According to the article, he and the university have been negotiating an early retirement package and have reached a stumbling block. Under the agreement, Professor Taylor is to receive a lump-sum payment equal to one year's salary in exchange for his retirement and the release of any and all rights associated with his tenure status. While recognizing that the payment would be subject to income tax, Taylor contends that the amount is not earned income and thus should not be subject to the FICA tax. The university negotiators say that they are not aware of any authority that supports Taylor's view. In fact, they have learned that other universities in the state system have been withholding amounts for FICA for years in situations involving early retirement buyout packages for high-level administrators. The university's position is that lacking the authority to not withhold for FICA and given the precedent set in similar early retirement packages at other universities, they are obligated to withhold FICA from the payment. You want to come to the aid of Professor Taylor. Obviously, if the payments are considered wages subject to the FICA tax, the value of the offer to Professor Taylor will be significantly reduced. Can you find any authority for his position?

Decision Making

Research Problem 4. George and Louise's dependent daughter, Jamie, is a full-time university student who recently completed her first semester. The tuition expense for Jamie's first semester was $11,000. George and Louise have read about various education credits that are generally available to offset the cost of higher education, but they have concluded that they do not qualify because their AGI is too high.

Nonetheless, George asks you about a tax strategy that he recently overheard being discussed. According to his recollection of the discussion, if he and Louise would forgo claiming Jamie as a dependent on their joint income tax return, Jamie could claim the HOPE scholarship credit on her income tax return. What do you tell George about this strategy? Under what conditions should George and Louise take advantage of this approach if it is available?

Partial list of research aids:
Reg. § 1.25A–1(f).

 Internet *Activity*

Use the tax resources of the Internet to address the following questions. Do not restrict your search to the World Wide Web, but include a review of newsgroups and general reference materials, practitioner sites and resources, primary sources of the tax law, chat rooms and discussion groups, and other opportunities.

Research Problem 5. The IRS has unveiled a Web-based tool to help taxpayers determine whether they or their clients are eligible for the earned income credit. Locate this tool at the IRS Web site and then apply the facts related to a hypothetical taxpayer and determine if the earned income credit is available.

Research Problem 6. Find several news stories or government reports that document the incentive effect of the research activities credit.

Research Problem 7. Download a copy of Form W–4 and complete the accompanying worksheet. File the worksheet with your employer if you discover that you currently are being under- or overwithheld.

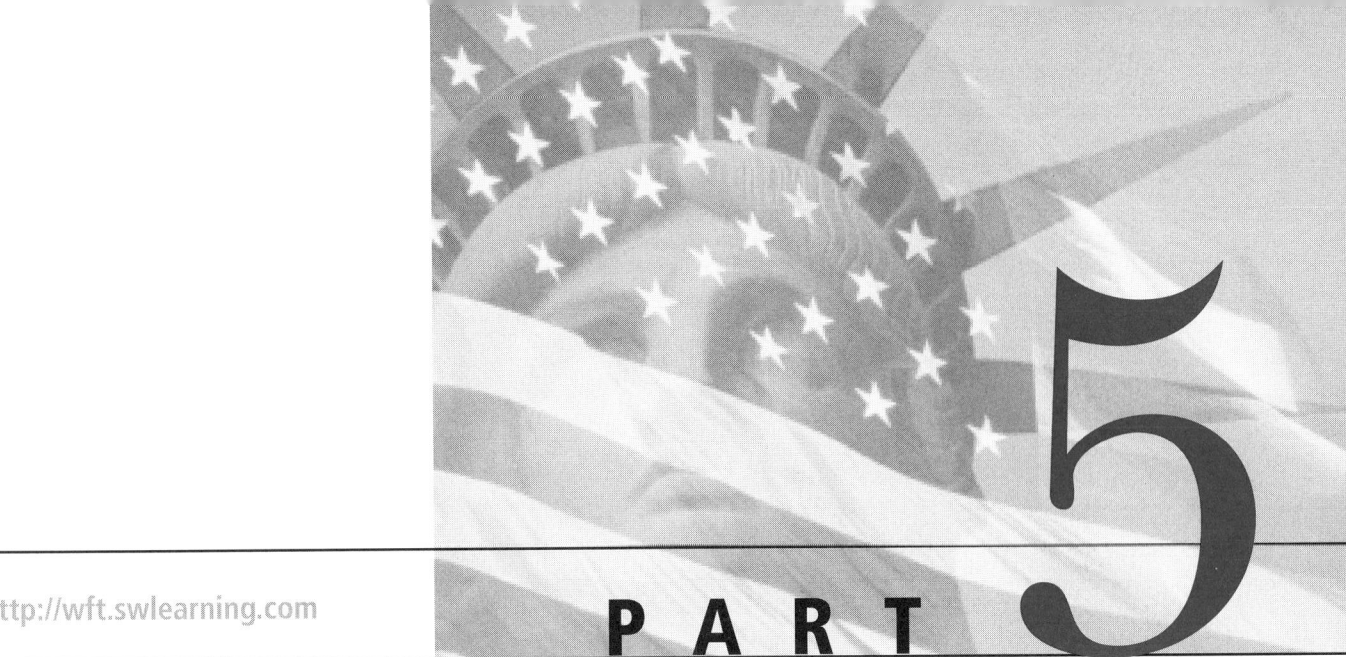

PART 5

Property Transactions

Part V presents the tax treatment of sales, exchanges, and other dispositions of property. Included are the determination of the realized gain or loss, recognized gain or loss, and the classification of the recognized gain or loss as capital or ordinary. The topic of basis is evaluated both in terms of its effect on the calculation of the gain or loss and in terms of the determination of the basis of any contemporaneous or related subsequent acquisitions of property.

CHAPTER 14

Property Transactions: Determination of Gain or Loss and Basis Considerations

LEARNING OBJECTIVES

After completing Chapter 14, you should be able to:

LO.1
Understand the computation of realized gain or loss on property dispositions.

LO.2
Distinguish between realized and recognized gain or loss.

LO.3
Apply the recovery of capital doctrine.

LO.4
Explain how basis is determined for various methods of asset acquisition.

LO.5
Describe various loss disallowance provisions.

LO.6
Identify tax planning opportunities related to selected property transactions.

This chapter and the following three chapters are concerned with the income tax consequences of property transactions (the sale or other disposition of property). The following questions are considered with respect to the sale or other disposition of property:

* Is there a realized gain or loss?
* If so, is the gain or loss recognized?
* If the gain or loss is recognized, is it ordinary or capital?
* What is the basis of any replacement property that is acquired?

EXAMPLE 1

Alice owns a house that she received from her mother seven months ago. Her mother's cost for the house was $75,000. Alice is considering selling the house to her favorite nephew, Dan, for $75,000. Alice anticipates she will have no gain or loss on the transaction. She comes to you for advice.

As Alice's tax adviser, you need answers to the following questions:

* You are aware that Alice's mother died around the time Alice indicates she received the house from her mother. Did Alice receive the house by gift prior to her mother's death? If so, what was the mother's adjusted basis? Did Alice instead inherit the house from her mother? If so, what was the fair market value of the house on the date of her mother's death?
* Has the house been Alice's principal residence during the period she has owned it? Was it her principal residence before she received it from her mother?
* How long did Alice's mother own the house?
* What is the fair market value of the house?
* Does Alice intend for the transaction with Dan to be a sale or part sale and part gift?
* What does Alice intend to do with the sale proceeds?

Once you have the answers to these questions, you can advise Alice on the tax consequences of the proposed transaction. ■

Chapters 14 and 15 discuss the determination of realized and recognized gain or loss and the basis of property. Chapters 16 and 17 cover the classification of the recognized gain or loss as ordinary or capital.

Determination of Gain or Loss

LO.1

Understand the computation of realized gain or loss on property dispositions.

Realized Gain or Loss

Realized gain or loss is the difference between the amount realized from the sale or other disposition of property and the property's adjusted basis on the date of disposition. If the amount realized exceeds the property's adjusted basis, the result is a **realized gain**. Conversely, if the property's adjusted basis exceeds the amount realized, the result is a **realized loss**.[1]

EXAMPLE 2

Tab sells Swan Corporation stock with an adjusted basis of $3,000 for $5,000. Tab's realized gain is $2,000. If Tab had sold the stock for $2,000, he would have had a realized loss of $1,000. ■

Sale or Other Disposition. The term *sale or other disposition* is defined broadly in the tax law and includes virtually any disposition of property. Thus, transactions such as trade-ins, casualties, condemnations, thefts, and bond retirements are treated as dispositions of property. The most common disposition of property is through a sale or exchange. Usually, the key factor in determining whether a disposition has taken place is whether an identifiable event has occurred[2] as opposed to a mere fluctuation in the value of the property.[3]

EXAMPLE 3

Lori owns Tan Corporation stock that cost $3,000. The stock has appreciated in value by $2,000 since Lori purchased it. Lori has no realized gain since mere fluctuation in value is not a disposition or identifiable event for tax purposes. Nor would Lori have a realized loss had the stock declined in value by $2,000. ■

Amount Realized. The **amount realized** from a sale or other disposition of property is the sum of any money received plus the fair market value of other property received. The amount realized also includes any real property taxes treated as imposed on the seller that are actually paid by the buyer.[4] The reason for including these taxes in the amount realized is that by paying the taxes, the purchaser is, in effect, paying an additional amount to the seller of the property.

The amount realized also includes any liability on the property disposed of, such as a mortgage debt, if the buyer assumes the mortgage or the property is sold subject to the mortgage.[5] The amount of the liability is included in the amount realized even if the debt is nonrecourse and the amount of the debt is greater than the fair market value of the mortgaged property.[6]

EXAMPLE 4

Barry sells property on which there is a mortgage of $20,000 to Cole for $50,000 cash. Barry's amount realized from the sale is $70,000 if Cole assumes the mortgage or takes the property subject to the mortgage. ■

The **fair market value** of property received in a sale or other disposition has been defined by the courts as the price at which property will change hands between a willing seller and a willing buyer when neither is compelled to sell or buy.[7] Fair market value is determined by considering the relevant factors in each case.[8] An expert appraiser is often required to evaluate these factors in arriving at

---

[1]§ 1001(a) and Reg. § 1.1001–1(a).

[2]Reg. § 1.1001–1(c)(1).

[3]*Lynch v. Turrish*, 1 USTC ¶18, 3 AFTR 2986, 38 S.Ct. 537 (USSC, 1918).

[4]§ 1001(b) and Reg. § 1.1001–1(b). Refer to Chapter 10 for a discussion of this subject.

[5]*Crane v. Comm.*, 47–1 USTC ¶9217, 35 AFTR 776, 67 S.Ct. 1047 (USSC, 1947). Although a legal distinction exists between the direct assumption of a

mortgage and taking property subject to a mortgage, the tax consequences in calculating the amount realized are the same.

[6]*Comm. v. Tufts*, 83–1 USTC ¶9328, 51 AFTR2d 83–1132, 103 S.Ct. 1826 (USSC, 1983).

[7]*Comm. v. Marshman*, 60–2 USTC ¶9484, 5 AFTR2d 1528, 279 F.2d 27 (CA–6, 1960).

[8]*O'Malley v. Ames*, 52–1 USTC ¶9361, 42 AFTR 19, 197 F.2d 256 (CA–8, 1952).

fair market value. When the fair market value of the property received cannot be determined, the value of the property given up by the taxpayer may be used.[9]

In calculating the amount realized, selling expenses such as advertising, commissions, and legal fees relating to the disposition are deducted. The amount realized is the net amount that the taxpayer received directly or indirectly, in the form of cash or anything else of value, from the disposition of the property.

Adjusted Basis. The **adjusted basis** of property disposed of is the property's original basis adjusted to the date of disposition.[10] Original basis is the cost or other basis of the property on the date the property is acquired by the taxpayer. Considerations involving original basis are discussed later in this chapter. *Capital additions* increase and *recoveries of capital* decrease the original basis so that on the date of disposition the adjusted basis reflects the unrecovered cost or other basis of the property.[11] Adjusted basis is determined as follows:

Cost (or other adjusted basis) on date of acquisition

+ Capital additions

− Capital recoveries

= Adjusted basis on date of disposition

Capital Additions. Capital additions include the cost of capital improvements and betterments made to the property by the taxpayer. These expenditures are distinguishable from expenditures for the ordinary repair and maintenance of the property, which are neither capitalized nor added to the original basis (refer to Chapter 6). The latter expenditures are deductible in the current taxable year if they are related to business or income-producing property. Amounts representing real property taxes treated as imposed on the seller but paid or assumed by the buyer are part of the cost of the property.[12] Any liability on property that is assumed by the buyer is also included in the buyer's original basis of the property. The same rule applies if property is acquired subject to a liability. Amortization of the discount on bonds increases the adjusted basis of the bonds.[13]

[9]*U.S. v. Davis*, 62–2 USTC ¶9509, 9 AFTR2d 1625, 82 S.Ct. 1190 (USSC, 1962).
[10]§ 1011(a) and Reg. § 1.1011–1.
[11]§ 1016(a) and Reg. § 1.1016–1.
[12]Reg. §§ 1.1001–1(b)(2) and 1.1012–1(b). Refer to Chapter 10 for a discussion of this subject.
[13]See Chapter 16 for a discussion of bond discount and the related amortization.

Capital Recoveries. Capital recoveries decrease the adjusted basis of property. The following are examples of capital recoveries:

1. *Depreciation and cost recovery allowances.* The original basis of depreciable property is reduced by the annual depreciation charges (or cost recovery allowances) while the property is held by the taxpayer. The amount of depreciation that is subtracted from the original basis is the greater of the *allowed* or *allowable* depreciation calculated on an annual basis.[14] In most circumstances, the allowed and allowable depreciation amounts are the same (refer to Chapter 8).

2. *Casualties and thefts.* A casualty or theft may result in the reduction of the adjusted basis of property.[15] The adjusted basis is reduced by the amount of the deductible loss. In addition, the adjusted basis is reduced by the amount of insurance proceeds received. However, the receipt of insurance proceeds may result in a recognized gain rather than a deductible loss. The gain increases the adjusted basis of the property.[16]

EXAMPLE 5

An insured truck used in a trade or business is destroyed in an accident. The adjusted basis is $8,000, and the fair market value is $6,500. Insurance proceeds of $6,500 are received. The amount of the casualty loss is $1,500 ($6,500 insurance proceeds − $8,000 adjusted basis). The adjusted basis is reduced by the $1,500 casualty loss and the $6,500 of insurance proceeds received. ∎

EXAMPLE 6

An insured truck used in a trade or business is destroyed in an accident. The adjusted basis is $6,500, and the fair market value is $8,000. Insurance proceeds of $8,000 are received. The amount of the casualty gain is $1,500 ($8,000 insurance proceeds − $6,500 adjusted basis). The adjusted basis is increased by the $1,500 casualty gain and is reduced by the $8,000 of insurance proceeds received ($6,500 basis before casualty + $1,500 casualty gain − $8,000 insurance proceeds = $0 basis). ∎

---

3. *Certain corporate distributions.* A corporate distribution to a shareholder that is not taxable is treated as a return of capital, and it reduces the basis of the shareholder's stock in the corporation.[17] For example, if a corporation makes a cash distribution to its shareholders and has no earnings and profits, the distributions are treated as a return of capital. Once the basis of the stock is reduced to zero, the amount of any subsequent distributions is a capital gain if the stock is a capital asset. These rules are illustrated in Example 23 of Chapter 20.

4. *Amortizable bond premium.* The basis in a bond purchased at a premium is reduced by the amortizable portion of the bond premium.[18] Investors in taxable bonds may *elect* to amortize the bond premium, but the premium on tax-exempt bonds *must be* amortized.[19] The amount of the amortized premium on taxable bonds is permitted as an interest deduction. Therefore, the election enables the taxpayer to take an annual interest deduction to offset ordinary income in exchange for a larger capital gain or smaller capital loss on the disposition of the bond. No such interest deduction is permitted for tax-exempt bonds.

    The amortization deduction is allowed for taxable bonds because the premium is viewed as a cost of earning the taxable interest from the bonds. The reason the basis of taxable bonds is reduced is that the amortization deduction is a recovery of the cost or basis of the bonds. The basis of tax-exempt bonds is reduced even though the amortization is not allowed as a deduction. No amortization deduction is permitted on tax-exempt bonds because the interest

---

[14]§ 1016(a)(2) and Reg. § 1.1016–3(a)(1)(i).
[15]Refer to Chapter 7 for the discussion of casualties and thefts.
[16]Reg. § 1.1016–6(a).
[17]§ 1016(a)(4) and Reg. § 1.1016–5(a).

[18]§ 1016(a)(5) and Reg. § 1.1016–5(b). The accounting treatment of bond premium amortization is the same as for tax purposes. The amortization results in a decrease in the bond investment account.
[19]§ 171(c).

CONCEPT SUMMARY 14–1

Recognized Gain or Loss

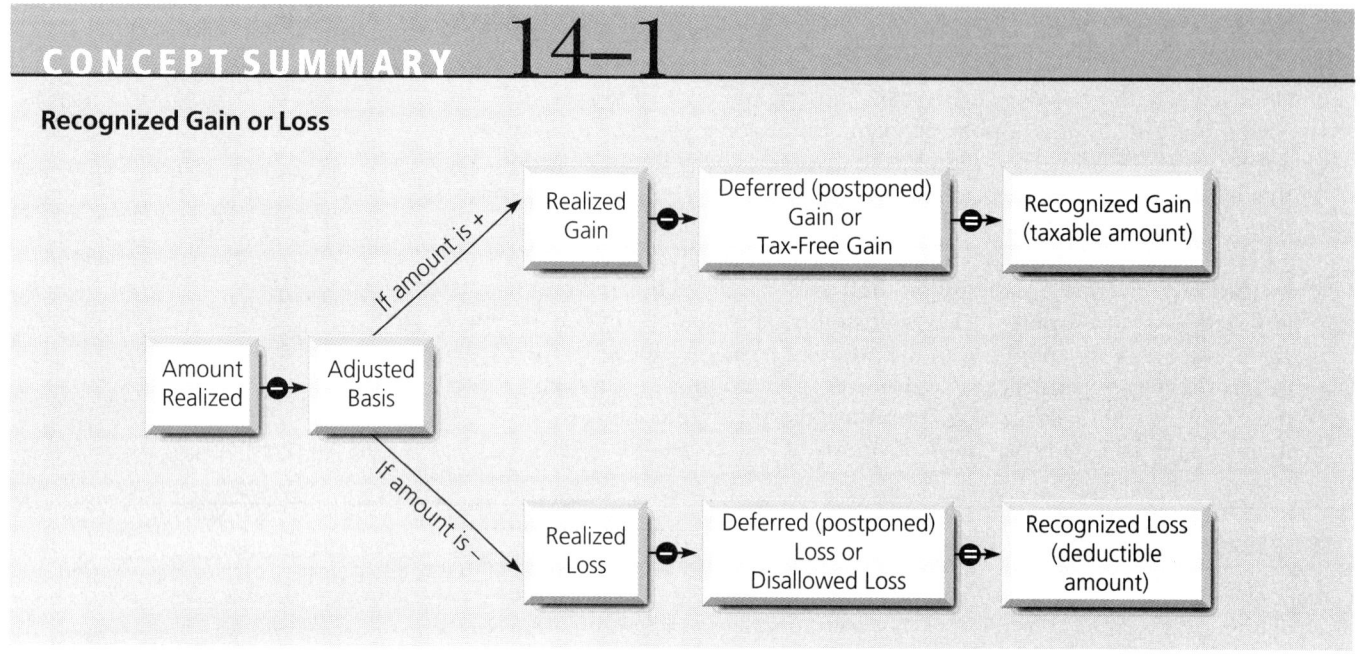

income is exempt from tax and the amortization of the bond premium merely represents an adjustment of the effective amount of such income.

EXAMPLE 7

Antonio purchases Eagle Corporation taxable bonds with a face value of $100,000 for $110,000, thus paying a premium of $10,000. The annual interest rate is 7%, and the bonds mature 10 years from the date of purchase. The annual interest income is $7,000 (7% × $100,000). If Antonio elects to amortize the bond premium, the $10,000 premium is deducted over the 10-year period. Antonio's basis for the bonds is reduced each year by the amount of the amortization deduction. Note that if the bonds were tax-exempt, amortization of the bond premium and the basis adjustment would be mandatory. However, no deduction would be allowed for the amortization. ∎

5. *Easements.* An easement is the legal right to use another's land for a special purpose. Historically, easements were commonly used to obtain rights-of-way for utility lines and roads. In recent years, grants of conservation easements have become a popular means of obtaining charitable contribution deductions and reducing the value of real estate for transfer tax (i.e., estate and gift) purposes. Likewise, scenic easements are used to reduce the value of land as assessed for ad valorem property tax purposes.

If the taxpayer does not retain any right to the use of the land, all of the basis is assigned to the easement. However, if the use of the land is only partially restricted, an allocation of some of the basis to the easement is appropriate.

LO.2

Distinguish between realized and recognized gain or loss.

Recognized Gain or Loss

Recognized gain is the amount of the realized gain that is included in the taxpayer's gross income.[20] A **recognized loss**, on the other hand, is the amount of a realized loss that is deductible for tax purposes.[21] As a general rule, the entire amount of a realized gain or loss is recognized.[22]

Concept Summary 14–1 summarizes the realized gain or loss and recognized gain or loss concepts.

[20]§ 61(a)(3) and Reg. § 1.61–6(a).
[21]§ 165(a) and Reg. § 1.165–1(a).
[22]§ 1001(c) and Reg. § 1.1002–1(a).

Nonrecognition of Gain or Loss

In certain cases, a realized gain or loss is not recognized upon the sale or other disposition of property. One such case involves nontaxable exchanges, which are covered in Chapter 15. Others include losses realized upon the sale, exchange, or condemnation of personal use assets (as opposed to business or income-producing property) and gains realized upon the sale of a residence (see Chapter 15). In addition, realized losses from the sale or exchange of business or income-producing property between certain related parties are not recognized.[23]

Sale, Exchange, or Condemnation of Personal Use Assets.
A realized loss from the sale, exchange, or condemnation of personal use assets (e.g., a personal residence or an automobile not used at all for business or income-producing purposes) is not recognized for tax purposes. An exception exists for casualty or theft losses from personal use assets (see Chapter 7). In contrast, any gain realized from the sale or other disposition of personal use assets is, generally, fully taxable.

EXAMPLE 8

Freda sells an automobile, which she has held exclusively for personal use, for $6,000. The adjusted basis of the automobile is $5,000. Freda has a realized and recognized gain of $1,000. ∎

EXAMPLE 9

Freda sells the automobile in Example 8 for $4,000. She has a realized loss of $1,000, but the loss is not recognized. ∎

ETHICAL *Considerations*   **AVOIDING THE DISALLOWANCE OF LOSSES ON PERSONAL USE ASSETS**

Meg owns a personal residence that she inherited from her mother five years ago. For estate tax purposes, the house was valued at $625,000. (Her mother's adjusted basis was $50,000.)

Meg, who has purchased another house in a resort community, has been offered $500,000 for the inherited house. Her brother advises Meg that losses on the sale of personal use assets are not deductible, but that losses on the sale of rental property are deductible. He suggests that she rent the house to the prospective buyer with the option to buy it for

$500,000 at the end of the one-year rental period. By doing so, she will be able to claim a deduction for the loss. The loss on the sale would be $125,000, reduced by the amount of depreciation deducted on the rental house. If necessary, Meg's brother can arrange for an appraisal to reflect that the house is currently worth $625,000.

Meg follows her brother's advice and takes a deduction for the loss when she sells the house in one year. Has Meg acted appropriately?

Recovery of Capital Doctrine

Doctrine Defined. The **recovery of capital doctrine** pervades all the tax rules relating to property transactions. The doctrine derives its roots from the very essence of the income tax—a tax on income. Under the doctrine, as a general rule, a taxpayer is entitled to recover the cost or other original basis of property acquired and is not taxed on that amount.

The cost or other original basis of depreciable property is recovered through annual depreciation deductions. The basis is reduced as the cost is recovered over the

<table>
<tr><td>**LO.3**</td></tr>
<tr><td>Apply the recovery of capital doctrine.</td></tr>
</table>

---

[23]§ 267(a)(1).

period the property is held. Therefore, when property is sold or otherwise disposed of, it is the adjusted basis (unrecovered cost or other basis) that is compared with the amount realized from the disposition to determine realized gain or loss.

Relationship of the Recovery of Capital Doctrine to the Concepts of Realization and Recognition. If a sale or other disposition results in a realized gain, the taxpayer has recovered more than the adjusted basis of the property. Conversely, if a sale or other disposition results in a realized loss, the taxpayer has recovered less than the adjusted basis.

The general rules for the relationship between the recovery of capital doctrine and the realized and recognized gain and loss concepts are summarized as follows:

Rule 1. A realized gain that is *never recognized* results in the *permanent recovery* of more than the taxpayer's cost or other basis for tax purposes. For example, all or a portion of the realized gain on the sale of a personal residence can be excluded from gross income under § 121.

Rule 2. A realized gain on which *recognition is postponed* results in the *temporary recovery* of more than the taxpayer's cost or other basis for tax purposes. For example, an exchange of like-kind property under § 1031 and an involuntary conversion under § 1033 are both eligible for postponement treatment.

Rule 3. A realized loss that is *never recognized* results in the *permanent recovery* of less than the taxpayer's cost or other basis for tax purposes. For example, a loss on the sale of an automobile held for personal use is not deductible.

Rule 4. A realized loss on which *recognition is postponed* results in the *temporary recovery* of less than the taxpayer's cost or other basis for tax purposes. For example, the realized loss on the exchange of like-kind property under § 1031 is postponed.

These rules are illustrated in discussions to follow in this and the next chapter.

LO.4

Explain how basis is determined for various methods of asset acquisition.

Basis Considerations

Determination of Cost Basis

As noted earlier, the basis of property is generally the property's cost. Cost is the amount paid for the property in cash or other property.[24] This general rule follows logically from the recovery of capital doctrine; that is, the cost or other basis of property is to be recovered tax-free by the taxpayer.

A *bargain purchase* of property is an exception to the general rule for determining basis. A bargain purchase may result when an employer transfers property to an employee at less than the property's fair market value (as compensation for services) or when a corporation transfers property to a shareholder at less than the property's fair market value (a dividend). The amount included in income either as compensation for services or dividend income is the difference between the bargain purchase price and the property's fair market value. The basis of property acquired in a bargain purchase is the property's fair market value.[25] If the basis of the property were not increased by the bargain amount, the taxpayer would be taxed on this amount again at disposition.

E X A M P L E   1 0

Wade buys land from his employer for $10,000 on December 30. The fair market value of the land is $15,000. Wade must include the $5,000 difference between the cost and the

---

[24]§ 1012 and Reg. § 1.1012–1(a).

[25]Reg. §§ 1.61–2(d)(2)(i) and 1.301–1(j). See the discussion in Chapter 5 of the circumstances under which what appears to be a taxable bargain purchase is an excludible qualified employee discount.

TAX *in the News*   WHAT'S YOUR STOCK BASIS?

AT&T has 2.7 million shareholders. Some of these are other corporations and wealthy investors, but many are widows and orphans. Each of these shareholders may encounter the same problem: What is the basis of their AT&T stock?

Under SBC Communications' proposal to buy AT&T (approved by the shareholders to be completed in 2006), the shareholders will need to know their stock basis in order to calculate their realized gain or loss. This is likely to be a complicated process. A shareholder who bought AT&T stock before the government broke up the Ma Bell monopoly in 1984 could face substantial difficulties in making this calculation. Such a shareholder who held onto those shares could have owned, at one time or another, shares of 20 different companies. Even with subsequent mergers and acquisitions,

that same shareholder today would own stock in nearly a dozen corporations. The key issue then will be to allocate the shareholder's original basis for the AT&T stock among the shares of the various corporations. This assumes, however, that the shareholder knows the amount of the original stock basis.

Chuck Carlson, who runs a Web site that sells software to aid in such basis allocations, refers to the AT&T shareholder basis situation as a "train wreck." There is some good news, though: the train wreck can be postponed to the future. Since SBC's acquisition of AT&T will be a tax-free reorganization, the shareholder will not need to make the basis determinations until the SBC stock is sold later.

Source: *Adapted from Jane J. Kim, "AT&T Investors Face Tax Headache,"* Wall Street Journal, *February 3, 2005, p. D1.*

---

fair market value of the land in gross income for the taxable year. The bargain element represents additional compensation to Wade. His basis for the land is $15,000, the land's fair market value. ∎

Identification Problems. Cost identification problems are frequently encountered in securities transactions. For example, the Regulations require that the taxpayer adequately identify the particular stock that has been sold.[26] A problem arises when the taxpayer has purchased separate lots of stock on different dates or at different prices and cannot adequately identify the lot from which a particular sale takes place. In this case, the stock is presumed to come from the first lot or lots purchased (a FIFO presumption).[27] When securities are left in the custody of a broker, it may be necessary to provide specific instructions and receive written confirmation as to which securities are being sold.

EXAMPLE 11

Polly purchases 100 shares of Olive Corporation stock on July 1, 2004, for $5,000 ($50 a share) and another 100 shares of Olive stock on July 1, 2005, for $6,000 ($60 a share). She sells 50 shares of the stock on January 2, 2006. The cost of the stock sold, assuming Polly cannot adequately identify the shares, is $50 a share, or $2,500. This is the cost Polly will compare with the amount realized in determining the gain or loss from the sale. ∎

Allocation Problems. When a taxpayer acquires *multiple assets in a lump-sum purchase,* the total cost must be allocated among the individual assets.[28] Allocation is necessary for several reasons:

- Some of the assets acquired may be depreciable (e.g., buildings), while others may not be (e.g., land).
- Only a portion of the assets acquired may be sold.
- Some of the assets may be capital or § 1231 assets that receive special tax treatment upon subsequent sale or other disposition.

The lump-sum cost is allocated on the basis of the fair market values of the individual assets acquired.

---

[26]Reg. § 1.1012–1(c)(1).
[27]*Kluger Associates, Inc.*, 69 T.C. 925 (1978).
[28]Reg. § 1.61–6(a).

EXAMPLE 12

Harry purchases a building and land for $800,000. Because of the depressed nature of the industry in which the seller was operating, Harry was able to negotiate a very favorable purchase price. Appraisals of the individual assets indicate that the fair market value of the building is $600,000 and that of the land is $400,000. Harry's basis for the building is $480,000 [($600,000/$1,000,000) × $800,000], and his basis for the land is $320,000 [($400,000/$1,000,000) × $800,000]. ■

If a business is purchased and **goodwill** is involved, a special allocation rule applies. Initially, the purchase price is assigned to the assets, excluding goodwill, to the extent of their total fair market value. This assigned amount is allocated among the assets on the basis of the fair market value of the individual assets acquired. Goodwill is then assigned the residual amount of the purchase price. The resultant allocation is applicable to both the buyer and the seller.[29]

EXAMPLE 13

Rocky sells his business to Paul. They agree that the values of the individual assets are as follows:

Inventory	$ 50,000
Building	500,000
Land	200,000 *not depreciated*
Goodwill	150,000

After negotiations, Rocky and Paul agree on a sales price of $1 million. Applying the residual method with respect to goodwill results in the following allocation of the $1 million purchase price:

Inventory	$ 50,000
Building	500,000
Land	200,000
Goodwill	250,000

The residual method requires that all of the excess of the purchase price over the fair market value of the assets ($1,000,000 − $900,000 = $100,000) be allocated to goodwill. Without this requirement, the purchaser could allocate the excess pro rata to all of the assets, including goodwill, based on their respective fair market values. This would have resulted in only $166,667 [$150,000 + ($150,000 ÷ $900,000 × $100,000)] being assigned to goodwill. ■

In the case of *nontaxable stock dividends*, the allocation depends on whether the dividend is a common stock dividend on common stock or a preferred stock dividend on common stock. If the dividend is common on common, the cost of the original common shares is allocated to the total shares owned after the dividend.[30]

EXAMPLE 14

Susan owns 100 shares of Sparrow Corporation common stock for which she paid $1,100. She receives a 10% common stock dividend, giving her a new total of 110 shares. Before the stock dividend, Susan's basis was $11 per share ($1,100 ÷ 100 shares). The basis of each share after the stock dividend is $10 ($1,100 ÷ 110 shares). ■

If the nontaxable stock dividend is preferred stock on common, the cost of the original common shares is allocated between the common and preferred shares on the basis of their relative fair market values on the date of distribution.[31]

EXAMPLE 15

Fran owns 100 shares of Cardinal Corporation common stock for which she paid $1,000. She receives a nontaxable stock dividend of 50 shares of preferred stock on her common stock.

---

[29]§ 1060.
[30]§§ 305(a) and 307(a).
[31]Reg. § 1.307–1(a).

The fair market values on the date of distribution of the preferred stock dividend are $30 a share for common stock and $40 a share for preferred stock.

Fair market value of common ($30 × 100 shares)	$3,000
Fair market value of preferred ($40 × 50 shares)	2,000
	$5,000
Basis of common: 3/5 × $1,000	$ 600
Basis of preferred: 2/5 × $1,000	$ 400

The basis per share for the common stock is $6 ($600/100 shares). The basis per share for the preferred stock is $8 ($400/50 shares). ■

The holding period for a nontaxable stock dividend, whether received in the form of common stock or preferred stock, includes the holding period of the original shares.[32] The significance of the holding period for capital assets is discussed in Chapter 16.

In the case of *nontaxable stock rights*, the basis of the rights is zero unless the taxpayer elects or is required to allocate a portion of the cost of the stock already held to the newly received stock rights. If the fair market value of the rights is 15 percent or more of the fair market value of the stock, the taxpayer is required to allocate. If the value of the rights is less than 15 percent of the fair market value of the stock, the taxpayer may elect to allocate.[33] When allocation is required or elected, the cost of the stock on which the rights are received is allocated between the stock and the rights on the basis of their relative fair market values.

EXAMPLE 16

Donald receives nontaxable stock rights with a fair market value of $1,000. The fair market value of the stock on which the rights were received is $8,000 (cost $10,000). Donald does not elect to allocate. The basis of the rights is zero. If he exercises the rights, the basis of the new stock is the exercise (subscription) price. ■

EXAMPLE 17

Assume the same facts as in Example 16, except the fair market value of the rights is $3,000. Donald must allocate because the value of the rights ($3,000) is 15% or more of the value of the stock ($3,000/$8,000 = 37.5%).

- The basis of the stock is $7,273 [($8,000/$11,000) × $10,000].
- The basis of the rights is $2,727 [($3,000/$11,000) × $10,000].

If Donald exercises the rights, the basis of the new stock is the exercise (subscription) price plus the basis of the rights. If he sells the rights, he recognizes gain or loss equal to the difference between the amount realized and the basis of the rights. This allocation rule applies only when the rights are exercised or sold. Therefore, if the rights are allowed to lapse (expire), they have no basis, and the basis of the original stock is the stock's cost, $10,000. ■

The holding period of nontaxable stock rights includes the holding period of the stock on which the rights were distributed. However, if the rights are exercised, the holding period of the newly acquired stock begins with the date the rights are exercised.[34]

Gift Basis

When a taxpayer receives property as a gift, there is no cost to the donee (recipient). Thus, under the cost basis provision, the donee's basis would be zero. However, this would violate the statutory intent that gifts not be subject to the income tax.[35] With a zero basis, if the donee sold the property, all of the amount realized

---

[32]§ 1223(5) and Reg. § 1.1223–1(e).
[33]§ 307(b).
[34]§ 1223(5) and Reg. §§ 1.1223–1(e) and (f).
[35]§ 102(a).

TAX *in the News*   FREQUENT-FLYER MILES AND BASIS

There are many ways to get frequent-flyer miles. Perhaps the most logical is to fly on an airplane, but staying in a hotel, renting a car, and using your credit card can also generate frequent-flyer miles. A more novel approach is to buy shares in a mutual fund.

Always watch out for the tax consequences, though. In a letter ruling, the IRS held that taxpayers who receive frequent-flyer miles for buying mutual fund shares must reduce their mutual fund basis by the fair market value of the miles received. The mutual fund must notify its shareholders of the fair market value, which is based on the cost of buying frequent-flyer miles from the airlines.

would be treated as realized gain. Therefore, a basis is assigned to the property received depending on the following:

- The date of the gift.
- The basis of the property to the donor.
- The amount of the gift tax paid.
- The fair market value of the property.

Gift Basis Rules if No Gift Tax Is Paid. Property received by gift can be referred to as *dual basis* property; that is, the basis for gain and the basis for loss might not be the same amount. The present basis rules for gifts of property are as follows:

- If the donee disposes of gift property in a transaction that results in a gain, the basis to the donee is the same as the donor's adjusted basis.[36] The donee's basis in this case is referred to as the *gain basis*. Therefore, a *realized gain* results if the amount realized from the disposition exceeds the donee's gain basis.

EXAMPLE 18

Melissa purchased stock in 2005 for $10,000. She gave the stock to her son, Joe, in 2006, when the fair market value was $15,000. No gift tax is paid on the transfer, and Joe subsequently sells the property for $15,000. Joe's basis is $10,000, and he has a realized gain of $5,000. ∎

- If the donee disposes of gift property in a transaction that results in a loss, the basis to the donee is the *lower* of the donor's adjusted basis or the fair market value on the date of the gift. The donee's basis in this case is referred to as the *loss basis*. Therefore, a *realized loss* results if the amount realized from the disposition is less than the donee's loss basis.

EXAMPLE 19

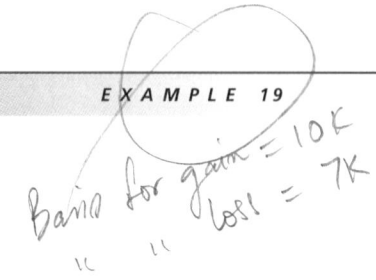

Burt purchased stock in 2005 for $10,000. He gave the stock to his son, Cliff, in 2006, when the fair market value was $7,000. No gift tax is paid on the transfer. Cliff later sells the stock for $6,000. Cliff's basis is $7,000 (fair market value is less than donor's adjusted basis of $10,000), and the realized loss from the sale is $1,000 ($6,000 amount realized − $7,000 basis). ∎

The amount of the loss basis will *differ* from the amount of the gain basis only if, at the date of the gift, the adjusted basis of the property exceeds the property's fair market value. Note that the loss basis rule prevents the donee from receiving a tax benefit from a decline in value that occurred while the donor held the property. Therefore, in Example 19, Cliff has a loss of only $1,000 rather than a loss of $4,000. The $3,000 difference represents the decline in value that occurred while Burt held the property. Ironically, however, the gain basis rule may result in

---

[36]§ 1015(a) and Reg. § 1.1015–1(a)(1). See Reg. § 1.1015–1(a)(3) for cases in which the facts necessary to determine the donor's adjusted basis are unknown. Refer to Example 24 for the effect of depreciation deductions by the donee.

the donee being subject to income tax on the appreciation that occurred while the donor held the property, as illustrated in Example 18.

If the amount realized from a sale or other disposition is *between* the basis for loss and the basis for gain, no gain or loss is realized.

EXAMPLE 20

Assume the same facts as in Example 19, except that Cliff sells the stock for $8,000. Application of the gain basis rule produces a loss of $2,000 ($8,000 − $10,000). Application of the loss basis rule produces a gain of $1,000 ($8,000 − $7,000). Because the amount realized is between the gain basis and the loss basis, Cliff recognizes neither a gain nor a loss. ■

Adjustment for Gift Tax. If gift taxes are paid by the donor, the donee's gain basis may exceed the adjusted basis of the property to the donor. This occurs only if the fair market value of the property at the date of the gift is greater than the donor's adjusted basis (the property has appreciated in value). The portion of the gift tax paid that is related to the appreciation is added to the donor's basis in calculating the donee's gain basis for the property. In this circumstance, the following formula is used for calculating the donee's gain basis:[37]

Donee's gain basis = Donor's adjusted basis + (Unrealized appreciation / Taxable gift*) × Gift tax paid

*The taxable gift is the fair market value of the gift less the per donee annual exclusion.

EXAMPLE 21

In 2006, Bonnie made a gift of stock (adjusted basis of $15,000) to Peggy. The stock had a fair market value of $50,000, and the transfer resulted in a gift tax of $4,000. The unrealized appreciation of the stock is $35,000 ($50,000 fair market value − $15,000 adjusted basis), and the taxable gift is $38,000 ($50,000 fair market value of gift − $12,000 annual exclusion). Peggy's basis in the stock is $18,680, determined as follows:

Cost 15K
FMV 50K
Gift tax 4K
35K

Donor's adjusted basis	$15,000
Gift tax attributable to appreciation—	
$35,000/$38,000 = 92% (rounded) × $4,000	3,680
Donee's gain basis	$18,680

■

EXAMPLE 22

Don made a gift of stock to Matt in 2006, when the fair market value of the stock was $50,000. Don paid gift tax of $4,000. Don had purchased the stock in 1987 for $65,000. Because there is no unrealized appreciation at the date of the gift, none of the gift tax paid is added to Don's basis in calculating Matt's gain basis. Therefore, Matt's gain basis is $65,000. ■

Buy $65K
FMV $50K < $65K.

For *gifts made before 1977,* the full amount of the gift tax paid is added to the donor's basis. However, the ceiling on this total is the fair market value of the property at the date of the gift. Thus, in Example 21, if the gift had been made before 1977, the basis of the property would be $19,000 ($15,000 + $4,000). In Example 22, the gain basis would still be $65,000 ($65,000 + $0).

Holding Period. The **holding period** for property acquired by gift begins on the date the donor acquired the property if the gain basis rule applies.[38] The holding period starts on the date of the gift if the loss basis rule applies.[39] The significance of the holding period for capital assets is discussed in Chapter 16.

[37]§ 1015(d)(6) and Reg. § 1.1015–5(c)(2).
[38]§ 1223(2) and Reg. § 1.1223–1(b).
[39]Rev.Rul. 59–86, 1959–1 C.B. 209.

The following example summarizes the basis and holding period rules for gift property:

EXAMPLE 23

Jill acquired 100 shares of Wren Corporation stock on December 30, 1988, for $40,000. On January 3, 2006, when the stock has a fair market value of $38,000, Jill gives it to Dennis and pays gift tax of $4,000. The basis is not increased by a portion of the gift tax paid because the property has not appreciated in value at the time of the gift, Therefore, Dennis's gain basis is $40,000. Dennis's basis for determining loss is $38,000 (fair market value) because the fair market value on the date of the gift is less than the donor's adjusted basis.

- If Dennis sells the stock for $45,000, he has a recognized gain of $5,000. The holding period for determining whether the capital gain is short term or long term begins on December 30, 1988, the date Jill acquired the property.
- If Dennis sells the stock for $36,000, he has a recognized loss of $2,000. The holding period for determining whether the capital loss is short term or long term begins on January 3, 2006, the date of the gift.
- If Dennis sells the property for $39,000, there is no loss because the amount realized is less than the gain basis of $40,000 and more than the loss basis of $38,000. ∎

Basis for Depreciation. The basis for depreciation on depreciable gift property is the donee's gain basis.[40] This rule is applicable even if the donee later sells the property at a loss and uses the loss basis rule in calculating the amount of the realized loss.

EXAMPLE 24

Vito gave a machine to Tina in 2006. At that time, the adjusted basis was $32,000 (cost of $40,000 − accumulated depreciation of $8,000), and the fair market value was $26,000. No gift tax was paid. Tina's gain basis at the date of the gift is $32,000, and her loss basis is $26,000. During 2006, Tina deducts depreciation (cost recovery) of $6,400 ($32,000 × 20%). (Refer to Chapter 8 for the cost recovery tables.) At the end of 2006, Tina's gain basis and loss basis are calculated as follows:

	Gain Basis	Loss Basis
Donor's basis or fair market value	$32,000	$26,000
Depreciation	(6,400)	(6,400)
	$25,600	$19,600

∎

Property Acquired from a Decedent

General Rules. The basis of property acquired from a decedent is generally the property's fair market value at the date of death (referred to as the *primary valuation amount*).[41] The property's basis is the fair market value six months after the date of death if the executor or administrator of the estate *elects* the alternate valuation date for estate tax purposes. This amount is referred to as the *alternate valuation amount.*

EXAMPLE 25

Linda and various other family members inherited property from Linda's father, who died in 2006. At the date of death, her father's adjusted basis for the property Linda inherited was $35,000. The property's fair market value at the date of death was $50,000. The alternate valuation date was not elected. Linda's basis for income tax purposes is $50,000. This is commonly referred to as a *stepped-up basis.* ∎

---

[40]§ 1011 and Reg. §§ 1.1011–1 and 1.167(g)–1.   [41]§ 1014(a).

Assume the same facts as in Example 25, except the property's fair market value at the date of death was $20,000. Linda's basis for income tax purposes is $20,000. This is commonly referred to as a *stepped-down basis.* ∎

EXAMPLE 26

No estate tax return must be filed for estates below a threshold amount. In such cases, the alternate valuation date and amount are not available. Even if an estate tax return is filed and the executor elects the alternate valuation date, the six months after death date is available only for property that the executor has not distributed before this date. For any property distributed or otherwise disposed of by the executor during the six-month period preceding the alternate valuation date, the adjusted basis to the beneficiary will equal the fair market value on the date of distribution or other disposition.[42]

gross value of estate, not indiv property's value.

The alternate valuation date can be *elected only* if, as a result of the election, both the value of the gross estate and the estate tax liability are lower than they would have been if the primary valuation date had been used. This provision prevents the alternate valuation election from being used to increase the basis of the property to the beneficiary for income tax purposes without simultaneously increasing the estate tax liability (because of estate tax deductions or credits).[43]

Nancy inherited all the property of her father, who died in 2006. Her father's adjusted basis for the property at the date of death was $650,000. The property's fair market value was $2,750,000 at the date of death and $2,760,000 six months after death. The alternate valuation date cannot be elected because the value of the gross estate has increased during the six-month period. Nancy's basis for income tax purposes is $2,750,000. ∎

EXAMPLE 27

Assume the same facts as in Example 27, except the property's fair market value six months after death was $2,745,000. If the executor elects the alternate valuation date, Nancy's basis for income tax purposes is $2,745,000. ∎

EXAMPLE 28

Assume the same facts as in the previous example, except the property is distributed four months after the date of the decedent's death. At the distribution date, the property's fair market value is $2,747,500. Since the executor elected the alternate valuation date, Nancy's basis for income tax purposes is $2,747,500. ∎

EXAMPLE 29

For inherited property, both unrealized appreciation and decline in value are taken into consideration in determining the basis of the property for income tax purposes. Contrast this with the carryover basis rules for property received by gift.

Deathbed Gifts. The Code contains a provision designed to eliminate a tax avoidance technique referred to as *deathbed gifts.* With this technique, a donor makes a gift of appreciated property to a dying person with the understanding that the donor (or the donor's spouse) will inherit the property on the donee's death. If the time period between the date of the gift and the date of the donee's death is not longer than one year, the usual basis rule (stepped-up basis) for inherited property may not apply. The adjusted basis of such property inherited by the donor or his or her spouse from the donee is the same as the decedent's adjusted basis for the property rather than the fair market value at the date of death or the alternate valuation date.[44]

---

[42]§ 2032(a)(1) and Rev.Rul. 56–60, 1956–1 C.B. 443.   [44]§ 1014(e).
[43]§ 2032(c).

EXAMPLE 30

Ned gives stock to his uncle, Vern, in 2006. Ned's basis for the stock is $1,000, and the fair market value is $9,000. No gift tax is paid. Eight months later, Ned inherits the stock from Vern. At the date of Vern's death, the fair market value of the stock is $12,000. Ned's adjusted basis for the stock is $1,000. ∎

Survivor's Share of Property. Both the decedent's share and the survivor's share of *community property* have a basis equal to the fair market value on the date of the decedent's death.[45] This result applies to the decedent's share of the community property because the property flows to the surviving spouse from the estate (fair market value basis is assigned to inherited property). Likewise, the surviving spouse's share of the community property is deemed to be acquired by bequest, devise, or inheritance from the decedent. Therefore, it also has a basis equal to the fair market value.

EXAMPLE 31

Floyd and Vera reside in a community property state. They own as community property 200 shares of Crow stock acquired in 1982 for $100,000. Floyd dies in 2006, when the securities are valued at $300,000. One-half of the Crow stock is included in Floyd's estate. If Vera inherits Floyd's share of the community property, the basis for determining gain or loss is $300,000, determined as follows:

Vera's one-half of the community property (stepped up from $50,000 to $150,000 due to Floyd's death)	$150,000
Floyd's one-half of the community property (stepped up from $50,000 to $150,000 due to inclusion in his gross estate)	150,000
Vera's new basis	$300,000

∎

In a *common law* state, only one-half of jointly held property of spouses (tenants by the entirety or joint tenants with rights of survivorship) is included in the estate.[46] In such a case, no adjustment of the basis is permitted for the excluded property interest (the surviving spouse's share).

EXAMPLE 32

Assume the same facts as in the previous example, except that the property is jointly held by Floyd and Vera who reside in a common law state. Floyd purchased the property and made a gift of one-half of the property to Vera when the stock was acquired. No gift tax was paid. Only one-half of the Crow stock is included in Floyd's estate. Vera's basis for determining

[45]§ 1014(b)(6). See the listing of community property states in Chapter 4.   [46]§ 2040(b).

gain or loss in the excluded half is not adjusted upward for the increase in value to date of death. Therefore, Vera's basis is $200,000, determined as follows:

Vera's one-half of the jointly held property (carryover basis of $50,000)	$ 50,000
Floyd's one-half of the jointly held property (stepped up from $50,000 to $150,000 due to inclusion in his gross estate)	150,000
Vera's new basis	$200,000

Holding Period of Property Acquired from a Decedent. The holding period of property acquired from a decedent is *deemed to be long term* (held for the required long-term holding period). This provision applies regardless of whether the property is disposed of at a gain or at a loss.[47]

Disallowed Losses

LO.5

Describe various loss disallowance provisions.

Related Taxpayers. Section 267 provides that realized losses from sales or exchanges of property, directly or indirectly, between certain related parties are not recognized. This loss disallowance provision applies to several types of related-party transactions. The most common involve (1) members of a family and (2) an individual and a corporation in which the individual owns, directly or indirectly, more than 50 percent in value of the corporation's outstanding stock. Section 707 provides a similar loss disallowance provision where the related parties are a partner and a partnership in which the partner owns, directly or indirectly, more than 50 percent of the capital interests or profits interests in the partnership. The rules governing the relationships covered by § 267 were discussed in Chapter 6. See Chapter 15 for the discussion of the special rules under § 1041 for property transfers between spouses or incident to divorce.

If income-producing or business property is transferred to a related taxpayer and a loss is disallowed, the basis of the property to the recipient is the property's cost to the transferee. However, if a subsequent sale or other disposition of the property by the original transferee results in a realized gain, the amount of gain is reduced by the loss that was previously disallowed.[48] This *right of offset* is not applicable if the original sale involved the sale of a personal use asset (e.g., the sale of a personal residence between related taxpayers). Furthermore, the right of offset is available only to the original transferee (the related-party buyer).

EXAMPLE 33

Pedro sells business property with an adjusted basis of $50,000 to his daughter, Josefina, for its fair market value of $40,000. Pedro's realized loss of $10,000 is not recognized.

- How much gain does Josefina recognize if she sells the property for $52,000? Josefina recognizes a $2,000 gain. Her realized gain is $12,000 ($52,000 less her basis of $40,000), but she can offset Pedro's $10,000 loss against the gain.
- How much gain does Josefina recognize if she sells the property for $48,000? Josefina recognizes no gain or loss. Her realized gain is $8,000 ($48,000 less her basis of $40,000), but she can offset $8,000 of Pedro's $10,000 loss against the gain. Note that Pedro's loss can only offset Josefina's gain. It cannot create a loss for Josefina.
- How much loss does Josefina recognize if she sells the property for $38,000? Josefina recognizes a $2,000 loss, the same as her realized loss ($38,000 less $40,000 basis). Pedro's loss does not increase Josefina's loss. His loss can be offset only against a gain. Since Josefina has no realized gain, Pedro's loss cannot be used and is never recognized. This part of the example assumes that the property is business or income-producing property to Josefina. If not, her $2,000 loss is personal and is not recognized. ■

---

[47]§ 1223(11).   [48]§ 267(d) and Reg. § 1.267(d)–1(a).

The loss disallowance rules are designed to achieve two objectives. First, the rules prevent a taxpayer from directly transferring an unrealized loss to a related taxpayer in a higher tax bracket who could receive a greater tax benefit from recognition of the loss. Second, the rules eliminate a substantial administrative burden on the Internal Revenue Service as to the appropriateness of the selling price (fair market value or not). The loss disallowance rules are applicable even where the selling price is equal to the fair market value and can be validated (e.g., listed stocks).

The holding period of the buyer for the property is not affected by the holding period of the seller. That is, the buyer's *holding period* includes only the period of time he or she has held the property.[49]

ETHICAL *Considerations*   TRANSACTIONS BETWEEN SPOUSES

At the time of their marriage, Ted and Lisa each had substantial assets. Consequently, they signed a premarital agreement to keep their assets separate and avoid any commingling. They do, however, own some undeveloped land jointly, with each having contributed $500,000 toward the $1 million purchase price. Though the value of the land is currently depressed, considerable profit would result if they could successfully have the land rezoned from residential to commercial use. Lisa has serious doubts that a rezoning request would be approved, but Ted thinks otherwise.

Ted has offered to buy Lisa's 50 percent interest in the land for $300,000. Lisa's CPA informs her that her realized loss of $200,000 on the sale would be disallowed under § 267

as a transaction between related parties. He also informs her that Ted, but not Lisa, could use this disallowed loss to reduce any recognized gain he might have on a subsequent sale of the land.

Horrified by these results, Lisa concludes that their marriage relationship is producing too many negative tax consequences. She proposes to Ted that they get a divorce "for tax purposes" and continue to live together as man and wife. Only Lisa, Ted, and their attorney would know that they are no longer married. Being no longer legally married, she could carry out the sale to Ted and avoid the related-party disallowance of loss rules of § 267. Comment on the propriety of Lisa's proposal.

Sell @ loss and buy back in 30 days.

Wash Sales. Section 1091 stipulates that in certain cases, a realized loss on the sale or exchange of stock or securities is not recognized. Specifically, if a taxpayer sells or exchanges stock or securities and within 30 days before *or* after the date of the sale or exchange acquires substantially identical stock or securities, any loss realized from the sale or exchange is not recognized because the transaction is a **wash sale**.[50] The term *acquire* means acquire by purchase or in a taxable exchange and includes an option to purchase substantially identical securities. *Substantially identical* means the same in all important particulars. Corporate bonds and preferred stock are normally not considered substantially identical to the corporation's common stock. However, if the bonds and preferred stock are convertible into common stock, they may be considered substantially identical under certain circumstances.[51] Attempts to avoid the application of the wash sales rules by having a related taxpayer repurchase the securities have been unsuccessful.[52] The wash sales provisions do *not* apply to gains.

Recognition of the loss is disallowed because the taxpayer is considered to be in substantially the same economic position after the sale and repurchase as before the sale and repurchase. This disallowance rule does not apply to taxpayers engaged in the business of buying and selling securities.[53] Investors, however, are not allowed to create losses through wash sales to offset income for tax purposes.

---

[49]§§ 267(d) and 1223(2) and Reg. § 1.267(d)–1(c)(3).

[50]§ 1091(a) and Reg. §§ 1.1091–1(a) and (f).

[51]Rev.Rul. 56–406, 1956–2 C.B. 523.

[52]*McWilliams v. Comm.*, 47–1 USTC ¶9289, 35 AFTR 1184, 67 S.Ct. 1477 (USSC, 1947).

[53]Reg. § 1.1091–1(a).

Realized loss that is not recognized is added to the *basis* of the substantially identical stock or securities whose acquisition resulted in the nonrecognition of loss.[54] In other words, the basis of the replacement stock or securities is increased by the amount of the unrecognized loss. If the loss were not added to the basis of the newly acquired stock or securities, the taxpayer would never recover the entire basis of the old stock or securities.

The basis of the new stock or securities includes the unrecovered portion of the basis of the formerly held stock or securities. Therefore, the *holding period* of the new stock or securities begins on the date of acquisition of the old stock or securities.[55]

EXAMPLE 34

Bhaskar owns 100 shares of Green Corporation stock (adjusted basis of $20,000). He sells 50 shares for $8,000. Ten days later, he purchases 50 shares of the same stock for $7,000. Bhaskar's realized loss of $2,000 ($8,000 amount realized − $10,000 adjusted basis of 50 shares) is not recognized because it resulted from a wash sale. Bhaskar's basis in the newly acquired stock is $9,000 ($7,000 purchase price + $2,000 unrecognized loss from the wash sale). ∎

A taxpayer may acquire fewer shares than the number sold in a wash sale. In this case, the loss from the sale is prorated between recognized and unrecognized loss on the basis of the ratio of the number of shares acquired to the number of shares sold.[56]

Conversion of Property from Personal Use to Business or Income-Producing Use

As discussed previously, losses from the sale of personal use assets are not recognized for tax purposes, but losses from the sale of business and income-producing assets are deductible. Can a taxpayer convert a personal use asset that has declined in value to business or income-producing use and then sell the asset to recognize a business or income-producing loss? The tax law prevents this practice by specifying that the *original basis for loss* on personal use assets converted to business or income-producing use is the *lower* of the property's adjusted basis or fair market value on the date of conversion.[57] The *gain basis* for converted property is the property's adjusted basis on the date of conversion. The tax law is not concerned with gains on converted property because gains are recognized regardless of whether property is business, income-producing, or personal use.

[handwritten margin note: Loss basis is lower of: – Adj basis – FMV]

EXAMPLE 35

Diane's personal residence has an adjusted basis of $175,000 and a fair market value of $160,000. Diane converts the personal residence to rental property. Her basis for loss is $160,000 (lower of $175,000 adjusted basis and fair market value of $160,000). The $15,000 decline in value is a personal loss and can never be recognized for tax purposes. Diane's basis for gain is $175,000. ∎

The basis for loss is also the *basis for depreciating* the converted property.[58] This is an exception to the general rule that the basis for depreciation is the gain basis (e.g., property received by gift). This exception prevents the taxpayer from recovering a personal loss indirectly through depreciation of the higher original basis. After the property is converted, both its basis for loss and its basis for gain are adjusted for depreciation deductions from the date of conversion to the date of disposition. These rules apply only if a conversion from personal to business or income-producing use has actually occurred.

---

[54]§ 1091(d) and Reg. § 1.1091–2(a).

[55]§ 1223(4) and Reg. § 1.1223–1(d).

[56]§ 1091(b) and Reg. § 1.1091–1(c).

[57]Reg. § 1.165–9(b)(2).

[58]Reg. § 1.167(g)–1.

EXAMPLE 36

At a time when his personal residence (adjusted basis of $140,000) is worth $150,000, Keith converts one-half of it to rental use. Assume the property is not MACRS recovery property. At this point, the estimated useful life of the residence is 20 years, and there is no estimated salvage value. After renting the converted portion for five years, Keith sells the property for $144,000. All amounts relate only to the building; the land has been accounted for separately. Keith has a $2,000 realized gain from the sale of the personal use portion of the residence and a $19,500 realized gain from the sale of the rental portion. These gains are computed as follows:

	Personal Use	Rental
Original basis for gain and loss—adjusted basis on date of conversion (fair market value is greater than the adjusted basis)	$70,000	$70,000
Depreciation—five years	None	17,500
Adjusted basis—date of sale	$70,000	$52,500
Amount realized	72,000	72,000
Realized gain	$ 2,000	$19,500

As discussed in Chapter 15, Keith may be able to exclude the $2,000 realized gain from the sale of the personal use portion of the residence under § 121. If the § 121 exclusion applies, only $17,500 (equal to the depreciation deducted) of the $19,500 realized gain from the rental portion is recognized.

EXAMPLE 37

Assume the same facts as in the previous example, except that the fair market value on the date of conversion is $130,000 and the sales proceeds are $90,000. Keith has a $25,000 realized loss from the sale of the personal use portion of the residence and a $3,750 realized loss from the sale of the rental portion. These losses are computed as follows:

	Personal Use	Rental
Original basis for loss—fair market value on date of conversion (fair market value is less than the adjusted basis)	*	$65,000
Depreciation—five years	None	16,250
Adjusted basis—date of sale	$70,000	$48,750
Amount realized	45,000	45,000
Realized loss	($25,000)	($ 3,750)

* Not applicable.

The $25,000 loss from the sale of the personal use portion of the residence is not recognized. The $3,750 loss from the rental portion is recognized. ∎

Additional Complexities in Determining Realized Gain or Loss

Amount Realized. The calculation of the amount realized may appear to be one of the least complex areas associated with property transactions. However, because numerous positive and negative adjustments may be required, this calculation can be complex and confusing. In addition, determining the fair market value of the items received by the taxpayer can be difficult. The following example provides insight into various items that can affect the amount realized.

EXAMPLE 38

Ridge sells an office building and the associated land on October 1, 2006. Under the terms of the sales contract, Ridge is to receive $600,000 in cash. The purchaser is to assume Ridge's mortgage of $300,000 on the property. To enable the purchaser to obtain adequate financing, Ridge is to pay the $15,000 in points charged by the lender. The broker's commission on the sale is $45,000. The purchaser agrees to pay the $12,000 in property taxes for the entire year. The amount realized by Ridge is calculated as follows:

Selling price		
Cash	$600,000	
Mortgage assumed by purchaser	300,000	
Seller's property taxes paid by		
purchaser ($12,000 × $^9/_{12}$)	9,000	$909,000
Less		
Broker's commission	$ 45,000	
Points paid by seller	15,000	(60,000)
Amount realized		$849,000	∎

Adjusted Basis. Three types of issues tend to complicate the determination of adjusted basis. First, the applicable tax provisions for calculating the adjusted basis depend on how the property was acquired (e.g., purchase, taxable exchange, nontaxable exchange, gift, inheritance). Second, if the asset is subject to depreciation, cost recovery, amortization, or depletion, adjustments must be made to the basis during the time period the asset is held by the taxpayer. Upon disposition of the asset, the taxpayer's records for both of these items may be deficient. For example, the donee does not know the amount of the donor's basis or the amount of gift tax paid by the donor, or the taxpayer does not know how much depreciation he or she has deducted. Third, the complex positive and negative adjustments encountered in calculating the amount realized are also involved in calculating the adjusted basis.

EXAMPLE 39

Jane purchased a personal residence in 1997. The purchase price and the related closing costs were as follows:

Purchase price	$125,000
Recording costs	140
Title fees and title insurance	815
Survey costs	115
Attorney's fees	750
Appraisal fee	60

Other relevant tax information for the house during the time Jane owned it is as follows:

- Constructed a swimming pool for medical reasons. The cost was $10,000, of which $3,000 was deducted as a medical expense.
- Added a solar heating system. The cost was $15,000.
- Deducted home office expenses of $6,000. Of this amount, $3,200 was for depreciation.

The adjusted basis for the house is calculated as follows:

Purchase price	$125,000
Recording costs	140
Title fees and title insurance	815
Survey costs	115
Attorney's fees	750
Appraisal fee	60

Swimming pool ($10,000 − $3,000)	7,000
Solar heating system	15,000
	$148,880
Less: Depreciation deducted on home office	(3,200)
Adjusted basis	$145,680

Summary of Basis Adjustments

Some of the more common items that either increase or decrease the basis of an asset appear in Concept Summary 14–2.

In discussing the topic of basis, a number of specific techniques for determining basis have been presented. Although the various techniques are responsive to and mandated by transactions occurring in the marketplace, they do possess enough common characteristics to be categorized as follows:

- The basis of the asset may be determined by reference to the asset's cost.
- The basis of the asset may be determined by reference to the basis of another asset.
- The basis of the asset may be determined by reference to the asset's fair market value.
- The basis of the asset may be determined by reference to the basis of the asset to another taxpayer.

LO.6

Identify tax planning opportunities related to selected property transactions.

TAX PLANNING
Considerations

Tax Consequences of Alice's Proposed Transaction

In Example 1 earlier in the chapter, Alice's tax adviser asked a number of questions in order to advise her on a proposed transaction. Alice provided the following answers:

- Alice inherited the house from her mother. The fair market value of the house at the date of her mother's death, based on the estate tax return, was $225,000. Based on an appraisal, the house is worth $230,000. Alice's mother lived in the house for 48 years. According to the mother's attorney, her adjusted basis for the house was $75,000.
- As a child, Alice lived in the house for 10 years. She has not lived there during the 35 years she has been married.

CONCEPT SUMMARY 14–2

Adjustments to Basis

Item	Effect	Refer to Chapter	Explanation
Amortization of bond discount.	Increase	16	Amortization is mandatory for certain taxable bonds and elective for tax-exempt bonds.
Amortization of bond premium.	Decrease	14	Amortization is mandatory for tax-exempt bonds and elective for taxable bonds.
Amortization of covenant not to compete.	Decrease	16	Covenant must be for a definite and limited time period. The amortization period is a statutory period of 15 years.
Amortization of intangibles.	Decrease	8	Intangibles are amortized over a 15-year period.
Assessment for local benefits.	Increase	10	To the extent not deductible as taxes (e.g., assessment for streets and sidewalks that increase the value of the property versus one for maintenance or repair or for meeting interest charges).
Bad debts.	Decrease	7	Only the specific charge-off method is permitted.
Capital additions.	Increase	14	Certain items, at the taxpayer's election, can be capitalized or deducted (e.g., selected medical expenses).
Casualty.	Decrease	7	For a casualty loss, the amount of the adjustment is the summation of the deductible loss and the insurance proceeds received. For a casualty gain, the amount of the adjustment is the insurance proceeds received reduced by the recognized gain.
Condemnation.	Decrease	15	See casualty explanation.
Cost recovery.	Decrease	8	§ 168 is applicable to tangible assets placed in service after 1980 whose useful life is expressed in terms of years.
Depletion.	Decrease	8	Use the greater of cost or percentage depletion. Percentage depletion can still be deducted when the basis is zero.
Depreciation.	Decrease	8	§ 167 is applicable to tangible assets placed in service before 1981 and to tangible assets not depreciated in terms of years.
Easement.	Decrease	14	If the taxpayer does not retain any use of the land, all of the basis is allocable to the easement transaction. However, if only part of the land is affected by the easement, only part of the basis is allocable to the easement transaction.
Improvements by lessee to lessor's property.	Increase	5	Adjustment occurs only if the lessor is required to include the fair market value of the improvements in gross income under § 109.
Imputed interest.	Decrease	18	Amount deducted is not part of the cost of the asset.
Inventory: lower of cost or market.	Decrease	18	Not available if the LIFO method is used.
Limited expensing under § 179.	Decrease	8	Occurs only if the taxpayer elects § 179 treatment.
Medical capital expenditure permitted as a medical expense.	Decrease	10	Adjustment is the amount of the deduction (the effect on basis is to increase it by the amount of the capital expenditure net of the deduction).

Item	Effect	Refer to Chapter	Explanation
Real estate taxes: apportionment between the buyer and seller.	Increase or decrease	10	To the extent the buyer pays the seller's pro rata share, the buyer's basis is increased. To the extent the seller pays the buyer's pro rata share, the buyer's basis is decreased.
Rebate from manufacturer.	Decrease		Since the rebate is treated as an adjustment to the purchase price, it is not included in the buyer's gross income.
Stock dividend.	Decrease	5	Adjustment occurs only if the stock dividend is nontaxable. While the basis per share decreases, the total stock basis does not change.
Stock rights.	Decrease	14	Adjustment to stock basis occurs only for nontaxable stock rights and only if the fair market value of the rights is at least 15% of the fair market value of the stock or, if less than 15%, the taxpayer elects to allocate the basis between the stock and the rights.
Theft.	Decrease	7	See casualty explanation.

- The house has been vacant during the seven months that Alice has owned it. She has been trying to decide whether she should sell it for its fair market value or sell it to her nephew for $75,000. Alice has suggested a $75,000 price for the sale to Dan because she believes this is the amount at which she will have no gain or loss.
- Alice intends to invest the $75,000 in stock.

You advise Alice that her adjusted basis for the house is the $225,000 fair market value on the date of her mother's death. If Alice sells the house for $230,000 (assuming no selling expenses), she would have a recognized gain of $5,000 ($230,000 amount realized − $225,000 adjusted basis). The house is a capital asset, and Alice's holding period is long term since she inherited the house. Thus, the gain would be classified as a long-term capital gain. If, instead, Alice sells the house to her nephew for $75,000, she will have a part sale and part gift. The realized gain on the sale of $1,630 is recognized.

Amount realized	$ 75,000
Less: Adjusted basis	(73,370)*
Realized gain	$ 1,630
Recognized gain	$ 1,630

* [($75,000/$230,000) × $225,000] = $73,370.

The gain is classified as a long-term capital gain. Alice is then deemed to have made a gift to Dan of $155,000 ($230,000 − $75,000).

With this information, Alice can make an informed selection between the two options.

Cost Identification and Documentation Considerations

When multiple assets are acquired in a single transaction, the contract price must be allocated for several reasons. First, some of the assets may be depreciable, while others are not. From the different viewpoints of the buyer and the seller, this may produce a tax conflict that needs to be resolved. That is, the seller prefers a high allocation for nondepreciable assets, whereas the purchaser prefers a high allocation for depreciable assets (see Chapters 16 and 17). Second, the seller needs to know the amount realized on the sale of the capital assets and the ordinary income assets so that the recognized gains and losses can be classified as capital or ordinary. For example, an allocation to goodwill or to a covenant not to compete (see Chapters 8, 16, and 17) produces different tax consequences to the seller. Third, the buyer needs the adjusted basis of each asset to calculate the realized gain or loss on a subsequent sale or other disposition of each asset.

Selection of Property for Making Gifts

A donor can achieve several tax advantages by making gifts of appreciated property. The donor avoids income tax on the unrealized gain that would have occurred had the donor sold the property. A portion of this amount can be permanently avoided because the donee's adjusted basis is increased by part or all of any gift tax paid by the donor. Even without this increase in basis, the income tax liability on the sale of the property by the donee can be less than the income tax liability that would have resulted from the donor's sale of the property, if the donee is in a lower tax bracket than the donor. In addition, any subsequent appreciation during the time the property is held by the lower tax bracket donee results in a tax savings on the sale or other disposition of the property. Such gifts of appreciated property can be an effective tool in family tax planning.

Taxpayers should generally not make gifts of depreciated property (property that, if sold, would produce a realized loss) because the donor does not receive an income tax deduction for the unrealized loss element. In addition, the donee receives no benefit from this unrealized loss upon the subsequent sale of the property because of the loss basis rule. The loss basis rule provides that the donee's basis is the lower of the donor's basis or the fair market value at the date of the gift. If the donor anticipates that the donee will sell the property upon receiving it, the donor should sell the property and take the loss deduction, assuming the loss is deductible. The donor can then give the proceeds from the sale to the donee.

Selection of Property for Making Bequests

A taxpayer should generally make bequests of appreciated property in his or her will. Doing so enables both the decedent and the heir to avoid income tax on the unrealized gain because the recipient takes the fair market value as his or her basis.

Taxpayers generally should not make bequests of depreciated property (property that, if sold, would produce a realized loss) because the decedent does not receive an income tax deduction for the unrealized loss element. In addition, the heir will receive no benefit from this unrealized loss upon the subsequent sale of the property.

EXAMPLE 40

On the date of her death, Marta owned land held for investment purposes. The land had an adjusted basis of $130,000 and a fair market value of $100,000. If Marta had sold the property before her death, the recognized loss would have been $30,000. If Roger inherits the property and later sells it for $90,000, the recognized loss is $10,000 (the decline in value since Marta's death). In addition, regardless of the period of time Roger holds the property, the holding period is long term (see Chapter 16). ∎

From an income tax perspective, it is preferable to transfer appreciated property as a bequest rather than as a gift. The reason is that inherited property receives a step-up in basis, whereas property received by gift has a carryover basis to the donee. However, in making this decision, the estate tax consequences of the bequest should also be weighed against the gift tax consequences of the gift.

Disallowed Losses

Section 267 Disallowed Losses. Taxpayers should be aware of the desirability of avoiding transactions that activate the loss disallowance provisions for related parties. This is so even in light of the provision that permits the related-party buyer to offset his or her realized gain by the related-party seller's disallowed loss. Even with this offset, several inequities exist. First, the tax benefit associated with the disallowed loss ultimately is realized by the wrong party (the related-party buyer rather than the related-party seller). Second, the tax benefit of this offset to the related-party buyer does not occur until the buyer disposes of the property. Therefore, the longer the time period between the purchase and disposition of the property by the related-party buyer, the less the economic benefit. Third, if the property does not appreciate to at least its adjusted basis to the related-party seller during the time period the related-party buyer holds it, part or all of the disallowed loss is permanently lost. Fourth, since the right of offset is available only to the original transferee (the related-party buyer), all of the disallowed loss is permanently lost if the original transferee subsequently transfers the property by gift or bequest.

EXAMPLE 41

Tim sells property with an adjusted basis of $35,000 to Wes, his brother, for $25,000, the fair market value of the property. The $10,000 realized loss to Tim is disallowed by § 267. If Wes subsequently sells the property to an unrelated party for $37,000, he has a recognized gain of $2,000 (realized gain of $12,000 reduced by disallowed loss of $10,000). Therefore, from the perspective of the family unit, the original $10,000 realized loss ultimately is recognized. However, if Wes sells the property for $29,000, he has a recognized gain of $0 (realized gain of $4,000 reduced by disallowed loss of $4,000 necessary to offset the realized gain). From the perspective of the family unit, $6,000 of the realized loss of $10,000 is permanently wasted ($10,000 realized loss − $4,000 offset permitted). ■

Wash Sales. The wash sales provisions can be avoided if the security that was sold is replaced within the statutory time period with a similar rather than a substantially identical security. For example, a sale of Dell, Inc. common stock accompanied by a purchase of Hewlett-Packard common stock is not treated as a wash sale. Such a procedure can enable the taxpayer to use an unrealized capital loss to offset a recognized capital gain. The taxpayer can sell the security before the end of the taxable year, offset the recognized capital loss against the capital gain, and invest the sales proceeds in a similar security.

Because the wash sales provisions do not apply to gains, it may be desirable to engage in a wash sale before the end of the taxable year. The recognized capital gain may be used to offset capital losses or capital loss carryovers from prior years. Since the basis of the replacement stock or securities will be the purchase price, the taxpayer in effect has exchanged a capital gain for an increased basis for the stock or securities.

KEY TERMS

Adjusted basis, 14–4	Holding period, 14–13	Recognized loss, 14–6
Amount realized, 14–3	Realized gain, 14–3	Recovery of capital doctrine, 14–7
Fair market value, 14–3	Realized loss, 14–3	
Goodwill, 14–10	Recognized gain, 14–6	Wash sale, 14–18

P R O B L E M   M A T E R I A L S

DISCUSSION QUESTIONS

1. Upon the sale or other disposition of property, what four questions should be considered for income tax purposes?

2. A realized gain occurs when the amount realized is greater than the adjusted basis, and a realized loss occurs when the adjusted basis is greater than the amount realized. Evaluate this statement.

3. Which of the following would be treated as a "sale or other disposition"?
   a. Sale for cash.
   b. Sale on credit.
   c. Exchange.
   d. Involuntary conversion.
   e. Bond retirement.

4. Ivan invests in land and Grace invests in taxable bonds. The land appreciates by $8,000 each year, and the bonds earn interest of $8,000 each year. After holding the land and bonds for five years, Ivan and Grace sell them. There is a $40,000 realized gain on the sale of the land and no realized gain or loss on the sale of the bonds. Are the tax consequences to Ivan and Grace the same for each of the five years? Explain.

   Decision Making

5. Carol and Dave each purchase 100 shares of stock of Burgundy, Inc., a publicly owned corporation, in July for $10,000 each. Carol sells her stock on December 31 for $8,000. Since Burgundy's stock is listed on a national exchange, Dave is able to ascertain that his shares are worth $8,000 on December 31. Does the tax law treat the decline in value of the stock differently for Carol and Dave? Explain.

6. If a taxpayer sells property for cash, the amount realized consists of the net proceeds from the sale. For each of the following, indicate the effect on the amount realized:
   a. The property is sold on credit.
   b. A mortgage on the property is assumed by the buyer.
   c. The buyer acquires the property subject to a mortgage of the seller.
   d. The seller pays real property taxes that are treated as imposed on the purchaser.
   e. Stock that has a basis to the purchaser of $6,000 and a fair market value of $10,000 is received by the seller as part of the consideration.

7. If the buyer pays real property taxes that are treated as imposed on the seller, what are the effects on the seller's amount realized and the buyer's adjusted basis for the property? If the seller pays real property taxes that are treated as imposed on the buyer, what are the effects on the seller's amount realized and the buyer's adjusted basis for the property?

8. Tad is negotiating to buy some land. Under the first option, Tad will give Sandra $120,000 and assume her mortgage on the land for $80,000. Under the second option, Tad will give Sandra $200,000, and she will immediately pay off the mortgage. Tad wants his basis for the land to be as high as possible. Given this objective, which option should Tad select?

   Decision Making

9. Eve purchases land from Gillen. Eve gives Gillen $100,000 in cash and agrees to pay Gillen an additional $400,000 one year later plus interest at 6%.
   a. What is Eve's adjusted basis for the land at the acquisition date?
   b. What is Eve's adjusted basis for the land one year later?

10. A taxpayer owns land and a building with an adjusted basis of $75,000 and a fair market value of $240,000. The property is subject to a mortgage of $360,000. Since the taxpayer is in arrears on the mortgage payments, the creditor is willing to accept the property in return for canceling the amount of the mortgage.
    a. How can the adjusted basis of the property be less than the amount of the mortgage?

b.   If the creditor's offer is accepted, what are the effects on the amount realized, the adjusted basis, and the realized gain or loss?

c.   Does it matter in (b) if the mortgage is recourse or nonrecourse?

11.   Discuss the effect of capital additions and capital recoveries on adjusted basis.

12.   On August 16, 2006, Todd acquires land and a building for $300,000 to use in his sole proprietorship. Of the purchase price, $200,000 is allocated to the building, and $100,000 is allocated to the land. Cost recovery of $1,926 is deducted in 2006 for the building.

a.   What is the adjusted basis for the land and the building at the acquisition date?

b.   What is the adjusted basis for the land and the building at the end of 2006?

13.   Abby owns stock in Orange Corporation and Blue Corporation. She receives a $1,000 distribution from both corporations. The instructions from Orange state that the $1,000 is a dividend. The instructions from Blue state that the $1,000 is not a dividend. What could cause the instructions to differ as to the tax consequences?

14.   A taxpayer who acquires a taxable bond at a premium may elect to amortize the premium, whereas a taxpayer who acquires a tax-exempt bond at a premium must amortize the premium.

a.   Why would a taxpayer make the amortization election for taxable bonds?

b.   What effect does the mandatory amortization of tax-exempt bonds have on taxable income?

Decision Making

15.   Rachel owns her personal use automobile, which has an adjusted basis of $26,000. Since she is interested in purchasing a newer model, she sells her car to Mason for $12,000.

a.   What are Rachel's realized and recognized loss resulting from this transaction?

b.   Could Rachel achieve better tax consequences if she traded her old car in for the newer model rather than selling it to Mason?

Issue ID

16.   Ron sold his sailboat for a $5,000 loss in the current year because he was diagnosed as having skin cancer. His spouse wants him to sell his Harley Davidson motorcycle because her brother broke his leg while riding his motorcycle. Since Ron no longer has anyone to ride with, he is seriously considering accepting his wife's advice. Because the motorcycle is a classic, Ron has received two offers. Each offer would result in a $5,000 gain. Joe would like to purchase the motorcycle before Christmas, and Jeff would like to purchase it after New Year's. Identify the relevant tax issues Ron faces in making his decision.

17.   Lee owns a life insurance policy that will pay $100,000 to Rita, his spouse, on his death. At the date of Lee's death, he had paid total premiums of $65,000 on the policy. In accordance with § 101(a)(1), Rita excludes the $100,000 of insurance proceeds. Discuss the relationship, if any, between the § 101 exclusion and the recovery of capital doctrine.

18.   In the case of a bargain purchase, why is the adjusted basis to the buyer the fair market value of the property rather than its purchase price?

19.   When a business is purchased and goodwill is involved, why is the basis of goodwill determined by the residual method rather than by using the amount assigned under the purchase contract?

20.   Discuss how the tax treatment differs when stock rights are allocated a cost basis versus when stock rights have no cost basis. When does each of these situations occur?

21.   Explain how a donee can sell investment property received by gift and recognize neither gain nor loss even though the selling price differs from the donee's adjusted basis.

Issue ID

22.   Simon, who is retired, owns Teal, Inc. stock that has declined in value since he purchased it. He has decided either to give the stock to his nephew, Fred, who is a high school teacher, or to sell the stock and give the proceeds to Fred. Because nearly all of his wealth is invested in tax-exempt bonds, Simon is in the 15% tax bracket. If Fred receives the stock, he will sell it himself. In either case, he will use the cash or the proceeds from his sale of the stock to make the down payment on the purchase of a house. Based on a recent conversation, Simon is aware that Fred is in the 25% bracket. Identify the tax issues relevant to Simon in deciding whether to give the stock or the sale proceeds to Fred.

23. Harold receives a gift from Rose, his aunt. The fair market value of the property on the date of the gift is $15,000 (adjusted basis of $16,500), and Rose pays a gift tax of $1,250. If Harold sells the property, describe circumstances in which the following will occur:
    a. A recognized gain results.
    b. A recognized loss results.
    c. Neither a recognized gain nor a recognized loss results.

24. Immediately before his death in 2006, Karl sells securities (adjusted basis of $95,000) for their fair market value of $20,000. The sale was not to a related party. Karl is survived by his wife, Zoe, who inherits all of his property.
    a. Did Karl act wisely? Why or why not?
    b. Suppose the figures are reversed (sale for $95,000 of property with an adjusted basis of $20,000). Would the sale be wise? Why or why not?

25. Gary makes a gift of an appreciated building to Carmen. She dies three months later, and Gary inherits the building from her. During the period that Carmen held the building, she deducted depreciation and made a capital expenditure. What effect might these items have on Gary's basis for the inherited building?

26. a. In a community property state, what effect does the death of one spouse have on the adjusted basis of the surviving spouse's one-half interest in the community property?
    b. Presuming the property is jointly owned, would the result be different in a common law state?

27. Mort owns 500 shares of Pear, Inc. stock with an adjusted basis of $22,000. On July 28, 2006, he sells 100 of these shares for $3,000. On August 16, 2006, he purchases another 100 shares for $3,400. Mort's realized loss of $1,400 ($3,000 − $4,400) on the July 28 sale is not recognized, and his adjusted basis for the 100 shares purchased on August 16 is $4,800. Explain.

28. Losses on the disposition of property used in a trade or business or held for investment are recognized, whereas losses on the disposition of personal use property are disallowed. Is it possible to avoid this disallowance of the personal loss by converting the property to either trade or business or investment property prior to its disposition?

PROBLEMS

29. Anne sold her home for $260,000 in 2006. Selling expenses were $15,000. She had purchased it in 1999 for $190,000. During the period of ownership, Anne had done the following:

    - Deducted $50,500 office-in-home expenses, which included $4,500 in depreciation. (Refer to Chapter 9.)
    - Deducted a casualty loss for residential trees destroyed by a hurricane. The total loss was $19,000 (after the $100 floor and the 10%-of-AGI floor), and Anne's insurance company reimbursed her for $13,500. (Refer to Chapter 7.)
    - Paid street paving assessment of $7,000 and added sidewalks for $11,000.
    - Installed an elevator for medical reasons. The total cost was $20,000, and Anne deducted $12,000 as medical expenses. (Refer to Chapter 10.)

    What is Anne's realized gain?

30. Kareem bought a rental house in October 2001 for $250,000, of which $50,000 is allocated to the land and $200,000 to the building. Early in 2003, he had a tennis court built in the backyard at a cost of $5,000. Kareem has deducted $30,900 for depreciation on the house and $1,300 for depreciation on the court. In January 2006, he sells the house and tennis court for $400,000 cash.
    a. What is Kareem's realized gain or loss?
    b. If an original mortgage of $75,000 is still outstanding and the buyer assumes the mortgage in addition to the cash payment, what is Kareem's realized gain or loss?
    c. If the buyer takes the property subject to the mortgage, what is Kareem's realized gain or loss?

31. Norm is negotiating the sale of a tract of his land to Pat. Use the following classification scheme to classify each of the items contained in the proposed sales contract:

Legend		
DARN	=	Decreases amount realized by Norm
IARN	=	Increases amount realized by Norm
DABN	=	Decreases adjusted basis to Norm
IABN	=	Increases adjusted basis to Norm
DABP	=	Decreases adjusted basis to Pat
IABP	=	Increases adjusted basis to Pat

   a. Norm is to receive cash of $50,000.
   b. Norm is to receive Pat's note payable for $25,000, payable in three years.
   c. Pat assumes Norm's mortgage of $5,000 on the land.
   d. Pat agrees to pay the realtor's sales commission of $8,000.
   e. Pat agrees to pay the property taxes on the land for the entire year. If each party paid his or her respective share, Norm's share would be $1,000, and Pat's share would be $3,000.
   f. Pat pays legal fees of $500.
   g. Norm pays legal fees of $750.

32. Gayla owns a building (adjusted basis of $375,000 on January 1, 2006) that she rents to Len who operates a restaurant in the building. The municipal health department closed the restaurant for two months during 2006 because of health code violations. Under MACRS, the cost recovery deduction for 2006 would be $24,000. However, Gayla deducted cost recovery only for the 10 months the restaurant was open since she waived the rent income during the two-month period the restaurant was closed.
   a. What is the amount of the cost recovery deduction that Gayla should report on her 2006 income tax return?
   b. Calculate the adjusted basis of the building at the end of 2006.

33. Nina owns a personal use boat that has a fair market value of $12,500 and an adjusted basis of $17,000. Nina's AGI is $60,000. Calculate the realized and recognized loss if:
   a. Nina sells the boat for $12,500.
   b. Nina exchanges the boat for another boat worth $12,500.
   c. The boat is stolen and Nina receives insurance proceeds of $12,500.

34. Alton owns stock in Dove Corporation. His adjusted basis for the stock is $85,000. During the year, he receives a distribution from the corporation of $65,000 that is labeled a return of capital (i.e., Dove has no earnings and profits).
   a. Determine the tax consequences to Alton.
   b. Assume instead that the amount of the distribution is $100,000. Determine the tax consequences to Alton.
   c. Assume instead in (a) that the $65,000 distribution is labeled a taxable dividend (i.e., Dove has earnings and profits of at least $65,000).

35. Chee purchases Tan, Inc. bonds for $110,000 on January 2, 2006. The face value of the bonds is $100,000, the maturity date is December 31, 2010, and the annual interest rate is 8%. Chee will amortize the premium only if he is required to do so. Chee sells the bonds on July 1, 2008, for $109,000.
   a. Determine the interest income Chee should report for 2006.
   b. Calculate Chee's recognized gain or loss on the sale of the bonds in 2008.

36. Tiffany sells the following assets during the year. All are held for personal use.

   • Car with an adjusted basis of $19,000 for $7,000.
   • Used clothing with an adjusted basis of $600 for $100.
   • Sailboat with an adjusted basis of $3,500 for $3,600.
   • Antique Chippendale chest with an adjusted basis of $10,000 for $14,000.

   Calculate Tiffany's realized and recognized gain or loss.

37. Hubert's personal residence is condemned as part of an urban renewal project. His adjusted basis for the residence is $325,000. He receives condemnation proceeds of $300,000 and invests the proceeds in stock.
    a. Calculate Hubert's realized and recognized gain or loss.
    b. If the condemnation proceeds are $355,000, what are Hubert's realized and recognized gain or loss?
    c. What are Hubert's realized and recognized gain or loss if the house was rental property?

38. Walt Barnes is a real estate agent for Governor's Estates, a residential real estate development. Because of his outstanding sales performance, Walt is permitted to buy a lot that normally would sell for $350,000 for $225,000. Walt is the only real estate agent for Governor's Estates who is permitted to do so.

    Communications

    a. Does Walt have gross income from the transaction?
    b. What is Walt's adjusted basis for the land?
    c. Write a letter to Walt informing him of the tax consequences of his acquisition of the lot. His address is 100 Tower Road, San Diego, CA 92182.

39. Karen makes the following purchases and sales of stock:

Transaction	Date	Number of Shares	Company	Price per Share
Purchase	1–1–2004	300	MDG	$ 75
Purchase	6–1–2004	150	GRU	300
Purchase	11–1–2004	60	MDG	70
Sale	12–3–2004	180	MDG	70
Purchase	3–1–2005	120	GRU	375
Sale	8–1–2005	90	GRU	330
Sale	1–1–2006	150	MDG	90
Sale	2–1–2006	75	GRU	500

    Assuming that Karen is unable to identify the particular lots that are sold with the original purchase, what is the recognized gain or loss on each type of stock as of the following dates:
    a. 7–1–2004.
    b. 12–31–2004.
    c. 12–31–2005.
    d. 7–1–2006.

40. Kevin purchases 1,000 shares of Bluebird Corporation stock on October 3, 2006, for $200,000. On December 12, 2006, Kevin purchases an additional 500 shares of Bluebird stock for $112,500. According to market quotations, Bluebird stock is selling for $240 per share on December 31, 2006. Kevin sells 400 shares of Bluebird stock on March 1, 2007, for $100,000.
    a. What is the adjusted basis of Kevin's Bluebird stock on December 31, 2006?
    b. What is Kevin's recognized gain or loss from the sale of Bluebird stock on March 1, 2007, assuming the shares sold are from the shares purchased on December 12, 2006?
    c. What is Kevin's recognized gain or loss from the sale of Bluebird stock on March 1, 2007, assuming Kevin cannot adequately identify the shares sold?

41. Rod Mitchell purchases Agnes's sole proprietorship for $975,000 on August 15, 2006. The assets of the business are as follows:

    Communications

Asset	Agnes's Adjusted Basis	FMV
Accounts receivable	$ 70,000	$ 70,000
Inventory	90,000	100,000
Equipment	150,000	160,000
Furniture and fixtures	95,000	130,000
Building	190,000	250,000
Land	25,000	75,000

Rod and Agnes agree that $50,000 of the purchase price is for Agnes's five-year covenant not to compete.
a.   Calculate Agnes's realized and recognized gain.
b.   Determine Rod's basis for each of the assets.
c.   Write a letter to Rod informing him of the tax consequences of the purchase. His address is 300 Riverview Drive, Delaware, OH 43015.

42. Diane owns 1,000 shares of Robin, Inc. common stock with an adjusted basis of $100,000. During the year, she receives the following distributions associated with the stock:

- $3,000 taxable cash dividend in March.
- 2% stock dividend in the form of 20 shares of preferred stock in July. The fair market value of the common stock was $110,000, and the fair market value of the preferred stock was $2,000. Shareholders do not have the option to receive cash.
- 5% stock dividend in the form of 50 shares of common stock in November. The fair market value of the 1,000 shares of common stock was $115,000. Shareholders do not have the option to receive cash.

a.   Determine the amount of gross income Diane must recognize.
b.   Calculate Diane's adjusted basis for her 1,050 shares of common stock and her 20 shares of preferred stock.

43. Sherry owns 1,000 shares of Taupe Corporation stock with a basis of $15,000 and a fair market value of $20,000. She receives nontaxable stock rights to purchase additional shares. The rights have a fair market value of $2,000.
a.   What are the basis of the stock and the basis of the stock rights?
b.   What is the holding period for the stock rights?
c.   What is the recognized gain or loss if the stock rights are sold for $2,000?
d.   What is the recognized gain or loss if the stock rights are allowed to lapse?

44. Rick has received various gifts over the years. He has decided to dispose of the following assets that he received as gifts:
a.   In 1950, he received land worth $25,000. The donor's adjusted basis was $30,000. Rick sells the land for $87,000 in 2006.
b.   In 1955, he received stock in Gold Company. The donor's adjusted basis was $10,000. The fair market value on the date of the gift was $28,000. Rick sells the stock for $40,000 in 2006.
c.   In 1961, he received land worth $12,000. The donor's adjusted basis was $25,000. Rick sells the land for $8,000 in 2006.
d.   In 1994, he received stock worth $30,000. The donor's adjusted basis was $45,000. Rick sells the stock for $39,000 in 2006.

What is the recognized gain or loss from each of the preceding transactions? Assume for each of the gift transactions that no gift tax was paid.

45. Beth receives a car from Sam as a gift. Sam paid $18,000 for the car. He had used it for business purposes and had deducted $8,000 for depreciation up to the time he gave the car to Beth. The fair market value of the car is $6,000.
a.   Assuming Beth uses the car for business purposes, what is her basis for depreciation?
b.   If the estimated useful life is two years (from the date of the gift), what is her depreciation deduction for each year? Assume Beth elects the straight-line method.
c.   If Beth sells the car for $900 one year after receiving it, what is her gain or loss?
d.   If Beth sells the car for $6,000 one year after receiving it, what is her gain or loss?

46. In 2006, Felix receives a gift of property with a fair market value of $111,000 (adjusted basis to the donor of $40,000). Assume the donor paid gift tax of $30,000 on the transfer.
a.   What is Felix's basis for gain and loss and for depreciation?
b.   If the gift occurred in 1975, what is Felix's basis for gain and loss and for depreciation?

47. On September 18, 2006, Gerald received land and a building from his Uncle Frank as a gift. Uncle Frank's adjusted basis and the fair market value at the date of the gift were as follows:

Asset	Adjusted Basis	FMV
Land	$100,000	$212,000
Building	80,000	100,000

Uncle Frank paid gift tax of $45,000.

a. Determine Gerald's adjusted basis for the land and building.

b. Assume instead that the fair market value of the land was $87,000 and that of the building was $65,000. Determine Gerald's adjusted basis for the land and building.

48. Ira Cook is planning to make a charitable contribution of Crystal, Inc. stock worth $20,000 to the Boy Scouts. The stock has an adjusted basis of $15,000. A friend has suggested that Ira sell the stock and contribute the $20,000 in proceeds rather than contribute the stock.

Decision Making

Communications

a. Should Ira follow the friend's advice? Why?

b. Assume the fair market value is only $13,000. In this case, should Ira follow the friend's advice? Why?

c. Rather than make a charitable contribution to the Boy Scouts, Ira is going to make a gift to Nancy, his niece. Advise Ira regarding (a) and (b).

d. Write a letter to Ira regarding whether in (a) he should sell the stock and contribute the cash or contribute the stock. He has informed you that he purchased the stock six years ago. Ira's address is 500 Ireland Avenue, De Kalb, IL 60115.

49. Catherine died in March 2006 leaving real estate (adjusted basis of $500,000) to her niece, Amanda. The fair market value of the real estate at the date of Catherine's death is $1,825,000. The executor of the estate does not distribute the real estate to Amanda until November 2006, when its fair market value is $1,813,000. The fair market value of the real estate six months after Catherine's death is $1,815,000.

a. What are the possibilities as to Amanda's adjusted basis in the real estate?

b. What purpose does the alternate valuation date serve?

c. Assume instead that the fair market value six months after Catherine's death is $1,860,000. What is Amanda's basis in the real estate?

50. Dan bought a hotel for $2,600,000 in January 2003. In May 2006, he died and left the hotel to Ed. Dan had deducted $289,000 of cost recovery on the hotel before his death. The fair market value in January 2006 was $2,800,000. The fair market value six months later was $2,850,000.

a. What is the basis of the property to Ed?

b. What is the basis of the property to Ed if the fair market value six months later was $2,500,000 and the objective of the executor was to minimize the estate tax liability?

51. Emily makes a gift of 100 shares of appreciated stock to her uncle, George, on January 5, 2006. The basis of the stock is $3,150, and the fair market value is $5,250. George dies on October 8, 2006. During the period that George held the stock, he received a 5% nontaxable stock dividend. Under the provisions of George's will, Emily inherits 100 shares of the stock. The value of the stock for Federal estate tax purposes is $55 per share.

a. What is the basis of the inherited stock to Emily?

b. What would have been the basis of the inherited stock to Emily if she had given the stock to George on January 5, 2005?

52. Larry and Grace live in Arizona, a community property state. They own land (community property) that has an adjusted basis to them of $150,000. When Grace dies, Larry inherits her share of the land. At the date of Grace's death, the fair market value of the land is $200,000. Six months after Grace's death, the land is worth $220,000.

a. What is Larry's basis for the land?

b. What would Larry's basis for the land be if he and Grace lived in Kansas, a common law state, and Larry inherited Grace's share?

53. Sheila sells land to Elane, her sister, for the fair market value of $40,000. Six months later when the land is worth $42,000, Elane gives it to Jacob, her son. No gift taxes are paid. Shortly thereafter, Jacob sells the land for $43,000.

a. Assuming Sheila's adjusted basis for the land is $25,000, what are Sheila's and Jacob's recognized gain or loss on their respective sales?

    b. Assuming Sheila's adjusted basis for the land is $50,000, what are Sheila's and Jacob's recognized gain or loss on their respective sales?

54. TJ Partnership sells property (adjusted basis of $200,000) to Thad (a partner who owns a 60% capital and profits interest) for its fair market value of $165,000.
    a. Calculate the realized and recognized loss to the partnership.
    b. Calculate the basis of the property to Thad.
    c. If Thad subsequently sells the property for $187,000, calculate his realized and recognized gain or loss.
    d. If Thad gives the property to his daughter, Donna, who subsequently sells it for $187,000, calculate Donna's realized and recognized gain or loss. (Assume no gift tax is paid and the fair market value on the date of the gift is $180,000.)
    e. Determine the tax consequences in (a) through (d) if Thad is a shareholder and TJ is a corporation.

Decision Making

55. Justin owns 1,000 shares of Oriole Corporation common stock (adjusted basis of $9,800). On April 27, 2006, he sells 300 of these shares for $2,800. On May 5, 2006, Justin purchases 200 shares of Oriole Corporation common stock for $2,500.
    a. What is Justin's recognized gain or loss resulting from these transactions?
    b. What is Justin's basis for the stock acquired on May 5?
    c. Could Justin have obtained different tax consequences in (a) and (b) if he had sold the 300 shares on December 27, 2006, and purchased the 200 shares on January 5, 2007?

Decision Making

56. Kristy owns 100 shares of stock in Magenta Corporation. Her adjusted basis for the stock is $5,000. On December 21, Kristy sells the stock for $12,000. She purchases 100 shares of Magenta stock on January 5 of the following year for $12,200.
    a. What is Kristy trying to achieve from a tax perspective?
    b. Will she succeed?
    c. Using the same data, except that Kristy's adjusted basis for the stock is $15,000, respond to (a) and (b).
    d. Advise Kristy on how she can avoid any negative tax consequences encountered in (c).

57. Jeffrey leaves a public accounting firm to enter private practice. He had bought a home two years earlier for $300,000 (ignore land). When starting his business, he converts one-fourth of the home into an office. The fair market value of the home on the date of the conversion (January 1, 2001) is $350,000, while the adjusted basis remains at $300,000. Jeffery lives and works in the home for six years and sells it at the end of the sixth year. He deducted $11,400 of cost recovery (using the statutory percentage method). How much gain or loss is recognized if Jeffrey sells the home for:
    a. $280,000?
    b. $400,000?

58. Surendra's personal residence originally cost $180,000 (ignore land). After living in the house for five years, he converts it to rental property. At the date of conversion, the fair market value of the house is $150,000. As to the rental property, calculate Surendra's basis for:
    a. Loss.
    b. Depreciation.
    c. Gain.

Decision Making

59. Hun, age 93, has accumulated substantial assets during his life. Among his many assets are the following, which he is considering giving to Koji, his grandson.

Asset	Adjusted Basis	Fair Market Value
Red Corporation stock	$900,000	$700,000
Silver Corporation stock	70,000	71,000
Emerald Corporation stock	200,000	500,000

Hun has been in ill health for the past five years. His physician has informed him that he probably will not live for more than six months. Advise Hun on which of the stocks should be transferred as gifts and which as bequests.

CUMULATIVE PROBLEMS

Tax Return Problem

60. Albert Sims, age 67, is married and files a joint return with his wife, Carol, age 65. Albert and Carol are both retired, and during 2005, they received Social Security benefits of $14,000. Albert's Social Security number is 366–55–1111, and Carol's is 555–66–2222. They reside at 210 College Drive, Columbia, SC 29201.

   Albert, who retired on January 1, 2005, receives benefits from a qualified pension plan of $700 a month for life. His total contributions to the plan (none of which were deductible) were $71,000. In January 2005, he received a bonus of $2,500 from his former employer for service performed in 2004. Although the former employer accrued the bonus in 2004, it was not paid until 2005.

   Carol, who retired on December 31, 2004, started receiving benefits of $850 a month on January 1, 2005. Her contributions to the qualified pension plan (none of which were deductible) were $69,940.

   Albert has been paying alimony of $9,000 each year to his former wife, Nancy. As Nancy died on September 1, the payments for 2005 were limited to $6,000. Nancy's Social Security number is 400–60–1234.

   Carol had casino winnings for the year of $5,500 and casino losses of $150, while Albert won $20,000 on a $1 lottery ticket.

   On September 27, 2005, Albert and Carol received a 10% stock dividend on 60 shares of stock they owned. They had bought the stock on March 5, 1998, for $11 a share. On December 16, 2005, they sold the 6 dividend shares for $45 a share.

   On January 10, 2005, Carol sold the car she had used in commuting to and from work for $8,000. She had paid $24,000 for the car in 1999.

   On July 14, 1996, Albert and Carol received a gift of 600 shares of stock from their son, Thomas. Thomas's basis in the stock was $25 a share (fair market value at the date of gift was $21). No gift tax was paid on the transfer. Albert and Carol sold the stock on October 8, 2005, for $20 a share.

   On May 1, 2005, Carol's mother died, and Carol inherited her personal residence. The residence had a fair market value of $190,000 and an adjusted basis to the mother of $130,000. Carol listed the house with a realtor, who estimated it was worth $210,000 as of December 31, 2005.

   Carol received rent income of $3,000 on a beach house she inherited three years ago from her Uncle Chuck. She had rented the property for one week during the July 4th weekend and one week during the Thanksgiving holidays. Uncle Chuck's adjusted basis in the beach house was $150,000, and its fair market value on the date of his death was $225,000. Carol and Albert used the beach house for personal purposes for 42 days during the year. Expenses associated with the house were $3,400 for utilities, maintenance, and repairs and $2,000 for property taxes. There are no mortgages on the property.

   Albert and Carol paid estimated Federal income tax of $3,100 and had itemized deductions of $9,500 (excluding any itemized deductions associated with the beach house). If they have overpaid their Federal income tax, they want the amount refunded. Both Albert and Carol wish to have $3 go to the Presidential Election Campaign Fund.

   Compute their net tax payable or refund due for 2005. If you use tax forms for your computations, you will need Form 1040 and Schedules A and D. Suggested software: TurboTax.

Tax Return Problem

Decision Making

Communications

61. John Custer, age 35, is single. His Social Security number is 443–11–2222, and he resides at 150 Highway 51, Tangipahoa, LA 70443.

   John has a five-year-old child, Kendra, who lives with her mother, Katy. John pays alimony of $15,000 per year to Katy and child support of $12,500. The $12,500 of child support covers 70% of Katy's costs of rearing Kendra. Kendra's Social Security number is 432–60–1000, and Katy's is 444–00–1234. John expected to receive alimony of $12,000 during the year from his second wife, Debra. However, she died in October, and John received only $10,000.

   John's mother, Sally, lived with him until her death in early September 2006. He incurred and paid medical expenses for her of $8,500 and other support payments of $6,000. Sally's only sources of income were $3,500 of interest income on certificates of deposit and

$3,600 of Social Security benefits, which she spent on her medical expenses and helping to maintain John's household. Sally's Social Security number was 400–10–2000.

John is employed by the Highway Department of the State of Louisiana in an executive position. His salary is $85,000. The appropriate amounts of Social Security tax ($5,270) and Medicare tax ($1,232) were withheld. In addition, $13,000 was withheld for Federal income taxes, and $3,500 was withheld for state income taxes.

In addition to his salary, John's employer provides him with the following fringe benefits:

* Group term life insurance with a maturity value of $45,000. The cost of the premiums for the employer was $300.
* Group health insurance plan. John's employer paid premiums of $1,500 for his coverage. The plan paid $900 for John's medical expenses during the year.

Upon the death of his Aunt Josie in December 2005, John, her only recognized heir, inherited the following assets:

Asset	Josie's Adjusted Basis	FMV at Date of Death
Car	$ 22,000	$ 15,000
Land—300 acres	150,000	500,000
IBM stock	80,000	135,000
Cash	42,000	42,000

Six months prior to her death, Josie gave John a mountain cabin. Her adjusted basis for the mountain cabin was $270,000, and the fair market value was $325,000. She paid gift tax of $18,000.

During the year, John had the following transactions:

* On February 1, 2006, he sold for $46,000 Microsoft stock that he inherited from his father four years ago. His father's adjusted basis was $49,000, and the fair market value at the date of the father's death was $38,000.
* The car John inherited from Josie was destroyed in a wreck on October 1, 2006. He had loaned the car to Katy to use for a two-week period while the engine in her car was being replaced. Fortunately, neither Katy nor Kendra was injured. John received insurance proceeds of $13,000, the fair market value of the car on October 1.
* On October 30, 2006, John gambled away the $42,000 he inherited at a casino in Biloxi. He had hoped this activity would help with the bouts of depression he had been suffering since Sally's death.
* On December 28, 2006, John sold the 300 acres of land to his brother, James, for its fair market value of $475,000. James planned on using the land for his dairy farm.

Other sources of income for John were as follows:

Dividend income	$22,000
Interest income:	
Guaranty Bank	9,000
City of Kentwood water bonds	20,000
Award from State of Louisiana for outstanding suggestion for highway beautification	5,000

Potential itemized deductions for John, in addition to items already mentioned, were as follows:

Property taxes paid on his residence	$4,500
Property taxes paid on personalty	2,500
Estimated Federal income taxes paid	4,300
Estimated state income taxes paid	2,300
Charitable contributions	5,500
Mortgage interest on his residence	6,400
Orthodontic expenses for Kendra	4,000
Psychiatric expenses for John	3,500
Sales taxes paid	6,000

Part 1—Tax Computation
Compute John's net tax payable or refund due for 2006.

Part 2—Tax Planning
Assume that rather than selling the land to James, John is considering leasing it to him for $30,000 annually with the lease beginning on October 1, 2006. James would prepay the lease payments through December 31, 2006. Thereafter, he would make monthly lease payments at the beginning of each month. What effect would this have on John's 2006 tax liability? What potential problem might John encounter? Write a letter to John in which you advise him of the tax consequences of leasing versus selling. Also, prepare a memo for the tax files.

RESEARCH PROBLEMS

Note: Solutions to Research Problems can be prepared by using the **RIA Checkpoint**® **Student Edition** online research product, which is available to accompany this text. It is also possible to prepare solutions to the Research Problems by using tax research materials found in a standard tax library.

Research Problem 1. Mitchell died on April 13, 2003. The executor of his estate made the § 2032(a) election to use the alternate valuation date in filing Mitchell's estate tax return. Using the primary valuation date and amount, the estate assets would have been valued at $1.5 million. With the election, the estate assets were valued at $1.25 million.

A major asset of the estate consisted of shares of BFI Corporation. The shares of BFI were traded on an established securities market. Since the estate owned 2% of BFI's stock, the executor secured the services of a major brokerage firm to calculate the blockage discount on the BFI stock. Shortly before the estate tax return due date of January 13, 2004, the executor filed a Form 4768 (Application for Extension of Time To File a Return and/or Pay U.S. Estate Taxes) requesting an extension for filing to July 13, 2004. At this time, the estate paid estimated estate taxes of $400,000. In early June, a representative of the brokerage firm notified the executor that it would not be able to finish the valuation on time. Another firm was engaged, and it completed the valuation as of November 29, 2004. Mitchell's executor finally filed the return on January 19, 2006, and made the § 2032(a) election.

The IRS determined that a § 2032(a) election cannot be made unless the estate tax return is timely filed. A deficiency was assessed based on an asset valuation of $1.5 million rather than $1.25 million. Evaluate the position of the IRS.

Research Problem 2. Terry owns real estate with an adjusted basis of $600,000 and a fair market value of $1.1 million. The amount of the nonrecourse mortgage on the property is $2.5 million. Because of substantial past and projected future losses associated with the real estate development (occupancy rate of only 37% after three years), Terry deeds the property to the creditor.
a. What are the tax consequences to Terry?
b. Assume the data are the same, except the fair market value of the property is $2,525,000. Therefore, when Terry deeds the property to the creditor, she also receives $25,000 from the creditor. What are the tax consequences to Terry?

Research Problem 3. Abner gives stock worth $400,000 to Hattie. Abner's adjusted basis in the stock is $95,000, and the gift taxes generated as a result of the transfer are $122,400. As a condition for receiving the stock, Hattie agrees to pay the gift tax. The stock is transferred to Hattie on February 5, 2006.
a. What are the income tax consequences to Abner?
b. What are the income tax consequences to Abner if the gift was made on February 5, 1981?

Research Problem 4. Ruth Ames died on January 10, 2006. In filing the estate tax return, her executor, Melvin Sims, elects the primary valuation date and amount (fair market value on the date of death). On March 12, 2006, Melvin invests $30,000 of cash that Ruth had in her money market account in acquiring 1,000 shares of Orange, Inc. ($30 per share). On January 10, 2006, Orange was selling for $29 per share. The stock is distributed to a beneficiary, Annette Rust, on June 1, 2006, when it is selling for $33 per share. Melvin wants you to determine the amount at which the Orange shares should appear on the estate tax return and the amount of Annette's adjusted basis for the stock. Write a letter to Melvin in which you respond to his inquiry and prepare a memo for the tax files. His address is 100 Center Lane, Miami, FL 32124.

Research Problem 5.   Amanda purchased the following lots of stock of Pearl, Inc. (a pharmaceutical company) during 2003:

Date	Number of Shares	Cost per Share
February 1	100	$150
July 25	100	140
November 3	100	130

On December 20, 2005, Amanda sold the 300 shares for $145 each.

In early January 2006, the Food and Drug Administration granted approval for a new drug developed by Pearl. Expecting the stock to continue to increase in value, Amanda purchased 300 shares on January 5, 2006, for $175 per share.

Amanda calculated her recognized gain as $1,500 ($43,500 amount realized − $42,000 adjusted basis). The IRS contends that the transaction must be treated as the sale of three lots of stock because of the wash sale rules. As a result, the $500 realized gain on the sale of the second lot and the $1,500 realized gain on the sale of the third lot must be recognized, and the $500 realized loss on the sale of the first lot is disallowed under § 1091. Who is correct?

Internet
Activity

Communications

Use the tax resources of the Internet to address the following questions. Do not restrict your search to the World Wide Web, but include a review of newsgroups and general reference materials, practitioner sites and resources, primary sources of the tax law, chat rooms and discussion groups, and other opportunities.

Research Problem 6.   Many see the "step-up in basis at death" rule of § 1014 as an expensive tax loophole enjoyed by the wealthy. Find the latest estimates of the revenue loss to the Treasury that is attributable to this rule.

a. How does Canada's tax law determine the basis of property acquired from a decedent?

b. Send an e-mail message to a member of the House Ways and Means Committee expressing a preference for the preservation of the current § 1014 rule or the modifications made to it by the Tax Relief Reconciliation Act of 2001.

Research Problem 7.   The specific identification method is important when one invests in mutual funds. When taxpayers sell part of their holdings, the basis of the surrendered shares can be difficult to compute. Go to the site of an investment adviser or mutual fund to find instructions on how to compute the basis of the shares sold. What options are available to the taxpayer according to this information? Illustrate each of the alternatives.

CHAPTER 15

Property Transactions: Nontaxable Exchanges

LEARNING OBJECTIVES

After completing Chapter 15, you should be able to:

LO.1

Understand the rationale for nonrecognition (postponement) of gain or loss in certain property transactions.

LO.2

Apply the nonrecognition provisions and basis determination rules for like-kind exchanges.

LO.3

Explain the nonrecognition provisions available on the involuntary conversion of property.

LO.4

Describe the provision for the permanent exclusion of gain on the sale of a personal residence.

LO.5

Identify other nonrecognition provisions contained in the Code.

LO.6

Identify tax planning opportunities related to the nonrecognition provisions discussed in the chapter.

LO.1

Understand the rationale for nonrecognition (postponement) of gain or loss in certain property transactions.

General Concept of a Nontaxable Exchange

A taxpayer who is going to replace a productive asset (e.g., machinery) used in a trade or business may structure the transactions as a sale of the old asset and the purchase of a new asset. When this approach is used, any realized gain or loss on the asset sale is recognized. The basis of the new asset is its cost. Alternatively, the taxpayer may be able to trade the old asset for the new asset. This exchange of assets may produce beneficial tax consequences by qualifying for nontaxable exchange treatment.

The tax law recognizes that nontaxable exchanges result in a change in the *form* but not in the *substance* of the taxpayer's relative economic position. The replacement property received in the exchange is viewed as substantially a continuation of the old investment.[1] Additional justification for nontaxable exchange treatment is that this type of transaction does not provide the taxpayer with the wherewithal to pay the tax on any realized gain.

The nonrecognition provisions for nontaxable exchanges do not apply to realized losses from the sale or exchange of personal use assets. Such losses are not recognized (are disallowed) because they are personal in nature and not because of any nonrecognition provision.

In a **nontaxable exchange**, realized gains or losses are not recognized. However, the nonrecognition is usually temporary. The recognition of gain or loss is *postponed* (deferred) until the property received in the nontaxable exchange is subsequently disposed of in a taxable transaction. This is accomplished by assigning a carryover basis to the replacement property.

EXAMPLE 1

Debra exchanges property with an adjusted basis of $10,000 and a fair market value of $12,000 for property with a fair market value of $12,000. The transaction qualifies for nontaxable exchange treatment. Debra has a realized gain of $2,000 ($12,000 amount realized − $10,000 adjusted basis). Her recognized gain is $0. Her basis in the replacement property is a

---

[1]Reg. § 1.1002–1(c).

carryover basis of $10,000. Assume the replacement property is nondepreciable and Debra subsequently sells it for $12,000. Her realized and recognized gain will be the $2,000 gain that was postponed (deferred) in the nontaxable transaction. If the replacement property is depreciable, the carryover basis of $10,000 is used in calculating depreciation. ■

In some nontaxable exchanges, only part of the property involved in the transaction qualifies for nonrecognition treatment. If the taxpayer receives cash or other nonqualifying property, part or all of the realized gain from the exchange is recognized. In these instances, gain is recognized because the taxpayer has changed or improved his or her relative economic position and has the wherewithal to pay income tax to the extent of cash or other property received.

It is important to distinguish between a nontaxable disposition, as the term is used in the statute, and a tax-free transaction. First, a direct exchange is not required in all circumstances (e.g., replacement of involuntarily converted property). Second, as previously mentioned, the term *nontaxable* refers to postponement of recognition via a carryover basis. In a *tax-free* transaction, the nonrecognition is permanent (e.g., see the discussion later in the chapter of the § 121 exclusion of realized gain on the sale of a personal residence). Therefore, the basis of any property acquired in a tax-free transaction does not depend on the basis of the property disposed of by the taxpayer.

Like-Kind Exchanges—§ 1031

LO.2

Apply the nonrecognition provisions and basis determination rules for like-kind exchanges.

Section 1031 provides for nontaxable exchange treatment if the following requirements are satisfied:[2]

- The form of the transaction is an exchange.
- Both the property transferred and the property received are held either for productive use in a trade or business or for investment.
- The property is like-kind property.

Like-kind exchanges include business for business, business for investment, investment for business, or investment for investment property. Property held for personal use, inventory, and partnership interests (both limited and general) do not qualify under the like-kind exchange provisions. Securities, even though held for investment, do not qualify for like-kind exchange treatment.

The nonrecognition provision for like-kind exchanges is *mandatory* rather than elective. A taxpayer who wants to recognize a realized gain or loss will have to structure the transaction in a form that does not satisfy the statutory requirements for a like-kind exchange. This topic is discussed further under Tax Planning Considerations.

Like-Kind Property

[handwritten: factory for factory, not factory for car.]

"The words 'like-kind' refer to the nature or character of the property and not to its grade or quality. One kind or class of property may not . . . be exchanged for property of a different kind or class."[3]

The term *like-kind* is intended to be interpreted very broadly. However, three categories of exchanges are not included. First, livestock of different sexes do not qualify as like-kind property. Second, real estate can be exchanged only for other real estate, and personalty can be exchanged only for other personalty. For example, the exchange of a machine (personalty) for an office building (realty) is not a like-kind exchange. *Real estate* (or realty) includes principally rental buildings, office and store buildings, manufacturing plants, warehouses, and land. It is immaterial whether real estate is improved or unimproved. Thus, unimproved land can be exchanged for an apartment house. Personalty includes principally machines,

---

[2]§ 1031(a) and Reg. § 1.1031(a)–1(a).   [3]Reg. § 1.1031(a)–1(b).

equipment, trucks, automobiles, furniture, and fixtures. Third, real property located in the United States exchanged for foreign real property (and vice versa) does not qualify as like-kind property.

EXAMPLE 2

Wade made the following exchanges during the taxable year:

N   a.   Inventory for a machine used in business.
Y   b.   Land held for investment for a building used in business.
N   c.   Stock held for investment for equipment used in business.
Y   d.   A business truck for a business truck.
N   e.   An automobile used for personal transportation for an automobile used in business.
N   f.   Livestock for livestock of a different sex.
N   g.   Land held for investment in New York for land held for investment in London.

Exchanges (b), investment real property for business real property, and (d), business personalty for business personalty, qualify as exchanges of like-kind property. Exchanges (a), inventory; (c), stock; (e), personal use automobile (not held for business or investment purposes); (f), livestock of different sexes; and (g), U.S. and foreign real estate do not qualify. ∎

A special provision relates to the location where personal property is used. Personal property used predominantly within the United States and personal property used predominantly outside the United States are not like-kind property. The location of use for the personal property given up is its location during the two-year period ending on the date of disposition of the property. The location of use for the personal property received is its location during the two-year period beginning on the date of the acquisition.

EXAMPLE 3

In October 2005, Walter exchanges a machine used in his factory in Denver for a machine that qualifies as like-kind property. In January 2006, the factory, including the machine, is moved to Berlin, Germany. As of January 2006, the exchange is not an exchange of like-kind property. The predominant use of the original machine was in the United States, whereas the predominant use of the new machine is foreign. ∎

Another special provision applies if the taxpayers involved in the exchange are *related parties* under § 267(b). To qualify for like-kind exchange treatment, the taxpayer and the related party must not dispose of the like-kind property received in the exchange within the two-year period following the date of the exchange. If such an early disposition does occur, the postponed gain is recognized as of the date of the early disposition. Dispositions due to death, involuntary conversions, and certain non-tax avoidance transactions are not treated as early dispositions.

ETHICAL *Considerations*   AN ASSUMPTION FOR A RELATED-PARTY EXCHANGE

Marcie owns a 10 percent interest in a shopping mall located in Portland, Maine. Her adjusted basis for her interest is $250,000, and its fair market value is $900,000. She exchanges it for undeveloped land in York, Pennsylvania, that is held by her sister, Sandra. Marcie is aware of the § 1031 related-party requirement that neither she nor Sandra dispose of the property received for a two-year period. Both Marcie and Sandra intend to hold the property as long-term investments. However, they agree to notify each other if a disposition does take place within two years of the exchange.

During the next six months, the land that Marcie received in the exchange continues to appreciate. Due to poor management, however, the value of Sandra's interest in the shopping mall declines to $700,000. As a result, Sandra is angry with Marcie and vows "never to speak to Marcie, her husband, or any of Marcie's children again."

As Marcie receives no communication from Sandra during the next 18 months, she assumes that her gain of $650,000 will continue to be deferred. Evaluate Marcie's assumption.

Regulations dealing with § 1031 like-kind exchange treatment provide that if the exchange transaction involves multiple assets of a business (e.g., a television station for another television station), the determination of whether the assets qualify as like-kind property will not be made at the business level.[4] Instead, the underlying assets must be evaluated.

The Regulations also provide for greater specificity in determining whether depreciable tangible personal property is of a like kind or class. Such property held for productive use in a business is of a like class only if the exchanged property is within the same *general business asset class* (as specified by the IRS in Revenue Procedure 87–57 or as subsequently modified) or the same *product class* (as specified by the Department of Commerce). Property included in a general business asset class is evaluated under this system rather than under the product class system.

The following are examples of general business asset classes:

- Office furniture, fixtures, and equipment.
- Information systems (computers and peripheral equipment).
- Airplanes.
- Automobiles and taxis.
- Buses.
- Light general-purpose trucks.
- Heavy general-purpose trucks.

These Regulations have made it more difficult for depreciable tangible personal property to qualify for § 1031 like-kind exchange treatment. For example, the exchange of office equipment for a computer does not qualify as an exchange of like-kind property. Even though both assets are depreciable tangible personal property, they are not like-kind property because they are in different general business asset classes.

Exchange Requirement

The transaction must involve a direct exchange of property to qualify as a like-kind exchange. The sale of old property and the purchase of new property, even though like kind, is generally not an exchange. However, if the two transactions are mutually dependent, the IRS may treat them as a like-kind exchange. For example, if the taxpayer sells an old business machine to a dealer and purchases a new one from the same dealer, like-kind exchange treatment could result.[5]

[handwritten: Must have same FMV]

The taxpayer may want to avoid nontaxable exchange treatment. Recognition of gain gives the taxpayer a higher basis for depreciation (see Example 33). To the extent that such gains would, if recognized, either receive favorable capital gain treatment or be passive activity income that could offset passive activity losses, it might be preferable to avoid the nonrecognition provisions through an indirect exchange transaction. For example, a taxpayer may sell property to one individual, recognize the gain, and subsequently purchase similar property from another individual. The taxpayer may also want to avoid nontaxable exchange treatment so that a realized loss can be recognized.

If the exchange is a delayed (nonsimultaneous) exchange, there are time limits on its completion. In a delayed like-kind exchange, one party fails to take immediate title to the new property because it has not yet been identified. The Code provides that the delayed swap will qualify as a like-kind exchange if the following requirements are satisfied:

- *Identification period.* The new property must be identified within 45 days of the date when the old property was transferred.

---

[4]Reg. § 1.1031(j)–1.   [5]Rev.Rul. 61–119, 1961–1 C.B. 395.

TAX *in the News*   AVOIDING TAXES ON THE DISPOSITION OF A VACATION HOME

Your client, Sandra, would like to dispose of her vacation home at the beach, which has appreciated substantially. She would prefer to acquire vacation property in the mountains. Even though the vacation home is personal use property, it is not eligible for § 121 exclusion treatment because it is not her principal residence.

If Sandra sells the beach house and uses the proceeds to purchase a mountain house, she will have to pay taxes at a 15 percent rate on the recognized gain. She would like to avoid paying taxes on the disposition, as she would merely be replacing her current vacation home with another in a different location. She has heard about § 1031 like-kind exchanges and wonders if her property would be eligible.

You inform Sandra that § 1031 deferral treatment does not apply to personal use property; instead, it must involve property that is either used in a trade or business or held for investment. However, she could convert her

beach house to rental property. After a suitable rental period, it could be disposed of in a delayed like-kind exchange under § 1031. The proceeds from the disposition of the beach house would be held by a third-party intermediary (e.g., a bank trust department). Sandra would then have 45 days after the date of sale to designate the mountain property she would like to acquire and 180 days after such date to complete the acquisition. The acquired mountain house should then be held as rental property with limited personal use. Conversion to personal use property would follow later.

You should be careful to point out to Sandra the potential danger of the 45-day rule with respect to identifying the replacement property. In today's volatile real estate market, a premium might have to be paid on the like-kind property acquired. A buyer who is under a time deadline (i.e., the 45-day rule) may have reduced negotiating ability.

- *Exchange period.* The new property must be received by the earlier of the following:
  - Within 180 days of the date when the old property was transferred.
  - The due date (including extensions) for the tax return covering the year of the transfer.

Are these time limits firm, or can they be extended due to unforeseen circumstances? Indications are that the IRS will allow no deviation from either the identification period or the exchange period even when events outside the taxpayer's control preclude strict compliance.

Boot

If the taxpayer in a like-kind exchange gives or receives some property that is not like-kind property, recognition may occur. Property that is not like-kind property, including cash, is referred to as **boot**. Although the term *boot* does not appear in the Code, tax practitioners commonly use it rather than saying "property that is not like-kind property."

The *receipt* of boot will trigger recognition of gain if there is realized gain. The amount of the recognized gain is the *lesser* of the boot received or the realized gain (realized gain serves as the ceiling on recognition).

[handwritten margin note: Exchange + Cash [value] (boot). Holding period of boot = day of transaction.]

EXAMPLE 4

Emily and Fran exchange machinery, and the exchange qualifies as like kind under § 1031. Since Emily's machinery (adjusted basis of $20,000) is worth $24,000 and Fran's machine has a fair market value of $19,000, Fran also gives Emily cash of $5,000. Emily's recognized gain is $4,000, the lesser of the realized gain ($24,000 amount realized − $20,000 adjusted basis = $4,000) or the fair market value of the boot received ($5,000). ∎

EXAMPLE 5

Assume the same facts as in the previous example, except that Fran's machine is worth $21,000 (not $19,000). Under these circumstances, Fran gives Emily cash of $3,000 to make up the difference. Emily's recognized gain is $3,000, the lesser of the realized gain of $4,000

($24,000 amount realized − $20,000 adjusted basis) or the fair market value of the boot received of $3,000. ■

The receipt of boot does not result in recognition if there is realized loss.

EXAMPLE 6

Assume the same facts as in Example 4, except that the adjusted basis of Emily's machine is $30,000. Emily's realized loss is $6,000 ($24,000 amount realized − $30,000 adjusted basis). The receipt of the boot of $5,000 does not trigger recognition. Therefore, the recognized loss is $0. ■

The *giving* of boot usually does not trigger recognition. If the boot given is cash, no realized gain or loss is recognized.

EXAMPLE 7

Fred and Gary exchange equipment in a like-kind exchange. Fred receives equipment with a fair market value of $25,000 and transfers equipment worth $21,000 (adjusted basis of $15,000) and cash of $4,000. Fred's realized gain is $6,000 ($25,000 amount realized − $15,000 adjusted basis − $4,000 cash). However, none of the realized gain is recognized. ■

If, however, the boot given is appreciated or depreciated property, gain or loss is recognized to the extent of the difference between the adjusted basis and the fair market value of the boot. For this purpose, *appreciated or depreciated property* is defined as property whose adjusted basis is not equal to the fair market value.

EXAMPLE 8

Assume the same facts as in the previous example, except that Fred transfers equipment worth $10,000 (adjusted basis of $12,000) and boot worth $15,000 (adjusted basis of $9,000). Fred's realized gain appears to be $4,000 ($25,000 amount realized − $21,000 adjusted basis). Since realization previously has served as a ceiling on recognition, it appears that the recognized gain is $4,000 (lower of realized gain of $4,000 or amount of appreciation on boot of $6,000). However, the recognized gain actually is $6,000 (full amount of the appreciation on the boot). In effect, Fred must calculate the like-kind and boot parts of the transaction separately. That is, the realized loss of $2,000 on the like-kind property is not recognized ($10,000 fair market value − $12,000 adjusted basis), and the $6,000 realized gain on the boot is recognized ($15,000 fair market value − $9,000 adjusted basis). ■

Basis and Holding Period of Property Received

If an exchange does not qualify as nontaxable under § 1031, gain or loss is recognized, and the basis of property received in the exchange is the property's fair market value. If the exchange qualifies for nonrecognition, the basis of property received must be adjusted to reflect any postponed (deferred) gain or loss. The *basis of like-kind property* received in the exchange is the property's fair market value less postponed gain or plus postponed loss. If the exchange partially qualifies for nonrecognition (if recognition is associated with boot), the basis of like-kind property received in the exchange is the property's fair market value less postponed gain or plus postponed loss. The *basis* of any *boot* received is the boot's fair market value.

If there is a postponed loss, nonrecognition creates a situation in which the taxpayer has recovered *less* than the cost or other basis of the property exchanged in an amount equal to the unrecognized loss. If there is a postponed gain, the taxpayer has recovered *more* than the cost or other basis of the property exchanged in an amount equal to the unrecognized gain.

EXAMPLE 9

Jaime exchanges a building (used in his business) with an adjusted basis of $30,000 and a fair market value of $38,000 for land with a fair market value of $38,000. The land is to be held as an investment. The exchange qualifies as like kind (an exchange of business real property for investment real property). Thus, the basis of the land is $30,000 (the land's fair market value of $38,000 less the $8,000 postponed gain on the building). If the land is later sold for its fair market value of $38,000, the $8,000 postponed gain is recognized. ∎

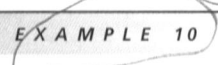
EXAMPLE 10

Assume the same facts as in the previous example, except that the building has an adjusted basis of $48,000 and a fair market value of only $38,000. The basis in the newly acquired land is $48,000 (fair market value of $38,000 plus the $10,000 postponed loss on the building). If the land is later sold for its fair market value of $38,000, the $10,000 postponed loss is recognized. ∎

The Code provides an alternative approach for determining the basis of like-kind property received:

Adjusted basis of like-kind property surrendered
+ Adjusted basis of boot given
+ Gain recognized
− Fair market value of boot received
− Loss recognized
= *Basis of like-kind property received*

This approach is logical in terms of the recovery of capital doctrine. That is, the unrecovered cost or other basis is increased by additional cost (boot given) or decreased by cost recovered (boot received). Any gain recognized is included in the basis of the new property. The taxpayer has been taxed on this amount and is now entitled to recover it tax-free. Any loss recognized is deducted from the basis of the new property. The taxpayer has received a tax benefit on that amount.

The holding period of the property surrendered in the exchange carries over and *tacks on* to the holding period of the like-kind property received.[6] See Chapter 16 for a discussion of the relevance of the holding period.

Depreciation recapture potential carries over to the property received in a like-kind exchange.[7] See Chapter 17 for a discussion of this topic.

The following comprehensive example illustrates the like-kind exchange rules.

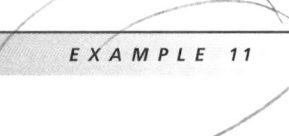
EXAMPLE 11

Vicki exchanged the following old machines for new machines in five independent like-kind exchanges:

Exchange	Adjusted Basis of Old Machine	Fair Market Value of New Machine	Adjusted Basis of Boot Given	Fair Market Value of Boot Received
1	$4,000	$9,000	$ –0–	$ –0–
2	4,000	9,000	3,000	–0–
3	4,000	9,000	6,000	–0–
4	4,000	9,000	–0–	3,000
5	4,000	3,500	–0–	300

Vicki's realized and recognized gains and losses and the basis of each of the like-kind properties received are as follows:

[6]§ 1223(1) and Reg. § 1.1223–1(a). For this carryover holding period rule to apply to like-kind exchanges after March 1, 1954, the like-kind property surrendered must have been either a capital asset or § 1231 property. See Chapters 16 and 17 for the discussion of capital assets and § 1231 property.

[7]Reg. §§ 1.1245–2(a)(4) and 1.1250–2(d)(1).

Exchange	Realized Gain (Loss)	Recognized Gain (Loss)	New Basis Calculation								
			Old Adj. Basis	+	Boot Given	+	Gain Recognized	−	Boot Received	=	New Basis
1	$5,000	$–(0)–	$4,000	+	$ –0–	+	$ –0–	−	$ –0–	=	$ 4,000*
2	2,000	–(0)–	4,000	+	3,000	+	–0–	−	–0–	=	7,000*
3	(1,000)	–(0)–	4,000	+	6,000	+	–0–	−	–0–	=	10,000**
4	8,000	3,000	4,000	+	–0–	+	3,000	−	3,000	=	4,000
5	(200)	–(0)–	4,000	+	–0–	+	–0–	−	300	=	3,700**

*Basis may be determined in gain situations under the alternative method by subtracting the gain not recognized from the fair market value of the new property:

$9,000 − $5,000 = $4,000 for exchange 1.
$9,000 − $2,000 = $7,000 for exchange 2.
$9,000 − $5,000 = $4,000 for exchange 4.

**In loss situations, basis may be determined by adding the loss not recognized to the fair market value of the new property:

$9,000 + $1,000 = $10,000 for exchange 3.
$3,500 + $200 = $3,700 for exchange 5.
The basis of the boot received is the boot's fair market value. ■

If the taxpayer either assumes a liability or takes property subject to a liability, the amount of the liability is treated as boot given. For the taxpayer whose liability is assumed or whose property is taken subject to the liability, the amount of the liability is treated as boot received. Example 12 illustrates the effect of such a liability. In addition, the example illustrates the tax consequences for both parties involved in the like-kind exchange.

EXAMPLE 12

Jane and Leo exchange real estate investments. Jane gives up property with an adjusted basis of $250,000 (fair market value of $400,000) that is subject to a mortgage of $75,000 (assumed by Leo). In return for this property, Jane receives property with a fair market value of $300,000 (adjusted basis of $200,000) and cash of $25,000.

- Jane's realized gain is $150,000. She gave up property with an adjusted basis of $250,000. Jane received $400,000 from the exchange ($300,000 fair market value of like-kind property plus $100,000 boot received). The boot received consists of the $25,000 cash received from Leo and Jane's mortgage of $75,000, which Leo assumes.
- Jane's recognized gain is $100,000. The realized gain of $150,000 is recognized to the extent of boot received.
- Jane's basis in the real estate received from Leo is $250,000. This basis can be computed by subtracting the postponed gain ($50,000) from the fair market value of the real estate received ($300,000). It can also be computed by adding the recognized gain ($100,000) to the adjusted basis of the real estate given up ($250,000) and subtracting the boot received ($100,000).
- Leo's realized gain is $100,000. Leo gave up property with an adjusted basis of $200,000 plus boot of $100,000 ($75,000 mortgage assumed + $25,000 cash) or a total of $300,000. Leo received $400,000 from the exchange (fair market value of like-kind property received).
- Leo has no recognized gain because he did not receive any boot. The entire realized gain of $100,000 is postponed.
- Leo's basis in the real estate received from Jane is $300,000. This basis can be computed by subtracting the postponed gain ($100,000) from the fair market value of the real estate received ($400,000). It can also be computed by adding the boot given ($75,000 mortgage assumed by Leo + $25,000 cash) to the adjusted basis of the real estate given up ($200,000).[8] ■

---

[8]Example (2) of Reg. § 1.1031(d)–2 illustrates a special situation in which both the buyer and the seller transfer liabilities that are assumed by the other party or both parties acquire property that is subject to a liability.

LO.3

Explain the nonrecognition provisions available on the involuntary conversion of property.

Involuntary Conversions—§ 1033

Section 1033 provides that a taxpayer who suffers an involuntary conversion of property may postpone recognition of *gain* realized from the conversion. The objective of this provision is to provide relief to the taxpayer who has suffered hardship and does not have the wherewithal to pay the tax on any gain realized from the conversion. Postponement of realized gain is permitted to the extent that the taxpayer *reinvests* the amount realized from the conversion in replacement property. The rules for nonrecognition of gain are as follows:

- If the amount reinvested in replacement property *equals or exceeds* the amount realized, realized gain is *not recognized.*
- If the amount reinvested in replacement property is *less than* the amount realized, realized gain *is recognized* to the extent of the deficiency.

If a *loss* occurs on an involuntary conversion, § 1033 does not modify the normal rules for loss recognition. That is, if a realized loss would otherwise be recognized, § 1033 does not change the result.

Involuntary Conversion Defined

An **involuntary conversion** results from the destruction (complete or partial), theft, seizure, requisition or condemnation, or sale or exchange under threat or imminence of requisition or condemnation of the taxpayer's property.[9] To prove the existence of a threat or imminence of condemnation, the taxpayer must obtain confirmation that there has been a decision to acquire the property for public use. In addition, the taxpayer must have reasonable grounds to believe the property will be taken.[10] The property does not have to be sold to the authority threatening to condemn it to qualify for § 1033 postponement. If the taxpayer satisfies the confirmation and reasonable grounds requirements, he or she can sell the property to another party.[11] Likewise, the sale of property to a condemning authority by a taxpayer who acquired the property from its former owner with the knowledge that the property was under threat of condemnation also qualifies as an involuntary conversion under § 1033.[12] A voluntary act, such as a taxpayer destroying the property by arson, is not an involuntary conversion.[13]

Computing the Amount Realized

The amount realized from the condemnation of property usually includes only the amount received as compensation for the property.[14] Any amount received that is designated as severance damages by both the government and the taxpayer is not included in the amount realized. *Severance awards* usually occur when only a portion of the property is condemned (e.g., a strip of land is taken to build a highway). Severance damages are awarded because the value of the taxpayer's remaining property has declined as a result of the condemnation. Such damages reduce the basis of the property. However, if either of the following requirements is satisfied, the nonrecognition provision of § 1033 applies to the severance damages:

- The severance damages are used to restore the usability of the remaining property.
- The usefulness of the remaining property is destroyed by the condemnation, and the property is sold and replaced at a cost equal to or exceeding the sum of the condemnation award, severance damages, and sales proceeds.

[9]§ 1033(a) and Reg. §§ 1.1033(a)–1(a) and –2(a).
[10]Rev.Rul. 63–221, 1963–2 C.B. 332, and *Joseph P. Balistrieri*, 38 TCM 526, T.C.Memo. 1979–115.
[11]Rev.Rul. 81–180, 1981–2 C.B. 161.
[12]Rev.Rul. 81–181, 1981–2 C.B. 162.
[13]Rev.Rul. 82–74, 1982–1 C.B. 110.
[14]*Pioneer Real Estate Co.*, 47 B.T.A. 886 (1942), *acq.* 1943 C.B. 18.

TAX *in the News* — A COURT UPHOLDS THE GOVERNMENT'S TAKING OF PROPERTY

Under eminent domain, governmental units have the right to take private property for public use. As fair compensation must be paid, disagreement often arises over the fair market value of condemned property.

In recent years, there has also been controversy over what constitutes "public use." Courts have expanded the definition of public use beyond the traditional public projects (such as roads, bridges, schools, hospitals, and slum clearance) to allow the taking of unblighted property for commercial development purposes. The objective in taking such property is to create jobs and increase tax revenues by means of new office parks, big box stores, racetracks, and other businesses.

The U.S. Supreme Court addressed this issue of what constitutes "public use" in its 2005 decision in *Kelo v. City of New London* (125 S.Ct. 2655 [USSC, 2005]). The Court, in a 5-to-4 decision, ruled that the "takings clause" in the Fifth Amendment to the U.S. Constitution permits the condemnation of private property for uses that are primarily commercial, as long as such use serves a demonstrated "public use." Here, the City of New London condemned 15 properties to enable the construction of a resort hotel and facilities for a major pharmaceutical company. "Public use" in this case was deemed to occur because benefits would accrue to the city in the form of new jobs and increased tax revenues.

Some have criticized the decision because it leaves few limits on the ability of local governments to take private property. In addition, for those property owners whose property is either condemned or threatened with condemnation, the decision may impair their ability to receive fair compensation. It appears that the only way now available to limit this government condemnation power is for the states to enact laws restricting its use.

EXAMPLE 13

The government condemns a portion of Ron's farmland to build part of an interstate highway. Because the highway denies his cattle access to a pond and some grazing land, Ron receives severance damages in addition to the condemnation proceeds for the land taken. Ron must reduce the basis of the property by the amount of the severance damages. If the amount of the severance damages received exceeds the adjusted basis, Ron recognizes gain. ∎

EXAMPLE 14

Assume the same facts as in the previous example, except that Ron uses the proceeds from the condemnation and the severance damages to build another pond and to clear woodland for grazing. Therefore, all the proceeds are eligible for § 1033 treatment. There is no possibility of gain recognition as the result of the amount of the severance damages received exceeding the adjusted basis. ∎

Replacement Property

The requirements for replacement property generally are more restrictive than those for like-kind property under § 1031. The basic requirement is that the replacement property be similar or related in service or use to the involuntarily converted property.[15]

Different interpretations of the phrase *similar or related in service or use* apply depending on whether the involuntarily converted property is held by an *owner-user* or by an *owner-investor* (e.g., lessor). A taxpayer who uses the property in his or her trade or business is subject to a more restrictive test in terms of acquiring replacement property. For an owner-user, the *functional use test* applies, and for an owner-investor, the *taxpayer use test* applies.

Taxpayer Use Test. The taxpayer use test for owner-investors provides the taxpayer with more flexibility in terms of what qualifies as replacement property than does the functional use test for owner-users. Essentially, the properties must be used by the taxpayer (the owner-investor) in similar endeavors. For example, rental property held by an owner-investor qualifies if replaced by other rental property,

---

[15]§ 1033(a) and Reg. § 1.1033(a)–1.

regardless of the type of rental property involved. The test is met when an investor replaces a manufacturing plant with a wholesale grocery warehouse if both properties are held for the production of rent income.[16] The replacement of a rental residence with a personal residence does not meet the test.[17]

Functional Use Test. The functional use test applies to owner-users (e.g., a manufacturer whose manufacturing plant is destroyed by fire is required to replace the plant with another facility of similar functional use). Under this test, the taxpayer's use of the replacement property and of the involuntarily converted property must be the same. Replacing a manufacturing plant with a wholesale grocery warehouse does not meet this test. Neither does replacing a rental residence with a personal residence.

Special Rules. Under one set of circumstances, the broader replacement rules for like-kind exchanges are substituted for the narrow replacement rules normally used for involuntary conversions. This beneficial provision applies if business real property or investment real property is condemned. This provision gives the taxpayer substantially more flexibility in selecting replacement property. For example, improved real property can be replaced with unimproved real property.

The rules concerning the nature of replacement property are illustrated in Concept Summary 15–1.

Time Limitation on Replacement

The taxpayer normally has a two-year period after the close of the taxable year in which gain is realized from an involuntary conversion to replace the property (*the latest date*).[18] This rule affords as much as three years from the date of realization of gain to replace the property if the realization of gain took place on the first day of the taxable year.[19] If the involuntary conversion involved the condemnation of real property used in a trade or business or held for investment, a three-year period is substituted for the normal two-year period. In this case, the taxpayer can actually have as much as four years from the date of realization of gain to replace the property.

EXAMPLE 15

Megan's warehouse is destroyed by fire on December 16, 2005. The adjusted basis is $325,000. Megan receives $400,000 from the insurance company on January 10, 2006. She is a calendar year taxpayer. The latest date for replacement is December 31, 2008 (the end of the taxable year in which realized gain occurred plus two years). The critical date is not the date the involuntary conversion occurred, but rather the date of gain realization. ∎

EXAMPLE 16

Assume the same facts as in the previous example, except that Megan's warehouse is condemned. The latest date for replacement is December 31, 2009 (the end of the taxable year in which realized gain occurred plus three years). ∎

The *earliest date* for replacement typically is the date the involuntary conversion occurs. However, if the property is condemned, it is possible to replace the condemned property before this date. In this case, the earliest date is the date of the threat or imminence of requisition or condemnation of the property. The purpose of this provision is to enable the taxpayer to make an orderly replacement of the condemned property.

---

[16]*Loco Realty Co. v. Comm.*, 62–2 USTC ¶9657, 10 AFTR2d 5359, 306 F.2d 207 (CA–8, 1962).

[17]Rev.Rul. 70–466, 1970–2 C.B. 165.

[18]§§ 1033(a)(2)(B) and (g)(4) and Reg. § 1.1033(a)–2(c)(3).

[19]The taxpayer can apply for an extension of this time period anytime before its expiration [Reg. § 1.1033(a)–2(c)(3)]. Also, the period for filing the application for extension can be extended if the taxpayer shows reasonable cause.

CONCEPT SUMMARY 15–1

Replacement Property Tests

Type of Property and User	Like-Kind Test	Taxpayer Use Test	Functional Use Test
Land used by a manufacturing company is condemned by a local government authority.	X		
Apartment and land held by an investor are sold due to the threat or imminence of condemnation.	X		
An investor's rented shopping mall is destroyed by fire; the mall may be replaced by other rental properties (e.g., an apartment building).		X	
A manufacturing plant is destroyed by fire; replacement property must consist of another manufacturing plant that is functionally the same as the property converted.			X
Personal residence of taxpayer is condemned by a local government authority; replacement property must consist of another personal residence.			X

EXAMPLE 17

Assume the same facts as in Example 16. Megan can replace the warehouse before December 16, 2005 (the condemnation date). The earliest date for replacement is the date of the threat or imminence of requisition or condemnation of the warehouse. ■

Nonrecognition of Gain

Nonrecognition of gain can be either mandatory or elective, depending on whether the conversion is direct (into replacement property) or indirect (into money).

Direct Conversion. If the conversion is directly into replacement property rather than into money, nonrecognition of realized gain is *mandatory*. In this case, the basis of the replacement property is the same as the adjusted basis of the converted property. Direct conversion is rare in practice and usually involves condemnations.

EXAMPLE 18

Lupe's property, with an adjusted basis of $20,000, is condemned by the state. Lupe receives property with a fair market value of $50,000 as compensation for the property taken. Since the nonrecognition of realized gain is mandatory for direct conversions, Lupe's realized gain of $30,000 is not recognized, and the basis of the replacement property is $20,000 (adjusted basis of the condemned property). ■

Conversion into Money. If the conversion is into money, at the election of the taxpayer, the realized gain is recognized only to the extent the amount realized from the involuntary conversion exceeds the cost of the qualifying replacement property.[20] This is the usual case, and nonrecognition (postponement) is *elective*. If the election is not made, the realized gain is recognized.

The basis of the replacement property is the property's cost less postponed (deferred) gain.[21] If the election to postpone gain is made, the holding period of the replacement property includes the holding period of the converted property.

---

[20]§ 1033(a)(2)(A) and Reg. § 1.1033(a)–2(c)(1).   [21]§ 1033(b).

Section 1033 applies *only to gains* and *not to losses*. Losses from involuntary conversions are recognized if the property is held for business or income-producing purposes. Personal casualty losses are recognized, but condemnation losses related to personal use assets (e.g., a personal residence) are neither recognized nor postponed.

EXAMPLE 19

Walt's building (used in his trade or business), with an adjusted basis of $50,000, is destroyed by fire on October 5, 2006. Walt is a calendar year taxpayer. On November 17, 2006, he receives an insurance reimbursement of $100,000 for the loss. Walt invests $80,000 in a new building.

- Walt has until December 31, 2008, to make the new investment and qualify for the non-recognition election.
- Walt's realized gain is $50,000 ($100,000 insurance proceeds received − $50,000 adjusted basis of old building).
- Assuming the replacement property qualifies as similar or related in service or use, Walt's recognized gain is $20,000. He reinvested $20,000 less than the insurance proceeds received ($100,000 proceeds − $80,000 reinvested). Therefore, his realized gain is recognized to that extent.
- Walt's basis in the new building is $50,000. This is the building's cost of $80,000 less the postponed gain of $30,000 (realized gain of $50,000 − recognized gain of $20,000).
- The computation of realization, recognition, and basis would apply even if Walt was a real estate dealer and the building destroyed by fire was part of his inventory. Unlike § 1031, § 1033 generally does not exclude inventory. ∎

EXAMPLE 20

Assume the same facts as in the previous example, except that Walt receives only $45,000 of insurance proceeds. He has a realized and recognized loss of $5,000. The basis of the new building is the building's cost of $80,000. If the destroyed building had been held for personal use, the recognized loss would have been subject to the following additional limitations.[22] The loss of $5,000 would have been limited to the decline in fair market value of the property, and the amount of the loss would have been reduced first by $100 and then by 10% of adjusted gross income (refer to Chapter 7). ∎

Involuntary Conversion of a Personal Residence

The tax consequences of the involuntary conversion of a personal residence depend on whether the conversion is a casualty or condemnation and whether a realized loss or gain results.

Loss Situations. If the conversion is a condemnation, the realized loss is not recognized. Loss from the condemnation of a personal use asset is never recognized. If the conversion is a casualty (a loss from fire, storm, etc.), the loss is recognized subject to the personal casualty loss limitations (refer to Chapter 7).

Gain Situations. If the conversion is a casualty, theft, or condemnation, the gain may be postponed under § 1033 or excluded under § 121. That is, the taxpayer may treat the involuntary conversion as a sale under the exclusion of gain rules relating to the sale of a personal residence under § 121 (presented subsequently).

Under certain circumstances, the taxpayer may use both the § 121 exclusion of gain and the § 1033 postponement of gain provisions. See the discussion under Involuntary Conversion and Using §§ 121 and 1033 later in this chapter.

---

[22]§ 165(c)(3) and Reg. § 1.165–7.

Reporting Considerations

Involuntary conversions from casualty and theft are reported first on Form 4684, Casualties and Thefts. Casualty and theft losses on personal use property for the individual taxpayer are carried from Form 4684 to Schedule A of Form 1040. For other casualty and theft items, the Form 4684 amounts are generally reported on Form 4797, Sales of Business Property, unless Form 4797 is not required. In the latter case, the amounts are reported directly on the tax return involved.

Except for personal use property, recognized gains and losses from involuntary conversions other than by casualty and theft are reported on Form 4797. As stated previously, if the property involved in the involuntary conversion (other than by casualty and theft) is personal use property, any realized loss is not recognized. Any realized gain is treated as gain on a voluntary sale.

Sale of a Residence—§ 121

> **LO.4**
> Describe the provision for the permanent exclusion of gain on the sale of a personal residence.

A taxpayer's **personal residence** is a personal use asset. Therefore, a realized loss from the sale of a personal residence is not recognized.[23]

A realized gain from the sale of a personal residence is subject to taxation. However, favorable relief from recognition of gain is provided in the form of the **§ 121 exclusion**. Under this provision, a taxpayer can exclude up to $250,000 of realized gain on the sale.[24]

Joint return : $500K.   2 out of 5 yrs living

Requirements for Exclusion Treatment

To qualify for exclusion treatment, at the date of the sale, the residence must have been *owned* and *used* by the taxpayer as the principal residence for at least two years during the five-year period ending on the date of the sale.[25]

EXAMPLE 21

Alice sells her principal residence on September 18, 2006. She had purchased it on July 5, 2004, and lived in it since then. The sale of Alice's residence qualifies for the § 121 exclusion. ∎

The five-year window enables the taxpayer to qualify for the § 121 exclusion even though the property is not his or her principal residence at the date of the sale.

EXAMPLE 22

Benjamin sells his principal residence on August 16, 2006. He had purchased it on April 1, 1998, and lived in it until July 1, 2005, when he converted it to rental property. Even though the property is rental property on August 16, 2006, rather than Benjamin's principal residence, the sale qualifies for the § 121 exclusion.[26] During the five-year period from August 16, 2001, to August 16, 2006, Benjamin owned and used the property as his principal residence for at least two years. ∎

Taxpayers might be tempted to make liberal use of the § 121 exclusion as a means of speculating when the price of residential housing is rising. Without any time restriction on its use, § 121 would permit the exclusion of realized gain on multiple sales of principal residences. The Code curbs this approach by denying the application of the § 121 exclusion to sales occurring within two years of its last use.[27]

---

[23]§ 165(c).
[24]§ 121(b).
[25]§ 121(a). However, § 121(d)(10) provides that exclusion treatment does not apply if the residence was acquired in a like-kind exchange within the prior five years of the sale of the residence.

[26]However, any realized gain on the sale that is attributable to depreciation is not eligible for the § 121 exclusion. See Example 38.
[27]§ 121(b)(3).

EXAMPLE 23

Seth sells his principal residence (the first residence) in June 2005 for $150,000 (realized gain of $60,000). He then buys and sells the following (all of which qualify as principal residences):

	Date of Purchase	Date of Sale	Amount Involved
Second residence	July 2005		$160,000
Second residence		April 2006	180,000
Third residence	May 2006		200,000

Because multiple sales have taken place within a period of two years, § 121 does not apply to the sale of the second residence. Thus, the realized gain of $20,000 [$180,000 (selling price) − $160,000 (purchase price)] must be recognized. ∎

Exceptions to the Two-Year Ownership Rule

The two-year ownership and use requirement and the "only once every two years" provision could create a hardship for taxpayers in certain situations that are beyond their control. Thus, under the following special circumstances, the requirements are waived:[28]

- Change in place of employment.
- Health.
- To the extent provided in the Regulations, other unforeseen circumstances.

These three exceptions have recently been amplified by the IRS and are discussed in the sections that follow.

Change in Place of Employment. In order for this exception to apply, the distance requirements applicable to the deductibility of moving expenses must be satisfied (see Chapter 9).[29] Consequently, the location of the taxpayer's new employment must be at least 50 miles further from the old residence than the old residence was from the old job. The house must be used as the principal residence of the taxpayer at the time of the change in the place of employment. Employment includes the commencement of employment with a new employer, the continuation of employment with the same employer, and the commencement or continuation of self-employment.

[28]§ 121(c)(2)(B).   [29]Reg. § 1.121–3T(c).

Assume the same facts as in the previous example, except that in March 2006, Seth's employer transfers him to a job in another state that is 400 miles away. Thus, the sale of the second residence and the purchase of the third residence were due to relocation of employment. Consequently, the § 121 exclusion is partially available on the sale of the second residence. ∎

Keep in mind, however, that the change in place of employment exception, or any of the other exceptions noted below, does not make the full amount of the exclusion available. See the discussion under Relief Provision later in this chapter for determining the amount of the partial exclusion allowed.

Health Considerations. For the health exception to apply, health must be the primary reason for the sale or exchange of the residence.[30] A sale or exchange that is merely beneficial to the general health or well-being of the individual will not qualify. A safe harbor applies if there is a physician's recommendation for a change of residence (1) to obtain, provide, or facilitate the diagnosis, cure, mitigation, or treatment of disease, illness, or injury or (2) to obtain or provide medical or personal care for an individual suffering from a disease, illness, or injury. If the safe harbor is not satisfied, then the determination is made using a facts and circumstances approach. Examples that qualify include the following:

- A taxpayer who is injured in an accident is unable to care for herself. She sells her residence and moves in with her daughter.
- A taxpayer's father has a chronic disease. The taxpayer sells his house in order to move into the father's house to provide the care the father requires as a result of the disease.
- A taxpayer's son suffers from a chronic disease. The taxpayer sells his house and moves his family so the son can begin a new treatment recommended by the son's physician that is available at a medical facility 100 miles away.
- A taxpayer suffers from chronic asthma. Her physician recommends that she move to a warm, dry climate. She moves from Minnesota to Arizona.

Unforeseen Circumstances. For the unforeseen circumstances exception to apply, the primary reason for the sale or exchange of the residence must be an event that the taxpayer did not anticipate before purchasing and occupying the residence.[31] This requirement is satisfied under a safe-harbor provision by any of the following:

- Involuntary conversion of the residence.
- Natural or human-made disasters or acts of war or terrorism resulting in a casualty to the residence.
- Death of a qualified individual.
- Cessation of employment that results in eligibility for unemployment compensation.
- Change in employment or self-employment that results in the taxpayer being unable to pay housing costs and reasonable basic living expenses for the taxpayer's household.
- Divorce or legal separation.
- Multiple births resulting from the same pregnancy.

If the safe harbor is not satisfied, then the determination is made using a facts and circumstances approach.

Debra and Roy are engaged and buy a house (sharing the mortgage payments) and live in it as their personal residence. Eighteen months after the purchase, they cancel their wedding plans, and Roy moves out of the house. Because Debra cannot afford to make the payments

---

[30]Reg. § 1.121–3T(d).   [31]Reg. § 1.121–3T(e).

alone, they sell the house. While the sale does not fit under the safe harbor, the sale does qualify under the unforeseen circumstances exception. ∎

Calculation of the Amount of the Exclusion

General Provisions. The amount of the available § 121 exclusion on the sale of a principal residence is $250,000.[32] If the realized gain does not exceed $250,000, there is no recognized gain.

Realized gain is calculated in the normal manner. The *amount realized* is the selling price less the selling expenses, which include items such as the cost of advertising the property for sale, real estate broker commissions, legal fees in connection with the sale, and loan placement fees paid by the taxpayer as a condition of arranging financing for the buyer. Repairs and maintenance performed by the seller to aid in selling the property are treated neither as selling expenses nor as adjustments to the taxpayer's adjusted basis for the residence.

EXAMPLE 26

Mandy, who is single, sells her personal residence (adjusted basis of $130,000) for $290,000. She has owned and lived in the residence for three years. Her selling expenses are $18,000. Three weeks prior to the sale, Mandy paid a carpenter and a painter $1,000 to make some repairs and paint the two bathrooms. Her recognized gain is calculated as follows:

Amount realized ($290,000 − $18,000)	$ 272,000
Adjusted basis	(130,000)
Realized gain	$ 142,000
§ 121 exclusion	(142,000)
Recognized gain	$ –0–

Since the available § 121 exclusion of $250,000 exceeds Mandy's realized gain of $142,000, her recognized gain is $0. ∎

EXAMPLE 27

Assume the same facts as in the previous example, except that the selling price is $490,000.

Amount realized ($490,000 − $18,000)	$ 472,000
Adjusted basis	(130,000)
Realized gain	$ 342,000
§ 121 exclusion	(250,000)
Recognized gain	$ 92,000

Since the realized gain of $342,000 exceeds the § 121 exclusion amount of $250,000, Mandy's recognized gain is $92,000 ($342,000 − $250,000). ∎

Effect on Married Couples. If a married couple files a joint return, the $250,000 amount is increased to $500,000 if the following requirements are satisfied:[33]

- Either spouse meets the at-least-two-years *ownership* requirement.
- Both spouses meet the at-least-two-years *use* requirement.
- Neither spouse is ineligible for the § 121 exclusion on the sale of the current principal residence because of the sale of another principal residence within the prior two years.

---

[32]§ 121(b)(1).   [33]§ 121(b)(2).

Margaret sells her personal residence (adjusted basis of $150,000) for $650,000. She has owned and lived in the residence for six years. Her selling expenses are $40,000. Margaret is married to Ted, and they file a joint return. Ted has lived in the residence since they were married two and one-half years ago.

Amount realized ($650,000 − $40,000)	$ 610,000
Adjusted basis	(150,000)
Realized gain	$ 460,000
§ 121 exclusion	(460,000)
Recognized gain	$ –0–

Since the realized gain of $460,000 is less than the available § 121 exclusion amount of $500,000, no gain is recognized. ■

If each spouse owns a qualified principal residence, each spouse can separately qualify for the $250,000 exclusion on the sale of his or her own residence even if the couple files a joint return.[34]

Anne and Samuel are married on August 1, 2006. Each owns a residence that is eligible for the § 121 exclusion. Anne sells her residence on September 7, 2006, and Samuel sells his residence on October 9, 2006. Relevant data on the sales are as follows:

	Anne	Samuel
Selling price	$320,000	$425,000
Selling expenses	20,000	25,000
Adjusted basis	190,000	110,000

Anne and Samuel intend to rent a condo in Florida or Arizona and to travel. The recognized gain of each is calculated as follows:

	Anne	Samuel
Amount realized	$ 300,000	$ 400,000
Adjusted basis	(190,000)	(110,000)
Realized gain	$ 110,000	$ 290,000
§ 121 exclusion	(110,000)	(250,000)
Recognized gain	$ –0–	$ 40,000

Anne has no recognized gain because the available $250,000 exclusion amount exceeds her realized gain of $110,000. Samuel's recognized gain is $40,000 as his realized gain of $290,000 exceeds the $250,000 exclusion amount. The recognized gains calculated above result regardless of whether Anne and Samuel file a joint return or separate returns. ■

Relief Provision. As discussed earlier in Requirements for Exclusion Treatment, partial § 121 exclusion treatment may be available when not all of the statutory requirements are satisfied. Under the relief provision, the § 121 exclusion amount ($250,000 or $500,000) is multiplied by a fraction, the numerator of which is the number of qualifying months and the denominator of which is 24 months. The resulting amount is the excluded gain.[35]

[34]§ 121(b)(1).   [35]§ 121(c)(1).

EXAMPLE 30

On October 1, 2005, Rich and Audrey, who file a joint return and live in Chicago, sell their personal residence, which they have owned and lived in for eight years. The realized gain of $325,000 is excluded under § 121. They purchase another personal residence for $525,000 on October 2, 2005. Audrey's employer transfers her to the Denver office in August 2006. Rich and Audrey sell their Chicago residence on August 2, 2006, and purchase a residence in Denver shortly thereafter. The realized gain on the sale is $300,000.

The $325,000 gain on the first Chicago residence is excluded under § 121. The sale of the second Chicago residence is within the two-year window of the prior sale, but because it resulted from a change in employment, Rich and Audrey can qualify for partial § 121 exclusion treatment as follows:

Realized gain	$ 300,000
§ 121 exclusion:	
$\dfrac{10 \text{ months}}{24 \text{ months}} \times \$500,000 = \$208,333$	(208,333)
Recognized gain	$ 91,667

Basis of New Residence. Because § 121 is an exclusion provision rather than a postponement of gain provision, the basis of a new residence is its cost.[36]

Principal Residence

To be eligible for the § 121 exclusion, the residence must have been owned and used by the taxpayer as the principal residence for at least two years during the five-year window (subject to partial exclusion treatment under the relief provision). Whether property is the taxpayer's principal residence "depends upon all of the facts and circumstances in each case."[37]

EXAMPLE 31

Mitch graduates from college and moves to Boston, where he is employed. He decides to rent an apartment in Boston because of its proximity to his place of employment. He purchases a beach condo in the Cape Cod area that he occupies most weekends. Mitch does not intend to live at the beach condo except on weekends. The apartment in Boston is his principal residence. ■

A residence does not have to be a house. For example, a houseboat, a house trailer, or a motor home can qualify.[38] Land, under certain circumstances, can qualify for exclusion treatment. The lot on which a house is built obviously qualifies. An adjacent lot can qualify if it is regularly used by the owner as part of the residential property. To qualify, the land must be sold along with the residence or within two years before or after the sale of the residence.

Involuntary Conversion and Using §§ 121 and 1033

As mentioned earlier (see Involuntary Conversion of a Personal Residence), a taxpayer can use both the § 121 exclusion of gain provision and the § 1033 postponement of gain provision.[39] The taxpayer initially can elect to exclude realized gain under § 121 to the extent of the statutory amount. Then a qualified replacement of the residence under § 1033 can be used to postpone the remainder of the realized gain. In applying § 1033, the amount of the required reinvestment is reduced by the amount of the § 121 exclusion.

---

[36]§ 1012.

[37]Regulation § 1.121–1(b)(2) includes factors to be considered in determining a taxpayer's principal residence.

[38]Reg. § 1.1034–1(c)(3)(i).

[39]§ 121(d)(5).

Angel's principal residence is destroyed by a tornado. Her adjusted basis for the residence is $140,000. She receives insurance proceeds of $480,000.

If Angel does not elect to use the § 121 exclusion, her realized gain on the involuntary conversion of her principal residence is $340,000 ($480,000 amount realized − $140,000 adjusted basis). Thus, to postpone the $340,000 realized gain under § 1033, she would need to acquire qualifying property costing at least $480,000.

Using the § 121 exclusion enables Angel to reduce the amount of the required reinvestment for § 1033 purposes from $480,000 to $230,000. That is, by using § 121 in conjunction with § 1033, the amount realized, for § 1033 purposes, is reduced to $230,000 ($480,000 − $250,000 § 121 exclusion).

Note that if Angel does not acquire qualifying replacement property for § 1033 purposes, her recognized gain is $90,000 ($480,000 − $140,000 adjusted basis − $250,000 § 121 exclusion). ■

EXAMPLE 32

§1033: buy other property to delay gain

If § 1033 is used in conjunction with the § 121 exclusion on an involuntary conversion of a principal residence, the holding period of the replacement residence includes the holding period of the involuntarily converted residence. This can be beneficial in satisfying the § 121 two-out-of-five-years ownership and use requirement on a subsequent sale of the replacement residence.

Other Nonrecognition Provisions

The typical taxpayer experiences the sale of a personal residence or an involuntary conversion more frequently than the other types of nontaxable exchanges. Several less common nonrecognition provisions are treated briefly in the remainder of this chapter.

Exchange of Stock for Property—§ 1032

Under § 1032, a corporation does not recognize gain or loss on the receipt of money or other property in exchange for its stock (including treasury stock). In other words, a corporation does not recognize gain or loss when it deals in its own stock. This provision is consistent with the accounting treatment of such transactions.

Certain Exchanges of Insurance Policies—§ 1035

Under § 1035, no gain or loss is recognized from the exchange of certain insurance contracts or policies. The rules relating to exchanges not solely in kind and the basis of the property acquired are the same as under § 1031. Exchanges qualifying for nonrecognition include the following:

- The exchange of life insurance contracts.
- The exchange of a life insurance contract for an endowment or annuity contract.
- The exchange of an endowment contract for another endowment contract that provides for regular payments beginning at a date not later than the date payments would have begun under the contract exchanged.
- The exchange of an endowment contract for an annuity contract.
- The exchange of annuity contracts.

Exchange of Stock for Stock of the Same Corporation—§ 1036

Section 1036 provides that a shareholder does not recognize gain or loss on the exchange of common stock solely for common stock in the same corporation or from the exchange of preferred stock for preferred stock in the same corporation. Exchanges between individual shareholders as well as between a shareholder and the corporation are included. The rules relating to exchanges not solely in kind and the basis of the property acquired are the same as under § 1031. For example, a nonrecognition exchange occurs when common stock with different rights, such as voting for nonvoting, is exchanged. A shareholder usually recognizes gain or loss from the exchange of common for preferred or preferred for common even though the stock exchanged is in the same corporation.

Certain Reacquisitions of Real Property—§ 1038

Under § 1038, no loss is recognized from the repossession of real property sold on an installment basis. Gain is recognized to a limited extent.

Transfers of Property between Spouses or Incident to Divorce—§ 1041

Section 1041 provides that transfers of property *between spouses or former spouses incident to divorce* are nontaxable transactions. Therefore, the basis to the recipient is a carryover basis. To be treated as incident to the divorce, the transfer must be related to the cessation of marriage or occur within one year after the date on which the marriage ceases.

Section 1041 also provides for nontaxable exchange treatment on property transfers *between spouses during marriage*. The basis to the recipient spouse is a carryover basis.

ETHICAL *Considerations*   **INCIDENT TO DIVORCE OR NOT?**

Randy and Judy are divorced on December 28, 2005, after being married for 10 years. Several years ago they purchased a beach lot for $150,000 and planned to construct a beach house there for vacation purposes.

On December 26, 2006, Randy transfers his interests in the beach lot to Judy for $200,000 (i.e., 50 percent of the fair market value of $400,000). According to both Randy and Judy, the sale was not associated with the divorce but was made to enable Randy to invest the cash in a business he is starting. They treat the transaction as the sale of Randy's one-half interest to Judy. Accordingly, Randy recognizes a capital gain of $125,000 ($200,000 − $75,000), which is eligible for the 15 percent alternative tax rate. Judy considers her adjusted basis to be $275,000 ($75,000 + $200,000).

Evaluate Randy and Judy's treatment of this transaction.

Rollovers into Specialized Small Business Investment Companies—§ 1044

A postponement opportunity is available for some sellers of publicly traded securities under § 1044. If the amount realized is reinvested in the common stock or partnership interest of a specialized small business investment company (SSBIC), the realized gain is not recognized. Any amount not reinvested will trigger recognition of the realized gain to the extent of the deficiency. The taxpayer must reinvest the proceeds within 60 days of the date of sale in order to qualify. In calculating the basis of the SSBIC stock, the amount of the purchase price is reduced by the amount of the postponed gain.

Statutory ceilings are imposed on the amount of realized gain that can be postponed for any taxable year as follows:

- For an individual taxpayer, the lesser of:
  - $50,000 ($25,000 for married filing separately).
  - $500,000 ($250,000 for married filing separately) reduced by the amount of such nonrecognized gain in prior taxable years.
- For a corporate taxpayer, the lesser of:
  - $250,000.
  - $1 million reduced by the amount of such nonrecognized gain in prior taxable years.

Investors *ineligible* for this postponement treatment include partnerships, S corporations, estates, and trusts.

Rollover of Gain from Qualified Small Business Stock into Another Qualified Small Business Stock—§ 1045

Under § 1045, realized gain from the sale of qualified small business stock held for more than six months may be postponed if the taxpayer acquires other qualified small business stock within 60 days. Any amount not reinvested will trigger the recognition of the realized gain on the sale to the extent of the deficiency. In calculating the basis of the acquired qualified small business stock, the amount of the purchase price is reduced by the amount of the postponed gain.

Qualified small business stock is stock of a qualified small business that is acquired by the taxpayer at its original issue in exchange for money or other property (excluding stock) or as compensation for services. A qualified small business is a domestic corporation that satisfies the following requirements:

- The aggregate gross assets prior to the issuance of the small business stock do not exceed $50 million.
- The aggregate gross assets immediately after the issuance of the small business stock do not exceed $50 million.

Like-Kind Exchanges

Since application of the like-kind exchange provisions is mandatory rather than elective, in certain instances it may be preferable to avoid qualifying for § 1031 nonrecognition. If the like-kind exchange provisions do not apply, the end result may be the recognition of capital gain in exchange for a higher basis in the newly acquired asset. Also, the immediate recognition of gain may be preferable in certain situations. Examples where immediate recognition is beneficial include the following:

- Taxpayer has unused net operating loss carryovers.
- Taxpayer has unused general business credit carryovers.
- Taxpayer has suspended or current passive activity losses.
- Taxpayer expects his or her effective tax rate to increase in the future.

> **LO.6**
>
> Identify tax planning opportunities related to the nonrecognition provisions discussed in the chapter.

TAX PLANNING
Considerations

EXAMPLE 33

Alicia disposes of a machine (used in her business) with an adjusted basis of $3,000 for $4,000. She also acquires a new business machine for $9,000. If § 1031 applies, the $1,000 realized gain is not recognized, and the basis of the new machine is reduced by $1,000 (from $9,000 to $8,000). If § 1031 does not apply, a $1,000 gain is recognized and may receive favorable capital gain treatment to the extent that the gain is not recognized as ordinary income due to the depreciation recapture provisions (see Chapter 17). In addition, the basis for depreciation on the new machine is $9,000 rather than $8,000 since there is no unrecognized gain. ■

The application of § 1031 nonrecognition treatment should also be avoided when the adjusted basis of the property being disposed of exceeds the fair market value.

EXAMPLE 34

Assume the same facts as in the previous example, except that the fair market value of the machine is $2,500. If § 1031 applies, the $500 realized loss is not recognized. To recognize the loss, Alicia should sell the old machine and purchase the new one. The purchase and sale transactions should be with different taxpayers. ∎

On the other hand, the like-kind exchange procedure can be utilized to control the amount of recognized gain.

EXAMPLE 35

Rex has property with an adjusted basis of $40,000 and a fair market value of $100,000. Sandra wants to buy Rex's property, but Rex wants to limit the amount of recognized gain on the proposed transaction. Sandra acquires other like-kind property (from an outside party) for $80,000. She then exchanges this property and $20,000 cash for Rex's property. Rex has a realized gain of $60,000 ($100,000 amount realized − $40,000 adjusted basis). His recognized gain is only $20,000, the lower of the $20,000 boot received or the $60,000 realized gain. Rex's basis for the like-kind property is $40,000 ($40,000 adjusted basis + $20,000 gain recognized − $20,000 boot received). If Rex had sold the property to Sandra for its fair market value of $100,000, the result would have been a $60,000 recognized gain ($100,000 amount realized − $40,000 adjusted basis) to him. It is permissible for Rex to identify the like-kind property that he wants Sandra to purchase.[40] ∎

Involuntary Conversions

In certain cases, a taxpayer may prefer to recognize gain from an involuntary conversion. Keep in mind that § 1033, unlike § 1031 (dealing with like-kind exchanges), generally is an elective provision.

EXAMPLE 36

Ahmad has a $40,000 realized gain from the involuntary conversion of an office building. He reinvests the entire proceeds of $450,000 in a new office building. He does not elect to postpone gain under § 1033, however, because of an expiring net operating loss carryover that is offset against the gain. Therefore, none of the realized gain of $40,000 is postponed. Because Ahmad did not elect § 1033 postponement, his basis in the replacement property is the property's cost of $450,000 rather than $410,000 ($450,000 reduced by the $40,000 realized gain). ∎

Sale of a Principal Residence

Election to Forgo. The § 121 exclusion automatically applies if the taxpayer is eligible. That is, the taxpayer does not have to make an election. However, if the taxpayer wishes to avoid § 121 exclusion treatment on an otherwise eligible sale, the taxpayer may elect to do so.[41]

EXAMPLE 37

George owns two personal residences that satisfy the two-year ownership and use test with respect to the five-year window. The Elm Street residence has appreciated by $25,000, and the Maple Street residence has appreciated by $230,000. He intends to sell both of them and move into rental property. He sells the Elm Street residence in December 2006 and expects to sell the Maple Street residence early next year.

Unless George elects not to apply the § 121 exclusion to the sale of the Elm Street residence, he will exclude the $25,000 realized gain on that residence in 2006. In 2007, however, he will have a recognized gain of $230,000 on the sale of the Maple Street residence.

If George makes the election to forgo, he will report a recognized gain of $25,000 on the sale of the Elm Street residence in 2006. But by using the § 121 exclusion in 2007, he will eliminate the recognized gain of $230,000 on the sale of the Maple Street residence. ∎

---

[40]*Franklin B. Biggs*, 69 T.C. 905 (1978); Rev.Rul. 73–476, 1973–2 C.B. 300; and *Starker v. U.S.*, 79–2 USTC ¶9541, 44 AFTR2d 79–5525, 602 F.2d 1341 (CA–9, 1979).

[41]§ 121(f).

| TAX *in the News* | SALE OF A RESIDENCE AND THE HOME OFFICE DEDUCTION |

If various requirements are satisfied, a taxpayer who uses his or her residence for business may claim a deduction for the expenses attributable to such use. But what effect, if any, does claiming an office in the home deduction have on a later sale of the residence? Do the sale proceeds still qualify for nonrecognition of gain treatment under § 121?

Until recently, the answers to these questions were unknown. In fact, concern that the § 121 exclusion might be denied may have deterred some taxpayers from claiming legitimate office in the home deductions. Such caution appears to have been unnecessary. The IRS has clarified its position. Only the depreciation deducted on the office portion of the residence after May 5, 1997, is not eligible for the § 121 exclusion.

Negative Effect of Renting or Using as a Home Office. The residence does not have to be the taxpayer's principal residence at the date of sale to qualify for the § 121 exclusion. During part of the five-year window, it could have been rental property (e.g., either a vacation home or entirely rental property). In addition, the taxpayer can have used part of the principal residence as a qualifying home office.

In either the rental or the home office setting, the taxpayer will have deducted depreciation. Any realized gain on the sale that is attributable to depreciation claimed after May 5, 1997, is not eligible for the § 121 exclusion.[42]

EXAMPLE 38

On December 5, 2006, Amanda sells her principal residence, which qualifies for the § 121 exclusion. Her realized gain is $190,000. From January through November 2005, she was temporarily out of town on a job assignment in another city and rented the residence to a college student. For this period, she deducted MACRS cost recovery of $7,000. Without the depreciation provision, Amanda could exclude the $190,000 realized gain. However, the depreciation taken requires her to recognize $7,000 of the realized gain. ∎

Qualification for § 121 Exclusion. The key requirement for the § 121 exclusion is that the taxpayer must have *owned* and *used* the property as a principal residence for at least two years during the five-year window. As taxpayers advance in age, they quite frequently make decisions such as the following:

• Sell the principal residence and buy a smaller residence or rent the principal residence.
• Sell vacation homes they own.
• Sell homes they are holding as rental property.

These properties may have experienced substantial appreciation during the ownership period. Clearly, the sale of the principal residence is eligible for the § 121 exclusion. Less clear, however, is that proper planning can make it possible for a vacation home or rental property to qualify for the exclusion. Although this strategy may require taxpayers to be flexible about where they live, it can result in substantial tax savings.

EXAMPLE 39

Thelma and David are approaching retirement. They have substantial appreciation on their principal residence and on a house they own at the beach (about two hours away). After retirement, they plan to move to Florida. They have owned and lived in the principal residence for 28 years and have owned the beach house for 9 years. If they sell their principal residence, it qualifies for the § 121 exclusion. At retirement, they could move into their beach house for two years and make it eligible for the exclusion. If the beach house were not so far

---

[42]§ 121(d)(6).

away, they could sell the principal residence now and move into the beach house to start the running of the two-year use period. Note that any realized gain on the beach house attributable to depreciation is not eligible for the § 121 exclusion. ∎

Record Keeping. Since the amount of the available exclusion ($250,000 or $500,000) for most taxpayers will exceed the realized gain on the sale of the residence, the IRS has discontinued the form that previously was used to report the sale of a principal residence. If the sale of the residence does result in a gain that is not excluded from gross income, the gain is reported on Schedule D of Form 1040 (Capital Gains and Losses).

However, it is a good idea for all taxpayers who own residences to continue to maintain records on the adjusted basis of the residence including the original cost, any capital improvements, and any deductions that decrease basis (e.g., depreciation on a home office or on rental use) for the following reasons:

- The sale of the residence may not qualify for the § 121 exclusion.
- The realized gain may exceed the § 121 exclusion amount.
- The residence may be converted to rental or business use.
- If part of the residence has been rental or business use property (e.g., a qualifying home office) and depreciation has been deducted, the realized gain is recognized to the extent of the depreciation deducted.

Chapter 15 has covered certain situations in which realized gains or losses are not recognized (nontaxable exchanges). Chapters 16 and 17 are concerned with the *classification* of recognized gains and losses. That is, if a gain or loss is recognized, is it an ordinary or a capital gain or loss? Chapter 16 discusses the tax consequences of capital gains and losses.

KEY TERMS

Boot, 15–6	Like-kind exchanges, 15–3	Personal residence, 15–15
Involuntary conversion, 15–10	Nontaxable exchange, 15–2	§ 121 exclusion, 15–15

PROBLEM MATERIALS

DISCUSSION QUESTIONS

1. What is the justification for nontaxable exchange treatment?

2. Distinguish between a loss that is not recognized on a nontaxable exchange and a loss that is not recognized on the sale or exchange of a personal use asset.

3. What are the three requirements that must be satisfied for a transaction to qualify for nontaxable exchange treatment under § 1031?

4. Can the exchange of personal use property for property held for productive use in a trade or business qualify for like-kind exchange treatment? Explain.

5. Amos owns a lathe (adjusted basis of $40,000) that he uses in his business. He exchanges the lathe and $20,000 in cash for a new lathe worth $50,000. May Amos avoid like-kind exchange treatment in order to recognize his realized loss of $10,000?

6. Which of the following qualify as like-kind exchanges under § 1031?
   a. Improved for unimproved real estate.
   b. Vending machine (used in business) for inventory.
   c. Rental house for personal residence.
   d. Business equipment for securities.
   e. Warehouse for office building (both used for business).
   f. Truck for computer (both used in business).
   g. Rental house for land (both held for investment).
   h. Ten shares of stock in Blue Corporation for 10 shares of stock in Red Corporation.
   i. Office furniture for office equipment (both used in business).
   j. Unimproved land in Jackson, Mississippi, for unimproved land in Toledo, Spain.

7. Melissa owns a residential lot in Spring Creek that has appreciated substantially in value. She holds the lot for investment. She is considering exchanging the lot with her father for a residential lot in McComb that she also will hold for investment. Identify the relevant tax issues for Melissa.

Issue ID

8. Ross would like to dispose of some land that he acquired five years ago because he believes that it will not continue to appreciate. Its value has increased by $50,000 over the five-year period. He also intends to sell stock that has declined in value by $50,000 during the eight-month period he has owned it. Ross has four offers to acquire the stock and land:

Issue ID

Buyer number 1:	Exchange land.
Buyer number 2:	Purchase land for cash.
Buyer number 3:	Exchange stock.
Buyer number 4:	Purchase stock for cash.

Identify the tax issues relevant to Ross in disposing of this land and stock.

9. Waldo owns a 20% interest in the AMW Partnership. He exchanges it with Karen for her 20% interest in the JKT Partnership. Does the trade qualify for nontaxable treatment as a like-kind exchange? Explain.

10. What is boot, and how does it affect the recognition of gain or loss on a like-kind exchange when received by the taxpayer? How is the recognition of gain or loss affected when boot is given?

11. In connection with like-kind exchanges, discuss each of the following:
    a. Realized gain.
    b. Realized loss.
    c. Recognized gain.
    d. Recognized loss.
    e. Postponed gain.
    f. Postponed loss.
    g. Basis of like-kind property received.
    h. Basis of boot received.

12. Edith exchanges a machine used in her business for another machine and stock of Teal, Inc. If Edith had sold her machine, she would have had a realized gain. Explain why the new machine will have a carryover holding period while the stock will have a new (date of exchange) holding period.

13. Mortgaged real estate may be received in a like-kind exchange. If the taxpayer's mortgage is assumed, what effect does the mortgage have on the recognition of realized gain? On the basis of the real estate received?

14. A taxpayer's appreciated property is involuntarily converted. She receives insurance proceeds equal to the fair market value of the property. What is the minimum amount the taxpayer must reinvest in qualifying property to defer recognition of realized gain?

15. What constitutes an involuntary conversion?

16. Ed receives severance damages from the state government for a public road built across his property. Under what circumstances can the § 1033 involuntary conversion provision apply to prevent the recognition of gain?

17. Distinguish between the taxpayer use test and the functional use test for involuntary conversions. When does each test apply?

18. On June 5, 2006, Tan, Inc., a calendar year taxpayer, receives cash of $520,000 from the county upon condemnation of its office building (adjusted basis of $250,000 and fair market value of $520,000).
    a. What must Tan do to qualify for § 1033 postponement of gain treatment?
    b. How would your advice to Tan differ if the adjusted basis were $550,000?

19. In January 2006, Stanley's warehouse (basis of $570,000) is destroyed by fire. Two months later, Stanley collects insurance proceeds of $610,000.
    a. If Stanley is a calendar year taxpayer, what is the latest date that he can reinvest the insurance proceeds and avoid recognition of gain?
    b. Suppose the warehouse was condemned by the city (instead of being destroyed by fire). What would be the latest date for reinvestment to avoid recognition of gain?

20. Bob is notified by the city public housing authority on May 3, 2006, that his apartment building is going to be condemned as part of an urban renewal project. On June 1, 2006, Carol offers to buy the building from Bob. Bob sells the building to Carol on June 30, 2006. Condemnation occurs on September 1, 2006, and Carol receives the condemnation proceeds from the city. Assume both Bob and Carol are calendar year taxpayers.
    a. What is the earliest date on which Bob can dispose of the building and qualify for § 1033 postponement treatment?
    b. Does the sale to Carol qualify as a § 1033 involuntary conversion?
    c. What is the latest date on which Carol can acquire qualifying replacement property and qualify for postponement of the realized gain?
    d. What type of property will be qualifying replacement property?

Issue ID

21. A warehouse owned by Martha and used in her business (i.e., to store inventory) is being condemned by the city to provide a right of way for a highway. The warehouse has appreciated by $100,000 based on Martha's estimate of its fair market value. In the negotiations, the city is offering $40,000 less than what Martha believes the property is worth. Alan, a real estate broker, has offered to purchase Martha's property for $25,000 more than the city's offer. Martha plans to invest the proceeds she will receive in an office building that she will lease to various tenants. Identify the relevant tax issues for Martha.

22. When does the holding period begin for replacement property acquired in an involuntary conversion? For property received in a like-kind exchange?

23. What requirements must be satisfied to qualify for the § 121 exclusion on the sale of a principal residence?

24. Arnold, who is single, sold his principal residence on April 10, 2006, and excluded the realized gain under § 121 (exclusion on the sale of a principal residence). On April 12, 2006, he purchased another principal residence, which he sells on January 12, 2007, for a realized gain of $80,000. Can Arnold exclude the $80,000 realized gain on the January 2007 sale if his reason for selling was:
    a. His noisy neighbors?
    b. A job transfer to another city?

Issue ID

25. Sandy owns a personal residence in which she has lived since she acquired it. It has appreciated by $90,000 during this period. Now, however, the school board has redrawn the boundaries for the school districts, and her son will have to transfer to a different high school for his senior year. Sandy is considering selling her residence and buying another one that will enable her son to remain in the same high school. Without this reason, she would not sell the house. Identify the relevant tax issues for Sandy.

26. Define each of the following items that are associated with the sale of a principal residence:
    a. Amount realized.
    b. Selling expenses.
    c. Realized gain.
    d. Recognized gain.
    e. § 121 excluded gain.
    f. Basis of a new residence.
    g. Principal residence.

27. To qualify for exclusion treatment on the sale of a principal residence, the residence must have been owned and used by the taxpayer for at least two years during the five-year period ending on the date of the sale. Are there any exceptions to this provision?

28. On May 5, 2006, Nancy sells her stock (adjusted basis of $13,000) in Lime, Inc., a publicly traded company, for $17,000. On May 31, 2006, she pays $20,000 for stock in Rose, Inc., a specialized small business investment company. Nancy believes that her adjusted basis for the Rose stock is $10,000. Evaluate Nancy's calculation of the adjusted basis for her Rose stock.

PROBLEMS

29. Catherine owns undeveloped land with an adjusted basis of $250,000. She exchanges it for other undeveloped land worth $310,000.
    a. What are Catherine's realized and recognized gain or loss?
    b. What is Catherine's basis in the undeveloped land she receives?

30. Kareem owns an automobile that he uses exclusively in his business. The adjusted basis is $19,000, and the fair market value is $16,000. Kareem exchanges the car for a car that he will use exclusively in his business.
    a. What are Kareem's realized and recognized gain or loss?
    b. What is his basis in the new car?
    c. What are the tax consequences to Kareem in (a) and (b) if he used the old car and will use the new car exclusively for personal purposes?

31. Tex Watson owns undeveloped land (basis of $350,000) held as an investment. On October 7, 2006, he exchanges the land with his 27-year-old daughter, Porchia, for other undeveloped land also to be held as an investment. The appraised value of Porchia's land is $500,000. *Decision Making* *Communications*
    a. On February 15, 2007, Tex sells the land to Baxter, a real estate broker, for $600,000. Calculate Tex's realized and recognized gain or loss from the exchange with Porchia and on the subsequent sale of the land to Baxter.
    b. Calculate Tex's realized and recognized gain or loss on the exchange with Porchia if Tex does not sell the land. Instead, on February 15, 2007, Porchia sells the land received from Tex. Calculate Tex's basis for the land on October 7, 2006, and on February 15, 2007.
    c. Write a letter to Tex advising him on how he could avoid any recognition of gain associated with the October 7, 2006 exchange. His address is The Corral, El Paso, TX 79968.

32. Bonnie owns a personal computer (adjusted basis of $3,000) that she uses exclusively in her business. Bonnie transfers the computer and cash of $1,500 to Green Computers for a laser printer (worth $5,500) also to be used in her business.
    a. Calculate Bonnie's recognized gain or loss on the exchange.
    b. Calculate Bonnie's basis for the printer.

33. Clarence exchanges a light-duty truck used in his business for one to be similarly used. The adjusted basis of the old truck is $17,000 (fair market value of $11,000). *Decision Making*
    a. Calculate Clarence's recognized gain or loss on the exchange.
    b. What is Clarence's basis in the new truck?
    c. How could the transaction have been structured to produce better tax results?
    d. How would your answers in (a), (b), and (c) change if the fair market value of the original truck was $19,000 and the fair market value of the replacement truck was $25,000 (i.e., cash payment of $6,000 was required from Clarence)?

34. Susan owns a car that she uses exclusively for personal purposes. Its original cost was $26,000, and the fair market value is $12,000. She exchanges the car and $18,000 cash for a new car.
    a. Calculate Susan's realized and recognized gain or loss.
    b. Calculate Susan's basis for the new car.
    c. Determine when Susan's holding period for the new car begins.

35. Stephanie owns a machine (adjusted basis of $60,000; fair market value of $95,000) that she uses in her business. She exchanges it for another machine (worth $70,000) and stock (worth $25,000). Determine Stephanie's:
    a. Realized and recognized gain or loss on the exchange.
    b. Basis in the new machine.
    c. Basis in the stock she received.

36. Ed owns investment land with an adjusted basis of $35,000. Polly has offered to purchase the land from Ed for $175,000 for use in a real estate development. The amount offered by Polly is $10,000 in excess of what Ed perceives as the fair market value of the land. Ed would like to dispose of the land to Polly but does not want to incur the tax liability that would result. He identifies an office building with a fair market value of $175,000 that he would like to acquire. Polly purchases the office building and then exchanges the office building for Ed's land.
    a. Calculate Ed's realized and recognized gain on the exchange and his basis for the office building.
    b. Calculate Polly's realized and recognized gain on the exchange and her basis in the land.

37. What is the basis of the new property in each of the following exchanges?
    a. Apartment building held for investment (adjusted basis $145,000) for office building to be held for investment (fair market value $225,000).
    b. Land and building used as a barber shop (adjusted basis $190,000) for land and building used as a grocery store (fair market value $350,000).
    c. Office building (adjusted basis $45,000) for bulldozer (fair market value $42,000), both held for business use.
    d. IBM common stock (adjusted basis $20,000) for ExxonMobil common stock (fair market value $28,000).
    e. Rental house (adjusted basis $90,000) for mountain cabin to be held for rental use (fair market value $225,000).

Decision Making

38. Norm owns Machine A (adjusted basis of $12,000; fair market value of $18,000), which he uses in his business. Norm is considering two options for the disposal of Machine A. Under the first option, he will transfer Machine A and $3,000 cash to Joan, a dealer, in exchange for Machine B (fair market value of $21,000). Under the second option, he will sell Machine A for $18,000 to Tim, another dealer, and then purchase Machine B from Joan for $21,000. Machines A and B qualify as like-kind property.
    a. Calculate Norm's recognized gain or loss and the basis of Machine B under the first option.
    b. Calculate Norm's recognized gain or loss and the basis of Machine B under the second option.
    c. Advise Norm on which option is preferable.

39. Gene exchanges real estate held for investment plus stock for real estate to be held for investment. The stock transferred has an adjusted basis of $30,000 and a fair market value of $20,000. The real estate transferred has an adjusted basis of $30,000 and a fair market value of $90,000. The real estate acquired has a fair market value of $110,000.
    a. What is Gene's realized gain or loss?
    b. His recognized gain or loss?
    c. The basis of the newly acquired real estate?

Decision Making

40. Audrey exchanges a warehouse with Dixon for an office building. Audrey's adjusted basis for her warehouse is $500,000. The fair market value of Dixon's office building is $545,000. Audrey's property has a $100,000 mortgage that Dixon assumes.
    a. Calculate Audrey's realized and recognized gain or loss.
    b. What is her adjusted basis for the office building?
    c. As an alternative, Dixon has proposed that he will transfer cash of $100,000 rather than assume the mortgage. Audrey would use the cash to pay off the mortgage. Advise Audrey on whether this alternative would be beneficial to her from a tax perspective.

41. Determine the realized, recognized, and postponed gain or loss and the new basis for each of the following like-kind exchanges:

	Adjusted Basis of Old Machine	Boot Given	Fair Market Value of New Asset	Boot Received
a.	$ 7,000	$ –0–	$12,000	$4,000
b.	14,000	2,000	15,000	–0–
c.	3,000	7,000	8,000	500
d.	22,000	–0–	32,000	–0–
e.	10,000	–0–	11,000	1,000
f.	10,000	–0–	8,000	–0–

42. Shontelle owns an apartment house that has an adjusted basis of $950,000 but is subject to a mortgage of $240,000. She transfers the apartment house to Dave and receives from him $150,000 in cash and an office building with a fair market value of $975,000 at the time of the exchange. Dave assumes the $240,000 mortgage on the apartment house.
    a. What is Shontelle's realized gain or loss?
    b. What is her recognized gain or loss?
    c. What is the basis of the newly acquired office building?

43. Melanie's office building (adjusted basis of $210,000) is destroyed by a tornado. Since Melanie has excess office space, she decides not to replace the building. Instead, she adds the proceeds to the working capital of her business. What is Melanie's recognized gain or loss if the insurance proceeds are:
    a. $300,000?
    b. $200,000?

44. Albert owns 100 acres of land on which he grows spruce Christmas trees. His adjusted basis for the land is $100,000. He receives condemnation proceeds of $10,000 when the city's new beltway takes 5 acres along the eastern boundary of his property. He also receives a severance award of $6,000 associated with the possible harmful effects of exhaust fumes on his Christmas trees. Albert invests the $16,000 in a growth mutual fund. Determine the tax consequences to Albert of the:
    a. Condemnation proceeds.
    b. Severance award.

45. For each of the following involuntary conversions, indicate whether the property acquired qualifies as replacement property, the recognized gain, and the basis for the property acquired:
    a. Frank owns a warehouse that is destroyed by a tornado. The space in the warehouse was rented to various tenants. The adjusted basis was $470,000. Frank uses all of the insurance proceeds of $700,000 to build a shopping mall in a neighboring community where no property has been damaged by tornadoes. The shopping mall is rented to various tenants.
    b. Ivan owns a warehouse that he uses in his business. The adjusted basis is $300,000. The warehouse is destroyed by fire. Because of economic conditions in the area, Ivan decides not to rebuild the warehouse. Instead, he uses all of the insurance proceeds of $400,000 to build a warehouse to be used in his business in another state.
    c. Ridge's personal residence is condemned as part of a local government project to widen the highway from two lanes to four lanes. The adjusted basis is $170,000. Ridge uses all of the condemnation proceeds of $200,000 to purchase another personal residence.
    d. Juanita owns a building that she uses in her retail business. The adjusted basis is $250,000. The building is destroyed by a hurricane. Because of an economic downturn in the area caused by the closing of a military base, Juanita decides to rent space for her retail outlet rather than to replace the building. She uses all of the insurance proceeds of $300,000 to buy a four-unit apartment building in another city. A realtor in that city will handle the rental of the apartments for her.
    e. Susan and Rick's personal residence is destroyed by a tornado. The adjusted basis was $170,000. Since they would like to travel, they decide not to acquire a replacement residence. Instead, they invest all of the insurance proceeds of $200,000 in a duplex, which they rent to tenants.

46. The building that houses LaToya's designer clothing store is destroyed in a mud slide associated with a flood on June 27, 2006. LaToya had anticipated the flood and moved her inventory, furniture, and fixtures to a warehouse outside the floodplain on June 20, 2006. Her adjusted basis for the building is $215,000, and she receives insurance proceeds of $240,000 on July 15, 2006. LaToya intends to purchase another building for her store, but would like to have time to find one in a safer location. Her taxable year ends on March 31.

    a. What are the earliest and latest dates that LaToya can make a qualified replacement?

    b. Assuming LaToya makes a qualified replacement costing $240,000, what are her realized gain, recognized gain, and basis for the replacement property?

    c. What are the earliest and latest dates that LaToya can make a qualified replacement if the form of the involuntary conversion is a condemnation by a governmental authority? She was officially notified of the pending condemnation on June 1, 2006, and the condemnation occurred on June 27, 2006.

47. Leslie's office building (adjusted basis of $325,000) is destroyed by a hurricane in November 2006. Leslie, a calendar year taxpayer, receives insurance proceeds of $450,000 in January 2007. Calculate Leslie's realized gain or loss, recognized gain or loss, and basis for the replacement property if she:

    a. Acquires a new office building for $460,000 in January 2007.

    b. Acquires a new office building for $430,000 in January 2007.

    c. Does not acquire replacement property.

Decision Making

48. Carlos's warehouse, which has an adjusted basis of $300,000 and a fair market value of $420,000, is condemned by an agency of the Federal government to make way for a highway interchange. The initial condemnation offer is $400,000. After substantial negotiations, the agency agrees to transfer to Carlos a surplus warehouse that he believes is worth $420,000.

    a. What are the recognized gain or loss and the basis of the replacement warehouse if Carlos's objective is to recognize as much gain as possible?

    b. Advise Carlos regarding what he needs to do by what date in order to achieve his objective.

49. What are the *maximum* postponed gain or loss and the basis for the replacement property for the following involuntary conversions?

	Property	Type of Conversion	Amount Realized	Adjusted Basis	Amount Reinvested
a.	Drugstore (business)	Casualty	$160,000	$130,000	$110,000
b.	Apartments (investment)	Condemned	100,000	125,000	175,000
c.	Grocery store (business)	Casualty	400,000	300,000	450,000
d.	Residence (personal)	Casualty	16,000	18,000	17,000
e.	Vacant lot (investment)	Condemned	240,000	160,000	220,000
f.	Residence (personal)	Casualty	20,000	18,000	19,000
g.	Residence (personal)	Condemned	18,000	20,000	26,000
h.	Apartments (investment)	Condemned	150,000	100,000	200,000

Decision Making

50. Rental property owned by Faye, a calendar year taxpayer, is destroyed by a tornado on January 1, 2006. Faye had originally paid $150,000 for the property ($125,000 allocated to the building and $25,000 allocated to the land). During the time Faye owned the property, MACRS deductions of $46,250 were claimed. MACRS deductions of $57,500 would have been claimed, except that Faye chose to forgo $11,250 one year when she had a net operating loss. Faye receives insurance proceeds of $60,000 in November 2006. As a result of continuing negotiations with the insurance company, Faye receives additional proceeds of $35,000 in August 2007.

    a. What is Faye's adjusted basis for the property?

    b. What is Faye's realized gain or loss on the involuntary conversion in 2006? In 2007?

c. What is the latest date that Faye can replace the involuntarily converted property to qualify for § 1033 postponement?

d. What is the latest date that Faye can replace the involuntarily converted property to qualify for § 1033 postponement if the form of the involuntary conversion is a condemnation?

e. What should Faye do regarding the omitted MACRS deductions of $11,250?

51. Karl purchased his residence on January 2, 2005, for $260,000 after having lived in it during 2004 as a tenant under a lease with an option to buy clause. On June 1, 2006, Karl sells the residence for $315,000. On June 13, 2006, Karl purchases a new residence for $360,000.

Decision Making

a. What is Karl's recognized gain? His basis for the new residence?

b. Assume instead that Karl purchased his original residence on January 2, 2004 (rather than on January 2, 2005). What is Karl's recognized gain? His basis for the new residence?

c. In (a), what could Karl do to minimize his recognized gain?

52. Taylor has owned and occupied her personal residence (adjusted basis of $190,000) for four years. In April 2006, she sells the residence for $300,000 (selling expenses are $20,000). On the same day as the sale, Taylor purchases another house for $350,000. Because of noisy neighbors, she sells the new house after just 10 months. The selling price is $483,000 (selling expenses are $18,000).

a. What is Taylor's recognized gain on the sale of the first residence?

b. What is Taylor's basis for her second residence?

c. What is Taylor's recognized gain on the sale of the second residence?

d. Assume instead that the sale of the second residence was due to Taylor's job transfer to another state. What is her recognized gain on the sale of the second residence?

53. Milton, who is single, listed his personal residence with a realtor on March 3, 2006, at a price of $250,000. He rejected several offers in the $200,000 range during the summer. Finally, on August 16, 2006, he and the purchaser signed a contract to sell for $245,000. The sale (i.e., closing) took place on September 7, 2006. The closing statement showed the following disbursements:

Realtor's commission	$ 14,000
Appraisal fee	500
Exterminator's certificate	300
Recording fees	400
Mortgage to First Bank	180,000
Cash to seller	49,800

Milton's adjusted basis for the house is $150,000. He owned and occupied the house for eight years. On October 1, 2006, Milton purchases another residence for $210,000.

a. Calculate Milton's recognized gain on the sale.

b. What is Milton's adjusted basis for the new residence?

c. Assume instead that the selling price is $735,000. What is Milton's recognized gain? His adjusted basis for the new residence?

54. Assuming § 121 applies, what are the realized, recognized, and excluded gain or loss and the new basis in each of the following cases?

a. Susan sold her residence for $390,000. The adjusted basis was $55,000. The selling expenses were $15,000. Repair expenses incurred to get the house ready to sell were $3,000. She did not reinvest in a new residence.

b. Rocky sold his residence for $270,000. The adjusted basis was $120,000. The selling expenses were $9,000. Repair expenses incurred to get the house ready to sell were $6,000. Rocky reinvested $260,000 in a new residence.

c. Veneia sold her residence for $465,000. The adjusted basis was $35,000. The selling expenses were $17,000. Repair expenses incurred to get the house ready to sell were $2,000. She reinvested $400,000 in a new residence.

d. Barry sold his residence for $70,000. The adjusted basis was $65,000. The selling expenses were $6,000. He reinvested $80,000 in a new residence.

e. Carl sold his residence for $100,000 in cash, and his mortgage is assumed by the buyer. The adjusted basis was $80,000; the mortgage, $50,000. The selling expenses were $4,000. Repair expenses incurred to get the house ready to sell were $2,000. He reinvested $120,000 in a new residence.

55. Pedro, age 57, is the sole owner of his principal residence. He has owned and occupied it for 10 years. Maria, his spouse, has also lived there for 10 years. He sells the house for a realized gain of $340,000. Pedro does not intend to acquire a replacement residence.
   a. Can Pedro use the § 121 exclusion if he and Maria file a joint return? If so, what are the available amount of the exclusion and the recognized gain?
   b. Can Pedro use the § 121 exclusion if he files a separate return? If so, what are the available amount of the exclusion and the recognized gain?
   c. Assume instead that the realized gain is $550,000 and a joint return is filed.
   d. Assume instead that the realized gain is $550,000 and separate returns are filed.
   e. Assume instead that Maria and Pedro have been married for only 18 months and that she has lived in his house only since their marriage. They file a joint return.

Decision Making

56. Meg and Walt are going to be married in three months. Meg has owned and lived in her home for 42 years, and Walt has owned and occupied his home for 35 years. They both have listed their homes for sale. They anticipate the sales results will be as follows:

	Meg	Walt
Selling price	$450,000	$190,000
Selling expenses	40,000	19,000
Adjusted basis	75,000	60,000

They intend to purchase a residence in an extended care facility for $400,000. They have come to you for advice regarding the following:
   a. What is their recognized gain if they marry before they sell their residences?
   b. What is their recognized gain if they marry after they sell their residences?
   c. Walt would prefer to invest his sales proceeds in the stock market. Does it matter whether the new residence is jointly owned or owned only by Meg?
   d. Should Meg and Walt delay their marriage if they have not yet sold their residences?

Communications

57. Nell, Nina, and Nora Sanders, who are sisters, sell their principal residence (owned as tenants in common) in which they have lived for the past 20 years. The youngest of the sisters is age 58. The selling price is $750,000, selling expenses and legal fees are $75,000, and the adjusted basis is $60,000 (the fair market value of the residence when inherited from their parents 20 years ago). Since the sisters are going to live in rental housing, they do not plan to acquire another residence. Nell has contacted you on behalf of the three sisters regarding the tax consequences of the sale.
   a. Write a letter to Nell advising her of the tax consequences and how taxes can be minimized. Nell's address is 100 Oak Avenue, Billings, MT 59101.
   b. Prepare a memo for the tax files.

Decision Making

58. Cisco, a calendar year taxpayer who is age 63, owns a residence in which he has lived for 28 years. The residence is destroyed by fire on August 8, 2006. The adjusted basis is $130,000, and the fair market value is $300,000. Cisco receives insurance proceeds of $300,000 for the residence on September 1, 2006. He is trying to decide whether to purchase a comparable house. He anticipates that he will retire in two years and will move to a warmer climate where he will rent in case he decides to live in different places.
   a. Advise Cisco of the tax consequences of replacing versus not replacing the residence.
   b. Which do you recommend to him?
   c. How would your answer in (a) change if the fair market value and insurance proceeds received were $500,000?

Decision Making

59. Jeff and Jill are divorced on August 1, 2006. According to the terms of the divorce decree, Jeff's ownership interest in the house is to be transferred to Jill in exchange for the release of marital rights. The house was separately owned by Jeff and on the date of the transfer has an adjusted basis of $175,000 and a fair market value of $200,000.

a.   Does the transfer cause recognized gain to either Jeff or Jill?

b.   What is the basis of the house to Jill?

c.   If instead Jeff sold the house to Jill for $200,000 two months prior to the divorce, would either Jeff or Jill have recognized gain?

d.   Which transaction, (a) or (c), would be preferable for Jeff?

CUMULATIVE PROBLEMS

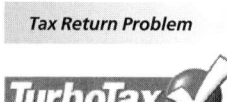

Tax Return Problem

60. Arnold Young, age 39, is single. He lives at 1507 Iris Lane, Albuquerque, NM 87131. His Social Security number is 999–55–2000. Arnold does not wish to have $3 go to the Presidential Election Campaign Fund.

Arnold was divorced in 2001 after 15 years of marriage. He pays alimony of $32,000 a year to his former spouse, Carol. Carol's Social Security number is 999–33–3000. Arnold's son, Tom, who is age 13, resides with Carol. Arnold pays child support of $9,000 per year. Carol has provided Arnold with a signed Form 8332 in which she releases the dependency deduction to him for 2005. Tom's Social Security number is 999–09–1000.

Arnold owns a sole proprietorship for which he uses the accrual method of accounting. His revenues and expenses for 2005 are as follows:

Sales revenue	$680,000
Cost of goods sold	405,000
Salary expense	85,000
Rent expense	29,000
Utilities	5,000
Telephone	3,000
Advertising	4,000
Bad debts	8,000
Depreciation	21,000
Health insurance*	10,000
Accounting and legal fees	4,000
Supplies	1,000

*$6,000 for employees and $4,000 for Arnold.

Other income received by Arnold includes the following:

Dividend income:	
Swan, Inc.	$ 9,000
Wren, Inc.	4,000
Interest income:	
First Bank	5,000
Second Bank	2,500
City of Asheville bonds	11,000
Lottery winnings (tickets purchased cost $1,000)	9,000

During the year, Arnold and his sole proprietorship had the following property transactions:

a.   Sold Blue, Inc. stock for $32,000 on March 12, 2005. He had purchased the stock on September 5, 2002, for $36,000.

b.   Received an inheritance of $105,000 from his Uncle Henry. Arnold used the $105,000 to purchase Green, Inc. stock on May 15, 2005.

c.   Received Orange, Inc. stock worth $9,500 as a gift from his Aunt Jane on June 17, 2005. Her adjusted basis for the stock was $5,000. No gift taxes were paid on the transfer. Aunt Jane had purchased the stock on April 1, 1999. Arnold sold the stock on July 1, 2005, for $20,000.

d.   On July 15, 2005, Arnold sold one-half of the Green, Inc. stock for $24,000.

e.   Arnold was notified on August 1, 2005, that Yellow, Inc. stock he purchased from a colleague on September 1, 2004, for $17,500 had become worthless. While he perceived that the investment was risky, he did not anticipate that the corporation would declare bankruptcy.

f. On August 15, 2005, Arnold received a parcel of land in Phoenix worth $180,000 in exchange for a parcel of land he owned in Tucson. Since the Tucson parcel was worth $200,000, he also received $20,000 cash. Arnold's adjusted basis for the Tucson parcel was $175,000. He originally purchased it on September 18, 2002.

g. On December 1, 2005, Arnold sold the condominium in which he had been living for the past 10 years. The sales price was $425,000, selling expenses were $25,500, and repair expenses related to the sale were $5,000. Arnold and Carol had purchased the condominium as joint owners for $142,000. Arnold had received Carol's ownership interest as part of the divorce proceedings. The fair market value at that time was $200,000.

Arnold's potential itemized deductions, exclusive of the aforementioned information, are as follows:

Medical expenses (before the 7.5% floor)	$ 8,000
Property taxes on residence	5,500
State income taxes	3,000
Charitable contributions	11,000
Mortgage interest on residence	8,500
Sales taxes paid	4,000

During the year, Arnold makes estimated Federal income tax payments of $25,000.

Compute Arnold's lowest net tax payable or refund due for 2005, assuming he makes any available elections that will reduce the tax. If you use tax forms for your computations, you will need Forms 1040, 8332, and 8824 and Schedules A, B, C, D, and SE. Suggested software: TurboTax.

Tax Return Problem

Decision Making

Communications

61. Tammy Walker, age 37, is a self-employed accountant. Tammy's Social Security number is 333–40–1111. Her address is 101 Glass Road, Richmond, VA 23236. Her income and expenses associated with her accounting practice for 2006 are as follows:

Revenues (cash receipts during 2006)	$320,000
Expenses	
Salaries	$ 85,000
Office supplies	2,100
Postage	2,900
Depreciation of equipment	30,000
Telephone	800
	$120,800

Since Tammy is a cash method taxpayer, she does not record her receivables as revenue until she receives cash payment. At the beginning of 2006, her accounts receivable were $90,000, and the balance had decreased to $35,000 by the end of the year. The balance on December 31, 2006, would have been $40,000, except that an account for $5,000 had become uncollectible in November.

Tammy used one room in her 10-room house as the office for her accounting practice (300 square feet out of a total square footage of 3,000). She paid the following expenses related to the house during 2006:

Utilities	$3,600
Insurance	1,000
Property taxes	5,000
Repairs	2,700

Tammy had purchased the house on September 1, 2005, for $275,000 (exclusive of land cost).

Tammy has one child, Thomas, age 16. Thomas lives with his father during the summer and with Tammy for the rest of the year. Tammy can document that she spent $16,000 during 2006 for the child's support. The father normally provides about $8,000 per year, but this year he gave Thomas a new car for Christmas. The cost of the car was $25,000. The divorce decree is silent regarding the dependency exemption for Thomas. Tammy does not provide her former spouse with a signed Form 8332 for 2006.

Under the terms of the divorce decree, Tammy is to receive alimony of $10,000 per month. The payments will terminate at Tammy's death or at her remarriage.

Tammy provides part of the support of her mother, age 67. The total support in 2006 for her mother was as follows:

Social Security benefits	$5,200
From Tammy	2,900
From Bob, Tammy's brother	2,000
From Susan, Tammy's sister	1,900

Bob and Susan have both indicated their willingness to sign a multiple support waiver form if it will benefit Tammy.

Tammy's deductible itemized deductions during 2006, excluding any itemized deductions related to the house, were $16,000. She made estimated tax payments of $98,000.

Part 1—Tax Computation
Compute Tammy's lowest net tax payable or refund due for 2006.

Part 2—Tax Planning
Tammy and her former husband have been discussing the $10,000 alimony he pays her each month. Because his new wife has a health problem, he does not feel that he can afford to continue to pay the $10,000 each month. He is in the 15% tax bracket. If Tammy will agree to decrease the amount by 25%, he will agree that the amount paid is not alimony for tax purposes. Assume that the other data used in calculating Tammy's taxable income for 2006 will apply for her 2007 tax return. Write a letter to Tammy that contains your advice on whether she should agree to her former husband's proposal. Also prepare a memo for the tax files.

RESEARCH PROBLEMS

Note: Solutions to Research Problems can be prepared by using the **RIA Checkpoint**® **Student Edition** online research product, which is available to accompany this text. It is also possible to prepare solutions to the Research Problems by using tax research materials found in a standard tax library.

Research Problem 1. Penelope and Stuart have been married for nine years. For the past six years, they have lived in the house Penelope owns at 100 Oriena Avenue. In July 2005, Stuart purchases the house from Penelope for $350,000. Her adjusted basis for the house is $130,000. No closing costs are incurred.

Penelope and Stuart continue to live in the house until February 2006 when Stuart sells it for $390,000. Selling expenses are $12,000. Penelope and Stuart file separate returns in 2006. Determine if Stuart is eligible for the § 121 exclusion and, if so, the amount of the exclusion. Also determine his recognized gain.

Partial list of research aids:
§ 121(d)(3)(A).

Research Problem 2. For three years, Amos, a calendar year taxpayer, has owned stock that is qualified small business stock under § 1045. The stock has an adjusted basis of $10,000. On July 2, 2006, he sells the stock for $100,000. On August 3, 2006, he uses the sales proceeds of $100,000 to purchase other qualified small business stock. If possible, Amos would like to defer any recognized gain on the sale of the stock. Advise Amos on the tax consequences of the sale and the subsequent purchase and the procedure he must follow to achieve his deferral objective.

Research Problem 3. Brown Construction, Inc., is in the road construction business. Brown exchanges a grader used in its business and $45,000 in cash for a scraper to be used in its business. The adjusted basis of the grader is $50,000, and the fair market value of the scraper is $102,000. What are the tax consequences to Brown of the exchange?

Research Problem 4. Asa operated his business in a building on Mason Drive. Due to changing residential housing patterns in the city, he decided to move the business to a new location on Leigh Lane. His adjusted basis for the Mason Drive property is $120,000, and the fair market value is $500,000. He purchased the Leigh Lane property for $500,000 on September 1, 2006. Asa quitclaimed title to the Leigh Lane property to Ivory Enterprises on September 1, 2006, in exchange for a nonrecourse and non-interest-bearing single payment note for $500,000 (to be paid at the second closing). Ivory was to have a building constructed on the Leigh Lane property in accordance with specifications provided by Asa. The construction of the building was financed by a $700,000 note that was guaranteed by Asa and was nonrecourse to Ivory.

Another agreement provided that Asa would convey the Mason Drive property to Ivory on completion of the building in exchange for the Leigh Lane property and the new building. At that time, Asa would assume the $700,000 note.

On December 1, the Leigh Lane property was conveyed to Asa, the Mason Drive property was conveyed to Ivory, and Ivory paid the $500,000 note to Asa (the second closing). Asa assumed the $700,000 note associated with the construction and reported his recognized gain as follows:

	Exchange of Mason Drive	Sale of Leigh Lane
Amount realized	$ 500,000	$ 1,210,000
Basis	(120,000)	(1,200,000)
Realized gain	$ 380,000	$ 10,000
Recognized gain	$ –0–*	$ 10,000

*§ 1031 like-kind exchange.

An IRS agent treated the transactions as the sale of the Mason Drive property and a § 1031 exchange of the Leigh Lane property, producing a recognized gain of $380,000 rather than $10,000.

Evaluate the position of the IRS and of Asa.

Research Problem 5. Frank and Karen Ames owned an auto dealership in Trenton. The Trenton Redevelopment Authority (TRA) prepared a redevelopment plan for the eastern part of Trenton that included an auto mall.

Believing that it needed a domestic auto dealer as the mall anchor, the TRA proposed that the Ames auto dealership relocate to the mall. Frank and Karen declined the TRA's proposal and indicated that they were going to relocate their dealership to Newark. Subsequently, however, their negotiations with Newark terminated.

At this time, TRA officials approved the use of threats of condemnation against the Ames dealership to get them to relocate to the auto mall. On several occasions, the officials told Frank and Karen that the TRA would condemn their current auto dealership unless they agreed to sell the property to the TRA and relocate to the mall. In addition, the TRA sent them a letter that included the following: "As you are aware, the TRA is authorized to acquire property by the use of eminent domain. If these negotiations are unsuccessful, staff will recommend to the TRA board that they continue with proceedings for the acquisition of your property through the exercise of the power of eminent domain." Although the subsequent negotiations were hostile, Frank and Karen ultimately sold their property to the TRA. They used the proceeds to purchase land in the auto mall and relocated their business there. Realized gain of $600,000 was deferred through the use of a § 1033 election.

An IRS agent has concluded that the sale and subsequent acquisition do not qualify for § 1033 deferral treatment. According to the agent, condemnation did not take place, and Frank and Karen did not sell the property under a "threat of condemnation."

Frank and Karen Ames have come to you for tax advice.

Use the tax resources of the Internet to address the following questions. Do not restrict your search to the World Wide Web, but include a review of newsgroups and general reference materials, practitioner sites and resources, primary sources of the tax law, chat rooms and discussion groups, and other opportunities.

 Internet *Activity*

Research Problem 6. Find two newspaper stories about transactions to which you believe the involuntary conversion rules could apply. Do not limit your search to individual taxpayers.

Research Problem 7. A number of public policy think tanks, taxpayer unions, and other private interest groups have proposed changes to the tax rules that apply to like-kind exchanges of realty. Summarize several of these proposals, including your assessment of the motivations underlying the suggested changes.

Research Problem 8. Find and print a Form 8824, Like Kind Exchanges. Fill in the form as part of the requirements for Problem 35.

Property Transactions: Capital Gains and Losses

LEARNING OBJECTIVES

After completing Chapter 16, you should be able to:

LO.1
Understand the rationale for separate reporting of capital gains and losses.

LO.2
Distinguish capital assets from ordinary assets.

LO.3
Understand the relevance of a sale or exchange to classification as a capital gain or loss and apply the special rules for the capital gain or loss treatment of the retirement of corporate obligations, options, patents, franchises, and lease cancellation payments.

LO.4
Determine whether the holding period for a capital asset is long term or short term.

LO.5
Describe the beneficial tax treatment for capital gains and the detrimental tax treatment for capital losses for noncorporate taxpayers.

LO.6
Describe the tax treatment for capital gains and the detrimental tax treatment for capital losses for corporate taxpayers.

LO.7
Identify tax planning opportunities arising from the sale or exchange of capital assets.

LO.1

Understand the rationale for separate reporting of capital gains and losses.

General Considerations

Rationale for Separate Reporting of Capital Gains and Losses

Fourteen years ago, a taxpayer purchased 100 shares of IBM stock for $17 a share. This year the taxpayer sells the shares for $80 a share. Should the $63 per share gain receive any special tax treatment? The $63 gain has built up over 14 years, so it may not be fair to tax it the same as income that was all earned this year.

What if the stock had been purchased for $80 per share and sold for $17 a share? Should the loss be fully deductible? The tax law has an intricate approach to answering these investment activity–related questions.

As you study this chapter, keep in mind that how investment-related gains and losses are taxed can dramatically affect whether taxpayers make investments and which investments are made. Except for a brief discussion in Chapter 3, earlier chapters dwelt on how to determine the amount of gain or loss from a property disposition, but did not discuss the classification of gains and losses. This chapter will focus on that topic.

The tax law requires **capital gains** and **capital losses** to be separated from other types of gains and losses. There are two reasons for this treatment. First, long-term capital gains may be taxed at a lower rate than ordinary gains. An *alternative tax computation* is used to determine the tax when taxable income includes net long-term capital gain. Capital gains and losses must therefore be matched with one another to see if a net long-term capital gain exists. The alternative tax computation is discussed later in the chapter under Tax Treatment of Capital Gains and Losses of Noncorporate Taxpayers.

The second reason the Code requires separate reporting of gains and losses and a determination of their tax character is that a net capital loss is only deductible up to $3,000 per year. Excess loss over the annual limit carries over and may be deductible in a future tax year. Capital gains and losses must be matched with one another to see if a net capital loss exists.

TAX *in the News*   **AVOIDING A RECOGNIZED GAIN**

Until recently the New York Stock Exchange (NYSE) was not a corporation. Instead, it was a partnership owned by its members. A membership in the NYSE was sold for $3 million during 2005. In early 2006, the NYSE merged with Archipelago Holdings, Inc. The members of the NYSE exchanged their membership interests in the NYSE for shares in the new corporation resulting from the merger of these two entities. If proper tax planning was done, the NYSE members did not have a *recognized* gain or loss from this transaction.

For these reasons, capital gains and losses must be distinguished from other types of gains and losses. Most of this chapter and the next chapter describe the intricate rules for determining what type of gains and losses the taxpayer has.

As a result of the need to distinguish and separately match capital gains and losses, the individual tax forms include very extensive reporting requirements for capital gains and losses. This chapter explains the principles underlying the forms. The forms are illustrated with an example at the end of the chapter.

General Scheme of Taxation

Recognized gains and losses must be properly classified. Proper classification depends upon three characteristics:

- The tax status of the property.
- The manner of the property's disposition.
- The holding period of the property.

The three possible tax statuses are capital asset, § 1231 asset, or ordinary asset. Property disposition may be by sale, exchange, casualty, theft, or condemnation.

There are two holding periods: short term and long term. The short-term holding period is one year or less. The long-term holding period is more than one year.

The major focus of this chapter is capital gains and losses. Capital gains and losses usually result from the disposition of a capital asset. The most common disposition is a sale of the asset. Capital gains and losses can also result from the disposition of § 1231 assets, which is discussed in Chapter 17.

Capital Assets

Definition of a Capital Asset

LO.2

Distinguish capital assets from ordinary assets.

Personal use assets and investment assets are the most common capital assets owned by individual taxpayers. Personal use assets usually include items such as clothing, recreational equipment, a residence, and automobiles. Investment assets usually include investments in mutual funds, corporate stocks and bonds, government bonds, and vacant land. Remember, however, that losses from the sale or exchange of personal use assets are not recognized. Therefore, the classification of such losses as capital losses can be ignored.

Due to the historical preferential treatment of capital gains, taxpayers have preferred that gains be capital gains rather than ordinary gains. As a result, a great many statutes, cases, and rulings have accumulated in the attempt to define what is and what is not a capital asset.

Capital assets are not directly defined in the Code. Instead, § 1221(a) defines what is *not* a capital asset. A **capital asset** is property held by the taxpayer (whether or not it is connected with the taxpayer's business) that is *not* any of the following:

- Inventory or property held primarily for sale to customers in the ordinary course of a business. The Supreme Court, in *Malat v. Riddell,* defined *primarily* as meaning *of first importance* or *principally.*[1]
- Accounts and notes receivable acquired from the sale of inventory or acquired for services rendered in the ordinary course of business.
- Depreciable property or real estate used in a business.
- Certain copyrights; literary, musical, or artistic compositions; or letters, memoranda, or similar property held by (1) a taxpayer whose efforts created the property; (2) in the case of a letter, memorandum, or similar property, a taxpayer for whom it was produced; or (3) a taxpayer in whose hands the basis of the property is determined, for purposes of determining gain from a sale or exchange, in whole or in part by reference to the basis of such property in the hands of a taxpayer described in (1) or (2).
- U.S. government publications that are (1) received by a taxpayer from the U.S. government other than by purchase at the price at which they are offered for sale to the public or (2) held by a taxpayer whose basis, for purposes of determining gain from a sale or exchange, is determined by reference to a taxpayer described in (1).
- Supplies of a type regularly used or consumed in the ordinary course of a business.

The Code defines what is not a capital asset. From the preceding list, it is apparent that inventory, accounts and notes receivable, supplies, and most fixed assets of a business are not capital assets. Often, the only business asset that is a capital asset is goodwill. The following discussion provides further detail on each part of the capital asset definition.

Inventory.   What constitutes inventory is determined by the taxpayer's business.

EXAMPLE 1

Green Company buys and sells used cars. Its cars are inventory. Its gains from the sale of the cars are ordinary income. ∎

EXAMPLE 2

Soong sells her personal use automobile at a $500 gain. The automobile is a personal use asset and, therefore, a capital asset. The gain is a capital gain. ∎

Accounts and Notes Receivable.   Collection of an accrual basis account receivable usually does not result in a gain or loss because the amount collected equals the receivable's basis. The sale of an account or note receivable may generate a gain or loss, and the gain or loss is ordinary because the receivable is not a capital asset. The sale of an accrual basis receivable may result in a gain or loss because it will probably be sold for more or less than its basis. A cash basis account receivable has no basis. Sale of such a receivable generates a gain. Collection of a cash basis receivable generates ordinary income rather than a gain. A gain usually requires a sale of the receivable. See the discussion of Sale or Exchange later in this chapter.

EXAMPLE 3

Oriole Company has accounts receivable of $100,000. Because it needs working capital, it sells the receivables for $83,000 to a financial institution. If Oriole is an accrual basis taxpayer, it has a $17,000 ordinary loss. Revenue of $100,000 would have been recorded and a $100,000 basis would have been established when the receivable was created. If Oriole is a

---

[1]66–1 USTC ¶9317, 17 AFTR2d 604, 86 S.Ct. 1030 (USSC, 1966).

cash basis taxpayer, it has $83,000 of ordinary income because it would not have recorded any revenue earlier; thus, the receivable has no tax basis. ∎

Business Fixed Assets. Depreciable personal property and real estate (both depreciable and nondepreciable) used by a business are not capital assets. Thus, *business fixed assets* are generally not capital assets.

The Code has a very complex set of rules pertaining to such property. One of these rules is discussed under Real Property Subdivided for Sale in this chapter; the remainder of the rules are discussed in Chapter 17. Although business fixed assets are not capital assets, a long-term capital gain can sometimes result from their sale. Chapter 17 discusses the potential capital gain treatment for business fixed assets under § 1231.

Copyrights and Creative Works. Generally, the person whose efforts led to the copyright or creative work has an ordinary asset, not a capital asset. *Creative works* include the works of authors, composers, and artists. Also, the person for whom a letter, memorandum, or other similar property was created has an ordinary asset. Finally, a person receiving a copyright, creative work, letter, memorandum, or similar property by gift from the creator or the person for whom the work was created has an ordinary asset.

EXAMPLE 4

Wanda is a part-time music composer. A music publisher purchases one of her songs for $5,000. Wanda has a $5,000 ordinary gain from the sale of an ordinary asset. ∎

EXAMPLE 5

Ed received a letter from the President of the United States in 1982. In the current year, Ed sells the letter to a collector for $300. Ed has a $300 ordinary gain from the sale of an ordinary asset (because the letter was created for Ed). ∎

EXAMPLE 6

Isabella gives a song she composed to her son. The son sells the song to a music publisher for $5,000. The son has a $5,000 ordinary gain from the sale of an ordinary asset. If the son inherits the song from Isabella, his basis for the song is its fair market value at Isabella's death. The song is a capital asset because the son's basis is not related to Isabella's basis for the song. ∎

(Patents are subject to special statutory rules discussed later in the chapter.)

ETHICAL *Considerations*   **INVENTORY OR CAPITAL ASSET?**

Mathias has been the sole proprietor of a clothing store for many years. He intends to retire after holding a "liquidation sale." He wants to avoid ordinary income from the sale of the business inventory, so he shuts down the store for one month and then begins the liquidation sale. Mathias tells you (his tax return preparer) to report the liquidation sale proceeds as capital gain because he was no longer using those assets in a business at the time of the sale, but was holding them for investment. Evaluate the propriety of Mathias's plan.

U.S. Government Publications. U.S. government publications received from the U.S. government (or its agencies) for a reduced price are not capital assets. This prevents a taxpayer from later donating the publications to charity and claiming a charitable contribution equal to the fair market value of the publications. A charitable contribution of a capital asset generally yields a deduction equal to the fair market value. A charitable contribution of an ordinary asset generally yields a deduction equal to less than the fair market value. If such property is received by gift from the original purchaser, the property is not a capital asset to the donee. (For a more comprehensive explanation of charitable contributions of property, refer to Chapter 10.)

Effect of Judicial Action

Court decisions play an important role in the definition of capital assets. Because the Code only lists categories of what are *not* capital assets, judicial interpretation is sometimes required to determine whether a specific item fits into one of those categories. The Supreme Court follows a literal interpretation of the categories. For instance, corporate stock is not mentioned in § 1221. Thus, corporate stock is *usually* a capital asset. However, what if corporate stock is purchased for resale to customers? Then it is *inventory* and not a capital asset because inventory is one of the categories in § 1221. (See the discussion of Dealers in Securities below.)

A Supreme Court decision was required to distinguish between capital asset and non-capital asset status when a taxpayer who did not normally acquire stock for resale to customers acquired stock with the intention of resale.[2] The Court decided that since the stock was not acquired primarily for sale to customers (the taxpayer did not sell the stock to its regular customers), the stock was a capital asset.

Often the crux of the capital asset determination hinges on whether the asset is held for investment purposes (capital asset) or business purposes (ordinary asset). The taxpayer's *use* of the property often provides objective evidence.

EXAMPLE 7

David's business buys an expensive painting. If the painting is used to decorate David's office and is not of investment quality, the painting is depreciable and, therefore, not a capital asset. If David's business is buying and selling paintings, the painting is inventory and, therefore, an ordinary asset. If the painting is of investment quality and the business purchased it for investment, the painting is a capital asset, even though it serves a decorative purpose in David's office. *Investment quality* generally means that the painting is expected to appreciate in value. If David depreciates the painting, that would be objective evidence that the painting is held for use in his business, is not being held for investment or as inventory, and is not a capital asset. ∎

Because of the uncertainty associated with capital asset status, Congress has enacted several Code Sections to clarify the definition. These statutory expansions of the capital asset definition are discussed in the following section.

Statutory Expansions

Congress has often expanded the § 1221 general definition of what is *not* a capital asset.

Dealers in Securities. As a general rule, securities (stocks, bonds, and other financial instruments) held by a dealer are considered to be inventory and are, therefore, not subject to capital gain or loss treatment. A *dealer in securities* is a merchant (e.g., a brokerage firm) that regularly engages in the purchase and resale of securities to customers. The dealer must identify any securities being held for investment. Generally, if a dealer clearly identifies certain securities as held for investment purposes by the close of business on the acquisition date, gain from the securities' sale will be capital gain. However, the gain will not be capital gain if the dealer ceases to hold the securities for investment prior to the sale. Losses are capital losses if at any time the securities have been clearly identified by the dealer as held for investment.[3]

---

[2]*Arkansas Best v. Comm.*, 88–1 USTC ¶9210, 61 AFTR2d 88–655, 108 S.Ct. 971 (USSC, 1988).

[3]§§ 1236(a) and (b) and Reg. § 1.1236–1(a).

Tracy is a securities dealer. She purchases 100 shares of Swan stock. If Tracy takes no further action, the stock is inventory and an ordinary asset. If she designates in her records that the stock is held for investment, the stock is a capital asset. Tracy must designate the investment purpose by the close of business on the acquisition date. If Tracy maintains her investment purpose and later sells the stock, the gain or loss is capital gain or loss. If Tracy redesignates the stock as held for resale (inventory) and then sells it, any gain is ordinary, but any loss is capital loss. Stock designated as held for investment and then sold at a loss always yields a capital loss. ■

EXAMPLE 8

Real Property Subdivided for Sale. Substantial real property development activities may result in the owner being considered a dealer for tax purposes. Income from the sale of real estate property lots is treated as the sale of inventory (ordinary income) if the owner is considered to be a dealer. However, § 1237 allows real estate investors capital gain treatment if they engage *only* in *limited* development activities. To be eligible for § 1237 treatment, the following requirements must be met:

- The taxpayer may not be a corporation.
- The taxpayer may not be a real estate dealer.
- No substantial improvements may be made to the lots sold. *Substantial* generally means more than a 10 percent increase in the value of a lot. Shopping centers and other commercial or residential buildings are considered substantial, while filling, draining, leveling, and clearing operations are not.
- The taxpayer must have held the lots sold for at least 5 years, except for inherited property. The substantial improvements test is less stringent if the property is held at least 10 years.

qualified to be capital assets.

If the preceding requirements are met, all gain is capital gain until the tax year in which the *sixth* lot is sold. Sales of contiguous lots to a single buyer in the same transaction count as the sale of one lot. Beginning with the tax year the *sixth* lot is sold, some of the gain may be ordinary income. Five percent of the revenue from lot sales is potential ordinary income. That potential ordinary income is offset by any selling expenses from the lot sales. Practically, sales commissions often are at least 5 percent of the sales price, so none of the gain is treated as ordinary income.

Section 1237 does not apply to losses. A loss from the sale of subdivided real property is an ordinary loss unless the property qualifies as a capital asset under § 1221. The following example illustrates the application of § 1237.

EXAMPLE 9

Jack owns a large tract of land and subdivides it for sale. Assume Jack meets all the requirements of § 1237 and during the tax year sells the first 10 lots to 10 different buyers for $10,000 each. Jack's basis in each lot sold is $3,000, and he incurs total selling expenses of $4,000 on the sales. Jack's gain is computed as follows:

Selling price (10 × $10,000)	$100,000	
Less: Selling expenses (10 × $400)	(4,000)	
Amount realized		$ 96,000
Basis (10 × $3,000)		(30,000)
Realized and recognized gain		$ 66,000
Classification of recognized gain:		
Ordinary income		
Five percent of selling price (5% × $100,000)	$ 5,000	
Less: Selling expenses	(4,000)	
Ordinary gain		1,000
Capital gain		$ 65,000

← gain

— ordinary gain
— capital gain

Nonbusiness Bad Debts. A loan not made in the ordinary course of business is classified as a nonbusiness receivable. In the year the receivable becomes completely worthless, it is a *nonbusiness bad debt*, and the bad debt is treated as a short-term capital loss. Even if the receivable was outstanding for more than one year, the loss is still a short-term capital loss. Chapter 7 discusses nonbusiness bad debts more thoroughly.

Sale or Exchange

Recognition of capital gain or loss usually requires a sale or exchange of a capital asset. The Code uses the term **sale or exchange**, but does not define it. Generally, a property sale involves the receipt of money by the seller and/or the assumption by the purchaser of the seller's liabilities. An exchange involves the transfer of property for other property. Thus, an involuntary conversion (casualty, theft, or condemnation) is not a sale or exchange. In several situations, the determination of whether a sale or exchange has taken place has been clarified by the enactment of Code Sections that specifically provide for sale or exchange treatment.

Recognized gains or losses from the cancellation, lapse, expiration, or any other termination of a right or obligation with respect to personal property (other than stock) that is or would be a capital asset in the hands of the taxpayer are capital gains or losses.[4] See the discussion under Options later in the chapter for more details.

Worthless Securities and § 1244 Stock

Occasionally, securities such as stock and, especially, bonds may become worthless due to the insolvency of their issuer. If such a security is a capital asset, the loss is deemed to have occurred as the result of a sale or exchange on the *last day* of the tax year.[5] This last-day rule may have the effect of converting what otherwise would have been a short-term capital loss into a long-term capital loss. See Treatment of Capital Losses later in this chapter.

Section 1244 allows an ordinary deduction on disposition of stock at a loss. The stock must be that of a small business company, and the ordinary deduction is limited to $50,000 ($100,000 for married individuals filing jointly) per year. For a more detailed discussion, refer to Chapter 7.

Special Rule—Retirement of Corporate Obligations

A debt obligation (e.g., a bond or note payable) may have a tax basis in excess of or less than its redemption value because it may have been acquired at a premium or discount. Consequently, the collection of the redemption value may result in a loss

---

[4]§ 1234A.   [5]§ 165(g)(1).

or gain. Generally, the collection of a debt obligation is *treated* as a sale or exchange.[6] Therefore, any loss or gain can be a capital loss or capital gain because a sale or exchange has taken place. However, if the debt obligation was issued by a human being prior to June 9, 1997, and/or purchased by the taxpayer prior to June 9, 1997, the collection of the debt obligation is not a sale or exchange.

EXAMPLE 10

Fran acquires $1,000 of Osprey Corporation bonds for $980 in the open market. If the bonds are held to maturity, the $20 difference between Fran's collection of the $1,000 redemption value and her cost of $980 is treated as capital gain. If the obligation had been issued to Fran by an individual prior to June 9, 1997, her $20 gain would be ordinary, since she did not sell or exchange the debt. ∎

Original Issue Discount. The benefit of the sale or exchange exception that allows a capital gain from the collection of certain obligations is reduced when the obligation has original issue discount. **Original issue discount (OID)** arises when the issue price of a debt obligation is less than the maturity value of the obligation. OID must generally be amortized over the life of the debt obligation using the effective interest method. The OID amortization increases the basis of the bond. Most new publicly traded bond issues do not carry OID since the stated interest rate is set to make the market price on issue the same as the bond's face amount. In addition, even if the issue price is less than the face amount, the difference is not considered to be OID if the difference is less than one-fourth of 1 percent of the redemption price at maturity multiplied by the number of years to maturity.[7]

In the case where OID does exist, it may or may not have to be amortized, depending upon the date the obligation was issued. When OID is amortized, the amount of gain upon collection, sale, or exchange of the obligation is correspondingly reduced. The obligations covered by the OID amortization rules and the method of amortization are presented in §§ 1272–1275. Similar rules for other obligations can be found in §§ 1276–1288.

EXAMPLE 11

Jerry purchases $10,000 of newly issued White Corporation bonds for $6,000. The bonds have OID of $4,000. Jerry must amortize the discount over the life of the bonds. The OID amortization *increases* his interest income. (The bonds were selling at a discount because the market rate of interest was greater than the bonds' interest rate.) After Jerry has amortized $1,800 of OID, he sells the bonds for $8,000. Jerry has a capital gain of $200 [$8,000 − ($6,000 cost + $1,800 OID amortization)]. The OID amortization rules prevent him from converting ordinary interest income into capital gain. Without the OID amortization, Jerry would have capital gain of $2,000 ($8,000 − $6,000 cost). ∎

Options

Frequently, a potential buyer of property wants some time to make the purchase decision, but wants to control the sale and/or the sale price in the meantime. **Options** are used to achieve these objectives. The potential purchaser (grantee) pays the property owner (grantor) for an option on the property. The grantee then becomes the option holder. The option usually sets a price at which the grantee can buy the property and expires after a specified period of time.

Sale of an Option. A grantee may sell or exchange the option rather than exercising it or letting it expire. Generally, the grantee's sale or exchange of the option results in capital gain or loss if the option property is (or would be) a capital asset to the grantee.[8]

---

[6]§ 1271.
[7]§ 1273(a)(3).

[8]§ 1234(a) and Reg. § 1.1234–1(a)(1). Stock options are discussed in Chapter 19.

EXAMPLE 12

Rosa wants to buy some vacant land for investment purposes. She cannot afford the full purchase price. Instead, she convinces the landowner (grantor) to sell her the right to purchase the land for $100,000 anytime in the next two years. Rosa (grantee) pays $3,000 to obtain this option to buy the land. The option is a capital asset for Rosa because if she actually purchased the land, the land would be a capital asset. Three months after purchasing the option, Rosa sells it for $7,000. She has a $4,000 ($7,000 − $3,000) short-term capital gain on this sale since she held the option for one year or less. ■

Failure to Exercise Options. If an option holder (grantee) fails to exercise the option, the lapse of the option is considered a sale or exchange on the option expiration date. Thus, the loss is a capital loss if the property subject to the option is (or would be) a capital asset in the hands of the grantee.

The grantor of an option on *stocks, securities, commodities, or commodity futures* receives short-term capital gain treatment upon the expiration of the option. Options on property other than stocks, securities, commodities, or commodity futures result in ordinary income to the grantor when the option expires. For example, an individual investor who owns certain stock (a capital asset) may sell a call option, entitling the buyer of the option to acquire the stock at a specified price higher than the value at the date the option is granted. The writer of the call receives a premium (e.g., 10 percent) for writing the option. If the price of the stock does not increase during the option period, the option will expire unexercised. Upon the expiration of the option, the grantor must recognize short-term capital gain. These provisions do not apply to options held for sale to customers (the inventory of a securities dealer).

Exercise of Options by Grantee. If the option is exercised, the amount paid for the option is added to the optioned property's selling price. This increases the gain (or reduces the loss) to the grantor resulting from the sale of the property. The grantor's gain or loss is capital or ordinary depending on the tax status of the property. The grantee adds the cost of the option to the basis of the property purchased.

EXAMPLE 13

On September 1, 2002, Wes purchases 100 shares of Eagle Company stock for $5,000. On April 1, 2006, he writes a call option on the stock, giving the grantee the right to buy the stock for $6,000 during the following six-month period. Wes (the grantor) receives a call premium of $500 for writing the call.

- If the call is exercised by the grantee on August 1, 2006, Wes has $1,500 ($6,000 + $500 − $5,000) of long-term capital gain from the sale of the stock. The grantee has a $6,500 ($500 option premium + $6,000 purchase price) basis for the stock.
- Assume that Wes decides to sell his stock prior to exercise for $6,000 and enters into a closing transaction by purchasing a call on 100 shares of Eagle Company stock for $5,000. Since the Eagle stock is selling for $6,000, Wes must pay a call premium of $1,000. He recognizes a $500 short-term capital loss [$1,000 (call premium paid) − $500 (call premium received)] on the closing transaction. On the actual sale of the Eagle stock, Wes has a long-term capital gain of $1,000 [$6,000 (selling price) − $5,000 (cost)]. The grantee is not affected by Wes's closing transaction. The original option is still in existence, and the grantee's tax consequences will depend on what action the grantee takes—exercising the option, letting the option expire, or selling the option.
- Assume that the original option expired unexercised. Wes has a $500 short-term capital gain equal to the call premium received for writing the option. This gain is not recognized until the option expires. The grantee has a loss from expiration of the option. The nature of the loss will depend upon whether the option was a capital asset or an ordinary asset. ■

Concept Summary 16–1 summarizes the rules for options.

CONCEPT SUMMARY   16–1

Options

Event	Effect on	
	Grantor	**Grantee**
Option is granted.	Receives value and has a contract obligation (a liability).	Pays value and has a contract right (an asset).
Option expires.	Has a short-term capital gain if the option property is stocks, securities, commodities, or commodity futures. Otherwise, gain is ordinary income.	Has a loss (capital loss if option property would have been a capital asset for the grantee).
Option is exercised.	Amount received for option increases proceeds from sale of the option property.	Amount paid for option becomes part of the basis of the option property purchased.
Option is sold or exchanged by grantee.	Result depends upon whether option later expires or is exercised (see above).	Could have gain or loss (capital gain or loss if option property would have been a capital asset for the grantee).

Patents

Transfer of a **patent** is treated as the sale or exchange of a long-term capital asset when all substantial rights to the patent (or an undivided interest that includes all such rights) are transferred by a holder.[9] The transferor/holder may receive payment in virtually any form. Lump-sum or periodic payments are most common. The amount of the payments may also be contingent on the transferee/purchaser's productivity, use, or disposition of the patent. If the transfer meets these requirements, any gain or loss is *automatically a long-term* capital gain or loss. Whether the asset was a capital asset for the transferor, whether a sale or exchange occurred, and how long the transferor held the patent are not relevant.

This special long-term capital gain or loss treatment for patents is intended to encourage technological progress. Ironically, authors, composers, and artists are not eligible for capital gain treatment when their creations are transferred. Books, songs, and artists' works may be copyrighted, but copyrights and the assets they represent are not capital assets. Thus, the disposition of those assets by their creators usually results in ordinary gain or loss. The following example illustrates the special treatment for patents.

EXAMPLE 14

Diana, a druggist, invents a pill-counting machine, which she patents. In consideration of a lump-sum payment of $200,000 plus $10 per machine sold, Diana assigns the patent to Drug Products, Inc. Assuming Diana has transferred all substantial rights, the question of whether the transfer is a sale or exchange of a capital asset is not relevant. Diana automatically has a long-term capital gain from both the lump-sum payment and the $10 per machine royalty to the extent these proceeds exceed her basis for the patent. ∎

Substantial Rights. To receive favorable capital gain treatment, all *substantial rights* to the patent (or an undivided interest in it) must be transferred. All substantial rights to a patent means all rights (whether or not then held by the grantor) that are valuable at the time the patent rights (or an undivided interest in the

---

[9]§ 1235.

patent) are transferred. All substantial rights have not been transferred when the transfer is limited geographically within the issuing country or when the transfer is for a period less than the remaining life of the patent. The circumstances of the entire transaction, rather than merely the language used in the transfer instrument, are to be considered in deciding whether all substantial rights have been transferred.[10]

EXAMPLE 15

Assume Diana, the druggist in Example 14, only licensed Drug Products, Inc., to manufacture and sell the invention in Michigan. She retained the right to license the machine elsewhere in the United States. Diana has retained a substantial right and is not eligible for automatic long-term capital gain treatment. ∎

Holder Defined. The *holder* of a patent must be an *individual* and is usually the invention's creator. A holder may also be an individual who purchases the patent rights from the creator before the patented invention is reduced to practice. However, the creator's employer and certain parties related to the creator do not qualify as holders. Thus, in the common situation where an employer has all rights to an employee's inventions, the employer is not eligible for long-term capital gain treatment. More than likely, the employer will have an ordinary asset because the patent was developed as part of its business.

Franchises, Trademarks, and Trade Names

A mode of operation, a widely recognized brand name (trade name), and a widely known business symbol (trademark) are all valuable assets. These assets may be licensed (commonly known as franchising) by their owner for use by other businesses. Many fast-food restaurants (such as McDonald's and Taco Bell) are franchises. The franchisee usually pays the owner (franchisor) an initial fee plus a contingent fee. The contingent fee is often based upon the franchisee's sales volume.

For Federal income tax purposes, a **franchise** is an agreement that gives the franchisee the right to distribute, sell, or provide goods, services, or facilities within a specified area.[11] A franchise transfer includes the grant of a franchise, a transfer by one franchisee to another person, or the renewal of a franchise.

A franchise transfer is generally not a sale or exchange of a capital asset. Section 1253 provides that a transfer of a franchise, trademark, or trade name is not a transfer of a capital asset when the transferor retains any significant power, right, or continuing interest in the property transferred.

Significant Power, Right, or Continuing Interest. *Significant powers, rights, or continuing interests* include control over assignment, quality of products and services, and sale or advertising of other products or services, and the right to require that substantially all supplies and equipment be purchased from the transferor. Also included are the right to terminate the franchise at will and the right to substantial contingent payments. Most modern franchising operations involve some or all of these powers, rights, or continuing interests.

In the unusual case where no significant power, right, or continuing interest is retained by the transferor, a sale or exchange may occur, and capital gain or loss treatment may be available. For capital gain or loss treatment to be available, the asset transferred must qualify as a capital asset.

EXAMPLE 16

Orange, Inc., a franchisee, sells the franchise to a third party. Payments to Orange are not contingent, and all significant powers, rights, and continuing interests are transferred. The gain (payments − adjusted basis) on the sale is a capital gain to Orange. ∎

---

[10]Reg. § 1.1235–2(b)(1).   [11]§ 1253(b)(1).

Noncontingent Payments. When the transferor retains a significant power, right, or continuing interest, the transferee's noncontingent payments to the transferor are ordinary income to the transferor. The franchisee capitalizes the payments and amortizes them over 15 years. The amortization is subject to recapture under § 1245.[12]

EXAMPLE 17

Grey Company signs a 10-year franchise agreement with DOH Donuts. Grey (the franchisee) makes payments of $3,000 per year for the first 8 years of the franchise agreement—a total of $24,000. Grey cannot deduct $3,000 per year as the payments are made. Instead, Grey may amortize the $24,000 total over 15 years. Thus, Grey may deduct $1,600 per year for each of the 15 years of the amortization period. The same result would occur if Grey made a $24,000 lump-sum payment at the beginning of the franchise period. Assuming DOH Donuts (the franchisor) retains significant powers, rights, or a continuing interest, it will have ordinary income when it receives the payments from Grey. ∎

Contingent Payments. Whether or not the transferor retains a significant power, right, or continuing interest, contingent franchise payments are ordinary income for the franchisor and an ordinary deduction for the franchisee. For this purpose, a payment qualifies as a contingent payment only if the following requirements are met:

- The contingent amounts are part of a series of payments that are paid at least annually throughout the term of the transfer agreement.
- The payments are substantially equal in amount or are payable under a fixed formula.

EXAMPLE 18

TAK, a spicy chicken franchisor, transfers an eight-year franchise to Otis. TAK retains a significant power, right, or continuing interest. Otis, the franchisee, agrees to pay TAK 15% of sales. This contingent payment is ordinary income to TAK and a business deduction for Otis as the payments are made. ∎

Sports Franchises. Professional sports franchises (e.g., the Detroit Tigers) are covered by § 1253.[13] Player contracts are usually one of the major assets acquired with a sports franchise. These contracts last only for the time stated in the contract. By being classified as § 197 intangibles, the player contracts and other intangible assets acquired in the purchase of the sports franchise are amortized over a statutory 15-year period.[14]

Concept Summary 16–2 summarizes the rules for franchises.

Lease Cancellation Payments

The tax treatment of payments received for canceling a lease depends on whether the recipient is the **lessor** or the **lessee** and whether the lease is a capital asset or not.

Lessee Treatment. Lease cancellation payments received by a lessee are treated as an exchange.[15] Thus, these payments are capital gains if the lease is a capital asset. Generally, a lessee's lease is a capital asset if the property (either personalty or realty) is used for the lessee's personal use (e.g., his or her residence). A lessee's lease is an ordinary asset if the property is used in the lessee's trade or business and the lease has existed for one year or less when it is canceled. A lessee's lease is a

---

[12]See Chapter 17 for a discussion of the recapture provisions.
[13]§ 1253(e).
[14]§ 197(a).
[15]§ 1241 and Reg. § 1.1241–1(a).

CONCEPT SUMMARY   16–2

Franchises

| | Effect on | |
Event	Franchisor	Franchisee
Franchisor Retains Significant Powers and Rights		
Noncontingent payment	Ordinary income.	Capitalized and amortized over 15 years as an ordinary deduction; if franchise is sold, amortization is subject to recapture under § 1245.
Contingent payment	Ordinary income.	Ordinary deduction.
Franchisor Does *Not* Retain Significant Powers and Rights		
Noncontingent payment	Ordinary income if franchise rights are an ordinary asset; capital gain if franchise rights are a capital asset (unlikely).	Capitalized and amortized over 15 years as an ordinary deduction; if the franchise is sold, amortization is subject to recapture under § 1245.
Contingent payment	Ordinary income.	Ordinary deduction.

§ 1231 asset if the property is used in the lessee's trade or business and the lease has existed for more than a year when it is canceled.[16]

EXAMPLE 19

Mark owns an apartment building that he is going to convert into an office building. Vicki is one of the apartment tenants and receives $1,000 from Mark to cancel the lease. Vicki has a capital gain of $1,000 (which is long term or short term depending upon how long she has held the lease). Mark has an ordinary deduction of $1,000. ∎

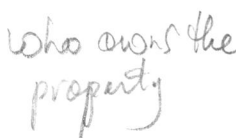

Lessor Treatment. Payments received by a lessor for a lease cancellation are always ordinary income because they are considered to be in lieu of rental payments.[17]

EXAMPLE 20

Floyd owns an apartment building near a university campus. Hui-Fen is one of the tenants. Hui-Fen is graduating early and offers Floyd $800 to cancel the apartment lease. Floyd accepts the offer. Floyd has ordinary income of $800. Hui-Fen has a nondeductible payment since the apartment was personal use property. ∎

L0.4

Determine whether the holding period for a capital asset is long term or short term.

Holding Period

Property must be held more than one year to qualify for long-term capital gain or loss treatment.[18] Property not held for the required long-term period results in short-term capital gain or loss. To compute the **holding period**, start counting on the day after the property was acquired and include the day of disposition.

---

[16]Reg. § 1.1221–1(b) and PLR 200045019.

[17]*Hort v. Comm.*, 41–1 USTC ¶9354, 25 AFTR 1207, 61 S.Ct. 757 (USSC, 1941).

[18]§ 1222.

> **TAX** *in the News*   **HOW LONG WAS THE HOLDING PERIOD FOR THAT PROPERTY?**
>
> An individual taxpayer exchanged rental real estate in Michigan that she had owned for 16 years for rental real estate in Florida. The transaction qualified as a nontaxable like-kind exchange. Within eight months of acquiring the Florida property, the taxpayer sold it when she received a very substantial unsolicited offer for the property. The local newspaper highlighted the transaction as an example of how out-of-state taxpayers were driving up real estate prices by buying and quickly reselling Florida property. Even though the taxpayer actually owned the Florida property for only eight months, her holding period for Federal income tax purposes was 16 years and eight months because the holding period of the property given up in the like-kind exchange is tacked on to the holding period of the property acquired in the exchange.

EXAMPLE 21

Marge purchases a capital asset on January 15, 2005, and sells it on January 16, 2006. Marge's holding period is more than one year. If Marge had sold the asset on January 15, 2006, the holding period would have been exactly one year, and the gain or loss would have been short term. ■

To be held for more than one year, a capital asset acquired on the last day of any month must not be disposed of until on or after the first day of the thirteenth succeeding month.[19]

EXAMPLE 22

Leo purchases a capital asset on February 28, 2005. If Leo sells the asset on February 28, 2006, the holding period is one year, and Leo will have a short-term capital gain or loss. If Leo sells the asset on March 1, 2006, the holding period is more than one year, and he will have a long-term capital gain or loss. ■

Review of Special Holding Period Rules

There are several special holding period rules.[20] The application of these rules depends on the type of asset and how it was acquired.

Nontaxable Exchanges. The holding period of property received in a like-kind exchange includes the holding period of the former asset if the property that has been exchanged is a capital asset or a § 1231 asset. In certain nontaxable transactions involving a substituted basis, the holding period of the former property is *tacked on* to the holding period of the newly acquired property.

EXAMPLE 23

Vern exchanges a business truck for another truck in a like-kind exchange. The holding period of the exchanged truck tacks on to the holding period of the new truck. ■

Certain Nontaxable Transactions Involving a Carryover of Another Taxpayer's Basis. A former owner's holding period is tacked on to the present owner's holding period if the transaction is nontaxable and the former owner's basis carries over to the present owner.

EXAMPLE 24

Kareem acquires 100 shares of Robin Corporation stock for $1,000 on December 31, 2002. He transfers the shares by gift to Megan on December 31, 2005, when the stock is worth $2,000. Kareem's basis of $1,000 becomes the basis for determining gain or loss on a subsequent sale by Megan. Megan's holding period begins with the date the stock was acquired by Kareem. ■

---

[19]Rev.Rul. 66–7, 1966–1 C.B. 188.   [20]§ 1223.

| EXAMPLE 25 | Assume the same facts as in Example 24, except that the fair market value of the shares is only $800 on the date of the gift. The holding period begins on the date of the gift if Megan sells the stock for a loss. The value of the shares at the date of the gift is used in the determination of her basis for loss. If she sells the shares for $500 on April 1, 2006, Megan has a $300 recognized capital loss, and the holding period is from December 31, 2005, to April 1, 2006 (thus, the loss is short term). ∎ |

Certain Disallowed Loss Transactions. Under several Code provisions, realized losses are disallowed. When a loss is disallowed, there is no carryover of holding period. Losses can be disallowed under § 267 (sale or exchange between related taxpayers) and § 262 (sale or exchange of personal use assets) as well as other Code Sections. Taxpayers who acquire property in a disallowed loss transaction will have a new holding period begin and will have a basis equal to the purchase price.

| EXAMPLE 26 | Janet sells her personal automobile at a loss. She may not deduct the loss because it arises from the sale of personal use property. Janet purchases a replacement automobile for more than the selling price of her former automobile. Janet has a basis equal to the cost of the replacement automobile, and her holding period begins when she acquires the replacement automobile. ∎ |

Inherited Property. The holding period for inherited property is treated as long term no matter how long the property is actually held by the heir. The holding period of the decedent or the decedent's estate is not relevant for the heir's holding period.[21]

| EXAMPLE 27 | Shonda inherits Blue Company stock from her father. She receives the stock on April 1, 2006, and sells it on November 1, 2006. Even though Shonda did not hold the stock more than one year, she receives long-term capital gain or loss treatment on the sale. ∎ |

Special Rules for Short Sales

General. The Code provides special rules for determining the holding period of property sold short.[22] A **short sale** occurs when a taxpayer sells borrowed property and repays the lender with substantially identical property either held on the date of the sale or purchased after the sale. Short sales usually involve corporate stock. The seller's objective is to make a profit in anticipation of a decline in the stock's price. If the price declines, the seller in a short sale recognizes a profit equal to the difference between the sales price of the borrowed stock and the price paid for the replacement stock.

A *short sale against the box* occurs when the stock is borrowed from a broker by a seller who already owns the same stock. The box is the safe deposit box where stock owners routinely used to keep stock certificates. Although today stockbrokers generally keep stock certificates for their customers, the terminology short sale against the box is still used.

| EXAMPLE 28 | Chris does not own any shares of Brown Corporation. However, Chris sells 30 shares of Brown. The shares are borrowed from Chris's broker and must be replaced within 45 days. Chris has a short sale because he was short the shares he sold. He will *close* the short sale by purchasing Brown shares and delivering them to his broker. If the original 30 shares were sold for $10,000 and Chris later purchases 30 shares for $8,000, he has a gain of $2,000. Chris's hunch that the price of Brown stock would decline was correct. Chris was able to profit from selling high and buying low. If Chris had to purchase Brown shares for $13,000 to |

---

[21]In 2010, there will be no estate tax, and not all inherited assets will receive an automatic long-term holding period. Some inherited assets will have a "carryover" basis and holding period that are calculated similarly to the basis and holding period for property received by gift. See § 1022 after the effective date for this provision in the Tax Relief Reconciliation Act of 2001.
[22]§ 1233.

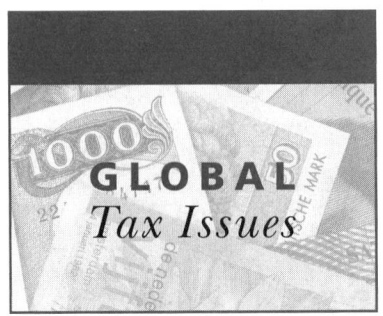

TRADING ADRs ON U.S. STOCK EXCHANGES

Many non-U.S. companies now have subsidiaries that were formerly U.S. companies. For instance, Chrysler Corporation is now a subsidiary of DaimlerChrysler (formed when the German company Daimler-Benz acquired Chrysler). Shares in such foreign companies generally cannot be traded directly on U.S. stock exchanges. Instead, the foreign companies issue instruments called American Depository Receipts (ADRs) that can be traded on U.S. stock exchanges. Purchases and sales of ADRs are treated for tax purposes as though the ADRs were shares in the corporation that issued them.

GLOBAL Tax Issues

close the short sale, he would have a loss of $3,000. In this case, Chris would have sold low and bought high—not the result he wanted! Chris would be making a short sale against the box if he borrowed shares from his broker to sell and then closed the short sale by delivering other Brown shares he owned at the time he made the short sale. ∎

A short sale gain or loss is a capital gain or loss to the extent that the short sale property constitutes a capital asset of the taxpayer. The gain or loss is not recognized until the short sale is closed. Generally, the holding period of the short sale property is determined by how long the property used to close the short sale was held. However, if *substantially identical property* (e.g., other shares of the same stock) is held by the taxpayer, the short-term or long-term character of the short sale gain or loss may be affected:

- If substantially identical property has *not* been held for the long-term holding period on the short sale date, the short sale *gain or loss* is short term.
- If substantially identical property has *been* held for the long-term holding period on the short sale date, the short sale *gain* is long term if the substantially identical property is used to close the short sale and short term if it is not used to close the short sale.
- If substantially identical property has *been* held for the long-term holding period on the short sale date, the short sale *loss* is long term whether or not the substantially identical property is used to close the short sale.
- If substantially identical property is acquired *after* the short sale date and on or before the closing date, the short sale *gain or loss* is short term.

Concept Summary 16–3 summarizes the short sale rules. These rules are intended to prevent the conversion of short-term capital gains into long-term capital gains and long-term capital losses into short-term capital losses.

Disposition Rules for Short Sales against the Box. In a short sale against the box, the taxpayer either owns securities that are substantially identical to the securities sold short at the short sale date or acquires such securities before the closing date. To remove the taxpayer's flexibility as to when the short sale gain must be reported, a constructive sale approach is used. If the taxpayer has not closed the short sale by delivering the short sale securities to the broker *before* January 31 of the year following the short sale, the short sale is deemed to have been closed on the *earlier* of two events:

- On the short sale date if the taxpayer owned substantially identical securities at that time.
- On the date during the year of the short sale that the taxpayer acquired substantially identical securities.[23]

The basis of the shares in the deemed transfer of shares is used to compute the gain or loss on the short sale. Later, when shares are *actually* transferred to the

---

[23]§ 1259.

CONCEPT SUMMARY 16-3

Short Sales of Securities

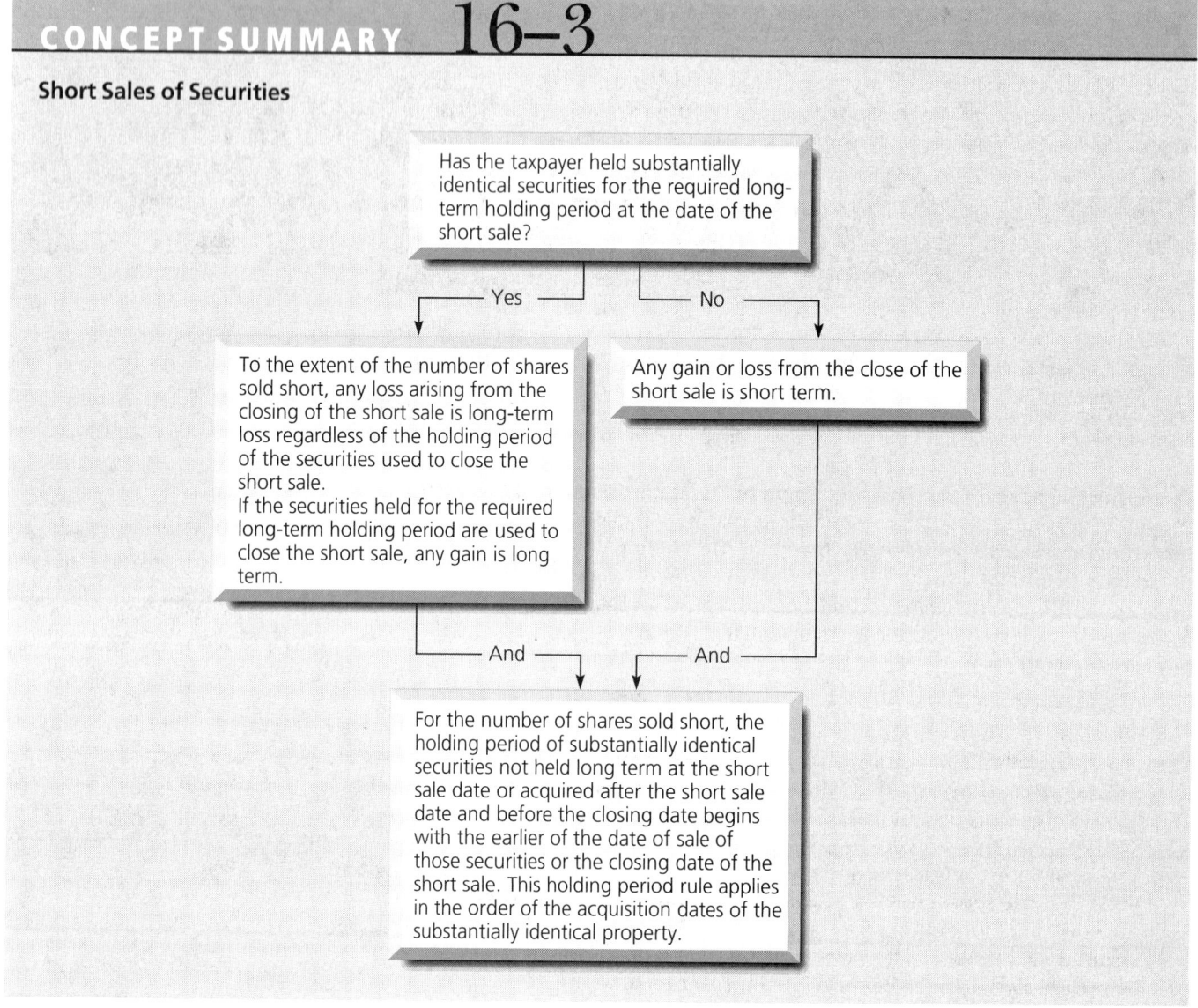

broker to close the short sale, there may be a gain or loss because the shares transferred will have a basis equal to the short sale date price and the value at the *actual* short sale closing date may be different from the short sale date price.

Illustrations. The following examples illustrate the treatment of short sales and short sales against the box.

EXAMPLE 29

On January 4, 2006, Donald purchases five shares of Osprey Corporation common stock for $100. On April 14, 2006, he engages in a short sale of five shares of the same stock for $150. On August 15, Donald closes the short sale by repaying the borrowed stock with the five shares purchased on January 4. Donald has a $50 short-term capital gain from the short sale because he had not held substantially identical shares for the long-term holding period on the short sale date. ∎

EXAMPLE 30

Assume the same facts as in the previous example, except that Donald closes the short sale on January 28, 2007, by repaying the borrowed stock with five shares purchased on January 27, 2007, for $200. The stock used to close the short sale was not the property purchased on January 4,

2006, but since Donald held short-term property at the April 14, 2006 short sale date, the gain or loss from closing the short sale is short term. Donald has a $50 short-term capital loss ($200 cost of stock purchased on January 27, 2007, and a short sale selling price of $150). ■

EXAMPLE 31

On January 18, 2005, Rita purchases 200 shares of Owl Corporation stock for $1,000. On November 11, 2006, she sells short for $1,300 200 shares of Owl Corporation stock that she borrows from her broker. On February 10, 2007, Rita closes the short sale by delivering the 200 shares of Owl Corporation stock that she had acquired in 2005. On that date, Owl Corporation stock had a market price of $3 per share. Since Rita owned substantially identical stock on the date of the short sale and did not close the short sale before January 31, 2007, she is *deemed* to have closed the short sale on November 11, 2006 (the date of the short sale). On her 2006 tax return, she reports a $300 long-term capital gain ($1,300 short sale price − $1,000 basis). On February 10, 2007, Rita has a $700 short-term capital loss [$600 short sale closing date price (200 shares × $3 per share) − $1,300 basis] because the holding period of the shares used to close the short sale commences with the date of the short sale. ■

EXAMPLE 32

Assume the same facts as in Example 31, except that Rita did not own any Owl Corporation stock on the short sale date and acquired the 200 shares of Owl Corporation stock for $1,000 on December 12, 2006 (after the November 11, 2006 short sale date). The *deemed* closing of the short sale is December 12, 2006, because Rita held substantially identical shares at the end of 2006 and did not close the short sale before January 31, 2007. Her 2006 short sale gain is a *short-term* gain of $300 ($1,300 short sale price − $1,000 basis), and she still has a short-term capital loss of $700 on February 10, 2007. ■

Tax Treatment of Capital Gains and Losses of Noncorporate Taxpayers

LO.5

Describe the beneficial tax treatment for capital gains and the detrimental tax treatment for capital losses for noncorporate taxpayers.

All taxpayers net their capital gains and losses. Short-term gains and losses (if any) are netted against one another, and long-term gains and losses (if any) are netted against one another. The results will be net short-term gain or loss and net long-term gain or loss. If these two net positions are of opposite sign (one is a gain and one is a loss), they are netted against one another.

Six possibilities exist for the result after all possible netting has been completed. Three of these final results are gains, and three are losses. One possible result is a net long-term capital gain (NLTCG). Net long-term capital gains of noncorporate taxpayers are subject to beneficial treatment. A second possibility is a net short-term capital gain (NSTCG). Third, the netting may result in both NLTCG and NSTCG.

The NLTCG portion of these results is eligible for an alternative tax calculation. As many as four different tax rates may be used in the calculation—5, 15, 25, and 28 percent. The tax savings from the alternative tax calculation range from a low of 5 percentage points (10 percent regular tax rate − 5 percent alternative tax rate) to a high of 20 percentage points (35 percent regular tax rate − 15 percent alternative tax rate). The alternative tax computation is discussed later in the chapter under Alternative Tax on Net Capital Gain.

The last three results of the capital gain and loss netting process are losses. Thus, a fourth possibility is a net long-term capital loss (NLTCL). A fifth result is a net short-term capital loss (NSTCL). Finally, a sixth possibility includes both an NLTCL and an NSTCL. Neither NLTCLs nor NSTCLs are treated as ordinary losses. Treatment as an ordinary loss generally is preferable to capital loss treatment since ordinary losses are deductible in full while the deductibility of capital losses is subject to certain limitations. An individual taxpayer may deduct a maximum of $3,000 of net capital losses for a taxable year.[24]

---

[24]§ 1211(b).

Capital Gain and Loss Netting Process

Holding Periods for Capital Gain and Loss Netting Purposes. As mentioned earlier in this chapter, there are two holding periods for purposes of the capital gain and loss netting process:

- *Short term*—Assets held one year or less.
- *Long term*—Assets held more than one year.

Net short-term capital gain is not eligible for any special tax rate. It is taxed at the same rate as the taxpayer's other taxable income. *Net long-term capital gain* is eligible for one or more of *four* alternative tax rates: 5 percent, 15 percent, 25 percent, and 28 percent. The 25 percent and 28 percent rates are used only in somewhat unusual circumstances, so the discussion below concentrates more heavily on the other two rates. The net long-term capital gain components are referred to as the *5%/15% gain*, the *25% gain*, and the *28% gain*.

The *25% gain* is technically called the **unrecaptured § 1250 gain** and is related to gain from disposition of § 1231 assets. Gains and losses from disposition of § 1231 assets are discussed in Chapter 17. In this chapter, the discussion will focus only on how the *25% gain* is taxed and not how it is determined. The *28% gain* relates to collectibles and § 1202 gain (see Chapter 5). Collectibles gain is discussed later in this chapter.

The *5% gain* portion of the *5%/15% gain* applies when the taxable income before taxing the *5%/15% gain* does not put the taxpayer out of the 15 percent bracket. Once the taxable income (including any portion of the *5%/15% gain* taxed at 5 percent) puts the taxpayer above the 15 percent bracket, the remaining portion of the *5%/15% gain* is taxed at 15 percent rather than at the regular tax rate.

When the long-term capital gain exceeds short-term capital loss, a **net capital gain (NCG)** exists. Net capital gain qualifies for beneficial alternative tax treatment (see the coverage later in the chapter).[25]

Since there are both short- and long-term capital gains and losses and because the long-term capital gains may be taxed at various rates, an *ordering procedure* is required. The ordering procedure tends to preserve the lowest tax rate long-term capital gain when there is a net long-term capital gain. This ordering procedure is explained in the steps below and then illustrated by several examples.

Step 1. Group all gains and losses into short term and 28%, 25%, and 5%/15% long term.

Step 2. Net the gains and losses within each group.

Step 3. Offset the net 28% and net 25% amounts if they are of opposite sign.

Step 4. Offset the results after step 3 against the 5%/15% amount if they are of opposite sign. If the 5%/15% amount is a loss, offset it against the *highest taxed gain first*. After this step, there is a net long-term capital gain or loss. If there is a net long-term capital gain, it may consist of only 28% gain, only 25% gain, only 5%/15% gain, or some combination of all of these gains. If there is a net long-term capital loss, it is simply a net long-term capital loss.

Step 5. Offset the net short-term amount against the results of step 4 if they are of opposite sign. The netting rules offset net short-term capital loss against the *highest taxed gain first*. Consequently, if there is a net short-term capital loss and a net gain from step 4, the short-term capital loss offsets first the 28% gain, then the 25% gain, and finally the 5%/15% gain.

If the result of step 5 is *only* a short-term capital gain, the taxpayer is not eligible for a reduced tax rate. If the result of step 5 is a loss, the taxpayer may be eligible for a *capital loss deduction* (discussed later in this chapter). If there was no offsetting in step 5 because the short-term and step 4 results were both gains *or* if the result of

---

[25]§ 1222(11).

the offsetting is a long-term gain, a net capital gain exists, and the taxpayer may be eligible for a reduced tax rate. The net capital gain may consist of *28% gain, 25% gain*, and/or *5%/15% gain*.

The five steps outlined above can have many unique final results. See Concept Summary 16–5 later in the chapter for a summary of the netting rules and how capital gains and losses are taxed. The following series of examples illustrates the capital gain and loss netting process.

EXAMPLE 33

This example shows how a net short-term capital gain may result from the netting process.

Step	Short Term	Long-Term Gains and Losses 28%	25%	5%/15%	Comment
1	$13,000	$ 12,000		$ 3,000	
	(2,000)	(20,000)			
2	$11,000	($ 8,000)		$ 3,000	
3					No 28%/25% netting because no opposite sign.
4		3,000 →		(3,000)	Netted because of opposite sign.
		($ 5,000)		$ –0–	
5	(5,000) ←	5,000			The net short-term capital gain is taxed as ordinary income.
	$ 6,000	$ –0–			
	Net short-term capital gain				

■

EXAMPLE 34

This example shows how a net long-term capital gain may result from the netting process.

Step	Short Term	Long-Term Gains and Losses 28%	25%	5%/15%	Comment
1	$ 3,000	$15,000	$4,000	$ 3,000	
	(5,000)	(7,000)		(8,000)	
2	($ 2,000)	$ 8,000	$4,000	($ 5,000)	
3					No 28%/25% netting because no opposite sign.
4		(5,000)	←	5,000	Netted because of opposite sign. Net 5%/15% loss is netted against 28% gain first.
		$ 3,000		$ –0–	
5	2,000 →	(2,000)			The net short-term capital loss is netted against 28% gain first. The net long-term capital gain is $5,000 ($1,000 + $4,000).
	$ –0–	$ 1,000	$4,000		
		Net 28% gain	Net 25% gain		

■

EXAMPLE 35

This example shows how a net long-term capital loss may result from the netting process.

Step	Short Term	Long-Term Gains and Losses 28%	25%	5%/15%	Comment
1	$ 3,000	$ 1,000		$ 3,000	
				(8,000)	
2	$ 3,000	$ 1,000		($ 5,000)	
3					No 28%/25% netting because no opposite sign.
4		(1,000)	→	1,000	Netted because of opposite sign.
		$ –0–		($ 4,000)	
5	(3,000)	→	→	3,000	The net short-term capital gain is netted against the net long-term capital loss, and the remaining loss is eligible for the capital loss deduction.
	$ –0–			($ 1,000)	
				Net long-term capital loss	

Use of Capital Loss Carryovers. A short-term capital loss carryover to the current year retains its character as short term and is combined with the short-term items of the current year. A long-term net capital loss carries over as a long-term capital loss and is combined with the current-year long-term items. The long-term loss carryover is first offset with 28% gain of the current year, then 25% gain, and then 5%/15% gain until it is absorbed.

EXAMPLE 36

In 2006, Abigail has a $4,000 short-term capital gain, a $36,000 28% long-term capital gain, and a $13,000 5%/15% long-term capital gain. She also has a $3,000 short-term capital loss carryover and a $2,000 long-term capital loss carryover from 2005. This produces a $1,000 net short-term capital gain ($4,000 − $3,000), a $34,000 net 28% long-term capital gain ($36,000 − $2,000), and a $13,000 net 5%/15% long-term capital gain for 2006. ■

Definition of Collectibles. Capital assets that are collectibles, even though they are held long term, are not eligible for the 5%/15% alternative tax rate. Instead, a 28 percent alternative tax rate applies.

For capital gain or loss purposes, **collectibles** include:[26]

- Any work of art.
- Any rug or antique.
- Any metal or gem.
- Any stamp.
- Any alcoholic beverage.
- Most coins.
- Any historical objects (documents, clothes, etc.).

[26]§ 408(m) and Reg. § 1.408–10(b).

ETHICAL
Considerations   IS THAT CAPITAL GAIN TAXABLE?

In 2006, a U.S. taxpayer has a capital gain from the disposition of shares of a Japanese mutual fund. The mutual fund invested in securities of Japanese banks. The taxpayer's practitioner recommends that the taxpayer not report the capital gain because a special tax treaty with Japan allows such capital gains to be excluded from U.S. taxable income. None of the documents that the taxpayer has received from the mutual fund mentions this exclusion. Evaluate the practitioner's advice.

Qualified Dividend Income

Dividends paid from current or accumulated earnings and profits of domestic and certain foreign corporations are eligible to be taxed at the 5%/15% long-term capital gain rates if they are **qualified dividend income**. The question of which dividends constitute qualified dividend income is discussed more fully in Chapter 4. Here the discussion focuses on how the qualified dividend income is taxed.

After the net capital gain or loss has been determined, the qualified dividend income is added to the net long-term capital gain portion of the net capital gain and is taxed as 5%/15% gain. If there is a net capital loss, the net capital loss is still deductible *for* AGI up to $3,000 per year with the remainder of the loss (if any) carrying forward. In this case, the qualified dividend income is still eligible to be treated as *5%/15% gain* in the alternative tax calculation (it is *not* offset by the net capital loss).

Refer to Example 34, but assume there is qualified dividend income of $2,500 in addition to the items shown. The qualified dividend income *is not* netted against the capital gains and losses. Instead, the taxpayer has $1,000 of 28% gain, $4,000 of 25% gain, *and* $2,500 of qualified dividend income taxed at 5%/15%. ∎

EXAMPLE 37

Refer to Example 35, but assume there is qualified dividend income of $2,500 in addition to the items shown. The qualified dividend income *is not* netted against the net capital loss. The taxpayer has a $1,000 capital loss deduction *and* $2,500 of qualified dividend income taxed at 5%/15%. ∎

EXAMPLE 38

Alternative Tax on Net Capital Gain

Section 1 contains the statutory provisions that enable the *net capital gain* to be taxed at special rates (5, 15, 25, and 28 percent). This calculation is referred to as the **alternative tax** on net capital gain.[27] The alternative tax applies only if taxable income includes some long-term capital gain (there is net capital gain). Taxable income includes *all* of the net capital gain unless taxable income is less than the net capital gain. In addition, the net capital gain is taxed *last*, after other taxable income (including any short-term capital gain).

Joan, an unmarried taxpayer, has 2006 taxable income of $88,000, including a $12,000 net capital gain. The last $12,000 of her $88,000 taxable income is the layer related to the net capital gain. The first $76,000 ($88,000 − $12,000) of her taxable income is not subject to any special tax rate, so it is taxed using the regular tax rates. ∎

EXAMPLE 39

Regular inc tax first, then 5%/15% — special rate applied.

---

[27]§ 1(h) Note: Examples 40, 41, and 42 use the 2006 Tax Rate Schedules rather than the 2006 Tax Table to calculate the tax on the non-long-term capital gain portion of taxable income. This approach is used to better illustrate the concepts under discussion. The actual tax on the non-long-term portion of taxable income would be calculated using the Tax Tables since that income is less than $100,000.

Since the net capital gain may be made up of various *rate layers*, it is important to know in what order those layers will be taxed. For *each* of the layers, the taxpayer compares the regular tax rate on that layer of income and the alternative tax rate on that portion of the net capital gain. The layers are taxed in the following order: *25% gain, 28% gain*, the 5 percent portion of the *5%/15% gain*, and then the 15 percent portion of the *5%/15% gain*. As a result of this layering, the taxpayer will benefit from the 5 percent portion of the net capital gain if the taxpayer is still in the 10 percent or 15 percent regular rate bracket after taxing other taxable income and the 25 percent and 28 percent portions of the net capital gain.

EXAMPLE 40

Assume that Joan's $12,000 net capital gain in Example 39 is made up of $10,000 *25% gain* and $2,000 *5%/15% gain*. Examination of the 2006 tax rates reveals that $76,000 of taxable income for a single individual puts Joan at a marginal tax rate of 28%. Consequently, she will use the alternative tax on both the $10,000 gain and the $2,000 gain. Her alternative tax liability for 2006 is $18,412 [$15,612 (tax on $76,000 of taxable income) + $2,500 ($10,000 × .25) + $300 ($2,000 × .15)]. Since the combination of the $76,000 taxable income and her $10,000 25% gain puts her above the 15% regular tax bracket, none of the $2,000 *5%/15% gain* is taxed at 5%. Her regular tax liability on $88,000 would be $18,972. Thus, Joan saves $560 ($18,972 − $18,412) by using the alternative tax computation. ∎

EXAMPLE 41

Joan, an unmarried taxpayer, has 2006 taxable income of $25,000. Of this amount, $12,000 is net capital gain, and $13,000 is other taxable income. The net capital gain is made up of $8,300 of *25% gain* and $3,700 of *5%/15% gain* (including $1,000 of qualified dividend income). Her tax liability using the alternative tax calculation is $3,003 [$1,573 (tax on $13,000 of taxable income) + $1,245 (tax on $8,300 *25% gain* at 15%) + $185 (tax on $3,700 *5%/15% gain* at 5%)]. Since her marginal rate is still 15% after taxing the $13,000 of other taxable income, she uses the 15% regular tax rate rather than the 25% alternative tax rate on the $8,300 *25% gain*. After taxing the $13,000 and the $8,300, a total of $21,300 of the $25,000 taxable income has been taxed. Since her marginal rate is still 15%, she uses the 5% alternative rate for the $3,700 of *5%/15% gain*. The $1,000 qualified dividend income is included in the $3,700 and, thus, is also taxed at 5%. Joan's regular tax liability on $25,000 would be $3,373. Thus, she saves $370 ($3,373 − $3,003) by using the alternative tax calculation. ∎

The alternative tax computation allows the taxpayer to receive the *lower of* the regular tax or the alternative tax on *each layer* of net capital gain or *portion of each layer* of net capital gain.

EXAMPLE 42

Assume the same facts as in Example 41 except that Joan's taxable income is $31,000, consisting of $12,000 of net capital gain and $19,000 of other taxable income. Not all of the $3,700 of *5%/15% gain* is taxed at 5% because Joan's taxable income exceeds $30,650, taking her out of the 15% bracket. Consequently, the last $350 ($31,000 − $30,650) of the $3,700 *5%/15% gain* is taxed at 15% rather than 5%. Her tax liability using the alternative tax computation is $3,939 [$2,473 (tax on $19,000 of taxable income) + $1,245 (tax on $8,300 *25% gain* at 15%) + $168 (tax on $3,350 *5%/15% gain* at 5%) + $53 (tax on $350 *5%/15% gain* at 15%)]. Joan's regular tax liability on $31,000 would be $4,308. Thus, she saves $369 ($4,308 − $3,939) by using the alternative tax calculation. ∎

Concept Summary 16–4 summarizes the alternative tax computation.

Treatment of Capital Losses

Computation of Net Capital Loss.
A net capital loss (NCL) results if capital losses exceed capital gains for the year. An NCL may be all long term, all short term, or

CONCEPT SUMMARY   16–4

Income Layers for Alternative Tax on Capital Gain Computation

Compute tax on:	Ordinary taxable income (including net short-term capital gain) using the regular tax rates.
Compute tax on:	Each of the layers below using the *lower* of the alternative tax rate or the regular tax rate for that layer (or portion of a layer) of taxable income.

+ 25% long-term capital gain (unrecaptured § 1250 gain) portion of taxable income

+ 28% long-term capital gain

+ 5% long-term capital gain (portion of 5%/15% capital gain that is taxed at 5%; available only if ordinary taxable income plus 25% and 28% capital gain layers do not put the taxpayer above the 15% bracket; 5% rate is no longer available once income including the portion of the gain taxed at 5% puts the taxpayer out of the 15% bracket)*

+ 15% long-term capital gain (remaining portion of 5%/15% capital gain)*

= Alternative tax on taxable income

*May include qualified dividend income.

part long and part short term.[28] The characterization of an NCL as long or short term is important in determining the capital loss deduction (discussed later in this chapter).

EXAMPLE 43

Three different individual taxpayers have the following capital gains and losses during the year:

Taxpayer	LTCG	LTCL	STCG	STCL	Result of Netting	Description of Result
Robert	$1,000	($ 2,800)	$1,000	($ 500)	($ 1,300)	NLTCL
Carlos	1,000	(500)	1,000	(2,800)	(1,300)	NSTCL
Troy	400	(1,200)	500	(1,200)	(1,500)	NLTCL ($800)
						NSTCL ($700)

Robert's NCL of $1,300 is all long term. Carlos's NCL of $1,300 is all short term. Troy's NCL is $1,500, $800 of which is long term and $700 of which is short term. ∎

Treatment of Net Capital Loss. An NCL is deductible from gross income to the extent of $3,000 per tax year.[29] Capital losses exceeding the loss deduction limits carry forward indefinitely. Thus, although there may or may not be beneficial treatment for capital gains, there is *unfavorable* treatment for capital losses in terms of the $3,000 annual limitation on deducting NCL against ordinary income. If the NCL includes both long-term and short-term capital loss, the short-term capital loss is counted first toward the $3,000 annual limitation.

EXAMPLE 44

Burt has an NCL of $5,500, of which $2,000 is STCL and $3,500 is LTCL. Burt has a capital loss deduction of $3,000 ($2,000 of STCL and $1,000 of LTCL). He has an LTCL carryforward of $2,500 ($3,500 − $1,000). ∎

[28]Section 1222(10) defines a net capital loss as the net loss after the capital loss deduction. However, that definition confuses the discussion of net capital loss. Therefore, net capital loss is used here to mean the result after netting capital gains and losses and before considering the capital loss deduction.

The capital loss deduction is discussed under Treatment of Net Capital Loss in this chapter.

[29]§ 1211(b)(1). Married persons filing separate returns are limited to a $1,500 deduction per tax year.

Carryovers. Taxpayers are allowed to carry over unused capital losses indefinitely. The short-term capital loss (STCL) retains its character as STCL. Likewise the long-term capital loss retains its character as LTCL.

EXAMPLE 45

In 2006, Mark incurred $1,000 of STCL and $11,000 of LTCL. In 2007, Mark has a $400 LTCG.

- Mark's NCL for 2006 is $12,000. Mark deducts $3,000 ($1,000 STCL and $2,000 LTCL). He has $9,000 of LTCL carried forward to 2007.
- Mark combines the $9,000 LTCL carryforward with the $400 LTCG for 2007. He has an $8,600 NLTCL for 2007. Mark deducts $3,000 of LTCL in 2007 and carries forward $5,600 of LTCL to 2008. ∎

When a taxpayer has both a capital loss deduction and negative taxable income, a special computation of the capital loss carryover is required.[30] Specifically, the capital loss carryover is the NCL minus the lesser of:

- The capital loss deduction claimed on the return.
- The negative taxable income increased by the capital loss deduction claimed on the return and the personal and dependency exemption deduction.

Without this provision, some of the tax benefit of the capital loss deduction would be wasted when the deduction drives taxable income below zero. However, the capital loss deduction is not reduced if taxable income before the exemption deduction is a positive number or zero. In that situation, it is the exemption deduction, and not the capital loss deduction, that is creating the negative taxable income.

EXAMPLE 46

In 2006, Joanne has a $13,000 NCL (all long term), a $3,300 personal exemption deduction, and $4,000 negative taxable income. The negative taxable income includes a $3,000 capital loss deduction. The capital loss carryover to 2007 is $10,700 computed as follows:

- The $4,000 negative taxable income is treated as a negative number, but the capital loss deduction and personal exemption deduction are treated as positive numbers.
- The normal ceiling on the capital loss deduction is $3,000.
- However, if the $3,000 capital loss deduction and the $3,300 exemption deduction are added back to the $4,000 negative taxable income, only $2,300 of the $3,000 capital loss deduction is needed to make taxable income equal to zero.
- Therefore, this special computation results in only $2,300 of the $13,000 NCL being consumed. The LTCL carryforward is $10,700 ($13,000 − $2,300). ∎

Concept Summary 16–5 summarizes the rules for noncorporate taxpayers' treatment of capital gains and losses.

CONCEPT SUMMARY 16–5

Some Possible Final Results of the Capital Gain and Loss Netting Process and How They Are Taxed

Result	Maximum Tax Rate	Comments
Net short-term capital loss	—	Eligible for capital loss deduction ($3,000 maximum per year).
Net long-term capital loss	—	Eligible for capital loss deduction ($3,000 maximum per year).
Net short-term capital loss *and* net long-term capital loss	—	Eligible for capital loss deduction ($3,000 maximum per year). Short-term capital losses are counted first toward the deduction.
Net short-term capital gain	10–35%	Taxed as ordinary income.
Net long-term capital gain	5–28%	The net long-term capital gain may have as many as four tax rate components: 25%, 28%, and 5%/15%.
• The net long-term capital gain is the *last* portion of taxable income.		The components are taxed in the following order: 25%, 28%, 5%, 15%. They are taxed *after* the non-long-term capital gain portion of taxable income has been taxed. The 5%/15% component may include qualified dividend income.
• Each net long-term capital gain component of taxable income is taxed at the the *lower of* the regular tax on that component or the alternative tax.		The alternative tax on net long-term capital gain can never increase the tax on taxable income, but it can reduce the tax on taxable income.
Net short-term capital gain *and* net long-term capital gain	10–35% on net short-term capital gain; 5–28% on net long-term capital gain	The net short-term capital gain is taxed as ordinary income; the net long-term capital gain is taxed as discussed above for just net long-term capital gain.

Reporting Procedures

The following discusses the 2005 tax forms because the 2006 tax forms were not available at the time of this writing.

Capital gains and losses are reported on Schedule D of the 2005 Form 1040 (reproduced on pages 16–28 and 16–29 using the data from Example 47). Part I of Schedule D is used to report short-term capital gains and losses. Part II of Schedule D is used to report long-term capital gains and losses. Part III summarizes the results of Parts I and II and indicates whether the taxpayer has a net capital gain or a net capital loss. Part III then helps determine which alternative tax worksheet is used to calculate the alternative tax on long-term capital gains and qualified dividends. If the taxpayer has a net long-term capital gain that does not include any 28% or 25% long-term capital gain, then the alternative tax is calculated using the Qualified Dividends and Capital Gain Worksheet from the Form 1040 instructions. If the taxpayer has a net long-term capital gain that does include either 28% or 25% long-term capital gain, then the alternative tax is calculated using the Schedule D Tax Worksheet from the Schedule D instructions. These worksheets do not have to be filed with the tax return, but are kept for the taxpayer's records.

SCHEDULE D
(Form 1040)

Department of the Treasury
Internal Revenue Service   (99)

Capital Gains and Losses

▶ Attach to Form 1040.   ▶ See Instructions for Schedule D (Form 1040).

▶ Use Schedule D-1 to list additional transactions for lines 1 and 8.

OMB No. 1545-0074

20**05**

Attachment
Sequence No. **12**

Name(s) shown on Form 1040
Joan Rapson

Your social security number
467 : 37 : 8383

Part I   Short-Term Capital Gains and Losses—Assets Held One Year or Less

	(a) Description of property (Example: 100 sh. XYZ Co.)	**(b)** Date acquired (Mo., day, yr.)	**(c)** Date sold (Mo., day, yr.)	**(d)** Sales price (see page D-6 of the instructions)	**(e)** Cost or other basis (see page D-6 of the instructions)	**(f)** Gain or (loss) Subtract (e) from (d)
1	*100 shares Blue stock*	*01/21/05*	*11/11/05*	*11,000*	*17,000*	*(6,000)*

2	Enter your short-term totals, if any, from Schedule D-1, line 2	**2**		
3	**Total short-term sales price amounts.** Add lines 1 and 2 in column (d)	**3**	*11,000*	
4	Short-term gain from Form 6252 and short-term gain or (loss) from Forms 4684, 6781, and 8824	**4**		
5	Net short-term gain or (loss) from partnerships, S corporations, estates, and trusts from Schedule(s) K-1	**5**		
6	Short-term capital loss carryover. Enter the amount, if any, from line 8 of your **Capital Loss Carryover Worksheet** on page D-6 of the instructions	**6**	(	)
7	**Net short-term capital gain or (loss).** Combine lines 1 through 6 in column (f)	**7**	*(6,000)*	

Part II   Long-Term Capital Gains and Losses—Assets Held More Than One Year

	(a) Description of property (Example: 100 sh. XYZ Co.)	**(b)** Date acquired (Mo., day, yr.)	**(c)** Date sold (Mo., day, yr.)	**(d)** Sales price (see page D-6 of the instructions)	**(e)** Cost or other basis (see page D-6 of the instructions)	**(f)** Gain or (loss) Subtract (e) from (d)
8	*100 shares Yellow stock*	*09/12/00*	*10/12/05*	*36,000*	*20,000*	*16,000*
	100 shares Purple stock	*03/14/03*	*10/12/05*	*14,000*	*12,000*	*2,000*

9	Enter your long-term totals, if any, from Schedule D-1, line 9	**9**		
10	**Total long-term sales price amounts.** Add lines 8 and 9 in column (d)	**10**	*50,000*	
11	Gain from Form 4797, Part I; long-term gain from Forms 2439 and 6252; and long-term gain or (loss) from Forms 4684, 6781, and 8824	**11**		
12	Net long-term gain or (loss) from partnerships, S corporations, estates, and trusts from Schedule(s) K-1	**12**		
13	Capital gain distributions. See page D-1 of the instructions	**13**		
14	Long-term capital loss carryover. Enter the amount, if any, from line 13 of your **Capital Loss Carryover Worksheet** on page D-6 of the instructions	**14**	(	)
15	**Net long-term capital gain or (loss).** Combine lines 8 through 14 in column (f). Then go to Part III on the back	**15**	*18,000*	

For Paperwork Reduction Act Notice, see Form 1040 instructions.   Cat. No. 11338H   **Schedule D (Form 1040) 2005**

Part III	Summary

16 Combine lines 7 and 15 and enter the result. If line 16 is a loss, skip lines 17 through 20, and go to line 21. If a gain, enter the gain on Form 1040, line 13, and then go to line 17 below . .

16	*12,000*

17 Are lines 15 and 16 **both** gains?
☒ **Yes.** Go to line 18.
☐ **No.** Skip lines 18 through 21, and go to line 22.

18 Enter the amount, if any, from line 7 of the **28% Rate Gain Worksheet** on page D-7 of the instructions .   .   .   .   ▶

18	*0*

19 Enter the amount, if any, from line 18 of the **Unrecaptured Section 1250 Gain Worksheet** on page D-8 of the instructions   .   .   .   .   ▶

19	*0*

20 Are lines 18 and 19 **both** zero or blank?
☒ **Yes.** Complete Form 1040 through line 43, and then complete the **Qualified Dividends and Capital Gain Tax Worksheet** on page 38 of the Instructions for Form 1040. **Do not** complete lines 21 and 22 below.
☐ **No.** Complete Form 1040 through line 43, and then complete the **Schedule D Tax Worksheet** on page D-9 of the instructions. **Do not** complete lines 21 and 22 below.

21 If line 16 is a loss, enter here and on Form 1040, line 13, the **smaller** of:

• The loss on line 16 or
• ($3,000), or if married filing separately, ($1,500) } .   .   .   .

21	(	)

Note. When figuring which amount is smaller, treat both amounts as positive numbers.

22 Do you have qualified dividends on Form 1040, line 9b?
☐ **Yes.** Complete Form 1040 through line 43, and then complete the **Qualified Dividends and Capital Gain Tax Worksheet** on page 38 of the Instructions for Form 1040.
☐ **No.** Complete the rest of Form 1040.

Schedule D (Form 1040) 2005

E X A M P L E 47

During 2005, Joan Rapson (Social Security number 467–37–8383) had the following sales of capital assets. In addition, she has other taxable income of $66,000, including $300 of qualified dividend income.

Description	Acquired On	Date Sold	Sales Price	Tax Basis	Gain or Loss	Character
100 shares Blue stock	1/21/05	11/11/05	$11,000	$17,000	($ 6,000)	STCL
100 shares Yellow stock	9/12/00	10/12/05	36,000	20,000	16,000	LTCG
100 shares Purple stock	3/14/03	10/12/05	14,000	12,000	2,000	LTCG

Qualified Dividends and Capital Gain Tax Worksheet—Line 44

Keep for Your Records

Before you begin:	✓	See the instructions for line 44 on page 37 to see if you can use this worksheet to figure your tax.
	✓	If you do not have to file Schedule D and you received capital gain distributions, be sure you checked the box on line 13 of Form 1040.

1. Enter the amount from Form 1040, line 43 .... **1.** | 78,000
2. Enter the amount from Form 1040, line 9b .... **2.** | 300
3. Are you filing Schedule D?
   - ☒ **Yes.** Enter the **smaller** of line 15 or 16 of Schedule D, but do not enter less than -0-
   - ☐ **No.** Enter the amount from Form 1040, line 13 ⟩ **3.** | 12,000
4. Add lines 2 and 3 .... **4.** | 12,300
5. If you are claiming investment interest expense on Form 4952, enter the amount from line 4g of that form. Otherwise, enter -0- .... **5.** | 0
6. Subtract line 5 from line 4. If zero or less, enter -0-..................... **6.** | 12,300
7. Subtract line 6 from line 1. If zero or less, enter -0-..................... **7.** | 65,700
8. Enter the **smaller** of:
   - The amount on line 1, or
   - $29,700 if single or married filing separately, $59,400 if married filing jointly or qualifying widow(er), $39,800 if head of household. ⟩ .... **8.** | 29,700
9. Is the amount on line 7 equal to or more than the amount on line 8?
   - ☒ **Yes.** Skip lines 9 through 11; go to line 12 and check the "No" box.
   - ☐ **No.** Enter the amount from line 7 .... **9.** |
10. Subtract line 9 from line 8 .... **10.** |
11. Multiply line 10 by 5% (.05)................................**11.** |
12. Are the amounts on lines 6 and 10 the same?
   - ☐ **Yes.** Skip lines 12 through 15; go to line 16.
   - ☒ **No.** Enter the **smaller** of line 1 or line 6 .... **12.** | 12,300
13. Enter the amount from line 10 (if line 10 is blank, enter -0-) .... **13.** | 0
14. Subtract line 13 from line 12..................... **14.** | 12,300
15. Multiply line 14 by 15% (.15) ....**15.** | 1,845
16. Figure the tax on the amount on line 7. Use the Tax Table or Tax Computation Worksheet, whichever applies ....**16.** | 13,096
17. Add lines 11, 15, and 16................................**17.** | 14,941
18. Figure the tax on the amount on line 1. Use the Tax Table or Tax Computation Worksheet, whichever applies ....**18.** | 16,354
19. **Tax on all taxable income.** Enter the **smaller** of line 17 or line 18. Also include this amount on Form 1040, line 44 ....**19.** | 14,941

Joan has a net capital gain of $12,000 ($16,000 5%/15% gain + $2,000 5%/15% gain − $6,000 short-term capital loss). Consequently, all of the net capital gain is composed of 5%/15% gain. Joan's $78,000 taxable income includes $65,700 ($66,000 − $300) of other taxable income. This example is filled in on the Schedule D on pages 16–28 through 16–30. Joan's total stock sales were reported to her on Form 1099–B by her stockbroker. ∎

Tax Treatment of Capital Gains and Losses of Corporate Taxpayers

The treatment of a corporation's net capital gain or loss differs from the rules for individuals. Briefly, the differences are as follows:

[handwritten: Carry back 3 yrs; forward 5 yrs]

[handwritten: Indiv cannot carry back.]

- There is an NCG alternative tax rate of 35 percent.[31] However, since the maximum corporate tax rate is 35 percent, the alternative tax is not beneficial.
- Capital losses offset only capital gains. No deduction of capital losses is permitted against ordinary taxable income (whereas a $3,000 deduction is allowed to individuals).[32]
- Corporations may carry back net capital losses (whether long term or short term) as short-term capital losses for three years; if losses still remain after the carryback, the remaining losses may be carried forward five years.[33] Individuals may carry forward unused capital losses indefinitely, but there is no carryback.

Sparrow Corporation has a $15,000 NLTCL for the current year and $57,000 of ordinary taxable income. Sparrow may not offset the $15,000 NLTCL against its ordinary income by taking a capital loss deduction. The $15,000 NLTCL becomes a $15,000 STCL for carryback and carryover purposes. This amount may be offset by capital gains in the three-year carryback period or, if not absorbed there, offset by capital gains in the five-year carryforward period. ∎

The rules applicable to corporations are discussed in greater detail in Chapter 20.

Importance of Capital Asset Status

Why is capital asset status important? Capital asset status enables the taxpayer to be eligible for the alternative tax on net capital gain. For a taxpayer in the 25, 28, 33, or 35 percent regular tax bracket, a 15 percent rate is available on assets held longer than one year. For a taxpayer in the 10 or 15 percent regular tax bracket, a 5 percent rate is available on assets held longer than one year. Thus, individuals who can receive income in the form of long-term capital gains or qualified dividend income have an advantage over taxpayers who cannot receive income in these forms.

TAX PLANNING
Considerations

Capital asset status is also important because capital gains must be offset by capital losses. If a net capital loss results, the maximum deduction is $3,000 per year.

Consequently, capital gains and losses must be segregated from other types of gains and losses and must be reported separately on Schedule D of Form 1040.

Planning for Capital Asset Status

It is important to keep in mind that capital asset status often is a question of objective evidence. Thus, property that is not a capital asset to one party may qualify as a capital asset to another party.

Diane, a real estate dealer, transfers by gift a tract of land to Jeff, her son. The land was recorded as part of Diane's inventory (it was held for resale) and was therefore not a capital asset to her. Jeff, however, treats the land as an investment. The land is a capital asset in Jeff's hands, and any later taxable disposition of the property by him will yield a capital gain or loss. ∎

If proper planning is carried out, even a dealer may obtain long-term capital gain treatment on the sale of the type of property normally held for resale.

---

[31]§ 1201.
[32]§ 1211(a).

[33]§ 1212(a)(1).

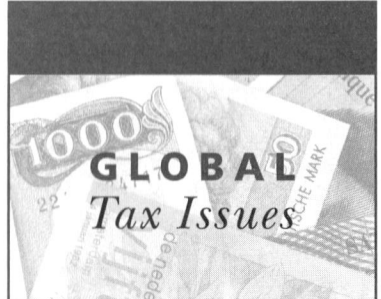

CAPITAL GAIN TREATMENT IN THE UNITED STATES AND OTHER COUNTRIES

The United States currently requires a very complex tax calculation when taxable income includes net long-term capital gain. However, the alternative tax on net long-term capital gain can generate tax savings even when the taxpayer is in the lowest regular tax bracket (10 percent) because there is an alternative tax rate of 5 percent. Many other countries do not have an alternative tax rate on long-term capital gains. Instead, those gains are taxed the same as other income. Consequently, even though the U.S. system is complex, it may be preferable because of the lower tax rates and because the lower rates are available to taxpayers in all tax brackets.

EXAMPLE 50

Jim, a real estate dealer, segregates tract A from the real estate he regularly holds for resale and designates the property as being held for investment purposes. The property is not advertised for sale and is disposed of several years later. The negotiations for the subsequent sale were initiated by the purchaser and not by Jim. Under these circumstances, it would appear that any gain or loss from the sale of tract A should be a capital gain or loss.[34] ∎

When a business is being sold, one of the major decisions usually concerns whether a portion of the sales price is for goodwill. For the seller, goodwill generally represents the disposition of a capital asset. Goodwill has no basis and represents a residual portion of the selling price that cannot be allocated reasonably to the known assets. The amount of goodwill thus represents capital gain.

From a legal perspective, the buyer may prefer that the residual portion of the purchase price be allocated to a covenant not to compete (a promise that the seller will not compete against the buyer by conducting a business similar to the one that the buyer has purchased). Both purchased goodwill and a covenant not to compete are § 197 intangibles. Thus, both must be capitalized and can be amortized over a 15-year statutory period.

To the seller, a covenant produces ordinary income. Thus, the seller would prefer that the residual portion of the selling price be allocated to goodwill—a capital asset. If the buyer does not need the legal protection provided by a covenant, the buyer is neutral regarding whether the residual amount be allocated to a covenant or to goodwill. Since the seller would receive a tax advantage from labeling the residual amount as goodwill, the buyer should factor this into the negotiation of the purchase price.

EXAMPLE 51

Marcia is buying Jack's dry cleaning proprietorship. An appraisal of the assets indicates that a reasonable purchase price would exceed the value of the known assets by $30,000. If the purchase contract does not specify the nature of the $30,000, the amount will be for goodwill, and Jack will have a long-term capital gain of $30,000. Marcia will have a 15-year amortizable $30,000 asset. If Marcia is paying the extra $30,000 to prevent Jack from conducting another dry cleaning business in the area (a covenant not to compete), Jack will have $30,000 of ordinary income. Marcia will have a $30,000 deduction over the statutory 15-year amortization period rather than over the actual life of the covenant (e.g., 5 years). ∎

Effect of Capital Asset Status in Transactions Other Than Sales

The nature of an asset (capital or ordinary) is important in determining the tax consequences that result when a sale or exchange occurs. It may, however, be just as

---

[34]*Toledo, Peoria & Western Railroad Co.*, 35 TCM 1663, T.C.Memo. 1976–366.

significant in circumstances other than a taxable sale or exchange. When a capital asset is disposed of, the result is not always a capital gain or loss. Rather, in general, the disposition must be a sale or exchange. Collection of a debt instrument having a basis less than the face value results in a capital gain if the debt instrument is a capital asset. The collection is a sale or exchange. Sale of the debt shortly before the due date for collection will produce a capital gain.[35] If selling the debt in such circumstances could produce a capital gain but collecting could not, the consistency of what constitutes a capital gain or loss would be frustrated. Another illustration of the sale or exchange principle involves a donation of certain appreciated property to a qualified charity. Recall that in certain circumstances, the measure of the charitable contribution is fair market value when the property, if sold, would have yielded a long-term capital gain [refer to Chapter 10 and the discussion of § 170(e)].

EXAMPLE 52

Sharon wants to donate a tract of unimproved land (basis of $40,000 and fair market value of $200,000) held for the required long-term holding period to State University (a qualified charitable organization). However, Sharon currently is under audit by the IRS for capital gains she reported on certain real estate transactions during an earlier tax year. Although Sharon is not a licensed real estate broker, the IRS agent conducting the audit is contending that she has achieved dealer status by virtue of the number and frequency of the real estate transactions she has conducted. Under these circumstances, Sharon would be well-advised to postpone the donation to State University until her status is clarified. If she has achieved dealer status, the unimproved land may be inventory (refer to Example 50 for another possible result), and Sharon's charitable contribution deduction would be limited to $40,000. If not, and if the land is held as an investment, Sharon's deduction is $200,000 (the fair market value of the property). ∎

Stock Sales

The following rules apply in determining the date of a stock sale:

- The date the sale is executed is the date of the sale. The execution date is the date the broker completes the transaction on the stock exchange.
- The settlement date is the date the cash or other property is paid to the seller of the stock. This date is *not* relevant in determining the date of sale.

EXAMPLE 53

Lupe, a cash basis taxpayer, sells stock that results in a gain. The sale was executed on December 30, 2005. The settlement date is January 2, 2006. The date of sale is December 30, 2005 (the execution date). The holding period for the stock sold ends with the execution date. ∎

Maximizing Benefits

Ordinary losses generally are preferable to capital losses because of the limitations imposed on the deductibility of net capital losses and the requirement that capital losses be used to offset capital gains. The taxpayer may be able to convert what would otherwise have been capital loss to ordinary loss. For example, business (but not nonbusiness) bad debts, losses from the sale or exchange of small business investment company stock, and losses from the sale or exchange of small business company stock all result in ordinary losses.[36]

Although capital losses can be carried over indefinitely, *indefinite* becomes definite when a taxpayer dies. Any loss carryovers not used by the taxpayer are permanently lost. That is, no tax benefit can be derived from the carryovers subsequent to death.[37] Therefore, the potential benefit of carrying over capital losses diminishes when dealing with older taxpayers.

[35]§ 1271(b).
[36]§§ 166(d), 1242, and 1244. Refer to the discussion in Chapter 7.
[37]Rev.Rul. 74–175, 1974–1 C.B. 52.

It is usually beneficial to spread gains over more than one taxable year. In some cases, this can be accomplished through the installment sales method of accounting.

Year-End Planning

The following general rules can be applied for timing the recognition of capital gains and losses near the end of a taxable year:

- If the taxpayer already has recognized more than $3,000 of capital loss, sell assets to generate capital gain equal to the excess of the capital loss over $3,000.

EXAMPLE 54

Kevin has already incurred a $7,000 STCL. Kevin should generate $4,000 of capital gain. The gain will offset $4,000 of the loss. The remaining loss of $3,000 can be deducted against ordinary income. ■

- If the taxpayer already has recognized capital gain, sell assets to generate capital loss equal to the capital gain. The gain will not be taxed, and the loss will be fully *deductible* against the gain.
- Generally, if the taxpayer has a choice between recognizing short-term capital gain or long-term capital gain, long-term capital gain should be recognized because it has the lower tax rate.

KEY TERMS

Alternative tax, 16–23	Holding period, 16–14	Original issue discount (OID), 16–9
Capital asset, 16–3	Lessee, 16–13	Patent, 16–11
Capital gains, 16–2	Lessor, 16–13	Qualified dividend income, 16–23
Capital losses, 16–2	Net capital gain (NCG), 16–20	Sale or exchange, 16–8
Collectibles, 16–22	Net capital loss (NCL), 16–24	Short sale, 16–16
Franchise, 16–12	Options, 16–9	Unrecaptured § 1250 gain, 16–20

PROBLEM MATERIALS

DISCUSSION QUESTIONS

Issue ID 1. An individual taxpayer sells some used assets at a garage sale. Why are none of the proceeds taxable in most situations?

Issue ID 2. Jeremy is a sole proprietor running a video store. A large national chain has made an offer to purchase all of his store assets. What issues does Jeremy face in determining what the results of this sale would be?

Issue ID 3. Melissa is a songwriter part-time and a waitress full-time. To her great surprise, a "song broker" has offered to purchase all of Melissa's rights to a song she wrote. What issues does Melissa face if she accepts this offer?

4. Anwar owns vacant land that he purchased many years ago as an investment. After getting approval to subdivide it into 35 lots, he made minimal improvements and then sold the entire property to a real estate developer. Anwar's recognized gain on the sale was $1.2 million. Is this transaction eligible for the "real property subdivided for sale" provisions?

5. Feng-Shu purchased an original issue discount bond several years ago. He paid $68,000 for the $100,000 face value bond. He sold the bond this year for $83,000. Is all of Feng-Shu's gain long-term capital gain? Why or why not?

6. Katrina was the grantee of an option that would have allowed her to purchase a tract of land for $5 million. She paid $50,000 for the option. She intended to hold the land as an investment if she exercised the option. However, the value of the land did not increase as she had expected, so she let the option lapse after holding it for 14 months. What is the nature of Katrina's gain or loss from this transaction?

7. Juan purchased corporate stock for $10,000 on April 10, 2004. On July 14, 2006, when the stock was worth $7,000, he gave it to his son, Miguel. What has to happen to the value of the property while Miguel holds it if Miguel is to tack Juan's holding period on to his own holding period?

Issue ID

8. Near the end of 2006, Byron realizes that he has a net short-term capital loss of $13,000 for the year. Byron has taxable income (not including the loss) of $123,000 and is single. He owns numerous stocks that could be sold for a long-term capital gain. What should he do before the end of 2006?

Issue ID

PROBLEMS

9. During the year, Eric had the four property transactions summarized below. Eric is a collector of antique automobiles and occasionally sells one to get funds to buy another. What are the amount and nature of the gain or loss from each of these transactions?

Property	Date Acquired	Date Sold	Adjusted Basis	Sale Price
Antique truck	06/18/98	05/23/06	$47,000	$35,000
Blue Growth Fund (100 shares)	12/23/00	11/22/06	12,000	23,000
Orange bonds	02/12/01	04/11/06	34,000	42,000*
Green stock (100 shares)	02/14/06	11/23/06	13,000	11,000

*The sales price included $750 of accrued interest.

10. Revez owns an antique shop. He buys property from estates, often at much less than the retail value of the property. Recently, Revez sold for $4,000 an antique desk for which he had paid $1,250. Revez had held the desk in his shop for 36 months before selling it. Revez would like the gain on the sale of the desk to be a long-term capital gain. How can he achieve that objective?

Decision Making

11. All of the following assets are held by Chuck, who is not in business. Which ones are capital assets?
    a. Ten shares of Green Motors common stock.
    b. A note Chuck received when he loaned $3,000 to a friend.
    c. Chuck's personal use automobile.
    d. A letter written by Abraham Lincoln that Chuck purchased at an auction. Chuck is a collector of Lincoln memorabilia.

12. Brenda Reynolds is a dealer in securities. She has spotted a fast-rising company and would like to buy and hold its stock for investment. The stock is currently selling for $145 per share, and Brenda thinks it will climb to $200 a share within two years. Brenda's co-workers have told her that there is "no way" she can get long-term capital gain treatment when she purchases stock because she is a securities dealer. Brenda has asked you to calculate her potential gain and tell her whether her co-workers are right. Draft a letter to Brenda responding to her request. Her address is 200 Morningside Drive, Hattiesburg, MS 39406.

Communications

13. Sue Ellen meets all the requirements of § 1237 (subdivided realty). In 2006, she begins selling lots and sells four separate lots to four different purchasers. She also sells two contiguous lots to another purchaser. The sale price of each lot is $20,000. Sue Ellen's basis for each lot is $15,000. Selling expenses are $500 per lot.
    a. What are the realized and recognized gain?
    b. Explain the nature of the gain (i.e., ordinary income or capital gain).
    c. Would your answers change if, instead, the lots sold to the fifth purchaser were not contiguous? If so, how?

Decision Making

14. Sue has had a bad year with her investments. She lent a friend $3,700; the friend did not repay the loan when it was due, and then declared bankruptcy. The loan is totally uncollectible. Sue also was notified by her broker that the Willow corporate bonds she owned became worthless on October 13, 2006. She had purchased the bonds for $12,000 on November 10, 2005. Sue also had a $30,000 loss on the disposition of § 1244 corporate stock that she purchased several years ago. Sue is single.
    a. What are the nature and amount of Sue's losses?
    b. What is Sue's AGI for 2006 assuming she has $65,000 of ordinary gross income from sources other than those discussed above?
    c. What are the nature and amount of Sue's loss carryforwards?

15. Sivu purchased $600,000 face value of publicly traded Brown corporate bonds for $530,000 three years ago when the bonds were issued. Sivu had amortized $17,000 of original issue discount when he sold the bonds for $401,000 this year. What is Sivu's adjusted basis for the bonds when he sells them, and what are the amount and nature of his loss from disposition of the bonds?

Decision Making

16. Frank is an investor in vacant land. When he thinks he has identified property that would be a good investment, he approaches the landowner, pays the landowner for a "right of first refusal" to purchase the land, records this right in the property records, and then waits to see if the land increases in value. The right of first refusal is valid for four years. Fourteen months ago, Frank paid a landowner $4,000 for a right of first refusal. The land was selected as the site of a new shopping center, and the landowner was offered $4 million for the land. In its title search on the land, the buyer discovered Frank's right of first refusal and involved him in the purchase negotiations. Ultimately, the landowner paid Frank $120,000 to give up his right of first refusal; the landowner then sold the land to the buyer for $4,120,000. Frank has a marginal tax rate of 35%.
    a. What difference does it make whether or not Frank treats the right of first refusal as an option to purchase the land?
    b. What difference does it make whether or not Frank is a "dealer" in land?

17. Celia was the owner of vacant land she was holding for investment. She paid $1 million for the land in 1999. Frank is an investor in vacant land. Fourteen months ago, Frank paid Celia $10,000 for a "right of first refusal" to purchase the land. The right of first refusal was valid for four years. The land was selected as the site of a new shopping center, and Celia was offered $4 million for the land. In its title search on the land, the buyer discovered Frank's right of first refusal and involved him in the purchase negotiations. Ultimately, Celia paid Frank $120,000 to give up his right of first refusal; she then sold the land to the buyer for $4,120,000. Celia has a marginal tax rate of 35%. What are the amount and nature of Celia's gain or loss from disposition of the land?

Decision Making

18. Mateen, an inventor, obtained a patent on a chemical process to clean old aluminum siding so that it can be easily repainted. Mateen has no tax basis in the patent. Mateen does not have the capital to begin manufacturing and selling this product, so he has done nothing with the patent since obtaining it two years ago. Now a group of individuals has approached him and offered two alternatives. Under one alternative, they will pay Mateen $600,000 (payable evenly over the next 15 years) for the exclusive right to manufacture and sell the product. Under the other, they will form a business and contribute capital to it to begin manufacturing and selling the product; Mateen will receive 20% of the company's shares of stock in exchange for all of his patent rights. Discuss which alternative is better for Mateen.

19. Freys, Inc., sells a 12-year franchise to Reynaldo. The franchise contains many restrictions on how Reynaldo may operate his store. For instance, Reynaldo cannot use less than Grade 10 Idaho potatoes, must fry the potatoes at a constant 410 degrees, dress

store personnel in Freys-approved uniforms, and have a Freys sign that meets detailed specifications on size, color, and construction. When the franchise contract is signed, Reynaldo makes a noncontingent $160,000 payment to Freys. During the same year, Reynaldo pays Freys $300,000—14% of Reynaldo's sales. How does Freys treat each of these payments? How does Reynaldo treat each of the payments?

20. Tricia owns numerous office buildings. A major tenant of one of the buildings wished to cancel its lease because it was moving to another city. After lengthy negotiations, the tenant paid Tricia $500,000 to cancel its obligations under the lease. If the tenant had fulfilled the lease terms, Tricia would have received rent of $1.8 million. What factors should Tricia consider to determine the amount and character of her income from these circumstances?

Issue ID

21. Faleh exchanges a business copying machine for another copier in a § 1031 like-kind exchange. Faleh acquired the relinquished machine on March 1, 2003, and the exchange occurred on July 3, 2006. When does the holding period of the replacement machine begin?

22. Dennis sells short 100 shares of ARC stock at $20 per share on January 15, 2006. He buys 200 shares of ARC stock on April 1, 2006, at $25 per share. On May 2, 2006, he closes the short sale by delivering 100 of the shares purchased on April 1.
    a. What are the amount and nature of Dennis's loss upon closing the short sale?
    b. When does the holding period for the remaining 100 shares begin?
    c. If Dennis sells (at $27 per share) the remaining 100 shares on January 20, 2007, what will be the nature of his gain or loss?

23. Elaine Case (single with no dependents) has the following transactions in 2006:

Communications

AGI (exclusive of capital gains and losses)	$240,000
Long-term capital gain	22,000
Long-term capital loss	(5,000)
Short-term capital gain	19,000
Short-term capital loss	(23,000)

What is Elaine's net capital gain or loss? Draft a letter to Elaine describing how the net capital gain or loss will be treated on her tax return. Assume Elaine's income from other sources puts her in the 35% bracket. Elaine's address is 300 Ireland Avenue, Shepherdstown, WV 25443.

24. In 2006, Betty (head of household with three dependents) had an $18,000 loss from the sale of a personal residence. She also purchased from an individual inventor for $8,000 (and resold in two months for $7,000) a patent on a rubber bonding process. The patent had not yet been reduced to practice. Betty purchased the patent as an investment. Additionally, she had the following capital gains and losses from stock transactions:

Communications

Long-term capital loss	($ 3,000)
Long-term capital loss carryover from 2005	(12,000)
Short-term capital gain	21,000
Short-term capital loss	(6,000)

What is Betty's net capital gain or loss? Draft a letter to Betty explaining the tax treatment of the sale of her personal residence. Assume Betty's income from other sources puts her in the 35% bracket. Betty's address is 1120 West Street, Ashland, OR 97520.

25. Bridgette is known as the "doll lady." She started collecting dolls as a child, always received one or more dolls as gifts on her birthday, never sold any dolls, and eventually owned 600 dolls. She is retiring and moving to a small apartment and has decided to sell her collection. She lists the dolls on an Internet auction site and, to her great surprise, receives an offer from another doll collector of $45,000 for the entire collection. Bridgette sells the entire collection, except for five dolls that she purchased during the last year. She had owned all the dolls sold for more than a year. What tax factors should Bridgette consider in deciding how to report the sale?

Issue ID

26. For 2006, Ramon has a net long-term capital loss of $45,000, a net short-term capital gain of $39,000, and $4,000 of qualified dividend income. Not including these items, he has $566,000 of taxable income from other sources.
    a. What is Ramon's net capital gain or loss?
    b. What is Ramon's taxable income?
    c. How much of Ramon's taxable income is eligible for the alternative 5%/15% tax rate?

27. Sateesh, a single taxpayer filing as head of household, had a $45,000 net capital loss in 2006. He used the standard deduction and had three exemptions (one personal exemption and two dependency exemptions). His properly determined taxable income was negative $6,000. What is his capital loss carryforward to 2007?

28. For 2006, Wilma has properly determined taxable income of $36,000, including $3,000 of unrecaptured § 1250 gain and $6,200 of 5%/15% gain. Wilma qualifies for head-of-household filing status. Compute Wilma's tax liability and the tax savings from the alternative tax on net capital gain.

29. Asok's AGI for 2006 is $133,050. Included in this AGI is a $45,000 25% long-term capital gain and a $13,000 5%/15% long-term capital gain. Asok is single, uses the standard deduction, and has only his personal exemption. Compute his taxable income, the tax liability, and the tax savings from the alternative tax on net capital gain.

30. Chartreuse, Inc., a C corporation, has taxable income from operations of $1,432,000 for 2006. It also has a net long-term capital loss of $455,000 from the sale of a subsidiary's stock. The year 2006 is the first year in the last 10 years that Chartreuse has not had at least $500,000 per year of net long-term capital gains. What is Chartreuse's 2006 taxable income, and what, if anything, can it do with any unused capital losses?

Decision Making

31. Hsui, who is single, is the owner of a sole proprietorship. Two years ago, Hsui developed a process for preserving fresh fruit that gives the fruit a much longer shelf life. The process is not patented or copyrighted, but only Hsui knows how it works. Hsui has been approached by a company that would like to buy the process. Hsui insists that she receive a long-term employment contract with the acquiring company as well as be paid for the rights to the process. The acquiring company offers Hsui a choice of two options: (1) $850,000 in cash for the process and a 10-year covenant not to compete at $45,000 per year or (2) $850,000 in cash for a 10-year covenant not to compete and $45,000 per year for 10 years in payment for the process. Which option should Hsui accept? What is the tax effect on the acquiring company of each approach?

CUMULATIVE PROBLEMS

Tax Return Problem

32. Sue Lowe lives at 1310 Meadow Lane, Lima, OH 23412, and her Social Security number is 312–55–8000. Sue is single and has a 20-year-old son, Kania. His Social Security number is 480–01–9030. Kania lives with Sue, and she fully supports him. Kania spent 2005 traveling in Europe and was not a college student. He had gross income of $4,355 in 2005.

    Sue owns the Lowe Enterprises sole proprietorship, a data processing service (38–1234567), which is located at 456 Hill Street, Lima, OH 23401. The business activity code is 514210. Her 2005 Form 1040, Schedule C for Lowe Enterprises shows revenues of $155,000, office expenses of $46,759, employee salaries of $23,000, employee payroll taxes of $1,760, meals and entertainment expenses (before the 50% reduction) of $18,000, and rent expense of $44,000. The rent expense includes payments related to renting an office ($32,000) and payments related to renting various equipment ($12,000). There is no depreciation because all depreciable equipment owned has been fully depreciated in previous years. No fringe benefits are provided to the employee. Sue personally purchases health insurance on herself and Kania. The premiums are $3,000 per year.

Sue has an extensive stock portfolio and has prepared the following analysis:

Stock	Number of Shares	Date Purchased	Date Sold	Per Share Cost	Per Share Selling Price	Total Dividends
Blue	10	10/18/04	10/11/05	$80	$ 72	$30
Green	30	10/11/96	10/11/05	43	157	70
Purple	15	3/10/05	8/11/05	62	33	45

Note: The per share cost includes commissions, and the per share selling price is net of commissions. Also, the dividends are the actual dividends received in 2005.

Sue had $800 of interest income from State of Ohio bonds and $600 of interest income on her Lima Savings Bank account. She also received $5,000 of alimony payments.

Sue itemizes her deductions and had the following items, which may be relevant to her return:

Item	Amount	Comment
Unreimbursed medical expenses for Sue (all for visits to doctors)	$1,786	Does not include health insurance premiums.
State income taxes paid	1,830	
Real property taxes on personal residence	3,230	
Interest paid on home mortgage (Form 1098)	8,137	The loan is secured by the residence and was incurred when the home was purchased.
Charitable contributions	940	Cash paid to Sue's church.
Sales taxes	619	Amount per sales tax table.

Sue made a $6,500 estimated Federal income tax payment, does not wish any of her taxes to finance presidential elections, has no foreign bank accounts or trusts, and wishes any refund to be applied against her 2006 taxes.

Compute Sue's net tax payable or refund due for 2005. If you use tax forms for your computations, you will need Forms 1040 and 4952 and Schedules A, B, C, D, and SE. Suggested software: TurboTax.

33. Paul Barrone is a graduate student at State University. His 10-year-old son, Jamie, lives with him, and Paul is Jamie's sole support. Paul's wife died in 2005, and Paul has not remarried. Paul received $320,000 of life insurance proceeds (related to his wife's death) in early 2006 and immediately invested the entire amount as shown below:

Tax Return Problem

Communications

Item	Date Acquired	Cost	Date Sold	Selling Price	Dividends/ Interest
1,000 shares Blue	01/23/06	$ 14,000	12/03/06	$ 3,500	None
400 shares Magenta	01/23/06	23,000			$ 750
600 shares Orange	01/23/06	230,000			2,300
100 shares Brown	06/23/02	2,800	01/23/06	14,000	None
Green bonds	01/23/06	23,000			1,200
Gold money market fund	01/23/06	30,000			600

Paul had $32,000 of taxable graduate assistant earnings from State University and also received a $10,000 scholarship. He used $8,000 of the scholarship to pay his tuition and fees for the year and $2,000 for Jamie's day care. Jamie attended Little Kids Daycare Center, a state certified child care facility. Paul received a statement related to the

Green bonds saying that there was $45 of original issue discount amortization during 2006. Paul maintains the receipts for the sales taxes he paid of $735.

Paul lives at 1610 Cherry Lane, State College, MD 34212, and his Social Security number is 452–78–0004. Jamie's Social Security number is 480–01–9030. The university withheld $3,000 of Federal income tax from Paul's salary. Paul is not itemizing his deductions.

Part 1—Tax Computation
Compute Paul's lowest tax liability for 2006.

Part 2—Tax Planning
Paul is concerned because the Green bonds were worth only $18,000 at the end of 2006, $5,000 less than he paid for them. He is an inexperienced investor and wants to know if this $5,000 is deductible. The bonds had original issue discount of $2,000 when he purchased them, and he is also curious about how that affects his investment in the bonds. The bonds had 20 years left to maturity when he purchased them. Draft a brief letter to Paul explaining how to handle these items. Also, prepare a memo for Paul's tax file.

RESEARCH PROBLEMS

Note: Solutions to Research Problems can be prepared by using the **RIA Checkpoint**® **Student Edition** online research product, which is available to accompany this text. It is also possible to prepare solutions to the Research Problems by using tax research materials found in a standard tax library.

Research Problem 1.   Ali owns 100 shares of Brown Corporation stock. He purchased the stock at five different times and at five different prices per share as indicated:

Share Block	Number of Shares	Per Share Price	Purchase Date
A	10	$60	10/10/94
B	20	20	8/11/95
C	15	15	10/24/95
D	35	30	4/23/97
E	20	25	7/28/97

On April 28, 2006, Ali will sell 40 shares of Brown stock for $40 per share. All of Ali's shares are held by his stockbroker. The broker's records track when the shares were purchased. May Ali designate the shares he sells, and, if so, which shares should he sell? Assume Ali wants to maximize his gain because he has a capital loss carryforward.

Communications

Research Problem 2.   Clean Corporation runs a chain of dry cleaners. Borax is used heavily in Clean's dry cleaning process and has been in short supply several times in the past. Clean Corporation buys a controlling interest in Dig Corporation—a borax mining concern. Clean's sole reason for purchasing the Dig stock is to assure Clean of a continuous supply of borax if another shortage develops. Although borax must be refined before it is usable for dry cleaning purposes, a well-established commodities market exists for trading unrefined borax for refined borax. After owning the Dig stock for several years, Clean sells the stock at a loss because Dig is in difficult financial straits. Clean no longer needs to own Dig because Clean has obtained an alternative source of borax. What is the nature of Clean's loss on the disposition of the Dig Corporation stock? Write a letter to the controller, Salvio Guitterez, that contains your advice and prepare a memo for the tax files. The mailing address of Clean Corporation is 4455 Whitman Way, San Mateo, CA 44589.

Research Problem 3.   Siva Nathaniel owns various plots of land in Fulton County, Georgia. He acquired the land at various times during the last 20 years. About every fourth year, Siva subdivides one of the properties he owns into lots. He then has water, sewer, natural gas, and electricity hookups put in on each lot and paves the streets. Siva has always treated his sales of such lots as sales of capital assets. His previous tax returns were prepared by an accountant whose practice you recently purchased. Has the proper tax treatment been used on the prior tax returns?

Partial list of research aids:
§§ 1221 and 1237
Jesse W. and Betty J. English, 65 TCM 2160, T.C.Memo. 1993–111.

Research Problem 4.   Mobley is a retired high school teacher. He has $65,000 of AGI from his retirement income. He is an avid player of the stock market. During 2006, he made 3,000 transactions buying and selling stocks. All the sales involved stocks held short term. His net loss for the year was $17,000. He incurred $7,000 of expenses for subscriptions to various publications dealing with how to buy and sell stocks. He has two questions. (1) Is the loss a short-term capital loss or an ordinary loss? (2) Is the $7,000 of expenses deductible *for* or from AGI?

Partial list of research aids:
Marlowe King, 89 T.C. 445 (1987), *acq.* 1988–2 C.B. 1.
Frederick Mayer, T.C.Memo. 1994–209 (1994), 67 TCM 2949.

Use the tax resources of the Internet to address the following questions. Do not restrict your search to the World Wide Web, but include a review of newsgroups and general reference materials, practitioner sites and resources, primary sources of the tax law, chat rooms and discussion groups, and other opportunities.

 Internet *Activity*

Research Problem 5.   Find a Web site that discusses the income tax in England. Determine whether England has an alternative tax on net long-term capital gains similar to that in the United States.

Research Problem 6.   Find a Web site, other than the IRS Web site, that discusses the taxation of subdivided real property.

CHAPTER 17

Property Transactions: § 1231 and Recapture Provisions

LEARNING OBJECTIVES

After completing Chapter 17, you should be able to:

LO.1
Understand the rationale for and the nature and treatment of gains and losses from the disposition of business assets.

LO.2
Distinguish § 1231 assets from ordinary assets and capital assets and calculate the § 1231 gain or loss.

LO.3
Determine when § 1245 recapture applies and how it is computed.

LO.4
Determine when § 1250 recapture applies and how it is computed.

LO.5
Understand considerations common to §§ 1245 and 1250.

LO.6
Apply the special recapture provisions for related parties and IDC and be aware of the special recapture provision for corporations.

LO.7
Describe and apply the reporting procedures for §§ 1231, 1245, and 1250.

LO.8
Identify tax planning opportunities associated with §§ 1231, 1245, and 1250.

Generic Motors Corporation sold machinery, office furniture, and unneeded production plants for $100 million last year. The corporation's disposition of these assets resulted in $60 million of gains and $13 million of losses. How are these gains and losses treated for tax purposes? Do any special tax rules apply? Could any of the gains and losses receive capital gain or loss treatment? This chapter answers these questions by explaining how to *classify* gains and losses from the disposition of assets that are used in the business rather than held for resale. Chapter 8 discussed how to *depreciate* such assets. Chapters 14 and 15 discussed how to determine the *adjusted basis* and the *amount* of gain or loss from their disposition.

A long-term capital gain was defined in Chapter 16 as the recognized gain from the sale or exchange of a capital asset held for the required long-term holding period.[1] Long-term capital assets are capital assets held more than one year.

This chapter is concerned with classification under § 1231, which applies to the sale or exchange of business properties and to certain involuntary conversions. The business properties are not capital assets because they are depreciable and/or real property used in business or for the production of income. Section 1221(a)(2) provides that such assets are not capital assets. Nonetheless, these business properties may be held for long periods of time and may be sold at a gain. Congress decided many years ago that such assets deserved *limited* capital gain–type treatment. Unfortunately, this limited capital gain–type treatment is very complex and difficult to understand.

Because the limited capital gain–type treatment sometimes gives too much tax advantage if assets are eligible for depreciation (or cost recovery), certain recapture rules may prevent the capital gain treatment when depreciation is taken. Thus, this chapter also covers the recapture provisions that tax as ordinary income certain gains that might otherwise qualify for long-term capital gain treatment.

---

[1]§ 1222(3). To be eligible for any beneficial tax treatment, the holding period must be more than one year.

Section 1231 Assets

Relationship to Capital Assets

Depreciable property and real property used in business are not capital assets.[2] Thus, the recognized gains from the disposition of such property (principally machinery, equipment, buildings, and land) would appear to be ordinary income rather than capital gain. Due to § 1231, however, *net gain* from the disposition of such property is sometimes *treated* as *long-term capital gain*. A long-term holding period requirement must be met; the disposition must generally be from a sale, exchange, or involuntary conversion; and certain recapture provisions must be satisfied for this result to occur. Section 1231 may also apply to involuntary conversions of capital assets. Since an involuntary conversion is not a sale or exchange, such a disposition normally would not result in a capital gain.

If the disposition of depreciable property and real property used in business results in a *net loss*, § 1231 *treats* the *loss* as an *ordinary loss* rather than as a capital loss. Ordinary losses are fully deductible *for* adjusted gross income (AGI). Capital losses are offset by capital gains, and, if any loss remains, the loss is deductible to the extent of $3,000 per year for individuals and currently is not deductible at all by regular corporations. It seems, therefore, that § 1231 provides the *best* of both potential results: net gain may be treated as long-term capital gain, and net loss is treated as ordinary loss.

> **EXAMPLE 1**
>
> Roberto sells business land and a building at a $5,000 gain and business equipment at a $3,000 loss. Both properties were held for the long-term holding period. Roberto's net gain is $2,000, and that net gain may (depending on various recapture rules discussed later in this chapter) be treated as a long-term capital gain under § 1231. ∎

> **EXAMPLE 2**
>
> Samantha sells business equipment at a $10,000 loss and business land at a $2,000 gain. Both properties were held for the long-term holding period. Samantha's net loss is $8,000, and that net loss is an ordinary loss. ∎

The rules regarding § 1231 treatment do *not* apply to *all* business property. Important in this regard are the holding period requirements and the fact that the property must be either depreciable property or real estate used in business. Nor is § 1231 necessarily limited to business property. Transactions involving certain capital assets may fall into the § 1231 category. Thus, § 1231 singles out only some types of business property.

As discussed in Chapter 16, long-term capital gains receive beneficial tax treatment. Section 1231 requires netting of § **1231 gains and losses**. If the result is a gain, it may be treated as a long-term capital gain. The net gain is added to the "real" long-term capital gains (if any) and netted with capital losses (if any). Thus,

[2]§ 1221(a)(2).

LO.1

Understand the rationale for and the nature and treatment of gains and losses from the disposition of business assets.

the net § 1231 gain may eventually be eligible for beneficial capital gain treatment or help avoid the unfavorable net capital loss result. The § 1231 gain and loss netting may result in a loss. In this case, the loss is an ordinary loss and is deductible *for* AGI. Finally, § 1231 assets are treated the same as capital assets for purposes of the appreciated property charitable contribution provisions (refer to Chapter 10).

Justification for Favorable Tax Treatment

The favorable capital gain/ordinary loss treatment sanctioned by § 1231 can be explained by examining several historical developments. Before 1938, business property had been included in the definition of capital assets. Thus, if such property was sold for a loss (not an unlikely possibility during the depression years of the 1930s), a capital loss resulted. If, however, the property was depreciable and could be retained for its estimated useful life, much (if not all) of its costs could be recovered in the form of depreciation. Because the allowance for depreciation was fully deductible whereas capital losses were not, the tax law favored those who did not dispose of an asset. Congress recognized this inequity when it removed business property from the capital asset classification. During the period 1938–1942, therefore, all such gains and losses were ordinary gains and losses.

With the advent of World War II, two developments in particular forced Congress to reexamine the situation regarding business assets. First, the sale of business assets at a gain was discouraged because the gain would be ordinary income. Gains were common because the war effort had inflated prices. Second, taxpayers who did not want to sell their assets often were required to because the government acquired them through condemnation. Often, as a result of the condemnation awards, taxpayers who were forced to part with their property experienced large gains and were deprived of the benefits of future depreciation deductions. Of course, the condemnations constituted involuntary conversions, so taxpayers could defer the gain by timely reinvestment in property that was "similar or related in service or use." But where was such property to be found in view of wartime restrictions and other governmental condemnations? The end result did not seem equitable: a large ordinary gain due to government action and no possibility of deferral due to government restrictions.

In recognition of these conditions, in 1942, Congress eased the tax bite on the disposition of some business property by allowing preferential capital gain treatment. Thus, the present scheme of § 1231 and the dichotomy of capital gain/ordinary loss treatment evolved from a combination of economic considerations existing in 1938 and 1942.

LO.2
Distinguish § 1231 assets from ordinary assets and capital assets and calculate the § 1231 gain or loss.

Property Included

Section 1231 property generally includes the following assets if they are held for more than one year:

- Depreciable or real property used in business or for the production of income (principally machinery and equipment, buildings, and land).
- Timber, coal, or domestic iron ore to which § 631 applies.
- Livestock held for draft, breeding, dairy, or sporting purposes.
- Unharvested crops on land used in business.
- Certain *purchased* intangible assets (such as patents and goodwill) that are eligible for amortization.

These assets are ordinary assets until they have been held for more than one year. Only then do they become § 1231 assets.

Property Excluded

Section 1231 property generally does *not* include the following:

- Property not held for the long-term holding period. Since the benefit of § 1231 is long-term capital gain treatment, the holding period must correspond to the more-than-one-year holding period that applies to capital assets. Livestock must be held at least 12 months (24 months in some cases). Unharvested crops do not have to be held for the required long-term holding period, but the land must be held for the long-term holding period.
- Nonpersonal use property where casualty losses exceed casualty gains for the taxable year. If a taxpayer has a net casualty loss, the individual casualty gains and losses are treated as ordinary gains and losses.
- Inventory and property held primarily for sale to customers.
- Copyrights; literary, musical, or artistic compositions, etc.; and certain U.S. government publications.
- Accounts receivable and notes receivable arising in the ordinary course of the trade or business.

Special Rules for Certain § 1231 Assets

A rather diverse group of assets is included under § 1231. The following discussion summarizes the special rules for some of those assets.

Timber. Congress has provided preferential treatment relative to the natural growth value of timber, which takes a relatively long time to mature. Congress believed that this preferential treatment would encourage reforestation of timber lands. A taxpayer disposing of timber held for the long-term holding period has a long-term capital gain or loss if the timber was held for investment, has a § 1231 gain or loss if the timber was used in a trade or business, but, without special statutory treatment, would have ordinary income or loss if the timber was held as inventory. Section 631(a) allows the taxpayer to *elect* to treat the cutting of timber as a sale or exchange and, if the election is made, to treat the sale as the disposition of a § 1231 asset.[3]

taxpayer elects.

The recognized § 1231 gain or loss is determined at the time the timber is cut and is equal to the difference between the timber's fair market value as of the *first day* of the taxable year and the adjusted basis for depletion. If a taxpayer sells the timber for more or less than the fair market value as of the first day of the taxable year in which it is cut, the difference is ordinary income or loss.

EXAMPLE 3

Several years ago, Tom, a timber dealer, purchased a tract of land with a substantial stand of trees on it. The land cost $40,000, and the timber cost $100,000. On the first day of 2006, the timber was appraised at $250,000. In August 2006, Tom cut the timber and sold it for $265,000. Tom elects to treat the cutting as a sale or exchange under § 1231. He has a $150,000 § 1231 gain ($250,000 − $100,000) and a $15,000 ordinary gain ($265,000 − $250,000).

What if the timber had been sold for $235,000? Tom would still have a $150,000 § 1231 gain, but he would also have a $15,000 ordinary loss. The price for computing § 1231 gain is the price at the beginning of the tax year. Any difference between that price and the sales price is ordinary gain or loss. Here, since the price declined by $15,000, Tom has an ordinary loss in that amount. ∎

---

[3]§ 631(a) and Reg. § 1.631–1. To receive § 631 treatment, the holding period for the timber must be greater than one year.

Livestock. Cattle and horses must be held 24 months or more and other livestock must be held 12 months or more to qualify under § 1231.[4] The primary reason for enacting this provision was the considerable amount of litigation over the character of livestock [whether livestock was held primarily for sale to customers (ordinary income) or for use in a trade or business (§ 1231 property)]. Poultry is not livestock for purposes of § 1231.

Section 1231 Assets Disposed of by Casualty or Theft. When § 1231 assets are disposed of by casualty or theft, a special netting rule is applied. For simplicity, the term *casualty* is used to mean both casualty and theft dispositions. First, the casualty gains and losses from § 1231 assets *and* the casualty gains and losses from long-term nonpersonal use capital assets are determined. A nonpersonal use capital asset might be an investment painting or a baseball card collection held by a non-dealer in baseball cards.

Next, the § 1231 asset casualty gains and losses and the nonpersonal use capital asset casualty gains and losses are netted together (see Concept Summary 17–1) . If the result is a *net loss*, the § 1231 casualty gains and the nonpersonal use capital asset casualty gains are treated as ordinary gains, the § 1231 casualty losses are deductible *for* AGI, and the nonpersonal use capital asset casualty losses are deductible *from* AGI subject to the 2 percent-of-AGI limitation.

If the result of the netting is a *net gain*, the net gain is treated as a § 1231 gain. Thus, a § 1231 asset disposed of by casualty may or may not get § 1231 treatment, depending on whether the netting process results in a gain or a loss. Also, a nonpersonal use capital asset disposed of by casualty may get § 1231 treatment or ordinary treatment, but will not get capital gain or loss treatment!

Personal use property casualty gains and losses are not subject to the § 1231 rules. If the result of netting these gains and losses is a gain, the net gain is a capital gain. If the netting results in a loss, the net loss is a deduction *from* AGI to the extent it exceeds 10 percent of AGI.

Casualties, thefts, and condemnations are *involuntary conversions*. Involuntary conversion gains may be deferred if conversion proceeds are reinvested; involuntary conversion losses are recognized currently (refer to Chapter 15) regardless of whether the conversion proceeds are reinvested. Thus, the special netting process discussed above for casualties and thefts would not include gains that are not currently recognizable because the insurance proceeds are reinvested.

The special netting process for casualties and thefts also does not include condemnation gains and losses. Consequently, a § 1231 asset disposed of by condemnation will receive § 1231 treatment. This variation between recognized casualty and

---

[4]Note that the holding period is "12 months or more" and not "more than 12 months."

CONCEPT SUMMARY   17–1

Section 1231 Netting Procedure

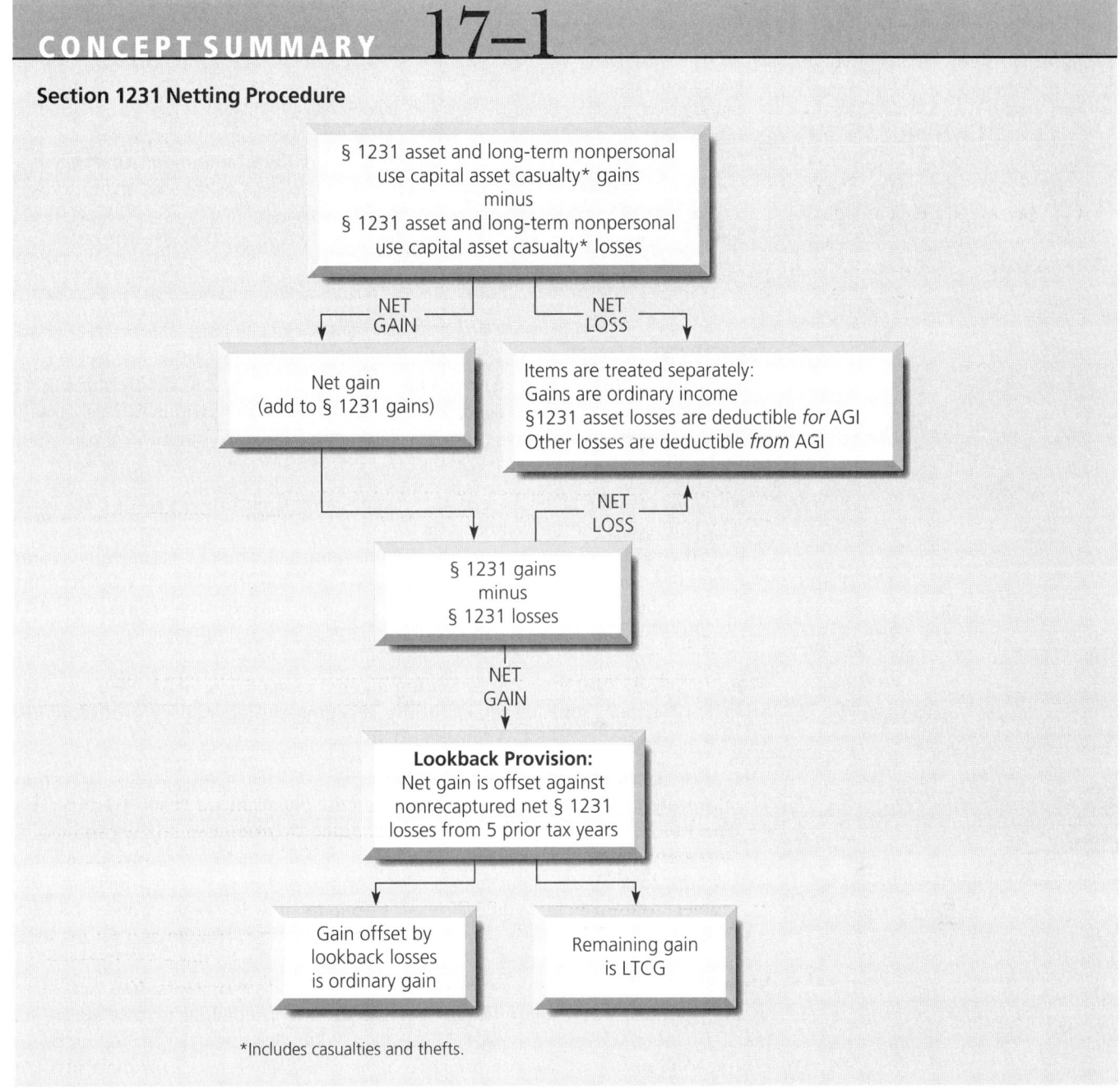

*Includes casualties and thefts.

condemnation gains and losses sheds considerable light on what § 1231 is all about. Section 1231 has no effect on whether or not *realized* gain or loss is recognized. Instead, § 1231 merely dictates how such *recognized* gain or loss is *classified* (ordinary, capital, or § 1231) under certain conditions.

Personal use property condemnation gains and losses are not subject to the § 1231 rules. The gains are capital gains (because personal use property is a capital asset), and the losses are nondeductible because they arise from the disposition of personal use property.

General Procedure for § 1231 Computation

The tax treatment of § 1231 gains and losses depends on the results of a rather complex *netting* procedure. The steps in this netting procedure are as follows.

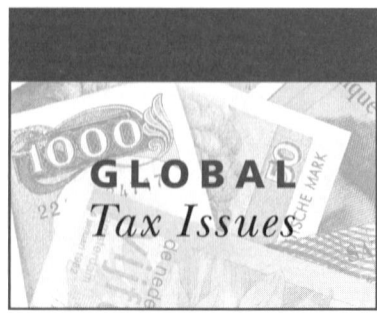

CANADIAN SLOW DEPRECIATION

A manufacturer has a division in Canada that manufactures auto components. The components are shipped to Detroit and become part of U.S.-manufactured automobiles. Due to slow auto sales, the manufacturer closes the Canadian plant and moves its machinery to the United States. Later, the manufacturer sells the machinery and has a tax loss because the machinery's adjusted basis is much higher than that of similar equipment that was used exclusively in the United States. The adjusted basis of the formerly Canadian equipment is higher because straight-line tax depreciation was required for the Canadian property (see Chapter 8).

Step 1: Casualty Netting. Net all recognized long-term gains and losses from casualties of § 1231 assets and nonpersonal use capital assets. Casualty gains result when insurance proceeds exceed the adjusted basis of the property. This casualty netting is beneficial because if there is a net gain, the gain may receive long-term capital gain treatment. If there is a net loss, it receives ordinary loss treatment.

  a. If the casualty gains exceed the casualty losses, add the excess to the other § 1231 gains for the taxable year.
  b. If the casualty losses exceed the casualty gains, exclude all casualty losses and gains from further § 1231 computation. If this is the case, all casualty gains are ordinary income. Section 1231 asset casualty losses are deductible *for* AGI. Other casualty losses are deductible *from* AGI.

Step 2: § 1231 Netting. After adding any net casualty gain from Step 1a to the other § 1231 gains and losses (including recognized § 1231 asset condemnation gains and losses), net all § 1231 gains and losses.

  a. If the gains exceed the losses, the net gain is offset by the "lookback" nonrecaptured § 1231 losses (see below) from the five prior tax years. To the extent of this offset, the net § 1231 gain is classified as ordinary gain. Any remaining gain is long-term capital gain.
  b. If the losses exceed the gains, all gains are ordinary income. Section 1231 asset losses are deductible *for* AGI. Other casualty losses are deductible *from* AGI.

Step 3: § 1231 Lookback Provision. The net § 1231 gain from Step 2a is offset by the nonrecaptured net § 1231 losses for the five preceding taxable years. For 2006, the lookback years are 2001, 2002, 2003, 2004, and 2005. To the extent of the nonrecaptured net § 1231 loss, the current-year net § 1231 gain is ordinary income. The *nonrecaptured* net § 1231 losses are those that have not already been used to offset net § 1231 gains. Only the net § 1231 gain exceeding this net § 1231 loss carryforward is given long-term capital gain treatment. Concept Summary 17–1 summarizes the § 1231 computational procedure. Examples 6 and 7 illustrate the **§ 1231 lookback** provision.

   Examples 4 through 7 illustrate the application of the § 1231 computation procedure.

EXAMPLE 4

During 2006, Ross had $125,000 of AGI before considering the following recognized gains and losses:

Capital Gains and Losses

Long-term capital gain	$3,000
Long-term capital loss	(400)
Short-term capital gain	1,000
Short-term capital loss	(200)

Casualties

Theft of diamond ring (owned four months)	($ 800)*
Fire damage to personal residence (owned 10 years)	(400)*
Gain from insurance recovery on fire loss to business building (owned two years)	200

§ 1231 Gains and Losses from Depreciable Business Assets Held Long Term

Asset A	$ 300
Asset B	1,100
Asset C	(500)

Gains and Losses from Sale of Depreciable Business Assets Held Short Term

Asset D	$ 200
Asset E	(300)

*As adjusted for the $100 floor on personal casualty losses.

Ross had no net § 1231 losses in tax years before 2006.

Disregarding the recapture of depreciation (discussed later in the chapter), Ross's gains and losses receive the following tax treatment:

- The diamond ring and the residence are personal use assets. Therefore, these casualties are not § 1231 transactions. The $800 (ring) plus $400 (residence) losses are potentially deductible *from* AGI. However, the total loss of $1,200 does not exceed 10% of AGI. Thus, only the business building (a § 1231 asset) casualty gain remains. The netting of the § 1231 asset and nonpersonal use capital asset casualty gains and losses contains only one item—the $200 gain from the business building. Consequently, there is a net gain and that gain is treated as a § 1231 gain (added to the § 1231 gains).
- The gains from § 1231 transactions (Assets A, B, and C and the § 1231 asset casualty gain) exceed the losses by $1,100 ($1,600 − $500). This excess is a long-term capital gain and is added to Ross's other long-term capital gains.
- Ross's net long-term capital gain is $3,700 ($3,000 + $1,100 from § 1231 transactions − $400 long-term capital loss). Ross's net short-term capital gain is $800 ($1,000 − $200). The result is capital gain net income of $4,500. The $3,700 net long-term capital gain portion is eligible for beneficial capital gain treatment [assume all the gain is 5%/15% gain (see the discussion in Chapter 16)]. The $800 net short-term capital gain is subject to tax as ordinary income.[5]
- Ross treats the gain and loss from Assets D and E (depreciable business assets held for less than the long-term holding period) as ordinary gain and loss.

Results of the Gains and Losses on Ross's Tax Computation

NLTCG	$ 3,700
NSTCG	800
Ordinary gain from sale of Asset D	200
Ordinary loss from sale of Asset E	(300)
AGI from other sources	125,000
AGI	$129,400

---

[5]Ross's taxable income (unless the itemized deductions and the personal exemption and dependency deductions are extremely large) will put him in at least the 28% bracket. Thus, the alternative tax computation will yield a lower tax. See Example 40 Chapter 16.

- Ross will have personal use property casualty losses of $1,200 [$800 (diamond ring) + $400 (personal residence)]. A personal use property casualty loss is deductible only to the extent it exceeds 10% of AGI. Thus, none of the $1,200 is deductible ($129,400 × 10% = $12,940). ■

EXAMPLE 5

§1231 loss ɾ̲ɾɾɾ = (100)
=> deduction for AGI.

Assume the same facts as in Example 4, except the loss from Asset C was $1,700 instead of $500.

- The treatment of the casualty losses is the same as in Example 4.
- The losses from § 1231 transactions now exceed the gains by $100 ($1,700 − $1,600). As a result, the gains from Assets A and B and the § 1231 asset casualty gain are ordinary income, and the loss from Asset C is a deduction *for* AGI (a business loss). The same result can be achieved by simply treating the $100 net loss as a deduction *for* AGI.
- Capital gain net income is $3,400 ($2,600 long term + $800 short term). The $2,600 net long-term capital gain portion is eligible for beneficial capital gain treatment, and the $800 net short-term capital gain is subject to tax as ordinary income.

Results of the Gains and Losses on Ross's Tax Computation	
NLTCG	$ 2,600
NSTCG	800
Net ordinary loss on Assets A, B, and C and § 1231 casualty gain	(100)
Ordinary gain from sale of Asset D	200
Ordinary loss from sale of Asset E	(300)
AGI from other sources	125,000
AGI	$128,200

- None of the personal use property casualty losses will be deductible since $1,200 does not exceed 10% of $128,200. ■

EXAMPLE 6

net w/ nonrecapture ∧ prev. year. from

Assume the same facts as in Example 4, except that Ross has a $700 nonrecaptured net § 1231 loss from 2005.

- The treatment of the casualty losses is the same as in Example 4.
- The 2006 net § 1231 gain of $1,100 is treated as ordinary income to the extent of the 2005 nonrecaptured § 1231 loss of $700. The remaining $400 net § 1231 gain is a long-term capital gain and is added to Ross's other long-term capital gains.
- Ross's net long-term capital gain is $3,000 ($3,000 + $400 from § 1231 transactions − $400 long-term capital loss). Ross's net short-term capital gain is still $800 ($1,000 − $200). The result is capital gain net income of $3,800. The $3,000 net long-term capital gain portion is eligible for beneficial capital gain treatment, and the $800 net short-term capital gain is subject to tax as ordinary income.

Results of the Gains and Losses on Ross's Tax Computation	
NLTCG	$ 3,000
NSTCG	800
Ordinary gain from recapture of § 1231 losses	700
Ordinary gain from sale of Asset D	200
Ordinary loss from sale of Asset E	(300)
AGI from other sources	125,000
AGI	$129,400

- None of the personal use property casualty losses will be deductible since $1,200 does not exceed 10% of $129,400. ∎

Assume the same facts as in Example 4, except that Ross had a net § 1231 loss of $2,700 in 2004 and a net § 1231 gain of $300 in 2005.

EXAMPLE 7

- The treatment of the casualty losses is the same as in Example 4.
- The 2004 net § 1231 loss of $2,700 will have carried over to 2005 and been offset against the 2005 net § 1231 gain of $300. Thus, the $300 gain will have been classified as ordinary income, and $2,400 of nonrecaptured 2004 net § 1231 loss will carry over to 2006. The 2006 net § 1231 gain of $1,100 will be offset against this loss, resulting in $1,100 of ordinary income. The nonrecaptured net § 1231 loss of $1,300 ($2,400 − $1,100) carries over to 2007.
- Capital gain net income is $3,400 ($2,600 net long-term capital gain + $800 net short-term capital gain). The $2,600 net long-term capital gain portion is eligible for beneficial capital gain treatment, and the $800 net short-term capital gain is subject to tax as ordinary income.

[Handwritten annotations:]
2004 : (2700)
2005 : 300
Carryover (2400)
2006 1100
carry over (1300)
and not offset LTCG
b/c $1231 loss is ord. L.
Why not use as ordinary Loss.

Results of the Gains and Losses on Ross's Tax Computation	
NLTCG	$ 2,600
NSTCG	800
Ordinary gain from recapture of § 1231 losses	1,100
Ordinary gain from sale of Asset D	200
Ordinary loss from sale of Asset E	(300)
AGI from other sources	125,000
AGI	$129,400

- None of the personal use property casualty losses will be deductible since $1,200 does not exceed 10% of $129,400. ∎

Section 1245 Recapture

LO.3

Determine when § 1245 recapture applies and how it is computed.

Now that the basic rules of § 1231 have been introduced, it is time to add some complications. The Code contains two major *recapture* provisions—§§ 1245 and 1250. These provisions cause *gain* to be treated *initially* as ordinary gain. Thus, what may appear to be a § 1231 gain is ordinary gain instead. These recapture provisions may also cause a gain in a nonpersonal use casualty to be *initially* ordinary gain rather than casualty gain. Classifying gains (and losses) properly initially is important because improper initial classification may lead to incorrect mixing and matching of gains and losses. This section discusses the § 1245 recapture rules, and the next section discusses the § 1250 recapture rules.

ETHICAL *Considerations* **PREPARING TAX RETURNS WITHOUT PROPER INFORMATION**

Your CPA firm is preparing the tax return of a new client who says he has had numerous transactions involving the sale of depreciable business property in prior years. The client lost all his tax records in a recent hurricane. His transactions for the current year result in a net § 1231 gain. Your supervisor instructs you to complete this return without further information. Should you do so?

TAX *in the News*   ASK THE CPA ABOUT RECAPTURE

A local newspaper includes a column called "Ask the CPA." A subscriber asked whether there were any differences between § 1245 recapture related to depreciable tangible personal property and that related to amortizable intangible personal property. The CPA wrote back that accelerated depreciation is usually used for tangible personal property, whereas straight-line amortization is used for intangible per-

sonal property. Consequently, the adjusted basis for the tangible personal property tends to be lower than that of the intangible personal property. If the properties had the same original cost and the same fair market value when they were sold, the tangible personal property would result in the larger gain and, therefore, the larger amount subject to recapture as ordinary income under § 1245.

Treat as ordinary gain on depreciation amt. Then, gain is §1231 gain

Section 1245 requires taxpayers to treat all gain as ordinary gain unless the property is disposed of for more than was paid for it. This result is accomplished by requiring that all gain be treated as ordinary gain to the extent of the depreciation taken on the property disposed of. Section 1231 gain results only when the property is disposed of for more than its original cost. The excess of the sales price over the original cost is § 1231 gain. Section 1245 applies *primarily* to non-real-estate property such as machinery, trucks, and office furniture. Section 1245 does not apply if property is disposed of at a loss. Generally, the loss will be a § 1231 loss unless the form of the disposition is a casualty.

EXAMPLE 8

cost 100,000
dep.   70,000
adj basis 30,000

sell   80,000
gain   50,000

50K < 70K
⟹ ordinary income.

Alice purchased a $100,000 business machine and deducted $70,000 depreciation before selling it for $80,000. If it were not for § 1245, the $50,000 gain would be § 1231 gain ($80,000 amount realized − $30,000 adjusted basis). Section 1245 prevents this potentially favorable result by treating as ordinary income (not as § 1231 gain) any gain to the extent of depreciation taken. In this example, the entire $50,000 gain would be ordinary income. If Alice had sold the machine for $120,000, she would have a gain of $90,000 ($120,000 amount realized − $30,000 adjusted basis). The § 1245 gain would be $70,000 (equal to the depreciation taken), and the § 1231 gain would be $20,000 (equal to the excess of the sales price over the original cost). ∎

Section 1245 recapture provides, in general, that the portion of recognized gain from the sale or other disposition of § 1245 property that represents depreciation (including § 167 depreciation, § 168 cost recovery, § 179 immediate expensing, and § 197 amortization) is *recaptured* as ordinary income. Thus, in Example 8, $50,000 of the $70,000 depreciation taken is recaptured as ordinary income when the business machine is sold for $80,000. Only $50,000 is recaptured rather than $70,000 because Alice is only required to recognize § 1245 recapture ordinary gain equal to the lower of the depreciation taken or the gain recognized.

The method of depreciation (e.g., accelerated or straight-line) does not matter. All depreciation taken is potentially subject to recapture. Thus, § 1245 recapture is often referred to as *full recapture*. Any remaining gain after subtracting the amount recaptured as ordinary income will usually be § 1231 gain. If the property is disposed of in a casualty event, however, the remaining gain will be casualty gain. If the business machine in Example 8 had been disposed of by casualty and the $80,000 received had been an insurance recovery, Alice would still have a gain of $50,000, and the gain would still be recaptured by § 1245 as ordinary gain. The § 1245 recapture rules apply before there is any casualty gain. Since all the $50,000 gain is recaptured, no casualty gain arises from the casualty.

If gain is due to casualty remaining gain is casualty gain

The following examples illustrate the general application of § 1245.

On January 1, 2006, Gary sold for $13,000 a machine acquired several years ago for $12,000. He had taken $10,000 of depreciation on the machine.   *Basis = 2k*

- The recognized gain from the sale is $11,000. This is the amount realized of $13,000 less the adjusted basis of $2,000 ($12,000 cost − $10,000 depreciation taken).
- Depreciation taken is $10,000. Therefore, since § 1245 recapture gain is the lower of depreciation taken or gain recognized, $10,000 of the $11,000 recognized gain is ordinary income, and the remaining $1,000 gain is § 1231 gain.
- The § 1231 gain of $1,000 is also equal to the excess of the sales price over the original cost of the property ($13,000 − $12,000 = $1,000 § 1231 gain). ∎

EXAMPLE 9

cost   12000
dep.   (10000)
adj basis   2000
sell   13000
gain   11000
ord. inc :   10000
1231 gain   1000

Assume the same facts as in the previous example, except the asset is sold for $9,000 instead of $13,000.

- The recognized gain from the sale is $7,000. This is the amount realized of $9,000 less the adjusted basis of $2,000.
- Depreciation taken is $10,000. Therefore, since the $10,000 depreciation taken exceeds the recognized gain of $7,000, the entire $7,000 recognized gain is ordinary income.
- The § 1231 gain is zero. There is no § 1231 gain because the selling price ($9,000) does not exceed the original purchase price ($12,000). ∎

EXAMPLE 10

Assume the same facts as in Example 9, except the asset is sold for $1,500 instead of $13,000.

- The recognized loss from the sale is $500. This is the amount realized of $1,500 less the adjusted basis of $2,000.
- Since there is a loss, there is no depreciation recapture. All of the loss is § 1231 loss. ∎

EXAMPLE 11

Recapture depreciation first, then other type of gain.

If § 1245 property is disposed of in a transaction other than a sale, exchange, or involuntary conversion, the maximum amount recaptured is the excess of the property's fair market value over its adjusted basis. See the discussion under Considerations Common to §§ 1245 and 1250 later in the chapter.

Section 1245 Property

Generally, **§ 1245 property** includes all depreciable personal property (e.g., machinery and equipment), including livestock. Buildings and their structural components generally are not § 1245 property. The following property is *also* subject to § 1245 treatment:

- Amortizable personal property such as goodwill, patents, copyrights, and leaseholds of § 1245 property. Professional baseball and football player contracts are § 1245 property.
- Amortization of reforestation expenditures.
- Expensing of costs to remove architectural and transportation barriers that restrict the handicapped and/or elderly.
- Section 179 immediate expensing of depreciable tangible personal property costs.
- Elevators and escalators acquired before January 1, 1987.
- Certain depreciable tangible real property (other than buildings and their structural components) employed as an integral part of certain activities such as manufacturing and production. For example, a natural gas storage tank where the gas is used in the manufacturing process is § 1245 property.
- Pollution control facilities, railroad grading and tunnel bores, on-the-job training, and child care facilities on which amortization is taken.
- Single-purpose agricultural and horticultural structures and petroleum storage facilities (e.g., a greenhouse or silo).

- Fifteen-year, 18-year, and 19-year nonresidential real estate for which accelerated cost recovery is used is subject to the § 1245 recapture rules, although it is technically not § 1245 property. Such property would have been placed in service after 1980 and before 1987.

EXAMPLE 12

James acquired nonresidential real property on December 1, 1986, for $100,000. He used the statutory percentage method to compute the ACRS cost recovery. He sells the asset on January 15, 2006, for $120,000. The amount and nature of James's gain are computed as follows:

Amount realized		$120,000
Adjusted basis		
Cost	$ 100,000	
Less cost recovery: 1986–2005	(100,000)	
2006	(–0–)	
January 15, 2006, adjusted basis		(–0–)
Gain realized and recognized		$120,000

The gain of $120,000 is treated as ordinary income to the extent of *all* depreciation taken because the property is 19-year nonresidential real estate for which accelerated depreciation was used. Thus, James reports ordinary income of $100,000 and § 1231 gain of $20,000 ($120,000 − $100,000). ∎

Observations on § 1245

- In most instances, the total depreciation taken will exceed the recognized gain. Therefore, the disposition of § 1245 property usually results in ordinary income rather than § 1231 gain. Thus, generally, no § 1231 gain will occur unless the § 1245 property is disposed of for more than its original cost. Refer to Examples 9 and 10.
- Recapture applies to the total amount of depreciation allowed or allowable regardless of the depreciation method used.
- Recapture applies regardless of the holding period of the property. Of course, the entire recognized gain would be ordinary income if the property were held for less than the long-term holding period because § 1231 would not apply.
- Section 1245 does not apply to losses, which receive § 1231 treatment.
- Gains from the disposition of § 1245 assets may also be treated as passive activity gains (see Chapter 11).

LO.4

Determine when § 1250 recapture applies and how it is computed.

Section 1250 Recapture

Generally, § 1250 property is depreciable real property (principally buildings and their structural components) that is not subject to § 1245.[6] Intangible real property, such as leaseholds of § 1250 property, is also included.

Section 1250 recapture rarely applies since only the amount of *additional depreciation* is subject to recapture. To have additional depreciation, accelerated depreciation must have been taken on the asset. Straight-line depreciation is not recaptured (except for property held one year or less). Since depreciable real property placed in service after 1986 can only be depreciated using the straight-line method, there will be *no § 1250 depreciation recapture* on such property. Nor does § 1250 apply if the real property is sold at a loss.

---

[6]As noted above, in one limited circumstance, § 1245 does apply to nonresidential real estate. If the nonresidential real estate was placed in service after 1980 and before 1987 and accelerated depreciation was used, the § 1245 recapture rules rather than the § 1250 recapture rules apply.

If depreciable real property has been held for many years before it is sold, however, the § 1250 recapture rules may apply and are therefore discussed here. **Additional depreciation** is the excess of the accelerated depreciation actually deducted over depreciation that would have been deductible if the straight-line method had been used. Section 1250 recapture may apply when either (1) residential rental real property was acquired after 1975 and before 1987 and accelerated depreciation was taken or (2) nonresidential real property was acquired before 1981 and accelerated depreciation was taken after December 31, 1969.

If § 1250 property with additional depreciation is disposed of in a transaction other than a sale, exchange, or involuntary conversion, the depreciation recapture is limited to the excess of the property's fair market value over the adjusted basis. For instance, if a corporation distributes real property to its shareholders as a dividend and the fair market value of the real property is greater than its adjusted basis, the corporation will recognize a gain. If accelerated depreciation was taken on the property, § 1250 recapture will apply.

It is important to know what assets are defined as § 1250 property because even when there is no additional depreciation, the gain from such property may be subject to a special 25 percent tax rate. See the discussion of Unrecaptured § 1250 Gain later in this chapter.

The discussion below describes the computational steps when § 1250 recapture applies and indicates how that recapture is reflected on Form 4797 (Sales of Business Property).

Computing Recapture on Nonresidential Real Property

For § 1250 property other than residential rental property, the potential recapture is equal to the amount of additional depreciation taken since December 31, 1969. This nonresidential real property includes buildings such as offices, warehouses, factories, and stores. (The definition of and rules for residential rental housing are discussed later in the chapter.) The lower of the potential § 1250 recapture amount or the recognized gain is ordinary income. The following general rules apply:

- Additional depreciation is depreciation taken in excess of straight-line after December 31, 1969, on property that was acquired before 1981.
- If the property is held for one year or less (usually not the case), all depreciation taken, even under the straight-line method, is additional depreciation.

The following procedure is used to compute recapture on nonresidential real property that was acquired before 1981 and for which accelerated depreciation was taken after December 31, 1969, under § 1250:

- Determine the recognized gain from the sale or other disposition of the property.
- Determine the additional depreciation (if any).
- The lower of the recognized gain or the additional depreciation is ordinary income.
- If any recognized gain remains (total recognized gain less recapture), it is § 1231 gain. However, it would be casualty gain if the disposition was by casualty.

The following example shows the application of the § 1250 computational procedure.

EXAMPLE 13

On January 3, 1980, Larry acquired a new building at a cost of $200,000 for use in his business. The building had an estimated useful life of 50 years and no estimated salvage value. Depreciation has been taken under the 150% declining-balance method through December 31, 2005. Pertinent information with respect to depreciation taken follows:

Year	Undepreciated Balance (Beginning of the Year)	Current Depreciation Provision	Straight-Line Depreciation	Additional Depreciation
1980–2004	$200,000	$106,880	$100,000	$6,880
2005	93,120	3,070	4,000	(930)
Total 1980–2005		$109,950	$104,000	$5,950

On January 2, 2006, Larry sold the building for $180,000. Compute the amount of his § 1250 ordinary income and § 1231 gain.

- Larry's recognized gain from the sale is $89,950. This is the difference between the $180,000 amount realized and the $90,050 adjusted basis ($200,000 cost − $109,950 depreciation taken).
- Additional depreciation is $5,950.
- The amount of ordinary income is $5,950. Since the additional depreciation of $5,950 is less than the recognized gain of $89,950, the entire gain is not recaptured.
- The remaining $84,000 ($89,950 − $5,950) gain is § 1231 gain. ∎

Computing Recapture on Residential Rental Housing

Section 1250 recapture sometimes applies to the sale or other disposition of residential rental housing. Property qualifies as *residential rental housing* only if at least 80 percent of gross rent income is rent income from dwelling units.[7] The rules are the same as for other § 1250 property, except that only the post-1975 additional depreciation may be recaptured on property acquired before 1987. If any of the recognized gain is not absorbed by the recapture rules pertaining to the post-1975 period, the remaining gain is § 1231 gain.

EXAMPLE 14

Assume the same facts as in the previous example, except the building is residential rental housing.

- Post-1975 ordinary income is $5,950 (post-1975 additional depreciation of $5,950).
- The remaining $84,000 ($89,950 − $5,950) gain is § 1231 gain. ∎

Under § 1250, when straight-line depreciation is used, there is no § 1250 recapture potential unless the property is disposed of in the first year of use. Generally, however, the § 1250 recapture rules do not apply to depreciable real property unless the property is disposed of in the first year of use.

EXAMPLE 15

Sanjay acquires a residential rental building on January 1, 2005, for $300,000. He receives an offer of $450,000 for the building in 2006 and sells it on December 23, 2006.

- Sanjay takes $20,909 {($300,000 × .03485) + [$300,000 × .03636 × (11.5/12)] = $20,909} of total depreciation for 2005 and 2006, and the adjusted basis of the property is $279,091 ($300,000 − $20,909).
- Sanjay's recognized gain is $170,909 ($450,000 − $279,091).
- All of the gain is § 1231 gain. ∎

Section 1250 Recapture Situations

The § 1250 recapture rules apply to the following property for which accelerated depreciation was used:

---

[7]§ 168(e)(2)(A). Note that there may be residential, nonrental housing (e.g., a bunkhouse on a cattle ranch). Such property is commonly regarded as "non-residential real estate." The rules for such property were discussed in the previous section.

CONCEPT SUMMARY 17–2

Comparison of § 1245 and § 1250 Depreciation Recapture

	§ 1245	§ 1250
Property affected	All depreciable personal property, but also nonresidential real property acquired after December 31, 1980, and before January 1, 1987, for which accelerated cost recovery was used. Also includes miscellaneous items such as § 179 expense and § 197 amortization of intangibles such as goodwill, patents, and copyrights.	Nonresidential real property acquired after December 31, 1969, and before January 1, 1981, on which accelerated depreciation was taken. Residential rental real property acquired after December 31, 1975, and before January 1, 1987, on which accelerated depreciation was taken.
Depreciation recaptured	Potentially all depreciation taken. If the selling price is greater than or equal to the original cost, all depreciation is recaptured. If the selling price is between the adjusted basis and the original cost, only some depreciation is recaptured.	Additional depreciation (the excess of accelerated cost recovery over straight-line cost recovery or the excess of accelerated depreciation over straight-line depreciation).
Limit on recapture	Lower of depreciation taken or gain recognized.	Lower of additional depreciation or gain recognized.
Treatment of gain exceeding recapture gain	Usually § 1231 gain.	Usually § 1231 gain.
Treatment of loss	No depreciation recapture; loss is usually § 1231 loss.	No depreciation recapture; loss is usually § 1231 loss.

- Residential rental real estate acquired before 1987.
- Nonresidential real estate acquired before 1981.
- Real property used predominantly outside the United States.
- Certain government-financed or low-income housing.[8]

Concept Summary 17–2 compares and contrasts the § 1245 and § 1250 depreciation recapture rules.

Unrecaptured § 1250 Gain (Real Estate 25% Gain)

This section will explain what gain is eligible for the 25 percent tax rate on **unrecaptured § 1250 gain**. This gain is used in the alternative tax computation for net capital gain discussed in Chapter 16. Unrecaptured § 1250 gain (25% gain) is some or all of the § 1231 gain that is treated as long-term capital gain and relates to a sale of depreciable real estate.

The maximum amount of this 25% gain is the depreciation taken on real property sold at a recognized gain. That maximum amount is reduced in one or more of the following ways:

- The recognized gain from disposition is less than the depreciation taken. The 25% gain is reduced to the recognized gain amount. Refer to Example 13. The depreciation taken was $109,950, but the recognized gain was only

---

[8]Described in § 1250(a)(1)(B).

$89,950. Consequently, *all* of the recognized gain is potential 25% § 1231 gain.

- There is § 1250 depreciation recapture because the property is residential real estate acquired before 1987 on which accelerated depreciation was taken. The § 1250 recapture reduces the 25% gain. Refer to Example 14. Of the $89,950 recognized gain, $5,950 was recaptured by § 1250 as ordinary income, leaving $84,000 of the potential 25% § 1231 gain.

- There is § 1245 depreciation recapture because the property is nonresidential real estate acquired in 1981–1986 on which accelerated depreciation was taken. No 25% § 1231 gain will be left because § 1245 will recapture all of the depreciation or the recognized gain, whichever is less. Refer to Example 12. Depreciation of $100,000 was taken, but all of it was recaptured as ordinary income by § 1245. Thus, there is no remaining potential 25% § 1231 gain. The entire $20,000 § 1231 gain in Example 12 is potential 5%/15% gain.

- Section 1231 loss from disposition of other § 1231 assets held long term reduces the gain from real estate.

- Section 1231 lookback losses convert some or all of the potential 25% § 1231 gain to ordinary income.

Special 25% Gain Netting Rules. Where there is a § 1231 gain from real estate and that gain includes both potential *25% gain* and potential *5%/15% gain*, any § 1231 loss from disposition of other § 1231 assets *first offsets* the *5%/15%* portion of the § 1231 gain and then offsets the *25%* portion of the § 1231 gain. Also, any § 1231 lookback loss *first recharacterizes* the *25%* portion of the § 1231 gain and then recharacterizes the *5%/15%* portion of the § 1231 gain as ordinary income.

Net § 1231 Gain Limitation. The amount of unrecaptured § 1250 gain may not exceed the net § 1231 gain that is eligible to be treated as long-term capital gain. The unrecaptured § 1250 gain is the *lesser of* the unrecaptured § 1250 gain or the net § 1231 gain that is treated as capital gain. Thus, if there is a net § 1231 gain, but it is all recaptured by the five-year § 1231 lookback loss provision, there is no surviving § 1231 gain or unrecaptured § 1250 gain.

Refer to Example 6. There was $200 of § 1231 gain from the building fire that would also be potential *25%* gain if at least $200 of depreciation was taken. The net § 1231 gain was $1,100 including the $200 building gain. (The $500 loss from Asset C would offset the potential *5%/15%* § 1231 gain and not the potential *25%* gain, so all of the potential *25%* gain of $200 is in the $1,100 net § 1231 gain.) However, the $700 of § 1231 lookback losses would *first* absorb the $200 building gain, so the $400 of § 1231 gain that is treated as long-term capital gain includes no *25%* gain.

Section 1250 Property for Purposes of the Unrecaptured § 1250 Gain. Section 1250 property includes any real property (other than § 1245 property) that is or has been depreciable. Land is *not* § 1250 property because it is not depreciable.

EXAMPLE 16

Bill is a single taxpayer with 2006 taxable income of $84,000 composed of:

- $64,000 ordinary taxable income,
- $3,000 short-term capital loss,
- $15,000 long-term capital gain from sale of stock, and
- $8,000 § 1231 gain that is all unrecaptured § 1250 gain (the actual unrecaptured gain was $11,000, but net § 1231 gain is only $8,000).

Bill's net capital gain is $20,000 ($15,000 long-term capital gain + $8,000 unrecaptured § 1250 gain/net § 1231 gain − $3,000 short-term capital loss). The $3,000 short-term capital loss is offset against the $8,000 unrecaptured § 1250 gain, reducing that gain to $5,000 (see the discussion in Chapter 16 concerning netting of capital losses). Bill's adjusted net capital

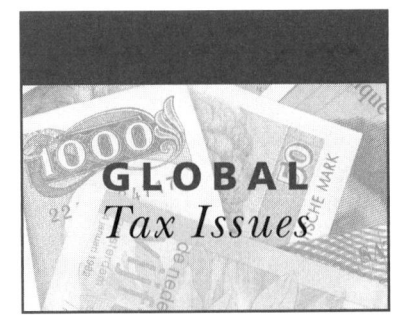

EXCHANGE FOR FOREIGN PROPERTY YIELDS RECOGNIZED RECAPTURE GAIN

Tangible personal property used in a trade or business may be the subject of a § 1031 like-kind exchange, and the postponed gain is most likely postponed § 1245 gain. However, tangible personal property used predominantly within the United States cannot be exchanged for tangible personal property used predominantly outside the United States. Thus, such an exchange would cause recognized gain, and, as long as the fair market value of the property given up does not exceed its original cost, all of the gain is § 1245 depreciation recapture gain.

GLOBAL Tax Issues

gain is $15,000 ($20,000 net capital gain − $5,000 unrecaptured § 1250 gain). Bill's total tax (using the alternative tax calculation discussed in Chapter 16) is $16,058 [$12,558 (tax on ordinary taxable income) + $1,250 ($5,000 unrecaptured § 1250 gain × 25%) + $2,250 ($15,000 adjusted net capital gain × 15%)]. ∎

Considerations Common to §§ 1245 and 1250

LO.5

Understand considerations common to §§ 1245 and 1250.

Exceptions

Recapture under §§ 1245 and 1250 does not apply to the following transactions.

Gifts. The recapture potential carries over to the donee.[9]

Wade gives his daughter, Helen, § 1245 property with an adjusted basis of $1,000. The amount of recapture potential is $700. Helen uses the property in her business and claims further depreciation of $100 before selling it for $1,900. Helen's recognized gain is $1,000 ($1,900 amount realized − $900 adjusted basis), of which $800 is recaptured as ordinary income ($100 depreciation taken by Helen + $700 recapture potential carried over from Wade). The remaining gain of $200 is § 1231 gain. Even if Helen used the property for personal purposes, the $700 recapture potential would still be carried over. ∎

EXAMPLE 17

Death. Although not a very attractive tax planning approach, death eliminates all recapture potential.[10] In other words, any recapture potential does not carry over from a decedent to an estate or heir.

Assume the same facts as in Example 17, except Helen receives the property as a result of Wade's death. The $700 recapture potential from Wade is extinguished. Helen has a basis for the property equal to the property's fair market value (assume $1,700) at Wade's death. She will have a $300 gain when the property is sold because the selling price ($1,900) exceeds the property's adjusted basis of $1,600 ($1,700 original basis to Helen − $100 depreciation) by $300. Because of § 1245, $100 is ordinary income. The remaining gain of $200 is § 1231 gain. ∎

EXAMPLE 18

Charitable Transfers. The recapture potential reduces the amount of the charitable contribution deduction under § 170.[11]

Kanisha donates to her church § 1245 property with a fair market value of $10,000 and an adjusted basis of $7,000. Assume that the amount of recapture potential is $2,000 (the

EXAMPLE 19

---

[9]§§ 1245(b)(1) and 1250(d)(1) and Reg. §§ 1.1245–4(a)(1) and 1.1250–3(a)(1).
[10]§§ 1245(b)(2) and 1250(d)(2).

[11]§ 170(e)(1)(A) and Reg. § 1.170A–4(b)(1). In certain circumstances, § 1231 gain also reduces the amount of the charitable contribution. See § 170(e)(1)(B).

amount of recapture that would occur if the property were sold). Her charitable contribution deduction (subject to the limitations discussed in Chapter 10) is $8,000 ($10,000 fair market value − $2,000 recapture potential). ∎

Certain Nontaxable Transactions.

In certain transactions, the transferor's adjusted basis of property carries over to the transferee.[12] The recapture potential also carries over to the transferee.[13] Included in this category are transfers of property pursuant to the following:

- Nontaxable incorporations under § 351.
- Certain liquidations of subsidiary companies under § 332.
- Nontaxable contributions to a partnership under § 721.
- Nontaxable reorganizations.

Gain may be recognized in these transactions if boot is received. If gain is recognized, it is treated as ordinary income to the extent of the recapture potential or recognized gain, whichever is lower.[14]

Like-Kind Exchanges (§ 1031) and Involuntary Conversions (§ 1033).

Realized gain will be recognized to the extent of boot received under § 1031. Realized gain also will be recognized to the extent the proceeds from an involuntary conversion are not reinvested in similar property under § 1033. Such recognized gain is subject to recapture as ordinary income under §§ 1245 and 1250. The remaining recapture potential, if any, carries over to the property received in the exchange. Realized losses are not recognized in like-kind exchanges, but are recognized in involuntary conversions (see Chapter 15).

EXAMPLE 20

Anita exchanges § 1245 property with an adjusted basis of $300 for § 1245 property with a fair market value of $6,000. The exchange qualifies as a like-kind exchange under § 1031. Anita also receives $1,000 cash (boot). Her realized gain is $6,700 ($7,000 amount realized − $300 adjusted basis of property). Assuming the recapture potential is $7,500, Anita recognizes § 1245 gain of $1,000 because she received boot of $1,000. The remaining recapture potential of $6,500 carries over to the like-kind property received. ∎

Other Applications

Sections 1245 and 1250 apply notwithstanding any other provisions in the Code.[15] That is, the recapture rules under these Sections *override* all other Sections. Special applications include installment sales and property dividends.

Installment Sales.

Recapture gain is recognized in the year of the sale regardless of whether gain is otherwise recognized under the installment method.[16] All gain is ordinary income until the recapture potential is fully absorbed. Nonrecapture (§ 1231) gain is recognized under the installment method as cash is received.

EXAMPLE 21

Seth sells § 1245 property for $20,000, to be paid in 10 annual installments of $2,000 each plus interest at 10%. Seth realizes a $6,000 gain from the sale, of which $4,000 is attributable to depreciation taken. If Seth uses the installment method, he recognizes the entire $4,000 of recapture gain as ordinary income in the year of the sale. The $2,000 of nonrecapture (§ 1231) gain will be recognized at the rate of $200 per year for 10 years. ∎

---

[12]§§ 1245(b)(3) and 1250(d)(3) and Reg. §§ 1.1245–4(c) and 1.1250–3(c).

[13]Reg. §§ 1.1245–2(a)(4) and –2(c)(2) and 1.1250–2(d)(1) and (3) and –3(c)(3).

[14]§§ 1245(b)(3) and 1250(d)(3) and Reg. §§ 1.1245–4(c) and 1.1250–3(c). Some of these special corporate problems are discussed in Chapter 20. Partnership contributions are also discussed in Chapter 20.

[15]§§ 1245(d) and 1250(i).

[16]§ 453(i). The installment method of reporting gains on the sale of property is discussed in Chapter 18.

Gain is also recognized on installment sales in the year of the sale in an amount equal to the § 179 (immediate expensing) deduction taken with respect to the property sold.

Property Dividends. A corporation generally recognizes gain if it distributes appreciated property as a dividend. Recapture under §§ 1245 and 1250 applies to the extent of the lower of the recapture potential or the excess of the property's fair market value over the adjusted basis.[17]

EXAMPLE 22

Emerald Corporation distributes § 1245 property as a dividend to its shareholders. The amount of the recapture potential is $300, and the excess of the property's fair market value over the adjusted basis is $800. Emerald recognizes $300 of ordinary income and $500 of § 1231 gain. ∎

Concept Summary 17–3 integrates the depreciation recapture rules with the § 1231 netting process. It is an expanded version of Concept Summary 17–1.

Special Recapture Provisions

Special Recapture for Corporations

> **LO.6**
>
> Apply the special recapture provisions for related parties and IDC and be aware of the special recapture provision for corporations.

Corporations selling depreciable real estate may have ordinary income in addition to that required by § 1250.[18] See the discussion of this topic in Chapter 20.

Gain from Sale of Depreciable Property between Certain Related Parties

When the sale or exchange of property, which in the hands of the *transferee* is depreciable property (principally machinery, equipment, and buildings, but not land), is between certain related parties, any gain recognized is ordinary income.[19] This provision applies to both direct and indirect sales or exchanges. A **related party** is defined as an individual and his or her controlled corporation or partnership or a taxpayer and any trust in which the taxpayer (or the taxpayer's spouse) is a beneficiary.

EXAMPLE 23

Isabella sells a personal use automobile (therefore nondepreciable) to her controlled corporation. The automobile, which was purchased two years ago, originally cost $5,000 and is sold for $7,000. The automobile is to be used in the corporation's business. If the related-party provision did not exist, Isabella would realize a $2,000 long-term capital gain. The income tax consequences would be favorable because Isabella's controlled corporation is entitled to depreciate the automobile based upon the purchase price of $7,000. Under the related-party provision, Isabella's $2,000 gain is ordinary income. ∎

Intangible Drilling Costs

Taxpayers may elect to either *expense or capitalize* intangible drilling and development costs for oil, gas, or geothermal properties.[20] **Intangible drilling and development costs (IDC)** include operator (one who holds a working or operating interest in any tract or parcel of land) expenditures for wages, fuel, repairs, hauling, and supplies. These expenditures must be incident to and necessary for the drilling of wells and preparation of wells for production. In most instances, taxpayers elect to expense IDC to maximize tax deductions during drilling.

---

[17] § 311(b) and Reg. §§ 1.1245–1(c) and –6(b) and 1.1250–1(a)(4), –1(b)(4), and –1(c)(2).
[18] § 291(a)(1).
[19] § 1239.
[20] § 263(c).

CONCEPT SUMMARY   17–3

Depreciation Recapture and § 1231 Netting Procedure

*Includes casualties and thefts.

Intangible drilling and development costs are subject to § 1254 recapture when the property is disposed of. The gain on the disposition of the property is subject to recapture as ordinary income.

<table>
<tr><td>**LO.7**</td></tr>
<tr><td>Describe and apply the reporting procedures for §§ 1231, 1245, and 1250.</td></tr>
</table>

Reporting Procedures

Noncapital gains and losses are reported on Form 4797, Sales of Business Property. Before filling out Form 4797, however, Form 4684, Casualties and Thefts, Part B, must be completed to determine whether any casualties will enter into the § 1231 computation procedure. Recall that gains from § 1231 asset casualties may be recaptured by § 1245 or § 1250. These gains will not appear on Form 4684. The § 1231 gains and nonpersonal use long-term capital gains are netted against § 1231

DEPRECIATION RECAPTURE IN OTHER COUNTRIES

The rules for dispositions of depreciated property are more complex in the United States than in any other country. Most countries treat the gain or loss from the disposition of business depreciable assets as ordinary income or loss. Consequently, although the U.S. rules are more complex, they can be more beneficial than those of other countries because at least some gains from the disposition of depreciable business property may be taxed at the lower capital gain rates.

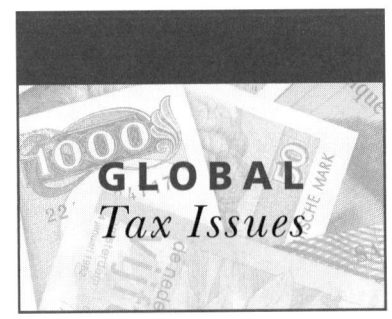

GLOBAL
Tax Issues

losses and nonpersonal use long-term capital losses on Form 4684 to determine if there is a net gain to transfer to Form 4797, Part I.

Because the 2006 tax forms were unavailable at this writing, 2005 tax forms are used in the remainder of the discussion.

Form 4797 is divided into four parts, summarized as follows:

Part	Function
I	To report regular § 1231 gains and losses [including recognized gains and losses from certain involuntary conversions (condemnations)].
II	To report ordinary gains and losses.
III	To determine the portion of the gain that is subject to recapture (e.g., §§ 1245 and 1250 gain).
IV	Computation of recapture amounts under §§ 179 and 280F when business use of depreciable property drops to 50% or less.

Generally, the best approach to completing Form 4797 is to start with Part III. Once the recapture amount has been determined, it is transferred to Part II. The balance of any gain remaining after the recapture has been accounted for is transferred from Part III to Part I. Also transferred to Part I is any net gain from certain casualties and thefts as reported on Form 4684, Part B (refer to above and Chapter 15). If the netting process in Form 4797, Part I, results in a gain, it is reduced by the nonrecaptured net § 1231 losses from prior years (line 8 of Part I). Any remaining gain is shifted to Schedule D, Capital Gains and Losses, of Form 1040. If the netting process in Part I of Form 4797 results in a loss, it goes to Part II to be treated as an ordinary loss.

The complex rules for the alternative tax on net capital gain for individuals, estates, and trusts affect the reporting of gains and losses from the disposition of business and rental assets. S corporations, partnerships, individuals, estates, and trusts that use Form 4797 must provide information sufficient to determine what portion of the gain surviving Form 4797, Part I (the gain that goes to Schedule D) is 28% gain, 25% gain, or 5%/15% gain.

The process explained below is based upon an analysis of Form 1040, Schedule D, and Form 4797 and their instructions. One key point to remember is that all the gains and losses that end up being treated as ordinary gains and losses (and, therefore, end up in Part II of Form 4797) are not eligible for any of the special tax rates for net capital gain. Another key point is that the gain that goes from Part I of Form 4797 to Schedule D will go to line 11 of Schedule D (long-term capital gains and losses). The entire gain from Form 4797 goes in column 11(f).

The 25% gain (if any) from Form 4797 is part of the Schedule D, line 11(f) gain. *Nothing on the face of Form 4797 or Schedule D identifies this gain.* Only when the alternative tax on net capital gain is computed is the 25% gain portion of the Form 4797 net gain specifically mentioned on line 19.

Also remember that § 1231 assets are assets held more than one year. Therefore, no gain or loss is reportable on Form 4797, Part I, unless that holding period requirement is satisfied.

EXAMPLE 24

For 2005, Troy Williams, a single taxpayer (Social Security number 467–85–3036), has taxable income of $133,000 *including* the following recognized gains and losses (a 2005 example has been used since 2006 forms were unavailable):

Sale of Depreciable Business Assets Held Long Term	
Asset A (Note 1)	$36,500
Asset B (Note 2)	20,126
Asset C (Note 3)	(880)
Sale of Depreciable Business Assets Held Short Term	
Asset D (Note 4)	($ 600)
Capital Assets	
Long-term gain (Note 5)	$ 3,000
Short-term loss (Note 6)	(200)

Note 1. Asset A was acquired on June 23, 2002, for $50,000. It was five-year MACRS property, and four years' cost recovery allowances totaled $38,480. The property was sold for $48,020 on August 31, 2005.

Note 2. Asset B was purchased on May 10, 1995, for $37,000. It was 27.5-year residential rental real estate, and straight-line depreciation totaled $14,126. Asset B was sold for $43,000 on November 10, 2005.

Note 3. Asset C was purchased on December 9, 2002, for $16,000. It was five-year MACRS property, and four years' cost recovery totaled $12,314. The property was sold for $2,806 on December 30, 2005.

Note 4. Asset D was purchased for $7,000 on July 27, 2005. It was five-year MACRS property but proved unsuitable to Troy's business. Troy sold it for $6,400 on November 3, 2005.

Note 5. The LTCG resulted from the sale of 100 shares of Orange Corporation stock purchased for $10,000 on April 5, 2003. The shares were sold on October 21, 2005, for $13,223. Expenses of sale were $223.

Note 6. The STCL resulted from the sale of 50 shares of Blue Corporation stock purchased for $350 on March 14, 2005. The shares were sold for $170 on August 20, 2005. Expenses of sale were $20.

The sale of asset A at a gain results in the recapture of cost recovery deductions. That recapture is shown in Part III of Form 4797. The gain from the sale of asset B is carried from line 32 to Part I, line 6, of Form 4797. On line 2, the loss from asset C appears. Part I is where the § 1231 netting process takes place. Assume Troy Williams has no nonrecaptured net § 1231 losses from prior years. The net gain on line 7 is transferred to Schedule D, line 11. In Part II of Form 4797, the ordinary gains are accumulated. On line 13, the recapture from line 31 (Part III) is shown. On line 10, the loss from asset D is shown. The net gain on line 18 is ordinary income and is transferred to Form 1040, line 14.

Schedule D, Part I, line 1, reports the short-term capital loss from the Blue Corporation stock. Part II of Schedule D has the net § 1231 gain transferred from Form 4797 on line 11 and the Orange Corporation gain on line 8. The net capital gain is determined on line 16, Part III. The capital gain is then carried to line 13 of Form 1040.

On Form 4797, Part III, the $20,126 § 1231 gain from Asset B is made up of $14,126 (equals depreciation taken) of potential 25% gain and $6,000 of potential 5%/15% gain. The $880 § 1231 loss from Form 4797, Part I, line 2, offsets the potential 5%/15% portion of the $20,126 § 1231 gain on Form 4797, Part I, line 6. Consequently, of the $19,246 § 1231 gain that goes from Form 4797, Part I, line 7, to Schedule D, line 11, $14,126 is 25% gain and $5,120 is 5%/15% gain. Schedule D, Part III, line 19, shows an unrecaptured § 1250 gain of

$13,926. This gain results from the $14,126 25% gain being reduced by the $200 short-term capital loss from Schedule D, line 7. Troy's 2005 tax liability is $30,274 using the alternative tax on net capital gain method. ■

The 2005 tax form solution for Example 24 appears on the following pages.

ETHICAL *Considerations* | **FORM 4797, DEPRECIATION RECAPTURE, AND CORPORATIONS**

Regular corporations are not eligible for lower tax rates on net long-term capital gain. However, such corporations are still required to complete Form 4797 when they dispose of a § 1231 asset. Quite often, the corporation's tax liability will be the same whether the depreciation recapture provisions are properly applied or not. Therefore, is it not logical and practical for the tax return preparer to simply ignore the recapture rules and the completion of Form 4797 and report all property dispositions on the corporation's Schedule D?

Timing of § 1231 Gain

Although §§ 1245 and 1250 recapture much of the gain from the disposition of business property, sometimes § 1231 gain is still substantial. For instance, land held as a business asset will generate either § 1231 gain or § 1231 loss. If the taxpayer already has a capital loss for the year, the sale of land at a gain should be postponed so that the net § 1231 gain is not netted against the capital loss. The capital loss deduction will therefore be maximized for the current tax year, and the capital loss carryforward (if any) may be offset against the gain when the land is sold. If the taxpayer already has a § 1231 loss, § 1231 gains might be postponed to maximize the ordinary loss deduction this year. However, the carryforward of unrecaptured § 1231 losses will make the § 1231 gain next year an ordinary gain.

LO.8

Identify tax planning opportunities associated with §§ 1231, 1245, and 1250.

TAX PLANNING *Considerations*

EXAMPLE 25

Mark has a $2,000 net STCL for 2006. He could sell business land held 27 months for a $3,000 § 1231 gain. He will have no other capital gains and losses or § 1231 gains and losses in 2006 or 2007. He has no nonrecaptured § 1231 losses from prior years. Mark is in the 28% tax bracket in 2006 and will be in the 25% bracket in 2007. If he sells the land in 2006, he will have a $1,000 net LTCG ($3,000 § 1231 gain − $2,000 STCL) and will pay a tax of $150 ($1,000 × 15%). If Mark sells the land in 2007, he will have a 2006 tax savings of $560 ($2,000 capital loss deduction × 28% tax rate on ordinary income). In 2007, he will pay tax of $450 ($3,000 × 15%). By postponing the sale for a year, Mark will have the use of $710 ($560 + $150). ■

EXAMPLE 26

Beth has a $15,000 § 1231 loss in 2006. She could sell business equipment held 30 months for a $20,000 § 1231 gain and a $12,000 § 1245 gain. Beth is in the 28% tax bracket in 2006 and will be in the 25% bracket in 2007. She has no nonrecaptured § 1231 losses from prior years. If she sells the equipment in 2006, she will have a $5,000 net § 1231 gain and $12,000 of ordinary gain. Her tax would be $4,110 [($5,000 § 1231 gain × 15%) + ($12,000 ordinary gain × 28%)].

If Beth postpones the equipment sale until 2007, she would have a 2006 ordinary loss of $15,000 and tax savings of $4,200 ($15,000 × 28%). In 2007, she would have $5,000 of § 1231 gain (the 2006 § 1231 loss carries over and recaptures $15,000 of the 2007 § 1231 gain as ordinary income) and $27,000 of ordinary gain. Her tax would be $7,500 [($5,000 § 1231 gain × 15%) + ($27,000 ordinary gain × 25%)]. By postponing the equipment sale, Beth has the use of $8,310 ($4,200 + $4,110). ■

Form **4797**

Department of the Treasury
Internal Revenue Service (99)

Sales of Business Property

(Also Involuntary Conversions and Recapture Amounts
Under Sections 179 and 280F(b)(2))

▶Attach to your tax return. ▶See separate instructions.

OMB No. 1545-0184

20**05**

Attachment
Sequence No. **27**

Name(s) shown on return	Identifying number
Troy Williams	*467 - 85 - 3036*

1 Enter the gross proceeds from sales or exchanges reported to you for 2005 on Form(s) 1099-B or 1099-S (or substitute statement) that you are including on line 2, 10, or 20 (see instructions). . . . . | **1** |

Part I **Sales or Exchanges of Property Used in a Trade or Business and Involuntary Conversions From Other Than Casualty or Theft—Most Property Held More Than 1 Year** (see instructions)

(a) Description of property	**(b)** Date acquired (mo., day, yr.)	**(c)** Date sold (mo., day, yr.)	**(d)** Gross sales price	**(e)** Depreciation allowed or allowable since acquisition	**(f)** Cost or other basis, plus improvements and expense of sale	**(g)** Gain or (loss) Subtract (f) from the sum of (d) and (e)
2 *Asset C*	*12/9/02*	*12/30/05*	*2,806*	*12,314*	*16,000*	*(880)*

3 Gain, if any, from Form 4684, line 42	**3**	
4 Section 1231 gain from installment sales from Form 6252, line 26 or 37	**4**	
5 Section 1231 gain or (loss) from like-kind exchanges from Form 8824	**5**	
6 Gain, if any, from line 32, from other than casualty or theft	**6**	*20,126*
7 Combine lines 2 through 6. Enter the gain or (loss) here and on the appropriate line as follows:	**7**	*19,246*

Partnerships (except electing large partnerships) and S corporations. Report the gain or (loss) following the instructions for Form 1065, Schedule K, line 10, or Form 1120S, Schedule K, line 9. Skip lines 8, 9, 11, and 12 below.

Individuals, partners, S corporation shareholders, and all others. If line 7 is zero or a loss, enter the amount from line 7 on line 11 below and skip lines 8 and 9. If line 7 is a gain and you did not have any prior year section 1231 losses, or they were recaptured in an earlier year, enter the gain from line 7 as a long-term capital gain on the Schedule D filed with your return and skip lines 8, 9, 11, and 12 below.

→to Sch. D

8 Nonrecaptured net section 1231 losses from prior years (see instructions)	**8**	
9 Subtract line 8 from line 7. If zero or less, enter -0-. If line 9 is zero, enter the gain from line 7 on line 12 below. If line 9 is more than zero, enter the amount from line 8 on line 12 below and enter the gain from line 9 as a long-term capital gain on the Schedule D filed with your return (see instructions).	**9**	

Part II **Ordinary Gains and Losses** (see instructions)

10 Ordinary gains and losses not included on lines 11 through 16 (include property held 1 year or less):

Asset D	*7/27/05*	*11/3/05*	*6,400*	*0*	*7,000*	*(600)*

11 Loss, if any, from line 7	**11** ( )
12 Gain, if any, from line 7 or amount from line 8, if applicable	**12**	
13 Gain, if any, from line 31	**13**	*36,500*
14 Net gain or (loss) from Form 4684, lines 34 and 41a	**14**	
15 Ordinary gain from installment sales from Form 6252, line 25 or 36	**15**	
16 Ordinary gain or (loss) from like-kind exchanges from Form 8824	**16**	
17 Combine lines 10 through 16	**17**	*35,900*
18 For all except individual returns, enter the amount from line 17 on the appropriate line of your return and skip lines a and b below. For individual returns, complete lines a and b below:		
a If the loss on line 11 includes a loss from Form 4684, line 38, column (b)(ii), enter that part of the loss here. Enter the part of the loss from income-producing property on Schedule A (Form 1040), line 27, and the part of the loss from property used as an employee on Schedule A (Form 1040), line 22. Identify as from "Form 4797, line 18a." See instructions	**18a**	
b Redetermine the gain or (loss) on line 17 excluding the loss, if any, on line 18a. Enter here and on Form 1040, line 14	**18b**	*35,900*

For Paperwork Reduction Act Notice, see separate instructions.

Cat. No. 13086I

Form **4797** (2005)

→1040 line 14

Form 4797 (2005) | | Page **2**

Part III Gain From Disposition of Property Under Sections 1245, 1250, 1252, 1254, and 1255 (see instructions)

19 **(a)** Description of section 1245, 1250, 1252, 1254, or 1255 property:

		(b) Date acquired (mo., day, yr.)	(c) Date sold (mo., day, yr.)
A	*Asset A*	*6/23/02*	*8/31/05*
B	*Asset B*	*5/10/95*	*11/10/05*
C			
D			

These columns relate to the properties on lines 19A through 19D. ▶		Property A	Property B	Property C	Property D
20 Gross sales price (**Note:** See line 1 before completing.)	**20**	*48,020*	*43,000*		
21 Cost or other basis plus expense of sale	**21**	*50,000*	*37,000*		
22 Depreciation (or depletion) allowed or allowable	**22**	*38,480*	*14,126*		
23 Adjusted basis. Subtract line 22 from line 21	**23**	*11,520*	*22,874*		
24 Total gain. Subtract line 23 from line 20	**24**	*36,500*	*20,126*		
25 If section 1245 property:					
a Depreciation allowed or allowable from line 22	**25a**	*38,480*			
b Enter the **smaller** of line 24 or 25a	**25b**	*36,500*			
26 If section 1250 property: If straight line depreciation was used, enter -0- on line 26g, except for a corporation subject to section 291.					
a Additional depreciation after 1975 (see instructions)	**26a**				
b Applicable percentage multiplied by the **smaller** of line 24 or line 26a (see instructions)	**26b**				
c Subtract line 26a from line 24. If residential rental property **or** line 24 is not more than line 26a, skip lines 26d and 26e	**26c**				
d Additional depreciation after 1969 and before 1976	**26d**				
e Enter the **smaller** of line 26c or 26d	**26e**				
f Section 291 amount (corporations only)	**26f**				
g Add lines 26b, 26e, and 26f	**26g**		*0*		
27 If section 1252 property: Skip this section if you did not dispose of farmland or if this form is being completed for a partnership (other than an electing large partnership).					
a Soil, water, and land clearing expenses	**27a**				
b Line 27a multiplied by applicable percentage (see instructions)	**27b**				
c Enter the **smaller** of line 24 or 27b	**27c**				
28 If section 1254 property:					
a Intangible drilling and development costs, expenditures for development of mines and other natural deposits, and mining exploration costs (see instructions)	**28a**				
b Enter the **smaller** of line 24 or 28a	**28b**				
29 If section 1255 property:					
a Applicable percentage of payments excluded from income under section 126 (see instructions)	**29a**				
b Enter the **smaller** of line 24 or 29a (see instructions)	**29b**				

Summary of Part III Gains. Complete property columns A through D through line 29b before going to line 30.

30 Total gains for all properties. Add property columns A through D, line 24	**30**	*56,626* ✓
31 Add property columns A through D, lines 25b, 26g, 27c, 28b, and 29b. Enter here and on line 13	**31**	*36,500*
32 Subtract line 31 from line 30. Enter the portion from casualty or theft on Form 4684, line 36. Enter the portion from other than casualty or theft on Form 4797, line 6	**32**	*20,126*

Part IV Recapture Amounts Under Sections 179 and 280F(b)(2) When Business Use Drops to 50% or Less (see instructions)

		(a) Section 179	(b) Section 280F(b)(2)
33 Section 179 expense deduction or depreciation allowable in prior years	**33**		
34 Recomputed depreciation (see instructions)	**34**		
35 Recapture amount. Subtract line 34 from line 33. See the instructions for where to report	**35**		

Form **4797** (2005)

SCHEDULE D (Form 1040)	Capital Gains and Losses	OMB No. 1545-0074

| SCHEDULE D (Form 1040)
Department of the Treasury
Internal Revenue Service   (99) | **Capital Gains and Losses**
▶ Attach to Form 1040.   ▶ See Instructions for Schedule D (Form 1040).
▶ Use Schedule D-1 to list additional transactions for lines 1 and 8. | OMB No. 1545-0074
20**05**
Attachment
Sequence No. **12** |

Name(s) shown on Form 1040 *Troy Williams*	Your social security number *467 85 3036*

Part I   Short-Term Capital Gains and Losses—Assets Held One Year or Less

	(a) Description of property (Example: 100 sh. XYZ Co.)	(b) Date acquired (Mo., day, yr.)	(c) Date sold (Mo., day, yr.)	(d) Sales price (see page D-6 of the instructions)	(e) Cost or other basis (see page D-6 of the instructions)	(f) Gain or (loss) Subtract (e) from (d)
1	*Blue Corp. (50 shares)*	*3/14/05*	*8/20/05*	*170*	*370*	*(200)*

2	Enter your short-term totals, if any, from Schedule D-1, line 2	**2**		
3	**Total short-term sales price amounts.** Add lines 1 and 2 in column (d)	**3**	*170*	
4	Short-term gain from Form 6252 and short-term gain or (loss) from Forms 4684, 6781, and 8824	**4**		
5	Net short-term gain or (loss) from partnerships, S corporations, estates, and trusts from Schedule(s) K-1	**5**		
6	Short-term capital loss carryover. Enter the amount, if any, from line 8 of your **Capital Loss Carryover Worksheet** on page D-6 of the instructions	**6**	(	)
7	**Net short-term capital gain or (loss).** Combine lines 1 through 6 in column (f)	**7**	*(200)*	

Part II   Long-Term Capital Gains and Losses—Assets Held More Than One Year

	(a) Description of property (Example: 100 sh. XYZ Co.)	(b) Date acquired (Mo., day, yr.)	(c) Date sold (Mo., day, yr.)	(d) Sales price (see page D-6 of the instructions)	(e) Cost or other basis (see page D-6 of the instructions)	(f) Gain or (loss) Subtract (e) from (d)
8	*Orange Corp. (100 shares)*	*4/5/03*	*10/21/05*	*13,223*	*10,223*	*3,000*

9	Enter your long-term totals, if any, from Schedule D-1, line 9	**9**		
10	**Total long-term sales price amounts.** Add lines 8 and 9 in column (d)	**10**	*13,223*	
11	Gain from Form 4797, Part I; long-term gain from Forms 2439 and 6252; and long-term gain or (loss) from Forms 4684, 6781, and 8824	**11**	*19,246*	
12	Net long-term gain or (loss) from partnerships, S corporations, estates, and trusts from Schedule(s) K-1	**12**		
13	Capital gain distributions. See page D-1 of the instructions	**13**		
14	Long-term capital loss carryover. Enter the amount, if any, from line 13 of your **Capital Loss Carryover Worksheet** on page D-6 of the instructions	**14**	(	)
15	**Net long-term capital gain or (loss).** Combine lines 8 through 14 in column (f). Then go to Part III on the back	**15**	*22,246*	

For Paperwork Reduction Act Notice, see Form 1040 instructions.   Cat. No. 11338H   **Schedule D (Form 1040) 2005**

Part III   **Summary**

16	Combine lines 7 and 15 and enter the result. If line 16 is a loss, skip lines 17 through 20, and go to line 21. If a gain, enter the gain on Form 1040, line 13, and then go to line 17 below . .	**16**	*22,046*

17   Are lines 15 and 16 **both** gains?
☒ **Yes.** Go to line 18.
☐ **No.** Skip lines 18 through 21, and go to line 22.

18	Enter the amount, if any, from line 7 of the **28% Rate Gain Worksheet** on page D-7 of the instructions . . . . ▶	**18**	*0*
19	Enter the amount, if any, from line 18 of the **Unrecaptured Section 1250 Gain Worksheet** on page D-8 of the instructions . . . . ▶	**19**	*13,926*

20   Are lines 18 and 19 **both** zero or blank?
☐ **Yes.** Complete Form 1040 through line 43, and then complete the **Qualified Dividends and Capital Gain Tax Worksheet** on page 38 of the Instructions for Form 1040. **Do not** complete lines 21 and 22 below.
☒ **No.** Complete Form 1040 through line 43, and then complete the **Schedule D Tax Worksheet** on page D-9 of the instructions. **Do not** complete lines 21 and 22 below.

21	If line 16 is a loss, enter here and on Form 1040, line 13, the **smaller** of: • The loss on line 16 or • ($3,000), or if married filing separately, ($1,500) . . . . **Note.** When figuring which amount is smaller, treat both amounts as positive numbers.	**21**	( )

22   Do you have qualified dividends on Form 1040, line 9b?
☐ **Yes.** Complete Form 1040 through line 43, and then complete the **Qualified Dividends and Capital Gain Tax Worksheet** on page 38 of the Instructions for Form 1040.
☐ **No.** Complete the rest of Form 1040.

Schedule D (Form 1040) 2005

Timing of Recapture

Since recapture is usually not triggered until the property is sold or disposed of, it may be possible to plan for recapture in low-bracket or loss years. If a taxpayer has net operating loss carryovers that are about to expire, the recognition of ordinary income from recapture may be advisable to absorb the loss carryovers.

E X A M P L E   27

Ahmad has a $15,000 net operating loss carryover that will expire this year. He owns a machine that he plans to sell in the early part of next year. The expected gain of $17,000 from the sale of the machine will be recaptured as ordinary income under § 1245. Ahmad sells the machine before the end of this year and offsets $15,000 of the ordinary income against the net operating loss carryover. ■

Postponing and Shifting Recapture

It is also possible to postpone recapture or to shift the burden of recapture to others. For example, recapture is avoided upon the disposition of a § 1231 asset if the taxpayer replaces the property by entering into a like-kind exchange. In this instance, recapture potential is merely carried over to the newly acquired property (refer to Example 20).

Recapture can be shifted to others through the gratuitous transfer of § 1245 or § 1250 property to family members. A subsequent sale of such property by the donee will trigger recapture to the donee rather than the donor (refer to Example 17). This procedure would be advisable only if the donee is in a lower income tax bracket than the donor.

Avoiding Recapture

The immediate expensing election (§ 179) is subject to § 1245 recapture. If the election is not made, the § 1245 recapture potential will accumulate more slowly (refer to Chapter 8). Since using the immediate expense deduction complicates depreciation and book accounting for the affected asset, not taking the deduction may make sense even though the time value of money might indicate it should be taken.

KEY TERMS

Additional depreciation, 17–15

Intangible drilling and development costs (IDC), 17–21

Long-term nonpersonal use capital assets, 17–6

Related party, 17–21

Section 1231 gains and losses, 17–3

Section 1231 lookback, 17–8

Section 1231 property, 17–4

Section 1245 property, 17–13

Section 1245 recapture, 17–12

Section 1250 property, 17–14

Section 1250 recapture, 17–14

Unrecaptured Section 1250 gain, 17–17

PROBLEM MATERIALS

DISCUSSION QUESTIONS

1. What types of transactions involving capital assets are included under § 1231? Why would they not qualify for long-term capital gain treatment without § 1231?

2. Does § 1231 treatment apply to all business property?

3. The disposition of depreciable business property results in a net loss. How is this net loss treated for tax purposes?

4. What two developments near the start of World War II caused Congress to reexamine the tax treatment of business assets?

Issue ID
5. A taxpayer has owned a painting for five years. What would have to be true of this painting for it to be a § 1231 asset?

Issue ID
6. Aretha has a loss of $4,000 on a § 1231 asset and a gain of $16,000 on sale of vacant land. Under what circumstances could the gain from the sale of the land offset the loss?

Issue ID
7. Sally lives in an area that was hit hard by a hurricane. She has correctly determined that she has a $15,000 business property long-term casualty loss and an $11,000 business property long-term casualty gain. What tax issues must Sally deal with?

8. Does § 1231 have any effect on whether *realized* gain or loss is *recognized*?

9. Tangible personal property held more than one year and used in a trade or business is disposed of at a loss as a result of a condemnation. Is the loss subject to § 1231 treatment?

Issue ID
10. An individual taxpayer had a net § 1231 loss in 2003 and a net § 1231 gain in 2004, 2005, and 2006. What factors will influence whether any of the 2006 net § 1231 gain will be treated as long-term capital gain?

11. Review Examples 4 and 6 in the text. In both examples, the taxpayer's AGI is $129,400 even though in Example 6 there is $700 of nonrecaptured § 1231 loss from 2005. Explain why the two AGI amounts are the same.

12. A taxpayer owns depreciable business equipment held for the long-term holding period. What would have to be true for the equipment to generate a § 1231 loss when it is sold?

13. A depreciable business machine has been owned for four years and is no longer useful to the taxpayer. What would have to be true for the disposition of the machine to generate at least some § 1231 gain?

14. Sylvia owns two items of business equipment. They were both purchased in 2002 for $100,000, both have a seven-year recovery period, and both have an adjusted basis of $37,490. Sylvia is considering selling these assets in 2006. One of them is worth $40,000, and the other is worth $23,000. Since both items were used in her business, Sylvia simply assumes that the loss on one will be offset against the gain from the other and the net gain or loss will increase or reduce her business income. Is she correct?

Issue ID

15. If depreciable equipment used in a business is sold at a recognized gain on July 10, 2006, and it was purchased on August 21, 2005, does § 1245 depreciation recapture apply to the asset?

16. A professional football player's contract is sold at a gain after it has been held for two years. What issues should the team consider in determining the nature of this gain?

Issue ID

17. A farmer's silo is destroyed by a tornado, but is insured for its replacement cost. Consequently, the farmer has a $40,000 gain after receiving the insurance proceeds. The silo is not replaced because the farmer spends the insurance proceeds on additional cattle. What is the nature of the gain if the silo originally cost $100,000 three years ago and had an adjusted basis of $60,000 at the time of its destruction?

18. Residential real estate is sold at a gain. In what year(s) would it have to have been acquired in order for some of the gain to be recaptured as ordinary income by § 1250?

19. Residential real estate was acquired in 1992. What is the maximum amount of unrecaptured § 1250 gain from the disposition of the real estate if the real estate is sold at a gain?

20. Nonresidential real estate was acquired in 2004. What is the maximum amount of unrecaptured § 1250 gain from the disposition of the real estate if the building is sold for a loss and the land is sold for a gain?

21. An individual taxpayer has $25,000 of § 1231 gain from the disposition of nonresidential real estate. Straight-line depreciation of $43,000 was deducted on the real estate. The taxpayer also has a § 1231 loss of $56,000 from the sale of equipment. How much of the § 1231 gain is taxed as unrecaptured § 1250 gain?

22. Abigail sells one § 1231 asset during the year at a gain of $45,000. The asset was depreciable real estate she had held for seven years. She wants to know what her maximum unrecaptured § 1250 gain might be.

23. An individual taxpayer has a net § 1231 gain from disposition of depreciable real estate. The net § 1231 gain is treated as a long-term capital gain. The net § 1231 gain is less than the depreciation taken on the real estate. The taxpayer also has a net short-term capital loss that is less than the net § 1231 gain. Does the taxpayer have any unrecaptured § 1250 gain subject to tax at 25% in the alternative tax on net capital gain calculation?

24. An individual taxpayer receives tangible personal property by gift. The property had been depreciated by the donor and had a fair market value greater than the donor's adjusted basis at the date of the gift. Does the § 1245 depreciation recapture potential carry over from the donor to the donee?

25. An individual taxpayer receives tangible personal property by inheritance. The property had been depreciated by the decedent and had a fair market value greater than the decedent's adjusted basis at the date of the decedent's death. Does the § 1245 depreciation recapture potential carry over from the decedent to the beneficiary?

26. A corporation distributes a truck it has owned for three years to its sole shareholder. The shareholder will use the truck for personal use activity. The truck's fair market value at the time of the distribution is greater than its adjusted basis, but less than its original cost. Does the corporation recognize a gain? If so, what is the character of the gain?

27. A corporation distributes a truck it has owned for three years to its sole shareholder. The shareholder will use the truck for business activity. The truck's fair market value at the time of the distribution is greater than its adjusted basis, but less than its original cost. Does the corporation recognize a gain? If so, what is the character of the gain?

28. Refer to Form 4797 at the end of this chapter. Where would a § 1231 loss be entered on the form?

29. Refer to Form 4797 at the end of this chapter. Where would a § 1231 gain on the disposition of business land be entered on the form?

30. Refer to Form 4797 at the end of this chapter. Where would a § 1231 lookback loss be entered on the form?

PROBLEMS

31. Sue-Jen purchased timber on a 100-acre tract of land in South Dakota in March 2004 for $100,000. On January 1, 2005, the timber had a fair market value of $110,000. Because of careless cutting in November 2005, when the fair market value was $115,000, the wood was sold on January 30, 2006, for $78,000.
    a. What gain (loss) was recognized in 2004, 2005, and 2006 if Sue-Jen elects to treat the cutting as a sale?
    b. What was the nature of the gains (losses) in (a)?
    c. Does the answer change if the timber was sold in December 2005? Why?
    d. If the timber was worth only $48,000 on January 1, 2005, was cut in November when worth $21,000, and was sold in December for $49,000, how would the answers to (a) and (b) change?

32. Bob owns a farming sole proprietorship. During the year, Bob sold a milk cow that he had owned for 15 months and a workhorse that he had owned for 66 months. The cow had an adjusted basis of $18,000 and was sold for $15,000. The horse had an adjusted basis of $350 and was sold for $4,000. Bob also has a $200 long-term capital loss from the sale of corporate stock. He has $55,000 of other AGI (not associated with the items above) for the year. He has $4,000 nonrecaptured § 1231 losses from the previous five years. What is the nature of the gains or losses from the disposition of the farm animals, and what is Bob's AGI for the year?

Communications

33. A painting that Kwan Lee held for investment was destroyed in a flood. The painting was insured, and Kwan had a $30,000 gain from this casualty. He also had a $17,000 loss from an uninsured antique vase that was destroyed by the flood. The vase was also held for investment. Kwan had no other property transactions during the year and has no nonrecaptured § 1231 losses from prior years. Both the painting and the vase had been held more than one year when the flood occurred. Compute Kwan's net gain or loss and identify how it would be treated. Also, write a letter to Kwan explaining the nature of the gain or loss. Kwan's address is 2367 Meridian Road, Hannibal Point, MO 34901.

34. Vicki has the following net § 1231 results for each of the years shown. What would be the nature of the net gains in 2005 and 2006?

Tax Year	Net § 1231 Loss	Net § 1231 Gain
2001	$16,000	
2002	33,000	
2003	32,000	
2004		$42,000
2005		30,000
2006		39,000

35. Yoshida owns two parcels of business land (§ 1231 assets). One parcel can be sold at a loss of $30,000, and the other parcel can be sold at a gain of $40,000. Yoshida has no nonrecaptured § 1231 losses from prior years. The parcels could be sold at any time because potential purchasers are abundant. Yoshida has a $25,000 short-term capital loss carryover from a prior tax year and no capital assets that could be sold to generate long-term capital gains. Both the land parcels have been held more than one year. What should Yoshida do based upon these facts? (Assume tax rates are constant and ignore the present value of future cash flow.)   *Decision Making*

36. Gray Industries (a sole proprietorship) sold three § 1231 assets during 2006. Data on these property dispositions are as follows:

Asset	Cost	Acquired	Depreciation	Sold for	Sold on
Rack	$100,000	10/10/02	$60,000	$75,000	10/10/06
Forklift	35,000	10/16/03	23,000	5,000	10/10/06
Bin	87,000	03/12/05	34,000	60,000	10/10/06

a. Determine the amount and the character of the recognized gain or loss from the disposition of each asset.
b. Assuming Gray has no nonrecaptured net § 1231 losses from prior years, how much of the 2006 recognized gains is treated as capital gains?

37. Green Industries (a sole proprietorship) sold three § 1231 assets during 2006. Data on these property dispositions are as follows:

Asset	Cost	Acquired	Depreciation	Sold for	Sold on
Rack	$100,000	10/10/02	$60,000	$135,000	10/10/06
Forklift	35,000	10/16/03	23,000	5,000	10/10/06
Bin	87,000	03/12/05	34,000	60,000	10/10/06

a. Determine the amount and the character of the recognized gain or loss from the disposition of each asset.
b. Assuming Green has $5,000 nonrecaptured net § 1231 losses from the five prior years, how much of the 2006 recognized gains is treated as capital gains?

38. Magenta Industries (a sole proprietorship) sold three § 1231 assets during 2006. Data on these property dispositions are as follows:

Asset	Cost	Acquired	Depreciation	Sold for	Sold on
Rack	$110,000	10/10/03	$60,000	$55,000	10/10/06
Forklift	45,000	10/16/02	23,000	15,000	10/10/06
Bin	97,000	03/12/05	34,000	60,000	10/10/06

a. Determine the amount and the character of the recognized gain or loss from the disposition of each asset.
b. Assuming Magenta has $2,000 nonrecaptured net § 1231 losses from prior years, how much of the 2006 recognized gains is treated as capital gains?

39. On December 1, 2004, Gray Manufacturing Company (a corporation) purchased another company's assets, including a patent. The patent was used in Gray's manufacturing operations; $40,500 was allocated to the patent, and it was amortized at the rate of $225 per month. On July 30, 2006, Gray sold the patent for $70,000. Twenty months of amortization had been taken on the patent. What are the amount and nature of the gain Gray recognizes on the disposition of the patent? Write a letter to Gray discussing the treatment of the gain. Gray's address is 6734 Grover Street, Back Bay Harbor, ME 23890. The letter should be addressed to Siddim Sadatha, Controller.   *Communications*

40. On June 1, 2002, Sparrow Enterprises (not a corporation) acquired a retail store for $500,000 (with $100,000 being allocated to the land). The store was 39-year real property, and the straight-line cost recovery method was used. The property was sold on June 21, 2006, for $385,000.
    a. Compute the cost recovery and adjusted basis for the store using Table 8–6 from Chapter 8.
    b. What are the amount and nature of Sparrow's gain or loss from disposition of the store? What amount, if any, of the gain is unrecaptured § 1250 gain?

41. On May 2, 1986, Moad acquired residential rental real estate for $450,000. Of the cost, $100,000 was allocated to the land and $350,000 to the building. On January 20, 2006, the building, which then had an adjusted basis of $0, was sold for $345,000 and the land for $500,000.
    a. Determine the amount and character of the recognized gain from the sale of the building.
    b. Determine the amount and character of the recognized gain from the sale of the land.

42. Dave is the sole proprietor of a trampoline shop. During 2006, the following transactions occurred:

    • Unimproved land adjacent to the store was condemned by the city on February 1. The condemnation proceeds were $25,000. The land, acquired in 1983, had an allocable basis of $40,000. Dave has additional parking across the street and plans to use the condemnation proceeds to build his inventory.
    • A truck used to deliver trampolines was sold on January 2 for $3,500. The truck was purchased on January 2, 2002, for $6,000. On the date of sale, the adjusted basis was $2,509.
    • Dave sold an antique rowing machine at an auction. Net proceeds were $3,900. The rowing machine was purchased as used equipment 17 years ago for $5,200 and is fully depreciated.
    • Dave sold an apartment building for $200,000 on September 1. The rental property was purchased on September 1, 2003, for $150,000 and was being depreciated over a 27.5-year life using the straight-line method. At the date of sale, the adjusted basis was $124,783.
    • Dave's personal yacht was stolen on September 5. The yacht had been purchased in August at a cost of $25,000. The fair market value immediately preceding the theft was $20,000. Dave was insured for 50% of the original cost, and he received $12,500 on December 1.
    • Dave sold a Buick on May 1 for $9,600. The vehicle had been used exclusively for personal purposes. It was purchased on September 1, 2002, for $20,800.
    • Dave's trampoline stretching machine (owned two years) was stolen on May 5, but the business's insurance company will not pay any of the machine's value because Dave failed to pay the insurance premium. The machine had a fair market value of $8,000 and an adjusted basis of $6,000 at the time of theft.
    • Dave had AGI of $402,000 from sources other than those described above.
    • Dave has no nonrecaptured § 1231 lookback losses.

    a. For each transaction, what are the amount and nature of recognized gain or loss?
    b. What is Dave's 2006 AGI?

Communications

43. On January 1, 1997, Cora Hassant acquired depreciable real property for $50,000. She used straight-line depreciation to compute the asset's cost recovery. The asset was sold for $89,000 on January 3, 2006, when its adjusted basis was $38,000.
    a. What are the amount and nature of the gain if the real property was residential?
    b. Cora is curious about how the recapture rules differ for residential rental real estate acquired in 1986 and for residential rental real estate acquired in 1987 and thereafter. Write a letter to Cora explaining the differences. Her address is 2345 Westridge Street #23, Homer, MT 67342.

Decision Making

44. Joanne is in the 35% tax bracket and owns depreciable business equipment that she purchased several years ago for $135,000. She has taken $100,000 of depreciation on the equipment, and it is worth $85,000. Joanne's niece, Susan, is starting a new business and

is short of cash. Susan has asked Joanne to gift the equipment to her so that Susan can use it in her business. Joanne no longer needs the equipment. Identify the alternatives available to Joanne if she wishes to help Susan and the tax effects of those alternatives. (Assume all alternatives involve the business equipment in one way or another, and ignore the gift tax.)

45. Paul owned a § 1245 asset with an adjusted basis of $5,000. He had deducted depreciation of $6,000, so his original cost was $11,000. On May 23, 2004, when the property's fair market value was $22,500, Paul gifted the asset to his daughter, Caroline. She used the asset for business purposes for two years and took another $2,000 of depreciation. She then sold the asset for $36,000 on June 1, 2006.
    a. What is Caroline's basis for the asset on May 23, 2004?
    b. What are the amount and character of Caroline's recognized gain or loss when she sells the asset?

46. Seko owned a § 1245 asset with an adjusted basis of $5,000. He had deducted depreciation of $6,000, so his original cost was $11,000. On May 23, 2004, when the property's fair market value was $22,500, Seko died, and the asset was inherited by his son, Tonji. Tonji used the asset for business purposes for two years and took $5,500 of depreciation. He then sold the asset for $36,000 on June 1, 2006.
    a. What is Tonji's basis for the asset on May 23, 2004?
    b. What are the amount and character of Tonji's recognized gain or loss when he sells the asset?

47. In 2006, Jerat donated to charity depreciable equipment used in his business. If Jerat had sold the equipment, he would have had a gain of $45,000. The equipment was worth $67,000 at the time of its contribution. Jerat had taken $33,000 of depreciation on the equipment. What is the amount of Jerat's charitable contribution from the donation of the equipment?

48. In 2006, Cicely sold depreciable equipment used in her business for a gain of $45,000. Cicely had taken $33,000 of depreciation on this equipment. She had also taken $27,000 of depreciation on like-kind equipment she had traded in on the equipment she sold this year. What is the nature of Cicely's gain from the disposition of the equipment?

49. Emily is the sole shareholder of Brown Corporation. Brown has a zero basis for a printing machine that Emily would like to use in a personal activity. The machine's fair market value is $4,500. Brown distributes the machine as a property dividend to Emily. Brown has accumulated earnings and profits of $3 million. What are the amount and nature of the gain recognized by Brown? What are the amount and nature of the distribution received by Emily?

50. Terri provided depreciable furniture in a furnished rental apartment she owned. She sold the furniture after owning it for two years and had a $4,000 loss on the disposition. What is the nature of the loss, and where is it reported on Form 4797?

51. Is a § 1245 gain that is reported on Form 4797, Part II, line 18(b) included on Form 1040, Schedule D? Is it included in AGI?

52. Jay sold three items of business equipment for a total of $300,000. None of the equipment was appraised to determine its value. Jay's cost and adjusted basis for the assets are as follows:

Decision Making

Asset	Cost	Adjusted Basis
Skidder	$230,000	$ 40,000
Driller	120,000	60,000
Platform	620,000	–0–
Total	$970,000	$100,000

Jay has been unable to establish the fair market values of the three assets. All he can determine is that combined they were worth $300,000 to the buyer in this arm's length transaction. How should Jay allocate the sales price and figure the gain or loss on the sale of the three assets?

CUMULATIVE PROBLEMS

Tax Return Problem

53. Justin Stone was an employee of DataCare Services, Inc. His salary was $187,000 through November 10, 2005, when he was laid off. He received $14,000 of unemployment compensation from November 11, 2005, through December 31, 2005. FICA withholdings were as follows: Social Security of $5,580 ($90,000 × 6.2%) and Medicare of $2,712 ($187,000 × 1.45%). Justin lives at 112 Green Road, Sandusky, ID 45623. His Social Security number is 567–89–1234. Justin owned an apartment building until November 22, 2005, when he sold it for $400,000. For 2005, he had rent revenue of $30,000. He incurred and paid expenses as follows: $4,568 of repairs, $12,000 of mortgage interest, and $1,000 of miscellaneous expenses. He had purchased the building on January 2, 1999, for $125,000. The building generated an operating profit each year that Justin owned it.

Other information follows:

- On November 22, 2005, Justin sold for $14,000 equipment that had been used for repairing various items in the apartments. The equipment was purchased for $25,000 on July 10, 1998, and was fully depreciated prior to 2005.
- Justin has no unrecaptured § 1231 losses from prior years.
- Justin is age 38, single, divorced, and has custody of his nine-year-old son, Flint. Justin provides more than 50% of Flint's support. Flint's Social Security number is 098–77–6543.
- Justin had $5,000 interest income from Blue Corporation bonds.
- Justin had $3,000 interest income from a State Bank certificate of deposit.
- Justin had a $2,000 5%/15% long-term capital gain distribution from the Brown Stock Investment Fund.
- Justin had the following itemized deductions: $5,600 real estate taxes on his home; $8,900 mortgage interest on his home; $760 charitable contributions (all in cash, properly documented, and no single contribution exceeded $25); $2,300 state income tax withholding during 2005; $2,000 state estimated income tax payments during 2005; $2,600 sales taxes paid.
- Justin does not wish to donate to the Presidential Election Campaign Fund.
- He had $15,000 of Federal income tax withholding during 2005 and made total Federal estimated income tax payments of $95,000 during 2005.

Compute Justin's 2005 net tax payable or refund due. If you use tax forms for your computations, you will need Form 1040 and Schedules A, B, D, and E. You will also need Forms 4562 and 4797, but ignore Form 6251. Suggested software: TurboTax.

Tax Return Problem

Communications

54. Glen and Diane Okumura are married, file a joint return, and live at 39 Kaloa Street, Honolulu, HI 56790. Glen's Social Security number is 777–88–2000 and Diane's is 888–77–1000. The Okumuras have two dependent children, Amy (age 15) and John (age 9). Glen works for the Hawaii Public Works Department, and Diane works in a retail dress shop. The Okumuras had the following transactions during 2006:

a. Glen earned $97,000 in wages and had Federal income tax withholding of $13,000.

b. Diane earned $68,000 in wages from the dress shop and had Federal income tax withholding of $11,000.

c. The Okumuras sold a small apartment building for $199,980 on November 15, 2006. The building was acquired in October 2000 for $300,000; cost recovery was $86,820.

d. The Okumuras received $3,000 in qualified dividends on various domestic corporation stocks that they own.

e. The Okumuras sold stock on November 5 for a $7,000 long-term capital gain and other stock on December 10 at a $2,000 short-term capital loss.

f. The Okumuras had the following itemized deductions: $11,000 unreimbursed medical expenses; $10,500 personal use real property taxes; $7,000 qualified residence interest; $1,500 of Glen's unreimbursed employee business expenses; $535 of investment-related expenses; $2,700 of state income taxes paid; and $1,061 of sales taxes from the sales tax table.

g. The Okumuras spent $3,000 on qualifying child care expenses during the year.

Compute the Okumuras' 2006 net tax payable or refund due. Also write a letter to the Okumuras describing how the sale of the apartment building affects their return.

RESEARCH PROBLEMS

Note: Solutions to Research Problems can be prepared by using the **RIA Checkpoint**® **Student Edition** online research product, which is available to accompany this text. It is also possible to prepare solutions to the Research Problems by using tax research materials found in a standard tax library.

Communications

Research Problem 1.   Sidney owns a professional football franchise. He has received an offer of $80 million for the franchise, all the football equipment, the rights to concession receipts, the rights to a stadium lease, and the rights to all the player contracts he owns. Most of the players have been with the team for quite a long time and have contracts that were signed several years ago. The contracts have been substantially depreciated. Sidney is concerned about potential § 1245 recapture when the contracts are sold. He has heard about "previously unrecaptured depreciation with respect to initial contracts" and would like to know more about it. Find a definition for that phrase and write an explanation of it.

Research Problem 2.   Walter is both a real estate developer and the owner and manager of residential rental real estate. Walter is retiring and is going to sell both the land he is holding for future development and the rental properties he owns. Straight-line depreciation was used to depreciate the rental real estate. The rental properties will be sold at a substantial loss, and the development property will be sold at a substantial gain. What is the nature of these gains and losses?

Partial list of research aids:
§§ 1221 and 1231.
Zane R. Tollis, 65 TCM 1951, T.C.Memo. 1993–63.

Research Problem 3.   An individual cash basis taxpayer sells rental real estate on the installment basis. The gain from the disposition is $45,000. Of this amount, $30,000 is potential 25% gain, and $15,000 is potential 5%/15% gain. In what sequence are these gains recognized as gain is recognized on the installment sale?

Research Problem 4.   Brown Corporation, a software development company, was formed in 1996 and has always been a C corporation. In 2003, it acquired all the assets of another software company, including $400,000 worth of copyrights developed by the acquired company. Brown treated these copyrights as § 197 intangible assets and amortized 30 months' worth of the 180-month life of the assets before selling the copyrights for $1.2 million on June 28, 2005. What was the tax status of these copyrights, and what is the nature of the gain or loss from their disposition?

Use the tax resources of the Internet to address the following questions. Do not restrict your search to the World Wide Web, but include a review of newsgroups and general reference materials, practitioner sites and resources, primary sources of the tax law, chat rooms and discussion groups, and other opportunities.

Internet
Activity

Research Problem 5.   Summarize tax planning strategies related to each of the following topics that are presented on the Internet by tax advisers looking for clients:

a. A strategy for maximizing gains that are eligible for the 5%/15% alternative tax rate rather than the 25% rate.
b. A strategy for maximizing gains that are eligible for the 5%/15% alternative tax rate rather than the 28% rate.

Research Problem 6.   Determine whether Australia has an equivalent to § 1231 treatment for gains from the disposition of business depreciable assets.

Research Problem 7.   Find a state Web site that has tax forms and instructions for that state. Let's call that state "X." Find a discussion in those sources that reveals whether state X taxes gains from the sale of real estate that is located in state Y when the taxpayer is an individual and is a full-time resident of state X.

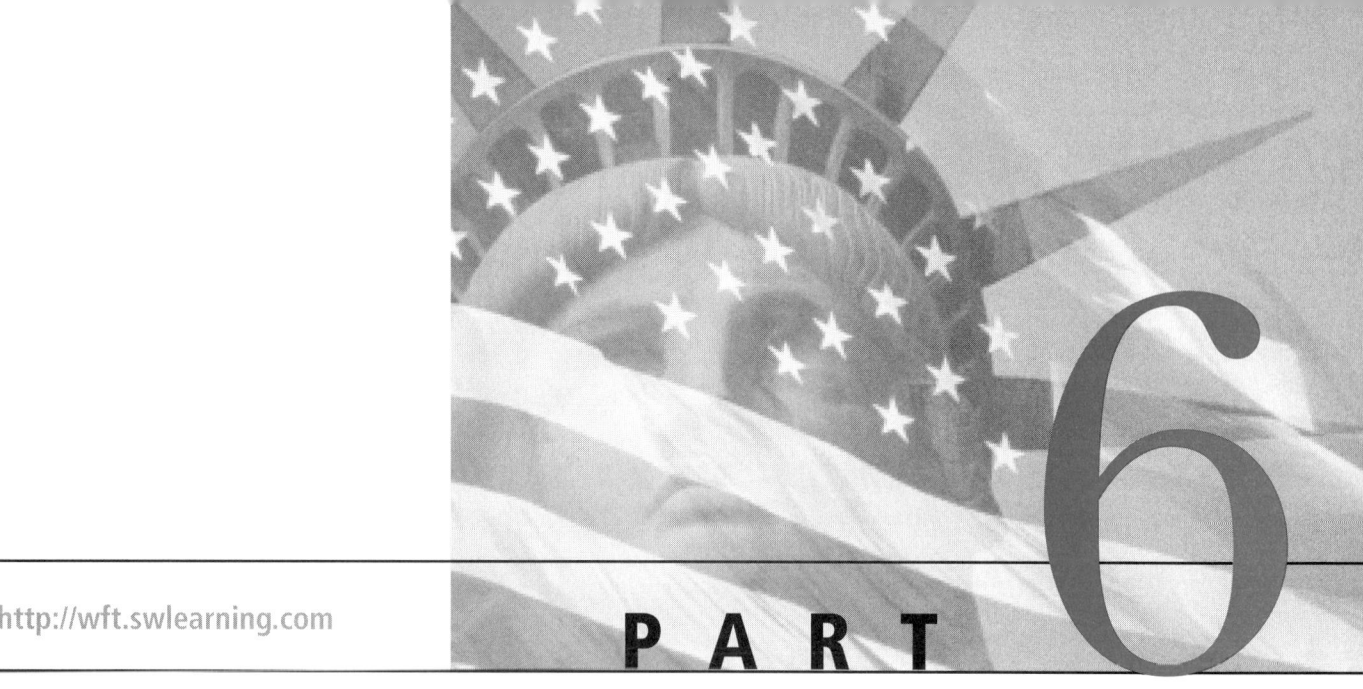

PART 6

Accounting Periods, Accounting Methods, and Deferred Compensation

Part VI provides a more comprehensive examination of the accounting periods and accounting methods that were introduced in Part II. A discussion of special accounting methods is also included. Part VI concludes with an analysis of the tax consequences of deferred compensation transactions.

CHAPTER 18
Accounting Periods and Methods

CHAPTER 19
Deferred Compensation

Accounting Periods and Methods

LEARNING OBJECTIVES

After completing Chapter 18, you should be able to:

LO.1

Understand the relevance of the accounting period concept, the different types of accounting periods, and the limitations on their use.

LO.2

Apply the cash method, accrual method, and hybrid method of accounting.

LO.3

Utilize the procedure for changing accounting methods.

LO.4

Determine when the installment method of accounting can be utilized and apply the related calculation techniques.

LO.5

Understand the alternative methods of accounting for long-term contracts (the completed contract method and the percentage of completion method) including the limitations on the use of the completed contract method.

LO.6

Know when accounting for inventories must occur, recognize the types of costs that must be included in inventories, and apply the LIFO method.

LO.7

Identify tax planning opportunities related to accounting periods and accounting methods.

Tax practitioners must deal with the issue of *when* particular items of income and expense are recognized as well as the basic issue of *whether* the items are includible in taxable income. Earlier chapters discussed the types of income subject to tax (gross income and exclusions) and allowable deductions (the *whether* issue).[1] This chapter focuses on the related issue of the periods in which income and deductions are reported (the *when* issue). Generally, a taxpayer's income and deductions must be assigned to particular 12-month periods—calendar years or fiscal years.

Income and deductions are placed within particular years through the use of tax accounting methods. The basic accounting methods are the cash method, accrual method, and hybrid method. Other special purpose methods, such as the installment method and the methods used for long-term construction contracts, are available for specific circumstances or types of transactions.

Over the long run, the accounting period used by a taxpayer will not affect the aggregate amount of reported taxable income. However, taxable income for any particular year may vary significantly due to the use of a particular reporting period. Also, through the choice of accounting methods or accounting periods, it is possible to postpone the recognition of taxable income and to enjoy the benefits from deferring the related tax. This chapter discusses the taxpayer's alternatives for accounting periods and accounting methods.

TAX *in the News* | **PRODUCTION ACTIVITIES DEDUCTION CREATES TAX PLANNING OPPORTUNITIES**

Under the American Jobs Creation Act of 2004, producers are allowed a deduction equal to a percentage of their income from qualified production activities: 3 percent in 2005 and 2006, 6 percent in 2007 through 2009, and 9 percent in 2010. Thus, assuming the tax rate is the same between years, a producer would prefer to take the deduction in 2007, rather than in 2006. Taking the deduction in 2006 reduces the producer's taxable income by $.03 for each dollar of production activities income whereas taking the deduction in 2007 reduces the producer's taxable income by $.06 on the dollar.

---

[1]See Chapters 4, 5, and 6.

Accounting Periods

In General

LO.1

Understand the relevance of the accounting period concept, the different types of accounting periods, and the limitations on their use.

A taxpayer who keeps adequate books and records may be permitted to elect a **fiscal year**, a 12-month period ending on the *last day* of a month other than December, for the **accounting period**. Otherwise, a *calendar year* must be used.[2] Frequently, corporations can satisfy the record-keeping requirements and elect to use a fiscal year.[3] Often the fiscal year conforms to a natural business year (e.g., a summer resort's fiscal year may end on September 30, after the close of the season). Individuals seldom use a fiscal year because they do not maintain the necessary books and records and because complications can arise as a result of changes in the tax law (e.g., often the transition rules and effective dates differ for fiscal year taxpayers).

Generally, a taxable year may not exceed 12 calendar months. However, if certain requirements are met, a taxpayer may elect to use an annual period that varies from 52 to 53 weeks.[4] In that case, the year-end must be on the same day of the week (e.g., the Tuesday falling closest to October 31 or the last Tuesday in October). The day of the week selected for ending the year will depend upon business considerations. For example, a retail business that is not open on Sundays may end its tax year on a Sunday so that it can take an inventory without interrupting business operations.

EXAMPLE 1

Wade is in the business of selling farm supplies. His natural business year terminates at the end of October with the completion of harvesting. At the end of the fiscal year, Wade must take an inventory, which is most easily accomplished on a Tuesday. Therefore, Wade could adopt a 52–53 week tax year ending on the Tuesday closest to October 31. If Wade selects this method, the year-end date may fall in the following month if that Tuesday is closer to October 31. The tax year ending in 2006 will contain 52 weeks beginning on Wednesday, November 2, 2005, and ending on Tuesday, October 31, 2006. The tax year ending in 2007 will have 52 weeks beginning on Wednesday, November 1, 2006, and ending on Tuesday, October 30, 2007. ■

Specific Provisions for Partnerships, S Corporations, and Personal Service Corporations

Partnerships and S Corporations. When a partner's tax year and the partnership's tax year differ, the partner will enjoy a deferral of income. This results because the partner reports his or her share of the partnership's income and deductions for the partnership's tax year ending within or with the partner's tax year.[5] For example, if the tax year of the partnership ends on January 31, a calendar year partner will not report partnership profits for the first 11 months of the partnership tax year until the following year. Therefore, partnerships are subject to special tax year requirements.

In general, the partnership tax year must be the same as the tax year of the majority interest partners. The **majority interest partners** are the partners who own a greater-than-50 percent interest in the partnership capital and profits. If there are no majority interest partners, the partnership must adopt the same tax year as its principal partners. A **principal partner** is a partner with a 5 percent or more interest in the partnership capital or profits.[6]

---

[2] § 441(c) and Reg. § 1.441–1(b)(1)(ii).
[3] Reg. § 1.441–1(e)(2).
[4] § 441(f).

[5] Reg. § 1.706–1(a).
[6] §§ 706(b)(1)(B) and 706(b)(3).

EXAMPLE 2

The RST Partnership is owned equally by Rose Corporation, Silver Corporation, and Tom. The partners have the following tax years.

	Partner's Tax Year Ending
Rose	June 30
Silver	June 30
Tom	December 31

The partnership's tax year must end on June 30. If Silver Corporation's as well as Tom's year ended on December 31, the partnership would be required to adopt a calendar year. ∎

If the principal partners do not all have the same tax year and no majority of partners have the same tax year, the partnership must use a year that results in the *least aggregate deferral* of income.[7] Under the **least aggregate deferral method**, the different tax years of the principal partners are tested to determine which produces the least aggregate deferral. This is calculated by first multiplying the combined percentages of the principal partners with the same tax year by the months of deferral for the test year. Once this is done for each set of principal partners with the same tax year, the resulting products are summed to produce the aggregate deferral. After calculating the aggregate deferral for each of the test years, the test year with the smallest summation (the least aggregate deferral) is the tax year for the partnership.

EXAMPLE 3

The DE Partnership is owned equally by Diane and Emily. Diane's fiscal year ends on March 31, and Emily's fiscal year ends on August 31. The partnership must use the partner's fiscal year that will result in the least aggregate deferral of income. Therefore, the fiscal years ending March 31 and August 31 must both be tested.

Test for Fiscal Year Ending March 31				
Partner	Year Ends	Profit %	Months of Deferral	Product
Diane	3–31	50	0	0
Emily	8–31	50	5	2.5
Aggregate deferral months				2.5

Thus, with a year ending March 31, Emily would be able to defer her half of the income for five months. That is, Emily's share of the partnership income for the fiscal year ending March 31, 2007, would not be included in her income until August 31, 2007.

Test for Fiscal Year Ending August 31				
Partner	Year Ends	Profit %	Months of Deferral	Product
Diane	3–31	50	7	3.5
Emily	8–31	50	0	0
Aggregate deferral months				3.5

[7]Temp.Reg. § 1.706–1T(a)(2).

Thus, with a year ending August 31, Diane would be able to defer her half of the income for seven months. That is, Diane's share of the partnership income for the fiscal year ending August 31, 2007, would not be included in her income until March 31, 2008.

The year ending March 31 must be used because it results in the least aggregate deferral of income. ■

Generally, S corporations must adopt a calendar year.[8] However, partnerships and S corporations may *elect* an otherwise *impermissible year* under any of the following conditions:

- A business purpose for the year can be demonstrated.[9]
- The partnership's or S corporation's year results in a deferral of not more than three months' income, and the entity agrees to make required tax payments.[10]
- The entity retains the same year as was used for the fiscal year ending in 1987, provided the entity agrees to make required tax payments.

Business Purpose. The only business purpose for a fiscal year that the IRS has acknowledged is the need to conform the tax year to the natural business year of a business.[11] Generally, only seasonal businesses have a natural business year. For example, the natural business year for a department store may end on January 31, after Christmas returns have been processed and clearance sales have been completed.

Required Tax Payments. Under the required payments system, tax payments are due from a fiscal year partnership or S corporation by April 15 of each tax year.[12] The amount due is computed by applying the highest individual tax rate plus 1 percentage point to an estimate of the deferral period income. The deferral period runs from the close of the fiscal year to the end of the calendar year. Estimated income for this period is based on the average monthly earnings for the previous fiscal year. The amount due is reduced by the amount of required tax payments for the previous year.[13]

EXAMPLE 4

Brown, Inc., an S corporation, elected a fiscal year ending September 30. Bob is the only shareholder. For the fiscal year ending September 30, 2006, Brown earned $100,000. The required tax payment for the previous year was $5,000. The corporation must pay $4,000 by April 15, 2007, calculated as follows:

$$(\$100,000 \times {}^{3}/_{12} \times 36\%^*) - \$5,000 = \$4,000$$

*Maximum § 1 rate of 35% + 1%. ■

| **ETHICAL** *Considerations* | **WHO BENEFITS FROM THE CHANGE IN TAX YEAR?** |

A public accounting sole practitioner has reached a breaking point. All of his clients use the calendar year to report income. Many of the clients are S corporations and partnerships. His workload the first four months of the year is so heavy that it is putting the quality of his work at risk. He is considering asking some of his S corporations and partnerships to switch to a fiscal year ending September 30. The accountant believes that he can convince the shareholders and partners to make the change. Although the shareholders and partners would be subject to the "required tax payments" rules, the accountant will sell the plan by promising better service. Evaluate the plan proposed by the accountant.

---

[8]§§ 1378(a) and (b).
[9]§§ 706(b)(1)(C) and 1378(b)(2).
[10]§ 444.
[11]Rev.Rul. 87–57, 1987–2 C.B. 117.

[12]§§ 444(c) and 7519. No payment is required if the calculated amount is $500 or less.
[13]§ 7519(b).

Personal Service Corporations. A **personal service corporation** (**PSC**) is a corporation whose shareholder-employees provide personal services (e.g., medical, dental, legal, accounting, engineering, actuarial, consulting, or performing arts). Generally, a PSC must use a calendar year.[14] However, a PSC can *elect* a fiscal year under any of the following conditions:

- A business purpose for the year can be demonstrated.
- The PSC year results in a deferral of not more than three months' income, the corporation pays the shareholder-employee's salary during the portion of the calendar year after the close of the fiscal year, and the salary for that period is at least proportionate to the shareholder-employee's salary received for the preceding fiscal year.[15]
- The PSC retains the same year it used for the fiscal year ending in 1987, provided it satisfies the latter two requirements in the preceding option.

EXAMPLE 5

Nancy's corporation paid Nancy a salary of $120,000 during its fiscal year ending September 30, 2006. The corporation cannot satisfy the business purpose test for a fiscal year. The corporation can continue to use its fiscal year without any negative tax effects, provided Nancy receives at least $30,000 [(3 months/12 months) × $120,000] as salary during the period October 1 through December 31, 2006. ■

If the salary test is not satisfied, the PSC can retain the fiscal year, but the corporation's deduction for salary for the fiscal year is limited to the following:

$$A + A \ (F/N)$$

Where A = Amount paid after the close of the fiscal year.
       F = Number of months in the fiscal year minus number of months from the end of the fiscal year to the end of the ongoing calendar year.
       N = Number of months from the end of the fiscal year to the end of the ongoing calendar year.

EXAMPLE 6

Assume the corporation in the previous example paid Nancy $10,000 of salary during the period October 1 through December 31, 2006. The deduction for Nancy's salary for the corporation's fiscal year ending September 30, 2007, is thus limited to $40,000 calculated as follows:

$$\$10,000 + \left[\$10,000\left(\frac{12-3}{3}\right)\right] = \$10,000 + \$30,000 = \$40,000$$ ■

Making the Election

A taxpayer elects to use a calendar or fiscal year by the timely filing of his or her initial tax return. For all subsequent years, the taxpayer must use this same period unless approval for change is obtained from the IRS.[16]

Changes in the Accounting Period

A taxpayer must obtain consent from the IRS before changing the tax year.[17] This power to approve or not to approve a change is significant in that it permits the IRS to issue authoritative administrative guidelines that must be met by taxpayers who wish to change their accounting period. An application for permission to change

---

[14]§ 441(i).
[15]§§ 444 and 280H.
[16]Reg. §§ 1.441–1(b)(3) and 1.441–1(b)(4).

[17]§ 442. Under certain conditions, corporations are allowed to change tax years without obtaining IRS approval. See Reg. § 1.442–1(c)(1).

tax years must be made on Form 1128, Application for Change in Accounting Period. The application must be filed on or before the fifteenth day of the second calendar month following the close of the short period that results from the change in accounting period.[18]

Beginning in 2006, Gold Corporation, a calendar year taxpayer, would like to switch to a fiscal year ending March 31. The corporation must file Form 1128 by May 15, 2006. ∎

IRS Requirements. The IRS will not grant permission for the change unless the taxpayer can establish a substantial business purpose for the request. One substantial business purpose is to change to a tax year that coincides with the *natural business year* (the completion of an annual business cycle). The IRS applies an objective gross receipts test to determine if the entity has a natural business year. At least 25 percent of the entity's gross receipts for the 12-month period must be realized in the final two months of the 12-month period for three consecutive years.[19]

A Virginia Beach motel had gross receipts as follows:

	2004	2005	2006
July–August receipts	$ 300,000	$250,000	$ 325,000
September 1–August 31 receipts	1,000,000	900,000	1,250,000
Receipts for 2 months divided by receipts for 12 months	30.0%	27.8%	26.0%

Since it satisfies the natural business year test, the motel will be allowed to use a fiscal year ending August 31. ∎

The IRS usually establishes certain conditions that the taxpayer must accept if the approval for change is to be granted. In particular, if the taxpayer has a net operating loss (NOL) for the short period, the IRS requires that the loss be carried forward; the loss cannot be carried back to prior years.[20] As you may recall (refer to Chapter 7), NOLs are ordinarily carried back for 2 years and forward for 20 years.

Parrot Corporation changed from a calendar year to a fiscal year ending September 30. The short-period return for the nine months ending September 30, 2006, reflected a $60,000 NOL. The corporation had taxable income for 2004 and 2005. As a condition for granting approval, the IRS requires Parrot to carry the loss forward rather than carrying the loss back to the two preceding years (the usual order for applying an NOL). ∎

Taxable Periods of Less Than One Year

A **short taxable year** (or **short period**) is a period of less than 12 calendar months. A taxpayer may have a short year for (1) the first income tax return, (2) the final income tax return, or (3) a change in the tax year. If the short period results from a change in the taxpayer's annual accounting period, the taxable income for the period must be annualized. Due to the progressive tax rate structure, taxpayers

---

[18]Reg. § 1.442–1(b)(1). In Example 7, the first period after the change in accounting period (January 1, 2006 through March 31, 2006) is less than a 12-month period and is referred to as a *short period*.

[19]Rev.Proc. 87–32, 1987–1 C.B. 131, and Rev.Rul. 87–57, 1987–2 C.B. 117.
[20]Rev.Proc. 2002–39, 2002–1 C.B. 1046.

could reap benefits from a short-period return if some adjustments were not required. Thus, the taxpayer is required to do the following:

1. Annualize the short-period income.

$$\text{Annualized income} = \text{Short-period income} \times \frac{12}{\text{Number of months in the short period}}$$

2. Compute the tax on the annualized income.
3. Convert the tax on the annualized income to a short-period tax.

$$\text{Short-period income} = \text{Tax on annualized income} \times \frac{\text{Number of months in the short period}}{12}$$

EXAMPLE 10

Gray Corporation obtained permission to change from a calendar year to a fiscal year ending September 30, beginning in 2006. For the short period January 1 through September 30, 2006, the corporation's taxable income was $48,000. The relevant tax rates and the resultant short-period tax are as follows:

Amount of Taxable Income	Tax Rates
$1–$50,000	15% of taxable income
$50,001–$75,000	$7,500 plus 25% of taxable income in excess of $50,000

Calculation of Short-Period Tax

Annualized income
  ($48,000 × $^{12}/_9$) = $64,000
Tax on annualized income
  $7,500 + .25($64,000 − $50,000) =
  $7,500 + $3,500 = $11,000
Short-period tax = ($11,000 × $^9/_{12}$) = $8,250
Annualizing the income increased the tax by $1,050:

Tax with annualizing	$ 8,250
Tax without annualizing (.15 × $48,000)	(7,200)
	$ 1,050

Rather than annualize the short-period income, the taxpayer can (1) elect to calculate the tax for a 12-month period beginning on the first day of the short period and (2) convert the tax in (1) to a short-period tax as follows:[21]

$$\frac{\text{Taxable income for short period}}{\text{Taxable income for the 12-month period}} \times \text{Tax on the 12 months of income}$$

EXAMPLE 11

Assume Gray Corporation's taxable income for the calendar year 2006 was $60,000. The tax on the full 12 months of income would have been $10,000 [$7,500 + .25($60,000 − $50,000)]. The short-period tax would be $8,000 [($48,000/$60,000) × $10,000]. Thus, if the corporation utilized this option, the tax for the short period would be $8,000 (rather than $8,250, as calculated in Example 10). ■

[21]§§ 443(b)(1) and (2).

For individuals, annualizing requires some special adjustments:[22]

- Deductions must be itemized for the short period (the standard deduction is not allowed).
- Personal and dependency exemptions must be prorated.

Fortunately, individuals rarely change tax years.

Mitigation of the Annual Accounting Period Concept

Several provisions in the Code are designed to give the taxpayer relief from the seemingly harsh results that may be produced by the combined effects of an arbitrary accounting period and a progressive rate structure. For example, under the NOL carryback and carryover rules, a loss in one year can be carried back and offset against taxable income for the preceding two years. Unused NOLs are then carried over for 20 years.[23] In addition, the Code provides special relief provisions for casualty losses pursuant to a disaster and for the reporting of insurance proceeds from destruction of crops.[24]

Restoration of Amounts Received under a Claim of Right. The court-made **claim of right doctrine** applies when the taxpayer receives property as income and treats it as his or her own but a dispute arises over the taxpayer's rights to the income.[25] According to the doctrine, the taxpayer must include the amount as income in the year of receipt. The rationale for the doctrine is that the Federal government cannot await the resolution of all disputes before exacting a tax. As a corollary to the doctrine, if the taxpayer is later required to repay the funds, generally a deduction is allowed in the year of repayment.[26]

> *EXAMPLE 12*
>
> In 2006, Pedro received a $5,000 bonus computed as a percentage of profits. In 2007, Pedro's employer determined that the 2006 profits had been incorrectly computed, and Pedro had to refund the $5,000 in 2007. Pedro was required to include the $5,000 in his 2006 gross income, but he can claim a $5,000 deduction in 2007. ∎

In Example 12 the transactions were a wash; that is, the income and deduction were the same ($5,000). Suppose, however, that Pedro was in the 35 percent tax bracket in 2006 but in the 15 percent bracket in 2007. Without some relief provision, the mistake would be costly to Pedro. He paid $1,750 tax in 2006 (.35 × $5,000), but the deduction reduced his tax liability in 2007 by only $750 (.15 × $5,000). The Code does provide the needed relief in such cases. Under § 1341, when income that has been taxed under the claim of right doctrine must later be repaid, in effect, the taxpayer gets to apply to the deduction the tax rate of the year that will produce the greatest tax benefit. Thus, in Example 12, the repayment in 2007 would reduce Pedro's 2007 tax liability by the greater 2006 rate (.35) applied to the $5,000. However, relief is provided only in cases where the tax is significantly different; that is, when the deduction for the amount previously included in income exceeds $3,000.

Accounting Methods

Permissible Methods

Section 446 requires the taxpayer to compute taxable income using the method of accounting regularly employed in keeping his or her books, provided the method

> **LO.2**
>
> Apply the cash method, accrual method, and hybrid method of accounting.

---

[22]§ 443(b)(3), § 443(c), and Reg. § 1.443–1(b).

[23]§ 172. Refer to Chapter 7. Losses incurred in 2001 or 2002 can be carried back for five years.

[24]§§ 165(i) and 451(d). Refer to Chapter 7.

[25]*North American Consolidated Oil Co. v. Burnet,* 3 USTC ¶943, 11 AFTR 16, 52 S.Ct. 613 (USSC, 1932).

[26]*U.S. v. Lewis,* 51–1 USTC ¶9211, 40 AFTR 258, 71 S.Ct. 522 (USSC, 1951).

clearly reflects income. The Code recognizes the following as generally permissible **accounting methods**:

- The cash receipts and disbursements method.
- The accrual method.
- A hybrid method (a combination of cash and accrual).

The Regulations refer to these alternatives as *overall methods* and add that the term *method of accounting* includes not only the taxpayer's overall method of accounting but also the accounting treatment of any item.[27]

Generally, any of the three methods of accounting may be used if the method is consistently employed and clearly reflects income. However, in most cases the taxpayer is required to use the accrual method for sales and cost of goods sold if inventories are an income-producing factor to the business.[28] Other situations in which the accrual method is required are discussed later. Special methods are also permitted for installment sales, long-term construction contracts, and farmers.

A taxpayer who has more than one trade or business may use a different method of accounting for each trade or business activity. Furthermore, a taxpayer may use one method of accounting to determine income from a trade or business and use another method to compute nonbusiness items of income and deductions.[29]

EXAMPLE 13

Linda operates a grocery store and owns stock and bonds. The sales and cost of goods sold from the grocery store must be computed by the accrual method because inventories are material. However, Linda can report her dividends and interest from the stocks and bonds under the cash method. ∎

The Code grants the IRS broad powers to determine whether the taxpayer's accounting method *clearly reflects income.* Thus, if the method employed does not clearly reflect income, the IRS has the power to prescribe the method to be used by the taxpayer.[30]

Cash Receipts and Disbursements Method—Cash Basis

Most individuals and many businesses use the cash basis to report income and deductions. The popularity of this method can largely be attributed to its simplicity and flexibility.

Under the **cash method**, income is not recognized until the taxpayer actually receives, or constructively receives, cash or its equivalent. Cash is constructively received if it is available to the taxpayer.[31] Generally, a cash equivalent is anything with a fair market value, including a note receivable from a customer.

EXAMPLE 14

Don, a dentist, does not accept credit cards. He requires that his patients either pay cash at the time the services are performed or give him a note receivable with interest at the market rate. Generally, the notes can be sold to the local banks for 95% of their face amount. At the end of 2006, Don has $60,000 in notes receivable from patients. The notes receivable are a cash equivalent and have a fair market value of $57,000 ($60,000 × 95%). Therefore, Don must include the $57,000 in his gross income for 2006. ∎

Deductions are generally permitted in the year of payment. Thus, year-end accounts receivable, accounts payable, and accrued income and deductions are not included in the determination of taxable income.

[27]Reg. § 1.446–1(a)(1).
[28]Reg. § 1.446–1(a)(4)(i).
[29]§ 446(d) and Reg. § 1.446–1(c)(1)(iv)(b).
[30]§ 446(b).
[31]Reg. § 1.451–1(a). Refer to Chapter 4 for a discussion of constructive receipt.

In many cases, a taxpayer using the cash method can choose the year in which a deduction is claimed simply by postponing or accelerating the payment of expenses. For fixed assets, however, the cash basis taxpayer claims deductions through depreciation or amortization, the same as an accrual basis taxpayer does. In addition, prepaid expenses must be capitalized and amortized if the life of the asset extends substantially beyond the end of the tax year.[32] Most courts have applied the one-year rule (**one-year rule for prepaid expenses**) to determine whether capitalization and amortization are required. According to this rule, capitalization is required only if the asset has a life that extends beyond the tax year following the year of payment.[33]

Restrictions on Use of the Cash Method.

Using the cash method to measure income from a merchandising or manufacturing operation would often yield a distorted picture of the results of operations. Income for the period would largely be a function of when payments were made for goods or materials. Thus, the Regulations prohibit the use of the cash method (and require the accrual method) to measure sales and cost of goods sold if inventories are material to the business.[34]

The prohibition on the use of the cash method if inventories are material and the rules regarding prepaid expenses (discussed above) are intended to assure that annual income is clearly reflected. However, certain taxpayers may not use the cash method of accounting for Federal income tax purposes regardless of whether inventories are material. The accrual basis must be used to report the income earned by (1) a corporation (other than an S corporation), (2) a partnership with a corporate partner, and (3) a tax shelter.[35] This accrual basis requirement has three exceptions:[36]

- A farming business.
- A qualified personal service corporation (a corporation performing services in health, law, engineering, architecture, accounting, actuarial science, performing arts, or consulting).
- An entity that is not a tax shelter whose average annual gross receipts for the most recent three-year period are $5 million or less.

As a matter of administrative convenience, the IRS will permit any entity with average annual gross receipts of not more than $1 million for the most recent three-year period to use the cash method. This applies even if the taxpayer is buying and selling inventory. Also as a matter of administrative convenience, the IRS will permit certain entities whose average annual gross receipts are greater than $1 million but are not more than $10 million for the most recent three-year period to use the cash method. However, under the $10 million exception, inventory on

[32]Reg. § 1.461–1(a)(1).

[33]*Zaninovich v. Comm.,* 80–1 USTC ¶9342, 45 AFTR2d 80–1442, 616 F.2d 429 (CA–9, 1980), *rev'g* 69 T.C. 605 (1978); *U.S. Freightways Corp. v. Comm.,* 2001–2 USTC ¶50,731, 88 AFTR2d 2001–6703, 270 F.3d 1137 (CA–7, 2001), *rev'g* 113 T.C. 329 (1999). Refer to Chapter 6 for further discussion of the one-year rule. See also Reg. § 1.263(a)–4(f) for the application of the one-year rule to prepayments for intangibles.

[34]Reg. § 1.446–1(a)(4)(i).

[35]§ 448(a). For this purpose, the hybrid method of accounting is considered the same as the cash method.

[36]§ 448(b).

hand at the end of the tax year cannot be deducted until the inventory is sold (i.e., must be capitalized). Not eligible for the cash method under the $10 million exception are entities whose principal business activity (the activity producing the largest percentage of gross receipts) is selling goods, manufacturing, mining, and certain publishing activities. Also not eligible are the C corporations, partnerships, and tax shelters discussed above that must use the accrual method. The major beneficiaries of the $10 million exception are small construction companies and small service businesses that sell some goods in conjunction with the services provided.[37]

Farming. Although inventories are material to farming operations, the IRS long ago created an exception to the general rule that allows farmers to use the cash method of accounting.[38] The purpose of the exception is to relieve the small farmer from the bookkeeping burden of accrual accounting. However, tax shelter promoters recognized, for example, that by deducting the costs of a crop in one tax year and harvesting the crop in a later year, income could be deferred from tax. Thus, §§ 447 and 464 were enacted to prevent certain farming corporations and limited partnerships (farming syndicates) from using the cash method.[39]

Cash method farmers must nevertheless capitalize their costs of raising trees that have a preproduction period of more than two years.[40] Thus, an apple farmer generally must capitalize the costs of raising the trees until they produce apples in merchantable quantities. However, to simplify the farmer's tax accounting, the cash method farmer is given an option: the preproduction cost of the trees can be expensed if the taxpayer elects to use the alternative depreciation system (refer to Chapter 8) for all the farming assets.

Generally, a cash basis farmer must capitalize the purchase price of an animal, whether it is acquired for sale or for breeding. However, the cost of raising the animal can be expensed.[41]

Accrual Method

All Events Test for Income. Under the **accrual method**, an item is generally included in gross income for the year in which it is earned, regardless of when the income is collected. An item of income is earned when (1) all the events have occurred to fix the taxpayer's right to receive the income and (2) the amount of income (the amount the taxpayer has a right to receive) can be determined with reasonable accuracy.[42]

E X A M P L E   15

Andre, a calendar year taxpayer who uses the accrual basis of accounting, was to receive a bonus equal to 6% of Blue Corporation's net income for its fiscal year ending each June 30. For the fiscal year ending June 30, 2006, Blue Corporation had net income of $240,000, and for the six months ending December 31, 2006, the corporation's net income was $150,000. Andre will report $14,400 (.06 × $240,000) for 2006 because his right to the amount became fixed when Blue Corporation's year closed. However, Andre would not accrue income based on the corporation's profits for the last six months of 2006 since his right to the income does not accrue until the close of the corporation's tax year. ∎

An accrual basis taxpayer's amount of income and the tax year the income is recognized are based on his or her right to receive the income. Thus, the fair market value of a receivable is irrelevant.

---

[37]Rev.Proc. 2001–10, 2001–1 C.B. 272 and Rev.Proc. 2002–28, 2002–1 C.B. 815.

[38]Reg. § 1.471–6(a).

[39]Section 447(c) contains counterexceptions that allow certain closely held corporations to use the cash method. See also § 464(c).

[40]§ 263A(d).

[41]Reg. § 1.162–12(a).

[42]Reg. § 1.451–1(a). Refer to Chapter 4 for further discussion of the accrual basis.

TAX ACCOUNTING METHODS AS AN INCENTIVE TO GO FOREIGN

Some foreign countries allow a corporation to defer income by using tax accounting methods that are not permitted in the United States. For example, a producer or retailer may be allowed to use the cash method of accounting even though inventory is present. Under the cash method, the cost of goods sold is deducted in the tax year the goods are paid for, and income is not recognized until receivables are collected. Thus, if a U.S. corporation creates a foreign subsidiary to produce in a country that permits the cash method in association with inventory, tax savings occur that would not be available in the United States. The corporation obtains additional deductions in the first year equal to the ending inventory and additional deferrals equal to the ending accounts receivable. The company would continue to benefit until it has no more receivables or inventory.

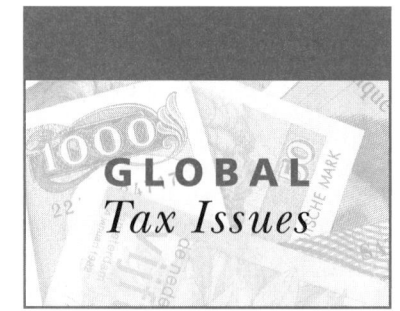

GLOBAL *Tax Issues*

EXAMPLE 16

Marcey, an accrual basis taxpayer, has provided services to clients and has the right to receive $60,000. The clients have signed notes receivable to Marcey that have a fair market value of $57,000. Marcey must include $60,000, the amount she has the right to receive, in her gross income, rather than the fair market value of the notes of $57,000. ■

As discussed in Chapter 4, when an accrual basis taxpayer receives prepaid income that will not all be earned by the end of the tax year following the tax year of receipt, generally the income that is not earned by the end of the year of receipt must be allocated to the following year.

EXAMPLE 17

Troy sells computers and two-year service contracts on the computers. On November 1, 2006, Troy sold a 24-month service contract and received $240. He recognizes $20 gross income in 2006 ($240 × $\frac{2}{24}$) and $220 ($240 − $20) in 2007. ■

However, the deferral of prepaid income is not available for prepaid rent and prepaid interest.

In a situation where the accrual basis taxpayer's right to income is being contested and the income has not yet been collected, generally no income is recognized until the dispute has been settled.[43] Before the settlement, "all of the events have not occurred that fix the right to receive the income."

All Events and Economic Performance Tests for Deductions. An **all events test** applies to accrual basis deductions. A deduction cannot be claimed until (1) all the events have occurred to create the taxpayer's liability and (2) the amount of the liability can be determined with reasonable accuracy.[44] Once these requirements are satisfied, the deduction will be permitted only if economic performance has occurred.[45]

The **economic performance test** addresses situations in which the taxpayer has either of the following obligations:

1. To pay for services or property to be provided in the future.
2. To provide services or property (other than money) in the future.

When services or property are to be provided to the taxpayer in the future (situation 1), economic performance occurs when the property or services are actually provided by the other party.

---

[43]*Burnet v. Sanford & Brooks Co.*, 2 USTC ¶636, 9 AFTR 603, 51 S.Ct. 150 (USSC, 1931).

[44]§ 461(h)(4).

[45]§ 461(h).

EXAMPLE 18

An accrual basis calendar year taxpayer, JAB, Inc., promoted a boxing match held in the company's arena on December 31, 2006. CLN, Inc., had contracted to clean the arena for $5,000, but did not actually perform the work until January 1, 2007. JAB, Inc., did not pay the $5,000 until 2008. Although financial accounting would require JAB, Inc., to accrue the $5,000 cleaning expense in 2006 to match the revenues from the fight, the economic performance test was not satisfied until 2007, when CLN, Inc., performed the service. Thus, JAB, Inc., must deduct the expense in 2007. ■

If the taxpayer is obligated to provide property or services (situation 2), economic performance occurs (and thus the deduction is allowed) in the year the taxpayer provides the property or services.

EXAMPLE 19

Copper Corporation, an accrual basis taxpayer, is in the strip mining business. According to the contract with the landowner, the company must reclaim the land. The estimated cost of reclaiming land mined in 2006 was $500,000, but the land was not actually reclaimed until 2008. The all events test was satisfied in 2006. The obligation existed, and the amount of the liability could be determined with reasonable accuracy. However, the economic performance test was not satisfied until 2008. Therefore, the deduction is not allowed until 2008.[46] ■

The economic performance test is waived, and thus year-end accruals can be deducted, if all the following conditions (*recurring item exception*) are met:

* The obligation exists and the amount of the liability can be reasonably estimated.
* Economic performance occurs within a reasonable period (but not later than 8½ months after the close of the taxable year).
* The item is recurring in nature and is treated consistently by the taxpayer.
* Either the accrued item is not material, or accruing it results in a better matching of revenues and expenses.

EXAMPLE 20

Green Corporation often sells goods that are on hand but cannot be shipped for another week. Thus, the sales account usually includes revenues for some items that have not been shipped at year-end. Green Corporation is obligated to pay shipping costs. Although the company's obligation for shipping costs can be determined with reasonable accuracy, economic performance is not satisfied until Green (or its agent) actually delivers the goods. However, accruing shipping costs on sold items will better match expenses with revenues for the period. Therefore, the company should be allowed to accrue the shipping costs on items sold but not shipped at year-end. ■

The economic performance test as set forth in the Code does not address all possible accrued expenses. That is, in some cases, the taxpayer incurs cost even though no property or services were received. In these instances, according to the Regulations, economic performance generally is not satisfied until the liability is paid. The following liabilities are cases in which payment is generally the only means of satisfying economic performance:[47]

1. Workers' compensation.
2. Torts.
3. Breach of contract.
4. Violation of law.
5. Rebates and refunds.
6. Awards, prizes, and jackpots.

[46]See § 468 for an elective method for reporting reclamation costs.   [47]Reg. §§ 1.461–4(g)(2)–(6) and 1.461–5(c).

TAX *in the News*	**ECONOMIC PERFORMANCE AND BREACH OF CONTRACT: WHICH CONTRACT?**

In a recent Tax Court decision, the taxpayer was a contractor who failed to properly perform on a construction contract. When the contractor was removed from the contract, the contractor's surety company was obligated to complete the construction. The contractor in turn was liable to the surety company.

By the end of the tax year, the surety company had spent substantial amounts to complete the contract, and the contractor admitted liability to the surety company for at least $2.5 million. Nevertheless, at the end of the tax year, the exact amount of the contractor's liability was still in dispute, and the contractor had not paid the $2.5 million.

Source: *Denis H. Dieker, et al.*, T.C.Memo. 2005–225 (2005).

The IRS argued that the contractor's liability was for breach of contract. Therefore, economic performance was not satisfied until the liability had been paid. The Tax Court agreed with the taxpayer that the liability arose out of the agreement with the surety company, rather than the contract with the customer, and that the surety contract had been breached. Therefore, the all events test was satisfied when the surety company performed, creating the contractor's obligation to the surety company.

7. Insurance, warranty, and service contracts.[48]
8. Taxes.

EXAMPLE 21

Yellow Corporation sold defective merchandise that injured a customer. Yellow admitted liability in 2006, but did not pay the claim until January 2007. The customer's tort claim cannot be deducted until it is paid. ■

However, items (5) through (8) above are eligible for the aforementioned recurring item exception.

EXAMPLE 22

Pelican Corporation filed its 2006 state income tax return in March 2007. At the time the return was filed, Pelican was required to pay an additional $5,000. The state taxes are eligible for the recurring item exception. Thus, the $5,000 of state income taxes can be deducted on the corporation's 2006 Federal tax return. The deduction is allowed because all the events had occurred to fix the liability as of the end of 2006, the payment was made within 8½ months after the end of the tax year, the item is recurring in nature, and allowing the deduction in 2006 produces a good matching of revenues and expenses. ■

Reserves. Generally, the all events and economic performance tests will prevent the use of reserves (e.g., for product warranty expense) frequently used in financial accounting to match expenses with revenues. However, small banks are allowed to use a bad debt reserve.[49] Furthermore, an accrual basis taxpayer in a service business is permitted to not accrue revenue that appears uncollectible based on experience. In effect, this approach indirectly allows a reserve.[50]

Hybrid Method

A **hybrid method** of accounting involves the use of more than one method. For example, a taxpayer who uses the accrual basis to report sales and cost of goods sold but uses the cash basis to report other items of income and expense is employing a hybrid method. The Code permits the use of a hybrid method provided the

[48]This item applies to contracts the taxpayer enters into for his or her own protection, rather than the taxpayer's liability as insurer, warrantor, or service provider.

[49]§ 585.
[50]§ 448(d)(5).

taxpayer's income is clearly reflected.[51] A taxpayer who uses the accrual method for business expenses must also use the accrual method for business income (the cash method may not be used for income items if the taxpayer's expenses are accounted for under the accrual method).

It may be preferable for a business that is required to report sales and cost of goods sold on the accrual method to report other items of income and expense under the cash method. The cash method permits greater flexibility in the timing of income and expense recognition.

Change of Method

LO.3

Utilize the procedure for changing accounting methods.

The taxpayer, in effect, makes an election to use a particular accounting method when an initial tax return is filed using that method. If a subsequent change in method is desired, the taxpayer must obtain the permission of the IRS. The request for change is made on Form 3115, Application for Change in Accounting Method. Generally, the form must be filed within the taxable year of the desired change.[52]

As previously mentioned, the term *accounting method* encompasses not only the overall accounting method used by the taxpayer (the cash or accrual method) but also the treatment of any material item of income or deduction.[53] Thus, a change in the method of deducting property taxes from a cash basis to an accrual basis that results in a deduction for taxes in a different year constitutes a change in an accounting method. Another example of an accounting method change is a change involving the method or basis used in the valuation of inventories. However, a change in treatment resulting from a change in the underlying facts does not constitute a change in the taxpayer's method of accounting.[54] For example, a change in employment contracts so that an employee accrues one day of vacation pay for each month of service rather than 12 days of vacation pay for a full year of service is a change in the underlying facts and is therefore not an accounting method change.

Correction of an Error.

A change in accounting method should be distinguished from the *correction of an error.* The taxpayer can correct an error (by filing amended returns) without permission, and the IRS can simply adjust the taxpayer's liability if an error is discovered on audit of the return. Some examples of errors are incorrect postings, errors in the calculation of tax liability or tax credits, deductions of business expense items that are actually personal, and omissions of income and deductions.[55] Unless the taxpayer or the IRS corrects the error within the statute of limitations, the taxpayer's total lifetime taxable income will be overstated or understated by the amount of the error.

Change from an Incorrect Method.

An *incorrect accounting method* is the consistent (year-after-year) use of an incorrect rule to report an item of income or expense. The incorrect accounting method generally will not affect the taxpayer's total lifetime income (unlike the error). That is, an incorrect method has a self-balancing mechanism. For example, deducting freight on inventory in the year the goods are purchased, rather than when the inventory is sold, is an incorrect accounting method. The total cost of goods sold over the life of the business is not affected, but the year-to-year income is incorrect.[56]

If a taxpayer is employing an incorrect method of accounting, permission must be obtained from the IRS to change to a correct method. An incorrect method is not treated as a mechanical error that can be corrected by merely filing an amended tax return.

---

[51]§ 446(c).
[52]Rev.Proc. 99–49, 1999–2 C.B. 725.
[53]Reg. § 1.446–1(a)(1).
[54]Reg. § 1.446–1(e)(2)(ii).

[55]Reg. § 1.446–1(e)(2)(ii)(b).
[56]But see *Korn Industries v. U.S.,* 76–1 USTC ¶9354, 37 AFTR2d 76–1228, 532 F.2d 1352 (Ct.Cls., 1976).

The tax return preparer as well as the taxpayer will be subject to penalties if the tax return is prepared using an incorrect method of accounting and permission for a change to a correct method has not been requested.[57]

Net Adjustments Due to Change in Accounting Method. In the year of a change in accounting method, some items of income and expense may have to be adjusted to prevent the change from distorting taxable income.

EXAMPLE 23

In 2006, White Corporation, with consent from the IRS, switched from the cash to the accrual basis for reporting sales and cost of goods sold. The corporation's accrual basis gross profit for the year was computed as follows:

Sales		$100,000
Beginning inventory	$ 15,000	
Purchases	60,000	
Less: Ending inventory	(10,000)	
Cost of goods sold		(65,000)
Gross profit		$ 35,000

At the end of the previous year, White Corporation had accounts receivable of $25,000 and accounts payable for merchandise of $34,000. The accounts receivable from the previous year in the amount of $25,000 were never included in gross income since White was on the cash basis and did not recognize the uncollected receivables. In the current year, the $25,000 was not included in the accrual basis sales since the sales were made in a prior year. Therefore, a $25,000 adjustment to income is required to prevent the receivables from being omitted from income.

The corollary of the failure to recognize a prior year's receivables is the failure to recognize a prior year's accounts payable. The beginning of the year's accounts payable were not included in the current or prior year's purchases. Thus, a deduction for the $34,000 was not taken in either year and is therefore included as an adjustment to income for the period of change.

An adjustment is also required to reflect the $15,000 beginning inventory that White deducted (due to the use of a cash method of accounting) in the previous year. In this instance, the cost of goods sold during the year of change was increased by the beginning inventory and resulted in a double deduction.

The net adjustment due to the change in accounting method is computed as follows:

Beginning inventory (deducted in prior and current year)	$ 15,000
Beginning accounts receivable (omitted from income)	25,000
Beginning accounts payable (omitted from deductions)	(34,000)
Net increase in taxable income	$ 6,000	∎

Disposition of the Net Adjustment. Required changes in accounting methods are the result of an IRS examination. The IRS usually will examine all years that are open under the statute of limitations. Generally, this means that the three preceding years are examined. The IRS will not require a change unless the net adjustment is positive. That adjustment generally must be included in gross income for the year of the change. Additional tax and interest on the tax will be due. However, if the adjustment is greater than $3,000, the taxpayer can elect to calculate the tax by spreading the adjustment over one or more previous years.[58] The election is beneficial if the taxpayer's marginal tax rate for the prior years is lower than the marginal tax rate for the year of the change.

---

[57]§ 446(f). See *West Federal Taxation: Corporations, Partnerships, Estates, and Trusts,* Chapter 16.

[58]§ 481(b). See also Notice 98–31, 1998–1 C.B. 1165.

To encourage taxpayers to *voluntarily* change from incorrect methods and to facilitate changes from one correct method to another, the IRS generally allows the taxpayer to spread a positive adjustment into future years. One-fourth of the adjustment is applied to the year of the change, and one-fourth of the adjustment is applied to each of the next three taxable years. A negative adjustment can be deducted in the year of the change.[59]

EXAMPLE 24

White Corporation in Example 23 voluntarily changed from an incorrect method (the cash basis was incorrect because inventories were material to the business) to a correct method. The company must add $1,500 (¼ × $6,000 positive adjustment) to its 2006, 2007, 2008, and 2009 income. ∎

Special Accounting Methods

Generally, accrual basis taxpayers recognize income when goods are sold and shipped to the customer. Cash basis taxpayers generally recognize income from a sale on the collection of cash from the customer. The tax law provides special accounting methods for certain installment sales and long-term contracts. These special methods were enacted, in part, to assure that the tax will be due when the taxpayer is best able to pay the tax.

LO.4

Determine when the installment method of accounting can be utilized and apply the related calculation techniques.

Installment Method

Under the general rule for computing the gain or loss from the sale of property, the taxpayer recognizes the entire amount of gain or loss upon the sale or other disposition of the property.

EXAMPLE 25

Mark sells property to Fran for $10,000 cash plus Fran's note (fair market value and face amount of $90,000). Mark's basis for the property was $15,000. Gain or loss is computed under either the cash or accrual basis as follows:

Selling price		
Cash down payment	$ 10,000	
Note receivable	90,000	
	$100,000	
Basis in the property	(15,000)	
Realized gain	$ 85,000	

∎

In Example 25, the general rule for recognizing gain or loss requires Mark to pay a substantial amount of tax on the gain in the year of sale even though he received only $10,000 cash. Congress enacted the installment sales provisions to prevent this sort of hardship by allowing the taxpayer to spread the gain from installment sales over the collection period. The installment method is a very important planning tool because of the tax deferral possibilities.

Eligibility and Calculations. The **installment method** applies to *gains* (but not losses) from the sale of property by a taxpayer who will receive at least one payment *after* the year of sale. For many years, practically all gains from the sale of property were eligible for the installment method. However, over the years, the Code has been amended to *deny* the use of the installment method for the following:[60]

[59]Rev.Proc. 99–49, 1999–2 C.B. 725 and Rev.Proc. 2002–19, 2002–1 C.B. 696.   [60]§§ 453(b), (i), and (l).

- Gains on property held for sale in the ordinary course of business.
- Depreciation recapture under § 1245 or § 1250.
- Gains on stocks or securities traded on an established market.

As an exception to the first item, the installment method may be used to report gains from sales of the following:[61]

- Time-share units (e.g., the right to use real property for two weeks each year).
- Residential lots (if the seller is not to make any improvements).
- Any property used or produced in the trade or business of farming.

The Nonelective Aspect. As a general rule, eligible sales *must* be reported by the installment method.[62] A special election is required to report the gain by any other method of accounting (see the discussion in a subsequent section of this chapter).

Computing the Gain for the Period. The gain reported on each sale is computed by the following formula:

$$\frac{\text{Total gain}}{\text{Contract price}} \times \text{Payments received} = \text{Recognized gain}$$

The taxpayer must compute each variable as follows:

1. *Total gain* is the selling price reduced by selling expenses and the adjusted basis of the property. The selling price is the total consideration received by the seller, including notes receivable from the buyer and the seller's liabilities assumed by the buyer.
2. *Contract price* is the selling price less the seller's liabilities that are assumed by the buyer. Generally, the contract price is the amount, other than interest, the seller will receive from the purchaser.
3. *Payments received* are the collections on the contract price received in the tax year. This generally is equal to the cash received less the interest income collected for the period. If the buyer pays any of the seller's expenses, the seller regards the amount paid as a payment received.

The seller is not a dealer, and the facts are as follows:

Sales price		
Cash down payment	$ 1,000	
Seller's mortgage assumed	3,000	
Notes payable to the seller	13,000	$ 17,000
Selling expenses		(500)
Seller's basis		(10,000)
Total gain		$ 6,500

The contract price is $14,000 ($17,000 − $3,000). Assuming the $1,000 is the only payment in the year of sale, the recognized gain in that year is computed as follows:

$$\frac{\$6,500 \text{ total gain}}{\$14,000 \text{ contract price}} \times \$1,000 = \$464 \text{ (gain recognized in year of sale)}$$ ∎

If the sum of the seller's basis and selling expenses is less than the liabilities assumed by the buyer, the difference must be added to the contract price and to the payments (treated as *deemed payments*) received in the year of sale.[63] This adjustment to the contract price is required so that the ratio of total gain to contract price will not be greater than one. The adjustment also accelerates the reporting of income from the deemed payments.

---

[61]§ 453(l)(2).
[62]§ 453(a).

[63]Temp.Reg. § 15a.453–1(b)(2)(iii).

EXAMPLE 27

Assume the same facts as in Example 26, except that the seller's basis in the property is only $2,000. The total gain, therefore, is $14,500 [$17,000 − ($2,000 + $500)]. Payments in the year of sale are $1,500 and are calculated as follows:

Down payment	$1,000
Excess of mortgage assumed over seller's basis and selling expenses ($3,000 − $2,000 − $500)	500
	$1,500

The contract price is $14,500 [$17,000 (selling price) − $3,000 (seller's mortgage assumed) + $500 (excess of mortgage assumed over seller's basis and selling expenses)]. The gain recognized in the year of sale is computed as follows:

$$\frac{\$14,500 \text{ total gain}}{\$14,500 \text{ contract price}} \times \$1,500 = \$1,500$$

In subsequent years, all amounts the seller collects on the note principal ($13,000) will be recognized gain ($13,000 × 100%). ∎

As previously discussed, gains attributable to ordinary income recapture under §§ 1245 and 1250 are *ineligible* for installment reporting. Therefore, the § 1245 or § 1250 gain realized must be recognized in the year of sale, and the installment sale gain is the remaining gain.

EXAMPLE 28

Olaf sold an apartment building for $50,000 cash and a $75,000 note due in two years. Olaf's basis in the property was $25,000, and he recaptured $40,000 ordinary income under § 1250.

Olaf's realized gain is $100,000 ($125,000 − $25,000), and the $40,000 recapture must be recognized in the year of sale. Of the $60,000 remaining § 1231 gain, $24,000 must be recognized in the year of sale:

$$\frac{\S\ 1231 \text{ gain}}{\text{Contract price}} \times \text{Payments received} = \frac{\$125,000 - \$25,000 - \$40,000}{\$125,000} \times \$50,000$$

$$= \frac{\$60,000}{\$125,000} \times \$50,000 = \$24,000$$

The remaining realized gain of $36,000 ($60,000 − $24,000) will be recognized as the $75,000 note is collected. ∎

Imputed Interest. If a deferred payment contract for the sale of property with a selling price greater than $3,000 does not contain a reasonable interest rate, a reasonable rate is imputed.[64] The imputing of interest effectively restates the selling price of the property to equal the sum of the payments at the date of the sale and the discounted present value of the future payments. The difference between the present value of a future payment and the payment's face amount is taxed as interest income, as discussed in the following paragraphs. Thus, the **imputed interest** rules prevent sellers of capital assets from increasing the selling price to reflect the equivalent of unstated interest on deferred payments and thereby converting ordinary (interest) income into long-term capital gains. In addition, the imputed interest rules are important because they affect the timing of income recognition.

Generally, if the contract does not charge at least the Federal rate, interest will be imputed at the Federal rate. The Federal rate is the interest rate the Federal government pays on new borrowing and is published monthly by the IRS.[65]

---

[64]§§ 483 and 1274.

[65]§ 1274(d)(1). There are three Federal rates: short term (not over three years), midterm (over three years but not over nine years), and long term (over nine years).

As a general rule, the buyer and seller must account for interest on the accrual basis with semiannual compounding.[66] Requiring the use of the accrual basis assures that the seller's interest income and the buyer's interest expense are reported in the same tax year. Under pre-1984 law, the cash basis seller did not report interest income until it was actually collected, but an accrual basis buyer could deduct the interest as it accrued. The following example illustrates the calculation and amortization of imputed interest.

EXAMPLE 29

Peggy, a cash basis taxpayer, sold land on January 1, 2006, for $200,000 cash and $6 million due on December 31, 2007, with 5% interest payable December 31, 2006, and December 31, 2007. At the time of the sale, the Federal rate was 8% (compounded semiannually). Because Peggy did not charge at least the Federal rate, interest will be imputed at 8% (compounded semiannually).

Date	Payment	Present Value (at 8%) on 1/1/2006	Imputed Interest
12/31/2006	$ 300,000	$ 277,500	$ 22,500
12/31/2007	6,300,000	5,386,500	913,500
	$6,600,000	$5,664,000	$936,000

Thus, the selling price will be restated to $5,864,000 ($200,000 + $5,664,000) rather than $6,200,000 ($200,000 + $6,000,000), and Peggy will recognize interest income in accordance with the following amortization schedule:

	Beginning Balance	Interest Income (at 8%)*	Received	Ending Balance
2006	$5,664,000	$462,182	$ 300,000	$5,826,182
2007	5,826,182	473,818	6,300,000	–0–

*Compounded semiannually. ∎

Congress has created several exceptions regarding the rate at which interest is imputed and the method of accounting for the interest income and expense. The general rules and exceptions are summarized in Concept Summary 18–1.

Related-Party Sales of Nondepreciable Property.

If the Code did not contain special rules, a taxpayer could make an installment sale of property to a related party (e.g., a family member) who would obtain a basis in the property equal to the purchase price (the fair market value of the property). Then, the purchasing family member could immediately sell the property to an unrelated party for cash with no recognized gain or loss (the amount realized would equal the basis). The related-party purchaser would not pay the installment note to the selling family member until a later year or years. The net result would be that the family has the cash, but no taxable gain is recognized until the intrafamily transfer of the cash (when the purchasing family member makes payments on the installment note).

Under special rules designed to combat the scheme described above, the proceeds from the subsequent sale (the second sale) by the purchasing family member are treated as though they were used to pay the installment note due the selling family member (the first sale). As a result, the recognition of gain from the original sale between the related parties is accelerated.[67]

However, even with these special rules, Congress did not eliminate the benefits of all related-party installment sales.

[66]§§ 1274(a), 1273(a), and 1272(a).   [67]§ 453(e).

CONCEPT SUMMARY   18–1

Interest on Installment Sales

	Imputed Interest Rate
General rule	Federal rate
Exceptions:	
• Principal amount not over $2.8 million.[1]	Lesser of Federal rate or 9%
• Sale of land (with a calendar year ceiling of $500,000) between family members (the seller's spouse, brothers, sisters, ancestors, or lineal descendants).[2]	Lesser of Federal rate or 6%

	Method of Accounting for Interest	
	Seller's Interest Income	Buyer's Interest Expense
General rule[3]	Accrual	Accrual
Exceptions:		
• Total payments under the contract are $250,000 or less.[4]	Taxpayer's overall method	Taxpayer's overall method
• Sale of a farm (sales price of $1 million or less).[5]	Taxpayer's overall method	Taxpayer's overall method
• Sale of a principal residence.[6]	Taxpayer's overall method	Taxpayer's overall method
• Sale for a note with a principal amount of not over $2 million, the seller is on the cash basis, the property sold is not inventory, and the buyer agrees to report expense by the cash method.[7]	Cash	Cash

[1] § 1274A(b). This amount is adjusted annually for inflation. For 2006, the amount is $4,630,300.
[2] §§ 1274(c)(3)(F) and 483(e).
[3] §§ 1274(a) and 1272(a)(3).
[4] §§ 1274(c)(3)(C) and 483.
[5] §§ 1274(c)(3)(A) and 483.
[6] §§ 1274(c)(3)(B) and 483.
[7] § 1274A(c). This amount is adjusted annually for inflation. For 2006, the amount is $3,307,400.

- Related parties include the first seller's brothers, sisters, ancestors, lineal descendants, controlled corporations, and partnerships, trusts, and estates in which the seller has an interest.[68]
- There is no acceleration if the second disposition occurs more than two years after the first sale.[69]

Thus, if the taxpayer can sell the property to an unrelated party (not a related party) or patient family member, the intrafamily installment sale is still a powerful tax planning tool. Other exceptions also can be applied in some circumstances.[70]

Related-Party Sales of Depreciable Property. The installment method cannot be used to report a gain on the sale of depreciable property to a controlled entity. The purpose of this rule is to prevent the seller from deferring gain (until collections are received) while the related purchaser is enjoying a stepped-up basis for depreciation purposes.[71]

---

[68]§ 453(f)(1), cross-referencing §§ 267(b) and 318(a). Although spouses are related parties, the exemption of gain between spouses (§ 1041) makes the second-disposition rules inapplicable when the first sale was between spouses.

[69]§ 453(e)(2). But see § 453(e)(2)(B) for extensions of the two-year period.
[70]See §§ 453(e)(6) and (7).
[71]§ 453(g).

The prohibition on the use of the installment method applies to sales between the taxpayer and a partnership or corporation in which the taxpayer holds a more-than-50 percent interest. Constructive ownership rules are used in applying the ownership test (e.g., the taxpayer is considered to own stock owned by a spouse and certain other family members).[72] However, if the taxpayer can establish that tax avoidance was not a principal purpose of the transaction, the installment method can be used to report the gain.

EXAMPLE 30

Alan purchased an apartment building from his controlled corporation, Emerald Corporation. Alan was short of cash at the time of the purchase (December 2006), but was to collect a large cash payment in January 2007. The agreement required Alan to pay the entire arm's length price in January 2007. Alan had good business reasons for acquiring the building. Emerald Corporation should be able to convince the IRS that tax avoidance was not a principal purpose for the installment sale because the tax benefits are not overwhelming. The corporation will report all of the gain in the year following the year of sale, and the building must be expensed over 27.5 years (the cost recovery period). ■

Disposition of Installment Obligations

Generally, a taxpayer must recognize the deferred profit from an installment sale when the obligation is transferred to another party or otherwise relinquished. The rationale for accelerating the gain is that the deferral should continue for no longer than the taxpayer owns the installment obligation.[73]

The gift or cancellation of an installment note is treated as a taxable disposition by the donor. The amount realized from the cancellation is the face amount of the note if the parties (obligor and obligee) are related to each other.[74]

EXAMPLE 31

Liz cancels a note issued by Tina (Liz's daughter) that arose in connection with the sale of property. At the time of the cancellation, the note had a basis to Liz of $10,000, a face amount of $25,000, and a fair market value of $20,000. Presuming the initial sale by Liz qualified as an installment sale, the cancellation results in gain of $15,000 ($25,000 − $10,000) to Liz. ■

Certain exceptions to the recognition of gain provisions are provided for transfers of installment obligations pursuant to tax-free incorporations under § 351, contributions of capital to a partnership, certain corporate liquidations, transfers due to the taxpayer's death, and transfers between spouses or incident to divorce.[75] In such situations, the deferred profit is merely shifted to the transferee, who is responsible for the payment of tax on the subsequent collections of the installment obligations.

Interest on Deferred Taxes

With the installment method, the seller earns interest on the receivable. The receivable includes the deferred gain. Thus, one could argue that the seller is earning interest on the deferred taxes. Some commentators reason that the government is, in effect, making interest-free loans to taxpayers who report gains by the installment method. Following the argument that the amount of the deferred taxes is a loan, the taxpayer is required to pay interest on the deferred taxes in some situations.[76]

The taxpayer is required to pay interest on the deferred taxes only if *both* of the following requirements are met:

- The installment obligation arises from the sale of property (other than farming property) for more than $150,000.
- Such installment obligations outstanding at the close of the tax year exceed $5 million.

---

[72]§§ 1239(b) and (c).
[73]§ 453B(a).
[74]§ 453B(f)(2).

[75]§§ 453B(c), (d), and (g). See Chapter 20 for a discussion of some of these subjects.
[76]§ 453A.

ETHICAL
Considerations

ELECTING OUT OF ELECTING OUT OF THE INSTALLMENT SALE METHOD

The general rule is that gain on a transaction eligible to use the installment sale method is to be reported by that method. However, the taxpayer can elect not to use the installment method. What if the taxpayer elects not to use the installment method but later discovers he or she has made an improvident election (e.g., the taxpayer thought he or she would have a loss to offset the gain)? Generally, the taxpayer cannot revoke the election.

If the election was "inadvertent," however, the IRS will grant permission to amend the return and to use the installment method. For example, the IRS has frequently allowed revocation when the taxpayer's accountant prepared the tax return without using the installment method (reporting the entire gain in the year of sale), and the taxpayer filed the

return not realizing that the election to forgo the use of the installment method had been made.

Martha, the tax adviser for Swan Partnership, analyzed Swan's situation and incorrectly concluded that the partnership should elect out of the installment method. Martha had discussed the tax return with Swan's CFO when she presented the tax return to him. Upon discovering her error in "electing out," Martha contacts Swan's new CFO (the CFO with whom she discussed the tax return has died), informs him of the benefit of amending the election out, and tells him that when she tried to discuss the tax return with the deceased CFO, he said, "I have complete confidence in you and do not need to discuss any aspect of the tax return." Evaluate what Martha has done.

Interest on the deferred taxes is payable only for the portion of the taxes that relates to the installment obligations in *excess* of $5 million. The interest is calculated using the underpayment rate in § 6621.

Electing Out of the Installment Method

A taxpayer can *elect not to use* the installment method. The election is made by reporting on a timely filed return the gain computed by the taxpayer's usual method of accounting (cash or accrual).[77] However, the Regulations provide that the amount realized by a cash basis taxpayer cannot be less than the value of the property sold. This rule differs from the usual cash basis accounting rules (discussed earlier),[78] which measure the amount realized in terms of the fair market value of the property received. The net effect of the Regulations is to allow the cash basis taxpayer to report his or her gain as an accrual basis taxpayer. The election is frequently applied to year-end sales by taxpayers who expect to be in a higher tax bracket in the following year.

EXAMPLE 32

On December 31, 2006, Kurt sold land to Jodie for $20,000 (fair market value). The cash was to be paid on January 4, 2007. Kurt is a cash basis taxpayer, and his basis in the land is $8,000. Kurt has a large casualty loss and very little other income in 2006. Thus, his marginal tax rate in 2006 is 15%. He expects his rate to increase to 35% in 2007.

The transaction constitutes an installment sale because a payment will be received in a tax year after the tax year of disposition. Jodie's promise to pay Kurt is an installment obligation, and under the Regulations, the value of the installment obligation is equal to the value of the property sold ($20,000). If Kurt elects out of the installment method, he would shift $12,000 of gain ($20,000 − $8,000) from the expected higher rate in 2007 to the 15% rate in 2006. The expected tax savings based on the rate differentials may exceed the benefit of the tax deferral available with the installment method. ■

Revocation of the Election. Permission of the IRS is required to revoke an election not to use the installment method.[79] The stickiness of the election is an added peril.

---

[77]§ 453(d) and Temp.Reg. § 15a.453–1(d). See also Rev.Rul. 82–227, 1982–2 C.B. 89.

[78]Refer to Chapter 4, Example 4–6.

[79]§ 453(d)(3) and Temp.Reg. § 15a.453–1(d)(4).

Long-Term Contracts

LO.5

Understand the alternative methods of accounting for long-term contracts (the completed contract method and the percentage of completion method) including the limitations on the use of the completed contract method.

A **long-term contract** is a building, installation, construction, or manufacturing contract that is entered into but not completed within the same tax year. However, a *manufacturing* contract is long term *only* if the contract is to manufacture (1) a unique item not normally carried in finished goods inventory or (2) items that normally require more than 12 calendar months to complete.[80] An item is *unique* if it is designed to meet the customer's particular needs and is not suitable for use by others. A contract to perform services (e.g., auditing or legal services) is not considered a contract for this purpose and thus cannot qualify as a long-term contract.

EXAMPLE 33

Rocky, a calendar year taxpayer, entered into two contracts during the year. One contract was to construct a building foundation. Work was to begin in October 2006 and was to be completed by June 2007. The contract is long term because it will not be entered into and completed in the same tax year. The fact that the contract requires less than 12 calendar months to complete is not relevant because the contract is not for manufacturing. The second contract was for architectural services to be performed over two years. These services will not qualify for long-term contract treatment because the taxpayer will not build, install, construct, or manufacture a product. ■

Generally, the taxpayer must accumulate all of the direct and indirect costs incurred under a contract. This means the production costs must be accumulated and allocated to individual contracts. Furthermore, mixed services costs, costs that benefit contracts as well as the general administrative operations of the business, must be allocated to production. Exhibit 18–1 lists the types of costs that must be accumulated and allocated to contracts. The taxpayer must develop reasonable bases for cost allocations.[81]

EXAMPLE 34

Falcon, Inc., uses detailed cost accumulation records to assign labor and materials to its contracts in progress. The total cost of fringe benefits is allocated to a contract on the following basis:

$$\frac{\text{Labor on the contract}}{\text{Total salaries and labor}} \times \text{Total cost of fringe benefits}$$

Similarly, storage and handling costs for materials are allocated to contracts on the following basis:

$$\frac{\text{Contract materials}}{\text{Materials purchases}} \times \text{Storage and handling costs}$$

The cost of the personnel operations, a mixed services cost, is allocated between production and general administration based on the number of employees in each function. The personnel cost allocated to production is allocated to individual contracts on the basis of the formula used to allocate fringe benefits. ■

The accumulated costs are deducted when the revenue from the contract is recognized. Generally, two methods of accounting are used in varying circumstances to determine when the revenue from a contract is recognized:[82]

- The completed contract method.
- The percentage of completion method.

The *completed contract method may be used* for (1) home construction contracts (contracts in which at least 80 percent of the estimated costs are for dwelling units in buildings with four or fewer units) and (2) certain other real estate construction

---

[80]§ 460(f) and Reg. § 1.451–3(b).
[81]Reg. §§ 1.263A–1T(b)(3)(iii)(A)(1) and 1.451–3(d)(9).

[82]§ 460.

EXHIBIT 18–1	Contract Costs, Mixed Services Costs, and Current Expense Items for Contracts

	Contracts Eligible for the Completed Contract Method	Other Contracts
Contract costs:		
Direct materials (a part of the finished product).	Capital	Capital
Indirect materials (consumed in production but not in the finished product, e.g., grease and oil for equipment).	Capital	Capital
Storage, handling, and insurance on materials.	Expense	Capital
Direct labor (worked on the product).	Capital	Capital
Indirect labor (worked in the production process but not directly on the product, e.g., a construction supervisor).	Capital	Capital
Fringe benefits for direct and indirect labor (e.g., vacation, sick pay, unemployment, and other insurance).	Capital	Capital
Pension costs for direct and indirect labor:		
• Current cost.	Expense	Capital
• Past service costs.	Expense	Capital
Depreciation on production facilities:		
• For financial statements.	Capital	Capital
• Tax depreciation in excess of financial statements.	Expense	Capital
Depreciation on idle facilities.	Expense	Expense
Property taxes, insurance, rent, and maintenance on production facilities.	Capital	Capital
Bidding expenses—successful.	Expense	Capital
Bidding expenses—unsuccessful.	Expense	Expense
Interest to finance real estate construction.	Capital	Capital
Interest to finance personal property:		
• Production period of one year or less.	Expense	Expense
• Production period exceeds one year and costs exceed $1 million.	Capital	Capital
• Production period exceeds two years.	Capital	Capital
Mixed services costs:		
• Personnel operations.	Expense	Allocate
• Data processing.	Expense	Allocate
• Purchasing.	Expense	Allocate
Selling, general, and administrative expenses (including an allocated share of mixed services).	Expense	Expense
Losses.	Expense	Expense

contracts. Other real estate contracts can qualify for the completed contract method if the following requirements are satisfied:

- The contract is expected to be completed within the two-year period beginning on the commencement date of the contract.
- The contract is performed by a taxpayer whose average annual gross receipts for the three taxable years preceding the taxable year in which the contract is entered into do not exceed $10 million.

All other contractors must use the percentage of completion method.

Completed Contract Method. Under the completed contract method, no revenue from the contract is recognized until the contract is completed and accepted. However, a taxpayer may not delay completion of a contract for the principal purpose of deferring tax.[83]

In some situations, the original contract price may be disputed, or the buyer may want additional work to be done on a long-term contract. If the disputed amount is substantial (it is not possible to determine whether a profit or loss will ultimately be realized on the contract), the Regulations provide that no amount of income or loss is recognized until the dispute is resolved. In all other cases, the profit or loss (reduced by the amount in dispute) is recognized in the current period on completion of the contract. However, additional work may need to be performed with respect to the disputed contract. In this case, the difference between the amount in dispute and the actual cost of the additional work is recognized in the year the work is completed rather than in the year in which the dispute is resolved.[84]

EXAMPLE 35

Ted, a calendar year taxpayer utilizing the completed contract method of accounting, constructed a building for Brad under a long-term contract. The gross contract price was $500,000. Ted finished construction in 2006 at a cost of $475,000. When Brad examined the building, he insisted that the building be repainted or the contract price be reduced. The estimated cost of repainting is $10,000. Since under the terms of the contract, Ted is assured of a profit of at least $15,000 ($500,000 − $475,000 − $10,000) even if the dispute is ultimately resolved in Brad's favor, Ted must include $490,000 ($500,000 − $10,000) in gross income and is allowed deductions of $475,000 for 2006.

In 2007, Ted and Brad resolve the dispute, and Ted repaints certain portions of the building at a cost of $6,000. Ted must include $10,000 in 2007 gross income and may deduct the $6,000 expense in that year. ■

EXAMPLE 36

Assume the same facts as in the previous example, except the estimated cost of repainting the building is $50,000. Since the resolution of the dispute completely in Brad's favor would mean a net loss on the contract for Ted ($500,000 − $475,000 − $50,000 = $25,000 loss), Ted does not recognize any income or loss until the year the dispute is resolved. ■

Frequently, a contractor receives payment at various stages of completion. For example, when the contract is 50 percent complete, the contractor may receive 50 percent of the contract price less a retainage. The taxation of these payments is generally governed by Regulation § 1.451–5 "advance payments for goods and long-term contracts" (discussed in Chapter 4). Generally, contractors are permitted to defer the advance payments until the payments are recognized as income under the taxpayer's method of accounting.

Percentage of Completion Method. The percentage of completion method must be used to account for long-term contracts unless the taxpayer qualifies for one of the two exceptions that permit the completed contract method to be used (home construction contracts and certain other real estate construction contracts).[85] Under the percentage of completion method, a portion of the gross contract price is included in income during each period as the work progresses. The revenue accrued each period (except for the final period) is computed as follows:[86]

$$\frac{C}{T} \times P$$

---

[83]Reg. § 1.451–3(b)(2).

[84]Reg. §§ 1.451–3(d)(2)(ii)–(vii), Example (2).

[85]Certain residential construction contracts that do not qualify for the completed contract method may nevertheless use that method to account for 30% of the profit from the contract, with the remaining 70% reported by the percentage of completion method.

[86]§ 460(b)(1)(A).

Where   C = Contract costs incurred during the period.
        T = Estimated total cost of the contract.
        P = Contract price.

All of the costs allocated to the contract during the period are deductible from the accrued revenue.[87] The revenue reported in the final period is simply the unreported revenue from the contract. Because T in this formula is an estimate that frequently differs from total actual costs, which are not known until the contract has been completed, the profit on a contract for a particular period may be overstated or understated.

EXAMPLE 37

Tan, Inc., entered into a contract that was to take two years to complete, with an estimated cost of $2,250,000. The contract price was $3,000,000. Costs of the contract for 2005, the first year, totaled $1,350,000. The gross profit reported by the percentage of completion method for 2005 was $450,000 [($1,350,000/$2,250,000 × $3,000,000) − $1,350,000]. The contract was completed at the end of 2006 at a total cost of $2,700,000. In retrospect, 2005 profit should have been $150,000 [($1,350,000/$2,700,000 × $3,000,000) − $1,350,000]. Thus, taxes were overpaid for 2005. ■

A *de minimis* rule enables the contractor to delay the recognition of income for a particular contract under the percentage of completion method. If less than 10 percent of the estimated contract costs have been incurred by the end of the taxable year, the taxpayer can elect to defer the recognition of income and the related costs until the taxable year in which cumulative contract costs are at least 10 percent of the estimated contract costs.[88]

Lookback Provisions. In the year a contract is completed, a *lookback* provision requires the recalculation of annual profits reported on the contract under the percentage of completion method. Interest is paid to the taxpayer if taxes were overpaid, and interest is payable by the taxpayer if there was an underpayment.[89] For a corporate taxpayer, the lookback interest paid by the taxpayer is deductible, but for an individual taxpayer, it is nondeductible personal interest associated with a tax liability.

EXAMPLE 38

Assume Tan, Inc., in Example 37, was in the 35% tax bracket in both years and the relevant interest rate was 10%. For 2005, the company paid excess taxes of $105,000 [($450,000 − $150,000) × .35]. When the contract is completed at the end of 2006, Tan, Inc., should receive interest of $10,500 for one year on the tax overpayment ($105,000 × .10). ■

LO.6

Know when accounting for inventories must occur, recognize the types of costs that must be included in inventories, and apply the LIFO method.

Inventories

Generally, tax accounting and financial accounting for inventories are much the same:

- The use of inventories is necessary to clearly reflect the income of any business engaged in the production and sale or purchase and sale of goods.[90]
- The inventories should include all finished goods, goods in process, and raw materials and supplies that will become part of the product (including containers).
- Inventory rules must give effect to the *best* accounting practice of a particular trade or business, and the taxpayer's method should be consistently followed from year to year.

---

[87]Reg. § 1.451–3(c)(3).
[88]§ 460(b)(5).
[89]§§ 460(b)(2) and (b)(6). The taxpayer can elect to not apply the lookback method in situations where the cumulative taxable income as of the close of each prior year is within 10% of the correct income for each prior year.

[90]§ 471(a) and Reg. §§ 1.471–1 and –2.

- All items included in inventory should be valued at either (1) cost or (2) the lower of cost or market value.

The following are *not* acceptable methods or practices in valuing inventories:

- A deduction for a reserve for anticipated price changes.
- The use of a constant price or nominal value for a so-called normal quantity of materials or goods in stock (e.g., the base stock method).
- The inclusion in inventory of stock in transit to which title is not vested in the taxpayer.
- The direct costing approach (excluding fixed indirect production costs from inventory).
- The prime costing approach (excluding all indirect production costs from inventory).

The reason for the similarities between tax and financial accounting for inventories is that § 471 sets forth what appears to be a two-prong test. Under this provision "inventories shall be taken . . . on such basis . . . as conforming as nearly as may be to the *best accounting practice* in the trade or business and as most *clearly reflecting the income.*" The best accounting practice is synonymous with generally accepted accounting principles (hereafter referred to as GAAP). However, the IRS determines whether an inventory method clearly reflects income.

In *Thor Power Tool Co. v. Comm.*, there was a conflict between the two tests.[91] The taxpayer's method of valuing obsolete parts was in conformity with GAAP. The IRS, however, successfully argued that the clear reflection of income test was not satisfied because the taxpayer's procedures for valuing its inventories were contrary to the Regulations. Under the taxpayer's method, inventories for parts in excess of estimated future sales were written off (expensed), although the parts were kept on hand and their asking prices were not reduced. [Under Regulation § 1.471–4(b), inventories cannot be written down unless the selling prices also are reduced.] The taxpayer contended that conformity to GAAP creates a presumption that the method clearly reflects income. The Supreme Court disagreed, concluding that the clear reflection of income test was *paramount.* Moreover, it is the opinion of the IRS that controls in determining whether the method of inventory clearly reflects income. Thus, the best accounting practice test was rendered practically meaningless. It follows that the taxpayer's method of inventory must strictly conform to the Regulations regardless of what GAAP may require.

Determining Inventory Cost

For merchandise purchased, cost is the invoice price less trade discounts plus freight and other handling charges.[92] Cash discounts approximating a fair interest rate can be deducted or capitalized at the taxpayer's option, providing the method used is consistently applied.

Uniform Capitalization (UNICAP).
Section 263A provides that for inventory and property produced by the taxpayer, "(A) the direct cost of such property, and (B) such property's share of those indirect costs (including taxes) part or all of which are allocable to such property" must be capitalized. The Committee Reports observe that Congress is attempting to achieve a set of capitalization rules that will apply to all types of businesses: contractors, manufacturers, farmers, wholesalers, and retailers.[93] Congress has labeled the system the uniform capitalization (UNICAP) rules, and practitioners refer to the rules as a *super-full absorption costing system.*

---

[91]79–1 USTC ¶9139, 43 AFTR2d 79–362, 99 S.Ct. 773 (USSC, 1979).
[92]Reg. § 1.471–3(b).

[93]H. Rep. 99–841, 99th Cong., 2nd Sess., 1986, pp. 302–309. See also Reg. § 1.263A–1(a).

To value inventory under the UNICAP rules, a *producer* must apply the following steps:

- Classify all costs into three categories: (1) production, (2) general administrative expense, and (3) mixed services.
- Allocate mixed services costs to production and general administrative expenses.[94]
- Allocate the production costs between the cost of goods sold and the ending inventory.

Exhibit 18–1 (see the "Other Contracts" column) lists typical items that are included in the three classes of costs. The mixed services costs should be allocated to production on a rational basis. For example, the costs of operating the personnel department may be allocated between production and general administration based on the number of applications processed or the number of employees. In lieu of allocating each mixed services cost, the taxpayer can elect a *simplified method* whereby the total of all mixed services costs is allocated to production as follows:[95]

$$MSP = \frac{TP}{TC} \times TMS$$

Where   MSP = Mixed services costs allocated to production.
        TP = Total production costs, other than interest and mixed services.
        TC = Total costs, other than interest; state, local, or foreign income taxes; and mixed services costs.
        TMS = Total mixed services costs.

The usual cost accounting techniques (e.g., average cost per equivalent unit) can be used to allocate the costs between the cost of goods sold and the ending inventory.

Alternatively, the producer can elect to allocate mixed services costs to production on the basis of labor charges only (production labor as a percentage of total labor costs).

The costs included in the inventory of *wholesalers and retailers* are comparable to those of the producer. However, many of these costs are captured in the price these taxpayers pay for the goods. The following additional costs must be capitalized by these taxpayers:

- All storage costs for wholesalers.
- Offsite storage costs for retailers.
- Purchasing costs (e.g., buyers' wages or salaries).
- Handling, processing, assembly, and repackaging.
- The portion of mixed services costs allocable to these functions.

Mixed services costs must be allocated to offsite storage, purchasing, and packaging on the basis of direct labor costs of these departments as a percentage of total payroll. Thus, the storage, purchasing, and packaging costs allocated to ending inventory include some mixed services costs.

The UNICAP rules may result in some costs being capitalized for tax purposes but not for financial accounting purposes. For example, a wholesaler's or a manufacturer's storage costs are generally expensed for financial reporting purposes, but are capitalized for tax purposes. Also, the taxpayer may capitalize straight-line depreciation of production equipment for financial accounting purposes, but the total tax depreciation must be capitalized under uniform capitalization.

[94]Producers with mixed services costs of less than $200,000 for the year are not required to allocate mixed services costs if the simplified method is used to allocate their production costs. Reg. § 1.263A–1(b)(12).

[95]Reg. § 1.263A–1(h)(5).

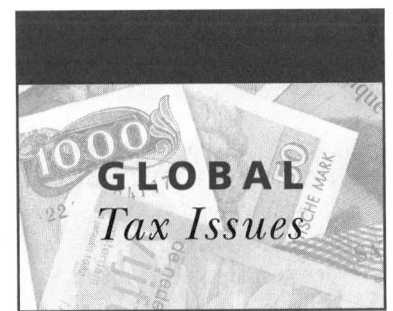

INVENTORY ACQUIRED FROM A FOREIGN SUBSIDIARY

Generally, a parent corporation and its foreign subsidiaries are treated as separate corporations. If a foreign subsidiary is producing goods in a country whose tax rates are lower than the U.S. tax rates, tax savings can accrue to the group if the foreign subsidiary's prices to the U.S. parent are as high as permissible. This will increase the income in the foreign country, but will reduce taxable income subject to the higher U.S. rates. Section 482 is the IRS's weapon against such income shifting. Under § 482, the prices charged on transactions between related parties must be equal to an "arm's length price."

GLOBAL Tax Issues

Lower of Cost or Market. Except for those taxpayers who use the LIFO method, inventories may be valued at the **lower of cost or market (replacement cost)**.[96] Taxpayers using LIFO must value inventory at cost. However, the write-down of damaged or shopworn merchandise and goods that are otherwise unsalable at normal prices is not considered to be an application of the lower of cost or market method. Such items should be valued at bona fide selling price less direct cost of disposal.[97]

In the case of excess inventories (as in *Thor Power Tool Co.*, discussed above), the goods can be written down only to the taxpayer's offering price. If the offering price on the goods is not reduced, the goods must be valued at cost.

EXAMPLE 39

The Cardinal Publishing Company invested $50,000 in printing 10,000 copies of a book. Although only 7,000 copies were sold in the first 3 years and none in the next 5 years, management is convinced that the book will become a classic in 20 years. Cardinal leaves the price the same as it was when the book was first distributed ($15 per copy). The remaining 3,000 books must be valued at cost ($15,000). Note that the tax law provides an incentive for the taxpayer to destroy or abandon its excess inventory and obtain an immediate deduction rather than wait for the event of future sales. ■

In applying the lower of cost or market method, *each* item included in the inventory must be valued at the lower of its cost or market value.[98]

EXAMPLE 40

The taxpayer's ending inventory is valued as follows:

Item	Cost	Market	Lower of Cost or Market
A	$5,000	$ 4,000	$4,000
B	3,000	2,000	2,000
C	1,500	6,000	1,500
	$9,500	$12,000	$7,500

Under the lower of cost or market method, the taxpayer's inventory is valued at $7,500 rather than $9,500. ■

Inventory Shrinkage. The difference between the inventory per physical count and according to the company's records is referred to as *inventory shrinkage*. Inventory shrinkage is the result of accidents, theft, and errors in recording. Many companies take physical inventories at times other than the last day of the tax year and

---

[96]Reg. § 1.472–4.
[97]Reg. § 1.471–2(c).
[98]Reg. § 1.471–4(c).

TAX *in the News*   **ENVIRONMENTAL MESS SPILLS ONTO INVENTORY VALUATION**

Generally, costs are capitalized so that revenues and expenses will be matched—the costs associated with producing the revenue will be deducted in the same period the revenue is taken into gross receipts. In a recent Revenue Ruling, the taxpayer had operated a manufacturing plant for several years and in the process had contaminated the surrounding land. The IRS ruled that because the contamination arose out of the production process, the costs of removing the contaminants were a production cost. The IRS then applied its uniform capitalization regulations to require the cost of the environmental cleanup to be included in the cost of goods produced in the period the cleanup was performed. The net result was a classic mismatching: The cost of the cleanup was not matched with the revenues from the goods that created the contamination. Rather, the cost of the cleanup was allocated to the cost of goods that happened to be produced in the period the cleanup occurred.

---

adjust their inventory per books to agree with the physical count. The inventory of the last day of the tax year, which is used to compute cost of goods sold, is based on the perpetual records. Such companies often adjust the ending inventory for the estimated shrinkage that has occurred between the date of the physical inventory and the last day of the tax year. The adjustment is often based on the historical relationship between inventory shrinkage and sales.[99]

Determining Cost—Specific Identification, FIFO, and LIFO. In some cases, it is feasible to determine the cost of the particular item sold. For example, an automobile dealer can easily determine the specific cost of each automobile that has been sold. However, in most businesses it is necessary to resort to a flow of goods assumption such as *first in, first out* (*FIFO*), *last in, first out* (*LIFO*), or an *average cost* method. A taxpayer may use any of these methods, provided the method selected is consistently applied from year to year.

During a period of rising prices, LIFO will generally produce a lower ending inventory valuation and will result in a greater cost of goods sold than would be obtained under the FIFO method. The following example illustrates how LIFO and FIFO affect the computation of the cost of goods sold.

EXAMPLE 41

On January 1, 2006, the taxpayer opened a retail store to sell refrigerators. At least 10 refrigerators must be carried in inventory to satisfy customer demands. The initial investment in the 10 refrigerators is $5,000. During the year, 10 refrigerators were sold at $750 each and were replaced at a cost of $6,000 ($600 each). Gross profit under the LIFO and FIFO methods is computed as follows:

		FIFO		LIFO
Sales (10 × $750)		$ 7,500		$ 7,500
Beginning inventory	$ 5,000		$ 5,000	
Purchases	6,000		6,000	
	$11,000		$11,000	
Ending inventory				
10 × $600	(6,000)			
10 × $500			(5,000)	
Cost of goods sold		(5,000)		(6,000)
Gross profit		$ 2,500		$ 1,500 ∎

---

[99]§ 471(b).

Dollar-Value LIFO. In the previous example, the taxpayer was buying and selling a single product, a particular model of a refrigerator. The taxpayer employed the specific goods LIFO technique. Under the specific goods approach, if the identical items are not on hand at the end of the period, the LIFO inventory is depleted, and all of the deferred profit must be recaptured. Thus, taxpayers who frequently change the items carried in inventory would realize little benefit from LIFO. However, the dollar-value LIFO technique avoids the LIFO depletion problem associated with the specific goods technique.

Under **dollar-value LIFO**, each inventory item is assigned to a pool. A *pool* is a collection of similar items and is treated as a separate inventory. Determining whether items are similar involves considerable judgment. In general, however, the taxpayer would prefer broad pools so that when a particular item is sold out, it can be replaced by increases in other items in the same pool. Generally, all products manufactured at a particular plant can be treated as a pool.[100] A department store may have a separate pool for each department. An automobile dealer may have separate pools for new cars, lightweight trucks, heavy-duty trucks, and car and truck parts.

At the end of the period, the ending inventory must be valued at the current-year prices and then at the LIFO base period (the year LIFO was adopted). The ratio of the ending inventory at current prices to the ending inventory at base period prices is the *LIFO index*. If the total current inventory at base period prices is greater than the base period inventory at base period prices, a LIFO layer must be added. The LIFO index is applied to the LIFO layer to convert it to current prices.

E X A M P L E   42

Black Company adopted LIFO effective January 1, 2006. The base LIFO inventory (from December 31, 2005) was $1,000,000. On December 31, 2006, the inventory was $1,320,000 at end-of-2006 prices and $1,200,000 at end-of-2005 (the base period) prices. Thus, Black added a 2006 layer of $200,000 ($1,200,000 − $1,000,000) at base period prices. The layer must be converted to 2006 prices as follows:

$$\text{LIFO index} = \$1,320,000/\$1,200,000 = 1.10$$

$$2006 \text{ layer} \times \text{LIFO index} = \$200,000 \times 1.10 = \$220,000$$

Therefore, the 2006 ending inventory is $1,000,000 + $220,000 = $1,220,000.

The inventory on December 31, 2007, is $1,325,000 using 2007 prices and $1,250,000 using base period prices. Thus, the LIFO index for 2007 is $1,325,000/$1,250,000 = 1.06. The LIFO inventory is $1,273,000, computed as follows:

BLACK COMPANY
LIFO Inventory
December 31, 2007

	Base Period Cost	LIFO Index	LIFO Layers
Base inventory	$1,000,000	1.00	$1,000,000
2006 layer	200,000	1.10	220,000
2007 layer	50,000	1.06	53,000
	$1,250,000		$1,273,000

---

[100]See, generally, Reg. § 1.472–8.

Blanch Corporation has been using the dollar-value LIFO inventory method for 20 years. The company maintains one inventory pool that includes raw materials, goods in process, and finished goods. The LIFO deferral is several million dollars. At the end of the current year, the corporation's inventory of finished goods was almost depleted because the company's major competitor had to recall a substantial portion of its products. Blanch's management is aware that if the inventory is not replenished, the corporation will be required to recognize income that has been deferred for the past 20 years. The controller has suggested that the company buy sufficient raw materials to substitute for the depleted finished goods. This will require having on hand at the end

of the year the raw materials required for the next 18 months, when ordinarily the company has only a three-month supply on hand. The controller argues that the cost of carrying the additional inventory is much less than the additional taxes that will be due if the inventories are allowed to decrease.

The operations manager has suggested that the company buy the raw materials before the end of the year and have the supplier store the materials. Furthermore, the supplier would act as Blanch's agent to sell the excess materials. This would minimize the actual investment in inventory. Do you think the corporation should follow either proposal?

The LIFO Election

A taxpayer may adopt LIFO by merely using the method in the tax return for the year of the change and by attaching Form 970 (Application to Use LIFO Inventory Method) to the tax return. Thus, a taxpayer does not have to request approval for the change. Once the election is made, it cannot be revoked. However, a prospective change from LIFO to any other inventory method can be made only if the consent of the IRS is obtained.[101]

The beginning inventory valuation for the first year LIFO is used is computed by the costing method employed in the preceding year. Thus, the beginning LIFO inventory is generally the same as the closing inventory for the preceding year. However, since lower of cost or market cannot be used in conjunction with LIFO, previous write-downs to market for items included in the beginning inventory must be restored to income. The amount the inventories are written up is an adjustment due to a change in accounting method.[102] However, the usual rules for disposition of the adjustments under Revenue Procedure 99–49 are not applicable.[103] The taxpayer is allowed to spread the adjustment ratably over the year of the change and the two succeeding years.

EXAMPLE 43   In 2005, Paul used the lower of cost or market FIFO inventory method. The FIFO cost of his ending inventory was $30,000, and the market value of the inventory was $24,000. Therefore, the ending inventory for 2005 was $24,000. Paul switched to LIFO in 2006 and was required to write up the beginning inventory to $30,000. Paul must add $2,000 ($6,000 ÷ 3) to his income for each of the years 2006, 2007, and 2008. ∎

Congress added this provision to the Code to overrule the previous IRS policy of requiring the taxpayer to include the entire adjustment in income for the year preceding the change to LIFO.[104]

Once the LIFO election is made for tax purposes, the taxpayer's financial reports to owners and creditors must also be prepared on the basis of LIFO.[105] The

[101]Reg. §§ 1.472–3(a) and 1.472–5 and Rev.Proc. 84–74, 1984–2 C.B. 736 at 742.
[102]Reg. § 1.472–2(c). In Rev.Rul. 76–282, 1976–2 C.B. 137, the IRS required the restoration of write-downs for damaged and shopworn goods when the taxpayer switched to LIFO.
[103]1999–2 C.B. 725.
[104]§ 472(d), overruling the IRS position cited in Footnote 102.
[105]§ 472(c).

conformity of financial reports to tax reporting is specifically required by the Code and is strictly enforced by the IRS. However, the Regulations permit the taxpayer to make a footnote disclosure of the net income computed by another method of inventory valuation (e.g., FIFO).[106]

Taxable Year

Under the general rules for tax years, partnerships and S corporations frequently will be required to use a calendar year. However, if the partnership or S corporation can demonstrate a business purpose for a fiscal year, the IRS will allow the entity to use the requested year. The advantage to a fiscal year is that the calendar year partners and S corporation shareholders may be able to defer from tax the income earned from the close of the fiscal year until the end of the calendar year. Tax advisers for these entities should apply the IRS's gross receipts test described in Revenue Procedure 87–32 to determine if permission for the fiscal year will be granted.[107]

TAX PLANNING
Considerations

Cash Method of Accounting

The cash method of accounting gives the taxpayer considerable control over the recognition of expenses and some control over the recognition of income. This method can be used by proprietorships, partnerships, and small corporations (gross receipts of $5 million or less) that provide services (inventories are not material to the service business). Farmers (except certain farming corporations) can also use the cash method.

Installment Method

Unlike the cash and accrual methods, the installment method often results in an interest-free loan (of deferred taxes) from the government. The installment method is not available for the sale of inventory. Nevertheless, the installment method is an important tax planning technique and should be considered when a sale of eligible property is being planned. That is, if the taxpayer can benefit from deferring the tax, the terms of sale can be arranged so that the installment method rules apply. If, on the other hand, the taxpayer expects to be in a higher tax bracket when the payments will be received, he or she can elect not to use the installment method.

Related Parties. Intrafamily installment sales can still be a useful family tax planning tool. If the related party holds the property more than two years, a subsequent sale will not accelerate the gain from the first disposition. Patience and forethought are rewarded.

The 6 percent limitation on imputed interest on sales of land between family members (see Concept Summary 18–1) enables the seller to convert ordinary income into capital gain or make what is, in effect, a nontaxable gift. If the selling price is raised to adjust for the low interest rate charges on an installment sale, the seller has more capital gain but less ordinary income than would be realized from a sale to an unrelated party. If the selling price is not raised and the specified interest of 6 percent is charged, the seller enables the relative to have the use of the property without having to pay its full market value. As an additional benefit, the bargain sale is not a taxable gift.

Disposition of Installment Obligations. A disposition of an installment obligation is also a serious matter. Gifts of the obligations will accelerate income to the seller. The list of taxable and nontaxable dispositions of installment obligations should not be trusted to memory. In each instance where transfers of installment

---

[106]Reg. § 1.472–2(e).   [107]See also Rev.Proc. 2002–38, 2002–1 C.B. 1037.

obligations are contemplated, the practitioner should conduct research to be sure he or she knows the consequences.

Completed Contract Method

Generally, large contractors must use the percentage of completion method of accounting for reporting the income from long-term contracts. Under the percentage of completion method, the taxpayer must recognize profit in each period costs are incurred. Profit is reported in proportion to the cost incurred for the period as a proportion of the total contract cost. However, small contractors (average annual gross receipts do not exceed $10 million) working on contracts that are completed within a two-year period can elect to use the completed contract method and defer profit until the year in which the contract is completed.

Inventories

Lower of Cost or Market. Generally, under tax accounting rules, a deduction cannot be taken for a loss before the loss is realized. Inventories with a replacement cost below their original cost are the major exception to this rule. The rationale for the lower of cost or market method is that when the replacement cost of the goods has decreased, the taxpayer's selling price must likewise be reduced. Under the lower of cost or market method, the taxpayer is allowed to anticipate a reduction in the expected selling price of the goods by taking a deduction in the period the replacement cost decreases, rather than waiting until the goods are actually sold. Thus, the lower of cost or market method is a tax deferral technique.

LIFO. While the lower of cost or market method defers tax when replacement costs are declining, LIFO defers tax when prices are rising. However, when some goods are increasing in value while others are decreasing, the taxpayer cannot use the lower of cost or market method for the goods declining in value and LIFO for the goods whose replacement costs are rising. That is, LIFO cannot be used in conjunction with the lower of cost or market method. Assuming that prices generally are rising, the taxpayer generally should elect LIFO. The only major disadvantage to LIFO is the financial-tax conformity requirement. However, even this disadvantage can be overcome through footnote disclosure of earnings as computed under FIFO.

KEY TERMS

Accounting methods, 18–10

Accounting period, 18–3

Accrual method, 18–12

All events test, 18–13

Cash method, 18–10

Claim of right doctrine, 18–9

Completed contract method, 18–27

Dollar-value LIFO, 18–33

Economic performance test, 18–13

Fiscal year, 18–3

Hybrid method, 18–15

Imputed interest, 18–20

Installment method, 18–18

Least aggregate deferral method, 18–4

Long-term contract, 18–25

Lower of cost or market (replacement cost), 18–31

Majority interest partners, 18–3

One-year rule for prepaid expenses, 18–11

Percentage of completion method, 18–27

Personal service corporation (PSC), 18–6

Principal partner, 18–3

Short taxable year (short period), 18–7

Uniform capitalization (UNICAP) rules, 18–29

P R O B L E M   M A T E R I A L S

DISCUSSION QUESTIONS

1. Why would December 31 be an inappropriate year-end for a ski resort?

2. Your client, an individual whose accounting period is the calendar year, recently formed an S corporation. The business of the S corporation is to sell materials used in planting farm crops in the spring and early summer. The business will be dormant during the remainder of the year. The business is expected to generate losses for each of the first two years of operations and thereafter to produce profits. Should the corporation use a calendar year, or should the client seek permission to use a fiscal year ending in the summer?

3. A medical practice was incorporated on January 1, 2006, and expects to earn $25,000 per month before deducting the doctor's salary. The doctor owns 100% of the stock. The corporation and the doctor both use the cash method of accounting. The corporation does not need to retain any of the earnings in the business; thus, the salary of the doctor (a calendar year taxpayer) will equal the corporation's net income before salary expense. If the corporation could choose any tax year it wished and pay the doctor's salary at the time that would be the most tax efficient (but at least once every 12 months), what tax year should the corporation choose, and when should the salary be paid each year?
   Decision Making

4. Pale Motel, Inc., was a C corporation using a fiscal year ending April 30 for tax purposes for all tax years through April 30, 2006. In May 2006, the corporation made an S election. What are the implications of the election for Pale's tax year?

5. Freda is a cash basis farmer. She was in the 35% marginal tax bracket in 2005, the 15% marginal tax bracket in 2006, and the 35% marginal tax bracket in 2007. In 2005, she received $10,000 from the sale of produce. The customer complained that the produce was unfit for consumption, and in 2006 Freda refunded the $10,000. Also in 2006, Freda paid her farmers' cooperative $50,000 for seeds and fertilizer. In 2007, the cooperative paid Freda a dividend of $5,000 based on the cooperative's 2006 earnings.
   a. What are the tax consequences of the payment to the customer in 2006?
   b. What are the tax consequences of the refund from the cooperative in 2007?
   c. Were the tax accounting rules "kind" to Freda?

6. The Cardinal Insurance Agency is a newly formed corporation, and its gross receipts will probably never exceed $2 million in a year. Generally, it takes approximately two months to collect accounts receivable. Accounts payable generally equal expenses for one month. Cardinal does not expect accounts payable and accounts receivable to increase significantly. It prepares monthly financial statements using the accrual method of accounting. Given that the accounts receivable and accounts payable will not significantly change, would Cardinal derive any benefit from filing its tax return using the cash method of accounting?
   Decision Making

7. A cash basis taxpayer owns rental properties. The insurance on the properties is renewed each January 1. On December 30, 2006, the taxpayer paid the premium of $24,000 for the period January 1, 2007, through December 31, 2007. Can the taxpayer deduct the premium of $24,000 in 2006?

8. In 2006, the IRS determined that the taxpayer must change from the cash to the accrual method. At the beginning of 2006, the company had accounts receivable of $250,000, inventory of $200,000, and $100,000 of accounts payable. What is the amount of the adjustment due to the change in accounting method?

9. Osprey Corporation, an accrual basis taxpayer, had taxable income for 2006. However, Osprey's accountant was ill, and the taxable income for 2006 was not computed until July 2007. The state income tax return for 2006 was filed on August 13, 2007, and state income taxes of $3,000 were paid at that time. Can the 2006 state income taxes be deducted in calculating the corporation's 2006 Federal taxable income?

10. Compare the cash basis and accrual basis of accounting as applied to the following:
    a. Fixed assets.
    b. Prepaid rent income.
    c. Prepaid interest expense.
    d. A note received for services performed if the market value and face amount of the note differ.

Decision Making

11. Edgar uses the cash method to report the income from his software consulting business. A large publicly held corporation has offered to invest in Edgar's business as a limited partner. What tax accounting complications would be created if Edgar and the corporation become partners?

12. In June 2006, a cash basis and calendar year corporation paid insurance premiums of $1,800 for the period July 1, 2006, through June 30, 2007. Assuming that 2006 is the first year of the corporation's operations, how much can the corporation deduct for the insurance premiums in 2006?

13. Ruby, Inc., manufactures consumer products and provides a 12-month warranty. The company can accurately predict the cost of services to be provided under the warranty. Therefore, the company's financial statements reflect an estimated future cost of warranty services. Discuss the tax accounting principle that prevents the company from accruing the estimated costs of services to be provided under the warranty.

Decision Making

14. Irene has made Sara an offer on the purchase of a capital asset. Irene will pay (1) $200,000 cash or (2) $50,000 cash and a 6% installment note for $150,000 guaranteed by City Bank of New York. If Sara sells for $200,000 cash, she will invest the after-tax proceeds in certificates of deposit yielding 6% interest. Sara's cost of the asset is $25,000. Why would Sara prefer the installment sale?

15. Warren owns property with a basis of $100,000 that is subject to a mortgage of $60,000. Felix is willing to pay Warren $140,000 cash and assume the mortgage. Alternatively, Felix is willing to pay Warren $200,000, and Warren will pay off the mortgage. Compare the tax consequences to Warren under the two options.

16. A seller and buyer agree that the sales/purchase price for land is $100,000 down and five payments of $50,000 each. In addition, the seller would like the contract to read that the total selling price is $322,600 and that the five payments of $50,000 each include interest at 4%, which is the current Federal intermediate-term rate. The buyer counters that the price should be stated as $310,600, with a 6% stated rate on the five payments of $50,000 each. The land is a capital asset to the seller, and the holding period is four years. Because the total amount received by the seller and the amount paid by the buyer are the same [$100,000 + 5($50,000) = $350,000], why does it matter how the price and interest rate are stated in the contract?

Decision Making

17. On June 1, 2004, Father sold land to Son for $200,000. Father reported the gain by the installment method, with the gain to be spread over five years. In May 2006, Son received an offer of $300,000 for the land, to be paid over three years. What would be the tax consequences of Son's sale? How could the tax consequences be improved?

Decision Making

18. In December 2006, Juan Corporation sold land it held as an investment. The corporation received $50,000 in 2006 and a note payable (with adequate interest) for $150,000 to be paid in 2008. Juan Corporation's cost of the land was $80,000. The corporation has a $90,000 net capital loss carryover that will expire in 2006. Should Juan Corporation report the sale in 2006 or use the installment method to report the income as payments are received?

19. What long-term contract method generally results in the greatest deferral of income? Explain. What are the limitations on using that method for tax purposes?

20. Your client is a real estate contractor who builds commercial and industrial buildings. When she began her business, you advised her to report income by the completed contract method. The business has grown rapidly, and the gross receipts are approaching $10 million per year. Your client is considering bidding on a large contract with very little risk but a very low profit margin. What might be an accounting method implication of accepting the new contract?

21. Nathan used the percentage of completion method to report income from a contract that began in the previous year and was completed in the current year. The actual total cost of completing the contract was greater than the estimate of total cost made at the end of the previous year. How will the lookback rules affect Nathan?

22. The Eagle Corporation builds yachts. All vessels are practically identical and sell for more than $2 million. Production does not begin until the company has a contract to sell the vessel. The company has recently changed its production techniques to reduce the time for producing a yacht from 15 months to 9 months. What are the accounting method implications of the change?

23. Largo Company is an engineering consulting business that uses the accrual method of accounting for its services. Mango Company manufactures nuts and bolts and also uses the accrual method to account for its sales. Each company has a personnel department. How should the cost of personnel operations be treated by each of the two companies?

24. For over 20 years, Pearl Parts Company has produced parts using brass as the only material. This year the company started making some of the component parts from plastic. This change substantially reduced production costs. What are the inventory valuation issues for Pearl, which has used the dollar-value LIFO inventory method for 10 years?

Issue ID

25. How can a company using LIFO for tax purposes disclose to shareholders the net income for the tax year computed under FIFO without violating the LIFO conformity provisions?

26. Blue and Gold are competitors in the automotive supply business. In calculating its ending inventory at the end of the tax year, Blue includes an estimate of inventory shrinkage, but Gold does not. What could account for this difference?

Issue ID

PROBLEMS

27. Red, White, and Blue are unrelated corporations engaged in real estate development. The three corporations formed a joint venture (treated as a partnership) to develop a tract of land. Assuming the venture does not have a natural business year, what tax year must the joint venture adopt under the following circumstances?

		Tax Year Ending	Interest in Joint Venture
a.	Red	March 31	60%
	Blue	June 30	20%
	White	October 31	20%
b.	Red	October 31	30%
	White	June 30	40%
	Blue	January 31	30%

28. The Cardinal Wholesale Company is an S corporation that began business on March 1, 2006. Robert, a calendar year taxpayer, owns 100% of the Cardinal stock. He has $400,000 taxable income from other sources each year. Robert will work approximately 30 hours a week for the corporation. Cardinal sells swimming pool supplies, and its natural business year ends in September. Approximately 80% of Cardinal's gross receipts occur in June through September.
   a. What tax year should Cardinal elect, assuming that Robert anticipates the company will produce a net profit for all years?
   b. What tax year should Cardinal elect, assuming it will lose $10,000 a month for the first 12 months and an average of $5,000 a month for the next 12 months? In the third year, the corporation will earn taxable income.

Decision Making

29. Zack conducted his professional practice through Zack, Inc. The corporation uses a fiscal year ending September 30 even though the business purpose test for a fiscal year cannot be satisfied. For the year ending September 30, 2006, the corporation paid Zack

Decision Making

a salary of $180,000, and during the period January through September 2006, the corporation paid him a salary of $150,000.

    a. How much salary should Zack receive during the period October 1 through December 31, 2006?

    b. Assume Zack received only $30,000 salary during the period October 1 through December 31, 2006. What would be the consequences to Zack, Inc.?

30. Mauve Corporation began operations as a farm supplies business and used a fiscal year ending September 30. The company gradually went out of the farm supplies business and into the mail-order Christmas gifts business. The company has received permission from the IRS to change to a fiscal year ending January 31, effective for the year ending January 31, 2006. For the short period October 1, 2005, through January 31, 2006, Mauve earned $25,000. Calculate Mauve's tax liability for the short period October 1, 2005, through January 31, 2006.

31. Turquoise, Inc., is a cash basis consulting firm. In 2006, the company reimbursed a client $15,000 because of an overcharge for services that was collected in 2005. The overcharge related to work done by one of Turquoise's subcontractors. Turquoise had paid the subcontractor the $15,000 in 2005 as part of total payments to the subcontractor of $150,000. The subcontractor felt that he was entitled to his full charges, but settled by refunding $7,000 to Turquoise in 2006. Turquoise was in the 35% marginal tax bracket in 2005 and is in the 15% marginal tax bracket in 2006.

    a. What are the tax consequences to Turquoise of these contract adjustments?

    b. Did Turquoise receive equitable tax treatment from these adjustments?

Communications   32. Gold, Inc., is an accrual basis taxpayer. In 2006, an employee accidentally spilled hazardous chemicals on leased property. The chemicals destroyed trees on neighboring property, resulting in $30,000 of damages. In 2006, the owner of the property sued Gold, Inc., for the $30,000. Gold's attorney feels that it is liable and the only issue is whether the neighbor will also seek punitive damages that could be as much as three times the actual damages. In addition, as a result of the spill, Gold was in violation of its lease and was therefore required to pay the landlord $15,000. However, the amount due for the lease violation is not payable until the termination of the lease in 2009. None of these costs were covered by insurance. Jeff Stuart, the president of Gold, Inc., is generally familiar with the accrual basis tax accounting rules and is concerned about when the company will be allowed to deduct the amounts the company is required to pay as a result of this environmental disaster. Write Mr. Stuart a letter explaining these issues. Gold's address is 200 Elm Avenue, San Jose, CA 95192.

33. Compute the taxpayer's income or deductions for 2006 using (1) the cash basis and (2) the accrual basis for each of the following:

    a. In March 2006, the taxpayer purchased a copying machine for $250,000. The taxpayer paid $25,000 in cash and gave a $225,000 interest-bearing note for the balance. The copying machine has an MACRS cost recovery period of five years, and the § 179 election was not made.

    b. In December 2006, the taxpayer collected $10,000 for January 2007 rents. In January 2007, the taxpayer collected $2,000 for December 2006 rents.

    c. In December 2006, the taxpayer paid office equipment insurance premiums of $30,000 for January–June 2007.

    d. In June 2006, the taxpayer purchased office furniture for $180,000. The taxpayer paid $36,000 in cash and gave a $144,000 interest-bearing note for the balance. The office furniture has an MACRS cost recovery period of seven years. The taxpayer made the § 179 election.

34. What accounting method (cash or accrual) would you recommend for the following businesses?

    a. An incorporated medical practice with annual gross receipts of $12 million.

    b. A hardware store with annual gross receipts of less than $1 million.

    c. A building contractor, who builds single-family houses, with annual gross receipts of $3 million.

    d. A grocery store with annual gross receipts of $4.5 million.

Decision Making   35. Pink Company, an architectural firm, has a bookkeeper who maintains a cash receipts and disbursements journal. At the end of the year, the company hires you to convert the cash receipts and disbursements into accrual basis revenues and expenses. The total cash receipts are summarized as follows:

Cash sales	$ 90,000
Collections on accounts receivable	300,000
Bank loan	30,000
Total cash receipts	$420,000

The accounts receivable from customers at the end of the year are $190,000. You note that the accounts receivable at the beginning of the year were $130,000. The cash sales included $30,000 of prepayments for services to be provided over the next 36 months (i.e., 12 months of such services relate to 2006).

a. Compute the company's accrual basis gross income for 2006.

b. Would you recommend that Pink use the cash method or the accrual method?

c. The company does not maintain an allowance for uncollectible accounts. Would you recommend that such an allowance be established for tax purposes?

36. How do the all events and economic performance requirements apply to the following transactions by an accrual basis taxpayer?

a. The company guarantees its products for six months. At the end of 2006, customers had made valid claims for $600,000 that were not paid until 2007. Also, the company estimates that another $400,000 in claims from 2006 sales will be filed and paid in 2007.

b. The accrual basis taxpayer reported $200,000 in corporate taxable income for 2006. The state income tax rate was 6%. The corporation paid $7,000 in estimated state income taxes in 2006 and paid $2,000 on 2005 state income taxes when it filed its 2005 state income tax return in March 2006. The company filed its 2006 state income return in March 2007 and paid the remaining $5,000 of its 2006 state income tax liability.

c. An employee was involved in an accident while making a sales call. The company paid the injured victim $15,000 in 2006 and agreed to pay the victim $15,000 a year for the next nine years.

37. Moss Company is a computer consulting firm. The company also sells equipment to its clients. The sales of equipment account for approximately 40% of the company's gross receipts. The company has consistently used the cash method to report its income from services and the accrual method to report its income from the sale of inventory. In June of the current year, Moss's accountant discovered that as a small business the company qualifies to use the cash method for all of its activities. The company is a calendar year taxpayer. As of the beginning of the current year, the company had $60,000 of inventory on hand and $50,000 of accounts receivable from the sales of equipment and $40,000 of receivables from the consulting services.

a. Compute the adjustment due to the change in accounting method.

b. Is the adjustment positive or negative? Explain.

c. When can the adjustment be taken into account in computing taxable income?

38. Crow Finance Company experiences bad debts of about 2% of its outstanding loans. At the end of the year, the company had outstanding receivables of $32 million. This balance included $3 million of accrued interest receivable. Crow's loan loss reserve for the year was computed as follows:

Decision Making

Balance, January 1, 2006	$600,000
Accounts written off as uncollectible	
Loans made in 2006	(60,000)
Loans made in prior years	(12,000)
Collections on loans previously written off	25,000
Adjustment to required balance	87,000
Balance, December 31, 2006	$640,000

a. Determine the effects of the above on Crow's taxable income for 2006.

b. Assume that Crow has used the reserve method to compute its taxable income for the 10 years the company has been in existence. In 2006, you begin preparing Crow's tax return. What should be done with regard to the reserve?

Communications

39. Jeffrey Boyd, the president of Eagle Furniture Company (average annual gross receipts of $4 million), has prepared the company's financial statements and income tax returns for the past 15 years. In July 2007, however, he hired you to prepare the 2006 corporate income tax return because he has not studied taxes for over 20 years and suspects the rules may have changed. Eagle uses the accrual method of accounting. Based on an initial examination of Eagle's trial balance and some account analyses, you have determined that the following items may require adjustments:

    - The company uses the FIFO inventory method, as valued at cost. However, all freight expenses on incoming merchandise have been expensed for the 15 years the company has been in business.
    - The company experiences inventory shrinkage (due to breakage and theft) of about 1% of sales each year. The shrinkage is not taken into account until the company takes a physical inventory each October, but the corporation's fiscal year ends January 31.
    - The company has used an allowance for uncollectible accounts, which has a balance of $60,000. In the past, the company has been able to accurately predict its actual bad debt expense.
    - The company sells a three-year service contract on its appliances. The company treats $1/36$ of the contract price as earned each month. At the beginning of the year, the company had $120,000 in its account for unearned revenues from the service contracts.
    - The company deducts its state income tax in the year paid. Thus, the 2006 state income tax expense includes the estimated taxes paid in 2006 and the additional amount paid in 2006 on 2005 taxes.

    Write a letter to Mr. Boyd explaining what adjustments will be required and how they will be implemented. The address of Eagle Furniture Company is 1000 East Maryland Street, Evansville, IL 47722.

Decision Making

40. Floyd, a cash basis taxpayer, has received an offer to purchase his land. The buyer will either pay him $100,000 at closing or pay $50,000 at closing and $52,000 one year after the date of closing. If Floyd recognizes the entire gain in the current year, his marginal tax rate will be 35% (combined Federal and state rates). However, if he spreads the gain over the two years, his marginal tax rate on the gain will be only 25%. Floyd does not consider the buyer a credit risk, but he realizes that the deferred payment will, in effect, earn only 4% interest ($2,000/$50,000 = 4%). Floyd believes he can earn a 10% before-tax rate of return on his after-tax cash. Floyd's adjusted basis for the land is $25,000, the buyer is also a cash basis taxpayer, and the short-term Federal rate is 4%. Floyd has asked you to evaluate the two alternatives on an after-tax basis.

41. Tom, a cash basis taxpayer, sold his unincorporated accounting practice for $600,000. The bases and fair market values of the assets sold were as follows:

Assets	Fair Market Value	Basis	
Office equipment	$ 50,000	Cost	$ 120,000
		Less: Depreciation	(100,000)
Office building	180,000	Cost	220,000
		Less: Depreciation	(100,000)
Land	100,000	Cost	40,000
Goodwill	270,000	Cost	–0–
Total	$600,000	Total	$ 180,000

The buyer paid $240,000 at closing and agreed to pay the balance with interest at 8% (exceeds the Federal rate) over 10 years. The office building was depreciated using the straight-line method. Thus, there is no § 1250 gain.
    a. Compute Tom's recognized gain in the year of the sale.
    b. Determine the character of the gain recognized in the year of the sale.

42. Kay, who is not a dealer, sold an apartment house to Polly during the current year (2006). The closing statement for the sale is as follows:

Total selling price		$ 150,000
Add: Polly's share of property taxes (6 months) paid by Kay		2,500
Less: Kay's 8% mortgage assumed by Polly	$55,000	
Polly's refundable binder ("earnest money") paid in 2005	1,000	
Polly's 8% installment note given to Kay	80,000	
Kay's real estate commissions and attorney's fees	7,500	(143,500)
Cash paid to Kay at closing		$ 9,000
Cash due from Polly = $9,000 + $7,500 expenses		$ 16,500

During 2006, Kay collected $4,000 in principal on the installment note and $2,000 of interest. Kay's basis in the property was $70,000 [$85,000 − $15,000 (depreciation)], and there was $9,000 in potential depreciation recapture under § 1250. The Federal rate is 6%.

    a.   Compute the following:
- 1. Total gain.
- 2. Contract price.
- 3. Payments received in the year of sale.
- 4. Recognized gain in the year of sale and the character of such gain.

        (*Hint:* Think carefully about the manner in which the property taxes are handled before you begin your computations.)

    b.   Same as (a)(2) and (3), except Kay's basis in the property was $45,000.

43. On June 30, 2006, Kelly sold property for $250,000 cash on the date of sale and a $750,000 note due on September 30, 2007. No interest was stated in the contract. The present value of the note (using 6.5%, which was the Federal rate) was $692,625. Kelly's basis in the property was $400,000, and $40,000 of the gain was depreciation recapture under § 1245. Expenses of the sale totaled $10,000, and Kelly was not a dealer in the property sold.

    a.   Compute Kelly's gain to be reported in 2006.

    b.   Compute Kelly's interest income for 2007.

44. On December 30, 2006, Father sold land to Son for $10,000 cash and a 7% installment note with a face amount of $260,000. In 2007, after paying $60,000 on the principal of the note, Son sold the land. In 2008, Son paid Father $40,000 on the note principal. Father's basis in the land was $90,000. Assuming Son sold the land for $350,000, compute Father's taxable gain in 2007.

45. George sold land to an unrelated party in 2005. His basis in the land was $40,000, and the selling price was $100,000—$25,000 payable at closing and $25,000 (plus 10% interest) due January 1, 2006, 2007, and 2008. What would be the tax consequences of the following? [Treat each part independently and assume (1) George did not elect out of the installment method and (2) the installment obligations have values equal to their face amounts.]

    a.   In 2006, George gave to his daughter the right to collect all future payments on the installment obligations.

    b.   In 2006, after collecting the payment due on January 1, George transferred the installment obligation to his 100%-controlled corporation in exchange for additional shares of stock.

    c.   On December 31, 2006, George received the payment due on January 1, 2007. On December 15, 2007, George died, and the remaining installment obligation was transferred to his estate. The estate collected the amount due on January 1, 2008.

46. The Dove Construction Company reports its income by the completed contract method. At the end of 2006, the company completed a contract to construct a building at a total cost of $750,000. The contract price was $1.2 million. However, the customer refused to accept the work and would not pay anything on the contract because he claimed the roof did not meet specifications. Dove's engineers estimated it would cost $140,000 to bring the roof up to the customer's standards. In 2007, the dispute was settled in the customer's favor; the roof was improved at a cost of $170,000, and the customer accepted the building and paid the $1.2 million.

    a.   What would be the effects of the above on Dove's taxable income for 2006 and 2007?

    b.   Same as (a), except Dove had $1.1 million accumulated cost under the contract at the end of 2006.

47. Rust Company is a real estate construction company with average annual gross receipts of $4 million. Rust uses the completed contract method, and the contracts require 18 months to complete.
    a. Which of the following costs would be allocated to construction in progress by Rust?
       1. The payroll taxes on direct labor.
       2. The current services pension costs for employees whose wages are included in direct labor.
       3. Accelerated depreciation on equipment used on contracts.
       4. Freight charges on materials assigned to contracts.
       5. The past service costs for employees whose wages are included in direct labor.
       6. Bidding expenses for contracts awarded.
    b. Assume that Rust generally builds commercial buildings under contracts with the owners and reports the income by the completed contract method. The company is considering building a series of similar stores for a retail chain. The gross profit margin would be a low percentage, but the company's gross receipts would triple. Write a letter to your client, Rust Company, explaining the tax accounting implications of entering into these contracts. Rust's mailing address is P.O. Box 1000, Harrisonburg, VA 22807.

48. Explain why the taxpayer may not be required to use the percentage of completion method in each of the following situations:
    a. The taxpayer agrees to build six aircraft. It takes six months to complete each aircraft, the price is $1.5 million per aircraft, and it will take 18 months to complete all six aircraft.
    b. A contract to produce and sell hot dogs at the Superbowl for the next two years.
    c. A contract to build an office building. The contractor's average annual gross receipts are approximately $3 million.

49. Ostrich Company makes gasoline storage tanks. Everything produced is under contract (that is, the company does not produce until it gets a contract for a product). Ostrich makes three basic models. However, the tanks must be adapted to each individual customer's location and needs (e.g., the location of the valves, the quality of the materials and insulation). Discuss the following issues relative to Ostrich's operations:
    a. An examining IRS agent contends that each of the company's contracts is to produce a "unique product." What difference does it make whether the product is unique or a "shelf item"?
    b. Producing one of the tanks takes over one year from start to completion, and the total cost is in excess of $1 million. What costs must be capitalized for this contract that are not subject to capitalization for a contract with a shorter duration and lower cost?
    c. What must Ostrich do with the costs of bidding on contracts?
    d. Ostrich frequently makes several cost estimates for a contract, using various estimates of materials costs. These costs fluctuate almost daily. Assuming Ostrich must use the percentage of completion method to report the income from the contract, what will be the consequence if the company uses the highest estimate of a contract's cost and the actual cost is closer to the lowest estimated cost?

50. Swallow Company is a large real estate construction company that reports its income by the percentage of completion method. In 2007, the company completed a contract at a total cost of $1.9 million. The contract price was $2.4 million. At the end of 2006, the year the contract was begun, Swallow estimated the total cost of the contract would be $2.1 million, and total accumulated costs on the contract at the end of 2006 were $1.4 million. The relevant tax rate is 34%, and the relevant Federal interest rate is 7%. Assume that all returns were filed and taxes were paid on March 15 following the close of the calendar tax year.
    a. Compute the gross profit on the contract for 2006 and 2007.
    b. Compute the lookback interest due with the 2007 return.
    c. Before bidding on a contract, Swallow generally makes three estimates of total contract costs: (1) optimistic, (2) pessimistic, and (3) most likely (based on a blending of optimistic and pessimistic assumptions). The company has asked you to write a letter explaining which of these estimates should be used for percentage of

completion purposes. In writing your letter, you should consider the fact that Swallow is incorporated and has made an S corporation election; therefore, the income and deductions flow through to the shareholders who are all individuals in the 35% marginal tax bracket. The relevant Federal interest rate is 8%. Swallow's mailing address is 400 Front Avenue, Ashland, OR 97520.

51. Bluebird Company is a furniture retailer whose average annual gross receipts for the three preceding years exceeded $10 million. In the current tax year, the company purchased merchandise with an invoice price of $12 million, less a 2% discount for early payment. However, the company had to borrow on a bank line of credit to take advantage of the discount for early payment. Freight on the merchandise totaled $360,000. The company has three stores and operates a warehouse where it stores goods. The cost of operating the warehouse was $300,000. The $300,000 includes labor, depreciation, taxes, and insurance on the building. The cost of the purchasing operations totaled $420,000. The jurisdiction where the company operates imposes a tax on inventories on hand as of January 1. The inventory tax for this year is $24,000. The invoice cost of goods on hand at the end of the year is $3 million. Compute Bluebird's ending inventory using the FIFO method.

52. Lavender Manufacturing Company began business in the current year. The company uses the simplified method to allocate mixed services costs to production. The company's costs and expenses for the year were as follows:

Decision Making

Direct labor	$1,750,000
Direct materials	2,500,000
Factory supervision	400,000
Personnel department	125,000
Computer operations	120,000
General administration	150,000
Marketing	100,000
Interest	25,000
	$5,170,000

a. Determine Lavender's total production costs for the year.
b. What suggestions can you offer regarding the allocation of the company's mixed services costs?

53. Copper Corporation is a calendar year taxpayer and uses the LIFO inventory method. In November a fire destroyed 25% of the company's raw materials inventory. The LIFO value of the company's inventory was $800,000, and its current replacement cost is $1 million. The company could continue operations until January without replacing the destroyed goods. Alternatively, it could acquire the replacement goods by the end of December. The latter option would increase storage costs. What would be the tax implications of this decision?

Decision Making

54. In 2006, Gail changed from the lower of cost or market FIFO method to the LIFO inventory method. The ending inventory for 2005 was computed as follows:

Item	FIFO Cost	Replacement Cost	Lower of Cost or Market
A	$21,000	$15,000	$15,000
B	50,000	66,000	50,000
C	30,000	3,000	3,000
			$68,000

Item C was damaged goods, and the replacement cost used was actually the estimated selling price of the goods. The actual cost to replace item C was $32,000.

a. What is the correct beginning inventory for 2006 under the LIFO method?
b. What immediate tax consequences (if any) will result from the switch to LIFO?

55. Amber Company has used the dollar-value LIFO technique for the past three years. The company has only one inventory pool. Its beginning inventory for the current year was computed as follows:

	Base Period Cost	LIFO Index	LIFO Layer
Base inventory	$1,250,000	1.0	$1,250,000
Year 1 layer	500,000	1.05	525,000
Year 2 layer	200,000	1.08	216,000
	$1,950,000		$1,991,000

The ending inventory is $1,955,000 at current period prices and $1,750,000 at base period prices. Determine the company's LIFO inventory value as of the end of the current year.

Decision Making

Communications

56. Your client, Bob Young, is negotiating a sale of investment real estate for $12 million. Bob believes that the buyer would pay cash of $8 million and a note for $4 million, or $3 million cash and a note for $9 million. The notes will pay interest at slightly above the market rate. Bob realizes that the second option involves more risks of collection, but he is willing to accept that risk if the tax benefits of the installment sale are substantial. Write a letter to Bob advising him of the tax consequences of choosing the lower down payment and larger note option, assuming he has no other installment receivables. Bob's address is 200 Jerdone, Gettysburg, PA 17325.

RESEARCH PROBLEMS

Note: Solutions to Research Problems can be prepared by using the **RIA Checkpoint® Student Edition** online research product, which is available to accompany this text. It is also possible to prepare solutions to the Research Problems by using tax research materials found in a standard tax library.

Research Problem 1.   Your client, a major supplier to a chain of grocery stores, needs funds for expansion. The client's major customer has offered to lend the funds with the condition that the principal amount will be reduced if the client supplies certain dollar amounts of products each year for the next four years. When you become aware of the negotiations between your client and the customer, you recall that sometimes what taxpayers consider a loan is treated as income for tax purposes. You are also aware of the *Indianapolis Power and Light* decision in which the Supreme Court held that amounts received from customers would be treated as loans.

Locate some cases describing conditions under which the funds received from the customer will be treated as income in the year of receipt rather than as a loan, and thus should be avoided.

Research Problem 2.   Your client is an accrual basis taxpayer. For 2006 the company had a $600,000 net operating loss, which can be carried back to 2004. The loss can also be carried back to the 2004 state income tax return and will create a $36,000 refund of state income taxes for that year. The IRS agent insists that the state income tax refund must be included in 2006 gross income (under the tax benefit rule) and thus will reduce the 2006 Federal income tax loss available for carryback by $36,000. When does the income from the state tax refund accrue?

Research Problem 3.   Your client, April, is a real estate developer. Usually, she begins development immediately after purchasing land. Recently, however, she purchased some property and has decided to wait at least one year before beginning development. April would like to know if she can deduct the costs of holding the property (insurance, taxes, and interest) while she is awaiting the appropriate time to begin development.

Partial list of research aids:
Von-Lusk, 104 T.C. 207 (1995).

Research Problem 4.   Your client is a manufacturer. For several years, the company buried empty paint cans on its property. The paint was used in the production process. Recently, a state environmental agency informed the company that it was required to dig up the paint cans and decontaminate the land. The company spent a substantial amount for this environmental cleanup in the current year. An IRS agent contends that the cost must be added to the basis in the land because the cleanup improved the land. The company's CFO has asked you to determine if any authority exists that would support a current deduction for these costs.

Research Problem 5.   In 2006, your client, Clear Corporation, changed from the cash to the accrual method of accounting for its radio station. The company had a positive § 481 adjustment of $2.4 million as a result of the change and began amortizing the adjustment in 2006. In 2007, Clear received an offer to purchase the assets of the radio station business (this would be considered a sale of a trade or business under § 1060). If the offer is accepted, Clear plans to purchase a satellite television business. Clear has asked you to explain the consequences of the sale of the radio station on the amortization of the § 481 adjustment.

Use the tax resources of the Internet to address the following questions. Do not restrict your search to the World Wide Web, but include a review of newsgroups and general reference materials, practitioner sites and resources, primary sources of the tax law, chat rooms and discussion groups, and other opportunities.

Internet
Activity

Research Problem 6.   What are the number and title of the IRS publication on accounting periods and methods?

Research Problem 7.   Your new client is an S corporation engaged in construction and is required to use the percentage of completion method. Your supervisor has informed you that the client should use the "simplified marginal impact method" to compute lookback interest on completed contracts. You are not familiar with the method. Using a search engine, locate a short explanation of this method.

CHAPTER 19

Deferred Compensation

LEARNING OBJECTIVES

After completing Chapter 19, you should be able to:

LO.1
Distinguish between qualified (defined contribution and defined benefit) and nonqualified compensation arrangements.

LO.2
Identify the qualification requirements for qualified plans.

LO.3
Discuss the tax consequences of qualified plans.

LO.4
Calculate the limitations on contributions to and benefits from qualified plans.

LO.5
Understand the qualified plan (Keogh plan) available to a self-employed person.

LO.6
Describe the benefits of the different types of Individual Retirement Accounts (IRAs).

LO.7
Understand the rationale for nonqualified deferred compensation plans and the related tax treatment.

LO.8
Explain the value of restricted property plans.

LO.9
Differentiate the tax treatment of qualified and nonqualified stock options.

LO.10
Identify tax planning opportunities available with deferred compensation.

OUTLINE

Compensation is important in any type of organization. If you have not chosen a career, consider becoming a professional basketball player. According to *Forbes*, 4 of the 10 highest-paid athletes in 2004 were basketball players: Michael Jordan ($35 million), Shaquille O'Neal ($31.9 million), Kevin Garnett ($29.7 million), and Kobe Bryant ($26.1 million).[1] At the top of this list, however, was golfer Tiger Woods ($80.3 million), followed by German auto racer Michael Schumacher ($80 million) and football quarterback Peyton Manning ($42 million). In 2004, Manning signed a seven-year $99 million contract that included a $34.5 million signing bonus to be received in the first year. For comparison, a second lieutenant in the U.S. Army receives approximately $40,000 (after factoring in the exclusion benefit for the meal and housing allowance), and an entry-level accountant earns approximately $45,000.

But consider the plight of the Texas Rangers who signed pitcher Chan Ho Park to a five-year $65 million contract in 2002. In his first three seasons, he pitched in only 40 games. For his first $32 million, Park produced these performance statistics:

Cost per victory earned	$2.7 million
Cost per inning pitched	$142,222
Cost per strikeout	$184,971

Before he was traded to the San Diego Padres in 2005, Park had pitched 109.2 innings in 20 games, with an ERA of 5.66. Thus, high compensation does not always produce outstanding results. As New York Yankees manager Joe Torre says, "Players often lose their humanity in inverse proportion to their salaries. The higher the salary, the lower the allowance for human frailties."

Before you decide to give up your future career in accounting, education, or the military and jump into major league sports, also consider the tax consequences. A professional athlete's lifetime sports income is compressed into about 10 years. For example, tennis star Pete Sampras, a 14-time Grand Slam winner, retired in

[1]"The Best Paid Athletes," http://www.Forbes.com/2004/06/23/04_athletes/and.html.

2003 at the age of 32. Yet income averaging is not allowed for Federal income tax purposes. As a result, the athlete will lose a larger portion of lifetime earned income in the form of taxes than someone with a comparable amount of earned income over a typical worklife cycle. The athlete does, however, have a method available for reducing the Federal income tax liability in the form of deferred compensation.

This chapter discusses the various types of deferred compensation arrangements available to employees and self-employed individuals. With deferred compensation, an employee receives compensation for services in a later period than that in which the services were performed—quite often during retirement years. The tax law encourages employers to offer deferred compensation plans to their employees to supplement the Federal Social Security retirement system.

Qualified deferred compensation plans receive particularly favorable tax treatment. The amounts that may be deferred under these plans are limited, so they might not be perfect for Tiger Woods or Peyton Manning. For employers and more traditional employees, however, they provide tax advantages that are exceedingly helpful. For example, contributors to qualified pension, profit sharing, or stock bonus plans receive three major tax advantages:

- Contributions are immediately deductible by the employer.
- Employees are not taxed until these funds are made available to them.
- Income earned by the plan trust, which has received the contributions, is not subject to tax until made available to the employees.

A variety of deferred compensation arrangements are being offered to employees, including the following:

- Qualified profit sharing plans.
- Qualified pension plans.
- Cash or deferred arrangement plans.
- SIMPLE IRAs and § 401(k) plans.
- Tax-deferred annuities.
- Incentive stock option plans.
- Nonqualified deferred compensation plans.
- Restricted property plans.
- Cafeteria benefit plans.

In addition to the various types of deferred compensation, employees may receive other valuable fringe benefits, some of which may be tax-free. Examples of such benefits include group term life insurance, medical reimbursement plans, company-supplied automobiles, education expense reimbursement plans, employee stock purchase plans, and group legal services.[2]

Qualified Pension, Profit Sharing, and Stock Bonus Plans

LO.1

Distinguish between qualified (defined contribution and defined benefit) and nonqualified compensation arrangements.

To ensure that retired people will not be dependent solely on government programs, the Federal government encourages private pension and profit sharing plans. Therefore, the Federal tax law provides substantial tax benefits for plans that meet certain requirements (qualified plans). The major requirement for qualification is that a plan not discriminate in favor of highly compensated employees.

Types of Plans

The tax law defines four types of qualified plans: pension, profit sharing, stock bonus, and cash balance plans.

---

[2]Refer to the discussions in Chapters 4 and 5.

TAX *in the News*   **COMPENSATION AND PERFORMANCE**

When one or several employees have huge salaries compared to the other employees, the business may not succeed in achieving its mission. Matt Bloom, a management professor at the University of Notre Dame, says that the bigger the pay difference between a major league baseball team's stars and scrubs, the worse its record. According to Bloom, more parity in performance pay will result in a better baseball team. Big pay differentials sow the seeds of discord rather than promoting team unity.

Big pay differentials may also sow the seeds of discord rather than promoting a team's success in other sports. Once again, in 2005 high salaries did not guarantee success in professional basketball. The N.Y. Knicks, with the highest payroll of $94 million, did not even make the playoffs and were ranked 27th out of 30 teams in terms of efficiency (lowest cost per regular season win). Only one team in the top five payroll rankings made the playoffs (the Dallas Mavericks). The San Antonio Spurs won it all and were the second most efficient team. The Detroit Pistons who lost to San Antonio in seven games were ranked 4th in terms of efficiency. In other words, Detroit and San Antonio were, respectively, 18th and 21st in payroll salary out of 30 teams. The two teams had only one player in the top 25 highest-paid players. Tim Duncan with San Antonio was ranked 20th with a salary of $14.2 million.

Payroll Rankings (in Millions)	Regular Season Games Won	Cost per Regular Season Win
1. N.Y. Knicks ($94)	45	$2,088,889
2. Dallas Mavericks ($87.4)	34	2,570,588
3. Portland Trail Blazers ($80.2)	54	1,485,185
4. Minnesota Timberwolves ($70.1)	45	1,557,778
5. Orlando Magic ($68.1)	42	1,621,429
6. Indiana Pacers ($66.3)	59	1,123,729
7. Los Angeles Lakers ($65.1)	30	2,170,000
8. Philadelphia 76ers ($63.8)	37	1,724,324
9. Sacramento Kings ($60.6)	49	1,236,735
10. Miami Heat ($59.5)	26	2,288,462
18. Detroit Pistons ($49.3)	54	912,963
21. San Antonio Spurs ($47.4)	59	803,390
29. Phoenix Suns ($35.3)	62	569,355
30. Charlotte Bobcats ($23.1)	18	1,283,333

Source: *Adapted from Gordon Fairclough, "Listen Up, Managers; Fat Paychecks Don't Always Guarantee Success,"* Wall Street Journal, *March 23, 1999, p. B1;* **http://asp.usatoday.com/sports/basketball/nba/salaries/default.aspx.**

Pension Plans. A **pension plan** is a deferred compensation arrangement that provides for systematic payments of definitely determinable retirement benefits to employees who meet the requirements set forth in the plan. Benefits are generally measured by and based on such factors as years of service and employee compensation. Employer contributions under a qualified pension plan must *not* depend on profits. In addition, they must be sufficient to provide definitely determinable benefits on some actuarial basis (except for a defined contribution pension plan).

There are basically two types of qualified pension plans: defined benefit plans and defined contribution plans.

A **defined benefit plan** includes a formula that defines the benefits employees are to receive.[3] Under such a plan, an employer must make annual contributions based upon actuarial computations that will be sufficient to pay the required retirement benefits. If a plan document permits, employees may make contributions to

---

[3]§ 414(j).

the pension fund. A separate account is not maintained for each participant. A defined benefit plan provides some sense of security for employees since the benefits may be expressed in fixed dollar amounts.

A defined contribution pension plan (or money purchase plan) defines the amount the employer is required to contribute (e.g., a flat dollar amount, an amount based on a special formula, or an amount equal to a certain percentage of compensation). A separate account must be maintained for each participant. Benefits are based solely on (1) the amount contributed and (2) income from the fund that accrues to the participant's account.[4] Consequently, actuarial calculations are not required to determine the employer's annual contribution. Upon retirement, an employee's pension amount depends on the value of his or her account. Although it is not mandatory, a plan may require or permit employee contributions to the pension fund.

EXAMPLE 1

The qualified pension plan of Rose Company calls for both the employer and the employee to contribute annually to the pension trust an amount equal to 5% of the employee's compensation. Since the employer's rate of contribution is fixed, this pension plan is a defined contribution plan. If the plan called for contributions sufficient to provide retirement benefits equal to 30% of the employee's average salary for the last five years of employment, it would be a defined benefit plan. ■

Concept Summary 19–1 compares and contrasts a defined benefit plan and a defined contribution plan.

Profit Sharing Plans. A profit sharing plan is a deferred compensation arrangement established and maintained by an employer to provide for employee participation in the company's profits. Contributions are paid from the employer's current or accumulated profits to a trustee and are commingled in a single trust fund. Thus, an employer does not have to have a profit for the current year to make a contribution (the contribution can be from accumulated profits).

In a profit sharing plan, a separate account is maintained for each participant. The plan must provide a definite, predetermined formula for allocating the contributions made to the trustee among the participants. Likewise, it must include a definite, predetermined formula for distributing the accumulated funds after a fixed number of years, on the attainment of a stated age, or on the occurrence of certain events such as illness, layoff, or retirement. A company is not required to contribute a definite, predetermined amount to the plan, although substantial and recurring contributions must be made to meet the permanency requirement. Forfeitures arising under this plan do not have to be used to reduce the employer's contribution. Instead, forfeitures may be used to increase the individual accounts of the remaining participants as long as these increases do not result in prohibited discrimination.[5] Since a profit sharing plan does not necessarily emphasize retirement income, benefits to employees may normally be distributed through lump-sum payouts.

Stock Bonus Plans. A stock bonus plan is another form of deferred compensation. The employer establishes and maintains the plan in order to contribute shares of its stock. The contributions need not be dependent on the employer's profits. A stock bonus plan is subject to the same requirements as a profit sharing plan for purposes of allocating and distributing the stock among the employees.[6] Any benefits of the plan are distributable in the form of stock of the employer company, except that distributable fractional shares may be paid in cash.

Cash Balance Plans. A cash balance plan is a controversial hybrid form of pension plan that is similar in many aspects to a defined benefit plan. These new plans

---

[4]§ 414(i).
[5]Reg. §§ 1.401–1(b) and 1.401–4(a)(1)(iii).

[6]Reg. § 1.401–1(b)(1)(iii).

CONCEPT SUMMARY   19–1

Defined Benefit Plan and Defined Contribution Plan Compared

Defined Benefit Plan	Defined Contribution Plan
Includes a pension plan.	Includes profit sharing, stock bonus, money purchase, target benefit, qualified cash or deferred compensation, employee stock ownership plans, and some pension plans.
Determinable benefits based upon years of service and average compensation. Benefits calculated by a formula.	An account for each participant. Ultimate benefits depend upon contributions and investment performance.
Maximum annual *benefits* payable may not exceed the smaller of (1) $175,000 (in 2006)* or (2) 100% of the participant's average earnings in the three highest years of employment.	Maximum annual *contribution* to an account may not exceed the smaller of (1) $44,000** (in 2006) or (2) 100% of the participant's compensation (25% for a profit sharing plan, money purchase plan, or stock bonus plan).
Forfeitures must reduce subsequent funding costs and cannot increase the benefits any participant can receive under the plan.	Forfeitures may be allocated to the accounts of remaining participants.
Subject to minimum funding requirement in order to avoid penalties.	Exempt from funding requirements.
Greater administrative and actuarial costs and greater reporting requirements.	Costs and reporting requirements less burdensome.
Subject to plan termination insurance.	Not subject to plan termination insurance.
More favorable to employees who are older when plan is adopted since it is possible to fund higher benefits over a shorter period.	More favorable to younger employees since, over a longer period, higher benefits may result.

*This amount is subject to indexing annually in $5,000 increments.

**This amount is subject to indexing annually in $1,000 increments.

are funded by the employer, and the employer bears the investment risks and rewards. Thus, the employer bears the mortality risk if an employee elects to receive benefits in the form of an annuity and lives beyond normal life expectancy. But like defined contribution plans, a cash balance plan establishes allocations to individual accounts. The payout for an employee depends on how much builds up over time in the employee's account and not on a formula based on years of service and pre-retirement pay. Cash balance plans are better for younger, mobile employees, but the companies save money by reducing pension payouts for older and longer-service employees.

ETHICAL Considerations   DO CASH BALANCE PLANS DISCRIMINATE AGAINST OLDER EMPLOYEES?

Older employees often suffer under both state and Federal laws when employers convert traditional pension plans to cash balance plans. Under a traditional pension plan, a company adopts a formula that calculates pension benefits by multiplying years of service by a factor based on average salary, which causes benefits to escalate rapidly in value in later years. Should companies be allowed to reduce a long-term employee's benefits significantly by converting to a cash balance plan?

Qualification Requirements

To be *qualified*, and thereby to receive favorable tax treatment, a plan must satisfy the following requirements:

- Exclusive benefit requirement.
- Nondiscrimination requirements.
- Participation and coverage requirements.
- Vesting requirements.
- Distribution requirements.

These qualification rules are highly technical and numerous. Thus, an employer should submit a retirement plan to the IRS for a determination letter regarding the qualified status of the plan and trust. A favorable determination letter may be expected within 6 to 12 months, indicating that the plan meets the qualification requirements and that the trust is tax-exempt. However, the continued qualification of the plan depends upon its actual operations. Therefore, the operations of the plan should be reviewed periodically.

Nondiscrimination Requirements. The contributions and benefits under a plan must *not discriminate* in favor of highly compensated employees. A plan is not considered discriminatory merely because contributions and benefits are proportional to compensation.[7] For example, a pension plan that provides for the allocation of employer contributions based upon a flat 3 percent of each employee's compensation would not be discriminatory even though highly paid employees receive greater benefits.

Participation and Coverage Requirements. A qualified plan must provide, at a minimum, that all employees in the covered group who are 21 years of age are eligible to participate after completing one year of service. A year of service is generally defined as the completion of 1,000 hours of service within a measuring period of 12 consecutive months. As an alternative, where the plan provides that 100 percent of an employee's accrued benefits will be vested upon entering the plan, the employee's participation may be postponed until the later of age 21 or two years from the date of employment. Once the age and service requirements are met, an employee must begin participating no later than the *earlier* of the following:

- The first day of the first plan year beginning after the date on which the requirements were satisfied.
- Six months after the date on which the requirements were satisfied.[8]

EXAMPLE 2

Coffee Corporation has a calendar year retirement plan covering its employees. The corporation adopts the most restrictive eligibility rules permitted. Wilma, age 21, is hired on January 31, 2005, and meets the service requirement over the next 12 months (completes at least 1,000 hours by January 31, 2006). Wilma must be included in this plan no later than July 31, 2006, because the six-month limitation would be applicable. If the company had adopted the two-year participation rule, Wilma must be included in the plan no later than July 31, 2007. ∎

Since a qualified plan must be primarily for the benefit of employees and be nondiscriminatory, the plan has to cover a reasonable percentage of the company employees. A plan will be qualified only if it satisfies one of the following tests:[9]

- The plan benefits at least 70 percent of all non-highly compensated employees (the *percentage test*).

---

[7]§§ 401(a)(4) and (5).
[8]§§ 410(a)(1)(A) and (B) and 410(a)(4).
[9]§ 410(b).

- The plan benefits a percentage of non-highly compensated employees equal to at least 70 percent of the percentage of highly compensated employees benefiting under the plan (the *ratio test*).
- The plan meets the *average benefits test*, which is described below.

If a company has no highly compensated employees, the retirement plan will automatically satisfy the coverage rules.

To satisfy the *average benefits test*, the plan must benefit any employees who qualify under a classification set up by the employer and found by the Secretary of the Treasury not to be discriminatory in favor of highly compensated employees (the *classification test*). In addition, the average benefit percentage for non-highly compensated employees must be at least 70 percent of the average benefit percentage for highly compensated employees. The *average benefit percentage* means, with respect to any group of employees, the average of the benefit percentages calculated separately for each employee in the group. The term *benefit percentage* means the employer-provided contributions (including forfeitures) or benefits of an employee under all qualified plans of the employer, expressed as a percentage of that employee's compensation.

An employee is a **highly compensated employee** if, at any time during the year or the preceding year, the employee satisfies *either* of the following:[10]

- Was a 5 percent owner of the company.
- Received more than $100,000 (in 2006) in annual compensation from the employer *and* was a member of the top-paid group of the employer.[11] The top-paid group clause is applicable only if the employer elects to have it apply. An employee whose compensation is in the top 20 percent of the employees is a member of the top-paid group.

An additional *minimum participation test* must also be met. A plan must cover at least 40 percent of all employees or, if fewer, at least 50 employees on one representative day of the plan year. In determining all employees, nonresident aliens, certain union members, and employees not fulfilling the minimum age or years-of-service requirement of the plan may be excluded.[12]

EXAMPLE 3

Rust Corporation's retirement plan meets the 70% test (the percentage test) because 70% of all non-highly compensated employees are benefited. The company has 100 employees, but only 38 of these employees are covered by the plan. Therefore, this retirement plan does not meet the minimum participation requirement. ∎

Vesting Requirements. The purpose of the **vesting requirements** is to protect an employee who has worked a reasonable period of time for an employer from losing employer contributions because of being fired or changing jobs. An employee's right to accrued benefits derived from his or her own contributions must be nonforfeitable from the date of contribution. The accrued benefits derived from employer contributions must be nonforfeitable in accordance with one of *two alternative minimum vesting schedules* [except for § 401(m) arrangements].

To satisfy the *first alternative*, a participant must have a nonforfeitable right to 100 percent of his or her accrued benefits derived from employer contributions upon completion of not more than five years of service (five-year or cliff vesting). The *second alternative* is satisfied if a participant has a nonforfeitable right at least equal to a percentage of the accrued benefits derived from employer contributions as depicted in Table 19–1 (graded vesting). Of the two alternatives, cliff vesting minimizes administration expenses for a company and provides more vesting for a long-term employee.

---

[10]§§ 401(a)(4) and 414(q).

[11]The $100,000 amount is indexed annually.

[12]§§ 401(a)(26) and 410(b)(3) and (4).

TABLE 19–1	Three- to Seven-Year Vesting

Years of Service	Nonforfeitable Percentage
3	20%
4	40%
5	60%
6	80%
7 or more	100%

TABLE 19–2	Two- to Six-Year Vesting

Years of Service	Nonforfeitable Percentage
2	20%
3	40%
4	60%
5	80%
6	100%

EXAMPLE 4

Mitch has six years of service completed as of February 2, 2006, his employment anniversary date. If his defined benefit plan has a five-year (cliff) vesting schedule, 100% of Mitch's accrued benefits are vested. If the plan uses the graded vesting rule, Mitch's nonforfeitable percentage is 80%. ∎

Certain § 401(k) plans must meet faster minimum vesting schedules (i.e., two- to six-year graded vesting, as shown in Table 19–2, or three-year cliff vesting). These faster minimum vesting schedules apply to defined contribution plans that include a "§ 401(m) arrangement." In such an arrangement, an employee may make voluntary after-tax contributions, and the employer may provide matching contributions with respect to the employee's elective deferrals. Any amounts attributable to the employer matching contributions must vest at least as rapidly as a three-year cliff vesting schedule or the six-year graded vesting schedule.

EXAMPLE 5

Assume the same facts as in Example 4, except that Mitch has a § 401(k) plan with a § 401(m) arrangement. Here Mitch must be 100% vested with six years of service under the six-year graded vesting schedule. ∎

Distribution Requirements. Uniform *minimum distribution rules* exist for all qualified defined benefit and defined contribution plans, traditional Individual Retirement Accounts (IRAs) and annuities, unfunded deferred compensation plans of state and local governments and tax-exempt employers, and tax-sheltered custodial accounts and annuities. Distributions to a participant must begin by April 1 of the calendar year *following the later* of (1) the calendar year in which the employee attains age 70½ or (2) the calendar year in which the employee retires. Thus, an employee can delay receiving distributions until retirement. However, distributions to a 5 percent owner or a traditional IRA holder must begin no later than April 1 of the calendar year *following* the year in which the 5 percent owner or the

---

TAX *in the News*   **UNDERFUNDED PENSION PLANS MULTIPLY**

In May 2005, UAL, the parent of United Airlines, terminated four of its underfunded defined benefit plans with the permission of a bankruptcy court. Thus, UAL transferred the plans' liabilities of $6.6 billion to the Pension Benefit Guaranty Corporation (PBGC). The PBGC is a government corporation under the Employee Retirement Security Act (ERISA), but it is not backed by the Federal government. In 2000, the PBGC had a surplus of $9.7 billion, but UAL's liabilities created an immediate cumulative deficit of $23.3 billion for the corporation. Other financially distressed airlines (e.g., Delta) may also transfer their pension obligations to the PBGC. Near the end of 2004, the PBGC had a potential exposure of another $96 billion.

Source: *Adapted from Solvency of the Pension Benefit Guaranty Corporation—Current Financial Condition and Potential Risks: Hearing before the Senate Committee on the Budget (Statement of Dr. Douglas Holtz-Eakin, 109th Cong. 1st Sess., 2005), available at* **http://www.senate.gov/~budget/republican/hearingarchive/testimonies/2005/20050615-CBO.pdf**.

IRA holder reaches age 70½.[13] A holder of a Roth IRA does *not* have to take a distribution by April 1 of the calendar year following the calendar year in which the holder attains age 70½. That is, there is no point in time at which the holder of a Roth IRA must begin receiving distributions.

Minimum annual distributions must be made over the life of the participant or the lives of the participant and a designated individual beneficiary. The amount of the required minimum distribution for a particular year is determined by dividing the account balance as of December 31 of the prior year by the applicable life expectancy. The life expectancy of the owner and his or her beneficiary is based upon the expected return multiples in the Regulations, using ages attained within the calendar year the participant reaches age 70½.[14]

EXAMPLE 6

Beth reaches age 70½ in 2006, and she will also be age 71 in 2006. Her retirement account has a balance of $120,000 on December 31, 2005. If Beth is retired, a 5% owner, or the holder of a traditional IRA, she must withdraw $7,843 for the 2006 calendar year, assuming her multiple is 15.3 ($120,000 ÷ 15.3). This distribution need not be made until April 1, 2007, but a second distribution must be made by December 31, 2007. ■

Failure to make a minimum required distribution to a particular participant results in a *50 percent nondeductible excise tax* on the excess in any taxable year of the amount that should have been distributed over the amount that actually was distributed. The tax is imposed on the individual required to take the distribution (the payee).[15] The Secretary of the Treasury is authorized to waive the tax for a given taxpayer year if the taxpayer is able to establish that the shortfall is due to reasonable error and that reasonable steps are being taken to remedy the shortfall.

If a taxpayer receives an *early distribution* from a qualified retirement plan, a 10 percent additional tax is levied on the full amount of any distribution includible in gross income.[16] For this purpose, the term *qualified retirement plan* includes a qualified defined benefit plan or defined contribution plan, a tax-sheltered annuity or custodial account, or a traditional IRA. The following distributions, however, are *not* treated as early distributions:

- Distributions made on or after the date the employee attains age 59½.
- Distributions made to a beneficiary (or the estate of an employee) on or after the death of the employee.

---

[13]§ 401(a)(9).
[14]Reg. § 1.72–9. Refer to Chapter 4.
[15]§ 4974(a).
[16]§ 72(t). See Ltr.Rul. 8837071.

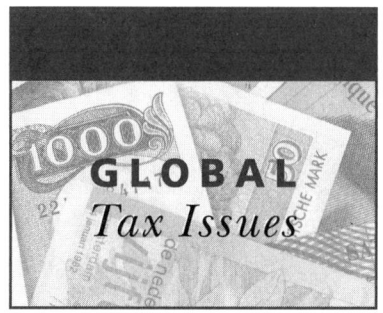

> **COVERING EXPATRIATE EMPLOYEES**
>
> Can an employer cover individuals employed outside the United States in a qualified retirement plan? This question often arises when an employee is transferred from the United States to a foreign affiliate of the employer.
>
> The hurdle to overcome is the exclusive benefit rule in § 401(a): the qualified plan must be maintained for the exclusive benefit of the employees of the company that sponsors the plan.
>
> If a company conducts its foreign operations through branches that are part of the U.S. entity, the employee can qualify for the plan. Likewise, all employees of all corporations that are members of a controlled group of corporations can be covered. A controlled group would include both a brother-sister group and a parent-subsidiary group.

GLOBAL Tax Issues

- Distributions attributable to the employee's being disabled.
- Distributions made as part of a scheduled series of substantially equal periodic payments (made not less frequently than annually) for the life of the participant (or the joint lives of the participant and the participant's beneficiary).
- Distributions made to an employee after separation from service because of early retirement under the plan after attaining age 55. This exception to early distribution treatment does not apply to a traditional IRA.
- Distributions used to pay medical expenses to the extent that the expenses are deductible under § 213 (determined regardless of whether or not the taxpayer itemizes deductions).
- IRA distributions that are used to pay qualified higher education expenses of the taxpayer, the spouse, or any child or grandchild of the taxpayer or the taxpayer's spouse.
- IRA distributions up to $10,000 that are used to pay expenses incurred by qualified first-time home buyers.

Tax Consequences to the Employee and Employer

LO.3

Discuss the tax consequences of qualified plans.

In General. Although employer contributions to qualified plans are generally deductible immediately (subject to contribution and deductibility rules), these amounts are not subject to taxation until distributed to employees.[17] If benefits are paid with respect to an employee (to a creditor of the employee, a child of the employee, etc.), the benefits paid are treated as if paid to the employee. When benefits are distributed to employees, or paid with respect to an employee, the employer does not receive another deduction.

The tax benefit to the employee amounts to a substantial tax deferral and may be viewed as an interest-free loan from the government to the trust fund. Another advantage of a qualified plan is that any income earned by the trust is not taxable to the trust.[18] Employees, in effect, are taxed on such earnings when they receive the retirement benefits.

The taxation of amounts received by employees in periodic or installment payments is generally subject to the annuity rules in § 72 (refer to Chapter 4). In most situations, employee contributions have been subject to tax previously and are therefore included in the employee's *investment in the contract.* Two other alternative options are available for benefit distributions. A taxpayer may (1) receive the distribution in a lump-sum payment or (2) roll over the benefits into an IRA or another qualified employer retirement plan.

---

[17]§ 402(a)(1).   [18]§ 501(a).

Lump-Sum Distributions from Qualified Plans.

A lump-sum distribution occurs when an employee receives his or her entire payout from a qualified plan in a single payment rather than receiving the amount in installments. The annuity rules do not apply to a lump-sum distribution. All such payments are taxed in one year. Since lump-sum payments have been accumulated over a number of years, bunching retirement benefits into one taxable year may impose a high tax burden because of progressive rates. To overcome this bunching effect, for many years the tax law has provided favorable treatment for certain lump-sum distributions. Major changes were made in the lump-sum distribution rules by TRA of 1986. Transitional provisions allow a participant who reached age 50 before January 1, 1986 (born before 1936), to elect the pre-1987 rules on a limited basis.

Under the *pre-1987 rules*, the taxable amount is allocated between a capital gain portion and an ordinary income portion (which may be subject to a special 10-year averaging treatment).[19] That portion attributable to the employee's service before 1974 qualifies for capital gain treatment. That portion attributable to the employee's service after 1973 is included as ordinary income when received and may be taxed under the 10-year averaging provision. An employee must be a plan participant for at least 5 years to take advantage of the 10-year averaging option.

An employee may *elect* to forgo the capital gain treatment and treat all of the distribution as ordinary income subject to the 10-year forward averaging provision.[20] In some instances, ordinary income treatment is preferable to long-term capital gain treatment because of the favorable averaging technique.

Special preferential 10-year averaging treatment of qualified lump-sum distributions can be used *only once* during a recipient's lifetime. In the case of a small lump-sum distribution, a recipient may prefer to pay ordinary income tax on the amount and save the averaging election for a possible larger lump-sum distribution in the future.

To determine the tax on a lump-sum distribution, it is necessary to compute the taxable portion of the distribution by subtracting employee contributions and the net unrealized appreciation in the value of any distributed securities of the employer corporation.[21] The taxable amount is then reduced by a minimum distribution allowance to arrive at the amount that is eligible for the 10-year income averaging provisions.[22] The following portion of the lump-sum distribution is treated as a long-term capital gain:

$$\text{Taxable amount} \times \frac{\text{Years of service before 1974}}{\text{Total years of service}}$$

(computed without being reduced by the minimum distribution allowance)

The applicable capital gain rate is 20 percent.

A five-year forward averaging rule that was available for recipients born either before 1936 or after 1935 has been repealed for tax years beginning after December 31, 1999.[23]

EXAMPLE 7

Esteban, age 71 and married, retires at the end of 2006 and receives a lump-sum distribution of $100,000 from his company's profit sharing plan. This plan includes $5,000 of his own contributions and $10,000 of unrealized appreciation on his employer's common stock. Esteban was a participant in the plan for 35 years. Since Esteban attained age 50 before January 1, 1986, he is

---

[19]§ 402(e)(1)(C) of the IRC of 1954.

[20]§ 402(e)(4)(L).

[21]Section 402(e)(4)(J) provides that before any distribution a taxpayer may elect not to have this subtraction associated with employer securities apply.

[22]Section 402(e)(1)(D) defines the *minimum distribution allowance* as the smaller of $10,000 or one-half of the total taxable amount of the lump-sum distribution,

reduced by 20% of the amount, if any, by which such total taxable amount exceeds $20,000. Thus, for lump-sum distributions of $70,000 or more, there will be no minimum distribution allowance.

[23]The grandfathered 10-year averaging and capital gains provisions for participants who attained age 50 by January 1, 1986, are retained.

CONCEPT SUMMARY 19–2

Model for Lump-Sum Distribution Computation

1. Start with the total lump-sum distribution and deduct any employee contributions and unrealized appreciation in employer securities.
2. Divide the result into the capital gain portion and the ordinary income portion.*
3. Multiply the capital gain portion by the capital gain rate of 20%.
4. Reduce the ordinary income portion by the minimum distribution allowance.
5. Divide the ordinary income portion into 10 equal portions.
6. Compute the tax on the result in step 5 using the 1986 Tax Rate Schedule for single taxpayers.
7. Multiply the resulting tax by 10.
8. Add the results in steps 3 and 7.

*In certain circumstances, none of the taxable amount of the distribution will be eligible for capital gain treatment. In other circumstances, the taxpayer may choose to treat none of the taxable amount as capital gain even though part could qualify.

eligible to elect the pre-1987 10-year forward averaging technique (using 1986 rates and the **zero bracket amount**). Refer to the computation model in Concept Summary 19–2.

Taxable portion of the lump-sum distribution		$85,000
Less: Minimum distribution allowance (½ of the taxable amount up to $20,000)	$10,000	
Less: 20% of the taxable amount in excess of $20,000: 20% × ($85,000 − $20,000)	(13,000)	
Minimum distribution allowance		–0–
Taxable amount		$85,000
Computation of tax under 10-year averaging:		
Long-term capital gain portion:		

$$\$85{,}000 \times \frac{2 \text{ (service before 1974)}}{35 \text{(total service years)}} = \$4{,}857 \times .20 = \qquad \$\ \ \ 971$$

Ordinary income portion:		
10 times the tax on $10,494[24]		
[1/10 ($85,000 − $4,857) + $2,480]		11,127
Tax on lump-sum distribution		$12,098

Thus, Esteban's capital gain on the distribution is $4,857 and is subject to a 20% capital gain rate. Here Esteban may wish to elect to treat the entire distribution as ordinary income using the 10-year forward averaging approach rather than taxing the capital gain portion at the 20% capital gain rate. The tax liability of $11,905 would be less than the previously calculated tax liability of $12,098. The capital gain on the unrealized appreciation in the employer's common stock is not taxable until Esteban sells the stock. In essence, the cost basis of the securities to the trust becomes the tax basis to the employee.[25] If Esteban keeps the securities until he dies, there may be some income tax savings on this gain to the extent his estate or heirs obtain a step-up in basis. ∎

---

[24]In making the tax computation, it is necessary to use the 1986 Tax Rate Schedule for single taxpayers and to add $2,480 (the zero bracket amount) to the taxable income. Thus, the tax was computed on $10,494, which is $8,014 (1/10 of $80,143) plus $2,480. Note that the tax rates provided in the instructions for Form 4972 (Tax on Lump-Sum Distributions) have already

been adjusted for the zero bracket amount (i.e., it is not necessary to add the zero bracket amount in making the calculation if Form 4972 is used).
[25]§ 402(e)(4)(J).

Rollover Treatment. A taxpayer who receives a distribution can avoid current taxation by rolling the distribution into another qualified employer retirement plan or into an IRA.[26] The taxation of the distribution is deferred until distributions are made from the recipient's qualified employer retirement plan or IRA. The rollover can be *direct* with the balance in the account going directly from a qualified employer retirement plan to another qualified employer retirement plan or an IRA. The rollover can be *indirect* with the proceeds going to the taxpayer who has 60 days to transfer the proceeds into another qualified employer retirement plan or an IRA. A benefit of the direct rollover is that it is not subject to the 20 percent withholding applicable to indirect rollovers.[27]

LO.4
Calculate the limitations on contributions to and benefits from qualified plans.

Limitations on Contributions to and Benefits from Qualified Plans

In General. The limitations on contributions to and benefits from qualified plans appearing in § 415 must be written into a qualified plan. The plan terminates if these limits are exceeded. Section 404 sets the limits on deductibility applicable to the employer. The limit on the amount deductible under § 404 may have an impact on the amount the employer is willing to contribute. In fact, a defined benefit plan or defined contribution plan is not allowed a deduction for the amount that exceeds the § 415 limitations.[28]

Defined Contribution Plans. Under a *defined contribution plan*, the annual addition to an employee's account cannot exceed the smaller of $44,000 (in 2006) or 100 percent of the employee's compensation.[29] However, this individual percentage limitation of 100 percent normally is not attainable because the employer's deduction limit cannot exceed 25 percent of eligible compensation. The $44,000 amount is indexed (in $1,000 increments).[30]

Defined Benefit Plans. Under a *defined benefit plan*, the annual benefit payable to an employee is limited to the smaller of $175,000 (in 2006)[31] or 100 percent of the employee's average compensation for the highest three years of employment. This benefit limit is subject to a $10,000 *de minimis* floor. The $175,000 limitation is reduced actuarially if the benefits begin before the Social Security normal retirement age (currently age 65 and four months) and is increased actuarially if the benefits begin after the Social Security normal retirement age. The dollar limit on annual benefits ($175,000) is reduced by one-tenth for each year of *participation* under 10 years by the employee. Furthermore, the 100 percent of compensation limitation and the $10,000 *de minimis* floor are reduced proportionately for a participant who has less than 10 years of *service* with the employer.[32]

EXAMPLE 8

Adam's average compensation for the highest three years of employment is $87,000. The defined benefit plan would not qualify if the plan provides for benefits in excess of the smaller of (1) $87,000 or (2) $175,000 for Adam in 2006 (assuming normal retirement age). ∎

EXAMPLE 9

Peggy has participated for four years in a defined benefit plan and has six years of service with her employer. Her average compensation for the three highest years is $60,000. Her four years of participation reduce her dollar limitation to $70,000 ($175,000 × 4/10). Her six years of service reduce her 100% of compensation limitation to 60%. Therefore, her limit on annual benefits is $36,000 ($60,000 × 60%). ∎

---

[26]§ 402(c).
[27]§ 3405(c).
[28]§ 404(j).
[29]§§ 415(c) and (d).

[30]§ 415(d)(4).
[31]This amount is indexed annually.
[32]§ 415(b).

The amount of compensation that may be taken into account under any plan is limited to $220,000 (in 2006).[33] Thus, the benefits highly compensated individuals receive may be smaller as a percentage of their pay than those received by non-highly compensated employees.

---

*E X A M P L E   **10***

Swan Corporation has a defined contribution plan with a 10% contribution formula. An employee earning less than $220,000 in 2006 would not be affected by this includible compensation limitation. However, an employee earning $440,000 in 2006 would have only 5% of compensation allocated to his or her account because of the $220,000 limit on includible compensation. ∎

The maximum deduction a corporation is permitted for contributions to pension plans may be determined by either of two methods. First, an aggregate cost method allows an actuarially determined deduction based on a level amount, or a level percentage, of compensation over the remaining future service of covered participants. Second, the employer is permitted to deduct the so-called normal cost plus no more than 10 percent of the past service costs. The *normal cost* represents the estimated contribution required associated with work performed by employees in the current year. *Past service costs* are costs relating to the inception of the plan and costs that result from changes in the retirement plan.

The employer's contribution is deductible in the tax year such amounts are paid to the pension trust. However, both cash and accrual basis employers may defer the payment of contributions with respect to any tax year until the date fixed for filing the taxpayer's Federal income tax return for that year (including extensions).[34] In effect, the corporation is allowed a deduction to the extent it is compelled to make such contributions to satisfy the funding requirement. If an amount in excess of the allowable amount is contributed in any tax year, the excess may be carried forward and deducted in succeeding tax years (to the extent the carryover plus the succeeding year's contribution does not exceed the deductible limitation for that year).[35]

---

*E X A M P L E   **11***

During 2006, Green Corporation contributes $17,500 to its qualified pension plan. Normal cost for this year is $7,200, and the amount necessary to pay retirement benefits on behalf of employee services before 2006 is $82,000 (past service costs). The corporation's maximum deduction is $15,400. This amount consists of the $7,200 normal cost plus 10% ($8,200) of the past service costs. The corporation has a $2,100 [$17,500 (contribution) − $15,400 (deduction)] contribution carryover. ∎

---

*E X A M P L E   **12***

Assume in the previous example that Green Corporation has normal cost of $7,200 in 2007 and contributes $10,000 to the pension trust. The corporation's maximum deduction would be $15,400. Green Corporation may deduct $12,100, composed of this year's contribution ($10,000) plus the $2,100 contribution carryover. ∎

A 10 percent excise tax is imposed on nondeductible contributions. The tax is levied on the employer making the contribution. The tax applies to nondeductible contributions for the current year and any nondeductible contributions for the preceding year that have not been eliminated by the end of the current year (as a carryover or by being returned to the employer in the current year).[36]

Profit Sharing and Stock Bonus Plan Limitations.
The maximum deduction permitted to an employer each year for contributions to profit sharing and stock bonus plans is 25 percent of the compensation paid or accrued with respect

---

[33]§§ 401(a)(17) and 404(l). This amount is indexed in $5,000 increments.
[34]§§ 404(a)(1) and (6).

[35]§ 404(a)(1)(D).
[36]§ 4972.

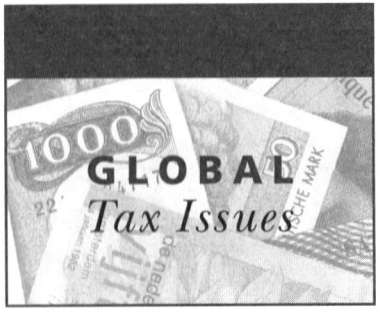

GLOBAL REMUNERATION APPROACH

A multinational firm may find it desirable to develop a global remuneration strategy. According to Bowker Consulting International, a nonglobal remuneration approach has several disadvantages:

- U.S. compensation and benefit programs are imposed worldwide, without regard to local laws, employee expectations, and competitive practices.
- U.S. compensation and benefit programs are layered on top of local programs, resulting in a confusing and often overly generous total remuneration package.
- Perceived "U.S." philosophy and principles that might have important global application if properly communicated may be rejected in favor of local programs that do not reflect overall business objectives, performance standards, and corporate values.
- An "us against them" attitude may develop between the corporation and local employees, preventing constructive dialogue in creating and implementing an appropriate rewards structure for a particular country.

Source: *Adapted from* **http://www.bowkerconsulting.com/services**.

to plan participants. The maximum amount of compensation that may be taken into account under a plan for an employee is $220,000 (in 2006). Any nondeductible excess, a so-called contribution carryover, may be carried forward indefinitely and deducted in subsequent years. The maximum deduction in any succeeding year is 25 percent of all compensation paid or accrued during that taxable year.[37]

§ 401(k) Plans

General. A **§ 401(k) plan** allows participants to elect either to receive up to $15,000 (in 2006)[38] in cash (taxed currently) or to have a contribution made on their behalf to a profit sharing or stock bonus plan. The plan may also be in the form of a salary-reduction agreement between an eligible participant and an employer under which a contribution will be made only if the participant elects to reduce his or her compensation or to forgo an increase in compensation.

Any pretax amount elected by the employee as a plan contribution is not includible in gross income and is 100 percent vested. Any employer contributions are tax deferred, as are earnings on contributions in the plan.

E X A M P L E   13

Sam participates in a § 401(k) plan of his employer. The plan permits the participants to choose between a full salary or a reduced salary where the reduction becomes a before-tax contribution to a retirement plan. Sam elects to contribute 10% of his annual compensation of $30,000 to the plan. Income taxes are paid on only $27,000. No income taxes are paid on the $3,000—or on any earnings—until it is distributed from the plan to Sam. The main benefit of a § 401(k) plan is that Sam can shift a portion of his income to a later taxable year. ∎

The maximum employee annual elective contribution to a § 401(k) plan is $15,000 (in 2006), but that amount is reduced dollar for dollar by other salary-reduction contributions to tax-sheltered annuities and simplified employee pension plans. Elective contributions in excess of the maximum limitation are taxable in the year of

---

[37]§§ 404(a)(3)(A) and (a)(7).
[38]§§ 402(g)(1) and (4). Starting in 2003, this amount was increased in $1,000 increments until it reached $15,000 in 2006. It will be indexed in $500

increments in years after 2006. For 2003, the amount was $12,000, for 2004, it was $13,000, and for 2005, it was $14,000.

deferral. These amounts may be distributed from the plan tax-free before April 15 of the following year. Excess amounts not timely distributed will be taxable in the year of distribution, even though they were included in income in the year of deferral. Annual elective contributions are also limited by complicated nondiscrimination requirements and the defined contribution plan limitations.

A person who has attained age 50 by the end of the tax year can make catch-up contributions of $1,000 for 2002, $2,000 for 2003, $3,000 for 2004, $4,000 for 2005, and $5,000 for 2006 and thereafter.[39]

Heather is age 57 in 2006. Heather is able to make additional catch-up elective deferrals of $1,000 for 2002 (beyond the $11,000 limit), $2,000 for 2003 (beyond the $12,000 limit), $3,000 for 2004 (beyond the $13,000 limit), $4,000 for 2005 (beyond the $14,000 limit), and $5,000 for 2006 (beyond the $15,000 limit). ■

EXAMPLE 14

A 10 percent excise tax is imposed on the employer for excess contributions not withdrawn from the plan within 2½ months after the close of the plan year. The plan will lose its qualified status if these excess contributions (and any related income) are not withdrawn by the end of the plan year following the plan year in which the excess contributions were made.[40]

Carmen, age 36, is an employee of a manufacturing corporation. She defers $17,000 in a § 401(k) plan in 2006. The $2,000 excess over the $15,000 limit, along with the appropriate earnings, must be returned to Carmen by April 15, 2007. This $2,000 excess amount plus related income is taxable to her in 2006 and will be taxed again upon distribution (if made after April 15, 2007). There will be a 10% tax on Carmen's employer on any excess contributions not returned within 2½ months after the close of the plan year. ■

EXAMPLE 15

SIMPLE Plans. Employers with 100 or fewer employees who do not maintain another qualified retirement plan may establish a *savings incentive match plan for employees* (SIMPLE plan).[41] The plan can be in the form of a § 401(k) plan or an IRA. The SIMPLE plan is not subject to the nondiscrimination rules that are normally applicable to § 401(k) plans.

All employees who received at least $5,000 in compensation from the employer during any two preceding years and who reasonably expect to receive at least $5,000 in compensation during the current year must be eligible to participate in the plan. The decision to participate is up to the employee. A self-employed individual may also participate in the plan.

The contributions made by the employee (a salary-reduction approach) must be expressed as a percentage of compensation rather than as a fixed dollar amount. The plan must not permit the elective employee contribution for the year to exceed $10,000 (in 2006).[42] The elective deferral limit is increased under the catch-up provision for employees age 50 and over. The amount is $500 for 2002, $1,000 for 2003, $1,500 for 2004, $2,000 for 2005, and $2,500 for 2006 and thereafter. The $2,500 amount is indexed for inflation in $500 increments beginning in 2007.

Generally, the employer must either match elective employee contributions up to 3 percent of the employee's compensation or provide nonmatching contributions of 2 percent of compensation for each eligible employee. Thus, the maximum amount that may be contributed to the plan for 2006 is $16,600 [$10,000 employee contributions + $6,600 ($220,000 compensation ceiling × 3%) employer match].

---

[39]The $5,000 amount will be indexed in $500 increments in 2007 and thereafter.

[40]§ 4979(a).

[41]§ 408(p).

[42]For 2004, the limit was $9,000. The $10,000 amount for 2005 is indexed for inflation in $500 increments in 2006 and thereafter. For 2006, the amount remains at $10,000. § 408(p)(2)(E)(i).

No other contributions may be made to the plan other than the employee elective contribution and the required employer matching contribution (or nonmatching contribution under the 2 percent rule). All contributions are fully vested. An employer is required to make contributions to a SIMPLE § 401(k) plan once it is established, whereas an employer's contributions to a traditional § 401(k) plan are optional.

An employer's deduction for contributions to a SIMPLE § 401(k) plan is limited to the greater of 25 percent of the compensation paid or accrued or the amount that the employer is required to contribute to the plan. Thus, an employer may deduct contributions to a SIMPLE § 401(k) plan in excess of 25 percent of the $220,000 salary cap. A traditional § 401(k) plan is limited to 25 percent of the total compensation of plan participants for the year.

An employer is allowed a deduction for matching contributions only if the contributions are made by the due date (including extensions) for the employer's tax return. Contributions to a SIMPLE plan are excludible from the employee's gross income, and the SIMPLE plan is tax-exempt.

EXAMPLE 16

The Mauve Company has a SIMPLE plan for its employees under which it provides nonmatching contributions of 2% of compensation for each eligible employee. The maximum amount that can be added to each participant's account in 2006 is $14,400, composed of the $10,000 employee salary reduction plus an employer contribution of $4,400 ($220,000 × 2%). ∎

Distributions from a SIMPLE plan are taxed under the IRA rules. Tax-free rollovers can be made from one SIMPLE account to another. A SIMPLE account can be rolled over to an IRA tax-free after the expiration of a two-year period since the individual first participated in the plan. Withdrawals of contributions during the two-year period beginning on the date an employee first participates in the SIMPLE plan are subject to a 25 percent early withdrawal tax rather than the 10 percent early withdrawal tax that otherwise would apply.

Retirement Plans for Self-Employed Individuals

LO.5

Understand the qualified plan (Keogh plan) available to a self-employed person.

Self-employed individuals (e.g., partners and sole proprietors) and their employees are eligible to receive qualified retirement benefits under the SIMPLE plans described above or under what are known as **H.R. 10 (Keogh) plans**. Because of contribution limitations and other restrictions, self-employed plans previously were less attractive than corporate plans. Contributions and benefits of a self-employed person now are subject to the general corporate provisions, putting self-employed persons on a parity with corporate employees. Consequently, Keogh plans can provide a self-employed person with an adequate retirement base.

A variety of funding vehicles can be used for Keogh investments, such as mutual funds, annuities, real estate shares, certificates of deposit, debt instruments, commodities, securities, and personal properties. Investment in most collectibles is not allowed in a self-directed plan. When an individual decides to make all investment decisions, a self-directed retirement plan is established. However, the individual may prefer to invest the funds with a financial institution such as a broker, a bank, or a savings and loan institution.

Coverage Requirements

Generally, the corporate coverage rules apply to Keogh plans. Thus, the percentage, ratio, and average benefits tests previously discussed also apply to self-employed plans.[43] An individual covered under a qualified corporate plan as an employee may also establish a Keogh plan for earnings from self-employment.

Contribution Limitations

A self-employed individual may annually contribute the smaller of $44,000 (in 2006) or 100 percent of earned income to a *defined contribution* Keogh plan.[44] However, if the defined contribution plan is a profit sharing plan or stock bonus plan, a 25 percent deduction limit applies. Under a *defined benefit* Keogh plan, the annual benefit payable to an employee is limited to the smaller of $175,000 (in 2006) or 100 percent of the employee's average compensation for the three highest years of employment.[45] An employee includes a self-employed person.

Earned income refers to net earnings from self-employment as defined in § 1402(a).[46] Net earnings from self-employment means the gross income derived by an individual from any trade or business carried on by that individual, less appropriate deductions, plus the distributive share of income or loss from a partnership.[47] Earned income is reduced by contributions to a Keogh plan on the individual's behalf and by 50 percent of any self-employment tax.[48]

EXAMPLE 17

Pat, a partner, has earned income of $150,000 in 2006 (after the deduction for one-half of self-employment tax). The maximum contribution Pat may make to a defined contribution Keogh plan is $44,000, the lesser of $150,000 or $44,000. ■

For discrimination purposes, the 25 percent limitation on the employee contribution to a profit sharing plan or stock bonus plan is computed on the first $220,000 (in 2006) of earned income. Thus, the maximum contribution in 2006 is $44,000 ($220,000 − .25X=X; X=$176,000). Therefore, $220,000 − $176,000 = $44,000. Alternatively, this can be calculated by multiplying $220,000 by 20 percent.

EXAMPLE 18

Terry, a self-employed accountant, has a profit sharing plan with a contribution rate of 15% of compensation. Terry's earned income after the deduction of one-half of self-employment tax, but before the Keogh contribution, is $250,000. Terry's contribution is limited to $28,696 ($220,000 − .15X=X), since X= $191,304 and .15 × $191,304 = $28,696. ■

Although a Keogh plan must be established before the end of the year in question, contributions may be made up to the normal filing date for that year.

Individual Retirement Accounts (IRAs)

General Rules

Employees not covered by another qualified plan can establish their own tax-deductible **Individual Retirement Accounts (IRAs)**. The contribution ceiling is the smaller of $4,000 (or $8,000 for spousal IRAs) for years 2005–2007 or 100 percent of compensation.[49]

An individual who attains the age of 50 by the end of the tax year can make additional catch-up IRA contributions. The maximum contribution limit is increased by $500 for the period 2002 through 2005 and $1,000 for years after 2005.

> **LO.6**
>
> Describe the benefits of the different types of Individual Retirement Accounts (IRAs).

---

[43]§ 401(d).
[44]§ 415(c)(1).
[45]§ 415(b)(1). This amount is indexed annually.
[46]§ 401(c)(2).
[47]§ 1402(a).

[48]§§ 401(c)(2)(A)(v) and 164(f).
[49]§§ 219(b)(1) and (c)(2). The ceiling was $3,000 for 2002–2004. It will increase to $5,000 for 2008. After 2008, the limit is adjusted annually for inflation in $500 increments.

TABLE 19–3	Phaseout of IRA Deduction of an Active Participant in 2006	
AGI Filing Status	**Phaseout Begins***	**Phaseout Ends**
Single and head of household	$50,000	$60,000
Married, filing joint return	75,000	85,000
Married, filing separate return	–0–	10,000

*The starting point for the phaseout is increased each year through 2007 for married filing jointly and through 2005 for other filing statuses.

The amount accumulated in an IRA can be substantial. For example, if a husband and wife each contribute only $4,000 annually to an IRA from age 25 to age 65 (and earn 6 percent annually), their account balances together would be approximately $1.4 million at retirement. If the taxpayer is an *active participant* in a qualified plan, the traditional IRA deduction limitation is phased out *proportionately* between certain adjusted gross income (AGI) ranges, as shown in Table 19–3.[50]

AGI is calculated taking into account any § 469 passive losses and § 86 taxable Social Security benefits and ignoring any § 911 foreign income exclusion, § 135 savings bonds interest exclusion, and the IRA deduction. There is a $200 floor on the IRA deduction limitation for individuals whose AGI is not above the phaseout range.

EXAMPLE 19

Dan, who is single, has compensation income of $56,000 in 2006. He is an active participant in his employer's qualified retirement plan. Dan contributes $4,000 to a traditional IRA. The deductible amount is reduced from $4,000 by $2,400 because of the phaseout mechanism:

$$\frac{\$6,000}{\$10,000} \times \$4,000 = \$2,400 \text{ reduction}$$

Therefore, of the $4,000 contribution, Dan can deduct only $1,600 ($4,000 − $2,400). ∎

EXAMPLE 20

Ben, an unmarried individual, is an active participant in his employer's qualified retirement plan. With AGI of $59,800, he would normally have an IRA deduction limit of $80 {$4,000 − [($59,800 − $50,000)/$10,000 × $4,000]}. However, because of the special floor provision, Ben is allowed a $200 IRA deduction. ∎

An individual is not considered an active participant in a qualified plan merely because the individual's spouse is an active participant in such a plan for any part of a plan year. Thus, most homemakers may take a full $4,000 deduction regardless of the participation status of their spouse, unless the couple has AGI above $150,000. If their AGI is above $150,000, the phaseout of the deduction begins at $150,000 and ends at $160,000 (phaseout over the $10,000 range) rather than beginning and ending at the phaseout amounts in Table 19–3.[51]

EXAMPLE 21

Nell is covered by a qualified employer retirement plan at work. Her husband, Nick, is not an active participant in a qualified plan. If Nell and Nick's combined AGI is $135,000, Nell cannot make a deductible IRA contribution because she exceeds the income threshold for an active participant in Table 19–3. However, since Nick is not an active participant, and their combined AGI does not exceed $150,000, he can make a deductible contribution of $4,000 to an IRA. ∎

---

[50]§ 219(g).

[51]§ 219 (g)(7). However, a special rule in § 219(g)(4) allows a married person filing a separate return to avoid the phaseout rules even though the spouse is an active participant. The individual must live apart from the spouse at all times during the taxable year and must not be an active participant in another qualified plan.

To the extent that an individual is ineligible to make a deductible contribution to an IRA, *nondeductible contributions* can be made to separate accounts.[52] The nondeductible contributions are subject to the same dollar limits as deductible contributions ($4,000 of earned income, $8,000 for a spousal IRA). Income in the account accumulates tax-free until distributed. Only the account earnings are taxed upon distribution because the account basis equals the contributions made by the taxpayer. A taxpayer may elect to treat deductible IRA contributions as nondeductible. If an individual has no taxable income for the year after taking into account other deductions, the election would be beneficial. The election is made on the individual's tax return for the taxable year to which the designation relates.

Starting in 2002 and continuing through 2006, there is a nonrefundable credit for contributions to a traditional IRA or elective deferrals for a § 401(k) plan (see Chapter 13).

Roth IRAs. Introduced by Congress to encourage individual savings, a **Roth IRA** is a *nondeductible* alternative to the traditional deductible IRA. Earnings inside a Roth IRA are not taxable, and all qualified distributions from a Roth IRA are tax-free.[53] The maximum allowable annual contribution to a Roth IRA is the smaller of $4,000 ($8,000 for spousal IRAs) or 100 percent of the individual's compensation for the year. Contributions to a Roth IRA must be made by the due date (excluding extensions) of the taxpayer's tax return. Roth IRAs are not subject to the minimum distribution rules that apply to traditional IRAs.

A taxpayer can make tax-free withdrawals from a Roth IRA after an initial five-year holding period if any of the following requirements is satisfied:

- The distribution is made on or after the date on which the participant attains age 59½.
- The distribution is made to a beneficiary (or the participant's estate) on or after the participant's death.
- The participant becomes disabled.
- The distribution is used to pay for qualified first-time home buyer's expenses (statutory ceiling of $10,000).

EXAMPLE 22

Edith establishes a Roth IRA at age 42 and contributes $4,000 per year for 20 years. The account is now worth $129,400, consisting of $80,000 of nondeductible contributions and $49,400 in accumulated earnings that have not been taxed. Edith may withdraw the $129,400 tax-free from the Roth IRA because she is over age 59½ and has met the five-year holding period requirement. ∎

If the taxpayer receives a distribution from a Roth IRA and does not satisfy the aforementioned requirements, the distribution may be taxable. If the distribution represents a return of capital, it is not taxable. Conversely, if the distribution represents a payout of earnings, it is taxable. Under the ordering rules for Roth IRA distributions, distributions are treated as first made from contributions (return of capital).

EXAMPLE 23

Assume the same facts as in the previous example, except that Edith is only age 50 and receives a distribution of $55,000. Since her adjusted basis for the Roth IRA is $80,000 (contributions made), the distribution is tax-free, and her adjusted basis is reduced to $25,000 ($80,000 − $55,000). ∎

Roth IRAs are subject to income limits. The maximum annual contribution of $4,000 is phased out beginning at AGI of $95,000 for single taxpayers and $150,000 for married couples who file a joint return. The phaseout range is $10,000 for married filing jointly and $15,000 for single taxpayers. For a married taxpayer filing

---

[52]§ 408(o).   [53]§ 408A.

separately, the phaseout begins with AGI of $0 and is phased out over a $10,000 range.

Bev, who is single, would like to contribute $4,000 to her Roth IRA. However, her AGI is $105,000, so her contribution is limited to $1,333 ($4,000 − $2,667) calculated as follows:

$$\frac{\$10,000}{\$15,000} \times \$4,000 = \$2,667 \text{ reduction}$$ ■

Coverdell Education Savings Accounts (CESAs).

Distributions from a **Coverdell Education Savings Account (CESA)** to pay for qualified education expenses receive favorable tax treatment.[54] Qualified education expenses include tuition, fees, books, supplies, and related equipment. Room and board qualify if the student's course load is at least one-half of the full-time course load. If the CESA is used to pay the qualified education expenses of the designated beneficiary, the withdrawals are tax-free. To the extent the distributions during a tax year exceed qualified education expenses, part of the excess is treated as a return of capital (the contributions), and part is treated as a distribution of earnings under the § 72 annuity rules. Thus, the distribution is presumed to be pro rata from each category. The exclusion for the distribution of earnings part is calculated as follows:

$$\frac{\text{Qualified education expenses}}{\text{Total distributions}} \times \text{Earnings} = \text{Exclusion}$$

Meg receives a $2,500 distribution from her CESA. She uses $2,000 to pay for qualified education expenses. On the date of the distribution, Meg's CESA balance is $10,000, $6,000 of which represents her contributions. Since 60% ($6,000/$10,000) of her account balance represents her contributions, $1,500 ($2,500 × 60%) of the distribution is a return of capital, and $1,000 ($2,500 × 40%) is a distribution of earnings. The excludible amount of the earnings is calculated as follows:

$$\frac{\$2,000}{\$2,500} \times \$1,000 = \$800$$

Thus, Meg must include $200 ($1,000 − $800) in her gross income. ■

The maximum amount that can be contributed annually to a CESA for a beneficiary is $2,000. A beneficiary must be an individual and cannot be a group of children or an unborn child. The contributions are not deductible. A CESA is subject to income limits. The maximum annual contribution is phased out beginning at $95,000 for single taxpayers and $190,000 for married couples who file a joint return. The phaseout range is $30,000 for married filing jointly and $15,000 for single taxpayers. Contributions cannot be made to a CESA after the date on which the designated beneficiary attains age 18. Thus, a total of up to $36,000 can be contributed for each beneficiary—$2,000 in the year of birth and in each of the following 17 years. A 6 percent excise tax is imposed on excess contributions to a CESA. A 10 percent excise tax is imposed on any distributions that are included in gross income.

The balance in a CESA must be distributed within 30 days after the death of the beneficiary or within 30 days after the beneficiary reaches age 30. Any balance at the close of either 30-day period is considered to be distributed at such time, and the earnings portion is included in the beneficiary's gross income. Before a beneficiary reaches age 30, any balance can be rolled over tax-free into another CESA for a member of the beneficiary's family who is under age 30.

---

[54]§ 530.

CONCEPT SUMMARY   19–3

Keogh Plan and SEP Compared

	Keogh	SEP
Form	Trust.	IRA.
Establishment	By end of year.	By extension due date of employer.
Type of plan	Qualified.	Qualified.
Contributions to plan	By extension due date.	By extension due date of employer.
Vesting rules	Qualified plan rules.	100% immediately.
Participants' rules	Flexible.	Stricter.
Lump-sum distributions and averaging	Yes, favorable 10-year forward averaging.	No, ordinary income.
Deduction limitation	Varies.*	Smaller of $44,000 (in 2006) or 25% of earned income.**
Self as trustee	Yes.	No.

*For a defined contribution pension plan, the limit is the smaller of $44,000 (in 2006) or 100% of self-employment income (after one-half of self-employment tax is deducted). A defined contribution profit sharing plan has a 25% deduction limit. A defined benefit Keogh plan's limit is the smaller of $175,000 (in 2006) or 100% of the employee's average compensation for the highest three years of employment.

**Only $220,000 of income can be taken into consideration.

The CESA exclusion may be available in a tax year in which the beneficiary claims the HOPE credit or the lifetime learning credit (see Chapter 13). However, any excluded amount of the CESA distribution cannot be used for the same educational expenses for which the HOPE credit or the lifetime learning credit is claimed.

Contributions cannot be made to a beneficiary's CESA during any year in which contributions are made to a qualified tuition program on behalf of the same beneficiary (see Chapter 5).

Simplified Employee Pension Plans. An employer may contribute to an IRA covering an employee an amount equal to the lesser of $44,000 (in 2006) or 25 percent of the employee's earned income. In such a plan, the employer must make contributions for *each* employee who has reached age 21, has performed service for the employer during the calendar year and at least three of the five preceding calendar years, and has received at least $450 (in 2006) in compensation from the employer for the year.[55] Known as **simplified employee pension (SEP) plans**, these plans are subject to many of the same restrictions applicable to qualified plans (e.g., age and period-of-service requirements, and nondiscrimination limitations). Concept Summary 19–3 compares a SEP with a Keogh plan.

EXAMPLE 26

In 2006, Ryan's compensation before his employer's contribution to a SEP is $30,000. Ryan's employer may contribute and deduct up to $7,500 ($30,000 × 25%) for 2006. ∎

The amounts contributed to a SEP by an employer on behalf of an employee and the elective deferrals of an employee under a SEP are excludible from gross income. Elective deferrals under a SEP are subject to a statutory ceiling of $15,000

---

[55]§§ 408(j) and (k)(2). This amount is indexed annually. For 2005, the amount was $450.

(in 2006),[56] which is increased under the catch-up provision for employees at least 50 years of age by the end of the tax year. Only $220,000 (in 2006) in compensation may be taken into account in making the SEP computation. An employer is permitted to elect to use its taxable year rather than the calendar year for purposes of determining contributions to a SEP.[57]

Simple IRA. A SIMPLE plan can be in the form of an IRA. See the earlier discussion under SIMPLE Plans.

Spousal IRA. If both spouses work, each can individually establish an IRA. Deductible IRA contributions of up to $4,000 may be made by each spouse if the combined compensation of both spouses is at least equal to the contributed amount. Thus, if each spouse has compensation of at least $4,000, they each may contribute a maximum of $4,000. Likewise, if only one spouse is employed, they each may contribute a maximum of $4,000 if the employed spouse has compensation of at least $8,000. Finally, if both spouses are employed, but one has compensation of less than $4,000, they each may contribute a maximum of $4,000 if their combined compensation is at least $8,000.

For the spousal IRA provision to apply, a joint return must be filed.[58] The spousal IRA deduction is also proportionately reduced for active participants whose AGI exceeds the above target ranges.

EXAMPLE 27

Tony, who is married, is eligible to establish an IRA. He received $30,000 in compensation in 2006, and his spouse does not work outside the home. Tony can contribute up to $8,000 to two IRAs, to be divided in any manner between the two spouses, except that no more than $4,000 can be allocated to either spouse. ∎

EXAMPLE 28

Assume the same facts as in the previous example, except that Tony's wife has compensation income of $2,200. Without the spousal IRA provision, Tony could contribute $4,000 to his IRA, and his spouse could contribute only $2,200 to her IRA. With the spousal IRA provision, they both can contribute $4,000 to their IRAs. ∎

Alimony is considered to be earned income for purposes of IRA contributions. Thus, a person whose only income is alimony can contribute to an IRA.

Timing of Contributions. Contributions (both deductible and nondeductible) can be made to an IRA anytime before the due date of the individual's tax return.[59] For example, an individual can establish and contribute to an IRA through April 15, 2007 (the return due date), and deduct this amount on his or her tax return for 2006. IRA contributions that are made during a tax return extension period do not satisfy the requirement of being made by the return due date. An employer can make contributions up until the time of the due date for filing the return (including extensions) and treat those amounts as a deduction for the prior year.[60] As noted earlier, a similar rule applies to Keogh plans. However, the Keogh plan must be established before the end of the tax year. Contributions to the Keogh plan may then be made anytime before the due date of the individual's tax return.

---

[56]Elective deferrals by an employee were repealed by the Small Business Job Protection Act of 1996 effective after December 31, 1996. However, if the employer plan was established before January 1, 1997, contributions can continue to be made under the pre-repeal provisions.

[57]§ 404(h)(1)(A). The $15,000 and $220,000 amounts are indexed annually. The $15,000 amount was increased in $1,000 annual increments until it reached $15,000 and then became subject to indexing.

[58]§ 219(c).
[59]§ 219(f)(3).
[60]§ 404(h)(1)(B).

Penalty Taxes for Excess Contributions

A cumulative, nondeductible 6 percent excise penalty tax is imposed on the smaller of (1) any excess contributions or (2) the market value of the plan assets determined as of the close of the tax year. *Excess contributions* are any contributions that exceed the maximum limitation and contributions that are made to a traditional IRA during or after the tax year in which the individual reaches age 70½.[61] Contributions can be made to a Roth IRA during or after the tax year in which the individual reaches age 70½. A taxpayer is not allowed a deduction for excess contributions. If the excess is corrected by contributing less than the deductible amount for a later year, a deduction then is allowable in the later year as a *makeup* deduction.

An excess contribution is taxable annually until returned to the taxpayer or reduced by the underutilization of the maximum contribution limitation in a subsequent year. The 6 percent penalty tax can be avoided if the excess amounts are returned.[62]

E X A M P L E 2 9

Nancy, age 45, establishes a traditional IRA in 2006 and contributes $4,300 in cash to the plan. She has earned income of $22,000. Nancy is allowed a $4,000 deduction *for* AGI for 2006. Assuming the market value of the plan assets is at least $300, there is a nondeductible 6% excise penalty tax of $18 ($300 × 6%). The $300 may be subject to an additional penalty tax in future years if it is not returned to Nancy or reduced by underutilization of the $4,000 maximum contribution limitation (ignoring any catch-up contributions). ∎

Taxation of Benefits

A participant has a zero basis in the *deductible* contributions of a traditional IRA because the contributions were deducted.[63] Therefore, all withdrawals from a deductible IRA are taxed as ordinary income in the year of receipt. They are not eligible for the 10-year averaging allowed for certain lump-sum distributions.

A participant has a basis equal to the contributions made for a *nondeductible* traditional IRA. Therefore, only the earnings component of withdrawals is included in gross income. Such amounts are taxed as ordinary income in the year of receipt and are not eligible for the 10-year averaging allowed for certain lump-sum distributions.

In addition to being included in gross income, payments from IRAs made to a participant before age 59½ are subject to a nondeductible 10 percent penalty tax on such actual, or constructive, payments.[64] However, an individual may make penalty-free withdrawals to pay for medical expenses in excess of 7.5 percent of AGI, to pay for qualified higher education expenses, and to pay for qualified, first-time home buyer expenses (up to $10,000). Note that a qualified first-time home buyer is defined as an individual (and spouse) who has not owned a principal residence in the two-year period preceding the date of acquisition of a principal residence. Further, an individual who has received unemployment compensation for at least 12 consecutive weeks may use IRA withdrawals to pay for health insurance for himself or herself, the spouse, and dependents without incurring the 10 percent penalty tax.[65]

All traditional IRAs of an individual are treated as one contract, and all distributions during a taxable year are treated as one distribution. See the earlier discussion of the special rules for distributions from Roth IRAs and traditional IRAs. If an individual who previously has made both deductible and nondeductible IRA

---

[61]§§ 4973(a)(1) and (b).

[62]§§ 408(d)(4) and 4973(b)(2).

[63]§ 408(d)(1).

[64]§ 72(t). There are limited exceptions to the penalty on early distributions.

[65]§§ 72(t)(2)(B), (D), (E), and (F). For purposes of the unemployment provision, a self-employed individual who otherwise would have been eligible for unemployment compensation will qualify.

contributions makes a withdrawal from a traditional IRA during a taxable year, the excludible amount must be calculated. The amount excludible from gross income for the taxable year is calculated by multiplying the amount withdrawn by a percentage. The percentage is calculated by dividing the individual's aggregate nondeductible IRA contributions by the aggregate balance of all of his or her traditional IRAs (including rollover IRAs and SEPs).[66]

EXAMPLE 30

Carl, age 59, has a $12,000 deductible traditional IRA and a $2,000 nondeductible traditional IRA (without any earnings). Carl withdraws $1,000 from the nondeductible IRA. The excludible portion is $143 [($2,000/$14,000) × $1,000], and the includible portion is $857 [($12,000/$14,000) × $1,000]. Carl must also pay a 10% penalty tax on the prorated portion considered withdrawn from the deductible IRA and earnings in either type of IRA. Thus, the 10% penalty tax is $85.70 (10% × $857). ∎

Rollovers: General Provisions. As introduced earlier, an IRA may be the recipient of a rollover from another qualified plan, including another IRA. Such a distribution from a qualified plan is not included in gross income if it is transferred within 60 days of receipt to an IRA or another qualified plan. For a series of distributions that constitute a lump-sum distribution, the 60-day period does not begin until the last distribution. Amounts received from IRAs may be rolled over tax-free only once in a 12-month period. If a person has more than one IRA, the one-year waiting period applies separately to each IRA.[67]

EXAMPLE 31

Nonemployer stock worth $60,000 is distributed to an employee from a qualified retirement plan. Hubert, the employee, sells the stock within 60 days for $60,000 and transfers one-half of the proceeds to a traditional IRA. Hubert has $30,000 of ordinary income, which is not eligible for 10-year forward averaging or for the capital gain treatment for pre-1974 contributions. One-half of the distribution, or $30,000, does escape taxation because of the rollover. ∎

A tax-free rollover for distributions from qualified plans is an alternative to the taxable 10-year forward averaging technique. Any rollover amount in a traditional IRA may later be rolled over into another qualified plan if the IRA consists of only the amounts from the original plan. The amount of nondeductible employee contributions included in a distribution may not be rolled over, but that amount is tax-free because the contributions were made with after-tax dollars. Partial rollovers are allowed, but the maximum amount that may be rolled over may not exceed the portion of the distribution that is otherwise includible in gross income. Rollovers are not available for required distributions under the minimum distribution rules once age 70½ is reached.

EXAMPLE 32

Jane withdraws $1,500 from her traditional IRA on May 2, 2006, but she redeposits it in the same IRA on June 28, 2006. Although the withdrawal and redeposit was a partial rollover and Jane may have used the funds for a limited time, this is a tax-free rollover.[68] ∎

A rollover is different from a direct transfer of funds from a qualified plan to an IRA or another qualified plan by a trustee or issuer. A direct transfer is not subject to the one-year waiting period and the withholding rules.[69] Further, in many states, IRA amounts are subject to claims of creditors, which is not the case for some employer plans.

---

[66]§ 408(d)(2).
[67]§ 408(d)(3)(B) and Reg. § 1.408–4(b)(4).

[68]Ltr.Rul. 9010007.
[69]Reg. § 35.3405–1.

CONCEPT SUMMARY 19–4

Comparison of IRAs

	Traditional		Roth IRA	Coverdell Education Savings Account (CESA)
	Deductible IRA	Nondeductible IRA		
Maximum contribution (per year)	$4,000*	$4,000*	$4,000*	$2,000
Tax-deductible contribution	Yes	No	No	No
Tax-free growth of income	Yes	Yes	Yes	Yes
Beginning of AGI phaseout for active participant (2006)	$50,000 single, $75,000 joint	N/A	$95,000 single, $150,000 joint	$95,000 single, $190,000 joint
Income tax on distributions	Yes, for entire distribution	Yes, for the earnings portion	No, if satisfy 5-year holding period**	No, if used for education expenses
50% excise tax: age 70½ minimum distributions	Yes	Yes	No	No
10% early withdrawal penalty (before age 59½)	Yes, with exceptions†	Yes, with exceptions†	Yes, with exceptions†	Yes‡

*The total of deductible, nondeductible, and Roth IRA contributions may not exceed $4,000 per year.

**In addition, the distribution must satisfy one of the following: after age 59½, for qualified first-time home buyer expenses, participant is disabled, or made to a beneficiary on or after the participant's death.

†Qualified education and first-time home buyer costs (up to $10,000) avoid the 10% penalty.

‡On early withdrawals not used for education costs. Qualified first-time home buyer costs (up to $10,000) avoid 10% penalty.

An employer must withhold 20 percent of any lump-sum distributions unless the transfer is a direct transfer to an IRA or another qualified plan.[70]

EXAMPLE 33

Kay receives a distribution from a qualified retirement plan. The amount of the distribution would have been $20,000, but Kay receives only $16,000 ($20,000 − $4,000) as a result of the 20% withholding provision. After several weeks, Kay decides to contribute $20,000 (the gross amount of the distribution) to her traditional IRA. Since she received only $16,000, she will need to contribute $4,000 from another source in order to make a $20,000 contribution. Kay will be able to claim a refund for the $4,000 that was withheld when she files her tax return for the year. ■

Distributions from a traditional IRA are generally not eligible for 10-year averaging or capital gain treatment. An exception applies in the case of a *conduit IRA*, where the sole assets of a plan are rolled over into an IRA, and the assets are then rolled into a qualified plan. With a conduit IRA, the lump-sum distribution from the original plan is still eligible for the special tax treatments.

Rollovers and Conversions: Roth IRAs. A Roth IRA may be rolled over tax-free into another Roth IRA.[71]

A traditional IRA may be rolled over or converted to a Roth IRA. A conversion occurs when the taxpayer notifies the IRA trustee that the IRA is now a Roth IRA. A rollover or conversion of a traditional IRA to a Roth IRA can occur only if the following requirements are satisfied:[72]

[70]§ 3405(c).
[71]§ 408A(c)(3)(B).
[72]§ 408A(c)(3)(B).

- The participant's AGI does not exceed $100,000 (excluding the amount included in gross income resulting from the rollover or conversion).
- The participant is not married filing a separate return.
- The rollover occurs within 60 days of the IRA distribution.

If a traditional IRA is rolled over or converted to a Roth IRA, the tax consequences depend on whether the traditional IRA was deductible or nondeductible. If deductible, then the basis for the IRA is zero. Thus, the entire amount of the rollover or conversion is included in gross income. If nondeductible, then the basis for the IRA is equal to the sum of the contributions. Thus, only the IRA earnings included in the rollover or conversion are included in gross income. The 10 percent penalty tax will not apply in either case.[73]

LO.7

Understand the rationale for nonqualified deferred compensation plans and the related tax treatment.

Nonqualified Deferred Compensation Plans

Underlying Rationale for Tax Treatment

Nonqualified deferred compensation (NQDC) plans provide a flexible way for taxpayers, particularly those in the 35 percent tax bracket, to defer income taxes on income payments until a possible lower tax bracket year. Where the deferred compensation is credited with annual earnings until payment, the entire deferred compensation, not the after-tax amount, is generating investment income. Also, most NQDC plans do not have to meet the discrimination, funding, coverage, and other requirements of qualified plans. In addition to these advantages for the employee, the employer may not have a current cash outflow.

Starting in 2005, an NQDC plan is taxed on the vesting date unless the plan is unfunded and satisfies the requirements of § 409A. In general, these amounts are included in gross income unless they are subject to a substantial risk of forfeiture or were previously included in gross income. If a plan does not satisfy the requirements of § 409A, any deferred compensation is subject to current taxation, a 20 percent penalty tax, and retroactive interest from the date of the deferral to the date of vesting (IRS underpayment rate plus 1 percentage point).[74]

A plan is unfunded if the employer merely promises to pay this deferred compensation at some future date and does not set aside the deferred funds in a separate account (Type 1). An employer may place the assets in a trust, annuity, escrow, or some other funded arrangement as long as the funds are subject to the claims of the employer's creditors in the event of bankruptcy or insolvency (Type 2). This Type 2 arrangement includes annuity contracts, Rabbi trusts, surety bonds, escrow arrangements, third-party guarantees, and other arrangements.

E X A M P L E   3 4

Eagle Corporation and Bill, a cash basis employee, enter into an employment agreement that provides an annual salary of $120,000 to Bill. Of this amount, $100,000 is to be paid in current monthly installments, and $20,000 is to be paid in 10 annual installments beginning at Bill's retirement or death. Although Eagle Corporation maintains a separate account for Bill, that account is not funded (Bill is merely an unsecured creditor of the corporation). The $20,000 is not considered constructively received and is deferred. Compensation of $100,000 is currently taxable to Bill and deductible to Eagle. The other $20,000 will be taxable and deductible when paid in future years. ∎

Tax Treatment to the Employer and Employee

The tax treatment of an NQDC plan depends on whether it is *funded* or *unfunded* and whether it is *forfeitable* or *nonforfeitable*. In an unfunded NQDC plan, the employee

---

[73]§ 408A(d)(3)(A)(ii).   [74]§ 409A(a)(1).

relies upon the company's mere promise to make the compensation payment in the future. An unfunded, unsecured promise to pay, not represented by a negotiable note, effectively defers the recognition of income if the § 409A requirements are satisfied. Thus, if deferral is available, the employee is taxed later when the compensation is actually paid or made available.[75] Similarly, the employer is allowed a deduction when the employee recognizes income.[76]

The employer can set up an escrow account to accumulate deferred payments on behalf of the employee. These funds may be invested by the escrow agent for the benefit of the employee.[77] By avoiding income recognition until the benefits from the escrow custodial account are received, the employee postpones the tax. An escrow arrangement can be appropriate for a professional athlete or entertainer whose income is earned in a few peak years.

E X A M P L E   35

Ted, a professional athlete, is to receive a bonus for signing an employment contract. An NQDC plan is established to defer the income beyond Ted's peak income years. His employer transfers the bonus to an escrow agent who invests the funds in securities, etc., which may act as a hedge against inflation. Assume the requirements of § 409A are satisfied. The bonus is deferred for 10 years and becomes payable gradually in years 11 through 15. The bonus is taxable to Ted and deductible by his employer when Ted receives the payments in years 11 through 15. ■

Generally, funded NQDC plans must be forfeitable to keep the compensation payments from being taxable immediately. In most instances, employees prefer to have some assurance that they will ultimately receive benefits from the NQDC (that the plan provides for nonforfeitable benefits). In such instances, the plan will have to be unfunded to prevent immediate taxation to the employee. Note that most funded NQDC plans are subject to many of the provisions that apply to qualified plans.

To be effective, an unfunded deferred compensation plan must meet and comply with the following requirements under § 409A:[78]

- The NQDC plan may not distribute the deferred compensation to the employee without penalty except in these six situations: separation of service, disability, death, specified time or fixed schedule, change in employer control, or unforeseeable emergency.
- The plan must not permit any participant to accelerate the time or scheduled date of distributions (subject to some exceptions).
- A participant must elect to postpone the compensation for the current year no later than the close of the preceding tax year.
- The employee must decide on the form and time of the benefits (e.g., installment payments or lump sum) when the deferral election is made. Or the NQDC plan may specify the form and time of distribution when there is a permissible distribution event.
- A participant must not change the time or form of benefits unless the employee does so at least 12 months before the scheduled distribution date and also postpones the scheduled distribution date by at least five years.

There are funded and vested NQDC plans, funded and nonvested NQDC plans, plans that fail to qualify with § 409A, and plans adopted prior to 2005. Often an employee is better off receiving the compensation, paying ordinary income taxes on it, and then investing the remainder. Dividends and appreciation on the investments are taxed at the 15 percent rate rather than the top rate of 35 percent on the deferred compensation (including interest and appreciation).

---

[75]Rev.Rul. 60–31, 1960–1 C.B. 174; Reg. § 1.451–2(a); *U.S. v. Basye*, 73–1 USTC ¶9250, 31 AFTR2d 73–802, 93 S.Ct. 1080 (USSC, 1973).

[76]§§ 404(a) and (d).

[77]Rev.Rul. 55–525, 1955–2 C.B. 543.

[78]§§ 409A(a)(2), (3), and (4).

When to Use an NQDC Arrangement. As a general rule, NQDC plans are more appropriate for executives in a financially secure company. Because of the need for currently disposable income, such plans are usually not appropriate for young employees.

An NQDC plan can reduce an employee's overall tax payments by deferring the taxation of income to later years (possibly when the employee is in a lower tax bracket). In effect, these plans may produce a form of income averaging. Further, NQDC plans may discriminate in favor of shareholders, officers, specific highly compensated key employees, or a single individual.

Certain disadvantages should be noted. As noted earlier, nonqualified plans are usually required to be unfunded, which means that an employee is not assured that funds ultimately will be available to pay the benefits. Also, the employer's tax deduction is postponed until the employee is taxed on those payments.

Golden Parachute Arrangements. Golden parachute arrangements promise monetary benefits to key employees if they lose their jobs as a result of a change in ownership of the corporation. These payments may be unreasonable or not really for services rendered. The term **golden parachute payments**, as used in the Code, means *excess severance pay*.

These excessive severance payments to employees are penalized. The Code denies a deduction to an employer who makes a payment of cash or property to an employee or independent contractor that satisfies both of the following conditions:

- The payment is contingent on a change of ownership of a corporation through a stock or asset acquisition.
- The aggregate present value of the payment equals or exceeds three times the employee's (or independent contractor's) average annual compensation.[79]

The disallowed amount is the excess of the payment over a statutory base amount (a five-year average of taxable compensation if the taxpayer was an employee for the entire five-year period). Further, a 20 percent excise tax is imposed on the recipient on the receipt of these parachute payments; the tax is withheld at the time of payment.[80]

E X A M P L E   3 6

Irene, an executive, receives a golden parachute payment of $380,000 from her employer. Her average annual compensation for the most recent five tax years is $120,000. The corporation will be denied a deduction for $260,000 ($380,000 payment − $120,000 base amount). Irene's excise tax is $52,000 ($260,000 × 20%). ∎

Golden parachute payments do not include payments to or from qualified pension, profit sharing, stock bonus, annuity, or simplified employee pension plans. Also excluded is the amount of the payment that, in fact, represents reasonable compensation for personal services actually rendered or to be rendered. Such excluded payments are not taken into account when determining whether the threshold (the aggregate present value calculation) is exceeded.

S corporations are not subject to the golden parachute rules. Generally, corporations that do not have stock that is readily tradable on an established securities market or elsewhere are also exempt.

Publicly Held Companies' Compensation Limitation. For purposes of both the regular income tax and the alternative minimum tax, the deductible compensation for the top five executives of publicly traded companies is limited to $1 million for each executive. A company is publicly held if the corporation has common stock listed on a national securities exchange.[81] This $1 million deduction limitation is

---

[79]§ 280G.
[80]§ 4999.

[81]§ 162(m).

decreased by any nondeductible golden parachute payments made to the employee during the same year.

This deduction limitation applies when the compensation deduction would otherwise be taken. For example, in the case of a nonqualified stock option (NQSO), which is discussed later in this chapter, the deduction is normally taken in the year the NQSO is exercised, even though the option was granted with respect to services performed in a prior year.

Certain types of compensation are *not* subject to this deduction limit and are not taken into account in determining whether other compensation exceeds $1 million:

- Compensation payable on a commission basis.
- Compensation payable solely on account of the attainment of one or more performance goals when certain requirements involving the approval of outside directors and shareholders are met.
- Payments to a tax-qualified retirement plan (including salary-reduction contributions).
- Amounts that are excludible from an executive's gross income (such as employer-provided health benefits and miscellaneous fringe benefits).

The most important exception is performance-based compensation. Compensation qualifies for this exception only if the following conditions are satisfied:

- The compensation is paid solely on account of the attainment of one or more performance goals.
- The performance goals are established by a compensation committee consisting solely of two or more outside directors.
- The material terms under which the compensation is to be paid (including the performance goals) are disclosed to and approved by the shareholders in a separate vote prior to payment.
- Prior to payment, the compensation committee certifies that the performance goals and any other material terms were in fact satisfied.

Compensation (other than stock options or other stock appreciation rights) is not treated as paid solely on account of the attainment of one or more performance goals unless the compensation is paid to the particular executive under a pre-established objective performance formula or standard that precludes discretion. In essence, a third party with knowledge of the relevant performance results could calculate the amount to be paid to the particular executive. A performance goal is broadly defined and includes, for example, any objective performance standard that is applied to the individual executive, a business unit (e.g., a division or a line of business), or the corporation as a whole. Performance standards could include increases in stock price, market share, sales, or earnings per share.

ETHICAL *Considerations* THE JOCK TAX SPREADS

The Tax Foundation recently reported that jock taxes are spreading from professional athletes to trainers, scouts, lawyers (New Jersey), and even touring skateboarders (Cincinnati). The so-called jock tax requires traveling professional athletes and other team employees to pay income taxes in every state where games are played. At least 20 of the 24 states that have professional teams have a jock tax, as do six cities. According to David Hoffman, an adjunct Tax Foundation scholar and the coauthor of the report, the jock tax started when California tried to get revenge on Michael Jordan and the Chicago Bulls for beating the L.A. Lakers in 1991. To level the playing field, Illinois imposed a retaliatory tax the following year.

Evaluate the fairness of taxing the compensation of athletes and other traveling professionals (both the rich and the not-so-rich) who do not live in the particular city or state imposing the tax.

Restricted Property Plans

General Provisions

A **restricted property plan** is an arrangement whereby an employer transfers property (e.g., stock of the employer-corporation) to an employee or other provider of services at no cost or at a bargain price. The usual purpose of a restricted stock plan is to retain the services of key employees who might otherwise leave. The employer hopes that such compensation arrangements will encourage company growth and attainment of performance objectives. Section 83 was enacted in 1969 to provide rules for the taxation of incentive compensation arrangements, which previously were governed by judicial and administrative interpretations. Although the following discussion refers to an employee as the provider of the services, the services may be performed by an independent contractor.

As a general rule, if an employee performs services and receives property (e.g., stock), the fair market value of that property in excess of any amount paid by the employee is includible in his or her gross income. The time for inclusion is the earlier of (1) the time the property is no longer subject to a substantial risk of forfeiture or (2) the time the property is transferable by the employee. The fair market value of the property is determined without regard to any restriction, except a restriction that by its terms will never lapse.[82] Since the amount of the compensation is determined at the date that the restrictions lapse or when the property is transferable, the opportunity to generate capital gain treatment on the property is denied during a period when the ordinary income element is being deferred.

EXAMPLE 37

On October 1, 2002, Blue Corporation sold 100 shares of its stock to Ahmad, an employee, for $10 per share. At the time of the sale, the fair market value of the stock was $100 per share. Under the terms of the sale, each share of stock was nontransferable and subject to a substantial risk of forfeiture (which was not to lapse until October 1, 2006). Evidence of these restrictions was stamped on the face of the stock certificates. On October 1, 2006, the fair market value of the stock was $250 per share. Since the stock was nontransferable and was subject to a substantial risk of forfeiture, Ahmad did not include any compensation in gross income during 2002 (assuming no special election was made). Instead, Ahmad was required to include $24,000 of compensation in gross income [100 shares × ($250 − $10 per share)] during 2006. If for some reason the forfeiture had occurred (e.g., the plan required Ahmad to surrender the stock to the corporation if he voluntarily terminated his employment with the company before October 1, 2006) and Ahmad never received the stock certificates, he would have been allowed a capital loss of $1,000 (the extent of his investment). ■

Substantial Risk of Forfeiture

A **substantial risk of forfeiture** exists if a person's rights to full enjoyment of property are conditioned upon the future performance, or the refraining from the performance, of substantial services by that individual.[83] For example, if an employee must return the property (receiving only his or her original cost, if any) should there be a failure to complete a substantial period of service (for any reason), the property is subject to a substantial risk of forfeiture. Another such situation exists when an employer can compel an employee to return the property due to a breach of a substantial covenant not to compete. Any substantial risk of forfeiture should be stated on the face of the stock certificates. Assuming that a substantial risk of forfeiture does not exist, the property received is valued at its fair market value, ignoring any restrictions, except for one instance dealing with closely held stock.

---

[82]§ 83(a)(1); *Miriam Sakol*, 67 T.C. 986 (1977); *T. M. Horwith*, 71 T.C. 932 (1979).

[83]§ 83(c). Regulation § 1.83–3(c)(2) includes several examples of restricted property arrangements.

TAX *in the News* | **DIVIDEND BENEFITS OF RESTRICTED STOCK**

How would you like to receive dividends on stock you do not own? That is happening to many executives, who hold restricted stock shares before the shares have even vested. About 90 percent of publicly traded U.S. companies give dividends on restricted stock.

Consider Altria Group Chairman and CEO Louis C. Camilleri's windfall. When the tobacco company raised its quarterly dividend to 73 cents from 68 cents, he earned more than $1.5 million in dividends on his 575,000 unvested restricted shares.

Source: *Adapted from Phyllis Plitch, "Executives Find Restricted Stock Pays Dividends from the Get-Go," Wall Street Journal, February 28, 2005, p. C3.*

Special Election Available

An employee may elect within 30 days after the receipt of restricted property to recognize immediately as ordinary income the fair market value in excess of the amount paid for the property. Any appreciation in the value of the property after receipt is classified as capital gain instead of ordinary income. No deduction is allowed to the employee for taxes paid on the original amount included in income if the property is subsequently forfeited.[84] The employee is permitted to take a capital loss for any amounts that were actually paid for the property. Furthermore, in such a case, the employer must repay taxes saved by any compensation deduction taken in the earlier year.[85]

Any increase in value between the time the property is received and the time it becomes either nonforfeitable or transferable is taxed as ordinary income if the employee does not make this special election. However, if the employee elects to be taxed immediately on the difference between the cost and fair market value on the date of issue, any future appreciation is treated as capital gain. In determining whether the gain is long term or short term, the holding period starts when the employee is taxed on the ordinary income.[86]

EXAMPLE 38

On July 1, 1996, Sparrow Company sold 100 shares of its preferred stock, worth $15 per share, to Diane (an employee) for $5 per share. The sale was subject to Diane's agreement to resell the preferred shares to the company for $5 per share if she terminated her employment during the following 10 years. The stock had a value of $25 per share on July 1, 2006, and Diane sold the stock for $30 per share on October 10, 2006. Diane made the special election to include the original spread (between the value of $15 in 1996 and the amount paid of $5) in income for 1996. Diane was required to recognize $1,000 of compensation income in 1995 ($15 − $5 = $10 × 100 shares), at which time her holding period in her stock began. Diane's tax basis in the stock was $1,500 ($1,000 + $500). When the preferred stock was sold in 2006, Diane recognized a $1,500 long-term capital gain ($30 × 100 shares − $1,500). ∎

EXAMPLE 39

Assume the same facts as in the previous example, except that Diane sells the stock in 2007 (rather than 2006). She would not recognize any gain in 2006 when the substantial risk of forfeiture lapses. Instead, Diane would recognize the $1,500 long-term capital gain in 2007. ∎

This special provision is usually not elected since it results in an immediate recognition of income and adverse tax consequences result from a subsequent forfeiture. However, the special election may be attractive in the following situations:

- The bargain element is relatively small.
- Substantial appreciation is expected in the future.
- A high probability exists that the restrictions will be met.

---

[84]§ 83(b).
[85]Reg. §§ 1.83–6(c) and 2(a).
[86]§ 1223(6).

Employer Deductions

At the time the employee is required to include the compensation in income, the employer is allowed a tax deduction for the same amount. The employer must withhold on this amount in accordance with § 3402. In the no-election situation, the deduction is limited to the fair market value of the restricted property (without regard to the restrictions) at the time the restrictions lapse, reduced by the amount originally paid for the property by the employee.[87] When the employee elects to be taxed immediately, the corporate deduction also is accelerated and deductible in like amount. In cases of deferred income recognition, the employer can receive a sizable deduction if the property has appreciated.

E X A M P L E   40

On March 14, 2004, Gold Corporation sold to Harry, an employee, 10 shares of Gold common stock for $100 per share. Both the corporation and Harry were calendar year taxpayers. The common stock was subject to a substantial risk of forfeiture and was nontransferable; both conditions were to lapse on March 14, 2006. At the time of the sale, the fair market value of the common stock (without considering the restrictions) was $1,000 per share. On March 14, 2006, when the fair market value of the stock is $2,000 per share, the restrictions lapse. Harry did not make the special election. In 2006, Harry realizes ordinary income of $19,000 (10 shares at $2,000 per share less the $100 per share he had paid). Likewise, Gold Corporation is allowed a $19,000 compensation deduction in 2006. ■

E X A M P L E   41

In the previous example, assume that Harry had made the special election. Since he was taxed on $9,000 in 2004, the corporation was allowed to deduct a like amount in 2004. No deduction would be available in 2006. ■

LO.9

Differentiate the tax treatment of qualified and nonqualified stock options.

Stock Options

In General

Various equity types of stock option programs are available for an employee's compensation package. Some authorities believe that some form of *equity kicker* is needed to attract new management, convert key officers into *partners* by giving them a share of the business, and retain the services of executives who might otherwise leave. Encouraging the managers of a business to have a proprietary interest in its successful operation should provide executives with a key motive to expand the company and improve its profits. In addition, under certain conditions, stock options may fall outside the $1 million limitation on the salaries of the top five executives of publicly traded companies.

A **stock option** gives an individual the right to purchase a stated number of shares of stock from a corporation at a certain price within a specified period of time. The optionee must be under no obligation to purchase the stock, and the option may be revocable by the corporation. The option must be in writing, and its terms must be clearly expressed.[88]

Incentive Stock Options

An equity type of stock option called an *incentive stock option (ISO)* is available. There are no tax consequences for either the issuing corporation or the recipient when the option is granted. However, the *spread* (the excess of the fair market value of the share at the date of exercise over the option price)[89] is a tax preference item to the recipient for purposes of the alternative minimum tax. The determination of

---

[87]Reg. § 1.83–6(a).
[88]Reg. §§ 1.421–1(a)(1) and –7(a)(1).

[89]§§ 422(a), 421(a)(1), 57(a)(3), and 1234(a)(1) and (2).

fair market value is made without regard to any lapse restrictions (a restriction that will expire after a period of time). After the option is exercised and when the stock is sold, any gain from the sale is taxed as a long-term capital gain if certain holding period requirements are met. For a gain to qualify as a long-term capital gain, the employee must not dispose of the stock within two years after the option is granted or within one year after acquiring the stock.[90] If the employee meets the holding period requirements, none of these transactions generates any business deduction for the employer.[91] If the employee pays anything for the option and does not exercise the option, any amount paid is recognized as a capital loss.

EXAMPLE 42

Wren Corporation granted an ISO for 100 shares of its stock to Rocky, an employee, on March 18, 2003. The option price was $100, and the fair market value was $100 on the date of the grant. Rocky exercised the option on April 1, 2005, when the fair market value of the stock was $200 per share. He sells the stock on April 6, 2006, for $300 per share. Rocky did not recognize any ordinary income on the date of the grant or the exercise date since the option qualified as an ISO. Wren received no compensation deduction. Rocky has a $10,000 tax preference item on the exercise date. He has a long-term capital gain of $20,000 [($300 − $100) × 100] on the sale of the stock in 2006, because the one-year and two-year holding periods and other requirements have been met. ∎

As a further requirement for ISO treatment, the option holder must be an employee of the issuing corporation from the date the option is granted until 3 months (12 months if disabled) before the date of exercise. The holding period and the employee-status rules just described (the one-year, two-year, and three-month requirements) are waived in the case of the death of an employee.[92]

EXAMPLE 43

Assume the same facts as in the previous example, except that Rocky was not employed by Wren Corporation for six months before the date he exercised the options. Rocky must recognize ordinary income to the extent of the spread, assuming there was no substantial risk of forfeiture. Thus, Rocky recognizes $10,000 [($200 − $100) × 100] of ordinary income on the exercise date, because he was not an employee of Wren Corporation at all times during the period beginning on the grant date and ending three months before the exercise date. Wren is allowed a deduction at the same time that Rocky reports the ordinary income. ∎

If the holding period requirements are not satisfied but all other conditions are met, the tax is still deferred to the point of the sale. However, the difference between the option price and the value of the stock at the date the option was exercised is treated as ordinary income. The difference between the amount realized for the stock and the value of the stock at the date of exercise is short-term or long-term capital gain, depending on the holding period of the stock itself. The employer is allowed a deduction equal to the amount recognized by the employee as ordinary income. The employee does not have a tax preference for alternative minimum tax purposes.

EXAMPLE 44

Assume the same facts as in Example 42, except that Rocky sells the stock on March 22, 2006, for $290 per share. Since Rocky did not hold the stock itself for more than one year, $10,000 of the gain is treated as ordinary income in 2006, and Wren Corporation is allowed a $10,000 compensation deduction in 2006. The remaining $9,000 is a short-term capital gain ($29,000 − $20,000). ∎

---

[90]§ 422(a)(1).

[91]§ 421(a)(2).

[92]§§ 422(a)(2) and (c)(3). Exceptions are made for parent and subsidiary situations, corporate reorganizations, and liquidations. Also, in certain situations involving an insolvent employee, the holding period rules are modified.

Qualification Requirements for Incentive Stock Option Plans. An incentive stock option (ISO) is an option to purchase stock of a corporation granted to an individual for any reason connected with his or her employment.[93] The option is granted by the employer-corporation or by a parent or subsidiary corporation of the employer-corporation. When exercising an option, an employee can use company stock to pay for the stock without disqualifying the ISO plan.

For an option to qualify as an ISO, the terms of the option itself must meet the following conditions:

* The option must be granted under a plan specifying the number of shares of stock to be issued and the employees or class of employees eligible to receive the options. The plan must be approved by the shareholders of the corporation within 12 months before or after the plan is adopted.
* The option must be granted within 10 years of the date the plan is adopted or of the date the plan is approved by the shareholders, whichever date is earlier.
* The option must by its terms be exercisable only within 10 years of the date it is granted.
* The option price must equal or exceed the fair market value of the stock at the time the option is granted. This requirement is deemed satisfied if there has been a good faith attempt to value the stock accurately, even if the option price is less than the stock value.
* The option by its terms must be nontransferable other than at death and must be exercisable during the employee's lifetime only by the employee.
* The employee must not, immediately before the option is granted, own stock representing more than 10 percent of the voting power or value of all classes of stock in the employer-corporation or its parent or subsidiary. (Here, the attribution rules of § 267 are applied in modified form.) However, the stock ownership limitation will be waived if the option price is at least 110 percent of the fair market value (at the time the option is granted) of the stock subject to the option and the option by its terms is not exercisable more than five years from the date it is granted.[94]

An overall limitation is imposed on the amount of ISOs that can be exercised in one year by an employee. This limit is set at $100,000 per year based on the value of the stock determined at the time the option is granted.

Nonqualified Stock Options

A **nonqualified stock option (NQSO)** does not satisfy the statutory requirements for ISOs. In addition, a stock option that otherwise would qualify as an ISO will be treated as an NQSO if the terms of the stock option provide that it is not an ISO. If the NQSO has a readily ascertainable fair market value (e.g., the option is traded on an established exchange), the value of the option must be included in the employee's income at the date of grant. Thereafter, capital gain or loss is recognized only upon the disposal of the optioned stock. The employee's basis is the amount paid for the stock plus any amount reported as ordinary income. The employer obtains a corresponding tax deduction at the same time and to the extent that ordinary income is recognized by the employee.[95]

EXAMPLE 45

On February 1, 2005, Janet was granted an NQSO to purchase 100 shares of stock from her employer at $10 per share. On this date, the option was selling for $2 on an established exchange. Janet exercised the option on March 30, 2006, when the stock was worth $20 per share. On November 5, 2006, Janet sold the optioned stock for $22 per share.

---

[93]§ 422(b).
[94]§ 422(c)(5).

[95]Reg. §§ 1.421–6(c), (d), (e), and (f); Reg. § 1.83–7.

- Janet must report ordinary income of $200 ($2 × 100 shares) on the date of grant (February 1, 2005), because the option has a readily ascertainable fair market value.
- Janet's adjusted basis for the stock is $1,200 ($1,000 cost + $200 recognized gain).
- Upon the sale of the stock (November 5, 2006), Janet must report a long-term capital gain of $1,000 [($22 − $12) × 100 shares].
- At the date of grant (February 1, 2005), the employer receives a tax deduction of $200, the amount of ordinary income reported by Janet.   ■

If an NQSO does not have a readily ascertainable fair market value, an employee does not recognize income at the grant date. However, as a general rule, ordinary income must then be reported in the year of exercise (the difference between the fair market value of the stock at the exercise date and the option price).[96] The amount paid by the employee for the stock plus the amount reported as ordinary income becomes the basis. Any appreciation above that basis is taxed as a long-term capital gain upon disposition (assuming the stock is held for the required long-term holding period after exercise). The corporation receives a corresponding tax deduction at the same time and to the extent that ordinary income is recognized by the employee.

E X A M P L E   46

On February 3, 2004, Maria was granted an NQSO for 100 shares of common stock at $10 per share. On the date of the grant, there was no readily ascertainable fair market value for the option. Maria exercised the options on January 3, 2005, when the stock was selling for $15 per share. She sold one-half of the shares on April 15, 2005, and the other half on September 17, 2006. The sale price on both dates was $21 per share. Maria would not recognize any income on the grant date (February 3, 2004) but would recognize $500 ($1,500 − $1,000) of ordinary income on the exercise date (January 3, 2005). She would recognize a short-term capital gain of $300 on the sale of the first half in 2005 and a $300 long-term capital gain on the sale of the second batch of stock in 2006 [½($2,100 − $1,500)].   ■

The major *advantages* of NQSOs can be summarized as follows:

- A tax deduction is available to the corporation without a cash outlay.
- The employee receives capital gain treatment on any appreciation in the stock starting either at the exercise date if the option does not have a readily ascertainable fair market value or at the date of grant if the option has a readily ascertainable fair market value.
- Options can be issued at more flexible terms than under ISO plans (e.g., longer exercise period and discount on exercise price).

A major *disadvantage* is that the employee must recognize ordinary income on the exercise of the option or at the date of grant without receiving cash to pay the tax.

Deferred Compensation

With the individual tax rate being as high as 35 percent in 2006, taxpayers are motivated to try to lower their tax burden by participating in more deferred compensation arrangements. The $1 million annual limit on the compensation deduction for the top five executives of publicly traded companies may cause a shift into § 401(k) plans, qualified retirement plans, and especially nonqualified deferred compensation arrangements. However, only $220,000 of compensation can be taken into consideration for purposes of calculating contributions or benefits under a qualified pension or profit sharing plan. The $4,000 allowed for traditional IRAs and Roth IRAs should encourage more participation in retirement vehicles. The spousal IRA option should expand retirement coverage even further.

LO.10

Identify tax planning opportunities available with deferred compensation.

TAX PLANNING
Considerations

---

[96]Reg. § 1.83–7(a); Reg. § 1.421–6(d).

Qualified Plans

Qualified plans provide maximum tax benefits for employers, because the employer receives an immediate tax deduction for contributions to such plans and the income that is earned on the contributions is not taxable to the employer. The employer's contributions and the trust earnings are not taxed to the employees until those funds are made available to them.

Qualified plans are most appropriate where it is desirable to provide benefits for a cross section of employees. In some closely held corporations, the primary objective is to provide benefits for the officer-shareholder group and other highly paid personnel. The nondiscrimination requirements that must be met in a qualified plan may prevent such companies from attaining these objectives. Thus, a nonqualified arrangement may be needed as a supplement to, or used in lieu of, the qualified plan.

Cash balance plans are better for younger, mobile employees, and the converting company saves money by reducing pension payouts for older and longer-service employees. If a participant moves or retires, he or she can roll over the lump-sum payment into an IRA or another qualified plan.

Self-Employed Retirement Plans

A Keogh or traditional deductible IRA participant may make a deductible contribution for a tax year up to the time prescribed for filing the individual's tax return. A Keogh plan must have been established by the end of the tax year (e.g., December 31) to obtain a current deduction for the contribution made in the subsequent year. An individual can establish an IRA after the end of the tax year and still receive a current deduction for the contribution made in the subsequent year. However, since the deductibility of contributions to IRAs has been restricted for many middle-income and upper-income taxpayers, Keogh plans are likely to become more important.

Individual Retirement Accounts

Unlike a traditional IRA, which only defers taxes, a Roth IRA allows the tax-free accumulation of wealth. All ordinary income and capital gains earned inside a Roth IRA are never taxed (assuming the five-year holding period provision is satisfied). Thus, a Roth IRA runs contrary to the general principle that it is usually better for a taxpayer to postpone the payment of any tax. In many situations, a retirement plan participant will earn more wealth with a Roth IRA than with a traditional IRA. This potential for tax-free growth is so advantageous that taxpayers who have substantial traditional IRA balances and are eligible should evaluate converting at least some of their traditional IRA balances into a Roth IRA.

Comparison of § 401(k) Plan with IRA

Most employees will find a § 401(k) plan more attractive than an IRA. Probably the biggest limitation of an IRA is the $4,000 maximum shelter in 2006 (ignoring the catch-up provision). Under § 401(k), employees are permitted to shelter compensation up to $15,000 (in 2006).[97] The restrictions on deducting contributions to IRAs for many middle-income and upper-income taxpayers may cause many employees to utilize § 401(k) plans more frequently.

Another difference between § 401(k) plans and IRAs is the manner in which the money is treated. Money placed in an IRA may be tax deductible, whereas dollars placed in a § 401(k) plan are considered to be deferred compensation. Thus, a § 401(k) reduction may reduce profit sharing payments, group life insurance, and Social Security benefits. Concept Summary 19–5 compares a § 401(k) plan with an IRA.

---

[97]These amounts are being increased through a phase-in approach. See Footnotes 38 and 49.

CONCEPT SUMMARY   19–5

Section 401(k) Plan and IRA Compared

	§ 401(k) Plan	IRA
Deduction limitation	Smaller of $15,000 (in 2006) or approximately 100% of total earnings. Limited by antidiscrimination requirements of § 401(k)(3).	$4,000 or 100% of compensation.
Distributions	Early withdrawal possible if for early retirement (55 or over) or to pay medical expenses.	10% penalty for early withdrawals, except for withdrawals to pay for certain medical expenses and health insurance, qualified education expenses, and qualified first-time home buyer expenses.
Effect on gross earnings	Gross salary reduction, which may reduce profit sharing contributions, Social Security benefits, and group life insurance.	No effect.
Employer involvement	Must keep records; monitor for compliance with antidiscrimination test.	Minimal.
Lump-sum distributions	Favorable 10-year forward averaging.	Ordinary income.
Timing of contribution	Within 30 days of plan year-end or due date of employer's return.*	Grace period up to due date of tax return (not including extensions).
Loans from plan	Yes.	No.

*Elective contributions must be made to the plan no later than 30 days after the end of the plan year, and nonelective contributions no later than the due date of the tax return (including extensions).

Nonqualified Deferred Compensation (NQDC) Plans

Nonqualified deferred compensation arrangements such as restricted property plans can be useful to attract executive talent or to provide substantial retirement benefits for executives. A restricted property plan may be used to retain a key employee of a closely held company when management continuity problems are anticipated. Without such employees, the untimely death or disability of one of the owners might cause a disruption of the business with an attendant loss in value for his or her heirs. Such plans may discriminate in favor of officers and other highly paid employees. The employer, however, does not receive a tax deduction until the employee is required to include the deferred compensation in income (upon the lapse of the restrictions).

The principal advantage of NQDC plans over current compensation is that the employee can defer the recognition of income to future periods when his or her income tax bracket may be lower (e.g., during retirement years). The time value benefits from the deferral of income should also be considered. With the trend toward decreasing rates, an executive with a deferred compensation arrangement entered into in a prior year might wish to continue to delay the income into future years since individual tax rates in future years may be even lower.

The principal disadvantage of NQDC plans could be the bunching effect that takes place on the expiration of the period of deferral. In some cases, planning can alleviate this result.

CONCEPT SUMMARY 19–6

Incentive Stock Options and Nonqualified Stock Options Compared

	ISO	NQSO
Granted at any price	No	Yes
May have any duration	No	Yes
Governing Code Section	§ 422	§ 83
Spread subject to alternative minimum tax	Yes	No
Deduction to employer for spread	No	Yes
Type of gain/loss on disposal	Capital	Capital
Statutory amount ($100,000) limitation	Yes	No

EXAMPLE 47

During 2006, Kelly, an executive, enters into an agreement to postpone a portion of her payment for current services until retirement. The deferred amount is not segregated from the company's general assets and is subject to normal business risk. The entire payment, not the after-tax amount, is invested in securities and variable annuity contracts. Kelly is not taxed on the payment in 2006, and the company receives no deduction in 2006. If Kelly receives the deferred payment in a lump sum when she retires, the tax rates might be higher and more progressive than in 2006. Thus, Kelly may wish to arrange for a number of payments to be made to her or a designated beneficiary over a number of years. ■

Stock Options

Rather than paying compensation in the form of corporate stock, a corporation may issue options to purchase stock at a specific price to an employee. Stock option plans are used more frequently by publicly traded companies than by closely held companies. This difference is due to the problems of determining the value of the stock of a company that is not publicly held.

Nonqualified stock options (NQSOs) are more flexible and less restrictive than incentive stock options (ISOs). For example, the holding period for an NQSO is not as long as that for an ISO. Further, the option price of an NQSO may be less than the fair market value of the stock at the time the option is granted. An NQSO creates an employer deduction that lowers the cost of the NQSO to the employer. The employer may pass along this tax savings to the employee in the form of a cash payment. Both the employer and the employee may be better off by combining NQSOs with additional cash payments rather than using ISOs. See Concept Summary 19–6.

For tax purposes, most companies are able to deduct the expense of options and thereby reduce their taxes. For accounting purposes, most companies do not wish to take a hit to reported earnings, so the deduction is ignored. Thus, although options cost shareholders in dilution, they cost a company little to issue and actually can save it money on payroll costs.

Stock options are an effective compensation device as long as share prices are rising. When stock prices fall, the options become unexercisable and possibly worthless. In an upmarket, options are great. But during a downturn in the market, these underwater options can be ugly.

Flexible Benefit Plans

Employees may be permitted to choose from a package of employer-provided fringe benefits.[98] In these so-called **cafeteria benefit plans**, some of the benefits chosen by an employee may be taxable, and some may be statutory nontaxable benefits (e.g., health and accident insurance and group term life insurance).

Employer contributions made to a flexible plan are included in an employee's gross income only to the extent that the employee actually elects the taxable benefits. Certain nondiscrimination standards with respect to coverage, eligibility for participation, contributions, and benefits must be met. Thus, such a plan must cover a fair cross section of employees. Also, a flexible plan cannot include an election to defer compensation, and a key employee is not exempt from taxation on the taxable benefits made available where more than 25 percent of the statutory nontaxable benefits are provided to key employees.

KEY TERMS

Cafeteria benefit plans, 19–41
Cash balance plan, 19–5
Coverdell Education Savings Account (CESA), 19–22
Deferred compensation, 19–3
Defined benefit plan, 19–4
Defined contribution pension plan, 19–5
Golden parachute payments, 19–30
Highly compensated employee, 19–8

H.R. 10(Keogh) plans, 19–18
Incentive stock option (ISO), 19–36
Individual Retirement Accounts (IRAs), 19–19
Lump-sum distribution, 19–12
Nonqualified deferred compensation (NQDC) plans, 19–28
Nonqualified stock option (NQSO), 19–36
Pension plan, 19–4

Profit sharing plan, 19–5
Restricted property plan, 19–32
Roth IRA, 19–21
Section 401(k) plan, 19–16
Simplified employee pension (SEP) plans, 19–23
Stock bonus plan, 19–5
Stock option, 19–34
Substantial risk of forfeiture, 19–32
Vesting requirements, 19–8
Zero bracket amount, 19–13

PROBLEM MATERIALS

DISCUSSION QUESTIONS

1. What is the purpose of the private pension and profit sharing plan system?

2. List some types of deferred compensation arrangements.

3. Determine whether each of the following independent statements best applies to a defined contribution plan *(DCP)*, defined benefit plan *(DBP)*, both *(B)*, or neither *(N)*:
   a. The amount to be received at retirement depends on actuarial calculations.
   b. Forfeitures can be allocated to the remaining participants' accounts.
   c. Requires greater reporting requirements and more actuarial and administrative costs.
   d. Forfeitures can revert to the employer.
   e. More favorable to employees who are older at the time the plan is adopted.
   f. Employee forfeitures can be used to reduce future contributions by the employer.
   g. May exclude employees who begin employment within five years of normal retirement age.

[98]§ 125.

      h.   Annual addition to each employee's account may not exceed the smaller of $44,000 or 100% of the employee's salary.

      i.   The final benefit to a participant depends upon investment performance.

      j.   To avoid penalties, the amount of annual contributions must meet minimum funding requirements.

4. Indicate whether the following statements apply to a pension plan *(P)*, a profit sharing plan *(PS)*, both *(B)*, or neither *(N)*:

    a.   Forfeited amounts can be used to reduce future contributions by the employer.

    b.   Allocation of forfeitures may discriminate in favor of the prohibited group (highly compensated employees).

    c.   Forfeitures can revert to the employer.

    d.   Forfeitures can be allocated to participants and increase plan benefits.

    e.   An annual benefit of $60,000 could be payable on behalf of a participant.

    f.   More favorable to employees who are older at the time the qualified plan is adopted.

5. What is a profit sharing plan?

6. Describe a stock bonus plan.

7. Is a cash balance plan a defined benefit plan, a defined contribution plan, or neither? Who bears the investment risk in a cash balance plan?

8. List the requirements that must be satisfied in order for a retirement plan to be a qualified plan and receive favorable tax treatment.

9. Why is a determination letter needed for a new qualified retirement plan?

10. When must an employee be eligible to participate in a qualified retirement plan?

Issue ID

11. Jenny plans to retire in 2006 at age 70. Identify any issues facing Jenny with respect to distributions from her qualified retirement plan.

Issue ID

Communications

12. Harvey Maxwell, who is age 71, is going to receive a lump-sum distribution from a qualified plan in 2006. He has asked you to provide him with a description of the alternatives available to him for taxing the lump-sum distribution. Draft a letter to Harvey in which you respond. He resides at 3000 East Glenn, Tulsa, OK 74104.

13. Which of the following would be considered a tax benefit or advantage of a qualified retirement plan?

    a.   Certain lump-sum distributions may be subject to capital gain treatment.

    b.   Employer contributions are deductible by the employer in the year of contribution.

    c.   Employee contributions are deductible by the employee in the year of contribution.

    d.   The qualified trust is tax-exempt as to all income (other than unrelated business income).

    e.   In a lump-sum distribution, any capital gain tax on the portion attributable to any unrealized appreciation in the stock of the employer at the time of distribution is deferred until the time the employee disposes of the stock in a taxable transaction.

    f.   An election may be made to allow a lump-sum distribution to be subject to a 10-year forward averaging technique.

Decision Making

14. Sally is retiring and wishes to know her alternatives for receiving payments from her qualified retirement plan.

15. What are the differences between a § 401(k) plan and a pension plan?

Decision Making

16. Should a 29-year-old self-employed woman establish a traditional deductible IRA, a traditional nondeductible IRA, or a Roth IRA? She has two children, ages 11 and 9.

17. Nick is not covered by another qualified plan and earns $97,000 at his job. How much can he contribute to a traditional IRA or to a Roth IRA in 2006?

18. A beneficiary of a Coverdell Education Savings Account (CESA) reaches age 30 in 2006. The plan balance of $6,000 consists of $4,000 of contributions and $2,000 of earnings. Discuss any tax consequences.

19. Jerry Polk calls you and asks about the differences between a Roth IRA and a CESA. Prepare a memo for the tax files about your response.

Communications

20. For an unfunded nonqualified deferred compensation plan to be eligible for deferral treatment, what requirements must be satisfied under § 409A?

21. During his senior year in college, Mark is drafted by the Los Angeles Dodgers. When he graduates, he expects to sign a five-year contract in the range of $1.8 million per year. Mark plans to marry his girlfriend before he reports to the Dodger farm team in California. Identify the relevant tax issues facing this left-handed pitcher.

Issue ID

22. Under what circumstances may the special election to recognize income immediately with restricted stock be appropriate?

23. What are the tax consequences to the issuing corporation and to the recipient when incentive stock options (ISOs) are granted?

24. Indicate whether each of the following items is considered a nonqualified compensation plan *(N)*, a qualified compensation plan *(Q)*, or both *(B)*:
    a. Individual Retirement Account.
    b. Incentive stock option.
    c. Group term life insurance.
    d. Cafeteria plan.
    e. Pension plan.
    f. Profit sharing plan.
    g. Nonqualified stock option.
    h. Keogh plan.
    i. Simplified employee pension plan.

25. Red Corporation has a total of 1,000 employees, of whom 700 are non-highly compensated. The retirement plan covers 300 non-highly compensated employees and 200 highly compensated employees. Does this plan satisfy the minimum coverage test?

26. Cardinal Corporation's pension plan benefits 620 of its 1,000 highly compensated employees. How many of its 620 non-highly compensated employees must benefit to meet the ratio test for the minimum coverage requirement?

27. A retirement plan covers 72% of the non-highly compensated individuals. The plan benefits 48 of the 131 employees. Determine if the participation requirement is met.

28. Robin, Inc., uses a three- to seven-year graded vesting approach in its retirement plan. Calculate the nonforfeitable percentage for each of the following participants based upon the years of service completed:

Participant	Years of Service
Mary	2
Sam	4
Peter	6
Heather	7

29. Chipmunk, Inc., uses the two- to six-year graded vesting approach in its retirement plan. Calculate the nonforfeitable percentage for each of the following participants based upon the years of service completed:

Participant	Years of Service
Caleb	3
Daniel	4
Sloane	5
Ryan	7

Decision Making

Communications

30. Yvonne Blair receives a $165,000 lump-sum distribution from a contributory pension plan in 2006; the distribution includes employer common stock with net unrealized appreciation of $30,000. Yvonne contributed $25,000 to the qualified plan while she was an active participant from February 10, 1973, to February 10, 1978. Yvonne attained age 50 before January 1, 1986. Yvonne wishes to know her tax consequences with respect to the lump-sum distribution. Write a letter to Yvonne that includes your calculations. Her address is 209 Barrett Street, Laramie, WY 82071.

31. Wade has been an active participant in a defined benefit plan for 21 years. During his last 5 years of employment, Wade earned $27,000, $42,000, $55,000, $90,000, and $100,000, respectively (representing his highest-income years).
    a. Calculate Wade's maximum allowable benefits from this qualified plan (assume there are fewer than 100 participants).
    b. Assume that Wade's average compensation for his three high years is $142,000. Calculate Wade's maximum allowable benefits.

32. Determine the maximum annual benefits payable to an employee from a defined benefit plan in the following independent situations:
    a. Quincy, age 66, has been a participant for 13 years, and his highest average compensation for 3 years is $80,000.
    b. Wendy, age 67, has been a participant for 9 years (11 years of service), and her highest average compensation for 3 years is $110,000.

33. In 2006, Rabbit Corporation paid compensation of $39,400 to the participants in a profit sharing plan. During 2006, Rabbit Corporation contributed $11,000 to the plan.
    a. Calculate Rabbit Corporation's deductible amount for 2006.
    b. Calculate the amount of the contribution carryover from 2006.

Decision Making

34. Amber's employer, Lavender, Inc., has a § 401(k) plan that permits salary deferral elections by its employees. Amber's salary is $95,000, and her marginal tax rate is 33%.
    a. What is the maximum amount Amber can elect for salary deferral treatment for 2006?
    b. If Amber elects salary deferral treatment for the amount in (a), how much can she save in taxes?
    c. What amount would you recommend that Amber elect for salary deferral treatment for 2006?

35. Sally, a single individual, participates in her employer's SIMPLE § 401(k) plan. The plan permits participants to contribute a percentage of their salary. Sally elects to contribute 5% of her annual salary of $111,000 to the plan. On what amount of her salary does Sally pay income taxes in 2006?

36. In 2006, Susan's sole proprietorship earns $220,000 of self-employment net income (after the deduction for one-half of self-employment tax).
    a. Calculate the maximum amount that Susan can deduct for contributions to a defined contribution Keogh plan.
    b. Suppose Susan contributes more than the allowable amount to the Keogh plan. What are the consequences to her?
    c. Can Susan retire and begin receiving Keogh payments at age 55 without incurring a penalty?

37. Sammy is a self-employed accountant with earned income from the business of $130,000 (after the deduction for one-half of any self-employment tax). He has a profit sharing plan (i.e., defined contribution Keogh plan). What is the maximum amount Sammy can contribute to his retirement plan?

38. Molly is unmarried and is an active participant in a qualified retirement plan. Her modified AGI is $55,000 in 2006.
    a. Calculate the amount that Molly can contribute to a traditional IRA and the amount she can deduct.
    b. Assume instead that Molly is a participant in a SIMPLE IRA and that she elects to contribute 4% of her compensation to the account, while her employer contributes 3%. What amount will be contributed for 2006? What amount will be vested?

39. Answer the following independent questions with respect to a deductible IRA and § 401(k) contributions for 2006:
    a. Govind earns a salary of $26,000 and is not an active participant in any other qualified plan. His wife has $600 of compensation income. What is the maximum total deductible contribution to their IRAs?
    b. Danos is a participant in a SIMPLE § 401(k) plan. He contributes 6% of his salary of $31,000, and his employer contributes 3%. What amount will be contributed for the year? What amount will be vested?

40. Answer the following independent questions with respect to traditional IRA contributions for 2006:
    a. Juan earns a salary of $28,000 and is not an active participant in any other qualified plan. His wife, Agnes, has no earned income. What is the maximum total deductible contribution to their IRAs? Juan wishes to contribute as much as possible to his own IRA.
    b. Abby has earned income of $25,000, and her husband has earned income of $2,600. They are not active participants in any other qualified plan. What is the maximum contribution to their IRAs?
    c. Leo's employer makes a contribution of $3,500 to Leo's simplified employee pension plan. If Leo is single, has earned income of $32,000, and has AGI of $29,000, what amount, if any, can he contribute to an IRA?

41. Gleim establishes a Roth IRA at age 37 and contributes a total of $89,600 to it over 29 years. The account is now worth $112,000. How much of these funds may Gleim withdraw tax-free?

42. Donna, age 54, has a traditional deductible IRA with an account balance of $107,600, of which $77,300 represents contributions and $30,300 represents earnings. In 2006, she converts her traditional IRA into a Roth IRA. What amount must Donna include in her gross income in 2006?

43. Karli and Jacob have been married for 12 years and are both active participants in employer qualified retirement plans. Their total AGI in 2006 is $157,000, and they earn salaries of $78,000 and $73,000, respectively. What amount can Karli and Jacob:
    a. Contribute to traditional IRAs?
    b. Deduct for their contributions in (a)?
    c. Contribute to Roth IRAs?
    d. Deduct for their contributions in (c)?
    e. Contribute to Coverdell Education Savings Accounts for their two children?

44. Heather is a participant in a SIMPLE IRA plan of her employer. During 2006, she contributes 9% of her $52,000 salary, and her employer contributes 3%. What amount will be vested in her account at the end of 2006?

45. In 2013, Joyce receives a $4,000 distribution from her Coverdell Education Savings Account, which has a fair market value of $10,000. Total contributions to her CESA have been $7,000. Joyce's AGI is $25,000.
    a. Joyce uses the entire $4,000 to pay for qualified education expenses. What amount should she include in her gross income?
    b. Assume instead that Joyce uses only $2,500 of the $4,000 distribution for qualified education expenses. What amount should she include in her gross income?

46. Gene, age 34, and Beth, age 32, have been married for nine years. Gene, who is a college student, works part-time and earns $1,500. Beth is a high school teacher and earns a salary of $34,000. Their AGI is $37,000.
    a. What is the maximum amount Gene can contribute to an IRA in 2006?
    b. What is the maximum amount Beth can contribute to an IRA in 2006?

47. Samuel, age 32, loses his job in a corporate downsizing. As a result of his termination, he receives a distribution of the balance in his § 401(k) account of $20,000 ($25,000 − $5,000 withholding) on May 1, 2006. Samuel's marginal tax rate is 28%.

    Decision Making

    a. What effect will the distribution have on Samuel's gross income and tax liability if he invests the $20,000 received in a mutual fund?
    b. Same as (a) except that Samuel invests the $20,000 received in a traditional IRA within 60 days of the distribution.

     c. Same as (a) except that Samuel invests the $20,000 received in a Roth IRA within 60 days of the distribution.

     d. How could Samuel have received better tax consequences in (b)?

48. Ned, a professional basketball player, is to receive a bonus of $2 million for signing an employment contract. An NQDC plan is established to postpone the income beyond Ned's peak income years. In 2006, his employer transfers the bonus to an escrow agent, who then invests the funds in mutual funds. The funds are subject to the claims of the employer's creditors. The bonus is deferred for 10 years and becomes payable gradually in years 11 through 15. When is the bonus taxable to Ned and deductible by the employer?

49. Nancy is an officer of a local bank that merges with a national bank, resulting in a change of ownership. She loses her job as a result of the merger, but she receives a cash settlement of $590,000 from her employer under her golden parachute. Her average annual compensation for the past five tax years is $200,000.

     a. What are the tax consequences to Nancy and to the bank of the $590,000 payment?

     b. Assume instead that Nancy's five-year average annual compensation was $110,000, and she receives $390,000 in the settlement. What are the tax consequences to Nancy?

Decision Making

50. On February 20, 2006, Tim (an executive of Hawk Corporation) purchased 100 shares of Hawk stock (selling at $20 a share) for $10. A condition of the transaction was that Tim must resell the stock to Hawk at cost if he voluntarily leaves the company within five years of receiving the stock (assume this represents a substantial risk of forfeiture).

     a. Assuming that no special election is made under § 83(b), what amount, if any, is taxable to Tim in 2006?

     b. Five years later when the stock is selling for $40 a share, Tim is still employed by Hawk. What amount of ordinary income, if any, is taxable to Tim?

     c. What amount, if any, is deductible by Hawk as compensation expense five years later?

     d. Should Tim make the § 83(b) special election in 2006? What amount would be taxable in 2006 if he makes the special election?

     e. In (d), what amount would be deductible by Hawk five years later?

     f. Under (d), assume Tim sold all the stock six years later for $65 per share. How much capital gain is included in his gross income?

     g. In (d), what loss is available to Tim if he voluntarily resigns in 2009 before the five-year period and does not sell the stock back to the corporation?

     h. In (g), in the year Tim resigns, what amount, if any, would be taxable to Hawk Corporation?

51. On July 2, 2004, Black Corporation sold 1,000 of its common shares (worth $14 per share) to Earl, an employee, for $5 per share. The sale was subject to Earl's agreement to resell the shares to the corporation for $5 per share if his employment is terminated within the following four years. The shares had a value of $24 per share on July 2, 2008. Earl sells the shares for $31 per share on September 16, 2008. No special election under § 83(b) is made.

     a. What amount, if any, is taxed to Earl on July 2, 2004?

     b. On July 2, 2008?

     c. On September 16, 2008?

     d. What deduction, if any, will Black Corporation obtain? When?

     e. Assume the same facts, except that Earl makes an election under § 83(b). What amount, if any, will be taxed to Earl on July 2, 2004, July 2, 2008, and September 16, 2008?

     f. Will the assumption made in (e) have any effect on any deduction Black Corporation will receive? Explain.

52. Rosa exercises ISOs for 100 shares of Copper Corporation common stock at the option price of $100 per share on May 21, 2005, when the fair market value is $120 per share. She sells the 100 shares of common stock three and one-half years later for $140.

     a. Calculate the long-term capital gain and the ordinary income on the sale.

     b. Assume Rosa holds the stock only seven months and sells the shares for $140 per share. Calculate the capital gain and ordinary income on the sale.

c. In (b), what amount can Copper Corporation deduct? When?

d. Assume instead that Rosa holds the stock for two years and sells the shares for $115 per share. Calculate any capital gain and ordinary income on this transaction.

e. In (a), assume the options are nonqualified stock options with a nonascertainable fair market value on the date of the grant. Calculate the long-term capital gain and ordinary income on the date of the sale.

f. In (e), assume that each option has an ascertainable fair market value of $10 on the date of the grant and that no substantial risk of forfeiture exists. Calculate the long-term capital gain and the ordinary income on the date of the sale.

53. On November 19, 2004, Rex is granted a nonqualified stock option to purchase 100 shares of Tan Company. On that date, the stock is selling for $8 per share, and the option price is $9 per share. Rex exercises the option on August 21, 2005, when the stock is selling for $10 per share. Five months later, Rex sells the shares for $11.50 per share.

a. What amount is taxable to Rex in 2004?

b. What amount is taxable to Rex in 2005?

c. What amount and type of gain are taxable to Rex in 2006?

d. What amount, if any, is deductible by Tan Company in 2005?

e. What amount, if any, is recognized in 2006 if the stock is sold for $9.50 per share?

54. Sara Reid, age 35, is the owner of a small business. She is trying to decide whether to have a § 401(k) plan or a simplified employee pension plan. She is not interested in a SIMPLE § 401(k) plan. Her salary will be approximately $45,000, and she will have no employees. She asks you to provide her with information on the advantages and disadvantages of both types of plans and your recommendation. Draft a letter to Sara that contains your response. Her address is 1000 Canal Avenue, New Orleans, LA 70148.

Decision Making

Communications

55. Lou's employer provides a qualified cafeteria plan under which he can choose cash of $9,000 or health and accident insurance premiums worth approximately $7,000. If Lou is in the 35% tax bracket, advise him of his tax alternatives.

Decision Making

RESEARCH PROBLEMS

Note: Solutions to Research Problems can be prepared by using the **RIA Checkpoint**® **Student Edition** online research product, which is available to accompany this text. It is also possible to prepare solutions to the Research Problems by using tax research materials found in a standard tax library.

Communications

Research Problem 1. Mr. Sanjay Baker and his sister owned and operated a mail-order business in corporate form. The corporation used the homes of Mr. Baker and his sister for corporate mail-order activities (assembling, storing inventory, etc.). The corporation paid Mr. Baker and the sister rent for the use of the homes. The payments were deducted as rent and reported by the two parties on their tax returns. The IRS disallowed most of the deduction, contending that the rent was excessive. Is the excessive rent deductible as compensation? Write a letter to Mr. Baker that contains your advice and prepare a memo for the tax files. His address is 63 Rose Avenue, San Francisco, CA 94117.

Partial list of research aids:
Multnomah Operating Co. v. Comm., 57–2 USTC ¶9979, 52 AFTR 672, 248 F.2d 661 (CA–9, 1957).

Research Problem 2. Shelly and Austin were divorced in 2006. Since they lived in a community property state, the judgment dissolving the marriage ordered that Austin's traditional deductible IRA be divided equally between Shelly and him. Austin accordingly withdrew $125,000 from his IRA and transferred $112,000 to Shelly. Discuss the tax consequences for Shelly and for Austin.

Partial list of research aids:
§§ 72(t), 408(d)(1), 408(d)(6), 408(g), and 6662(a).

Research Problem 3.   New York City withdrew $177 million over seven years from municipal pension systems and used this money to pay its own operating expenses. The affected unions approved the withdrawals starting in 1988, and continuing through 1999, in exchange for additional benefits for retired police officers, firefighters, and other city workers. Have these withdrawals and agreements created any tax problems?

Research Problem 4.   Jim Raby transfers one-half of his compensatory stock options (ISOs and nonqualified stock options) to his ex-wife as part of a divorce settlement. Discuss the tax aspects of this transfer.

Research Problem 5.   Are stock appreciation rights covered by the new statutory framework for nonqualified deferred compensation in § 409A?

Internet
Activity

Use the tax resources of the Internet to address the following questions. Do not restrict your search to the World Wide Web, but include a review of newsgroups and general reference materials, practitioner sites and resources, primary sources of the tax law, chat rooms and discussion groups, and other opportunities.

Research Problem 6.   Locate and download an Internet retirement calculator. Use this program to help you answer the questions in Problems 38 and 39.

Research Problem 7.   Search the Internet for information about nonqualified deferred compensation plans. How can a Rabbi trust be used to defer taxation?

Research Problem 8.   Using newspapers and magazine articles, determine the latest positions of the AICPA, SEC, PCAOB, and other groups with respect to the deductibility of stock option expense for financial statement purposes.

PART 7

Corporations and Partnerships

The primary orientation of this text is toward basic tax concepts and the individual taxpayer. Although many of these tax concepts also apply to corporations and partnerships, numerous tax concepts apply specifically to corporations or partnerships. An overview of these provisions is presented in Part VII. Comprehensive coverage of these topics appears in West Federal Taxation: Corporations, Partnerships, Estates, & Trusts.

CHAPTER 20
Corporations and Partnerships

C H A P T E R **20**

Corporations and Partnerships

LEARNING OBJECTIVES

After completing Chapter 20, you should be able to:

LO.1

Identify those entities that are treated as corporations for Federal income tax purposes.

LO.2

Contrast the income tax treatment of individuals with that applicable to corporations.

LO.3

Recognize and calculate the tax deductions available only to corporations.

LO.4

Determine the corporate tax liability and comply with various procedural and reporting requirements.

LO.5

Understand the tax rules governing the formation of corporations.

LO.6

Work with the tax rules governing the operation of corporations.

LO.7

Recognize the tax rules governing the liquidation of corporations.

LO.8

Appreciate the utility and effect of the Subchapter S election.

LO.9

Understand the tax consequences of forming and operating a partnership.

LO.10

Evaluate the advantages and disadvantages of the various forms for conducting a business.

Until now this text has concentrated on the Federal income taxation of individual taxpayers. However, even the most basic business decisions require some awareness of the tax implications of other business forms.

EXAMPLE 1

Gina and Tom are contemplating entering into a new business venture that will require additional capital investment by other parties. As the venture will involve financial risk, both Gina and Tom are concerned about personal liability. Further, they would prefer to avoid any income taxes at the entity level. Both Gina and Tom would like to take advantage of any losses the venture may generate during its formative period. ∎

In choosing the form for the venture, Gina and Tom will have to consider using a corporation. The corporate form limits a shareholder's liability to the amount invested in the stock. Regular corporations, however, are subject to the corporate income tax. Furthermore, losses incurred by corporations do not pass through to the shareholders. Perhaps the ideal solution would be to use the corporate form and elect to be taxed as an S corporation. The election would avoid the corporate income tax and permit the pass-through of losses while providing limited liability for the shareholders.

Although the resolution of the problem posed by Example 1 seems simple enough, it did not consider the possible use of a partnership or limited liability company. More important, the decision required *some* knowledge of corporations and the S corporation election. This chapter is intended to provide such knowledge by briefly reviewing the tax consequences of the various forms of business organization.

LO.1

Identify those entities that are treated as corporations for Federal income tax purposes.

What Is a Corporation?

Compliance with State Law

A company must comply with the specific requirements for corporate status under state law. For example, it is necessary to draft articles of incorporation and file them with the state regulatory agency, be granted a charter, and issue stock to share-holders.

Compliance with state law, although important, is not the only requirement that must be met to qualify for corporate *tax* status. For example, a corporation qualifying under state law may be disregarded as a taxable entity if it is a mere sham lacking in economic substance. The key consideration is the degree of business activity conducted at the corporate level.

EXAMPLE 2

Gene and Mike are joint owners of a tract of unimproved real estate that they wish to protect from future creditors. Gene and Mike form Falcon Corporation and transfer the land to it in return for all of the corporation's stock. The corporation merely holds title to the land and conducts no other activities. In all respects, Falcon Corporation meets the legal requirements of a corporation under applicable state law. Nevertheless, Falcon might not be recognized as a separate entity for corporate tax purposes under these facts.[1] ■

EXAMPLE 3

Assume the same facts as in Example 2. In addition to holding title to the land, Falcon Corporation leases the property, collects rents, and pays the property taxes. Falcon probably would be treated as a corporation for Federal income tax purposes because of the scope of its activities. ■

In some instances, the IRS has attempted to disregard (or collapse) a corporation in order to make the income taxable directly to the shareholders.[2] In other cases, the IRS has asserted that the corporation is a separate taxable entity so as to assess tax at the corporate level and to tax corporate distributions to shareholders as dividend income (double taxation).[3]

Entity Classification prior to 1997

Can an organization not qualifying as a corporation under state law still be treated as such for Federal income tax purposes? Unfortunately, the tax law defines a corporation as including "associations, joint stock companies, and insurance companies."[4] As the Code contains no definition of an "association," the issue became the subject of frequent litigation.[5]

It was finally determined that an entity would be treated as a corporation if it had a majority of the characteristics common to corporations.[6] For this purpose, the relevant characteristics are:

- Continuity of life.
- Centralized management.
- Limited liability.
- Free transferability of interests.

These criteria did not resolve all of the problems that continued to arise over corporate classification. When a new type of business entity, the limited liability company, was developed, the IRS was deluged with inquiries about its tax status. As the limited liability company became increasingly popular with professional groups, all states enacted statutes allowing some form of this entity. The statutes invariably permitted the corporate characteristic of limited liability and, often, that of centralized management. Because continuity of life and free transferability of interests were absent, it was hoped that the entity would be classified as a partnership.

---

[1]See *Paymer v. Comm.*, 45–2 USTC ¶9353, 33 AFTR 1536, 150 F.2d 334 (CA–2, 1945).

[2]*Floyd Patterson*, 25 TCM 1230, T.C.Memo. 1966–239, *aff'd* in 68–2 USTC ¶9471, 22 AFTR2d 5810 (CA–2, 1968).

[3]*Raffety Farms Inc. v. U.S.*, 75–1 USTC ¶9271, 35 AFTR2d 75–811, 511 F.2d 1234 (CA–8, 1975).

[4]§ 7701(a)(3).

[5]See, for example, *U.S. v. Kintner*, 54–2 USTC ¶9626, 46 AFTR 995, 216 F.2d 418 (CA–5, 1954).

[6]See Reg. § 301.7701–2(a) prior to repeal.

This treatment would avoid the double taxation result inherent in the corporate form.

Entity Classification after 1996

In late 1996, the IRS issued its so-called **check-the-box Regulations.**[7] Effective beginning in 1997, these Regulations enable taxpayers to classify a business entity for tax purposes without regard to its corporate (or noncorporate) characteristics. These rules have simplified tax administration considerably and eliminated the litigation that arose with regard to association (corporation) status.

Under the rules, an entity with more than one owner can elect to be classified as either a partnership or a corporation. An entity with only one owner can elect to be classified as a corporation or a sole proprietorship. In the event of default (no election is made), entities with multiple owners will be classified as partnerships and single-person businesses as sole proprietorships.

The election is not available to entities that are actually incorporated under state law or to entities that are required to be corporations under Federal law (e.g., certain publicly traded partnerships). For purposes of these prohibitions, limited liability companies not incorporated under state law can elect either corporation or partnership status.

Eligible entities make the election as to tax status by filing Form 8832 (Entity Classification Election).[8] New elections are permitted, but only after a 60-month waiting period.

LO.2

Contrast the income tax treatment of individuals with that applicable to corporations.

Income Tax Considerations

General Tax Consequences of Different Forms of Business Entities

A business operation may be conducted as a sole proprietorship, as a partnership, or in corporate form.

- Sole proprietorships are not separate taxable entities. The owner of the business reports all business transactions on his or her individual income tax return.
- Partnerships are not subject to the income tax. Under the *conduit* concept, the various tax attributes of the partnership's operations flow through to the individual partners to be reported on their personal income tax returns.
- The regular corporate form (known as a **C corporation**) of doing business carries with it the imposition of the corporate income tax. The corporation is recognized as a separate taxpaying entity. Income is taxed to the corporation as earned and taxed again to the shareholders as dividends when distributed.
- A regular corporation (C corporation) may elect to be taxed as an S corporation. This special treatment is similar (although not identical) to the partnership rules. Income tax is generally avoided at the corporate level, and shareholders are taxed currently on the taxable income of the S corporation.

Individuals and Corporations Compared—An Overview

Similarities between Corporate and Individual Tax Rules. The gross income of a corporation is determined in much the same manner as for individuals. Both individuals and corporations are entitled to exclusions from gross income, such as interest on municipal bonds. Gains and losses from property transactions are also treated similarly. For example, whether a gain or loss is capital or

---

[7]Reg. §§ 301.7701–1 through –4, and –7.   [8]Reg. § 301.7701–3(c).

ordinary depends on the nature and use of the asset rather than the type of tax-payer. Upon the sale or other taxable disposition of depreciable personalty, the recapture rules of § 1245 make no distinction between corporate and noncorporate taxpayers. In the case of the recapture of depreciation on real property (§ 1250), however, corporate taxpayers experience more severe tax consequences. As illustrated later, corporations must recognize as additional ordinary income 20 percent of the excess of the amount that would be recaptured under § 1245 over the amount recaptured under § 1250.

The business deductions of corporations parallel those available to individuals. Corporate deductions are allowed for all ordinary and necessary expenses paid or incurred in carrying on a trade or business. Corporations may also deduct interest, certain taxes, losses, bad debts, depreciation, cost recovery, charitable contributions subject to corporate limitation rules, net operating losses, research and experimental expenditures, and other less common deductions.

ETHICAL *Considerations*   **WHO GETS THE DEDUCTION?**

Monica and DeWitt are the sole shareholders and key employees of Meadowlark Corporation, a calendar year taxpayer. As Meadowlark's business is sales related, Monica and DeWitt incur significant expenses in entertaining key customers. Typically, they pay these amounts and are subsequently reimbursed by Meadowlark. For year 2006, however, they determine that Meadowlark cannot receive any tax benefit from the entertainment expenses. Consequently, Monica and DeWitt do not seek any reimbursement. Instead, in January 2007, they have Meadowlark adopt a corporate resolution to the effect that all entertainment expenses are to be absorbed by its employees.

Pursuant to the new resolution, Monica and DeWitt deduct the entertainment expenditures for year 2006 on their individual income tax returns. Have Monica and DeWitt acted properly?

Many of the tax credits available to individuals, such as the foreign tax credit, can be claimed by corporations. Not available to corporations are certain credits that are personal in nature. Examples of credits not available to corporations include the credit for child and dependent care expenses, the credit for the elderly or disabled, and the earned income credit.

Corporations usually have the same choices of accounting periods as do individuals. Like an individual, a corporation may choose a calendar year or a fiscal year for reporting purposes. Corporations do enjoy greater flexibility in the election of a tax year. For example, corporations usually can have different tax years from those of their shareholders. Also, a newly formed corporation generally has a free choice of any approved accounting period without having to obtain the consent of the IRS. As noted in Chapter 18, however, personal service corporations are subject to severe restrictions on the use of a fiscal year.

In terms of methods of accounting, both individuals and corporations must use the *accrual* method in determining cost of goods sold if they maintain inventory for sale to customers. The *accrual* method must also be used by *large* corporations (annual gross receipts in excess of $5 million). The *cash method* of accounting, however, is available to *small* corporations and in the following additional situations:

- An S election is in effect.
- The trade or business is farming or timber.
- A qualified personal service corporation is involved.
- A qualified service provider (e.g., plumbing business) is involved, and annual gross receipts (for the past three years) do not exceed $10 million. This exception applies even if the service provider is buying and selling inventory.

Dissimilarities. Both noncorporate and corporate taxpayers are subject to progressive income tax rates. For individuals, the rates for 2006 are 10, 15, 25, 28, 33, and 35 percent. For corporations, the rates are 15, 25, 34, and 35 percent. Corporate taxpayers lose the benefits of the lower brackets (using a phaseout approach) once taxable income reaches a certain level. Noncorporate taxpayers, however, continue to enjoy the benefits of the lower brackets even though they have reached the higher taxable income levels.

Commencing in 2003, qualified dividends received by individual shareholders are subject to preferential tax rates. For those shareholders in the top four tax brackets (25, 28, 33, and 35 percent), the maximum rate is 15 percent; for those in the bottom two brackets (10 and 15 percent), the rate is 5 percent. As discussed later, corporate shareholders enjoy the alternative of the dividends received deduction.

Many corporate and all noncorporate taxpayers are subject to the alternative minimum tax (AMT). For AMT purposes, many adjustments and tax preference items are the same for both, but other adjustments and tax preferences apply only to corporations or only to individuals. Also, certain small business corporations are effectively exempt from the corporate AMT. Corporate tax rates are discussed later in the chapter. The AMT is discussed at length in Chapter 12. See also the coverage in *West Federal Taxation: Corporations, Partnerships, Estates, and Trusts.*

All allowable corporate deductions are treated as business expenses. The determination of adjusted gross income, so essential for individuals, has no relevance to corporations. Corporations need not be concerned with classifying deductions into *deduction for* and *deduction from* categories.

Specific Provisions Compared

Corporate and individual tax rules also differ in the following areas:

- Capital gains and losses.
- Recapture of depreciation.
- Charitable contributions.
- Production activities deduction.
- Net operating losses.
- Special deductions for corporations.

Capital Gains and Losses. Both corporate and noncorporate taxpayers are required to aggregate gains and losses from the taxable sale or exchange of capital assets. (Refer to Chapter 16 for a description of the netting process that takes place after the aggregation has been completed.) For long-term capital gains (including gains from collectibles and unrecaptured § 1250 gain), individuals enjoy an advantage. Called the alternative tax, the maximum applicable tax rate is 28 percent for collectibles, 25 percent for unrecaptured § 1250 gain, and 15 percent for other capital gains. For the last category, the tax rate is reduced to 5 percent if the taxpayer is in the 15 percent (or lower) tax bracket. In the case of corporations, all capital gains are taxed using the rates for ordinary income. Therefore, the net long-term capital gain of a corporation could be taxed at a rate of 35 percent (the highest rate applicable to corporations).

Significant differences exist in the treatment of capital losses for income tax purposes. Individuals, for example, can annually deduct up to $3,000 of net capital losses against ordinary income. If an individual has both net short-term and net long-term capital losses, the short-term capital losses are used first in arriving at the $3,000 ordinary loss deduction. Corporations are not permitted to use net capital losses to offset ordinary income. Net capital losses can be used only to offset past or future capital gains.[9] Unlike individuals, corporations are not allowed an unlimited

---

[9]§§ 1211(a) and (b).

carryover period for capital losses. Instead, they may carry back excess capital losses to the three preceding years, applying the losses initially to the earliest year. If not exhausted by the carryback, remaining unused capital losses may be carried forward for a period of five years from the year of the loss.[10]

When carried back or forward, *both* short-term capital losses and long-term capital losses are treated as short-term capital losses by corporate taxpayers. For noncorporate taxpayers, carryovers of capital losses retain their identity as short or long term.

EXAMPLE 4

Hawk Corporation, a calendar year taxpayer, incurs a long-term net capital loss of $5,000 for 2006. None of the capital loss may be deducted in 2006. Hawk may, however, carry the loss back to years 2003, 2004, and 2005 (in this order) and offset any capital gains recognized in these years. If the carryback does not exhaust the loss, the loss may be carried forward to 2007, 2008, 2009, 2010, and 2011 (in this order). Such capital loss carrybacks or carryovers are treated as short-term capital losses. ■

Recapture of Depreciation. Corporations selling depreciable real estate may have ordinary income in addition to that required by § 1250. Under § 291, the additional ordinary income element is 20 percent of the excess of the § 1245 recapture potential over the § 1250 recapture. As a result, the § 1231 gain is correspondingly decreased by the additional recapture.

Under § 1250, the excess of accelerated depreciation over straight-line depreciation is recaptured as ordinary income as to residential real property. Since all real property purchased since 1986 is depreciated using only the straight-line method, after 2005 the § 1250 amount is zero because the depreciation period (19 years in 1986) has expired and such buildings are fully depreciated.

EXAMPLE 5

Condor Corporation purchases residential real property on November 3, 1996, for $300,000. Straight-line cost recovery is taken in the amount of $99,992 before the property is sold on January 5, 2006, for $250,000.

First, determine the recognized gain:

Sales price		$ 250,000
Less adjusted basis:		
Cost of property	$300,000	
Less cost recovery	(99,992)	(200,008)
Recognized gain		$ 49,992

Second, determine the § 1245 recapture potential. This is the lesser of $49,992 (recognized gain) or $99,992 (cost recovery claimed).

Third, determine the § 1250 recapture amount:

Cost recovery taken	$ 99,992
Less straight-line cost recovery	(99,992)
§ 1250 ordinary income	$ –0–

Fourth, because the taxpayer is a corporation, determine the additional § 291 amount:

§ 1245 recapture potential	$ 49,992
Less § 1250 recapture amount	(–0–)
Excess § 1245 recapture potential	$ 49,992
Apply § 291 percentage	× 20%
Additional ordinary income under § 291	$ 9,998

---

[10]§ 1212(a).

Condor Corporation's recognized gain of $49,992 is accounted for as follows:

Ordinary income under § 1250	$ –0–
Ordinary income under § 291	9,998
§ 1231 gain	39,994
Total recognized gain	$49,992

■

Charitable Contributions. Generally, a charitable contribution deduction is allowed only for the tax year in which the payment is made. However, an important exception is made for accrual basis corporations. The deduction may be claimed in the tax year *preceding* payment if the following conditions are satisfied:

- The contribution is authorized by the board of directors by the end of that tax year *and*
- The contribution is paid on or before the fifteenth day of the third month of the next tax year.[11]

EXAMPLE 6

On December 29, 2006, the board of directors of Dove Corporation, a calendar year, accrual basis taxpayer, authorizes a $5,000 donation to a qualified charity. The donation is paid on March 14, 2007. Dove Corporation may claim the $5,000 donation as a deduction for 2006. As an alternative, Dove may claim the deduction in 2007 (the year of payment). ■

Like individuals, corporations are not permitted an unlimited charitable contribution deduction. In any one year, a corporate taxpayer is limited to 10 percent of taxable income. For this purpose, taxable income is computed without regard to the charitable contribution deduction, any net operating loss carryback or capital loss carryback, or the dividends received deduction.[12] Any contributions in excess of the 10 percent limitation are carried forward to the five succeeding tax years. Any carryover must be added to subsequent contributions and is subject to the 10 percent limitation. In applying the limitation, the most recent contributions must be deducted first.[13]

EXAMPLE 7

During 2006, Eagle Corporation (a calendar year taxpayer) had the following income and expenses:

Income from operations	$140,000
Expenses from operations	110,000
Dividends received	10,000
Charitable contributions made in 2006	5,000

For purposes of the 10% limitation only, Eagle's taxable income is $40,000 ($140,000 − $110,000 + $10,000). Consequently, the allowable charitable contribution deduction for 2006 is $4,000 (10% × $40,000). The $1,000 unused portion of the contribution is carried forward to 2007, 2008, 2009, 2010, and 2011 (in that order) until exhausted. ■

EXAMPLE 8

Assume the same facts as in Example 7. In 2007, Eagle Corporation has taxable income (after adjustments) of $50,000 and makes a charitable contribution of $4,800. The maximum deduction allowed for 2007 is $5,000 (10% × $50,000). The first $4,800 of the allowed deduction must be allocated to the 2007 contribution, and the $200 excess is allocated to the carryover from 2006. The remaining $800 of the 2006 contribution is carried over to 2008, etc. ■

---

[11]§ 170(a)(2).
[12]§ 170(b)(2).
[13]§ 170(d)(2).

As noted in Chapter 10, the deduction for charitable contributions of ordinary income property is limited to the lesser of the fair market value or the adjusted basis of the property. A special rule permits a corporation to contribute inventory (ordinary income property) to certain charitable organizations and receive a deduction equal to the adjusted basis plus one-half of the difference between the fair market value and the adjusted basis of the property.[14] In no event, however, may the deduction exceed twice the adjusted basis of the property. To qualify for this exception, the inventory must be used by the charity in its exempt purpose for the care of *children*, the *ill*, or the *needy*.

EXAMPLE 9

In the current year, Robin Company (a retail clothier) donates sweaters and overcoats to Sheltering Arms (a qualified charity caring for the homeless). The clothing is inventory and has a basis of $10,000 and a fair market value of $14,000. If Robin is a corporation, the charitable contribution that results is $12,000 [$10,000 (basis) + $2,000 (50% of the appreciation of $4,000)]. In contrast, if Robin is not a corporation, the charitable contribution is limited to $10,000 (basis). ∎

Production Activities Deduction. As noted in Chapter 7, new § 199 was designed to replace various export tax benefits that our world trading partners deemed discriminatory. Known as the production activities deduction, the provision is equally applicable to C corporations. In the case of C corporations, however, the limitation is based on taxable income, rather than AGI (both computed without considering the deduction). Thus, the deduction is 3 percent of the *lesser* of qualified production activities income (QPAI) or taxable income. (The deduction increases to 6 percent in 2007 and 9 percent in 2010.) As with individual taxpayers, the deduction cannot exceed 50 percent of the W-2 wages involved (those subject to withholding plus certain elective deferrals). Domestic gross receipts from manufacturing activities are a major source of QPAI. These gross receipts are adjusted by cost of goods sold and other assignable expenses to arrive at QPAI.

For corporations that are members of an affiliated group (based on 50 percent common control), the deduction is determined by treating the group as a single taxpayer. In effect, therefore, each member of the group is treated as being engaged in the activities of every other member. The deduction is then allocated among the members in proportion to each member's respective amount of QPAI.[15]

EXAMPLE 10

Mallard and Pintail Corporations are members of an affiliated group but do not file a consolidated return. Mallard manufactures a machine at a cost of $30 and sells it to Pintail for $50. Pintail incurs additional cost of $10 for marketing and then sells the machine to an unrelated customer for $70. The QPAI deduction is based on $30 ($70 − $30 − $10) even though the seller (Pintail) did not perform any manufacturing.[16] Note that this is the same result that would have been reached if Pintail had not been involved and Mallard had conducted its own marketing function. ∎

EXAMPLE 11

Assume the same facts as in Example 10 except that the parties are not related. Under these circumstances, Mallard has QPAI of $20 ($50 − $30) and Pintail has none. Pintail's activities, when considered alone, are not QPAI because they involve marketing and not manufacturing. ∎

---

[14]§ 170(e)(3).

[15]§ 199(d)(4).

[16]Notice 2005-14, 2005-1 C.B. 498, issued on February 14, 2005. Notice 2005-14 provides guides to action under § 199 and can be relied on until the Regulations are issued.

In the case of pass-through entities (e.g., partnerships, S corporations, trusts, and estates), special rules apply for handling the production activities deduction.[17] Because the deduction is determined at the owner level, each partner or shareholder must make the computation separately. Thus, the entity allocates to each owner his or her share of QPAI. The QPAI that is passed through is then combined with any qualifying activities that the owner has from other sources (e.g., a partner also conducts a manufacturing activity on his or her own).

In applying the wage limitation in the pass-through setting, the limitation is first applied at the entity level. Once this is done, the partner or shareholder will be treated as having been allocated the lesser of that person's actual share of the wages or two times 3 percent of his or her share of the QPAI. This last limitation precludes an owner from taking advantage of the entity's wages to cover QPAI from other sources. The partner or shareholder, however, may add any wages separately paid to the allocation from the entity.

The production activities deduction can be claimed in computing the alternative minimum tax (including adjusted current earnings). The deduction allowed is the lesser of QPAI or alternative minimum taxable income (AMTI). In the case of an individual taxpayer, AGI is substituted for AMTI in determining the limitation on the amount allowed as a deduction.[18]

Net Operating Losses. The computation of a net operating loss (NOL) for individuals was discussed in Chapter 7. Corporations are not subject to the complex adjustments required for individuals (e.g., a corporation has no adjustments for nonbusiness deductions or capital gains and losses). Corporations are subject to fewer adjustments than individuals are because a corporation's loss more clearly approximates a true economic loss. Artificial deductions (e.g., personal and dependency exemptions) that merely generate paper losses are not permitted for corporations.

In computing the NOL of a corporation, the dividends received deduction (discussed below) can be claimed in determining the amount of the loss. Generally, NOLs generated after 1997 may be carried back 2 years and forward 20 years (or taxpayers may elect to forgo the carryback period) to offset taxable income for those years.[19]

EXAMPLE 12

In 2006, Wren Corporation has gross income of $200,000 and deductions of $300,000, excluding the dividends received deduction. Wren received taxable dividends of $100,000 from ExxonMobil stock. Wren has an NOL of $170,000, computed as follows:

Gross income (including ExxonMobil dividends)		$ 200,000
Less: Business deductions	$300,000	
Dividends received deduction (70% × $100,000)	70,000	(370,000)
Taxable income (loss)		($ 170,000) ∎

EXAMPLE 13

Assume the same facts as in Example 12 and that Wren Corporation had taxable income of $40,000 in 2004. The NOL of $170,000 is carried back to 2004 (unless Wren elects not to carry back the loss to that year). The carryover to 2005 is $130,000, computed as follows:

Taxable income for 2004	$ 40,000
Less: NOL carryback from 2006	(170,000)
Carryover of unabsorbed 2006 loss	($ 130,000) ∎

---

[17]§ 199(d)(1).
[18]§ 199(d)(6).
[19]§ 172(b).

TAX *in the News* | **VARIATIONS IN MITIGATING THE EFFECT OF MULTIPLE TAXATION**

When a corporation receives a dividend from another corporation, multiple taxation of the same income is eased (or avoided) by allowing the corporate shareholder a dividends received deduction. But what happens when these funds are later passed through to the individual shareholders? Until recently, such distributions were fully taxed as ordinary income.

This problem of double taxation of corporate distributions at the individual shareholder level was addressed by Congress in JGTRRA of 2003. The solution arrived at,

however, is different from that used for corporate shareholders. Instead of allowing a deduction for some (or all) of the dividends received, relief is provided through the application of a lower tax rate. Thus, qualified dividends are taxed at the same preferential tax rate available to net capital gains.

In summary, the possible triple taxation of corporate-source income is mitigated by the combination of a deduction (available to corporate shareholders) and a lower tax rate (available to individual shareholders).

In Example 13, the carryback to 2004 might have been ill-advised if Wren Corporation had little, if any, taxable income in 2005 and if it anticipated large amounts of taxable income in the immediate future. In that case, the *election to forgo* the carryback might generate greater tax savings. In this regard, three points should be considered. First, the time value of the tax refund that is lost by not using the carryback procedure must be considered. Second, the election to forgo an NOL carryback is irrevocable. Thus, it cannot be changed later if the future high profits do not materialize. Third, future increases or decreases in corporate income tax rates that can reasonably be anticipated should be considered.

Deductions Available Only to Corporations

Dividends Received Deduction. The purpose of the **dividends received deduction** is to prevent triple taxation. Without the deduction, income paid to a corporation in the form of a dividend would be subject to taxation for a second time (after being taxed first to the distributing corporation) with no corresponding deduction to the distributing corporation. A third level of tax would be assessed on the shareholders when the recipient corporation distributed the income to its shareholders. Since the dividends received deduction may be less than 100 percent, the law provides only partial relief.

The amount of the dividends received deduction depends upon the percentage of ownership the recipient corporate shareholder holds in the corporation making the dividend distribution.[20] For dividends received or accrued, the *deduction percentage* is summarized as follows:

Percentage of Ownership by Corporate Shareholder	Deduction Percentage
Less than 20%	70%
20% or more (but less than 80%)	80%
80% or more	100%

The dividends received deduction may be limited to a percentage of the taxable income of a corporation computed without regard to the NOL deduction, the dividends received deduction, or any capital loss carryback to the current tax year. The percentage of taxable income limitation corresponds to the deduction percentage. Thus, if a corporate shareholder owns less than 20 percent of the stock in the

[20]§ 243(a).

distributing corporation, the dividends received deduction is limited to 70 percent of taxable income (as previously defined). However, this limitation does not apply if the corporation has an NOL for the current taxable year.[21]

In working with these myriad rules, the following steps need to be taken:

1. Multiply the dividends received by the deduction percentage.
2. Multiply the taxable income (as previously defined) by the deduction percentage.
3. The deduction is limited to the lesser of step 1 or step 2, unless subtracting the amount derived from step 1 from taxable income (as previously defined) generates a negative number. If so, the amount derived in step 1 should be used.

EXAMPLE 14

Crane, Osprey, and Gull Corporations, three unrelated calendar year corporations, have the following transactions for 2006:

	Crane Corporation	Osprey Corporation	Gull Corporation
Gross income from operations	$ 400,000	$ 320,000	$ 260,000
Expenses from operations	(340,000)	(340,000)	(340,000)
Dividends received from domestic corporations (less than 20% ownership)	200,000	200,000	200,000
Taxable income before the dividends received deduction	$ 260,000	$ 180,000	$ 120,000

In determining the dividends received deduction, use the step procedure just described:

	Crane Corporation	Osprey Corporation	Gull Corporation
Step 1: (70% × $200,000)	$140,000	$140,000	$140,000
Step 2:			
70% × $260,000 (taxable income)	$182,000		
70% × $180,000 (taxable income)		$126,000	
70% × $120,000 (taxable income)			$ 84,000
Step 3:			
Lesser of step 1 or step 2	$140,000	$126,000	
Generates an NOL			$140,000

Osprey Corporation is subject to the 70 percent of taxable income limitation. It does not qualify for the loss rule treatment, since subtracting $140,000 (step 1) from $180,000 does not yield a loss. Gull Corporation qualifies for the loss rule treatment because subtracting $140,000 (step 1) from $120,000 does yield a loss. In summary, each corporation has the following dividends received deduction for 2006: $140,000 for Crane, $126,000 for Osprey, and $140,000 for Gull. If a corporation already has an NOL before any dividends received deduction is claimed, the full dividends received deduction (as calculated in step 1) is allowed. ∎

---

[21]§ 246(b).

Deduction of Organizational Expenditures. Under § 248, a corporation may elect to amortize organizational expenses over a period of 15 years or more. A special exception allows the corporation to immediately expense the first $5,000 of these costs.[22] The exception, however, is phased out on a dollar-for-dollar basis when these expenses exceed $50,000.

EXAMPLE 15

Kingbird Corporation, a calendar year taxpayer, is formed on June 1, 2006. In connection with its formation, it incurs organizational expenditures of $52,000. If Kingbird wants to claim as much of these expenses as soon as possible, its deduction for 2006 is—

$$\text{Expense: } \$5,000 - (\$52,000 - \$50,000) = \$3,000$$

$$\text{Amortization: } \frac{\$52,000 - \$3,000}{180 \text{ months}} \times 7 \text{ (months)} = \$1,906$$

Kingbird deducts a total of $4,906 ($3,000 + $1,906) for 2006. ∎

If the election is not made on a timely basis, the expenditures cannot be deducted until the corporation ceases to conduct business and liquidates. The election is made in a statement attached to the corporation's return for its first taxable year. The election covers all qualifying expenses *incurred* in the corporation's first year. Thus, a cash basis taxpayer need not have paid the expenses as long as they were incurred.

Organizational expenditures include the following:

- Legal services incident to organization (e.g., drafting the corporate charter, bylaws, minutes of organizational meetings, terms of original stock certificates).
- Necessary accounting services.
- Expenses of temporary directors and of organizational meetings of directors and shareholders.
- Fees paid to the state of incorporation.

Expenditures connected with issuing or selling shares of stock or other securities (e.g., commissions, professional fees, and printing costs) or with the transfer of assets to a corporation do not qualify. These expenditures are generally added to the capital account and are not subject to amortization.

Determination of Corporate Tax Liability

Income Tax Rates. The rate brackets for corporations are as follows:[23]

Taxable Income	Tax Rate
Not over $50,000	15%
Over $50,000 but not over $75,000	25%
Over $75,000 but not over $100,000	34%
Over $100,000 but not over $335,000	39%*
Over $335,000 but not over $10,000,000	34%
Over $10,000,000 but not over $15,000,000	35%
Over $15,000,000 but not over $18,333,333	38%**
Over $18,333,333	35%

*Five percent of this rate represents a phaseout of the benefits of the lower tax rates on the first $75,000 of taxable income.

**Three percent of this rate represents a phaseout of the benefits of the lower tax rate (34% rather than 35%) on the first $10 million of taxable income.

> **LO.4**
>
> Determine the corporate tax liability and comply with various procedural and reporting requirements.

---

[22]Organizational expenditures incurred before October 23, 2004, could not be immediately expensed but could be amortized over a period of 60 months or more.

[23]§ 11(b).

EXAMPLE 16

A calendar year corporation has taxable income of $90,000 for the current year. The income tax liability is $18,850, determined as follows: $7,500 (15% × $50,000) + $6,250 (25% × $25,000) + $5,100 (34% × $15,000). ∎

Qualified personal service corporations are taxed at a flat 35 percent rate on all taxable income. They do not enjoy the tax savings of the lower brackets. For this purpose, a *qualified* **personal service corporation** is one that is substantially employee owned and engages in one of the following activities: health, law, engineering, architecture, accounting, actuarial science, performing arts, or consulting.

Alternative Minimum Tax. Corporations are subject to an alternative minimum tax (AMT) that is structured in the same manner as that applicable to individuals. The AMT for corporations, as for individuals, defines a more expansive tax base than for the regular tax. Like individuals, corporations are required to apply a minimum tax rate to the expanded base and pay the difference between the tentative AMT liability and the regular tax. Many of the adjustments and tax preference items necessary to arrive at alternative minimum taxable income (AMTI) are the same for individuals and corporations. Although the objective of the AMT is the same for individuals and for corporations, the rate and exemptions are different. As noted in Chapter 12, certain small business corporations are effectively exempt from the corporate AMT.

Corporate Filing Requirements

A corporation must file a return whether it has taxable income or not.[24] A corporation that was not in existence throughout an entire annual accounting period is required to file a return for the fraction of the year during which it was in existence. In addition, the corporation must file a return even though it has ceased to do business if it has valuable claims for which it will bring suit. It is relieved of filing returns once it ceases business and dissolves.

The corporate return is filed on Form 1120 unless the corporation is a small corporation entitled to file the shorter Form 1120–A. Among the *several* requirements for filing Form 1120–A are gross receipts (or sales) of less than $500,000 and total assets of less than $500,000. Corporations making the S corporation election (discussed later in the chapter) file on Form 1120S.

Corporations with less than $250,000 of gross receipts and less than $250,000 in assets do not have to complete Schedule L (balance sheet) and Schedules M–1 and M–2 (see below) of Form 1120. Similar omissions are allowed for Forms 1120–A and 1120S. These rules are intended to ease the compliance burden on small business.

The return must be filed on or before the fifteenth day of the third month following the close of the corporation's tax year. Corporations can receive an automatic extension of six months for filing the corporate return by filing Form 7004 by the due date of the return. However, the IRS may terminate an extension by mailing a 10-day notice to the taxpayer corporation.[25]

A corporation must make payments of estimated tax unless its tax liability can reasonably be expected to be less than $500.[26] For 2006, the payments must equal 100 percent of the corporation's final tax. These payments may be made in four installments due on or before the fifteenth day of the fourth, sixth, ninth, and twelfth months of the corporate taxable year. The full amount of the unpaid tax is due on the date of the return. Failure to make the required estimated tax prepayments will result in a nondeductible penalty being imposed on the corporation. The penalty can be avoided, however, if any of various exceptions apply.[27]

---

[24]§ 6012(a)(2).
[25]§ 6081.

[26]§ 6655(f).
[27]See § 6655 for the penalty involved and the various exceptions.

Reconciliation of Corporate Taxable Income and Accounting Income

Taxable income and accounting net income are seldom the same amount. For example, a difference may arise if the corporation uses accelerated depreciation for tax purposes and straight-line depreciation for accounting purposes.

Many items of income for accounting purposes, such as proceeds from a life insurance policy on the death of a corporate officer and interest on municipal bonds, may not be includible in calculating taxable income. Some expense items for accounting purposes, such as expenses to produce tax-exempt income, estimated warranty reserves, a net capital loss, and Federal income taxes, are not deductible for tax purposes.

Schedule M–1 on the last page of Form 1120 is used to reconcile accounting net income (net income after Federal income taxes) with taxable income (as computed on the corporate tax return before the deduction for an NOL and the dividends received deduction). In the left-hand column of Schedule M–1, net income per books is added to the following: the Federal income tax liability for the year, the excess of capital losses over capital gains (which cannot be deducted in the current year), income for tax purposes that is not income in the current year for accounting purposes, and expenses recorded on the books that are not deductible on the tax return. In the right-hand column, income recorded on the books that is not currently taxable or is tax-exempt and deductions for tax purposes that are not expenses for accounting purposes are totaled and subtracted from the left-hand column total to arrive at taxable income (before the NOL or dividends received deductions).

E X A M P L E   17

During the current year, Crow Corporation had the following transactions:

Net income per books (after tax)	$92,400
Taxable income	50,000
Federal income tax liability (15% × $50,000)	7,500
Interest income from tax-exempt bonds	5,000
Interest paid on loan, the proceeds of which were used to purchase the tax-exempt bonds	500
Life insurance proceeds received as a result of the death of a key employee	50,000
Premiums paid on key employee life insurance policy	2,600
Excess of capital losses over capital gains	2,000

For book and tax purposes, Crow determines depreciation under the straight-line method. Crow's Schedule M–1 for the current year follows.

Schedule M-1	**Reconciliation of Income (Loss) per Books With Income per Return**				
1	Net income (loss) per books	*92,400*	**7**	Income recorded on books this year not included on this return (itemize):	
2	Federal income tax per books	*7,500*			
3	Excess of capital losses over capital gains .	*2,000*		Tax-exempt interest $ *5,000*	
4	Income subject to tax not recorded on books this year (itemize): _____			*Life insurance proceeds on key employee $50,000*	*55,000*
	_____		**8**	Deductions on this return not charged against book income this year (itemize):	
5	Expenses recorded on books this year not deducted on this return (itemize):		**a**	Depreciation . . . . $_____	
a	Depreciation . . . $ _____		**b**	Charitable contributions $_____	
b	Charitable contributions $ _____			_____	
c	Travel and entertainment $ _____				
	Prem.–life ins. $2,600; Int.–exempt bonds $500	*3,100*	**9**	Add lines 7 and 8	*55,000*
6	Add lines 1 through 5	*105,000*	**10**	Income (page 1, line 28)—line 6 less line 9	*50,000*

■

Schedule M–2 reconciles unappropriated retained earnings at the beginning of the year with unappropriated retained earnings at year-end. Beginning balance plus net income per books, as entered on line 1 of Schedule M–1, less dividend distributions during the year equals ending retained earnings. Other sources of increases or decreases in retained earnings are also listed on Schedule M–2.

EXAMPLE 18

Assume the same facts as in Example 17. Crow Corporation's beginning balance in unappropriated retained earnings is $125,000, and Crow distributed a cash dividend of $30,000 to its shareholders during the year. Based on these further assumptions, Crow has the following Schedule M–2 for the current year.

Schedule M-2	**Analysis of Unappropriated Retained Earnings per Books (Line 25, Schedule L)**				
1	Balance at beginning of year	125,000	5	Distributions: a Cash	30,000
2	Net income (loss) per books	92,400		b Stock	
3	Other increases (itemize):			c Property	
	....		6	Other decreases (itemize):	
	....		7	Add lines 5 and 6	30,000
4	Add lines 1, 2, and 3	217,400	8	Balance at end of year (line 4 less line 7)	187,400

Effective for taxable years ending on or after December 31, 2004, a new **Schedule M–3** will have to be filed by certain corporations.[28] This schedule, designated "Net Income (Loss) Reconciliation for Corporations With Total Assets of $10 Million or More," will be in lieu of Schedule M–1. It will have to be filed when the assets reported on Schedule L of Form 1120 total or exceed $10 million. Because it will reveal significant differences between book and taxable income, Schedule M–3 will enable the IRS to more quickly identify possible abusive transactions (e.g., use of tax shelter schemes).

LO.5

Understand the tax rules governing the formation of corporations.

Forming the Corporation

Capital Contributions

The receipt of money or property in exchange for capital stock produces neither recognized gain nor loss to the recipient corporation.[29] Gross income of a corporation does not include shareholders' contributions of money or property to the capital of the corporation.[30] Contributions by nonshareholders are also excluded from the gross income of a corporation.[31] The basis of the property (capital transfers by nonshareholders) to the corporation is zero.

EXAMPLE 19

A city donates land worth $200,000 to Cardinal Corporation as an inducement for it to locate in the city. The receipt of the land does not represent gross income. The land's basis to the corporation is zero. ■

Thin Capitalization. The advantages of capitalizing a corporation with debt may be substantial. Interest on debt is deductible by the corporation, while dividend payments are not. Further, the shareholders are not taxed on loan repayments unless the payments exceed basis.

In certain instances, the IRS will contend that debt is really an equity interest (**thin capitalization**) and will deny the shareholders the tax advantages of debt

---

[28]Rev.Proc. 2004–45, 2004–2 C.B. 140. Schedule M–3 will satisfy some of the disclosure requirements set forth in Reg. § 1.6011–4 when significant book-tax differences occur.

[29]§ 1032.

[30]§ 118.

[31]*Edwards v. Cuba Railroad Co.*, 1 USTC ¶139, 5 AFTR 5398, 45 S.Ct. 614 (USSC, 1925).

CONCEPT SUMMARY   20–1

Summary of Income Tax Consequences

	Individuals	Corporations
Computation of gross income	§ 61.	§ 61.
Computation of taxable income	§§ 62, 63(b) through (h).	§ 63(a). Concept of AGI has no relevance.
Deductions	Trade or business (§ 162); nonbusiness (§ 212); some personal and employee expenses (generally deductible as itemized deductions).	Trade or business (§ 162).
Charitable contributions	Limited in any tax year to 50% of AGI; 30% for long-term capital gain property unless election is made to reduce fair market value of gift; 20% for long-term capital gain property contributed to private nonoperating foundations. Time of deduction—year in which payment is made.	Limited in any tax year to 10% of taxable income computed without regard to the charitable contribution deduction, net operating loss or capital loss carryback, and dividends received deduction. Time of deduction—year in which payment is made unless accrual basis taxpayer. Accrual basis corporation may take deduction in year preceding payment if contribution was authorized by board of directors by end of that year and contribution is paid by fifteenth day of third month of following year.
Casualty losses	$100 floor on nonbusiness casualty and theft losses; nonbusiness casualty and theft losses deductible only to extent losses exceed 10% of AGI.	Deductible in full.
Depreciation recapture for § 1250 property	Recaptured to extent accelerated depreciation exceeds straight-line.	20% of excess of amount that would be recaptured under § 1245 over amount recaptured under § 1250 is additional ordinary income under § 291.
Production activities deduction	3% of the lesser of QPAI or AGI.	3% of the lesser of QPAI or taxable income.
Net operating loss	Adjusted for nonbusiness deductions over nonbusiness income and for personal and dependency exemptions.	Generally no adjustments.
Dividends received	Qualified dividends are taxed at the same rate applicable to net long-term capital gains.	Deduction allowed (70%, 80%, or 100%) as to dividends received.
Long-term capital gains	Generally taxed at a rate no higher than 15% (5% if taxpayer is in the 15% or lower tax bracket).	Taxed using regular corporate rates.
Capital losses	Only $3,000 of capital loss can offset ordinary income; loss is carried forward indefinitely to offset capital gains or ordinary income up to $3,000; carryovers of short-term losses remain short term; long-term losses carry over as long term.	Can offset only capital gains; carried back three years and forward five years; carrybacks and carryovers are treated as short-term losses.

	Individuals	Corporations
Passive activity losses	Generally deductible only against income from passive activities.	For regular corporations, no limitation on deductibility. Personal service corporations and certain closely held corporations, however, are subject to same limitations as imposed on individuals. A closely held corporation is one where five or fewer individuals own more than 50% of the stock either directly or indirectly.
Alternative minimum tax	Applied at a graduated rate schedule of 26% and 28% to AMT base (taxable income as modified by certain adjustments plus preference items minus exemption amount); exemption allowed depending on filing status (e.g., $58,000 in 2006 for married filing jointly); exemption phaseout begins when AMTI reaches a certain amount (e.g., $150,000 for married filing jointly).	Applied at a 20% rate to AMT base (taxable income as modified by certain adjustments plus preference items minus exemption amount); $40,000 exemption allowed but phaseout begins once AMTI reaches $150,000; adjustments and tax preference items similar to those applicable to individuals but also include 75% of adjusted current earnings (ACE) over AMTI. Certain small business corporations are exempt from the AMT.
Tax rates	Progressive with six rates in 2006 (10%, 15%, 25%, 28%, 33%, and 35%).	Progressive with four rates (15%, 25%, 34%, and 35%); lower brackets phased out at higher levels.

financing. If the debt instrument has too many features of stock, it may be treated as a form of stock, and principal and interest payments are treated as dividends.[32]

The form of the instrument will not assure debt treatment, but failure to observe certain formalities in creating the debt may lead to an assumption that the purported debt is a form of stock. The debt should be in proper legal form, bear a legitimate rate of interest, have a definite maturity date, and be repaid on a timely basis. Payments should not be contingent upon earnings. Further, the debt should not be subordinated to other liabilities, and proportionate holdings of stock and debt should be avoided or minimized.

The preferential treatment allowed for qualified dividend income has added another dimension to the thin capitalization issue. Although a corporation would prefer to pay out profits in the form of interest (deductible as an expense) rather than as dividends (nondeductible), the shareholders have the opposite tax position. Interest income is ordinary income, while qualified dividends are subject to beneficial net capital gain rates. Nevertheless, the repayment of the debt is not taxed at all as it is a return of capital. Hence, the thin capitalization incentive will continue to exist.

Transfers to Controlled Corporations

Without special provisions in the Code, a transfer of property to a corporation in exchange for its stock would be a sale or exchange of property and would constitute a taxable transaction to the transferor shareholder. Section 351 provides for the

---

[32]Section 385 lists several factors that might be used to determine whether a debtor-creditor relationship or a shareholder-corporation relationship exists.

nonrecognition of gain or loss upon such transfers of property if the transferors are in control of the corporation immediately after the transfer. Gain or loss is merely postponed in a manner similar to a like-kind exchange (see Chapter 15). The following requirements must be met to qualify under § 351:

- The transferors must be in control of the corporation immediately after the exchange. *Control* is defined as ownership of at least 80 percent of the total combined voting power of all classes of stock entitled to vote and at least 80 percent of the total number of shares of all other classes of stock.[33]
- Realized gain (but not loss) is recognized to the extent that the transferors receive property other than stock. Such nonqualifying property is commonly referred to as *boot.*

If the requirements of § 351 are satisfied and no boot is involved, nonrecognition of gain or loss is *mandatory.*

Basis Considerations and Computation of Gain. The nonrecognition of gain or loss is accompanied by a carryover of basis. The basis of stock received in a §351 transfer is determined as follows:

- Start with the adjusted basis of the property transferred by the shareholder.
- Add any gain recognized by the shareholder as a result of the transfer.
- Subtract the fair market value of any boot received by the shareholder from the corporation.[34]

Shareholders who receive noncash boot have a basis in the property equal to the fair market value.

The basis of properties received by the corporation is the basis in the hands of the transferor increased by the amount of any gain recognized to the transferor shareholder.[35]

EXAMPLE 20

Ann and Lori form Bluejay Corporation. Ann transfers property with an adjusted basis of $30,000 and a fair market value of $60,000 for 50% of the stock. Lori transfers property with an adjusted basis of $40,000 and a fair market value of $60,000 for the remaining 50% of the stock. The realized gain ($30,000 for Ann and $20,000 for Lori) is not recognized on the transfer because the transfer qualifies under § 351. The basis of the stock to Ann is $30,000, and the basis of the stock to Lori is $40,000. Bluejay Corporation has a basis of $30,000 in the property transferred by Ann and a basis of $40,000 in the property transferred by Lori. ■

EXAMPLE 21

Mike and John form Condor Corporation with the following investments: Mike transfers property (adjusted basis of $30,000 and fair market value of $70,000), and John transfers cash of $60,000. Each receives 50 shares of the Condor stock, but Mike also receives $10,000 in cash. Assume each share of the Condor stock is worth $1,200. Mike's realized gain is $40,000, determined as follows:

Value of the Condor stock received	
[50 (shares) × $1,200 (value per share)]	$ 60,000
Cash received	10,000
Amount realized	$ 70,000
Less basis of property transferred	(30,000)
Realized gain	$ 40,000

Mike's recognized gain is $10,000, the lesser of the realized gain ($40,000) or the fair market value of the boot received ($10,000). Mike's basis in the Condor stock is $30,000, computed as follows:

---

[33]§ 368(c).
[34]§ 358(a).
[35]§ 362(a).

Basis in the property transferred	$ 30,000
Plus recognized gain	10,000
	$ 40,000
Less boot received	(10,000)
Basis to Mike of the Condor stock	$ 30,000

Condor Corporation's basis in the property transferred by Mike is $40,000 [$30,000 (basis of the property to Mike) + $10,000 (gain recognized by Mike)]. John neither realizes nor recognizes gain or loss and will have a basis of $60,000 in the Condor stock. ■

ETHICAL
Considerations

SELECTIVE INCORPORATION

Miguel, a cash basis taxpayer, owns and operates a home renovation business that he decides to incorporate. In forming the corporation, he transfers *most* of the business, which includes unrealized receivables and inventory items. However, he retains the land and building and the trade accounts payable.

For tax purposes, what is Miguel trying to accomplish by being selective in terms of what he transfers to the corporation? Will it work?

The receipt of stock for the performance of *services* always results in ordinary income to the transferor shareholder. An example might be an attorney who does not charge a fee for incorporating a business but instead receives the value equivalent in stock of the newly formed corporation. The basis of stock received for the performance of services is equal to the fair market value of the services.

LO.6

Work with the tax rules governing the operation of corporations.

Operating the Corporation

Dividend Distributions

Corporate distributions of cash or property to shareholders are treated as dividend income to the extent the corporation has accumulated *or* current earnings and profits (E & P).[36] In determining the source of the distribution, a dividend is deemed to have been made initially from current E & P.

EXAMPLE 22

As of January 1, 2006, Teal Corporation has a deficit in accumulated E & P of $30,000. For tax year 2006, it has current E & P of $10,000. In 2006, the corporation distributes $5,000 to its shareholders. The $5,000 distribution is treated as a dividend, since it is deemed to have been made from current E & P. This is the case even though Teal still has a deficit in its accumulated E & P at the end of 2006. ■

Qualified dividend income is taxed like net long-term capital gain.[37] Consequently, the tax rate on such income cannot exceed 15 percent (5 percent for individual shareholders in the 15 percent or lower tax bracket).[38]

If a corporate distribution is not covered by E & P (either current or past), it is treated as a return of capital (refer to the discussion of the recovery of capital doctrine in Chapter 4). This treatment allows the shareholder to apply the amount of the distribution against the basis of the stock investment and therefore represents a

---

[36]§ 316.

[37]Qualified dividend income is defined in § 1(h)(11)(B) and is discussed in Chapter 4.

[38]§ 1(h)(1). See the discussion in Chapter 3.

TRANSFERRING ASSETS TO FOREIGN CORPORATIONS—FORGET § 351?

Otherwise tax-deferred transfers to controlled corporations under § 351 may generate current taxation when those transfers cross national borders. When a U.S. person transfers appreciated assets to a foreign corporation, the United States may lose its ability to tax the deferred gain on those assets (as well as the future income generated by the assets). To protect the U.S. taxing jurisdiction, § 367 provides that transfers of assets outside the U.S. tax net are generally taxable, in spite of the provisions of § 351.

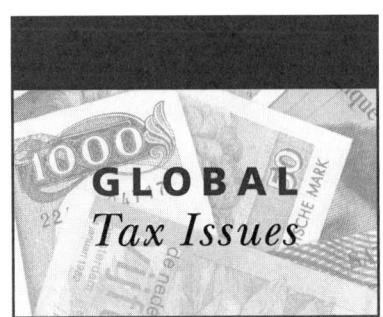

GLOBAL *Tax Issues*

nontaxable return of capital. Any amount received in excess of the stock basis is classified as a capital gain (if the stock is a capital asset in the hands of the shareholder).

EXAMPLE 23

When Mallard Corporation has no E & P (either current or accumulated), it distributes cash of $30,000 to its sole shareholder, Helen. The basis of Helen's stock investment is $20,000. Based on these facts, the $30,000 distribution Helen receives is accounted for as follows:

Return of capital (nontaxable)	$20,000
Capital gain	10,000
Total amount of distribution	$30,000

After the distribution, Helen has a basis of zero in her stock investment. ∎

Concept of Earnings and Profits. The term **earnings and profits** is not defined in the Code, but § 312 does include certain transactions that affect E & P. Although E & P and the accounting concept of retained earnings have certain similarities, they differ in numerous respects. For example, a nontaxable stock dividend is treated as a capitalization of retained earnings for accounting purposes, yet it does not decrease E & P for tax purposes. Taxable dividends do reduce E & P but cannot yield a deficit. Referring to Example 23, after the distribution Mallard Corporation's E & P remains zero rather than being a negative amount.

Generally, *current E & P* for a taxable year is taxable income plus or minus certain adjustments (e.g., an addition is made for tax-exempt income). Federal income taxes are subtracted from taxable income in arriving at current E & P. *Accumulated E & P* is the sum of the corporation's past current E & P that has not been distributed as dividends. A detailed discussion of the concept of E & P is beyond the scope of this chapter.

Property Dividends. A distribution of property to a shareholder is measured by the fair market value of the property on the date of distribution. The shareholder's basis in the property received is also the fair market value.[39]

EXAMPLE 24

Drake Corporation has E & P of $60,000. It distributes land with a fair market value of $50,000 (adjusted basis of $30,000) to its sole shareholder, Art. Art has a taxable dividend of $50,000 and a basis in the land of $50,000. ∎

A corporation that distributes appreciated property to its shareholders as a dividend must recognize the amount of the appreciation as gain.[40]

---

[39]§ 301.

[40]The tax consequences to a corporation of nonliquidating distributions to shareholders are covered in § 311.

| EXAMPLE 25 | Assume the same facts as in Example 24. Drake Corporation must recognize a gain of $20,000 on the distribution it made to Art. ∎ |

However, if the property distributed has a basis in excess of its fair market value, the distributing corporation cannot recognize any loss.

ETHICAL *Considerations*   **AN ART LOVER'S DREAM COME TRUE**

Imelda is the owner and operator of a large and prosperous incorporated automobile dealership. She is also an avid fan of American artists, particularly those who feature western landscapes. In 2004, the dealership purchased several paintings by Georgia O'Keefe and displayed them for several weeks at its main showroom. Since then, and purportedly for security reasons, the paintings have been kept in the living room of Imelda's personal residence.

Are there any tax risks in the procedure followed by Imelda and her dealership? Explain.

Constructive Dividends. Many taxpayers mistakenly assume that dividend consequences do not take place unless the distribution carries the formalities of a dividend (declaration date, record date, payment date). They further assume that dividends must be paid out to all shareholders on a pro rata basis. This may not be the case when closely held corporations are involved. Here, the key to dividend treatment depends upon whether the shareholders derive a benefit from the corporation that cannot be otherwise classified (e.g., as reasonable salary). The following are examples of **constructive dividends**:

- Salaries paid to shareholder-employees that are not reasonable (refer to Example 6 in Chapter 6).
- Interest on debt owed by the corporation to shareholders that is reclassified as equity because the corporation is thinly capitalized (refer to the earlier discussion in this chapter).
- Excessive rent paid by a corporation for the use of shareholder property. The arm's length standard is used to test whether the rent is excessive (refer to Example 22 in Chapter 1) .
- Advances to shareholders that are not bona fide loans.
- Interest-free (or below-market) loans to shareholders. In this situation, the dividend component is the difference between the interest provided for, if any, and that calculated using the market rate.
- Shareholder use of corporate property for less than an arm's length rate.
- Absorption by the corporation of a shareholder's personal expenses.
- Bargain purchase of corporate property by shareholders.

Like regular dividends, constructive dividends must be covered by E & P to carry dividend income consequences to the shareholders. As noted above, however, constructive dividends need not be available to all shareholders on a pro rata basis.

Although dividends reduce the E & P of a corporation, they are not deductible for income tax purposes. In this regard, certain constructive dividends could have subtle tax consequences for all parties concerned.

| EXAMPLE 26 | Grouse Corporation makes a loan to one of its shareholders, Hal. No interest is provided for, but application of the market rate would produce $20,000 of interest for the term of the loan. Presuming the loan is bona fide, the following results occur: |

- Hal has dividend income of $20,000.
- Grouse Corporation has interest income of $20,000.
- Hal might obtain an interest deduction of $20,000.

Not only does Grouse Corporation have to recognize income of $20,000, but it also obtains no income tax deduction for the $20,000 constructive dividend. ■

EXAMPLE 27

Assume the same facts as in Example 26, except that the loan to Hal was not bona fide. In this event, the full amount of the loan is regarded as a dividend to Hal. Therefore, the interest element is not a factor since no bona fide loan ever existed. ■

Stock Redemptions

If a corporation redeems a shareholder's stock (a **stock redemption**), one of two possible outcomes occurs:

- The redemption may qualify as a sale or exchange under § 302 or § 303. In that case, capital gain or loss treatment usually applies to the qualifying shareholders.
- The redemption will be treated as a dividend under § 301, provided the distributing corporation has E & P.

EXAMPLE 28

Reba owns 300 shares of Snipe Corporation stock as an investment. The shares have a basis to Reba of $100 each, for a total of $30,000. When the fair market value of a share is $300, Snipe redeems 200 of Reba's shares. If the redemption qualifies for sale or exchange treatment, the result is a capital gain to Reba of $40,000 [$60,000 (redemption price) − $20,000 (basis in 200 shares)]. Reba's basis in the remaining 100 shares is $10,000 [$30,000 (basis in the original shares) − $20,000 (basis in the shares redeemed)]. ■

EXAMPLE 29

Assume the same facts as in Example 28, except that the redemption does not qualify for sale or exchange treatment. Presuming adequate E & P, the redemption results in $60,000 dividend income. Reba's basis in the remaining 100 shares now becomes $30,000, or $300 per share. ■

Because dividend income is taxed at the rate applicable to net long-term capital gain, the difference between Examples 28 and 29 is in the amount of recognized gain that is eligible for the beneficial capital gain rate. In Example 29, an extra $20,000 of such gain occurs, since the redeemed stock's basis of $20,000 is not part of the recognized gain calculation.

A stock redemption qualifies as a sale or exchange if it meets any of the safe harbors of § 302 or § 303.

Liquidating the Corporation

> **LO.7**
>
> Recognize the tax rules governing the liquidation of corporations.

Unlike dividend distributions or stock redemptions, where the distributing corporation continues its operations, **liquidating distributions** occur during the termination of the business. All debts are paid, and any remaining corporate assets are distributed pro rata to the shareholders in exchange for their stock. Once these distributions are completed, the corporation undergoing liquidation will cease to be a separate tax entity.

General Rule of § 331

Under the general rule, the shareholders recognize gain or loss in a corporate liquidation. The amount of recognized gain or loss is measured by the difference between the fair market value of the assets received from the corporation and the adjusted basis of the stock surrendered. The shareholders recognize capital gain or loss if the stock is a capital asset.[41]

EXAMPLE 30

Pursuant to a complete liquidation, Starling Corporation distributes $100,000 in cash to Edna, one of its shareholders. If Edna's basis in the stock surrendered is $40,000, she must recognize a gain of $60,000. If Edna held the stock as an investment, the $60,000 gain is capital gain—either short term or long term (depending on the holding period). ■

ETHICAL *Considerations*   ELIMINATING BURDENSOME PAPERWORK

For many years, Sophie has owned and operated several apartment buildings. In 1995 and upon the advice of her attorney, Sophie transferred the apartment buildings to a newly created corporation. Her main reason for incorporating the business was to achieve limited liability.

Every year since 1995, Sophie has prepared and filed a Form 1120 for the corporation. No corporate income tax has been paid because, after the deduction of various expenses

(including Sophie's "management fee"), the corporation has zero taxable income.

In 2006, Sophie decides that filing Form 1120 is a waste of time and serves no useful purpose. Instead, she plans to report all of the financial activities of the apartment business on her own individual Form 1040.

Comment on the propriety of what Sophie plans to do.

Exception to the General Rule

Section 332 is an exception to the general rule that the shareholder recognizes gain or loss on a corporate liquidation. If a parent corporation liquidates a subsidiary corporation in which it owns at least 80 percent of the voting power and value of the stock, no gain or loss is recognized by the parent company. The subsidiary must distribute all of its property in complete liquidation of all of its stock within the taxable year or within three years from the close of the tax year in which the first distribution occurred.

Basis Determination—§§ 334 and 338

General Rule. Where gain or loss is recognized upon the complete liquidation of a corporation, the basis of the property received by the shareholders is the property's fair market value.[42]

Subsidiary Liquidation Basis Rules. The general rule is that the property received by the parent corporation in a complete liquidation of its subsidiary under § 332 has the same basis it had in the hands of the subsidiary (a carryover basis).[43] The parent's basis in the stock of the liquidated subsidiary disappears.

EXAMPLE 31

Swallow, the parent corporation, has a basis of $20,000 in the stock of Shrike Corporation, a subsidiary in which it owns 85% of all classes of stock. Swallow purchased the stock of Shrike Corporation 10 years ago. In the current year, Swallow liquidates Shrike Corporation and receives assets worth $50,000 with a tax basis to Shrike of $40,000. Swallow Corporation will have a basis of $40,000 in the assets, with a potential gain upon sale of $10,000. Swallow's original $20,000 basis in the Shrike stock disappears. ■

---

[41]If the stock is held as an investment, which is usually the case, gain or loss will be capital. Stock owned by a broker probably will be inventory and therefore will not constitute a capital asset. Thus, the gain or loss on this type of stock is ordinary and not capital.

[42]§ 334(a).
[43]§ 334(b)(1).

An exception to the carryover of basis rule is provided in § 338. Under this exception, the parent company may elect to receive a basis for the assets equal to the adjusted basis of the stock of the subsidiary. In effect, the initial acquisition of the subsidiary is treated as if the parent company had acquired the assets (rather than the stock) of the subsidiary.

Effect of the Liquidation on the Corporation

At the corporate level, § 336 applies to dictate the tax consequences to the corporation being liquidated. Under § 336, the distributing corporation recognizes gain or loss upon complete liquidation. In this regard, it does not matter whether the corporation distributes the property in kind (*as is*) to the shareholders or first sells the property and then distributes the proceeds.

EXAMPLE 32

Pursuant to a complete liquidation, Grackle Corporation distributes the following assets to its shareholders: undeveloped land held as an investment (basis of $150,000 and fair market value of $140,000) and marketable securities (basis of $160,000 and fair market value of $200,000). Since Grackle is treated as if it had sold the property, a gain of $40,000 results from the securities, and a loss of $10,000 results from the land. ■

The deductibility of losses may be restricted by the related-party rules (refer to Chapter 6) if certain conditions exist (e.g., the distributions are not pro rata).[44]

A wholly owned subsidiary corporation does not recognize gain or loss when the parent corporation uses the carryover basis option of § 334(b)(1). The reason for the special treatment is that the subsidiary's basis (and all other tax attributes) in the assets carries over to the parent corporation.

The S Election

LO.8

Appreciate the utility and effect of the Subchapter S election.

Numerous nontax reasons exist for operating a business in the corporate form (e.g., limited liability). Consequently, the existence of income tax disadvantages (e.g., double taxation of corporate income and shareholder dividends) should not deter businesspeople from using the corporate form. To prevent tax considerations from interfering with the exercise of sound business judgment, Congress enacted Subchapter S of the Code. The Subchapter S election enables taxpayers to use the corporate form for conducting a business without being taxed as a corporation.

Qualification for S Status

To achieve S corporation status, the corporation must meet certain requirements and make an effective election.

Qualifying for the Election. To qualify for **S corporation** status, the corporation must be a **small business corporation.** This includes any corporation that has the following characteristics:

- Is a domestic corporation.
- Has no more than 100 shareholders.
- Has as its shareholders only individuals, estates, and certain trusts.
- Does not have a nonresident alien as a shareholder.
- Has only one class of stock outstanding.

Effective for tax years beginning after 2004, the members of a family who do, or will, own stock can agree to be treated as a single shareholder. Members of a family

---

[44]§ 336(d).

TAX *in the News*   **EXPLOSIVE GROWTH MAY LEAD TO INCREASED AUDITS**

In news release IR–2005–76, the IRS Commissioner has noted the enormous increase in the use of the S corporation as a form of doing business. In 1985, there were 724,749 S corporations; by 2002, that number had grown to 3,154,377. The number of big S structures has grown even faster. From 1985 to 2002, the number of S corporations with more than $10 million in assets grew more than tenfold, from 2,305 to 26,096. In fact, today S corporations are more common than C corporations and account for 59 percent of all corporate tax returns.

Because of this explosive growth, the IRS is reevaluating its audit procedures to ensure that a high level of taxpayer compliance is obtained. In other words, in the future S corporations can expect increased and more sophisticated audits by the IRS!

---

include all lineal descendants of a shareholder and spouse (or ex-spouse) and the spouses (or ex-spouses) of such lineal descendants.[45]

EXAMPLE 33

Harry, a shareholder in an S corporation dies, and under his will, his stock is distributed among three children and eight grandchildren. If an agreement is in effect, the 11 new shareholders are treated as one shareholder for purposes of the 100-shareholder limitation. ∎

These characteristics must continue to exist if an electing S corporation is to maintain S status.

Making the Election. The election is made by filing Form 2553, and *all* shareholders must consent. For this purpose, husbands and wives are counted as a single shareholder.

To be effective for the current year, the election must be filed anytime during the preceding taxable year or on or before the fifteenth day of the third month of the current year.[46]

EXAMPLE 34

Heron, a calendar year taxpayer, is a regular corporation that wishes to elect S status for 2006. If the election is filed anytime from January 1, 2005, through March 15, 2006, it will be effective for 2006. ∎

The IRS has the authority to waive invalid S elections (e.g., inadvertent failure to obtain all the necessary shareholder consents to the original election) and to treat late elections as timely.

Loss of the Election. The S election may be terminated *voluntarily* (a majority of the shareholders file to revoke the election) or *involuntarily*. An involuntary termination may occur in *any* of the following ways:

* The corporation ceases to qualify as a small business corporation (e.g., the number of shareholders exceeds 100, or a partnership becomes a shareholder).
* The corporation has passive investment income (e.g., interest, dividends) in excess of 25 percent of gross receipts for a period of three consecutive years. This possibility applies only if the corporation was previously a regular corporation and has E & P from that period.

---

[45]§ 1361(c)(1).   [46]§ 1362.

If the holders of a *majority* of the shares consent to a voluntary revocation of S status, the election to revoke must be made on or before the fifteenth day of the third month of the tax year to be effective for that year.

EXAMPLE 35

The shareholders of Stork Corporation, a calendar year S corporation, elect to revoke the election on January 3, 2006. Assuming the election is duly executed and timely filed, Stork will become a regular corporation for calendar year 2006. If the election to revoke is not made until June 2006, Stork will not become a regular corporation until calendar year 2007. ■

Suppose the shareholders in Example 35 file the election to revoke on January 3, 2006, but do not want the revocation to take place until 2007. If the election so specifies, Stork Corporation will cease to have S status as of January 1, 2007.

In the case where S status is lost because of a disqualifying act (involuntarily), the loss of the election takes effect as of the date on which the event occurs.

EXAMPLE 36

Crow Corporation has been a calendar year S corporation for several years. On August 14, 2006, one of its shareholders sells her stock to Kite Corporation. Since Crow Corporation no longer satisfies the definition of a small business corporation (it has another corporation as a shareholder), the election has been involuntarily terminated. For calendar year 2006, therefore, Crow will be an S corporation through August 13 and a regular corporation from August 14 through December 31, 2006. ■

In the event the election is lost through a violation of the passive investment income limitation, the loss of S status starts at the beginning of the next tax year.

Barring certain exceptions, the loss of the election places the corporation in a five-year holding period before S status can be reelected.

Operational Rules

The S corporation is primarily a tax-reporting rather than a taxpaying entity. In this respect, the entity is taxed much like a partnership.[47] Under the conduit concept, the taxable income and losses of an S corporation flow through to the shareholders who report them on their personal income tax returns.

To ascertain the annual tax consequences to each shareholder, it is necessary to carry out two steps at the S corporation level. First, all corporate transactions that will flow through to the shareholders on an *as is* basis under the conduit approach must be set aside. Second, what remains is aggregated as the taxable income of the S corporation and is allocated to each shareholder on a per-share and per-day of stock ownership basis.[48]

Separately Stated Items. The following are some of the items that do not lose their identity as they pass through the S corporation and are therefore picked up by each shareholder on an *as is* basis:

- Tax-exempt income.
- Long-term and short-term capital gains and losses.
- Section 1231 gains and losses.
- Charitable contributions.
- Production activities deduction.
- Qualified dividend income.
- Foreign tax credits.
- Depletion.

---

[47]This is not to imply that an S corporation is always free from the income tax. For example, a tax may be imposed on certain built-in gains or certain excessive passive investment income.

[48]§ 1366.

TAX *in the News*

S CORPORATIONS AND SALARIES: MORE TRAUMA ON THE WAY!

Devising the most beneficial salary structure has always presented a supreme challenge for many S corporations. The owner-shareholders may want to receive enough salary to be covered under Social Security and private retirement plans. Too much, however, will aggravate the employment tax cost (particularly the Medicare portion, which does not have a cap). (Note that nonsalary distributions to a shareholder are not subject to self-employment tax.) Not infrequently, common sense disappears, and shareholders work for free just to avoid payroll taxes.

Finding the right salary mix has become even more complicated with the enactment of the production activities deduction. Two new variables have been added with both detrimental and beneficial effects. The bad news is that salary is an expense and will reduce the QPAI that passes through. The good news is that salary is a Form W–2 item and will increase the wage limitation on deducting QPAI.

When the benefits of the production activities deduction are fully phased in at 9 percent, the salary structure of an S corporation will become even more significant.

- Nonbusiness income or loss under § 212.
- Intangible drilling costs.
- Investment interest, income, and expenses covered under § 163(d).
- Certain portfolio income.
- Passive activity gains, losses, and credits under § 469.
- AMT adjustments and tax preference items.

In the case of the production activities deduction, the individual components needed to determine the deduction at the shareholder level must be broken out. These components include each shareholder's pro rata portion of QPAI and the W–2 wages paid by the corporation. This information is listed on line 12 of Schedule K–1 (Form 1120S) and is picked up by the shareholder on his or her Form 8903 (Domestic Production Activities Deduction).

The items listed above are separately stated because each may lead to a different tax result when combined with a particular shareholder's other transactions.

EXAMPLE 37

Arnold and Jean are equal shareholders in Lark Corporation (an S corporation). For calendar year 2006, each must account for one-half of a corporate short-term capital gain of $6,000. Arnold has no other capital asset transactions, and Jean has a short-term capital loss of $3,000 from the sale of stock in IBM Corporation. In terms of overall effect, the difference between the two taxpayers is significant. Although both must report the short-term capital gain pass-through, Jean will neutralize its inclusion in gross income by offsetting it with the $3,000 short-term capital loss from the sale of the IBM stock. For Arnold, the short-term capital gain pass-through results in a $3,000 increase in his taxable income. ■

Taxable Income. After the separately stated items have been removed, the balance represents the taxable income of the S corporation. In arriving at taxable income, the dividends received deduction and the NOL deduction are not allowed. An S corporation does come under the regular corporate rules, however, for purposes of amortization of organizational expenditures.

Once taxable income has been determined, it passes through to each shareholder as of the last day of the S corporation's tax year.

EXAMPLE 38

Harrier Corporation, a calendar year S corporation, had the following transactions during the current year:

Sales		$ 40,000
Cost of goods sold		(23,000)
Other income		
*Tax-exempt interest	$ 300	
*Long-term capital gain	500	800
Other expenses		
*Charitable contributions	$ 400	
Advertising expense	1,500	
Other operating expenses	2,000	
*Short-term capital loss	150	(4,050)
Net income per books		$ 13,750

When the items that are to be separately stated (those preceded by an asterisk [*]) and shown *as is* by each shareholder are withdrawn, Harrier has the following taxable income:

Sales		$ 40,000
Cost of goods sold		(23,000)
Other expenses		
Advertising expense	$1,500	
Other operating expenses	2,000	(3,500)
Taxable income		$ 13,500

EXAMPLE 39

If Oscar owned 10% of the stock in Harrier Corporation (refer to Example 38) during all of the current year, he must account for the following:

Separately stated items	
Tax-exempt interest	$ 30
Long-term capital gain	50
Charitable contributions	40
Short-term capital loss	15
Taxable income (10% of $13,500)	1,350

Some of the separately stated items need not be reported on Oscar's individual income tax return (e.g., the tax-exempt interest). Others must be reported but may not lead to tax consequences. Oscar picks up his share of Harrier's taxable income ($1,350) as ordinary income. ■

Treatment of Losses. As previously noted, separately stated loss items (e.g., capital losses, § 1231 losses) flow through to the shareholders on an *as is* basis. Their treatment by a shareholder depends on the shareholder's individual income tax position. If the S corporation's taxable income determination results in an operating loss, it also passes through to the shareholders. As is the case with separately stated items, the amount of the loss each shareholder receives depends on the stock ownership during the year.

EXAMPLE 40

In 2006, Oriole Corporation (a calendar year S corporation) incurred an operating loss of $36,500. During 2006, Jason's ownership in Oriole was as follows: 20% for 200 days and 30% for 165 days. Jason's share of the loss is determined as follows:

[$36,500 × (200/365)] × 20% =	$4,000
[$36,500 × (165/365)] × 30% =	4,950
Total loss for Jason	$8,950

Presuming the basis limitation does not come into play (see the following discussion), Jason deducts $8,950 in arriving at adjusted gross income. ■

Basis Determination. A shareholder's *basis* in the stock of an S corporation, like that of a regular corporation, is the original investment plus additional capital contributions less return of capital distributions. At this point, however, the symmetry disappears. Generally, basis is increased by the pass-through of income items (including those separately stated) and decreased by the loss items (including those separately stated).[49]

EXAMPLE 41

In 2006, Warbler Corporation is formed with an investment of $100,000, of which Janice contributed $20,000 for a 20% stock interest. A timely S election is made, and for 2006, Warbler earns taxable income of $15,000. Janice's basis in her stock investment now becomes $23,000 [$20,000 (original capital contribution) + $3,000 (the 20% share of the corporation's taxable income assigned to Janice)]. ■

Distributions by an S corporation reduce the basis of a shareholder's stock investment. However, if the amount of the distribution exceeds basis, the excess normally receives capital gain treatment.

As previously noted, operating losses of an S corporation pass through to the shareholders and reduce the basis in their stock investment. Because the basis of the stock cannot fall below zero, an excess loss is then applied against the basis of any loans the shareholder may have made to the corporation.

EXAMPLE 42

Flamingo Corporation, a calendar year S corporation, has an operating loss of $60,000 for 2006. Norman, a 50% shareholder, has an adjusted basis of $25,000 in his stock investment and has made loans to the corporation of $5,000. Based on these facts, Norman may take full advantage of the $30,000 loss (50% of $60,000) on his 2006 individual income tax return. Norman's basis in the stock and the loans must be reduced accordingly, and both will be zero after the pass-through. ■

In the event the basis limitation precludes an operating loss from being absorbed, the loss can be carried forward and deducted when and if it is covered by basis.

EXAMPLE 43

Assume the same facts as in Example 42, except that Norman had not made any loans to Flamingo Corporation. Further assume that Flamingo has taxable income of $15,000 in the following year (2007). Norman's tax situation for 2006 and 2007 is summarized as follows:

Ordinary loss for 2006	$25,000
Income to be reported in 2007 (50% of $15,000)	7,500
Restoration of stock basis in 2007 (50% of $15,000)	7,500
Loss allowed for 2007 ($30,000 − $25,000)	5,000
Basis in stock account after 2007 ($7,500 − $5,000)	2,500

Thus, Norman's unabsorbed loss of $5,000 from 2006 carries over to 2007 and is applied against the $7,500 of ordinary income for that year. ■

LO.9

Understand the tax consequences of forming and operating a partnership.

Partnerships

Nature of Partnership Taxation

Unlike corporations, partnerships are not considered separate taxable entities. Each member of a partnership is subject to income tax on his or her distributive share of the partnership's income, even if an actual distribution is not made. The

---

[49]§ 1367.

tax return (Form 1065) required of a partnership serves only to provide information necessary in determining the character and amount of each partner's distributive share of the partnership's income and expense. Because a partnership acts as a conduit, items that pass through to the partners do not lose their identity. For example, tax-exempt income earned by a partnership is picked up by the partners as tax-exempt income. In this regard, partnerships function in much the same fashion as S corporations, which also serve as conduits.

A partnership is considered a separate taxable entity for purposes of making various elections and selecting its taxable year, method of depreciation, and accounting method. A partnership is also treated as a separate legal entity under civil law with the right to own property in its own name and to transact business free from the personal debts of its partners.

Partnership Formation

Recognition of Gain or Loss. The general rule is that no gain or loss is recognized by a partnership or any of its partners on the contribution of property in exchange for a capital interest in the partnership.[50] The general rule also applies to all subsequent contributions of property.

There are certain exceptions to the nonrecognition of gain or loss rule including the following:

- If a partner transfers property to the partnership and receives money or other consideration (boot) as a result, the transaction will be treated as a sale or exchange rather than as a contribution of capital. Realized gain is recognized to the extent of the fair market value of the boot received.
- If a partnership interest is received in exchange for services rendered or to be rendered by the partner to the partnership, the fair market value of the transferred capital interest is regarded as compensation for services rendered. In such cases, the recipient of the capital interest must recognize the amount as ordinary income in the year actually or constructively received.
- If property that is subject to a liability in excess of its basis is contributed to a partnership, the contributing partner may recognize gain.

Basis of a Partnership Interest. The contributing *partner's basis* in the partnership interest received is the sum of money contributed plus the adjusted basis of any other property transferred to the partnership.[51]

EXAMPLE 44

In return for the contribution of property (with a basis of $50,000 and a fair market value of $80,000) and cash of $10,000 to the Brown Partnership, Marcia receives a 10% capital interest worth $90,000. Although Marcia has a realized gain of $30,000 ($90,000 − $60,000) on the transfer, none of the gain is recognized. The basis of her interest in the Brown Partnership is $60,000 [$50,000 (basis of property contributed) + $10,000 (cash contribution)]. ■

A partner's basis in the partnership interest is determined without regard to any amount reflected on the partnership's books as capital, equity, or a similar account.

EXAMPLE 45

Marge and Clyde form the equal Blue Partnership with a cash contribution of $30,000 from Marge and a property contribution (adjusted basis of $18,000 and fair market value of $30,000) from Clyde. Although the books of the Blue Partnership may reflect a credit of $30,000 to each partner's capital account, only Marge has a tax basis of $30,000 in her partnership interest. Clyde's tax basis in his partnership interest is $18,000, the amount of his tax basis in the property contributed to the partnership. ■

---

[50]§ 721. [51]§ 722.

After its initial determination, the basis of a partnership interest is subject to continuous fluctuations. A partner's basis is increased by additional contributions and the sum of his or her current and prior years' distributive share of the following:

- Taxable income of the partnership, including capital gains.
- Tax-exempt income of the partnership.
- The excess of the deductions for depletion over the basis of the partnership's property subject to depletion.[52]

Similarly, the basis of a partner's interest is decreased, but not below zero, by distributions of partnership property and by the sum of the current and prior years' distributive share of the following:

- Partnership losses, including capital losses.
- Partnership expenditures that are not deductible in computing taxable income or loss and that are not capital expenditures.

Changes in the liabilities (including trade accounts payable, bank loans, etc.) of a partnership also affect the basis of a partnership interest. A partner's basis is increased by his or her assumption of partnership liabilities and by his or her pro rata share of liabilities incurred by the partnership. Likewise, the partner's basis is decreased by the amount of any personal liabilities assumed by the partnership and by the pro rata share of any decreases in the liabilities of the partnership.

EXAMPLE 46

Tony, Martha, and Carolyn form the Orange Partnership with the following contributions: cash of $50,000 from Tony for a 50% interest in capital and profits, cash of $25,000 from Martha for a 25% interest, and property valued at $33,000 from Carolyn for a 25% interest. The property contributed by Carolyn has an adjusted basis of $15,000 and is subject to a mortgage of $8,000, which is assumed by the partnership. Carolyn's basis in her interest in the Orange Partnership is $9,000, determined as follows:

Adjusted basis of Carolyn's contributed property	$15,000
Less portion of mortgage assumed by Tony and Martha and treated as a distribution of money to Carolyn (75% of $8,000)	(6,000)
Basis of Carolyn's interest in Orange Partnership	$ 9,000

■

EXAMPLE 47

Assuming the same facts as in Example 46, Tony and Martha have a basis in their partnership interests of $54,000 and $27,000, respectively.

	Tony	Martha
Cash contribution	$50,000	$25,000
Plus portion of mortgage assumed and treated as an additional cash contribution:		
(50% of $8,000)	4,000	
(25% of $8,000)		2,000
Basis of interest in Orange Partnership	$54,000	$27,000

■

Partnership's Basis in Contributed Property. The *basis of property* contributed to a partnership by a partner is the adjusted basis of the property to the contributing partner at the time of the contribution.[53] Additionally, the holding period of the property for the partnership includes the period during which the property

[52]§ 705(a).   [53]§ 723.

was held by the contributing partner. This is logical, since the partnership's basis in the property is the same basis the property had in the hands of the partner.[54]

In 2006, Roger contributed equipment with an adjusted basis of $10,000 and fair market value of $30,000 to the Red Partnership in exchange for a one-third interest in the partnership. No gain or loss is recognized by Roger. The Red Partnership's basis in the equipment is $10,000. If Roger had acquired the equipment in 1998, the partnership's holding period would include the period from 1998 through 2006. ∎

Partnership Operation

Measuring and Reporting Partnership Income.

Although a partnership is not subject to Federal income taxation, it is required to determine its taxable income and file an income tax return for information purposes.[55] The tax return, Form 1065, is due on the fifteenth day of the fourth month following the close of the taxable year of the partnership.

In measuring and reporting partnership income, certain transactions must be segregated and reported separately on the partnership return. Items such as charitable contributions, the production activities deduction, capital gains and losses, qualified dividend income, and foreign taxes are excluded from partnership taxable income and are allocated separately to the partners.[56] These items must be segregated and allocated separately because they affect the computation of various exclusions, deductions, and credits at the individual partner level. For example, one of the partners may have made personal charitable contributions in excess of the ceiling limitations on his or her individual tax return. Therefore, partnership charitable contributions are excluded from partnership taxable income and are reported separately on the partnership return.

Similar to the procedure for an S corporation, the individual components needed to determine the production activities deduction at the partner level must be separated. These components include each partner's pro rata portion of QPAI and the W–2 wages paid by the partnership. This information is listed on line 13 of Schedule K–1 (Form 1065) and is picked up by the partner on his or her Form 8903 (Domestic Production Activities Deduction).

A second step in the measurement and reporting process is the computation of the partnership's ordinary income or loss. The taxable income of a partnership is computed in the same manner as the taxable income of an individual taxpayer. However, a partnership is not allowed the following deductions:[57]

- The deduction for personal and dependency exemptions.
- The deduction for taxes paid to foreign countries or possessions of the United States.
- The deduction for charitable contributions.
- The deduction for net operating losses.
- The additional itemized deductions allowed individuals in §§ 211 through 219.

The partnership's ordinary income or loss and each of the items requiring separate treatment are reported in the partnership's information return and allocated to the partners in accordance with their distributive shares.

Limitation on Partner's Share of Losses.

A partner's deduction of the distributive share of partnership losses (including capital losses) could be limited. The limitation is the adjusted basis of the partnership interest at the end of the partnership year in which the losses were incurred.

---

[54] § 1223(2).
[55] § 6031.

[56] § 702(a).
[57] § 703(a).

The limitation for partnership loss deductions is similar to that applicable to losses of S corporations. Like S corporation losses, partnership losses may be carried forward by the partner and utilized against future increases in the basis of the partnership interest. Such increases might result from additional capital contributions to the partnership, from additional partnership liabilities, or from future partnership income.

EXAMPLE 49	Florence and Donald do business as the Green Partnership, sharing profits and losses equally. All parties use the calendar year for tax purposes. As of January 1, 2006, Florence's basis in her partnership interest is $25,000. The partnership sustained an operating loss of $80,000 in 2006 and earned a profit of $70,000 in 2007. For the calendar year 2006, Florence may claim only $25,000 of her $40,000 distributive share of the partnership loss (one-half of the $80,000 loss). As a result, the basis in her partnership interest is reduced to zero as of January 1, 2007, and she must carry forward the remaining $15,000 of partnership losses. ■
EXAMPLE 50	Assuming the same facts as in Example 49, what are the income tax consequences for Florence in 2007? Since the partnership earned a profit of $70,000 for the calendar year 2007, Florence reports income from the partnership of $20,000 ($35,000 distributive share of income for 2007 less the $15,000 loss not allowed for 2006). The adjusted basis of her partnership interest now becomes $20,000. ■

Transactions between Partner and Partnership. A partner engaging in a transaction with the partnership is generally regarded as a nonpartner or outsider. However, the Code includes certain exceptions to prevent unwarranted tax avoidance in related-party situations. For instance, losses from the sale or exchange of property are disallowed if they arise in either of the following cases:

- Between a partnership and a person whose direct or indirect interest in the capital or profits of the partnership is more than 50 percent.
- Between two partnerships in which the same persons own more than a 50 percent interest in the capital or profits.[58]

An indirect interest includes those owned by family members (e.g., parents, children, brothers, and sisters).

EXAMPLE 51	Michael, Samantha, and Sarah (brother and sisters) are equal partners in the Beige Partnership. For purposes of the 50% related-party rules described above, each partner indirectly owns the interests of the others. Thus, Michael has a 100% interest (i.e., his one-third *direct* interest plus the two-thirds *indirect* interests of his sisters) in the Beige Partnership. ■

In a related-party situation, if one of the purchasers later sells the property, any gain realized will be recognized only to the extent that it exceeds the loss previously disallowed.

EXAMPLE 52	Pat owns a 60% interest in the capital and profits of the Rose Partnership. In the current year, Pat sells property with an adjusted basis of $50,000 to the partnership for its fair market value of $35,000. The $15,000 loss is not deductible since Pat's ownership interest is more than 50%. If the Rose Partnership later sells the property for $40,000, none of the $5,000 gain (sale price of $40,000 less adjusted basis to partnership of $35,000) will be recognized since it is offset by $5,000 of the previously disallowed loss of $15,000. The unused loss of $10,000, however, is of no tax benefit either to the partnership or to Pat. ■

Payments made by a partnership to one of its partners for services rendered or for the use of capital, to the extent they are determined without regard to the

---

[58]§ 707(b)(1).

income of the partnership, are treated by the partnership in the same manner as payments made to a person who is not a partner. Referred to as **guaranteed payments,** these are generally deductible by the partnership as a business expense.[59] The payments must be reported as ordinary income by the receiving partner. Their deductibility distinguishes guaranteed payments from a partner's distributive share of income that is not deductible by the partnership.

Under the terms of the Silver Partnership agreement, Kim is entitled to a fixed annual salary of $18,000 without regard to the income of the partnership. He is also to share in the profits and losses of the partnership as a one-third partner. After deducting the guaranteed payment, the partnership has $36,000 of ordinary income. Kim must include $30,000 as ordinary income on his income tax return for his tax year with or within which the partnership tax year ends ($18,000 guaranteed payment + $12,000 one-third distributive share of partnership income). ■

Other Partnership Considerations. Complex tax provisions involving liquidating and nonliquidating distributions and the sale of a partnership interest are beyond the scope of this text and are discussed in depth in *West Federal Taxation: Corporations, Partnerships, Estates, and Trusts.*

Corporate versus Noncorporate Forms of Business Organization

> **LO.10**
>
> Evaluate the advantages and disadvantages of the various forms for conducting a business.

Nontax Considerations. The decision of which entity to use in conducting a trade or business must be weighed carefully. Of prime importance are nontax considerations, including the legal attributes of the business entity chosen. For the corporate form, those commonly include limited liability, continuity of life, free transferability of interests, and centralized management. Many, if not all, of these attributes can also be obtained through the use of a limited liability company. When evaluating nontax considerations, close attention must be paid to applicable state law. Many states, for example, place severe restrictions on the use of corporations to practice certain professions (e.g., medicine, law). Likewise, the legal attributes of a limited liability company may vary from one state to another and may not be identical to those of corporations.

TAX PLANNING *Considerations*

Tax Considerations. The applicable income tax rates will affect the choice of the form of doing business. Because of the wide range of possibilities (10 to 35 percent for individuals in 2006 and 15 to 35 percent for corporations), this factor must be evaluated on a case-by-case basis. For example, the corporate form is very appealing if the anticipated taxable income falls within the 25 percent corporate bracket and the shareholder's individual bracket is 35 percent. Here, the time value of the taxes saved could make operating a business as a corporation advantageous. Do not, moreover, overlook the potential impact of state and local income taxes applicable to individuals and corporations. Also, in those states that do not have an income tax, a franchise tax can pose an added tax burden on corporations (see Chapter 1).

Unless an election is made under Subchapter S, operating as a corporation yields a potential double tax result. Corporate-source income will be taxed twice—once as earned by the corporation and again when distributed to the shareholders. The payment of a dividend does not result in a deduction to the corporation, and the receipt of a dividend generally results in ordinary income to a shareholder who is an individual. In the case of closely held corporations, therefore, a strong incentive exists to avoid the payment of dividends. Instead, a premium is put on bailing

---

[59]§ 707(c).

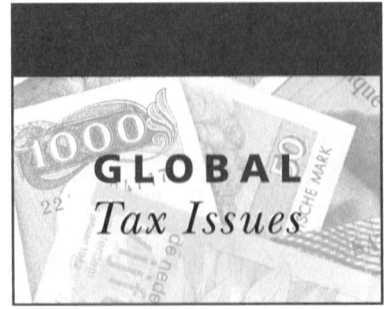

TAXING THE INCOME OF FOREIGN CORPORATIONS

Are foreign corporations subject to the U.S. corporate income tax? If the income is from U.S. sources, the answer is *yes*! This presumes that the income is not insulated from U.S. taxation by a provision in a tax treaty between the United States and the country of incorporation.

The manner of taxation depends upon the nature of the income involved. If the income is fixed, determinable, annual, or periodic (known as FDAP income), it is taxed at 30 percent on the *gross* amount. The tax is collected by virtue of required withholding imposed on the payor. FDAP income generally includes passive income (e.g., dividends, interest, rents, royalties, annuities) that is not effectively connected with a U.S. trade or business.

If, however, the income comes from the conduct of a U.S. trade or business, it is taxed at *net* in much the same manner as the income of domestic corporations. Any FDAP income effectively connected with the trade or business is taxed in the same manner as the business *net* income.

out profits in some manner that is deductible by the corporation. This can be accomplished by categorizing the distributions as salaries, interest, or rent—all of which are deductible by the corporation. If not properly structured, however, these devices can generate a multitude of problems. Excessive debt, for example, can lead to its reclassification as equity (under the thin capitalization approach) with a resulting disallowance of any interest deduction. Large salaries could fail the reasonableness test, and rent payments must meet an arm's length standard.

Changes in the tax treatment of qualified dividends have interjected an additional variable that must be taken into account when structuring corporation-shareholder dealings. Prior to JGTRRA of 2003, it made little tax difference to an individual shareholder whether a corporate distribution was classified as a dividend, interest, salary, or rent—all were fully taxed as ordinary income. After 2002, however, qualified dividends are taxed in the same manner as net long-term capital gain.[60] Thus, the maximum rate cannot exceed 15 percent (5 percent in some cases). In light of this preferential treatment of qualified dividends, effective planning becomes a matter of deciding who most needs the tax benefit. If it is the corporation, try to pay out profits in a deductible form (i.e., interest, salaries, rents). If it is the shareholder, distribute the profits as dividends. These rules apply only to *qualified* dividends and are subject to a sunset provision.[61]

Other tax considerations having a bearing on the choice of the corporate form to operate a business are summarized below:

- Corporate-source income loses its identity as it passes through the corporation to the shareholders. Thus, items possessing preferential tax treatment (e.g., interest on municipal bonds) are not taxed as such to the shareholders.
- As noted earlier, it may be difficult for shareholders to recover some or all of their investment in the corporation without a dividend income result. Recall that most corporate distributions are treated as dividends to the extent of the corporation's E & P. Structuring the capital of the corporation to include debt is a partial solution to this problem. Thus, the shareholder-creditor could recoup part of his or her investment through the tax-free payment of principal. Too much debt, however, may lead to the debt being reclassified as equity.
- Corporate losses cannot be passed through to the shareholders.

---

[60]§ 1(h)(3)(B).

[61]After December 31, 2008, dividend income will be taxed as ordinary income (i.e., pre-2003 tax treatment is reinstated).

- The production activities deduction generated by the corporation is not available to its shareholders. The deduction will become even more attractive as the applicable rate progresses from 3 percent to 9 percent.
- The liquidation of a corporation may generate tax consequences to both the corporation and its shareholders.
- The corporate form provides the shareholders with the opportunity to be treated as employees for tax purposes if they render services to the corporation. This status makes a number of attractive tax-sheltered fringe benefits available (e.g., group term life insurance). These benefits are not available to partners and sole proprietors.

Regular Corporation versus S Status

Due to the pass-through concept, the use of S status generally avoids the income tax at the corporate level, bringing the individual income tax into play. As noted in the previous section, the differential between the rates applicable to noncorporate and corporate taxpayers makes this a factor to be considered. The S election enables a business to operate in the corporate form, avoid the corporate income tax, and, depending on taxable income, possibly take advantage of the lower rates usually applicable to individuals. Also, losses incurred at the corporate level pass through to the shareholders, who will utilize them on their individual returns.

Electing S status can present several problems, however. First, the election is available only to small business corporations. Consequently, many corporations will not qualify for the election. Second, S corporations are subject to the rules governing regular corporations unless otherwise specified in the Code. For example, § 351 applies on the formation of an S corporation. Likewise, if the S corporation later carries out a stock redemption or is liquidated, the rules governing regular corporations apply. Third, some states do not recognize S status for purposes of state and local taxation. Therefore, an S corporation might be subject to a state franchise tax or a state or local income tax.

Use of an Entity to Reduce the Family Income Tax Burden

One objective of tax planning is to keep the income from a business within the family unit but to disperse the income in such a manner as to minimize the overall tax burden. To the extent feasible, therefore, income should be shifted from higher-bracket to lower-bracket family members.

Unfortunately, the income from property (a business) cannot be shifted to another without also transferring an interest in the property. If, for example, a father wants to assign income from his sole proprietorship to his children, he must form a partnership or incorporate the business.[62] In either case, the transfer of the interest may be subject to the Federal gift tax. But any potential gift tax can be eliminated or controlled through judicious use of the annual exclusion, the election to split gifts (for married donors), and the unified tax credit (refer to the discussion of the Federal gift tax in Chapter 1).

Consequently, the first problem to be resolved becomes which form of business organization will best fit the objective of income shifting. For the partnership form, one major obstacle arises. Family partnership rules preclude the assignment of income to a family member unless capital is a material income-producing factor.[63] If not, the family member must contribute substantial or vital services. Ordinarily, capital is not a material income-producing factor if the income of the business consists principally of compensation for personal services performed by members or

---

[62]Income shifting will not work, however, if the minor is under 14 years of age. In such cases, net unearned income (refer to the discussion in Chapter 3) of the child is taxed at the parents' tax rate. § 1(g).

[63]§ 704(e).

employees of the partnership. Conversely, capital is a material income-producing factor if the operation of the business entails a substantial investment in physical assets (e.g., inventory, plant, machinery, or equipment).

Income shifting through the use of a partnership, therefore, may be ineffectual if a personal service business is involved. In fact, it could be hopeless if the assignees are minors. The use of the corporate form usually involves no such impediment. Regardless of the nature of the business, a gift of stock carries with it the attributes of ownership. Thus, dividends paid on stock are taxed to the owner of the stock.

But what if the corporate form is utilized and the S election is made? A new hurdle arises. The Code authorizes the IRS to make adjustments in situations where shareholders are not being adequately compensated for the value of their services or capital provided to an S corporation in a family setting.[64] Thus, an S corporation suffers from the same vulnerability that exists with family partnerships.

A further factor that favors the corporate form (either a regular or an S corporation) as a device for income splitting is the ease with which it can be carried out. Presuming the entity already exists, the transfer of stock merely requires an entry in the corporation's stock ledger account. In contrast, a gift of a partnership interest probably requires an amendment to the articles of copartnership. If minors are to be the assignees (donees), a state's Uniform Gifts to Minors Act (or Uniform Transfers to Minors Act) provides a useful and flexible means of holding a stock interest until the assignees become adults.[65] In the case of a partnership interest, however, a guardianship may have to be set up to achieve the same flexibility. In summary, the transfer of stock is more convenient and, since it usually avoids legal problems, can be less expensive.

Regardless of the form of organization used for the business, income shifting will not take place unless the transfer is complete.[66] If the donor continues to exercise control over the interest transferred and does not recognize and protect the ownership rights of the donee, the IRS may argue that the transfer is ineffective for tax purposes. In that case, the income from the transferred interest continues to be taxed to the donor.

KEY TERMS

C corporation, 20–4	Guaranteed payments, 20–35	S corporation, 20–25
Check-the-box Regulations, 20–4	Limited liability company, 20–3	Schedule M–1, 20–15
Constructive dividends, 20–22	Liquidating distributions, 20–23	Schedule M–3, 20–16
Dividends received deduction, 20–11	Organizational expenditures, 20–13	Small business corporation, 20–25
Earnings and profits, 20–21	Personal service corporation, 20–14	Stock redemption, 20–23
		Thin capitalization, 20–16

---

[64]§ 1366(e).

[65]The Uniform Gifts to Minors Act is explained in Chapter 4.

[66]*Ginsberg v. Comm.*, 74–2 USTC ¶9660, 34 AFTR2d 74–5760, 502 F.2d 965 (CA–6, 1974), and *Michael F. Beirne*, 61 T.C. 268 (1973).

P R O B L E M   M A T E R I A L S

D I S C U S S I O N   Q U E S T I O N S

1. What is the role of state law in determining whether an entity will be classified as a corporation for Federal income tax purposes?

2. Under what circumstances might the disregard of the corporate entity produce a favorable result for the IRS?

3. Why are limited liability companies advantageous?

4. What purpose is served by the check-the-box Regulations?

5. In the event of a "default" under the check-the-box Regulations, how will the following be classified as to business form?
   a. A one-person entity not incorporated under state law.
   b. A multi-owner entity not incorporated under state law.

6. In 1997, Harrison incorporated his sole proprietorship. In 2006, he wants to use the check-the-box Regulations to convert the corporation back to a sole proprietorship. Can this be done? Why or why not?

7. Is the cash method of accounting available to all C corporations? Explain.

8. Compare the income tax treatment of individuals and C corporations as to each of the following:
   a. The tax rates that apply.
   b. The tax year (i.e., fiscal, calendar) allowed.
   c. The special treatment of qualified dividend income.
   d. The allowance of deductions *from* AGI (i.e., itemized deductions).
   e. The availability of the production activities deduction.

9. Shearwater Corporation, a real estate developer, sells a tract of land for a substantial gain. Since the land was held both for resale and as an investment, the gain could arguably be classified as either ordinary or capital.   *Issue ID*
   a. In most cases, would the classification of the gain make any difference for tax purposes? Why?
   b. Under what circumstances might the classification of the gain as capital be preferable?

10. The treatment of excess capital losses for individuals and corporations is different in many respects. As far as the tax effect on individuals is concerned, how are these differences: *Issue ID*
    a. Favorable?
    b. Unfavorable?

11. What are the limitations, if any, on the deductible amount allowed on appreciated inventory donated to charity?

12. Regarding the 10% limitation on the charitable contributions of a corporation, how do the following affect the determination of taxable income?
    a. Charitable contribution deduction.
    b. Net operating loss carryback.
    c. Capital loss carryback.
    d. Dividends received deduction.

13. At the end of 2006, Olive Corporation, a calendar year, accrual basis C corporation, would like to make a generous donation to a hurricane relief fund. However, it is hesitant to do so because it has not yet determined its taxable income for 2006 and cash-flow needs for early 2007. How could this dilemma be resolved?   *Issue ID*

14. How is the production activities deduction determined for an affiliated group of corporations?

15. In connection with the dividends received deduction, comment on the following:
    a. Reason for the deduction.
    b. How the deduction percentage is determined.
    c. The percentage of taxable income limitation—when applicable and not applicable.

Issue ID

16. Mallard Corporation was formed in December 2005 and plans to use the cash basis of accounting. Mallard incurred one-half of its organizational expenses in December 2005 and one-half in January 2006. The payment of these expenses also occurred in these two months. Do you recognize any income tax problem?

Issue ID

17. Personal service corporations frequently pay out all of their profits to their shareholder-employees in the form of salaries. Is there a reason for doing this? Explain.

18. Concerning the filing requirements for C corporations, comment on the following:
    a. When an income tax return must be filed.
    b. The Form 1120–A option to Form 1120.
    c. The purpose of Schedules M–1, M–2, and M–3 of Form 1120.

19. Under what circumstances might a nonshareholder make a contribution to the capital of a corporation? What income tax consequences, if any, would such a contribution have to the corporation?

20. In view of changes made by JGTRRA of 2003, the thin capitalization procedure is no longer as tax advantageous as it was previously.
    a. Why is this so?
    b. In what respects, if any, is thin capitalization still advantageous?

Decision Making

21. A group of developers is planning to form a new corporation to construct and operate a shopping center. Rachel, who is to contribute a specific tract of land to the venture, would like to recognize the gain on its appreciation. In view of the rules governing the application of § 351, what do you suggest?

22. When a corporation is formed pursuant to § 351, the shareholders will have the same basis in the stock received as the corporation has in the property transferred to it. Comment on the validity of this statement.

23. How do the following transactions affect the E & P of a corporation?
    a. A nontaxable stock dividend issued to the shareholders.
    b. Receipt of interest on municipal bonds.
    c. Federal corporate income tax liability.

24. A corporation makes a cash distribution to its shareholders. Describe the tax effect on the shareholders if the distribution is:
    a. A qualified dividend.
    b. A return of capital that does not exceed the basis in the stock investment.
    c. A return of capital that exceeds the basis in the stock investment.

25. When a corporation distributes property as a dividend, what are the tax effects on the corporation and its shareholders under the following assumptions?
    a. The property has declined in value.
    b. The property has appreciated in value.

Issue ID

26. The stock of Grouse Corporation is owned equally by a sister and two brothers: Mary, Rex, and Orson. During the year, the following transactions occur:
    a. Mary sells property to Grouse Corporation.
    b. Rex leases property to Grouse Corporation.
    c. All shareholders drive automobiles owned by Grouse Corporation.
    d. Orson borrows money from Grouse Corporation.
    e. All shareholders are paid salaries by Grouse Corporation.
    f. Grouse Corporation pays interest on bonds issued to its shareholders.

    Discuss any potential tax problems that these transactions might present.

27. Regarding constructive dividends, comment on the accuracy of the following observations:
    a. Must be distributed to the shareholders on a pro rata basis.
    b. Formalities of a dividend (declaration, record, and payment dates) must be preserved.
    c. Need not be covered by E & P to carry dividend income consequences.
    d. Do not reduce a corporation's E & P.

28. Angie is the sole shareholder of Rust Corporation. If the corporation is liquidated, what are the tax effects on:
    a. Rust Corporation?
    b. Angie?

29. In terms of *electing* and *terminating* Subchapter S status, contrast the following:
    a. Number of shareholders required.
    b. Effective date of election (or termination).

30. Norm, Ashton, and Fritz are equal shareholders in Auburn, a calendar year S corporation. For 2006, Auburn Corporation received qualified dividends, had a short-term capital loss, and made a charitable contribution. As to these transactions, explain the following results:
    a. Norm's share of the dividends is taxed at a lower rate than are Ashton's and Fritz's shares.
    b. Ashton cannot (for 2006) deduct her share of the capital loss.
    c. Fritz cannot deduct his share of the charitable contribution.

    Issue ID

31. Compare the nonrecognition of gain or loss on contributions to a partnership with the similar provision found in corporate formation (§ 351). What are the major differences and similarities?

32. Under what circumstances does the receipt of a partnership interest result in the recognition of ordinary income? What is the effect of this on the partnership and the other partners?

33. How do changes in the liabilities of a partnership affect the basis of a partnership interest?

34. Indicate whether each of the following will increase (+), decrease (−), or have no effect (*NE*) on a partner's basis in a partnership interest:
    a. Taxable income of the partnership.
    b. Capital losses of the partnership.
    c. Tax-exempt income of the partnership.
    d. Partnership expenditures that are not deductible in computing taxable income.

35. How is the production activities deduction handled at the partnership level? The partner level?

36. To what extent can a partner deduct his or her distributive share of partnership losses? What happens to any unused losses?

37. Blanche and her two brothers are equal partners in the Rose Partnership. During the year, Blanche sells land (adjusted basis of $220,000) to Rose for its fair market value of $200,000. Do you perceive any tax problems as to this transfer? Explain.

    Issue ID

38. What are guaranteed payments? When might such payments be used?

PROBLEMS

39. Robin has the following capital asset transactions during 2006:

Long-term capital gain	$10,000
Short-term capital gain	8,000

Further, Robin has an excess capital loss carryforward of $4,000 from 2005.
a.   What are the tax consequences of these transactions if the $4,000 loss is long term and Robin is an individual? Robin is a C corporation?
b.   What are the tax consequences of these transactions if the $4,000 loss is short term and Robin is an individual? Robin is a C corporation?

40. Avocet Corporation has net short-term capital gains of $10,000 and long-term capital losses of $60,000 during 2006. Taxable income from other sources is $300,000. Prior years' capital transactions include the following:

2002	Net short-term capital gain	$20,000
2003	No capital asset transactions	–0–
2004	Net short-term capital gain	15,000
2005	Net long-term capital gain	25,000

a.   How are the capital gains and losses handled on Avocet's 2006 tax return?
b.   Compute the capital loss carryback and apply it to the carryback years.
c.   Compute the capital loss carryover, if any, and its nature. What years would be involved?

41. On December 30, 2006, Peacock Company (a calendar year taxpayer) authorized a cash contribution of $50,000 to the United Way of Little Rock, Arkansas. The contribution is made in 2007 as follows: $20,000 on March 6 and $30,000 on April 14. Regarding the year of deduction, what are the options if Peacock is:
a.   A cash basis partnership?
b.   A cash basis corporation?
c.   Would your answers to parts (a) and (b) change if Peacock uses the accrual basis?

42. During 2006, Kinglet Corporation had the following transactions:

Income from operations	$600,000
Expenses from operations	510,000
Dividends from domestic corporations (less than 20% ownership)	20,000
Dividends received deduction (70% × $20,000)	14,000
Unused short-term capital loss from 2004 (there are no capital gains in 2005 and 2006)	3,000
NOL carryover from 2005	30,000

In June 2006, Kinglet made a contribution to a qualified charitable organization of $11,000 in cash (not included in any of the items listed above).
a.   How much, if any, of the contribution can be claimed as a deduction for 2006?
b.   What happens to any portion not deductible for 2006?

43. Ivory Supply Company manufactures and sells furnishings for hospitals (e.g., adjustable beds). In the current year, it donates some of its inventory to a newly constructed hospice. The hospice is adjacent to a cancer treatment center and is intended to care for indigent and terminal patients. The property donated has an adjusted basis of $20,000 and a fair market value of $30,000. What is the amount of the charitable contribution deduction if Ivory is a:
a.   Sole proprietorship?
b.   C corporation?
c.   Would your answer to part (b) change if the fair market value of the property is $61,000 (not $30,000)?

44. In each of the following independent situations, determine the dividends received deduction. Assume the percentage of stock owned in the corporation paying the dividends is 25% for Owl Corporation and less than 20% for Pheasant and Partridge corporations.

	Owl Corporation	Pheasant Corporation	Partridge Corporation
Income from operations	$2,000,000	$2,000,000	$1,500,000
Expenses of operations	2,100,000	1,800,000	1,600,000
Qualified dividends received	500,000	400,000	50,000

45. Marson Corporation is formed on June 1, 2006, and incurs qualifying organizational expenditures. It uses a calendar year and wants to accelerate any deductions that are available. Based on this assumption, what is Marson Corporation's deduction for 2006 if its organizational expenditures are:
   a. $3,000.
   b. $30,000.
   c. $53,000.
   d. $56,000.

46. In each of the following independent situations, determine the corporation's Federal income tax liability. Assume that all corporations are on a calendar year and that the tax year involved is 2006.

Corporation	Taxable Income
Hummingbird	$ 10,000
Ostrich	56,000*
Loon	74,000**
Curlew	108,000
Tanager	390,000
Vireo (a personal service corporation)	110,000

 * Does not include a short-term capital loss of $7,000.
**Does not include a long-term capital gain of $2,000.

47. Using the legend provided below, classify each statement.

Legend
I = Applies *only* to the income taxation of individuals
C = Applies *only* to the income taxation of corporations
B = Applies to the income taxation of *both* individuals and corporations
N = Applies to the income taxation of *neither* individuals nor corporations

   a. The determination of AGI.
   b. The deduction of charitable contributions is subject to percentage limitation(s).
   c. Excess charitable contributions can be carried over indefinitely.
   d. Excess capital losses cannot be carried back.
   e. The lowest possible tax rate that can be imposed is 10%.
   f. A production activities deduction may be available.
   g. A net short-term capital gain is taxed at the same tax rate as ordinary income.
   h. A dividends received deduction may be available.
   i. Casualty losses may be subject to dollar and percentage limitations.
   j. No exemption amount is allowed for AMT purposes.

48. Carlton, Jessica, and Sheri form Peach Corporation with the following investments:

	Basis to Transferor	Fair Market Value	Number of Shares Issued
From Carlton—Cash	$300,000	$300,000	300
From Jessica—Land	660,000	700,000	650
From Sheri—Services		50,000	50

In addition to stock, Jessica receives cash of $50,000. Assume each share of stock is worth $1,000.
   a.   How much gain (or loss) must Jessica recognize?
   b.   What basis will Jessica have in the Peach stock?
   c.   What basis will Peach Corporation have in the land transferred by Jessica?
   d.   What are Sheri's tax consequences?

49. Elton, Neil, Courtney, and Zelma form Ecru Corporation with the following investments:

	Basis to Transferor	Fair Market Value	Number of Shares Issued
From Elton—Cash	$ 200,000	$ 200,000	200
From Neil—Inventory	230,000	270,000	260
From Courtney—Machinery and equipment	400,000	370,000	350
From Zelma—Land and building	1,270,000	1,300,000	1,200

In addition to its stock, Ecru distributes cash as follows: $10,000 to Neil, $20,000 to Courtney, and $100,000 to Zelma. Assume that each share of Ecru stock is worth $1,000. Regarding these transactions, provide the following information:
   a.   Neil's realized and recognized gain (or loss).
   b.   Neil's basis in the Ecru stock.
   c.   Ecru's basis in the inventory.
   d.   Courtney's realized and recognized gain (or loss).
   e.   Courtney's basis in the Ecru stock.
   f.   Ecru's basis in the machinery and equipment.
   g.   Zelma's realized and recognized gain (or loss).
   h.   Zelma's basis in the Ecru stock.
   i.   Ecru's basis in the land and building.

50. Amelia is the sole shareholder of Emerald Corporation. At a time when Emerald has a deficit in accumulated E & P of $80,000 and current E & P of $40,000, it distributes a cash dividend of $70,000. If Amelia's basis in her stock is $25,000, what are the tax consequences of the distribution to:
   a.   Amelia?
   b.   Emerald Corporation?

Decision Making

Communications

51. The stock of Sandpiper Corporation is held equally by Russ and Erlyne. The shareholders would like to receive, as a dividend, value of $100,000 each. The corporation has the following assets it can spare:

Asset	Adjusted Basis to Sandpiper Corporation	Fair Market Value
Land (parcel A)	$ 60,000	$100,000
Land (parcel B)	130,000	100,000

Both assets are held as investments. Sandpiper Corporation has a capital loss carryover from the previous year of $10,000 and has accumulated E & P in excess of $1 million.

   Russ and Erlyne have come to you for advice. Suggest an attractive tax plan to carry out what the parties want. Write a letter (addressed to Sandpiper Corporation at P.O. Box 1150, St. Louis, MO 63130) describing your plan and its tax consequences.

52. In the current year, Azure Corporation is liquidated under the general rule of § 331. It has cash of $100,000 and undeveloped land (basis of $75,000 and fair market value of $275,000). After taxes, Azure distributes all remaining assets to Faith, its sole shareholder. Faith's basis in the Azure stock is $50,000.
   a.   What are Azure Corporation's income tax consequences?
   b.   What are Faith's income tax consequences?
   c.   What basis will Faith have in the land?

53. Ten years ago, Rose Corporation purchased all of the stock of Fuchsia Corporation for $200,000. In the current year, Fuchsia has a basis in its assets of $600,000 and a fair market value of $800,000. Rose liquidates Fuchsia Corporation and receives all of its assets. The exception to the carryover basis rule does not apply.
    a. Does Rose Corporation recognize any gain as a result of the liquidation?
    b. What is Rose Corporation's basis for the assets it receives from Fuchsia Corporation?

54. During 2006, Pipit (a calendar year, accrual basis S corporation) has the following transactions:

Sales	$520,000
Cost of goods sold	230,000
Bad debts (trade accounts receivable deemed to be uncollectible)	21,000
Long-term capital gain	30,000
Short-term capital loss	12,000
Rent expense	36,000
Qualified dividends	15,000
Charitable contribution	9,000
Salaries	110,000
Interest on State of Maryland bonds	11,000
Organizational expenditures	1,800
Advertising expense	14,000
§ 1231 gain	18,000

    a. Determine Pipit Corporation's separately stated items.
    b. Determine Pipit Corporation's taxable income.

55. Julius Walker owns all of the stock of Mockingbird Corporation, a calendar year S corporation. For calendar year 2006, Mockingbird anticipates an operating loss of $20,000 and could, if deemed worthwhile, sell a stock investment that would generate a $3,000 long-term capital loss. Julius has an adjusted basis of $5,000 in the Mockingbird stock. He anticipates no capital asset transactions and expects to be in the 33% tax bracket in 2006.

    Decision Making

    Communication

    a. Can you recommend a course of action that can save Julius taxes for 2006?
    b. Write a letter to Julius explaining your recommendations. Julius's address is Box 429, Normal, AL 35762.

56. Pierce is a 40% shareholder in Beige, a calendar year S corporation. Beige's operations resulted in an operating loss of $250,000 in 2006 and an operating profit of $100,000 in 2007. Pierce withdrew $20,000 in cash from Beige in 2007. As of January 1, 2006, Pierce's basis in the Beige Corporation stock is $80,000.
    a. As to the Beige stock, what are Pierce's tax consequences for 2006? For 2007?
    b. What basis will Pierce have in his Beige stock as of January 1, 2008?

57. Guy, Alma, and Kara form the Rust Partnership. In exchange for a 30% capital interest, Guy transfers property (basis of $200,000; fair market value of $400,000) subject to a liability of $100,000. The liability is assumed by the partnership. Alma transfers property (basis of $350,000; fair market value of $300,000) for a 30% capital interest. Kara invests cash of $400,000 for the remaining 40% capital interest. Concerning these transactions, provide the following information:
    a. Guy's recognized gain.
    b. Guy's basis in the partnership interest.
    c. Alma's recognized loss.
    d. Alma's basis in the partnership interest.
    e. Kara's basis in the partnership interest.
    f. Rust Partnership's basis in the property transferred by Guy and Alma.

58. As of January 1, 2005, Victor had a basis of $26,000 in his 25% capital interest in the Gray Partnership. He and the partnership use the calendar year for tax purposes. The

    Decision Making

partnership incurred an operating loss of $120,000 for 2005 and a profit of $80,000 for 2006.

    a. How much, if any, loss may Victor recognize for 2005?

    b. How much income must Victor recognize for 2006?

    c. What basis will Victor have in his partnership interest as of January 1, 2006?

    d. What basis will Victor have in his partnership interest as of January 1, 2007?

    e. What year-end tax planning would you suggest to ensure that a partner could deduct all of his or her share of any partnership losses?

59. Stella owns a 60% interest in the capital and profits of the Grebe Partnership. In 2006, Stella sells property (adjusted basis of $200,000) to Grebe for its fair market value of $180,000. In 2007, Grebe Partnership sells the same property to an outside party for $205,000.

    a. What are Stella's tax consequences on the 2006 sale?

    b. What are Grebe Partnership's tax consequences on the 2007 sale?

    c. Would the answers to parts (a) and (b) change if Stella owns only a 40% interest and the other 60% interest is owned by her brother? Explain.

RESEARCH PROBLEMS

Note: Solutions to Research Problems can be prepared by using the **RIA Checkpoint® Student Edition** online research product, which is available to accompany this text. It is also possible to prepare solutions to the Research Problems by using tax research materials found in a standard tax library.

Research Problem 1. In 2001, Rhoda forms Madison Healthcare Center, LLC, to own and operate several nursing homes. Madison is a limited liability company with Rhoda as its sole owner. Rhoda *did not* elect under the "check-the-box" Regulations to have Madison treated as a corporation for Federal income tax purposes.

    In 2006 and after several years of Madison's failure to pay taxes, the IRS assesses Rhoda for the delinquency. Because Madison is a sole proprietorship, Rhoda is directly liable for the tax obligations of the business. Under the check-the-box Regulations, a one-owner limited liability company is a sole proprietorship in a default situation (i.e., failure to elect otherwise). [Reg. § 301.7701–3(b)(1)(iii)]

    Rhoda maintains that Madison is a corporation and that, as a shareholder, she is not liable for its obligations. She says that Madison is a corporation because it meets the definition of a corporation under § 7701(a)(2). Included in the definition is an "association," which is an entity that possesses a preponderance of corporate attributes—continuity of life, centralized management, limited liability, and free transferability of interests. Consequently, says Rhoda, the check-the-box Regulations are an unnecessary and invalid interpretation of the Code.

    Which party will prevail?

Partial list of research aids:
§§ 7701(a)(2) and (3).
Reg. § 301.7701–2. The "Kintner" Regulations issued in 1960 and effective prior to January 1, 1997.
Reg. §§ 301.7701–1 through –3. The check-the-box Regulations and effective after 1996.
Littriello v. U.S., 2005–1 USTC ¶50,385, 95 AFTR2d 2005–2581 (D.Ct.Ky., 2005).

Research Problem 2. Ashley is a retired professional who has accumulated considerable investment property. One of her choice properties is the Pine Ridge tract, which is contiguous to a growing metropolitan suburb. Ashley inherited Pine Ridge from her father in 1974 when it was worth $80,000. Just recently, Ashley mortgaged the property for $200,000 and used the proceeds to completely renovate her personal residence. At that time, the mortgage company appraised the Pine Ridge tract at $1 million.

In 2006, Ashley is approached by a real estate group regarding the development of the Pine Ridge tract. Under the proposed arrangement, a new corporation is to be formed to carry out the construction and sale of residential housing. The formation will satisfy the requirements of § 351, and in return for her transfer, Ashley will receive stock in accordance with the following options:

- $1 million in value if the tract has no mortgage; or
- $800,000 in value if the tract is subject to the mortgage.

a. Advise Ashley regarding the tax consequences of each option.
b. If Ashley decides to pay off the mortgage, do you have any suggestions as to where she should obtain the funds to do so?

Research Problem 3. Several years ago, Mike incorporated his sole proprietorship and immediately made an election under Subchapter S. Mike lives in El Paso, Texas, and is married to Consuela, a citizen of Mexico. Since Consuela's father is ill and requires constant care, she lives with him across the border in Ciudad Juarez.

This year, the IRS audits the Forms 1120S filed by Mike's corporation and disallows its Subchapter S status. What could be the cause of the disallowance?

Research Problem 4. In 1995, Claude received a distribution of $50,000 from Swallow Corporation that purported to be a return of capital. Since Claude's basis in the stock was $80,000, he reduced the basis to $30,000 and recognized no income as to the distribution. In 2002, it was determined that Swallow Corporation has been miscalculating its E & P for a number of years. As a result, the 1995 distribution it made should have been taxed to the shareholders as a dividend. Due to the expiration of the three-year statute of limitations, Claude made no adjustment to his income tax return for 1995.

In 2006, Claude sells his stock in Swallow for $300,000. He feels that he should recognize a gain of only $220,000 from the sale. Since the 1995 distribution was a dividend and not a return of capital, his stock basis should not have been reduced and should remain at the original $80,000. Claude seeks your advice on this matter.

Write a letter to Claude Romano, Box 1340, Clinton, MS 39058, explaining his position. Use layperson terminology, as your client is not well versed in tax matters.

Communications

Use the tax resources of the Internet to address the following questions. Do not restrict your search to the World Wide Web, but include a review of newsgroups and general reference materials, practitioner sites and resources, primary sources of the tax law, chat rooms and discussion groups, and other opportunities.

 Internet *Activity*

Research Problem 5. Does your state permit CPAs to practice public accounting in the corporate form? If not, can they form limited liability companies? What, if any, special restrictions are imposed?

Research Problem 6. If your state imposes an income tax, does it recognize the new production activities deduction? If your state does not levy an income tax, check on a contiguous state that does. [Note: Those in Alaska use Washington and those in Hawaii use California.]

Research Problem 7. Does your state recognize a Subchapter S election for state tax purposes? If so, does it treat out-of-state shareholders in the same way as resident shareholders?

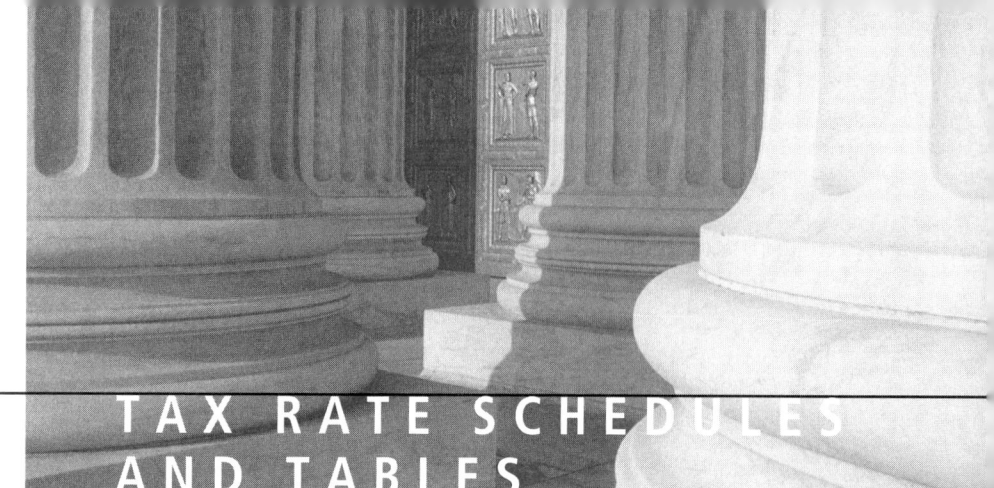

TAX RATE SCHEDULES AND TABLES

(The 2006 Tax Tables and 2006 Sales Tax Tables can be accessed at the IRS web site: [**http://www.irs.gov**] when released.)

2005 Tax Rate Schedules

Single—Schedule X

If taxable income is: Over—	But not over—	The tax is:	of the amount over—
$ 0	$ 7,300	.......10%	$ 0
7,300	29,700	$ 730.00 + 15%	7,300
29,700	71,950	4,090.00 + 25%	29,700
71,950	150,150	14,652.50 + 28%	71,950
150,150	326,450	36,548.50 + 33%	150,150
326,450	....	94,727.50 + 35%	326,450

Head of household—Schedule Z

If taxable income is: Over—	But not over—	The tax is:	of the amount over—
$ 0	$ 10,450	.......10%	$ 0
10,450	39,800	$ 1,045.00 + 15%	10,450
39,800	102,800	5,447.50 + 25%	39,800
102,800	166,450	21,197.50 + 28%	102,800
166,450	326,450	39,019.50 + 33%	166,450
326,450	....	91,819.50 + 35%	326,450

Married filing jointly or Qualifying widow(er)—Schedule Y–1

If taxable income is: Over—	But not over—	The tax is:	of the amount over—
$ 0	$ 14,600	.......10%	$ 0
14,600	59,400	$ 1,460.00 + 15%	14,600
59,400	119,950	8,180.00 + 25%	59,400
119,950	182,800	23,317.50 + 28%	119,950
182,800	326,450	40,915.50 + 33%	182,800
326,450	....	88,320.00 + 35%	326,450

Married filing separately—Schedule Y–2

If taxable income is: Over—	But not over—	The tax is:	of the amount over—
$ 0	$ 7,300	.......10%	$ 0
7,300	29,700	$ 730.00 + 15%	7,300
29,700	59,975	4,090.00 + 25%	29,700
59,975	91,400	11,658.75 + 28%	59,975
91,400	163,225	20,457.75 + 33%	91,400
163,225	....	44,160.00 + 35%	163,225

2006 Tax Rate Schedules

Single—Schedule X

If taxable income is: Over—	But not over—	The tax is:	of the amount over—
$ 0	$ 7,550	.......10%	$ 0
7,550	30,650	$ 755.00 + 15%	7,550
30,650	74,200	4,220.00 + 25%	30,650
74,200	154,800	15,107.50 + 28%	74,200
154,800	336,550	37,675.50 + 33%	154,800
336,550	....	97,653.00 + 35%	336,550

Head of household—Schedule Z

If taxable income is: Over—	But not over—	The tax is:	of the amount over—
$ 0	$ 10,750	.......10%	$ 0
10,750	41,050	$ 1,075.00 + 15%	10,750
41,050	106,000	5,620.00 + 25%	41,050
106,000	171,650	21,857.50 + 28%	106,000
171,650	336,550	40,239.50 + 33%	171,650
336,550	....	94,656.50 + 35%	336,550

Married filing jointly or Qualifying widow(er)—Schedule Y–1

If taxable income is: Over—	But not over—	The tax is:	of the amount over—
$ 0	$ 15,100	.......10%	$ 0
15,100	61,300	$ 1,510.00 + 15%	15,100
61,300	123,700	8,440.00 + 25%	61,300
123,700	188,450	24,040.00 + 28%	123,700
188,450	336,550	42,170.00 + 33%	188,450
336,550	....	91,043.00 + 35%	336,550

Married filing separately—Schedule Y–2

If taxable income is: Over—	But not over—	The tax is:	of the amount over—
$ 0	$ 7,550	.......10%	$ 0
7,550	30,650	$ 755.00 + 15%	7,550
30,650	61,850	4,220.00 + 25%	30,650
61,850	94,225	12,020.00 + 28%	61,850
94,225	168,275	21,085.00 + 33%	94,225
168,275	....	45,521.50 + 35%	168,275

2005 Tax Table

See the instructions for line 44 that begin on page 37 to see if you must use the Tax Table below to figure your tax.

Example. Mr. and Mrs. Brown are filing a joint return. Their taxable income on Form 1040, line 43, is $25,300. First, they find the $25,300–25,350 taxable income line. Next, they find the column for married filing jointly and read down the column. The amount shown where the taxable income line and filing status column meet is $3,069. This is the tax amount they should enter on Form 1040, line 44.

Sample Table

At least	But less than	Single	Married filing jointly*	Married filing separately	Head of a household
			Your tax is—		
25,200	25,250	3,419	3,054	3,419	3,261
25,250	25,300	3,426	3,061	3,426	3,269
25,300	25,350	3,434	(3,069)	3,434	3,276
25,350	25,400	3,441	3,076	3,441	3,284

If line 43 (taxable income) is— At least	But less than	Single	Married filing jointly*	Married filing separately	Head of a household
			Your tax is—		
0	5	0	0	0	0
5	15	1	1	1	1
15	25	2	2	2	2
25	50	4	4	4	4
50	75	6	6	6	6
75	100	9	9	9	9
100	125	11	11	11	11
125	150	14	14	14	14
150	175	16	16	16	16
175	200	19	19	19	19
200	225	21	21	21	21
225	250	24	24	24	24
250	275	26	26	26	26
275	300	29	29	29	29
300	325	31	31	31	31
325	350	34	34	34	34
350	375	36	36	36	36
375	400	39	39	39	39
400	425	41	41	41	41
425	450	44	44	44	44
450	475	46	46	46	46
475	500	49	49	49	49
500	525	51	51	51	51
525	550	54	54	54	54
550	575	56	56	56	56
575	600	59	59	59	59
600	625	61	61	61	61
625	650	64	64	64	64
650	675	66	66	66	66
675	700	69	69	69	69
700	725	71	71	71	71
725	750	74	74	74	74
750	775	76	76	76	76
775	800	79	79	79	79
800	825	81	81	81	81
825	850	84	84	84	84
850	875	86	86	86	86
875	900	89	89	89	89
900	925	91	91	91	91
925	950	94	94	94	94
950	975	96	96	96	96
975	1,000	99	99	99	99

1,000

At least	But less than	Single	Married filing jointly*	Married filing separately	Head of a household
1,000	1,025	101	101	101	101
1,025	1,050	104	104	104	104
1,050	1,075	106	106	106	106
1,075	1,100	109	109	109	109
1,100	1,125	111	111	111	111
1,125	1,150	114	114	114	114
1,150	1,175	116	116	116	116
1,175	1,200	119	119	119	119
1,200	1,225	121	121	121	121
1,225	1,250	124	124	124	124
1,250	1,275	126	126	126	126
1,275	1,300	129	129	129	129

If line 43 (taxable income) is— At least	But less than	Single	Married filing jointly*	Married filing separately	Head of a household
			Your tax is—		
1,300	1,325	131	131	131	131
1,325	1,350	134	134	134	134
1,350	1,375	136	136	136	136
1,375	1,400	139	139	139	139
1,400	1,425	141	141	141	141
1,425	1,450	144	144	144	144
1,450	1,475	146	146	146	146
1,475	1,500	149	149	149	149
1,500	1,525	151	151	151	151
1,525	1,550	154	154	154	154
1,550	1,575	156	156	156	156
1,575	1,600	159	159	159	159
1,600	1,625	161	161	161	161
1,625	1,650	164	164	164	164
1,650	1,675	166	166	166	166
1,675	1,700	169	169	169	169
1,700	1,725	171	171	171	171
1,725	1,750	174	174	174	174
1,750	1,775	176	176	176	176
1,775	1,800	179	179	179	179
1,800	1,825	181	181	181	181
1,825	1,850	184	184	184	184
1,850	1,875	186	186	186	186
1,875	1,900	189	189	189	189
1,900	1,925	191	191	191	191
1,925	1,950	194	194	194	194
1,950	1,975	196	196	196	196
1,975	2,000	199	199	199	199

2,000

At least	But less than	Single	Married filing jointly*	Married filing separately	Head of a household
2,000	2,025	201	201	201	201
2,025	2,050	204	204	204	204
2,050	2,075	206	206	206	206
2,075	2,100	209	209	209	209
2,100	2,125	211	211	211	211
2,125	2,150	214	214	214	214
2,150	2,175	216	216	216	216
2,175	2,200	219	219	219	219
2,200	2,225	221	221	221	221
2,225	2,250	224	224	224	224
2,250	2,275	226	226	226	226
2,275	2,300	229	229	229	229
2,300	2,325	231	231	231	231
2,325	2,350	234	234	234	234
2,350	2,375	236	236	236	236
2,375	2,400	239	239	239	239
2,400	2,425	241	241	241	241
2,425	2,450	244	244	244	244
2,450	2,475	246	246	246	246
2,475	2,500	249	249	249	249
2,500	2,525	251	251	251	251
2,525	2,550	254	254	254	254
2,550	2,575	256	256	256	256
2,575	2,600	259	259	259	259
2,600	2,625	261	261	261	261
2,625	2,650	264	264	264	264
2,650	2,675	266	266	266	266
2,675	2,700	269	269	269	269

If line 43 (taxable income) is— At least	But less than	Single	Married filing jointly*	Married filing separately	Head of a household
			Your tax is—		
2,700	2,725	271	271	271	271
2,725	2,750	274	274	274	274
2,750	2,775	276	276	276	276
2,775	2,800	279	279	279	279
2,800	2,825	281	281	281	281
2,825	2,850	284	284	284	284
2,850	2,875	286	286	286	286
2,875	2,900	289	289	289	289
2,900	2,925	291	291	291	291
2,925	2,950	294	294	294	294
2,950	2,975	296	296	296	296
2,975	3,000	299	299	299	299

3,000

At least	But less than	Single	Married filing jointly*	Married filing separately	Head of a household
3,000	3,050	303	303	303	303
3,050	3,100	308	308	308	308
3,100	3,150	313	313	313	313
3,150	3,200	318	318	318	318
3,200	3,250	323	323	323	323
3,250	3,300	328	328	328	328
3,300	3,350	333	333	333	333
3,350	3,400	338	338	338	338
3,400	3,450	343	343	343	343
3,450	3,500	348	348	348	348
3,500	3,550	353	353	353	353
3,550	3,600	358	358	358	358
3,600	3,650	363	363	363	363
3,650	3,700	368	368	368	368
3,700	3,750	373	373	373	373
3,750	3,800	378	378	378	378
3,800	3,850	383	383	383	383
3,850	3,900	388	388	388	388
3,900	3,950	393	393	393	393
3,950	4,000	398	398	398	398

4,000

At least	But less than	Single	Married filing jointly*	Married filing separately	Head of a household
4,000	4,050	403	403	403	403
4,050	4,100	408	408	408	408
4,100	4,150	413	413	413	413
4,150	4,200	418	418	418	418
4,200	4,250	423	423	423	423
4,250	4,300	428	428	428	428
4,300	4,350	433	433	433	433
4,350	4,400	438	438	438	438
4,400	4,450	443	443	443	443
4,450	4,500	448	448	448	448
4,500	4,550	453	453	453	453
4,550	4,600	458	458	458	458
4,600	4,650	463	463	463	463
4,650	4,700	468	468	468	468
4,700	4,750	473	473	473	473
4,750	4,800	478	478	478	478
4,800	4,850	483	483	483	483
4,850	4,900	488	488	488	488
4,900	4,950	493	493	493	493
4,950	5,000	498	498	498	498

(Continued on next page)

* This column must also be used by a qualifying widow(er).

2005 Tax Table—*Continued*

If line 43 (taxable income) is—		And you are—				If line 43 (taxable income) is—		And you are—				If line 43 (taxable income) is—		And you are—			
At least	But less than	Single	Married filing jointly *	Married filing sepa-rately	Head of a house-hold	At least	But less than	Single	Married filing jointly *	Married filing sepa-rately	Head of a house-hold	At least	But less than	Single	Married filing jointly *	Married filing sepa-rately	Head of a house-hold
		Your tax is—						Your tax is—						Your tax is—			
5,000						**8,000**						**11,000**					
5,000	5,050	503	503	503	503	8,000	8,050	839	803	839	803	11,000	11,050	1,289	1,103	1,289	1,131
5,050	5,100	508	508	508	508	8,050	8,100	846	808	846	808	11,050	11,100	1,296	1,108	1,296	1,139
5,100	5,150	513	513	513	513	8,100	8,150	854	813	854	813	11,100	11,150	1,304	1,113	1,304	1,146
5,150	5,200	518	518	518	518	8,150	8,200	861	818	861	818	11,150	11,200	1,311	1,118	1,311	1,154
5,200	5,250	523	523	523	523	8,200	8,250	869	823	869	823	11,200	11,250	1,319	1,123	1,319	1,161
5,250	5,300	528	528	528	528	8,250	8,300	876	828	876	828	11,250	11,300	1,326	1,128	1,326	1,169
5,300	5,350	533	533	533	533	8,300	8,350	884	833	884	833	11,300	11,350	1,334	1,133	1,334	1,176
5,350	5,400	538	538	538	538	8,350	8,400	891	838	891	838	11,350	11,400	1,341	1,138	1,341	1,184
5,400	5,450	543	543	543	543	8,400	8,450	899	843	899	843	11,400	11,450	1,349	1,143	1,349	1,191
5,450	5,500	548	548	548	548	8,450	8,500	906	848	906	848	11,450	11,500	1,356	1,148	1,356	1,199
5,500	5,550	553	553	553	553	8,500	8,550	914	853	914	853	11,500	11,550	1,364	1,153	1,364	1,206
5,550	5,600	558	558	558	558	8,550	8,600	921	858	921	858	11,550	11,600	1,371	1,158	1,371	1,214
5,600	5,650	563	563	563	563	8,600	8,650	929	863	929	863	11,600	11,650	1,379	1,163	1,379	1,221
5,650	5,700	568	568	568	568	8,650	8,700	936	868	936	868	11,650	11,700	1,386	1,168	1,386	1,229
5,700	5,750	573	573	573	573	8,700	8,750	944	873	944	873	11,700	11,750	1,394	1,173	1,394	1,236
5,750	5,800	578	578	578	578	8,750	8,800	951	878	951	878	11,750	11,800	1,401	1,178	1,401	1,244
5,800	5,850	583	583	583	583	8,800	8,850	959	883	959	883	11,800	11,850	1,409	1,183	1,409	1,251
5,850	5,900	588	588	588	588	8,850	8,900	966	888	966	888	11,850	11,900	1,416	1,188	1,416	1,259
5,900	5,950	593	593	593	593	8,900	8,950	974	893	974	893	11,900	11,950	1,424	1,193	1,424	1,266
5,950	6,000	598	598	598	598	8,950	9,000	981	898	981	898	11,950	12,000	1,431	1,198	1,431	1,274
6,000						**9,000**						**12,000**					
6,000	6,050	603	603	603	603	9,000	9,050	989	903	989	903	12,000	12,050	1,439	1,203	1,439	1,281
6,050	6,100	608	608	608	608	9,050	9,100	996	908	996	908	12,050	12,100	1,446	1,208	1,446	1,289
6,100	6,150	613	613	613	613	9,100	9,150	1,004	913	1,004	913	12,100	12,150	1,454	1,213	1,454	1,296
6,150	6,200	618	618	618	618	9,150	9,200	1,011	918	1,011	918	12,150	12,200	1,461	1,218	1,461	1,304
6,200	6,250	623	623	623	623	9,200	9,250	1,019	923	1,019	923	12,200	12,250	1,469	1,223	1,469	1,311
6,250	6,300	628	628	628	628	9,250	9,300	1,026	928	1,026	928	12,250	12,300	1,476	1,228	1,476	1,319
6,300	6,350	633	633	633	633	9,300	9,350	1,034	933	1,034	933	12,300	12,350	1,484	1,233	1,484	1,326
6,350	6,400	638	638	638	638	9,350	9,400	1,041	938	1,041	938	12,350	12,400	1,491	1,238	1,491	1,334
6,400	6,450	643	643	643	643	9,400	9,450	1,049	943	1,049	943	12,400	12,450	1,499	1,243	1,499	1,341
6,450	6,500	648	648	648	648	9,450	9,500	1,056	948	1,056	948	12,450	12,500	1,506	1,248	1,506	1,349
6,500	6,550	653	653	653	653	9,500	9,550	1,064	953	1,064	953	12,500	12,550	1,514	1,253	1,514	1,356
6,550	6,600	658	658	658	658	9,550	9,600	1,071	958	1,071	958	12,550	12,600	1,521	1,258	1,521	1,364
6,600	6,650	663	663	663	663	9,600	9,650	1,079	963	1,079	963	12,600	12,650	1,529	1,263	1,529	1,371
6,650	6,700	668	668	668	668	9,650	9,700	1,086	968	1,086	968	12,650	12,700	1,536	1,268	1,536	1,379
6,700	6,750	673	673	673	673	9,700	9,750	1,094	973	1,094	973	12,700	12,750	1,544	1,273	1,544	1,386
6,750	6,800	678	678	678	678	9,750	9,800	1,101	978	1,101	978	12,750	12,800	1,551	1,278	1,551	1,394
6,800	6,850	683	683	683	683	9,800	9,850	1,109	983	1,109	983	12,800	12,850	1,559	1,283	1,559	1,401
6,850	6,900	688	688	688	688	9,850	9,900	1,116	988	1,116	988	12,850	12,900	1,566	1,288	1,566	1,409
6,900	6,950	693	693	693	693	9,900	9,950	1,124	993	1,124	993	12,900	12,950	1,574	1,293	1,574	1,416
6,950	7,000	698	698	698	698	9,950	10,000	1,131	998	1,131	998	12,950	13,000	1,581	1,298	1,581	1,424
7,000						**10,000**						**13,000**					
7,000	7,050	703	703	703	703	10,000	10,050	1,139	1,003	1,139	1,003	13,000	13,050	1,589	1,303	1,589	1,431
7,050	7,100	708	708	708	708	10,050	10,100	1,146	1,008	1,146	1,008	13,050	13,100	1,596	1,308	1,596	1,439
7,100	7,150	713	713	713	713	10,100	10,150	1,154	1,013	1,154	1,013	13,100	13,150	1,604	1,313	1,604	1,446
7,150	7,200	718	718	718	718	10,150	10,200	1,161	1,018	1,161	1,018	13,150	13,200	1,611	1,318	1,611	1,454
7,200	7,250	723	723	723	723	10,200	10,250	1,169	1,023	1,169	1,023	13,200	13,250	1,619	1,323	1,619	1,461
7,250	7,300	728	728	728	728	10,250	10,300	1,176	1,028	1,176	1,028	13,250	13,300	1,626	1,328	1,626	1,469
7,300	7,350	734	733	734	733	10,300	10,350	1,184	1,033	1,184	1,033	13,300	13,350	1,634	1,333	1,634	1,476
7,350	7,400	741	738	741	738	10,350	10,400	1,191	1,038	1,191	1,038	13,350	13,400	1,641	1,338	1,641	1,484
7,400	7,450	749	743	749	743	10,400	10,450	1,199	1,043	1,199	1,043	13,400	13,450	1,649	1,343	1,649	1,491
7,450	7,500	756	748	756	748	10,450	10,500	1,206	1,048	1,206	1,049	13,450	13,500	1,656	1,348	1,656	1,499
7,500	7,550	764	753	764	753	10,500	10,550	1,214	1,053	1,214	1,056	13,500	13,550	1,664	1,353	1,664	1,506
7,550	7,600	771	758	771	758	10,550	10,600	1,221	1,058	1,221	1,064	13,550	13,600	1,671	1,358	1,671	1,514
7,600	7,650	779	763	779	763	10,600	10,650	1,229	1,063	1,229	1,071	13,600	13,650	1,679	1,363	1,679	1,521
7,650	7,700	786	768	786	768	10,650	10,700	1,236	1,068	1,236	1,079	13,650	13,700	1,686	1,368	1,686	1,529
7,700	7,750	794	773	794	773	10,700	10,750	1,244	1,073	1,244	1,086	13,700	13,750	1,694	1,373	1,694	1,536
7,750	7,800	801	778	801	778	10,750	10,800	1,251	1,078	1,251	1,094	13,750	13,800	1,701	1,378	1,701	1,544
7,800	7,850	809	783	809	783	10,800	10,850	1,259	1,083	1,259	1,101	13,800	13,850	1,709	1,383	1,709	1,551
7,850	7,900	816	788	816	788	10,850	10,900	1,266	1,088	1,266	1,109	13,850	13,900	1,716	1,388	1,716	1,559
7,900	7,950	824	793	824	793	10,900	10,950	1,274	1,093	1,274	1,116	13,900	13,950	1,724	1,393	1,724	1,566
7,950	8,000	831	798	831	798	10,950	11,000	1,281	1,098	1,281	1,124	13,950	14,000	1,731	1,398	1,731	1,574

* This column must also be used by a qualifying widow(er).

(Continued on next page)

2005 Tax Table—*Continued*

14,000

If line 43 (taxable income) is— At least	But less than	Single	Married filing jointly *	Married filing separately	Head of a household
			Your tax is—		
14,000	14,050	1,739	1,403	1,739	1,581
14,050	14,100	1,746	1,408	1,746	1,589
14,100	14,150	1,754	1,413	1,754	1,596
14,150	14,200	1,761	1,418	1,761	1,604
14,200	14,250	1,769	1,423	1,769	1,611
14,250	14,300	1,776	1,428	1,776	1,619
14,300	14,350	1,784	1,433	1,784	1,626
14,350	14,400	1,791	1,438	1,791	1,634
14,400	14,450	1,799	1,443	1,799	1,641
14,450	14,500	1,806	1,448	1,806	1,649
14,500	14,550	1,814	1,453	1,814	1,656
14,550	14,600	1,821	1,458	1,821	1,664
14,600	14,650	1,829	1,464	1,829	1,671
14,650	14,700	1,836	1,471	1,836	1,679
14,700	14,750	1,844	1,479	1,844	1,686
14,750	14,800	1,851	1,486	1,851	1,694
14,800	14,850	1,859	1,494	1,859	1,701
14,850	14,900	1,866	1,501	1,866	1,709
14,900	14,950	1,874	1,509	1,874	1,716
14,950	15,000	1,881	1,516	1,881	1,724

15,000

At least	But less than	Single	Married filing jointly *	Married filing separately	Head of a household
15,000	15,050	1,889	1,524	1,889	1,731
15,050	15,100	1,896	1,531	1,896	1,739
15,100	15,150	1,904	1,539	1,904	1,746
15,150	15,200	1,911	1,546	1,911	1,754
15,200	15,250	1,919	1,554	1,919	1,761
15,250	15,300	1,926	1,561	1,926	1,769
15,300	15,350	1,934	1,569	1,934	1,776
15,350	15,400	1,941	1,576	1,941	1,784
15,400	15,450	1,949	1,584	1,949	1,791
15,450	15,500	1,956	1,591	1,956	1,799
15,500	15,550	1,964	1,599	1,964	1,806
15,550	15,600	1,971	1,606	1,971	1,814
15,600	15,650	1,979	1,614	1,979	1,821
15,650	15,700	1,986	1,621	1,986	1,829
15,700	15,750	1,994	1,629	1,994	1,836
15,750	15,800	2,001	1,636	2,001	1,844
15,800	15,850	2,009	1,644	2,009	1,851
15,850	15,900	2,016	1,651	2,016	1,859
15,900	15,950	2,024	1,659	2,024	1,866
15,950	16,000	2,031	1,666	2,031	1,874

16,000

At least	But less than	Single	Married filing jointly *	Married filing separately	Head of a household
16,000	16,050	2,039	1,674	2,039	1,881
16,050	16,100	2,046	1,681	2,046	1,889
16,100	16,150	2,054	1,689	2,054	1,896
16,150	16,200	2,061	1,696	2,061	1,904
16,200	16,250	2,069	1,704	2,069	1,911
16,250	16,300	2,076	1,711	2,076	1,919
16,300	16,350	2,084	1,719	2,084	1,926
16,350	16,400	2,091	1,726	2,091	1,934
16,400	16,450	2,099	1,734	2,099	1,941
16,450	16,500	2,106	1,741	2,106	1,949
16,500	16,550	2,114	1,749	2,114	1,956
16,550	16,600	2,121	1,756	2,121	1,964
16,600	16,650	2,129	1,764	2,129	1,971
16,650	16,700	2,136	1,771	2,136	1,979
16,700	16,750	2,144	1,779	2,144	1,986
16,750	16,800	2,151	1,786	2,151	1,994
16,800	16,850	2,159	1,794	2,159	2,001
16,850	16,900	2,166	1,801	2,166	2,009
16,900	16,950	2,174	1,809	2,174	2,016
16,950	17,000	2,181	1,816	2,181	2,024

17,000

At least	But less than	Single	Married filing jointly *	Married filing separately	Head of a household
17,000	17,050	2,189	1,824	2,189	2,031
17,050	17,100	2,196	1,831	2,196	2,039
17,100	17,150	2,204	1,839	2,204	2,046
17,150	17,200	2,211	1,846	2,211	2,054
17,200	17,250	2,219	1,854	2,219	2,061
17,250	17,300	2,226	1,861	2,226	2,069
17,300	17,350	2,234	1,869	2,234	2,076
17,350	17,400	2,241	1,876	2,241	2,084
17,400	17,450	2,249	1,884	2,249	2,091
17,450	17,500	2,256	1,891	2,256	2,099
17,500	17,550	2,264	1,899	2,264	2,106
17,550	17,600	2,271	1,906	2,271	2,114
17,600	17,650	2,279	1,914	2,279	2,121
17,650	17,700	2,286	1,921	2,286	2,129
17,700	17,750	2,294	1,929	2,294	2,136
17,750	17,800	2,301	1,936	2,301	2,144
17,800	17,850	2,309	1,944	2,309	2,151
17,850	17,900	2,316	1,951	2,316	2,159
17,900	17,950	2,324	1,959	2,324	2,166
17,950	18,000	2,331	1,966	2,331	2,174

18,000

At least	But less than	Single	Married filing jointly *	Married filing separately	Head of a household
18,000	18,050	2,339	1,974	2,339	2,181
18,050	18,100	2,346	1,981	2,346	2,189
18,100	18,150	2,354	1,989	2,354	2,196
18,150	18,200	2,361	1,996	2,361	2,204
18,200	18,250	2,369	2,004	2,369	2,211
18,250	18,300	2,376	2,011	2,376	2,219
18,300	18,350	2,384	2,019	2,384	2,226
18,350	18,400	2,391	2,026	2,391	2,234
18,400	18,450	2,399	2,034	2,399	2,241
18,450	18,500	2,406	2,041	2,406	2,249
18,500	18,550	2,414	2,049	2,414	2,256
18,550	18,600	2,421	2,056	2,421	2,264
18,600	18,650	2,429	2,064	2,429	2,271
18,650	18,700	2,436	2,071	2,436	2,279
18,700	18,750	2,444	2,079	2,444	2,286
18,750	18,800	2,451	2,086	2,451	2,294
18,800	18,850	2,459	2,094	2,459	2,301
18,850	18,900	2,466	2,101	2,466	2,309
18,900	18,950	2,474	2,109	2,474	2,316
18,950	19,000	2,481	2,116	2,481	2,324

19,000

At least	But less than	Single	Married filing jointly *	Married filing separately	Head of a household
19,000	19,050	2,489	2,124	2,489	2,331
19,050	19,100	2,496	2,131	2,496	2,339
19,100	19,150	2,504	2,139	2,504	2,346
19,150	19,200	2,511	2,146	2,511	2,354
19,200	19,250	2,519	2,154	2,519	2,361
19,250	19,300	2,526	2,161	2,526	2,369
19,300	19,350	2,534	2,169	2,534	2,376
19,350	19,400	2,541	2,176	2,541	2,384
19,400	19,450	2,549	2,184	2,549	2,391
19,450	19,500	2,556	2,191	2,556	2,399
19,500	19,550	2,564	2,199	2,564	2,406
19,550	19,600	2,571	2,206	2,571	2,414
19,600	19,650	2,579	2,214	2,579	2,421
19,650	19,700	2,586	2,221	2,586	2,429
19,700	19,750	2,594	2,229	2,594	2,436
19,750	19,800	2,601	2,236	2,601	2,444
19,800	19,850	2,609	2,244	2,609	2,451
19,850	19,900	2,616	2,251	2,616	2,459
19,900	19,950	2,624	2,259	2,624	2,466
19,950	20,000	2,631	2,266	2,631	2,474

20,000

At least	But less than	Single	Married filing jointly *	Married filing separately	Head of a household
20,000	20,050	2,639	2,274	2,639	2,481
20,050	20,100	2,646	2,281	2,646	2,489
20,100	20,150	2,654	2,289	2,654	2,496
20,150	20,200	2,661	2,296	2,661	2,504
20,200	20,250	2,669	2,304	2,669	2,511
20,250	20,300	2,676	2,311	2,676	2,519
20,300	20,350	2,684	2,319	2,684	2,526
20,350	20,400	2,691	2,326	2,691	2,534
20,400	20,450	2,699	2,334	2,699	2,541
20,450	20,500	2,706	2,341	2,706	2,549
20,500	20,550	2,714	2,349	2,714	2,556
20,550	20,600	2,721	2,356	2,721	2,564
20,600	20,650	2,729	2,364	2,729	2,571
20,650	20,700	2,736	2,371	2,736	2,579
20,700	20,750	2,744	2,379	2,744	2,586
20,750	20,800	2,751	2,386	2,751	2,594
20,800	20,850	2,759	2,394	2,759	2,601
20,850	20,900	2,766	2,401	2,766	2,609
20,900	20,950	2,774	2,409	2,774	2,616
20,950	21,000	2,781	2,416	2,781	2,624

21,000

At least	But less than	Single	Married filing jointly *	Married filing separately	Head of a household
21,000	21,050	2,789	2,424	2,789	2,631
21,050	21,100	2,796	2,431	2,796	2,639
21,100	21,150	2,804	2,439	2,804	2,646
21,150	21,200	2,811	2,446	2,811	2,654
21,200	21,250	2,819	2,454	2,819	2,661
21,250	21,300	2,826	2,461	2,826	2,669
21,300	21,350	2,834	2,469	2,834	2,676
21,350	21,400	2,841	2,476	2,841	2,684
21,400	21,450	2,849	2,484	2,849	2,691
21,450	21,500	2,856	2,491	2,856	2,699
21,500	21,550	2,864	2,499	2,864	2,706
21,550	21,600	2,871	2,506	2,871	2,714
21,600	21,650	2,879	2,514	2,879	2,721
21,650	21,700	2,886	2,521	2,886	2,729
21,700	21,750	2,894	2,529	2,894	2,736
21,750	21,800	2,901	2,536	2,901	2,744
21,800	21,850	2,909	2,544	2,909	2,751
21,850	21,900	2,916	2,551	2,916	2,759
21,900	21,950	2,924	2,559	2,924	2,766
21,950	22,000	2,931	2,566	2,931	2,774

22,000

At least	But less than	Single	Married filing jointly *	Married filing separately	Head of a household
22,000	22,050	2,939	2,574	2,939	2,781
22,050	22,100	2,946	2,581	2,946	2,789
22,100	22,150	2,954	2,589	2,954	2,796
22,150	22,200	2,961	2,596	2,961	2,804
22,200	22,250	2,969	2,604	2,969	2,811
22,250	22,300	2,976	2,611	2,976	2,819
22,300	22,350	2,984	2,619	2,984	2,826
22,350	22,400	2,991	2,626	2,991	2,834
22,400	22,450	2,999	2,634	2,999	2,841
22,450	22,500	3,006	2,641	3,006	2,849
22,500	22,550	3,014	2,649	3,014	2,856
22,550	22,600	3,021	2,656	3,021	2,864
22,600	22,650	3,029	2,664	3,029	2,871
22,650	22,700	3,036	2,671	3,036	2,879
22,700	22,750	3,044	2,679	3,044	2,886
22,750	22,800	3,051	2,686	3,051	2,894
22,800	22,850	3,059	2,694	3,059	2,901
22,850	22,900	3,066	2,701	3,066	2,909
22,900	22,950	3,074	2,709	3,074	2,916
22,950	23,000	3,081	2,716	3,081	2,924

* This column must also be used by a qualifying widow(er).

(Continued on next page)

2005 Tax Table—Continued

23,000 / 24,000 / 25,000

If line 43 (taxable income) is— At least	But less than	Single	Married filing jointly *	Married filing separately	Head of a household
23,000					
23,000	23,050	3,089	2,724	3,089	2,931
23,050	23,100	3,096	2,731	3,096	2,939
23,100	23,150	3,104	2,739	3,104	2,946
23,150	23,200	3,111	2,746	3,111	2,954
23,200	23,250	3,119	2,754	3,119	2,961
23,250	23,300	3,126	2,761	3,126	2,969
23,300	23,350	3,134	2,769	3,134	2,976
23,350	23,400	3,141	2,776	3,141	2,984
23,400	23,450	3,149	2,784	3,149	2,991
23,450	23,500	3,156	2,791	3,156	2,999
23,500	23,550	3,164	2,799	3,164	3,006
23,550	23,600	3,171	2,806	3,171	3,014
23,600	23,650	3,179	2,814	3,179	3,021
23,650	23,700	3,186	2,821	3,186	3,029
23,700	23,750	3,194	2,829	3,194	3,036
23,750	23,800	3,201	2,836	3,201	3,044
23,800	23,850	3,209	2,844	3,209	3,051
23,850	23,900	3,216	2,851	3,216	3,059
23,900	23,950	3,224	2,859	3,224	3,066
23,950	24,000	3,231	2,866	3,231	3,074
24,000					
24,000	24,050	3,239	2,874	3,239	3,081
24,050	24,100	3,246	2,881	3,246	3,089
24,100	24,150	3,254	2,889	3,254	3,096
24,150	24,200	3,261	2,896	3,261	3,104
24,200	24,250	3,269	2,904	3,269	3,111
24,250	24,300	3,276	2,911	3,276	3,119
24,300	24,350	3,284	2,919	3,284	3,126
24,350	24,400	3,291	2,926	3,291	3,134
24,400	24,450	3,299	2,934	3,299	3,141
24,450	24,500	3,306	2,941	3,306	3,149
24,500	24,550	3,314	2,949	3,314	3,156
24,550	24,600	3,321	2,956	3,321	3,164
24,600	24,650	3,329	2,964	3,329	3,171
24,650	24,700	3,336	2,971	3,336	3,179
24,700	24,750	3,344	2,979	3,344	3,186
24,750	24,800	3,351	2,986	3,351	3,194
24,800	24,850	3,359	2,994	3,359	3,201
24,850	24,900	3,366	3,001	3,366	3,209
24,900	24,950	3,374	3,009	3,374	3,216
24,950	25,000	3,381	3,016	3,381	3,224
25,000					
25,000	25,050	3,389	3,024	3,389	3,231
25,050	25,100	3,396	3,031	3,396	3,239
25,100	25,150	3,404	3,039	3,404	3,246
25,150	25,200	3,411	3,046	3,411	3,254
25,200	25,250	3,419	3,054	3,419	3,261
25,250	25,300	3,426	3,061	3,426	3,269
25,300	25,350	3,434	3,069	3,434	3,276
25,350	25,400	3,441	3,076	3,441	3,284
25,400	25,450	3,449	3,084	3,449	3,291
25,450	25,500	3,456	3,091	3,456	3,299
25,500	25,550	3,464	3,099	3,464	3,306
25,550	25,600	3,471	3,106	3,471	3,314
25,600	25,650	3,479	3,114	3,479	3,321
25,650	25,700	3,486	3,121	3,486	3,329
25,700	25,750	3,494	3,129	3,494	3,336
25,750	25,800	3,501	3,136	3,501	3,344
25,800	25,850	3,509	3,144	3,509	3,351
25,850	25,900	3,516	3,151	3,516	3,359
25,900	25,950	3,524	3,159	3,524	3,366
25,950	26,000	3,531	3,166	3,531	3,374

26,000 / 27,000 / 28,000

If line 43 (taxable income) is— At least	But less than	Single	Married filing jointly *	Married filing separately	Head of a household
26,000					
26,000	26,050	3,539	3,174	3,539	3,381
26,050	26,100	3,546	3,181	3,546	3,389
26,100	26,150	3,554	3,189	3,554	3,396
26,150	26,200	3,561	3,196	3,561	3,404
26,200	26,250	3,569	3,204	3,569	3,411
26,250	26,300	3,576	3,211	3,576	3,419
26,300	26,350	3,584	3,219	3,584	3,426
26,350	26,400	3,591	3,226	3,591	3,434
26,400	26,450	3,599	3,234	3,599	3,441
26,450	26,500	3,606	3,241	3,606	3,449
26,500	26,550	3,614	3,249	3,614	3,456
26,550	26,600	3,621	3,256	3,621	3,464
26,600	26,650	3,629	3,264	3,629	3,471
26,650	26,700	3,636	3,271	3,636	3,479
26,700	26,750	3,644	3,279	3,644	3,486
26,750	26,800	3,651	3,286	3,651	3,494
26,800	26,850	3,659	3,294	3,659	3,501
26,850	26,900	3,666	3,301	3,666	3,509
26,900	26,950	3,674	3,309	3,674	3,516
26,950	27,000	3,681	3,316	3,681	3,524
27,000					
27,000	27,050	3,689	3,324	3,689	3,531
27,050	27,100	3,696	3,331	3,696	3,539
27,100	27,150	3,704	3,339	3,704	3,546
27,150	27,200	3,711	3,346	3,711	3,554
27,200	27,250	3,719	3,354	3,719	3,561
27,250	27,300	3,726	3,361	3,726	3,569
27,300	27,350	3,734	3,369	3,734	3,576
27,350	27,400	3,741	3,376	3,741	3,584
27,400	27,450	3,749	3,384	3,749	3,591
27,450	27,500	3,756	3,391	3,756	3,599
27,500	27,550	3,764	3,399	3,764	3,606
27,550	27,600	3,771	3,406	3,771	3,614
27,600	27,650	3,779	3,414	3,779	3,621
27,650	27,700	3,786	3,421	3,786	3,629
27,700	27,750	3,794	3,429	3,794	3,636
27,750	27,800	3,801	3,436	3,801	3,644
27,800	27,850	3,809	3,444	3,809	3,651
27,850	27,900	3,816	3,451	3,816	3,659
27,900	27,950	3,824	3,459	3,824	3,666
27,950	28,000	3,831	3,466	3,831	3,674
28,000					
28,000	28,050	3,839	3,474	3,839	3,681
28,050	28,100	3,846	3,481	3,846	3,689
28,100	28,150	3,854	3,489	3,854	3,696
28,150	28,200	3,861	3,496	3,861	3,704
28,200	28,250	3,869	3,504	3,869	3,711
28,250	28,300	3,876	3,511	3,876	3,719
28,300	28,350	3,884	3,519	3,884	3,726
28,350	28,400	3,891	3,526	3,891	3,734
28,400	28,450	3,899	3,534	3,899	3,741
28,450	28,500	3,906	3,541	3,906	3,749
28,500	28,550	3,914	3,549	3,914	3,756
28,550	28,600	3,921	3,556	3,921	3,764
28,600	28,650	3,929	3,564	3,929	3,771
28,650	28,700	3,936	3,571	3,936	3,779
28,700	28,750	3,944	3,579	3,944	3,786
28,750	28,800	3,951	3,586	3,951	3,794
28,800	28,850	3,959	3,594	3,959	3,801
28,850	28,900	3,966	3,601	3,966	3,809
28,900	28,950	3,974	3,609	3,974	3,816
28,950	29,000	3,981	3,616	3,981	3,824

29,000 / 30,000 / 31,000

If line 43 (taxable income) is— At least	But less than	Single	Married filing jointly *	Married filing separately	Head of a household
29,000					
29,000	29,050	3,989	3,624	3,989	3,831
29,050	29,100	3,996	3,631	3,996	3,839
29,100	29,150	4,004	3,639	4,004	3,846
29,150	29,200	4,011	3,646	4,011	3,854
29,200	29,250	4,019	3,654	4,019	3,861
29,250	29,300	4,026	3,661	4,026	3,869
29,300	29,350	4,034	3,669	4,034	3,876
29,350	29,400	4,041	3,676	4,041	3,884
29,400	29,450	4,049	3,684	4,049	3,891
29,450	29,500	4,056	3,691	4,056	3,899
29,500	29,550	4,064	3,699	4,064	3,906
29,550	29,600	4,071	3,706	4,071	3,914
29,600	29,650	4,079	3,714	4,079	3,921
29,650	29,700	4,086	3,721	4,086	3,929
29,700	29,750	4,096	3,729	4,096	3,936
29,750	29,800	4,109	3,736	4,109	3,944
29,800	29,850	4,121	3,744	4,121	3,951
29,850	29,900	4,134	3,751	4,134	3,959
29,900	29,950	4,146	3,759	4,146	3,966
29,950	30,000	4,159	3,766	4,159	3,974
30,000					
30,000	30,050	4,171	3,774	4,171	3,981
30,050	30,100	4,184	3,781	4,184	3,989
30,100	30,150	4,196	3,789	4,196	3,996
30,150	30,200	4,209	3,796	4,209	4,004
30,200	30,250	4,221	3,804	4,221	4,011
30,250	30,300	4,234	3,811	4,234	4,019
30,300	30,350	4,246	3,819	4,246	4,026
30,350	30,400	4,259	3,826	4,259	4,034
30,400	30,450	4,271	3,834	4,271	4,041
30,450	30,500	4,284	3,841	4,284	4,049
30,500	30,550	4,296	3,849	4,296	4,056
30,550	30,600	4,309	3,856	4,309	4,064
30,600	30,650	4,321	3,864	4,321	4,071
30,650	30,700	4,334	3,871	4,334	4,079
30,700	30,750	4,346	3,879	4,346	4,086
30,750	30,800	4,359	3,886	4,359	4,094
30,800	30,850	4,371	3,894	4,371	4,101
30,850	30,900	4,384	3,901	4,384	4,109
30,900	30,950	4,396	3,909	4,396	4,116
30,950	31,000	4,409	3,916	4,409	4,124
31,000					
31,000	31,050	4,421	3,924	4,421	4,131
31,050	31,100	4,434	3,931	4,434	4,139
31,100	31,150	4,446	3,939	4,446	4,146
31,150	31,200	4,459	3,946	4,459	4,154
31,200	31,250	4,471	3,954	4,471	4,161
31,250	31,300	4,484	3,961	4,484	4,169
31,300	31,350	4,496	3,969	4,496	4,176
31,350	31,400	4,509	3,976	4,509	4,184
31,400	31,450	4,521	3,984	4,521	4,191
31,450	31,500	4,534	3,991	4,534	4,199
31,500	31,550	4,546	3,999	4,546	4,206
31,550	31,600	4,559	4,006	4,559	4,214
31,600	31,650	4,571	4,014	4,571	4,221
31,650	31,700	4,584	4,021	4,584	4,229
31,700	31,750	4,596	4,029	4,596	4,236
31,750	31,800	4,609	4,036	4,609	4,244
31,800	31,850	4,621	4,044	4,621	4,251
31,850	31,900	4,634	4,051	4,634	4,259
31,900	31,950	4,646	4,059	4,646	4,266
31,950	32,000	4,659	4,066	4,659	4,274

* This column must also be used by a qualifying widow(er).

(Continued on next page)

2005 Tax Table—*Continued*

32,000 / 35,000 / 38,000

If line 43 (taxable income) is— At least	But less than	Single	Married filing jointly *	Married filing separately	Head of a house-hold
32,000					
32,000	32,050	4,671	4,074	4,671	4,281
32,050	32,100	4,684	4,081	4,684	4,289
32,100	32,150	4,696	4,089	4,696	4,296
32,150	32,200	4,709	4,096	4,709	4,304
32,200	32,250	4,721	4,104	4,721	4,311
32,250	32,300	4,734	4,111	4,734	4,319
32,300	32,350	4,746	4,119	4,746	4,326
32,350	32,400	4,759	4,126	4,759	4,334
32,400	32,450	4,771	4,134	4,771	4,341
32,450	32,500	4,784	4,141	4,784	4,349
32,500	32,550	4,796	4,149	4,796	4,356
32,550	32,600	4,809	4,156	4,809	4,364
32,600	32,650	4,821	4,164	4,821	4,371
32,650	32,700	4,834	4,171	4,834	4,379
32,700	32,750	4,846	4,179	4,846	4,386
32,750	32,800	4,859	4,186	4,859	4,394
32,800	32,850	4,871	4,194	4,871	4,401
32,850	32,900	4,884	4,201	4,884	4,409
32,900	32,950	4,896	4,209	4,896	4,416
32,950	33,000	4,909	4,216	4,909	4,424
33,000					
33,000	33,050	4,921	4,224	4,921	4,431
33,050	33,100	4,934	4,231	4,934	4,439
33,100	33,150	4,946	4,239	4,946	4,446
33,150	33,200	4,959	4,246	4,959	4,454
33,200	33,250	4,971	4,254	4,971	4,461
33,250	33,300	4,984	4,261	4,984	4,469
33,300	33,350	4,996	4,269	4,996	4,476
33,350	33,400	5,009	4,276	5,009	4,484
33,400	33,450	5,021	4,284	5,021	4,491
33,450	33,500	5,034	4,291	5,034	4,499
33,500	33,550	5,046	4,299	5,046	4,506
33,550	33,600	5,059	4,306	5,059	4,514
33,600	33,650	5,071	4,314	5,071	4,521
33,650	33,700	5,084	4,321	5,084	4,529
33,700	33,750	5,096	4,329	5,096	4,536
33,750	33,800	5,109	4,336	5,109	4,544
33,800	33,850	5,121	4,344	5,121	4,551
33,850	33,900	5,134	4,351	5,134	4,559
33,900	33,950	5,146	4,359	5,146	4,566
33,950	34,000	5,159	4,366	5,159	4,574
34,000					
34,000	34,050	5,171	4,374	5,171	4,581
34,050	34,100	5,184	4,381	5,184	4,589
34,100	34,150	5,196	4,389	5,196	4,596
34,150	34,200	5,209	4,396	5,209	4,604
34,200	34,250	5,221	4,404	5,221	4,611
34,250	34,300	5,234	4,411	5,234	4,619
34,300	34,350	5,246	4,419	5,246	4,626
34,350	34,400	5,259	4,426	5,259	4,634
34,400	34,450	5,271	4,434	5,271	4,641
34,450	34,500	5,284	4,441	5,284	4,649
34,500	34,550	5,296	4,449	5,296	4,656
34,550	34,600	5,309	4,456	5,309	4,664
34,600	34,650	5,321	4,464	5,321	4,671
34,650	34,700	5,334	4,471	5,334	4,679
34,700	34,750	5,346	4,479	5,346	4,686
34,750	34,800	5,359	4,486	5,359	4,694
34,800	34,850	5,371	4,494	5,371	4,701
34,850	34,900	5,384	4,501	5,384	4,709
34,900	34,950	5,396	4,509	5,396	4,716
34,950	35,000	5,409	4,516	5,409	4,724

If line 43 (taxable income) is— At least	But less than	Single	Married filing jointly *	Married filing separately	Head of a house-hold
35,000					
35,000	35,050	5,421	4,524	5,421	4,731
35,050	35,100	5,434	4,531	5,434	4,739
35,100	35,150	5,446	4,539	5,446	4,746
35,150	35,200	5,459	4,546	5,459	4,754
35,200	35,250	5,471	4,554	5,471	4,761
35,250	35,300	5,484	4,561	5,484	4,769
35,300	35,350	5,496	4,569	5,496	4,776
35,350	35,400	5,509	4,576	5,509	4,784
35,400	35,450	5,521	4,584	5,521	4,791
35,450	35,500	5,534	4,591	5,534	4,799
35,500	35,550	5,546	4,599	5,546	4,806
35,550	35,600	5,559	4,606	5,559	4,814
35,600	35,650	5,571	4,614	5,571	4,821
35,650	35,700	5,584	4,621	5,584	4,829
35,700	35,750	5,596	4,629	5,596	4,836
35,750	35,800	5,609	4,636	5,609	4,844
35,800	35,850	5,621	4,644	5,621	4,851
35,850	35,900	5,634	4,651	5,634	4,859
35,900	35,950	5,646	4,659	5,646	4,866
35,950	36,000	5,659	4,666	5,659	4,874
36,000					
36,000	36,050	5,671	4,674	5,671	4,881
36,050	36,100	5,684	4,681	5,684	4,889
36,100	36,150	5,696	4,689	5,696	4,896
36,150	36,200	5,709	4,696	5,709	4,904
36,200	36,250	5,721	4,704	5,721	4,911
36,250	36,300	5,734	4,711	5,734	4,919
36,300	36,350	5,746	4,719	5,746	4,926
36,350	36,400	5,759	4,726	5,759	4,934
36,400	36,450	5,771	4,734	5,771	4,941
36,450	36,500	5,784	4,741	5,784	4,949
36,500	36,550	5,796	4,749	5,796	4,956
36,550	36,600	5,809	4,756	5,809	4,964
36,600	36,650	5,821	4,764	5,821	4,971
36,650	36,700	5,834	4,771	5,834	4,979
36,700	36,750	5,846	4,779	5,846	4,986
36,750	36,800	5,859	4,786	5,859	4,994
36,800	36,850	5,871	4,794	5,871	5,001
36,850	36,900	5,884	4,801	5,884	5,009
36,900	36,950	5,896	4,809	5,896	5,016
36,950	37,000	5,909	4,816	5,909	5,024
37,000					
37,000	37,050	5,921	4,824	5,921	5,031
37,050	37,100	5,934	4,831	5,934	5,039
37,100	37,150	5,946	4,839	5,946	5,046
37,150	37,200	5,959	4,846	5,959	5,054
37,200	37,250	5,971	4,854	5,971	5,061
37,250	37,300	5,984	4,861	5,984	5,069
37,300	37,350	5,996	4,869	5,996	5,076
37,350	37,400	6,009	4,876	6,009	5,084
37,400	37,450	6,021	4,884	6,021	5,091
37,450	37,500	6,034	4,891	6,034	5,099
37,500	37,550	6,046	4,899	6,046	5,106
37,550	37,600	6,059	4,906	6,059	5,114
37,600	37,650	6,071	4,914	6,071	5,121
37,650	37,700	6,084	4,921	6,084	5,129
37,700	37,750	6,096	4,929	6,096	5,136
37,750	37,800	6,109	4,936	6,109	5,144
37,800	37,850	6,121	4,944	6,121	5,151
37,850	37,900	6,134	4,951	6,134	5,159
37,900	37,950	6,146	4,959	6,146	5,166
37,950	38,000	6,159	4,966	6,159	5,174

If line 43 (taxable income) is— At least	But less than	Single	Married filing jointly *	Married filing separately	Head of a house-hold
38,000					
38,000	38,050	6,171	4,974	6,171	5,181
38,050	38,100	6,184	4,981	6,184	5,189
38,100	38,150	6,196	4,989	6,196	5,196
38,150	38,200	6,209	4,996	6,209	5,204
38,200	38,250	6,221	5,004	6,221	5,211
38,250	38,300	6,234	5,011	6,234	5,219
38,300	38,350	6,246	5,019	6,246	5,226
38,350	38,400	6,259	5,026	6,259	5,234
38,400	38,450	6,271	5,034	6,271	5,241
38,450	38,500	6,284	5,041	6,284	5,249
38,500	38,550	6,296	5,049	6,296	5,256
38,550	38,600	6,309	5,056	6,309	5,264
38,600	38,650	6,321	5,064	6,321	5,271
38,650	38,700	6,334	5,071	6,334	5,279
38,700	38,750	6,346	5,079	6,346	5,286
38,750	38,800	6,359	5,086	6,359	5,294
38,800	38,850	6,371	5,094	6,371	5,301
38,850	38,900	6,384	5,101	6,384	5,309
38,900	38,950	6,396	5,109	6,396	5,316
38,950	39,000	6,409	5,116	6,409	5,324
39,000					
39,000	39,050	6,421	5,124	6,421	5,331
39,050	39,100	6,434	5,131	6,434	5,339
39,100	39,150	6,446	5,139	6,446	5,346
39,150	39,200	6,459	5,146	6,459	5,354
39,200	39,250	6,471	5,154	6,471	5,361
39,250	39,300	6,484	5,161	6,484	5,369
39,300	39,350	6,496	5,169	6,496	5,376
39,350	39,400	6,509	5,176	6,509	5,384
39,400	39,450	6,521	5,184	6,521	5,391
39,450	39,500	6,534	5,191	6,534	5,399
39,500	39,550	6,546	5,199	6,546	5,406
39,550	39,600	6,559	5,206	6,559	5,414
39,600	39,650	6,571	5,214	6,571	5,421
39,650	39,700	6,584	5,221	6,584	5,429
39,700	39,750	6,596	5,229	6,596	5,436
39,750	39,800	6,609	5,236	6,609	5,444
39,800	39,850	6,621	5,244	6,621	5,454
39,850	39,900	6,634	5,251	6,634	5,466
39,900	39,950	6,646	5,259	6,646	5,479
39,950	40,000	6,659	5,266	6,659	5,491
40,000					
40,000	40,050	6,671	5,274	6,671	5,504
40,050	40,100	6,684	5,281	6,684	5,516
40,100	40,150	6,696	5,289	6,696	5,529
40,150	40,200	6,709	5,296	6,709	5,541
40,200	40,250	6,721	5,304	6,721	5,554
40,250	40,300	6,734	5,311	6,734	5,566
40,300	40,350	6,746	5,319	6,746	5,579
40,350	40,400	6,759	5,326	6,759	5,591
40,400	40,450	6,771	5,334	6,771	5,604
40,450	40,500	6,784	5,341	6,784	5,616
40,500	40,550	6,796	5,349	6,796	5,629
40,550	40,600	6,809	5,356	6,809	5,641
40,600	40,650	6,821	5,364	6,821	5,654
40,650	40,700	6,834	5,371	6,834	5,666
40,700	40,750	6,846	5,379	6,846	5,679
40,750	40,800	6,859	5,386	6,859	5,691
40,800	40,850	6,871	5,394	6,871	5,704
40,850	40,900	6,884	5,401	6,884	5,716
40,900	40,950	6,896	5,409	6,896	5,729
40,950	41,000	6,909	5,416	6,909	5,741

* This column must also be used by a qualifying widow(er).

(Continued on next page)

2005 Tax Table—Continued

If line 43 (taxable income) is— At least	But less than	Single	Married filing jointly*	Married filing separately	Head of a household
41,000					
41,000	41,050	6,921	5,424	6,921	5,754
41,050	41,100	6,934	5,431	6,934	5,766
41,100	41,150	6,946	5,439	6,946	5,779
41,150	41,200	6,959	5,446	6,959	5,791
41,200	41,250	6,971	5,454	6,971	5,804
41,250	41,300	6,984	5,461	6,984	5,816
41,300	41,350	6,996	5,469	6,996	5,829
41,350	41,400	7,009	5,476	7,009	5,841
41,400	41,450	7,021	5,484	7,021	5,854
41,450	41,500	7,034	5,491	7,034	5,866
41,500	41,550	7,046	5,499	7,046	5,879
41,550	41,600	7,059	5,506	7,059	5,891
41,600	41,650	7,071	5,514	7,071	5,904
41,650	41,700	7,084	5,521	7,084	5,916
41,700	41,750	7,096	5,529	7,096	5,929
41,750	41,800	7,109	5,536	7,109	5,941
41,800	41,850	7,121	5,544	7,121	5,954
41,850	41,900	7,134	5,551	7,134	5,966
41,900	41,950	7,146	5,559	7,146	5,979
41,950	42,000	7,159	5,566	7,159	5,991
42,000					
42,000	42,050	7,171	5,574	7,171	6,004
42,050	42,100	7,184	5,581	7,184	6,016
42,100	42,150	7,196	5,589	7,196	6,029
42,150	42,200	7,209	5,596	7,209	6,041
42,200	42,250	7,221	5,604	7,221	6,054
42,250	42,300	7,234	5,611	7,234	6,066
42,300	42,350	7,246	5,619	7,246	6,079
42,350	42,400	7,259	5,626	7,259	6,091
42,400	42,450	7,271	5,634	7,271	6,104
42,450	42,500	7,284	5,641	7,284	6,116
42,500	42,550	7,296	5,649	7,296	6,129
42,550	42,600	7,309	5,656	7,309	6,141
42,600	42,650	7,321	5,664	7,321	6,154
42,650	42,700	7,334	5,671	7,334	6,166
42,700	42,750	7,346	5,679	7,346	6,179
42,750	42,800	7,359	5,686	7,359	6,191
42,800	42,850	7,371	5,694	7,371	6,204
42,850	42,900	7,384	5,701	7,384	6,216
42,900	42,950	7,396	5,709	7,396	6,229
42,950	43,000	7,409	5,716	7,409	6,241
43,000					
43,000	43,050	7,421	5,724	7,421	6,254
43,050	43,100	7,434	5,731	7,434	6,266
43,100	43,150	7,446	5,739	7,446	6,279
43,150	43,200	7,459	5,746	7,459	6,291
43,200	43,250	7,471	5,754	7,471	6,304
43,250	43,300	7,484	5,761	7,484	6,316
43,300	43,350	7,496	5,769	7,496	6,329
43,350	43,400	7,509	5,776	7,509	6,341
43,400	43,450	7,521	5,784	7,521	6,354
43,450	43,500	7,534	5,791	7,534	6,366
43,500	43,550	7,546	5,799	7,546	6,379
43,550	43,600	7,559	5,806	7,559	6,391
43,600	43,650	7,571	5,814	7,571	6,404
43,650	43,700	7,584	5,821	7,584	6,416
43,700	43,750	7,596	5,829	7,596	6,429
43,750	43,800	7,609	5,836	7,609	6,441
43,800	43,850	7,621	5,844	7,621	6,454
43,850	43,900	7,634	5,851	7,634	6,466
43,900	43,950	7,646	5,859	7,646	6,479
43,950	44,000	7,659	5,866	7,659	6,491

If line 43 (taxable income) is— At least	But less than	Single	Married filing jointly*	Married filing separately	Head of a household
44,000					
44,000	44,050	7,671	5,874	7,671	6,504
44,050	44,100	7,684	5,881	7,684	6,516
44,100	44,150	7,696	5,889	7,696	6,529
44,150	44,200	7,709	5,896	7,709	6,541
44,200	44,250	7,721	5,904	7,721	6,554
44,250	44,300	7,734	5,911	7,734	6,566
44,300	44,350	7,746	5,919	7,746	6,579
44,350	44,400	7,759	5,926	7,759	6,591
44,400	44,450	7,771	5,934	7,771	6,604
44,450	44,500	7,784	5,941	7,784	6,616
44,500	44,550	7,796	5,949	7,796	6,629
44,550	44,600	7,809	5,956	7,809	6,641
44,600	44,650	7,821	5,964	7,821	6,654
44,650	44,700	7,834	5,971	7,834	6,666
44,700	44,750	7,846	5,979	7,846	6,679
44,750	44,800	7,859	5,986	7,859	6,691
44,800	44,850	7,871	5,994	7,871	6,704
44,850	44,900	7,884	6,001	7,884	6,716
44,900	44,950	7,896	6,009	7,896	6,729
44,950	45,000	7,909	6,016	7,909	6,741
45,000					
45,000	45,050	7,921	6,024	7,921	6,754
45,050	45,100	7,934	6,031	7,934	6,766
45,100	45,150	7,946	6,039	7,946	6,779
45,150	45,200	7,959	6,046	7,959	6,791
45,200	45,250	7,971	6,054	7,971	6,804
45,250	45,300	7,984	6,061	7,984	6,816
45,300	45,350	7,996	6,069	7,996	6,829
45,350	45,400	8,009	6,076	8,009	6,841
45,400	45,450	8,021	6,084	8,021	6,854
45,450	45,500	8,034	6,091	8,034	6,866
45,500	45,550	8,046	6,099	8,046	6,879
45,550	45,600	8,059	6,106	8,059	6,891
45,600	45,650	8,071	6,114	8,071	6,904
45,650	45,700	8,084	6,121	8,084	6,916
45,700	45,750	8,096	6,129	8,096	6,929
45,750	45,800	8,109	6,136	8,109	6,941
45,800	45,850	8,121	6,144	8,121	6,954
45,850	45,900	8,134	6,151	8,134	6,966
45,900	45,950	8,146	6,159	8,146	6,979
45,950	46,000	8,159	6,166	8,159	6,991
46,000					
46,000	46,050	8,171	6,174	8,171	7,004
46,050	46,100	8,184	6,181	8,184	7,016
46,100	46,150	8,196	6,189	8,196	7,029
46,150	46,200	8,209	6,196	8,209	7,041
46,200	46,250	8,221	6,204	8,221	7,054
46,250	46,300	8,234	6,211	8,234	7,066
46,300	46,350	8,246	6,219	8,246	7,079
46,350	46,400	8,259	6,226	8,259	7,091
46,400	46,450	8,271	6,234	8,271	7,104
46,450	46,500	8,284	6,241	8,284	7,116
46,500	46,550	8,296	6,249	8,296	7,129
46,550	46,600	8,309	6,256	8,309	7,141
46,600	46,650	8,321	6,264	8,321	7,154
46,650	46,700	8,334	6,271	8,334	7,166
46,700	46,750	8,346	6,279	8,346	7,179
46,750	46,800	8,359	6,286	8,359	7,191
46,800	46,850	8,371	6,294	8,371	7,204
46,850	46,900	8,384	6,301	8,384	7,216
46,900	46,950	8,396	6,309	8,396	7,229
46,950	47,000	8,409	6,316	8,409	7,241

If line 43 (taxable income) is— At least	But less than	Single	Married filing jointly*	Married filing separately	Head of a household
47,000					
47,000	47,050	8,421	6,324	8,421	7,254
47,050	47,100	8,434	6,331	8,434	7,266
47,100	47,150	8,446	6,339	8,446	7,279
47,150	47,200	8,459	6,346	8,459	7,291
47,200	47,250	8,471	6,354	8,471	7,304
47,250	47,300	8,484	6,361	8,484	7,316
47,300	47,350	8,496	6,369	8,496	7,329
47,350	47,400	8,509	6,376	8,509	7,341
47,400	47,450	8,521	6,384	8,521	7,354
47,450	47,500	8,534	6,391	8,534	7,366
47,500	47,550	8,546	6,399	8,546	7,379
47,550	47,600	8,559	6,406	8,559	7,391
47,600	47,650	8,571	6,414	8,571	7,404
47,650	47,700	8,584	6,421	8,584	7,416
47,700	47,750	8,596	6,429	8,596	7,429
47,750	47,800	8,609	6,436	8,609	7,441
47,800	47,850	8,621	6,444	8,621	7,454
47,850	47,900	8,634	6,451	8,634	7,466
47,900	47,950	8,646	6,459	8,646	7,479
47,950	48,000	8,659	6,466	8,659	7,491
48,000					
48,000	48,050	8,671	6,474	8,671	7,504
48,050	48,100	8,684	6,481	8,684	7,516
48,100	48,150	8,696	6,489	8,696	7,529
48,150	48,200	8,709	6,496	8,709	7,541
48,200	48,250	8,721	6,504	8,721	7,554
48,250	48,300	8,734	6,511	8,734	7,566
48,300	48,350	8,746	6,519	8,746	7,579
48,350	48,400	8,759	6,526	8,759	7,591
48,400	48,450	8,771	6,534	8,771	7,604
48,450	48,500	8,784	6,541	8,784	7,616
48,500	48,550	8,796	6,549	8,796	7,629
48,550	48,600	8,809	6,556	8,809	7,641
48,600	48,650	8,821	6,564	8,821	7,654
48,650	48,700	8,834	6,571	8,834	7,666
48,700	48,750	8,846	6,579	8,846	7,679
48,750	48,800	8,859	6,586	8,859	7,691
48,800	48,850	8,871	6,594	8,871	7,704
48,850	48,900	8,884	6,601	8,884	7,716
48,900	48,950	8,896	6,609	8,896	7,729
48,950	49,000	8,909	6,616	8,909	7,741
49,000					
49,000	49,050	8,921	6,624	8,921	7,754
49,050	49,100	8,934	6,631	8,934	7,766
49,100	49,150	8,946	6,639	8,946	7,779
49,150	49,200	8,959	6,646	8,959	7,791
49,200	49,250	8,971	6,654	8,971	7,804
49,250	49,300	8,984	6,661	8,984	7,816
49,300	49,350	8,996	6,669	8,996	7,829
49,350	49,400	9,009	6,676	9,009	7,841
49,400	49,450	9,021	6,684	9,021	7,854
49,450	49,500	9,034	6,691	9,034	7,866
49,500	49,550	9,046	6,699	9,046	7,879
49,550	49,600	9,059	6,706	9,059	7,891
49,600	49,650	9,071	6,714	9,071	7,904
49,650	49,700	9,084	6,721	9,084	7,916
49,700	49,750	9,096	6,729	9,096	7,929
49,750	49,800	9,109	6,736	9,109	7,941
49,800	49,850	9,121	6,744	9,121	7,954
49,850	49,900	9,134	6,751	9,134	7,966
49,900	49,950	9,146	6,759	9,146	7,979
49,950	50,000	9,159	6,766	9,159	7,991

* This column must also be used by a qualifying widow(er).

(Continued on next page)

2005 Tax Table—*Continued*

Left column group:

At least	But less than	Single	Married filing jointly*	Married filing separately	Head of a household
50,000					
50,000	50,050	9,171	6,774	9,171	8,004
50,050	50,100	9,184	6,781	9,184	8,016
50,100	50,150	9,196	6,789	9,196	8,029
50,150	50,200	9,209	6,796	9,209	8,041
50,200	50,250	9,221	6,804	9,221	8,054
50,250	50,300	9,234	6,811	9,234	8,066
50,300	50,350	9,246	6,819	9,246	8,079
50,350	50,400	9,259	6,826	9,259	8,091
50,400	50,450	9,271	6,834	9,271	8,104
50,450	50,500	9,284	6,841	9,284	8,116
50,500	50,550	9,296	6,849	9,296	8,129
50,550	50,600	9,309	6,856	9,309	8,141
50,600	50,650	9,321	6,864	9,321	8,154
50,650	50,700	9,334	6,871	9,334	8,166
50,700	50,750	9,346	6,879	9,346	8,179
50,750	50,800	9,359	6,886	9,359	8,191
50,800	50,850	9,371	6,894	9,371	8,204
50,850	50,900	9,384	6,901	9,384	8,216
50,900	50,950	9,396	6,909	9,396	8,229
50,950	51,000	9,409	6,916	9,409	8,241
51,000					
51,000	51,050	9,421	6,924	9,421	8,254
51,050	51,100	9,434	6,931	9,434	8,266
51,100	51,150	9,446	6,939	9,446	8,279
51,150	51,200	9,459	6,946	9,459	8,291
51,200	51,250	9,471	6,954	9,471	8,304
51,250	51,300	9,484	6,961	9,484	8,316
51,300	51,350	9,496	6,969	9,496	8,329
51,350	51,400	9,509	6,976	9,509	8,341
51,400	51,450	9,521	6,984	9,521	8,354
51,450	51,500	9,534	6,991	9,534	8,366
51,500	51,550	9,546	6,999	9,546	8,379
51,550	51,600	9,559	7,006	9,559	8,391
51,600	51,650	9,571	7,014	9,571	8,404
51,650	51,700	9,584	7,021	9,584	8,416
51,700	51,750	9,596	7,029	9,596	8,429
51,750	51,800	9,609	7,036	9,609	8,441
51,800	51,850	9,621	7,044	9,621	8,454
51,850	51,900	9,634	7,051	9,634	8,466
51,900	51,950	9,646	7,059	9,646	8,479
51,950	52,000	9,659	7,066	9,659	8,491
52,000					
52,000	52,050	9,671	7,074	9,671	8,504
52,050	52,100	9,684	7,081	9,684	8,516
52,100	52,150	9,696	7,089	9,696	8,529
52,150	52,200	9,709	7,096	9,709	8,541
52,200	52,250	9,721	7,104	9,721	8,554
52,250	52,300	9,734	7,111	9,734	8,566
52,300	52,350	9,746	7,119	9,746	8,579
52,350	52,400	9,759	7,126	9,759	8,591
52,400	52,450	9,771	7,134	9,771	8,604
52,450	52,500	9,784	7,141	9,784	8,616
52,500	52,550	9,796	7,149	9,796	8,629
52,550	52,600	9,809	7,156	9,809	8,641
52,600	52,650	9,821	7,164	9,821	8,654
52,650	52,700	9,834	7,171	9,834	8,666
52,700	52,750	9,846	7,179	9,846	8,679
52,750	52,800	9,859	7,186	9,859	8,691
52,800	52,850	9,871	7,194	9,871	8,704
52,850	52,900	9,884	7,201	9,884	8,716
52,900	52,950	9,896	7,209	9,896	8,729
52,950	53,000	9,909	7,216	9,909	8,741

Middle column group:

At least	But less than	Single	Married filing jointly*	Married filing separately	Head of a household
53,000					
53,000	53,050	9,921	7,224	9,921	8,754
53,050	53,100	9,934	7,231	9,934	8,766
53,100	53,150	9,946	7,239	9,946	8,779
53,150	53,200	9,959	7,246	9,959	8,791
53,200	53,250	9,971	7,254	9,971	8,804
53,250	53,300	9,984	7,261	9,984	8,816
53,300	53,350	9,996	7,269	9,996	8,829
53,350	53,400	10,009	7,276	10,009	8,841
53,400	53,450	10,021	7,284	10,021	8,854
53,450	53,500	10,034	7,291	10,034	8,866
53,500	53,550	10,046	7,299	10,046	8,879
53,550	53,600	10,059	7,306	10,059	8,891
53,600	53,650	10,071	7,314	10,071	8,904
53,650	53,700	10,084	7,321	10,084	8,916
53,700	53,750	10,096	7,329	10,096	8,929
53,750	53,800	10,109	7,336	10,109	8,941
53,800	53,850	10,121	7,344	10,121	8,954
53,850	53,900	10,134	7,351	10,134	8,966
53,900	53,950	10,146	7,359	10,146	8,979
53,950	54,000	10,159	7,366	10,159	8,991
54,000					
54,000	54,050	10,171	7,374	10,171	9,004
54,050	54,100	10,184	7,381	10,184	9,016
54,100	54,150	10,196	7,389	10,196	9,029
54,150	54,200	10,209	7,396	10,209	9,041
54,200	54,250	10,221	7,404	10,221	9,054
54,250	54,300	10,234	7,411	10,234	9,066
54,300	54,350	10,246	7,419	10,246	9,079
54,350	54,400	10,259	7,426	10,259	9,091
54,400	54,450	10,271	7,434	10,271	9,104
54,450	54,500	10,284	7,441	10,284	9,116
54,500	54,550	10,296	7,449	10,296	9,129
54,550	54,600	10,309	7,456	10,309	9,141
54,600	54,650	10,321	7,464	10,321	9,154
54,650	54,700	10,334	7,471	10,334	9,166
54,700	54,750	10,346	7,479	10,346	9,179
54,750	54,800	10,359	7,486	10,359	9,191
54,800	54,850	10,371	7,494	10,371	9,204
54,850	54,900	10,384	7,501	10,384	9,216
54,900	54,950	10,396	7,509	10,396	9,229
54,950	55,000	10,409	7,516	10,409	9,241
55,000					
55,000	55,050	10,421	7,524	10,421	9,254
55,050	55,100	10,434	7,531	10,434	9,266
55,100	55,150	10,446	7,539	10,446	9,279
55,150	55,200	10,459	7,546	10,459	9,291
55,200	55,250	10,471	7,554	10,471	9,304
55,250	55,300	10,484	7,561	10,484	9,316
55,300	55,350	10,496	7,569	10,496	9,329
55,350	55,400	10,509	7,576	10,509	9,341
55,400	55,450	10,521	7,584	10,521	9,354
55,450	55,500	10,534	7,591	10,534	9,366
55,500	55,550	10,546	7,599	10,546	9,379
55,550	55,600	10,559	7,606	10,559	9,391
55,600	55,650	10,571	7,614	10,571	9,404
55,650	55,700	10,584	7,621	10,584	9,416
55,700	55,750	10,596	7,629	10,596	9,429
55,750	55,800	10,609	7,636	10,609	9,441
55,800	55,850	10,621	7,644	10,621	9,454
55,850	55,900	10,634	7,651	10,634	9,466
55,900	55,950	10,646	7,659	10,646	9,479
55,950	56,000	10,659	7,666	10,659	9,491

Right column group:

At least	But less than	Single	Married filing jointly*	Married filing separately	Head of a household
56,000					
56,000	56,050	10,671	7,674	10,671	9,504
56,050	56,100	10,684	7,681	10,684	9,516
56,100	56,150	10,696	7,689	10,696	9,529
56,150	56,200	10,709	7,696	10,709	9,541
56,200	56,250	10,721	7,704	10,721	9,554
56,250	56,300	10,734	7,711	10,734	9,566
56,300	56,350	10,746	7,719	10,746	9,579
56,350	56,400	10,759	7,726	10,759	9,591
56,400	56,450	10,771	7,734	10,771	9,604
56,450	56,500	10,784	7,741	10,784	9,616
56,500	56,550	10,796	7,749	10,796	9,629
56,550	56,600	10,809	7,756	10,809	9,641
56,600	56,650	10,821	7,764	10,821	9,654
56,650	56,700	10,834	7,771	10,834	9,666
56,700	56,750	10,846	7,779	10,846	9,679
56,750	56,800	10,859	7,786	10,859	9,691
56,800	56,850	10,871	7,794	10,871	9,704
56,850	56,900	10,884	7,801	10,884	9,716
56,900	56,950	10,896	7,809	10,896	9,729
56,950	57,000	10,909	7,816	10,909	9,741
57,000					
57,000	57,050	10,921	7,824	10,921	9,754
57,050	57,100	10,934	7,831	10,934	9,766
57,100	57,150	10,946	7,839	10,946	9,779
57,150	57,200	10,959	7,846	10,959	9,791
57,200	57,250	10,971	7,854	10,971	9,804
57,250	57,300	10,984	7,861	10,984	9,816
57,300	57,350	10,996	7,869	10,996	9,829
57,350	57,400	11,009	7,876	11,009	9,841
57,400	57,450	11,021	7,884	11,021	9,854
57,450	57,500	11,034	7,891	11,034	9,866
57,500	57,550	11,046	7,899	11,046	9,879
57,550	57,600	11,059	7,906	11,059	9,891
57,600	57,650	11,071	7,914	11,071	9,904
57,650	57,700	11,084	7,921	11,084	9,916
57,700	57,750	11,096	7,929	11,096	9,929
57,750	57,800	11,109	7,936	11,109	9,941
57,800	57,850	11,121	7,944	11,121	9,954
57,850	57,900	11,134	7,951	11,134	9,966
57,900	57,950	11,146	7,959	11,146	9,979
57,950	58,000	11,159	7,966	11,159	9,991
58,000					
58,000	58,050	11,171	7,974	11,171	10,004
58,050	58,100	11,184	7,981	11,184	10,016
58,100	58,150	11,196	7,989	11,196	10,029
58,150	58,200	11,209	7,996	11,209	10,041
58,200	58,250	11,221	8,004	11,221	10,054
58,250	58,300	11,234	8,011	11,234	10,066
58,300	58,350	11,246	8,019	11,246	10,079
58,350	58,400	11,259	8,026	11,259	10,091
58,400	58,450	11,271	8,034	11,271	10,104
58,450	58,500	11,284	8,041	11,284	10,116
58,500	58,550	11,296	8,049	11,296	10,129
58,550	58,600	11,309	8,056	11,309	10,141
58,600	58,650	11,321	8,064	11,321	10,154
58,650	58,700	11,334	8,071	11,334	10,166
58,700	58,750	11,346	8,079	11,346	10,179
58,750	58,800	11,359	8,086	11,359	10,191
58,800	58,850	11,371	8,094	11,371	10,204
58,850	58,900	11,384	8,101	11,384	10,216
58,900	58,950	11,396	8,109	11,396	10,229
58,950	59,000	11,409	8,116	11,409	10,241

* This column must also be used by a qualifying widow(er).

(Continued on next page)

2005 Tax Table—*Continued*

59,000 / 60,000 / 61,000

If line 43 (taxable income) is— At least	But less than	Single	Married filing jointly *	Married filing separately	Head of a household
59,000					
59,000	59,050	11,421	8,124	11,421	10,254
59,050	59,100	11,434	8,131	11,434	10,266
59,100	59,150	11,446	8,139	11,446	10,279
59,150	59,200	11,459	8,146	11,459	10,291
59,200	59,250	11,471	8,154	11,471	10,304
59,250	59,300	11,484	8,161	11,484	10,316
59,300	59,350	11,496	8,169	11,496	10,329
59,350	59,400	11,509	8,176	11,509	10,341
59,400	59,450	11,521	8,186	11,521	10,354
59,450	59,500	11,534	8,199	11,534	10,366
59,500	59,550	11,546	8,211	11,546	10,379
59,550	59,600	11,559	8,224	11,559	10,391
59,600	59,650	11,571	8,236	11,571	10,404
59,650	59,700	11,584	8,249	11,584	10,416
59,700	59,750	11,596	8,261	11,596	10,429
59,750	59,800	11,609	8,274	11,609	10,441
59,800	59,850	11,621	8,286	11,621	10,454
59,850	59,900	11,634	8,299	11,634	10,466
59,900	59,950	11,646	8,311	11,646	10,479
59,950	60,000	11,659	8,324	11,659	10,491
60,000					
60,000	60,050	11,671	8,336	11,673	10,504
60,050	60,100	11,684	8,349	11,687	10,516
60,100	60,150	11,696	8,361	11,701	10,529
60,150	60,200	11,709	8,374	11,715	10,541
60,200	60,250	11,721	8,386	11,729	10,554
60,250	60,300	11,734	8,399	11,743	10,566
60,300	60,350	11,746	8,411	11,757	10,579
60,350	60,400	11,759	8,424	11,771	10,591
60,400	60,450	11,771	8,436	11,785	10,604
60,450	60,500	11,784	8,449	11,799	10,616
60,500	60,550	11,796	8,461	11,813	10,629
60,550	60,600	11,809	8,474	11,827	10,641
60,600	60,650	11,821	8,486	11,841	10,654
60,650	60,700	11,834	8,499	11,855	10,666
60,700	60,750	11,846	8,511	11,869	10,679
60,750	60,800	11,859	8,524	11,883	10,691
60,800	60,850	11,871	8,536	11,897	10,704
60,850	60,900	11,884	8,549	11,911	10,716
60,900	60,950	11,896	8,561	11,925	10,729
60,950	61,000	11,909	8,574	11,939	10,741
61,000					
61,000	61,050	11,921	8,586	11,953	10,754
61,050	61,100	11,934	8,599	11,967	10,766
61,100	61,150	11,946	8,611	11,981	10,779
61,150	61,200	11,959	8,624	11,995	10,791
61,200	61,250	11,971	8,636	12,009	10,804
61,250	61,300	11,984	8,649	12,023	10,816
61,300	61,350	11,996	8,661	12,037	10,829
61,350	61,400	12,009	8,674	12,051	10,841
61,400	61,450	12,021	8,686	12,065	10,854
61,450	61,500	12,034	8,699	12,079	10,866
61,500	61,550	12,046	8,711	12,093	10,879
61,550	61,600	12,059	8,724	12,107	10,891
61,600	61,650	12,071	8,736	12,121	10,904
61,650	61,700	12,084	8,749	12,135	10,916
61,700	61,750	12,096	8,761	12,149	10,929
61,750	61,800	12,109	8,774	12,163	10,941
61,800	61,850	12,121	8,786	12,177	10,954
61,850	61,900	12,134	8,799	12,191	10,966
61,900	61,950	12,146	8,811	12,205	10,979
61,950	62,000	12,159	8,824	12,219	10,991

62,000 / 63,000 / 64,000

If line 43 (taxable income) is— At least	But less than	Single	Married filing jointly *	Married filing separately	Head of a household
62,000					
62,000	62,050	12,171	8,836	12,233	11,004
62,050	62,100	12,184	8,849	12,247	11,016
62,100	62,150	12,196	8,861	12,261	11,029
62,150	62,200	12,209	8,874	12,275	11,041
62,200	62,250	12,221	8,886	12,289	11,054
62,250	62,300	12,234	8,899	12,303	11,066
62,300	62,350	12,246	8,911	12,317	11,079
62,350	62,400	12,259	8,924	12,331	11,091
62,400	62,450	12,271	8,936	12,345	11,104
62,450	62,500	12,284	8,949	12,359	11,116
62,500	62,550	12,296	8,961	12,373	11,129
62,550	62,600	12,309	8,974	12,387	11,141
62,600	62,650	12,321	8,986	12,401	11,154
62,650	62,700	12,334	8,999	12,415	11,166
62,700	62,750	12,346	9,011	12,429	11,179
62,750	62,800	12,359	9,024	12,443	11,191
62,800	62,850	12,371	9,036	12,457	11,204
62,850	62,900	12,384	9,049	12,471	11,216
62,900	62,950	12,396	9,061	12,485	11,229
62,950	63,000	12,409	9,074	12,499	11,241
63,000					
63,000	63,050	12,421	9,086	12,513	11,254
63,050	63,100	12,434	9,099	12,527	11,266
63,100	63,150	12,446	9,111	12,541	11,279
63,150	63,200	12,459	9,124	12,555	11,291
63,200	63,250	12,471	9,136	12,569	11,304
63,250	63,300	12,484	9,149	12,583	11,316
63,300	63,350	12,496	9,161	12,597	11,329
63,350	63,400	12,509	9,174	12,611	11,341
63,400	63,450	12,521	9,186	12,625	11,354
63,450	63,500	12,534	9,199	12,639	11,366
63,500	63,550	12,546	9,211	12,653	11,379
63,550	63,600	12,559	9,224	12,667	11,391
63,600	63,650	12,571	9,236	12,681	11,404
63,650	63,700	12,584	9,249	12,695	11,416
63,700	63,750	12,596	9,261	12,709	11,429
63,750	63,800	12,609	9,274	12,723	11,441
63,800	63,850	12,621	9,286	12,737	11,454
63,850	63,900	12,634	9,299	12,751	11,466
63,900	63,950	12,646	9,311	12,765	11,479
63,950	64,000	12,659	9,324	12,779	11,491
64,000					
64,000	64,050	12,671	9,336	12,793	11,504
64,050	64,100	12,684	9,349	12,807	11,516
64,100	64,150	12,696	9,361	12,821	11,529
64,150	64,200	12,709	9,374	12,835	11,541
64,200	64,250	12,721	9,386	12,849	11,554
64,250	64,300	12,734	9,399	12,863	11,566
64,300	64,350	12,746	9,411	12,877	11,579
64,350	64,400	12,759	9,424	12,891	11,591
64,400	64,450	12,771	9,436	12,905	11,604
64,450	64,500	12,784	9,449	12,919	11,616
64,500	64,550	12,796	9,461	12,933	11,629
64,550	64,600	12,809	9,474	12,947	11,641
64,600	64,650	12,821	9,486	12,961	11,654
64,650	64,700	12,834	9,499	12,975	11,666
64,700	64,750	12,846	9,511	12,989	11,679
64,750	64,800	12,859	9,524	13,003	11,691
64,800	64,850	12,871	9,536	13,017	11,704
64,850	64,900	12,884	9,549	13,031	11,716
64,900	64,950	12,896	9,561	13,045	11,729
64,950	65,000	12,909	9,574	13,059	11,741

65,000 / 66,000 / 67,000

If line 43 (taxable income) is— At least	But less than	Single	Married filing jointly *	Married filing separately	Head of a household
65,000					
65,000	65,050	12,921	9,586	13,073	11,754
65,050	65,100	12,934	9,599	13,087	11,766
65,100	65,150	12,946	9,611	13,101	11,779
65,150	65,200	12,959	9,624	13,115	11,791
65,200	65,250	12,971	9,636	13,129	11,804
65,250	65,300	12,984	9,649	13,143	11,816
65,300	65,350	12,996	9,661	13,157	11,829
65,350	65,400	13,009	9,674	13,171	11,841
65,400	65,450	13,021	9,686	13,185	11,854
65,450	65,500	13,034	9,699	13,199	11,866
65,500	65,550	13,046	9,711	13,213	11,879
65,550	65,600	13,059	9,724	13,227	11,891
65,600	65,650	13,071	9,736	13,241	11,904
65,650	65,700	13,084	9,749	13,255	11,916
65,700	65,750	13,096	9,761	13,269	11,929
65,750	65,800	13,109	9,774	13,283	11,941
65,800	65,850	13,121	9,786	13,297	11,954
65,850	65,900	13,134	9,799	13,311	11,966
65,900	65,950	13,146	9,811	13,325	11,979
65,950	66,000	13,159	9,824	13,339	11,991
66,000					
66,000	66,050	13,171	9,836	13,353	12,004
66,050	66,100	13,184	9,849	13,367	12,016
66,100	66,150	13,196	9,861	13,381	12,029
66,150	66,200	13,209	9,874	13,395	12,041
66,200	66,250	13,221	9,886	13,409	12,054
66,250	66,300	13,234	9,899	13,423	12,066
66,300	66,350	13,246	9,911	13,437	12,079
66,350	66,400	13,259	9,924	13,451	12,091
66,400	66,450	13,271	9,936	13,465	12,104
66,450	66,500	13,284	9,949	13,479	12,116
66,500	66,550	13,296	9,961	13,493	12,129
66,550	66,600	13,309	9,974	13,507	12,141
66,600	66,650	13,321	9,986	13,521	12,154
66,650	66,700	13,334	9,999	13,535	12,166
66,700	66,750	13,346	10,011	13,549	12,179
66,750	66,800	13,359	10,024	13,563	12,191
66,800	66,850	13,371	10,036	13,577	12,204
66,850	66,900	13,384	10,049	13,591	12,216
66,900	66,950	13,396	10,061	13,605	12,229
66,950	67,000	13,409	10,074	13,619	12,241
67,000					
67,000	67,050	13,421	10,086	13,633	12,254
67,050	67,100	13,434	10,099	13,647	12,266
67,100	67,150	13,446	10,111	13,661	12,279
67,150	67,200	13,459	10,124	13,675	12,291
67,200	67,250	13,471	10,136	13,689	12,304
67,250	67,300	13,484	10,149	13,703	12,316
67,300	67,350	13,496	10,161	13,717	12,329
67,350	67,400	13,509	10,174	13,731	12,341
67,400	67,450	13,521	10,186	13,745	12,354
67,450	67,500	13,534	10,199	13,759	12,366
67,500	67,550	13,546	10,211	13,773	12,379
67,550	67,600	13,559	10,224	13,787	12,391
67,600	67,650	13,571	10,236	13,801	12,404
67,650	67,700	13,584	10,249	13,815	12,416
67,700	67,750	13,596	10,261	13,829	12,429
67,750	67,800	13,609	10,274	13,843	12,441
67,800	67,850	13,621	10,286	13,857	12,454
67,850	67,900	13,634	10,299	13,871	12,466
67,900	67,950	13,646	10,311	13,885	12,479
67,950	68,000	13,659	10,324	13,899	12,491

* This column must also be used by a qualifying widow(er).

(Continued on next page)

2005 Tax Table—_Continued_

Column headers for each section:

At least	But less than	Single	Married filing jointly *	Married filing separately	Head of a household

Your tax is—

68,000

At least	But less than	Single	Married filing jointly	Married filing separately	Head of a household
68,000	68,050	13,671	10,336	13,913	12,504
68,050	68,100	13,684	10,349	13,927	12,516
68,100	68,150	13,696	10,361	13,941	12,529
68,150	68,200	13,709	10,374	13,955	12,541
68,200	68,250	13,721	10,386	13,969	12,554
68,250	68,300	13,734	10,399	13,983	12,566
68,300	68,350	13,746	10,411	13,997	12,579
68,350	68,400	13,759	10,424	14,011	12,591
68,400	68,450	13,771	10,436	14,025	12,604
68,450	68,500	13,784	10,449	14,039	12,616
68,500	68,550	13,796	10,461	14,053	12,629
68,550	68,600	13,809	10,474	14,067	12,641
68,600	68,650	13,821	10,486	14,081	12,654
68,650	68,700	13,834	10,499	14,095	12,666
68,700	68,750	13,846	10,511	14,109	12,679
68,750	68,800	13,859	10,524	14,123	12,691
68,800	68,850	13,871	10,536	14,137	12,704
68,850	68,900	13,884	10,549	14,151	12,716
68,900	68,950	13,896	10,561	14,165	12,729
68,950	69,000	13,909	10,574	14,179	12,741

69,000

At least	But less than	Single	Married filing jointly	Married filing separately	Head of a household
69,000	69,050	13,921	10,586	14,193	12,754
69,050	69,100	13,934	10,599	14,207	12,766
69,100	69,150	13,946	10,611	14,221	12,779
69,150	69,200	13,959	10,624	14,235	12,791
69,200	69,250	13,971	10,636	14,249	12,804
69,250	69,300	13,984	10,649	14,263	12,816
69,300	69,350	13,996	10,661	14,277	12,829
69,350	69,400	14,009	10,674	14,291	12,841
69,400	69,450	14,021	10,686	14,305	12,854
69,450	69,500	14,034	10,699	14,319	12,866
69,500	69,550	14,046	10,711	14,333	12,879
69,550	69,600	14,059	10,724	14,347	12,891
69,600	69,650	14,071	10,736	14,361	12,904
69,650	69,700	14,084	10,749	14,375	12,916
69,700	69,750	14,096	10,761	14,389	12,929
69,750	69,800	14,109	10,774	14,403	12,941
69,800	69,850	14,121	10,786	14,417	12,954
69,850	69,900	14,134	10,799	14,431	12,966
69,900	69,950	14,146	10,811	14,445	12,979
69,950	70,000	14,159	10,824	14,459	12,991

70,000

At least	But less than	Single	Married filing jointly	Married filing separately	Head of a household
70,000	70,050	14,171	10,836	14,473	13,004
70,050	70,100	14,184	10,849	14,487	13,016
70,100	70,150	14,196	10,861	14,501	13,029
70,150	70,200	14,209	10,874	14,515	13,041
70,200	70,250	14,221	10,886	14,529	13,054
70,250	70,300	14,234	10,899	14,543	13,066
70,300	70,350	14,246	10,911	14,557	13,079
70,350	70,400	14,259	10,924	14,571	13,091
70,400	70,450	14,271	10,936	14,585	13,104
70,450	70,500	14,284	10,949	14,599	13,116
70,500	70,550	14,296	10,961	14,613	13,129
70,550	70,600	14,309	10,974	14,627	13,141
70,600	70,650	14,321	10,986	14,641	13,154
70,650	70,700	14,334	10,999	14,655	13,166
70,700	70,750	14,346	11,011	14,669	13,179
70,750	70,800	14,359	11,024	14,683	13,191
70,800	70,850	14,371	11,036	14,697	13,204
70,850	70,900	14,384	11,049	14,711	13,216
70,900	70,950	14,396	11,061	14,725	13,229
70,950	71,000	14,409	11,074	14,739	13,241

71,000

At least	But less than	Single	Married filing jointly	Married filing separately	Head of a household
71,000	71,050	14,421	11,086	14,753	13,254
71,050	71,100	14,434	11,099	14,767	13,266
71,100	71,150	14,446	11,111	14,781	13,279
71,150	71,200	14,459	11,124	14,795	13,291
71,200	71,250	14,471	11,136	14,809	13,304
71,250	71,300	14,484	11,149	14,823	13,316
71,300	71,350	14,496	11,161	14,837	13,329
71,350	71,400	14,509	11,174	14,851	13,341
71,400	71,450	14,521	11,186	14,865	13,354
71,450	71,500	14,534	11,199	14,879	13,366
71,500	71,550	14,546	11,211	14,893	13,379
71,550	71,600	14,559	11,224	14,907	13,391
71,600	71,650	14,571	11,236	14,921	13,404
71,650	71,700	14,584	11,249	14,935	13,416
71,700	71,750	14,596	11,261	14,949	13,429
71,750	71,800	14,609	11,274	14,963	13,441
71,800	71,850	14,621	11,286	14,977	13,454
71,850	71,900	14,634	11,299	14,991	13,466
71,900	71,950	14,646	11,311	15,005	13,479
71,950	72,000	14,660	11,324	15,019	13,491

72,000

At least	But less than	Single	Married filing jointly	Married filing separately	Head of a household
72,000	72,050	14,674	11,336	15,033	13,504
72,050	72,100	14,688	11,349	15,047	13,516
72,100	72,150	14,702	11,361	15,061	13,529
72,150	72,200	14,716	11,374	15,075	13,541
72,200	72,250	14,730	11,386	15,089	13,554
72,250	72,300	14,744	11,399	15,103	13,566
72,300	72,350	14,758	11,411	15,117	13,579
72,350	72,400	14,772	11,424	15,131	13,591
72,400	72,450	14,786	11,436	15,145	13,604
72,450	72,500	14,800	11,449	15,159	13,616
72,500	72,550	14,814	11,461	15,173	13,629
72,550	72,600	14,828	11,474	15,187	13,641
72,600	72,650	14,842	11,486	15,201	13,654
72,650	72,700	14,856	11,499	15,215	13,666
72,700	72,750	14,870	11,511	15,229	13,679
72,750	72,800	14,884	11,524	15,243	13,691
72,800	72,850	14,898	11,536	15,257	13,704
72,850	72,900	14,912	11,549	15,271	13,716
72,900	72,950	14,926	11,561	15,285	13,729
72,950	73,000	14,940	11,574	15,299	13,741

73,000

At least	But less than	Single	Married filing jointly	Married filing separately	Head of a household
73,000	73,050	14,954	11,586	15,313	13,754
73,050	73,100	14,968	11,599	15,327	13,766
73,100	73,150	14,982	11,611	15,341	13,779
73,150	73,200	14,996	11,624	15,355	13,791
73,200	73,250	15,010	11,636	15,369	13,804
73,250	73,300	15,024	11,649	15,383	13,816
73,300	73,350	15,038	11,661	15,397	13,829
73,350	73,400	15,052	11,674	15,411	13,841
73,400	73,450	15,066	11,686	15,425	13,854
73,450	73,500	15,080	11,699	15,439	13,866
73,500	73,550	15,094	11,711	15,453	13,879
73,550	73,600	15,108	11,724	15,467	13,891
73,600	73,650	15,122	11,736	15,481	13,904
73,650	73,700	15,136	11,749	15,495	13,916
73,700	73,750	15,150	11,761	15,509	13,929
73,750	73,800	15,164	11,774	15,523	13,941
73,800	73,850	15,178	11,786	15,537	13,954
73,850	73,900	15,192	11,799	15,551	13,966
73,900	73,950	15,206	11,811	15,565	13,979
73,950	74,000	15,220	11,824	15,579	13,991

74,000

At least	But less than	Single	Married filing jointly	Married filing separately	Head of a household
74,000	74,050	15,234	11,836	15,593	14,004
74,050	74,100	15,248	11,849	15,607	14,016
74,100	74,150	15,262	11,861	15,621	14,029
74,150	74,200	15,276	11,874	15,635	14,041
74,200	74,250	15,290	11,886	15,649	14,054
74,250	74,300	15,304	11,899	15,663	14,066
74,300	74,350	15,318	11,911	15,677	14,079
74,350	74,400	15,332	11,924	15,691	14,091
74,400	74,450	15,346	11,936	15,705	14,104
74,450	74,500	15,360	11,949	15,719	14,116
74,500	74,550	15,374	11,961	15,733	14,129
74,550	74,600	15,388	11,974	15,747	14,141
74,600	74,650	15,402	11,986	15,761	14,154
74,650	74,700	15,416	11,999	15,775	14,166
74,700	74,750	15,430	12,011	15,789	14,179
74,750	74,800	15,444	12,024	15,803	14,191
74,800	74,850	15,458	12,036	15,817	14,204
74,850	74,900	15,472	12,049	15,831	14,216
74,900	74,950	15,486	12,061	15,845	14,229
74,950	75,000	15,500	12,074	15,859	14,241

75,000

At least	But less than	Single	Married filing jointly	Married filing separately	Head of a household
75,000	75,050	15,514	12,086	15,873	14,254
75,050	75,100	15,528	12,099	15,887	14,266
75,100	75,150	15,542	12,111	15,901	14,279
75,150	75,200	15,556	12,124	15,915	14,291
75,200	75,250	15,570	12,136	15,929	14,304
75,250	75,300	15,584	12,149	15,943	14,316
75,300	75,350	15,598	12,161	15,957	14,329
75,350	75,400	15,612	12,174	15,971	14,341
75,400	75,450	15,626	12,186	15,985	14,354
75,450	75,500	15,640	12,199	15,999	14,366
75,500	75,550	15,654	12,211	16,013	14,379
75,550	75,600	15,668	12,224	16,027	14,391
75,600	75,650	15,682	12,236	16,041	14,404
75,650	75,700	15,696	12,249	16,055	14,416
75,700	75,750	15,710	12,261	16,069	14,429
75,750	75,800	15,724	12,274	16,083	14,441
75,800	75,850	15,738	12,286	16,097	14,454
75,850	75,900	15,752	12,299	16,111	14,466
75,900	75,950	15,766	12,311	16,125	14,479
75,950	76,000	15,780	12,324	16,139	14,491

76,000

At least	But less than	Single	Married filing jointly	Married filing separately	Head of a household
76,000	76,050	15,794	12,336	16,153	14,504
76,050	76,100	15,808	12,349	16,167	14,516
76,100	76,150	15,822	12,361	16,181	14,529
76,150	76,200	15,836	12,374	16,195	14,541
76,200	76,250	15,850	12,386	16,209	14,554
76,250	76,300	15,864	12,399	16,223	14,566
76,300	76,350	15,878	12,411	16,237	14,579
76,350	76,400	15,892	12,424	16,251	14,591
76,400	76,450	15,906	12,436	16,265	14,604
76,450	76,500	15,920	12,449	16,279	14,616
76,500	76,550	15,934	12,461	16,293	14,629
76,550	76,600	15,948	12,474	16,307	14,641
76,600	76,650	15,962	12,486	16,321	14,654
76,650	76,700	15,976	12,499	16,335	14,666
76,700	76,750	15,990	12,511	16,349	14,679
76,750	76,800	16,004	12,524	16,363	14,691
76,800	76,850	16,018	12,536	16,377	14,704
76,850	76,900	16,032	12,549	16,391	14,716
76,900	76,950	16,046	12,561	16,405	14,729
76,950	77,000	16,060	12,574	16,419	14,741

* This column must also be used by a qualifying widow(er).

(Continued on next page)

2005 Tax Table—Continued

77,000 / 78,000 / 79,000

If line 43 (taxable income) is— At least	But less than	Single	Married filing jointly *	Married filing separately	Head of a household
77,000					
77,000	77,050	16,074	12,586	16,433	14,754
77,050	77,100	16,088	12,599	16,447	14,766
77,100	77,150	16,102	12,611	16,461	14,779
77,150	77,200	16,116	12,624	16,475	14,791
77,200	77,250	16,130	12,636	16,489	14,804
77,250	77,300	16,144	12,649	16,503	14,816
77,300	77,350	16,158	12,661	16,517	14,829
77,350	77,400	16,172	12,674	16,531	14,841
77,400	77,450	16,186	12,686	16,545	14,854
77,450	77,500	16,200	12,699	16,559	14,866
77,500	77,550	16,214	12,711	16,573	14,879
77,550	77,600	16,228	12,724	16,587	14,891
77,600	77,650	16,242	12,736	16,601	14,904
77,650	77,700	16,256	12,749	16,615	14,916
77,700	77,750	16,270	12,761	16,629	14,929
77,750	77,800	16,284	12,774	16,643	14,941
77,800	77,850	16,298	12,786	16,657	14,954
77,850	77,900	16,312	12,799	16,671	14,966
77,900	77,950	16,326	12,811	16,685	14,979
77,950	78,000	16,340	12,824	16,699	14,991
78,000					
78,000	78,050	16,354	12,836	16,713	15,004
78,050	78,100	16,368	12,849	16,727	15,016
78,100	78,150	16,382	12,861	16,741	15,029
78,150	78,200	16,396	12,874	16,755	15,041
78,200	78,250	16,410	12,886	16,769	15,054
78,250	78,300	16,424	12,899	16,783	15,066
78,300	78,350	16,438	12,911	16,797	15,079
78,350	78,400	16,452	12,924	16,811	15,091
78,400	78,450	16,466	12,936	16,825	15,104
78,450	78,500	16,480	12,949	16,839	15,116
78,500	78,550	16,494	12,961	16,853	15,129
78,550	78,600	16,508	12,974	16,867	15,141
78,600	78,650	16,522	12,986	16,881	15,154
78,650	78,700	16,536	12,999	16,895	15,166
78,700	78,750	16,550	13,011	16,909	15,179
78,750	78,800	16,564	13,024	16,923	15,191
78,800	78,850	16,578	13,036	16,937	15,204
78,850	78,900	16,592	13,049	16,951	15,216
78,900	78,950	16,606	13,061	16,965	15,229
78,950	79,000	16,620	13,074	16,979	15,241
79,000					
79,000	79,050	16,634	13,086	16,993	15,254
79,050	79,100	16,648	13,099	17,007	15,266
79,100	79,150	16,662	13,111	17,021	15,279
79,150	79,200	16,676	13,124	17,035	15,291
79,200	79,250	16,690	13,136	17,049	15,304
79,250	79,300	16,704	13,149	17,063	15,316
79,300	79,350	16,718	13,161	17,077	15,329
79,350	79,400	16,732	13,174	17,091	15,341
79,400	79,450	16,746	13,186	17,105	15,354
79,450	79,500	16,760	13,199	17,119	15,366
79,500	79,550	16,774	13,211	17,133	15,379
79,550	79,600	16,788	13,224	17,147	15,391
79,600	79,650	16,802	13,236	17,161	15,404
79,650	79,700	16,816	13,249	17,175	15,416
79,700	79,750	16,830	13,261	17,189	15,429
79,750	79,800	16,844	13,274	17,203	15,441
79,800	79,850	16,858	13,286	17,217	15,454
79,850	79,900	16,872	13,299	17,231	15,466
79,900	79,950	16,886	13,311	17,245	15,479
79,950	80,000	16,900	13,324	17,259	15,491

80,000 / 81,000 / 82,000

If line 43 (taxable income) is— At least	But less than	Single	Married filing jointly *	Married filing separately	Head of a household
80,000					
80,000	80,050	16,914	13,336	17,273	15,504
80,050	80,100	16,928	13,349	17,287	15,516
80,100	80,150	16,942	13,361	17,301	15,529
80,150	80,200	16,956	13,374	17,315	15,541
80,200	80,250	16,970	13,386	17,329	15,554
80,250	80,300	16,984	13,399	17,343	15,566
80,300	80,350	16,998	13,411	17,357	15,579
80,350	80,400	17,012	13,424	17,371	15,591
80,400	80,450	17,026	13,436	17,385	15,604
80,450	80,500	17,040	13,449	17,399	15,616
80,500	80,550	17,054	13,461	17,413	15,629
80,550	80,600	17,068	13,474	17,427	15,641
80,600	80,650	17,082	13,486	17,441	15,654
80,650	80,700	17,096	13,499	17,455	15,666
80,700	80,750	17,110	13,511	17,469	15,679
80,750	80,800	17,124	13,524	17,483	15,691
80,800	80,850	17,138	13,536	17,497	15,704
80,850	80,900	17,152	13,549	17,511	15,716
80,900	80,950	17,166	13,561	17,525	15,729
80,950	81,000	17,180	13,574	17,539	15,741
81,000					
81,000	81,050	17,194	13,586	17,553	15,754
81,050	81,100	17,208	13,599	17,567	15,766
81,100	81,150	17,222	13,611	17,581	15,779
81,150	81,200	17,236	13,624	17,595	15,791
81,200	81,250	17,250	13,636	17,609	15,804
81,250	81,300	17,264	13,649	17,623	15,816
81,300	81,350	17,278	13,661	17,637	15,829
81,350	81,400	17,292	13,674	17,651	15,841
81,400	81,450	17,306	13,686	17,665	15,854
81,450	81,500	17,320	13,699	17,679	15,866
81,500	81,550	17,334	13,711	17,693	15,879
81,550	81,600	17,348	13,724	17,707	15,891
81,600	81,650	17,362	13,736	17,721	15,904
81,650	81,700	17,376	13,749	17,735	15,916
81,700	81,750	17,390	13,761	17,749	15,929
81,750	81,800	17,404	13,774	17,763	15,941
81,800	81,850	17,418	13,786	17,777	15,954
81,850	81,900	17,432	13,799	17,791	15,966
81,900	81,950	17,446	13,811	17,805	15,979
81,950	82,000	17,460	13,824	17,819	15,991
82,000					
82,000	82,050	17,474	13,836	17,833	16,004
82,050	82,100	17,488	13,849	17,847	16,016
82,100	82,150	17,502	13,861	17,861	16,029
82,150	82,200	17,516	13,874	17,875	16,041
82,200	82,250	17,530	13,886	17,889	16,054
82,250	82,300	17,544	13,899	17,903	16,066
82,300	82,350	17,558	13,911	17,917	16,079
82,350	82,400	17,572	13,924	17,931	16,091
82,400	82,450	17,586	13,936	17,945	16,104
82,450	82,500	17,600	13,949	17,959	16,116
82,500	82,550	17,614	13,961	17,973	16,129
82,550	82,600	17,628	13,974	17,987	16,141
82,600	82,650	17,642	13,986	18,001	16,154
82,650	82,700	17,656	13,999	18,015	16,166
82,700	82,750	17,670	14,011	18,029	16,179
82,750	82,800	17,684	14,024	18,043	16,191
82,800	82,850	17,698	14,036	18,057	16,204
82,850	82,900	17,712	14,049	18,071	16,216
82,900	82,950	17,726	14,061	18,085	16,229
82,950	83,000	17,740	14,074	18,099	16,241

83,000 / 84,000 / 85,000

If line 43 (taxable income) is— At least	But less than	Single	Married filing jointly *	Married filing separately	Head of a household
83,000					
83,000	83,050	17,754	14,086	18,113	16,254
83,050	83,100	17,768	14,099	18,127	16,266
83,100	83,150	17,782	14,111	18,141	16,279
83,150	83,200	17,796	14,124	18,155	16,291
83,200	83,250	17,810	14,136	18,169	16,304
83,250	83,300	17,824	14,149	18,183	16,316
83,300	83,350	17,838	14,161	18,197	16,329
83,350	83,400	17,852	14,174	18,211	16,341
83,400	83,450	17,866	14,186	18,225	16,354
83,450	83,500	17,880	14,199	18,239	16,366
83,500	83,550	17,894	14,211	18,253	16,379
83,550	83,600	17,908	14,224	18,267	16,391
83,600	83,650	17,922	14,236	18,281	16,404
83,650	83,700	17,936	14,249	18,295	16,416
83,700	83,750	17,950	14,261	18,309	16,429
83,750	83,800	17,964	14,274	18,323	16,441
83,800	83,850	17,978	14,286	18,337	16,454
83,850	83,900	17,992	14,299	18,351	16,466
83,900	83,950	18,006	14,311	18,365	16,479
83,950	84,000	18,020	14,324	18,379	16,491
84,000					
84,000	84,050	18,034	14,336	18,393	16,504
84,050	84,100	18,048	14,349	18,407	16,516
84,100	84,150	18,062	14,361	18,421	16,529
84,150	84,200	18,076	14,374	18,435	16,541
84,200	84,250	18,090	14,386	18,449	16,554
84,250	84,300	18,104	14,399	18,463	16,566
84,300	84,350	18,118	14,411	18,477	16,579
84,350	84,400	18,132	14,424	18,491	16,591
84,400	84,450	18,146	14,436	18,505	16,604
84,450	84,500	18,160	14,449	18,519	16,616
84,500	84,550	18,174	14,461	18,533	16,629
84,550	84,600	18,188	14,474	18,547	16,641
84,600	84,650	18,202	14,486	18,561	16,654
84,650	84,700	18,216	14,499	18,575	16,666
84,700	84,750	18,230	14,511	18,589	16,679
84,750	84,800	18,244	14,524	18,603	16,691
84,800	84,850	18,258	14,536	18,617	16,704
84,850	84,900	18,272	14,549	18,631	16,716
84,900	84,950	18,286	14,561	18,645	16,729
84,950	85,000	18,300	14,574	18,659	16,741
85,000					
85,000	85,050	18,314	14,586	18,673	16,754
85,050	85,100	18,328	14,599	18,687	16,766
85,100	85,150	18,342	14,611	18,701	16,779
85,150	85,200	18,356	14,624	18,715	16,791
85,200	85,250	18,370	14,636	18,729	16,804
85,250	85,300	18,384	14,649	18,743	16,816
85,300	85,350	18,398	14,661	18,757	16,829
85,350	85,400	18,412	14,674	18,771	16,841
85,400	85,450	18,426	14,686	18,785	16,854
85,450	85,500	18,440	14,699	18,799	16,866
85,500	85,550	18,454	14,711	18,813	16,879
85,550	85,600	18,468	14,724	18,827	16,891
85,600	85,650	18,482	14,736	18,841	16,904
85,650	85,700	18,496	14,749	18,855	16,916
85,700	85,750	18,510	14,761	18,869	16,929
85,750	85,800	18,524	14,774	18,883	16,941
85,800	85,850	18,538	14,786	18,897	16,954
85,850	85,900	18,552	14,799	18,911	16,966
85,900	85,950	18,566	14,811	18,925	16,979
85,950	86,000	18,580	14,824	18,939	16,991

* This column must also be used by a qualifying widow(er).

(Continued on next page)

2005 Tax Table—*Continued*

If line 43 (taxable income) is— At least	But less than	Single	Married filing jointly *	Married filing separately	Head of a household
86,000					
86,000	86,050	18,594	14,836	18,953	17,004
86,050	86,100	18,608	14,849	18,967	17,016
86,100	86,150	18,622	14,861	18,981	17,029
86,150	86,200	18,636	14,874	18,995	17,041
86,200	86,250	18,650	14,886	19,009	17,054
86,250	86,300	18,664	14,899	19,023	17,066
86,300	86,350	18,678	14,911	19,037	17,079
86,350	86,400	18,692	14,924	19,051	17,091
86,400	86,450	18,706	14,936	19,065	17,104
86,450	86,500	18,720	14,949	19,079	17,116
86,500	86,550	18,734	14,961	19,093	17,129
86,550	86,600	18,748	14,974	19,107	17,141
86,600	86,650	18,762	14,986	19,121	17,154
86,650	86,700	18,776	14,999	19,135	17,166
86,700	86,750	18,790	15,011	19,149	17,179
86,750	86,800	18,804	15,024	19,163	17,191
86,800	86,850	18,818	15,036	19,177	17,204
86,850	86,900	18,832	15,049	19,191	17,216
86,900	86,950	18,846	15,061	19,205	17,229
86,950	87,000	18,860	15,074	19,219	17,241
87,000					
87,000	87,050	18,874	15,086	19,233	17,254
87,050	87,100	18,888	15,099	19,247	17,266
87,100	87,150	18,902	15,111	19,261	17,279
87,150	87,200	18,916	15,124	19,275	17,291
87,200	87,250	18,930	15,136	19,289	17,304
87,250	87,300	18,944	15,149	19,303	17,316
87,300	87,350	18,958	15,161	19,317	17,329
87,350	87,400	18,972	15,174	19,331	17,341
87,400	87,450	18,986	15,186	19,345	17,354
87,450	87,500	19,000	15,199	19,359	17,366
87,500	87,550	19,014	15,211	19,373	17,379
87,550	87,600	19,028	15,224	19,387	17,391
87,600	87,650	19,042	15,236	19,401	17,404
87,650	87,700	19,056	15,249	19,415	17,416
87,700	87,750	19,070	15,261	19,429	17,429
87,750	87,800	19,084	15,274	19,443	17,441
87,800	87,850	19,098	15,286	19,457	17,454
87,850	87,900	19,112	15,299	19,471	17,466
87,900	87,950	19,126	15,311	19,485	17,479
87,950	88,000	19,140	15,324	19,499	17,491
88,000					
88,000	88,050	19,154	15,336	19,513	17,504
88,050	88,100	19,168	15,349	19,527	17,516
88,100	88,150	19,182	15,361	19,541	17,529
88,150	88,200	19,196	15,374	19,555	17,541
88,200	88,250	19,210	15,386	19,569	17,554
88,250	88,300	19,224	15,399	19,583	17,566
88,300	88,350	19,238	15,411	19,597	17,579
88,350	88,400	19,252	15,424	19,611	17,591
88,400	88,450	19,266	15,436	19,625	17,604
88,450	88,500	19,280	15,449	19,639	17,616
88,500	88,550	19,294	15,461	19,653	17,629
88,550	88,600	19,308	15,474	19,667	17,641
88,600	88,650	19,322	15,486	19,681	17,654
88,650	88,700	19,336	15,499	19,695	17,666
88,700	88,750	19,350	15,511	19,709	17,679
88,750	88,800	19,364	15,524	19,723	17,691
88,800	88,850	19,378	15,536	19,737	17,704
88,850	88,900	19,392	15,549	19,751	17,716
88,900	88,950	19,406	15,561	19,765	17,729
88,950	89,000	19,420	15,574	19,779	17,741

If line 43 (taxable income) is— At least	But less than	Single	Married filing jointly *	Married filing separately	Head of a household
89,000					
89,000	89,050	19,434	15,586	19,793	17,754
89,050	89,100	19,448	15,599	19,807	17,766
89,100	89,150	19,462	15,611	19,821	17,779
89,150	89,200	19,476	15,624	19,835	17,791
89,200	89,250	19,490	15,636	19,849	17,804
89,250	89,300	19,504	15,649	19,863	17,816
89,300	89,350	19,518	15,661	19,877	17,829
89,350	89,400	19,532	15,674	19,891	17,841
89,400	89,450	19,546	15,686	19,905	17,854
89,450	89,500	19,560	15,699	19,919	17,866
89,500	89,550	19,574	15,711	19,933	17,879
89,550	89,600	19,588	15,724	19,947	17,891
89,600	89,650	19,602	15,736	19,961	17,904
89,650	89,700	19,616	15,749	19,975	17,916
89,700	89,750	19,630	15,761	19,989	17,929
89,750	89,800	19,644	15,774	20,003	17,941
89,800	89,850	19,658	15,786	20,017	17,954
89,850	89,900	19,672	15,799	20,031	17,966
89,900	89,950	19,686	15,811	20,045	17,979
89,950	90,000	19,700	15,824	20,059	17,991
90,000					
90,000	90,050	19,714	15,836	20,073	18,004
90,050	90,100	19,728	15,849	20,087	18,016
90,100	90,150	19,742	15,861	20,101	18,029
90,150	90,200	19,756	15,874	20,115	18,041
90,200	90,250	19,770	15,886	20,129	18,054
90,250	90,300	19,784	15,899	20,143	18,066
90,300	90,350	19,798	15,911	20,157	18,079
90,350	90,400	19,812	15,924	20,171	18,091
90,400	90,450	19,826	15,936	20,185	18,104
90,450	90,500	19,840	15,949	20,199	18,116
90,500	90,550	19,854	15,961	20,213	18,129
90,550	90,600	19,868	15,974	20,227	18,141
90,600	90,650	19,882	15,986	20,241	18,154
90,650	90,700	19,896	15,999	20,255	18,166
90,700	90,750	19,910	16,011	20,269	18,179
90,750	90,800	19,924	16,024	20,283	18,191
90,800	90,850	19,938	16,036	20,297	18,204
90,850	90,900	19,952	16,049	20,311	18,216
90,900	90,950	19,966	16,061	20,325	18,229
90,950	91,000	19,980	16,074	20,339	18,241
91,000					
91,000	91,050	19,994	16,086	20,353	18,254
91,050	91,100	20,008	16,099	20,367	18,266
91,100	91,150	20,022	16,111	20,381	18,279
91,150	91,200	20,036	16,124	20,395	18,291
91,200	91,250	20,050	16,136	20,409	18,304
91,250	91,300	20,064	16,149	20,423	18,316
91,300	91,350	20,078	16,161	20,437	18,329
91,350	91,400	20,092	16,174	20,451	18,341
91,400	91,450	20,106	16,186	20,466	18,354
91,450	91,500	20,120	16,199	20,483	18,366
91,500	91,550	20,134	16,211	20,499	18,379
91,550	91,600	20,148	16,224	20,516	18,391
91,600	91,650	20,162	16,236	20,532	18,404
91,650	91,700	20,176	16,249	20,549	18,416
91,700	91,750	20,190	16,261	20,565	18,429
91,750	91,800	20,204	16,274	20,582	18,441
91,800	91,850	20,218	16,286	20,598	18,454
91,850	91,900	20,232	16,299	20,615	18,466
91,900	91,950	20,246	16,311	20,631	18,479
91,950	92,000	20,260	16,324	20,648	18,491

If line 43 (taxable income) is— At least	But less than	Single	Married filing jointly *	Married filing separately	Head of a household
92,000					
92,000	92,050	20,274	16,336	20,664	18,504
92,050	92,100	20,288	16,349	20,681	18,516
92,100	92,150	20,302	16,361	20,697	18,529
92,150	92,200	20,316	16,374	20,714	18,541
92,200	92,250	20,330	16,386	20,730	18,554
92,250	92,300	20,344	16,399	20,747	18,566
92,300	92,350	20,358	16,411	20,763	18,579
92,350	92,400	20,372	16,424	20,780	18,591
92,400	92,450	20,386	16,436	20,796	18,604
92,450	92,500	20,400	16,449	20,813	18,616
92,500	92,550	20,414	16,461	20,829	18,629
92,550	92,600	20,428	16,474	20,846	18,641
92,600	92,650	20,442	16,486	20,862	18,654
92,650	92,700	20,456	16,499	20,879	18,666
92,700	92,750	20,470	16,511	20,895	18,679
92,750	92,800	20,484	16,524	20,912	18,691
92,800	92,850	20,498	16,536	20,928	18,704
92,850	92,900	20,512	16,549	20,945	18,716
92,900	92,950	20,526	16,561	20,961	18,729
92,950	93,000	20,540	16,574	20,978	18,741
93,000					
93,000	93,050	20,554	16,586	20,994	18,754
93,050	93,100	20,568	16,599	21,011	18,766
93,100	93,150	20,582	16,611	21,027	18,779
93,150	93,200	20,596	16,624	21,044	18,791
93,200	93,250	20,610	16,636	21,060	18,804
93,250	93,300	20,624	16,649	21,077	18,816
93,300	93,350	20,638	16,661	21,093	18,829
93,350	93,400	20,652	16,674	21,110	18,841
93,400	93,450	20,666	16,686	21,126	18,854
93,450	93,500	20,680	16,699	21,143	18,866
93,500	93,550	20,694	16,711	21,159	18,879
93,550	93,600	20,708	16,724	21,176	18,891
93,600	93,650	20,722	16,736	21,192	18,904
93,650	93,700	20,736	16,749	21,209	18,916
93,700	93,750	20,750	16,761	21,225	18,929
93,750	93,800	20,764	16,774	21,242	18,941
93,800	93,850	20,778	16,786	21,258	18,954
93,850	93,900	20,792	16,799	21,275	18,966
93,900	93,950	20,806	16,811	21,291	18,979
93,950	94,000	20,820	16,824	21,308	18,991
94,000					
94,000	94,050	20,834	16,836	21,324	19,004
94,050	94,100	20,848	16,849	21,341	19,016
94,100	94,150	20,862	16,861	21,357	19,029
94,150	94,200	20,876	16,874	21,374	19,041
94,200	94,250	20,890	16,886	21,390	19,054
94,250	94,300	20,904	16,899	21,407	19,066
94,300	94,350	20,918	16,911	21,423	19,079
94,350	94,400	20,932	16,924	21,440	19,091
94,400	94,450	20,946	16,936	21,456	19,104
94,450	94,500	20,960	16,949	21,473	19,116
94,500	94,550	20,974	16,961	21,489	19,129
94,550	94,600	20,988	16,974	21,506	19,141
94,600	94,650	21,002	16,986	21,522	19,154
94,650	94,700	21,016	16,999	21,539	19,166
94,700	94,750	21,030	17,011	21,555	19,179
94,750	94,800	21,044	17,024	21,572	19,191
94,800	94,850	21,058	17,036	21,588	19,204
94,850	94,900	21,072	17,049	21,605	19,216
94,900	94,950	21,086	17,061	21,621	19,229
94,950	95,000	21,100	17,074	21,638	19,241

* This column must also be used by a qualifying widow(er).

(Continued on next page)

2005 Tax Table—*Continued*

If line 43 (taxable income) is—		And you are—				If line 43 (taxable income) is—		And you are—			
At least	But less than	Single	Married filing jointly *	Married filing separately	Head of a household	At least	But less than	Single	Married filing jointly *	Married filing separately	Head of a household
		Your tax is—						Your tax is—			
95,000						**98,000**					
95,000	95,050	21,114	17,086	21,654	19,254	98,000	98,050	21,954	17,836	22,644	20,004
95,050	95,100	21,128	17,099	21,671	19,266	98,050	98,100	21,968	17,849	22,661	20,016
95,100	95,150	21,142	17,111	21,687	19,279	98,100	98,150	21,982	17,861	22,677	20,029
95,150	95,200	21,156	17,124	21,704	19,291	98,150	98,200	21,996	17,874	22,694	20,041
95,200	95,250	21,170	17,136	21,720	19,304	98,200	98,250	22,010	17,886	22,710	20,054
95,250	95,300	21,184	17,149	21,737	19,316	98,250	98,300	22,024	17,899	22,727	20,066
95,300	95,350	21,198	17,161	21,753	19,329	98,300	98,350	22,038	17,911	22,743	20,079
95,350	95,400	21,212	17,174	21,770	19,341	98,350	98,400	22,052	17,924	22,760	20,091
95,400	95,450	21,226	17,186	21,786	19,354	98,400	98,450	22,066	17,936	22,776	20,104
95,450	95,500	21,240	17,199	21,803	19,366	98,450	98,500	22,080	17,949	22,793	20,116
95,500	95,550	21,254	17,211	21,819	19,379	98,500	98,550	22,094	17,961	22,809	20,129
95,550	95,600	21,268	17,224	21,836	19,391	98,550	98,600	22,108	17,974	22,826	20,141
95,600	95,650	21,282	17,236	21,852	19,404	98,600	98,650	22,122	17,986	22,842	20,154
95,650	95,700	21,296	17,249	21,869	19,416	98,650	98,700	22,136	17,999	22,859	20,166
95,700	95,750	21,310	17,261	21,885	19,429	98,700	98,750	22,150	18,011	22,875	20,179
95,750	95,800	21,324	17,274	21,902	19,441	98,750	98,800	22,164	18,024	22,892	20,191
95,800	95,850	21,338	17,286	21,918	19,454	98,800	98,850	22,178	18,036	22,908	20,204
95,850	95,900	21,352	17,299	21,935	19,466	98,850	98,900	22,192	18,049	22,925	20,216
95,900	95,950	21,366	17,311	21,951	19,479	98,900	98,950	22,206	18,061	22,941	20,229
95,950	96,000	21,380	17,324	21,968	19,491	98,950	99,000	22,220	18,074	22,958	20,241
96,000						**99,000**					
96,000	96,050	21,394	17,336	21,984	19,504	99,000	99,050	22,234	18,086	22,974	20,254
96,050	96,100	21,408	17,349	22,001	19,516	99,050	99,100	22,248	18,099	22,991	20,266
96,100	96,150	21,422	17,361	22,017	19,529	99,100	99,150	22,262	18,111	23,007	20,279
96,150	96,200	21,436	17,374	22,034	19,541	99,150	99,200	22,276	18,124	23,024	20,291
96,200	96,250	21,450	17,386	22,050	19,554	99,200	99,250	22,290	18,136	23,040	20,304
96,250	96,300	21,464	17,399	22,067	19,566	99,250	99,300	22,304	18,149	23,057	20,316
96,300	96,350	21,478	17,411	22,083	19,579	99,300	99,350	22,318	18,161	23,073	20,329
96,350	96,400	21,492	17,424	22,100	19,591	99,350	99,400	22,332	18,174	23,090	20,341
96,400	96,450	21,506	17,436	22,116	19,604	99,400	99,450	22,346	18,186	23,106	20,354
96,450	96,500	21,520	17,449	22,133	19,616	99,450	99,500	22,360	18,199	23,123	20,366
96,500	96,550	21,534	17,461	22,149	19,629	99,500	99,550	22,374	18,211	23,139	20,379
96,550	96,600	21,548	17,474	22,166	19,641	99,550	99,600	22,388	18,224	23,156	20,391
96,600	96,650	21,562	17,486	22,182	19,654	99,600	99,650	22,402	18,236	23,172	20,404
96,650	96,700	21,576	17,499	22,199	19,666	99,650	99,700	22,416	18,249	23,189	20,416
96,700	96,750	21,590	17,511	22,215	19,679	99,700	99,750	22,430	18,261	23,205	20,429
96,750	96,800	21,604	17,524	22,232	19,691	99,750	99,800	22,444	18,274	23,222	20,441
96,800	96,850	21,618	17,536	22,248	19,704	99,800	99,850	22,458	18,286	23,238	20,454
96,850	96,900	21,632	17,549	22,265	19,716	99,850	99,900	22,472	18,299	23,255	20,466
96,900	96,950	21,646	17,561	22,281	19,729	99,900	99,950	22,486	18,311	23,271	20,479
96,950	97,000	21,660	17,574	22,298	19,741	99,950	100,000	22,500	18,324	23,288	20,491
97,000											
97,000	97,050	21,674	17,586	22,314	19,754						
97,050	97,100	21,688	17,599	22,331	19,766						
97,100	97,150	21,702	17,611	22,347	19,779						
97,150	97,200	21,716	17,624	22,364	19,791						
97,200	97,250	21,730	17,636	22,380	19,804						
97,250	97,300	21,744	17,649	22,397	19,816						
97,300	97,350	21,758	17,661	22,413	19,829						
97,350	97,400	21,772	17,674	22,430	19,841						
97,400	97,450	21,786	17,686	22,446	19,854						
97,450	97,500	21,800	17,699	22,463	19,866						
97,500	97,550	21,814	17,711	22,479	19,879						
97,550	97,600	21,828	17,724	22,496	19,891						
97,600	97,650	21,842	17,736	22,512	19,904						
97,650	97,700	21,856	17,749	22,529	19,916						
97,700	97,750	21,870	17,761	22,545	19,929						
97,750	97,800	21,884	17,774	22,562	19,941						
97,800	97,850	21,898	17,786	22,578	19,954						
97,850	97,900	21,912	17,799	22,595	19,966						
97,900	97,950	21,926	17,811	22,611	19,979						
97,950	98,000	21,940	17,824	22,628	19,991						

$100,000 or over — use the Tax Rate Schedules on page A-2

* This column must also be used by a qualifying widow(er).

2005 Optional Sales Tax Tables

When Used. The election to deduct state and local general sales taxes requires that the taxpayer forgo any deduction for state and local income taxes. Whether this is advisable or not depends on a comparison of the amounts involved. In making the choice, however, the outcome could be influenced by the additional sales tax incurred due to any "big ticket" purchases that were made. For example, a taxpayer who chose to deduct state and local income taxes for 2004 might well prefer the sales tax deduction in 2005 if a new family SUV was purchased during the year. To make the sales tax election, the taxpayer must check **box b** on **line 5** of Schedule A to Form 1040.

If the sales tax election is made, the amount of the deduction can be determined by use of the *actual expense method* or the *optional sales tax tables* issued by the IRS. The actual expense method can be used only when the taxpayer has actual receipts to support the deduction claimed. In the absence of receipts, the usual case with most taxpayers, resort to the optional sales tax tables is necessary. Under neither method, however, is the purchase of items used in a taxpayer's trade or business to be considered.

Adjustments Necessary. The optional sales tax tables are based on a number of assumptions that require adjustments to be made. As the starting point for the use of the tables is AGI, nontaxable receipts have not been included. Examples of receipts that should be added include: tax-exempt interest, veterans' benefits, workers' compensation, nontaxable Social Security and other retirement benefits. But do not include any large nontaxable items that are not likely to be spent. For example, a $100,000 inheritance should not be added if it was invested in a certificate of deposit.

The tables represent the sales tax on the average (and recurring) expenditures based on level of income by family size and do not include exceptional purchases. Therefore, add to the table amount any sales taxes on major purchases (such as motor vehicles, aircraft, boats, and home building materials, etc.).

When the optional sales tax tables are utilized, special adjustments may be needed when a taxpayer has lived in more than one taxing jurisdiction (e.g., state, county, city) during the year. The adjustments involve apportionment of taxes based on days involved and are illustrated in the 2005 Instructions for Schedules A & B (Form 1040), pages A-3 to A-5.

Local Sales Taxes. Local sales taxes (i.e., those imposed by counties, cities, transit authorities) may or may not require a separate determination. In those states where they are not imposed (such as Connecticut, Hawaii, Indiana, and others), no further computations are necessary. This is also the case where the local taxes are uniform and are incorporated into the state sales tax table (Virginia). In other situations, another step is necessary to arrive at the optional sales tax table deduction. Depending on where the taxpayer lives, one of two procedures need be used. In one procedure, the local sales tax is arrived at by using the **state table** amount—see the Example 1 worksheet. In the other procedure, special **local tables** issued by the IRS for enumerated state and local jurisdictions are modified (if necessary) and used—see the Example 2 worksheet.

Use Illustrated.

EXAMPLE 1 The Archers file a joint return for 2005 reflecting AGI of $88,000 and claiming three exemptions. They have tax-exempt interest of $3,000, and during the year they incurred sales tax of $1,650 on the purchase of an automobile for their dependent teenage son. They live in Bellaire, Texas, where the general sales tax rates are 6.25% for state and 2% for local. Since the IRS *has not issued* optional local sales tax tables for Texas, use the Worksheet below to arrive at the Archers' general sales tax deduction of $3,057.

Sales Tax Deduction Worksheet
(To be used when *no* IRS Optional Local Sales Tax Table Available)

Adjusted Gross Income (AGI) as listed on line 37 of Form 1040	$88,000
Add nontaxable items	3,000
Table income to be used for purposes of line 1 below	$91,000

1. Use table income to determine table amount—go to state of residence and find applicable range of table income and exemption column* for *state* sales tax ... $ 1,066

2a. Enter local general sales tax rate — 2.0

2b. Enter state general sales tax rate — 6.25

2c. Divide 2a by 2b — 0.32

2d. Multiply line 1 by line 2c for the local sales tax — 341

3. Enter general sales tax on large purchases — 1,650

4. Deduction for general sales tax (add lines 1 + 2d + 3) and report on line 5 of Schedule A of Form 1040 — $ 3,057

* Use total of personal and dependency exemptions as reported in item 6d of Form 1040.

EXAMPLE 2 The Hardys file a joint return for 2005, reporting AGI of $40,000 and claiming four exemptions (two personal and two dependency). They received $30,000 in nontaxable pension benefits. Although the Hardys do not keep sales tax receipts, they can prove that they paid $4,800 in sales tax on the purchase of a new RV in 2005. The Hardys are residents of Georgia and live in a jurisdiction that imposes a 2% local sales tax. Since the IRS *has issued* optional local sales tax tables for Georgia, use the Worksheet below to arrive at the Hardys' general sales tax deduction of $5,686.

Sales Tax Deduction Worksheet
[To be used for Alaska, Arizona, Arkansas (Texarkana), California (Los Angeles County), Colorado, Georgia, Illinois, Louisiana, New York (New York City) and North Carolina]

Adjusted Gross Income (AGI) as listed on line 37 of Form 1040	$40,000
Add nontaxable income	30,000
Table income to be used for purpose of line 1 below	$70,000

1. Use the table income to determine *state* sales tax amount—go to table for state of residence and find applicable income range and exemption column* ... $ 552

2a. Enter local general sales tax rate — 2.0

2b. Enter IRS *local* sales tax table amount (based on 1%) — $167

2c. Multiply line 2b by 2a for the local sales tax — 334

3. Enter general sales tax on large purchases — 4,800

4. Deduction for general sales tax (add lines 1 + 2c + 3) and report on line 5 of Schedule A of Form 1040 — $ 5,686

* Use total of personal and dependency exemptions as reported in item 6d of Form 1040

2005 Optional State Sales Tax Tables

Alabama 4.0000% · Arizona 5.6000% · Arkansas 6.0000% · California¹ 7.2500% · Colorado 2.9000%

Income	Alabama Exemptions 1	2	3	4	5	Over 5	Arizona 1	2	3	4	5	Over 5	Arkansas 1	2	3	4	5	Over 5	California 1	2	3	4	5	Over 5	Colorado 1	2	3	4	5	Over 5
$0–$20,000	195	236	265	288	307	333	183	212	231	245	257	274	297	358	399	432	459	498	195	227	249	265	279	298	93	107	117	124	130	138
20,000–30,000	299	361	404	437	466	506	324	374	407	432	453	482	478	573	638	690	732	793	346	401	438	467	491	524	155	179	194	206	216	229
30,000–40,000	351	423	473	512	545	591	400	462	502	533	559	595	570	683	760	821	871	943	427	495	541	576	605	646	188	216	235	249	261	277
40,000–50,000	396	476	532	575	612	663	468	539	587	623	653	694	650	777	865	933	991	1072	499	578	631	672	706	753	217	249	270	287	300	318
50,000–60,000	436	524	584	632	671	728	530	610	664	705	738	785	721	862	959	1034	1098	1187	565	655	715	761	799	852	243	279	303	321	335	356
60,000–70,000	472	567	632	683	725	786	587	676	735	781	818	869	787	940	1044	1126	1195	1292	627	726	792	843	885	943	267	306	332	352	368	391
70,000–80,000	507	607	676	731	776	841	643	740	804	853	894	950	848	1013	1125	1213	1287	1391	686	794	866	921	967	1031	290	332	360	382	399	423
80,000–90,000	538	645	718	775	823	891	694	799	868	922	965	1026	906	1080	1200	1294	1372	1483	741	858	935	995	1044	1113	312	357	387	409	428	454
90,000–100,000	568	680	757	817	867	939	744	856	930	987	1034	1099	960	1145	1271	1370	1453	1569	794	919	1002	1066	1119	1192	332	380	412	436	456	483
100,000–120,000	608	726	808	872	925	1001	810	932	1013	1074	1125	1196	1032	1229	1364	1470	1559	1684	865	1000	1090	1160	1217	1297	359	411	445	471	492	522
120,000–140,000	662	790	878	947	1005	1086	903	1038	1127	1196	1252	1330	1130	1346	1493	1608	1705	1841	964	1114	1214	1291	1355	1444	397	453	491	519	543	575
140,000–160,000	709	845	939	1012	1074	1161	984	1132	1229	1303	1365	1450	1216	1447	1605	1729	1832	1978	1052	1215	1324	1407	1477	1573	430	491	531	562	587	622
160,000–180,000	756	901	1000	1077	1142	1234	1067	1226	1331	1412	1478	1571	1302	1548	1717	1849	1958	2114	1137	1317	1434	1525	1600	1704	463	529	572	605	632	670
180,000–200,000	799	950	1054	1136	1204	1300	1142	1313	1425	1511	1582	1680	1380	1640	1818	1957	2073	2237	1221	1410	1535	1632	1712	1823	493	563	609	644	673	712
200,000 or more	1010	1198	1326	1426	1510	1628	1530	1755	1905	2019	2113	2244	1769	2097	2321	2496	2643	2849	1637	1887	2053	2181	2287	2435	646	736	795	841	878	929

Connecticut² 6.0000% · District of Columbia² 5.7500% · Florida 6.0000% · Georgia 4.0000% · Hawaii² 4.0000%

Income	Connecticut 1	2	3	4	5	Over 5	D.C. 1	2	3	4	5	Over 5	Florida 1	2	3	4	5	Over 5	Georgia 1	2	3	4	5	Over 5	Hawaii 1	2	3	4	5	Over 5
$0–$20,000	179	202	217	228	238	250	153	175	190	201	210	223	192	226	249	266	281	301	137	156	169	179	187	197	207	250	279	302	321	349
20,000–30,000	317	358	384	404	421	443	273	312	337	357	373	396	335	393	431	462	486	521	230	261	282	298	311	328	333	401	447	483	513	556
30,000–40,000	392	442	475	499	520	548	338	386	417	442	462	489	411	482	529	566	596	639	287	316	341	360	376	397	398	477	532	575	611	661
40,000–50,000	458	516	555	584	607	640	395	451	488	517	540	572	479	561	615	658	693	743	321	364	393	414	432	457	453	544	605	654	694	752
50,000–60,000	519	585	628	661	687	724	448	511	553	585	612	648	541	632	694	742	782	837	359	408	439	464	483	511	503	603	671	725	769	833
60,000–70,000	575	648	696	732	762	803	497	567	614	649	678	719	598	699	767	820	863	924	394	448	482	509	530	560	549	657	731	789	838	906
70,000–80,000	629	709	761	801	833	878	544	621	672	710	742	787	653	763	837	894	941	1008	428	486	523	552	575	607	592	708	788	850	902	976
80,000–90,000	680	766	823	865	900	949	588	671	726	768	802	850	704	822	902	964	1015	1086	460	521	562	592	617	651	632	756	840	907	962	1040
90,000–100,000	729	821	881	927	965	1016	631	720	778	823	860	911	753	880	964	1030	1085	1161	490	555	598	630	657	693	670	801	890	960	1019	1101
100,000–120,000	793	894	960	1009	1050	1106	687	784	848	897	937	992	819	956	1047	1119	1178	1260	540	600	646	681	710	749	720	860	956	1031	1093	1182
120,000–140,000	884	996	1069	1124	1169	1232	766	874	945	999	1044	1105	910	1061	1163	1242	1307	1398	585	662	713	751	783	826	789	941	1045	1127	1195	1292
140,000–160,000	964	1086	1165	1226	1275	1343	836	953	1031	1090	1138	1206	990	1155	1265	1351	1421	1520	634	717	772	813	847	893	849	1012	1124	1212	1285	1388
160,000–180,000	1044	1176	1263	1328	1381	1455	907	1034	1117	1181	1234	1307	1072	1249	1368	1460	1536	1643	682	772	831	875	911	961	909	1083	1202	1296	1374	1484
180,000–200,000	1118	1259	1351	1421	1478	1557	971	1107	1197	1265	1321	1399	1146	1335	1462	1560	1641	1755	727	822	884	931	970	1023	963	1147	1273	1372	1454	1570
200,000 or more	1495	1684	1807	1900	1976	2081	1302	1484	1603	1694	1769	1873	1524	1773	1940	2069	2176	2326	952	1075	1155	1216	1265	1334	1235	1467	1626	1750	1854	2001

Idaho 5.5000% · Illinois 6.2500% · Indiana² 6.0000% · Iowa 5.0000% · Kansas 5.3000%

Income	Idaho 1	2	3	4	5	Over 5	Illinois 1	2	3	4	5	Over 5	Indiana 1	2	3	4	5	Over 5	Iowa 1	2	3	4	5	Over 5	Kansas 1	2	3	4	5	Over 5
$0–$20,000	266	323	363	394	420	458	199	233	256	273	288	308	208	243	266	283	298	318	177	204	223	237	248	264	256	313	352	383	409	446
20,000–30,000	408	494	553	599	638	693	346	403	442	472	497	531	343	398	435	463	487	519	308	355	387	411	431	458	408	495	556	604	644	702
30,000–40,000	479	579	647	701	746	810	424	494	542	578	608	650	413	479	523	556	584	623	378	436	474	504	528	562	485	588	659	716	763	831
40,000–50,000	540	651	727	787	838	909	493	574	629	671	706	755	474	549	599	637	669	713	440	507	551	585	614	653	551	667	748	811	865	941
50,000–60,000	595	716	799	865	919	997	556	648	709	756	795	850	529	612	668	710	745	794	496	572	622	660	692	736	611	738	827	897	956	1040
60,000–70,000	644	774	864	934	993	1077	615	715	783	835	878	938	580	671	731	777	815	869	548	631	687	729	764	813	665	803	899	975	1039	1129
70,000–80,000	691	830	925	1000	1063	1152	671	780	853	910	957	1022	628	726	791	841	882	939	598	689	749	795	833	886	716	864	967	1048	1117	1214
80,000–90,000	734	881	981	1061	1127	1221	723	841	920	980	1031	1101	673	777	846	900	944	1005	645	742	807	857	898	955	763	921	1030	1116	1189	1292
90,000–100,000	775	929	1035	1118	1187	1286	773	899	983	1048	1101	1176	716	826	900	956	1002	1067	689	794	863	916	959	1020	808	975	1090	1181	1257	1366
100,000–120,000	829	992	1105	1193	1267	1372	840	976	1067	1137	1195	1276	773	891	970	1030	1080	1150	749	862	937	994	1042	1107	868	1045	1168	1265	1347	1463
120,000–140,000	903	1079	1200	1295	1375	1488	933	1083	1184	1261	1326	1415	851	981	1067	1133	1188	1264	831	956	1039	1103	1155	1228	949	1142	1276	1381	1470	1596
140,000–160,000	967	1155	1284	1385	1470	1590	1015	1178	1287	1371	1441	1538	920	1059	1152	1223	1282	1364	904	1040	1130	1199	1256	1335	1020	1227	1370	1482	1577	1712
160,000–180,000	1031	1230	1366	1474	1563	1690	1098	1274	1391	1482	1557	1662	989	1138	1237	1313	1376	1464	978	1124	1222	1296	1358	1443	1091	1311	1463	1583	1684	1827
180,000–200,000	1089	1298	1441	1554	1648	1781	1173	1360	1486	1583	1662	1774	1052	1210	1315	1395	1462	1554	1044	1201	1305	1384	1450	1541	1155	1387	1547	1674	1780	1931
200,000 or more	1378	1635	1812	1950	2066	2230	1558	1805	1969	2096	2201	2347	1369	1571	1705	1808	1892	2010	1386	1592	1729	1833	1920	2040	1475	1766	1967	2125	2258	2447

Kentucky² 6.0000% · Louisiana 4.0000% · Maine² 5.0000% · Maryland² 5.0000% · Massachusetts² 5.0000%

Income	Kentucky 1	2	3	4	5	Over 5	Louisiana 1	2	3	4	5	Over 5	Maine 1	2	3	4	5	Over 5	Maryland 1	2	3	4	5	Over 5	Massachusetts 1	2	3	4	5	Over 5
$0–$20,000	202	234	255	271	285	303	141	161	175	185	194	205	129	151	165	177	186	199	158	184	202	215	227	242	145	164	177	187	196	207
20,000–30,000	335	387	421	447	469	499	245	281	304	322	336	356	228	266	291	311	327	350	275	319	349	372	391	418	250	284	306	323	337	356
30,000–40,000	405	466	507	539	564	600	302	345	373	395	413	437	282	328	359	383	403	431	338	392	428	456	479	512	307	348	375	395	412	436
40,000–50,000	465	536	582	618	647	688	351	401	434	459	480	508	329	383	419	447	470	503	394	456	498	530	557	594	357	404	435	459	478	505
50,000–60,000	520	599	650	690	723	768	396	452	490	518	541	573	373	433	474	506	532	568	445	514	561	597	627	670	402	456	490	517	539	569
60,000–70,000	571	656	713	756	792	841	438	500	541	572	598	633	413	480	525	560	589	629	492	568	620	660	693	739	444	503	541	571	595	628
70,000–80,000	619	711	772	819	857	910	478	545	590	624	652	691	452	525	574	612	643	687	537	620	676	719	755	806	485	548	590	622	648	684
80,000–90,000	664	762	827	877	918	975	515	588	636	673	703	744	489	567	620	661	695	742	580	669	729	775	814	868	522	591	636	670	698	737
90,000–100,000	707	811	880	933	976	1037	551	629	680	719	751	796	524	608	664	708	744	794	620	715	779	829	870	927	558	631	679	716	746	787
100,000–120,000	763	876	950	1007	1053	1118	598	683	739	781	816	864	570	662	723	770	809	864	674	777	846	900	944	1006	606	685	737	777	809	854
120,000–140,000	842	965	1046	1108	1159	1230	664	758	820	867	905	959	635	737	805	857	901	961	749	863	939	999	1048	1116	673	760	818	861	897	946
140,000–160,000	911	1043	1131	1198	1253	1329	723	825	892	943	984	1042	693	803	877	934	981	1048	816	939	1022	1086	1139	1214	732	827	889	936	975	1028
160,000–180,000	980	1122	1216	1287	1346	1428	782	892	964	1019	1064	1127	751	870	950	1012	1063	1134	883	1016	1105	1174	1231	1311	791	893	960	1011	1053	1110
180,000–200,000	1043	1193	1293	1369	1431	1518	835	953	1030	1088	1137	1203	805	932	1017	1083	1137	1214	945	1086	1181	1254	1315	1400	845	954	1025	1080	1124	1185
200,000 or more	1361	1555	1682	1779	1859	1970	1109	1264	1365	1443	1506	1594	1078	1247	1359	1447	1519	1619	1259	1444	1568	1664	1743	1855	1121	1264	1357	1428	1486	1567

Michigan² 6.0000% · Minnesota 6.5000% · Mississippi² 7.0000% · Missouri 4.2250% · Nebraska 5.5000%

Income	Michigan 1	2	3	4	5	Over 5	Minnesota 1	2	3	4	5	Over 5	Mississippi 1	2	3	4	5	Over 5	Missouri 1	2	3	4	5	Over 5	Nebraska 1	2	3	4	5	Over 5
$0–$20,000	196	228	250	266	280	299	184	210	228	242	253	269	347	418	466	505	536	581	153	179	196	209	220	236	194	223	242	256	268	285
20,000–30,000	340	395	431	460	483	515	323	369	400	424	443	470	558	669	745	805	855	926	252	293	321	343	360	385	340	390	422	446	466	494
30,000–40,000	417	484	528	563	591	631	398	455	493	522	546	579	666	797	887	958	1017	1101	303	353	386	411	433	462	414	475	515	546	571	606
40,000–50,000	485	562	614	653	686	732	465	531	575	608	636	674	759	908	1010	1090	1156	1251	348	405	442	471	495	529	482	553	599	635	664	705
50,000–60,000	546	633	691	736	773	824	526	600	650	688	719	762	842	1007	1119	1207	1281	1385	389	451	493	525	552	589	540	623	676	716	749	794
60,000–70,000	604	700	763	812	853	909	582	665	719	761	795	843	918	1097	1219	1315	1395	1508	426	494	540	575	604	644	601	689	747	791	827	877
70,000–80,000	659	763	832	885	929	991	636	726	786	831	869	921	990	1182	1313	1416	1502	1623	461	535	584	622	653	696	656	751	814	862	902	957
80,000–90,000	710	822	896	954	1001	1067	687	784	848	897	937	992	1057	1261	1401	1510	1601	1730	494	573	625	665	699	745	710	810	878	929	972	1031
90,000–100,000	759	879	958	1019	1070	1140	736	839	908	960	1003	1063	1121	1336	1483	1599	1695	1831	526	609	664	707	742	791	756	866	938	994	1039	1102
100,000–120,000	825	954	1040	1106	1161	1237	801	913	987	1044	1091	1156	1204	1435	1592	1716	1819	1965	567	657	716	762	800	853	821	940	1019	1079	1128	1196
120,000–140,000	915	1058	1154	1227	1287	1371	891	1016	1098	1161	1213	1285	1319	1570	1742	1877	1989	2148	625	723	788	838	879	937	912	1044	1131	1197	1252	1327
140,000–160,000	996	1151	1254	1333	1399	1490	971	1107	1196	1264	1321	1399	1420	1689	1873	2017	2137	2307	676	781	851	905	949	1011	992	1135	1230	1302	1361	1443
160,000–180,000	1077	1244	1355	1441	1511	1610	1052	1198	1295	1369	1429	1514	1520	1807	2003	2157	2285	2466	726	839	914	971	1019	1085	1073	1227	1329	1407	1471	1560
180,000–200,000	1151	1329	1447	1539	1614	1718	1126	1282	1385	1464	1529	1619	1611	1914	2121	2283	2418	2610	772	891	971	1032	1082	1152	1146	1311	1420	1503	1571	1666
200,000 or more	1528	1762	1917	2037	2135	2273	1504	1710	1846	1950	2036	2155	2065	2447	2708	2913	3083	3324	1005	1157	1258	1336	1400	1490	1521	1739	1882	1991	2081	2206

(Continued)

2005 Optional State Sales Tax Tables (Continued)

Nevada³ 6.5000%

Income At least	But less than	1	2	3	4	5	Over 5
$0	$20,000	213	246	269	286	300	320
20,000	30,000	368	426	464	493	517	550
30,000	40,000	451	521	568	603	633	673
40,000	50,000	525	605	659	700	734	781
50,000	60,000	592	682	742	789	827	880
60,000	70,000	654	753	820	871	912	971
70,000	80,000	713	821	893	949	994	1057
80,000	90,000	768	885	962	1022	1071	1139
90,000	100,000	821	946	1028	1092	1144	1216
100,000	120,000	892	1027	1116	1185	1241	1320
120,000	140,000	990	1139	1238	1314	1376	1463
140,000	160,000	1077	1239	1346	1428	1496	1590
160,000	180,000	1164	1339	1454	1543	1616	1717
180,000	200,000	1244	1430	1553	1647	1725	1833
200,000 or more		1651	1895	2056	2180	2282	2423

New Jersey²,⁴ 6.0000%

Income At least	But less than	1	2	3	4	5	Over 5
$0	$20,000	178	202	217	229	239	253
20,000	30,000	314	356	384	405	422	446
30,000	40,000	388	440	474	500	521	551
40,000	50,000	453	514	554	584	609	643
50,000	60,000	513	582	627	661	689	728
60,000	70,000	569	645	694	732	763	806
70,000	80,000	622	705	759	800	834	881
80,000	90,000	672	761	820	865	901	952
90,000	100,000	720	815	878	926	965	1019
100,000	120,000	784	888	956	1008	1050	1109
120,000	140,000	872	988	1064	1122	1169	1234
140,000	160,000	951	1077	1160	1222	1274	1345
160,000	180,000	1030	1167	1256	1324	1380	1457
180,000	200,000	1103	1249	1344	1417	1476	1559
200,000 or more		1473	1668	1795	1892	1971	2081

New Mexico 5.0000%

Income At least	But less than	1	2	3	4	5	Over 5
$0	$20,000	184	213	231	246	257	274
20,000	30,000	321	369	401	426	446	475
30,000	40,000	393	453	492	522	547	582
40,000	50,000	458	527	572	607	636	676
50,000	60,000	516	594	645	685	717	762
60,000	70,000	571	656	713	756	792	841
70,000	80,000	622	716	777	824	863	917
80,000	90,000	671	771	838	888	930	988
90,000	100,000	717	824	895	950	994	1056
100,000	120,000	779	895	972	1031	1079	1146
120,000	140,000	865	994	1079	1144	1197	1272
140,000	160,000	941	1080	1173	1243	1302	1382
160,000	180,000	1017	1167	1267	1344	1406	1494
180,000	200,000	1087	1247	1354	1435	1502	1595
200,000 or more		1441	1653	1793	1900	1988	2111

New York 4.1034%

Income At least	But less than	1	2	3	4	5	Over 5
$0	$20,000	140	163	177	189	198	211
20,000	30,000	246	284	309	329	345	367
30,000	40,000	302	349	380	404	423	451
40,000	50,000	352	406	442	470	493	525
50,000	60,000	397	459	499	530	556	592
60,000	70,000	439	507	552	586	615	654
70,000	80,000	480	553	602	640	671	714
80,000	90,000	518	597	650	690	723	770
90,000	100,000	554	638	695	738	774	823
100,000	120,000	602	694	755	802	840	894
120,000	140,000	669	771	838	890	933	993
140,000	160,000	728	839	912	969	1015	1080
160,000	180,000	788	907	987	1048	1098	1168
180,000	200,000	842	970	1054	1119	1173	1248
200,000 or more		1119	1288	1400	1486	1557	1655

North Carolina 4.5000%

Income At least	But less than	1	2	3	4	5	Over 5
$0	$20,000	152	179	197	211	222	239
20,000	30,000	262	307	337	361	380	408
30,000	40,000	321	375	412	441	464	497
40,000	50,000	372	435	478	511	538	576
50,000	60,000	419	490	537	574	605	648
60,000	70,000	463	540	593	633	667	714
70,000	80,000	504	589	645	689	726	777
80,000	90,000	543	634	695	742	781	835
90,000	100,000	580	677	742	792	834	892
100,000	120,000	629	734	804	859	904	966
120,000	140,000	698	813	891	951	1001	1070
140,000	160,000	758	884	968	1033	1086	1161
160,000	180,000	819	954	1045	1115	1172	1253
180,000	200,000	875	1018	1115	1189	1251	1337
200,000 or more		1158	1346	1472	1569	1649	1762

North Dakota 5.0000%

Income At least	But less than	1	2	3	4	5	Over 5
$0	$20,000	163	191	210	225	237	254
20,000	30,000	281	328	360	385	406	435
30,000	40,000	345	402	441	471	496	531
40,000	50,000	401	467	511	546	575	616
50,000	60,000	452	526	576	615	647	693
60,000	70,000	499	581	635	678	714	764
70,000	80,000	545	633	692	739	777	831
80,000	90,000	587	682	746	795	837	895
90,000	100,000	628	729	797	850	894	955
100,000	120,000	682	791	864	922	969	1036
120,000	140,000	757	877	958	1022	1074	1148
140,000	160,000	824	954	1042	1110	1167	1246
160,000	180,000	891	1031	1125	1199	1260	1346
180,000	200,000	952	1101	1202	1280	1345	1436
200,000 or more		1266	1460	1590	1692	1777	1896

Ohio 5.7500%

Income At least	But less than	1	2	3	4	5	Over 5
$0	$20,000	204	236	258	274	288	306
20,000	30,000	351	405	441	469	492	524
30,000	40,000	429	495	539	573	600	639
40,000	50,000	497	574	624	663	695	740
50,000	60,000	559	645	702	746	782	832
60,000	70,000	617	711	774	822	862	917
70,000	80,000	672	774	842	895	938	997
80,000	90,000	723	833	906	962	1009	1073
90,000	100,000	772	890	967	1027	1076	1145
100,000	120,000	838	964	1049	1113	1166	1240
120,000	140,000	928	1068	1161	1232	1291	1373
140,000	160,000	1008	1159	1260	1337	1401	1490
160,000	180,000	1088	1251	1360	1443	1512	1607
180,000	200,000	1161	1335	1450	1539	1612	1713
200,000 or more		1531	1759	1910	2026	2122	2254

Oklahoma 4.5000%

Income At least	But less than	1	2	3	4	5	Over 5
$0	$20,000	205	246	274	297	315	342
20,000	30,000	333	398	443	478	508	549
30,000	40,000	399	477	530	571	606	655
40,000	50,000	457	544	604	651	691	747
50,000	60,000	509	605	672	724	767	829
60,000	70,000	556	661	733	790	837	904
70,000	80,000	601	714	791	852	903	975
80,000	90,000	643	763	846	910	964	1041
90,000	100,000	683	810	897	965	1022	1103
100,000	120,000	736	872	965	1038	1099	1186
120,000	140,000	809	957	1058	1138	1205	1299
140,000	160,000	873	1031	1140	1226	1297	1398
160,000	180,000	937	1106	1222	1313	1389	1497
180,000	200,000	995	1174	1296	1392	1473	1586
200,000 or more		1288	1513	1668	1789	1891	2034

Pennsylvania 6.0000%

Income At least	But less than	1	2	3	4	5	Over 5
$0	$20,000	176	201	219	232	242	257
20,000	30,000	307	352	381	404	423	449
30,000	40,000	378	432	468	496	519	551
40,000	50,000	440	503	545	578	604	641
50,000	60,000	497	568	616	652	682	723
60,000	70,000	549	628	681	721	754	800
70,000	80,000	600	686	743	786	822	872
80,000	90,000	647	740	801	848	887	941
90,000	100,000	692	791	857	907	948	1006
100,000	120,000	752	860	931	985	1030	1093
120,000	140,000	836	955	1033	1094	1144	1213
140,000	160,000	909	1039	1124	1190	1244	1319
160,000	180,000	984	1124	1216	1287	1345	1427
180,000	200,000	1052	1201	1299	1375	1437	1524
200,000 or more		1397	1594	1725	1825	1907	2022

Rhode Island² 7.0000%

Income At least	But less than	1	2	3	4	5	Over 5
$0	$20,000	201	230	249	264	276	293
20,000	30,000	352	402	435	460	481	510
30,000	40,000	433	494	534	565	591	626
40,000	50,000	504	575	622	658	687	728
50,000	60,000	570	650	702	743	776	822
60,000	70,000	631	719	777	821	858	909
70,000	80,000	689	785	848	896	936	991
80,000	90,000	744	847	915	967	1010	1069
90,000	100,000	796	906	979	1034	1080	1143
100,000	120,000	865	985	1064	1124	1174	1242
120,000	140,000	962	1095	1182	1249	1304	1380
140,000	160,000	1048	1192	1287	1359	1419	1501
160,000	180,000	1135	1290	1392	1470	1535	1624
180,000	200,000	1213	1379	1488	1572	1640	1735
200,000 or more		1617	1835	1979	2089	2180	2305

South Carolina 5.0000%

Income At least	But less than	1	2	3	4	5	Over 5
$0	$20,000	235	288	324	353	378	412
20,000	30,000	374	456	512	557	595	648
30,000	40,000	445	541	608	660	705	768
40,000	50,000	506	614	689	749	799	870
50,000	60,000	561	680	763	828	883	961
60,000	70,000	611	740	829	900	959	1044
70,000	80,000	658	796	892	968	1032	1122
80,000	90,000	702	849	951	1031	1099	1195
90,000	100,000	744	899	1006	1091	1162	1263
100,000	120,000	798	964	1079	1169	1245	1353
120,000	140,000	874	1054	1179	1277	1360	1477
140,000	160,000	940	1133	1266	1371	1459	1585
160,000	180,000	1006	1211	1353	1465	1559	1692
180,000	200,000	1066	1282	1432	1550	1649	1789
200,000 or more		1366	1637	1824	1972	2096	2272

South Dakota 4.0000%

Income At least	But less than	1	2	3	4	5	Over 5
$0	$20,000	199	240	269	291	310	337
20,000	30,000	320	385	430	466	495	537
30,000	40,000	382	460	513	554	589	639
40,000	50,000	436	523	583	631	670	726
50,000	60,000	484	581	647	699	743	804
60,000	70,000	528	633	705	761	809	876
70,000	80,000	570	682	760	820	871	943
80,000	90,000	608	728	810	875	929	1006
90,000	100,000	645	771	858	927	984	1065
100,000	120,000	693	829	922	995	1056	1142
120,000	140,000	759	907	1009	1088	1155	1249
140,000	160,000	817	976	1085	1170	1241	1342
160,000	180,000	875	1044	1160	1251	1327	1435
180,000	200,000	928	1106	1229	1325	1405	1519
200,000 or more		1190	1415	1570	1691	1792	1935

Tennessee 7.0000%

Income At least	But less than	1	2	3	4	5	Over 5
$0	$20,000	322	386	430	465	494	534
20,000	30,000	525	627	697	752	798	863
30,000	40,000	629	751	835	900	954	1032
40,000	50,000	719	858	953	1027	1089	1177
50,000	60,000	801	955	1059	1142	1210	1307
60,000	70,000	876	1043	1157	1246	1321	1426
70,000	80,000	946	1126	1249	1345	1425	1539
80,000	90,000	1012	1203	1334	1437	1522	1643
90,000	100,000	1074	1277	1416	1524	1614	1742
100,000	120,000	1156	1374	1523	1639	1736	1873
120,000	140,000	1270	1508	1670	1797	1903	2052
140,000	160,000	1369	1625	1799	1935	2049	2209
160,000	180,000	1469	1741	1927	2073	2194	2366
180,000	200,000	1558	1847	2044	2198	2326	2507
200,000 or more		2009	2376	2626	2822	2985	3214

Texas 6.2500%

Income At least	But less than	1	2	3	4	5	Over 5
$0	$20,000	216	250	273	291	305	325
20,000	30,000	377	436	475	505	530	565
30,000	40,000	464	536	584	621	651	693
40,000	50,000	540	624	679	722	757	806
50,000	60,000	610	704	767	815	854	909
60,000	70,000	674	778	847	900	944	1005
70,000	80,000	736	849	924	982	1030	1096
80,000	90,000	794	916	997	1059	1110	1181
90,000	100,000	849	979	1066	1132	1187	1263
100,000	120,000	923	1064	1158	1230	1289	1372
120,000	140,000	1025	1181	1285	1365	1431	1523
140,000	160,000	1115	1285	1398	1485	1556	1656
160,000	180,000	1206	1390	1512	1606	1683	1790
180,000	200,000	1289	1485	1615	1715	1798	1912
200,000 or more		1713	1972	2143	2275	2384	2535

Utah 4.7500%

Income At least	But less than	1	2	3	4	5	Over 5
$0	$20,000	232	282	315	342	365	397
20,000	30,000	371	448	501	543	578	627
30,000	40,000	442	533	595	645	686	744
40,000	50,000	503	606	676	732	778	844
50,000	60,000	558	671	749	810	861	934
60,000	70,000	608	730	815	881	937	1015
70,000	80,000	655	787	877	948	1008	1092
80,000	90,000	699	839	935	1010	1073	1163
90,000	100,000	741	888	989	1069	1136	1230
100,000	120,000	795	953	1061	1146	1218	1319
120,000	140,000	871	1042	1160	1253	1330	1440
140,000	160,000	936	1120	1246	1345	1428	1546
160,000	180,000	1002	1197	1332	1437	1526	1651
180,000	200,000	1061	1268	1409	1521	1614	1746
200,000 or more		1358	1617	1795	1935	2052	2218

Vermont 6.0000%

Income At least	But less than	1	2	3	4	5	Over 5
$0	$20,000	116	130	139	146	152	160
20,000	30,000	216	243	260	273	284	298
30,000	40,000	273	306	327	344	357	376
40,000	50,000	323	363	388	408	424	446
50,000	60,000	370	415	445	467	485	511
60,000	70,000	414	465	498	523	543	571
70,000	80,000	457	513	549	576	599	630
80,000	90,000	497	558	597	627	652	686
90,000	100,000	536	601	644	676	703	739
100,000	120,000	589	660	707	742	771	811
120,000	140,000	662	742	795	835	867	912
140,000	160,000	728	816	874	917	953	1003
160,000	180,000	794	891	954	1001	1040	1094
180,000	200,000	856	959	1027	1079	1121	1179
200,000 or more		1175	1318	1410	1481	1539	1618

Virginia⁵ 5.0000%

Income At least	But less than	1	2	3	4	5	Over 5
$0	$20,000	168	196	214	228	240	256
20,000	30,000	278	323	352	375	394	420
30,000	40,000	336	389	424	451	474	500
40,000	50,000	386	446	487	518	543	579
50,000	60,000	431	498	543	578	606	646
60,000	70,000	473	546	595	633	664	707
70,000	80,000	512	592	644	685	718	765
80,000	90,000	549	634	690	733	769	819
90,000	100,000	585	674	734	780	817	870
100,000	120,000	631	728	792	841	882	939
120,000	140,000	696	802	872	926	970	1032
140,000	160,000	753	867	942	1000	1048	1114
160,000	180,000	810	932	1012	1074	1126	1197
180,000	200,000	862	991	1076	1142	1196	1271
200,000 or more		1124	1290	1399	1483	1552	1649

Washington 6.5000%

Income At least	But less than	1	2	3	4	5	Over 5
$0	$20,000	229	266	291	310	325	347
20,000	30,000	395	458	500	532	559	596
30,000	40,000	484	560	611	650	683	728
40,000	50,000	562	650	709	754	792	844
50,000	60,000	633	732	798	849	891	949
60,000	70,000	698	808	880	936	982	1046
70,000	80,000	761	880	959	1019	1069	1139
80,000	90,000	820	947	1032	1097	1151	1226
90,000	100,000	876	1012	1102	1172	1229	1309
100,000	120,000	950	1097	1195	1270	1331	1419
120,000	140,000	1053	1216	1324	1407	1476	1572
140,000	160,000	1144	1321	1438	1528	1603	1706
160,000	180,000	1236	1426	1552	1650	1730	1842
180,000	200,000	1319	1522	1657	1760	1846	1965
200,000 or more		1744	2009	2186	2322	2434	2590

West Virginia² 6.0000%

Income At least	But less than	1	2	3	4	5	Over 5
$0	$20,000	299	358	399	432	458	496
20,000	30,000	480	574	639	689	731	791
30,000	40,000	573	684	760	820	870	940
40,000	50,000	653	779	865	933	989	1068
50,000	60,000	724	864	959	1034	1096	1183
60,000	70,000	790	941	1045	1126	1193	1288
70,000	80,000	852	1015	1126	1212	1285	1387
80,000	90,000	910	1083	1201	1293	1370	1479
90,000	100,000	964	1147	1272	1369	1450	1565
100,000	120,000	1036	1232	1365	1470	1557	1679
120,000	140,000	1135	1348	1494	1607	1702	1836
140,000	160,000	1222	1450	1606	1728	1829	1973
160,000	180,000	1308	1552	1718	1848	1956	2109
180,000	200,000	1386	1644	1819	1956	2070	2231
200,000 or more		1777	2102	2323	2496	2640	2843

Wisconsin 5.0000%

Income At least	But less than	1	2	3	4	5	Over 5
$0	$20,000	177	203	220	233	244	259
20,000	30,000	308	353	383	406	424	450
30,000	40,000	379	434	470	498	521	552
40,000	50,000	441	505	547	579	606	642
50,000	60,000	498	570	617	653	683	724
60,000	70,000	550	630	682	722	755	800
70,000	80,000	600	687	744	787	823	873
80,000	90,000	647	741	802	849	887	941
90,000	100,000	692	792	857	907	949	1005
100,000	120,000	752	860	931	986	1030	1092
120,000	140,000	835	955	1034	1094	1143	1212
140,000	160,000	909	1039	1124	1190	1243	1318
160,000	180,000	983	1123	1216	1286	1344	1424
180,000	200,000	1051	1200	1299	1374	1436	1521
200,000 or more		1395	1592	1722	1822	1903	2016

Wyoming 4.0000%

Income At least	But less than	1	2	3	4	5	Over 5
$0	$20,000	195	236	264	287	305	332
20,000	30,000	312	377	421	456	485	527
30,000	40,000	372	448	501	542	577	626
40,000	50,000	424	510	569	616	655	711
50,000	60,000	470	565	631	682	725	786
60,000	70,000	513	616	687	742	789	855
70,000	80,000	553	663	739	799	849	920
80,000	90,000	590	707	788	852	905	981
90,000	100,000	625	749	835	902	958	1038
100,000	120,000	671	804	896	967	1028	1113
120,000	140,000	735	880	979	1058	1123	1216
140,000	160,000	791	946	1052	1136	1206	1306
160,000	180,000	847	1012	1125	1215	1289	1395
180,000	200,000	897	1071	1191	1285	1364	1476
200,000 or more		1149	1368	1519	1637	1736	1877

1 The California table includes the 1% uniform local sales tax rate in addition to the 6.25% state sales tax rate.
2 This state does not have a local general sales tax.
3 The Nevada table includes the 2.25% uniform local sales tax rate in addition to the 4.25% state sales tax rate.
4 Residents of Salem County, NJ should deduct only half of the amount in the state table.
5 The state and local general sales taxes are combined in the Virginia table.

2005 Optional Local Sales Tax Tables

Which Optional Local Sales Tax Table Should I Use?

IF you live in the state of...	AND you live in...	THEN use Local Table...
Alaska	Any locality	C
Arizona	Any locality	B
Arkansas	Texarkana	B
California	Los Angeles County	B
Colorado	Aurora, Greeley, Longmont, or City of Pueblo	B
	Arvada, City of Boulder, Fort Collins, Lakewood, Thornton, or Westminster	C
	Boulder County, Pueblo County, or any other locality	A
Georgia	Any locality	B
Illinois	Arlington Heights, Aurora, Bloomington, Champaign, Chicago, Cicero, Decatur, Elgin, Evanston, Joliet, Palatine, Peoria, Schaumburg, Skokie, Springfield, or Waukegan	B
	Any other locality	A
Louisiana	Any locality	C
New York	New York City	B
North Carolina	Any locality	C

2005 Optional Local Sales Tax Tables A, B, and C

(Based on a local sales tax rate of 1 percent)

Income At least	But less than	Local Table A Exemptions 1	2	3	4	5	Over 5	Local Table B Exemptions 1	2	3	4	5	Over 5	Local Table C Exemptions 1	2	3	4	5	Over 5
$0	$20,000	32	37	40	43	45	48	41	48	53	57	60	65	50	60	67	72	77	83
20,000	30,000	54	62	67	71	75	79	66	78	87	93	98	105	80	96	107	115	122	132
30,000	40,000	65	75	81	86	90	96	80	94	104	111	118	126	96	114	127	137	145	157
40,000	50,000	75	86	93	99	103	110	92	108	119	127	134	144	109	130	144	155	165	178
50,000	60,000	84	96	104	111	116	123	102	120	132	142	149	161	121	144	160	172	182	197
60,000	70,000	92	106	115	121	127	135	112	131	145	155	163	175	132	157	174	187	198	214
70,000	80,000	100	115	124	132	138	146	121	142	156	167	176	189	142	169	187	202	214	230
80,000	90,000	107	123	133	141	148	157	129	152	167	179	189	202	151	180	200	215	228	245
90,000	100,000	114	131	142	150	157	167	137	161	177	190	200	215	160	191	211	227	241	260
100,000	120,000	124	141	153	162	170	180	148	174	191	204	216	231	172	205	227	244	258	279
120,000	140,000	137	156	169	179	187	198	163	191	210	225	237	254	189	224	248	267	282	304
140,000	160,000	148	169	183	194	202	214	176	206	226	242	255	273	203	241	266	286	303	327
160,000	180,000	159	182	197	208	218	231	189	221	243	260	274	293	217	257	285	306	324	349
180,000	200,000	170	194	210	222	232	245	201	235	258	276	290	311	230	273	301	324	343	369
200,000 or more		222	253	274	289	302	320	260	304	333	356	374	401	295	348	384	413	436	470

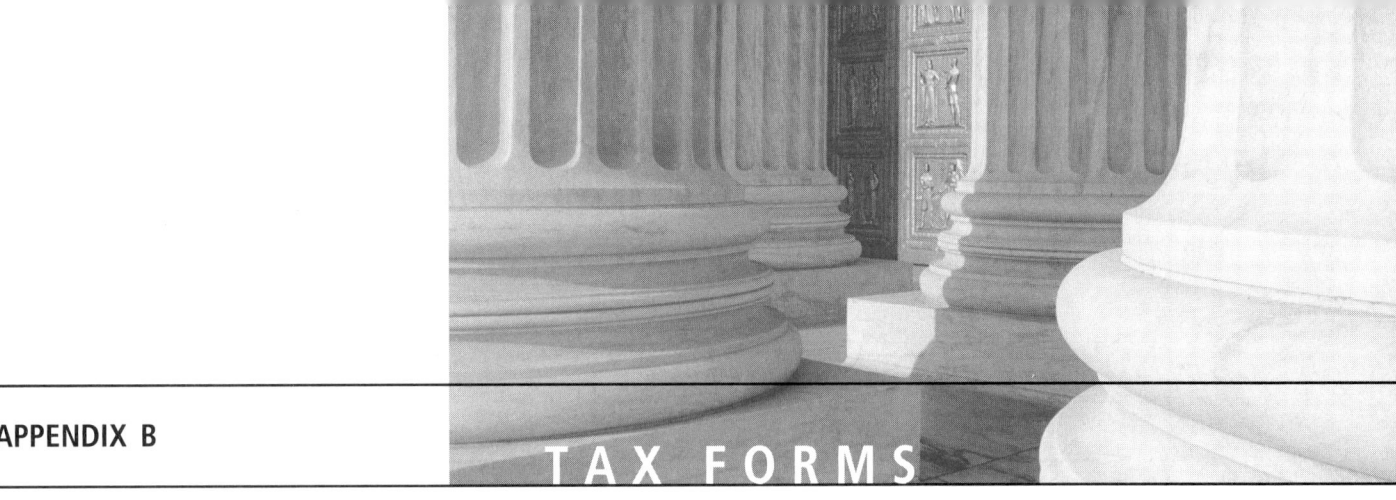

APPENDIX B

(Tax forms can be obtained from the IRS web site: http://www.irs.gov)

Form 1040

Department of the Treasury—Internal Revenue Service

U.S. Individual Income Tax Return 2005 (99) IRS Use Only—Do not write or staple in this space.

For the year Jan. 1–Dec. 31, 2005, or other tax year beginning , 2005, ending , 20   OMB No. 1545-0074

Label (See instructions on page 16.) **Use the IRS label.** Otherwise, please print or type.

Your first name and initial | Last name | Your social security number

If a joint return, spouse's first name and initial | Last name | Spouse's social security number

Home address (number and street). If you have a P.O. box, see page 16. | Apt. no.

▲ You **must** enter your SSN(s) above. ▲

City, town or post office, state, and ZIP code. If you have a foreign address, see page 16.

Checking a box below will not change your tax or refund.

Presidential Election Campaign ▶ Check here if you, or your spouse if filing jointly, want $3 to go to this fund (see page 16) ▶ ☐ You ☐ Spouse

Filing Status — Check only one box.

1 ☐ Single
2 ☐ Married filing jointly (even if only one had income)
3 ☐ Married filing separately. Enter spouse's SSN above and full name here. ▶
4 ☐ Head of household (with qualifying person). (See page 17.) If the qualifying person is a child but not your dependent, enter this child's name here. ▶
5 ☐ Qualifying widow(er) with dependent child (see page 17)

Exemptions

6a ☐ **Yourself.** If someone can claim you as a dependent, **do not** check box 6a
b ☐ **Spouse**
c Dependents:

(1) First name Last name	(2) Dependent's social security number	(3) Dependent's relationship to you	(4)✓ if qualifying child for child tax credit (see page 19)
			☐
			☐
			☐
			☐

If more than four dependents, see page 19.

Boxes checked on 6a and 6b ___
No. of children on 6c who:
• lived with you ___
• did not live with you due to divorce or separation (see page 20) ___
Dependents on 6c not entered above ___
Add numbers on lines above ▶ ☐

d Total number of exemptions claimed

Income

Attach Form(s) W-2 here. Also attach Forms W-2G and 1099-R if tax was withheld.

If you did not get a W-2, see page 22.

Enclose, but do not attach, any payment. Also, please use Form 1040-V.

7 Wages, salaries, tips, etc. Attach Form(s) W-2 | 7
8a **Taxable** interest. Attach Schedule B if required | 8a
b **Tax-exempt** interest. **Do not** include on line 8a | 8b
9a Ordinary dividends. Attach Schedule B if required | 9a
b Qualified dividends (see page 23) | 9b
10 Taxable refunds, credits, or offsets of state and local income taxes (see page 23) | 10
11 Alimony received | 11
12 Business income or (loss). Attach Schedule C or C-EZ | 12
13 Capital gain or (loss). Attach Schedule D if required. If not required, check here ▶ ☐ | 13
14 Other gains or (losses). Attach Form 4797 | 14
15a IRA distributions | 15a | b Taxable amount (see page 25) | 15b
16a Pensions and annuities | 16a | b Taxable amount (see page 25) | 16b
17 Rental real estate, royalties, partnerships, S corporations, trusts, etc. Attach Schedule E | 17
18 Farm income or (loss). Attach Schedule F | 18
19 Unemployment compensation | 19
20a Social security benefits | 20a | b Taxable amount (see page 27) | 20b
21 Other income. List type and amount (see page 29) | 21
22 Add the amounts in the far right column for lines 7 through 21. This is your **total income** ▶ | 22

Adjusted Gross Income

23 Educator expenses (see page 29) | 23
24 Certain business expenses of reservists, performing artists, and fee-basis government officials. Attach Form 2106 or 2106-EZ | 24
25 Health savings account deduction. Attach Form 8889 | 25
26 Moving expenses. Attach Form 3903 | 26
27 One-half of self-employment tax. Attach Schedule SE | 27
28 Self-employed SEP, SIMPLE, and qualified plans | 28
29 Self-employed health insurance deduction (see page 30) | 29
30 Penalty on early withdrawal of savings | 30
31a Alimony paid b Recipient's SSN ▶ | 31a
32 IRA deduction (see page 31) | 32
33 Student loan interest deduction (see page 33) | 33
34 Tuition and fees deduction (see page 34) | 34
35 Domestic production activities deduction. Attach Form 8903 | 35
36 Add lines 23 through 31a and 32 through 35 | 36
37 Subtract line 36 from line 22. This is your **adjusted gross income** ▶ | 37

For Disclosure, Privacy Act, and Paperwork Reduction Act Notice, see page 78.   Cat. No. 11320B   Form **1040** (2005)

Form 1040 (2005)   Page **2**

Tax and Credits	38	Amount from line 37 (adjusted gross income)	38	
	39a	Check if: ☐ **You** were born before January 2, 1941, ☐ Blind. / ☐ **Spouse** was born before January 2, 1941, ☐ Blind. } **Total boxes** checked ▶ 39a		
Standard Deduction for—	b	If your spouse itemizes on a separate return or you were a dual-status alien, see page 35 and check here ▶39b ☐		
	40	**Itemized deductions** (from Schedule A) **or** your **standard deduction** (see left margin) . .	40	
	41	Subtract line 40 from line 38	41	
• People who checked any box on line 39a or 39b **or** who can be claimed as a dependent, see page 36.	42	If line 38 is over $109,475, or you provided housing to a person displaced by Hurricane Katrina, see page 37. Otherwise, multiply $3,200 by the total number of exemptions claimed on line 6d	42	
	43	**Taxable income.** Subtract line 42 from line 41. If line 42 is more than line 41, enter -0-	43	
	44	**Tax** (see page 37). Check if any tax is from: **a** ☐ Form(s) 8814 **b** ☐ Form 4972 . . .	44	
• All others:	45	**Alternative minimum tax** (see page 39). Attach Form 6251	45	
Single or Married filing separately, $5,000	46	Add lines 44 and 45 . . . . ▶	46	

Married filing jointly or Qualifying widow(er), $10,000	47	Foreign tax credit. Attach Form 1116 if required	47		
	48	Credit for child and dependent care expenses. Attach Form 2441	48		
	49	Credit for the elderly or the disabled. Attach Schedule R . .	49		
	50	Education credits. Attach Form 8863	50		
Head of household, $7,300	51	Retirement savings contributions credit. Attach Form 8880 . .	51		
	52	Child tax credit (see page 41). Attach Form 8901 if required .	52		
	53	Adoption credit. Attach Form 8839	53		
	54	Credits from: **a** ☐ Form 8396 **b** ☐ Form 8859 . .	54		
ANTI credit ▶	55	Other credits. Check applicable box(es): **a** ☐ Form 3800 **b** ☐ Form 8801 **c** ☐ Form ____6251____	55		
	56	Add lines 47 through 55. These are your **total credits**	56		
	57	Subtract line 56 from line 46. If line 56 is more than line 46, enter -0- . . . . . ▶	57		

Other Taxes	58	Self-employment tax. Attach Schedule SE	58	
	59	Social security and Medicare tax on tip income not reported to employer. Attach Form 4137 . .	59	
	60	Additional tax on IRAs, other qualified retirement plans, etc. Attach Form 5329 if required .	60	
	61	Advance earned income credit payments from Form(s) W-2	61	
	62	Household employment taxes. Attach Schedule H	62	
	63	Add lines 57 through 62. This is your **total tax** . . . . ▶	63	

Payments	64	Federal income tax withheld from Forms W-2 and 1099 . .	64		
	65	2005 estimated tax payments and amount applied from 2004 return	65		
If you have a qualifying child, attach Schedule EIC.	66a	**Earned income credit (EIC)**	66a		
	b	Nontaxable combat pay election ▶	66b		
	67	Excess social security and tier 1 RRTA tax withheld (see page 59)	67		
	68	Additional child tax credit. Attach Form 8812	68		
	69	Amount paid with request for extension to file (see page 59)	69		
	70	Payments from: **a** ☐ Form 2439 **b** ☐ Form 4136 **c** ☐ Form 8885	70		
	71	Add lines 64, 65, 66a, and 67 through 70. These are your **total payments** . . . . ▶	71		

Refund	72	If line 71 is more than line 63, subtract line 63 from line 71. This is the amount you **overpaid**	72	
Direct deposit? See page 59 and fill in 73b, 73c, and 73d.	73a	Amount of line 72 you want **refunded to you** . . . . ▶	73a	
	▶ b	Routing number		
	▶ d	Account number		
		▶ **c** Type: ☐ Checking ☐ Savings		
	74	Amount of line 72 you want **applied to your 2006 estimated tax** ▶	74	
Amount You Owe	75	**Amount you owe.** Subtract line 71 from line 63. For details on how to pay, see page 60 ▶	75	
	76	Estimated tax penalty (see page 60)	76	

Third Party Designee	Do you want to allow another person to discuss this return with the IRS (see page 61)? ☐ **Yes.** Complete the following. ☐ **No** Designee's name ▶ / Phone no. ▶ ( ) / Personal identification number (PIN) ▶

Sign Here Joint return? See page 17. Keep a copy for your records.	Under penalties of perjury, I declare that I have examined this return and accompanying schedules and statements, and to the best of my knowledge and belief, they are true, correct, and complete. Declaration of preparer (other than taxpayer) is based on all information of which preparer has any knowledge.
	Your signature / Date / Your occupation / Daytime phone number ( )
	Spouse's signature. If a joint return, **both** must sign. / Date / Spouse's occupation

Paid Preparer's Use Only	Preparer's signature ▶ / Date / Check if self-employed ☐ / Preparer's SSN or PTIN
	Firm's name (or yours if self-employed), address, and ZIP code ▶ / EIN / Phone no. ( )

Form **1040** (2005)

SCHEDULES A&B
(Form 1040)

Department of the Treasury
Internal Revenue Service   (99)

Schedule A—Itemized Deductions

(Schedule B is on back)

▶ **Attach to Form 1040.**   ▶ **See Instructions for Schedules A&B (Form 1040).**

OMB No. 1545-0074

20**05**

Attachment
Sequence No. **07**

Name(s) shown on Form 1040

Your social security number

Medical and Dental Expenses		Caution. Do not include expenses reimbursed or paid by others.		
	1	Medical and dental expenses (see page A-2) . . .	**1**	
	2	Enter amount from Form 1040, line 38 **2**		
	3	Multiply line 2 by 7.5% (.075).	**3**	
	4	Subtract line 3 from line 1. If line 3 is more than line 1, enter -0-		**4**
Taxes You Paid (See page A-2.)	5	State and local (check only one box):		
		a ☐ Income taxes, **or**	**5**	
		b ☐ General sales taxes (see page A-3)		
	6	Real estate taxes (see page A-5)	**6**	
	7	Personal property taxes	**7**	
	8	Other taxes. List type and amount ▶ _____		
			8	
	9	Add lines 5 through 8		**9**
Interest You Paid (See page A-5.)	10	Home mortgage interest and points reported to you on Form 1098	**10**	
	11	Home mortgage interest not reported to you on Form 1098. If paid to the person from whom you bought the home, see page A-6 and show that person's name, identifying no., and address ▶		
Note. Personal interest is not deductible.			**11**	
	12	Points not reported to you on Form 1098. See page A-6 for special rules	**12**	
	13	Investment interest. Attach Form 4952 if required. (See page A-6.)	**13**	
	14	Add lines 10 through 13		**14**
Gifts to Charity If you made a gift and got a benefit for it, see page A-7.	15a	Total gifts by cash or check. If you made any gift of $250 or more, see page A-7	**15a**	
	b	Gifts by cash or check after August 27, 2005, that you elect to treat as qualified contributions (see page A-7) **15b**		
	16	Other than by cash or check. If any gift of $250 or more, see page A-7. You **must** attach Form 8283 if over $500	**16**	
	17	Carryover from prior year	**17**	
	18	Add lines 15a, 16, and 17		**18**
Casualty and Theft Losses	19	Casualty or theft loss(es). Attach Form 4684. (See page A-8.)		**19**
Job Expenses and Certain Miscellaneous Deductions (See page A-8.)	20	Unreimbursed employee expenses—job travel, union dues, job education, etc. Attach Form 2106 or 2106-EZ if required. (See page A-8.) ▶ _____	**20**	
	21	Tax preparation fees.	**21**	
	22	Other expenses—investment, safe deposit box, etc. List type and amount ▶ _____		
			22	
	23	Add lines 20 through 22	**23**	
	24	Enter amount from Form 1040, line 38 **24**		
	25	Multiply line 24 by 2% (.02)	**25**	
	26	Subtract line 25 from line 23. If line 25 is more than line 23, enter -0-		**26**
Other Miscellaneous Deductions	27	Other—from list on page A-9. List type and amount ▶ _____		
				27
Total Itemized Deductions	28	Is Form 1040, line 38, over $145,950 (over $72,975 if married filing separately)?		
		☐ **No.** Your deduction is not limited. Add the amounts in the far right column for lines 4 through 27. Also, enter this amount on Form 1040, line 40.	▶	**28**
		☐ **Yes.** Your deduction may be limited. See page A-9 for the amount to enter.		
	29	If you elect to itemize deductions even though they are less than your standard deduction, check here ▶ ☐		

For Paperwork Reduction Act Notice, see Form 1040 instructions.   Cat. No. 11330X   **Schedule A (Form 1040) 2005**

Schedules A&B (Form 1040) 2005   OMB No. 1545-0074   Page **2**

Name(s) shown on Form 1040. Do not enter name and social security number if shown on other side. | Your social security number

Schedule B—Interest and Ordinary Dividends

Attachment Sequence No. **08**

			Amount

Part I
Interest

(See page B-1 and the instructions for Form 1040, line 8a.)

1 List name of payer. If any interest is from a seller-financed mortgage and the buyer used the property as a personal residence, see page B-1 and list this interest first. Also, show that buyer's social security number and address ▶

Note. If you received a Form 1099-INT, Form 1099-OID, or substitute statement from a brokerage firm, list the firm's name as the payer and enter the total interest shown on that form.

| | 1 | |

2 Add the amounts on line 1 . . . . | 2 |

3 Excludable interest on series EE and I U.S. savings bonds issued after 1989. Attach Form 8815 . . . . | 3 |

4 Subtract line 3 from line 2. Enter the result here and on Form 1040, line 8a ▶ | 4 |

Note. If line 4 is over $1,500, you must complete Part III.

			Amount

Part II
Ordinary Dividends

(See page B-1 and the instructions for Form 1040, line 9a.)

5 List name of payer ▶

Note. If you received a Form 1099-DIV or substitute statement from a brokerage firm, list the firm's name as the payer and enter the ordinary dividends shown on that form.

| | 5 | |

6 Add the amounts on line 5. Enter the total here and on Form 1040, line 9a . ▶ | 6 |

Note. If line 6 is over $1,500, you must complete Part III.

Part III
Foreign Accounts and Trusts

(See page B-2.)

You must complete this part if you **(a)** had over $1,500 of taxable interest or ordinary dividends; or **(b)** had a foreign account; or **(c)** received a distribution from, or were a grantor of, or a transferor to, a foreign trust. | Yes | No

7a At any time during 2005, did you have an interest in or a signature or other authority over a financial account in a foreign country, such as a bank account, securities account, or other financial account? See page B-2 for exceptions and filing requirements for Form TD F 90-22.1. . . . .

b If "Yes," enter the name of the foreign country ▶

8 During 2005, did you receive a distribution from, or were you the grantor of, or transferor to, a foreign trust? If "Yes," you may have to file Form 3520. See page B-2 . . . .

For Paperwork Reduction Act Notice, see Form 1040 instructions.   Schedule B (Form 1040) 2005

SCHEDULE C
(Form 1040)

Department of the Treasury
Internal Revenue Service   (99)

Profit or Loss From Business

(Sole Proprietorship)

▶ Partnerships, joint ventures, etc., must file Form 1065 or 1065-B.

▶ **Attach to Form 1040 or 1041.**   ▶ **See Instructions for Schedule C (Form 1040).**

OMB No. 1545-0074

2005

Attachment
Sequence No. **09**

Name of proprietor   Social security number (SSN)

A Principal business or profession, including product or service (see page C-2 of the instructions)	B Enter code from pages C-8, 9, & 10 ▶
C Business name. If no separate business name, leave blank.	D Employer ID number (EIN), if any

E Business address (including suite or room no.) ▶ --
     City, town or post office, state, and ZIP code

F Accounting method: **(1)** ☐ Cash   **(2)** ☐ Accrual   **(3)** ☐ Other (specify) ▶ ----------------------------

G Did you "materially participate" in the operation of this business during 2005? If "No," see page C-3 for limit on losses   ☐ Yes ☐ No

H If you started or acquired this business during 2005, check here   .   .   .   .   ▶ ☐

Part I Income

1	Gross receipts or sales. **Caution.** If this income was reported to you on Form W-2 and the "Statutory employee" box on that form was checked, see page C-3 and check here . . . . . . ▶ ☐	1
2	Returns and allowances	2
3	Subtract line 2 from line 1	3
4	Cost of goods sold (from line 42 on page 2)	4
5	**Gross profit.** Subtract line 4 from line 3	5
6	Other income, including Federal and state gasoline or fuel tax credit or refund (see page C-3) . . .	6
7	**Gross income.** Add lines 5 and 6 . . . . ▶	7

Part II Expenses. Enter expenses for business use of your home **only** on line 30.

8	Advertising	8	18	Office expense . . .	18
9	Car and truck expenses (see page C-3)	9	19	Pension and profit-sharing plans	19
10	Commissions and fees . .	10	20	Rent or lease (see page C-5):	
11	Contract labor (see page C-4)	11	a	Vehicles, machinery, and equipment .	20a
12	Depletion	12	b	Other business property. . .	20b
13	Depreciation and section 179 expense deduction (not included in Part III) (see page C-4)	13	21	Repairs and maintenance . .	21
			22	Supplies (not included in Part III) .	22
			23	Taxes and licenses	23
			24	Travel, meals, and entertainment:	
			a	Travel	24a
14	Employee benefit programs (other than on line 19). .	14	b	Deductible meals and entertainment (see page C-5)	24b
15	Insurance (other than health) .	15	25	Utilities	25
16	Interest:		26	Wages (less employment credits) .	26
a	Mortgage (paid to banks, etc.) .	16a	27	Other expenses (from line 48 on page 2)	27
b	Other	16b			
17	Legal and professional services	17			

28	**Total expenses** before expenses for business use of home. Add lines 8 through 27 in columns . . ▶	28
29	Tentative profit (loss). Subtract line 28 from line 7	29
30	Expenses for business use of your home. Attach **Form 8829**	30
31	**Net profit or (loss).** Subtract line 30 from line 29.	
	● If a profit, enter on **Form 1040, line 12,** and also on **Schedule SE, line 2** (statutory employees, see page C-6). Estates and trusts, enter on Form 1041, line 3.	31
	● If a loss, you **must** go to line 32.	
32	If you have a loss, check the box that describes your investment in this activity (see page C-6).	
	● If you checked 32a, enter the loss on **Form 1040, line 12,** and also on **Schedule SE, line 2** (statutory employees, see page C-6). Estates and trusts, enter on Form 1041, line 3.	32a ☐ All investment is at risk.
	● If you checked 32b, you **must** attach **Form 6198.** Your loss may be limited.	32b ☐ Some investment is not at risk.

For Paperwork Reduction Act Notice, see page C-7 of the instructions.   Cat. No. 11334P   Schedule C (Form 1040) 2005

Schedule C (Form 1040) 2005   Page **2**

Part III   **Cost of Goods Sold** (see page C-6)

| 33 | Method(s) used to value closing inventory: | **a** ☐ Cost | **b** ☐ Lower of cost or market | **c** ☐ Other (attach explanation) |

34   Was there any change in determining quantities, costs, or valuations between opening and closing inventory? If "Yes," attach explanation . . . .   ☐ **Yes**   ☐ **No**

35	Inventory at beginning of year. If different from last year's closing inventory, attach explanation . .	**35**	
36	Purchases less cost of items withdrawn for personal use	**36**	
37	Cost of labor. Do not include any amounts paid to yourself	**37**	
38	Materials and supplies	**38**	
39	Other costs	**39**	
40	Add lines 35 through 39	**40**	
41	Inventory at end of year	**41**	
42	**Cost of goods sold.** Subtract line 41 from line 40. Enter the result here and on page 1, line 4 . .	**42**	

Part IV   **Information on Your Vehicle.** Complete this part **only** if you are claiming car or truck expenses on line 9 and are not required to file Form 4562 for this business. See the instructions for line 13 on page C-4 to find out if you must file Form 4562.

43   When did you place your vehicle in service for business purposes? (month, day, year) ▶ ..../.........../...... .

44   Of the total number of miles you drove your vehicle during 2005, enter the number of miles you used your vehicle for:

a Business .... **b** Commuting (see instructions) .... **c** Other ....

45   Do you (or your spouse) have another vehicle available for personal use?. . . . .   ☐ **Yes**   ☐ **No**

46   Was your vehicle available for personal use during off-duty hours?   . . . .   ☐ **Yes**   ☐ **No**

47a Do you have evidence to support your deduction?   . . . .   ☐ **Yes**   ☐ **No**

 b If "Yes," is the evidence written? . . . .   ☐ **Yes**   ☐ **No**

Part V   **Other Expenses.** List below business expenses not included on lines 8–26 or line 30.

--		
--		
--		
--		
--		
--		
--		
--		
48 **Total other expenses.** Enter here and on page 1, line 27	**48**	

Schedule C (Form 1040) 2005

SCHEDULE D (Form 1040)	Capital Gains and Losses	OMB No. 1545-0074

SCHEDULE D (Form 1040)

Department of the Treasury
Internal Revenue Service   (99)

Capital Gains and Losses

▶ Attach to Form 1040.   ▶ See Instructions for Schedule D (Form 1040).

▶ Use Schedule D-1 to list additional transactions for lines 1 and 8.

OMB No. 1545-0074

2005

Attachment Sequence No. **12**

Name(s) shown on Form 1040

Your social security number

Part I Short-Term Capital Gains and Losses—Assets Held One Year or Less

(a) Description of property (Example: 100 sh. XYZ Co.)	**(b)** Date acquired (Mo., day, yr.)	**(c)** Date sold (Mo., day, yr.)	**(d)** Sales price (see page D-6 of the instructions)	**(e)** Cost or other basis (see page D-6 of the instructions)	**(f)** Gain or (loss) Subtract (e) from (d)
1					

2 Enter your short-term totals, if any, from Schedule D-1, line 2 . . . . **2**

3 **Total short-term sales price amounts.** Add lines 1 and 2 in column (d) **3**

4 Short-term gain from Form 6252 and short-term gain or (loss) from Forms 4684, 6781, and 8824 **4**

5 Net short-term gain or (loss) from partnerships, S corporations, estates, and trusts from Schedule(s) K-1 . . . . **5**

6 Short-term capital loss carryover. Enter the amount, if any, from line 8 of your **Capital Loss Carryover Worksheet** on page D-6 of the instructions . . . . **6** (   )

7 **Net short-term capital gain or (loss).** Combine lines 1 through 6 in column (f) **7**

Part II Long-Term Capital Gains and Losses—Assets Held More Than One Year

(a) Description of property (Example: 100 sh. XYZ Co.)	**(b)** Date acquired (Mo., day, yr.)	**(c)** Date sold (Mo., day, yr.)	**(d)** Sales price (see page D-6 of the instructions)	**(e)** Cost or other basis (see page D-6 of the instructions)	**(f)** Gain or (loss) Subtract (e) from (d)
8					

9 Enter your long-term totals, if any, from Schedule D-1, line 9 . . . . **9**

10 **Total long-term sales price amounts.** Add lines 8 and 9 in column (d) **10**

11 Gain from Form 4797, Part I; long-term gain from Forms 2439 and 6252; and long-term gain or (loss) from Forms 4684, 6781, and 8824 . . . . **11**

12 Net long-term gain or (loss) from partnerships, S corporations, estates, and trusts from Schedule(s) K-1 . . . . **12**

13 Capital gain distributions. See page D-1 of the instructions **13**

14 Long-term capital loss carryover. Enter the amount, if any, from line 13 of your **Capital Loss Carryover Worksheet** on page D-6 of the instructions . . . . **14** (   )

15 **Net long-term capital gain or (loss).** Combine lines 8 through 14 in column (f). Then go to Part III on the back **15**

For Paperwork Reduction Act Notice, see Form 1040 instructions.   Cat. No. 11338H   **Schedule D (Form 1040) 2005**

Part III   **Summary**

16 Combine lines 7 and 15 and enter the result. If line 16 is a loss, skip lines 17 through 20, and go to line 21. If a gain, enter the gain on Form 1040, line 13, and then go to line 17 below . . | **16** |

17 Are lines 15 and 16 **both** gains?
☐ **Yes.** Go to line 18.
☐ **No.** Skip lines 18 through 21, and go to line 22.

18 Enter the amount, if any, from line 7 of the **28% Rate Gain Worksheet** on page D-7 of the instructions . . . . ▶ | **18** |

19 Enter the amount, if any, from line 18 of the **Unrecaptured Section 1250 Gain Worksheet** on page D-8 of the instructions . . . . ▶ | **19** |

20 Are lines 18 and 19 **both** zero or blank?
☐ **Yes.** Complete Form 1040 through line 43, and then complete the **Qualified Dividends and Capital Gain Tax Worksheet** on page 38 of the Instructions for Form 1040. **Do not** complete lines 21 and 22 below.

☐ **No.** Complete Form 1040 through line 43, and then complete the **Schedule D Tax Worksheet** on page D-9 of the instructions. **Do not** complete lines 21 and 22 below.

21 If line 16 is a loss, enter here and on Form 1040, line 13, the **smaller** of:

- The loss on line 16 or
- ($3,000), or if married filing separately, ($1,500)   } . . . . | **21** | (|) |

Note. When figuring which amount is smaller, treat both amounts as positive numbers.

22 Do you have qualified dividends on Form 1040, line 9b?
☐ **Yes.** Complete Form 1040 through line 43, and then complete the **Qualified Dividends and Capital Gain Tax Worksheet** on page 38 of the Instructions for Form 1040.
☐ **No.** Complete the rest of Form 1040.

SCHEDULE E (Form 1040)	Supplemental Income and Loss	OMB No. 1545-0074
Department of the Treasury Internal Revenue Service (99)	(From rental real estate, royalties, partnerships, S corporations, estates, trusts, REMICs, etc.) ► **Attach to Form 1040 or Form 1041.** ► **See Instructions for Schedule E (Form 1040).**	20**05** Attachment Sequence No. **13**

Name(s) shown on return — Your social security number

Part I   Income or Loss From Rental Real Estate and Royalties   Note. If you are in the business of renting personal property, use **Schedule C** or **C-EZ** (see page E-3). Report farm rental income or loss from **Form 4835** on page 2, line 40.

1 List the type and location of each **rental real estate property:**

A ....

B ....

C ....

2 For each rental real estate property listed on line 1, did you or your family use it during the tax year for personal purposes for more than the greater of:
- 14 days **or**
- 10% of the total days rented at fair rental value?
(See page E-3.)

	Yes	No
A		
B		
C		

Income:		Properties			Totals (Add columns A, B, and C.)	
		A	B	C		
3 Rents received	**3**				**3**	
4 Royalties received	**4**				**4**	
Expenses:						
5 Advertising	**5**					
6 Auto and travel (see page E-4)	**6**					
7 Cleaning and maintenance	**7**					
8 Commissions	**8**					
9 Insurance	**9**					
10 Legal and other professional fees	**10**					
11 Management fees	**11**					
12 Mortgage interest paid to banks, etc. (see page E-4)	**12**				**12**	
13 Other interest	**13**					
14 Repairs	**14**					
15 Supplies	**15**					
16 Taxes	**16**					
17 Utilities	**17**					
18 Other (list) ►	**18**					
19 Add lines 5 through 18	**19**				**19**	
20 Depreciation expense or depletion (see page E-4)	**20**				**20**	
21 Total expenses. Add lines 19 and 20	**21**					
22 Income or (loss) from rental real estate or royalty properties. Subtract line 21 from line 3 (rents) or line 4 (royalties). If the result is a (loss), see page E-5 to find out if you must file **Form 6198**	**22**					
23 Deductible rental real estate loss. **Caution.** Your rental real estate loss on line 22 may be limited. See page E-5 to find out if you must file **Form 8582.** Real estate professionals must complete line 43 on page 2	**23**	( )	( )	( )		

24	**Income.** Add positive amounts shown on line 22. **Do not** include any losses	**24**	
25	**Losses.** Add royalty losses from line 22 and rental real estate losses from line 23. Enter total losses here	**25**	( )
26	**Total rental real estate and royalty income or (loss).** Combine lines 24 and 25. Enter the result here. If Parts II, III, IV, and line 40 on page 2 do not apply to you, also enter this amount on Form 1040, line 17. Otherwise, include this amount in the total on line 41 on page 2	**26**	

For Paperwork Reduction Act Notice, see page E-7 of the instructions.   Cat. No. 11344L   **Schedule E (Form 1040) 2005**

Schedule E (Form 1040) 2005 — Attachment Sequence No. **13** — Page **2**

Name(s) shown on return. Do not enter name and social security number if shown on other side.

Your social security number

Caution. The IRS compares amounts reported on your tax return with amounts shown on Schedule(s) K-1.

Part II **Income or Loss From Partnerships and S Corporations** **Note.** If you report a loss from an at-risk activity for which **any** amount is **not** at risk, you **must** check the box in column **(e)** on line 28 and attach **Form 6198.** See page E-1.

27 Are you reporting any loss not allowed in a prior year due to the at-risk or basis limitations, a prior year unallowed loss from a passive activity (if that loss was not reported on Form 8582), or unreimbursed partnership expenses? ☐ **Yes** ☐ **No**
If you answered "Yes," see page E-6 before completing this section.

28	(a) Name	(b) Enter P for partnership; S for S corporation	(c) Check if foreign partnership	(d) Employer identification number	(e) Check if any amount is not at risk
A			☐		☐
B			☐		☐
C			☐		☐
D			☐		☐

	Passive Income and Loss		Nonpassive Income and Loss		
	(f) Passive loss allowed (attach **Form 8582** if required)	(g) Passive income from **Schedule K-1**	(h) Nonpassive loss from **Schedule K-1**	(i) Section 179 expense deduction from **Form 4562**	(j) Nonpassive income from **Schedule K-1**
A					
B					
C					
D					
29a Totals					
b Totals					

30 Add columns (g) and (j) of line 29a **30**
31 Add columns (f), (h), and (i) of line 29b . . . . **31** (   )
32 **Total partnership and S corporation income or (loss).** Combine lines 30 and 31. Enter the result here and include in the total on line 41 below **32**

Part III **Income or Loss From Estates and Trusts**

33	(a) Name	(b) Employer identification number
A		
B		

	Passive Income and Loss		Nonpassive Income and Loss	
	(c) Passive deduction or loss allowed (attach **Form 8582** if required)	(d) Passive income from **Schedule K-1**	(e) Deduction or loss from **Schedule K-1**	(f) Other income from **Schedule K-1**
A				
B				
34a Totals				
b Totals				

35 Add columns (d) and (f) of line 34a **35**
36 Add columns (c) and (e) of line 34b . . . . **36** (   )
37 **Total estate and trust income or (loss).** Combine lines 35 and 36. Enter the result here and include in the total on line 41 below **37**

Part IV **Income or Loss From Real Estate Mortgage Investment Conduits (REMICs) — Residual Holder**

38	(a) Name	(b) Employer identification number	(c) Excess inclusion from **Schedules Q,** line 2c (see page E-6)	(d) Taxable income (net loss) from **Schedules Q,** line 1b	(e) Income from **Schedules Q,** line 3b

39 Combine columns (d) and (e) only. Enter the result here and include in the total on line 41 below **39**

Part V **Summary**

40 Net farm rental income or (loss) from **Form 4835.** Also, complete line 42 below **40**
41 **Total income or (loss).** Combine lines 26, 32, 37, 39, and 40. Enter the result here and on Form 1040, line 17 ▶ **41**

42 **Reconciliation of farming and fishing income.** Enter your **gross** farming and fishing income reported on Form 4835, line 7; Schedule K-1 (Form 1065), box 14, code B; Schedule K-1 (Form 1120S), box 17, code N; and Schedule K-1 (Form 1041), line 14, code F (see page E-7) **42**

43 **Reconciliation for real estate professionals.** If you were a real estate professional (see page E-1), enter the net income or (loss) you reported anywhere on Form 1040 from all rental real estate activities in which you materially participated under the passive activity loss rules **43**

Schedule E (Form 1040) 2005

SCHEDULE SE (Form 1040) Department of the Treasury Internal Revenue Service (99)	**Self-Employment Tax** ▶ **Attach to Form 1040.** ▶ **See Instructions for Schedule SE (Form 1040).**	OMB No. 1545-0074 2005 Attachment Sequence No. **17**

Name of person with **self-employment** income (as shown on Form 1040)	Social security number of person with **self-employment** income ▶

Who Must File Schedule SE

You must file Schedule SE if:

- You had net earnings from self-employment from **other than** church employee income (line 4 of Short Schedule SE or line 4c of Long Schedule SE) of $400 or more, **or**

- You had church employee income of $108.28 or more. Income from services you performed as a minister or a member of a religious order **is not** church employee income (see page SE-1).

Note. Even if you had a loss or a small amount of income from self-employment, it may be to your benefit to file Schedule SE and use either "optional method" in Part II of Long Schedule SE (see page SE-3).

Exception. If your only self-employment income was from earnings as a minister, member of a religious order, or Christian Science practitioner **and** you filed Form 4361 and received IRS approval not to be taxed on those earnings, **do not** file Schedule SE. Instead, write "Exempt–Form 4361" on Form 1040, line 58.

May I Use Short Schedule SE or Must I Use Long Schedule SE?

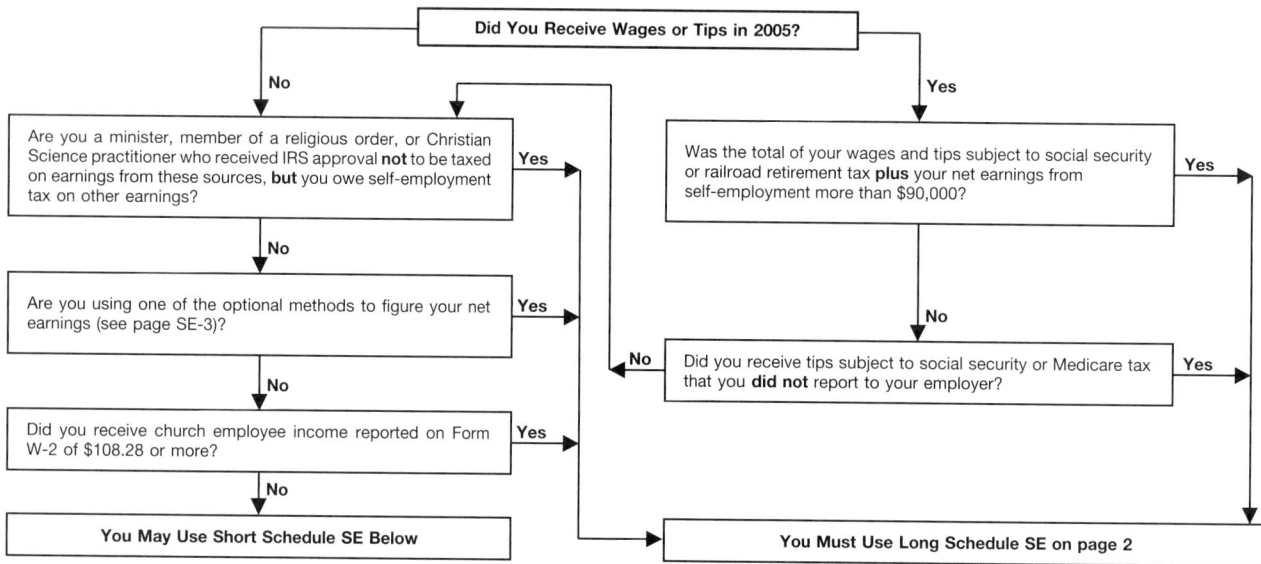

Section A—Short Schedule SE. Caution. Read above to see if you can use Short Schedule SE.

1	Net farm profit or (loss) from Schedule F, line 36, and farm partnerships, Schedule K-1 (Form 1065), box 14, code A	**1**	
2	Net profit or (loss) from Schedule C, line 31; Schedule C-EZ, line 3; Schedule K-1 (Form 1065), box 14, code A (other than farming); and Schedule K-1 (Form 1065-B), box 9. Ministers and members of religious orders, see page SE-1 for amounts to report on this line. See page SE-2 for other income to report	**2**	
3	Combine lines 1 and 2	**3**	
4	**Net earnings from self-employment.** Multiply line 3 by 92.35% (.9235). If less than $400, **do not** file this schedule; you do not owe self-employment tax . . . . ▶	**4**	
5	**Self-employment tax.** If the amount on line 4 is: • $90,000 or less, multiply line 4 by 15.3% (.153). Enter the result here and on **Form 1040, line 58.** • More than $90,000, multiply line 4 by 2.9% (.029). Then, add $11,160.00 to the result. Enter the total here and on **Form 1040, line 58.**	**5**	
6	**Deduction for one-half of self-employment tax.** Multiply line 5 by 50% (.5). Enter the result here and on **Form 1040, line 27**	**6**	

For Paperwork Reduction Act Notice, see Form 1040 instructions.   Cat. No. 11358Z   **Schedule SE (Form 1040) 2005**

Schedule SE (Form 1040) 2005   Attachment Sequence No. **17**   Page **2**

Name of person with **self-employment** income (as shown on Form 1040)	Social security number of person with **self-employment** income ▶	

Section B—Long Schedule SE

Part I Self-Employment Tax

Note. If your only income subject to self-employment tax is **church employee income,** skip lines 1 through 4b. Enter -0- on line 4c and go to line 5a. Income from services you performed as a minister or a member of a religious order **is not** church employee income. See page SE-1.

A If you are a minister, member of a religious order, or Christian Science practitioner **and** you filed Form 4361, but you had $400 or more of **other** net earnings from self-employment, check here and continue with Part I . . . . . . ▶ ☐

1	Net farm profit or (loss) from Schedule F, line 36, and farm partnerships, Schedule K-1 (Form 1065), box 14, code A. **Note.** Skip this line if you use the farm optional method (see page SE-4)	**1**		
2	Net profit or (loss) from Schedule C, line 31; Schedule C-EZ, line 3; Schedule K-1 (Form 1065), box 14, code A (other than farming); and Schedule K-1 (Form 1065-B), box 9. Ministers and members of religious orders, see page SE-1 for amounts to report on this line. See page SE-2 for other income to report. **Note.** Skip this line if you use the nonfarm optional method (see page SE-4)	**2**		
3	Combine lines 1 and 2	**3**		
4a	If line 3 is more than zero, multiply line 3 by 92.35% (.9235). Otherwise, enter amount from line 3	**4a**		
b	If you elect one or both of the optional methods, enter the total of lines 15 and 17 here . . .	**4b**		
c	Combine lines 4a and 4b. If less than $400, **stop;** you do not owe self-employment tax. **Exception.** If less than $400 and you had **church employee income,** enter -0- and continue. . . . . . ▶	**4c**		
5a	Enter your **church employee income** from Form W-2. See page SE-1 for definition of church employee income **5a**			
b	Multiply line 5a by 92.35% (.9235). If less than $100, enter -0-	**5b**		
6	**Net earnings from self-employment.** Add lines 4c and 5b	**6**		
7	Maximum amount of combined wages and self-employment earnings subject to social security tax or the 6.2% portion of the 7.65% railroad retirement (tier 1) tax for 2005	**7**	90,000	00
8a	Total social security wages and tips (total of boxes 3 and 7 on Form(s) W-2) and railroad retirement (tier 1) compensation. If $90,000 or more, skip lines 8b through 10, and go to line 11 . . . . **8a**			
b	Unreported tips subject to social security tax (from Form 4137, line 9) **8b**			
c	Add lines 8a and 8b	**8c**		
9	Subtract line 8c from line 7. If zero or less, enter -0- here and on line 10 and go to line 11 . ▶	**9**		
10	Multiply the **smaller** of line 6 or line 9 by 12.4% (.124)	**10**		
11	Multiply line 6 by 2.9% (.029)	**11**		
12	**Self-employment tax.** Add lines 10 and 11. Enter here and on **Form 1040, line 58**	**12**		
13	**Deduction for one-half of self-employment tax.** Multiply line 12 by 50% (.5). Enter the result here and on **Form 1040, line 27** **13**			

Part II Optional Methods To Figure Net Earnings (see page SE-3)

Farm Optional Method. You may use this method **only** if **(a)** your gross farm income[1] was not more than $2,400 **or (b)** your net farm profits[2] were less than $1,733.

14	Maximum income for optional methods	**14**	1,600	00
15	Enter the **smaller** of: two-thirds (⅔) of gross farm income[1] (not less than zero) or $1,600. Also include this amount on line 4b above	**15**		

Nonfarm Optional Method. You may use this method **only** if **(a)** your net nonfarm profits[3] were less than $1,733 and also less than 72.189% of your gross nonfarm income[4] **and (b)** you had net earnings from self-employment of at least $400 in 2 of the prior 3 years.

Caution. You may use this method no more than five times.

16	Subtract line 15 from line 14	**16**		
17	Enter the **smaller** of: two-thirds (⅔) of gross nonfarm income[4] (not less than zero) or the amount on line 16. Also include this amount on line 4b above	**17**		

[1] From Sch. F, line 11, and Sch. K-1 (Form 1065), box 14, code B.

[2] From Sch. F, line 36, and Sch. K-1 (Form 1065), box 14, code A.

[3] From Sch. C, line 31; Sch. C-EZ, line 3; Sch. K-1 (Form 1065), box 14, code A; and Sch. K-1 (Form 1065-B), box 9.

[4] From Sch. C, line 7; Sch. C-EZ, line 1; Sch. K-1 (Form 1065), box 14, code C; and Sch. K-1 (Form 1065-B), box 9.

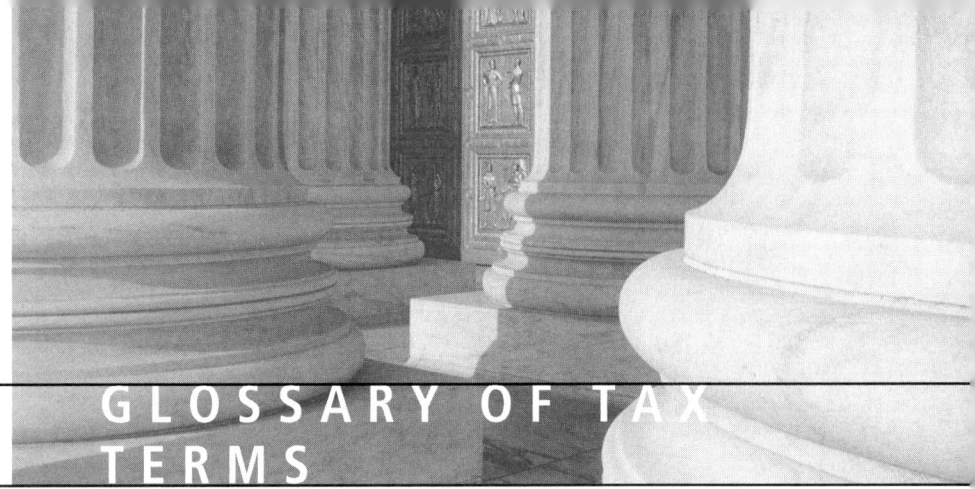

GLOSSARY OF TAX TERMS

The words and phrases in this glossary have been defined to reflect their conventional use in the field of taxation. The definitions may therefore be incomplete for other purposes.

A

Abandoned spouse. The abandoned spouse provision enables a married taxpayer with a dependent child whose spouse did not live in the taxpayer's home during the last six months of the tax year to file as a head of household rather than as married filing separately.

Accelerated cost recovery system (ACRS). A method in which the cost of tangible property is recovered over a prescribed period of time. Enacted by the Economic Recovery Tax Act (ERTA) of 1981 and substantially modified by the Tax Reform Act (TRA) of 1986 (the modified system is referred to as MACRS), the approach disregards salvage value, imposes a period of cost recovery that depends upon the classification of the asset into one of various recovery periods, and prescribes the applicable percentage of cost that can be deducted each year. § 168.

Accelerated death benefits. The amount received from a life insurance policy by the insured who is terminally ill or chronically ill. Any realized gain may be excluded from the gross income of the insured if the policy is surrendered to the insurer or is sold to a licensed viatical settlement provider. § 101(g).

Accelerated depreciation. Various methods of depreciation that yield larger deductions in the earlier years of the life of an asset than the straight-line method. Examples include the double declining-balance and the sum-of-the-years' digits methods of depreciation. § 167.

Accident and health benefits. Employee fringe benefits provided by employers through the payment of health and accident insurance premiums or the establishment of employer-funded medical reimbursement plans. Employers generally are entitled to a deduction for such payments, whereas employees generally exclude the fringe benefits from gross income. §§ 105 and 106.

Accountable plan. An accountable plan is a type of expense reimbursement plan that requires an employee to render an adequate accounting to the employer and return any excess reimbursement or allowance. If the expense qualifies, it will be treated as a deduction *for* AGI.

Accounting income. The accountant's concept of income is generally based upon the realization principle. Financial accounting income may differ from taxable income (e.g., accelerated depreciation might be used for Federal income tax and straight-line depreciation for financial accounting purposes). Differences are included in a reconciliation of taxable and accounting income on Schedule M–1 or Schedule M–3 of Form 1120 for corporations. Seventy-five percent of the excess of adjusted current earnings over alternative minimum taxable income is an adjustment for alternative minimum tax purposes for a corporation. See also *alternative minimum tax* and *economic income.*

Accounting method. The method under which income and expenses are determined for tax purposes. Major accounting methods are the cash basis and the accrual basis. Special methods are available for the reporting of gain on installment sales, recognition of income on construction projects (the completed contract and percentage of completion methods), and the valuation of inventories (last-in, first-out and first-in, first-out). §§ 446–474. See also *accrual method, cash receipts method, completed contract method, percentage of completion method,* etc.

Accounting period. The period of time, usually a year, used by a taxpayer for the determination of tax liability. Unless a fiscal year is chosen, taxpayers must determine and pay their income tax liability by using the calendar year (January 1 through December 31) as the period of measurement. An example of a fiscal year is July 1 through June 30. A change in accounting period (e.g., from a calendar year to a fiscal year) generally requires the consent of the IRS. A new taxpayer, such as a newly formed corporation or an estate created upon the death of an individual taxpayer, is free to select either a calendar or a fiscal year without the consent of the IRS. Limitations exist on the accounting period that may be selected by a partnership, an S corporation, and a personal service corporation. §§ 441–444.

Accrual basis. See *accrual method.*

Accrual method. A method of accounting that reflects expenses incurred and income earned for any one tax year. In contrast to the cash basis of accounting, expenses do not have to be paid to be deductible nor does income have to be received to be taxable. Unearned income (e.g., prepaid interest and rent) generally is taxed in the year of receipt regardless of the method of accounting used by the taxpayer. § 446(c)(2). See also *accounting method, cash receipts method,* and *unearned income.*

Accumulated earnings tax. A special tax imposed on corporations that accumulate (rather than distribute) their earnings beyond the reasonable needs of the business. The tax is imposed on accumulated taxable income and is imposed in addition to the corporate income tax. §§ 531–537.

ACE adjustment. See *adjusted current earnings (ACE) adjustment.*

Acquiescence. In agreement with the result reached. The IRS follows a policy of either acquiescing (*A, Acq.*) or nonacquiescing (*NA, Nonacq.*) in the results reached in certain judicial decisions.

Acquisition indebtedness. Debt incurred in acquiring, constructing, or substantially improving a qualified residence of the taxpayer. The interest on such loans is deductible as *qualified residence interest.* However, interest on such debt is deductible only on the portion of the indebtedness that does not exceed $1,000,000 ($500,000 for married persons filing separate returns). § 163(h)(3). See also *home equity loans.*

ACRS. See *accelerated cost recovery system.*

Active income. Active income includes wages, salary, commissions, bonuses, profits from a trade or business in which the taxpayer is a material participant, gain on the sale or other disposition of assets used in an active trade or business, and income from intangible property if the taxpayer's personal efforts significantly contributed to the creation of the property. The passive activity loss rules require classification of income and losses into three categories with active income being one of them.

Active participation. A term that is relevant for both the at-risk rules and the passive activity loss rules associated with rental real estate activities. For the at-risk rules, the following factors indicate active participation: (1) making decisions involving the operation or management of the activity, (2) performing services for the activity, and (3) hiring and discharging employees. For the passive activity loss rules, the taxpayer must participate in the making of management decisions in a significant and bona fide sense.

Ad valorem tax. A tax imposed on the value of property. The most familiar ad valorem tax is that imposed by states, counties, and cities on real estate. Ad valorem taxes can, however, be imposed upon personal property (e.g., a motor vehicle tax based on the value of an automobile). §§ 164(a)(1) and (2).

Additional depreciation. The excess of the amount of depreciation actually deducted over the amount that would have been deducted had the straight-line method been used. § 1250(b). See also *Section 1250 recapture.*

Adjusted basis. The cost or other basis of property reduced by depreciation (cost recovery) allowed or allowable and increased by capital improvements. See also *basis* and *realized gain or loss.*

Adjusted current earnings (ACE) adjustment. An adjustment in computing corporate alternative minimum taxable income (AMTI), computed at 75 percent of the excess of adjusted current earnings and profits computations over unadjusted AMTI. ACE computations reflect longer and slower cost recovery deductions and other restrictions on the timing of certain recognition events. Exempt interest, life insurance proceeds, and other receipts that are included in earnings and profits but not in taxable income also increase the ACE adjustment. If unadjusted AMTI exceeds adjusted current earnings and profits, the ACE adjustment is negative. The negative adjustment is limited to the aggregate of the positive adjustments under ACE for prior years, reduced by any previously claimed negative adjustments. See also *alternative minimum tax* and *earnings and profits.*

Adjusted gross income (AGI). A determination peculiar to individual taxpayers. Generally, it represents gross income less business expenses, expenses attributable to the production of rent or royalty income, the allowed capital loss deduction, and certain personal expenses (deductions *for* AGI). § 62. See also *gross income.*

Adoption expenses credit. A provision intended to assist taxpayers who incur nonrecurring costs directly associated with the adoption process such as legal costs, social service review costs, and transportation costs. Up to $10,960 ($10,960 for a child with special needs regardless of the actual adoption expenses) of costs incurred to adopt an eligible child qualify for the credit. A taxpayer may claim the credit in the year qualifying expenses are paid or incurred if the expenses are paid during or after the year in which the adoption is finalized. For qualifying expenses paid or incurred in a tax year prior to the year the adoption is finalized, the credit must be claimed in the tax year following the tax year during which the expenses are paid or incurred. § 23.

Advance payments. In general, prepayments for services or goods are includible in gross income upon receipt of the advance payments (for both accrual and cash basis taxpayers). However, Revenue Procedure 2004–34, I.R.B. No. 22, 991, provides guidelines for the deferral of tax on certain advance payments providing specific conditions are met.

AFTR. Published by Research Institute of America (formerly by Prentice-Hall), *American Federal Tax Reports* contains all of the Federal tax decisions issued by the U.S. District Courts, U.S. Court of Federal Claims, U.S. Courts of Appeals, and U.S. Supreme Court.

AFTR2d. The second series of the *American Federal Tax Reports.*

AFTR3d. The third series of the *American Federal Tax Reports.*

Alimony and separate maintenance payments. Alimony and separate maintenance payments are includible in the gross income of the recipient and are deductible by the payor. The payments must be made in discharge of a legal obligation arising from a marital or family relationship. Child support and voluntary payments are not treated as alimony. Alimony is deductible *for* AGI. §§ 62(10), 71, and 215. See also *child support payments.*

Alimony recapture. The amount of alimony that previously has been included in the gross income of the recipient and deducted by the payor that now is deducted by the recipient and included in the gross income of the payor as the result of front-loading. § 71(f).

All events test. For accrual method taxpayers, income is earned when (1) all the events have occurred that fix the right to receive the income and (2) the amount can be determined with reasonable accuracy. Accrual of income cannot be postponed simply because a portion of the income may have to be returned in a subsequent period. The all events test also is utilized to determine when expenses can be deducted by an accrual basis taxpayer. The application of the test could cause a variation between the treatment of an item for accounting and for tax purposes. For example, a reserve for warranty expense may be properly accruable under generally accepted accounting principles but not be deductible under the Federal income tax law. Because of the application of the all events test, the deduction becomes available in the year the warranty obligation becomes fixed and the amount is determinable with reasonable certainty. See also *economic performance test.* Reg. §§ 1.446–1(c)(1)(ii) and 1.461–1a(2).

Alternate valuation date. Property passing from a person by reason of death may be valued for death tax purposes as of the date of death or the alternate valuation date. The alternate valuation date is six months from the date of death or the date the property is disposed of by the estate, whichever comes first. To use the alternate valuation date, the executor or administrator of the estate must make an affirmative election. The election of the alternate valuation date is not available unless it decreases both the amount of the gross estate *and* the estate tax liability. §§ 1014(a) and 2032.

Alternative depreciation system (ADS). A cost recovery system that produces a smaller deduction than would be calculated under ACRS or MACRS. The alternative system must be used in certain instances and can be elected in other instances. § 168(g). See also *cost recovery allowance.*

Alternative minimum tax (AMT). The alternative minimum tax is imposed only to the extent it exceeds the regular income tax (in effect, the tax liability is the greater of the tax liability calculated using the AMT rules and that calculated using the regular income tax rules). The AMT rates (26 and 28 percent for the individual taxpayer and 20 percent for the corporate taxpayer) are applied to the AMT base. The AMT base is calculated by modifying taxable income as follows: (1) add tax preferences, (2) add certain adjustments, (3) deduct certain adjustments, and (4) deduct the exemption amount. §§ 55–59. See also *adjusted current earnings (ACE) adjustment.*

Alternative minimum tax credit. The AMT can result from timing differences that give rise to positive adjustments in calculating the AMT base. To provide equity for the taxpayer when these timing differences reverse, the regular tax liability may be reduced by a tax credit for prior year's minimum tax liability attributable to timing differences. § 53.

Alternative tax. An option that is allowed in computing the tax on net capital gain. For the corporate taxpayer, the rate is 35 percent (the same as the highest regular corporate tax rate). Thus, for corporate taxpayers, the alternative tax does not produce a beneficial result. For noncorporate taxpayers, the rate is usually 15 percent (but it is 25 percent for unrecaptured § 1250 gain and is 28 percent for collectibles and § 1202 gain). However, if the noncorporate taxpayer is in either the 10 percent or the 15 percent tax bracket, the alternative tax rate is 5 percent (rather than 15 percent). §§ 1(h) and 1201. See also *collectibles, net capital gain* and *unrecaptured § 1250 gain (25 percent gain).*

Alternative tax NOL deduction (ATNOLD). In calculating the AMT, the taxpayer is allowed to deduct NOL carryovers and carrybacks. A special calculation, referred to as the ATNOLD, is required for this purpose. The regular income tax is modified for AMT adjustments and preferences to produce the ATNOLD. § 56(d).

Amortization. The allocation (and charge to expense) of the cost or other basis of an intangible asset over a statutory period of 15 years. Examples of amortizable intangibles include patents, copyrights, covenants not to compete, acquired goodwill, and leasehold interests. See also *estimated useful life* and *goodwill.* § 197.

Amount realized. The amount received by a taxpayer on the sale or other disposition of property. The amount realized is the sum of the cash and the fair market value of any property or services received, plus any related debt assumed by the buyer. Determining the amount realized is the starting point for arriving at realized gain or loss. The amount realized is defined in § 1001(b) and the related Regulations. See also *realized gain or loss* and *recognized gain or loss.*

AMT adjustments. In calculating AMTI, certain adjustments are added to or deducted from taxable income. These adjustments generally reflect timing differences. § 56.

AMT exclusions. A credit that can be used to reduce the regular tax liability in future tax years is available in connection with the AMT (*AMT credit*). The credit is applicable only with respect to the AMT that results from timing differences. It is not available in connection with AMT exclusions, which include the standard deduction, personal exemptions, medical expenses deductible in calculating the regular income tax that are not deductible in computing the AMT, other itemized deductions that are not allowable for AMT purposes, excess percentage depletion, and tax-exempt interest on specified private activity bonds.

Annuity. A fixed sum payable to a person at specified intervals for a specific period of time or for life. Payments represent a partial return of capital and a return (interest) on the capital investment. Therefore, an exclusion ratio must be used to compute the amount of nontaxable income. The exclusion ratio is used until the annuitant has recovered his or her investment in the annuity contract. Thereafter, all of the annuity payments received are included in gross income. If the annuitant dies before his or her investment is recovered, a deduction is allowed. § 72. See also *qualified pension or profit sharing plan.*

Appellate court. For Federal tax purposes, appellate courts include the Courts of Appeals and the Supreme Court. If the party losing in the trial (or lower) court is dissatisfied with the result, the dispute may be carried to the appropriate appellate court. See also *Court of Appeals* and *trial court.*

Archer medical savings account. See *medical savings account.*

Arm's length transaction. The standard under which unrelated parties would determine an exchange price for a transaction. Suppose, for example, Cardinal Corporation sells property to its sole shareholder for $10,000. In testing whether the $10,000 is an "arm's length" price, one would ascertain the price that would have been negotiated between the corporation and an unrelated party in a bargained exchange.

Asset Depreciation Range (ADR) system. A system of estimated useful lives for categories of tangible assets prescribed by the IRS. The system provides a range for each
category that extends from 20 percent above to 20 percent
below the guideline class lives prescribed by the IRS.

Assignment of income. A procedure whereby a taxpayer
attempts to avoid the recognition of income by assigning the
property that generates the income to another. Such a procedure will not avoid the recognition of income by the taxpayer making the assignment if it can be said that the
income was earned at the point of the transfer. In this
case, usually referred to as an anticipatory assignment of
income, the income will be taxed to the person who earns it.

Association. An organization treated as a corporation for Federal tax purposes even though it may not qualify as such
under applicable state law. An entity designated as a trust
or a partnership, for example, may be classified as an association if it clearly possesses corporate attributes. Corporate attributes include centralized management, continuity
of life, free transferability of interests, and limited
liability. When the check-the-box Regulations were finalized,
the association Regulations were withdrawn. Thus, for most
entities, reclassification as an association is unlikely.
§ 7701(a)(3). See also *check-the-box Regulations.*

At-risk limitation. Under the at-risk rules, a taxpayer's deductible losses from an activity for any taxable year are limited
to the amount the taxpayer has at risk at the end of the taxable year. The initial amount considered at risk is generally
the sum of the amount of cash and the adjusted basis of
property contributed to the activity and amounts borrowed
for use in the activity for which the taxpayer is personally
liable or has pledged as security property not used in the
activity. § 465.

Attribution. Under certain circumstances, the tax law applies
attribution (construction ownership) rules to assign to one
taxpayer the ownership interest of another taxpayer. If, for
example, the stock of Gold Corporation is held 60 percent
by Marsha and 40 percent by Sid, Marsha may be deemed
to own 100 percent of Gold Corporation if she and Sid are
mother and son. In that case, the stock owned by Sid is
attributed to Marsha. See, for example, §§ 267 and 318.

Audit. Inspection and verification of a taxpayer's return or
other transactions possessing tax consequences. See also
correspondence audit, field audit, and *office audit.*

Automatic mileage method. See *automobile expenses.*

Automobile expenses. Automobile expenses are generally
deductible only to the extent the automobile is used in business or for the production of income. Personal commuting
expenses are not deductible. The taxpayer may deduct
actual expenses (including depreciation and insurance), or
the standard (automatic) mileage rate may be used
(37.5 cents per mile for 2004, 40.5 cents per mile for 2005
for January–August and 48.5 cents per mile for September–
December, and 44.5 cents per mile for 2006) during any one
year. Automobile expenses incurred for medical purposes or
in connection with job-related moving expenses are deductible to the extent of actual out-of-pocket expenses or at the
rate of 18 cents per mile in 2006 (15 cents per mile in 2005
for January through August and 22 cents per mile for September through December). For charitable activities, the
rate is 14 cents per mile. See also *transportation expenses.*

B

Bad debts. A deduction is permitted if a business account
receivable subsequently becomes partially or completely
worthless, providing the income arising from the debt previously was included in income. Available methods are the
specific charge-off method and the reserve method. However, except for certain financial institutions, TRA of 1986
repealed the use of the reserve method for 1987 and thereafter. If the reserve method is used, partially or totally
worthless accounts are charged to the reserve. A nonbusiness bad debt deduction is allowed as a short-term capital
loss if the loan did not arise in connection with the creditor's trade or business activities. Loans between related
parties (family members) generally are classified as nonbusiness. § 166. See also *nonbusiness bad debts.*

Basis. The acquisition cost assigned to an asset for income tax
purposes. For assets acquired by purchase, the basis is the
cost (§ 1012). Special rules govern the basis of property
received by virtue of another's death (§ 1014) or by gift
(§ 1015), the basis of stock received on a transfer of property to a controlled corporation (§ 358), the basis of the
property transferred to the corporation (§ 362), and the
basis of property received upon the liquidation of a corporation (§§ 334 and 338). See also *adjusted basis.*

Book value. The net amount of an asset after reduction by a
related reserve. The book value of accounts receivable, for
example, is the face amount of the receivables less the
reserve for bad debts. The book value of a building is the
cost less the accumulated depreciation.

Boot. Cash or property of a type not included in the definition of a nontaxable exchange. The receipt of boot will
cause an otherwise nontaxable transfer to become taxable
to the extent of the lesser of the fair market value of such
boot or the realized gain on the transfer. Examples of nontaxable exchanges that could be partially or completely
taxable due to the receipt of boot include transfers to controlled corporations [§ 351(b)] and like-kind exchanges
[§ 1031(b)]. See also *realized gain or loss* and *recognized gain
or loss.*

Bribes and illegal payments. Section 162 denies a deduction
for bribes or kickbacks, fines, and penalties paid to a government official or employee for violation of law, and two-
thirds of the treble damage payments made to claimants
for violation of the antitrust law. Denial of a deduction for
bribes and illegal payments is based upon the judicially
established principle that allowing such payments would
be contrary to public policy.

B.T.A. The Board of Tax Appeals was a trial court that considered Federal tax matters. This court is now the U.S. Tax
Court.

Burden of proof. The requirement in a lawsuit to show the
weight of evidence and thereby gain a favorable decision.
Except in cases of tax fraud, the burden of proof in a tax
case generally is on the taxpayer.

Business bad debt. A debt created or acquired in connection
with a trade or business of the taxpayer, or a debt the loss
from the worthlessness of which is incurred in the taxpayer's trade or business. A business bad debt is deducted
as an ordinary deduction. § 166.

Business expenses. See *trade or business expenses.*

Business gifts. Business gifts are deductible only to the extent that each gift does not exceed $25 per person per year. Exceptions are made for gifts costing $4 or less and for certain employee awards. § 274(b).

C

C corporation. A corporation that has not elected conduit treatment under § 1361. See also *S corporation status*.

Cafeteria benefit plan. An employee benefit plan under which an employee is allowed to select from among a variety of employer-provided fringe benefits. Some of the benefits may be taxable and some may be statutory nontaxable benefits (e.g., health and accident insurance and group term life insurance). The employee is taxed only on the taxable benefits selected. A cafeteria benefit plan is also referred to as a flexible benefit plan. § 125.

Cafeteria plan. See *cafeteria benefit plan*.

Canons of taxation. Criteria used in the selection of a tax base that were originally discussed by Adam Smith in *The Wealth of Nations*. Canons of taxation include equality, convenience, certainty, and economy.

Capital asset. Broadly speaking, all assets are capital except those specifically excluded by the Code. Major categories of noncapital assets include property held for resale in the normal course of business (inventory), trade accounts and notes receivable, and depreciable property and real estate used in a trade or business (§ 1231 assets). § 1221. See also *capital gain* and *capital loss*.

Capital contributions. Various means by which a shareholder makes additional funds available to the corporation (placed at the risk of the business) without the receipt of additional stock. Such contributions are added to the basis of the shareholder's existing stock investment and do not generate income to the corporation. § 118.

Capital expenditure. An expenditure that should be added to the basis of the property improved. For income tax purposes, this generally precludes a full deduction for the expenditure in the year paid or incurred. Any capital recovery in the form of a tax deduction must come in the form of depreciation. § 263.

Capital gain. The gain from the sale or exchange of a capital asset. See also *capital asset* and *net capital gain*.

Capital gain net income. If the total capital gains for the tax year exceed the total capital losses, the result is capital gain net income. Note that the term does not distinguish between the long-term and short-term gains. § 1222(9). See also *net capital gain*.

Capital gain or loss holding period. The period of time that a capital asset is held by the taxpayer. To qualify for long-term treatment, the asset must be held for more than one year. If held for one year or less, the holding period is short term. See also *holding period*.

Capital gain property. Property contributed to a charitable organization that, if sold rather than contributed, would have resulted in long-term capital gain to the donor. See also *ordinary income property*.

Capital loss. The loss from the sale or exchange of a capital asset. See also *capital asset*.

Cash balance plan. A hybrid form of pension plan similar in some aspects to a defined benefit plan. Such a plan is funded by the employer, and the employer bears the investment risks and rewards. But like defined contribution plans, a cash balance plan establishes allocations to individual employee accounts, and the payout for an employee depends on investment performance.

Cash basis. See *accounting method* and *cash receipts method*.

Cash equivalent doctrine. Generally, a cash basis taxpayer does not report income until cash is constructively or actually received. Under the cash equivalent doctrine, cash basis taxpayers are required to report income if they receive the equivalent of cash (e.g., property is received) in a taxable transaction.

Cash method. See *cash receipts method*.

Cash receipts method. A method of accounting under which the taxpayer generally reports income when cash is collected and reports expenses when cash payments are made. However, for fixed assets, the cash basis taxpayer claims deductions through depreciation or amortization in the same manner as an accrual basis taxpayer. Prepaid expenses must be capitalized and amortized if the life of the asset extends "substantially beyond" the end of the tax year. See also *constructive receipt*.

Casualty loss. A casualty is defined as "the complete or partial destruction of property resulting from an identifiable event of a sudden, unexpected or unusual nature" (e.g., floods, storms, fires, auto accidents). Individuals may deduct a casualty loss only if the loss is incurred in a trade or business or in a transaction entered into for profit or arises from fire, storm, shipwreck, or other casualty or from theft. Individuals usually deduct personal casualty losses as itemized deductions subject to a $100 nondeductible amount and to an annual floor equal to 10 percent of adjusted gross income that applies after the $100 per casualty floor has been applied. Special rules are provided for the netting of certain casualty gains and losses. § 165. See also *disaster area loss* and *Section 1231 gains and losses*.

Cert. den. By denying the Writ of Certiorari, the U.S. Supreme Court refuses to accept an appeal from a U.S. Court of Appeals. The denial of certiorari does not, however, mean that the U.S. Supreme Court agrees with the result reached by the lower court.

Certiorari. Appeal from a U.S. Court of Appeals to the U.S. Supreme Court is by Writ of Certiorari. The Supreme Court does not have to accept the appeal and usually does not (*cert. den.*) unless there is a conflict among the lower courts that needs to be resolved or a constitutional issue is involved.

Change in accounting method. A change in the taxpayer's method of accounting (e.g., from FIFO to LIFO) generally requires prior approval from the IRS. Generally, a request must be filed within the taxable year of the desired change. In some instances, the permission for change will not be granted unless the taxpayer agrees to certain adjustments prescribed by the IRS.

Change in accounting period. A taxpayer must obtain the consent of the IRS before changing his or her tax year. Income for the short period created by the change must be annualized.

Charitable contributions. Contributions are deductible (subject to various restrictions and ceiling limitations) if made to qualified nonprofit charitable organizations. A cash basis taxpayer is entitled to a deduction solely in the year of payment. Accrual basis corporations may accrue contributions at year-end if payment is properly authorized before the end of the year and payment is made within two and one-half months after the end of the year. § 170.

Check-the-box Regulations. These Regulations enable taxpayers to classify the tax status of a business entity without regard to its corporate or noncorporate characteristics. An entity with more than one owner can elect to be classified either as a partnership or as a corporation. An entity with only one owner can elect to be classified as a sole proprietorship or as a corporation. These Regulations should simplify tax administration and taxpayer compliance and reduce tax litigation.

Child and dependent care expenses credit. A tax credit ranging from 20 percent to 35 percent of employment-related expenses (child and dependent care expenses) for amounts of up to $6,000 is available to individuals who are employed (or deemed to be employed) and maintain a household for a dependent child under age 13, disabled spouse, or disabled dependent. § 21.

Child support payments. Payments for child support do not constitute alimony and are therefore not includible in gross income by the recipient or deductible as alimony by the payor. Generally, none of the amounts paid are regarded as child support unless the divorce decree or separation agreement specifically calls for child support payments. However, if the amount of the payment to the former spouse would be reduced upon the happening of a contingency related to a child (e.g., the child attains age 21 or dies), the amount of the future reduction in the payment will be deemed child support for post-1984 agreements and decrees. § 71(c). See also *alimony and separate maintenance payments*.

Child tax credit. A tax credit based solely on the number of qualifying children under age 17. The maximum credit available is $1,000 per child through 2010. A qualifying child must be claimed as a dependent on a parent's tax return in order to qualify for the credit. Taxpayers who qualify for the child tax credit may also qualify for a supplemental credit. The supplemental credit is treated as a component of the earned income credit and is therefore refundable. The credit is phased out for higher-income taxpayers. § 24.

Circuit Court of Appeals. See *Court of Appeals*.

Circulation expenditures. Expenditures of establishing or increasing the circulation of a periodical that may be either expensed or capitalized. If such expenses are expensed, an adjustment will occur for AMT purposes, since the expenses are deducted over a three-year period for AMT purposes. Over the three-year period, both positive and negative AMT adjustments will be produced. § 173. See also *AMT adjustments*.

Citator. A tax research resource that presents the judicial history of a court case and traces the subsequent references to the case. When these references include the citing case's evaluations of the cited case's precedents, the research can obtain some measure of the efficacy and reliability of the original holding.

Claim of right doctrine. A judicially imposed doctrine applicable to both cash and accrual basis taxpayers that holds that an amount is includible in income upon actual or constructive receipt if the taxpayer has an unrestricted claim to the payment. For the tax treatment of amounts repaid when previously included in income under the claim of right doctrine, see § 1341.

Claims Court. One of three Federal trial courts that consider Federal tax controversies. Now known as the U.S. Court of Federal Claims, appeal from this court (formerly to the U.S. Supreme Court) now goes to the Court of Appeals for the Federal Circuit. See also *trial court*.

Clear reflection of income. The IRS has the authority to redetermine a taxpayer's income using a method that clearly reflects income if the taxpayer's method does not do so. § 446(b). In addition, the IRS may apportion or allocate income among various related businesses if income is not "clearly reflected." § 482.

Closely held corporation. A corporation where the stock ownership is not widely dispersed. Instead, a few shareholders are in control of corporate policy and are in a position to benefit personally from that policy.

Collectibles. A special type of capital asset, the gain from which is taxed at a maximum rate of 28 percent if the holding period is more than one year. Examples include art, rugs, antiques, gems, metals, stamps, some coins and bullion, and alcoholic beverages held for investment.

Community property. Louisiana, Texas, New Mexico, Arizona, California, Washington, Idaho, Nevada, and Wisconsin have community property systems. In Alaska, spouses can choose to have the community property rules apply. The rest of the states are classified as common law jurisdictions. The difference between common law and community property systems centers around the property rights possessed by married persons. In a common law system, each spouse owns whatever he or she earns. Under a community property system, one-half of the earnings of each spouse is considered owned by the other spouse. Assume, for example, Alice and Jeff are husband and wife and their only income is the $50,000 annual salary Jeff receives. If they live in New York (a common law state), the $50,000 salary belongs to Jeff. If, however, they live in Texas (a community property state), the $50,000 salary is divided equally, in terms of ownership, between Jeff and Alice. See also *separate property*.

Compensatory damages. Damages received or paid by the taxpayer can be classified as compensatory damages or as punitive damages. Compensatory damages are those paid to compensate one for harm caused by another. Compensatory damages are excludible from the recipient's gross income. See also *punitive damages*.

Completed contract method. A method of reporting gain or loss on certain long-term contracts. Under this method of accounting, gross income and expenses are recognized in the tax year in which the contract is completed. Reg. § 1.451–3. Limitations exist on a taxpayer's ability to use the completed contract method. § 460. See also *long-term contract* and *percentage of completion method*.

Component depreciation. The process of dividing an asset (e.g., a building) into separate components or parts for the purpose of calculating depreciation. The advantage of dividing an asset into components is to use shorter depreciation lives for selected components under § 167. Generally, the same cost recovery period must be used for all the components of an asset under § 168.

Condemnation. The taking of property by a public authority. The property is condemned as the result of legal action, and the owner is compensated by the public authority. The power to condemn property is known as the right of eminent domain.

Conduit concept. An approach assumed by the tax law in the treatment of certain entities and their owners. Specific tax characteristics pass through the entity without losing their identity. For example, items of income and expense, capital gains and losses, tax credits, etc., realized by a partnership pass through the partnership (a conduit) and are subject to taxation at the partner level. Also, in an S corporation, certain items pass through and are reported on the returns of the shareholders.

Constructive dividends. In addition to dividends formally declared by the board of directors of a corporation (i.e., declaration date, record date, and payment date), a shareholder may receive a distribution that does not have the formalities of a dividend but is treated as a dividend. Examples include salaries paid to shareholder-employees that are not reasonable and the shareholder use of corporate property for less than an arm's length rate.

Constructive ownership. See *attribution*.

Constructive receipt. If income is unqualifiedly available, it will be subject to the income tax even though it is not physically in the taxpayer's possession. An example is accrued interest on a savings account. Under the constructive receipt of income concept, the interest will be taxed to a depositor in the year it is available rather than the year actually withdrawn. The fact that the depositor uses the cash basis of accounting for tax purposes is irrelevant. See Reg. § 1.451–2.

Consumer interest. Interest expense of the taxpayer of a personal nature (not trade or business interest, investment interest, qualified residence interest, or passive activity interest) is not deductible. § 163(h). See also *interest on student loans* and *qualified residence interest*.

Contributions to the capital of a corporation. See *capital contributions*.

Convention expenses. Travel expenses incurred in attending a convention are deductible if the meetings are related to a taxpayer's trade or business or job-related activities. If, however, the convention trip is primarily for pleasure, no deduction is permitted for transportation expenses. Likewise, if the expenses are for attending a convention related to the production of income (§ 212), no deduction is permitted. Specific limitations are provided for foreign convention expenses. See § 274(n) for the limitations on the deductions for meals. § 274(h).

Correspondence audit. An audit conducted by the IRS by mail. Typically, the IRS writes to the taxpayer requesting the verification of a particular deduction, exemption, or credit. The completion of a special form or the remittance of copies of records or other support is all that is requested of the taxpayer. To be distinguished from a *field audit* or an *office audit*.

Cost depletion. Depletion that is calculated based on the adjusted basis of the asset. The adjusted basis is divided by the expected recoverable units to determine the depletion per unit. The depletion per unit is multiplied by the units sold during the tax year to calculate cost depletion. See also *percentage depletion*.

Cost recovery allowance. The portion of the cost of an asset written off under ACRS (or MACRS), which replaced the depreciation system as a method for writing off the cost of an asset for most assets placed in service after 1980 (after 1986 for MACRS). § 168. See also *alternative depreciation system* and *thirty percent additional first-year depreciation*.

Cost recovery period. A period specified in the Code for writing off the cost of an asset under ACRS or MACRS.

Court of Appeals. Any of 13 Federal courts that consider tax matters appealed from the U.S. Tax Court, U.S. Court of Federal Claims, or a U.S. District Court. Appeal from a U.S. Court of Appeals is to the U.S. Supreme Court by Writ of Certiorari. See also *appellate court*.

Court of Federal Claims. See *Claims Court*.

Court of original jurisdiction. The Federal courts are divided into courts of original jurisdiction and appellate courts. A dispute between a taxpayer and the IRS is first considered by a court of original jurisdiction (i.e., a trial court). The four Federal courts of original jurisdiction are the U.S. Tax Court, U.S. District Court, the Court of Federal Claims, and the Small Cases Division of the U.S. Tax Court. See also *Court of Appeals*.

Coverdell Education Savings Account (CESA). A savings account established to pay for qualified education expenses (i.e., tuition, fees, books, supplies, related equipment, room and board if the student's course load is at least one-half of the full-time course load). The maximum annual contribution to the savings account of a beneficiary is $2,000. The maximum annual contribution is subject to phaseout beginning at $95,000 for single taxpayers and $150,000 for married couples who file a joint return. Contributions are not deductible ad cannot be made to a savings account once the beneficiary attains age 18. Distributions used to pay for qualified education expenses for a designated beneficiary are tax free. § 530.

Credit for certain retirement plan contributions. A nonrefundable credit is available based on eligible contributions of up to $2,000 to certain qualified retirement plans, such as traditional and Roth IRAs and § 401(k) plans, for taxable years beginning after 2001 and before 2007. The benefit provided by this credit is in addition to any deduction or exclusion that otherwise is available resulting from the qualifying contribution. The amount of the credit depends on the taxpayer's AGI and filing status. § 25B.

Credit for child and dependent care expenses. See *child and dependent care expenses credit*.

Credit for employer-provided child care. A nonrefundable credit is available to employers who provide child care facilities to their employees during normal working hours. The credit, limited to $150,000, is comprised of two components. The portion of the credit for qualified child care expenses is equal to 25 percent of these expenses while the portion of the credit for qualified child care resource and referral services is equal to 10 percent of these expenses. Any qualifying expenses otherwise deductible by the taxpayer must be reduced by the amount of the credit. In addition, the taxpayer's basis for any property used for qualifying purposes is reduced by the amount of the credit. § 45F.

Credit for small employer pension plan startup costs. A non-refundable credit available to small businesses based on administrative costs associated with establishing and maintaining certain qualified plans. While such qualifying costs generally are deductible as ordinary and necessary business expenses, the availability of the credit is intended to lower the costs of starting a qualified retirement program, and therefore encourage qualifying businesses to establish retirement plans for their employees. The credit is available for eligible employers at the rate of 50 percent of qualified startup costs. The maximum credit is $500 (based on a maximum $1,000 of qualifying expenses). § 45E.

D

Death benefit. A payment made by an employer to the beneficiary or beneficiaries of a deceased employee on account of the death of the employee.

Death tax. See *estate tax.*

Declaration of estimated tax. A procedure whereby individuals and corporations are required to make quarterly installment payments of estimated tax. Individuals are required to make the declaration and file quarterly payments of the estimated tax if certain requirements are met. In 2006, a declaration is not required for an individual whose estimated tax is reasonably expected to be less than $1,000.

Deduction for qualified tuition and related expenses. Taxpayers are allowed a deduction of up to $4,000 for higher education expenses. Certain taxpayers are not eligible for the deduction: those whose AGI exceeds a specified amount and those who can be claimed as a dependent by another taxpayer. These expenses are classified as a deduction *for* AGI and they need not be employment related. § 222.

Deductions for adjusted gross income. See *adjusted gross income.*

Deductions from adjusted gross income. See *itemized deductions.*

Deferred compensation. Compensation that will be taxed when received or upon the removal of certain restrictions on receipt and not when earned. Contributions by an employer to a qualified pension or profit sharing plan on behalf of an employee are an example. The contributions will not be taxed to the employee until the funds are made available or distributed to the employee (e.g., upon retirement). See also *qualified pension or profit sharing plan.*

Deficiency. Additional tax liability owed by a taxpayer and assessed by the IRS. See also *statutory notice of deficiency.*

Defined benefit plan. Qualified plans can be dichotimized into defined benefit plans and defined contribution plans. Under a defined benefit plan, a formula defines the benefits employees are to receive. The formula usually includes years of service, employee compensation, and some stated percentage. The employer must make annual contributions based on actuarial computations that will be sufficient to pay the vested retirement benefits. See also *defined contribution plan* and *pension plan.*

Defined contribution plan. Qualified plans can be dichotimized into defined benefit plans and defined contribution plans. Under a defined contribution plan, a separate account is maintained for each covered employee. The employee's benefits under the plan are based solely on (1) the amount contributed and (2) income from the fund that accrues to the employee's account. The plan defines the amount the employer is required to contribute (e.g., a flat dollar amount, an amount based on a special formula, or an amount equal to a certain percentage of compensation). See also *defined benefit plan* and *pension plan.*

Defined contribution pension plan. See *defined contribution plan.*

De minimis fringe. Benefits provided to employees that are too insignificant to warrant the time and effort required to account for the benefits received by each employee and the value of those benefits. Such amounts are excludible from the employee's gross income. § 132.

Dependency exemption. See *personal and dependency exemptions.*

Depletion. The process by which the cost or other basis of a natural resource (e.g., an oil or gas interest) is recovered upon extraction and sale of the resource. The two ways to determine the depletion allowance are the cost and percentage (or statutory) methods. Under the cost method, each unit of production sold is assigned a portion of the cost or other basis of the interest. This is determined by dividing the cost or other basis by the total units expected to be recovered. Under the percentage (or statutory) method, the tax law provides a special percentage factor for different types of minerals and other natural resources. This percentage is multiplied by the gross income from the interest to arrive at the depletion allowance. §§ 613 and 613A.

Depreciation. The deduction of the cost or other basis of a tangible asset over the asset's estimated useful life. § 167. For intangible assets, see *amortization.* For natural resources, see *depletion.* Also see *estimated useful life.* The depreciation system was replaced by ACRS for most assets placed in service after 1980 (by MACRS for most assets placed in service after 1986) but still applies for assets placed in service before 1981. See also *recapture of depreciation.*

Determination letter. Upon the request of a taxpayer, a District Director will comment on the tax status of a completed transaction. Determination letters are most frequently used to clarify employee versus self-employed status, to determine whether a pension or profit sharing plan qualifies under the Code, and to determine the tax-exempt status of certain nonprofit organizations.

Direct charge-off method. See *specific charge-off method.*

Disabled access credit. A tax credit designed to encourage small businesses to make their facilities more accessible to disabled individuals. The credit is equal to 50 percent of the eligible expenditures that exceed $250 but do not exceed $10,250. Thus, the maximum amount for the credit is $5,000. The adjusted basis for depreciation is reduced by the amount of the credit. To qualify, the facility must have been placed in service before November 6, 1990. § 44. See also *general business credit.*

Disaster area loss. A casualty sustained in an area designated as a disaster area by the President of the United States. In such an event, the disaster loss may be treated as having occurred in the taxable year immediately preceding the year in which the disaster actually occurred. Thus, immediate tax benefits are provided to victims of a disaster. § 165(i). See also *casualty loss*.

Dissent. To disagree with the majority. If, for example, Judge Brown disagrees with the result reached by Judges Charles and Davis (all of whom are members of the same court), Judge Brown could issue a dissenting opinion.

District Court. A Federal District Court is a trial court for purposes of litigating (among others) Federal tax matters. It is the only trial court where a jury trial can be obtained. See also *trial court*.

Dividends received deduction. A deduction allowed a shareholder that is a corporation for dividends received from a domestic corporation. The percentage applied in calculating the dividends received deduction varies according to the percentage of stock ownership. If the stock ownership percentage is less than 20 percent, the percentage is 70 percent of the dividends received. If the stock ownership percentage is at least 20 percent but less than 80 percent, the percentage is 80 percent. If the stock ownership percentage is at least 80 percent, the percentage is 100 percent. §§ 243–246A.

Dollar value LIFO. An inventory technique that focuses on the dollars invested in the inventory rather than the particular items on hand each period. Each inventory item is assigned to a pool. A pool is a collection of similar items and is treated as a separate inventory. At the end of the period, each pool is valued in terms of prices at the time LIFO was adopted (base period prices), whether or not the particular items were actually on hand in the year LIFO was adopted, to compare with current prices to determine if there has been an increase or decrease in inventories.

Domestic production gross receipts (DPGR). A key component in computing the production activities deduction (PAD). Includes receipts from the sale and other disposition of qualified production property produced in significant part within the U.S. DPGR is defined in § 199(c)(4). See also *production activities deduction (PAD)*.

E

Earned income. Income from personal services as distinguished from income generated by property. See §§ 32 and 911 and the related Regulations.

Earned income credit. A refundable tax credit designed to provide assistance to certain low-income individuals. To receive the most beneficial treatment, the taxpayer must have qualifying children. However, it is possible to qualify for the credit without having a child. To calculate the credit for a taxpayer with one or more children for 2006, a statutory rate of 34.0 percent for one child (40.0 percent for two or more children) is multiplied by the earned income (subject to a statutory maximum of $8,080 with one qualifying child or $11,340 with two or more qualifying children). Once the earned income exceeds certain thresholds, the credit is phased out using a 15.98 percent rate for one qualifying child and a 21.06 percent rate for two or more qualifying children. For the qualifying taxpayer without children, the credit is calculated on a maximum earned income of $5,380 applying a 7.65 percent rate with the phaseout beginning at later applying the same rate. § 32.

Earnings and profits. A tax concept peculiar to corporate taxpayers that measures economic capacity to make a distribution to shareholders that is not a return of capital. Such a distribution will result in dividend income to the shareholders to the extent of the corporation's current and accumulated earnings and profits.

Economic income. The change in the taxpayer's net worth, as measured in terms of market values, plus the value of the assets the taxpayer consumed during the year. Because of the impracticality of this income model, it is not used for tax purposes. See also *accounting income*.

Economic performance test. One of the requirements that must be satisfied in order for an accrual basis taxpayer to deduct an expense. The accrual basis taxpayer first must satisfy the all events test. That test is not deemed satisfied until economic performance occurs. This occurs when property or services are provided to the taxpayer or, in the case in which the taxpayer is required to provide property or services, whenever the property or services are actually provided by the taxpayer. See also *all events test*.

Education expenses. Employees may deduct education expenses that are incurred either (1) to maintain or improve existing job-related skills or (2) to meet the express requirements of the employer or the requirements imposed by law to retain employment status. The expenses are not deductible if the education is required to meet the minimum educational standards for the taxpayer's job or if the education qualifies the individual for a new trade or business. Reg. § 1.162–5. See also *HOPE scholarship credit* and *lifetime learning credit*.

Educational savings bonds. U.S. Series EE bonds whose proceeds are used for qualified higher educational expenses for the taxpayer, the taxpayer's spouse, or a dependent. The interest may be excluded from gross income, provided the taxpayer's adjusted gross income does not exceed certain amounts. § 135.

e-file. The electronic filing of a tax return. The filing is either direct or indirect. As to direct, the taxpayer goes online using a computer and tax return preparation software. Indirect filing occurs when a taxpayer utilizes an authorized IRS e-file provider. The provider often is the tax return preparer.

Employee expenses. The deductions *for* adjusted gross income include reimbursed expenses and certain expenses of performing artists. All other employee expenses are deductible *from* AGI. § 62. See also *trade or business expenses*.

Employment taxes. Employment taxes are those taxes that an employer must pay on account of its employees. Employment taxes include FICA (Federal Insurance Contributions Act) and FUTA (Federal Unemployment Tax Act) taxes. Employment taxes are paid to the IRS in addition to income tax withholdings at specified intervals. Such taxes can be levied on the employees, the employer, or both. See also *FICA tax* and *FUTA tax*.

Entertainment expenses. These expenses are deductible only if they are directly related to or associated with a trade or business. Various restrictions and documentation requirements have been imposed upon the deductibility of entertainment expenses to prevent abuses by taxpayers. See, for example, the provision contained in § 274(n) that disallows 50 percent of entertainment expenses. § 274.

Estate tax. A tax imposed on the right to transfer property by reason of death. Thus, an estate tax is levied on the decedent's estate and not on the heir receiving the property. §§ 2001 and 2002. See also *inheritance tax.*

Estimated tax. The amount of tax (including alternative minimum tax and self-employment tax) an individual expects to owe for the year after subtracting tax credits and income tax withheld. The estimated tax must be paid in installments at designated intervals (e.g. for the individual taxpayer, by April 15, June 15, September 15, and January 15 of the following year).

Estimated useful life. The period over which an asset will be used by a particular taxpayer. Although the period cannot be longer than the estimated physical life of an asset, it could be shorter if the taxpayer does not intend to keep the asset until it wears out. Assets such as goodwill do not have an estimated useful life. The estimated useful life of an asset is essential to measuring the annual tax deduction for depreciation and amortization. An asset subject to ACRS or MACRS is written off over a specified cost recovery period rather than over its estimated useful life. In addition, most intangibles are now amortized over a 15-year statutory period.

Excise tax. A tax on the manufacture, sale, or use of goods or on the carrying on of an occupation or activity. Also, a tax on the transfer of property. Thus, the Federal estate and gift taxes are, theoretically, excise taxes.

Extraordinary personal services. These are services provided by individuals where the customers' use of the property is incidental to their receipt of the services. For example, a patient's use of a hospital bed is incidental to his or her receipt of medical services. This is one of the six exceptions to determine whether an activity is a passive rental activity. § 469.

F

Fair market value. The amount at which property would change hands between a willing buyer and a willing seller, neither being under any compulsion to buy or sell and both having reasonable knowledge of the relevant facts. Reg. §§ 1.1001–1(a) and 20.2031–1(b).

Federal district court. See *district court.*

FICA tax. An abbreviation for Federal Insurance Contributions Act, commonly referred to as the Social Security tax. The FICA tax is comprised of the Social Security tax (old age, survivors, and disability insurance) and the Medicare tax (hospital insurance) and is imposed on both employers and employees. The employer is responsible for withholding from the employee's wages the Social Security tax at a rate of 6.2 percent on a maximum wage base of $94,200 (for 2006) and the Medicare tax at a rate of 1.45 percent (no maximum wage base). The employer is required to match the employee's contribution. See also *employment taxes.*

Field audit. An audit by the IRS conducted on the business premises of the taxpayer or in the office of the tax practitioner representing the taxpayer. To be distinguished from a *correspondence audit* or an *office audit.*

Fifty percent additional first-year depreciation. This provision, which was effective for property acquired after May 5, 2003 and placed in service before January 1, 2005, provided for an additional cost recovery deduction of fifty percent in the tax year the qualified property is placed in service. Qualified property included most types of new property other than buildings. The taxpayer could elect to forgo this bonus depreciation. The taxpayer also could elect to use thirty percent bonus depreciation rather than the fifty percent bonus depreciation. See also *cost recovery allowance* and *thirty percent additional first-year depreciation.*

Finalized Regulation. See *regulations.*

First-in, first-out (FIFO). An accounting method for determining the cost of inventories. Under this method, the inventory on hand is deemed to be the sum of the cost of the most recently acquired units. See also *last-in, first-out (LIFO).*

Fiscal year. A fiscal year is a 12-month period ending on the last day of a month other than December. In certain circumstances, a taxpayer is permitted to elect a fiscal year instead of being required to use a calendar year. See also *accounting period* and *taxable year.*

Flat tax. In its pure form, it would replace the graduated income tax rates with a single rate (e.g., 17 percent). All deductions are eliminated, and a large personal exemption is allowed to remove low-income and many middle-income taxpayers from the application of the tax.

Flexible spending plan. An employee benefit plan that allows the employee to take a reduction in salary in exchange for the employer paying benefits that can be provided by the employer without the employee being required to recognize income (e.g., medical and child care benefits).

Foreign earned income exclusion. The foreign earned income exclusion is a relief provision that applies to U.S. citizens working in a foreign country. To qualify for the exclusion, the taxpayer must be either a bona fide resident of the foreign country or present in the country for 330 days during any 12 consecutive months. The exclusion is limited to $80,000 per year. § 911.

Foreign tax credit or deduction. Both individual taxpayers and corporations may claim a foreign tax credit on income earned and subject to tax in a foreign country or U.S. possession. As an alternative to the credit, a deduction may be taken for the foreign taxes paid. §§ 27, 164, and 901–905.

Franchise. An agreement that gives the transferee the right to distribute, sell, or provide goods, services, or facilities within a specified area. The cost of obtaining a franchise may be amortized over a statutory period of 15 years. In general, the franchisor's gain on the sale of franchise rights is an ordinary gain because the franchisor retains a significant power, right, or continuing interest in the subject of the franchise. §§ 197 and 1253.

Franchise tax. A tax levied on the right to do business in a state as a corporation. Although income considerations may come into play, the tax usually is based on the capitalization of the corporation.

Fringe benefits. Compensation or other benefits received by an employee that are not in the form of cash. Some fringe benefits (e.g., accident and health plans, group term life insurance) may be excluded from the employee's gross income and therefore are not subject to the Federal income tax.

Fruit and tree metaphor. The courts have held that an individual who earns income from property or services cannot assign that income to another. For example, a father cannot assign his earnings from commissions to his child and escape income tax on those amounts.

F.3d. An abbreviation for the Third Series of the *Federal Reporter*, the official series where decisions of the U.S. Claims Court (before October 1982) and the U.S. Courts of Appeals are published.

F.Supp. The abbreviation for the *Federal Supplement*, the official series where the reported decisions of the U.S. District Courts are published.

FUTA tax. An employment tax levied on employers. Jointly administered by the Federal and state governments, the tax provides funding for unemployment benefits. FUTA applies at a rate of 6.2 percent on the first $7,000 of covered wages paid during the year for each employee. The Federal government allows a credit for FUTA paid (or allowed under a merit rating system) to the state. The credit cannot exceed 5.4 percent of the covered wages. See also *employment taxes*.

G

General business credit. The summation of various nonrefundable business credits, including the tax credit for rehabilitation expenditures, business energy credit, welfare-to-work credit, work opportunity credit, research activities credit, low-income housing credit, and disabled access credit. The amount of general business credit that can be used to reduce the tax liability is limited to the taxpayer's net income tax reduced by the greater of (1) the tentative minimum tax or (2) 25 percent of the net regular tax liability that exceeds $25,000. Unused general business credits can be carried back 1 year and forward 20 years.

Gift. A transfer of property for less than adequate consideration. Gifts usually occur in a personal setting (such as between members of the same family). Gifts are excluded from the income tax but may be subject to the *gift tax*.

Gift tax. A tax imposed on the transfer of property by gift. The tax is imposed upon the donor of a gift and is based upon the fair market value of the property on the date of the gift. §§ 2501–2524.

Golden parachute payment. A severance payment to employees that meets the following requirements: (1) the payment is contingent on a change of ownership of a corporation through a stock or asset acquisition and (2) the aggregate present value of the payment equals or exceeds three times the employee's average annual compensation. To the extent the severance payment meets these conditions, a deduction is disallowed to the employer for the excess of the payment over a statutory base amount (a five-year average of compensation if the taxpayer was an employee for the entire five-year period). In addition, a 20 percent excise tax is imposed on the employee who receives the excess severance pay. §§ 280G and 4999.

Goodwill. The ability of a business to generate income in excess of a normal rate on assets due to superior managerial skills, market position, new product technology, etc. In the purchase of a business, goodwill represents the difference between the purchase price and the fair market value of the net assets acquired. Goodwill is an intangible asset that possesses an indefinite life. However, since acquired goodwill is a § 197 intangible asset, it is amortized over a 15-year statutory period. Self-created goodwill cannot be amortized. Reg. § 1.167(a)–3. See also *amortization*.

Government bonds issued at a discount. Certain U.S. government bonds (Series EE) are issued at a discount and do not pay interest during the life of the bonds. Instead, the bonds are redeemable at increasing fixed amounts. Thus, the difference between the purchase price and the amount received upon redemption represents interest income to the holder. A cash basis taxpayer may defer recognition of gross income until the bonds are redeemed. For Series EE savings bonds issued after 1989, the interest otherwise taxable at redemption can be excluded if the bonds are qualified educational savings bonds. As an alternative to deferring recognition of gross income until the bonds are redeemed, the taxpayer may elect to include in gross income on an annual basis the annual increase in the value of the bonds. § 454.

Gross income. Income subject to the Federal income tax. Gross income does not include income for which the Code permits exclusion treatment (e.g., interest on municipal bonds). For a manufacturing or merchandising business, gross income means gross profit (gross sales or gross receipts less cost of goods sold). § 61 and Reg. § 1.61–3(a).

Group term life insurance. Life insurance coverage permitted by an employer for a group of employees. Such insurance is renewable on a year-to-year basis and does not accumulate in value (i.e., no cash surrender value is built up). The premiums paid by the employer on the insurance are not taxed to an employee on coverage of up to $50,000 per person. § 79 and Reg. § 1.79–1(a).

Guaranteed payments. Payments made by a partnership to one of its partners for services rendered or for the use of capital, to the extent the payments are determined without regard to the income of the partnership. Such payments generally are deductible by the partnership as a business expense and are reported as ordinary income by the recipient partner. § 707(c).

H

Half-year convention. The half-year convention is a cost recovery convention that assumes all property is placed in service at mid-year and thus provides for a half-year's cost recovery for that year.

Head of household. An unmarried individual who maintains a household for another and satisfies certain conditions set forth in § 2(b). Such status enables the taxpayer to use a set of income tax rates [see § 1(b)] that are lower than those applicable to other unmarried individuals [§ 1(c)] but higher than those applicable to surviving spouses and married persons filing a joint return [§ 1(a)]. See also *tax rate schedules*.

Health savings account. A medical savings account created in legislation enacted in December 2003 that is designed to replace and expand Archer Medical Savings Accounts. See also *medical savings account*.

Highly compensated employee. The employee group is generally divided into two categories for fringe benefit (including pension and profit sharing plans) purposes. These are (1) highly compensated employees and (2) non-highly compensated employees. For most fringe benefits, if the fringe benefit plan discriminates in favor of highly compensated employees, it will not be a qualified plan with respect, at a minimum, to the highly compensated employees.

Hobby loss. A nondeductible loss arising from a personal hobby as contrasted with an activity engaged in for profit. Generally, the law provides a rebuttable presumption that an activity is engaged in for profit if profits are earned during any three or more years during a five-year period. § 183. See also *vacation home*.

Holding period. The period of time property has been held for income tax purposes. The holding period is crucial in determining whether gain or loss from the sale or exchange of a capital asset is long term or short term. § 1223. See also *capital gain or loss holding period*.

Home equity loans. Loans that utilize the personal residence of the taxpayer as security. The interest on such loans is deductible as *qualified residence interest*. However, interest is deductible only on the portion of the loan that does not exceed the lesser of (1) the fair market value of the residence, reduced by the *acquisition indebtedness*, or (2) $100,000 ($50,000 for married persons filing separate returns). A major benefit of a home equity loan is that there are no tracing rules regarding the use of the loan proceeds. § 163(h)(3).

Home office expenses. See *office-in-the-home expenses*.

HOPE scholarship credit. A tax credit for qualifying expenses paid for the first two years of postsecondary education. Room, board, and book costs are ineligible for the credit. The maximum credit available is $1,650 per year per student, computed as 100 percent of the first $1,100 of qualifying expenses, plus 50 percent of the second $1,100 of qualifying expenses. Eligible students include the taxpayer, taxpayer's spouse, and taxpayer's dependents. To qualify for the credit, a student must take at least one-half the full-time course load for at least one academic term at a qualifying educational institution. The credit is phased out for higher-income taxpayers. § 25A.

H.R 10 (Keogh) plan. See *self-employment retirement plan*.

Hybrid method. A combination of the accrual and cash methods of accounting. That is, the taxpayer may account for some items of income on the accrual method (e.g., sales and cost of goods sold) and other items (e.g., interest income) on the cash method.

I

Imputed interest. For certain long-term sales of property, the IRS can convert some of the gain from the sale into interest income if the contract does not provide for a minimum rate of interest to be paid by the purchaser. The application of this procedure has the effect of forcing the seller to recognize less long-term capital gain and more ordinary income (interest income). §§ 483 and 1274 and the Regulations thereunder. In addition, interest income and interest expense are imputed (deemed to exist) on interest-free or below-market rate loans between certain related parties. § 7872. See also *interest-free loans*.

Incentive stock option (ISO). A type of stock option that receives favorable tax treatment. If various qualification requirements can be satisfied, there are no recognition tax consequences when the stock option is granted. However, the spread (the excess of the fair market value at the date of exercise over the option price) is a tax preference item for purposes of the alternative minimum tax. The gain on disposition of the stock resulting from the exercise of the stock option will be classified as long-term capital gain if certain holding period requirements are met (the employee must not dispose of the stock within two years after the option is granted or within one year after acquiring the stock). § 422. See also *nonqualified stock option (NQSO)*.

Income. For tax purposes, an increase in wealth that has been realized.

Independent contractor. A self-employed person as distinguished from one who is employed as an employee.

Individual retirement account (IRA). A type of retirement plan to which an individual with earned income can contribute a maximum of $3,000 ($3,000 each in the case of a married couple with a spousal IRA) per tax year for 2002–2004. The maximum amount increases to $4,000 in 2005 and to $5,000 in 2008. IRAs can be classified as traditional IRAs or Roth IRAs. With a traditional IRA, an individual can contribute and deduct a maximum of $4,000 per tax year in 2006. The deduction is a deduction *for* AGI. However, if the individual is an active participant in another qualified retirement plan, the deduction is phased out proportionally between certain AGI ranges (note that the phase-out limits the amount of the deduction and not the amount of the contribution). With a Roth IRA, an individual can contribute a maximum of $4,000 per tax year in 2006. No deduction is permitted. However, if a five-year holding period requirement is satisfied and if the distribution is a qualified distribution, the taxpayer can make tax-free withdrawals from a Roth IRA. The maximum annual contribution is phased out proportionally between certain AGI ranges. §§ 219 and 408A. See also *simplified employee pension plan*.

Inheritance tax. An excise tax levied on the heir based on the value of property received from a decedent. See also *estate tax*.

Installment method. A method of accounting enabling a taxpayer to spread the recognition of gain on the sale of property over the payout period. Under this procedure, the seller computes the gross profit percentage from the sale (the gain divided by the contract price) and applies it to each payment received to arrive at the gain to be recognized. §§ 453 and 453A.

Intangible drilling and development costs (IDC). Taxpayers may elect to expense or capitalize (subject to amortization) intangible drilling and development costs. However, ordinary income recapture provisions apply to oil and gas properties on a sale or other disposition if the expense method is elected. §§ 263(c) and 1254(a).

Interest-free loans. Bona fide loans that carry no interest (or a below-market rate). If made in a nonbusiness setting, the imputed interest element is treated as a gift from the lender to the borrower. If made by a corporation to a shareholder, a constructive dividend could result. In either event, the lender may recognize interest income, and the borrower may be able to deduct interest expense. § 7872.

Interest on student loans. A limited ability exists to deduct interest on student loans used to pay qualified higher education expenses (i.e., tuition, fees, books, supplies, room and board). The ceiling on the deduction is $2,500. The deduction is a deduction *for* AGI. § 221. See also *consumer interest.*

Interpretive Regulation. A Regulation issued by the Treasury Department that purports to explain the meaning of a particular Code Section. An interpretive Regulation is given less deference than a legislative Regulation. See also *legislative regulation* and *procedural regulation.* § 7805.

Investigation of a new business. Expenditures incurred in the evaluation of prospective business activities by taxpayers who are not engaged in a trade or business (to acquire an existing business or enter into a new trade or business). If the expenditures are general, it is the position of the IRS that no deduction is permitted even if the investigation is abandoned because the taxpayer is not engaged in a trade or business. The courts, however, have permitted a loss deduction providing the expenditures were specific.

Investment income. Gross income from interest, dividends, annuities, and royalties not derived in the ordinary course of a trade or business. Net capital gain attributable to the disposition of property producing these types of income and qualified dividend income normally are not included in investment income. However, a taxpayer may elect to include the capital gains as investment income if the net capital gain qualifying for the *alternative tax* is reduced by an equivalent amount. A similar election can be made for qualified dividends. See also *investment interest.*

Investment indebtedness. If funds are borrowed by non-corporate taxpayers for the purpose of purchasing or continuing to hold investment property, some portion of the interest expense deduction may be disallowed. The interest deduction is generally limited to net investment income. Amounts that are disallowed may be carried forward and treated as investment interest of the succeeding year. § 163(d).

Investment interest. Payment for the use of funds used to acquire assets that produce investment income. The deduction for investment interest is limited to *net investment income* for the tax year. See also *investment income.*

Investment tax credit (ITC). A tax credit that usually was equal to 10 percent (unless a reduced credit was elected) of the qualified investment in tangible personalty used in a trade or business. If the tangible personalty had a recovery period of five years or more, the full cost of the property qualified for the credit. Only 60 percent of cost qualified for property with a recovery period of three years. However, the regular investment tax credit was repealed by TRA of 1986 for property placed in service after December 31, 1985. §§ 46–48. See also *general business credit and recapture of investment tax credit.*

Involuntary conversion. The loss or destruction of property through theft, casualty, or condemnation. Any gain realized on an involuntary conversion can, at the taxpayer's election, be postponed (deferred) for Federal income tax purposes if the owner reinvests the proceeds within a prescribed period of time in property that is similar or related in service or use. § 1033. See also *nontaxable exchange.*

IRA. See *individual retirement account.*

Itemized deductions. Certain personal expenditures allowed by the Code as deductions *from* adjusted gross income. Examples include certain medical expenses, interest on home mortgages, state income taxes, and charitable contributions. Itemized deductions are reported on Schedule A of Form 1040. Certain miscellaneous itemized deductions are reduced by 2 percent of the taxpayer's adjusted gross income. In addition, a taxpayer whose adjusted gross income exceeds $100,000 ($50,000 for married filing separately) must reduce the itemized deductions by 3 percent of the excess of adjusted gross income over $100,000. For 2006, the indexed amount for the $100,000 is $150,500, and the indexed amount for the $50,000 is $75,250. Medical, casualty and theft, and investment interest deductions arc not subject to the 3 percent reduction. The 3 percent reduction may not reduce itemized deductions that are subject to the reduction to below 20 percent of their initial amount. Beginning in 2006, this reduction is subject to partial phaseout. §§ 63(d), 67, and 68.

K

Keogh plan. See *self-employment retirement plan.*

Kiddie tax. To reduce the tax savings that result from shifting income from parents to children, the net unearned income of a child under age 14 is taxed at the marginal tax rate of the parent(s). For the provision to apply, the child must have at least one living parent and unearned income of more than $1,700 for the tax year. § 1(g). See also *unearned income.*

L

Last-in, first-out (LIFO). An accounting method for valuing inventories for tax purposes. Under this method, it is assumed that the inventory on hand is valued at the cost of the earliest acquired units. § 472 and the related Regulations. See also *first-in, first-out (FIFO).*

Least aggregate deferral method. An algorithm set forth in the Regulations to determine the tax year for a partnership with partners whose tax years differ. The tax year that produces the least aggregate deferral of income for the partners is selected.

Legislative Regulation. Some Code Sections give the Secretary of the Treasury or his delegate the authority to prescribe Regulations to carry out the details of administration or to otherwise complete the operating rules. Regulations issued pursuant to this type of authority truly possess the force and effect of law. In effect, Congress is almost delegating its legislative powers to the Treasury Department. See also *interpretive regulation* and *procedural regulation.*

Lessee. One who rents property from another. In the case of real estate, the lessee is also known as the tenant.

Lessor. One who rents property to another. In the case of real estate, the lessor is also known as the landlord.

Letter rulings. Issued upon a taxpayer's request, by the National Office of the IRS, they describe how the IRS will treat a proposed transaction for tax purposes. They apply only to the taxpayer who asks for and obtains the ruling, but post-1984 rulings may be substantial authority for purposes of avoiding the accuracy-related penalties. The IRS limits the issuance of letter rulings to restricted, preannounced areas of taxation.

Life insurance proceeds. Generally, life insurance proceeds paid to a beneficiary upon the death of the insured are exempt from Federal income tax. An exception is provided when a life insurance contract has been transferred for valuable consideration to another individual who assumes ownership rights. In that case, the proceeds are income to the assignee to the extent that the proceeds exceed the amount paid for the policy plus any subsequent premiums paid. Insurance proceeds may be subject to the Federal estate tax if the decedent retained any incidents of ownership in the policy before death or if the proceeds are payable to the decedent's estate. §§ 101 and 2042.

Lifetime learning credit. A tax credit for qualifying expenses for taxpayers pursuing education beyond the first two years of postsecondary education. Individuals who are completing their last two years of undergraduate studies, pursuing graduate or professional degrees, or otherwise seeking new job skills or maintaining existing job skills are all eligible for the credit. Eligible individuals include the taxpayer, taxpayer's spouse, and taxpayer's dependents. The maximum credit is 20 percent of the first $10,000 of qualifying expenses and is computed per taxpayer. The credit is phased out for higher-income taxpayers. § 25A.

Like-kind exchange. An exchange of property held for productive use in a trade or business or for investment (except inventory, stocks and bonds, and partnership interests) for other investment or trade or business property. Unless non-like-kind property is received (boot), the exchange will be nontaxable. § 1031. See also *boot* and *nontaxable exchange*.

Limited expensing. See *Section 179 expensing*.

Limited liability company. An organization that combines the corporate characteristic of limited liability with treatment as a partnership for Federal income tax purposes.

Liquidating distribution. A distribution of assets by a corporation associated with the termination of the business. See also *liquidation of a corporation*.

Liquidation of a corporation. In a complete or partial liquidation of a corporation, amounts received by the shareholders in exchange for their stock are usually treated as a sale or exchange of the stock resulting in capital gain or loss treatment. § 331. Special rules apply to the liquidation of a subsidiary under § 332. Generally, a liquidation is a taxable event to the corporation. § 336. Special rules apply to a parent corporation that is liquidating a subsidiary. § 337.

Listed property. The term listed property includes (1) any passenger automobile, (2) any other property used as a means of transportation, (3) any property of a type generally used for purposes of entertainment, recreation, or amusement, (4) any computer or peripheral equipment (with an exception for exclusive business use), (5) any cellular telephone (or other similar telecommunications equipment), and (6) any other property of a type specified in the Regulations. If listed property is predominantly used for business, the taxpayer is allowed to use the statutory percentage method of cost recovery. Otherwise, the straight-line cost recovery method must be used. § 280F.

Long-term care insurance. Insurance that helps pay the cost of care when the insured is unable to care for himself or herself. Such insurance is generally thought of as insurance against the cost of an aged person entering a nursing home. The employer can provide the insurance, and the premiums may be excluded from the employee's gross income. § 7702B.

Long-term contract. A building, installation, construction, or manufacturing contract that is entered into but not completed within the same tax year. A manufacturing contract is a long-term contract only if the contract is to manufacture (1) a unique item not normally carried in finished goods inventory or (2) items that normally require more than 12 calendar months to complete. The two available methods to account for long-term contracts are the percentage of completion method and the completed contract method. The completed contract method can be used only in limited circumstances. § 460. See also *completed contract method* and *percentage of completion method*.

Long-term nonpersonal use capital assets. Includes investment property with a long-term holding period. Such property disposed of by casualty or theft may receive § 1231 treatment. See also *Section 1231 gains and losses*.

Lower of cost or market. An elective inventory method, whereby the taxpayer may value inventories at the lower of the taxpayer's actual cost or the current replacement cost of the goods. This method cannot be used in conjunction with the LIFO inventory method.

Low-income housing. Low-income housing is rental housing that is a dwelling unit for low- or moderate-income individuals or families. Beneficial tax treatment is in the form of the *low-income housing credit*. § 42. See also *accelerated cost recovery system (ACRS)*.

Low-income housing credit. Beneficial treatment to owners of low-income housing is provided in the form of a tax credit. The calculated credit is claimed in the year the building is placed in service and in the following nine years. § 42. See also *general business credit*.

Lump-sum distribution. Payment of the entire amount due at one time rather than in installments. Such distributions often occur from qualified pension or profit sharing plans upon the retirement or death of a covered employee. The recipient of a lump-sum distribution may recognize both long-term capital gain and ordinary income upon the receipt of the distribution. The ordinary income portion may be subject to a special 10-year income averaging provision. § 402(e).

M

MACRS. See *accelerated cost recovery system (ACRS)*.

Majority interest partners. Partners who have more than a 50 percent interest in partnership profits and capital, counting only those partners who have the same taxable year, are referred to as majority interest partners. The term is of significance in determining the appropriate taxable year of a partnership. § 706(b). See also *accounting period* and *principal partner*.

Marital deduction. A deduction allowed upon the transfer of property from one spouse to another. The deduction is allowed under the Federal gift tax for lifetime (inter vivos) transfers or under the Federal estate tax for death (testamentary) transfers. §§ 2056 and 2523.

Marriage penalty. The additional tax liability that results for a married couple compared with what their tax liability would be if they were not married and filed separate returns.

Material participation. If an individual taxpayer materially participates in a nonrental trade or business activity, any loss from that activity is treated as an active loss that can be offset against active income. Material participation is achieved by meeting any one of seven tests provided in the Regulations. § 469(h).

Medical expenses. Medical expenses of an individual, spouse, and dependents are allowed as an itemized deduction to the extent that such amounts (less insurance reimbursements) exceed 7.5 percent of adjusted gross income. § 213.

Medical savings account. A plan available to employees of small firms (50 or fewer employees) with high-deductible health insurance. The employee can place money in the fund and then deduct the contributions (within limits) from gross income. If the employer contributes to the fund, the employee can exclude the contribution from gross income. Income earned from the fund and withdrawals for medical care are not subject to tax. §§ 106(b) and 220.

Mid-month convention. A cost recovery convention that assumes property is placed in service in the middle of the month that it is actually placed in service.

Mid-quarter convention. A cost recovery convention that assumes property placed in service during the year is placed in service at the middle of the quarter in which it is actually placed in service. The mid-quarter convention applies if more than 40 percent of the value of property (other than eligible real estate) is placed in service during the last quarter of the year.

Miscellaneous itemized deductions. A special category of itemized deductions that includes such expenses as professional dues, tax return preparation fees, job-hunting costs, unreimbursed employee business expenses, and certain investment expenses. Such expenses are deductible only to the extent they exceed 2 percent of adjusted gross income. § 67. See also *itemized deductions*.

Mitigation of the annual accounting period concept. Various tax provisions that provide relief from the effect of the finality of the annual accounting period concept. For example, the *net operating loss* provisions provide relief to a taxpayer whose business profits and losses for different taxable years fluctuate. See also *accounting period*.

Modified accelerated cost recovery system (MACRS). See *accelerated cost recovery system (ACRS)*.

Modified adjusted gross income. A key determinant in computing the production activities deduction (PAD). The deduction is limited to a percentage of the *lesser of* qualified production activities income (QPAI) or modified adjusted gross income. Aside from limited changes required by § 199(d)(2)(A), modified adjusted gross income is AGI as usually determined but without any production activities deduction (PAD). See also *production activities deduction (PAD)*.

Moving expenses. A deduction *for* AGI is permitted to employees and self-employed individuals provided certain tests are met. The taxpayer's new job must be at least 50 miles farther from the old residence than the old residence was from the former place of work. In addition, an employee must be employed on a full-time basis at the new location for 39 weeks in the 12-month period following the move. Deductible moving expenses include the cost of moving the household and personal effects, transportation, and lodging expenses during the move. The cost of meals during the move are not deductible. Qualified moving expenses that are paid (or reimbursed) by the employer can be excluded from the employee's gross income. In this case, the related deduction by the employee is not permitted. §§ 62(a)(15), 132(a)(6), and 217.

Multiple support agreement. To qualify for a dependency exemption, the support test must be satisfied. This requires that over 50 percent of the support of the potential dependent be provided by the taxpayer. Where no one person provides more than 50 percent of the support, a multiple support agreement enables a taxpayer to still qualify for the dependency exemption. Any person who contributed more than 10 percent of the support is entitled to claim the exemption if each person in the group who contributed more than 10 percent files a written consent (Form 2120). Each person who is a party to the multiple support agreement must meet all the other requirements for claiming the dependency exemption. § 152(c). See also *personal and dependency exemptions*.

N

National sales tax. Intended as a replacement for the current Federal income tax. Unlike a value added tax (VAT), which is levied on the manufacturer, it would be imposed on the consumer upon the final sale of goods and services. To keep the tax from being regressive, low-income taxpayers would be granted some kind of credit or exemption.

Necessary. Appropriate and helpful in furthering the taxpayer's business or income-producing activity. §§ 162(a) and 212. See also *ordinary*.

Net capital gain. The excess of the net long-term capital gain for the tax year over the net short-term capital loss. The net capital gain of an individual taxpayer is eligible for the alternative tax. § 1222(11). See also *alternative tax*.

Net capital loss. The excess of the losses from sales or exchanges of capital assets over the gains from sales or exchanges of such assets. Up to $3,000 per year of the net capital loss may be deductible by noncorporate taxpayers against ordinary income. The excess net capital loss carries over to future tax years. For corporate taxpayers, the net capital loss cannot be offset against ordinary income, but it can be carried back three years and forward five years to offset net capital gains. §§ 1211, 1212, and 1221(10).

Net investment income. The excess of *investment income* over investment expenses. Investment expenses are those deductible expenses directly connected with the production of investment income. Investment expenses do not include investment interest. The deduction for *investment interest* for the tax year is limited to net investment income. § 163(d).

Net operating loss. To mitigate the effect of the annual accounting period concept, § 172 allows taxpayers to use an excess loss of one year as a deduction for certain past or future years. In this regard, a carryback period of 2 years and a carryforward period of 20 years are allowed. See also *mitigation of the annual accounting period concept.*

Net worth method. An approach used by the IRS to reconstruct the income of a taxpayer who fails to maintain adequate records. Under this approach, the gross income for the year is the increase in net worth of the taxpayer (assets in excess of liabilities) with appropriate adjustment for nontaxable receipts and nondeductible expenditures. The net worth method often is used when tax fraud is suspected.

Ninety-day letter. See *statutory notice of deficiency.*

No-additional-cost services. Services that the employer may provide the employee at no additional cost to the employer. Generally, the benefit is the ability to utilize the employer's excess capacity (vacant seats on an airliner). Such amounts are excludible from the recipient's gross income. § 132.

Nonaccountable plan. An expense reimbursement plan that does not have an accountability feature. The result is that employee expenses must be claimed as deductions *from* AGI. An exception is moving expenses, which are deductions *for* AGI. See also *accountable plan.*

Nonacquiescence. Announcement of disagreement by the IRS on the result reached in certain judicial decisions. Sometimes abbreviated *Nonacq.* or *NA.* See also *acquiescence.*

Nonbusiness bad debts. A bad debt loss not incurred in connection with a creditor's trade or business. The loss is deductible as a short-term capital loss and is allowed only in the year the debt becomes entirely worthless. In addition to family loans, many investor losses fall into the classification of nonbusiness bad debts. § 166(d). See also *bad debts.*

Nonqualified deferred compensation (NQDC) plans. Compensation arrangements that are frequently offered to executives. Such plans may include stock options, restricted stock, etc. Often, an executive may defer the recognition of taxable income. The employer, however, does not receive a tax deduction until the employee is required to include the compensation in income. See also *restricted property plan.*

Nonqualified stock option (NQSO). A type of stock option that does not satisfy the statutory requirements of an incentive stock option. If the NQSO has a readily ascertainable fair market value (e.g., the option is traded on an established exchange), the value of the option must be included in the employee's gross income at the date of the grant. Otherwise, the employee does not recognize income at the grant date. Instead, ordinary income is recognized in the year of exercise of the option. See also *incentive stock option (ISO).*

Nonrecourse debt. An obligation on which the endorser is not personally liable. An example of a nonrecourse debt is a mortgage on real estate acquired by a partnership without the assumption of any liability on the mortgage by the partnership or any of the partners. The acquired property generally is pledged as collateral for the loan.

Nonrefundable credit. A nonrefundable credit is a credit that is not paid if it exceeds the taxpayer's tax liability. Some nonrefundable credits qualify for carryback and carryover treatment. See also *refundable credit.*

Nontaxable exchange. A transaction in which realized gains or losses are not recognized. The recognition of gain or loss is postponed (deferred) until the property received in the nontaxable exchange is subsequently disposed of in a taxable transaction. Examples are § 1031 like-kind exchanges and § 1033 involuntary conversions. See also *involuntary conversion* and *like-kind exchange.*

O

Occupational tax. A tax imposed on various trades or businesses. A license fee that enables a taxpayer to engage in a particular occupation.

Office audit. An audit by the IRS of a taxpayer's return that is conducted in the agent's office. To be distinguished from a *correspondence audit* or a *field audit.*

Office-in-the-home expenses. Employment and business-related expenses attributable to the use of a residence (e.g., den or office) are allowed only if the portion of the residence is exclusively used on a regular basis as a principal place of business of the taxpayer or as a place of business that is used by patients, clients, or customers. If the expenses are incurred by an employee, the use must be for the convenience of the employer as opposed to being merely appropriate and helpful. § 280A.

One-year rule for prepaid expenses. Taxpayers who use the cash method are required to use the accrual method for deducting certain prepaid expenses (i.e., must capitalize the item and can deduct only when used). If a prepayment will not be consumed or expire by the end of the tax year following the year of payment, the prepayment must be capitalized and prorated over the benefit period. Conversely, if the prepayment will be consumed by the end of the tax year following the year of payment, it can be expensed when paid. To obtain the current deduction under the one-year rule, the payment must be a required payment rather than a voluntary payment.

Open transaction. A judicially imposed doctrine that allows the taxpayer to defer all gain until he or she has collected an amount equal to the adjusted basis of assets transferred pursuant to an exchange transaction. This doctrine has been applied where the property received in an exchange has no ascertainable fair market value due to the existence of contingencies. The method is permitted only in very limited circumstances. See also *recovery of capital doctrine.*

Options. The sale or exchange of an option to buy or sell property results in capital gain or loss if the property is a capital asset. Generally, the closing of an option transaction results in short-term capital gain or loss to the writer of the call and the purchaser of the call option. § 1234.

Ordinary. Common and accepted in the general industry or type of activity in which the taxpayer is engaged. It comprises one of the tests for the deductibility of expenses incurred or paid in connection with a trade or business; for the production or collection of income; for the management, conservation, or maintenance of property held for the production of income; or in connection with the determination, collection, or refund of any tax. §§ 162(a) and 212. See also *necessary*.

Ordinary and necessary. See *necessary* and *ordinary*.

Ordinary income property. Property contributed to a charitable organization that, if sold rather than contributed, would have resulted in other than long-term capital gain to the donor (i.e., ordinary income property and short-term capital gain property). Examples are inventory and capital assets held for less than the long-term holding period.

Organizational expenditures. A corporation may elect to immediately expense the first $5,000 (subject to phaseout) of organizational expenses and generally amortize the balance over a period of 180 months or more. Certain expenses of organizing a company do not qualify for amortization (e.g., expenditures connected with issuing or selling stock or other securities). § 248.

Original issue discount (OID). The difference between the issue price of a debt obligation (e.g., a corporate bond) and the maturity value of the obligation when the issue price is *less than* the maturity value. OID represents interest and must be amortized over the life of the debt obligation using the effective interest method. The difference is not considered to be original issue discount for tax purposes when it is less than one-fourth of 1 percent of the redemption price at maturity multiplied by the number of years to maturity. §§ 1272 and 1273(a)(3).

Outside salesperson. An outside salesperson solicits business away from the employer's place of business on a full-time basis. The employment-related expenses of an outside salesperson are itemized deductions unless reimbursed by the employer. If reimbursed, such expenses are deductible *for* AGI.

P

Partnerships. A partnership is treated as a conduit and is not subject to taxation. Various items of partnership income, expenses, gains, and losses flow through to the individual partners and are reported on the partners' personal income tax returns. §§ 701 and 702.

Passive activity. A trade or business activity in which the taxpayer does not materially participate is subject to limitations on the deduction of losses and credits. Rental activities (subject to exceptions) and limited partnership interests are inherently passive. Relief from passive activity limitation treatment is provided in certain situations, such as for certain rental real estate, if the taxpayer actively participates in the activity. The annual ceiling on this rental real estate relief is $25,000. Relief also is provided for material participation in a real estate trade or business. § 469. See also *passive loss* and *portfolio income*.

Passive investment income. As defined in § 1362(d)(3)(D), passive investment income means gross receipts from royalties, certain rents, dividends, interest, annuities, and gains from the sale or exchange of stock and securities. Revocation of the S corporation election may occur in certain cases when the S corporation has passive investment income in excess of 25 percent of gross receipts for a period of three consecutive years.

Passive loss. Any loss from (1) activities in which the taxpayer does not materially participate or (2) rental activities (subject to certain exceptions). Net passive losses cannot be used to offset income from nonpassive sources. Rather, they are suspended until the taxpayer either generates net passive income (and a deduction of the losses is allowed) or disposes of the underlying property (at which time the loss deductions are allowed in full). One relief provision allows landlords who actively participate in the rental activities to deduct up to $25,000 of passive losses annually. However, a phaseout of the $25,000 amount commences when the landlord's AGI exceeds $100,000. Another relief provision applies for material participation in a real estate trade or business. See also *passive activity* and *portfolio income*.

Patent. A patent is an intangible asset that may be amortized over a statutory 15-year period as a § 197 intangible. The sale of a patent usually results in favorable long-term capital gain treatment. §§ 197 and 1235.

Pension plan. A type of deferred compensation arrangement that provides for systematic payments of definitely determinable retirement benefits to employees who meet the requirements set forth in the plan. See also *defined benefit plan* and *defined contribution plan*.

Percentage depletion. Percentage depletion is depletion based on a statutory percentage applied to the gross income from the property. The taxpayer deducts the greater of cost depletion or percentage depletion. § 613. See also *cost depletion*.

Percentage of completion method. A method of reporting gain or loss on certain long-term contracts. Under this method of accounting, the gross contract price is included in income as the contract is being completed. § 460 and Reg. § 1.451–3. See also *completed contract method* and *long-term contract*.

Permanent and total disability. A person is considered permanently and totally disabled if he or she is unable to engage in any substantial gainful activity due to a physical or mental impairment. In addition, this impairment must be one that can be expected to result in death or that has lasted or can be expected to last for a continuous period of not less than 12 months. The taxpayer generally must provide the IRS a physician's statement documenting this condition.

Personal and dependency exemptions. The tax law provides an exemption for each individual taxpayer and an additional exemption for the taxpayer's spouse if a joint return is filed. An individual may also claim a dependency exemption for each dependent, provided certain tests are met. The amount of the personal and dependency exemptions is $3,200 in 2005 and $3,300 in 2006. The amount is indexed for inflation. The exemption is subject to phaseout once adjusted gross income exceeds certain statutory threshold amounts. This phaseout provision is subject to partial phaseout beginning in 2006. §§ 151 and 152. See also *qualifying child* and *qualifying relative*.

Personal casualty gain. The recognized gain from any involuntary conversion of personal use property arising from fire, storm, shipwreck, or other casualty, or from theft. See also *personal casualty loss*.

Personal casualty loss. The recognized loss from any involuntary conversion of personal use property arising from fire, storm, shipwreck, or other casualty, or from theft. See also *personal casualty gain.*

Personal exemption. See *personal and dependency exemptions.*

Personal expenses. Expenses of an individual for personal reasons that are not deductible unless specifically provided for under the tax law. § 262.

Personal property. Generally, all property other than real estate. It is sometimes referred to as personalty when real estate is termed realty. Personal property also can refer to property that is not used in a taxpayer's trade or business or held for the production or collection of income. When used in this sense, personal property can include both realty (e.g., a personal residence) and personalty (e.g., personal effects such as clothing and furniture).

Personal residence. See *sale of principal residence.*

Personal service corporation (PSC). A corporation the principal activity of which is the performance of personal services (e.g., health, law, engineering, architecture, accounting, actuarial science, performing arts, or consulting), with such services being substantially performed by the employee-owners. The 35 percent statutory rate applies to PSCs.

Personalty. All property other than realty (real estate). Personalty usually is categorized as tangible or intangible property. Tangible personalty includes such assets as machinery and equipment, automobiles and trucks, and office equipment. Intangible personalty includes stocks and bonds, goodwill, patents, trademarks, and copyrights. See also *personal property.*

Points. Loan origination fees that may be deductible as interest by a buyer of property. A seller of property who pays points reduces the selling price by the amount of the points paid for the buyer. While the seller is not permitted to deduct this amount as interest, the buyer may do so. See *prepaid interest* for the timing of the interest deduction.

Pollution control facilities. A certified pollution control facility, the cost of which may be amortized over a 60-month period if the taxpayer elects. § 169.

Portfolio income. The term is relevant in applying the limitation on passive activity losses and credits. Although normally considered passive in nature, for this purpose portfolio income is treated as nonpassive. Therefore, net passive losses and credits cannot be offset against portfolio income. Examples of portfolio income are interest, dividends, annuities, and certain royalties. § 469. See also *passive activity.*

Precedent. A previously decided court decision that is recognized as authority for the disposition of future decisions.

Prepaid expenses. Cash basis as well as accrual basis taxpayers usually are required to capitalize prepayments for rent, insurance, etc., that cover more than one year. Deductions are taken during the period the benefits are received.

Prepaid interest. In effect, the Code places cash basis taxpayers on an accrual basis for purposes of recognizing a deduction for prepaid interest. Thus, interest paid in advance is deductible as an interest expense only as it accrues. The one exception to this rule involves the interest element when a cash basis taxpayer pays points to obtain financing for the purchase of a principal residence (or to make improvements thereto) if the payment of points is an established business practice in the area in which the indebtedness is incurred and the amount involved is not excessive. § 461(g). See also *points.*

Principal partner. A partner with a 5 percent or greater interest in partnership capital or profits. § 706(b)(3). See also *majority interest partners.*

Private activity bond. Interest on state and local bonds is excludible from gross income. § 103. Certain such bonds are labeled private activity bonds. Although the interest on such bonds is excludible for regular income tax purposes, it is treated as a tax preference in calculating the AMT. See also *alternative minimum tax (AMT).*

Prizes and awards. The fair market value of a prize or award generally is includible in gross income. However, exclusion is permitted if the prize or award is made in recognition of religious, charitable, scientific, educational, artistic, literary, or civic achievement, and the recipient transfers the award to a qualified governmental unit or a nonprofit organization. In that case, the recipient must be selected without any action on his or her part to enter a contest or proceeding, and the recipient must not be required to render substantial future services as a condition of receiving the prize or award. § 74.

Procedural Regulation. A Regulation issued by the Treasury Department that is a housekeeping-type instruction indicating information that taxpayers should provide the IRS as well as information about the internal management and conduct of the IRS itself. See also *interpretive regulation* and *legislative regulation.*

Production activities deduction (PAD). A deduction based on 3% of the lesser of qualified production activities income (QPAI) or modified adjusted gross income but not to exceed 50% of the W–2 wages paid. In the case of a corporate taxpayer, taxable income is substituted for modified AGI. The deduction rate increases to 6% for 2007 to 2009 and to 9% for 2010 and thereafter. §199. See also *qualified production activities income (QPAI).*

Profit sharing plan. A deferred compensation plan established and maintained by an employer to provide for employee participation in the company's profits. Contributions are paid from the employer's current or accumulated profits to a trustee. Separate accounts are maintained for each participant employee. The plan must provide a definite, predetermined formula for allocating the contributions among the participants. It also must include a definite, predetermined formula for distributing the accumulated funds after a fixed number of years, on the attainment of a stated age, or on the occurrence of certain events such as illness, layoff, or retirement.

Proposed Regulation. A Regulation issued by the Treasury Department in proposed, rather than final, form. The interval between the proposal of a Regulation and its finalization permits taxpayers and other interested parties to comment on the propriety of the proposal. See also *regulations* and *temporary regulation.*

Public policy limitation. See *bribes and illegal payments.*

Punitive damages. Damages received or paid by the taxpayer can be classified as compensatory damages or as punitive damages. Punitive damages are those awarded to punish the defendant for gross negligence or the intentional infliction of harm. Such damages are includible in gross income. § 104. See also *compensatory damages.*

Q

Qualified dividend income. Dividends that are eligible for the beneficial 5 percent or 15 percent tax rate. Excluded are certain dividends from foreign corporations, dividends from tax-exempt entities, and dividends that do not satisfy the holding period requirement. A dividend from a foreign corporation is eligible for qualified dividend status only if one of the following requirements are met: (1) the foreign corporation's stock is traded on an established U.S. securities market, or (2) the foreign corporation is eligible for the benefits of a comprehensive income tax treaty between its country of incorporation and the United States. To satisfy the holding period requirement, the stock on which the dividend is paid must have been held for more than 60 days during the 120-day period beginning 60 days before the ex-dividend date.

Qualified employee discounts. Discounts offered employees on merchandise or services that the employer ordinarily sells or provides to customers. The discounts must be generally available to all employees. In the case of property, the discount cannot exceed the employer's gross profit (the sales price cannot be less than the employer's cost). In the case of services, the discounts cannot exceed 20 percent of the normal sales price. § 132.

Qualified pension or profit sharing plan. An employer-sponsored plan that meets the requirements of § 401. If these requirements are met, none of the employer's contributions to the plan will be taxed to the employee until distributed to him or her (§ 402). The employer will be allowed a deduction in the year the contributions are made (§ 404). See also *annuity* and *deferred compensation.*

Qualified production activities income (QPAI). A key determinant in computing the production activities deduction (PAD). It consists of domestic production gross receipts (DPGR) reduced by cost of goods sold and other assignable expenses. Thus, QPAI represents the profit derived from production activities. § 199. See also *production activities deduction (PAD)* and *domestic production gross receipts (DPGR).*

Qualified real property business indebtedness. Indebtedness that was incurred or assumed by the taxpayer in connection with real property used in a trade or business and is secured by such real property. The taxpayer must not be a C corporation. For qualified real property business indebtedness, the taxpayer may elect to exclude some or all of the income realized from cancellation of debt on qualified real property. If the election is made, the basis of the property must be reduced by the amount excluded. The amount excluded cannot be greater than the excess of the principal amount of the outstanding debt over the fair market value (net of any other debt outstanding on the property) of the property securing the debt. § 108(c).

Qualified residence interest. A term relevant in determining the amount of interest expense the individual taxpayer may deduct as an itemized deduction for what otherwise would be disallowed as a component of personal interest (consumer interest). Qualified residence interest consists of interest paid on qualified residences (principal residence and one other residence) of the taxpayer. Debt that qualifies as qualified residence interest is limited to $1 million of debt to acquire, construct, or substantially improve qualified residences (acquisition indebtedness) plus $100,000 of other debt secured by qualified residences (home equity indebtedness). The home equity indebtedness may not exceed the fair market value of a qualified residence reduced by the acquisition indebtedness for that residence. § 163(h)(3). See also *consumer interest* and *home equity loans.*

Qualified transportation fringes. Transportation benefits provided by the employer to the employee. Such benefits include (1) transportation in a commuter highway vehicle between the employee's residence and the place of employment, (2) a transit pass, and (3) qualified parking. Qualified transportation fringes are excludible from the employee's gross income to the extent categories (1) and (2) above do not exceed $105 per month in 2006 and category (3) does not exceed $205 per month in 2006. These amounts are indexed annually for inflation. § 132.

Qualified tuition program. A program that allows college tuition to be prepaid for a beneficiary. When amounts in the plan are used, nothing is included in gross income provided they are used for qualified higher education expenses. § 529.

Qualified tuition reduction plan. A type of fringe benefit plan that is available to employees of nonprofit educational institutions. Such employees (and the spouse and dependent children) are allowed to exclude from gross income a tuition waiver pursuant to a qualified tuition reduction plan. The exclusion applies to undergraduate tuition. In limited circumstances, the exclusion also applies to the graduate tuition of teaching and research assistants. § 117(d).

Qualifying child. An individual who, as to the taxpayer, satisfies the relationship, abode, and age tests. To be claimed as a dependent, such an individual must also meet the citizenship and joint return tests and not be self-supporting. §§ 152(a)(1) and (c). See also *personal and dependency exemptions.*

Qualifying relative. An individual who, as to the taxpayer, satisfies the relationship, gross income, support, citizenship, and joint return tests. Such an individual can be claimed as a dependent of the taxpayer. §§ 152(a)(2) and (d). See also *personal and dependency exemptions.*

R

RAR. A Revenue Agent's Report, which reflects any adjustments made by the agent as a result of an audit of the taxpayer. The RAR is mailed to the taxpayer along with the 30-day letter, which outlines the appellate procedures available to the taxpayer.

Realized gain or loss. The difference between the amount realized upon the sale or other disposition of property and the adjusted basis of the property. § 1001. See also *adjusted basis* and *recognized gain or loss.*

Realty. All real estate, including land and buildings. Permanent improvements to a building (fixtures) become realty if their removal would cause significant damage to the property. An example of a fixture is the installation of a central air conditioning or heating system to a building.

Thus, personalty can become realty through the fixture reclassification.

Reasonable needs of the business. See *accumulated earnings tax.*

Reasonableness. The Code includes a reasonableness requirement with respect to the deduction of salaries and other compensation for services. What constitutes reasonableness is a question of fact. If an expense is unreasonable, the amount that is classified as unreasonable is not allowed as a deduction. The question of reasonableness generally arises with respect to closely held corporations where there is no separation of ownership and management. § 162(a)(1).

Recapture. To recover the tax benefit of a deduction or a credit previously taken.

Recapture of depreciation. Upon the disposition of depreciable property used in a trade or business, gain or loss is measured by the difference between the consideration received (the amount realized) and the adjusted basis of the property. Before the enactment of the recapture of depreciation provisions of the Code, any such gain recognized could be § 1231 gain and usually qualified for long-term capital gain treatment. The recapture provisions of the Code (e.g., §§ 1245 and 1250) may operate to convert some or all of the previous § 1231 gain into ordinary income. The justification for recapture of depreciation is that it prevents a taxpayer from deducting depreciation at ordinary income rates and having the related gain on disposition taxed at capital gain rates. The recapture of depreciation rules do not apply when the property is disposed of at a loss. See also *residential rental property, Section 1231 gains and losses, Section 1245 recapture,* and *Section 1250 recapture.*

Recapture of investment tax credit. When investment tax credit property is disposed of or ceases to be used in the trade or business of the taxpayer, some or all of the investment tax credit claimed on the property may be recaptured as additional tax liability. The amount of the recapture is the difference between the amount of the credit originally claimed and what should have been claimed in light of the length of time the property was actually held or used for qualifying purposes. § 50. See also *investment tax credit.*

Recapture potential. Reference is to property that, if disposed of in a taxable transaction, would result in the recapture of depreciation (§§ 1245 or 1250) and/or of the investment tax credit (§ 50).

Recognized gain or loss. The portion of realized gain or loss that is considered in computing taxable income. See also *realized gain or loss.*

Recovery of capital doctrine. When a taxable sale or exchange occurs, the seller may be permitted to recover his or her investment (or other adjusted basis) in the property before gain or loss is recognized. See also *open transaction.*

Refundable credit. A refundable credit is a credit that is paid to the taxpayer even if the amount of the credit (or credits) exceeds the taxpayer's tax liability. See also *nonrefundable credit.*

Regulations. Treasury Department Regulations represent the position of the IRS as to how the Internal Revenue Code is to be interpreted. Their purpose is to provide taxpayers and IRS personnel with rules of general and specific application to the various provisions of the tax law. Regulations are published in the *Federal Register* and in all tax services. See also *interpretive regulation, legislative regulation, procedural regulation,* and *proposed regulation.*

Rehabilitation expenditures credit. A credit that is based on expenditures incurred to rehabilitate industrial and commercial buildings and certified historic structures. The credit is intended to discourage businesses from moving from older, economically distressed areas to newer locations and to encourage the preservation of historic structures. § 47. See also *rehabilitation expenditures credit recapture.*

Rehabilitation expenditures credit recapture. When property that qualifies for the rehabilitation expenditures credit is disposed of or ceases to be used in the trade or business of the taxpayer, some or all of the tax credit claimed on the property may be recaptured as additional tax liability. The amount of the recapture is the difference between the amount of the credit claimed originally and what should have been claimed in light of the length of time the property was actually held or used for qualifying purposes. § 50. See also *rehabilitation expenditures credit.*

Related party. Includes certain family members and controlled entities (i.e., partnerships and corporations). §§ 267, 707(b), and 1239. See also *related-party transactions.*

Related-party transactions. The tax law places restrictions upon the recognition of gains and losses between related parties because of the potential for abuse. For example, restrictions are placed on the deduction of losses from the sale or exchange of property between related parties. In addition, under certain circumstances, related-party gains that would otherwise be classified as capital gain are classified as ordinary income. §§ 267, 707(b), and 1239. See also *related party.*

Rental activity. Any activity where payments are received principally for the use of tangible property is a rental activity. Temporary Regulations provide that in certain circumstances activities involving rentals of real and personal property are not to be *treated* as rental activities. The Temporary Regulations list six exceptions.

Research activities credit. A tax credit whose purpose is to encourage research and development. It consists of two components: the incremental research activities credit and the basic research credit. The incremental research activities credit is equal to 20 percent of the excess of qualified research expenditures over the base amount. The basic research credit is equal to 20 percent of the excess of basic research payments over the base amount. § 41. See also *general business credit.*

Research and experimental expenditures. The Code provides three alternatives for the tax treatment of research and experimentation expenditures. They may be expensed in the year paid or incurred, deferred subject to amortization, or capitalized. If the taxpayer does not elect to expense such costs or to defer them subject to amortization (over 60 months), the expenditures must be capitalized. § 174. Two types of research activities credits are available: the basic research credit and the incremental research activities credit. The rate for each type is 20 percent. § 41. See also *research activities credit.*

Reserve for bad debts. A method of accounting whereby an allowance is permitted for estimated uncollectible accounts. Actual write-offs are charged to the reserve, and recoveries of amounts previously written off are credited to the reserve. The Code permits only certain financial institutions to use the reserve method. § 166. See also *specific charge-off method.*

Reserve method. See *reserve for bad debts.*

Reserves for estimated expenses. Except in the limited case for bad debts, reserves for estimated expenses (e.g., warranty service costs) are not permitted for tax purposes even though such reserves are appropriate for financial accounting purposes. See also *all events test.*

Residential rental property. Buildings for which at least 80 percent of the gross rents are from dwelling units (e.g., an apartment building). This type of building is distinguished from nonresidential (commercial or industrial) buildings in applying the recapture of depreciation provisions. The term also is relevant in distinguishing between buildings that are eligible for a 27.5-year life versus a 39-year (or 31.5-year) life for MACRS purposes. Generally, residential buildings receive preferential treatment. §§ 168(e)(2) and 1250. See also *recapture of depreciation.*

Residential rental real estate. See *residential rental property.*

Restricted property plan. An arrangement whereby an employer transfers property (usually stock) to an employee at a bargain price (for less than the fair market value). If the transfer is accompanied by a substantial risk of forfeiture and the property is not transferable, no compensation results to the employee until the restrictions disappear. An example of a substantial risk of forfeiture would be a requirement that the employee return the property if his or her employment is terminated within a specified period of time. § 83. See also *nonqualified deferred compensation (NQDC) plans* and *substantial risk of forfeiture.*

Retirement of corporate obligations. The retirement of corporate and certain government obligations is considered to be a sale or exchange. Gain or loss, upon the retirement of a corporate obligation, therefore, is treated as capital gain or loss rather than as ordinary income or loss. §§ 1271–1275.

Return of capital doctrine. See *recovery of capital doctrine.*

Revenue neutrality. A description that characterizes tax legislation when it neither increases nor decreases the revenue result. Thus, any tax revenue losses are offset by tax revenue gains.

Revenue Procedure. A matter of procedural importance to both taxpayers and the IRS concerning the administration of the tax law is issued by the National Office of the IRS as a Revenue Procedure (abbreviated Rev.Proc.). A Revenue Procedure is first published in an *Internal Revenue Bulletin* (I.R.B.) and later transferred to the appropriate *Cumulative Bulletin* (C.B.). Both the *Internal Revenue Bulletin* and the *Cumulative Bulletin* are published by the U.S. Government Printing Office.

Revenue Ruling. A Revenue Ruling (abbreviated Rev.Rul.) is issued by the National Office of the IRS to express an official interpretation of the tax law as applied to specific transactions. It is more limited in application than a Regulation. A Revenue Ruling is first published in an *Internal Revenue Bulletin* (I.R.B.) and later transferred to the appropriate *Cumulative Bulletin* (C.B.). Both the *Internal Revenue*

Bulletin and the *Cumulative Bulletin* are published by the U.S. Government Printing Office.

S

S corporation. See *S corporation status.*

S corporation status. An elective provision permitting certain small business corporations (§ 1361) and their shareholders to elect (§ 1362) to be treated for income tax purposes in accordance with the operating rules of §§ 1363–1379. Of major significance are the facts that S status avoids the corporate income tax and corporate losses can be claimed by the shareholders. See also *C corporation.*

Sale of principal residence. If a residence has been owned and used by the taxpayer as the principal residence for at least two years during the five-year period ending on the date of sale, up to $250,000 of realized gain is excluded from gross income. For a married couple filing a joint return, the $250,000 is increased to $500,000 if either spouse satisfies the ownership requirement and both spouses satisfy the use requirement. § 121.

Sale or exchange. A requirement for the recognition of capital gain or loss. Generally, the seller of property must receive money or relief from debt in order to have sold the property. An exchange involves the transfer of property for other property. Thus, collection of a debt is neither a sale nor an exchange. The term *sale or exchange* is not defined by the Code.

Sales tax. A transaction tax imposed upon the sale of goods. It usually is based on a specified percentage of the value of the property sold. A sales tax differs from an excise tax, in that a sales tax applies to a broad variety of commodities.

Salvage value. The estimated amount a taxpayer will receive upon the disposition of an asset used in the taxpayer's trade or business. Salvage value is relevant in calculating depreciation under § 167, but is not relevant in calculating cost recovery under § 168.

Schedule M-1. On the Form 1120, a reconciliation of book net income with Federal taxable income. Accounts for timing and permanent differences in the two computations, such as depreciation differences, exempt income, and nondeductible items. On Forms 1120S and 1065, the Schedule M-1 reconciles book income with the owners' aggregate ordinary taxable income.

Schedule M-3. An *expanded* reconciliation of book net income with Federal taxable income (refer to *Schedule M-1* above). Applies to corporations with total assets of $10 million or more.

Scholarships. Scholarships are generally excluded from the gross income of the recipient unless the payments are a disguised form of compensation for services rendered. However, the Code imposes restrictions on the exclusion. The recipient must be a degree candidate. The excluded amount is limited to amounts used for tuition, fees, books, supplies, and equipment required for courses of instruction. Amounts received for room and board are not eligible for the exclusion. § 117.

Section 121 exclusion. See *sale of principal residence.*

Section 179 expensing. The ability to deduct a capital expenditure in the year an asset is placed in service rather than over the asset's useful life or cost recovery period. The annual ceiling on the deduction is $108,000 for 2006. However, the deduction is reduced dollar for dollar when § 179 property placed in service during the taxable year exceeds $430,000 in 2006. In addition, the amount expensed under § 179 cannot exceed the aggregate amount of taxable income derived from the conduct of any trade or business by the taxpayer.

Section 401(k) plan. A cash or deferred arrangement plan that allows participants to elect to receive up to $15,000 in 2006 ($14,000 in 2005) in cash (taxed currently) or to have a contribution made on their behalf to a profit sharing or stock bonus plan (excludible from gross income). The plan may also be in the form of a salary reduction agreement between the participant and the employer.

Section 1231 assets. Depreciable assets and real estate used in a trade or business and held for the required long-term holding period. Under certain circumstances, the classification also includes timber, coal, domestic iron ore, livestock (held for draft, breeding, dairy, or sporting purposes), and unharvested crops. § 1231(b).

Section 1231 gains and losses. If the net result of the combined gains and losses from the taxable dispositions of § 1231 assets plus the net gain from the involuntary conversion of nonpersonal use assets is a gain, the gains and losses from § 1231 assets are treated as long-term capital gains and losses. In arriving at § 1231 gains, however, the depreciation recapture provisions (e.g., §§ 1245 and 1250) are first applied to produce ordinary income. If the net result of the combination is a loss, the gains and losses from § 1231 assets are treated as ordinary gains and losses. § 1231(a). See also *recapture of depreciation*.

Section 1231 lookback. In order for gain to be classified as § 1231 gain, the gain must survive the § 1231 lookback. To the extent of nonrecaptured § 1231 losses for the five prior tax years, the gain is classified as ordinary income. § 1231(c).

Section 1231 property. See *Section 1231 assets*.

Section 1244 stock. Stock issued under § 1244 by qualifying small business corporations. If § 1244 stock is disposed of at a loss or becomes worthless, the shareholders may claim an ordinary loss rather than the usual capital loss. The annual ceiling on the ordinary loss treatment is $50,000 ($100,000 for married individuals filing jointly). See also *worthless securities*.

Section 1245 property. Property that is subject to the recapture of depreciation under § 1245. For a definition of § 1245 property, see § 1245(a)(3). See also *Section 1245 recapture*.

Section 1245 recapture. Upon a taxable disposition of § 1245 property, all depreciation claimed on the property is recaptured as ordinary income (but not to exceed the recognized gain from the disposition). See also *recapture of depreciation*.

Section 1250 property. Real estate that is subject to the recapture of depreciation under § 1250. For a definition of § 1250 property, see § 1250(c). See also *Section 1250 recapture*.

Section 1250 recapture. Upon a taxable disposition of § 1250 property, some or all of the additional depreciation claimed on the property may be recaptured as ordinary income. Various recapture rules apply depending upon the type of property (residential or nonresidential real estate) and the date acquired. Generally, the additional depreciation is recaptured in full to the extent of the gain recognized. See also *additional depreciation* and *recapture of depreciation*.

Self-employment retirement plan. A designation for retirement plans available to self-employed taxpayers. Also referred to as H.R. 10 and Keogh plans. Under such plans, in 2006, a taxpayer may deduct each year up to either 100 percent of net earnings from self-employment or $44,000, whichever is less. If the plan is a profit sharing plan, the percentage is 25 percent.

Self-employment tax. In 2006, a tax of 12.4 percent is levied on individuals with net earnings from self-employment (up to $94,200) to provide Social Security benefits (i.e., the old age, survivors, and disability insurance portion) for such individuals. In addition, in 2006, a tax of 2.9 percent is levied on individuals with net earnings from self-employment (with no statutory ceiling) to provide Medicare benefits (i.e., the hospital insurance portion) for such individuals. If a self-employed individual also receives wages from an employer that are subject to FICA, the self-employment tax will be reduced if total income subject to Social Security is more than $94,200 in 2006. A partial deduction is allowed in calculating the self-employment tax. Individuals with net earnings of $400 or more from self-employment are subject to this tax. §§ 1401 and 1402.

Separate property. In a community property jurisdiction, separate property is the property that belongs entirely to one of the spouses. Generally, it is property acquired before marriage or acquired after marriage by gift or inheritance. See also *community property*.

Severance tax. A tax imposed upon the extraction of natural resources.

Short sale. A short sale occurs when a taxpayer sells borrowed property (usually stock) and repays the lender with substantially identical property either held on the date of the short sale or purchased after the sale. No gain or loss is recognized until the short sale is closed, and such gain or loss is generally short term. § 1233.

Short taxable year (short period). A tax year that is less than 12 months. A short taxable year may occur in the initial reporting period, in the final tax year, or when the taxpayer changes tax years.

Significant participation activity. There are seven tests to determine whether an individual has achieved material participation in an activity, one of which is based on more than 500 hours of participation in significant participation activities. A significant participation activity is one in which the individual's participation exceeds 100 hours during the year. Reg. § 1.469–5T.

Simplified employee pension (SEP) plan. An employer may make contributions to an employee's IRA in amounts not exceeding the lesser of 15 percent of compensation or $44,000 per individual in 2006. These employer-sponsored simplified employee pensions are permitted only if the contributions are nondiscriminatory and are made on behalf of all employees who have attained age 21 and have worked for the employer during at least three of the five preceding calendar years. § 219(b). See also *individual retirement account (IRA)*.

Small business corporation. A corporation that satisfies the definition of § 1361(b), § 1244(c)(3), or both. Satisfaction of § 1361(b) permits an S corporation election, and satisfaction of § 1244 enables the shareholders of the corporation to claim an ordinary loss. See also *S corporation status* and *Section 1244 stock.*

Small business stock. See *small business corporation.*

Small cases division. A subsidiary division of the U.S. Tax Court. The jurisdiction of the Small Cases division is limited to small claims (i.e., claims of $50,000 or less). The proceedings of the Small Cases Division are informal, and the findings cannot be appealed.

Specific charge-off method. A method of accounting for bad debts in which a deduction is permitted only when an account becomes partially or completely worthless. See also *reserve for bad debts.*

Standard deduction. The individual taxpayer can either itemize deductions or take the standard deduction. The amount of the standard deduction depends on the taxpayer's filing status (single, head of household, married filing jointly, surviving spouse, or married filing separately). For 2006, the amount of the standard deduction ranges from $5,150 to $10,300. Additional standard deductions of either $1,000 (for married taxpayers) or $1,250 (for single taxpayers) are available if the taxpayer is either blind or age 65 or over. Limitations exist on the amount of the standard deduction of a taxpayer who is another taxpayer's dependent. The standard deduction amounts are adjusted for inflation each year. § 63(c). See also *zero bracket amount.*

Statute of limitations. Provisions of the law that specify the maximum period of time in which action may be taken on a past event. Code §§ 6501–6504 contain the limitation periods applicable to the IRS for additional assessments, and §§ 6511–6515 relate to refund claims by taxpayers.

Statutory employee. Statutory employees are considered self-employed independent contractors for purposes of reporting income and expenses on their tax returns. Generally, a statutory employee must meet three tests:

- It is understood from a service contract that the services will be performed by the person.
- The person does not have a substantial investment in facilities (other than transportation used to perform the services).
- The services involve a continuing relationship with the person for whom they are performed.

For further information on statutory employees, see Circular E, *Employer's Tax Guide*, IRS Publication 15.

Statutory notice of deficiency. Commonly referred to as the 90-day letter, this notice is sent to a taxpayer upon request, upon the expiration of the 30-day letter, or upon exhaustion by the taxpayer of his or her administrative remedies before the IRS. The notice gives the taxpayer 90 days in which to file a petition with the U.S. Tax Court. If a petition is not filed, the IRS will issue a demand for payment of the assessed deficiency. §§ 6211–6216. See also *thirty-day letter.*

Stock bonus plan. A type of deferred compensation plan in which the employer establishes and maintains the plan and contributes employer stock to the plan for the benefit of employees. The contributions need not be dependent on the employer's profits. Any benefits of the plan are distributable in the form of employer stock, except that distributable fractional shares may be paid in cash.

Stock option. The right to purchase a stated number of shares of stock from a corporation at a certain price within a specified period of time. §§ 421 and 422. See also *incentive stock option (ISO)* and *nonqualified stock option (NQSO).*

Stock redemption. The redemption of the stock of a shareholder by the issuing corporation is treated as a sale or exchange of the stock if the redemption is not a dividend. §§ 301 and 302.

Substantial risk of forfeiture. A term that is associated with a restricted property plan. Generally, an employee who receives property (e.g., stock of the employer-corporation) from the employer at a bargain price or at no cost must include the bargain element in gross income. However, the employee currently does not have to do so if there is a substantial risk of forfeiture. A substantial risk of forfeiture exists if a person's rights to full enjoyment of property are conditioned upon the future performance, or the refraining from the performance, of substantial services by the individual. § 83. See also *restricted property plan.*

Sunset provision. A provision attached to new tax legislation that will cause such legislation to expire at a specified date. Sunset provisions are attached to tax cut bills for long-term budgetary reasons in order to make their effect temporary. Once the sunset provision comes into play, the tax cut is rescinded and former law is reinstated. An example of a sunset provision is the one contained in the Tax Relief Reconciliation Act of 2001, which relates to the estate tax. After the estate tax is phased out by 2010, a sunset provision reinstates the estate tax as on January 1, 2011.

Super-full absorption costing rules. See *uniform capitalization rules.*

Surviving spouse. The joint return tax rates apply for a surviving spouse. Such rates apply for the two tax years after the tax year of the death of the spouse. To qualify as a surviving spouse, the taxpayer must maintain a household for a dependent child. § 2.

T

Targeted jobs tax credit. See *work opportunity tax credit.*

Taxable year. The annual period over which income is measured for income tax purposes. Most individuals use a calendar year, but many businesses use a fiscal year based on the natural business year. See also *accounting period* and *fiscal year.*

Tax avoidance. The minimization of one's tax liability by taking advantage of legally available tax planning opportunities. Tax avoidance can be contrasted with tax evasion, which entails the reduction of tax liability by illegal means.

Tax benefit rule. A provision that limits the recognition of income from the recovery of an expense or loss properly deducted in a prior tax year to the amount of the deduction that generated a tax benefit. § 111.

Tax Court. The U.S. Tax Court is one of three trial courts of original jurisdiction that decides litigation involving Federal income, estate, or gift taxes. It is the only trial court where the taxpayer need not first pay the deficiency assessed by the IRS. The Tax Court will not have jurisdiction over a case unless the statutory notice of deficiency (90-day letter) has been issued by the IRS and the taxpayer files the petition for hearing within the time prescribed.

Tax credits. Tax credits are amounts that directly reduce a taxpayer's tax liability. The tax benefit received from a tax credit is not dependent on the taxpayer's marginal tax rate, whereas the benefit of a tax deduction or exclusion is dependent on the taxpayer's tax bracket.

Tax credit for the elderly or disabled. An elderly (age 65 and over) or disabled taxpayer may receive a tax credit amounting to 15 percent of $5,000 ($7,500 for qualified married individuals filing jointly). This amount is reduced by Social Security benefits, excluded pension benefits, and one-half of the taxpayer's adjusted gross income in excess of $7,500 ($10,000 for married taxpayers filing jointly). § 22.

Tax-free exchange. Transfers of property specifically exempted from Federal income tax consequences. Examples are a transfer of property to a controlled corporation under § 351(a) and a like-kind exchange under § 1031(a). The recognition of gain or loss is postponed, rather than being permanently excluded, through the assignment of a carryover basis to the replacement property. See also *nontaxable exchange.*

Tax home. Since travel expenses of an employee are deductible only if the taxpayer is away from home, the deductibility of such expenses rests upon the definition of tax home. The IRS position is that tax home is the business location, post, or station of the taxpayer. If an employee is temporarily reassigned to a new post for a period of one year or less, the taxpayer's home should be his or her personal residence, and the travel expenses should be deductible. If the assignment is for more than two years, the IRS position is that it is indefinite or permanent and the taxpayer is therefore not in travel status. If the assignment is for between one and two years, the IRS position is that the location of the tax home will be determined on the basis of the facts and circumstances. The courts are in conflict regarding what constitutes a person's home for tax purposes. The taxpayer will not be treated as temporarily away from home if the employment period exceeds one year. Thus, in this situation, the tax home will be the place of employment. See also *travel expenses.*

Tax preferences. Those items set forth in § 57 that may result in the imposition of the alternative minimum tax. See also *alternative minimum tax (AMT).*

Tax rate schedules. Rate schedules appearing in Appendix A that are used by upper-income taxpayers and those not permitted to use the tax table. Separate rate schedules are provided for married individuals filing jointly, head of household, single taxpayers, estates and trusts, and married individuals filing separate returns. § 1.

Tax research. The method used to determine the best available solution to a situation that possesses tax consequences. Both tax and nontax factors are considered.

Tax shelters. The typical tax shelter generated large losses in the early years of the activity. Investors would offset these losses against other types of income and, therefore, avoid paying income taxes on this income. These tax shelter investments could then be sold after a few years and produce capital gain income, which is taxed at a lower rate than ordinary income. The passive activity loss rules and the at-risk rules now limit tax shelter deductions.

Tax table. A tax table appearing in Appendix A that is provided for taxpayers with less than $100,000 of taxable income. Separate columns are provided for single taxpayers, married taxpayers filing jointly, head of household, and married taxpayers filing separately. § 3.

Technical advice memoranda (TAMs). TAMs are issued by the National Office of the IRS in response to questions raised by IRS field personnel during audits. They deal with completed rather than proposed transactions and are often requested for questions related to exempt organizations and employee plans.

Temporary Regulation. A Regulation issued by the Treasury Department in temporary form. When speed is critical, the Treasury Department issues Temporary Regulations, which take effect immediately. These Regulations have the same authoritative value as final Regulations and may be cited as precedent for three years. Temporary Regulations are also issued as Proposed Regulations. See also *proposed regulation* and *regulations.*

Theft loss. A loss from larceny, embezzlement, and robbery. It does not include misplacement of items. See also *casualty loss.*

Thin capitalization. When debt owed by a corporation to its shareholders is large relative to its capital structure (stock and shareholder equity), the IRS may contend that the corporation is thinly capitalized. In effect, this means that some or all of the debt will be reclassified as equity. The immediate result is to disallow any interest deduction to the corporation on the reclassified debt. To the extent of the corporation's earnings and profits, interest payments and loan repayments on the reclassified debt are treated as dividends to the shareholders. § 385.

Thirty-day letter. A letter that accompanies a Revenue Agent's Report (RAR) issued as a result of an IRS audit of a taxpayer (or the rejection of a taxpayer's claim for refund). The letter outlines the taxpayer's appeal procedure before the IRS. If the taxpayer does not request any such procedures within the 30-day period, the IRS will issue a *statutory notice of deficiency* (the 90-day letter).

Thirty percent additional first-year depreciation. This provision, which was effective for property acquired after September 10, 2001 and before September 11, 2004, provided for an additional cost recovery deduction of 30 percent in the tax year that qualified property was placed in service. Qualified property included most types of new property other than buildings. The property had to be placed in service before January 1, 2005. § 168(k). See also *cost recovery allowance* and *fifty percent additional first-year depreciation.*

Timber. Special rules apply to the recognition of gain from the sale of timber. A taxpayer may elect to treat the cutting of timber that is held for sale or use in a trade or business as a sale or exchange. If the holding period requirements are met, the gain is recognized as § 1231 gain and may therefore receive long-term capital gain treatment. § 631.

Trade or business expenses. Deductions *for* AGI that are attributable to a taxpayer's business or profession. Some employee expenses may also be treated as trade or business expenses. See also *employee expenses.*

Transportation expenses. Transportation expenses for an employee include only the cost of transportation (taxi fares, automobile expenses, etc.) in the course of employment when the employee is not away from home in travel status. Commuting expenses are not deductible. See also *automobile expenses.*

Travel expenses. Travel expenses include meals (generally subject to a 50 percent disallowance) and lodging and transportation expenses while away from home in the pursuit of a trade or business (including that of an employee). See also *tax home.*

Trial court. The court of original jurisdiction; the first court to consider litigation. In Federal tax controversies, trial courts include U.S. District Courts, the U.S. Tax Court, and the U.S. Court of Federal Claims. See also *appellate court.*

U

Unearned income. Also referred to as investment income, it includes such income as interest, dividends, capital gains, rents, royalties, and pension and annuity income. See also *kiddie tax.*

Unearned (prepaid) income. For tax purposes, prepaid income (e.g., rent) is taxable in the year of receipt. In certain cases involving advance payments for goods and services, income may be deferred. See Revenue Procedure 2004–34 (2004–22 I.R.B. 13, 991) and Reg. § 1.451–5. See also *accrual method.*

Uniform capitalization (UNICAP) rules. Under § 263A, the Regulations provide a set of rules that all taxpayers (regardless of the particular industry) can use to determine the items of cost (and means of allocating those costs) that must be capitalized with respect to the production of tangible property.

Unreasonable compensation. Under § 162(a)(1), a deduction is allowed for "reasonable" salaries or other compensation for personal services actually rendered. To the extent compensation is excessive ("unreasonable"), no deduction will be allowed. The problem of unreasonable compensation usually is limited to closely held corporations where the motivation is to pay out profits in some form deductible to the corporation. Deductible compensation, therefore, becomes an attractive substitute for nondeductible dividends when the shareholders are also employees of the corporation.

Unrecaptured § 1250 gain (25 percent gain). Gain from the sale of depreciable real estate held more than one year. The gain is equal to or less than the depreciation taken on such property and is reduced by § 1245 gain and § 1250 gain. See also *alternative tax.*

U.S. Court of Federal Claims. See *Claims Court.*

U.S. Supreme Court. The highest appellate court or the court of last resort in the Federal court system and in most states. Only a small number of tax decisions of the U.S. Courts of Appeal are reviewed by the U.S. Supreme Court under its certiorari procedure. The Supreme Court usually grants certiorari to resolve a conflict among the Courts of Appeal (e.g., two or more appellate courts have assumed opposing positions on a particular issue) or when the tax issue is extremely important (e.g., size of the revenue loss to the Federal government).

U.S. Tax Court. See *Tax Court.*

Use tax. A use tax is an ad valorem tax, usually at the same rate as the sales tax, on the use or consumption of tangible personalty. The purpose of a use tax is to prevent the avoidance of a sales tax.

USTC. Published by Commerce Clearing House, *U.S. Tax Cases* contain all of the Federal tax decisions issued by the U.S. District Courts, U.S. Court of Federal Claims, U.S. Courts of Appeals, and the U.S. Supreme Court.

V

Vacation home. The Code places restrictions upon taxpayers who rent their residences or vacation homes for part of the tax year. The restrictions may result in a scaling down of expense deductions for the taxpayers. § 280A. See also *hobby loss.*

Value added tax (VAT). A national sales tax that taxes the increment in value as goods move through the production process. A VAT is much used in other countries, but has not yet been incorporated as part of the U.S. Federal tax structure.

Vesting requirements. A qualified deferred compensation arrangement must satisfy a vesting requirement. Under this provision, an employee's right to accrued plan benefits derived from employer contributions must be nonforfeitable in accordance with one of two vesting time period schedules (or two required alternate vesting schedules for certain employer matching contributions).

W

W–2 wages. The production activities deduction (PAD) cannot exceed 50% of the W–2 wages paid for any particular year. Prop.Reg. § 199–2(f)(2) provides several methods for calculating the W–2 wages, but the payments must involve common law employees. To qualify, however, they need not be involved in the production process. § 199. See also *production activities deduction (PAD).*

Wash sale. A loss from the sale of stock or securities that is disallowed because the taxpayer within 30 days before or after the sale has acquired stock or securities that are substantially identical to those sold. § 1091.

Welfare-to-work credit. A tax credit available to employers hiring individuals who have been long-term recipients of family assistance welfare benefits. In general, long-term recipients are those individuals who are certified by a designated local agency as being members of a family receiving assistance under a public aid program for at least an 18-month period ending on the hiring date. The welfare-to-work credit is available for qualified wages paid in the first two years of employment. The maximum credit is equal to $8,500 per qualified employee, computed as 35 percent of the first $10,000 of qualified wages paid in the first year of employment, plus 50 percent of the first $10,000 of qualified wages paid in the second year of employment. § 51A. See also *general business credit.*

Wherewithal to pay. This concept recognizes the inequity of taxing a transaction when the taxpayer lacks the means with which to pay the tax. Under it, there is a correlation between the imposition of the tax and the ability to pay the tax. It is particularly suited to situations in which the taxpayer's economic position has not changed significantly as a result of the transaction.

Withholding allowances. The number of withholding allowances serves as the basis for determining the amount of income taxes withheld from an employee's salary or wages. The more withholding allowances claimed, the less income tax withheld by an employer. An employee may claim withholding allowances for personal exemptions for self and spouse (unless claimed as a dependent of another person), dependency exemptions, and special withholding allowances.

Working condition fringe. A type of fringe benefit received by the employee that is excludible from the employee's gross income. It consists of property or services provided (paid or reimbursed) by the employer for which the employee could take a tax deduction if the employee had paid for them. § 132.

Work opportunity tax credit. Employers are allowed a tax credit equal to 40 percent of the first $6,000 of wages (per eligible employee) for the first year of employment. Eligible employees include certain hard-to-employ individuals (e.g., qualified ex-felons, high-risk youth, food stamp recipients, and veterans). For an employer to qualify for the 40 percent credit, the employees must (1) be certified by a designated local agency as being members of one of the targeted groups and (2) have completed at least 400 hours of service to the employer. For employees who meet the first condition but not the second, the credit rate is reduced to 25 percent provided the employees meet a minimum employment level of 120 hours of service to the employer. The employer's deduction for wages is reduced by the amount of the credit taken. For qualified summer youth employees, the 40 percent rate is applied to the first $3,000 of qualified wages. §§ 51 and 52.

Worthless securities. A loss (usually capital) is allowed for a security that becomes worthless during the year. The loss is deemed to have occurred on the last day of the year. Special rules apply to securities of affiliated companies and small business stock. § 165. See also *Section 1244 stock*.

Writ of certiorari. See *certiorari*.

Z

Zero bracket amount. A deduction that was generally available to all individual taxpayers in arriving at taxable income. It represented the equivalent of the standard deduction for taxable years before 1987. The taxpayer did not take a deduction for the zero bracket amount because it was built into the tax tables and tax rate schedules. Because the amount was built in, if the taxpayer itemized deductions, only the excess itemized deductions (amount of the itemized deductions in excess of the zero bracket amount) were deductible. TRA of 1986 repealed the zero bracket amount and replaced it with the standard deduction for 1987 and thereafter. The zero bracket amount for 1986 is currently used in the 10-year forward averaging calculation for lump-sum distributions. § 63(c). See also *standard deduction*.

[See Title 26 U.S.C.A.]

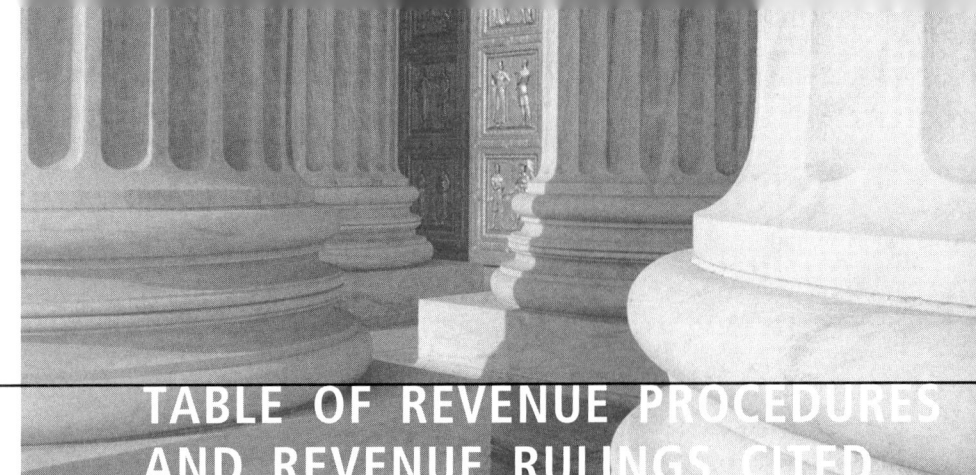

APPENDIX D–3

TABLE OF REVENUE PROCEDURES AND REVENUE RULINGS CITED

Revenue Rulings

Revenue Rulings

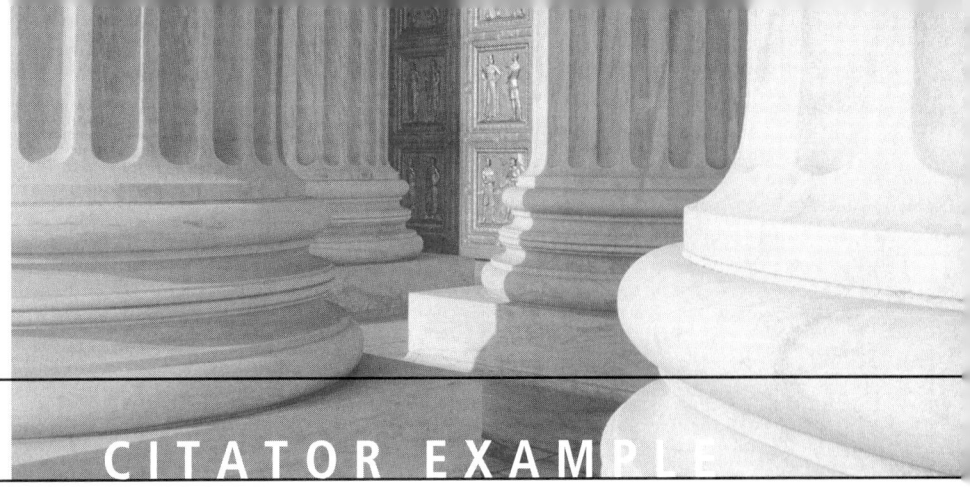

Illustration of the Use of the Citator

Background

A *Citator* provides the history of a legal case and lists subsequently published opinions that refer to the case being assessed. Reviewing these references enables the tax researcher to determine whether the decision in question has been reversed, affirmed, followed by other courts, or distinguished in some way. Chapter 2 introduces the *Citator* as an invaluable reference in tax research. The major citators are published by Commerce Clearing House (CCH), RIA, and Shepard's Citation, Inc. The use of the RIA citator is illustrated in the discussion that follows.

The *RIA Federal Tax Citator* is a separate multivolume service with monthly supplements that may be used to determine the tax status of tax case decisions, Revenue Rulings, and Revenue Procedures. A similar citation process is available with the online research system.[1] Cases that are traced by the *Citator* are divided into the issues involved. Since the researcher may be interested in only one issue, only those cases involving that issue need to be checked.

The *Citator* includes the following volumes, each of which covers a particular period of time:

- Volume 1 (1863–1941)
- Volume 2 (1942–1948)
- Volume 3 (1948–1954)
- Volume 1, Second Series (1954–1977)
- Volume 2, Second Series (1978–1989)
- Volume 3, Second Series (1990–1996)
- Volume 4, Second Series (1997–2002)
- Volume 5, Second Series (2003–2005).
- Annual and monthly cumulative paperback supplements

Through the use of symbols, the *Citator* indicates whether a decision has been followed, explained, criticized, questioned, or overruled by a later court decision. These symbols are reproduced in Figure E–1.

Example

Determine the background and validity of *Adda v. Comm.*, 37 AFTR 654, 171 F.2d 457 (CA–4, 1948).

---

[1]Features in the *RIA Citator* that do not appear in the CCH *Citator* include the following: (1) distinguishes between the various issues in the case, (2) lists all court decisions that cite the court decision being researched, (3) indicates the relationship (e.g., explained, criticized, followed, or overruled) between the court decision being researched and subsequent decisions, and (4) pinpoints the exact page on which one court decision is cited by another court decision. Prior to the acquisition of Prentice-Hall Information Services, the *Federal Tax Citator* was published by Prentice-Hall. The *Citator 2nd Series* is now published by Research Institute of America.

FIGURE E–1	RIA Citator Symbols

Citator Symbols*
COURT DECISIONS
Judicial History of the Case

a	affirmed (by decision of a higher court)
d	dismissed (appeal to a higher court dismissed)
m	modified (decision modified by a higher court, or on rehearing)
r	reversed (by a decision of a higher court)
s	same case (e.g., on rehearing)
rc	related case (companion cases and other cases arising out of the same subject matter are so designated)
x	certiorari denied (by the Supreme Court of the United States)
(C or G)	The Commissioner or Solicitor General has made the appeal
(T)	Taxpayer has made the appeal
(A)	decision acquiesced in by Commissioner
(NA)	decision nonacquiesced in by Commissioner
sa	same case affirmed (by the cited case)
sd	same case dismissed (by the cited case)
sm	same case modified (by the cited case)
sr	same case reversed (by the cited case)
sx	same case—certiorari denied

Syllabus of the Cited Case

iv	four (on all fours with the cited case)
f	followed (the cited case followed)
e	explained (comment generally favorable, but not to a degree that indicates the cited case is followed)
k	reconciled (the cited case reconciled)
n	dissenting opinion (cited in a dissenting opinion)
g	distinguished (the cited case distinguished either in law or on the facts)
l	limited (the cited case limited to its facts. Used when an appellate court so limits a prior decision, or a lower court states that in its opinion the cited case should be so limited)
c	criticized (adverse comment on the cited case)
q	questioned (the cited case not only criticized, but its correctness questioned)
o	overruled

*Reprinted from RIA *Citator 2nd Series* Volume 1 © 1992, RIA, 395 Hudson St., NY, NY 10014.

Solution

The headnote for *Adda* summarizes the holding of the court and lists the two main issues involved (designated "1" and "2") in the case. As noted previously, the issue designation procedure facilitates the use of the *Citator*.

Refer to Volume 3 of the First Series (covering the period from October 7, 1948, through July 29, 1954) of the *Citator*. Information about the case reference is located in the excerpt reproduced in Figure E–2.

FIGURE E–2	**Excerpt from Volume 3, First Series**

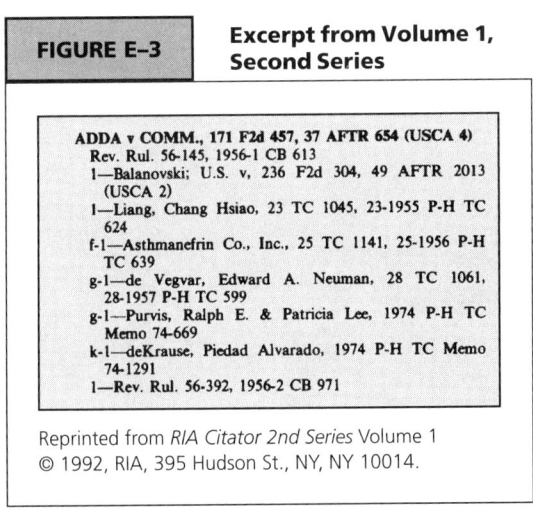

> **ADDA v COMM.**, 171 F (2d) 457, 37 AFTR 654,
>   1948 P.-H. ¶ 72,655 (CCA 4, Dec 3, 1948)
> Cert. filed, March 1, 1949 (T)
> No cert. (G) 1949 P-H ¶ 71,050
> x—Adda v Comm., 336 US 952, 69 S Ct 883,
>   93 L Ed 1107, April 18, 1949 (T)
> sa—Adda, Fernand C. A., 10 TC 273 (No.
>   33), ¶ 10.33 P.-H. TC 1948
> iv—Milner Hotels, Inc., N. Y., 173 F (2d)
>   567, 37 AFTR 1170, 1949 P.-H. page 72,528
>   (CCA 6)
> l—Nubar; Comm. v, 185 F(2d) 588, 39 AFTR
>   1315, 1950 P.-H. page 73,423 (CCA 4)
> g-1—Scottish Amer. Invest. Co., Ltd.,
>   The, 12 TC 59, 12-1949 P.-H. TC 32
> g-1—Nubar, Zareh, 13 TC 579, 13-1949
>   P.-H. TC 318

Reprinted from *RIA Citator 1st Series* Volume 3
© 1955, RIA, 395 Hudson St., NY, NY 10014.

Correlating the symbols in Figure E–1 with the excerpt in Figure E–2 reveals the following information about *Adda v. Comm.*:

- Application for certiorari (appeal to the U.S. Supreme Court) filed by the taxpayer (T) on March 1, 1949.
- Certiorari was denied (x) by the U.S. Supreme Court on April 18, 1949.
- The trial court decision is reported in 10 T.C. 273 and was affirmed on appeal (sa) to the Fourth Court of Appeals.
- During the time frame of Volume 3 of the *Citator* (October 7, 1948, through July 29, 1954), one decision (*Milner Hotels, Inc.*) has agreed "on all fours with the cited case" (iv). One decision (*Comm. v. Nubar*) has cited the first issue in *Adda* without comment and two decisions (*The Scottish American Investment Co., Ltd.* and *Zareh Nubar*) have distinguished the cited case on issue number one (g–1).

Reference to Volume 1 of the *Citator 2nd Series* (covering the period from 1954 through 1977) shows the *Adda v. Comm.* case which is reproduced in Figure E–3.

FIGURE E–3	**Excerpt from Volume 1, Second Series**

> **ADDA v COMM.**, 171 F2d 457, 37 AFTR 654 (USCA 4)
> Rev. Rul. 56-145, 1956-1 CB 613
> l—Balanovski; U.S. v, 236 F2d 304, 49 AFTR 2013
>   (USCA 2)
> l—Liang, Chang Hsiao, 23 TC 1045, 23-1955 P-H TC
>   624
> f-1—Asthmanefrin Co., Inc., 25 TC 1141, 25-1956 P-H
>   TC 639
> g-1—de Vegvar, Edward A. Neuman, 28 TC 1061,
>   28-1957 P-H TC 599
> g-1—Purvis, Ralph E. & Patricia Lee, 1974 P-H TC
>   Memo 74-669
> k-1—deKrause, Piedad Alvarado, 1974 P-H TC Memo
>   74-1291
> l—Rev. Rul. 56-392, 1956-2 CB 971

Reprinted from *RIA Citator 2nd Series* Volume 1
© 1992, RIA, 395 Hudson St., NY, NY 10014.

Correlating the symbols in Figure E–1 with the excerpt in Figure E–3 reveals the following additional information about *Adda v. Comm.*:

- The case was cited without comment in two rulings and two cases: Rev. Rul. 56–145, Rev.Rul. 56–392, *Balanovski*, and *Liang*.

FIGURE E–4	**Excerpt from Volume 2, Second Series**

> **ADDA v COMM., 171 F2d 457, 37 AFTR 654 (USCA 4)**
> 1—Connelly, Judith C., 1982 PH TC Memo 82-2866
> 1—Cleveland, Robert E., 1983 PH TC Memo 83-1223

Reprinted from *RIA Citator 2nd Series* Volume 2
© 1992, RIA, 395 Hudson St., NY, NY 10014.

- It was followed in *Asthmanefrin Co.* (f–1).
- It was distinguished in *de Vegvar* and *Purvis* (g–1).
- It was reconciled in *deKrause* (k–1).

Reference to the "Court Decisions" section of Volume 2, *Citator 2nd Series* (covering the period from 1978 through 1989) shows that *Adda v. Comm.* was cited in *Judith C. Connelly* and *Robert E. Cleveland*, as to the first issue in *Adda* without comment. See the excerpt which is reproduced in Figure E–4.

No citations appear in Volume 3, *Citator Second Series* (which covers the period from 1990 through 1996), in Volume 4, *Citator Second Series* (which covers 1997 through 2002), or in Volume 5, *Citator Second Series* (which covers 2003 through 2005) for *Adda v. Comm.*

The *Citator* includes a cumulative supplement, and a cumulative monthly paperback supplement is published each month. Be sure to refer to these supplements, or very recent citations might be overlooked. No citations appear in the supplements for *Adda v. Comm.*

Except as otherwise noted, it appears that *Adda v. Comm.* has withstood the test of time.

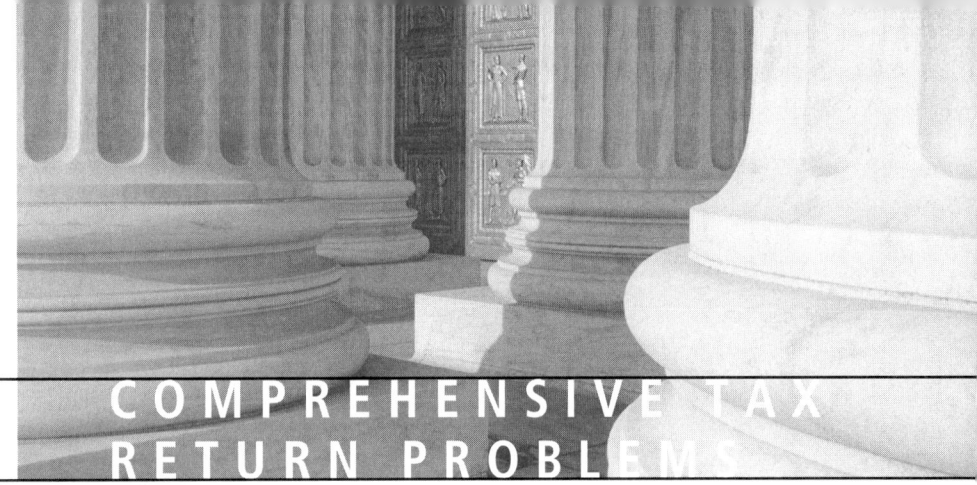

Problem 1

Fred C. and Brenda P. Archer, ages 46 and 47, are husband and wife and reside at 4282 Camellia Road, Jackson, MS 39205.

1. Fred is a civil engineer who specializes in the construction and maintenance of rural access roads (i.e., "farm-to-market" type). Although he does handle some private property projects, Fred deals mainly with county road commissioners on a per-job basis. However, at least two counties (Hinds and Rankin) pay him an annual retainer to be on call as needed. Fred is particularly adept at weatherizing roadbeds so as to minimize the damage from climatic variations. In all of his work (including the annual retainers), Fred considers himself to be an independent contractor. As noted below (see item 3), he conducts his consulting business from an office in his home.

2. Brenda is a registered nurse and is employed by the Bone and Joint Clinic of Jackson. On alternate weekends, she takes classes offered by a local medical school leading to a Master of Science in Nursing. In driving to work and school, Brenda uses the family Suburban.

3. The Archers constructed their residence on Camellia Road in 2004 at a cost of $320,000. They had acquired the lot from a grandparent several years before for $20,000. Of the 3,200 square feet of livable space, one-fourth (25%) is used as Fred's office. Besides the interest on the home mortgage and property taxes (see item 18 below), residential expenses for 2005 are as follows:

2nd
month?

Utilities	$4,200
Security system annual service fee	600
Homeowner's insurance	800
Carpeting of office area, 6/7/05	2,200

25%

100%

Fred's office furniture (e.g., desk, chairs, drafting tables) was expensed previously under § 179 when acquired. On May 16, 2005, however, he bought a new Xerox copier for $850.

7-yr → 179

4. In August of 2004, Fred purchased a Land Rover that he uses exclusively for business. No trade-in was involved and part of the purchase price of $45,000 was financed. For 2004, he did not choose to claim any § 179 expensing and did not elect any additional first-year depreciation. Under the actual operating cost method, he uses 200% declining-balance with half-year convention. His expenses relating to the Land Rover for 2005 are as follows:

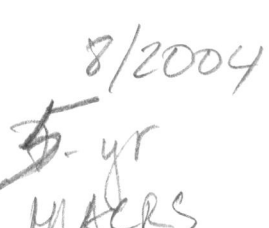

8/2004
5-yr
MACRS

Gasoline	$2,400
Oil and lubrication	120
Auto insurance	1,400
Interest on car loan	1,200
Repairs (not under warranty)	420

On rare occasions, Fred is able to "top off" his gas tank compliments of the county road district where he is working. During 2005, Fred drove the Land Rover 18,000 miles.

5. Except for the work he does for Hinds and Rankin Counties, which are in the Jackson area, Fred's consulting usually requires overnight stays. On a typical trip, he drives to the county seat and stays at a motel until the assignment is complete. In addition to the auto expense previously noted (see item 4), his business travel expenses for 2005 are summarized below:

Meals	$7,400
Lodging	8,200
Laundry	310
Parking	205

These expenses are billed as incurred and reimbursed by the county along with the statement for services that Fred submits.

6. To maintain good relations with the county road commissioners for whom he does work, Fred gives fruit baskets at Christmas. Each basket cost $23 with wrapping ($2) and shipping ($4), making the total $29. On December 19, 2005, Fred charged the fruit baskets order of $609 (21 baskets at $29 each) to his Visa credit card. [The Visa bill was paid in January 2006.]

7. Two of Fred's clients, Hinds County and Rankin County, pay him an annual retainer of $8,000 and $12,000, respectively. The retainers for a year are to be paid by December 31 of that year. For budgetary reasons, however, Hinds delayed its 2004 payment until February 2005. All other retainers were paid on schedule.

8. One private client, John Hood, retained Fred to design a better road leading to his hunting lodge near Tupelo, Mississippi. Regarding the fee of $6,000, John offered Fred a choice: cash or a Chevrolet Camaro (1998, V-6) listed for sale at $7,999. Hood owns several car dealerships and had taken the Camaro as a trade-in on a new car purchase. As the blue book value of a '98 Camaro ranges from $3,675 to $7,925 and Fred needed a car for his daughters, he took the Camaro. The manager of Hood's used-car lot indicates that all of his prices are "negotiable." No Form 1099 was issued by Hood's car dealership regarding this transaction.

9. Expenses incurred by Brenda during 2005 in pursuing the M.S. in Nursing are as follows:

Tuition (spring and fall 2005)	$7,100
Books, lab supplies, computer software	940
Campus parking	230

Mileage driven is 1,040 miles (500 miles, spring, and 540 miles after 8/31). For tax purposes, the Archers use the automatic mileage method as to the family Suburban, which was purchased on June 15, 2003.

10. For several years, Brenda has not been pleased with her job at the Bone and Joint Clinic. Although the fringe benefits are good (see items 18 and 19 below), her salary is too low. In 2005, therefore she retained the services of a professional medical recruitment agency. After considerable effort and multiple job interviews, she received several attractive job offers. When the clinic learned of her job search, it gave her a raise (effective in 2006), and she decided against any change. The job search effort cost Brenda $3,200, or slightly less than her salary increase.

11. In the summer of 2004 while on a family outing, the Archers had an auto accident. Although it was the other driver's fault, the Archers had to resort to their own insurance company (USAA) for the repairs to the Suburban. Consequently, they were charged the $1,000 deductible and were unable to deduct any of this amount on their income tax return due to the 10%-of-AGI floor. In 2005, USAA was able to collect from the other driver's carrier, and the Archers recovered the $1,000 deductible.

12. In late 2005, the Archers were audited by the Mississippi State Tax Commission. The agent checked their state income tax returns for tax years 2002, 2003, and 2004. She assessed deficiencies of $420 for 2002 and $310 for 2003 but did not add a charge for

interest. For year 2004, she accepted the return and made no change. Fred agreed to the assessments and immediately mailed a check for $730 to the state.

13. For several years Brenda's parents, John and Irene Porter, have been living with the Archers. Since they meet the dependency requirements, the Archers have claimed the parents on their tax returns. On December 30, 2004, Irene suffered a stroke, was taken to Memorial Hospital, and died in the ICU on January 2, 2005. In February 2005, Fred received and paid a bill from Memorial for $9,400 ($5,100 of which related to 2004). The Archers also paid for Irene's funeral expenses of $4,900. Irene owned her own cemetery lot.

14. Because John (Brenda's father) is physically handicapped and must use a wheelchair, Fred had some changes made to portions of the Camellia Road residence. A contractor was hired to add ramps to entrances, lower certain counters, widen several hallways, and add guardrails to the bathroom facilities. The contractor, Brenda's cousin and John's nephew, charged Fred only $6,000 for the job. This was about one-third of what he would ordinarily bill for the same work. A reasonable estimate is that the capital improvements increased the value of the residence by $10,000.

15. Several years ago, Brenda took out life insurance policies on the lives of her parents. The policies, face amount of $50,000 each, are issued by Cardinal Life and designate Brenda as the owner and beneficiary. After the death of her mother in 2005, Cardinal Life paid Brenda $50,000. Brenda had previously paid premiums of $18,200 on the policy. In 2005, Brenda paid Cardinal Life $1,400 in premiums on her father's policy.

16. The Archers have a $4,000 excess long-term capital loss carryover from 2004. Their property transactions for 2005 are summarized below:

Property	Date Acquired	Date Sold	Cost or Other Basis	Sale Price
Lot in Yazoo City	2/3/99	6/2/05	Inherited	$13,100
1,000 shares of Mallard Corporation common	8/10/98	5/20/05	Gift	14,000
600 shares of Pintail Corporation common	12/2/03	11/30/05	$11,000	12,000
Camper	4/25/02	9/2/05	$8,500	2,200

Fred inherited the Yazoo City lot from his grandmother, Lucy, who died in 1999. Lucy had paid $2,000 for the property in 1941, and it was worth $9,000 when she died. In the prior year (1998), Lucy had given Fred 1,000 shares of Mallard stock. The shares had cost Lucy $30,000 in 1996 and were worth $24,000 on the date of the gift. The Mallard Corporation declared a 2-for-1 stock split in early 2000. For sentimental reasons, Fred wanted to keep half of the Mallard stock. The camper was used by the Archers on family vacations. As their daughters are older now and Brenda attends classes on weekends, Fred decided to accept a neighbor's unsolicited offer to buy. Fred's broker, a cousin on his mother's side of the family, did not charge him a commission on the sale of the Mallard and Pintail stocks.

17. Besides the items already noted, the Archers had the following receipts during 2005:

Fred's consulting fees (including expense reimbursement but *not* including items 7 and 8 above)		$72,000
Brenda's salary		42,000
Interest income—		
City of Jackson bonds	$2,400	
General Electric bonds	800	
Bank of America CD	1,100	4,300
Qualified dividends—		
Mallard Corporation common	$400	
Pintail Corporation common	600	1,000
Income tax refunds (for tax year 2004)		
Federal	$1,500	
State	290	1,790

18. In addition to the items already mentioned, the Archers had the following expenditures for 2004: *2005*

Dental (orthodontist)	$1,400
Property taxes on personal residence	4,000
Interest on home mortgage	4,800
Work-related expenses (see item 19)	8,750
Tax return preparation fee (one-half of the preparer's time was devoted to Fred's business activities)	900
Payment of church pledge (includes $600 left over from 2004 pledge)	3,000
College donations (see item 20)	2,150

For medical purposes, the Archers are covered by Brenda's policy available through the Bone and Joint Clinic. No contribution from the employee is required, no co-pay or deductible features are involved, and spouse and children are included. Other dependents (e.g., parents) and dental bills are excluded from coverage.

19. Professional dues, journals, and license fees (nursing and engineering) are as follows:

	Brenda	Fred
Dues	$150	$300
Journals	75	100
Licenses	125	–0–

Fred contributed $8,000 to an H.R. 10 (Keogh) plan that he established several years ago. The administrator of the plan is Oriole Trust Company. Brenda is covered by a non-contributory retirement plan that the Bone and Joint Clinic maintains for its employees.

Brenda spent $370 on nursing uniforms and $205 on having them laundered. Fred spent $140 on safety glasses and $260 on safety boots.

20. Brenda and Fred attended the University of Mississippi and Mississippi State University, respectively, and belong to their alumni associations. Each paid $75 (for a total of $150) in annual dues. Also, they sent each athletic department $1,000 (for a total of $2,000) to give them preferred seating at home football games. The charge for seating preference does not include the cost of the tickets for games.

21. The Archers have three daughters who live with them. Amber (age 20) and Reba (age 18) are high school graduates and have part-time jobs earning $9,000 and $8,000, respectively. As they are saving most of their earnings for college, both receive almost all of their support from their parents. Tiffany (age 17) is a full-time student and does not work.

22. Brenda's Form W–2 from her employer shows withholding of $4,368 for Federal income tax and $1,536 for state income tax. The Archers made quarterly estimated payments of $12,800 ($3,200 each quarter) to the U.S. Treasury and $1,600 ($400 each quarter) to the state of Mississippi.

23. Social Security numbers for the parties involved are as follows:

Name	S.S. Number
Brenda P. Archer	426–81–7492
Fred C. Archer	426–53–5261
John Porter	425–89–6494
Irene Porter	425–74–5213
Amber Archer	427–52–3162
Reba Archer	427–43–2485
Tiffany Archer	427–37–4533

Requirements

Prepare a joint return (with appropriate schedules) for the Archers for 2005. In doing this, make the following assumptions:

✓ • The principal business code for Fred is 541330.
✓ • The Archers itemized their deductions *from* AGI for tax year 2004. In making the choice between deducting state and local sales taxes and state income taxes, they selected state income taxes.
✓ • The Archers drove 840 miles, all before 9/1, for medical (e.g., doctor and dentist visits, hospital trips) purposes and 280 miles for charitable (e.g., canvassing for annual church pledges) purposes in 2005. The family Suburban was used in both cases.
 • If a refund is due, they want it sent to them.
✓ • They do not want to contribute to the Presidential Election Campaign Fund.

Problem 2

Victor E. and Mary N. Polk, ages 56 and 54, are married and reside at 1480 Boheme Drive, Houston, TX 77024. Victor owns and operates a retail business as a sole proprietor, and Mary is a homemaker.

1. For many years, Victor was involved in the wholesale distribution of beer for various major breweries. In 2003, he sold his business and decided to open a retail liquor store. Called "Bayou Liquors," the store is located in a freestanding building adjacent to an upscale suburban shopping center. Victor had the building constructed on a lot he had acquired in 2002 at a cost of $90,000. The design of the building was customized to meet the needs of storage as well as sales activities (e.g., wine cellar, customer service facilities). Construction costs were as follows:

Architect fee	$ 12,000
Building, placed in service 6/20/03	820,000
Parking lot (paving, lighting)—cost recovery period of 15 years	24,000
Outdoor signs (marquee, etc.)—cost recovery period of 15 years	18,000

2. Furnishings acquired 6/20/03 for Bayou Liquors were as follows:

Computers (including price scanners)—cost recovery period of 5 years	$23,000
Fixtures (wine racks, counters, coolers)—cost recovery period of 7 years	38,000

Since Victor could not predict the profitability of the business, at least for the near future, he did not claim any additional first-year depreciation or § 179 expensing on his tax return for 2003. Further, he chose MACRS straight-line depreciation (assuming half-year convention) for the personalty and other assets acquired.

On July 1, 2003, Bayou Liquors opened its doors to the general public and began business.

3. Bayou Liquors uses a calendar year and, except for the computation of cost of goods sold, reports on a cash basis. Its gross profit for 2005 is summarized below:

Sales		$ 3,000,000
Cost of goods sold—		
Beginning inventory	$ 510,000	
Purchases	2,200,000	
Less final inventory	(506,000)	(2,204,000)
Gross profit		$ 796,000

Year-end inventories are determined on a physical count basis. Inventory is valued at the lower of cost or market. Losses due to spoilage and breakage are minimal and are not accounted for separately. Theft of goods by employees and customers is unknown. What is stolen, however, reduces the final inventory amount.

4. A partial list of expenditures for Bayou Liquors as to 2005 is as follows:

Depreciation (see items 1 and 2 above)	$?
Wages	180,000
Retirement plan for employees	32,000
Advertising	55,000
Utilities	61,000
Taxes and licenses	56,000
Premiums on health insurance for employees	44,000
Interest on mortgage (funds were used to construct the building)	39,000
Casualty and theft insurance	43,000
Business liability insurance (see item 8 below)	36,000
Legal and professional fees	24,000
Accounting services	20,000
Janitorial services	18,000
Office expenses	3,200
Supplies (shopping bags, carts, etc.)	3,300
Repairs and maintenance	900
Security alarm service	3,000

The amounts listed for accounting services and janitorial services are for contract labor. To avoid additional problems with payroll taxes (particularly FUTA), Victor tries not to hire part-time employees. Consequently, he contracts with a local bookkeeping group and a janitorial service to do this work.

The category of taxes and licenses includes payroll taxes (FICA and FUTA), property taxes, and various license fees (e.g., liquor sales permit).

5. On December 31, 2004, the store was burglarized, and $20,000 in cash was stolen. Victor filed a claim with Eagle Insurance Company. After an investigation, Eagle denied the claim because Victor's night manager could not remember whether he had activated the alarm system on the night of the burglary. As no insurance recovery was anticipated, Victor claimed a $20,000 theft loss on his 2004 income tax return. In October 2005, the Houston police arrested the persons who had committed the burglary. None of the cash was recovered, but it was revealed that the alarm system, though properly activated, had been bypassed by the burglars. Once informed of this fact, Eagle sent Victor a check for $20,000, which he received in early November. Eagle was so embarrassed over its prior rejection of Victor's claim that the reimbursement was not reduced by the 20% co-insurance feature of the policy—$4,000 in this case (20% of $20,000).

6. Victor's prior contacts from his wholesale liquor business are a major reason why Bayou Liquors has been profitable since its creation. Since Victor is willing to continue selling at wholesale to his former customers, many keep buying from him. One such prior contact who continued to be an exceptional customer was Sam Lyons, owner of Sam's Lounge. To help Sam renovate his bar in December 2003, Victor loaned him $25,000. A note was issued bearing 6% interest and payable in three years. In early 2005, Sam sold the business and disappeared with the sales proceeds for parts unknown. As Sam left no assets behind, Victor (and Sam's other creditors) do not expect to ever be paid.

7. To take advantage of his former contacts (see item 6 above), Victor is considering expanding Bayou Liquors to other cities. Using a trade publication, he investigated the possibility of acquiring several liquor stores that were listed as being for sale. On trips to Port Arthur and Austin, he incurred the following expenses:

Lodging	$ 610
Meals	520
Entertainment	220
Car rental	505
Consulting fees	2,100

The consulting fees were paid for abbreviated market surveys and cash-flow analysis. Victor decided against acquiring either business—the Port Arthur store was in a poor location (i.e., deteriorating neighborhood), while the Austin store was overpriced.

8. After repeated warnings from his attorney about the danger of ruinous damages awards, Victor decided to obtain business liability insurance. He acquired a policy from Falcon Insurance that provides protection for a wide range of hazards extending from personal injury to product liability damages. The policy cost $36,000 (see item 4 above) with coverage commencing on July 1, 2005, and extending through June 30, 2008.

9. Because of the past burglary (see item 5 above) and to forestall customer theft, Victor purchased a state-of-the-art electronic surveillance system. It was installed on the night of June 30, 2005, and cost $39,000. Due to the profitability of Bayou Liquors (early losses were expected), Victor has changed his mind about the tax treatment of capital expenditures. He no longer favors a conservative deferral approach to the write-off of these expenses.

10. Victor takes pride in his compliance with state and local liquor control laws. Despite his caution, however, one of his employees was duped into selling liquor to a minor with a false ID. Victor wanted to contest the charge, but his attorney warned that a court trial might generate negative publicity. With this in mind, Victor pleaded "no contest" to the charge and paid a fine of $2,000. The attorney billed Victor $500 for her services. Neither of these payments made in August 2005 is included in the expenses listed in item 4 above.

11. The City of Houston has established a Convention Bureau whose purpose is to attract business meetings and conventions to the area. The Bureau maintains several suites of rooms in a local hotel to accommodate visiting business prospects. These facilities include a hospitality room that Victor has agreed to stock with liquid refreshments at no cost to the city. For year 2005, Bayou Liquors furnished beer, wine, and liquor as promised in the amount of $20,500 cost ($35,000 retail) value. Since charitable contributions cannot be claimed on Schedule C, these transactions are not reflected in items 3 and 4 above.

12. On October 13, 1975, the Polks' first wedding anniversary, Mary's parents gave them a tract of undeveloped land as a present. Located in Brazos County, the property was purchased by the parents on June 4, 1960, for $12,000 and was worth $20,000 on the date of the gift. Title to the property was reregistered as "Victor and Mary Polk, joint tenants with right of survivorship." No gift tax was due on the transfer. On May 10, 2004, the Polks sold the Brazos County property to the First Baptist Church for $48,000, receiving $38,000 cash and a note for $10,000 payable in 2005 with 8% interest. The Polks did not elect out of the installment method. On June 30, 2005, the Polks received a check for $10,800 from First Baptist Church in full satisfaction of its obligation.

13. When Victor's father, Clarence, died on March 12, 2001, he left all of his property to his children. A portion of Victor's inheritance was a tract of undeveloped land in Montgomery County. Acquired in 1990 at a cost of $40,000, the land was worth $80,000 when Clarence died. In 2004, the state of Texas contacted Victor about buying the land for use as a rehabilitation facility for juvenile offenders. After considerable negotiations and just before eminent domain proceedings were commenced, on October 26, 2005, Victor accepted an offer of $130,000 for the property. Although he has not yet done so, Victor expects to reinvest the proceeds in an apartment project being planned near Galveston.

14. On February 4, 1997, Victor attended a land foreclosure auction. Upon the advice of his father, who was quite adept at recognizing real estate values, Victor purchased six contiguous lots in Katy for $60,000. On July 15, 2005, a real estate syndicate contacted Victor and offered $220,000 for the Katy property. After some deliberate hesitation on Victor's part, the offer was raised to $250,000. Victor consulted his accountant, and on September 1, 2005, the following transaction took place: in exchange for the Katy lots, Victor received $10,000 in cash and undeveloped land in Travis County worth $240,000.

15. In early 2004, Mary was badly injured when an escalator in a local department store stopped unexpectedly. Besides pain and suffering, she incurred medical bills (including hospitalization) in the amount of $32,000—Mary paid $8,000 and her insurance covered the balance. When the department store attributed the accident to Mary's negligence and refused to pay for damages, a lawsuit was filed. Due to the assistance of Sarah, Mary's daughter and a trained paralegal, no attorney was hired. On November

23, 2005, and just prior to the scheduled trial date, Mary received the following settlement:

Pain and suffering	$120,000
Medical expenses	32,000

Mary had $24,000 of the medical reimbursement sent directly to her insurance company. The settlement also included a letter of apology from the store manager with a $500 gift certificate enclosed. [Note that the Polks were not able to deduct any medical expenses on their 2004 Federal income tax return due to the 7.5%-of-AGI limitation.]

16. One of the assets that Victor inherited from his father (see item 13) was a collection of ivory figurines. Clarence had acquired the individual pieces over the years at a cost of $29,000. Because ivory objects are no longer held in high regard, the collection was appraised at only $35,000 as of Clarence's date of death. Victor has no interest in the collection, so he sold it to an art dealer on June 2, 2005, for $33,000.

17. On December 5, 2005, Mary sold 9,000 shares of Harrier Oil for $15,000 (net of $200 brokerage commission). She had purchased the stock on March 10, 1997, for $34,000 using her separate funds. As the company specializes in extracting oil from various hard minerals, Mary was convinced that it possessed tremendous growth potential. After eight years of waiting, Mary decided to cut her losses and look elsewhere.

18. In addition to the items already mentioned, the Polks had the following:

Contribution from Sarah Holt (see item 19 below)	$ 3,600
Repayment of loan from Jim Holt (see item 19 below)	3,400
Interest on City of San Francisco bonds	5,700
Bank of America CD	1,400
Qualified cash dividends on General Electric common stock	900
Cash gift from Mary's parents	22,000

19. In 2003, the Polks' only child, Sarah, filed for divorce. Although her husband, Jim, wanted to marry one of Sarah's former bridesmaids, the parting was amicable. In fact, Victor lent Jim $3,400 (interest-free) to help pay for court costs and attorney's fees. Under the decree, finalized in 2004, Sarah is granted custody of their two children, Emily (age 6) and Jacob (age 4), and Jim is required to pay $300 monthly in child support. The decree does not award the dependency exemptions to either parent, but Jim has not claimed either of the children and does not plan to do so. Since the divorce, Sarah and the children have lived with the Polks. Sarah is a full-time mother and does not work. She turns over to Victor the $3,600 she receives each year from Jim. Victor feels certain that the Polks furnish more than half of Sarah's support.

20. Besides what has been previously noted, the Polks had the following expenditures for 2005:

Payments to retirement plans (see item 21 below)		$12,000
Medical expenses (see item 21 below)		4,800
Taxes (see item 22 below):		
Property taxes on personal residence	$7,100	
Sales tax on auto purchase	4,125	11,225
Contributions:		
Reelection campaign of local state representative	1,000	
Cash donation (supported by receipts) to Salvation Army	500	1,500
Interest (see item 23 below):		
Interest on home mortgage	$3,000	
Interest on home equity loan	2,100	5,100

21. In 2005, Victor contributed $8,000 to an H.R. 10 (Keogh) plan, and Mary contributed $4,000 to a spousal IRA. Victor established his H.R. 10 plan many years ago but never had to cover any employees until he opened Bayou Liquors. Victor has been advised by

his attorney that the H.R. 10 plan and the plan established for the employees comply with the coverage and antidiscrimination requirements applicable to qualified retirement plans. The $4,800 medical expense is the annual premium on a health insurance policy the Polks maintain for themselves and their dependents. Except for the insurance premium, the Polks had no other medical expenses for 2005.

Neither the $12,000 ($4,000 for Mary) nor the $4,800 amount is included in the expenses listed in item 4 above.

22. Included in the property taxes of $7,100 is a paving assessment of $4,000. The city decided to repave the street where the Polks live, and the $4,000 was their share of the cost.

Texas has no income tax but imposes a general sales tax of 6.25%, with a local option of up to 2% additional (which Houston levies). The Polks do not keep track of how much sales tax they incur, but in January 2005, they paid a sales tax of $4,125 on a new Lincoln Navigator they purchased. The Navigator is used exclusively for personal purposes.

23. The purchase of the Navigator was partly financed with funds obtained from a home equity loan.

24. Victor made quarterly payments to the U.S. Treasury of $4,000 (for a total of $16,000). In addition, he had the $2,400 refund for 2004 applied toward his 2005 income tax liability.

25. The business address for Bayou Liquors is 14345 Memorial Drive, Houston, TX 77079. Its employer identification number is 53–4758905, and the business code is 445310.

26. Social Security numbers for the parties involved are:

Name	S.S. Number
Victor E. Polk	447–39–8213
Mary N. Polk	446–53–2894
Sarah Holt	451–66–8415
Emily Holt	462–92–5618
Jacob Holt	463–44–6572

Requirements

Prepare a joint return (with appropriate schedules) for the Polks for tax year 2005. In doing this, make the following assumptions:

- If a refund is due, apply it toward the 2006 liability.
- The Polks desire to contribute $3 each to the Presidential Election Campaign Fund.

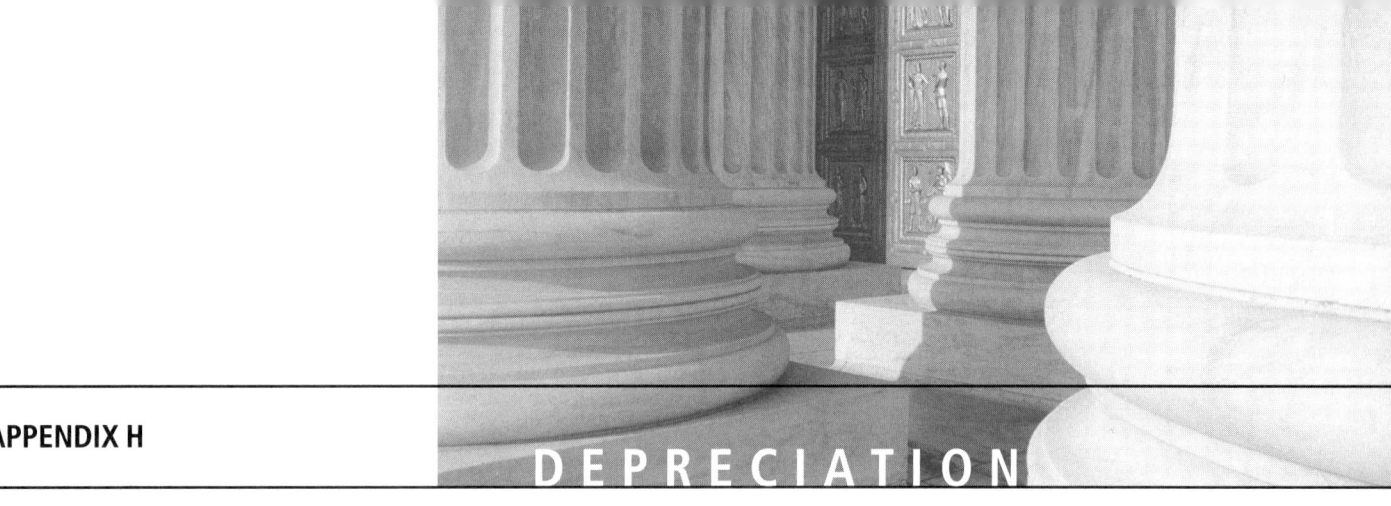

DEPRECIATION

Introduction

Cost recovery, amortization, and depletion are presented in Chapter 8. For most fixed assets (e.g., machinery, equipment, furniture, fixtures, buildings) placed in service after December 31, 1980, the Economic Recovery Tax Act of 1981 (ERTA) has replaced the depreciation system with the cost recovery system.[1] The general relationship between the depreciation system and the cost recovery system is summarized in Exhibit H–1.

Despite ERTA, a discussion of § 167 depreciation is still relevant for two reasons. First, assets that were placed in service prior to 1981 are still in use. Second, certain assets placed in service after 1980 are not eligible to use the cost recovery system (ACRS and MACRS) and therefore must be depreciated. They include property placed in service after 1980 whose life is not based on years (e.g., units-of-production method).

Depreciation

Section 167 permits a depreciation deduction in the form of a reasonable allowance for the exhaustion, wear and tear, and obsolescence of business property and property held for the production of income (e.g., rental property held by an investor).[2] Obsolescence refers to normal technological change due to reasonably foreseeable economic conditions. If rapid or abnormal obsolescence occurs, a taxpayer may change to a shorter estimated useful life if there is a "clear and convincing

EXHIBIT H–1	Depreciation and Cost Recovery: Relevant Time Periods
System	**Date Property Is Placed in Service**
§ 167 depreciation	Before January 1, 1981, and *certain* property placed in service after December 31, 1980.
Original accelerated cost recovery system (ACRS)	After December 31, 1980, and before January 1, 1987.
Modified accelerated cost recovery system (MACRS)	After December 31, 1986.

---

[1]Depreciation is covered in § 167, and cost recovery (ACRS and MACRS) is covered in § 168.

[2]§ 167(a) and Reg. § 1.167(a)–1.

basis for the redetermination." Depreciation deductions are *not* permitted for personal use property.

The taxpayer must adopt a reasonable and consistent plan for depreciating the cost or other basis of assets over the estimated useful life of the property (e.g., the taxpayer cannot arbitrarily defer or accelerate the amount of depreciation from one year to another). The basis of the depreciable property must be reduced by the depreciation allowed and by not less than the allowable amount.[3] The *allowed* depreciation is the depreciation actually taken, whereas the *allowable* depreciation is the amount that could have been taken under the applicable depreciation method. If the taxpayer does not claim any depreciation on property during a particular year, the basis of the property still must be reduced by the amount of depreciation that should have been deducted (the allowable depreciation).

EXAMPLE 1

On January 1, Ted paid $7,500 for a truck to be used in his business. He chose a five-year estimated useful life, no salvage value, and straight-line depreciation. Thus, the allowable depreciation deduction was $1,500 per year. However, depreciation actually taken (allowed) was as follows:

Year 1	$1,500
Year 2	–0–
Year 3	–0–
Year 4	1,500
Year 5	1,500

The adjusted basis of the truck must be reduced by the amount of allowable depreciation of $7,500 ($1,500 × 5 years) even though Ted claimed only $4,500 depreciation during the five-year period. Therefore, if Ted sold the truck at the end of Year 5 for $1,000, he would recognize a $1,000 gain, since the adjusted basis of the truck is zero. ∎

Qualifying Property and Basis for Depreciation

The use rather than the character of property determines whether a depreciation deduction is permitted. Property must be used in a trade or business or held for the production of income to qualify as depreciable.

EXAMPLE 2

Carol is a self-employed CPA who maintains her office in a room in her home. The room, which is used exclusively for her business, comprises 20% of the square footage of her house. Carol is permitted a depreciation deduction only for the business use part of the house. No depreciation deduction is permitted for the 80% of the square footage of her house that is used as her residence. ∎

The basis for depreciation generally is the adjusted cost basis used to determine gain if the property is sold or otherwise disposed of.[4] However, if personal use assets are converted to business or income-producing use, the basis for depreciation *and* for loss is the *lower* of the adjusted basis or fair market value at the time of the conversion of the property.[5] As a result of this lower of basis rule, losses that occurred while the property was personal use property will not be recognized for tax purposes through the depreciation of the property.

---

[3]§ 1016(a)(2) and Reg. § 1.167(a)–10(a).
[4]§ 167(c).

[5]Reg. § 1.167(g)–1.

Hans acquires a personal residence for $130,000. Four years later, when the fair market value is only $125,000, he converts the property to rental use. The basis for depreciation is $125,000, since the fair market value is less than the adjusted basis. The $5,000 decline in value is deemed to be personal (since it occurred while the property was held for personal use) and therefore nondeductible. ■

EXAMPLE 3

The Regulations provide that tangible property is depreciable only to the extent that the property is subject to wear and tear, decay or decline from natural causes, exhaustion, and obsolescence.[6] Thus, land and inventory are not depreciable, but land improvements are depreciable (e.g., paved surfaces, fences, landscaping).

Other Depreciation Considerations

In determining the amount of the depreciation deduction, the following additional considerations need to be addressed:

* The salvage value of the asset.
* The choice of depreciation methods.
* The useful life of the asset.

For property subject to depreciation under § 167, taxpayers generally must take into account the **salvage value** (assuming there is a salvage value) of an asset in calculating depreciation. An asset cannot be depreciated below its salvage value. However, the Code permits a taxpayer to disregard salvage value for amounts up to 10 percent of the basis in the property. This provision applies to tangible personal property (other than livestock) with an estimated useful life of three years or more.[7]

Green Company acquired a machine for $10,000 in 1980 with an estimated salvage value of $3,000 after 19 years. The company may disregard salvage value to the extent of $1,000 and compute the machine's depreciation based upon a cost of $10,000 less $2,000 salvage value. The adjusted basis may be reduced to $2,000 (depreciation of $8,000 may be taken) even though the actual salvage value is $3,000. ■

EXAMPLE 4

This provision was incorporated into the law to reduce the number of IRS-taxpayer disputes over the amount of the salvage value that should be used.

Another consideration is the *choice of depreciation methods* from among the several allowed. The following alternative depreciation methods are permitted for property placed into service before January 1, 1981, and for the aforementioned property placed in service after December 31, 1980, for which cost recovery is not permitted:

* The straight-line (SL) method (cost basis less salvage value ÷ estimated useful life).
* The declining-balance method (DB) using a rate not to exceed twice the straight-line rate. Common methods include 200 percent DB (double-declining balance), 150 percent DB, and 125 percent DB. Salvage value is not taken into account under any of the declining-balance methods. However, no further depreciation can be claimed once net book value (cost minus depreciation) and salvage value are the same.
* The sum-of-the-years' digits method (SYD).
* Any other consistent method that does not result in greater total depreciation being claimed during the first two-thirds of the useful life than would have been allowable under the double-declining balance method. Permissible methods include machine hours and the units-of-production method.

[6]Reg. § 1.167(a)–2.   [7]Reg. §§ 1.167(a)–1(c) and (f)–1.

EXAMPLE 5

On January 1, 1980, Diego acquired a new machine to be used in his business. The asset cost $10,000 with an estimated salvage value of $2,000 and a four-year estimated useful life.[8] The following amounts of depreciation could be deducted, depending on the method of depreciation used:

	1980	1981	1982	1983
1. Straight-line:				
$10,000 cost less ($2,000 salvage value reduced by 10% of cost) ÷ 4 years	$2,250	$2,250	$2,250	$2,250
2. Double-declining balance:				
a. $10,000 × 50% (twice the straight-line rate)	5,000			
b. ($10,000 − $5,000) × 50%		2,500		
c. ($10,000 − $5,000 − $2,500) × 50%			1,250	
d. ($10,000 − $5,000 − $2,500 − $1,250) × 50%				250[9]
3. Sum-of-the-years' digits:*				
$10,000 cost less ($2,000 salvage value reduced by 10% of cost) or $9,000				
a. $9,000 × 4/10	3,600			
b. $9,000 × 3/10		2,700		
c. $9,000 × 2/10			1,800	
d. $9,000 × 1/10				900

*The formula for the sum-of-the-years' digits (SYD) method is

$$\text{Cost} - \text{Salvage value} \times \frac{\text{Remaining life at the beginning of the year}}{\text{Sum-of-the-years' digits of the estimated life}}$$

In this example, the denominator for SYD is 1 + 2 + 3 + 4, or 10. The numerator is 4 for Year 1 (the number of years left at the beginning of Year 1), 3 for Year 2, etc. The denominator can be calculated by the following formula:

$$S = \frac{Y(Y + 1)}{2} \text{ where } Y = \text{estimated useful life}$$

$$S = \frac{4(4 + 1)}{2} = 10$$

■

EXAMPLE 6

Using the depreciation calculations in Example 5, the depreciation reserve (accumulated depreciation) and net book value at the end of 1983 are as follows:

	Cost	−	Depreciation	=	Net Book Value*
Straight-line	$10,000		$9,000		$1,000
Double-declining balance	10,000		9,000		1,000
Sum-of-the-years' digits	10,000		9,000		1,000

*Note that an asset may not be depreciated below its salvage value even when a declining-balance method is used.

■

In 1969, Congress placed certain restrictions on the use of accelerated methods for new and used realty that are subject to the depreciation rules under § 167. These restrictions were imposed to reduce the opportunities for using real estate

---

[8]A four-year life is used to illustrate the different depreciation methods. Note that an asset placed in service in 1980 must have a useful life of at least 27 years in order for depreciation to be deducted in 2006.

[9]Total depreciation taken cannot exceed cost minus estimated salvage value ($1,000 in this example).

investments as tax shelters. The use of accelerated depreciation frequently resulted in the recognition of ordinary tax losses on economically profitable real estate ventures.

The following methods were permitted for residential and nonresidential real property:

	Nonresidential Real Property (Commercial and Industrial Buildings, Etc.)	Residential Real Property (Apartment Buildings, Etc.)
New property acquired after July 24, 1969, and generally before January 1, 1981	150% DB, SL	200% DB, SYD, 150% DB, or SL
Used property acquired after July 24, 1969, and generally before January 1, 1981	SL	125% DB (if estimated useful life is 20 years or greater) or SL

Congress chose to permit accelerated methods (200 percent declining-balance and sum-of-the-years' digits) for new residential rental property. Presumably, the desire to stimulate construction of new housing units justified the need for such accelerated methods.

Restrictions on the use of accelerated methods were not imposed on new tangible personalty (e.g., machinery, equipment, and automobiles). However, the 200 percent declining-balance and sum-of-the-years' digits methods were not permitted for used tangible personal property. The depreciation methods permitted for *used* tangible personal property were as follows:

	Useful Life of Three Years or More	Useful Life of Less Than Three Years
Used tangible personal property acquired after July 24, 1969, and generally before January 1, 1981	150% DB, SL	SL

Since the acquisition of used property does not result in any net addition to gross private investment in our economy, Congress chose not to provide as rapid accelerated depreciation for used property.

The determination of a *useful life* for a depreciable asset often led to disagreement between taxpayers and the IRS. One source of information was the company's previous experience and policy with respect to asset maintenance and utilization. Another source was the guideline lives issued by the IRS.[10] In 1971, the IRS guideline life system was modified and liberalized by the enactment of the **Asset Depreciation Range (ADR) system.**[11]

KEY TERMS

Asset Depreciation Range (ADR) system, H–5

Salvage value, H–3

---

[10]Rev.Proc. 72–10, 1972–1 C.B. 721, superseded by Rev.Proc. 83–35, 1983–1 C.B. 745.   [11]Reg. § 1.167(a)–11.

G

Index   **I–13**

Net short-term capital gain (NSTCG), **16**:19, **16**:20

Net short-term capital loss (NSTCL), **3**:34, **16**:19

Net unearned income of a dependent child, **3**:23

Netting process, capital gain and loss, **16**:20–22
  capital loss carryovers, **16**:22
  definition of collectibles, **16**:22
  holding periods, **16**:20–22
  qualified dividend income, **16**:23

New York Stock Exchange (NYSE), **16**:3

No-additional-cost service, **5**:20–21, **5**:25

Nonaccountable plans, **9**:26
  failure to comply with accountable plan requirements, **9**:26
  unreimbursed employee expenses, **9**:26

Nonacquiescence, **2**:18

Nonbusiness bad debt, **7**:2, **7**:4–5, **16**:8

Nonbusiness deductions, **7**:21

Nonbusiness expenses, **3**:6

Nonbusiness income, **7**:21

Nonbusiness losses, **6**:7

Noncontingent payments, **16**:13

Noncorporate taxpayers, tax treatment of capital gains and losses of, **16**:19–30

Noncustodial parent, deductibility of medical expenses, **10**:5

Nondeductible contributions and IRAs, **19**:21

Nondeductible items, charitable contributions, **10**:21

Nondiscrimination provisions, employee fringe benefits, **5**:24

Nondiscrimination requirements, qualified plans, **19**:7

Nondiscrimination test, **5**:24

Nonoperating private foundations, **10**:24

Nonqualified deferred compensation (NQDC) plans, **19**:3, **19**:28–31
  tax planning for, **19**:39
  tax treatment to the employer and employee, **19**:28–31
  underlying rationale for tax treatment, **19**:28

Nonqualified stock options (NQSO), **19**:31, **19**:36–37
  and incentive stock options compared, **19**:40

Nonrecaptured net Section 1231 losses, **17**:8

Nonrecognition of gain
  conversion into money, **15**:13–14
  direct conversion, **15**:13

Nonrecourse financing, qualified, **11**:4

Nonrefundable credits, **13**:5
  carryover provision, **13**:5

Nonresidential real property, computing Section 1250 recapture on, **17**:15–16

Nontaxable economic benefits, tax planning for, **4**:34–35

Nontaxable exchange, **15**:2–3
  certain exchanges of insurance policies—Section 1035, **15**:21

certain reacquisitions of real property—Section 1038, **15**:22

exchange of stock for property—Section 1032, **15**:21

exchange of stock for stock of the same corporation—Section 1036, **15**:21–22

general concept of, **15**:2–3

holding period rules, **16**:15

involuntary conversions—Section 1033, **15**:10–15

like-kind exchanges—Section 1031, **15**:3–9

of a passive activity, **11**:23

other nonrecognition provisions of, **15**:21–23

rollover of gain from qualified small business stock into another qualified small business stock—Section 1045, **15**:23

rollovers into specialized small business investment companies—Section 1044, **15**:22–23

sale of personal residence, **15**:15–21

transfers of property between spouses or incident to divorce—Section 1041, **15**:22

Nontaxable stock dividends, **14**:10, **14**:11

Nontaxable stock rights, **14**:11

Nontaxable transactions, recapture exceptions, **17**:20

Normal cost, **19**:15

North American Free Trade Agreement of 1993, **5**:14

Nursing home care, deductible medical expenses, **10**:3

O

Obligations
  disposition of installment, **18**:23
  retirement of corporate (special rule), **16**:8–9
  tax planning for the disposition of installment, **18**:35–36
  to repay, amounts received under, **4**:11–12

Occupational taxes, **1**:17

OECD (Organization for Economic Cooperation and Development), **1**:18

Office audit, **1**:19

Office in the home expenses, **9**:20–22

Offset, right of, **14**:17–18

Old age, survivors, and disability insurance, **1**:16

$100 per event floor and a 10 percent-of-AGI aggregate floor, reduction for, **7**:11

One-year rule for prepaid expenses, **6**:9–10, **18**:11

Online systems, **2**:25

Online tax services, **2**:25

Options, **16**:9–10, **16**:11
  exercise of by grantee, **16**:10
  failure to exercise, **16**:10
  sale of, **16**:9–10

Ordering procedure, **16**:20

Ordinary and necessary, **6**:5–7

Ordinary asset, **16**:3

Ordinary income property, **10**:23–24

Ordinary loss, **7**:6–7, **17**:3–4

Organizational expenditures, **20**:13

Original issue discount (OID), **4**:10–11, **16**:9

Outsourcing of tax return preparation, **1**:24

P

Participation and coverage requirements, qualified plan, **19**:7–8

Partnership, **4**:16, **20**:4, **20**:30–35
  accounting period for, **18**:3–6
  basis of partnership interest, **20**:31–32
  formation of, **20**:31–33
  income from, **4**:16–17
  limitation on partner's share of losses, **20**:33–34
  measuring and reporting partnership income, **20**:33
  nature of taxation, **20**:30–31
  operation, **20**:33–35
  other partner considerations, **20**:35
  partnership's basis in contributed property, **20**:32–33
  recognition of gain or loss, **20**:31
  Subchapter K, **2**:6
  transactions between partner and partnership, **20**:34–35

Passenger automobiles, **8**:13

Passive activity loss rules
  general concepts, **11**:25
  individual AMT adjustments, **12**:14–15

Passive activity losses (PALs), **11**:23
  individual AMT adjustments, **12**:14–15

Passive income and losses
  carryovers of suspended losses, **11**:7–8
  classification of, **11**:5–10
  general impact, **11**:6
  impact of suspended losses, **11**:6–7
  passive activity changes to active, **11**:9
  passive credits, **11**:8

Passive income generators (PIGs), **11**:23

Passive income under Section 469, **11**:6

Passive interests, dispositions of, **11**:22–23

Passive loss, **11**:3

Passive loss rules limits, **11**:5–23
  classification and impact of passive income and losses, **11**:5–10
  closely held C corporations, **11**:9–10
  dispositions of passive interests, **11**:22–23
  identification of an activity, **11**:10–12
  interaction of the at-risk and passive activity limits, **11**:18–19
  material participation, **11**:12–16, **11**:19–20
  passive activities defined, **11**:10–18
  personal service corporations, **11**:9
  real estate rental activities, **11**:20–22
  regrouping of activities, **11**:11

AMT Formula for Individuals

Regular Taxable Income

Plus or minus:	Adjustments
Plus:	Tax preferences
Equals:	Alternative minimum taxable income
Minus:	Exemption
Equals:	Alternative minimum tax base
Times:	26% and 28% graduated rates
Equals:	Tentative minimum tax before foreign tax credit
Minus:	Alternative minimum tax foreign tax credit
Equals:	Tentative minimum tax
Minus:	Regular income tax liability
Equals:	Alternative minimum tax (if amount is positive)

AMT Exemption Phaseout for Individuals

		Phaseout	
Filing Status	**Exemption**	**Begins at**	**Ends at**
Married, filing jointly	$58,000	$150,000	$382,000
Single or head of household	40,250	112,500	273,500
Married, filing separately	29,000	75,000	191,000

AMT Formula for Corporations

Regular Taxable Income before NOL Deduction

Plus or minus:	Adjustments (except ACE adjustment)
Plus:	Tax preferences
Equals:	AMTI before ATNOL deduction and ACE adjustment
Plus or minus:	ACE adjustment
Equals:	Alternative minimum taxable income (AMTI) before ATNOL deduction
Minus:	ATNOL deduction (limited to 90% of AMTI before ATNOL deduction)
Equals:	Alternative minimum taxable income (AMTI)
Minus:	Exemption
Equals:	Alternative minimum tax base
Times:	20% rate
Equals:	Tentative AMT before AMT foreign tax credit
Minus:	AMT foreign tax credit
Equals:	Tentative minimum tax
Minus:	Regular income tax liability before credits minus regular foreign tax credit
Equals:	Alternative minimum tax (AMT) if positive